Dear Reader

With the aim of giving a maximum amount of information in a limited number of pages Michelin has adopted a system of symbols which is today known the world over.

Failing this system the present publication would run to six volumes.

Judge for yourselves by comparing the descriptive text below with the equivalent extract from the Guide in symbol form.

Astoria (Robert) , 21 32 43, Fax 21 32 49, ≤ lake, « Flowered garden », - , . AE E JCB BX **a**
March-November - **M** *(closed Sunday)* 350/650 - 75 - **25 rm** 500/800.
Spec. Goujonnettes de sole, Chartreuse de perdreau, Profiteroles. **Wines.** Chablis, Irancy.

A very comfortable hotel where you will enjoy a pleasant stay and be tempted to prolong your visit.

The very good quality of the cuisine, which is personally supervised by the proprietor Mr Robert, is worth a stop on your journey.

The hotel is in a quiet secluded setting, away from the built-up area.

To reserve phone 21 32 43 ; the Fax number is 21 32 49.

The hotel affords a fine view of the lake ; in good weather it is possible to eat out of doors. The hotel is enhanced by an attractive flowered garden and has an indoor swimming pool a private tennis court.

Smoking is not allowed in certain areas of the establishment.

Direct dialling telephone in room.

Parking facilities, under cover, are available to hotel guests.

The hotel accepts payment by American Express, Eurocard and Japan Card Bank credit cards.

Letters giving the location of the hotel on the town plan : BX **a**.

The establishment is open from March to November but the restaurant closes every Sunday.

The set meal prices range from 350 F for the lowest to 650 F for the highest.

The cost of continental breakfast served in the bedroom is 75 F.

25 bedroomed hotel. The charges vary from 500 F for a single to 800 F for the best twin bedded room.

Included for the gourmet are some culinary specialities, recommended by the hotelier : Small fillets of fried sole, Young partridge cooked with cabbage, Small round pastry poffs filled with ice cream and covered with chocolate sauce. In addition to the best quality wines you will find many of the local wines worth sampling : Chablis, Irancy.

This demonstration clearly shows that each entry contains a great deal of information. The symbols are easily learnt and to know them will enable you to understand the Guide and to choose those establishments that you require.

Contents

217 **Germany** – *Deutschland*

Berlin
Cologne, *Wittlich*
Dresden
Düsseldorf, *Essen-Kettwig, Grevenbroich*
Frankfurt on Main, *Guldental, Mannheim, Wertheim*
Leipzig
Hamburg
Hanover
Munich
Stuttgart, *Baiersbronn, Öhringen*

287 **Greece** – *Hellás*

Athens

295 **Hungary** – *Magyarország*

Budapest

303 **Ireland**, *Republic of*

Dublin

311 **Italy** – *Italia*

Rome
Florence
Milan, *Abbiategrasso, Malgrate, Ranco, Soriso*
Naples, *Island of Capri, Sant'Agata sui Due Golfi*
Palermo *(Sicily)*
Taormina *(Sicily)*
Turin, *Costigliole d'Asti*
Venice

369 **Norway** – *Norge*

Oslo

377 **Portugal**

Lisbon

387 **Spain** – *España*

Madrid
Barcelona, *San Celoni*
Málaga
Marbella
Sevilla
Valencia

429 **Sweden** - *Sverige*

Stockholm
Gothenburg

443 **Switzerland** - *Suisse* - *Schweiz*

Basle
Geneva
Zurich

463 **United Kingdom**

London, *Bray-on-Thames, Oxford, Reading*
Birmingham
Edinburgh
Glasgow
Leeds
Liverpool
Manchester

In addition to those situated in the main cities, restaurants renowned for their exceptional cuisine will be found in the towns printed in light type in the list above.

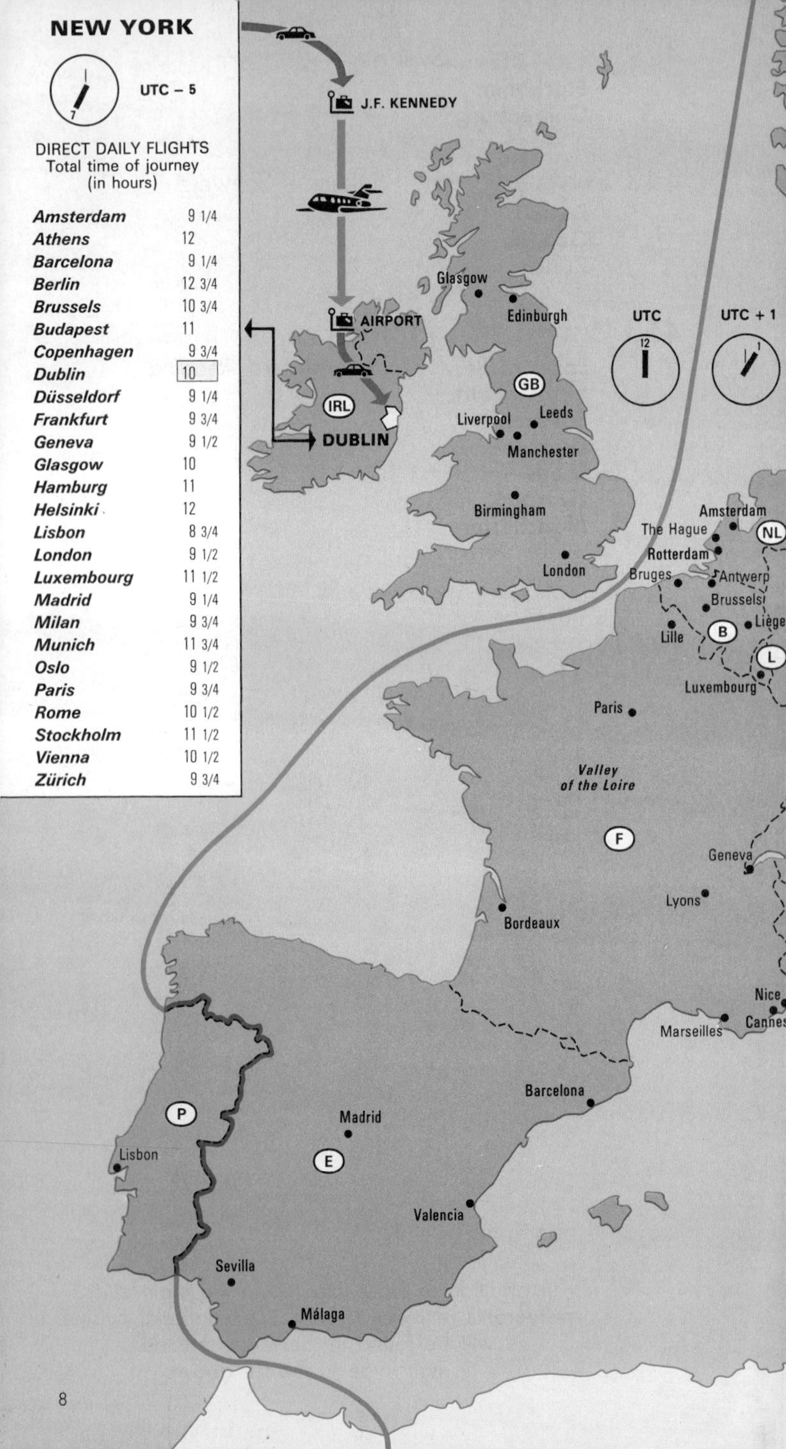

NEW YORK

UTC – 5

DIRECT DAILY FLIGHTS
Total time of journey
(in hours)

Amsterdam	9 1/4
Athens	12
Barcelona	9 1/4
Berlin	12 3/4
Brussels	10 3/4
Budapest	11
Copenhagen	9 3/4
Dublin	10
Düsseldorf	9 1/4
Frankfurt	9 3/4
Geneva	9 1/2
Glasgow	10
Hamburg	11
Helsinki	12
Lisbon	8 3/4
London	9 1/2
Luxembourg	11 1/2
Madrid	9 1/4
Milan	9 3/4
Munich	11 3/4
Oslo	9 1/2
Paris	9 3/4
Rome	10 1/2
Stockholm	11 1/2
Vienna	10 1/2
Zürich	9 3/4

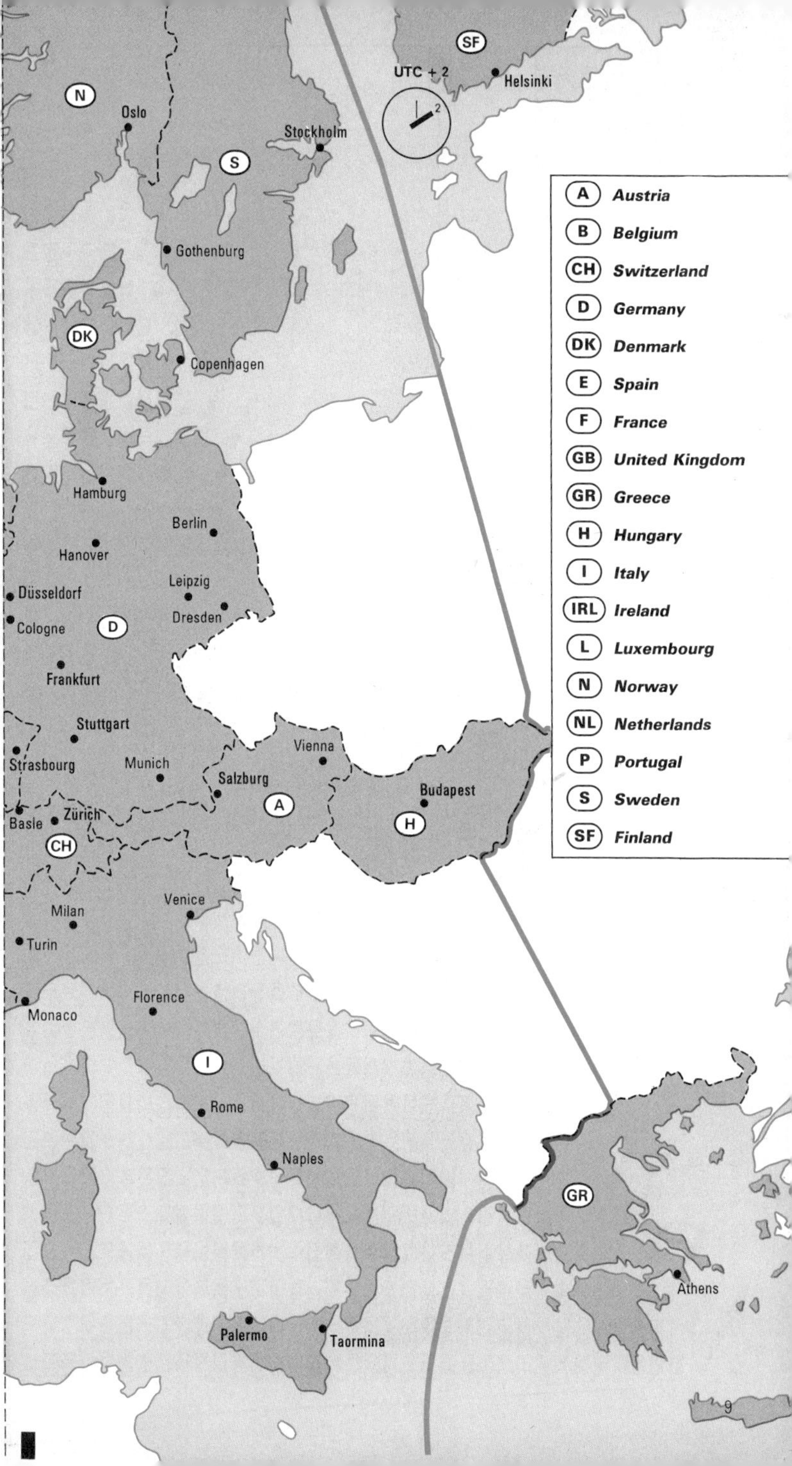

SF
UTC + 2
2
Helsinki
N
Oslo
Stockholm
S
Gothenburg
DK
Copenhagen
Hamburg
Berlin
Hanover
Leipzig
Düsseldorf
Dresden
Cologne
D
Frankfurt
Stuttgart
Strasbourg
Munich
Vienna
Salzburg
Budapest
A
H
Basle
Zürich
CH
Venice
Milan
Turin
Florence
Monaco
I
Rome
Naples
Palermo
Taormina
GR
Athens
A Austria
B Belgium
CH Switzerland
D Germany
DK Denmark
E Spain
F France
GB United Kingdom
GR Greece
H Hungary
I Italy
IRL Ireland
L Luxembourg
N Norway
NL Netherlands
P Portugal
S Sweden
SF Finland

DISTANCES BY ROAD

(in kilometres)

	Amsterdam	Athens	Barcelona	Berlin	Birmingham	Bordeaux	Brussels	Budapest	Cologne	Copenhagen	Dublin	Edinburgh	Frankfurt	Geneva	Glasgow	Hamburg	Helsinki	Lisbon	London	Luxembou.g	Lyons	Madrid	Manchester	Marseilles	Milan	Munich	Nice	Oslo	Paris	Rome	Stockholm	Strasbourg	Stuttgart	Venice	Vienna
Athens	2837																																		
Barcelona	1548	3091																																	
Berlin	670	2584	1854																																
Birmingham	783	3316	1488	1348																															
Bordeaux	1082	3240	634	1647	854																														
Brussels	205	2793	1366	782	592	886																													
Budapest	1394	1510	1352	883	1873	2041	1350																												
Cologne	265	2579	1342	575	803	1098	212	1136																											
Copenhagen	738	2938	2100	384	1475	1774	890	1293	723																										
Dublin	608	3587	1758	1493	248	1124	760	2144	1074	1620																									
Edinburgh	1290	3823	1995	1855	484	1361	1099	2380	1310	1982	417																								
Frankfurt	447	2396	1319	566	991	1159	403	953	189	785	1262	1498																							
Geneva	886	2446	771	1121	934	682	704	1308	747	1367	1365	1441	586																						
Glasgow	1288	3822	1993	1854	483	1359	1097	2379	1309	1981	343	75	1497	1440																					
Hamburg	441	2780	1803	289	1178	1477	593	1198	426	305	1449	1685	488	1070	1684																				
Helsinki	1205	2540	2389	505	1883	2182	1317	1630	1110	795	2154	2390	1101	1656	2389	776																			
Lisbon	2322	4320	1285	2888	2095	1233	2127	3182	2339	3015	2668	2602	2400	2000	2600	2718	3423																		
London	196	3253	1424	1054	196	790	315	1810	740	1180	434	613	928	926	669	1115	1820	2229																	
Luxembou.g	391	2637	1149	768	780	948	219	1165	194	916	980	1287	248	487	1285	619	1303	2189	540																
Lyons	917	2560	631	1223	857	538	735	1421	712	1469	1128	1364	688	142	1363	1179	1758	1860	794	518															
Madrid	1813	3761	680	2378	1585	723	1617	2622	1829	2505	2167	2092	1890	1441	2090	2208	2913	658	1728	1679	1301														
Manchester	945	3478	1650	1510	139	1016	754	2035	965	1637	200	357	1153	1096	356	1340	2045	2257	326	942	1019	1747													
Marseilles	1229	2622	494	1535	1169	648	1047	1483	1023	1781	1439	1676	1000	452	1674	1484	2070	1723	1105	830	313	1164	1331												
Milan	1089	2128	974	1040	1252	1123	894	990	831	1414	1522	1759	670	323	1757	1117	1575	2203	1188	677	437	1644	1414	505											
Munich	838	2063	1370	585	1236	1272	770	678	580	939	1507	1743	397	600	1742	781	1120	2513	1173	557	741	2040	1398	1054	560										
Nice	1388	2434	657	1355	1328	808	1206	1296	1146	1729	1598	1834	985	472	1833	1432	1890	1886	1264	989	472	1327	1490	187	317	866									
Oslo	1321	3521	2683	967	2058	2357	1473	1876	1306	583	2329	2565	1368	1950	2564	888	690	3598	1995	1499	2052	3088	2220	2364	1997	1522	2312								
Paris	504	2913	1091	1070	407	579	309	1470	520	1197	854	914	588	538	913	900	1605	1820	414	376	462	1310	569	773	855	833	932	1780							
Rome	1666	2389	1350	1506	1814	1499	1471	1251	1408	1860	2240	2321	1247	885	2319	1702	2041	2579	1801	1254	965	2020	1976	881	572	918	693	2443	1417						
Stockholm	1368	3568	2730	1014	2105	2404	1520	1923	1353	630	2250	2612	1415	1997	2611	935	165	3645	1810	1546	2099	3135	2267	2411	2044	1569	2359	525	1827	2490					
Strasbourg	635	2438	1110	751	892	922	440	1053	377	997	1186	1399	216	404	1398	700	1286	2163	746	223	480	1653	1054	791	488	358	803	1580	489	1065	1627				
Stuttgart	623	2302	1259	631	1034	1070	559	917	365	967	1305	1541	204	526	1540	670	1166	2311	971	346	628	1801	1196	940	523	222	838	1550	631	1098	1597	156			
Venice	1284	1878	1230	1080	1514	1379	1156	740	1026	1434	1784	2021	892	585	2019	1276	1615	2459	1450	939	699	1900	1676	761	267	492	573	2017	1117	528	2064	750	672		
Vienna	1151	1862	1834	642	1630	1798	1107	243	893	1052	1901	2137	710	1031	2136	957	924	3039	1567	922	1172	2504	1792	1365	871	435	1177	1635	1227	1110	1682	810	674	599	
Zürich	831	2417	1058	853	1036	917	637	989	574	1189	1307	1543	413	288	1542	892	1388	2158	973	420	429	1728	1198	739	294	315	609	1772	640	871	1819	231	230	556	746

Helsinki — Strasbourg: 1286

AIR LINKS (in hours)

31/2 not daily

	Amsterdam	Athens	Barcelona	Berlin	Birmingham	Bordeaux	Brussels	Budapest	Cologne	Copenhagen	Dublin	Edinburgh	Frankfurt	Geneva	Glasgow	Hamburg	Helsinki	Lisbon	London	Luxembourg	Lyons	Madrid	Manchester	Marseilles	Milan	Munich	Nice	Oslo	Paris	Rome	Stockholm	Strasbourg	Stuttgart	Venice	Vienna
Athens	5
Barcelona	33/4	41/2
Berlin	3	8	53/4
Birmingham	23/4	71/2	8	51/4
Bordeaux	23/4	9		81/2	53/4
Brussels	21/2	5	33/4	41/4	31/4	51/2
Budapest	4	33/4		31/2			4
Cologne		6	51/4	23/4	41/4	71/4		33/4
Copenhagen	3	5	41/2	4	41/2	6	31/4	33/4	41/4
Dublin	31/4	8	61/2	51/2	21/2	53/4	31/4		51/2	4
Edinburgh	33/4	81/2	61/4	6	23/4	51/2	43/4		51/4	51/2	23/4
Frankfurt	23/4	41/2	33/4	23/4	31/4	61/4	23/4	31/2	21/2	31/4	33/4	53/4
Geneva	3	41/2	3	41/2	5	3	3		41/2	33/4	4	51/2	3
Glasgow	31/4	8	63/4	63/4	23/4	6	43/4		51/2	31/2	21/2	21/4	51/2	51/2
Hamburg	23/4	61/2	51/2	21/2	5	53/4	3	4	23/4	21/2	51/2	61/4	23/4	43/4	6
Helsinki	51/4	91/2	71/2	5	12	91/4	41/2	41/2	6	31/4	73/4	83/4	41/4	6	8	33/4
Lisbon	41/2	91/2	31/4	71/2	7		41/2		71/2	51/2	63/4	71/4	43/4	31/4	7	61/4	8
London	23/4	53/4	41/4	7	3	33/4	31/4	5	31/2	4	31/4	31/2	31/2	31/2	31/2	33/4	51/4	43/4
Luxembourg	21/2	61/2	63/4	43/4	6	61/4	21/4		41/2	43/4	51/2		21/2	4	51/2	43/4	53/4	63/4	31/4
Lyons	31/2	71/4	3	4	43/4	3	31/4		5	4	6	6	31/4		6	51/2	8	41/4	4	
Madrid	3	61/4	23/4	61/4	61/4	3	4	5	51/2	43/4	4	6	41/4	31/2	61/4	6	73/4	23/4	41/4	6	43/4
Manchester	3	71/4	6	51/2	21/2	53/4	3		51/2	33/4	23/4	3	33/4	4	2	5	71/2	43/4	31/4	53/4	6	41/4
Marseilles	41/2	53/4	23/4	71/4	43/4	23/4	31/2		61/2	51/4	61/4	61/4	41/2	21/2	61/2	61/2	83/4	4	4	6	23/4	31/4	53/4
Milan	3	33/4	31/4	5	43/4	51/4	31/4	33/4	41/4	33/4	51/4	61/4	3	21/2	51/2	43/4	61/4	51/4	4	43/4	3	33/4	4	3
Munich	31/4	41/4	33/4	3	5	6	3	31/4	23/4	31/4	41/4	61/4	23/4	31/2	6	3	41/2	61/2	4	41/4	51/4	51/2	51/2	8	23/4
Nice	31/4	63/4	23/4	61/4	53/4	3	3		51/4	4	51/2	61/2	31/4	21/2	6	51/2	7	4	4	4	23/4	31/4	4	21/4	23/4	3
Oslo	3	83/4	61/4	41/2	43/4	71/4	43/4		63/4	31/2	6	71/2	31/2	51/4	41/4	23/4	4	71/4	3	6	53/4	61/2	51/4	7	51/4	5	53/4
Paris	2	5	31/2	43/4	3	3	23/4	41/4	3	33/4	33/4	5	31/4	3	33/4	31/2	5	41/2	31/2	23/4	3	33/4	31/4	3	31/4	31/2	31/4	4
Rome	3	33/4	31/2	51/4	61/4	81/4	4	4	53/4	41/2	41/4	63/4	33/4	31/2	71/4	53/4	71/4	43/4	43/4	33/4	5	41/4	5	3	3	31/2	23/4	61/2	41/4
Stockholm	4	61/4	73/4	5	51/4	63/4	51/4	61/4	61/2	31/4	7	71/4	4	6	7	31/2	23/4	91/4	5	63/4	61/2	7	6	73/4	6	53/4	6	23/4	43/4	7
Strasbourg	21/2	71/4	63/4		51/2	41/2	21/2			53/4	61/2	53/4		23/4	61/2		81/4	61/2	41/2		31/4	7	43/4	33/4	23/4		23/4	63/4	3	43/4	81/2
Stuttgart	33/4	8	33/4	3	5	8	33/4	31/2	21/2	31/4	51/2	63/4	21/2	33/4	6	3	61/4	43/4	33/4	41/4	5	41/4	5	61/4	23/4	21/2	23/4	5	31/4	51/2	51/2	
Venice	51/2	61/4	53/4	5	53/4		43/4		51/4	53/4	61/4		3	43/4	6	5	71/4	7	41/4	5	5	51/4	61/2	43/4	21/2	3	31/4	6	31/2	3	61/2		5
Vienna	31/2	4	4	5	43/4	6	31/2	23/4	41/2	31/4	53/4	61/4	3	31/4	6	43/4	6	61/2	41/2	43/4	51/2	43/4	53/4	6	3	23/4	31/4	5	33/4	31/2	41/4		3	31/4
Zürich	3	41/2	31/4	31/4	41/4	6	3	31/2	23/4	31/2	53/4	51/2	23/4	21/2	51/4	3	53/4	41/2	33/4	21/2	31/4	33/4	33/4	5	21/2	21/2	23/4	5	31/4	31/2	41/2	21/2	21/2	33/4	3

HAMBURG

FUHLSBÜTTEL

23/4

FORNEBU

OSLO

This revised edition from
Michelin Tyre Company's Tourism Department
offers you a selection of
hotels and restaurants in the main European cities.
The latter have been chosen for
their business or tourist interest.

In addition the guide indicates establishments,
located in other towns,
renowned for the excellence of their cuisine.

We hope that the guide will help you
with your choice of a hotel or restaurant
and prove useful for your sightseeing.
Have an enjoyable stay.

Hotels restaurants

CATEGORY, STANDARD OF COMFORT

Hotels		Restaurants
	Luxury in the traditional style	XXXXX
	Top class comfort	XXXX
	Very comfortable	XXX
	Comfortable	XX
	Quite comfortable	X
M	In its class, hotel with modern amenities	

ATMOSPHERE AND SETTING

...	Pleasant hotels
XXXXX ... X	Pleasant restaurants
« Park »	Particularly attractive feature
	Very quiet or quiet secluded hotel
	Quiet hotel
sea,	Exceptional view, Panoramic view
	Interesting or extensive view

CUISINE

	Exceptional cuisine in the country, worth a special journey
	Excellent cooking : worth a detour
	A very good restaurant in its category
M	Other recommended carefully prepared meals

HOTEL FACILITIES

30 rm	Number of rooms
	Lift (elevator) – Television in room
	Non-smoking areas
	Air conditioning
	Telephone in room: direct dialling for outside calls
	Telephone in room: outside calls connected by operator
	Hotel tenis court(s) – Outdoor or indoor swimming pool
	Sauna – Exercise room
	Garden – Beach with bathing facilities
	Meals served in garden or on terrace
	Garage – Car park
	Bedrooms accessible to disabled people
	Equipped conference hall
	Dogs are not allowed
without rest.	The hotel has no restaurant

PRICES

These prices are given in the currency of the country in question. Valid for 1993 the rates shown should only vary if the cost of living changes to any great extent.

	Meals
M 115/230	Set meal prices
M à la carte 150/280	"a la carte" meals
b.i.	House wine included
	Table wine available by the carafe
	Hôtels
30 rm 285/500	Lowest price for a comfortable single and highest price for the best double room.
30 rm 325/580	Price includes breakfast
	Breakfast
55	Price of breakfast
	Credit cards
AE GB JCB VISA	Credit cards accepted

SERVICE and TAXES

Except in Greece and Spain, prices shown are inclusive, that is to say service and V.A.T. included. In U.K. and Ireland, s = service only included, t = V.A.T. only included. In Italy, when not included, a percentage for service is shown after the meal prices, eg. (16 %).

Town Plans

Main conventional signs

	Tourist Information Centre
a	Hotel, restaurant – Reference letter on the town plan
	Place of interest and its main entrance } Reference letter on the town plan
B	Interesting church or chapel } Reference letter on the town plan
Thiers (R.)	Shopping street – Public car park
	Tram
	Underground station
	One-way street
	Church or chapel
	Poste restante, telegraph – Telephone
	Public buildings located by letters :
POL T M	Police (in large towns police headquaters) – Theatre – Museum
	Coach station – Airport – Hospital – Covered market
	Ruins – Monument, statue – Fountain
	Garden, park, wood – Cemetery, Jewish cemetery
9	Outdoor or indoor swimming pool – Racecourse – Golf course
	Cable-car – Funicular
	Sports ground, stadium – View – Panorama

Names shown on the street plans are in the language of the country to conform to local signposting.

SIGHTS

★★★	Worth a journey
★★	Worth a detour
★	Interesting

Avec cette nouvelle édition,
les Services de Tourisme du Pneu Michelin
vous proposent une sélection
d'hôtels et restaurants
des principales villes d'Europe,
choisies en raison de leur vocation internationale
sur le plan des affaires et du tourisme.

Vous y trouverez également les grandes tables
situées hors de ces grandes villes.

Nous vous souhaitons d'agréables séjours
et espérons que ce guide vous aidera utilement
pour le choix d'un hôtel,
d'une bonne table
et pour la visite des principales curiosités.

Hôtels restaurants

CLASSE ET CONFORT

⌂⌂⌂⌂⌂	Grand luxe et tradition	XXXXX
⌂⌂⌂⌂	Grand confort	XXXX
⌂⌂⌂	Très confortable	XXX
⌂⌂	Bon confort	XX
⌂	Assez confortable	X
[M]	Dans sa catégorie, hôtel d'équipement moderne	

L'AGRÉMENT

⌂⌂⌂⌂⌂ ... ⌂	Hôtels agréables
XXXXX ... X	Restaurants agréables
« Park »	Élément particulièrement agréable
🐦	Hôtel très tranquille, ou isolé et tranquille
🐦	Hôtel tranquille
⩽ sea, ✳	Vue exceptionnelle, panorama
⩽	Vue intéressante ou étendue

LA TABLE

✿✿✿	Une des meilleures tables du pays, vaut le voyage
✿✿	Table excellente, mérite un détour
✿	Une très bonne table dans sa catégorie
M	Autre table soignée

L'INSTALLATION

30 rm	Nombre de chambres
[symbols]	Ascenseur - Télévision dans la chambre
[symbol]	Non-fumeurs
[symbol]	Air conditionné
[symbol]	Téléphone dans la chambre direct avec l'extérieur
[symbol]	Téléphone dans la chambre relié par standard
[symbols]	Tennis - Piscine : de plein air ou couverte
[symbols]	Sauna - Salle de remise en forme
[symbols]	Jardin - Plage aménagée
[symbol]	Repas servis au jardin ou en terrasse
[symbols]	Garage - Parc à voitures
[symbol]	Chambres accessibles aux handicapés physiques
[symbol]	L'hôtel reçoit les séminaires
[symbol]	Accès interdit aux chiens
without rest.	L'hôtel n'a pas de restaurant

LES PRIX

Les prix sont indiqués dans la monnaie du pays. Établis pour l'année 1993, ils ne doivent être modifiés que si le coût de la vie subit des variations importantes.

	Au restaurant
M 115/230	Prix des repas à prix fixes
M à la carte 150/280	Prix des repas à la carte
b.i.	Boisson comprise
[symbol]	Vin de table en carafe
	A l'hôtel
30 rm 285/500	Prix minimum pour une chambre d'une personne et maximum pour la plus belle chambre occupée par deux personnes
30 rm [symbol] 325/580	Prix des chambres petit déjeuner compris
	Petit déjeuner
[symbol] 55	Prix du petit déjeuner
	Cartes de crédit
[symbol] AE GB [symbol] [symbol] E JCB VISA	Cartes de crédit acceptées

SERVICE ET TAXES

A l'exception de la Grèce et de l'Espagne, les prix indiqués sont nets. Au Royaume Uni et en Irlande, s = service compris, t = T.V.A. comprise. En Italie, le service est parfois compté en supplément aux prix des repas. Ex. : (16 %).

Les Plans

Principaux signes conventionnels

Information touristique

a — Hôtel, restaurant – Lettre les repérant sur le plan

B — Monument intéressant et entrée principale / Église ou chapelle intéressante — Lettre les repérant sur le plan

Thiers (R.) — Rue commerçante – Parc de stationnement public

Tramway

Station de métro

Sens unique

Église ou chapelle

Poste restante, télégraphe – Téléphone

Édifices publics repérés par des lettres :

POL T M — Police (dans les grandes villes commissariat central) – Théâtre – Musée

Gare routière – Aéroport – Hôpital – Marché couvert

Ruines – Monument, statue – Fontaine

Jardin, parc, bois – Cimetière, Cimetière israélite

Piscine de plein air, couverte – Hippodrome – Golf

Téléphérique – Funiculaire

Stade – Vue – Panorama

Les indications portées sur les plans sont dans la langue du pays, en conformité avec la dénomination locale.

LES CURIOSITÉS

★★★	Vaut le voyage
★★	Mérite un détour
★	Intéressante

Mit dieser Neuauflage
präsentieren Ihnen die Michelin-Touristikabteilungen
eine Auswahl von Hotels und Restaurants
in europäischen Hauptstädten
von internationaler Bedeutung
für Geschäftsreisende und Touristen.

Besonders gute Restaurants in der näheren Umgebung
dieser Städte wurden ebenfalls aufgenommen.

Wir wünschen einen angenehmen Aufenthalt
und hoffen, daß Ihnen dieser Führer
bei der Wahl eines Hotels, eines Restaurants
und beim Besuch der Hauptsehenswürdigkeiten
gute Dienste leisten wird.

Hotels restaurants

KLASSENEINTEILUNG UND KOMFORT

	Großer Luxus und Tradition	XXXXX
	Großer Komfort	XXXX
	Sehr komfortabel	XXX
	Mit gutem Komfort	XX
	Mit ausreichendem Komfort	X
M	Moderne Einrichtung	

ANNEHMLICHKEITEN

...	Angenehme Hotels
XXXXX ... X	Angenehme Restaurants
« Park »	Besondere Annehmlichkeit
	Sehr ruhiges oder abgelegenes und ruhiges Hotel
	Ruhiges Hotel
sea,	Reizvolle Aussicht, Rundblick
	Interessante oder weite Sicht

KÜCHE

	Eine der besten Küchen des Landes : eine Reise wert
	Eine hervorragende Küche : verdient einen Umweg
	Eine sehr hute Küche : verdient Ihre besondere Beachtung
M	Andere sorgfältig zubereitete Mahlzeiten

EINRICHTUNG

30 rm	Anzahl der Zimmer
	Fahrstuhl - Fernsehen im Zimmer
	Nichtraucher
	Klimaanlage
	Zimmertelefon mit direkter Außenverbindung
	Zimmertelefon mit Außenverbindung über Telefonzentrale
	Tennis - Freibad - Hallenbad
	Sauna - Fitneß Center
	Garten - Strandbad
	Garten-, Terrassenrestaurant
	Garage - Parkplatz
	Für Körperbehinderte leicht zugängliche Zimmer
	Konferenzraum
	Das Mitführen von Hunden ist unerwünscht
without rest.	Hotel ohne Restaurant

DIE PREISE

Die Preise sind in der jeweiligen Landeswährung angegeben. Sie gelten für das Jahr 1993 und können nur geändert werden, wenn die Lebenshaltungskosten starke Veränderungen erfahren.

	Im Restaurant
M 115/230	Feste Menupreise
M à la carte 150/280	Mahlzeiten "a la carte"
b.i.	Getränke inbegriffen
	Preiswerter Tischwein in Karaffen
	Im Hotel
30 rm 285/500	Mindestpreis für ein Einzelzimmer und Höchstpreis für das schönste Doppelzimmer für zwei Personen.
30 rm 325/580	Zimmerpreis inkl. Frühstück
	Frühstück
55	Preis des Frühstücks
	Kreditkarten
AE GB JCB VISA	Akzeptierte Kreditkarten

BEDIENUNGSGELD UND GEBÜHREN

Mit Ausnahme von Griechenland und Spanien sind die angegebenen Preise Inklusivpreise. In den Kapiteln über Großbritannien und Irland bedeutet s = Bedienungsgeld inbegriffen, t = MWSt inbegriffen. In Italien wird für die Bedienung gelegentlich ein Zuschlag zum Preis der Mahlzeit erhoben, zB (16 %).

Stadtpläne

Erklärung der wichtigsten Zeichen

Zeichen	Erklärung
	Informationsstelle
a	Hotel, Restaurant – Referenzbuchstabe auf dem Plan
	Sehenswertes Gebäude mit Haupteingang – Referenzbuchstabe auf dem Plan
B	Sehenswerte Kirche oder Kapelle – Referenzbuchstabe auf dem Plan
Thiers (R.)	Einkaufsstraße – Öffentlicher Parkplatz, Parkhaus
	Straßenbahn
	U-Bahnstation
	Einbahnstraße
	Kirche oder Kapelle
	Postlagernde Sendungen, Telegraph – Telefon
	Öffentliche Gebäude, durch Buchstaben gekennzeichnet :
POL T M	Polizei (in größeren Städten Polizeipräsidium) – Theater – Museum
	Autobusbahnhof – Flughafen
	Krankenhaus – Markthalle
	Ruine – Denkmal, Statue – Brunnen
	Garten, Park, Wald – Friedhof, Jüd. Friedhof
9	Freibad – Hallenbad – Pferderennbahn – Golfplatz und Lochzahl
	Seilschwebebahn – Standseilbahn
	Sportplatz – Aussicht – Rundblick

Die Angaben auf den Stadtplänen erfolgen, übereinstimmend mit der örtlichen Beschilderung, in der Landessprache.

SEHENSWÜRDIGKEITEN

★★★	Eine Reise wert
★★	Verdient einen Umweg
★	Sehenswert

この改訂版ガイドブックはミシュラン・タイヤ社観光部がおとどけするものです。

ビジネスに、観光に、国際的な拠点ヨーロッパ主要都市が誇る自慢のホテルとレストランを、そして郊外にたたずむ名うてのレストランをあわせて、御紹介いたします。

このガイドブックが、より快適なホテル、味わい深いレストランやあこがれの地と出逢うきっかけとなり、皆さまの旅をより素晴らしいものにするお手伝いができれば幸いです。

ホテル
レストラン

等級と快適さ

⌂⌂⌂⌂⌂	豪華で伝統的様式	XXXXX
⌂⌂⌂⌂	トップクラス	XXXX
⌂⌂⌂	たいへん快適	XXX
⌂⌂	快適	XX
⌂	割に快適	X
M	等級内での近代的設備のホテル	

居心地

⌂⌂⌂⌂⌂ ... ⌂	居心地よいホテル
XXXXX ... X	居心地よいレストラン
« Park »	特に魅力的な特徴
	大変静かなホテルまたは人里離れた静かなホテル
	静かなホテル
< sea ✳	見晴らしがよい展望(例：海)、パノラマ
<	素晴らしい風景

料理

✿✿✿	最上の料理、出かける価値あり
✿✿	素晴らしい料理、寄り道の価値あり
✿	等級内では大変おいしい料理
M	その他の心のこもった料理

設備

30 rm	ルームナンバー
	エレベーター、室内テレビ
	非喫煙室
	空調設備
	室内に電話あり、外線直通
	室内に電話あり、外線は交換台経由
	テニスコート。屋外プール。屋内プール。
	サウナ。トレーニングルーム。
	くつろげる庭。整備された海水浴場
	食事が庭またはテラスでできる。
P	駐車場、パーキング。
	体の不自由な方のための設備あり
	会議又は研修会の出来るホテル
	犬の連れ込みおことわり
without rest.	レストランの無いホテル

料金

料金は1993年のその国の貨幣単位で示してありますが、物価の変動などで変わる場合もあります。

レストラン

M 115/230 **M** à la carte 150/280	定食、ア・ラ・カルトそれぞれの最低料金と最高料金。
b.i.	飲物付
	デカンター入りテーブルワイン有ります。

ホテル

30 rm 285/500 **30 rm** 325/580	一人部屋の最低料金と二人部屋の最高料金。 朝食代は含まれています

朝食

55	朝食代

クレジット・カード

AE GB JCB VISA	クレジット・カード使用可

サービス料と税金

ギリシャ、ポルトガル、スペイン以外の国に関しては正価料金。英国及びアイルランドでは、s.：サービス料込み、t.：付加価値税込み、を意味する。イタリアでは、サービス料が料金に加算されることがある。例: (16%)

地図

主な記号

	ツーリストインフォメーション
a	ホテル・レストラン — 地図上での目印番号
	興味深い歴史的建造物と、その中央入口 } 地図上での目印番号
B	興味深い教会または聖堂 } 地図上での目印番号
Thiers (R.) P	商店街　公共駐車場
	路面電車
	地下鉄駅
	一方通行路
	教会または聖堂 —局留郵便、電報 — 電話
	公共建造物、記号は下記の通り
POL T M	警察（大都市では、中央警察署） — 劇場 — 美術観、博物館
	長距離バス発着所 — 空港 — 病院 — 屋内市場
	遺跡 — 歴史的建造物、像 — 泉
	庭園、公園、森林 — 墓地 — ユダヤ教の墓地
9	屋外プール、屋内プール — 競馬場 — ゴルフ場
	ロープウェイ — ケーブルカー
	スタジアム — 風景 — パノラマ

地図上の名称は、地方の標識に合わせてその国の言葉で表記されています。

名所

★★★	出かける価値あり
★★	立ち寄る価値あり
★	興味深い

Austria

Österreich

VIENNA – SALZBURG

PRACTICAL INFORMATION

LOCAL CURRENCY

Austrian Schilling; 100 S = 8.70 US $ = 7.31 Ecus (Jan. 93)

TOURIST INFORMATION

In Vienna: Österreich-Information, 1040 Wien, Margaretenstr. 1, ✆ (01) 5 87 20 00
Niedcrösterreich-Information, 1010 Wien, Heidenschuß 2, ✆ (01) 5 33 31 14 34
In Salzburg: Landesverkehrsamt, Sigmund-Haffner-Gasse 16, ✆ (0662) 80 42 23 27

AIRLINES

AUSTRIAN SWISSAIR: 1010 Wien, Kärtner Ring 18, ✆ (01) 7 17 99
AIR FRANCE: 1010 Wien, Kärntner Str. 49, ✆ (01) 5 14 19
BRITISH AIRWAYS: 1010 Wien, Kärntner Ring 10, ✆ (01) 505 76 91
DEUTSCHE LUFTHANSA: 1015 Wien, Kärntner Str. 42, ✆ (01) 5 88 36
JAPAN AIRLINES: Stephansplatz 1, ✆ (01) 535 51 25

FOREIGN EXCHANGE

Hotels, restaurants and shops do not always accept foreign currencies and it is wise, therefore, to change money and cheques at the banks and exchange offices which are found in the larger stations, airports and at the frontier.

SHOPPING and BANK HOURS

Shops are open from 9am to 6pm, but often close for a lunch break. They are closed Saturday afternoon, Sunday and Bank Holidays (except the shops in railway stations).
Branch offices of banks are open from Monday to Friday between 8am and 12.30pm (in Salzburg 12am) and from 1.30pm to 3pm (in Salzburg 2pm to 4.30pm), Thursday to 5.30pm (only in Vienna).
In the index of street names those printed in red are where the principal shops are found.

BREAKDOWN SERVICE

ÖAMTC: See addresses in the text of Vienna and Salzburg
ARBÖ: in Vienna: Mariahilfer Str. 180, ✆ (01) 85 35 35
in Salzburg: Münchner Bundesstr. 9, ✆ (0662) 3 36 01
In Austria the ÖAMTC (emergency number ✆ 120) and the ARBÖ (emergency number ✆ 123) make a special point of assisting foreign motorists. They have motor patrols covering main roads.

TIPPING

Service is generally included in hotel and restaurant bills. But in Austria, it is usual to give more than the expected tip in hotels, restaurants and cafés. Taxi-drivers, porters, barbers and theatre attendants also expect tips.

SPEED LIMITS

The speed limit in built up areas (indicated by place name signs at the beginning and end of such areas) is 50 km/h - 31 mph; on motorways 130 km/h - 80 mph and on all other roads 100 km/h - 62 mph.

SEAT BELTS

The wearing of seat belts in Austria is compulsory for drivers and all passengers.

Vienna

(WIEN) Austria 987 ⑩, 426 ⑫ – pop. 1 500 000 – alt. 156 m. – ✆ 01.

HOFBURG★★★ FGY

Imperial Palace of the Habsburgs (Kaiserpalast der Habsburger) : Swiss Court – Royal Chapel – Amalienhof – Stallburg – Leopold Wing – Ballhausplatz – Imperial Chancellery – Spanish Riding School – Neue Burg – Josefsplatz – Michaelerplatz – In der Burg – Capuchins Crypt – Church of the Augustinians. Art Collections : Imperial Treasury★★★ – Imperial Apartments★★ – Austrian National Library (Great Hall★ – Frescoes★★) – Collection of Court Porcelain and Silver★★ – Collection of Arms and Armour★★ – Collection of Old Musical Instruments★ – Albertina (Dürer Collection★) – Museum of Ephesian Sculpture (Reliefs of Ephesus★★).

BUILDINGS AND MONUMENTS

St Stephen's Cathedral★★★ (Stephansdom) GY – Schönbrunn★★★ (Apartments★★★, Park★★, Gloriette★★, Coach Room★★) AS – Upper and Lower Belvedere★★ (Oberes und Unteres Belvedere) (Terraced Gardens and Art Collections★) HZ and DV – Opera★ (Staatsoper)★ GY – Church of St Charles★★ (Karlskirche) GZ – Church of St Michael (Michaeler Kirche) GY – Church of the Minor Friars (Minoritenkirche) FY – Church of the Teutonic Order (Deutschordenskirche) (Altarpiece★, Treasure★) GY **E** – Church of the Jesuits (Jesuitenkirche) HY **H** – Church of Our Lady of the River Bank (Maria am Gestade) GX – Church of the Faithful Virgin (Maria Treu) AR – Mozart Memorial (Mozart-Gedenkstätte) GY **F** – Dreimäderlhaus FX **W** – Pavilion Otto Wagner★ GZ **Q** – Pavilion of the Secession★ GZ **S**.

STREETS, PLACES, PARKS

The Tour of the Ring★ – The Old Town (Altstadt)★ – Kärntner Straße GY – Graben (Plague Column) GY – Am Hof (Column to the Virgin) GY – Herrengasse★ GY – Maria-Theresien-Platz FY – Prater★ (Giant Whell, ⩽★) BR – Oberlaapark★ BS – Donner Fountain (Donnerbrunnen)★ GY **Y** – Heldenplatz FY – Burggarten GY – Volksgarten FY – Rathausplatz FY.

IMPORTANTS MUSEUMS (Hofburg and Belvedere see above)

Museum of Fine Arts★★★ (Kunsthistorisches Museum) FY – Historical Museum of the City of Vienna★★ (Historisches Museum der Stadt Wien) GZ **M6** – Austrian Folklore Museum★★ (Österreichisches Museum für Volkskunde) AR **M7** – Gallery of Painting and Fine Arts★ (Gemäldegalerie der Akademie der Bildenden Künste) GZ **M9** – Natural History Museum★ (Naturhistorisches Museum) FY **M1** – Birthplace of Schubert (Schubert-Museum) BR **M16** – Austrian Museum of Applied Arts★ (Österreichisches Museum für angewandte Kunst) HY **M10** – Clock Museum (Uhrenmuseum der Stadt Wien) GY **M3**.

EXCURSIONS

Danube Tower★★ (Donauturm) BR – Leopoldsberg ⩽★★ AR – Kahlenberg ⩽★ AR – Klosterneuburg Abbey (Stift Klosterneuburg) (Altarpiece by Nicolas of Verdun★) AR – Grinzing★ AR – Baden★ AS – Vienna Woods★ (Wienerwald) AS.

18 Freudenau 65a, ✆ 2 18 95 64

✈ Wien-Schwechat by ③, ✆ 711 10 and 711 10 22 31, Air Terminal, at Stadtpark (HY) ✆ 72 35 34

🚗 ✆ 58 00 29 89.

Exhibition Centre, Messeplatz 1, ✆ 521 20.

ℹ Tourist-information, ✉ A-1010, Kärtner Str. 38, ✆ 513 88 92 – ÖAMTC, ✉ A-1010, Schubertring 1, ✆ 71 19 90, Fax 7 13 18 07.

Budapest 208 ④ – München 435 ⑦ – Praha 292 ① – Salzburg 292 ⑦ – Zagreb 362 ⑥.

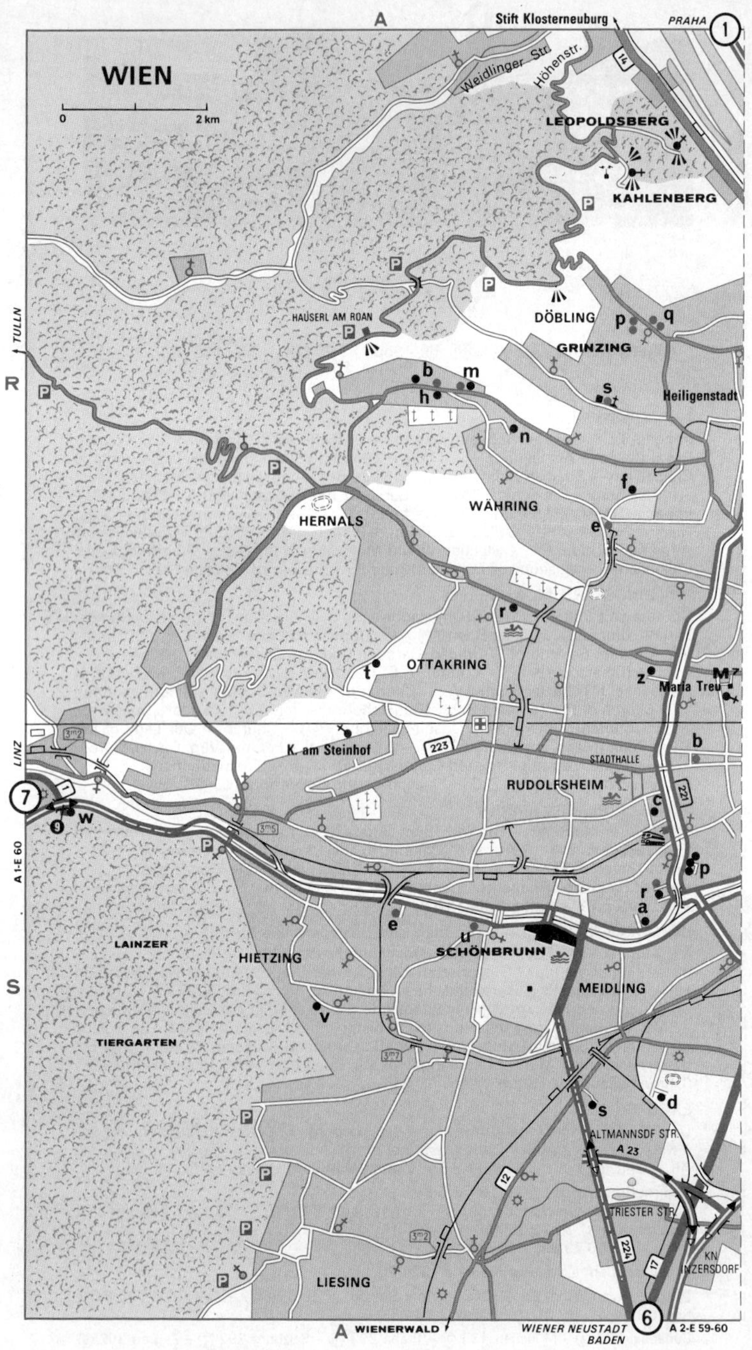
WIEN
0
2 km
A
Stift Klosterneuburg
PRAHA
1
Weidlinger Str.
Höhenstr.
14
LEOPOLDSBERG
KAHLENBERG
HAUSERL AM ROAN
DÖBLING
GRINZING
Heiligenstadt
TULLN
R
HERNALS
WÄHRING
OTTAKRING
Maria Treu
K. am Steinhof
223
STADTHALLE
RUDOLFSHEIM
221
LINZ
7
A1-E 60
LAINZER
HIETZING
SCHÖNBRUNN
MEIDLING
S
TIERGARTEN
ALTMANNSDF STR.
A 23
12
TRIESTER STR.
224
17
KN INZERSDORF
LIESING
A
WIENERWALD
WIENER NEUSTADT
BADEN
6
A 2-E 59-60

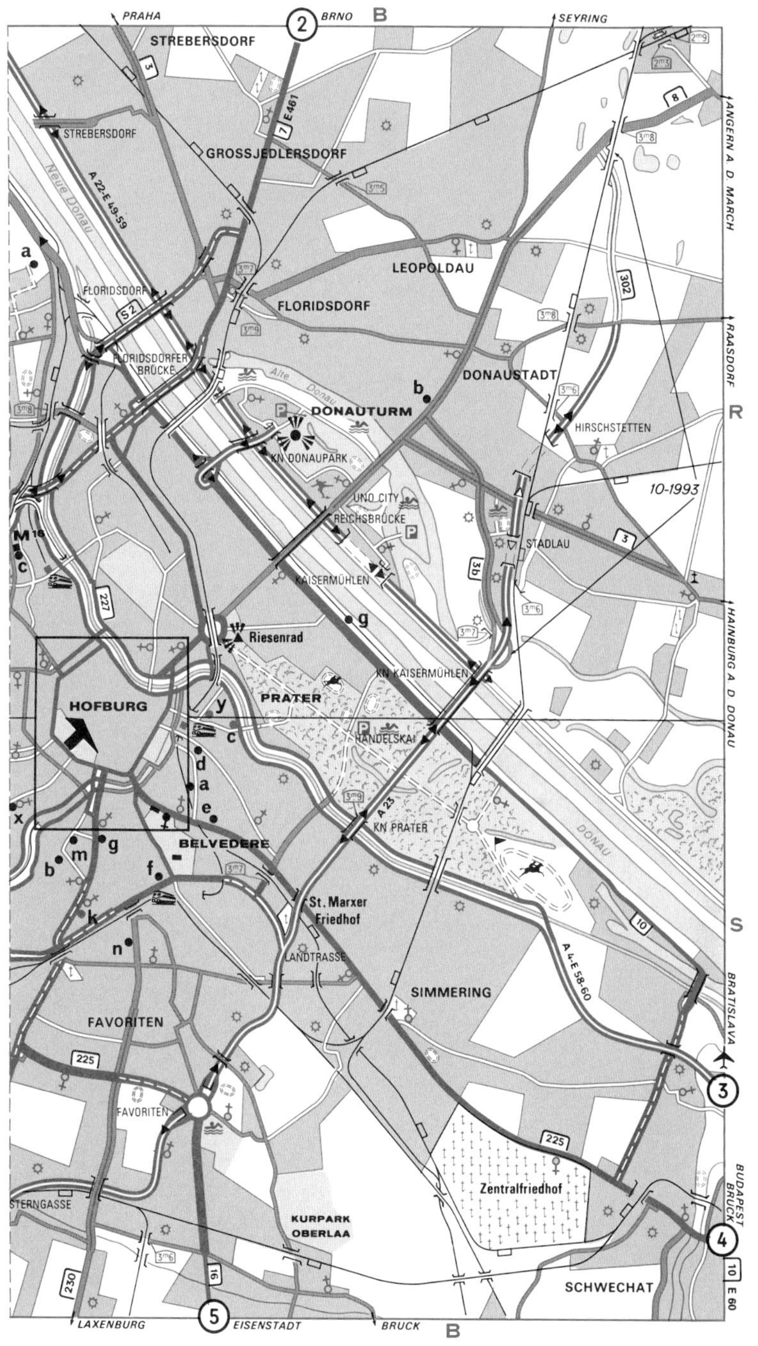
PRAHA
BRNO
SEYRING
STREBERSDORF
GROSSJEDLERSDORF
LEOPOLDAU
FLORIDSDORF
FLORIDSDORFER BRÜCKE
DONAUSTADT
DONAUTURM
KN DONAUPARK
HIRSCHSTETTEN
UNO CITY
REICHSBRÜCKE
STADLAU
KAISERMÜHLEN
10-1993
Riesenrad
HOFBURG
PRATER
KN KAISERMÜHLEN
HANDELSKAI
KN PRATER
BELVEDERE
St. Marxer Friedhof
LANDTRASSE
SIMMERING
FAVORITEN
Zentralfriedhof
STERNGASSE
KURPARK OBERLAA
SCHWECHAT
LAXENBURG
EISENSTADT
BRUCK
ANGERN A. D. MARCH
RAASDORF
HAINBURG A. D. DONAU
BRATISLAVA
BUDAPEST BRUCK
Neue Donau
Alte Donau
DONAU
A 22-E 49-59
A 23
A 4-E 58-60
E 461
E 60

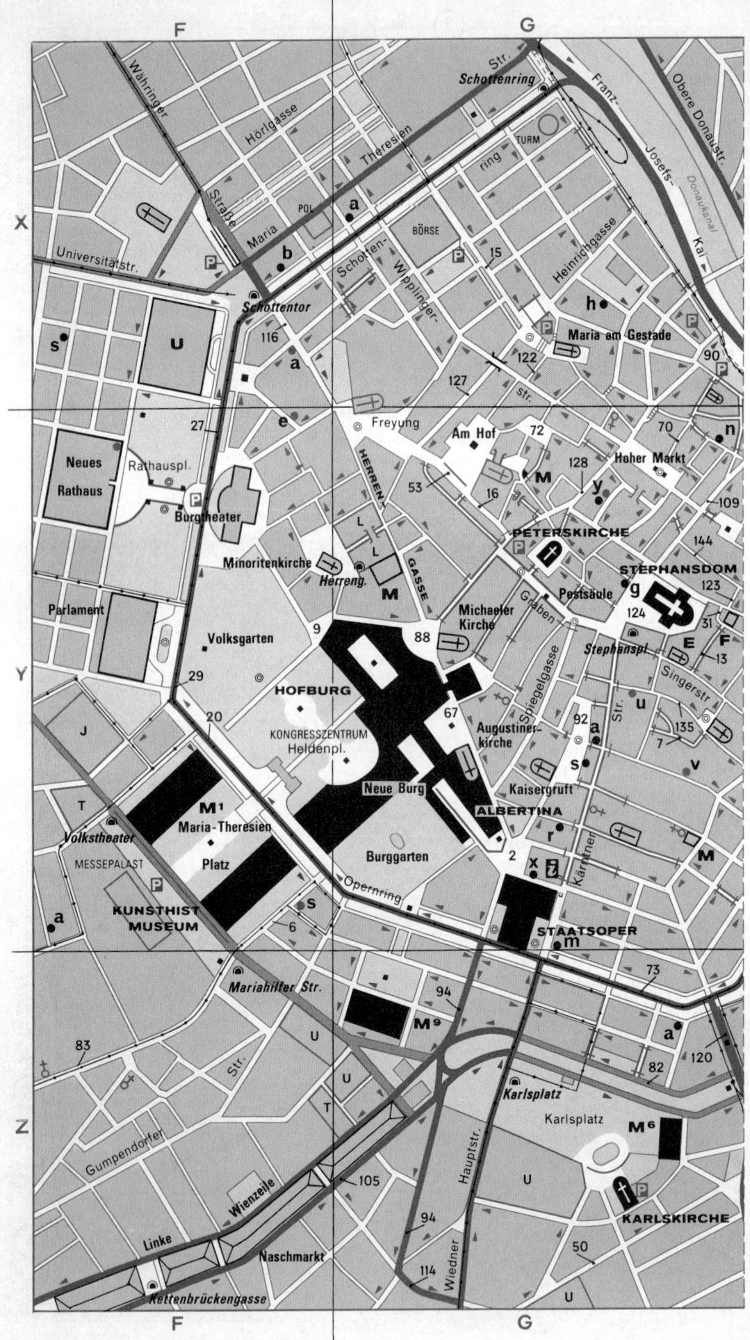
F
G
X
Y
Z
Währinger
Straße
Universitätstr.
Hörlgasse
Maria
Theresien
Str.
Schottenring
ring
TURM
POL
BÖRSE
Franz-
Josefs-
Kai
Obere Donaustr.
Donaukanal
Schotten-
Wipplinger-
Heinrichgasse
Schottentor
Maria am Gestade
U
Neues Rathaus
Rathauspl.
Burgtheater
Freyung
Am Hof
HERREN-
GASSE
Minoritenkirche
Herreng.
Hoher Markt
PETERSKIRCHE
STEPHANSDOM
Pestsäule
Graben
Stephanspl.
Singerstr.
Parlament
Volksgarten
Michaeler Kirche
HOFBURG
KONGRESSZENTRUM
Heldenpl.
Augustiner-kirche
Spiegelgasse
Neue Burg
Kaisergruft
ALBERTINA
Kärntner
Str.
Volkstheater
MESSEPALAST
Maria-Theresien
Platz
Burggarten
Opernring
KUNSTHIST MUSEUM
STAATSOPER
Mariahilfer Str.
Karlsplatz
Gumpendorfer
Wienzeile
Linke
Naschmarkt
Kettenbrückengasse
Hauptstr.
Wiedner
KARLSKIRCHE
34

WIEN

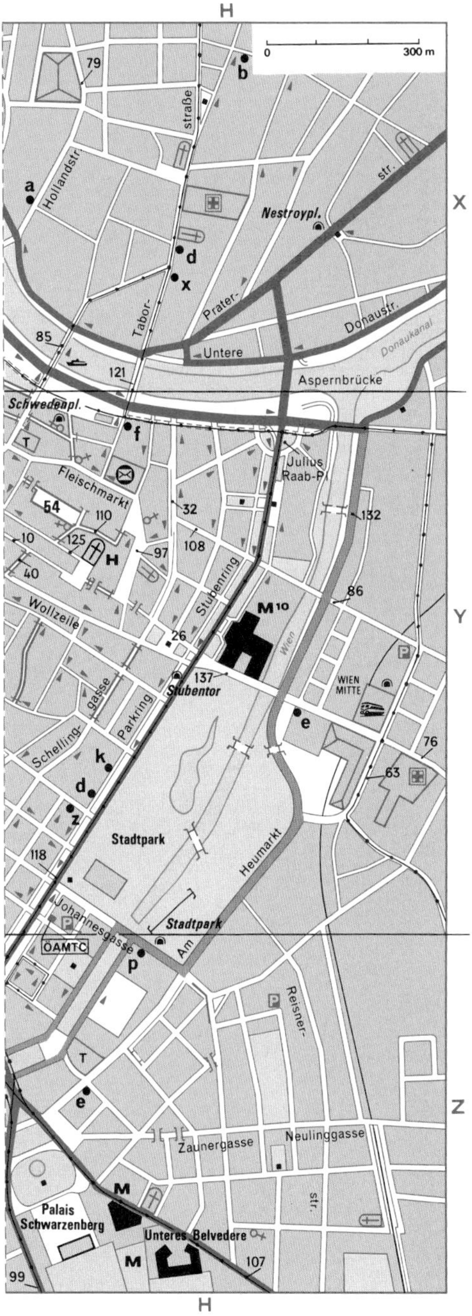

Babenbergestr	FY	6
Graben	GY	
Kärntner Straße	GY	
Landstraßer Hauptstr	HY	76
Mariahilfer Str.	FZ	83
Rotenturmstraße	GY	109
Stephansplatz	GY	124
Tuchlauben	GY	128
Wollzeile	GY	144
Albertinaplatz	GY	2
Ballgasse	GY	7
Ballhausplatz	FY	9
Bäckerstr	HY	10
Blutgasse	GY	13
Börsegasse	GX	15
Bognergasse	GY	16
Burgring	FY	20
Dr. Karl Lueger Platz	HY	26
Dr. Karl Lueger Ring	FY	27
Dr. Renner Ring	FY	29
Domgasse	GY	31
Dominikanerbastei	HY	32
Essiggasse	HY	40
Gußhausstr	GZ	50
Heidenschuß	GY	53
Heiligenkreuzerhof	HY	54
Invalidenstr	HY	63
Josefsplatz	GY	67
Judengasse	GY	70
Judenplatz	GY	72
Kärtner Ring	GZ	73
Leopoldsgasse	HX	79
Lothringerstr	GZ	82
Marienbrücke	HX	85
Marxergasse	HY	86
Michaelerplatz	GY	88
Morzinplatz	GX	90
Neuer Markt	GY	92
Operngasse	GZ	94
Postgasse	HY	97
Prinz Eugen Str.	HZ	99
Rechte Wienzeile	GZ	105
Rennweg	HZ	107
Rosenbursenstr	HY	108
Schönlaterngasse	HY	110
Schleifmühlgasse	GZ	114
Schottengasse	FX	116
Schubertring	HY	118
Schwarzenbergplatz	GZ	120
Schwedenbrücke	HX	121
Strobelgasse	GY	122
Sonnenfelsgasse	HY	125
Tiefer Graben	GX	127
Vordere Zollamtsstr	HY	132
Weihburggasse	GY	135
Weiskirchnerstr	HY	137

Write us...

If you have any comments on the contents of this guide.

Your praise as well as your criticisms will receive careful consideration and, with your assistance, we will be able to add to our stock of information and, where necessary, amend our judgments.

Thank you in advance!

Town Centre, city districts (Stadtbezirke) 1 - 9 :

Imperial (converted 19C palace), Kärntner Ring 16, ✉ A-1015, ℘ 50 11 00, Fax 50110410 - 🛗 ⇔ rm ▤ TV - 🚶 200. AE ⓓ E VISA. ✻ rest GZ **a**
- **Zur Majestät** (booking essential) *(dinner only)* **M** a la carte 500/780 - **Café Imperial M** a la carte 290/530 - **145 rm** ☕ 4350/7500, 22 suites.

✿ **Bristol - Restaurant Korso**, Kärntner Ring 1, ✉ A-1015, ℘ 51 51 60, Telex 112477, Fax 51516550 - 🛗 ⇔ rm ▤ TV - 🚶 150. AE ⓓ E VISA. ✻ rest GYZ **m**
M *(closed Saturday lunch)* a la carte 420/825 - **Rôtisserie Sirk M** a la carte 320/440 - **148 rm** ☕ 3570/5700, 13 suites
Spec. Marinierter Kalbskopf mit Ingwer und Balsamessig, Gebratene Seeforelle auf Petersilienschaum, Soufflierter Scheiterhaufen mit Calvados-Äpfeln.

✿ **Plaza Wien - Restaurant La Scala**, Schottenring 11, ✉ A-1010, ℘ 31 39 00, Telex 135859, Fax 31390160, Massage, Ƒ₅, ≘s - 🛗 ⇔ rm ▤ TV ♿ 🚗 - 🚶 180. AE ⓓ E VISA GX **a**
M *(closed lunch Saturday, Sunday and Bank Holidays)* a la carte 515/760 - **Le Jardin** *(lunch only)* **M** a la carte approx. 390 (buffet) - **223 rm** ☕ 3890/5180, 37 suites
Spec. Terrine von Taschenkrebsen mit Kaviarmousseline, Souffliertes Rehnüsschen "La Scala", Karamelisierte Wiliamsbirne im Strudelblatt mit Schokolade-Minzsorbet.

Sacher, Philharmonikerstr. 4, ✉ A-1010, ℘ 5 14 56, Telex 112520, Fax 51457810, « Collection of valuable furniture and paintings » - 🛗 ▤ TV. AE ⓓ E VISA. ✻ rest GY **x**
M a la carte 470/695 - **118 rm** ☕ 1700/4950, 3 suites.

Hotel im Palais Schwarzenberg, Schwarzenbergplatz 9, ✉ A-1030, ℘ 78 45 15, Telex 136124, Fax 784714, « Converted 1727 baroque palace, park », 🌳, 🎾 - 🛗 TV Ⓟ - 🚶 120. AE ⓓ E VISA. ✻ rest HZ
M a la carte 480/910 - **38 rm** ☕ 2350/7300.

Vienna Hilton, Landstraßer Hauptstr. 2 (near Stadtpark), ✉ A-1030, ℘ 7 17 00, Telex 136799, Fax 7130691 - 🛗 ⇔ rm ▤ TV ♿ 🚗 - 🚶 700. AE ⓓ E VISA. ✻ rest HY **e**
- **Prinz Eugen** (booking essential) *(Saturday and Sunday dinner only)* **M** a la carte 460/760 - **Café am Park M** a la carte 320/510 - **600 rm** ☕ 3110/4590, 25 suites.

Vienna Marriott Hotel, Parkring 12a, ✉ A-1010, ℘ 51 51 80, Telex 112249, Fax 515186736, Massage, ≘s, 🏊 - 🛗 ⇔ rm ▤ TV ♿ 🚗 - 🚶 400. AE ⓓ E VISA. ✻ rest HY **d**
- **Symphonika** *(dinner only, closed Sunday)* **M** a la carte 500/790 - **Parkring-Restaurant M** a la carte 290/600 - **310 rm** ☕ 3060/5380, 7 suites.

Intercontinental, Johannesgasse 28, ✉ A-1037, ℘ 71 12 20, Telex 131235, Fax 7134489, ≘s - 🛗 ⇔ rm ▤ TV ♿ 🚗 - 🚶 1000. AE ⓓ E VISA. ✻ rest HZ **p**
- **Vier Jahreszeiten** *(closed Saturday lunch and Sunday dinner)* **M** a la carte 355/765 - **Brasserie M** a la carte 260/540 - **492 rm** ☕ 2510/4300, 62 suites.

Penta Hotel (former imperial riding school with modern hotel wing), Ungargasse 60, ✉ A-1030, ℘ 71 17 50, Telex 112529, Fax 7117590, Massage, ≘s, 🏊, 🌳 - 🛗 ⇔ rm ▤ TV ♿ - 🚶 500. AE ⓓ E VISA BS **a**
M 290/buffet (lunch) and a la carte 260/450 - **342 rm** ☕ 1900/2900.

Scandic Crown Hotel, Handelskai 269, ✉ A-1020, ℘ 2 17 77/7 27 77, Telex 133318, Fax 21777199, ⛱, ≘s, 🏊 (heated), 🎾 - 🛗 ⇔ rm ▤ TV ♿ Ⓟ - 🚶 300. AE ⓓ E VISA. ✻ rest BR **g**
- **Scandirama** *(dinner only) (closed Monday and Bank Holidays)* **M** a la carte 380/550 - **Symphony M** a la carte 280/460 - **367 rm** ☕ 2125/4450.

SAS-Palais-Hotel, Parkring/Weihburggasse 32, ✉ A-1010, ℘ 51 51 70, Telex 136127, Fax 5122216, ≘s - 🛗 ⇔ rm ▤ TV ♿ - 🚶 100. AE ⓓ E VISA. ✻ rest HY **z**
M *(closed lunch Saturday and Sunday, July - August 2 weeks)* a la carte 470/680 - **149 rm** ☕ 2500/5000, 10 suites.

Hotel de France, Schottenring 3, ✉ A-1010, ℘ 34 35 40, Telex 114360, Fax 3195969, ≘s - 🛗 TV ♿ - 🚶 100. AE ⓓ E VISA. ✻ rest FX **b**
M *(closed Saturday)* a la carte 310/500 - **218 rm** ☕ 2400/3700, 10 suites.

Biedermeier, Landstraßer Hauptstr. 28 (at Sünnhof), ✉ A-1030, ℘ 71 67 10, Telex 111039, Fax 71671503, ⛱ - 🛗 TV 🚗 - 🚶 50. AE ⓓ E VISA BS **d**
M a la carte 360/470 - **204 rm** ☕ 1900/2250, 18 suites.

Ambassador, Neuer Markt 5, ✉ A-1010, ℘ 5 14 66, Telex 111906, Fax 5132999 - 🛗 ▤ TV. AE ⓓ E VISA GY **s**
M a la carte 425/830 - **107 rm** ☕ 1650/4300.

Europa, Neuer Markt 3, ✉ A-1015, ℘ 51 59 40, Telex 112292, Fax 5138138 - 🛗 ▤ TV ☎ - 🚶 60. AE ⓓ E VISA. ✻ rest GY **a**
M *(rest. closed July)* a la carte 350/490 - **102 rm** ☕ 1550/2600.

City-Central without rest, Taborstr. 8a, ✉ A-1020, ℘ 21 10 50, Telex 134570, Fax 21105140 - 🛗 TV ☎ ♿ Ⓟ. AE ⓓ E VISA HX **x**
58 rm ☕ 1540/2590.

Nestroy without rest, Rotensterngasse 12, ✉ A-1020, ☎ 2 11 40, Fax 211407, – rm – 120. AE E VISA HX **b**
62 rm 1550/2300, 7 suites.

Arkadenhof without rest, Viriotgasse 5, ✉ A-1090, ☎ 3 10 08 37, Fax 3107686 – rm – 30. AE E VISA BR **c**
45 rm 1380/1880, 10 suites.

K. u. K. Hotel Maria Theresia without rest, Kirchberggasse 6 - 8, ✉ A-1070, ☎ 5 21 23, Telex 111530, Fax 5212370 – rm – 50. AE E VISA FY **a**
123 rm 1360/2200, 3 suites.

Pannonia, Matrosengasse 6, ✉ A-1060, ☎ 59 90 10, Telex 132940, Fax 5976940 – rm – 80. AE E VISA AS **p**
M a la carte 210/415 – **210 rm** 1420/2210, 6 suites.

Rathauspark without rest, Rathausstr. 17, ✉ A-1010, ☎ 40 41 20, Telex 112817, Fax 40412761 – – 30. AE E VISA FX **s**
117 rm 1260/2300.

K u. K Palais Hotel without rest, Rudolfsplatz 11, ✉ A-1010, ☎ 5 33 13 53, Telex 134049, Fax 533135370 – rm – 50. AE E VISA GX **h**
66 rm 1390/1980.

Alba Palace, Margaretenstr. 92, ✉ A-1050, ☎ 55 46 86, Fax 55468686, – – 100. AE E VISA. rest BS **b**
M a la carte 240/370 – **117 rm** 1350/2600.

Stefanie, Taborstr. 12, ✉ A-1020, ☎ 21 15 00, Telex 134589, Fax 21150160, – – 200. AE E VISA HX **d**
M a la carte 260/400 – **130 rm** 1340/2280.

President, Wallgasse 23, ✉ A-1060, ☎ 5 99 90, Telex 112523, Fax 567646 – – 50. AE E VISA AS **p**
M *(closed Sunday)* a la carte 250/400 – **77 rm** 1350/2800.

Amadeus without rest, Wildpretmarkt 5, ✉ A-1010, ☎ 5 33 87 38, Fax 533873838 – . AE E VISA GY **y**
closed 22 to 26 December – **30 rm** 1030/1800.

Sofitel Hotel Belvedere, Am Heumarkt 35-37, ✉ A-1030, ☎ 71 61 60, Telex 111822, Fax 71616844 – – 30. AE E VISA. rest HZ **e**
M a la carte 230/340 – **211 rm** 1380/2800.

Alba-Accadia, Margaretenstr. 53, ✉ A-1050, ☎ 5 88 50, Telex 113264, Fax 58850899, , – – 80. AE E VISA BS **m**
M a la carte 285/425 – **104 rm** 1350/2600.

Astoria (19C period house with period interior), Führichgasse 1, ✉ A-1015, ☎ 51 57 70, Telex 112856, Fax 5157782 – . AE E VISA GY **r**
M *(closed Saturday and Sunday)* a la carte 400/580 – **108 rm** 1300/2600.

Am Parkring, Parkring 12, ✉ A-1015, ☎ 5 14 80, Telex 113420, Fax 5148040, ← – . AE E VISA. HY **k**
M *(closed Sunday dinner)* a la carte 295/505 – **64 rm** 1590/2280, 3 suites.

Erzherzog Rainer, Wiedner Hauptstr. 27, ✉ A-1040, ☎ 50 11 10, Telex 132329, Fax 50111350 – rest – 50. AE E VISA BS **g**
M *(closed Saturday and Sunday)* a la carte 320/490 – **84 rm** 1680/2260.

Capricorno without rest, Schwedenplatz 3, ✉ A-1010, ☎ 53 33 10 40, Telex 115266, Fax 53376714 – . AE E VISA HY **f**
46 rm 1220/2080.

Kummer, Mariahilfer Str. 71a, ✉ A-1060, ☎ 5 88 95, Telex 111417, Fax 5878133 – rm . AE E VISA BS **x**
M a la carte 215/350 – **103 rm** 1495/2200.

Mercure without rest, Hollandstr. 3, ✉ A-1020, ☎ 21 31 30, Telex 116197, Fax 21313230 – rm . AE E VISA HX **a**
63 rm 1280/2110

Mercure, Fleischmarkt 1a, ✉ A-1010, ☎ 53 46 00, Telex 112048, Fax 53460232 – rm . AE E VISA GY **n**
M a la carte 260/445 – **155 rm** 1280/2110.

Am Stephansplatz, Stephansplatz 9, ✉ A-1010, ☎ 53 40 50, Telex 114334, Fax 53405711 – rest . AE E VISA – (accepted by the hotel only) GY **g**
M *(closed 5 to 30 July)* a la carte 180/410 – **62 rm** 1350/2060.

Prinz Eugen, Wiedner Gürtel 14, ✉ A-1040, ☎ 5 05 17 41, Telex 132483, Fax 505174119 – rm . AE E VISA BS **f**
M a la carte 240/400 – **112 rm** 1495/2200.

Ibis, Mariahilfer Gürtel 22, ✉ A-1060, ☎ 56 56 26, Telex 133833, Fax 564368 – – 120. AE E VISA AS **p**
M a la carte 210/370 – **341 rm** 1050/1450.

Astra am Rennweg, Rennweg 51, ✉ A-1030, ☎ 7 13 25 21, Telex 131797, Fax 7145930 – . AE E VISA BS **e**
M *(closed Sunday dinner)* a la carte 240/440 – **168 rm** 1280/1880.

XXXX ✿✿ **Steirereck**, Rasumofskygasse 2 / Ecke Weißgerberlände, ✉ A-1030, ✆ 7 13 31 68, Fax 7135168 – AE VISA – *closed Saturday, Sunday and Bank Holidays* – **M** *(remarkable wine-list, visit of the wine-cellar possible)* (booking essential) a la carte 500/850 BS **c**
Spec. Kalbskopf in 3 Gängen serviert, Steinbutt in Apfelmostessigsauce mit Rauchlachs-Ravioli, Geeister Haselnußspitz mit Himbeeren.

XXX ✿ **Drei Husaren**, Weihburggasse 4, ✉ A-1010, ✆ 51 21 09 20, Fax 512109218 – AE DC E VISA GY **u**
closed mid July - mid August and 24 to 28 December – **M** a la carte 550/780
Spec. Hors d'œuvres vom Wagen, Gekochter Tafelspitz mit Apfelkren und Schnittlauchsauce, Gefüllte Kalbsniere mit glacierten Rübchen.

XXX ✿ **Gottfried**, Untere Viaduktgasse 45/Marxergasse, ✉ A-1030, ✆ 7 13 82 56, Fax 713355130 – AE VISA BRS **y**
closed Saturday lunch and Bank Holidays, May - September closed Saturday and Sunday – **M** *(booking essential)* (remarkable wine list) a la carte 440/750
Spec. Variationen von der Gänseleber, Gratinierter Steinbutt mit Hummer und Limettenbutter, Schokolademousseterrine mit Moccasabayon.

XXX **Grotta Azzurra** (Italian rest.), Babenberger Str. 5, ✉ A-1010, ✆ 5 86 10 44, Fax 586104415 – AE DC E VISA FY **s**
closed Sunday, mid July - mid August and 24 to 27 December – **M** a la carte 370/580.

XXX Kupferdachl, Schottengasse 7 (entrance Mölker Bastei), ✉ A-1010, ✆ 63 93 81, Fax 5354042 FX **a**

XXX **Steirer Stub'n**, Wiedner Hauptstr. 111, ✉ A-1050, ✆ 55 43 49, Fax 550888 – AE DC E VISA
closed Sunday and Bank Holidays – **M** *(booking essential)* a la carte 330/480. BS **k**

XX **Schubertstüberln**, Schreyvogelgasse 4, ✉ A-1010, ✆ 5 33 71 87, Fax 5353546, 🏖 – DC E VISA FXY **e**
closed Saturday, Sunday and 24 December - 6 January – **M** a la carte 300/565.

XX **Steinerne Eule**, Halbgasse 30, ✉ A-1070, ✆ 93 22 50, Fax 5233818, 🏖 – AE DC E VISA
closed Sunday and Monday – **M** a la carte 360/550. AS **b**

XX **Zum Kuckuck**, Himmelpfortgasse 15, ✉ A-1010, ✆ 5 12 84 70, Fax 5233818 – AE E VISA
closed Saturday, Sunday and 3 weeks July - August – **M** a la carte 350/570. GY **v**

XX **Wiener Rathauskeller** (vaults with murals), Rathausplatz 1, ✉ A-1010, ✆ 4 21 21 90, Fax 42121927 – AE DC E VISA FY
closed Sunday and Bank Holidays – **M** a la carte 290/480 🎵.

XX Salut, Wildpretmarkt 3, ✉ A-1010, ✆ 5 33 13 22 GY **y**

X Leupold, Schottengasse 7, ✉ A-1010, ✆ 5 33 93 81 FX **a**

City districts (Stadtbezirke) 10 - 15 :

🏨 **Wien Renaissance Hotel**, Ullmannstr. 71, ✉ A-1150, ✆ 8 50 40, Telex 112206, Fax 8504100, ≘s, 🏊 – |♦| ⇔ rm ▤ TV 🚗 – 🎪 200. AE DC E VISA. ✻ rest AS **a**
– **Orangerie** *(closed Saturday and Sunday)* **M** a la carte 370/730 – **Allegro M** 320 (buffet only) – **309 rm** ☕ 2100/2450, 3 suites.

🏨 **Bosei** 🐦, Gutheil-Schoder-Gasse 9, ✉ A-1100, ✆ 66 10 60, Fax 66106-99 – |♦| ⇔ rm TV ☎ P – 🎪 200. AE DC E VISA AS **d**
M a la carte 320/470 – **185 rm** ☕ 1700/2100, 8 suites.

🏨 **Trend-Hotel Favorita**, Laxenburger Str. 8-10, ✉ A-1100, ✆ 60 14 60, Fax 60146720, ≘s – |♦| TV ☎ 🚗 – 🎪 200. AE E VISA BS **n**
M a la carte 260/400 – **161 rm** ☕ 1290/1580, 4 suites.

🏨 **Gartenhotel Altmannsdorf** 🐦, Hoffingergasse 26, ✉ A-1120, ✆ 8 04 75 27, Telex 135327, Fax 804752751, 🏖, Park, ≘s – |♦| TV ☎ 🚗 – 🎪 120. AE DC E VISA
closed 23 to 29 December – **M** a la carte 255/415 – **41 rm** ☕ 1200/1550. AS **s**

🏨 **Austrotel**, Felberstr. 4, ✉ A-1150, ✆ 98 11 10, Fax 98111930, ≘s – |♦| ⇔ rm TV ☎ ♿ 🚗 – 🎪 260. AE DC E VISA AS **c**
M a la carte 245/470 – **254 rm** ☕ 1620/2900.

🏨 **Reither** without rest, Graumanngasse 16, ✉ A-1150, ✆ 85 61 65, Telex 136430, Fax 855244, ≘s, 🏊 – |♦| TV ☎ 🚗. AE DC E VISA AS **r**
closed 22 to 27 December – **50 rm** ☕ 1000/1500.

🏨 **Arabella - Hotel Jagdschloß** without rest, Jagdschloßgasse 79, ✉ A-1130, ✆ 8 04 35 08, Fax 8043500, 🏊 (heated), 🌳 – |♦| TV ☎ 🚗 AS **v**
closed 3 January - 19 February – **48 rm** ☕ 1080/1900.

XXX **Villa Hans Moser**, Auhofstr. 76 - 78, ✉ A-1130, ✆ 87 74 74 70, Fax 8776050, 🏖 – ▤ rest. AE DC E VISA. ✻ AS **e**
closed Sunday and Monday – **M** a la carte 490/740.

XXX **Altwienerhof** with rm, Herklotzgasse 6, ✉ A-1150, ✆ 8 92 60 00, Fax 89260008, « Winter garden, court terrace » – |♦| TV ☎. VISA AS **r**
M *(closed Saturday lunch, Sunday, Bank Holidays and 1 to 24 January)* (remarkable wine list) a la carte 445/695 – **23 rm** ☕ 580/1800.

XX **Hietzinger Bräu**, Auhofstr. 1, ✉ A-1130, ✆ 87 77 70 87, Fax 877708722 AS **u**
closed mid July - mid August and 24 to 27 December – **M** *(mainly boiled beef dishes)* a la carte 305/540.

City districts (Stadtbezirke) 16 - 19 :

Modul, Peter-Jordan-Str. 78, A-1190, 47 66 00, Telex 116736, Fax 47660117 - 100. AR f
M a la carte 310/470 - **43 rm** 1450/2500, 8 suites.

Clima Villenhotel, Nussberggasse 2c, A-1190, 37 15 16, Telex 115670, Fax 371392, « Rest. Bockkeller, vaulted cellar with Tyrolian farmhouse furniture », - 70. BR a
M *(closed Sunday)* a la carte 335/480 - **30 rm** 1750/2500.

Landhaus Fuhrgassl-Huber without rest, Rathstr. 24, A-1190, 44 30 33, Fax 442714, « Country house atmosphere », AR m
closed 2 weeks February - **22 rm** 1060/1550.

Schloß Wilhelminenberg, Savoyenstr. 2, A-1160, 45 85 03, Telex 132008, Fax 454876, « Terrace with ≤ Vienna, Park » - 120. AR t
M a la carte 230/390 - **90 rm** 890/1320.

Maté (with guest-house), Ottakringer Str. 34, A-1170, 4 04 55, Telex 115485, Fax 40455888, AR z
M a la carte 245/480 - **125 rm** 1380/2200.

Gartenhotel Glanzing without rest, Glanzinggasse 23, A-1190, 47 04 27 20, Fax 470427214, - **20 rm** 1180/2200. AR n

Jäger without rest, Hernalser Hauptstr. 187, A-1170, 4 66 62 00/48 66 62 00, Fax 48666208 - **18 rm** 950/1400. AR r

Celtes without rest, Celtesgasse 1a, A-1190, 44 41 51, Fax 444152116 - **16 rm**. AR b

Schild without rest, Neustift am Walde 97, A-1190, 4 42 19 10, Fax 44219153, - **33 rm** 840/1320. AR h

Eckel, Sieveringer Str. 46, A-1190, 32 32 18, Fax 326660, AR s
closed Sunday, Monday, August 2 weeks and 24 December - 18 January - **M** a la carte 230/570.

Sailer, Gersthofer Str. 14, A-1180, 47 21 21/47 92 12 12, Fax 4721214/47921214,
closed Sunday and Bank Holidays - **M** a la carte 280/470. AR e

City district (Stadtbezirk) 22 :

Trend Hotel Donauzentrum, Wagramer Str. 83, A-1220, 2 35 54 50, Telex 113785, Fax 235545183, - 60. BR b
M a la carte 210/380 - **137 rm** 1290/2200.

Heurigen and Buschen-Schänken (wine gardens) - (mostly self-service, hot and cold dishes from buffet, prices according to weight of chosen meals, therefore not shown below. Buschen-Schänken sell their own wines only) :

Oppolzer, Himmelstr. 22, A-1190, 32 24 16, Fax 3224160, « Garden » - AR p
closed Sunday and 23 December - 6 January - **M** (dinner only).

Altes Preßhaus, Cobenzlgasse 15, A-1190, 32 23 93, Telex 132211, Fax 32234285, « Old vaulted wine cellar » - AR p
closed January and February Sunday to Wednesday - **M** (dinner only) (buffet).

Wolff, Rathstr. 44, A-1190, 44 23 35, Fax 441403, « Terraced garden » AR m
M (buffet).

Fuhrgassl Huber, Neustift am Walde 68, A-1190, 44 14 05, Fax 442730, (wine-garden with Viennese Schrammelmusik), « Court-terrace » - AR b
closed February 3 weeks - **M** (buffet).

Grinzinger Hauermandl, Cobenzlgasse 20, A-1190, 3 22 04 44, Fax 32571322, - *closed Sunday* - **M** (dinner only) a la carte 180/380. AR q

Grinzinger Weinbottich, Cobenzlgasse 28, A-1190, 32 42 37, Fax 32571322, « Shady garden » - AR q
closed Monday - **M** (dinner only) a la carte 170/350.

at Auhof motorway station W : 8 km :

Novotel Wien-West, Wientalstraße, A-1140, (01) 9 72 54 20, Telex 135584, Fax 974140, (heated), rest - 300 - **115 rm**. AS w

at Perchtoldsdorf **A-2380** by B12 and Breitenfurter Str. AS :

Jahreszeiten, Hochstr. 17, (01) 8 65 31 29 - *closed Saturday lunch, Sunday dinner and Monday, February 1 week and July - August 4 weeks* - **M** a la carte 450/570.

at Vösendorf **A-2334** S : 11 km by ⑥ or A 2 AS :

Novotel Wien-Süd, Nordring 4 (Shopping City Süd), (01) 6 92 60 10, Telex 134793, Fax 694859, (heated) - rm rest - 250 - **102 rm**.

at Groß-Enzersdorf **A-2301** E : 16 km, by B 3 BR :

Am Sachsengang, Schloßhofer Str. 60 (B 3), (02249) 2 90 10, Fax 2905, « Terrace », Massage, - 200. - (accepted by the hotel only)
closed 22 to 26 December - **M** a la carte 375/550 - **102 rm** 900/1700.

SALZBURG **5020.** Austria 413 W 23, 426 K 5, 413 W 23 – pop. 140 000 – alt. 425 m – ☎ 0662.

See : < ★★ on the town (from the Mönchsberg) X and <★★ (from Hettwer Bastei)Y – Hohensalzburg ★★ X, Z : <★★ (from the Kuenburg Bastion), ✳★★ (from the Reck Tower), Museum (Burgmuseum)★ – St. Peter's Churchyard (Petersfriedhof)★★ Z – St. Peter's Church (Stiftskirche St. Peter)★★ Z – Residenz★★ Z – Natural History Museum (Haus der Natur)★★ Y **M2** – Franciscan's Church (Franziskanerkirche)★ Z **A** – Getreidegasse★ Y – Mirabell Gardens (Mirabellgarten)★ V (Grand Staircase ★★ of the castle) – Baroquemuseum ★ V **M 3** – Dom★ Z.

Envir. : Road to the Gaisberg (Gaisbergstraße)★★ (<★) by ① – Untersberg★ by ② : 10 km (with cable car) – Castle Hellbrunn (Schloß Hellbrunn) ★ by Nonntaler Hauptstraße X.

9 Salzburg-Wals, Schloß Klessheim, ☎ 85 08 51 ; 9 Hof (① : 20 km), ☎ (06229) 23 90 ; 18 St. Lorenz (① : 29 km), ☎ (06232) 38 35.

✈ Innsbrucker Bundesstr. 95 (by ③), ☎ 85 12 23 - City Air Terminal, Südtiroler Platz (Autobus Station) V 🚗 ☎ 71 54 14 22.

Exhibition Centre (Messegelände), Linke Glanzeile 65, ☎ 3 45 66.

ℹ Tourist Information, Mozartplatz 5, ☎ 84 75 68.

ÖAMTC, Alpenstr. 102 (by ②), ☎ 2 05 01, Fax 2050145.

Wien 292 ① – Innsbruck 177 ③ – München 140 ③.

SALZBURG

Auerspergstraße . . . . V 3
Bürglsteinstraße . . . . X 5
Erzabt-Klotz-Str. . . . . X 9
Gstättengasse . . . . X 12
Kaiserschützenstr. . . . . V 20
Nonntaler Hauptstr. . . . . X 29
Späthgasse . . . . X 37

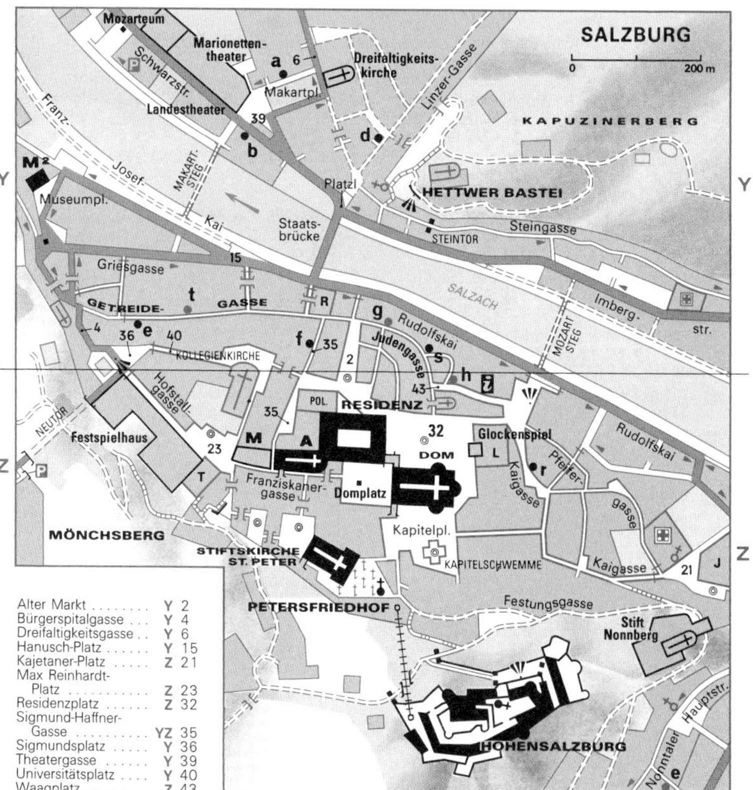

Österreichischer Hof, Schwarzstr. 5, ✆ 8 89 77, Telex 633590, Fax 8897714, « Salzach-side setting, terrace with ≤ old town and castle » – |₿| ⇆ rm ▤ TV ♿ 🚗 – 🏛 70. AE ⓓ E VISA — Y **b**
– **Zirbelzimmer M** a la carte 425/675 – **Salzach-Grill M** a la carte 230/455 – **119 rm** 2250/4900, 7 suites.

Salzburg Sheraton Hotel, Auerspergstr. 4, ✆ 88 99 90, Telex 632518, Fax 881776, « Terrace in spa gardens », entrance to the spa facilities – |₿| ⇆ rm ▤ TV ♿ 🚗 – 🏛 150. AE ⓓ E VISA. ✂ rest — V **s**
Mirabell M a la carte 470/850 – **Bistro M** a la carte 200/450 – **165 rm** ☕ 2800/5900, 9 suites.

Radisson Hotel Altstadt, Judengasse 15, ✆ 8 48 57 10, Fax 8485716, « Modernized 14C Patrician house, antique furnishings » – |₿| ⇆ rm TV – 🏛 35. AE ⓓ E VISA. ✂ rest — Y **s**
closed 3 weeks February – **M** a la carte 410/580 – **62 rm** ☕ 2800/6800, 16 suites.

Bristol, Makartplatz 4, ✆ 87 35 57, Telex 633337, Fax 8735576 – |₿| ▤ rest TV – 🏛 80. AE ⓓ E VISA. ✂ rest — Y **a**
closed early January - end March – **M** *(closed Sunday and Monday)* a la carte 370/700 – **75 rm** ☕ 2250/5200, 8 suites.

Salzburg Penta Hotel, Fanny-von-Lehnert-Str. 2, ✆ 4 68 80, Telex 632695, Fax 4688298, ⛲, Massage, ≘s, ▣ – |₿| ⇆ rm ▤ TV ♿ 🚗 – 🏛 750. AE ⓓ E VISA. ✂ rest
M *(closed Saturday lunch, Sunday dinner)* a la carte 290/470 – **257 rm** ☕ 2000/4800, 3 suites.
by Kaiserschützenstraße — V

Goldener Hirsch, Getreidegasse 37, ✆ 84 85 11, Telex 632967, Fax 848517845, « 15C Patrician house, tastefully furnished » – |₿| ⇆ rm ▤ TV – 🏛 40. AE ⓓ E VISA — Y **e**
M a la carte 450/650 – **71 rm** ☕ 2660/6500, 3 suites.

Schloß Mönchstein 🔇, Am Mönchsberg 26, ✆ 8 48 55 50, Telex 632080, Fax 848559, ≤ Salzburg and environs, ⛲, « Small castle with elegant, stylish furnishings, wedding chapel, park », 🌳, 🎾 – |₿| TV Ⓟ – 🏛 30. AE ⓓ E VISA. ✂ rest — X **e**
closed February – **M** a la carte 490/800 – **17 rm** ☕ 2400/8000.

Holiday Inn Crowne Plaza, Rainerstr. 6, 8 89 78, Telex 633532, Fax 878893, , , – – 200. V **n**
200 rm.

Rosenberger, Bessarabierstr. 94, 43 55 46, Telex 3622405, Fax 43951095, – rm – 450. by ④
M a la carte 210/380 – **120 rm** 1060/1850.

Mercure, Bayerhamerstr. 14, 8 81 43 80, Telex 632341, Fax 871111411, – rm – 150. V **t**
M a la carte 268/450 – **121 rm** 1800/2100.

Dorint-Hotel, Sterneckstr. 20, 88 20 31, Telex 631075, Fax 8820319, – rest – 200. V **z**
M 210/buffet (lunch) and a la carte 290/460 – **140 rm** 1260/2860.

Theater-Hotel, Schallmooser Hauptstr. 13, 8 81 68 10, Telex 632319, Fax 88168692, , – – 40. . rest V **y**
M *(closed Sunday)* a la carte 220/390 – **58 rm** 1550/2260, 11 suites.

Carlton without rest, Markus-Sittikus-Str. 3, 88 21 91, Fax 87478447, – . V **c**
40 rm 1400/2420, 13 suites.

Austrotel, Mirabellplatz 8, 88 16 88, Telex 632361, Fax 881687 – – 45 V **a**
73 rm.

Novotel Salzburg City, Franz-Josef-Str. 26, 88 20 41, Telex 632886, Fax 874240 – – 110. V **k**
M a la carte 260/430 – **140 rm** 1310/2220.

Europa without rest, Rainerstr. 31, 88 99 30, Telex 633424, Fax 889938 – – 80. V **b**
104 rm 1310/2100.

Schaffenrath, Alpenstr. 115, 23 15 30, Telex 633207, Fax 29314, , Massage, – – 80. by ②
M a la carte 200/400 – **50 rm** 1050/2800.

K u. K Hotel Stieglbräu, Rainerstr. 14, 8 89 92(hotel) 87 76 94(rest.), Telex 633671, Fax 8899271, – – 25 V **g**
50 rm.

Kasererhof, Alpenstr. 6, 2 12 65, Telex 633477, Fax 2126550, , – by ②
54 rm – 6 suites.

Zum Hirschen, St.-Julien-Str. 21, 88 90 30, Telex 632691, Fax 8890358, , Massage, – V **r**
70 rm – 5 suites.

Hohenstauffen without rest, Elisabethstr. 19, 87 76 69, Fax 87219351 – . V **e**
27 rm 1060/1960.

Fuggerhof without rest, Eberhard-Fugger-Str. 9, 6 41 29 00, Telex 632533, Fax 6412904, , , , – . by Bürglsteinstr. X
closed 20 December - 20 January – **20 rm** 950/2400.

Elefant, Sigmund-Haffner-Gasse 4, 84 33 97, Telex 632725, Fax 84010928 – . Y **f**
M *(closed Tuesday except August)* a la carte 200/390 – **38 rm** 770/2100.

Nußdorfer Hof without rest, Moosstr. 36, 82 48 38, Telex 632515, Fax 8249379, , (heatet), , – . X **k**
closed November – **35 rm** 680/2160.

Gablerbräu, Linzer Gasse 9, 8 89 65, Telex 631067, Fax 8896555, – – 60. Y **d**
M a la carte 180/390 – **52 rm** 1000/2220.

Wolf-Dietrich, Wolf-Dietrich-Str. 7, 87 12 75, Telex 633877, Fax 882320, , – . V **m**
closed early February - mid March – **M** *(closed Sunday)* (dinner only) a la carte 250/360 – **30 rm** 830/1880.

Mozart, Getreidegasse 22 (1st floor,), 84 37 46, Fax 846852 – Y **t**
closed Wednesday and Thursday – **M** *(booking essential)* (Monday - Friday dinner only) a la carte 390/600.

K u. K Restaurant am Waagplatz, Waagplatz 2 (1st floor), 84 21 56, Fax 84215633, , « Medieval dinner with period performance in the Freysauff-Keller (by arrangement) » Z **h**

Zum Mohren, Judengasse 9, 84 23 87 – Y **g**
closed Sunday, Bank Holidays and 1 to 30 June – **M** *(booking essential)* a la carte 280/430.

Riedenburg, Neutorstr. 31, 89 12 90, – . X **a**
closed Monday lunch, Sunday and 2 weeks June – **M** a la carte 320/550.

at Salzburg-Aigen **A-5026** by Bürglsteinstr. X :

Doktorwirt, Glaser Str. 9, ☎ 62 29 73, Telex 632938, Fax 62897524, (heated), – TV ☎ P. AE O E VISA. rest – *closed 9 to 25 February and mid October - November* – **M** *(closed Monday)* a la carte 200/400 – **39 rm** 800/1600.

XX **Gasthof Schloß Aigen**, Schwarzenbergpromenade 37, ☎ 62 12 84, Fax 621284, – P. AE O E VISA
closed Thursday lunch, Wednesday, 1 week February and 2 weeks September – **M** a la carte 280/490.

at Salzburg-Hellbrunn **A-5020** by Nonntaler Hauptstraße X :

Maria-Theresien-Schlößl, Morzger Str. 87, ☎ 82 01 91, Telex 633440, Fax 82019113, « Park » – TV ☎ P. AE O E VISA
closed early January - February – **M** *(closed Monday except festival)* a la carte 350/580 – **14 rm** 1200/2400.

at Salzburg-Liefering **A-5020** by ④ :

Brandstätter, Münchner Bundesstr. 69, ☎ 43 45 35, Fax 43453590, – TV ☎ P – 40
closed 22 to 27 December – **M** *(closed 2 to 16 January)* (booking essential) a la carte 280/570 – **36 rm** 1050/2800.

at Salzburg-Maria Plain **A-5101** by Plainstr. V :

Maria Plain (17C inn), Plainbergweg 41, ☎ 5 07 01, Telex 632801, Fax 5070119, « Garden with ≤ » – TV ☎ P – 40
30 rm – 5 suites.

at Salzburg-Parsch **A-5020** by Bürglsteinstr. X :

Fondachhof, Gaisbergstr. 46, ☎ 64 13 31, Fax 641576, ≤, « 18C manor house in a park », (heated), – TV P – 25. AE O E VISA. rest
April - October – **M** (residents only) – **28 rm** 1200/40000, 4 suites.

Villa Pace, Sonnleitenweg 9, ☎ 64 15 01, Telex 631141, Fax 6415015, ≤ town and Hohensalzburg, (heated), – TV ☎ P. AE O E VISA
March - October – **M** *(closed Sunday)* (booking essential) a la carte 490/740 – **12 rm** 2600/4500, 5 suites.

on the Heuberg NE : 3 km by ① – alt. 565 m

Schöne Aussicht, Heuberg 3, ✉ A-5023 Salzburg, ☎ (0662) 64 06 08, Fax 6406902, « Garden with ≤ Salzburg and Alps », – TV ☎ P – 30. AE O E VISA
April - October – **M** *(closed Sunday)* a la carte 285/530 – **30 rm** 900/2000.

on the Gaisberg by ① :

Kobenzl, Gaisberg 11, alt. 750 m, ✉ A-5020 Salzburg, ☎ (0662) 64 15 10, Telex 633833, Fax 642238, « Beautiful panoramic location with ≤ Salzburg and Alps », Massage, – TV P – 40. AE O E VISA. rest
closed 26 December - 4 January – **M** a la carte 350/560 – **35 rm** 1490/5550, 4 suites.

Romantik-Hotel Gersberg Alm, Gersberg 37, alt. 800, ✉ A-5023 Salzburg-Gnigl, ☎ (0662) 64 12 57, Fax 64125780, – TV ☎ P – 55. AE O E VISA
closed 8 January - February – **M** a la carte 280/550 – **36 rm** 1200/3100.

Beim Flughafen by ③ :

Airporthotel, Loigstr. 20a, ✉ A-5020 Salzburg-Loig, ☎ (0662) 85 00 20, Telex 633634, Fax 85002044, – rm TV ☎ P – 25. AE O E VISA
M (residents only) (dinner only) – **36 rm** 1200/2600.

at Anif **A-5081** ② : 7 km – 06246 :

Friesacher, ☎ 20 75, Fax 207549, – TV ☎ P – 25
closed 2 to 22 January – **M** *(closed Wednesday)* a la carte 230/400 – **70 rm** 800/1820.

Point Hotel, Berchtesgadener Str.364, ☎ 42 56, Telex 631003, Fax 4256443, Massage, (heated), (covered court) – TV ☎ P – 100
62 rm.

Hubertushof, Neu Anif 4 (near motorway exit Salzburg Süd), ☎ 24 78, Telex 632684, Fax 421768, – TV ☎ P – 60. AE VISA.
M *(closed Monday, 2 weeks February and 3 weeks July)* a la carte 275/445 – **68 rm** 830/1540.

Romantik-Hotel Schloßwirt (17C inn with Biedermeier furniture), Halleiner Bundesstr. 22, ☎ 21 75, Fax 217580, – TV ☎ P – 20 – **29 rm**.

at Elixhausen **A-5161** N : 8 km by ⑤ :

Romantik-Hotel Gmachl, Dorfstr. 14, ☎ (0662) 5 87 97, Fax 5879772, (indoor court), (indoor) – TV ☎ P – 40
closed 2 weeks June – **M** *(closed Monday lunch and Sunday)* a la carte 225/460 – **34 rm** 660/1950, 3 suites.

at Hof A-5322 ① : 20 km :

Schloß Fuschl (former 15C hunting seat with 3 guest-houses), (06229) 2 25 30, Telex 633454, Fax 2253531, ←, Massage, - 130. AE ① E VISA. rest
M a la carte 500/770 - **84 rm** 1800/3700, 12 suites.

Jagdhof am Fuschlsee (former 18C farmhouse with guest-house), (06229) 2 37 20, Telex 633454, Fax 2372413, ←, « Hunting museum », - - 180. AE ① E VISA
M a la carte 205/400 - **50 rm** 680/1500.

at Fuschl am See A-5330 ① : 26 km :

Parkhotel Waldhof, Seepromenade, (06226) 2 64, Fax 644, ←, Massage, - - 90. rest
closed November - 20 December - **M** (booking essential) a la carte 270/500 - **68 rm** 810/2400.

Brunnwirt, (06226) 2 36, - . AE ① E VISA.
dinner only except during the festival, closed Sunday and 7 to 31 January - **M** (booking essential) a la carte 395/620.

at Mondsee ① : 28 km (by motorway A 1) - 06232 :

Seehof, (SE : 7 km), A-5311 Loibichl, 2 55 00, Fax 255051, ←, Massage, -
31 rm - 10 suites.

Landhaus Eschlböck-Plomberg with rm, (S : 5 km), A-5310 St. Lorenz - Plomberg, 35 72, Fax 316620, ←, Landing Jetty - rest . AE ① E VISA
closed 3 weeks January - **M** *(closed September - June Tuesday and Wednesday)* (booking essential) a la carte 440/730 - **14 rm** 950/2500
Spec. Gänsestopfleberparfait, Fische aus dem Mondsee mit Veltiner Sauce, Marillenstrudel mit Marilleneis.

Weißes Kreuz - Restaurant Cantagallo (Italian rest.), Herzog-Odilo-Str. 25, A-5310 Mondsee, 22 54, Fax 225434, - . AE
closed Monday and 11 November - 15 December - **M** (booking essential) (remarkable wine list) a la carte 450/760
Spec. Gratinierter Tintenfisch mit Basilikum, Saibling im Schwammerlfond, Schokoladenblätter mit Cappuccinomus.

Benelux

Belgium

BRUSSELS - ANTWERP - BRUGES - LIÈGE

Grand Duchy of Luxembourg

LUXEMBOURG

Netherlands

AMSTERDAM - The HAGUE - ROTTERDAM

PRACTICAL INFORMATION

LOCAL CURRENCY

Belgian Franc: 100 F = 3.00 US $ = 2.49 Ecus (Jan. 93) can also be used in Luxembourg

Dutch Florin: 100 Fl. = 54.40 US $ = 45.66 Ecus (Jan. 93)

TOURIST INFORMATION

Telephone numbers and addresses of Tourist Offices are given in the text of each city under ℹ.

AIRLINES

SABENA : rue Cardinal Mercier 35, 1000 Bruxelles, ☎ (02) 511 90 30, 70, Grand-Rue, L-1660 Luxembourg, ☎ 22 12 12, Weteringschans 26, 1017 SG Amsterdam, ☎ (020) 626 29 66.

LUXAIR : Luxembourg Airport, L-2987 Luxembourg, ☎ 43 61 61.

KLM : avenue Marnix 28, 1050 Bruxelles, ☎ (02) 507 70 70, 1, rue du Potager, L-2347 Luxembourg, ☎ 42 48 42, Amsterdamseweg 55, 1182 GP Amsterdam, ☎ (020) 649 91 23.

FOREIGN EXCHANGE

In Belgium, banks close at 3.30pm and weekends;

in the Netherlands, banks close at 5.00pm and weekends, Schiphol Airport exchange offices open daily from 6.30am to 11.30pm.

TRANSPORT

Taxis: may be hailed in the street, at taxi ranks or called by telephone.

Bus, tramway: practical for long and short distances and good for sightseeing.

Brussels has a **Métro** (subway) network. In each station complete information and plans will be found.

POSTAL SERVICES

Post offices open Monday to Friday from 9am to 5pm in Benelux.

SHOPPING

Shops and boutiques are generally open from 9am to 7pm in Belgium and Luxembourg, and from 9am to 6pm in the Netherlands. The main shopping areas are:

in Brussels: Rue Neuve, Porte de Namur, Avenue Louise - Also Brussels antique market on Saturday from 9am to 3pm, and Sunday from 9am to 1pm (around place du Grand-Sablon) - Flower and Bird market (Grand-Place) on Sunday morning.

in Amsterdam: Kalverstraat, Leidsestraat, Nieuwendijk, P.C. Hoofstraat and Utrechtsestraat. Second-hand goods and antiques. Amsterdam Flea Market (near Waterlooplein).

BREAKDOWN SERVICE

24 hour assistance:

Belgium: TCB, Brussels ☎ (070) 34 47 77 – VTB-VAB, Antwerp ☎ (0 3) 253 63 63 – RACB, Brussels ☎ (0 2) 287 09 00.

Luxembourg: ACL ☎ 45 00 45.

Netherlands: ANWB, The Hague ☎ (0 70) 314 71 47.

TIPPING

In Benelux, prices include service and taxes.

SPEED LIMITS – SEAT BELTS

In Belgium and Luxembourg, the maximum speed limits are 120 km/h-74 mph on motorways and dual carriageways, 90 km/h-56 mph on all other roads and 50 km/h-31 mph in built-up areas. In the Netherlands, 100/120 km/h-62/74 mph on motorways and "autowegen", 80 km/h-50 mph on other roads and 50 km/h-31 mph in built-up areas. In each country, the wearing of seat belts is compulsory for driver and passengers.

Brussels

(BRUXELLES - BRUSSEL) 1000 Brabant 213 ⑱ and 409 ⑬ - Pop. 964 385 - ✆ 0 2.

See : Market Square★★★ (Grand Palace) LZ - Manneken Pis★★ KZ - Rue des Bouchers LZ - St Michael's Cathedral★★ : stained glass★ FU - Place du Grand-Sablon★ and the Church of Notre-Dame du Sablon★ FV **D** - St Hubert Arcades★ LZ - Place Royale★ FV - Statue★ in the Church of Notre-Dame de la Chapelle FV **A** - Square du Petit Sablon★ FV - Royal Palace : Ballroom★ GV - Palais de la Nation : Senate Chamber★ GU - St-Gilles and Ixelles : Notre Dame de la Cambre Abbey★ : Christ Reviled★ - La Cambre Wood★ - Heysel : Atomium★ - Anderlecht : Erasmus's House★ - Kockelberg : national basilica of Sacré-Cœur★.

Museums : Royal Museums of Belgian Fine Arts★★★ : Ancient Art★★★ (Brueghel) FV, Modern Art★★ FV **M3** - Royal Museum of Art and History★★★ (antiquities and Belgian decorative arts) - Musical Instruments★★ FV **M18** - Bellevue★ GV **M14** - Autoworld★★ - Natural Science (Royal Institute) : iguanodon skeletons★ HX **M8** - Belgian Centre of Comic Strips FU **M19** - Ixelles Municipal Museum★ - St-Gilles and Ixelles : Horta Museum : staircase★ - Uccle : David and Alice van Buuren Museum★.

Env. Forest of Soignes★★ - Tervuren Park★ - Arboretum★ - Royal Museum of Central Africa★★ ⑥ : 13 km : African art★, mineralogy★ - Beersel : castle★ S : 11 km - Gaasbeek : castle and grounds★, tapestrie★ SW : 12 km by rue de Lennick - Hoeilaart (Groenendaal) : site★ - Meise : Bouchout Estate★ ① : 13 km : Plant Houses★★ - Grimbergen ① : 18 km : confessional★ in the Abbey Church (Abdijkerk) - Vilvoorde : stalls in the Church of Our Lady (O.L.-Vrouwekerk).

18 9 at Tervuren by ⑥ : 14 km, Château de Ravenstein ✆ (0 2) 767 58 01, 18 at Melsbroek NE : 14 km, Steenwagenstraat 11 ✆ (0 2) 751 82 05 - 9 at Anderlecht, Sports Area of la Pede, Drève Olympique 1 ✆ (0 2) 521 16 87 - 9 at Watermael-Boitsfort, chaussée de la Hulpe 53a ✆ (0 2) 672 22 22 - 9 at Overijse by ⑦ : 16 km, Gemslaan 55 ✆ (0 2) 687 50 30 - 9 at Itterbeek by ⑪ : 8 km, J.M. van Lierdelaan 28 b ✆ (0 2) 567 00 38 - 18 at Kampenhout NE : 20 km, Wildersedreef 56 ✆ (016) 65 12 16.

National NE : 12 km ✆ 722 31 11 - Air Terminal : Air Terminus, r. du Cardinal Mercier 35 LZ ✆ 511 90 30. - ✆ 219 28 80.

(Closed Sundays from October to Easter) Town Hall (Hôtel de Ville), Grand'Place, ✉ 1000 ✆ 513 89 40 and (closed Sunday mornings from October to end March) r. Marché-aux-Herbes 63 ✉ 1000 ✆ 504 03 90 - Tourist Association of the Province (closed Sundays from October to Easter), r. Marché-aux-Herbes 61, ✉ 1000 ✆ 504 04 55.

Paris 308 ⑨ - Amsterdam 204 ① - Düsseldorf 222 ⑤ - Lille 116 ⑫ - Luxembourg 219 ⑦.

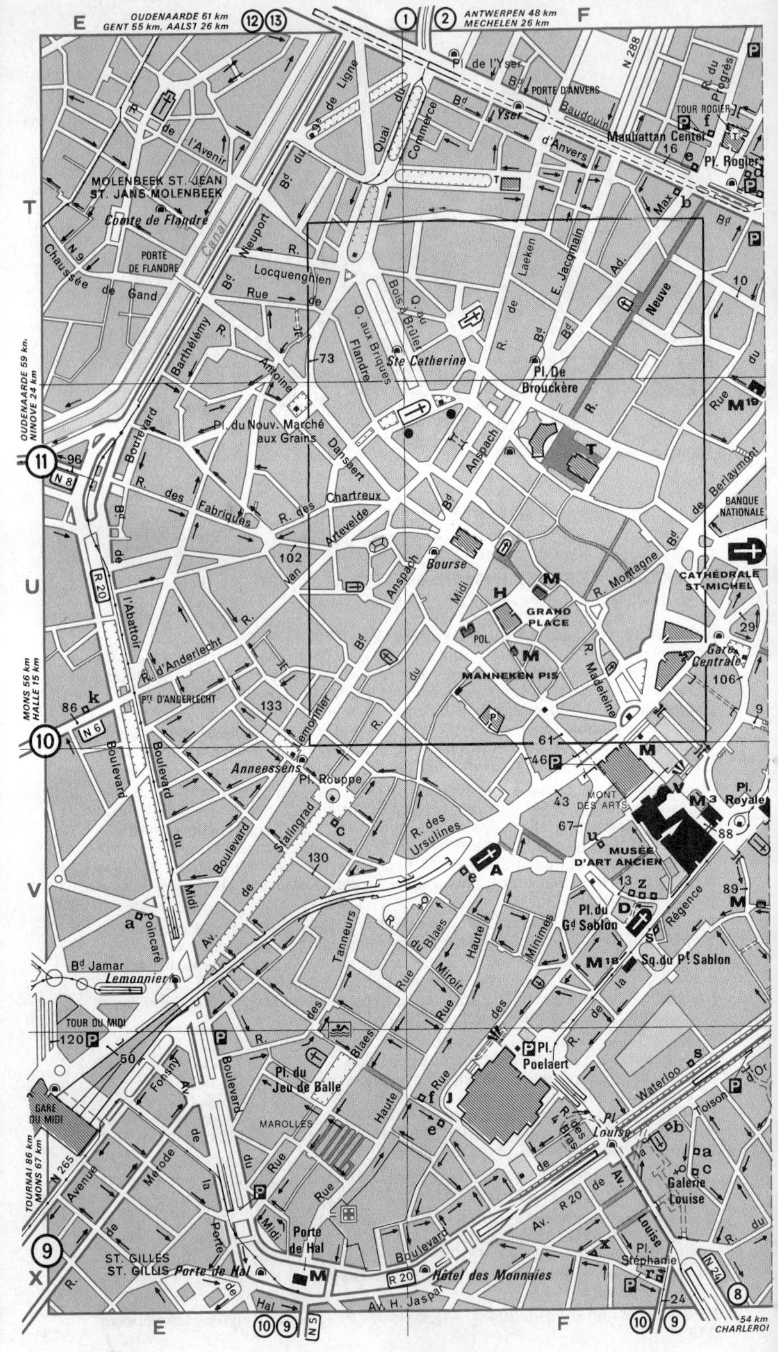

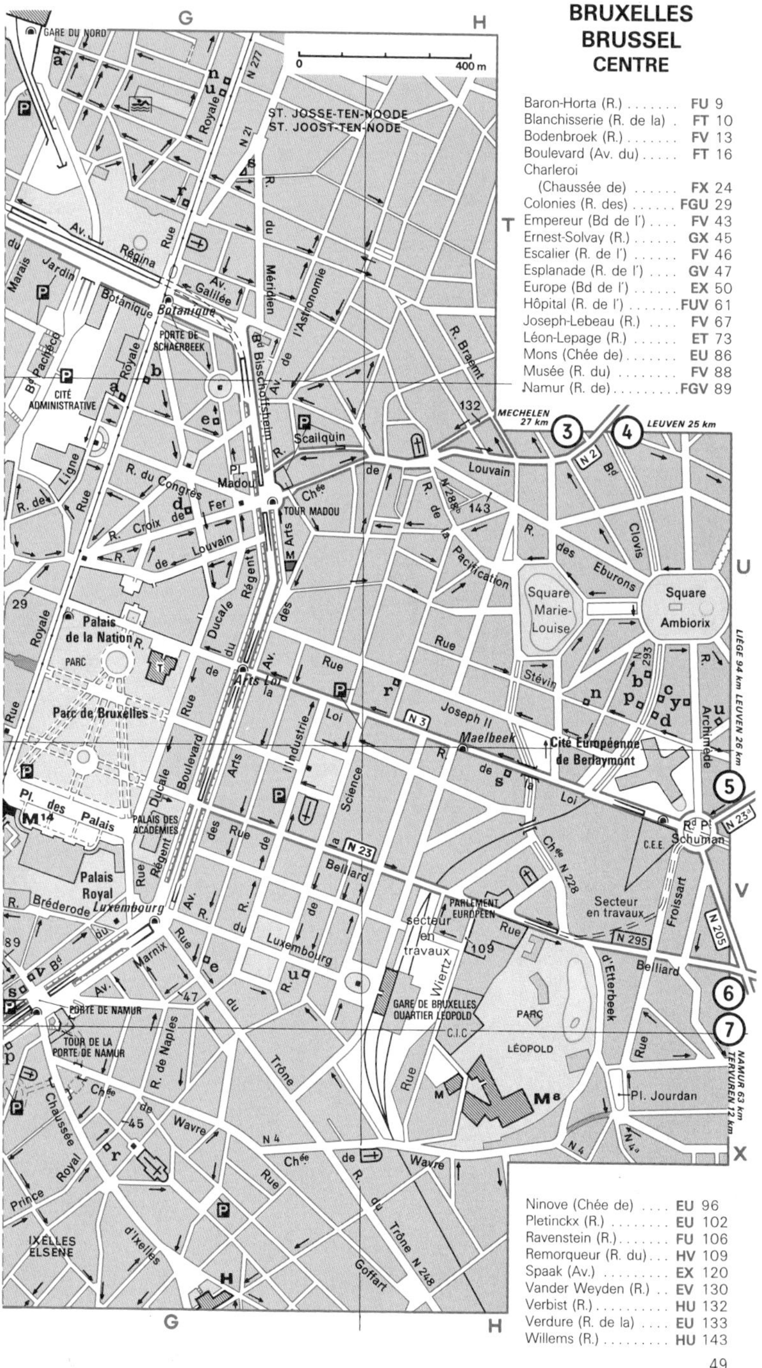

BRUXELLES BRUSSEL CENTRE

BRUXELLES (BRUSSEL)

🏨 **SAS Royal,** r. Fossé-aux-Loups 47, ✉ 1000, ✆ 219 28 28, Telex 22202, Fax 219 62 62, « Patio with remains of 12C City wall », Fб, ≘s – |$| ⇔ rm ▤ TV ☎ ⇌ P – 🏨 25-380. AE ⓞ E VISA LY **c**
M see rest **Sea Grill** below – **Atrium** (partly Scandinavian buffet) a la carte 1200/1500 – **263 rm** ☕ 9900/12500, 18 suites.

🏨 **Métropole,** pl. de Brouckère 31, ✉ 1000, ✆ 217 23 00, Telex 21234, Fax 218 02 20, « Late 19C hall and lounges », Fб, ≘s – |$| ⇔ rm ▤ rest TV ☎ – 🏨 25-600. AE ⓞ E VISA. ⚘ rest LY **r**
M **L'Alban Chambon** *(closed Saturday, Sunday and Bank Holidays)* 1350/1990 – **395 rm** ☕ 6000/10500, 5 suites.

🏨 **Pullman Astoria,** r. Royale 103, ✉ 1000, ✆ 217 62 90, Telex 25040, Fax 217 11 50, « Early 20C residence » – |$| ⇔ rm ▤ rest TV ☎ – 🏨 25-320. AE ⓞ E VISA GTU **b**
M **Le Palais Royal** a la carte approx. 1600 – ☕ 590 – **113 rm** 3850/6500, 12 suites.

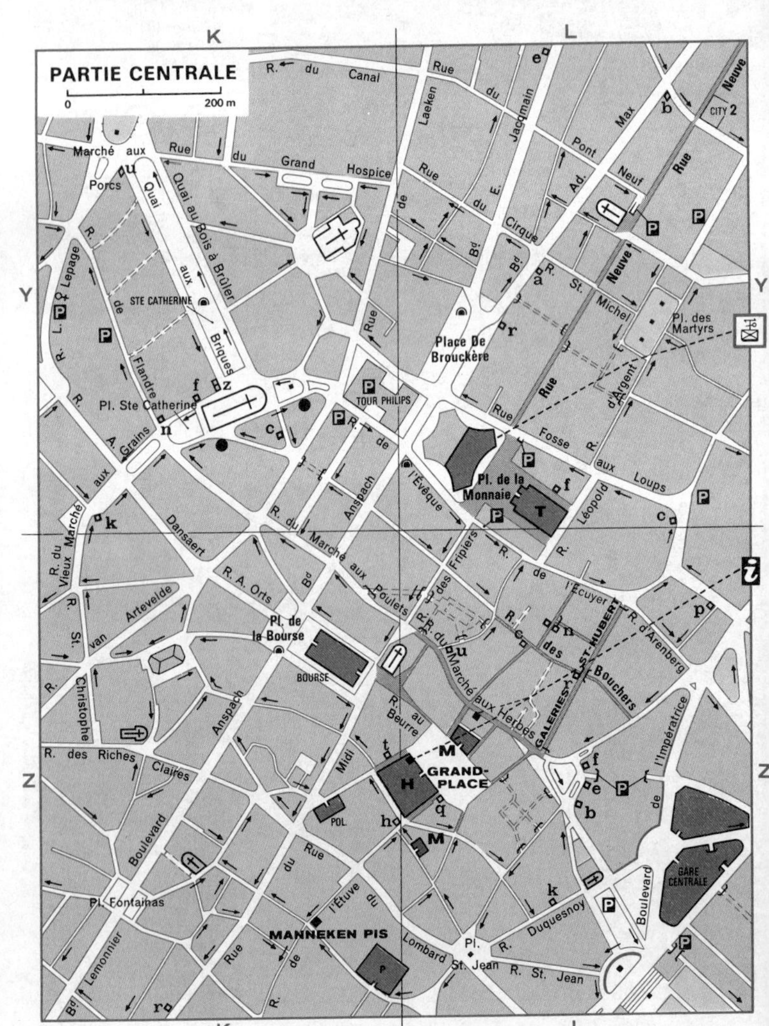

Bedford, r. Midi 135, ✉ 1000, ☎ 512 78 40, Telex 24059, Fax 514 17 59 – rm rest – 50-200. AE E VISA. KZ **r**
M *(closed Christmas and New Year)* 900 – **296 rm** 5400/7200.

Jolly Atlanta, bd A. Max 7, ✉ 1000, ☎ 217 01 20, Telex 21475, Fax 217 37 58 – rest – 25-50. AE E VISA. rest LY **a**
M a la carte 1500/2000 – **240 rm** 7700/8300, 1 suite.

Président Centre without rest, r. Royale 160, ✉ 1000, ☎ 219 00 65, Telex 26784, Fax 218 09 10 – . AE E VISA. GU **a**
73 rm 5400/6500.

Arenberg, r. Assaut 15, ✉ 1000, ☎ 511 07 70, Telex 25660, Fax 514 19 76 – rm rest – 25-90. AE E VISA LZ **p**
M a la carte 1000/1500 – **155 rm** 5800/6800.

Chambord without rest, r. Namur 82, ✉ 1000, ☎ 513 41 19, Telex 20373, Fax 514 08 47 – . AE E VISA. GV **v**
69 rm 3625/4825.

Queen Anne without rest, bd E. Jacqmain 110, ✉ 1000, ☎ 217 16 00, Telex 22676, Fax 217 18 38 – . AE E VISA LY **e**
60 rm 3000/3500.

Sabina without rest, r. Nord 78, ✉ 1000, ☎ 218 26 37, Fax 219 32 39 – . E VISA GU **e**
23 rm 1300/2100.

Sea Grill - (at SAS Royal H.), r. Fossé-aux-Loups 47, ✉ 1000, ☎ 217 92 25, Telex 22202, Fax 219 62 62, Seafood – . AE E VISA. LY **c**
closed Saturday lunch, Sunday, Bank Holidays, 12 to 18 April and 26 July-16 August – **M** a la carte 2250/2900
Spec. Saumon norvégien mariné à l'aneth et sauce moutarde, Salade de langoustines et foie gras poêlé, Turbot rôti, sauce Choron.

Comme Chez Soi (Wynants), pl. Rouppe 23, ✉ 1000, ☎ 512 29 21, Fax 511 80 52, « Belle Epoque atmosphere in an Horta decor » – . AE E VISA EV **c**
closed Sunday, Monday, 4 July-2 August and Christmas-New Year – **M** (booking essential) a la carte 2400/3350
Spec. Filets de sole et médaillon de homard cardinal, Canard des bois grillé à l'huile de truffes blanches, Crêpes caramélisées à l'orange.

Astrid "Chez Pierrot", r. Presse 21, ✉ 1000, ☎ 217 38 31, Fax 217 38 31 – AE E VISA GU **d**
closed Sunday, 1 week Easter and 15 July-15 August – **M** 875.

Roma, r. Princes 12, ✉ 1000, ☎ 218 34 30, Partly Italian cuisine – . AE E VISA. LY **f**
closed Sunday and Bank Holidays – **M** a la carte 1450/2000.

Bernard 1 st floor, r. Namur 93, ✉ 1000, ☎ 512 88 21, Fax 502 21 77 – . AE E VISA GV **s**
closed dinner Monday and July, Saturday, Sunday and Bank Holidays – **M** 1450.

Quartier de l'Europe

Europa, r. Loi 107, ✉ 1040, ☎ 230 13 33, Telex 25121, Fax 230 36 82, – rm – 25-350. AE E VISA. HV **s**
M Les Continents a la carte approx. 2000 – **240 rm** 8500/9500.

Archimède without rest, r. Archimède 22, ✉ 1040, ☎ 231 09 09, Telex 20420, Fax 230 33 71 – . AE E VISA. HU **y**
56 rm 5200/6500.

Euro-flat without rest, bd Charlemagne 50, ✉ 1040, ☎ 230 00 10, Telex 21120, Fax 230 36 83, – – 30. AE E VISA. HU **p**
121 rm 5700/7300, 12 suites.

Eurovillage, bd Charlemagne 80, ✉ 1040, ☎ 230 85 55, Telex 20927, Fax 230 56 35, – rm – 80-100. AE E VISA. HU **b**
M *(closed lunch Saturday and Sunday)* a la carte approx. 1200 – 450 – **80 rm** 5000/6000.

City Garden without rest, r. Joseph II 59, ✉ 1040, ☎ 230 09 45, Telex 63570, Fax 230 64 37 – . AE E VISA. GU **r**
96 rm 5000/6500.

Charlemagne without rest, bd Charlemagne 25, ✉ 1040, ☎ 230 21 35, Telex 22772, Fax 230 25 10 – – 30-60. AE E VISA HU **c**
475 – **66 rm** 3500/5600.

Le Gigotin, r. Stevin 102, ✉ 1040, ☎ 230 30 91, – AE E VISA HU **n**
closed Saturday, Sunday, Bank Holidays and 15 to 31 August – **M** 800/1200.

L'Atelier, r. Franklin 28, ✉ 1040, ☎ 734 91 40, Fax 735 35 98, – AE E VISA HU **u**
closed Saturday, Sunday, Bank Holidays, August and 24 December-3 January – **M** 980/1200.

Takesushi, bd Charlemagne 21, ✉ 1040, ☎ 230 56 27, , Japanese cuisine – AE E VISA HU **d**
closed Saturday and 2 weeks August – **M** a la carte 1150/1900.

Quartier Grand'Place (Ilot Sacré)

✿ **Royal Windsor,** r. Duquesnoy 5, ✉ 1000, ✆ 511 42 15, Telex 62905, Fax 511 60 04 – 🛗 ⇎ rm ▤ TV ☎ 🚗 – 🎤 25-250. AE ⓓ E VISA LZ **k**
M Les 4 Saisons *(closed Saturday lunch and 20 July-21 August)* a la carte 2400/2850 – **266 rm** ☕ 10825/15325, 9 suites
Spec. Barbue en croustillant de curry, beurre au gingembre, Sole farcie en croûte, Pigeon rôti et ses cuisses confites au Porto vieux.

Amigo, r. Amigo 1, ✉ 1000, ✆ 547 47 47, Telex 21618, Fax 513 52 77, « Collection of works of art » – 🛗 ▤ TV ☎ 🚗 – 🎤 25-150. AE ⓓ E VISA. ⚘ rest KZ **h**
M a la carte 1300/2000 – **165 rm** ☕ 6950/11950, 18 suites.

Carrefour de l'Europe, r. Marché-aux-Herbes 110, ✉ 1000, ✆ 504 94 00, Telex 22050, Fax 504 95 00 – 🛗 ⇎ rm ▤ TV ☎ – 🎤 25-120. AE ⓓ E VISA LZ **e**
M (Pub rest.) a la carte approx. 1000 – **58 rm** ☕ 9200, 5 suites.

Novotel Grand'Place, r. Marché-aux-Herbes 120, ✉ 1000, ✆ 514 33 33, Telex 20377, Fax 511 77 23 – 🛗 ⇎ rm ▤ TV ☎ ♿ – 🎤 25. AE ⓓ E VISA LZ **b**
M (open until midnight) a la carte approx. 1100 – ☕ 460 – **136 rm** 4970.

Ibis Center without rest, r. Marché-aux-Herbes 100, ✉ 1000, ✆ 514 40 40, Telex 25490, Fax 514 50 67 – 🛗 TV ☎ ♿ – 🎤 25-130. AE ⓓ E VISA LZ **f**
170 rm ☕ 3900/4200.

XXXX ✿ **La Maison du Cygne,** Grand'Place 9, ✉ 1000, ✆ 511 82 44, Fax 514 31 48, « Former 17C guildhouse » – ▤ Ⓟ. AE ⓓ E VISA. ⚘ LZ **q**
closed Saturday lunch, Sunday, 3 weeks August and late December – **M** a la carte 2250/2950
Spec. Filets de sole aux écrevisses, Turbot braisé au fenouil, Gibier façon "Cygne" (15 October-15 December).

XX **La Tête d'Or,** r. Tête d'Or 9, ✉ 1000, ✆ 511 02 01, Fax 502 44 91, « Ancient Brussels residence » – AE ⓓ E VISA KZ **t**
closed Saturday, Sunday, 19 to 24 July and 15 to 21 August – **M** a la carte 1750/2300.

XX **Aux Armes de Bruxelles,** r. Bouchers 13, ✉ 1000, ✆ 511 55 98, Fax 514 33 81, Brussels atmosphere, open until 11 p.m. – ▤. AE ⓓ E VISA. ⚘ LZ **c**
closed Monday and June – **M** 990.

XX **La Porte du Japon,** r. Fourche 9, ✉ 1000, ✆ 511 15 11, Fax 511 15 11, Japanese cuisine – ▤. AE ⓓ E VISA – *closed Monday* – **M** 1120/1690. LZ **u**

X **L'Ogenblik,** Galerie des Princes 1, ✉ 1000, ✆ 511 61 51, Fax 513 41 58, Open until midnight – AE ⓓ E VISA LZ **n**
closed Sunday – **M** a la carte 1600/2100.

X **Taverne du Passage,** Galerie de la Reine 30, ✉ 1000, ✆ 512 37 32, Fax 511 08 82, Brussels atmosphere, open until midnight – AE ⓓ E VISA LZ **r**
closed Wednesday and Thursday in June and July – **M** a la carte 900/1400.

X **Vincent,** r. Dominicains 8, ✉ 1000, ✆ 511 26 07, Fax 502 36 93, Brussels atmosphere, open until 11.30 p.m., « Original ceramics » – ▤. AE ⓓ E VISA LZ **n**
closed August – **M** 1000/1500.

Quartier Ste-Catherine (Marché-aux-Poissons)

Atlas without rest, r. Vieux Marché-aux-Grains 30, ✉ 1000, ✆ 502 60 06, Fax 502 69 35 – 🛗 TV ☎ ♿ 🚗 – 🎤 40. AE ⓓ E VISA KY **k**
☕ 300 – **88 rm** 3200/3500.

Sainte-Catherine without rest, r. Joseph Plateau 2, ✉ 1000, ✆ 513 76 20, Telex 22476, Fax 514 22 14 – 🛗 TV ☎ ♿ – 🎤 80. AE E VISA KY **c**
235 rm ☕ 3900, 1 suite.

XX **La Sirène d'Or,** pl. Ste-Catherine 1a, ✉ 1000, ✆ 513 51 98, Fax 502 13 05, Seafood – ▤. AE ⓓ E VISA KY **n**
closed Sunday, Monday, 20 July-9 August and 23 December-1 January – **M** 1500/1900.

XX **François,** quai aux Briques 2, ✉ 1000, ✆ 511 60 89, Fax 512 06 67, Seafood – ▤. AE ⓓ E VISA KY **z**
closed Monday and June – **M** a la carte 1700/2450.

XX **Au Cheval Marin,** Marché-aux-Porcs 25, ✉ 1000, ✆ 513 02 87, « Period decor » – Ⓟ. AE ⓓ E VISA KY **u**
closed Sunday and 2 weeks August – **M** 900/1750.

XX **La Belle Maraîchère,** pl. Ste-Catherine 11, ✉ 1000, ✆ 512 97 59, Fax 513 76 91, Seafood – ▤ Ⓟ. AE ⓓ E VISA KY **f**
closed Wednesday and Thursday –**M** 900/1600.

Quartier des Sablons

Jolly du Grand Sablon, r. Bodenbroek 2, ✉ 1000, ✆ 512 88 00, Telex 20397, Fax 512 67 66 – 🛗 ⇎ rm ▤ TV ☎ ♿ 🚗 – 🎤 25-100. AE ⓓ E VISA. ⚘ rest FV **z**
M a la carte 1550/2250 – **198 rm** ☕ 7350/9450, 5 suites.

XXX ✿✿ **L'Écailler du Palais Royal** (Basso), r. Bodenbroek 18, ✉ 1000, ✆ 512 87 51, Seafood – AE ⓓ E VISA FV **z**
closed Sunday, Bank Holidays, 8 to 14 April and 2 to 31 August – **M** a la carte 2500/2900
Spec. Langoustines poêlées, crème légère de haricots blancs au foie gras, Suprême de barbue à la moutarde de Meaux, Civet de homard au chou.

XX **Les Brigittines,** pl. de la Chapelle 5, ✉ 1000, ☎ 512 68 91, Fax 512 41 30, terrace, « Belle Epoque atmosphere » – AE ⓓ E VISA FV **e**
closed Saturday lunch, Sunday, Bank Holidays and August – **M** a la carte 1500/2100.

XX ✿ **Trente rue de la Paille** (Martiny), r. Paille 30, ✉ 1000, ☎ 512 07 15, Fax 514 23 33, Open until 11.30 p.m. – ▤. AE ⓓ E VISA FV **u**
closed Saturday, Sunday, Bank Holidays, July and Christmas-New Year – **M** a la carte 2100/2400
Spec. Canard sauvage aux lardons et oignons confits, sauce au Porto (mid August-10 February), Foie gras d'oie en cocotte, Glace à la cannelle au pain d'épices.

XX **En Provence "Chez Marius",** pl. du Petit Sablon 1, ✉ 1000, ☎ 511 12 08, Fax 512 27 89 – AE ⓓ E VISA. ✻ – *closed Sunday* – **M** 1100/1600. FV **s**

XX **Castello Banfi,** r. Bodenbroek 12, ✉ 1000, ☎ 512 87 94, Partly Italian cuisine – AE ⓓ E VISA
closed Sunday dinner, Monday, 15 to 31 August and 20 to 28 December – **M** a la carte 1500/1900. FV **z**

Quartier Palais de Justice

Hilton International, bd de Waterloo 38, ✉ 1000, ☎ 504 11 11, Telex 22744, Fax 504 21 11, ≦ – 🛗 ⇔ rm ▤ TV ☎ ♿ 🚗 – 🏛 45-600. AE ⓓ E VISA. ✻ rest FX **s**
M see rest **Maison du Bœuf** below – **Plein Ciel 27th floor** ≤ town *(closed Saturday and January)* (lunch only) 1090 – **Café d'Egmont** a la carte approx. 1500 – ☕ 780 – **437 rm** 9000/15000, 13 suites.

XXXX ✿ **Maison du Bœuf** - (at Hilton H.), 1st floor, bd de Waterloo 38, ✉ 1000, ☎ 504 11 11, Telex 22744, Fax 504 21 11, ≤ – ▤ Ⓟ. AE ⓓ E VISA. ✻ FX **s**
M a la carte 1900/2500
Spec. Ravioles d'escargots aux cèpes, Sole au plat aux asperges, Pigeonneau rôti, sauce aux truffes.

X **Les Larmes du Tigre,** r. Wynants 21, ✉ 1000, ☎ 512 18 77, Fax 502 10 03, terrace, Thaï cuisine – AE ⓓ E VISA FX **e**
closed Monday and Saturday lunch – **M** a la carte 900/1300.

X ✿ **Au Beurre Blanc** (Hella), r. Faucon 2a, ✉ 1000, ☎ 513 01 11 – AE ⓓ E VISA FX **f**
closed Saturday, Sunday, 1 week Easter, last 3 weeks August, Christmas and New Year – **M** a la carte 1600/2000
Spec. Foie de canard truffé au homard et son corail, Assiette du pêcheur au beurre blanc, Râble de lièvre poivrade aux mangues poêlées (15 October-December).

Quartier Léopold (see also at Ixelles)

Stanhope, r. Commerce 9, ✉ 1040, ☎ 506 91 11, Fax 512 17 08, terrace, Ⅎ₆, ≦ – 🛗 ▤ TV ☎ 🚗. AE ⓓ E VISA. ✻ GV **e**
M *(closed Saturday, Sunday, 15 July-15 August and Christmas-New Year)* a la carte 1500/2600 – **46 rm** ☕ 12500/14500, 4 suites.

Quartier Louise (see also at Ixelles)

Mayfair, av. Louise 381, ✉ 1050, ☎ 649 98 00, Telex 24821, Fax 640 17 64 – 🛗 ⇔ rm ▤ TV ☎ 🚗 – 🏛 30-60. AE ⓓ E VISA. ✻ rest
M Taishin (Japanese cuisine) *(closed Sunday)* a la carte approx. 1800 – ☕ 650 – **97 rm** 8200/8900, 2 suites.

Copthorne Stéphanie, av. Louise 91, ✉ 1050, ☎ 539 02 40, Telex 25558, Fax 538 03 07, 🏊 – 🛗 ⇔ ▤ TV ☎ 🚗 – 🏛 50-200. AE ⓓ E VISA. ✻ rest
M L'Avenue Louise *(closed Saturday, Sunday lunch, 2 to 22 August and 24 December-1 January)* a la carte 1600/2400 – ☕ 720 – **141 rm** 7450/9950, 1 suite.

Clubhouse without rest, r. Blanche 4, ✉ 1050, ☎ 537 92 10, Telex 62434, Fax 537 00 18 – 🛗 ⇔ TV ☎ 🚗 – 🏛 30. AE ⓓ E VISA
80 rm ☕ 5100/7100, 1 suite.

Brussels President without rest, av. Louise 315, ✉ 1050, ☎ 640 24 15, Telex 25075, Fax 647 34 63 – 🛗 TV ☎ 🚗. AE ⓓ E VISA
28 rm ☕ 4800/6320, 10 suites.

L'Agenda without rest, r. Florence 6, ✉ 1050, ☎ 539 00 31, Telex 63947, Fax 539 00 63 – 🛗 TV ☎ 🚗. AE ⓓ E VISA
☕ 325 – **38 rm** 3250/3550.

XX **La Porte des Indes,** av. Louise 455, ✉ 1050, ☎ 647 86 51, Fax 640 30 59, Indian cuisine, « Exotic decor » – AE ⓓ E VISA – *closed Sunday* – **M** a la carte 1200/2100.

XX **Myako Tagawa,** av. Louise 279, ✉ 1050, ☎ 640 50 95, Fax 648 41 36, Japanese cuisine – ▤ Ⓟ. AE ⓓ E VISA. ✻ – *closed Saturday lunch and Sunday* – **M** a la carte 1700/3500.

Quartier Bois de la Cambre

XXXXX ✿✿ **Villa Lorraine** (Van de Casserie), av. du Vivier d'Oie 75, ✉ 1180, ☎ 374 31 63, terrace – Ⓟ. AE ⓓ E VISA – *closed Sunday and 4 July-4 August* – **M** a la carte 2700/3500
Spec. St-Jacques au coulis de persil (October-April), Ecrevisses "Villa Lorraine", Soufflé au chocolat et jus de noix vertes.

XXX ✿ **La Truffe Noire,** bd de la Cambre 12, ✉ 1050, ☎ 640 44 22, Fax 647 97 04, « Elegant interior » – AE ⓓ E VISA – *closed Saturday lunch, Sunday, 1 week Easter, last 2 weeks August and 1 week late December* – **M** a la carte 2800/3200
Spec. Carpaccio aux truffes, Truffe blanche (October-late December), St-Pierre aux poireaux et truffes.

Quartier Botanique, Gare du Nord (see also at St-Josse-ten-Noode and at Schaerbeek)

Sheraton Towers, pl. Rogier 3, ✉ 1210, ☎ 224 31 11, Telex 26887, Fax 224 34 56, Ls, ≘s, ◻ - |‡| ⇔ rm ▤ TV ☎ P - 🏛 25-800. AE ⓓ E VISA. ✻ rest FT **e**
M Les Comtes de Flandre *(closed Saturday, Sunday and August)* a la carte 1600/2300 - ☐ 670 - **484 rm** 9600/13000, 44 suites.

President World Trade Center, bd E. Jacqmain 180, ✉ 1210, ☎ 217 20 20, Telex 21066, Fax 218 84 02, Ls, ≘s, ◻ - |‡| ⇔ rm ▤ rest TV ☎ ⇔ P - 🏛 25-350. AE ⓓ E VISA. ✻
M a la carte 1000/1750 - **309 rm** ☐ 7650, 1 suite.

Le Dome, bd du Jardin Botanique 12, ✉ 1000, ☎ 218 06 80, Telex 61317, Fax 218 41 12 - |‡| ▤ rest TV ☎ - 🏛 25-100. AE ⓓ E VISA. ✻ FT **b**
M *(closed Sunday and Monday dinner)* 1500 - **77 rm** ☐ 5800/8000.

Président Nord without rest, bd A. Max 107, ✉ 1000, ☎ 219 00 60, Telex 61417, Fax 218 12 69 - |‡| TV ☎. AE ⓓ E VISA. ✻ LY **b**
63 rm ☐ 4900/6900.

Quartier Atomium (Centenaire - Trade Mart)

XXX **Ming Dynasty,** av. de l'Esplanade BP 9, ✉ 1020, ☎ 475 23 45, Fax 475 23 50, Chinese cuisine, open until 11 p.m. - ▤ P. AE ⓓ E VISA
closed Sunday - **M** a la carte 1050/1500.

XXX **Le Centenaire,** av. J. Sobieski 84, ✉ 1020, ☎ 478 66 23, Fax 478 66 23 - AE ⓓ E VISA. ✻
closed Sunday, Monday, July and Christmas-New Year - **M** a la carte 1200/1650.

XX ✿ **Les Baguettes Impériales** (Mme Ma), av. J. Sobieski 70, ✉ 1020, ☎ 479 67 32, Fax 479 67 32, 🏖, Partly Vietnamese cuisine - AE. ✻
closed Tuesday, Sunday dinner, 2 weeks Easter and August - **M** a la carte 2100/2700
Spec. Pétale de bœuf cru aux fines épices, Pigeonneau farci aux nids d'hirondelles, Mangue chaude à la crème de soja.

X **Le Paradis de Chang,** r. De Wand 51, ✉ 1020, ☎ 268 18 45, Chinese cuisine - AE ⓓ E VISA. ✻
closed Monday except Bank Holidays - **M** 680.

ANDERLECHT

Le Prince de Liège, chaussée de Ninove 664, ✉ 1080, ☎ 522 16 00, Fax 520 81 85 - |‡| TV ☎ ⇔ - 🏛 25. AE ⓓ E VISA
M *(closed Sunday dinner and 9 July-7 August)* 750/1350 - **31 rm** ☐ 1950/2950.

Ustel, Square de l'Aviation 6, ✉ 1070, ☎ 520 60 53, Fax 520 33 28 - |‡| TV ☎ - 🏛 30. AE E VISA EV **a**
M *(closed Saturday lunch and Sunday dinner)* 595/795 - **28 rm** ☐ 3600/5900.

Gerfaut without rest, chaussée de Mons 115, ✉ 1070, ☎ 522 19 22, Fax 523 89 91 - |‡| ⇔ TV ☎ ♿ P. AE ⓓ E VISA EU **k**
48 rm ☐ 2400/3400.

XXX **Saint-Guidon** 2nd floor, av. Théo Verbeeck 2 (in the Constant Vanden Stock stadium), ✉ 1070, ☎ 520 55 36, Fax 523 38 27 - ▤ P - 🏛 25-400. ⓓ E VISA. ✻
closed July, Christmas-New Year, Saturday, Sunday, first league match days and Bank Holidays - **M** (lunch only) a la carte 1600/2150.

XX **La Réserve,** chaussée de Ninove 675, ✉ 1080, ☎ 411 26 53, Fax 411 66 67, 🏖 - AE ⓓ E VISA
M a la carte 1100/1600.

X **La Brouette,** bd Prince de Liège 61, ✉ 1070, ☎ 522 51 69 - AE ⓓ E VISA
closed Sunday dinner, Monday and 18 July-10 August - **M** 900/1450.

X **La Paix** r. Ropsy-Chaudron 49 (opposite slaughterhouse), ✉ 1070, ☎ 523 09 58, Pub rest - P. AE E VISA. ✻
closed Saturday, Sunday and last 2 weeks July - **M** (lunch only) a la carte 950/1450.

AUDERGHEM (OUDERGEM)

XX ✿ **La Grignotière** (Chanson), chaussée de Wavre 2041, ✉ 1160, ☎ 672 81 85, Fax 672 81 85 - AE ⓓ E VISA
closed Sunday, Monday and Bank Holidays - **M** 1700/1950
Spec. Composé gourmand de cailles et foie d'oie poêlé, Homard façon Thermidor, Gâteau fondant de canard sauvage à la moëlle (15 August-10 February).

XX **L'Abbaye de Rouge Cloître,** r. Rouge Cloître 8, ✉ 1160, ☎ 672 45 25, Fax 660 12 01, ≤, 🏖, « Forest-side setting » - P - 🏛 25-55. AE ⓓ E VISA
closed Saturday, Sunday and 23 December-6 January - **M** 870.

XX **New Asia,** chaussée de Wavre 1240, ✉ 1160, ☎ 660 62 06, 🏖, Chinese cuisine, « Terrace » - AE ⓓ E VISA. ✻
M 480/680.

ETTERBEEK

XX **Le Pavillon d'Été,** av. de Tervuren 107, ⊠ 1040, ☎ 732 03 59, Fax 732 10 56 – AE ⓓ E VISA
closed Sunday, Monday and 20 July-15 August – **M** a la carte 1450/1900.

X **Harry's Place,** r. Bataves 65, ⊠ 1040, ☎ 735 09 00 – AE ⓓ E VISA
closed Thursday dinner, Saturday lunch, Sunday, 20 July-12 August and 24 December-2 January – **M** a la carte approx. 1300.

Quartier Cinquantenaire

Park without rest, av. de l'Yser 21, ⊠ 1040, ☎ 735 74 00, Fax 735 19 67, – 25. AE ⓓ E VISA.
50 rm 5800/7100, 1 suite.

XX **La Fontaine de Jade,** av. de Tervuren 5, ⊠ 1040, ☎ 736 32 10, Chinese cuisine – AE ⓓ E VISA
closed Tuesday and August – **M** a la carte approx. 1100.

EVERE

Belson without rest, chaussée de Louvain 805, ⊠ 1140, ☎ 735 00 00, Telex 64921, Fax 735 60 43 – – 25. AE ⓓ E VISA
550 – **140 rm** 6050/6650, 3 suites.

Mercure, av. J. Bordet 74, ⊠ 1140, ☎ 242 53 35, Telex 65460, Fax 245 05 95, – rm – 25-60. AE ⓓ E VISA
M *(closed lunch Saturday and Sunday)* 1375 – 495 – **120 rm** 3750/7000.

Evergreen, av. V. Day 1, ⊠ 1140, ☎ 732 15 15, Fax 732 16 60 – . AE E VISA
M (Pub rest, open until midnight) 725/1200 – **20 rm** 2650/3150.

FOREST (VORST)

De Fierlant without rest, r. De Fierlant 67, ⊠ 1060, ☎ 538 60 70, Fax 538 91 99 – . AE ⓓ E VISA.
40 rm 2800/3550.

XXX **Le Chouan,** av. Brugmann 100, ⊠ 1060, ☎ 344 09 99, Seafood – . AE ⓓ E VISA
closed Saturday lunch, Sunday dinner and July – **M** a la carte 1600/2250.

XX **Les Jardins de l'Abbaye,** pl. Saint-Denis 9, ⊠ 1190, ☎ 332 11 59, Fax 332 11 59, ≤, – . AE ⓓ E VISA
closed Sunday dinner, Monday and August – **M** 795.

GANSHOREN

XXXX ✿✿✿ **Bruneau,** av. Broustin 75, ⊠ 1080, ☎ 427 69 78, Fax 425 97 26 – . AE ⓓ E VISA
closed lunch Saturday and Sunday, Monday and 8 July-4 August – **M** a la carte 2400/3500
Spec. Dos de barbue poêlé aux épices, Ravioles de céleri aux truffes, Croustillant au café.

XXX ✿✿ **Claude Dupont,** av. Vital Riethuisen 46, ⊠ 1080, ☎ 426 00 00, Fax 426 65 40 – AE ⓓ E VISA.
closed Monday, Tuesday and 5 July-10 August – **M** a la carte 2100/3400
Spec. Fricassée d'huîtres au Champagne et caviar (15 September-April), Méli-Mélo de homard aux golden et curry léger, Croustillant au Praslin en chaud-froid.

XXX **San Daniele,** av. Charles-Quint 6, ⊠ 1080, ☎ 426 79 23, Italian cuisine – . AE ⓓ E VISA
closed Sunday, Bank Holidays and mid July-mid August – **M** a la carte 1600/2150.

XX **Cambrils** 1st floor, av. Charles-Quint 365, ⊠ 1080, ☎ 465 35 82, Fax 465 76 63, – . AE E VISA
closed Thursday dinner, Sunday and 16 July-16 August – **M** 810/995.

X **Le Claudalain,** av. des Gloires Nationales 65, ⊠ 1080, ☎ 428 82 63 – AE ⓓ E
closed Sunday dinner, Monday, Tuesday, last 2 weeks August-first week September and last week January-first week February – **M** 740/1090.

IXELLES (ELSENE)

XX **Aub. de Boendael,** square du Vieux Tilleul 12, ⊠ 1050, ☎ 672 70 55, Fax 660 75 82, Grill rest, Rustic – . AE ⓓ E VISA
closed Saturday, Sunday, Bank Holidays, 31 July-22 August and 24 December-2 January – **M** a la carte 1500/2200.

XX **Les Foudres,** r. Eugène Cattoir 14, ⊠ 1050, ☎ 647 36 36, Fax 649 09 86, , « Former wine cellar » – . AE ⓓ E VISA
closed Saturday lunch and Sunday – **M** 1000/1450.

XX **Le Chalet Rose,** av. du Bois de la Cambre 49, ⊠ 1050, ☎ 672 78 64, Fax 672 78 64, – . AE ⓓ E VISA
closed Saturday lunch, Sunday and Bank Holidays – **M** a la carte 1650/1950.

X **La Pagode d'Or,** chaussée de Boondael 332, ⊠ 1050, ☎ 649 06 56, , Vietnamese cuisine – AE ⓓ E VISA.
closed after 8.30 p.m. – **M** 890/1350.

Quartier Bascule

Primevère, chaussée de Vleurgat 191, 1050, 646 64 20, Fax 646 33 14, - 25. AE E VISA
M 675 - **62 rm** 3150/3350.

La Mosaïque, r. Forestière 23, 1050, 649 02 35, Fax 647 11 49, - AE E VISA
closed Saturday lunch, Sunday and 15 July-15 August - **M** a la carte approx. 2100.

Maison Félix 1st floor, r. Washington 149 (square Henri Michaux), 1050, 345 66 93 - AE E VISA
closed Sunday and Monday - **M** a la carte 2150/2850.

La Thaïlande, av. Legrand 29, 1050, 640 24 62, , Thaï cuisine, open until 11 p.m. - AE E VISA
closed Sunday - **M** 900/1300.

Quartier Léopold (see also at Bruxelles)

Leopold, r. Luxembourg 35, 1040, 511 18 28, Telex 62804, Fax 514 19 39, - - 25-80. AE E VISA. rm GV **u**
M (Brasserie) a la carte approx. 1000 - **85 rm** 3350/5850 and 1 suite.

Quartier Louise (see also at Bruxelles)

Sofitel, av. de la Toison d'Or 40, 1060, 514 22 00, Telex 63547, Fax 514 57 44, - rm - 25-120. AE E VISA FX **b**
M 790 - 580 - **171 rm** 6900.

Cadettt, r. Paul Spaak 15, 1050, 645 61 11, Telex 20819, Fax 646 63 44, , - rest - 25. AE E VISA
M (open until 11 p.m.) a la carte 1000/1350 - 500 - **128 rm** 5600.

Argus without rest, r. Capitaine Crespel 6, 1050, 514 07 70, Telex 29393, Fax 514 12 22 - . AE E VISA. FX **a**
41 rm 3100/3400.

Le Criterion, av. de la Toison d'Or 7, 1060, 512 37 68, Pub rest, open until 11.30 p.m. - AE E VISA. GX **p**
M a la carte approx. 1500.

Shogun, r. Capitaine Crespel 10, 1050, 512 83 19, , Japanese cuisine, teppan-yaki, open until 11 p.m. - AE E VISA FX **c**
closed Saturday lunch and Sunday - **M** 1300/2000.

JETTE

Le Sermon (Kobs), av. Jacques Sermon 91, 1090, 426 89 35, Fax 426 70 90 - AE E VISA
closed Sunday, Monday and July - **M** a la carte 1600/2300
Spec. Moules au Champagne (August-March), Sole "Sermon", Caneton aux pommes et poivre vert.

Rôtiss. Le Vieux Pannenhuis, r. Léopold-Ier 317, 1090, 425 83 73, Fax 428 12 99, , Grill rest, « 17C inn » - . AE E VISA
closed Saturday lunch, Sunday and July - **M** 960.

MOLENBEEK-ST-JEAN (SINT-JANS-MOLENBEEK)

Le Béarnais, bd Louis Mettewie 318, 1080, 411 51 51, Fax 410 70 81 - . AE E VISA
closed Sunday, Monday dinner and last week July-first week August - **M** a la carte 1700/2200.

ST-GILLES (SINT-GILLIS)

Ramada, chaussée de Charleroi 38, 1060, 533 66 66, Telex 25539, Fax 538 90 14 - rm rm - 25-170. rest
201 rm.

Manos Stephanie without rest, chaussée de Charleroi 28, 1060, 539 02 50, Telex 20556, Fax 537 57 29 - . AE E VISA
550 - **50 rm** 4450/5750 and 5 suites.

Manos without rest, chaussée de Charleroi 102, 1060, 537 96 82, Telex 65369, Fax 539 36 55 - . AE E VISA
450 - **38 rm** 3175/4275.

Delta, chaussée de Charleroi 17, 1060, 539 01 60, Telex 63225, Fax 537 90 11 - rest - 25-100. AE E VISA FX **r**
M *(closed 25 December and 1 January)* a la carte 750/1300 - **246 rm** 5500/6500.

Diplomat without rest, r. Jean Stas 32, 1060, 537 42 50, Telex 61012, Fax 539 33 79 - . AE E VISA FX **x**
68 rm 5500/6500.

Forum without rest, av. du Haut-Pont 2, 1060, 343 01 00, Telex 62311, Fax 347 00 54 - - 25-100. AE E VISA
78 rm 3500/4300.

XX **Le Forcado,** chaussée de Charleroi 192, ✉ 1060, ☎ 537 92 20, Portuguese cuisine – ▤. AE ⓓ E VISA
closed Sunday, Bank Holidays, August and carnival week – **M** a la carte approx. 1300.

X **Inada,** r. Source 73, ✉ 1060, ☎ 538 01 13, Fax 646 11 01 – AE E VISA
closed Saturday lunch, Sunday and 15 July-15 August – **M** a la carte approx. 1800.

ST-JOSSE-TEN-NOODE (SINT-JOOST-TEN-NODE)

Quartier Botanique (see also at Bruxelles and at Schaerbeek)

Scandic Crown, r. Royale 250, ✉ 1210, ☎ 220 66 11, Telex 61871, Fax 217 84 44, – rm ▤ TV ☎ – 30-300. AE ⓓ E VISA. rest GT r
M *(closed Saturday and mid July-mid August)* a la carte 1850/2400 – **309 rm** 7100/7800, 6 suites.

Palace, r. Gineste 3, ✉ 1210, ☎ 217 62 00, Telex 65604, Fax 218 76 51 – rm TV ☎ – 25-300. AE ⓓ E VISA. rest FT d
M Le Bouquet a la carte 1200/1900 – **359 rm** 6000/7000 and 1 suite.

Alfa Rogier without rest, r. Brabant 80, ✉ 1210, ☎ 223 07 07, Telex 21155, Fax 223 03 24 – TV ☎. AE ⓓ E VISA GT a
73 rm 5600/6800.

New Siru, pl. Rogier 1, ✉ 1210, ☎ 217 75 80 and 217 83 08 (rest), Telex 21722, Fax 218 33 03, « Every room decorated by a contemporary Belgian artist » – ▤ rest TV ☎ – 25-70. AE ⓓ E VISA FT f
M (Pub rest, open until 11.30 p.m.) a la carte approx. 1200 – **101 rm** 3600/5900.

Albert Premier without rest, pl. Rogier 20, ✉ 1210, ☎ 217 21 25, Telex 27111, Fax 217 93 31 – TV ☎ – 25-70. AE ⓓ E VISA FT d
285 rm 3000/3500.

XX **De Ultieme Hallucinatie,** r. Royale 316, ✉ 1210, ☎ 217 06 14, Fax 217 72 40, « Art Nouveau interior » – AE ⓓ E VISA. GT u
closed Saturday lunch, Sunday and mid July-mid August – **M** 1450.

X **Les Dames Tartine,** chaussée de Haecht 58, ✉ 1030, ☎ 218 45 49, Fax 218 45 49 – AE ⓓ E VISA GT s
closed Saturday lunch, Sunday and Monday – **M** a la carte approx. 1400.

SCHAERBEEK (SCHAARBEEK)

Quartier Botanique (see also at Bruxelles and at St-Josse-ten-Noode)

XX **Den Botaniek,** r. Royale 328, ✉ 1210, ☎ 218 48 38, Fax 218 41 95, « 1900 decor, garden » – AE ⓓ E VISA GT n
closed Saturday lunch, Sunday and dinner Monday and Tuesday – **M** a la carte 1700/2150.

Quartier Meiser

Lambermont without rest, bd Lambermont 322, ✉ 1030, ☎ 242 55 95, Telex 27198, Fax 215 36 13 – TV ☎. AE ⓓ E VISA
42 rm 3100/3600.

Reyers without rest, bd Aug. Reyers 40, ✉ 1040, ☎ 732 42 42, Fax 732 41 82, – ☎ P. AE ⓓ E VISA
49 rm 2600/3400.

XX **Philippe Riesen** 1st floor, bd Aug. Reyers 163, ✉ 1040, ☎ 736 41 38, Fax 736 41 38 – AE ⓓ E VISA
closed Saturday in summer, Saturday lunch in winter, Sunday, 3 weeks August and Christmas-New Year – **M** a la carte 1700/2250.

XX **Au Cadre Noir,** av. Milcamps 158, ✉ 1040, ☎ 734 14 45 – AE ⓓ E VISA.
closed Saturday lunch, Sunday dinner, Monday and 1 to 21 July – **M** 870.

UCCLE (UKKEL)

County House, square des Héros 2, ✉ 1180, ☎ 375 44 20, Telex 22392, Fax 375 31 22 – ▤ rest TV ☎ – 25-140. AE ⓓ E VISA. rest
M a la carte approx. 1300 – **99 rm** 3150/5100.

XXX **Les Délices de la Mer,** chaussée de Waterloo 1020, ✉ 1180, ☎ 375 54 67, Fax 375 28 00 – P. AE ⓓ E VISA
closed Saturday lunch and Sunday – **M** 2275/2600.

XXX **Les Frères Romano,** av. de Fré 182, ✉ 1180, ☎ 374 70 98, – P. AE ⓓ E VISA
closed Sunday, Bank Holidays and August – **M** a la carte 1600/2300.

XX **L'Amandier,** av. de Fré 184, ✉ 1180, ☎ 374 03 95, Fax 374 86 92, Open until 11 p.m. – P. AE ⓓ E VISA
closed Saturday lunch – **M** a la carte 1500/1800.

XX ✿ **Villa d'Este,** r. Etoile 142, ✉ 1180, ☎ 376 48 48, « Terrace » – P. AE ⓓ E VISA
closed Sunday dinner, Monday, July and Christmas-New Year – **M** a la carte 1750/2600
Spec. Suprême de turbotin au basilic (summer), Sole farcie aux poireaux, Coquelet à la moutarde de Meaux.

XX **La Cité du Dragon,** chaussée de Waterloo 1024, ✉ 1180, ☎ 375 80 80, Fax 375 69 77, terrace, Chinese cuisine, open until 11.30 p.m., « Exotic garden with fountains » - P. AE ① E VISA
M 810/995.

XX **L'Éléphant Bleu,** chaussée de Waterloo 1120, ✉ 1180, ☎ 374 49 62, Fax 375 44 68, Thaï cuisine, « Exotic decor » - ▤ P. AE ① E VISA - *closed Saturday lunch, 24 December dinner, 25 December and 1 January* - **M** a la carte 1100/1900.

XX **Willy et Marianne,** chaussée d'Alsemberg 705, ✉ 1180, ☎ 343 60 09 - AE ① E VISA
closed Tuesday dinner, Wednesday, 2 weeks July and 2 weeks carnival - **M** 900.

X **Brasseries Georges,** av. Winston Churchill 259, ✉ 1180, ☎ 347 21 00, Fax 344 02 45, terrace, Open until midnight - ▤. AE ① E VISA
M a la carte 1000/1700.

X **De Hoef,** r. Edith Cavell 218, ✉ 1180, ☎ 374 34 17, Fax 375 30 84, terrace, Grill rest, « 17C inn » - AE ① E VISA
M 695.

WATERMAEL-BOITSFORT (WATERMAAL-BOSVOORDE)

XX **Host. Des 3 Tilleuls** ♨ with rm, Berensheide 8, ✉ 1170, ☎ 672 30 14, Fax 673 65 52, terrace - TV ☎. AE ① E VISA. ✻ rm
M *(closed Sunday and 15 July-15 August)* a la carte 1500/2500 - **7 rm** ☕ 2600/4350.

XX **Le Canard Sauvage,** chaussée de La Hulpe 194, ✉ 1170, ☎ 673 09 75, Fax 675 21 45 - AE ① E VISA. ✻
closed Saturday lunch, Sunday dinner and August - **M** a la carte approx. 1600.

XX **Nouveau Chez Nous,** r. Middelbourg 28, ✉ 1170, ☎ 673 53 93, Fax 673 53 93 - AE ① E VISA - *closed Sunday dinner, Monday and 2 to 26 August* - **M** 1190.

XX **Samambaïa,** r. Philippe Dewolfs 7, ✉ 1170, ☎ 672 87 20, Fax 675 20 74, Brazilian cuisine - AE ① E
closed Sunday, Monday and 25 July-25 August - **M** a la carte approx. 1300.

XX **Les Rives du Gange** with rm, av. de la Fauconnerie 1, ✉ 1170, ☎ 672 16 01, Telex 62661, Fax 672 43 30 - TV ☎. AE ① E VISA
M (Indian cuisine, open until 11 p.m.) a la carte 1100/1400 - **20 rm** ☕ 1880/2880.

WOLUWÉ-ST-LAMBERT (SINT-LAMBRECHTS-WOLUWE)

Sodehotel ♨, av. E. Mounier 5, ✉ 1200, ☎ 775 21 11, Telex 20170, Fax 770 47 80, terrace - |♦| ⇆ rm ▤ TV ☎ ♿ ⇔ P - 🏛 25-200. AE ① E VISA. ✻ rest
M a la carte 1400/1800 - ☕ 520 - **120 rm** 6200.

Lambeau without rest, av. Lambeau 150, ✉ 1200, ☎ 732 51 70, Fax 732 54 90 - |♦| TV ☎. AE E VISA
22 rm ☕ 2450/3250.

XXX ✿ **Mon Manège à Toi,** r. Neerveld 1, ✉ 1200, ☎ 770 02 38, Fax 762 95 80, « Floral garden » - P. AE ① E VISA - *closed Saturday, Sunday, Bank Holidays, 7 to 31 July and 23 December-1 January* - **M** a la carte 2100/2800
Spec. Terrine de foie gras landais, Rougets de roche poêlés, vinaigrette tomatée, Aiguillettes de canard sauvage aux figues confites (August-February).

XXX **Lindekemale,** av. J.F. Debecker 6, ✉ 1200, ☎ 770 90 57, Fax 770 90 57, terrace, « 15C watermill » - P. AE ① E VISA
closed Saturday, Sunday, Bank Holidays and August - **M** a la carte 1800/2200.

XX **Michel Servais,** r. Th. Decuyper 136, ✉ 1200, ☎ 762 62 95, Fax 771 20 32, terrace - AE ① E VISA - *closed Sunday, Monday and 21 July-21 August* - **M** a la carte 1400/2150.

XX **Le Relais de la Woluwe,** av. Georges Henri 1, ✉ 1200, ☎ 762 66 36, Fax 762 18 55, terrace, « Terrace and garden » - AE ① E VISA
closed Saturday lunch, Sunday, 1 week Easter and 1 week Christmas - **M** a la carte 1450/1800.

WOLUWÉ-ST-PIERRE (SINT-PIETERS-WOLUWE)

XXX ✿ **Des 3 Couleurs** (Tourneur), av. de Tervuren 453, ✉ 1150, ☎ 770 33 21, terrace, « Terrace » - E - *closed September, last 2 weeks December and Monday, Tuesday except Bank Holidays* - **M** (lunch only on Bank Holidays) a la carte 1800/2450
Spec. Pigeonneau aux champignons et jus de truffes, Saumon "Liliane", Terrine d'anguille et cervelle de veau.

BRUSSELS ENVIRONS

at Diegem Brussels-Zaventem motorway Diegem exit C Machelen pop. 11 250 - ✉ 1831 Diegem - ✆ 0 2 :

Holiday Inn, Holidaystraat 7 ☎ 720 58 65, Telex 24285, Fax 720 41 45, Fø, ≘s, ▣, ✂ - |♦| ⇆ rm ▤ TV ☎ P - 🏛 35-500. AE ① E VISA. ✻ rest
M (buffets) a la carte 1400/1700 - ☕ 575 - **309 rm** 8000.

Sofitel Airport, Bessenveldstraat 15 ☎ 725 11 60, Telex 26595, Fax 721 43 45, terrace, ≘s, ▣ - ⇆ rm ▤ TV ☎ P - 🏛 25-500. AE ① E VISA
M a la carte 1400/1950 - ☕ 575 - **125 rm** 6000.

Novotel Airport, Olmenstraat ✆ 725 30 50, Fax 721 39 58, rm rm - ⓟ - 25-250. AE ⓞ E VISA
M (open until midnight) a la carte approx. 1100 - 435 - **209 rm** 4500/4700.

Ibis Airport, Bessenveldstraat 17 ✆ 725 43 21, Telex 22062, Fax 725 40 40, - ⓟ - 25-50. AE ⓞ E VISA. rest - **M** 695 - **95 rm** 3550.

Fimotel Airport, Berkenlaan 5 ✆ 725 33 80, Telex 20906, Fax 725 38 10, - ⓟ - 25-200. AE ⓞ E VISA. rest
M 975 - **79 rm** 3200/3700.

Diegemhof, Calenbergstraat 51 ✆ 720 11 34, Fax 720 14 87, - AE ⓞ E VISA.
closed Saturday, Sunday, July and 1 week late December - **M** a la carte 1650/2000.

at Dilbeek by ⑪ : 7 km - pop. 36 647 - ✉ 1700 Dilbeek - 0 2 :

Relais Delbeccha, Bodegemstraat 158 ✆ 569 44 30, Fax 569 75 30, - ⓟ - 25-100. AE ⓞ E VISA. rest
M *(closed Sunday dinner)* a la carte 1600/1900 - 350 - **11 rm** 3400/4800 and 3 suites.

Host. d'Arconati with rm, d'Arconatistraat 77 ✆ 569 35 15, Fax 569 35 04, « Floral garden » - ⓟ - 60. AE E VISA.
closed February and 1 week July - **M** *(closed Sunday dinner, Monday and Tuesday)* a la carte approx. 1700 - **6 rm** 2000/2500.

at Dworp (Tourneppe) by ⑨ : 16 km Ⓒ Beersel pop. 21 995 - ✉ 1653 Dworp - 0 2 :

Kasteel Gravenhof, Alsembergsesteenweg 676 ✆ 380 44 99, Fax 380 40 60, « Woodland setting », - ⓟ - 25-120. AE ⓞ E VISA. rest
M (Pub rest) a la carte approx. 1200 - 395 - **24 rm** 3250/5950.

at Grimbergen - pop. 31 944 - ✉ 1850 Grimbergen - 0 2 :

Abbey, Kerkeblokstraat 5 ✆ 236 63 62, Fax 269 66 88, - rest ⓟ - 30-200. AE ⓞ E VISA. rm
M 't Wit Paard *(closed Saturday lunch and Sunday)* a la carte 1550/2000 - 300 - **28 rm** 4200/4800.

at Groot-Bijgaarden Ⓒ Dilbeek pop. 36 647 - ✉ 1702 Groot-Bijgaarden - 0 2 :

De Bijgaarden, I. Van Beverenstraat 20 (near castle) ✆ 466 44 85, Fax 463 08 11, - AE ⓞ E VISA
closed Saturday lunch, Sunday, 11 to 19 April and 15 August-6 September - **M** a la carte 2700/3600
Spec. Chou vert au caviar, Canette de Barbarie "à la presse", Soufflé chaud aux pistaches et chocolat amer.

Michel (Coppens), Schepen Gossetlaan 31 ✆ 466 65 91, Fax 466 90 07, - ⓟ. ⓞ E VISA
closed Sunday, Monday and August - **M** a la carte 2000/2450
Spec. Gratin d'huîtres au witlof et Champagne (September-March), Blanc de cabillaud rôti sur la peau, Faisan rôti à la feuille de vigne (15 October-December).

at Hoeilaart - pop. 9 437 - ✉ 1560 Hoeilaart - 0 2 :

Romeyer, Groenendaalsesteenweg 109 (at Groenendaal) ✆ 657 05 81, Fax 657 27 73, « forest, garden and private lake » - ⓟ. AE ⓞ E VISA
closed Sunday, Monday, 1 to 17 August and February - **M** a la carte 2800/4200
Spec. Homard au suc de céleri, Dos de turbot au four beurre au Bouzy, Tournedos aux échalotes confites.

Aloyse Kloos, Terhulpsesteenweg 2 (at Groenendaal) ✆ 657 37 37, - ⓟ. AE ⓞ E VISA
closed Sunday dinner, Monday, 2 weeks Easter and 10 August-6 September - **M** a la carte 1700/2200
Spec. Jambons de notre fumoir, Fricassée de champignons des bois, Noisettes de chevreuil poivrade (October-10 December).

at Huizingen by ⑨ : 12 km Ⓒ Beersel pop. 21 995 - ✉ 1654 Huizingen - 0 2 :

Terborght, Oud Dorp 16 (near E 19 - exit 15) ✆ 380 10 10, Fax 380 10 97, « Rustic » - ⓟ. AE ⓞ E VISA.
closed dinner Sunday and Tuesday, Monday, 21 July-15 August and carnival - **M** a la carte 1900/2200.

at Kobbegem by ⑬ : 11 km Ⓒ Asse pop. 27 047 - ✉ 1730 Kobbegem - 0 2 :

Chalet Rose, Brusselsesteenweg 331 ✆ 452 60 41, Fax 452 26 75, - ⓟ. AE ⓞ E VISA
closed Sunday dinner and Monday - **M** a la carte 1500/2000.

De Plezanten Hof, Broekstraat 2 ✆ 452 89 39, Fax 452 99 11, - ⓟ. AE ⓞ E VISA
closed Tuesday, Wednesday, Sunday, 22 July-20 August and 1 week February - **M** (dinner only) a la carte approx. 1900.

at Kraainem - pop. 12 356 - ✉ 1950 Kraainem - 0 2 :

d'Oude Pastorie, Pastoorkesweg 1 (Park Jourdain) ✆ 720 63 46, « Lakeside setting in park » - AE ⓞ E VISA.
closed Monday dinner, Thursday, 12 to 19 April and 16 August-6 September - **M** a la carte approx. 1700.

at Linkebeek - pop. 4 533 - ✉ 1630 Linkebeek - ☎ 0 2 :

XXX **Le Saint-Sébastien,** Square Maas 16 ☎ 380 54 90, Fax 380 54 41 - P. E VISA
closed Monday, Tuesday and 15 July-15 August - **M** a la carte 1700/2050.

at Machelen - pop. 11 250 - ✉ 1830 Machelen - ☎ 0 2 :

XXX ✿ **André D'Haese,** Heirbaan 210 ☎ 252 50 72, Fax 252 50 72 - P. AE E VISA.
closed Saturday lunch, Sunday, Bank Holidays, last 3 weeks July and 2 weeks January - **M** a la carte 2100/2750
Spec. Foie d'oie du gastronome, Soupe de homard norvégien au pistou, Ris de veau braisé à brun Zingara.

at Meise by ① : 14 km - pop. 16 661 - ✉ 1860 Meise - ☎ 0 2 :

XX **Aub. Napoléon,** Bouchoutlaan 1 ☎ 269 30 78, Fax 269 79 98, Grill rest - P. AE E VISA
closed August - **M** a la carte 1650/2300.

XX **Koen Van Loven,** Brusselsesteenweg 11 ☎ 270 05 77, Fax 270 05 46 - P - 40. AE E VISA.
closed Sunday dinner, Monday, 2 weeks September and 2 weeks February - **M** 1475/1750.

at Melsbroek C Steenokkerzeel pop. 9 925 - ✉ 1820 Melsbroek - ☎ 0 2 :

XX **Boetfort,** Sellaerstraat 42 ☎ 751 64 00, Fax 751 62 00, « 17C mansion, park » - P - 25. AE E VISA.
closed Wednesday dinner, Saturday lunch, Sunday and carnival week - **M** a la carte 1950/2200.

at Overijse by ⑦ : 16 km - pop. 22 665 - ✉ 3090 Overijse - ☎ 0 2 :

XXXX ✿ **Barbizon** (Deluc), Welriekendedreef 95 (at Jezus-Eik) ☎ 657 04 62, Fax 657 40 66, « Terrace and garden » - P. AE E VISA
closed Tuesday, Wednesday, 2 February-3 March and 13 July-4 August - **M** a la carte 2350/3250
Spec. Homard en chemise, beurre "Barbizon", Caneton au miel et poireaux confits, Tartare de loup et saumon à l'huile de noisettes.

X **Istas,** Brusselsesteenweg 652 (NW : 2 km at Jezus-Eik) ☎ 657 05 11, , Pub rest - P
closed Wednesday, Thursday and 1 to 30 August - **M** a la carte 750/1200.

at Schepdaal by ⑪ : 12 km C Dilbeek pop. 36 647 - ✉ 1703 Schepdaal - ☎ 0 2 :

Lienzana without rest, Ninoofsesteenweg 209 ☎ 569 65 25, Fax 569 64 64, , - TV ☎ P - 25. AE E VISA
closed 24 December-2 January - **19 rm** 2200/2800.

at Sint-Genesius-Rode (Rhode-St-Genèse) by ⑧ : 13 km - pop. 17 789 - ✉ 1640 Sint-Genesius-Rode - ☎ 0 2 :

Aub. de Waterloo without rest, chaussée de Waterloo 212 ☎ 358 35 80, Telex 24042, Fax 358 38 06 - TV ☎ P - 30-60. AE E VISA
84 rm 3000/5980.

at Strombeek-Bever C Grimbergen pop. 31 944 - ✉ 1853 Strombeek-Bever - ☎ 0 2 :

XX **Le Val Joli,** Leestbeekstraat 16 ☎ 460 65 43, Fax 460 04 00, , « Terrace and garden » - P. AE VISA
closed Monday and Tuesday - **M** 990/1490.

XX **'t Stoveke,** Jetsestraat 52 ☎ 267 67 25, , Seafood - AE E VISA
closed Sunday, Monday, Bank Holidays, 3 weeks June and Christmas-New Year - **M** a la carte 1600/2700.

at Vilvoorde (Vilvorde) - pop. 32 942 - ✉ 1800 Vilvoorde - ☎ 0 2 :

XX **Barbay,** Romeinsesteenweg 220 (SW : 4 km at Koningslo) ☎ 267 00 45, Fax 267 00 45, - AE E VISA
closed Saturday lunch, Sunday, 15 July-15 August and 1 week New Year - **M** a la carte 1500/2000.

at Vlezenbeek by ⑩ : 11 km C Sint-Pieters-Leeuw pop. 28 697 - ✉ 1602 Vlezenbeek - ☎ 0 2 :

XX **Philippe Verbaeys,** Dorp 49 ☎ 569 05 25, Fax 569 05 25, - AE E VISA
closed Monday, 5 to 20 April and 26 July-13 August - **M** 800/1600.

X **Aub. Le St-Esprit,** Postweg 250 (road to the castle of Gaasbeek) ☎ 532 42 18 - AE E VISA
closed dinner Sunday and Tuesday, Monday, first 2 weeks March and September - **M** a la carte 1600/1950.

at Wemmel - pop. 13 666 - ✉ 1780 Wemmel - ☎ 0 2 :

XX **Parkhof,** Parklaan 7 ☎ 460 42 89, Fax 460 25 10, , « Terrace » - P. AE E VISA
closed Wednesday, Thursday, 16 August-10 September and carnival week - **M** 1400.

at Wezembeek-Oppem by ⑤: 11 km – pop. 13 016 – ✉ 1970 Wezembeek-Oppem – ☎ 0 2 :

XXX **L'Aub. Saint-Pierre,** Sint-Pietersplein 8 ☎ 731 21 79, Fax 731 21 79 – AE ⓓ E VISA
closed Saturday lunch, Sunday, Bank Holidays, mid July-mid August and 24 December-3 January – **M** a la carte 1700/2050.

at Zaventem – pop. 25 856 – ✉ 1930 Zaventem – ☎ 0 2 :

Sheraton Airport, at airport (NE by A 201) ☎ 725 10 00, Telex 27085, Fax 725 11 55 – 🛗 ⇔ rm ▤ TV ☎ & 🚗 – 🏛 25-585. AE ⓓ E VISA. ✗ rest
M Concorde a la carte 1600/2250 – ☕ 690 – **290 rm** 8400/9400, 2 suites.

XX ✿ **Stockmansmolen** 1st floor, H. Henneaulaan 164 ☎ 725 34 34, Fax 725 75 05, Partly pub rest, « Former watermill » – Ⓟ. AE ⓓ E VISA. ✗
closed Saturday, Sunday and Bank Holidays – **M** a la carte 1900/2600
Spec. Gaspacho de crustacés, Turbot au corail d'oursin, Tarte landaise aux poires.

Berlare 9290 Oost-Vlaanderen 213 ⑤ and 409 ③ – pop. 12 674 – ☎ 0 52 – 38 km.

XXX ✿✿ **'t Laurierblad** (Van Cauteren) (new hotel planned in annexe), Dorp 4 ☎ 42 48 01, Fax 42 59 97, « Terrace with ornamental lake » – Ⓟ – 🏛 25-40. AE ⓓ E VISA
M a la carte 2000/2700
Spec. Gnocchi de pommes de terre et homard à l'huile de truffes, Salade de langoustines, foie de canard et filet d'Anvers, Fondant de ris et tête de veau aux truffes.

Genval 1322 Brabant Ⓒ Rixensart pop. 20 743 213 ⑲ and 409 ⑬ – ☎ 0 2 – 21 km.

Château du Lac ⛰, av. du Lac 87 ☎ 654 11 22, Fax 653 62 00, ≤ lake and woodland, ✗ – 🛗 TV ☎ Ⓟ – 🏛 30-1000. AE ⓓ E VISA
M see rest **Le Trèfle à 4** below – **37 rm** ☕ 7400/8600, 1 suite.

Le Manoir ⛰ without rest, av. Hoover 4 ☎ 655 63 11, Fax 655 64 55, ≤, « Park », ≘s, ✗ – TV ☎ Ⓟ – 🏛 25. AE ⓓ E VISA
12 rm ☕ 7400/8600.

XXXX ✿✿ **Le Trèfle à 4** (Haquin) - at Château du Lac H., av. du Lac 87 ☎ 654 07 98, Fax 653 31 31, ≤ lake and woodland – Ⓟ. AE ⓓ E VISA
closed Monday, Tuesday and late January-early February – **M** a la carte 2500/2950
Spec. Poêlée de langoustines, buisson de légumes et herbes frites, Homard à l'armoricaine, Poularde en croûte de sel, crème de cresson aux légumes.

ANTWERP (ANTWERPEN) 2000 212 ⑮ and 409 ④ – pop. 470 349 – ☎ 0 3.

See: Around the Market Square (Grote Markt) and the Cathedral★★★ : Vlaaikensgang★ FY, Cathedral★★★ FY – Rubens' House★★ (Rubenshuis) GZ – Butchers' House★ (Vleeshuis) : Musical instruments★ FY D - Hendrik Conscience Place★ GY – Interior★ of the St. James' church (St-Jacobskerk) GY – The port (Haven) ⛴ FY – Zoo★★ (Dierentuin) EU – St. Charles Borromeo's Church★ (St-Carolus Borromeuskerk) GY – St. Paul's Church (St-Pauluskerk) : interior★ FY.

Museums : Royal Art Gallery★★★ (Koninklijk Museum voor Schone Kunsten) CV – Plantin-Moretus★★★ (ancient printing-office) FZ – Mayer Van den Bergh★★ : Mad Meg★★ (Dulle Griet) GZ – Maritime "Steen"★ (Nationaal Scheepvaartmuseum Steen) FY M¹ – Rockox House★ (Rockoxhuis) GY M² – Etnographic Museum 1e FY M¹⁰ – Museum of Photography★ – Open-air Museum of Sculpture Middelheim★ (Openluchtmuseum voor Beeldhouwkunst).

⛳18 ⛳9 at Kapellen by ②: 15,5 km, G. Capiaulei 2 ☎ (0 3) 666 84 56 - ⛳18 at Aartselaar by ⑩: 10 km, Kasteel Cleydael ☎ (0 3) 887 00 79 - ⛳18 at Wommelgem by ⑥ : 10 km, Uilenbaan 15 ☎ (0 3) 353 02 92 - ⛳18 ⛳9 at Broechem by ⑥ : 16 km, Kasteel Bossenstein ☎ (0 3) 485 64 46.

🛈 Grote Markt 15 ☎ 232 01 03 – Tourist association of the province, Karel Oomsstraat 11, ✉ 2018, ☎ 216 28 10.

Brussels 48 ⑩ – Amsterdam 159 ④ – Luxemburg 261 ⑨ – Rotterdam 103 ④.

Plans on following pages

Old Antwerp

De Rosier ⛰ without rest, Rosier 23 ☎ 225 01 40, Telex 33697, Fax 231 41 11, « Former 17C residence », ≘s, 🏊, 🌳 – 🛗 TV ☎ 🚗. AE ⓓ E VISA — FZ **d**
closed 24, 25, 26 and 31 December-2 January – ☕ 600 – **8 rm** 6890/9010, 4 suites.

Alfa Theater, Arenbergstraat 30 ☎ 231 17 20, Telex 33910, Fax 233 88 58, ≘s – 🛗 ⇔ rm ▤ rest TV ☎ – 🏛 25. AE ⓓ E VISA — GZ **t**
M *(closed Saturday lunch, Sunday and Bank Holidays)* a la carte approx. 1200 – **127 rm** ☕ 5750/7550, 5 suites.

Villa Mozart, Handschoenmarkt 3 ☎ 231 30 31, Fax 231 56 85, 🌿, « Elegant interior », ≘s – 🛗 TV ☎ – 🏛 25. AE ⓓ E VISA — FY **e**
M (Pub rest) *(closed Tuesday)* a la carte approx. 1200 – **23 rm** ☕ 4500/6200, 2 suites.

Prinse ⛰ without rest, Keizerstraat 63 ☎ 226 40 50, Fax 225 11 48 – 🛗 ▤ TV ☎ 🚗 – 🏛 25-120. AE E VISA. ✗ — GY **a**
30 rm ☕ 3500/4000.

Rubens ⛰ without rest, Oude Beurs 29 ☎ 226 95 82, Fax 225 19 40 – 🛗 TV ☎ – 🏛 25-50. AE ⓓ E VISA — FY **f**
35 rm ☕ 3850/9000, 1 suite.

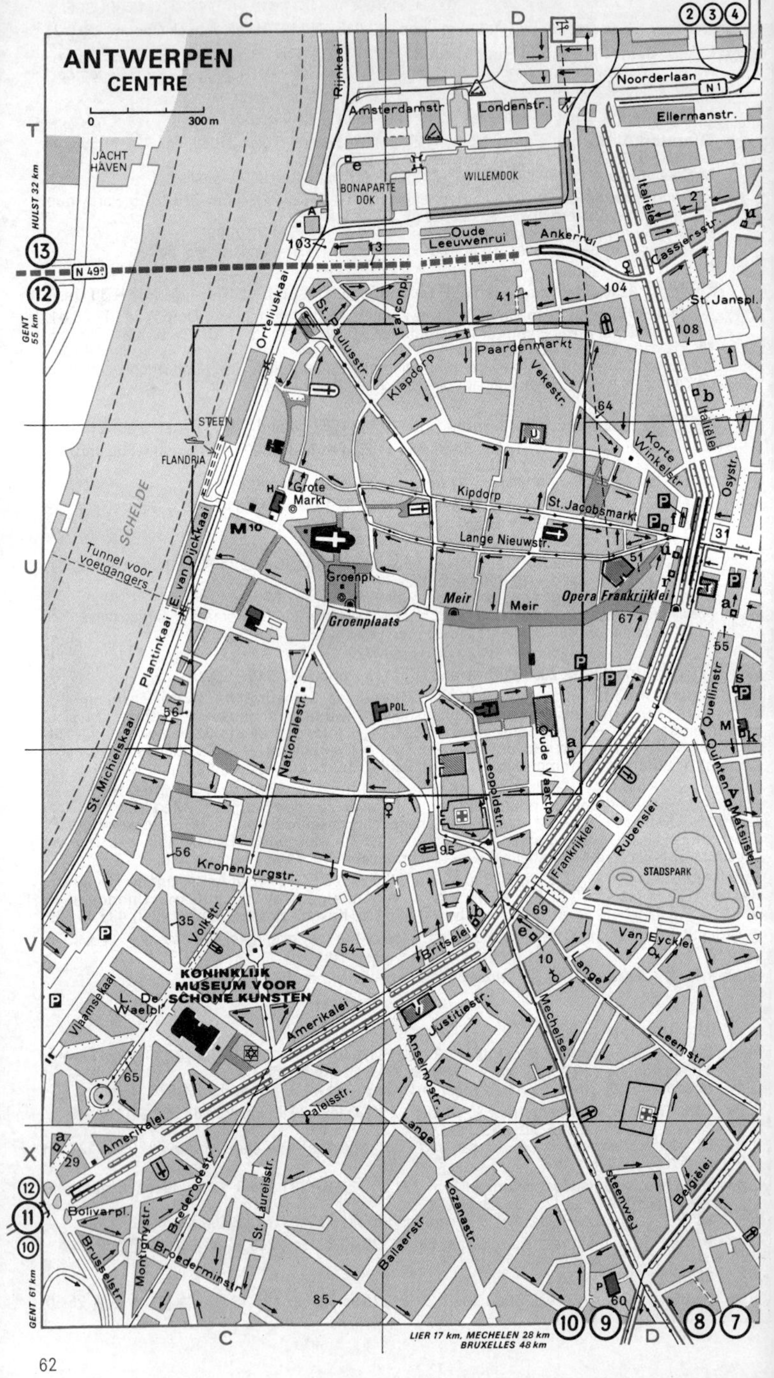
ANTWERPEN
CENTRE
0
300 m
JACHT HAVEN
BONAPARTE DOK
WILLEMDOK
Rijnkaai
Amsterdamstr.
Londenstr.
Noorderlaan
N 1
Ellermanstr.
Oude Leeuwenrui
Ankerrui
Italiëlei
Cassiersstr.
St. Janspl.
N 49a
HULST 32 km
GENT 55 km
Orteliuskaai
St. Paulusstr.
Falconpl.
Paardenmarkt
Klapdorp
Vekestr.
STEEN
FLANDRIA
SCHELDE
Korte Winkelstr.
Osystr.
Grote Markt
Kipdorp
St. Jacobsmarkt
M10
Lange Nieuwstr.
Tunnel voor voetgangers
E. van Dijckkaai
Groenpl.
Meir
Opera
Frankrijklei
Groenplaats
Plantinkaai
POL.
Quellinstr.
Quinten Matsijslei
St. Michielskaai
Nationalestr.
Oude Vaartpl.
Leopoldstr.
Kronenburgstr.
Frankrijklei
Rubenslei
STADSPARK
Volkstr.
Britselei
Van Eycklei
KONINKLIJK MUSEUM VOOR SCHONE KUNSTEN
Vlaamsekaai
L. De Waelpl.
Amerikalei
Justitiestr.
Lange
Mechelse-
Leemstr.
Anselmostr.
Paleisstr.
Lange
Bolivarpl.
Brederodestr.
Montignystr.
St. Laureisstr.
Lozanastr.
Steenweg
Belgiëlei
Brusselstr.
Broederminstr.
Ballaerstr.
GENT 61 km
LIER 17 km, MECHELEN 28 km
BRUXELLES 48 km
T
U
V
X
C
D

STREET INDEX TO ANTWERPEN TOWN PLANS

Carnotstr. . . . . EU
Dambruggestr. . . . . ETU
Gemeentestr. . . . . EU 33
Groenplaats . . . . . FZ
De Keyserlei . . . . . DEU 55
Klapdorp . . . . . GY

Leysstr. . . . . DU 67
Meir . . . . . GZ
Nationalestr. . . . . FZ
Offerandestr. . . . . EU
Paardenmarkt . . . . . GY
Pelikaanstr. . . . . EUV 81
Quellinstr. . . . . DU
Schoenmarkt . . . . . FZ
Turnhoutsebaan (BORGERHOUT) . . . . . EU

van Aerdtstr. . . . . DT 2
Amerikalei CVX
Amsterdamstr. . . . . CDT
Ankerrui . . . . . DT
Anselmostr. . . . . DV
Arenbergstr. . . . . GZ
Ballaerstr. . . . . DX
Belgiëlei . . . . . DX, EV
Bleekhofstr. . . . . EV
Blindestr. . . . . GY
Bolivarplaats CX
Borzestr. . . . . GY
Brederodestr. CX
van Breestr. . . . . DV 10
Brialmontlei . . . . . EV 12
Britselei . . . . . DV
Broederminstr. CX
Brouwersvliet . . . . . CT 13
Brusselstr. CX
Cassiersstr. . . . . DT
Charlottalei . . . . . EV 17
Diepestr. . . . . ET
Eiemarkt . . . . . FZ
Ellermanstr. . . . . DT
Emiel Banningstr. . . . . CX 29
Ernest van Dijckkaai . . . . . FY
van Eycklei . . . . . DV
Falconplein . . . . . DT
F. Rooseveltplein . . . . . DU 31
Frankrijklei . . . . . DUV
Gildekamersstr. . . . . FY
Graanmarkt . . . . . GZ
Graaf van Egmontstr. . . . . CV 35
Grote Markt . . . . . FY
Halenstr. . . . . ET
Handelsstr. . . . . ET
Handschoenmarkt . . . . . FY
H. Conscienceplein . . . . . GY
's Herenstr. . . . . EV
Hessenplein . . . . . DT 41
Hofstr. . . . . FY
Hollandstr. . . . . ET 43
Hoogstr. . . . . FZ
Huidevettersstr. . . . . GZ
Italïelei . . . . . DTU
Jezusstr. . . . . DU 51
Jordaenskaai . . . . . FY
Justitiestr. . . . . DV
Kaasrui . . . . . FY
Kammenstr. . . . . FZ
Kasteelpleinstr. . . . . CV 54
van Kerckhovenstr. . . . . ET
Kerkstr. . . . . EU
Kipdorp . . . . . GY
Kloosterstr. . . . . CUV 56
Koningin Astridplein . . . . . EU 59
Koningin Elisabethlei . . . . . DX 60
Korte Gasthuisstr. . . . . GZ
Korte Winkelstr. . . . . DU
Korte Zavelstr. . . . . ET 61
Kronenburgstr. CV
Kroonstr. . . . . EV
Lamorinièrestr. . . . . EVX
Lange Beeldekensstr. . . . . EU
Lange Gasthuisstr. . . . . GZ
Lange Klarenstr. . . . . GZ
Lange Koepoortstr. . . . . FY
Lange Leemstr. . . . . DV, EX
Lange Lozanastr. . . . . DX
Lange Nieuwstr. . . . . GY
Lange Riddersstr. . . . . FZ
Lange Winkelstr. . . . . DT 64
Leopold de Waelpl CV
Leopold de Waelstr. . . . . CV 65
Leopoldstr. . . . . DV
Lombardenvest . . . . . FZ
Londenstr. . . . . DT
Maria-Henriettalei . . . . . DV 69
Maria-Pijpelinckxstr. . . . . GZ
Marialei . . . . . EX
Mechelsesteenweg . . . . . DVX
Mercatorstr. . . . . EV 72
Minderbroedersrui . . . . . FGY

Continued on next page

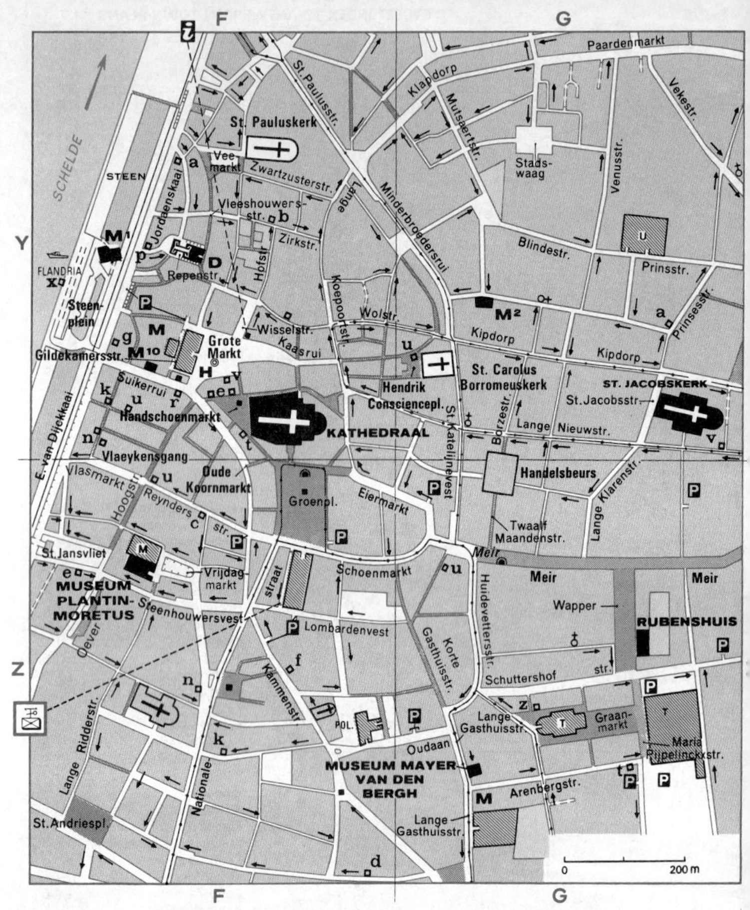

STREET INDEX TO ANTWERPEN TOWN PLANS (Concluded)

Antigone without rest, Jordaenskaai 11 ☎ 231 66 77, Fax 231 37 74 - |‡| TV ☎. AE ⓓ E VISA. ✻ FY a
15 rm ☐ 3000/3500 and 2 suites.

Cammerpoorte without rest, Nationalestraat 38 ☎ 231 97 36, Fax 226 29 68 - |‡| TV ☎ Ⓟ. AE ⓓ E VISA. ✻ FZ n
39 rm ☐ 2750/3350.

Arcade without rest, Meistraat 39 (Theaterplein) ☎ 231 88 30, Telex 31104, Fax 234 29 21 - |‡| TV ☎ ♿ - 25-75. AE E VISA DV a
150 rm ☐ 3100/3450.

XXXX ✿✿ **La Pérouse,** Steenplein (pontoon) ☎ 231 31 51, Fax 231 13 60, « Anchored vessel with ≤ » - ▤ Ⓟ. AE ⓓ E VISA. ✻ FY x
closed Sunday, Monday and Bank Holidays - **M** a la carte 2400/2750
Spec. Marbré de foie de canard et de filet d'Anvers, Marinière de barbue et de St-Jacques, Sole "La Pérouse".

XXX **Den Gulden Greffoen,** Hoogstraat 37 ☎ 231 50 46, Fax 233 20 39, « In a 15C residence » - ▤. AE ⓓ E VISA. ✻ - *closed Saturday lunch, Sunday, Bank Holidays and 2 weeks August*
M a la carte 2000/2650. FZ u

XXX **La Rade** 1st floor, E. Van Dijckkaai 8 ☎ 233 37 37, Fax 233 49 63, « Former 19C freemason's lodge » - AE ⓓ E VISA - *closed Saturday lunch, Sunday, Bank Holidays, carnival week and 5 to 25 July* - **M** a la carte 1950/2600. FY g

XXX ✿✿ **'t Fornuis** (Segers), Reyndersstraat 24 ☎ 233 62 70, « 17C residence, rustic interior » - AE ⓓ E VISA. ✻ - *closed Saturday, Sunday, Bank Holidays, last 3 weeks August and Christmas-New Year* - **M** a la carte 2300/2600 FZ c
Spec. Terrine de foie d'oie au beurre de Porto, Escalope de saumon au miel, Rognon de veau aux pommes et vinaigre de Cidre.

XX **Huis De Colvenier,** St-Antoniusstraat 8 ☎ 226 65 73, Fax 226 65 73, « Late 19C residence » - AE ⓓ E VISA. ✻ FZ k
closed Saturday lunch, Sunday dinner, Monday and 3 weeks August - **M** 1500/1800.

XX **Petrus,** Kelderstraat 1 ☎ 225 27 34, 🏠 - ▤. AE ⓓ E VISA GZ z
closed lunch Saturday and Sunday, Monday, 3 weeks July and 1 week February - **M** a la carte 1600/1950.

XX **De Kerselaar,** Grote Pieter Potstraat 22 ☎ 233 59 69, Fax 233 11 49 - ▤. AE ⓓ E VISA
closed lunch Saturday and Monday, Sunday, 5 to 26 July and 24 to 31 December - **M** a la carte approx. 2000. FY n

XX **'t Silveren Claverblat,** Grote Pieter Potstraat 16 ☎ 231 33 88 - AE ⓓ E VISA. ✻ FY k
closed Tuesday, Saturday lunch, first 2 weeks March and first 2 weeks September - **M** a la carte 1800/2100.

XX **De Manie,** H. Conscienceplein 3 ☎ 232 64 38 - AE ⓓ E VISA GY u
closed Wednesday, Sunday, 21 to 28 February, 12 to 18 April and 16 August-2 September - **M** a la carte 1600/1900.

XX **Zirk,** Zirkstraat 29 ☎ 225 25 86, Fax 226 51 77 - AE ⓓ E. ✻ FY b
closed Saturday lunch, Sunday, Monday, 1 week early September and 26 January-9 February - **M** a la carte 1300/1900.

XX **P. Preud'homme,** Suikerrui 28 ☎ 233 42 00, Fax 233 42 00, 🏠, Open until 11 p.m. - ▤. AE ⓓ E VISA. ✻ FY r
closed Tuesday and February - **M** a la carte 1500/2400.

XX **De Gulden Beer,** Grote Markt 14 ☎ 226 08 41, 🏠, Partly Italian cuisine - ▤. AE ⓓ E VISA. ✻ - *closed Wednesday and 1 to 15 October* - **M** a la carte 1150/1600. FY v

XX **De Koperen Ketel,** Wiegstraat 5 ☎ 233 12 74 - AE ⓓ E VISA GZ u
closed Saturday lunch, Sunday, Bank Holidays and July - **M** a la carte approx. 1600.

XX **Les Larmes du Tigre,** Vleeshuisstraat 1 ☎ 226 21 90, Thaï cuisine, « Elegant Asiatic installation » - AE ⓓ E VISA FY p
closed 26 July-16 August - **M** a la carte 1000/1550.

XX **VIP Diners,** Lange Nieuwstraat 95 ☎ 233 13 17 - AE ⓓ E VISA GY v
closed Saturday lunch, Sunday, Bank Holidays and last 2 weeks July - **M** a la carte approx. 1800.

XX **De Perelaer,** Kammenstraat 75 ☎ 233 42 73, Fax 226 28 51, « 16C residence » - AE ⓓ E VISA FZ f
closed lunch Saturday and Monday, Sunday and 2 to 15 August - **M** a la carte 1400/1950.

XX **Het Nieuwe Palinghuis,** St-Jansvliet 14 ☎ 231 74 45, Fax 231 50 53, Seafood - ▤. AE ⓓ E VISA - *closed Monday, Tuesday and June* - **M** 1150/1850. FZ e

XX **In de Schaduw van de Kathedraal,** Handschoenmarkt 17 ☎ 232 40 14, 🏠, Mussels in season - AE ⓓ E VISA. ✻ FY e
closed Monday September-Easter, Tuesday and February - **M** a la carte 1700/2050.

XX ✿ **De Matelote** (Garnich), Haarstraat 9 ☎ 231 32 07, Seafood - AE ⓓ E VISA FY u
closed Saturday, Sunday, July and first 2 weeks January - **M** a la carte 1900/2900
Spec. Terrine de crevettes grises et artichauts, Lotte poêlée aux mange-tout et lardons croquants, Crème brûlée à la cassonade.

X **Rooden Hoed,** Oude Koornmarkt 25 ☎ 233 28 44, Mussels in season, Antwerp atmosphere - AE VISA. ✻ FY t
closed Wednesday, Thursday, 15 June-15 July and carnival week - **M** a la carte 1100/1500.

Town Centre

Alfa De Keyser, De Keyserlei 66, ⊠ 2018, ✆ 234 01 35, Telex 34219, Fax 232 39 70, – – AE E VISA. EU **b**
M a la carte 1450/1800 - **115 rm** 5900/8100, 2 suites.

Switel, Copernicuslaan 2, ⊠ 2018, ✆ 231 67 80, Telex 33965, Fax 233 02 90, – rm – 25-1000. AE E VISA EV **a**
M a la carte 1300/2000 - 575 - **301 rm** 4220/6275, 9 suites.

Carlton with 11 apartments in annexe, Quinten Matsijslei 25, ⊠ 2018, ✆ 231 15 15, Telex 31072, Fax 225 30 90, – rm – 30-100. AE E VISA. rest
M *(closed dinner Friday and Sunday, Saturday lunch, 1 to 22 August and 21 December-3 January)* a la carte 850/1650 - **137 rm** 5400/9800, 1 suite. DV **v**

Alfa Empire without rest, Appelmansstraat 31, ⊠ 2018, ✆ 231 47 55, Telex 33909, Fax 233 40 60 – . AE E VISA DU **s**
70 rm 5550/6750.

Plaza without rest, Charlottalei 43, ⊠ 2018, ✆ 218 92 40, Telex 31531, Fax 218 88 23 – . AE E VISA EV **v**
350 - **80 rm** 3900/4900.

Residence without rest, St-Jacobsmarkt 85 ✆ 232 76 75, Fax 233 73 28 – . AE E VISA. DU **f**
400 - **19 rm** 3500/6000.

Colombus without rest, Frankrijklei 4 ✆ 233 03 90, Telex 71354, Fax 226 09 46, – . AE E VISA. DU **u**
32 rm 2900/3650.

Alfa Congress, Plantin en Moretuslei 136, ⊠ 2018, ✆ 235 30 00, Telex 31959, Fax 235 52 31 – rm – 30-70. AE E VISA. EV **s**
M *(closed Saturday, Sunday, Bank Holidays and Christmas-New Year)* a la carte approx. 1400 - **66 rm** 4050/4500.

Eden without rest, Lange Herentalsestraat 25, ⊠ 2018, ✆ 233 06 08, Telex 31132, Fax 233 12 28 – . AE E VISA DUV **k**
66 rm 2750/3250.

Christian V, Bonapartedok - St-Laureiskaai ✆ 226 83 17, Fax 226 03 28, , « Anchored merchant ship » – – 100. AE E VISA CT **e**
M *(closed Saturday lunch)* a la carte 1150/1750 - 400 - **54 rm** 2300/5950.

Fouquets 1st floor, De Keyserlei 17, ⊠ 2018, ✆ 233 97 42, Fax 226 16 88, , Open until 11 p.m. – . AE E VISA DU **a**
M a la carte 1500/1900.

Corum (De Koninck), Italiëlei 177 ✆ 232 23 44, Fax 232 24 41 – . AE E VISA.
closed lunch Saturday and Sunday, Monday, 15 to 31 July and late December – **M** a la carte 1750/2150 DT **b**
Spec. Sole vapeur aux champignons blancs, Suprêmes de pigeon au miel et gingembre, Marée du jour, sauce hollandaise.

De Barbarie, Van Breestraat 4, ⊠ 2018, ✆ 232 81 98, – AE E VISA DV **e**
closed Sunday, Monday and 1 to 15 September – **M** a la carte 1700/2200.

Blue Phoenix, Frankrijklei 14 ✆ 233 33 77, Fax 233 88 46, Chinese cuisine – . AE E VISA. DU **r**
closed Monday, Saturday lunch and August – **M** 750/1600.

De Zeste, Lange Dijkstraat 36, ⊠ 2060, ✆ 233 45 49 – . AE E VISA. DT **u**
closed Saturday lunch, Sunday, Monday, first 2 weeks August and last 2 weeks December – **M** a la carte 1650/2100.

Milano, Statiestraat 15, ⊠ 2018, ✆ 232 67 43, Partly Italian cuisine, open until 2 a.m. – . AE E VISA EU **q**
closed July – **M** a la carte 800/1700.

Osaka, Bollandusstraat 15 (angle Britselei) ✆ 233 16 22, Fax 231 47 08, Japanese cuisine – AE E VISA. DV **b**
closed Monday – **M** a la carte 1300/2000.

't Lammeke, Lange Lobroekstraat 51 (opposite slaughterhouse), ⊠ 2060, ✆ 236 79 86, Fax 271 05 16 – . AE E VISA
closed lunch Saturday and Monday, Sunday, Bank Holidays, 14 to 31 August and 23 to 31 December – **M** a la carte 1050/1700.

Panaché back room, Statiestraat 17, ⊠ 2018, ✆ 232 69 05, Fax 232 13 60 – AE E VISA
M 960. EU **q**

South Quarter

Holiday Inn Crowne Plaza, G. Legrellelaan 10, ⊠ 2020, ✆ 237 29 00, Telex 33843, Fax 216 02 96, – rm – 25-800. AE E VISA. rest
M *(closed 3 weeks July)* a la carte 1800/2300 - **256 rm** 7995/8995, 4 suites.

Pullman Park, Desguinlei 94, ⊠ 2018, ✆ 216 48 00, Telex 33368, Fax 216 47 12, – rm – 25-450. AE E VISA
M Tiffany's *(closed Saturday)* a la carte 1100/1600 - 550 - **213 rm** 3000/5500, 3 suites.

Firean (annexe 6 rm) without rest, Karel Oomsstraat 6, ✉ 2018, ☎ 237 02 60, Fax 238 11 68, « Period residence, Art-Deco style » – AE ① E VISA.
closed 31 July-16 August and 24 December-10 January – **10 rm** 3400/4600, 1 suite.

Industrie without rest, E. Banningstraat 52 ☎ 238 66 00, Fax 238 86 88 – AE ① E VISA. CX **a**
9 rm 2500/3500.

Vateli, Van Putlei 31, ✉ 2018, ☎ 238 72 52, Fax 238 25 88 – AE ① E VISA.
closed Saturday lunch, Sunday, Bank Holidays and last 2 weeks July – **M** a la carte 1850/2400.

Loncin, Markgravelei 127, ✉ 2018, ☎ 248 29 89, Fax 248 38 66, Open until midnight – ① E VISA.
closed lunch Saturday and Sunday, Tuesday and Wednesday – **M** 2600.

Liang's Garden, Markgravelei 141, ✉ 2018, ☎ 237 22 22, Fax 248 38 34, Chinese cuisine – AE ① E VISA.
closed Sunday and 2 to 18 August – **M** a la carte 1000/1650.

De Poterne, Desguinlei 186, ✉ 2018, ☎ 238 28 24, Fax 238 28 24 – AE ① E.
closed Saturday, Sunday, Bank Holidays, 21 July-15 August and 24 December-1 January – **M** a la carte 1950/2350.

Suburbs

North – ✉ 2030 :

Novotel, Luithagen-Haven 6 ☎ 542 03 20, Fax 541 70 93, – rm – 25-150. AE ① E VISA. rest
M (open until midnight) a la carte approx. 1100 – 400 – **119 rm** 3100.

at Borgerhout C Antwerpen – ✉ 2140 Borgerhout – 0 3 :

Scandic Crown, Luitenant Lippenslaan 66 ☎ 235 91 91, Telex 34479, Fax 235 08 96, – rm – 25-200. AE ① E VISA
M a la carte approx. 1600 – 575 – **203 rm** 4600/5000.

at Deurne C Antwerpen – ✉ 2100 Deurne – 0 3 :

Périgord, Turnhoutsebaan 273 ☎ 325 52 00 – AE ① E VISA.
closed Tuesday, Wednesday, Saturday lunch, July and carnival – **M** a la carte 1450/1900.

at Ekeren C Antwerpen – ✉ 2180 Ekeren – 0 3 :

Hof de Bist, Veltwijcklaan 258 ☎ 664 61 30, Fax 664 67 24 – AE ① E VISA
closed Sunday, Monday, August and Christmas-early January – **M** a la carte 2050/2550.

at Merksem C Antwerpen – ✉ 2170 Merksem – 0 3 :

Maritime, Bredabaan 978 ☎ 646 22 23, Fax 646 22 71, Seafood – AE ① E VISA
closed Sunday – **M** a la carte 1700/2050.

at Wilrijk C Antwerpen – ✉ 2610 Wilrijk – 0 3 :

Schans XV, Moerelei 155 ☎ 828 45 64, Fax 828 93 29, « Early 20C redoubt » – AE ① E VISA.
closed Thursday dinner, Saturday lunch, Sunday, Bank Holidays, 2 weeks August and 2 weeks February – **M** a la carte 2000/2400.

Bistrot, Doornstraat 186 ☎ 829 17 29 – AE ① E VISA
closed Monday, Tuesday, Saturday lunch, late July-late August and 1 week late December – **M** 895/1495.

Environs

at Aartselaar by ⑩ : 10 km – pop. 13 895 – ✉ 2630 Aartselaar – 0 3 :

Host. Kasteelhoeve Groeninghe with rm, Kontichsesteenweg 78 ☎ 457 95 86, Fax 458 13 68, « Restored Flemish farm, country atmosphere », – 25-150. AE ① E VISA.
closed 15 to 22 August and 23 December-6 January – **M** *(closed Saturday lunch, Sunday and Bank Holidays)* a la carte 1800/2300 – 500 – **7 rm** 3900/5250.

Lindenbos, Boomsesteenweg 139 ☎ 888 09 65, Fax 844 47 58, « Converted mansion with park and lake » – AE ① E VISA.
closed Monday and August – **M** a la carte 1750/2400.

at Brasschaat by ② and ③ : 11 km – pop. 34 540 – ✉ 2930 Brasschaat – 0 3 :

Het Villasdal (Van Raes), Kapelsesteenweg 480 ☎ 664 58 21, Fax 605 08 42, – AE ① E VISA
closed Saturday lunch, Sunday dinner, Monday, 19 July-9 August and 19 January-2 February – **M** a la carte 1950/2400
Spec. Fondant de ris de veau aux pointes vertes, Sole farcie aux poireaux, crevettes grises et moules au safran, Parfait aux amandes et pistaches.

Halewijn, Donksesteenweg 212 (Ekeren-Donk) ☎ 647 20 10, Fax 647 08 95, – ① E VISA
closed Monday – **M** a la carte approx. 1700.

at Hemiksem by ⑩, at West : 9 km – pop. 9 380 – ✉ 2620 Hemiksem – ✪ 0 3 :

Scheldeboord, Scheldestraat 151 ☎ 877 14 14, Fax 877 12 10, « Scheldt-side setting », – |♦| ▤ rest TV ☎ P – 25-60. AE ◑ E VISA.
M *(closed Saturday lunch)* 1460/1980 – **20 rm** ☐ 3300/3700.

at Kapellen by ② : 15,5 km – pop. 23 977 – ✉ 2950 Kapellen – ✪ 0 3 :

XXX ✿✿ **De Bellefleur** (Buytaert), Antwerpsesteenweg 253 ☎ 664 67 19, Fax 665 02 01, « Winter garden » – P. AE ◑ E VISA
closed Saturday, Sunday, July and 2 weeks February – **M** a la carte 1900/2650
Spec. Tagliatellini de homard au basilic, Rôti de turbot aux champignons des bois, Carré de porcelet aux herbes thaï.

at Kontich by ⑧ : 12 km – pop. 18 667 – ✉ 2550 Kontich – ✪ 0 3 :

XXX **Carême,** Koningin Astridlaan 114 ☎ 457 63 04, Fax 457 93 02, – P. AE ◑ E VISA
closed Saturday lunch, Sunday and Monday dinner – **M** a la carte 2050/2400.

XXX **Alexander's,** Mechelsesteenweg 318 ☎ 457 26 31, Fax 457 26 31 – P. AE ◑ E VISA
closed Sunday dinner, Monday, last 3 weeks July and late December – **M** a la carte 1450/1950.

at Schoten – pop. 31 037 – ✉ 2900 Schoten – ✪ 0 3 :

XXX **Uilenspiegel,** Brechtsebaan 277 (3 km on N 115) ☎ 651 61 45, Fax 652 08 08, « Terrace and garden » – P. AE E VISA
closed Sunday, Monday, last 3 weeks July and last week January – **M** a la carte 1200/2000.

XXX **Kleine Barreel,** Bredabaan 1147 ☎ 645 85 84, Fax 645 85 03 – ▤ P. AE ◑ E VISA.
closed 19 July-2 August – **M** 1950.

XX **De Witte Raaf,** Horstebaan 97 ☎ 658 86 64, Fax 658 86 64, – P. AE ◑ E VISA
closed Tuesday dinner, Wednesday and 16 August-9 September – **M** a la carte 1400/1850.

at Wijnegem by ⑤ : 10 km – pop. 8 391 – ✉ 2110 Wijnegem – ✪ 0 3 :

XXX **Ter Vennen,** Merksemsebaan 278 ☎ 326 20 60, Fax 326 38 47, « Small farmhouse with elegant interior » – P. AE ◑ E VISA
M a la carte 1600/2400.

Kruiningen Zeeland (Netherlands) C Reimerswaal pop. 19 633 212 ⑬ ⑭ and 408 ⑯ – ✪ 0 1130 – 56 km.

Le Manoir , Zandweg 2 (W : 1 km), ✉ 4416 NA, ☎ 8 17 53, Fax 8 17 63, ←, – TV ☎ P. AE ◑ E VISA
closed January – **M** see rest **Inter Scaldes** below – ☐ 28 – **10 rm** 250/450 and 2 suites.

XXXX ✿✿ **Inter Scaldes** (Mme Boudeling) - at Le Manoir H., Zandweg 2 (W : 1 km), ✉ 4416 NA, ☎ 8 17 53, Fax 8 17 63, « Terrace-veranda overlooking an English-style garden » – P. AE ◑ E VISA
closed Monday, Tuesday and January – **M** a la carte 148/195
Spec. Homard fumé, sauce au caviar, Bar légèrement fumé à la tomate, basilic et olives (May-November), Turbot en robe de truffes et son beurre.

BRUGES **(BRUGGE) 8000** West-Vlaanderen 213 ③ and 409 ② – pop. 117 460 – ✪ 0 50.

See : Trips on the canals★★★ (Boottocht) CY **E** – Historic centre and canals★★★ (Historisch centrum en grachten) – Procession of the Holy Blood★★★ (Heilig Bloedprocessie) – Market square★★ (Markt) : Belfry and Halles★★★ (Belfort en Hallen) ←★★ from the top CY **F** – Market-town★★ (Burg) CY **D** – Beguinage★★ (Begijnhof) CZ – Basilica of the Holy Blood★ (Basiliek van het Heilig Bloed) : low Chapel★ (beneden- of St-Basiliuskapel) CY **A** – Church of Our Lady★ (O.L. Vrouwekerk) : tower★★, statue of the Madonna★★, tombstone of Mary of Burgundy★★ CZ **S** – Rosery quay (Rozenhoedkaai) ←★★ CY – Dijver ←★★ CZ – St. Boniface bridge (Bonifaciusbrug) : site★★ CZ – Chimney of the "Brugse Vrije" in the Court of Justice (Gerechtshof) CY **B**.

Museums : Groeninge★★★ (Stedelijk Museum voor Schone Kunsten) CZ – Memling★★★ (St. John's Hospital) CZ – Gruuthuse★ : bust of Charles the Fifth★ (borstbeeld van Karel V) CZ **M**[1] – Brangwyn★ CZ **M**[4] – Folklore★ (Museum voor Volkskunde) DY **M**[2].

Envir : Zedelgem : baptismal font★ in the St. Lawrence's church by ⑥ : 10,5 km.

18 at Damme NE : 7 km, Doornstraat 16 ☎ (0 50) 33 35 72.

i (closed Sunday except April-end Sept.) Burg 11 ☎ 44 86 86 – Tourist association of the province, Kasteel Tillegem ✉ 8200 ☎ 38 02 96.

Brussels 96 ③ – Ghent 45 ③ – Lille 72 ⑪ – Ostend 28 ⑤.

Plans on following pages

Holiday Inn Crowne Plaza , Burg 10 ☎ 34 58 34, Telex 81461, Fax 34 56 15, ←, « Interesting medieval remains and objects in basement », – |♦| rm ▤ TV ☎ P – 65-420. AE ◑ E VISA. rest CY **z**
M 't Kapittel *(closed Sunday dinner and Monday)* a la carte 1400/1800 – ☐ 500 – **90 rm** 5300/6700, 6 suites.

Pullman, Boeveriestraat 2 ☎ 34 09 71, Telex 81369, Fax 34 40 53, – |♦| ▤ TV ☎ P – 35-200. AE ◑ E VISA CZ **a**
M 850/2150 – **155 rm** ☐ 4950/5400.

De Tuilerieën without rest, Dijver 7 ℘ 34 36 91, Fax 34 04 00, ←, - 45. AE E VISA CYZ **p**
26 rm ☐ 4950/9950, 1 suite.

Relais Oud Huis Amsterdam without rest, Spiegelrei 3 ℘ 34 18 10, Telex 83121, Fax 33 88 91, ←, « 17C residence, former Dutch trading post », - 25. AE E VISA. CY **v**
22 rm ☐ 4000/6250.

De Orangerie without rest, Karthuizerinnenstraat 10 ℘ 34 16 49, Telex 82443, Fax 33 30 16, « Period canalside residence » - AE E VISA CY **y**
18 rm ☐ 4950/7950.

Academie, Wijngaardstraat 7 ℘ 33 22 66, Fax 33 21 66 - rest - 30-300. AE E VISA. CZ **k**
M 750/2200 - **33 rm** ☐ 4850/5450, 1 suite.

Karos without rest, Hoefijzerlaan 37 ℘ 34 14 48, Telex 82377, Fax 34 00 91, - AE E VISA BY **r**
closed 3 January-15 February - **60 rm** ☐ 2500/4590.

de'Medici without rest, Potterierei 15 ℘ 33 98 33, Telex 82227, Fax 33 07 64, « Modern style », - - 35. AE E VISA. DX **b**
34 rm ☐ 4500/5000.

Novotel Centrum, Katelijnestraat 65b ℘ 33 75 33, Telex 81799, Fax 33 65 56, - rm - 50-400. AE E VISA. rest CZ **v**
M (open until midnight) 850 - ☐ 425 - **126 rm** 3800/4550.

Parkhotel without rest, Vrijdagmarkt 5 ℘ 33 33 64, Telex 81686, Fax 33 47 63 - - 25-115. AE E VISA CZ **g**
86 rm ☐ 4000/5400.

Portinari without rest, 't Zand 15 ℘ 34 10 34, Telex 82400, Fax 34 41 80 - - 80. AE E VISA CZ **x**
closed 3 to 23 January - **40 rm** ☐ 3000/4500.

Alfa Dante, Coupure 29a ℘ 34 01 94, Telex 81452, Fax 34 35 39, ← - - 25-60. AE E VISA DY **e**
M (vegetarian cuisine) *(closed Sunday, Monday and August)* a la carte approx. 950 - **22 rm** ☐ 3850/5900.

Acacia without rest, Korte Zilverstraat 3a ℘ 34 44 11, Fax 33 88 17, - - 40. AE E VISA. CY **m**
closed 2 to 23 January - **30 rm** ☐ 3600/5400.

Die Swaene, Steenhouwersdijk 1 ℘ 34 27 98, Telex 82446, Fax 33 66 74, ←, « Stylish furnishing » - - 30. AE E VISA CY **g**
M *(closed Wednesday, Thursday lunch and 2 weeks July)* a la carte 2000/2350 - **22 rm** ☐ 4050/5850, 2 suites.

Pandhotel without rest., Pandreitje 16 ℘ 34 06 66, Telex 81018, Fax 34 05 56 - . AE E VISA CY **u**
24 rm ☐ 3400/4490.

De Castillion, Heilige Geeststraat 1 ℘ 34 30 01, Telex 83252, Fax 33 94 75, - - 50. AE E VISA. rest CZ **w**
M *(closed Monday November-April)* 1895 - **18 rm** ☐ 3150/5300 and 2 suites.

Prinsenhof without rest, Ontvangersstraat 9 ℘ 34 26 90, Fax 34 23 21 - . AE E VISA CY **c**
16 rm ☐ 3200/6000.

Bryghia without rest, Oosterlingenplein 4 ℘ 33 80 59, Telex 81691, Fax 34 14 30 - . AE E VISA. CY **f**
18 rm ☐ 3500/4200.

Adornes without rest, St-Annarei 26 ℘ 34 13 36, Fax 34 20 85, ←, « Period vaulted cellars » - . AE E VISA. DY **r**
closed January-1 February - **20 rm** ☐ 2350/2550.

Aragon without rest, Naaldenstraat 24 ℘ 33 35 33, Telex 81593, Fax 34 28 05 - . AE E VISA CY **t**
closed 5 to 31 January - **18 rm** ☐ 3500/3950.

Biskajer without rest, Biskajersplein 4 ℘ 34 15 06, Telex 81874, Fax 34 39 11 - . AE E VISA CY **j**
17 rm ☐ 2700/3700.

Ter Duinen without rest, Langerei 52 ℘ 33 04 37, Fax 34 42 16 - . AE E VISA. CX **a**
closed January - **18 rm** ☐ 2200/3500.

Azalea without rest, Wulfhagestraat 43 ℘ 33 14 78, Fax 33 97 00 - . AE E VISA CY **d**
25 rm ☐ 3000/4100.

Europ without rest, Augustijnenrei 18 ℘ 33 79 75, Telex 82490, Fax 34 52 66 - - 30. AE E VISA. CY **b**
closed 2 January-2 February - **28 rm** ☐ 2800/3950.

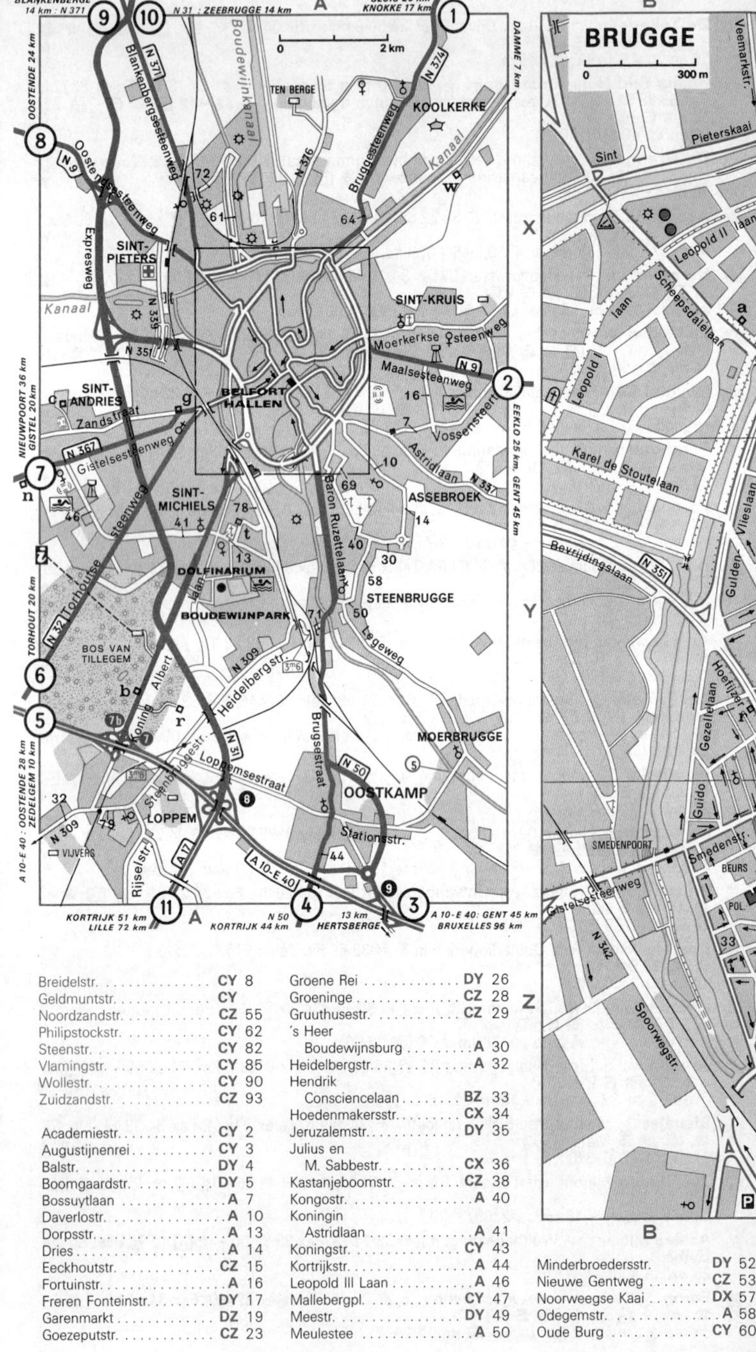

Breidelstr. . . . . **CY** 8
Geldmuntstr. . . . . **CY**
Noordzandstr. . . . . **CZ** 55
Philipstockstr. . . . . **CY** 62
Steenstr. . . . . **CY** 82
Vlamingstr. . . . . **CY** 85
Wollestr. . . . . **CY** 90
Zuidzandstr. . . . . **CZ** 93

Academiestr. . . . . **CY** 2
Augustijnenrei . . . . **CY** 3
Balstr. . . . . **DY** 4
Boomgaardstr. . . . . **DY** 5
Bossuytlaan . . . . **A** 7
Daverlostr. . . . . **A** 10
Dorpsstr. . . . . **A** 13
Dries . . . . **A** 14
Eeckhoutstr. . . . . **CZ** 15
Fortuinstr. . . . . **A** 16
Freren Fonteinstr. . . . . **DY** 17
Garenmarkt . . . . **DZ** 19
Goezeputstr. . . . . **CZ** 23

Groene Rei . . . . **DY** 26
Groeninge . . . . **CZ** 28
Gruuthusestr. . . . . **CZ** 29
's Heer
Boudewijnsburg . . . . **A** 30
Heidelbergstr. . . . . **A** 32
Hendrik
Consciencelaan . . . . **BZ** 33
Hoedenmakersstr. . . . . **CX** 34
Jeruzalemstr. . . . . **DY** 35
Julius en
M. Sabbestr. . . . . **CX** 36
Kastanjeboomstr. . . . . **CZ** 38
Kongostr. . . . . **A** 40
Koningin
Astridlaan . . . . **A** 41
Koningstr. . . . . **CY** 43
Kortrijkstr. . . . . **A** 44
Leopold III Laan . . . . **A** 46
Mallebergpl. . . . . **CY** 47
Meestr. . . . . **DY** 49
Meulestee . . . . **A** 50

Minderbroedersstr. . . . . . . **DY** 52
Nieuwe Gentweg . . . . **CZ** 53
Noorweegse Kaai . . . . **DX** 57
Odegemstr. . . . . **A** 58
Oude Burg . . . . **CY** 60

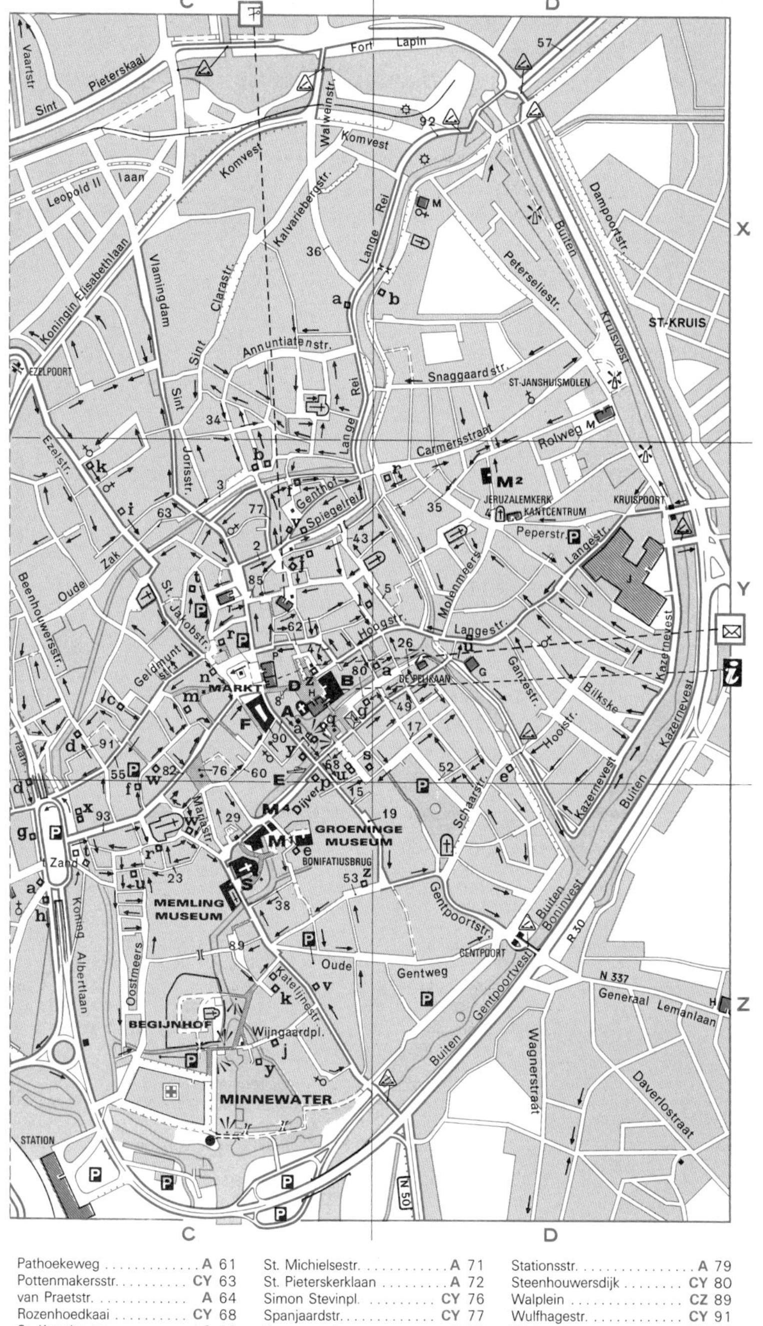

Ter Brughe without rest, Oost-Gistelhof 2 ☎ 34 03 24, Telex 82265, Fax 33 88 73 – TV ☎. AE ⓓ E VISA CY **b**
23 rm ☐ 2550/4400.

Boudewijn I ⛰, 't Zand 21 ☎ 33 69 62, Telex 81163, Fax 34 44 57 – |☰| TV ☎ – 🏛 25. AE ⓓ E VISA CZ **t**
closed 25 January-14 February – **M** *(closed Tuesday)* a la carte 750/1250 – **11 rm** ☐ 2000/3700.

Patritius without rest, Riddersstraat 11 ☎ 33 84 54, Fax 33 96 34, 🌳 – |☰| TV ☎ P – 🏛 25. AE ⓓ E VISA CY **l**
closed January-14 February – **16 rm** ☐ 4000/4500.

Bourgoensch Hof, Wollestraat 39 ☎ 33 16 45, Fax 34 63 78, ≤ canals and old Flemish houses – |☰| TV ☎. ✗ CY **a**
M (Pub rest) *(10 September-15 March closed Sunday dinner, Monday and Tuesday lunch)* a la carte approx. 900 – **11 rm** *(11 November-15 March open Friday, Saturday and school holidays only)* ☐ 2350/4800.

Albert I without rest, Koning Albertlaan 2 ☎ 34 09 30, Fax 33 84 18 – TV ☎. AE ⓓ E VISA
11 rm ☐ 2100/3200. CZ **h**

✿ **Maraboe** (De Smedt), Hoefijzerlaan 9 ☎ 33 81 55, Fax 33 29 28 – TV ☎. AE ⓓ E VISA
M *(closed Saturday lunch, Sunday dinner, Monday, 3 weeks after carnival, last week June and last week November)* (booking essential) a la carte 1600/2100 – **9 rm** *(closed 3 weeks after carnival, last week November and Sunday dinner and Monday out of season)* ☐ 1800/2600 CZ **d**
Spec. Terrine de foie gras, Homard au four au basilic (July-November), Suprême de pigeonneau à la crème de sauge (April-15 October).

Egmond ⛰ without rest, Minnewater 15 ☎ 34 14 45, Fax 34 29 40, « Garden setting » – TV ☎ P. AE E VISA CZ **y**
15 February-November – **9 rm** ☐ 3000/3400.

XXX ✿✿ **De Karmeliet** (Van Hecke), Langestraat 19 ☎ 33 82 59, Fax 33 10 11, 🍽, « Terrace » – P. AE ⓓ E VISA DY **u**
closed Sunday lunch July-August, Sunday dinner, Monday, 16 February-9 March and 23 August-7 September – **M** a la carte 2550/3100
Spec. Croustillant de pommes de terre, langoustines et foie d'oie, Pigeon au jus velouté de truffes, Ravioli à la vanille et pommes confites.

XXX ✿ **De Snippe** (Huysentruyt) ⛰ with rm, Nieuwe Gentweg 53 ☎ 33 70 70, Fax 33 76 62, « 18C residence with wall paintings » – |☰| TV ☎ P. AE ⓓ E VISA CZ **z**
M *(closed Sunday, Monday lunch and first 2 weeks March)* a la carte 2550/2900 – **9 rm** *(closed Sunday in winter and first 2 weeks March)* ☐ 4000/6000
Spec. Flan d'artichaut truffé aux queues de langoustines, Suprême de turbot à la persilllade de crabe, Civet de pigeonneau aux truffes et poires confites.

XXX **Vasquez,** Zilverstraat 38 ☎ 34 08 45, Fax 33 52 41, 🍽, « 15C residence, floral inner courtyard » – AE ⓓ E VISA CZ **f**
closed Wednesday and Thursday lunch – **M** 1980/2800.

XXX **De Witte Poorte,** Jan Van Eyckplein 6 ☎ 33 08 83, Fax 34 55 60, « Vaulted dining room, garden » – AE ⓓ E VISA CY **v**
closed Sunday, Monday, 2 weeks March and 2 weeks August – **M** a la carte 1800/2500.

XXX **Duc de Bourgogne** with rm, Huidenvettersplein 12 ☎ 33 20 38, Fax 34 40 37, ≤ canals, « Rustic decor and wall paintings of late medieval style » – ▤ rest TV ☎. AE ⓓ E VISA
closed 3 weeks July and January – **M** *(closed Monday and Tuesday lunch)* a la carte approx. 2400 – **9 rm** ☐ 3500/5000. CY **q**

XXX **Den Braamberg,** Pandreitje 11 ☎ 33 73 70, Fax 33 99 73 – AE E VISA CY **u**
closed Sunday dinner, Thursday, 10 to 31 July and 1 to 10 January – **M** a la carte 1750/2200.

XXX **Huyze Die Maene** 1st floor, Markt 17 ☎ 33 39 59, Fax 33 44 60 – AE ⓓ E VISA CY **n**
closed Tuesday, Wednesday, last week June-first 2 weeks July and 2 weeks February – **M** 1250.

XXX **Den Gouden Harynck,** Groeninge 25 ☎ 33 76 37, Fax 34 42 70 – P. AE ⓓ E VISA
closed Sunday, Monday, 1 week Easter, last week July-first week August and first week January – **M** a la carte 2250/2750. CZ **e**

XXX **'t Pandreitje,** Pandreitje 6 ☎ 33 11 90, Fax 34 00 70 – AE ⓓ E VISA CDY **s**
closed Wednesday, Sunday, 1 to 14 March, 28 June-11 July and 1 to 7 November – **M** a la carte 2150/2750.

XX **Patrick Devos,** Zilverstraat 41 ☎ 33 55 66, Fax 33 58 67, « Belle Epoque interior, patio » – AE ⓓ E VISA. ✗ CYZ **w**
closed Sunday, Monday lunch and Bank Holidays – **M** a la carte 1900/2150.

XX ✿ **Hermitage** (Dryepondt), Ezelstraat 18 ☎ 34 41 73 – ⓓ E VISA CY **i**
closed Sunday, Monday, July and August – **M** (dinner only) (booking essential) a la carte 1900/2200
Spec. Terrine de foie gras d'oie, Saumurade de filets de sole en goujonnette, Pavé de bœuf au Bouzy.

XX **'t Stil Ende,** Scheepsdalelaan 12 ☎ 33 92 03, 🍽 – AE ⓓ E VISA. ✗ BX **a**
closed Saturday lunch, Sunday dinner, Monday, last 2 weeks July-first week August and first week February – **M** a la carte 1850/2100.

XX **Ambrosius,** Arsenaalstraat 55 ☎ 34 41 57, «Rustic» - VISA. CZ **j**
closed Monday, Tuesday, 2 weeks September and 2 weeks February - **M** (dinner only) a la carte 1650/1900.

XX **'t Bourgoensche Cruyce,** Wollestraat 41 ☎ 33 79 26, Fax 34 19 68, ≤ canals and old Flemish houses - AE E VISA CY **a**
closed Tuesday, Wednesday lunch, late November-early December and February - **M** a la carte 2200/2600.

XX **René Van Puyenbroeck,** 't Zand 13 ☎ 33 30 35, Fax 33 30 35 - AE E VISA. CZ **x**
closed Sunday dinner, Monday and July - **M** a la carte 1200/1900.

XX **Kardinaalshof,** Sint-Salvatorkerkhof 14 ☎ 34 16 91, Fax 34 20 62, Seafood - AE E VISA CZ **r**
closed Wednesday, Saturday lunch and 1 to 21 January - **M** a la carte approx. 1800.

XX **Spinola,** Spinolarei 1 ☎ 34 17 85, Fax 39 12 01, «Rustic» - AE E VISA CY **j**
closed Sunday and Monday lunch except Bank Holidays and late June-early July - **M** a la carte 1200/1500.

XX **De Lotteburg,** Goezeputstraat 43 ☎ 33 75 35, Fax 33 04 04, - AE E VISA CZ **u**
closed Monday and Tuesday except Bank Holidays, last week July-first week August and last week January-first week February - **M** a la carte 1400/2000.

XX **De Zinc,** A. Van Ackerplein 2 ☎ 33 64 65, Open until midnight - AE E VISA CY **k**
closed Wednesday, Thursday, 2 weeks July and 1 week January - **M** a la carte approx. 1300.

X **Chez Olivier,** Meestraat 9 ☎ 33 36 59, Fax 34 15 79, ≤ - AE E VISA DY **a**
closed Thursday and Friday lunch - **M** 1450/1750.

X **Tanuki,** Noordstraat 3 ☎ 31 75 12, Fax 31 75 12, Japanese cuisine - E VISA. CZ **k**
closed Monday, Tuesday and 2 weeks July - **M** a la carte 1300/1700.

X **Malpertuus,** Eiermarkt 9 ☎ 33 30 38 - AE E VISA CY **r**
closed Wednesday dinner, Thursday and July - **M** 495/1050.

South - ✉ 8200 - ☎ 0 50 :

Novotel Zuid, Chartreuseweg 20 ☎ 38 28 51, Telex 81507, Fax 38 79 03, - rm rest - 25-230. AE E VISA A **r**
M (open until midnight) a la carte 1000/1300 - 425 - **101 rm** 3300/3900.

XXXX ✿ **Weinebrugge** (Galens), Koning Albertlaan 242 ☎ 38 44 40, Fax 38 72 67, Seafood - AE E VISA A **b**
closed Sunday dinner in winter, Wednesday, Thursday, 3 weeks September, Christmas and first 2 weeks January - **M** a la carte 2800/4100
Spec. Création de foie gras d'oie frais au "Vintage Port", Homard rôti au four aux épices douces, Javanais de saumon aux langoustines.

XXX **Casserole** (Hotel school), Groene Poortdreef 17 ☎ 38 38 88, Fax 39 09 37, «Garden setting» - AE E VISA A **t**
closed 30 June-20 August and 26 to 31 December - **M** (lunch only except Friday and Saturday) a la carte 1600/1900.

South-West - ✉ 8200 - ☎ 0 50 :

Host. Pannenhuis , Zandstraat 2 ☎ 31 19 07, Telex 82345, Fax 31 77 66, ≤, «Terrace and garden» - - 25. AE E VISA. rest A **g**
M *(closed Tuesday dinner, Wednesday, 1 to 16 July and 15 January-1 February)* a la carte 1600/2000 - **18 rm** *(closed 15 January-1 February)* 3200/4750, 1 suite.

XX **Vossenburg** with rm, Zandstraat 272 (Coude Ceucen) ☎ 31 70 26, ≤, «Converted mansion in a park» - AE E VISA. A **c**
closed 2 to 18 March and 16 to 25 November - **M** *(closed Monday dinner and Tuesday)* a la carte 1500/2100 - **7 rm** 2725/3950.

XX **Herborist** with rm, De Watermolen 15 (by ⑥ : 6 km, then on the right after E 40) ☎ 38 76 00, Fax 38 76 00, «Country atmosphere», - AE E VISA.
closed Sunday dinner, Monday and 1 to 21 January - **M** a la carte 2000/2550 - **4 rm** 2500/3800.

at Hertsberge by ④ : 12,5 km C Oostkamp pop. 20 203 - ✉ 8020 Hertsberge - ☎ 0 50 :

XXX **Manderley,** Kruisstraat 13 ☎ 27 80 51, «Terrace and garden» - AE E VISA
closed Thursday dinner September-April, Sunday dinner, Monday, first week October and last 3 weeks January - **M** a la carte 1550/2100.

at Ruddervoorde by ④ : 12 km C Oostkamp pop. 20 203 - ✉ 8020 Ruddervoorde - ☎ 0 50 :

XXX **Host. Leegendael** with rm, Kortrijkstraat 498 (N 50) ☎ 27 76 99, Fax 27 58 80, «Period residence, country atmosphere» - AE E VISA
closed 15 August-early September and carnival week - **M** *(closed Wednesday and Sunday dinner)* a la carte 1700/2000 - **7 rm** 1550/2550.

at Sint-Kruis by ② : 6 km 🄲 Bruges – ✉ 8310 Sint-Kruis – ☎ 0 50 :

Wilgenhof without rest, Polderstraat 151 ☎ 36 27 44, Fax 36 28 21, ←, « Country Polder surroundings » – TV ☎ P. AE ⓓ E VISA A **w**
closed last week January – **6 rm** ☐ 2400/4000.

XXX **Ronnie Jonkman,** Maalsesteenweg 438 ☎ 36 07 67, Fax 35 76 96, 帚, « Terrace » – P. AE ⓓ E VISA
closed Sunday, Monday, 1 week Easter, first week July and 1 to 15 October – **M** a la carte 2000/2550.

at Varsenare by ⑦ : 6,5 km 🄲 Jabbeke pop. 12 053 – ✉ 8490 Varsenare – ☎ 0 50 :

XXXX **Manoir Stuivenberg** with rm, Gistelsteenweg 27 ☎ 38 15 02, Fax 38 28 92, 帚 – 🛗 TV ☎ P. AE ⓓ E VISA. ✻ A **n**
closed 4 to 19 April – **M** *(closed Sunday dinner and Monday)* 1750/2150 – **8 rm** ☐ 4450/6500 and 1 suite.

at Waardamme by ④ : 11 km 🄲 Oostkamp pop. 20 203 – ✉ 8020 Waardamme – ☎ 0 50 :

XXX **Ter Talinge,** Rooiveldstraat 46 ☎ 27 90 61, Fax 27 90 61, « Terrace » – P. AE VISA
closed Wednesday, Thursday, 26 February-12 March and 23 August-3 September – **M** a la carte 1000/1650.

at Zedelgem by ⑥ : 10,5 km – pop. 20 171 – ✉ 8210 Zedelgem – ☎ 0 50 :

Zuidwege without rest, Torhoutsesteenweg 126 ☎ 20 13 39, Fax 20 17 39 – TV ☎ P. AE ⓓ E VISA. ✻
closed 23 December-4 January – **17 rm** ☐ 1680/2380.

XX **Ter Leepe,** Torhoutsesteenweg 168 ☎ 20 01 97 – P. AE ⓓ E VISA
closed Wednesday dinner, Sunday, 15 to 31 July and 25 January-5 February – **M** a la carte 1300/1700.

Kortrijk 8500 West-Vlaanderen 213 ⑮ and 409 ⑪ – pop. 76 081 – ☎ 0 56 – 51 km.

XXX ✿✿ **Filip Bogaert,** Minister Tacklaan 5 ☎ 20 30 34, Fax 20 30 75, « Late 19C residence » – AE ⓓ E VISA
closed Wednesday, Sunday dinner and 3 weeks August – **M** a la carte 2300/4450
Spec. Pomme nouvelle au caviar et sa vinaigrette, Pot-au-feu de St-Pierre aux choux et truffes, Canard rôti au four "mi-confit".

Waregem 8790 West-Vlaanderen 213 ⑮ and 409 ⑪ – pop. 34 555 – ☎ 0 56 – 47 km.

XXXX ✿✿ **'t Oud Konijntje** (Mme Desmedt), Bosstraat 53 (S : 2 km near E 17) ☎ 60 19 37, Fax 60 92 12, 帚, « Floral terrace » – P. AE ⓓ E VISA
closed dinner Thursday and Sunday, Friday, 22 July-13 August and 26 December-4 January – **M** a la carte 2000/2500
Spec. Ragoût d'asperges aux lardons et croûtons, Feuilleté de petits gris au fromage blanc et aux deux céleris, Estouffade de pigeonneau farci au foie gras.

LIÈGE 4000 213 ㉒ and 409 ⑮ – pop. 196 825 – ☎ 0 41.

See: Old town★★ – Baptismal font★★★ of St. Bartholomew's church DX – Citadel ←★★ DX – Treasury★★ of St. Paul's Cathedral : reliquary of Charles the Bold★★ FZ – Palace of the Prince-Bishops★ : court of honour★★ GY **J** – The Perron★ (market cross) GY **A** – Aquarium★ DY **D** – St. James church★★ : vaults of the nave★★ DY – Cointe Park ←★ CZ – Altarpiece★ in the St. Denis church GZ – Church of St. John : Wooden Calvary statues★ FZ.

Museums : Provincial Museum of Life in Wallonia★★ GY – Curtius and Glass Museum★ : evangelistary of Notger★★★, collection of glassware★ EX **M1** – Ansembourg★ DX **M2** – Arms★ DX **M3** – Religious and Roman Art Museum★ GY **M5**.

Envir: Blégny-Trembleur★★ by ① : 20 km – Baptismal font★ in the church★ of St. Severin-en-Condroz by ⑥ : 27 km.

18 at Ougrée by ⑥ : 7,5 km, rte du Condroz 541 ☎ (0 41) 36 20 21 - 18 at Gomzé-Andoumont by ⑤ : 18 km, r. Gomzé 30 ☎ (0 41) 60 92 07 – 🚗 ☎ 42 52 14.

ℹ En Féronstrée 92 ☎ 22 24 56 and Gare des Guillemins ☎ 52 44 19 – Tourist association of the province, bd de la Sauvenière 77 ☎ 22 42 10.

Brussels 97 ⑨ – Amsterdam 242 ① – Antwerp 119 ⑫ – Köln 122 ② – Luxemburg 159 ⑤.

Plans on following pages

Holiday Inn, Esplanade de l'Europe 2, ✉ 4020, ☎ 42 60 20, Telex 41156, Fax 43 48 10, ←, 🏋, ≘s, 🏊 – 🛗 ⇔ rm ▤ TV ☎ ♿ 🚗 P – 🏛 25-40. AE ⓓ E VISA. ✻ rest DY **n**
M Ile de Meuse (open until 11.30 p.m) a la carte 1300/1800 – **217 rm** ☐ 4950/6800, 2 suites.

Ramada, bd de la Sauveniere 100 ☎ 21 77 11, Telex 41896, Fax 21 77 01 – 🛗 ⇔ ▤ TV ☎ 🚗 – 🏛 25-100. AE ⓓ E VISA CX **u**
M a la carte 1100/1700 – ☐ 540 – **105 rm** 5000.

Simenon without rest, bd de l'Est 16, ✉ 4020, ☎ 42 86 90, Fax 44 26 69 – 🛗 TV ☎. AE ⓓ E VISA DX **b**
☐ 250 – **11 rm** 2000/3500.

XXX **Au Vieux Liège,** quai Goffe 41 ℘ 23 77 48, Fax 23 78 60, « 16C residence » - AE ⓓ E VISA GY **c**
closed Wednesday dinner, Sunday, Bank Holidays, 1 week Easter, mid July-mid August and 24 December - **M** a la carte 2000/2300.

XXX **L'Héliport,** bd Frère-Orban ℘ 52 13 21, ≤, 🍽 - Ⓟ. AE E VISA DY **q**
closed Sunday, Monday dinner and last 3 weeks July - **M** a la carte 1850/2550.

XX **As Ouhès,** pl. du Marché 21 ℘ 23 32 25, 🍽, Open until 11 p.m. - AE ⓓ E VISA GY **r**
closed Sunday and holiday Mondays - **M** a la carte 900/1600.

XX **Le Shanghai** 1st floor, Galeries Cathédrale 104 ℘ 22 22 63, Fax 23 00 50, Chinese cuisine - ▤. AE ⓓ E VISA. ✗ FZ **m**
closed Tuesday, 5 to 27 July and 19 to 27 January - **M** a la carte 750/1300.

X **Ma Maison,** r. Hors-Château 46 ℘ 23 30 91, Fax 21 11 31 - AE ⓓ E VISA GY **k**
closed Sunday, Monday and first week January - **M** 950.

X **Chez Max,** pl. de la République Française 12 ℘ 22 08 59, Fax 22 90 02, 🍽, Open until 11 p.m. - AE ⓓ E VISA FY **s**
closed Sunday - **M** a la carte 1300/1900.

X **L'Ecailler,** r. Dominicains 26 ℘ 22 17 49, Fax 21 10 09, Seafood - ▤. AE ⓓ E VISA FZ **e**
M a la carte 1200/1900.

X **Lalo's Bar,** r. Madeleine 18 ℘ 23 22 57, Italian cuisine - AE ⓓ E VISA. ✗ GY **d**
M 750/1190.

at Ans - pop. 27 637 - ✉ 4430 Ans - ✆ 0 41 :

XX **La Fontaine de Jade,** r. Yser 321 ℘ 46 49 72, Fax 63 69 53, Chinese cuisine, open until 11 p.m. - ▤. AE ⓓ E. ✗
closed Monday except Bank Holidays - **M** a la carte 950/1400.

X **Le Marguerite,** r. Walthère Jamar 171 ℘ 26 43 46 - AE ⓓ E VISA
closed Saturday lunch, Sunday, Monday and 15 July-15 August - **M** a la carte 1200/1700.

at Chênée Ⓒ Liège - ✉ 4032 Chênée - ✆ 0 41 :

XX **Le Gourmet,** r. Large 91 ℘ 65 87 97, Fax 65 38 12, 🍽 - AE ⓓ E VISA
closed Monday dinner, Wednesday, Saturday lunch except Bank Holidays and 15 to 30 July - **M** a la carte 1300/1800.

XX **Le Vieux Chênée,** r. Gravier 45 ℘ 67 00 92 - AE ⓓ E VISA
closed Thursday - **M** a la carte 1050/1400.

at Engis by ⑦ : 10 km - pop. 5 875 - ✉ 4480 Engis - ✆ 0 41 :

XX **La Ciboulette,** quai Herten 11 ℘ 75 19 65, 🍽 - AE ⓓ E VISA
closed Saturday lunch, dinner Sunday and Wednesday, Monday, 1 week Easter, 1 week September and 26 December-10 January - **M** 1550.

at Hermalle-sous-Argenteau by ① : 14 km Ⓒ Oupeye pop. 23 206 - ✉ 4681 Hermalle-sous-Argenteau - ✆ 0 41 :

🏨 **Mosa** 🐦 without rest, r. Préixhe 3 ℘ 79 71 71, Fax 79 85 00, ≤ - |‡| TV ☎ Ⓟ - 🏛 50. AE ⓓ E VISA. ✗
14 rm ☐ 2200/3900, 1 suite.

XXX **Au Comte de Mercy** 🐦 with rm, r. Tilleul 5 ℘ 79 35 35, 🍽, « Rustic » - ☎ Ⓟ. AE ⓓ E VISA. ✗ rm
closed Sunday, Monday, 3 days after Easter, July and early January - **M** a la carte 1350/2100 - ☐ 350 - **8 rm** 1500/1800.

at Herstal - pop. 36 356 - ✉ 4040 Herstal - ✆ 0 41 :

🏨 **Post House** 🐦, r. Hurbise (by motorway E 40 exit 34) ℘ 64 64 00, Telex 41103, Fax 48 06 90, 🍽, 🏊 - |‡| ▤ rest TV ☎ Ⓟ - 🏛 25-60. AE ⓓ E VISA
M 1150 - **94 rm** ☐ 3930/5115.

at Neuville-en-Condroz by ⑥ : 18 km Ⓒ Neupré pop. 8 748 - ✉ 4121 Neuville-en-Condroz - ✆ 0 41 :

XXXX ✿✿ **Le Chêne Madame** (Mme Tilkin), av. de la Chevauchée 70 (in Rognacs wood SE : 2 km) ℘ 71 41 27, Fax 71 29 43 - Ⓟ. AE ⓓ E VISA
closed Monday, dinner Sunday and Thursday, 3 days after Easter, August and late December-early January - **M** a la carte 2200/3000
Spec. Crêpes parmentières au saumon et caviar, Poêlée de langoustines aux fleurs de capucines (June-15 September), Gibiers en saison.

at Rotheux-Rimière by ⑥ : 16 km Ⓒ Neupré pop. 8 748 - ✉ 4120 Rotheux-Rimière - ✆ 0 41 :

XX **Le Vieux Chêne,** r. Bonry 146 (near N 63) ℘ 71 46 51 - Ⓟ. AE ⓓ E VISA. ✗
closed Wednesday, dinner Monday and Tuesday, August and 23 December-6 January - **M** a la carte 900/1450.

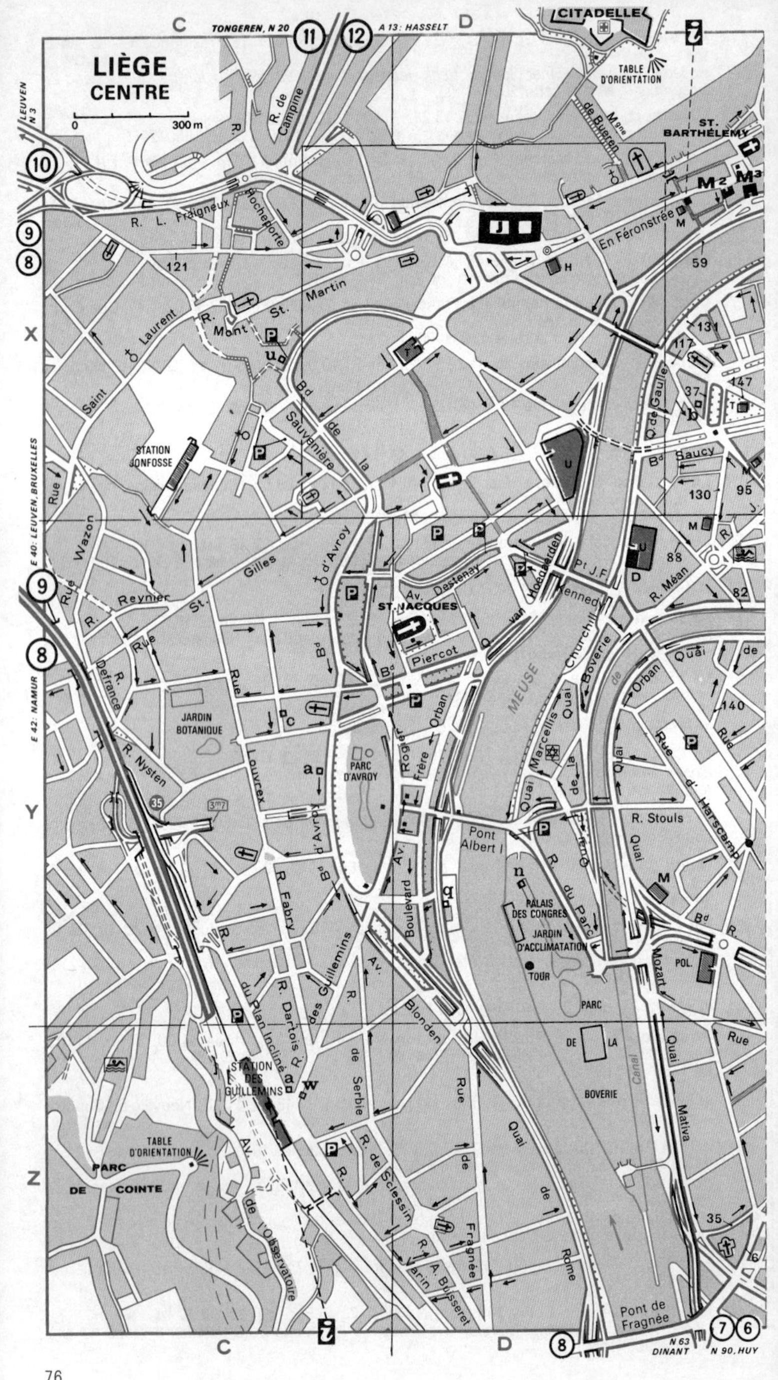

LIÈGE
CENTRE
0
300 m
TONGEREN, N 20
A 13: HASSELT
CITADELLE
TABLE D'ORIENTATION
ST. BARTHÉLEMY
LEUVEN N 3
E 40: LEUVEN, BRUXELLES
E 42: NAMUR
STATION JONFOSSE
JARDIN BOTANIQUE
ST. JACQUES
PARC D'AVROY
MEUSE
Pont Albert I
PALAIS DES CONGRES
JARDIN D'ACCLIMATATION
TOUR
PARC DE LA BOVERIE
STATION DES GUILLEMINS
TABLE D'ORIENTATION
PARC DE COINTE
Pont de Fragnée
N 63 DINANT
N 90, HUY

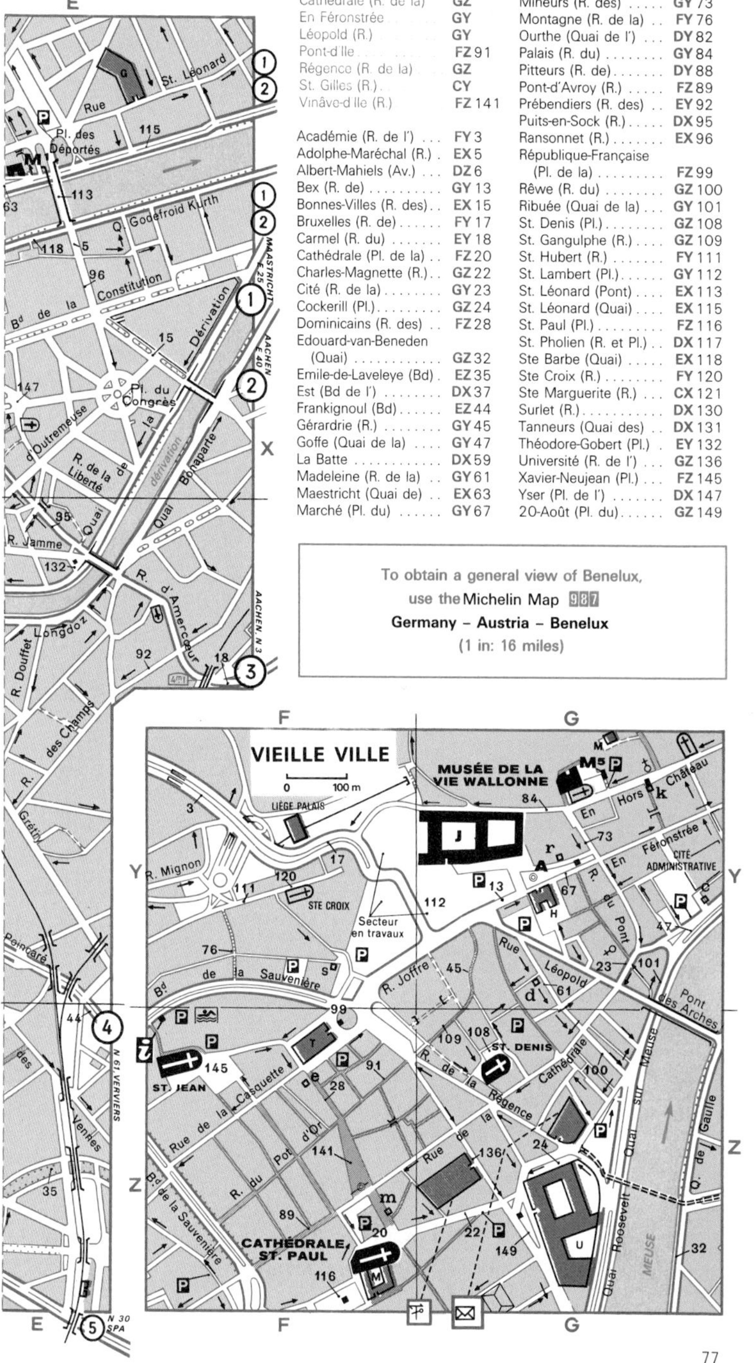

Cathédrale (R. de la)	GZ	
En Féronstrée	GY	
Léopold (R.)	GY	
Pont-d'Ile	FZ	91
Régence (R. de la)	GZ	
St. Gilles (R.)	CY	
Vinâve-d'Ile (R.)	FZ	141
Académie (R. de l')	FY	3
Adolphe-Maréchal (R.)	EX	5
Albert-Mahiels (Av.)	DZ	6
Bex (R. de)	GY	13
Bonnes-Villes (R. des)	EX	15
Bruxelles (R. de)	FY	17
Carmel (R. du)	EY	18
Cathédrale (Pl. de la)	FZ	20
Charles-Magnette (R.)	GZ	22
Cité (R. de la)	GY	23
Cockerill (Pl.)	GZ	24
Dominicains (R. des)	FZ	28
Edouard-van-Beneden (Quai)	GZ	32
Emile-de-Laveleye (Bd)	EZ	35
Est (Bd de l')	DX	37
Frankignoul (Bd)	EZ	44
Gérardrie (R.)	GY	45
Goffe (Quai de la)	GY	47
La Batte	DX	59
Madeleine (R. de la)	GY	61
Maestricht (Quai de)	EX	63
Marché (Pl. du)	GY	67
Mineurs (R. des)	GY	73
Montagne (R. de la)	FY	76
Ourthe (Quai de l')	DY	82
Palais (R. du)	GY	84
Pitteurs (R. de)	DY	88
Pont-d'Avroy (R.)	FZ	89
Prébendiers (R. des)	EY	92
Puits-en-Sock (R.)	DX	95
Ransonnet (R.)	EX	96
République-Française (Pl. de la)	FZ	99
Rêwe (R. du)	GZ	100
Ribuée (Quai de la)	GY	101
St. Denis (Pl.)	GZ	108
St. Gangulphe (R.)	GZ	109
St. Hubert (R.)	FY	111
St. Lambert (Pl.)	GY	112
St. Léonard (Pont)	EX	113
St. Léonard (Quai)	EX	115
St. Paul (Pl.)	FZ	116
St. Pholien (R. et Pl.)	DX	117
Ste Barbe (Quai)	EX	118
Ste Croix (R.)	FY	120
Ste Marguerite (R.)	CX	121
Surlet (R.)	DX	130
Tanneurs (Quai des)	DX	131
Théodore-Gobert (Pl.)	EY	132
Université (R. de l')	GZ	136
Xavier-Neujean (Pl.)	FZ	145
Yser (Pl. de l')	DX	147
20-Août (Pl. du)	GZ	149

To obtain a general view of Benelux,
use the Michelin Map 987
Germany – Austria – Benelux
(1 in: 16 miles)

at Tilff S : 12 km by N 633 © Esneux pop. 12 634 – ✉ 4130 Tilff – ☎ 0 41 :

XXX **Casino,** pl. du Roi Albert 3 ☎ 88 10 15, Fax 88 33 16, ←, « Terrace overlooking the lake » – AE ◑ E VISA. ✻
closed Monday and Saturday dinner – **M** 1250/1850.

Hasselt **3500 Limburg 213** ⑨ **and 409** ⑥ – **pop. 66 094 – ☎ 0 11 – 42 km.**

at Stevoort by N 2 : 5 km to Kermt, then road on the left © Hasselt – ✉ 3512 Stevoort – ☎ 0 11 :

✿✿ **Scholteshof** (Souvereyns) ⚐, Kermtstraat 130 ☎ 25 02 02, Telex 39684, Fax 25 43 28, ←, « 18C farmhouse with English-style garden in country atmosphere », ✻ – TV ☎ Ⓟ – 🏛 25-60. AE ◑ E VISA
closed 12 to 29 July and 3 to 20 January – **M** *(closed Wednesday)* a la carte 3350/3850 – ☕ 450 – **11 rm** 2600/14000, 7 suites
Spec. Langoustines en robe de poireaux grillés, Turbot Aïda, Ris de veau rôti au romarin.

St-Vith **4780 Liège 214** ⑨ **and 409** ⑯ – **pop. 8 567 – ☎ 0 80 – 78 km.**

XXX ✿✿ **Zur Post** (Pankert) with rm, Hauptstr. 39 ☎ 22 80 27, Fax 22 93 10 – TV ☎. E VISA. ✻
closed Sunday dinner and Monday except Bank Holidays, 29 June-9 July and January – **M** a la carte 2250/2900 – ☕ 350 – **8 rm** 1900/2700
Spec. Langoustines grillées aux graines de sésame, Mille-feuille aux pommes caramélisées, Côtelettes de pigeonneau farcies et foie gras.

Valkenburg Limburg (Netherlands) © Valkenburg aan de Geul pop. 18 116 **212** ① and **408** ㉖ – ☎ 0 4406 – 47 km.

✿✿ **Prinses Juliana** (annexe Residentie ⚐ - 3 rm 275 and 5 suites), **Broekhem 11**, ✉ 6301 HD, ☎ 1 22 44, Fax 1 44 05, « Terrace and floral garden » – |♦| ▤ rest TV ☎ 🚗 Ⓟ – 🏛 50. AE ◑ E VISA. ✻ rest
M *(closed Saturday lunch)* a la carte 115/135 – ☕ 25 – **17 rm** 250/300
Spec. Bouillabaisse à notre façon, Carré d'agneau au romarin, Pigeon fermier à l'estragon.

Weert Limburg (Netherlands) **212** ⑲ and **408** ⑲ – pop. 40 560 – ☎ 0 4950 – 90 km.

XX ✿✿ **L'Auberge** (Mertens) Parallelweg 101, ✉ 6001 HM, ☎ 3 10 57, Fax 3 10 57 – AE E VISA. ✻
closed Sunday, Monday, 16 July-6 August and 24 December-2 January – **M** a la carte 109/127
Spec. Tête de veau pressée à l'huile d'olives et truffes "croque-au-sel" (January-March), Carpaccio de bar fumé aux huîtres (October-May), Selle d'agneau cloutée à l'ail, fritots d'olives (May-October).

Luxembourg

215 ⑤ and 409 ㉖ - pop. 75 377.

See : Site★★ - Old Luxembourg★★ DY - "Chemin de la Corniche"★★, ≤★★ and the rocks DY **29** - The Bock cliff ≤★★, Bock Casemates★★ DY **A** - Place de la Constitution ≤★★ DY **28** - Grand-Ducal Palace★ DY **K** - Cathedral of Our Lady (Notre Dame)★ DY **L** - Grand-Duchess Charlotte Bridge★ DY - Boulevard Victor Thorn ≤★ DY **97** - The Trois Glands (Three Acorns) ≤★ DY **S** - ≤★★ from Plateau St. Esprit DZ.

Museum : National Museum of Art and History★, Gallo Romain section★, Luxembourg life section (decorative arts, arts and folk traditions)★★ DY **M**[1].

18 Hoehenhof Senningerberg (near Airport), ✉ 1736, ✆ 3 40 90.

✈ Findel by ③ : 6 km ✆ 40 08 08 - Air Terminal : pl. de la Gare ✆ 48 11 99.

ℹ pl. d'Armes. ✉ 2011, ✆ 22 28 09 - Air Terminus (closed Sunday from December to March), pl. de la Gare, ✉ 1616, ✆ 48 11 99 - Findel, Airport, ✉ 1010, ✆ 40 08 08.

Amsterdam 391 ⑧ - Bonn 190 ③ - Bruxelles 219 ⑧.

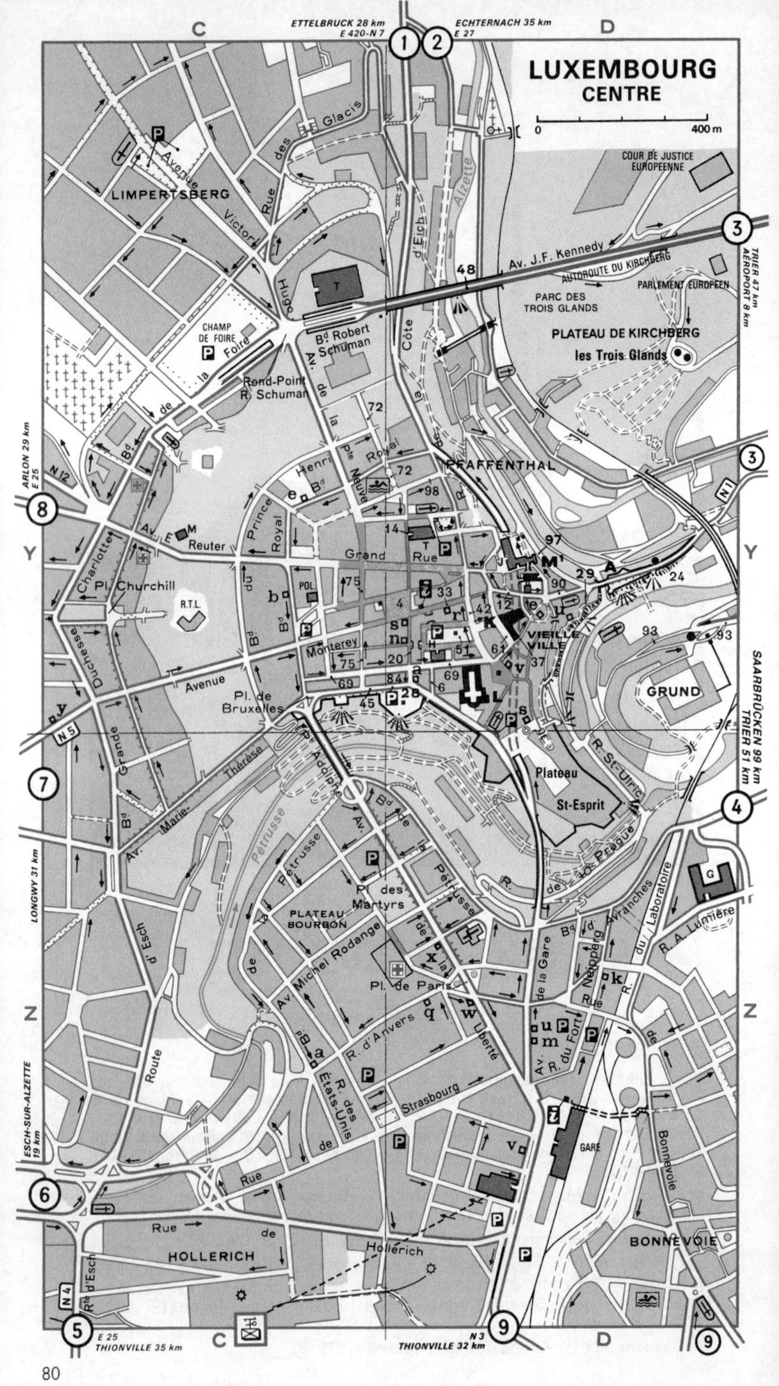
LUXEMBOURG
CENTRE
0
400 m
ETTELBRUCK 28 km
E 420-N 7
ECHTERNACH 35 km
E 27
TRIER 47 km
AÉROPORT 8 km
SAARBRÜCKEN 99 km
TRIER 51 km
ARLON 29 km
E 25
LONGWY 31 km
ESCH-SUR-ALZETTE 19 km
E 25
THIONVILLE 35 km
N 3
THIONVILLE 32 km
LIMPERTSBERG
CHAMP DE FOIRE
Rond-Point R. Schuman
Bd Robert Schuman
COUR DE JUSTICE EUROPEENNE
Av. J.F. Kennedy
AUTOROUTE DU KIRCHBERG
PARLEMENT EUROPEEN
PARC DES TROIS GLANDS
PLATEAU DE KIRCHBERG
les Trois Glands
PFAFFENTHAL
Alzette
Côte d'Eich
Rue des Glacis
Avenue Victor Hugo
Av. E. Reuter
Pl. Churchill
R.T.L.
Grand Rue
Monterey
VIEILLE VILLE
GRUND
Plateau St-Esprit
R. St-Ulric
Pl. de Bruxelles
Bd Prince Henri
Av. Marie-Thérèse
Pétrusse
Pl. des Martyrs
PLATEAU BOURBON
Av. Michel Rodange
Pl. de Paris
R. d'Anvers
Av. de la Liberté
Strasbourg
R. des États-Unis
Route d'Esch
Av. de la Gare
R. du Fort Neipperg
Bd d'Avranches
R. du Laboratoire
R. A. Lumière
GARE
Bonnevoie
BONNEVOIE
HOLLERICH
Rue de Hollerich
Rte d'Esch
N 4
N 5
N 12
N 1
C
D
Y
Z

Luxembourg-Centre :

Le Royal, bd Royal 12, ⊠ 2449, ☎ 4 16 16, Telex 2979, Fax 22 59 48, ... - rm ... - 25-350. AE ⓓ E VISA. rest CY **e**
M Le Relais Royal *(closed lunch Saturday and Sunday, Bank Holidays and 3 weeks August)* 2250 - **Le Jardin** a la carte 1200/1650 - **167 rm** 7400/11800, 3 suites.

Cravat, bd Roosevelt 29, ⊠ 2450, ☎ 22 19 75, Telex 2846, Fax 22 67 11 - ... - 25-70. AE ⓓ E VISA. rest DY **a**
M a la carte 1400/1700 - **59 rm** 5400/6500.

Rix without rest, bd Royal 20, ⊠ 2449, ☎ 47 16 66, Fax 22 75 35 - ... E VISA. CY **b**
closed 19 December-3 January - **21 rm** 4060/5760.

Clairefontaine, pl. de Clairefontaine 9, ⊠ 1341, ☎ 46 22 11, Fax 47 08 21 - ... AE ⓓ E VISA DY **v**
closed Saturday lunch, Sunday, Bank Holidays, 9 to 28 August, 1 to 6 November and 1 week February - **M** a la carte 2300/3000.

✿✿ **St-Michel** (Guillou) 1st floor, r. Eau 32, ⊠ 1449, ☎ 22 32 15, Fax 46 25 93, « In the old city, rustic interior » - AE ⓓ E VISA DY **e**
closed Saturday, Sunday, 1 to 23 August and 1 to 10 January - **M** (booking essential) a la carte 2550/3150
Spec. Carpaccio aux truffes d'été, Turbot rôti au four au curry doux, Aiguillettes de canard de Challans aux épices. Wines Pinot gris, Riesling, Koëppchen.

Astoria, av. du X-Septembre 14, ⊠ 2550, ☎ 44 62 23, Fax 45 82 96 - AE ⓓ E VISA
closed Saturday, 14 to 22 August and 27 December-2 January - **M** (lunch only) a la carte 1800/2300. CY **y**

Hemmen, Plateau du St-Esprit 5, ⊠ 1475, ☎ 47 00 23, Fax 46 64 02, ... - ... AE ⓓ E VISA DY **s**
closed Sunday dinner - **M** a la carte approx. 2100.

Speltz, r. Chimay 8, ⊠ 1333, ☎ 47 49 50, Fax 47 46 77 - AE ⓓ E VISA DY **n**
closed Saturday, Sunday, Bank Holidays, 5 to 12 April, 26 July-8 August and 24 December-2 January - **M** 1100/1450.

La Cigogne, r. Curé 24, ⊠ 1368, ☎ 22 82 50, Fax 46 51 21 - E VISA. DY **r**
closed Saturday, Sunday, Bank Holidays and August - **M** a la carte 1850/2150.

La Lorraine, pl. d'Armes 7, ⊠ 1136, ☎ 47 46 20, Fax 47 09 64, ..., Oyster bar and Seafood - ... AE ⓓ E VISA DY **s**
closed Saturday lunch and Sunday - **M** a la carte 2000/2800.

Brédewée, r. Large/Corniche 9, ⊠ 1917, ☎ 22 26 96, Fax 46 77 20, ... - AE ⓓ E VISA DY **u**
closed Sunday, last 2 weeks August and first 2 weeks January - **M** 1380.

Luxembourg-Station :

Président, pl. de la Gare 32, ⊠ 1616, ☎ 48 61 61, Telex 1510, Fax 48 61 80 - ... rm ... - 40. AE ⓓ E VISA. DZ **v**
M *(closed Sunday and August)* (dinner only) a la carte 1150/1800 - **38 rm** 4000/6400.

Arcotel without rest, av. de la Gare 43, ⊠ 1611, ☎ 49 40 01, Fax 40 56 24 - ... AE ⓓ E VISA. DZ **u**
30 rm 3800/4400.

Central Molitor, av. de la Liberté 28, ⊠ 1930, ☎ 48 99 11, Telex 2613, Fax 48 33 82 - ... AE ⓓ E VISA DZ **x**
M *(closed Sunday dinner, Monday and mid December-mid January)* a la carte 1000/1500 - **36 rm** 3200/4200.

Nobilis, av. de la Gare 47, ⊠ 1611, ☎ 49 49 71, Telex 3212, Fax 40 31 01 - ... - 70. AE ⓓ E VISA DZ **m**
M a la carte 1150/2150 - **43 rm** 3695/4320.

Du Coin, bd de la Pétrusse 2, ✉ 2320, ℘ 40 21 01, Fax 40 36 66 – |≡| TV ☎ – 30. AE ⓓ E VISA. ✻ rest CZ **a**
closed 15 December-15 January – **M** *(closed Sunday and Bank Holidays)* 1400 – **29 rm** 2500/3300.

Marco Polo without rest, r. Fort Neipperg 27, ✉ 2230, ℘ 406 41 41, Fax 40 48 84 – |≡| TV ☎. AE ⓓ E VISA DZ **k**
18 rm 2750/3750.

XXX **Cordial** 1st floor, pl. de Paris 1, ✉ 2314, ℘ 48 85 38, Fax 40 77 76 – E VISA DZ **w**
closed Friday, Saturday lunch, 19 July-14 August and 22 to 28 February – **M** 1400.

XX **Italia** with rm, r. Anvers 15, ✉ 1130, ℘ 48 66 26, Telex 3644, Fax 48 08 07, – TV ☎. AE ⓓ E VISA DZ **q**
M a la carte 1100/1800 – **20 rm** 2400/2800.

Airport by ③ : 8 km :

Sheraton Aérogolf, rte de Trèves, ✉ 1019, ℘ 3 45 71, Telex 2662, Fax 3 42 17, ≤ – |≡| rm ≡ TV ☎ P – 25-120. AE ⓓ E VISA
M Le Montgolfier (open until 11.30 p.m.) a la carte 1250/1900 – 530 – **146 rm** 6500/8200, 4 suites.

Ibis, rte de Trèves, ✉ 2632, ℘ 43 88 01, Telex 60790, Fax 43 88 02, ≤ – |≡| ≡ TV ☎ & P – 25-80. AE ⓓ E VISA
M 740 – **120 rm** 2800/3800.

XX **Le Grimpereau,** r. Cents 140, ✉ 1319, ℘ 43 67 87, Fax 42 60 26 – P. AE E VISA. ✻
closed Sunday dinner, Monday, 2 to 23 August, 1 to 8 November and 1 week carnival – **M** a la carte 1400/1900.

at Dommeldange C Luxembourg :

Inter.Continental, r. Jean Engling 12, ✉ 1466, ℘ 4 37 81, Telex 3754, Fax 43 60 95, ≤, – |≡| rm ≡ TV ☎ & P – 25-360. AE ⓓ E VISA. ✻ rest
M a la carte 2150/2900 – 570 – **313 rm** 7700/8950, 31 suites.

Parc, rte d'Echternach 120, ✉ 1453, ℘ 43 56 43, Telex 1418, Fax 43 69 03, – |≡| TV ☎ & P – 40-2000. AE ⓓ E VISA
M (open until midnight) a la carte 1100/1700 – **259 rm** 3500/4200, 12 suites.

Host. du Grünewald, rte d'Echternach 10, ✉ 1453, ℘ 43 18 82 and 42 03 14 (rest), Telex 60543, Fax 42 06 46, – |≡| TV ☎ P – 40. AE ⓓ E VISA. ✻ rest
M *(closed Saturday lunch, Sunday, Bank Holidays except weekends and 1 to 24 January)* a la carte 1700/2300 – **25 rm** 2850/4950, 3 suites.

at Hesperange – pop. 9 918 :

XXX ✿ **L'Agath** (Steichen) with rm, rte de Thionville 274 (Howald), ✉ 5884, ℘ 48 86 87, Fax 48 55 05, – TV ☎ P – 60. AE ⓓ E VISA
closed Sunday, Monday, Bank Holidays, 15 July-2 August and late December-early January – **M** a la carte 2400/2800 – **6 rm** 3300/3500
Spec. Gâteau de lapereau cuit au Riesling, Bouillon safrané de poissons de roches, Bœuf à moëlle. Wines Pinot gris, Riesling.

at Hostert by ③ : 12 km C Niederanven pop. 5 054 :

XX **Le Gastronome,** r. Andethana 90, ✉ 6970, ℘ 3 40 39, Fax 3 40 39, – P. AE ⓓ E VISA
closed Saturday lunch, Sunday, 3 weeks August and 2 weeks Christmas – **M** a la carte 1400/2000.

Upland of Kirchberg :

Pullman, r. Fort Niedergrünewald 6 (European Centre), ✉ 2226, ℘ 43 77 61, Telex 2751, Fax 43 86 58, – |≡| rm ≡ TV ☎ & P – 50-450. AE ⓓ E VISA. ✻ rest
M Les Trois Glands *(closed Saturday lunch and August)* a la carte approx. 1600 – **257 rm** 5500/7400, 3 suites.

at the skating-rink of Kockelscheuer :

XXX ✿✿ **Patin d'Or** (Berring), rte de Bettembourg 40, ✉ 1899, ℘ 22 64 99, Fax 40 40 11 – ≡ P. ⓓ E VISA. ✻
closed Saturday, Sunday, Bank Holidays, 1 week Easter, 1 week Whitsun, first week September and late December-early January – **M** a la carte 2000/2600
Spec. Tartare de saumon et œuf brouillé au caviar, Petite soupe de sole, langoustines et rouget aux ravioles de fines herbes, Pied de porc farci à l'ancienne et fricassée de lentilles vertes. Wines Pinot gris, Riesling.

at Sandweiler by ④ : 7 km – pop. 2 024 :

XX **Hoffmann,** r. Principale 21, ✉ 5240, ℘ 3 51 80, Fax 35 79 36, – AE E VISA. ✻
closed Monday dinner, Tuesday, 26 July-20 August and 27 December-20 January – **M** a la carte 1500/1950.

Echternach 215 ③ and 409 ㉗ - pop. 4 211 - 35 km.

at Geyershaff SW : 6,5 km by E 27 🄲 Bech pop. 787 :

XXX ✿✿ **La Bergerie** (Phal), ✉ 6251, ☎ 7 94 64, Fax 7 97 71, ≤, 🏠, « Floral country setting » - 🅿. AE ⓞ E VISA
closed Sunday dinner, Monday and 5 January-15 February - **M** a la carte 2500/3000
Spec. Foie d'oie au naturel, Galette de St-Jacques, Croustillant de pigeonneau. Wines Riesling Koëppchen, Pinot gris.

Paliseul 6850 Luxembourg belge (Belgium) 214 ⑯ and 409 ㉔ - pop. 4 818 - ☎ 061 - 94 km.

XXX ✿✿ **Au Gastronome** (Libotte) with rm, r. Bouillon 2 (Paliseul-Gare) ☎ 53 30 64, « Floral garden » - TV ☎ 🚗 🅿. AE ⓞ E VISA
closed Sunday dinner and Monday except Bank Holidays, last week January-February, carnival and last week June-first week July - **M** a la carte 2050/2600 - **9 rm** ☕ 2300/3000
Spec. Fricassée de langoustines en vinaigrette de poireaux, Dos de turbot rôti, mousseline au cresson, Cochon de lait au poivre, sauce à l'aigre-doux.

Amsterdam

Noord-Holland 408 ⑩ ㉗ ㉘ - Pop. 702 444 - ✪ 0 20.

See : Old Amsterdam★★★ : the canals★★★ (Grachten) : Singel ; Herengracht ; Cromhout Houses★ (Cromhouthuizen) ; Reguliersgracht ≤★ ; Keizersgracht - Boat trips★ (Rond-vaart) - Beguine Convent★★ (Begijnhof) LY - Dam : pulpit★ in the New Church★ (Nieuwe Kerk) LXY - Flower market★ (Bloemenmarkt) LY - Rembrandt Square (Rembrandtsplein) MY - Thin Bridge★ (Magere Brug) MZ - Leeuwenburg House ≤★ MX - Artis★ (Zoological Garden) - Royal Palace★ (Koninklijk Paleis) LY **B**.

Museums : Rijksmuseum★★★ KZ - Vincent van Gogh National Museum★★★ (Rijksmuseum) - Municipal★★ (Stedelijk Museum) : Modern Art - Amsterdam Historical Museum★★ (Amsterdams Historisch Museum) LY - Madame Tussaud's★ : wax museum LY **M¹** - Amstelkring Museum "Our Dear Lord in the Attic" (Museum Amstelkring Ons'Lieve Heer op Solder) : clandestine chapel MX **M⁴** - Rembrandt's House★ (Rembrandthuis) : works by the master MY **M⁵** - Netherlands Maritime History Museum★ (Nederlands Scheepvaart Museum) - Tropical Museum★ (Tropenmuseum) - Allard Pierson★ : antiquities LY **M²** - Jewish Museum★ (Joods Historisch Museum) MY **M¹⁵**.

Casino **KZ**, Max Euweplein 62 (near Leidseplein) ℘ 620 10 06

18 Bauduinlaan 35 at Halfweg ℘ (0 2907) 78 66 - 9 Zwarte Laantje 4 at Duivendrecht ℘ (0 20) 604 36 50 - 9 Abcouderstraatweg 46 at Holendrecht ℘ (020) 645 74 31.

✈ at Schiphol SW : 9,5 km ℘ (0 20) 601 09 66 (information) and 674 77 47 (reservations).

(Departure from's-Hertogenbosch) ℘ 620 22 66 and 601 05 41 (Schiphol).

to Göteborg : Scandinavian Seaways Cie ℘ 611 66 15.

Stationsplein, ✉ 1012 AB ℘ 06-34 03 40 66.

Bruxelles 204 - Düsseldorf 227 - Den Haag 60 - Luxembourg 419 - Rotterdam 76.

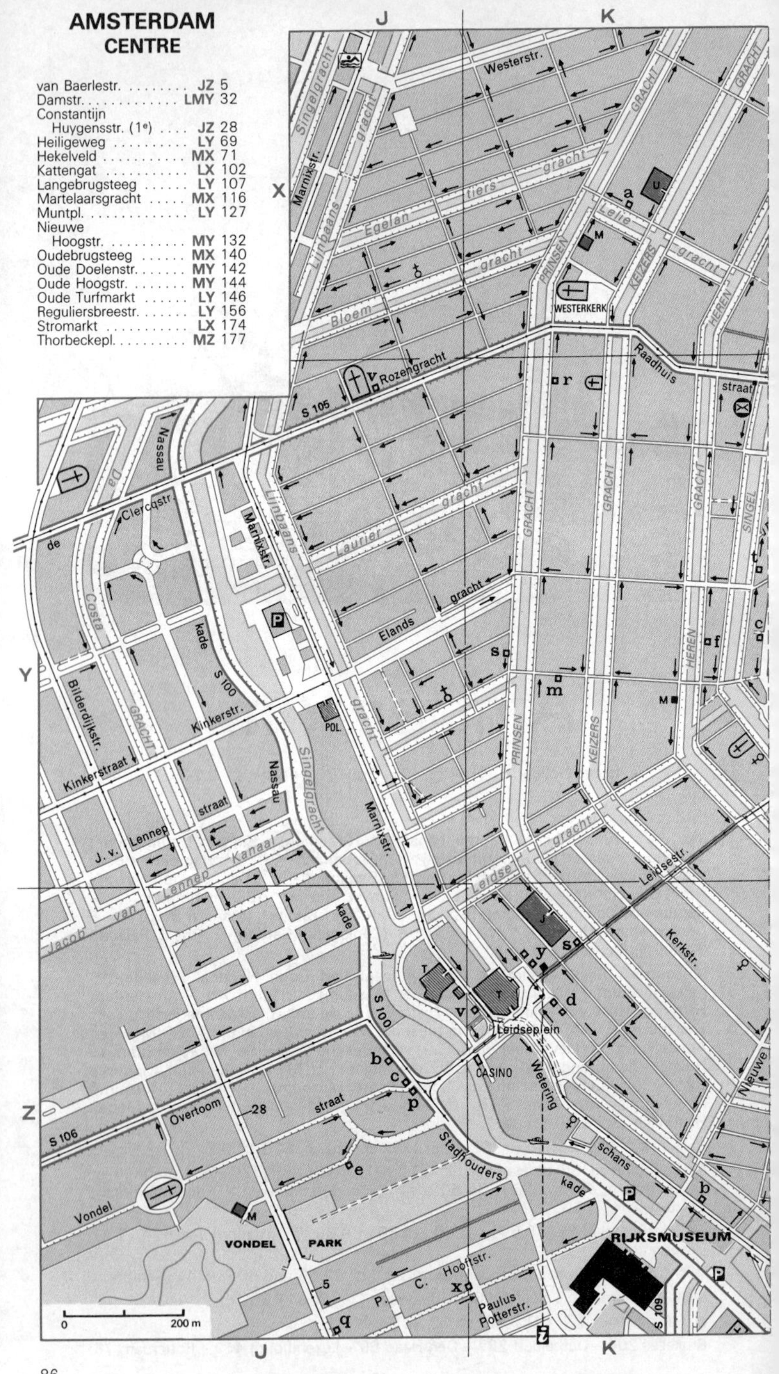
AMSTERDAM
CENTRE
van Baerlestr. . . . . JZ 5
Damstr. . . . . LMY 32
Constantijn
Huygensstr. (1e) . . . . JZ 28
Heiligeweg . . . . LY 69
Hekelveld . . . . MX 71
Kattengat . . . . LX 102
Langebrugsteeg . . . . . . LY 107
Martelaarsgracht . . . . . MX 116
Muntpl. . . . . LY 127
Nieuwe
Hoogstr. . . . . MY 132
Oudebrugsteeg . . . . . . MX 140
Oude Doelenstr. . . . . . . MY 142
Oude Hoogstr. . . . . MY 144
Oude Turfmarkt . . . . . . LY 146
Reguliersbreestr. . . . . . LY 156
Stromarkt . . . . LX 174
Thorbeckepl. . . . . MZ 177
J
K
X
Y
Z
Westerstr.
Singelgracht
Marnixstr.
Lijnbaansgracht
Egelantiersgracht
Lelie gracht
Bloemgracht
WESTERKERK
Rozengracht
S 105
Raadhuisstraat
Nassau
de Clercqstr.
da Costa
Laurier gracht
Elandsgracht
Bilderdijkstr.
Kinkerstr.
Kinkerstraat
Nassau straat
J. v. Lennep
Jacob van Lennep Kanaal
Leidse gracht
Leidsestr.
Kerkstr.
Leidseplein
CASINO
Wetering schans
Stadhouders kade
Overtoom
S 106
S 100
Vondel
VONDEL PARK
RIJKSMUSEUM
Hooftstr.
P. C.
Paulus Potterstr.
S 109
Nieuwe
PRINSEN GRACHT
KEIZERS GRACHT
HEREN GRACHT
SINGEL
0
200 m

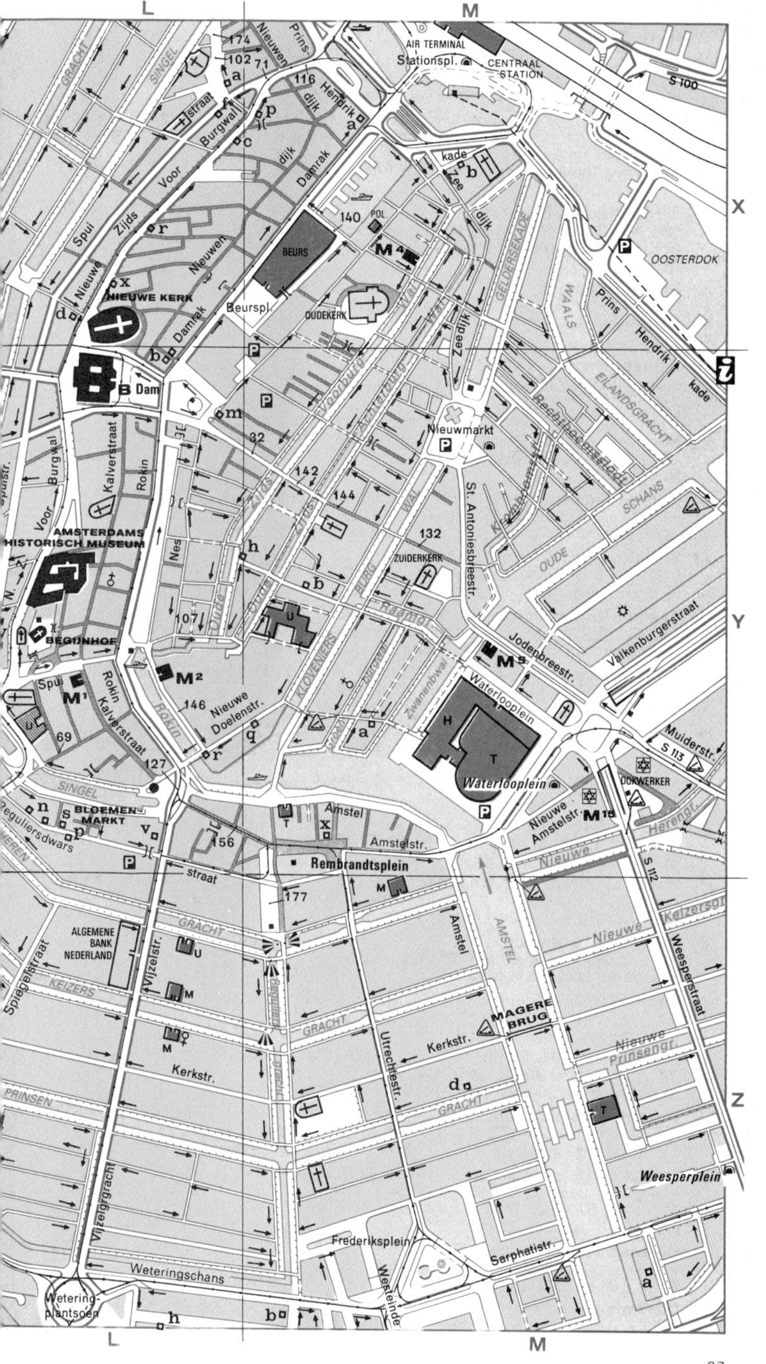

L
M
X
Y
Z
AIR TERMINAL
Stationspl.
CENTRAAL STATION
S 100
OOSTERDOK
BEURS
POL.
OUDEKERK
NIEUWE KERK
Beurspl.
Dam
Nieuwmarkt
AMSTERDAMS HISTORISCH MUSEUM
BEGIJNHOF
ZUIDERKERK
Waterlooplein
Jodenbreestr.
Valkenburgerstraat
Muiderstr.
DOKWERKER
Rembrandtsplein
BLOEMENMARKT
ALGEMENE BANK NEDERLAND
MAGERE BRUG
Weesperplein
Frederiksplein
Weteringschans
Weteringplantsoen
Sarphatistr.
Utrechtsestr.
Vijzelgracht
Vijzelstr.
Kerkstr.
Amstel
AMSTEL
Weesperstraat
Spiegelstraat
Reguliersdwars straat
Nieuwe Doelenstr.
Rokin
Kalverstraat
Nes
Zeedijk
St. Antoniesbreestr.
Damrak
Spui

Centre

Amstel, Prof. Tulpplein 1, 1018 GX, 622 60 60, Fax 520 32 37, - - 25-180. . MZ **a**
M see rest **La Rive** below - 35 - **77 rm** 850, 2 suites.

The Grand, O.Z. Voorburgwal 197, 1001 EX, 555 31 11, Telex 13074, Fax 555 32 22, « Historic building, authentic Art Nouveau lounges, inner garden », - rm rest - 25-320. . LMY **h**
M see rest **The Admiralty** below - **Café Roux** a la carte approx. 55 - 30 - **155 rm** 495/595, 11 suites.

Europe, Nieuwe Doelenstraat 2, 1012 CP, 623 48 36, Telex 12081, Fax 624 29 62, - - 25-250. LY **r**
M Excelsior (open until 11 p.m.) 85/135 - **Le Relais** (open until midnight) 40/50 - 29 - **91 rm** 395/620, 10 suites.

Barbizon Palace, Prins Hendrikkade 59, 1012 AD, 556 45 64, Telex 10187, Fax 624 33 53, - rm - 25-210. . rest
M see rest **Vermeer** below - **Brasserie Barbizon** a la carte 58/87 - 33 - **265 rm** 410/530, 3 suites. MX **b**

Ramada Renaissance, Kattengat 1, 1012 SZ, 621 22 23, Telex 17149, Fax 627 52 45, « Contemporary art collection », - - 25-400. LX **a**
M a la carte 64/84 - 33 - **418 rm** 525, 7 suites.

Marriott, Stadhouderskade 21, 1054 ES, 607 55 55, Telex 15087, Fax 607 55 11, - rm - 25-360. . JZ **p**
M (open until 11 p.m.) a la carte approx. 65 - 30 - **392 rm** 445, 3 suites.

Holiday Inn Crowne Plaza, N.Z. Voorburgwal 5, 1012 RC, 620 05 00, Telex 15183, Fax 620 11 73, - rm - 25-260. .
M 7-Seas a la carte 57/92 - 35 - **268 rm** 375/475, 2 suites. MX **p**

SAS Royal, Rusland 17, 1012 CK, 623 12 31, Telex 10365, Fax 520 82 00, - rm - 25-180. . MY **b**
M *(closed Sunday)* (dinner only) a la carte 70/89 - 37 - **246 rm** 410/510, 1 suite.

Scandic Crown Victoria, Damrak 1, 1012 LG, 623 42 55, Telex 16625, Fax 625 29 97, - rm rest - 25-250. MX **a**
M a la carte 55/88 - 28 - **305 rm** 325/395, 5 suites.

Gd H. Krasnapolsky, Dam 9, 1012 JS, 554 91 11, Telex 12262, Fax 622 86 07 - rm - 25-1500. LY **m**
M Le Reflet d'Or (open until 11 p.m.) 60 - 33 - **322 rm** 390/465.

Pulitzer, Prinsengracht 323, 1016 GZ, 523 52 35, Telex 16508, Fax 627 67 53, « Contemporary art collection », - rm rest - 25-160. . rest KY **r**
M De Goudsbloem *(closed first 2 weeks January)* (dinner only) a la carte 73/87 - 32 - **232 rm** 355/525, 2 suites.

Jolly Carlton, Vijzelstraat 4, 1017 HK, 622 22 66, Telex 11670, Fax 626 61 83 - rm - 25-80. . rest LY **v**
M 55/65 - 30 - **219 rm** 300/400.

Barbizon Centre, Stadhouderskade 7, 1054 ES, 685 13 51, Telex 12601, Fax 685 16 11, - rm - 150. . JZ **c**
M *(closed Sunday)* a la carte 40/94 - 32 - **234 rm** 450/525, 2 suites.

American, Leidsekade 97, 1017 PN, 624 53 22, Telex 12545, Fax 625 32 36, - - 80-200. . JKZ **v**
M Café Américain a la carte approx. 75 - 30 - **183 rm** 345/450, 5 suites.

Capitool, N.Z. Voorburgwal 67, 1012 RE, 627 59 00, Telex 14494, Fax 623 89 32, - rm - 30-100. . LX **r**
M (dinner only) 45 - **144 rm** 321, 4 suites.

Ascot, Damrak 95, 1012 LP, 626 00 66, Telex 16620, Fax 627 09 82 - rm - 25-70. . rest LY **b**
M a la carte 62/96 - 28 - **110 rm** 325/395.

Doelen, Nieuwe Doelenstraat 24, 1012 CP, 622 07 22, Telex 14399, Fax 622 10 84, - rm rest - 25-150. . rest MY **q**
M (dinner only) a la carte 60/75 - **85 rm** 275/350, 1 suite.

Dikker en Thijs, Prinsengracht 444, 1017 KE, 626 77 21, Telex 13161, Fax 625 89 86 - - 25. KZ **s**
M see rest **Dikker en Thijs** below - **De Prinsenkelder** *(closed Monday)* (dinner only) a la carte approx. 70 - 31 - **25 rm** 250/365.

Caransa, Rembrandtsplein 19, 1017 CT, 622 94 55, Telex 13342, Fax 622 27 73, - rm - 30-150. MY **x**
M 35 - **66 rm** 285/345.

Die Port van Cleve, N.Z. Voorburgwal 178, 1012 SJ, 624 48 60, Telex 13129, Fax 622 02 40 - - 25-50. . LX **d**
M see rest **De Blauwe Parade** below - **102 rm** 261/329.

Ambassade without rest, Herengracht 341, ✉ 1016 AZ, ✆ 626 23 33, Telex 10158, Fax 624 53 21, ≤ – AE E VISA KY **f**
43 rm 195/265, 3 suites.

Estheréa without rest, Singel 305, ✉ 1012 WJ, ✆ 624 51 46, Telex 14019, Fax 623 90 01 – AE E VISA. KY **t**
75 rm 275/325.

De Roode Leeuw, Damrak 93, ✉ 1012 LP, ✆ 624 03 96, Fax 620 47 16 – 25-50. AE E VISA. rest LXY **b**
M a la carte 42/75 – **78 rm** 175/285.

Avenue without rest, N.Z. Voorburgwal 27, ✉ 1012 RD, ✆ 623 83 07, Fax 638 39 46 – AE E VISA. LX **c**
50 rm 150/230.

Owl without rest, Roemer Visscherstraat 1, ✉ 1054 EV, ✆ 618 94 84, Telex 13360, Fax 618 94 41 – AE E VISA JZ **e**
34 rm 140/190.

Nicolaas Witsen without rest, Nicolaas Witsenstraat 4, ✉ 1017 ZH, ✆ 626 65 46, Fax 620 51 13 – E VISA MZ **b**
31 rm 110/200.

Wiechmann without rest, Prinsengracht 328, ✉ 1016 HX, ✆ 626 33 21, Fax 626 89 62 – KY **s**
38 rm 225.

Asterisk without rest, Den Texstraat 16, ✉ 1017 ZA, ✆ 626 23 96, Fax 638 27 90 – E VISA LZ **h**
26 rm 149/179.

La Rive - (at Amstel H.), Prof. Tulpplein 1, ✉ 1018 GX, ✆ 622 60 60, Fax 520 32 37, ≤, « On Amstel-side » – AE E VISA. MZ **a**
closed lunch Saturday and Sunday – **M** a la carte 100/175.

The Admiralty - (at The Grand H.), O.Z. Voorburgwal 197, ✉ 1001 EX, ✆ 555 31 11, Telex 13074, Fax 555 32 22, Seafood – AE E VISA. LMY **h**
closed Saturday lunch and Sunday – **M** a la carte 136/190.

Vermeer - (at Barbizon Palace H.), Prins Hendrikkade 59, ✉ 1012 AD, ✆ 556 48 85, Telex 10187, Fax 624 33 53 – AE E VISA. MX **b**
closed Sunday, 12 July-8 August and 27 December-1 January – **M** (dinner only) a la carte 92/116
Spec. Entrecôte grillée à la purée de truffes, Canard sauvage, beignets à l'ail, Soufflé chaud au mascarpone.

Dikker en Thijs 1st floor, Prinsengracht 444, ✉ 1017 KE, ✆ 626 77 21, Telex 13161, Fax 625 89 86 – AE E VISA KZ **s**
closed Sunday and 1 to 16 August – **M** (dinner only) 85/95.

D'Vijff Vlieghen, Spuistraat 294, ✉ 1012 VX, ✆ 624 83 69, Telex 12262, Fax 623 64 04, « Typical 17C houses » – AE E VISA. KY **c**
M (dinner only) a la carte 73/112.

Radèn Mas, Stadhouderskade 6, ✉ 1054 ES, ✆ 685 40 41, Fax 685 39 81, Indonesian cuisine, open until 11 p.m., « Exotic decor » – AE E VISA JZ **b**
closed lunch Saturday and Sunday – **M** a la carte 62/93.

De Blauwe Parade - (at Die Port van Cleve H.), N.Z. Voorburgwal 178, ✉ 1012 SJ, ✆ 624 00 47, Telex 13129, Fax 622 02 40, « Delftware » – AE E VISA. LX **d**
closed lunch Saturday and Sunday – **M** a la carte approx. 85.

Dynasty, Reguliersdwarsstraat 30, ✉ 1017 BM, ✆ 626 84 00, Fax 622 30 38, Oriental cuisine – AE E VISA. LY **p**
closed January – **M** (dinner only until 11 p.m.) a la carte approx. 95.

't Swarte Schaep 1st floor, Korte Leidsedwarsstraat 24, ✉ 1017 RC, ✆ 622 30 21, Fax 624 82 68, Open until 11 p.m., « 17C Dutch interior » – AE E VISA KZ **d**
closed 25, 26 and 31 December and 1 January – **M** a la carte 80/98.

Les Quatre Canetons, Prinsengracht 1111, ✉ 1017 JJ, ✆ 624 63 07, Fax 638 45 99 – AE E VISA. MZ **d**
closed Saturday lunch, Sunday and 31 December-1 January – **M** 62/83.

Tout Court, Runstraat 13, ✉ 1016 GJ, ✆ 625 86 37, Open until 11.30 p.m. – AE E VISA
M 50/90. KY **m**

Sichuan Food, Reguliersdwarsstraat 35, ✉ 1017 BK, ✆ 626 93 27, Chinese cuisine – AE E VISA. LY **s**
M (dinner only until 11.30 p.m.) a la carte 54/85
Spec. Dim Sum, Canard laqué.

De Oesterbar, Leidseplein 10, ✉ 1017 PT, ✆ 623 29 88, Fax 623 21 99, Seafood, open until 1 a.m. – AE E. KZ **y**
M a la carte 63/79.

Treasure, N.Z. Voorburgwal 115, ✉ 1012 RH, ✆ 626 09 15, Fax 640 12 02, Chinese cuisine – AE E VISA. LX **x**
M a la carte 40/71.

XX **Manchurian,** Leidseplein 10a, ✉ 1017 PT, ✆ 623 13 30, Fax 626 21 05, Oriental cuisine – ▤. AE ⓓ E VISA. ✻ KZ **y**
M a la carte approx. 55.

XX **La Camargue,** Reguliersdwarsstraat 7, ✉ 1017 BJ, ✆ 623 93 52 – ▤. AE ⓓ E VISA LY **n**
closed lunch Saturday and Sunday and 30 December-1 January – **M** 45/60.

XX **Het Amsterdamse Wijnhuis,** Reguliersdwarsstraat 23, ✉ 1017 BJ, ✆ 623 42 59 – AE ⓓ E VISA. ✻ LY **n**
closed Sunday, Monday, 25 July-9 August and 23 December-8 January – **M** a la carte approx. 75.

XX **Sea Palace,** Oosterdokskade 8, ✉ 1011 AE, ✆ 626 47 77, Fax 620 42 66, Asian cuisine, open until 11 p.m., « Floating restaurant with ≤ town » – AE ⓓ E VISA. ✻
M a la carte 40/64.

XX ✿ **Christophe** (Royer), Leliegracht 46, ✉ 1015 DH, ✆ 625 08 07, Fax 638 91 32 – ▤. AE ⓓ E VISA KX **a**
closed Sunday – **M** (dinner only until 11 p.m.) a la carte 95/118
Spec. Fondant d'aubergines au cumin, Homard rôti à l'ail doux et aux pommes de terre, Pigeonneau fermier rôti en croûte d'épices.

X **Le Provençal,** Weteringschans 91, ✉ 1017 RZ, ✆ 623 96 19 – ▤. AE ⓓ E VISA KZ **b**
M a la carte approx. 70.

X **Tom Yam,** Staalstraat 22, ✉ 1011 JM, ✆ 622 95 33, Fax 624 90 62, Thaï cuisine – AE ⓓ E VISA MY **a**
closed 31 December – **M** (dinner only) a la carte 64/83.

X **Bistro La Forge,** Korte Leidsedwarsstraat 26, ✉ 1017 RC, ✆ 624 00 95 – AE ⓓ E VISA KZ **d**
closed 24 and 31 December and 1 January – **M** (dinner only until midnight) 43/53.

X **Lucius,** Spuistraat 247, ✉ 1012 VP, ✆ 624 18 31, Fax 627 61 53, Seafood, open until midnight – AE ⓓ E VISA LY **e**
M 48/75.

X **Haesje Claes,** Spuistraat 273, ✉ 1012 VR, ✆ 624 99 98, Fax 627 48 17, « Typical atmosphere » – AE ⓓ E VISA. ✻ LY **y**
closed 31 December and 1 January – **M** a la carte 40/54.

X **Kantjil,** Spuistraat 291, ✉ 1012 VS, ✆ 620 09 94, Fax 623 21 66, ☂, Pub rest, Indonesian cuisine – AE ⓓ E VISA. ✻ LY **y**
closed 4 May and 31 December – **M** (dinner only until 11 p.m.) a la carte 40/89.

South and West Quarters

🏨 **Okura,** Ferdinand Bolstraat 333, ✉ 1072 LH, ✆ 678 71 11, Telex 16182, Fax 671 23 44, ⛱ – |‡| ▤ TV ☎ 🚗 P – 🎤 25-600. AE ⓓ E VISA. ✻
M see rest **Ciel Bleu** below – **Yamazato** (Japanese cuisine) a la carte 58/93 – ☕ 34 – **358 rm** 420/500, 12 suites.

🏨 **Garden,** Dijsselhofplantsoen 7, ✉ 1077 BJ, ✆ 664 21 21, Telex 15453, Fax 679 93 56 – |‡| ⇍ TV ☎ P – 🎤 25-150. AE ⓓ E VISA
M see rest **De Kersentuin** below – ☕ 35 – **95 rm** 360/445, 2 suites.

🏨 **Forte Crest Apollo,** Apollolaan 2, ✉ 1077 BA, ✆ 673 59 22, Telex 14084, Fax 570 57 44, ☂, « Terrace with ≤ canal » – |‡| ⇍ rm ▤ rm TV ☎ P – 🎤 25-200. AE ⓓ E VISA
M a la carte 41/75 – ☕ 30 – **225 rm** 385/475, 3 suites.

🏨 **Hilton,** Apollolaan 138, ✉ 1077 BG, ✆ 678 07 80, Telex 11025, Fax 662 66 88 – |‡| ⇍ rm ▤ rest TV ☎ P – 🎤 25-325. AE ⓓ E VISA. ✻
M a la carte 40/72 – ☕ 39 – **263 rm** 440/510, 11 suites.

🏨 **Novotel,** Europaboulevard 10, ✉ 1083 AD, ✆ 541 11 23, Telex 13375, Fax 646 28 23 – |‡| ⇍ rm ▤ rm TV ☎ P – 🎤 25-300. AE ⓓ E VISA
M (open until midnight) a la carte approx. 60 – ☕ 23 – **600 rm** 240/270.

🏨 **Altea,** Joan Muyskenweg 10, ✉ 1096 CJ, ✆ 665 81 81, Telex 13382, Fax 694 87 35, Fö, ⛱ – |‡| ⇍ rm ▤ rm TV ☎ ♿ P – 🎤 25-250. AE ⓓ E VISA. ✻
M a la carte 65/81 – **176 rm** ☕ 200/310, 2 suites.

🏨 **Memphis** without rest, De Lairessestraat 87, ✉ 1071 NX, ✆ 673 31 41, Telex 12450, Fax 673 73 12 – |‡| TV ☎ – 🎤 25-45. AE ⓓ E VISA
☕ 25 – **74 rm** 360/450.

🏨 **Lairesse** without rest, De Lairessestraat 7, ✉ 1071 NR, ✆ 671 95 96, Fax 671 17 56 – |‡| TV ☎. AE ⓓ E VISA
34 rm ☕ 240/290.

🏨 **Cok Hotels,** Koninginneweg 34, ✉ 1075 CZ, ✆ 664 61 11, Telex 11679, Fax 664 53 04 – |‡| TV ☎ – 🎤 25-80. AE ⓓ E VISA
M a la carte 40/58 – **159 rm** ☕ 150/325.

🏨 **Toro** 🐚 without rest, Koningslaan 64, ✉ 1075 AG, ✆ 673 72 23, Fax 675 00 31 – |‡| TV ☎. AE ⓓ E VISA
22 rm ☕ 170/200.

Jan Luyken without rest, Jan Luykenstraat 58, ✉ 1071 CS, ☏ 573 07 30, Telex 16254, Fax 676 38 41 – rm – 25-150. AE E VISA. JZ x
63 rm 290/350.

Villa Borgmann without rest, Koningslaan 48, ✉ 1075 AE, ☏ 673 52 52, Fax 676 25 80 – AE E VISA.
15 rm 115/205.

Apollofirst, Apollolaan 123, ✉ 1077 AP, ☏ 673 03 33 and 679 79 71 (rest), Fax 675 03 48, – rest AE E VISA. rest
M *(closed Saturday lunch, Sunday and 24 December-2 January)* (open until 11.30 p.m.) a la carte approx. 85 – **40 rm** 260/285.

Delphi without rest, Apollolaan 105, ✉ 1077 AN, ☏ 679 51 52, Fax 675 29 41 – AE E VISA
50 rm 175/240.

XXX **De Kersentuin** - (at Garden H.), Dijsselhofplantsoen 7, ✉ 1077 BJ, ☏ 664 21 21, Telex 15453, Fax 679 93 56 – AE E VISA.
closed Saturday lunch, Sunday, 31 December and 1 January – **M** a la carte 115/153

XXX **Ciel Bleu** 23rd floor - (at Okura H.), Ferdinand Bolstraat 333, ✉ 1072 LH, ☏ 678 71 11, Telex 16182, Fax 671 23 44, Partly Asian cuisine, ≤ town – AE E VISA.
closed 15 to 30 July – **M** (dinner only) a la carte 89/115.

XXX **Parkrest. Rosarium,** Amstelpark 1, Europaboulevard, ✉ 1083 HZ, ☏ 644 40 85, Fax 646 60 04, Open until midnight, « Floral park » – AE E VISA
closed Sunday – **M** a la carte 84/108.

XX ✿ **De Trechter** (de Wit), Hobbemakade 63, ✉ 1071 XL, ☏ 671 12 63, Fax 662 27 60 – AE E VISA.
closed Sunday, Monday, Bank Holidays, 13 July-4 August and 25 December-6 January – **M** (dinner only, booking essential) a la carte 98/111
Spec. St-Jacques grillées au jus de moules (October-May), Terrine de foie gras d'oie, filet de bœuf et persil, Soupe d'endives au Roquefort et noix.

XX ✿ **Halvemaan,** van Leyenberghlaan 20 (Gijsbrecht van Aemstelpark), ✉ 1082 GM, ☏ 644 03 48, Fax 644 17 77, « Terrace with ≤ private lake » – AE E VISA.
closed Saturday lunch, Sunday, Easter Monday, Whitsun Monday, 30 April and 24 December-2 January – **M** a la carte 100/132
Spec. Steak tartare maison, Saumon mariné au yaourt, Turbot avec mousseline de pommes de terre aux huîtres.

XX **Bartholdy,** Van Baerlestraat 35, ✉ 1071 AP, ☏ 662 26 55, Fax 671 09 19, – AE E VISA.
closed Monday – **M** a la carte 77/88.

XX **Le Garage,** Ruysdaelstraat 54, ✉ 1071 XE, ☏ 679 71 76, Fax 662 22 49, Open until 11 p.m. – AE E VISA
closed Sunday July-August and Bank Holidays – **M** a la carte approx. 60.

XX **Beddington's,** Roelof Hartstraat 6, ✉ 1071 VH, ☏ 676 52 01 – AE E VISA.
closed Saturday lunch, Sunday and last week December-first week January – **M** a la carte 62/75.

XX **Keyzer,** Van Baerlestraat 96, ✉ 1071 BB, ☏ 671 14 41, Fax 673 73 53 – AE E VISA.
closed Easter, Whitsun and Christmas – **M** 53.

XX **Het Bosch,** Jollenpad 10 (by Amstelveenseweg), ✉ 1081 KC, ☏ 644 58 00, Fax 644 19 64, ≤, « Terrace overlooking lake » – AE E VISA.
closed Saturday lunch – **M** a la carte approx. 80.

X **Ravel,** Gelderlandplein 2, ✉ 1082 LA, ☏ 644 16 43, Fax 642 86 84, Pub rest – AE E VISA
closed Sunday lunch – **M** 42/58.

X **Brasserie Van Baerle,** Van Baerlestraat 158, ✉ 1071 BG, ☏ 679 15 32, Fax 671 71 96, Pub rest, open until 11 p.m. – AE E VISA
closed Saturday and 25 December-2 January – **M** 55.

X **Oriënt,** Van Baerlestraat 21, ✉ 1071 AN, ☏ 673 49 58, Fax 676 82 57, Indonesian cuisine – AE E VISA JZ q
closed 12 to 31 December – **M** (dinner only except Saturday and Sunday) 40.

North

Galaxy, Distelkade 21, ✉ 1031 XP, ☏ 634 43 66, Telex 18607, Fax 636 03 45 – 25-250. AE E VISA. rest
M a la carte 44/60 – **276 rm** 215/250, 4 suites.

Bastion Noord without rest, Rode Kruisstraat 28 (by Nieuwe Purmerweg), ✉ 1025 KN, ☏ 632 31 31, Fax 634 44 96 – AE E VISA.
40 rm 108/131.

Environs

at Badhoevedorp Haarlemmermeer pop. 98 073 – 0 20 :

Dorint, Sloterweg 299, 1171 VB, 658 81 11, Telex 13117, Fax 659 71 01, – rm rest – 25-150. VISA. rest
M a la carte 52/68 – 25 – **200 rm** 275/330.

De Herbergh with rm, Sloterweg 259, 1171 CP, 659 26 00, Fax 659 83 90, – rest . VISA.
M *(closed 19 July-9 August)* a la carte 68/82 – 15 – **15 rm** 145/175.

at Schiphol (international airport) Haarlemmermeer pop. 98 073 – 0 20 :

Hilton International, Herbergierstraat 1, 1118 ZK, 603 45 67, Telex 15186, Fax 648 09 17, – rm – 25-110. VISA. rest
M a la carte 84/100 – 36 – **274 rm** 440/660, 1 suite.

by motorway The Hague (A 4) – 0 20 :

Mercure, Oude Haagseweg 20, 1066 BW, 617 90 05, Telex 15524, Fax 615 90 27 – rm rest – 25-250. VISA.
M a la carte 65/81 – **150 rm** 270/310, 1 suite.

Barbizon, Kruisweg 495, 2132 NA Hoofddorp (15 km), 655 05 50, Telex 74546, Fax 653 49 99, – rm – 25-500. VISA
M *(closed lunch Saturday and Sunday and late December)* (open until 11 p.m.) a la carte 75/104 – 29 – **244 rm** 350/395.

Blokzijl Overijssel Brederwiede pop. 11 980 408 ⑫ – 0 5272 – 102 km.

Kaatje bij de Sluis, Brouwerstraat 20, 8356 DV, 18 33, Fax 18 36, – rest VISA
closed Monday, Tuesday and February-1 March – **M** *(closed Monday, Tuesday and Saturday lunch)* a la carte 106/141 – 34 – **8 rm** 190/240
Spec. Anguille à l'aneth en pâte de riz (15 April-October), Feuillantines au chocolat et pamplemousse, Canard sauvage aux olives (August-15 November).

Haarlem Noord-Holland 408 ⑩ – pop. 149 474 – 0 23 – 24 km.

at Overveen W : 4 km Bloemendaal pop. 17 216 – 0 23 :

De Bokkedoorns, Zeeweg 53, 2051 EB, 26 36 00, Fax 27 31 43, « Terrace with dunes » – VISA.
closed Monday, Saturday lunch, 5, 24 and 31 December-13 January – **M** a la carte 114/140
Spec. Cocotte de foie d'oie, Salade de homard et de St-Jacques au caviar, Rognons de veau et ragoût d'abats.

Hoorn Noord-Holland 408 ⑩ ⑪ – pop. 58 225 – 0 2290 – 43 km.

De Oude Rosmolen (Fonk), Duinsteeg 1, 1621 ER, 1 47 52, Fax 1 49 38 – . VISA
closed Thursday, 15 August-1 September, 27 December-5 January and 2 weeks February – **M** (dinner only, booking essential) a la carte 97/125
Spec. Profiteroles à la mousse de foie gras, Bourride à ma façon, Pâtisseries maison.

Zaandam Noord-Holland Zaanstad pop. 130 705 408 ⑩ – 0 75 – 16 km.

De Hoop op d'Swarte Walvis, Kalverringdijk 15 (Zaanse Schans), 1509 BT, 16 55 40, Fax 16 24 76, « 18C residence in a museum village » – VISA
closed Saturday lunch November-April, Sunday and 27 December-2 January – **M** a la carte 102/120
Spec. Ris de veau en pâte de riz au beurre d'écrevisses, Turbot au beurre de moutarde et safran, Côte de veau rôtie au cassoulet.

The HAGUE (Den HAAG or 's-GRAVENHAGE) Zuid-Holland 408 ⑨ – pop. 444 242 – 0 70.

See : Scheveningen★★ – Binnenhof★ : The Knights' Room★ (Ridderzaal) JV **A** – Hofvijver (Court pool) ★ JV – Lange Voorhout★ JV – Panorama Mesdag★ HV **B** – Madurodam★.

Museums : Mauritshuis★★★ JV **D** – Municipal★★ (Gemeentemuseum) – Mesdag★ HU **M²** – Prince William V painting gallery★ (Schilderijengalerij Prins Willem V).

18 at Wassenaar NE : 11 km, Groot Haesebroekseweg 22 (0 1751) 7 96 07 and 9 Hoge klei 1 (0 1751) 1 78 46 - 18 at Rijswijk SE : 5 km, Delftweg 59 (0 70) 399 50 40.

Amsterdam-Schiphol NE : 37 km (0 20) 601 09 66 (information) and (0 20) 674 77 47 (reservations) – Rotterdam-Zestienhoven SE : 17 km (0 10) 446 34 44 (information) and 437 27 45 (reservations).

(departs from 's-Hertogenbosch) 347 16 81.

Kon. Julianaplein 30, 2595 AA, 354 62 00.

Amsterdam 55 – Brussels 182 – Rotterdam 24 – Delft 13.

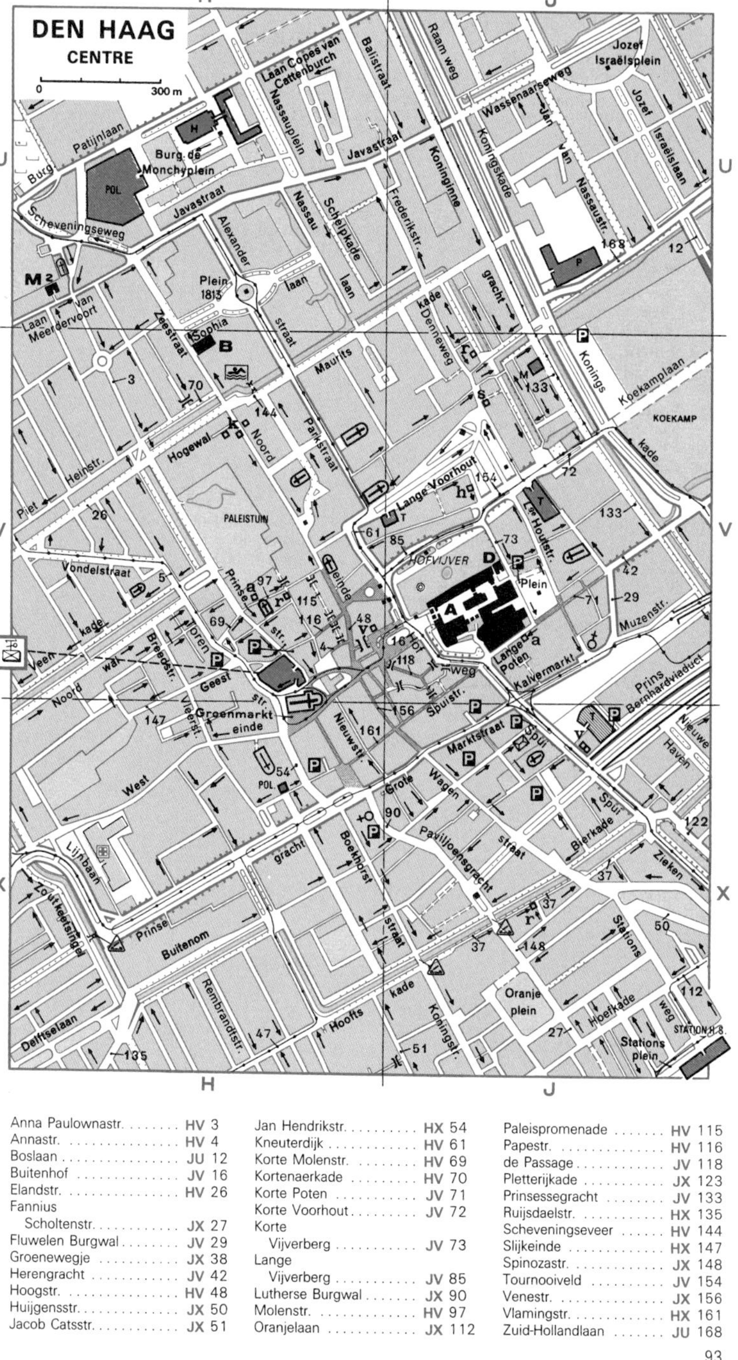

Anna Paulownastr.	HV 3	Jan Hendrikstr.	HX 54	Paleispromenade	HV 115
Annastr.	HV 4	Kneuterdijk	HV 61	Papestr.	HV 116
Boslaan	JU 12	Korte Molenstr.	HV 69	de Passage	JV 118
Buitenhof	JV 16	Kortenaerkade	HV 70	Pletterijkade	JX 123
Elandstr.	HV 26	Korte Poten	JV 71	Prinsessegracht	JV 133
Fannius Scholtenstr.	JX 27	Korte Voorhout	JV 72	Ruijsdaelstr.	HX 135
Fluwelen Burgwal	JV 29	Korte Vijverberg	JV 73	Scheveningseveer	HV 144
Groenewegje	JX 38	Lange Vijverberg	JV 85	Slijkeinde	HX 147
Herengracht	JV 42	Lutherse Burgwal	JX 90	Spinozastr.	JX 148
Hoogstr.	HV 48	Molenstr.	HV 97	Tournooiveld	JV 154
Huijgensstr.	JX 50	Oranjelaan	JX 112	Venestr.	JX 156
Jacob Catsstr.	JX 51			Vlamingstr.	HX 161
				Zuid-Hollandlaan	JU 168

Des Indes, Lange Voorhout 54, ⊠ 2514 EG, ✆ 363 29 32, Telex 31196, Fax 345 17 21, « Late 19C residence » – |♦| ⇎ rm ▤ rest TV ☎ P – 25-250. AE ⓓ E VISA. ✻ rest JV **s**
M Le Restaurant a la carte 89/108 – ☕ 35 – **76 rm** 380/480, 1 suite.

Sofitel, Koningin Julianaplein 35, ⊠ 2595 AA, ✆ 381 49 01, Telex 34001, Fax 382 59 27 – |♦| ⇎ rm ▤ TV ☎ ♿ – 25-100. AE ⓓ E VISA
M a la carte approx. 90 – ☕ 30 – **124 rm** 315, 20 suites.

Promenade, van Stolkweg 1, ⊠ 2585 JL, ✆ 352 51 61, Telex 34186, Fax 354 10 46, ≤, ☂, « Collection of modern Dutch paintings » – |♦| ▤ rest TV ☎ ⇔ P – 25-160. AE ⓓ E VISA
M La Cigogne a la carte 74/99 – ☕ 28 – **99 rm** 315/355, 2 suites.

Mercure Central, Spui 180, ⊠ 2511 BW, ✆ 363 67 00, Telex 32000, Fax 363 93 98, ⛹, ≘s – |♦| ⇎ rm ▤ rest TV ☎ ♿ P – 25-110. AE ⓓ E VISA JX **v**
M 40 – **156 rm** ☕ 230/270, 3 suites.

Corona, Buitenhof 42, ⊠ 2513 AH, ✆ 363 79 30, Telex 31418, Fax 361 57 85 – |♦| ▤ rest TV ☎ P – 100. AE ⓓ E VISA HV **v**
M *(closed last 2 weeks July)* a la carte 102/130 – ☕ 15 – **26 rm** 230/455.

Bel Air, Johan de Wittlaan 30, ⊠ 2517 JR, ✆ 350 20 21, Telex 31444, Fax 351 26 82, ≤, ▢ – |♦| TV ☎ P – 25-250. AE ⓓ E VISA
M a la carte 60/87 – ☕ 23 – **346 rm** 220/240, 4 suites.

Parkhotel without rest, Molenstraat 53, ⊠ 2513 BJ, ✆ 362 43 71, Telex 33005, Fax 361 45 25 – |♦| TV ☎ – 25-100. AE ⓓ E VISA HV **a**
114 rm ☕ 144/245.

Paleis without rest, Molenstraat 26, ⊠ 2513 BL, ✆ 362 46 21, Telex 34349, Fax 361 45 33, ≘s – |♦| TV ☎. AE ⓓ E VISA HV **r**
☕ 20 – **20 rm** 155/219.

Da Roberto, Noordeinde 196, ⊠ 2514 GS, ✆ 346 49 77, Italian cuisine – AE ⓓ E
closed Saturday lunch and Sunday – **M** a la carte approx. 90. HV **k**

De Hoogwerf, Zijdelaan 20 (by N 44), ⊠ 2594 BV, ✆ 347 55 14, Fax 381 95 96, ☂, « 17C farmhouse, garden » – AE ⓓ E VISA. ✻
closed Sunday and Bank Holidays except 30 April and Christmas – **M** 85.

Royal Dynasty, Noordeinde 123, ⊠ 2514 GG, ✆ 365 25 98, Asian cuisine – ▤. AE ⓓ E VISA HV **k**
closed 27 and 31 December – **M** a la carte approx. 65.

La Grande Bouffe, Maziestraat 10, ⊠ 2514 GT, ✆ 365 42 74, Fax 356 28 28 – AE E VISA
closed lunch Saturday and Sunday, Sunday dinner May-September, Monday and last week July-first 2 weeks August – **M** a la carte 74/90. HV **k**

Rousseau, Van Boetzelaerlaan 134, ⊠ 2581 AX, ✆ 355 47 43, ☂ – AE ⓓ E VISA
closed lunch Saturday and Sunday, Monday, 22 February-8 March and 30 August-20 September – **M** 55/115.

't Ganzenest, Groenewegje 115, ⊠ 2515 LP, ✆ 389 67 09 – AE ⓓ E. ✻ JX **r**
closed Sunday, Monday, 3 weeks August, late December-early January and carnival week – **M** (dinner only until 11.30 p.m.) 53/85.

Shirasagi, Spui 170, ⊠ 2511 BW, ✆ 346 47 00, Fax 346 26 01, Japanese cuisine, teppanyaki – ▤ P. AE ⓓ E VISA. ✻ JX **v**
closed lunch Saturday and Sunday – **M** 59/125.

The Ajoe, Lange Poten 31, ⊠ 2511 CM, ✆ 364 56 13, Fax 364 45 92, Indonesian cuisine – AE ⓓ E VISA. ✻ JV **a**
M a la carte 59/92.

Les Ombrelles, Hooistraat 4a, ⊠ 2514 BM, ✆ 365 87 89, ☂, Seafood, open until 11 p.m. – AE ⓓ E VISA. ✻ JV **r**
closed lunch Saturday and Sunday and 23 December-3 January – **M** a la carte 60/80.

Saur, Lange Voorhout 47, ⊠ 2514 EC, ✆ 346 25 65, Fax 365 86 14 – ▤. AE ⓓ E VISA. ✻
closed Sunday and Bank Holidays – **M** a la carte 69/119. JV **h**

at Scheveningen C 's-Gravenhage – ⚙ 0 70 – Seaside resort★★ – Casino Kurhaus, Gevers Deijnootplein ✆ 351 26 21.

ℹ Gevers Deijnootweg 1134, ⊠ 2586 BX, ✆ 354 62 00

Kurhaus, Gevers Deijnootplein 30, ⊠ 2586 CK, ✆ 352 00 52, Telex 33295, Fax 350 09 11, ≤, ☂, « Former late 19C concert hall », ⛱ – |♦| ⇎ rm TV ☎ ♿ P – 35-480. AE ⓓ E VISA. ✻ rest
M see rest. **Kandinsky** below – **Kurzaal** (Buffets) a la carte approx. 40 – ☕ 35 – **231 rm** 345/475, 8 suites.

Carlton Beach, Gevers Deijnootweg 201, ⊠ 2586 HZ, ✆ 354 14 14, Telex 33687, Fax 352 00 20, ≤, ⛹, ≘s, ▢ – |♦| TV ☎ P – 45-280. AE ⓓ E VISA
M (open until 11 p.m.) 40/103 – ☕ 20 – **182 rm** 205/245.

Europa, Zwolsestraat 2, ⊠ 2587 VJ, ✆ 351 26 51, Telex 33138, Fax 350 64 73, ⛹, ≘s, ▢ – |♦| ⇎ rm TV ☎ P – 400. AE ⓓ E VISA
M (dinner only until 11 p.m.) a la carte approx. 40 – ☕ 21 – **173 rm** 200/335, 1 suite.

XXXX **Kandinsky** - (at Kurhaus H.), Gevers Deijnootplein 30, ✉ 2586 CK, ☎ 352 00 52, Telex 33295, Fax 350 09 11, ≤ - ▤ P. AE ① E VISA. ✻
closed Saturday lunch and Sunday - **M** (dinner only July-August) a la carte 90/131.

XXX **Radèn Mas,** Gevers Deijnootplein 125, ✉ 2586 CR, ☎ 354 54 32, Fax 354 54 32, Indonesian cuisine - ▤. AE ① E VISA
closed lunch Saturday and Sunday - **M** a la carte 62/93.

XXX **Seinpost,** Zeekant 60, ✉ 2586 AD, ☎ 355 52 50, Fax 355 50 93, ≤, Seafood - ▤. AE ① E VISA
closed Saturday lunch, Sunday, 24 and 31 December and 1 January - **M** 50/60.

XX **China Delight,** Dr Lelykade 118, ✉ 2583 CN, ☎ 355 54 50, Fax 354 66 52, Chinese cuisine, open until 11 p.m. - ▤. ① E VISA - **M** a la carte 53/104.

XX **Ducdalf,** Dr Lelykade 5, ✉ 2583 CL, ☎ 355 76 92, Fax 355 15 28, ≤, Seafood, mussels in season - P. AE ① E VISA
closed 24 and 31 December - **M** 50.

XX **Bali,** Badhuisweg 1, ✉ 2587 CA, ☎ 350 24 34, Fax 354 03 63, Indonesian cuisine - P. AE ① E VISA. ✻
closed 31 December - **M** (dinner only) 58.

Environs

at Kijkduin W : 4 km C 's-Gravenhage - ☎ 0 70 :

Atlantic, Deltaplein 200, ✉ 2554 EJ, ☎ 325 40 25, Fax 368 67 21, ≤, 斧, Fā, ≘s, ▣ - |‡| TV ☎ P - ⚲ 25-300. AE ① E VISA
M 40 - **119 rm** ⊐ 233/283.

Zeehaghe without rest, Deltaplein 675, ✉ 2554 GK, ☎ 325 62 62, Telex 34186, Fax 325 40 69, ≤ - |‡| ⇔ TV ☎ P - ⚲ 30. AE ① E VISA
70 rm ⊐ 220, 5 suites.

at Leidschendam E : 6 km - pop. 33 192 - ☎ 0 70 :

Green Park, Weigelia 22, ✉ 2262 AB, ☎ 320 92 80, Telex 33090, Fax 327 49 07, ≤, Fā - |‡| ⇔ rm ▤ rest TV ☎ P - ⚲ 25-250. AE ① E VISA. ✻
M Brasserie The Greenery a la carte 51/69 - ⊐ 25 - **92 rm** 220/265, 4 suites.

XXX ✿ **Villa Rozenrust,** Veursestraatweg 104, ✉ 2265 CG, ☎ 327 74 60, Fax 327 50 62, 斧, « Terrace » - P. AE ① E VISA
closed Saturday lunch, Sunday and 1 to 15 August - **M** a la carte approx. 100
Spec. Lasagne de homard, Saltimbocca de ris de veau.

at Voorburg E : 5 km - pop. 39 813 - ☎ 0 70 :

XXXXX ✿ **Vreugd en Rust** (Savelberg) ⛰ with rm, Oosteinde 14, ✉ 2271 EH, ☎ 387 20 81, Fax 387 77 15, ≤, 斧, « 17C residence with terrace in public park » - |‡| ⇔ rm TV ☎ P - ⚲ 35. AE ① E VISA
M *(closed 24 December and lunch 31 December)* a la carte 117/164 - **14 rm** ⊐ 200/495
Spec. Salade de homard, Pigeon de Bresse à la sauge, Huîtres chaudes au safran (October-April).

XX **Villa la Ruche,** Prinses Mariannelaan 71, ✉ 2275 BB, ☎ 386 01 10, Fax 386 50 64 - ▤. AE ① E VISA. ✻
closed 28 December-3 January - **M** a la carte 79/104.

at Wassenaar NE : 11 km - pop. 26 218 - ☎ 0 1751 :

Aub. De Kieviet ⛰, Stoeplaan 27, ✉ 2243 CX, ☎ 1 92 32, Fax 1 09 69, 斧, « Floral terrace » - |‡| ⇔ rm ▤ TV ☎ ♿ P - ⚲ 50. AE ① E VISA
M a la carte 91/125 - ⊐ 25 - **24 rm** 295/450.

Wassenaar, Katwijkseweg 33 (N : 2 km), ✉ 2242 PC, ☎ 1 92 18, Fax 7 64 81 - |‡| ⇔ rm TV ☎ P - ⚲ 60. AE ① E VISA. ✻ rest
M a la carte approx. 65 - **57 rm** ⊐ 160/200.

ROTTERDAM Zuid-Holland 212 ⑤ and 408 ㉔ ㉕ - pop. 582 266 - ☎ 0 10 - Casino JKY, Weena 10 ☎ 414 77 99.

See : The harbour★★★ ⛴ KZ - Lijnbaan★ (Shopping centre) JKY - St. Laurence Church (Grote-of St. Laurenskerk) : interior★ KYD - Euromast★ (tower) (✻★★, ≤★) JZ.

Museums : Boymans-van Beuningen★★★ (History Museum) JZ - "De Dubbele Palmboom"★ - Het Schielandshuis★ (History Museum) KY.

Envir : SE : 15 km, Kinderdijk Windmills★★.

⛳9 Kralingseweg 200 ☎ 452 22 83 - ⛳18 at Rhoon SW : 11 km, Veerweg 2a ☎ (0 1890) 1 80 58.

✈ Zestienhoven ☎ 446 34 44 (information) and 437 27 45 (reservations).

🚗 (departs from 's-Hertogenbosch) ☎ 411 71 00.

⛴ Europoort to Kingston-upon-Hull : North Sea Ferries ☎ (0 1819) 5 55 00 (information) and 5 55 55 (reservations).

ℹ Coolsingel 67, ✉ 3012 AC, ☎ 0 6-34 03 40 65 and Central Station, Spoorsingel 10, ✉ 3033 GK, ☎ 413 60 06 - at Schiedam W : 6 km, Buitenhavenweg 9, ✉ 3113 BC, ☎ (0 10) 473 30 00.

Amsterdam 76 - The Hague 24 - Antwerp 103 - Brussels 149 - Utrecht 57.

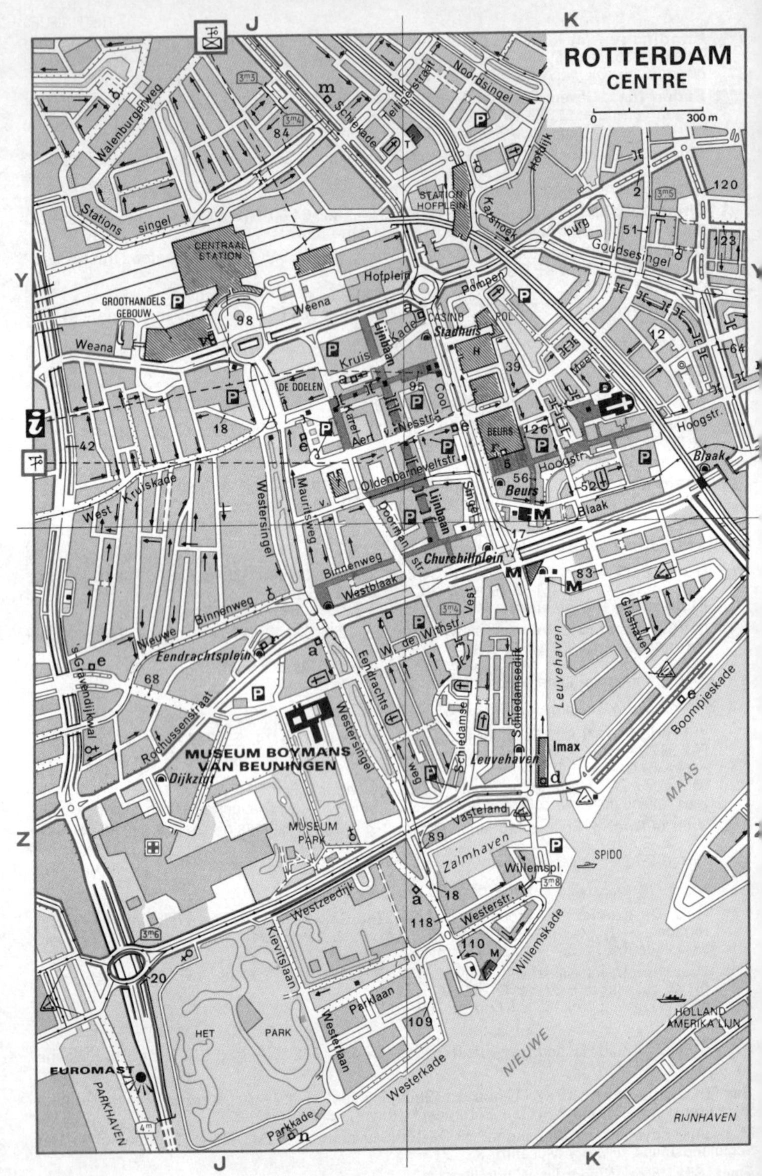

Beurspl.	KY	5
Binnenweg	JZ	
Hoogstr.	KY	
Karel Doormanstr.	JY	
Korte Hoogstr.	KY	56
Lijnbaan	KYZ	
Stadhuispl.	KY	95
Admiraal de Ruyterweg	KY	2
Botersloot	KY	12
Churchillpl.	KY	17
Diergaardesingel	JY	18
Droogleever Fortuynpl.	JZ	20
Haagsever	KY	39
Henegouwerlaan	JY	42
Jonker Fransstr.	KY	51
Keizerstr.	KY	52
Mariniersweg	KY	64
Mathenesserlaan	JZ	68
Posthoornstr.	KZ	83
Provenierssingel	JY	84
Scheepstimmermanslaan	KZ	89
Stationspl.	JY	98
Veerhaven	KZ	109
Veerkade	KZ	110
van Vollenhovenstr.	KZ	118
Vondelweg	KY	120
Warande	KY	123
Westewagenstr.	KY	126

Hilton International, Weena 10, ✉ 3012 CM, ☎ 414 40 44, Telex 22666, Fax 411 88 84 – |♦| ⇆ rm ▤ TV ☎ ♿ P – 🏛 80-250. AE ◑ E VISA. ✂
M a la carte 54/77 – ☕ 38 – **244 rm** 390/495, 8 suites. JKY **a**

Parkhotel, Westersingel 70, ✉ 3015 LB, ☎ 436 36 11, Telex 22020, Fax 436 42 12, Lб, ≘s, 🌳 – |♦| ⇆ rm ▤ TV ☎ P – 🏛 25-50. AE ◑ E VISA. ✂ JZ **a**
M a la carte 55/83 – **189 rm** ☕ 245/375, 3 suites.

Rijnhotel, Schouwburgplein 1, ✉ 3012 CK, ☎ 433 38 00, Telex 21640, Fax 414 54 82 – |♦| ▤ rest TV ☎ – 🏛 25-220. AE ◑ E VISA. ✂ JY **e**
M *(closed lunch Saturday and Sunday)* (dinner only July-August) a la carte approx. 70 – ☕ 28 – **98 rm** 265/350, 2 suites.

Atlanta, Aert van Nesstraat 4, ✉ 3012 CA, ☎ 411 04 20, Telex 21595, Fax 413 53 20 – |♦| ⇆ rm TV ☎ 🚗 – 🏛 25-400. AE ◑ E VISA KY **e**
M (dinner only) a la carte approx. 65 – ☕ 25 – **163 rm** 175/240, 1 suite.

Inntel, Leuvehaven 80, ✉ 3011 EA, ☎ 413 41 39, Fax 413 32 22, ≤, Lб, ≘s, 🏊 – |♦| ⇆ rm ▤ rest TV ☎ P – 🏛 25-220. AE ◑ E VISA KZ **d**
M (open until 11 p.m.) a la carte 53/68 – ☕ 20 – **150 rm** 210/260.

Zuiderparkhotel, Dordtsestraatweg 285, ✉ 3083 AJ, ☎ 485 00 55, Telex 28755, Fax 485 63 04, ≘s, 🏊 – |♦| ▤ rest TV ☎ P – 🏛 25-200. AE ◑ E VISA
M a la carte approx. 70 – ☕ 22 – **110 rm** 125/215, 3 suites.

Savoy, Hoogstraat 81, ✉ 3011 PJ, ☎ 413 92 80, Telex 21525, Fax 404 57 12 – |♦| TV ☎. AE ◑ E VISA KY **n**
M (dinner only) a la carte 55/75 – ☕ 20 – **94 rm** 155/170.

Pax without rest, Schiekade 658, ✉ 3032 AK, ☎ 466 33 44, Fax 467 52 78 – |♦| TV ☎ P. AE ◑ E VISA JY **m**
45 rm ☕ 145/250.

Van Walsum, Mathenesserlaan 199, ✉ 3014 HC, ☎ 436 32 75, Telex 20010, Fax 436 44 10 – |♦| TV ☎ P. AE ◑ E VISA. ✂ rest JZ **e**
closed 23 December-2 January – **M** (residents only) – **25 rm** ☕ 85/150.

XXXX ✿ **Parkheuvel** (Helder), Heuvellaan 21, ✉ 3016 GL, ☎ 436 07 66, Fax 436 71 40, ≤, 🍽, « Terrace » – P. AE ◑ E VISA JZ **n**
closed Sunday and 27 December-3 January – **M** a la carte 100/130
Spec. Spaghetti d'asperges au saumon mariné (May-June), Homard au four, Trois crèmes brûlées.

XXX **Old Dutch,** Rochussenstraat 20, ✉ 3015 EK, ☎ 436 03 44, Fax 436 78 26, 🍽 – ▤ P. AE ◑ E VISA JZ **r**
closed Saturday and Sunday – **M** a la carte 65/100.

XXX **World Trade Center** 23rd floor, Beursplein 37, ✉ 3011 AA, ☎ 405 44 65, Fax 405 51 20, ✳ city – |♦| ▤ P. AE ◑ E VISA. ✂ KY **r**
closed Saturday, Sunday and August – **M** a la carte approx. 80.

XXX **Radèn Mas** 1st floor, Kruiskade 72, ✉ 3012 EH, ☎ 411 72 44, Fax 411 72 44, Indonesian cuisine, « Exotic decor » – ▤. AE ◑ E VISA JY **a**
closed lunch Saturday and Sunday – **M** a la carte 62/93.

XXX **Le Coq d'Or** 1st floor, van Vollenhovenstraat 25, ✉ 3016 BG, ☎ 436 64 05, Fax 436 59 06, 🍽 – AE ◑ E VISA. ✂ KZ **a**
M a la carte 80/125.

XXX Regent Palace, Oosterkade 5, ✉ 3011 TV, ☎ 414 19 11, Fax 414 32 05, ≤, Chinese cuisine – ▤. ✂.

XX **Brasserie La Vilette,** Westblaak 160, ✉ 3012 KM, ☎ 414 86 92, Fax 414 33 91 – ▤. AE ◑ E VISA JZ **t**
closed Saturday lunch and Sunday – **M** 40/55.

XX **Boompjes,** Boompjes 701, ✉ 3011 XZ, ☎ 413 60 70, Fax 413 70 87, ≤ Nieuwe Maas (Meuse), Open until 11 p.m. – ▤. AE ◑ E VISA. ✂ KZ **e**
closed lunch Saturday and Sunday – **M** 65/78.

XX Silhouet, Euromast tower (Admission charge), Parkhaven 20, ✉ 3016 GM, ☎ 436 48 11, Fax 436 22 80, ✳ city and port – ▤ P. ✂ JZ

XX **Engels,** Stationsplein 45, ✉ 3013 AK, ☎ 411 95 50, Fax 413 94 21, Multinational cuisines – ▤ P – 🏛 25-800. AE ◑ E VISA JY **v**
M a la carte approx. 60.

Airport C Rotterdam – ✪ 0 10 :

Airport, Vliegveldweg 59, ✉ 3043 NT, ☎ 462 55 66, Telex 25785, Fax 462 22 66 – |♦| ⇆ rm TV ☎ ♿ P – 🏛 25-300. AE ◑ E VISA
M a la carte approx. 80 – **96 rm** ☕ 195/245 and 2 suites.

at Hillegersberg C Rotterdam – ✪ 0 10 :

XXX **Beau Rivage,** Weissenbruchlaan 149, ✉ 3054 LM, ☎ 418 40 40, Fax 418 64 65, ≤, 🍽, « Terrace overlooking lake » – AE ◑ E VISA. ✂
closed Saturday lunch, Sunday and Bank Holidays – **M** 70.

XX **Senang,** Grindweg 650, ✉ 3055 VD, ☎ 422 25 02, 🍽, Indonesian cuisine – ▤ P. AE ◑ E VISA
closed lunch Saturday and Sunday – **M** 34/63.

at Kralingen C Rotterdam - ☎ 0 10 :

Novotel, K.P. van der Mandelelaan 130 (near A 16), ✉ 3062 MB, ✆ 453 07 77, Telex 24109, Fax 453 15 03 - |♦| ⇆ rm ▤ TV ☎ ♿ P - 🎤 25-625. AE ⓓ E VISA
M (open until midnight) a la carte approx. 70 - ☕ 22 - **196 rm** 225/255.

XXX **In den Rustwat,** Honingerdijk 96, ✉ 3062 NX, ✆ 413 41 10, Fax 404 85 40, 🏠, « 16C residence » - P. AE ⓓ E VISA. ✻
closed Saturday lunch, Sunday and Bank Holidays - **M** a la carte 81/105.

at Ommoord C Rotterdam - ☎ 0 10 :

XXX **Keizershof,** Martin Luther Kingweg 7, ✉ 3069 EW, ✆ 455 13 33, Fax 456 80 23, 🏠 - ▤ P. AE ⓓ E VISA
closed 24 and 31 December - **M** 40/90.

at Rhoon C Albrandswaard pop. 14 121 - ☎ 0 1890 :

XX **Het Kasteel van Rhoon,** Dorpsdijk 63, ✉ 3161 KD, ✆ 1 88 84, ≤, 🏠, « In the grounds of the chateau » - P. AE ⓓ E VISA
closed 25 and 26 December - **M** a la carte 88/113.

at Schiedam - pop. 70 207 - ☎ 0 10 :

Novotel, Hargalaan 2 (near A 20), ✉ 3118 JA, ✆ 471 33 22, Telex 22582, Fax 470 06 56, 🏠, ⛱, 🌳 - |♦| ⇆ rm ▤ rest TV ☎ ♿ P - 🎤 25-150. AE ⓓ E VISA
M (open until midnight) a la carte 43/62 - ☕ 23 - **138 rm** 190/245.

XXX **La Duchesse,** Maasboulevard 9, ✉ 3114 HB, ✆ 426 46 26, Fax 473 25 01, ≤ Nieuwe Maas (Meuse), 🏠 - P. AE ⓓ E VISA
closed Saturday lunch, Sunday and 31 December - **M** a la carte 90/110.

XXX **Aub. Hosman Frères** 1st floor, Korte Dam 10, ✉ 3111 BG, ✆ 426 40 96, Fax 473 00 08 - ▤. AE ⓓ E VISA
closed Sunday, Monday and 24 and 31 December - **M** a la carte 80/115.

Europoort zone by ⑥ : 25 km - ☎ 0 1819 :

De Beer Europoort, Europaweg 210 (N 15), ✉ 3198 LD, ✆ 6 23 77, Telex 29979, Fax 6 29 23, ≤, 🏠, ⛱, 🎾 - |♦| TV ☎ P - 🎤 25-180. AE ⓓ E VISA
M a la carte 45/115 - **78 rm** ☕ 135/180.

Denmark

Danmark

COPENHAGEN

PRACTICAL INFORMATION

LOCAL CURRENCY

Danish Kroner: 100 D.Kr = 15.70 US $ = 13.21 Ecus (Jan. 93)

TOURIST INFORMATION

The telephone number and address of the Tourist Information office is given in the text under ℹ.

FOREIGN EXCHANGE

Banks are open between 9.30am and 4.00pm (6.00pm on Thursdays) on weekdays except Saturdays. The main banks in the centre of Copenhagen, the Central Station and the Airport have exchange facilities outside these hours.

MEALS

At lunchtime, follow the custom of the country and try the typical buffets of Scandinavian specialities.
At dinner, the a la carte and the menus will offer you more conventional cooking.

SHOPPING IN COPENHAGEN

Strøget (Department stores, exclusive shops, boutiques).
Kompagnistræde (Antiques).
See also in the index of street names, those printed in red are where the principal shops are found.

CAR HIRE

The international car hire companies have branches in Copenhagen – Your hotel porter should be able to give details and help you with your arrangements.

TIPPING

In Denmark, all hotels and restaurants include a service charge. As for the taxis, there is no extra charge to the amount shown on the meter.

SPEED LIMITS

The maximum permitted speed in cities is 50 km/h - 31mph, outside cities 80 km/h - 50mph and 110 km/h - 68mph on motorways. Cars towing caravans 70 km/h – 44 mph and buses 80 km/h – 50 mph also on motorways.
Local signs may indicate lower or permit higher limits. On the whole, speed should always be adjusted to prevailing circumstances. In case of even minor speed limit offences, drivers will be liable to heavy fines to be paid on the spot. If payment cannot be made, the car may be detained.

SEAT BELTS

The wearing of seat belts is compulsory for drivers and all passengers except children under the age of 3 and taxi passengers.

Copenhagen

(KØBENHAVN) Danmark 985 Q 9 – pop. 575 000, Greater Copenhagen 1 200 000.

See : Tivoli★★★ : May 1 to September 15 BZ – Harbour and Canal Tour★★★ (Kanaltur) : May to September 15 (Gammel Strand and Nyhavn) – Little Mermaid★★★ (Den Lille Havfrue) DX – Strøget★★ BCYZ – Nyhavn★★ DY – Amalienborg★★ : Changing of the Guard at noon DY – Rosenborg Castle★★ (Rosenborg Slot) CX – Christiansborg Palace★★ (Christiansborg Slot) CZ – Old Stock Exchange★★ (Børsen) CZ – Round Tower★★ (Rundetårn) CY **D** – Gråbrødretorv★ CY **28** – Gammel Strand★ CZ **26** – Marble Church★ (Marmorkirke) DY **E** – Royal Chapel and Naval Church★ (Holmen's Kirke) CZ **B** – King's Square★ (Kongens Nytorv) DY – Charlottenborg Palace★ (Charlottenborg Slot) DY **F** – Citadel★ (Kastellet) DX – Christianhavn★ DZ – Botanical Garden★ (Botanisk Have) BX – Frederiksberg Garden★ (Frederiksberg Have) AZ – Town Hall (Rådhus) : World Clock★ (Jens Olsen's Verdensur) BZ **H.** Breweries – Porcelain Factories.

Museums : Ny Carlsberg Glyptotek★★★ (Glyptoteket) BZ – National Museum★★ (Nationalmuseet) CZ – Royal Museum of Fine Arts★★ (Statens Museum for Kunst) CX – Thorvaldsen Museum★ CZ **M1** Royal Arsenal Museum★ (Tøjhusmuseet) CZ **M2** – Royal Theatre Museum★ (Teaterhistorisk Museum) CZ **M3** – Copenhagen City Museum★ (Bymuseet) AZ **M4**.

Outskirts : Open Air Museum★★ (Frilandsmuseet) NW : 12 km BX – Ordrupgaard Museum★ (Ordrupgaardsamlingen) N : 10 km CX – Dragør★ SW : 13 km DZ – Karen Blixen Museum★ (Karen Blixen Museet) N : 20 km AX – Louisiana Museum of Modern Art★ (Louisiana Museum for moderne kunst) N : 35 km AX.

18 Dansk Golf Union 56 ✆ 42 64 06 66.

Copenhagen/Kastrup SE : 10 km ✆ 31 54 17 01 – Air Terminal : main railway station.

Motorail for Southern Europe : ✆ 33 14 17 01.

Further information from the D S B, main railway station or tourist information centre (see below).

Danmarks Turistråd, Bernstorffsgade 1, København, 1577 V ✆ 33 11 13 25.

Berlin 385 – Hamburg 305 – Oslo 583 – Stockholm 630.

4

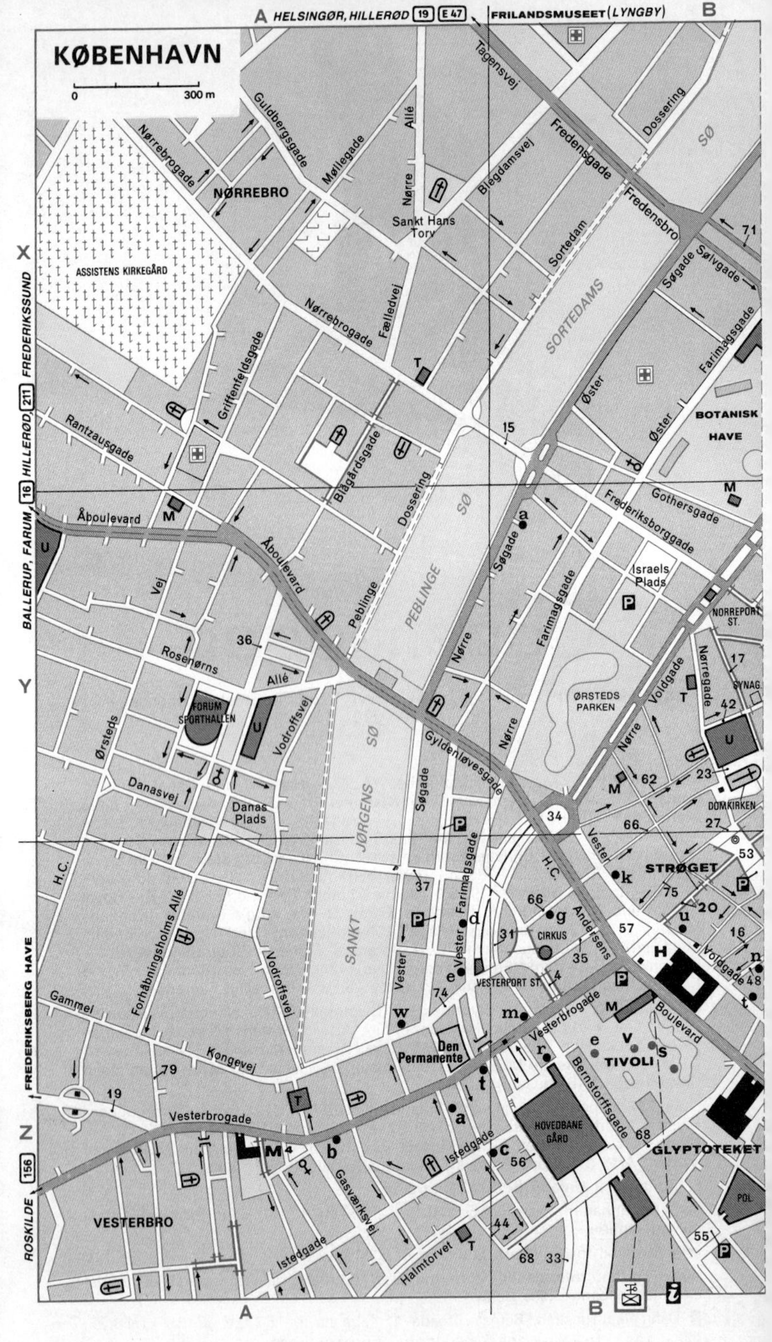
KØBENHAVN
0
300 m
HELSINGØR, HILLERØD
19
E 47
FRILANDSMUSEET (LYNGBY)
BALLERUP, FARUM
16
HILLERØD
211
FREDERIKSSUND
FREDERIKSBERG HAVE
ROSKILDE
156
NØRREBRO
ASSISTENS KIRKEGÅRD
SORTEDAMS SØ
PEBLINGE SØ
SANKT JØRGENS SØ
BOTANISK HAVE
ØRSTEDS PARKEN
Israels Plads
NØRREPORT ST.
DOMKIRKEN
STRØGET
TIVOLI
HOVEDBANE GÅRD
GLYPTOTEKET
CIRKUS
VESTERPORT ST.
Den Permanente
FORUM SPORTHALLEN
Danas Plads
Sankt Hans Torv
VESTERBRO
SYNAG.
POL.
Tagensvej
Guldbergsgade
Møllegade
Nørre Allé
Blegdamsvej
Fredensgade
Fredensbro
Dossering
Sortedam
Søgade
Sølvgade
Farimagsgade
Øster
Gothersgade
Frederiksborggade
Nørrebrogade
Fælledvej
Griffenfeldsgade
Rantzausgade
Åboulevard
Blågårdsgade
Peblinge
Rosenørns Allé
Vej
Vodroffsvej
Ørsteds
Danasvej
Gyldenløvesgade
Nørre Voldgade
Nørregade
Vester
H.C. Andersens Boulevard
Forhåbningsholms Allé
Gammel Kongevej
Vesterbrogade
Bernstorffsgade
Istedgade
Gasværksvej
Halmtorvet
Voldgade

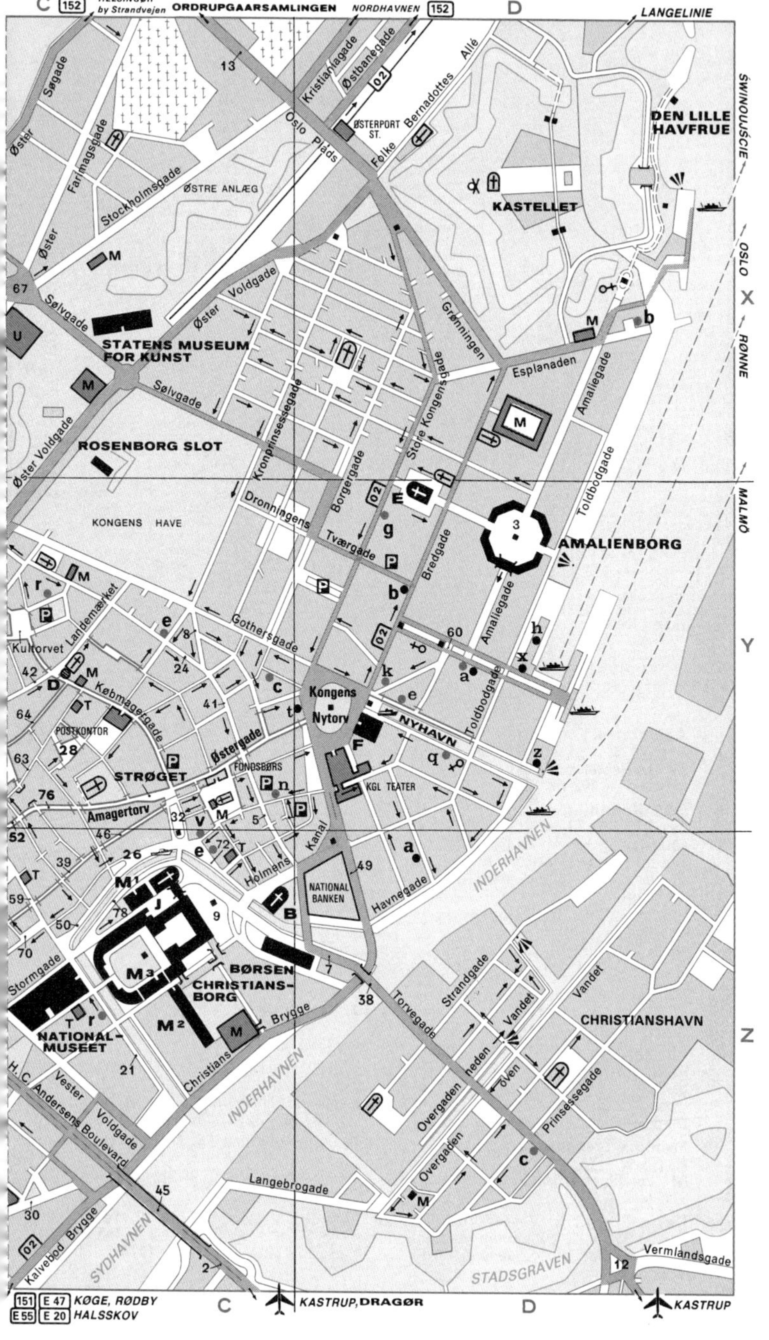

C
152
HELSINGØR by Strandvejen
ORDRUPGAARSAMLINGEN
NORDHAVNEN
152
D
LANGELINIE
Søgade
Øster Farimagsgade
Stockholmsgade
ØSTRE ANLÆG
Kristianiagade
Østbanegade
02
ØSTERPORT ST.
Oslo Plads
Folke Bernadottes Allé
KASTELLET
DEN LILLE HAVFRUE
ŚWINOUJŚCIE
OSLO
X
RØNNE
MALMÖ
Y
Z
Øster
M
67
Sølvgade
Øster Voldgade
U
STATENS MUSEUM FOR KUNST
Sølvgade
ROSENBORG SLOT
Øster Voldgade
Kronprinsessegade
Grønningen
Store Kongensgade
Esplanaden
Amaliegade
Toldbodgade
Borgergade
Dronningens Tværgade
Bredgade
AMALIENBORG
3
KONGENS HAVE
Gothersgade
Landemærket
Kultorvet
Købmagergade
POSTKONTOR
Kongens Nytorv
NYHAVN
Toldbodgade
Amaliegade
Østergade
FONDSBØRS
KGL TEATER
STRØGET
Amagertorv
Holmens Kanal
NATIONAL BANKEN
Havnegade
INDERHAVNEN
BØRSEN
CHRISTIANSBORG
NATIONALMUSEET
Stormgade
Christians Brygge
Torvegade
Strandgade
Vandet
Overgaden neden Vandet
Overgaden oven Vandet
Prinsessegade
CHRISTIANSHAVN
H.C. Andersens Boulevard
Vester Voldgade
Langebrogade
Kalvebod Brygge
SYDHAVNEN
STADSGRAVEN
Vermlandsgade
12
151
E 47
KØGE, RØDBY
E 55
E 20
HALSSKOV
KASTRUP, DRAGØR
KASTRUP

STREET INDEX TO KØBENHAVN TOWN PLAN

Amagertorv (Strøget) CY
Bredgade DY
Frederiksberggade (Strøget) BZ 20
Købmagergade CY
Nygade (Strøget) CYZ 52
Nørre Voldgade BY
Store Kongensgade DX
Vesterbrogade ABZ
Vimmelskaftet (Strøget) CY 76
Østergade (Strøget) CY

Amager Boulevard CZ 2
Amaliegade DXY
Amalienborg Plads DY 3
Axeltorv BZ 4
Bernstorffsgade BZ
Blegdamsvej BX
Blågårdsgåde AX
Borgergade DXY
Bremerholm CY 5
Børsgade DZ 7
Christan IX's Gade CY 8
Christiansborg Slotsplads CZ 9
Christians Brygge CZ
Christmas Møllers Plads DZ 12
Dag Hammarskjölds Allé CX 13
Danas Plads AY
Danasvej AY
Dronningens Tværgade CDY
Dronning Louises Bro BX 15
Esplanaden DX
Farvergade BZ 16
Fiolstræde BY 17
Folke Bernadottes Allé DX
Forhåbningsholms Allé AZ
Fredensbro BX
Fredensgade BX
Frederiksberg Allé AZ 19
Frederiksborggade BY
Frederiksholms Kanal CZ 21
Frue Plads BY 23
Fælledvej AX
Gammel Kongevej AZ
Gammel Mønt CY 24
Gammel Strand CZ 26
Gammeltorv BYZ 27
Gasværksvej AZ
Gothersgade BCY
Griffenfeldsgade AX
Grønningen DX
Gråbrødretorv CY 28
Guldbergsgade AX
Gyldenløvesgade AY
Halmtorvet AZ
Hambrosgade CZ 30
Hammerichsgade BZ 31
Havnegade DZ
H.C. Andersens Boulevard BCZ
H.C. Ørsteds Vej AY
Holmens Kanal CDZ
Højbro Plads CY 32
Ingerslevsgade BZ 33
Israels Plads BY
Istedgade AZ
Jarmers Plads BY 34
Jernbanegade BZ 35
Julius Thomsens Gade AY 36
Kalvebod Brygge CZ
Kampmannsgade AZ 37
Knippelsbro DZ 38
Kompagnistræde CZ 39
Kongens Nytorv DY
Kristen Bernikows Gade CY 41
Kristianiagade DX
Kronprinsessegade CXY
Krystalgade BCY 42
Kultorvet CY
Kvægtorvsgade ABZ 44
Landemaerket CY
Langebro CZ 45
Langebrogade CDZ
Læderstræde CYZ 46
Løngangstræde BZ 48
Møllegade AX
Niels Juels Gade DZ 49
Nybrogade CZ 50
Nyhavn DY
Nytorv BZ 53
Nørre Allé AX
Nørrebrogade AX
Nørre Farimagsgade BY
Nørregade BY
Nørre Søgade ABY
Oslo Plads DX
Overgaden neden Vandet DZ
Overgaden oven Vandet DZ
Peblinge Dossering AY
Polititorvet BZ 55
Prinsessegade DZ
Rantzausgade AX
Reventlowsgade BZ 56
Rosenørns Allé AY
Rådhuspladsen BZ 57
Rådhusstræde CZ 59
Sankt Annæ Plads DY 60
Sankt Hans Torv AX
Sankt Peders Stræde BY 62
Skindergade CY 63
Sortedam Dossering BX
Stockholmsgade CX
Store Kannikestræde CY 64
Stormgade CZ
Strandgade DZ
Studiestræde BYZ 66
Sølvgade BCX
Sølvtorvet CX 67
Tagensvej BX
Tietgensgade BZ 68
Toldbodgade DXY
Torvegade DZ
Vandkunsten CZ 70
Webersgade BX 71
Ved Stranden CZ 72
Ved Vesterport AZ 74
Vermlandsgade DZ
Vester Farimagsgade AZ
Vestergade BZ 75
Vester Søgade AYZ
Vester Voldgade BCZ
Vindebrogade CZ 78
Vodroffsvej AYZ
Værnedamsvej AZ 79
Østbanegade DX
Øster Farimagsgade BCX
Øster Søgade BCX
Øster Voldgade CX
Aboulevard AY

Angleterre, Kongens Nytorv 34, 1050 K, 33 12 00 95, Telex 15877, Fax 33 12 11 18 – – 400. CDY **t**
M – **Le Restaurant** a la carte 330/580 – **La Brasserie** *(closed Sunday)* 148/298 and a la carte – 120 – **102 rm** 1800/2850, 18 suites.

SAS Scandinavia, Amager Boulevard 70, 2300 S, 33 11 23 24, Telex 31330, Fax 31 57 01 93, Copenhagen, « Panoramic restaurant on 25th floor », squash – rm – 1 400. rest
closed 25 to 31 December and Bank Holidays – **M** a la carte 226/360 – **Top of Town** *(closed Sunday and Bank Holidays)* 305/495 – 115 – **506 rm** 1395/1595, 36 suites. by Amager Boulevard CZ

Sheraton Copenhagen, 6 Vester Søgade, 1601 K, 33 14 35 35, Telex 27450, Fax 33 32 12 23, – rm – 1 200. rest AZ **w**
M 395 (dinner) and a la carte 142/430 – **469 rm** 1100/1550, 2 suites.

SAS Royal, Hammerichsgade 1, 1611 V, 33 14 14 12, Telex 27155, Fax 33 14 14 21, « Panoramic restaurant on 20th floor », – rm – 300. BZ **m**
M 395 and a la carte – 115 – **264 rm** 1395/2395, 2 suites.

Plaza, Bernstorffsgade 4, 1577 V, 33 14 92 62, Telex 15330, Fax 33 93 93 62, « Library bar » – – 60. rest BZ **r**
closed 22 December-3 January – **M** – **Alexander Nevski** (dinner only) 218 and a la carte – **Flora Danica** (lunch only) 98 and a la carte – 105 – **87 rm** 1325/1925, 6 suites.

Phoenix, Bredgade 37, 1260 K, 33 95 95 00, Telex 40068, Fax 33 33 98 33 – rm – 100. DY **b**
M – **Von Plessen** *(closed 25 December and 1 January)* 198/225 – 95 Bb – **209 rm** 900/2050, 3 suites.

Kong Frederik, Vester Voldgade 25, 1552 V, 33 12 59 02, Telex 19702, Fax 33 93 59 01, « Victorian pub, antiques » – – 80. BZ **k**
closed 22 December-2 January – **M** 220/390 and a la carte – 100 – **107 rm** 1350/1900, 3 suites.

Imperial, Vester Farimagsgade 9, 1606 V, 33 12 80 00, Telex 15556, Fax 33 93 80 31 – rm – 100. AZ **e**
M *(closed 5 to 31 July)* 80/220 and a la carte – **163 rm** 1105/2200.

Palace, Raadhuspladsen 57, ✉ 1550 V, ☎ 33 14 40 50, Telex 19693, Fax 33 14 52 79, – |‡| TV ☎ – 60. AE ⓓ E VISA. BZ **u**
M 198/328 and a la carte – **155 rm** 1290/1690, 4 suites.

Kong Arthur, Nørre Søgade 11, ✉ 1370 K, ☎ 33 11 12 12, Telex 16512, Fax 33 32 61 30, – |‡| TV ☎ P – 60. AE ⓓ E VISA BY **a**
M *(closed Sunday)* a la carte 186/232 – **89 rm** 845/1095, 1 suite.

Copenhagen Admiral, Toldbodgade 24-28, ✉ 1253 K, ☎ 33 11 82 82, Telex 15941, Fax 33 32 55 42, ←, « Former 18C warehouse », – |‡| TV ☎ P – 180 DY **h**
M 135/405 and a la carte – 90 – **360 rm** 845/1090, 6 suites.

Neptun, Sankt Annae Plads 14-20, ✉ 1250 K, ☎ 33 13 89 00, Telex 19554, Fax 33 14 12 50 – |‡| TV ☎ – 50. AE ⓓ E VISA DY **a**
closed 23 December-4 January – **M** 160/240 and a la carte – **121 rm** 970/1500, 15 suites.

Mayfair without rest., Helgolandsgade 3-5, ✉ 1653 V, ☎ 31 31 48 01, Telex 27468, Fax 31 23 96 86, « English style decor » – |‡| TV ☎. AE ⓓ E VISA. AZ **a**
102 rm 895/1295, 4 suites.

Sophie Amalie, Sankt Annae Plads 21, ✉ 1250 K, ☎ 33 13 34 00, Telex 15815, Fax 33 11 77 07, – |‡| rm TV ☎ – 80. AE E VISA DY **x**
M (see **Copenhagen Admiral** H. above) – 90 – **130 rm** 845/1090, 4 suites.

Mercur, Vester Farimagsgade 17, ✉ 1780 V, ☎ 33 12 57 11, Telex 19767, Fax 33 12 57 17, – |‡| rm TV ☎. AE ⓓ E VISA AZ **d**
M *(closed Sunday and Bank Holidays)* 108/220 and a la carte – **108 rm** 995/1600, 1 suite.

Grand, Vesterbrogade 9, ✉ 1620 V, ☎ 31 31 36 00, Telex 15343, Fax 31 31 33 50 – |‡| rm rest TV ☎ – 100. AE ⓓ E VISA AZ **t**
M *(closed Sunday)* 158/208 and a la carte – **148 rm** 750/1280, 2 suites.

71 Nyhavn, Nyhavn 71, ✉ 1051 K, ☎ 33 11 85 85, Telex 27558, Fax 33 93 15 85, ←, « Former warehouse » – |‡| rest TV ☎ P – 25. AE ⓓ E VISA. DY **z**
M *(closed 24 to 26 December)* 168/295 and a la carte – 88 – **76 rm** 950/1750, 6 suites.

Copenhagen Crown without rest., Vesterbrogade 41, ✉ 1620 V, ☎ 31 21 21 66, Fax 31 21 00 66 – rm TV ☎ – 30 AZ **b**
78 rm, 2 suites.

City without rest., Peder Skramsgade 24, ✉ 1054 K, ☎ 33 13 06 66, Telex 19258, Fax 33 13 06 67 – |‡| TV ☎. AE ⓓ E VISA. DZ **a**
85 rm 870/1170.

Copenhagen Star without rest., Colbjørnsensgade 13, ✉ 1652 V, ☎ 31 22 11 00, Telex 21100, Fax 31 22 21 99 – TV ☎ – 35. AE ⓓ E VISA ABZ **c**
131 rm 890/1120, 3 suites.

Ascot without rest., Studiestraede 61, ✉ 1554 V, ☎ 33 12 60 00, Telex 15730, Fax 33 14 60 40 – |‡| TV ☎ P – 90. AE ⓓ E VISA BZ **g**
117 rm 670/1090, 3 suites.

Komfort, Løngangstraede 27, ✉ 1468 K, ☎ 33 12 65 70, Telex 16488, Fax 33 15 28 99 – |‡| TV ☎. AE ⓓ E VISA. BZ **n**
M 89/138 and a la carte – **201 rm** 780/1080.

Christian IV without rest., Dronningens Tvaergade 45, ✉ 1302 K, ☎ 33 32 10 44, Fax 33 32 07 06 – |‡| TV ☎. AE ⓓ E VISA CY **f**
closed 24 to 27 December – **42 rm** 810/925.

Danmark without rest., Vester Voldgade 89, ✉ 1552 V, ☎ 33 11 48 06, Telex 15518, Fax 33 14 36 30 – |‡| TV ☎. AE ⓓ E VISA BZ **t**
closed 23 December-3 January – **49 rm** 685/975, 2 suites.

XXX ✿ **Kong Hans Kaelder,** Vingardsstraede 6, ✉ 1070 K, ☎ 33 11 68 68, Telex 50404, Fax 33 32 67 68, « Vaulted Gothic cellar » – AE ⓓ E VISA CY **n**
closed Sunday, 5 July-2 August, Christmas-New Year and Bank Holidays – **M** (booking essential) (dinner only) 350/675 and a la carte 555/630
Spec. Home smoked salmon, Lobster "Tiger Lee", Escalopes of foie gras in a raspberry sauce.

XX ✿ **Nouvelle,** Gammel Strand 34 (1st floor), ✉ 1202 K, ☎ 33 13 50 18, Fax 33 32 07 97 – AE ⓓ E VISA CZ **a**
closed last 3 weeks July, 22 December-first week January and Bank Holidays – **M** *(closed lunch June and July, Saturday lunch and Sunday)* 225/425 and a la carte 365/480
Spec. Skagerak lobster bisque with Armagnac, Terrine of smoked Baltic salmon and eel, Sole medallions with small oyster sausages.

XX ✿ **Kommandanten,** NY Adelgade 7, ✉ 1104 K, ☎ 33 12 09 90, Fax 33 93 12 23, « 16C town house, contemporary furnishings » – AE ⓓ E VISA CY **c**
closed lunch in summer, Saturday lunch, Sunday, Christmas, New Year and Bank Holidays – **M** 255/475 and a la carte 340/505
Spec. Braised sweetbreads and lobster with a trout roe sauce, The fish menu.

XX **Restaurationen,** Møntergade 19, ✉ 1116 K, ☎ 33 14 94 95 – AE ⓓ E VISA CY **e**
closed Sunday, Monday, July, 23 December-5 January, Easter and Bank Holidays – **M** (dinner only) 305/375.

XX **Leonore Christine,** Nyhavn 9 (1st floor), ✉ 1051 K, ✆ 33 13 50 40, Fax 33 32 07 97 – AE ① E VISA DY **e**
closed 22 December-2 January – **M** 225/358 and a la carte.

XX **St. Gertruds Kloster,** 32 Hauser Plads, ✉ 1127 K, ✆ 33 14 66 30, Fax 33 93 93 65, « Part 14C monastic cellars » – ▤. AE ① E VISA CY **r**
closed 24 December-2 January – **M** (dinner only) a la carte 334/561.

XX **Era Ora,** Torvegade 62 (Christianshavn), ✉ 1400 K, ✆ 31 54 06 93, Fax 31 85 07 53, Italian rest. – AE ① E VISA. ✻ DZ **c**
closed Sunday, Christmas and New Year – **M** (dinner only) 295/550 and a la carte.

X **Lumskebugten,** Esplanaden 21, ✉ 1263 K, ✆ 33 15 60 29, Fax 33 32 87 18, 余, « Mid 19C café-pavilion » – AE ① E VISA DX **b**
closed Saturday lunch, Sunday, Christmas and Bank Holidays – **M** 220/420 and a la carte.

X **Els,** Store Strandstraede 3, ✉ 1255 K, ✆ 33 14 13 41, Fax 33 91 07 00, « 19C murals » – AE ① E VISA DY **k**
closed 24-25 and 31 December – **M** 176/296 and a la carte.

X **Den Sorte Ravn,** Nyhavn 14, ✉ 1051 K, ✆ 33 13 12 33, Fax 33 13 24 72 – ▤. AE ① E VISA
closed 8 to 12 April – **M** 175/450 and a la carte. DY **q**

X **Den Gyldne Fortun,** Ved Stranden 18, ✉ 1061 K, ✆ 33 12 20 11, Fax 33 93 35 11, Seafood – AE ① E VISA CZ **e**
closed 7, 20 and 29 to 31 May, 7 to 12 July, 24 to 26 December and 31 December-2 January – **M** *(closed lunch Saturday and Sunday)* a la carte 262/365.

X **Lille Laekkerbisken,** Gammel Strand 34 (ground floor), ✉ 1202 K, ✆ 33 32 04 00, Fax 33 32 07 97, 余 – AE ① E VISA CZ **a**
closed Sunday, 22 December-first week January and Bank Holidays – **M** (lunch only) 135/165 and a la carte.

in Tivoli : (Entrance fee payable)

XXX **Divan 2,** Vesterbrogade 3, ✉ 1620 V, ✆ 33 12 51 51, Fax 33 91 08 82, ≤, 余, « Floral decoration and terrace » – ① E VISA. ✻ BZ **a**
22 April-19 September – **M** 325/550 and a la carte.

XXX **Belle Terrasse,** Vesterbrogade 3, ✉ 1620 V, ✆ 33 12 11 36, Fax 33 15 00 31, ≤, 余, « Floral decoration and terrace » – AE ① E VISA BZ **s**
23 April-18 September – **M** (grill rest.) 295/495 and a la carte.

XXX **Divan 1,** Vesterbrogade 3, ✉ 1620 V, ✆ 33 11 42 42, Fax 33 11 74 07, ≤, 余, « 19C pavilion and terrace » – AE ① E VISA BZ **v**
22 April-19 September – **M** 255/395 and a la carte.

XX **La Crevette,** Vesterbrogade 3, ✉ 1620 V, ✆ 33 14 68 47, Fax 33 14 60 06, ≤, 余, Seafood, « Part mid 19C pavilion and terrace » – AE ① E VISA. ✻ BZ **e**
Easter-20 September – **M** 225/380 and a la carte.

SMØRREBRØD RESTAURANTS

The following list of simpler restaurants and cafés/bars specialize in Danish open sandwiches and are generally open from 10.00am to 4.00pm.

X **Ida Davidsen,** St. Kongensgade 70, ✉ 1264 K, ✆ 33 91 36 55, Fax 33 11 36 55 – ① E VISA. ✻ DY **g**
closed Saturday, Sunday, July and 2 weeks December – **M** approx. 170/555 and a la carte.

X **Slotskaelderen-Hos Gitte Kik,** Fortunstraede 4, ✉ 1065 K, ✆ 33 11 15 37, Fax 33 11 60 65 – ① E VISA CYZ **v**
closed Sunday, Monday and Easter – **M** (lunch only) 35/68 and a la carte.

X **Kanal Caféen,** Frederiksholms Kanal 18, ✉ 1220 K, ✆ 33 11 57 70, Fax 33 13 79 62 – ① E VISA CZ **r**
closed Saturday, Sunday, July and Bank Holidays – **M** (lunch only) 29/62 and a la carte.

X **Sankt Annae,** Sankt Annae Plads 12, ✉ 1250 K, ✆ 33 12 54 97 – ① E VISA DY **a**
closed Saturday and Sunday – **M** (lunch only) 20/65 and a la carte.

at Klampenborg N : 12 km by Østbanegade - DX - on coast rd :

X **Den Gule Cottage,** Staunings Plaene, Strandvejen 506, ✉ 2930, ✆ 31 64 06 91, ≤, « Thatched cottage beside the sea » – Ⓟ. AE ① E VISA. ✻
M (booking essential) 255/425 and a la carte.

at Søllerød N : 16 km by Tagensvej BX Lyngbyvej and Road 19 – ✉ 2840 Holte

XXX ✿ **Søllerød Kro,** Søllerødvej 35, ✉ 2840, ✆ 42 80 25 05, Fax 42 80 22 70, 余, « 17C thatched inn, terrace » – AE ① E VISA. ✻
M 370/525 and a la carte
Spec. Marbled duck liver with grilled yeast bread, Grilled salmon with tomatoes and a champagne butter sauce, Chocolate soufflé with caramel ice cream.

at Kastrup Airport SE : 10 km – ✉ 2300 S

🏨 SAS Globetrotter, Engvej 171, ✉ 2300 S, NW : 2 ½ km ✆ 31 55 14 33, Telex 31222, Fax 31 55 81 45, Fø, ≘s, ▣ – ▮ ⇔ rm ▣ Ⓟ – 🔬 350 by Amager Boulevard CZ
196 rm.

Finland

Suomi

HELSINKI

PRACTICAL INFORMATION

LOCAL CURRENCY

Finnish Mark: 100 FIM = 18.58 US $ = 15.60 Ecus (Jan. 93)

TOURIST INFORMATION

The Tourist Office is situated near the Market Square, Pohjoisesplanadi 19 ✆ 169 3757 and 174 088. Open from 16 May to 15 September, Monday to Friday 8.30am - 6pm, Saturday 8.30am - 1pm, and from 16 September to 15 May, Monday 8.30am - 4.30pm and Tuesday to Friday 8.30am - 4.00pm. Hotel bookings are possible from a reservation board situated in airport arrival lounge; information also available free.

FOREIGN EXCHANGE

Banks are open between 9.15am and 4.15pm on weekdays only. Exchange office at Helsinki-Vantaa airport and Helsinki harbour open daily between 6.30am and 11pm.

MEALS

At lunchtime, follow the custom of the country and try the typical buffets of Scandinavian specialities.
At dinner, the a la carte and the menus will offer you more conventionnal cooking.
A lot of city centre restaurants are closed for a few days over the Midsummer Day period.

SHOPPING IN HELSINKI

Furs, jewelry, china, glass and ceramics, Finnish handicraft and wood.
In the index of street names, those printed in red are where the principal shops are found. Your hotel porter will be able to help you and give you information.

THEATRE BOOKINGS

A ticket service - Lippupalvelu, Mannerheimintie 5, is selling tickets for cinema, concert and theatre performances - Telephone 970 004 700, open Mon-Fri 9am to 5pm, Sat. 9am to 2pm (except July).

CAR HIRE

The international car hire companies have branches in Helsinki city and at Vantaa airport. Your hotel porter should be able to help you with your arrangements.

TIPPING

Service is normally included in hotel and restaurant bills - Doormen, baggage porters etc. are generally given a gratuity; taxi drivers are usually not tipped.

SPEED LIMITS

The maximum permitted speed on motorways is 120 km/h - 74 mph (in winter 100 km/h - 62 mph), 80 km/h - 50 mph on other roads and 50 km/h - 31 mph in built-up areas.

SEAT BELTS

The wearing of seat belts in Finland is compulsory for drivers and for front and rear seat passagers.

Helsinki

Finland 985 L 21 - Pop. 491 777 - ☎ 90.

See : Senate Square★★★ (Senaatintori) DY 53 : Lutheran Cathedral (Tuomiokirkko) DY, University Library (Yliopiston kirjasto) CY **B**, Government Building (Valtioneuvosto) DY **C**, Sederholm House DY **E** - Market Square★★ (Kauppatori) DY **26** : Uspensky Cathedral (Uspenskin katedraali) DY, Presidential Palace (Presidentinlinna) DY **F**, Havis Amanda Fountain DY **K** - Spa Park★ (Kaivopuisto) DZ ; Esplanade★★ (Eteläesplanadi CY **8**, Pohjoisesplanadi CY **43** ; Aleksanterinkatu★ CDY **2** ; Atheneum Art Museum★★ (Ateneumintaidemuseo) CY **M¹** - Mannerheimintie★★ BCXY : Parliament House (Eduskuntatalo) BX, Rock Church (Temppeliaukion kirkko) BX, National Museum (Kansallismuseo) BX **M²**, Helsinki City Museum (Helsingin kaupunginmuseo) BX **M³**, Finlandia Hall (Finlandia-talo) BX - Sibelius Monument★★ (Sibeliuksen puisto) AX ; Stadium tower (Olympiastadion) BX : view★★.

Sightseeing by sea : Fortress of Suomenlinna★★ ; Seurasaari Open-Air Museum★ (from Kauppatori) ; Helsinki zoo★ (Korkeasaari).

Entertainment : Helsinki Festival★★ (20 August to 6 September).

18 Tali Manor ☎ 550 235.

✈ Helsinki-Vantaa N : 19 km ☎ 821 122 - Finnair Head Office, Mannerheimintie 102 ☎ 822 414, Telex 124 404, Fax 818 87 36 - Air Terminal : Hotel Intercontinental, Mannerheimintie 46.

⛴ To Sweden, Estonia and boat excursions : contact the City Tourist Office (see below) - Car Ferry : Silja Line - Finnjet Line ☎ 180 41.

ℹ City Tourist Office Pohjoisesplanadi 19 ☎ 169 37 57, Fax 169 38 39 - Automobile and Touring Club of Finland : Autoliitto ☎ 694 00 22, Telex 124 839, Fax 693 25 78.

Lahti 103 - Tampere 176 - Turku 165.

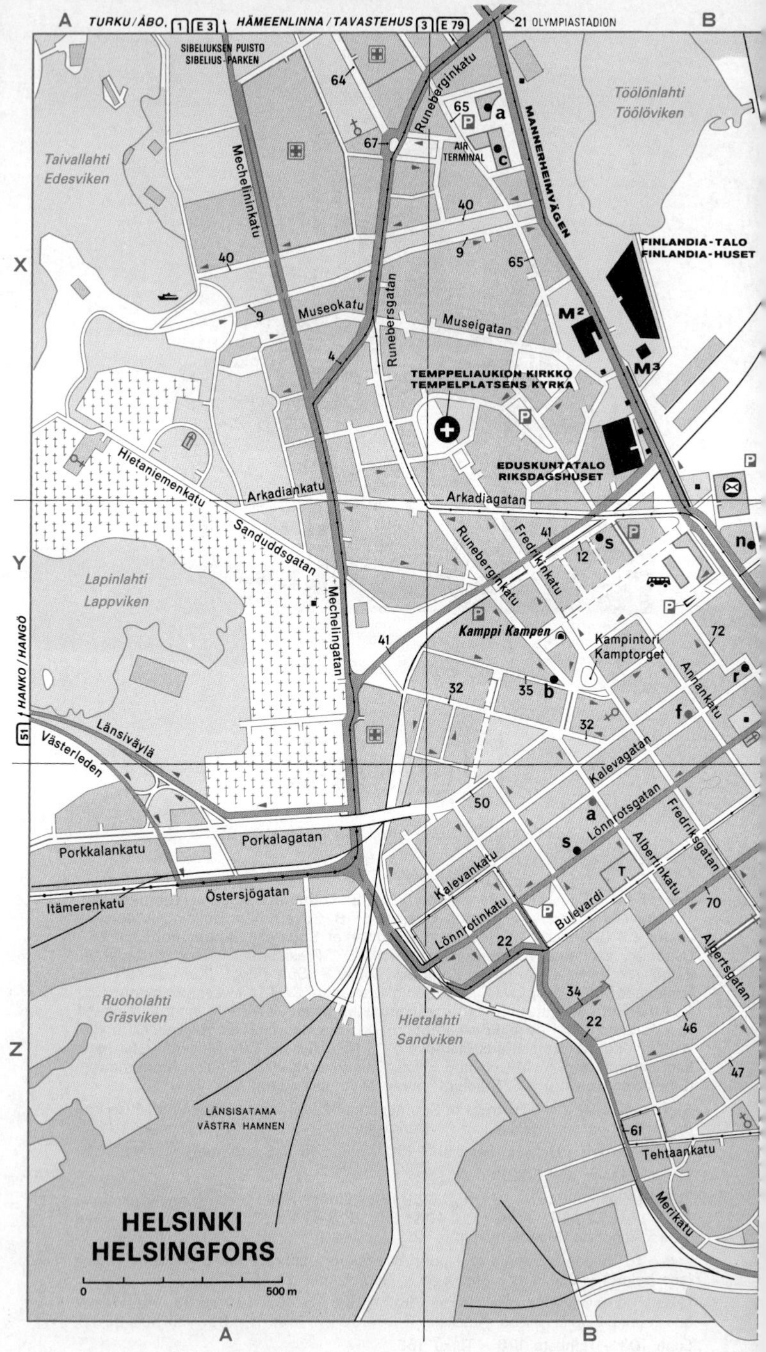

HELSINKI
HELSINGFORS
TURKU/ÅBO.
HÄMEENLINNA/TAVASTEHUS
21 OLYMPIASTADION
SIBELIUKSEN PUISTO
SIBELIUS-PARKEN
Töölönlahti
Tööloviken
Taivallahti
Edesviken
Mechelininkatu
Runeberginkatu
MANNERHEIMVÄGEN
AIR TERMINAL
FINLANDIA-TALO
FINLANDIA-HUSET
Museokatu
Museigatan
Runebersgatan
TEMPPELIAUKION KIRKKO
TEMPELPLATSENS KYRKA
EDUSKUNTATALO
RIKSDAGSHUSET
Hietaniemenkatu
Arkadiankatu
Arkadiagatan
Sandudsgatan
Fredrikinkatu
Lapinlahti
Lappviken
Mechelingatan
Kamppi Kampen
Kampintori
Kamptorget
Annankatu
HANKO/HANGÖ
Länsiväylä
Västerleden
Kalevagatan
Lönnrotsgatan
Fredriksgatan
Albertinkatu
Porkkalankatu
Porkalagatan
Itämerenkatu
Östersjögatan
Kalevankatu
Lönnrotinkatu
Bulevardi
Albertsgatan
Ruoholahti
Gräsviken
Hietalahti
Sandviken
LÄNSISATAMA
VÄSTRA HAMNEN
Tehtaankatu
Merikatu
0
500 m

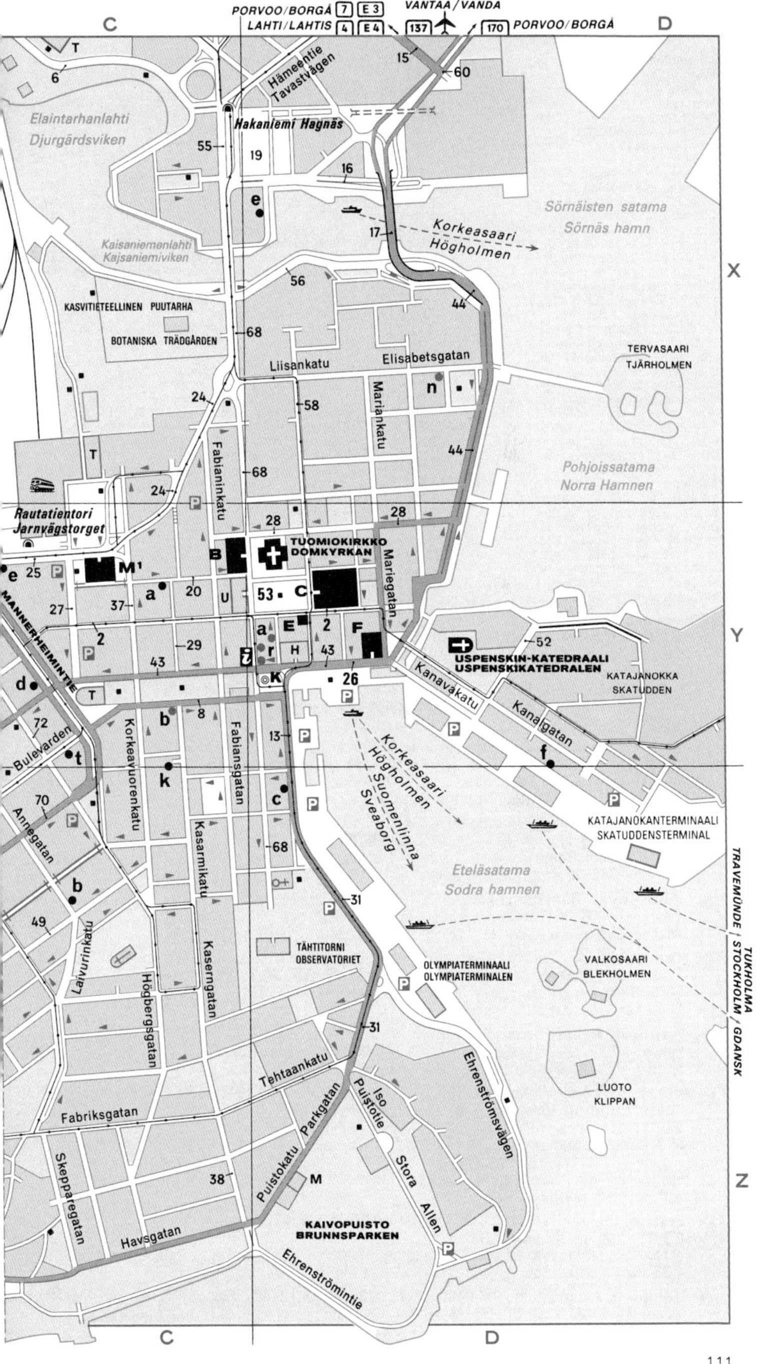
PORVOO/BORGÅ 7 E 3
LAHTI/LAHTIS 4 E 4
VANTAA/VANDA
137
170 PORVOO/BORGÅ
C
D
Hämeentie
Tavastvägen
Hakaniemi Hagnäs
Elaintarhanlahti
Djurgårdsviken
Kaisaniemenlahti
Kajsaniemiviken
Sörnäisten satama
Sörnäs hamn
Korkeasaari
Högholmen
KASVITIETEELLINEN PUUTARHA
BOTANISKA TRÄDGÅRDEN
Liisankatu
Elisabetsgatan
Mariankatu
TERVASAARI
TJÄRHOLMEN
Fabianinkatu
Pohjoissatama
Norra Hamnen
Rautatientori
Jarnvägstorget
TUOMIOKIRKKO
DOMKYRKAN
Mariegatan
MANNERHEIMINTIE
USPENSKIN-KATEDRAALI
USPENSKIKATEDRALEN
KATAJANOKKA
SKATUDDEN
Kanavakatu
Kanalgatan
Bulevarden
Korkeavuorenkatu
Fabiansgatan
Korkeasaari
Högholmen
Suomenlinna
Sveaborg
Annegatan
Kasarmikatu
KATAJANOKANTERMINAALI
SKATUDDENSTERMINAL
Eteläsatama
Sodra hamnen
TUKHOLMA
STOCKHOLM
TRAVEMÜNDE
GDANSK
Laivurinkatu
Kaserngatan
TÄHTITORNI
OBSERVATORIET
OLYMPIATERMINAALI
OLYMPIATERMINALEN
VALKOSAARI
BLEKHOLMEN
Högbergsgatan
Tehtaankatu
Iso Puistotie
Ehrenströmsvägen
LUOTO
KLIPPAN
Fabriksgatan
Puistokatu
Parkgatan
Skepparegatan
Stora Allen
KAIVOPUISTO
BRUNNSPARKEN
Havsgatan
Ehrenströmintie
X
Y
Z

STREET INDEX TO HELSINKI/HELSINGFORS TOWN PLAN

Strand Intercontinental, John Stenbergin Ranta 4, 00530, ℘ 39351, Telex 126202, Fax 3935255, ≤, « Contemporary decor, modern art collection », ⇌s, ⊡ - |‡| ⇆ rm ▤ ⊡ ☎ ♿ ⇔ - 🏆 300. AE ⓓ E VISA DX **e**
closed Christmas - **M** - **Atrium Plaza** a la carte 203/235 - **Pamir** *(closed Saturday, Sunday, Easter and 25 June-15 August)* (dinner only) 290/340 and a la carte - ☐ 65 - **192 rm** 940/1190, 8 suites.

Inter-Continental, Mannerheimintie 46, 00260, ℘ 40551, Telex 122159, Fax 4055255, ⇌s, ⊡ - |‡| ⇆ rm ▤ rm ⊡ ☎ ♿ ⇔ Ⓟ - 🏆 750. AE ⓓ E VISA BX **c**
M - **Galateia** (Seafood) *(closed weekends and 20 June-15 August)* (dinner only) 279 and a la carte - **Brasserie** 193/210 and a la carte - ☐ 45 - **540 rm** 780/1140, 12 suites.

Hesperia, Mannerheimintie 50, 00260, ℘ 43101, Telex 122117, Fax 4310995, ⇌s, ⊡ - |‡| ⇆ rm ▤ ⊡ ☎ ⇔ Ⓟ - 🏆 400. AE ⓓ E VISA BX **a**
M - **Russian Room** *(closed Saturday and Sunday)* (dinner only) 185/250 and a la carte - ☐ 40 - **372 rm** 880/1020, 4 suites.

SAS Royal, Runeberginkatu 2, 00100, ℘ 69580, Telex 122112, Fax 69587100, ⇌s - |‡| ⇆ rm ▤ ⊡ ☎ ♿ ⇔ - 🏆 160. AE ⓓ E VISA. ✂ BY **b**
M 160/235 and a la carte - ☐ 65 - **253 rm** 860/1220, 7 suites.

Grand Marina, Katajanokanlaituri 7, 00160, ℘ 16661, Telex 124878, Fax 664764, ⇌s - |‡| ⇆ rm ▤ ⊡ ☎ ♿ ⇔ Ⓟ - 🏆 450. AE ⓓ E VISA. ✂ rest DYZ **f**
M - **Bistro** 90/215 - **Baltic Room** a la carte 80/188 - ☐ 27 - **442 rm** 550/770, 20 suites.

Ramada Presidentti, Eteläinen Rautatiekatu 4, 00100, ℘ 6911, Telex 121953, Fax 6947886, ⇌s, ⊡ - |‡| ⇆ rm ▤ ⊡ ☎ ♿ - 🏆 400. AE ⓓ E VISA BY **s**
M 95/165 and a la carte - ☐ 40 - **490 rm** 800/920, 5 suites.

✿ **Lord** ⊗, Lönnrotinkatu 29, 00180, ℘ 680 1680, Fax 680 1315, « Part Jugendstil (Art Nouveau) building, fireplaces », ⇌s - |‡| ⇆ rm ⊡ ☎ ♿ ⇔ - 🏆 100. AE ⓓ E VISA BZ **s**
M *(closed Sunday and Bank Holidays)* 55/190 and a la carte 151/250 - **47 rm** ☐ 650/800, 1 suite
Spec. Warm quail salad, Stuffed breast of pheasant with a buckthorn berry sauce, Honey parfait with a warm poppy seed sauce.

Palace, Eteläranta 10, 00130, ℘ 134 561, Telex 121570, Fax 654 786, ⇌s - |‡| ⇆ rm ▤ ⊡ ☎ - 🏆 40. AE ⓓ E VISA DZ **c**
closed Christmas and Easter - **M** a la carte approx. 139 - (see also **Palace Gourmet** below) - **35 rm** ☐ 820/1160, 15 suites.

Vaakuna, Asema-aukio 2, 00100, ℘ 131 181, Telex 121381, Fax 13118234, ⇌s - |‡| ⇆ rm ▤ rm ⊡ ☎ ♿ - 🏆 50. AE ⓓ E VISA. ✂ rest BY **n**
M 59 (lunch) and a la carte 101/119 - ☐ 35 - **278 rm** 780/880, 10 suites.

Klaus Kurki, Bulevardi 2, 00120, 618 911, Telex 121670, Fax 608 538, – rm . AE E VISA. CY **t**
closed 23 to 26 December – **M** *(closed Saturday lunch, Sunday and Bank Holidays)* 35/148 (lunch) and dinner a la carte 117/153 – **134 rm** 680/840, 1 suite.

Arctia Hotel Marski, Mannerheimintie 10, 00100, 68061, Telex 121240, Fax 642377, – rm – 300. AE E VISA. rest CY **d**
M 65/140 and a la carte – **158 rm** 840/940, 6 suites.

Seurahuone-Socis without rest., Kaivokatu 12, 00100, 170 441, Telex 122234, Fax 664 170, – . AE E VISA CY **e**
40 – **118 rm** 540/1150.

Rivoli Jardin without rest., Kasarmikatu 40, 00130, 177 880, Telex 125881, Fax 656 988, <, – . AE E VISA CYZ **k**
53 rm 710/820, 1 suite.

Pasila, Maistraatinportti 3, 00240, 148 841, Telex 125809, Fax 143 771, , squash – rm rest – 80. AE E VISA. rest
M 165/215 and a la carte – 30 – **247 rm** 510/650, 6 suites.
N : 3 km by Mannerheimintie BX

Helsinki without rest., Hallituskatu 12, 00100, 131 401, Telex 121022, Fax 176 014, – rm – 30. AE E VISA CY **a**
closed 20 December-1 January – 30 – **129 rm** 540/850.

Torni, Yrjönkatu 26, 00100, 131 131, Telex 125153, Fax 1311361, – rm rest – 30. AE E VISA. rest BY **r**
closed Christmas – **M** – **Ritarisali** *(closed lunch Saturday, Sunday and Bank Holidays)* 150/230 (lunch) and a la carte 160/296 – 35 – **141 rm** 660/790, 9 suites.

Aurora without rest., Helsinginkatu 50, 00530, 717 400, Telex 125643, Fax 714 240, , , squash – – 80. AE E VISA
closed 23 December-1 January – **70 rm** 330/480. NE : 2 km by Helsinginkatu BX

Anna without rest., Annankatu 1, 00120, 648 011, Telex 125514, Fax 602 664, – . AE E VISA. CZ **b**
closed 24 December-6 January – **59 rm** 420/570, 1 suite.

Palace Gourmet, (at Palace H.), Eteläranta 10 (10th floor), 00130, 134 561, Telex 121570, Fax 657 474, < harbour and city – . AE E VISA DZ **c**
closed Saturday, Sunday, July and Bank Holidays – **M** 220/395 and dinner a la carte.

Savoy, Eteläesplanadi, 00130, 176571, Fax 628715, – AE E VISA. CY **b**
closed Saturday and Sunday – **M** 195/365 and a la carte 190/255.

Alexander Nevski, Pohjoisesplanadi 17, 00170, 639 610, Fax 6164252, Russian rest. – . AE E VISA. DY **r**
closed lunch in July, Sunday and Christmas – **M** 120/300 and a la carte.

Havis Amanda, Unioninkatu 23, 00170, 666 882, Fax 631 435, Seafood – AE E VISA. DY **r**
closed Saturday dinner September-May, Sunday and Bank Holidays – **M** (booking essential) 165/212 and a la carte.

Svenska Klubben, Maurinkatu 6, 00170, 135 4706, Fax 135 4896, « Scottish style house » – . AE E VISA. DX **n**
closed Sunday – **M** 145/360 and dinner a la carte.

Rivoli (Kala and Cheri), Albertinkatu 38, 00180, 643 455, Fax 647 780, « Nautical decor » – . AE E VISA BZ **a**
closed lunch Saturday and Sunday, 9 to 12 April, 25 to 27 June, 24 to 26 December and Bank Holidays – **M** a la carte 148/214.

Piekka, Sibeliuksenkatu 2, 00260, 493 591, Fax 495 664, Finnish rest. – AE E VISA.
by Mannerheimintie BX
closed mid summer, Easter and Christmas – **M** (dinner only) a la carte 100/240.

Amadeus, Sofiankatu 4, 00170, 626 676, Fax 636 064 – AE E VISA DY **a**
closed Saturday lunch, Sunday and Bank Holidays – **M** 170/293 and dinner a la carte.

on 137 N : 15 km – Vantaa – 90 Helsinki :

Holiday Inn Garden Court, Rälssitie 2, 01510, 870 900, Telex 126121, Fax 870 90101, – rm rest – 40. AE E VISA. rest
M 75/120 and a la carte – 25 – **313 rm** 520/620.

Airport Hotel Rantasipi, Robert Huberin Tie 4, Box 53, 01510, 87051, Telex 121812, Fax 822 846, , – rm – 150. AE E VISA. rest
M *(closed Sunday lunch)* 130 (lunch) and dinner a la carte 87/151 – **296 rm** 590, 4 suites. by Helsinginkatu BX

When in a hurry use the Michelin Main Road Maps :

970 Europe, 980 Greece, 984 Germany, 985 Scandinavia-Finland,

986 Great Britain and Ireland, 987 Germany-Austria-Benelux, 988 Italy,

989 France, 990 Spain-Portugal and 991 Yugoslavia.

France

PARIS AND ENVIRONS - BORDEAUX
CANNES - LILLE - LYONS
MARSEILLES - PRINCIPALITY OF MONACO
NICE - STRASBOURG
VALLEY OF THE LOIRE

PRACTICAL INFORMATION

LOCAL CURRENCY

French Franc: 100 F = 17.90 US $ = 15. Ecus (Jan. 93)

TOURIST INFORMATION IN PARIS

Paris "Welcome" Office (Office du Tourisme et des Congrès de Paris - Accueil de France): 127 Champs-Élysées, 8th, ✆ 49 52 53 54, Telex 645439
American Express 11 Rue Scribe, 9th, ✆ 47 77 70 00

AIRLINES

T.W.A.: 101 Champs-Élysées, 8th, ✆ 47 20 62 11
DELTA AIRLINES: 4 pl. des Vosges Immeuble Lavoisier Cédex 64 – Paris 92052 La défense ✆ 47 68 92 92
BRITISH AIRWAYS: 12 r. Castiglione, 1st, ✆ 47 78 14 14
AIR FRANCE: 119 Champs-Élysées, 8th, ✆ 45 35 61 61
AIR INTER: 49 Champs-Élysées, ✆ 45 46 90 00

FOREIGN EXCHANGE OFFICES

Banks: close at 5pm and at weekends
Orly Airport: daily 6.30am to 11.30pm
Roissy-Charles de Gaulle Airport: daily 7am to 11.30 mp

TRANSPORT IN PARIS

Taxis: may be hailed in the street when showing the illuminated sign-available day and night at taxi ranks or called by telephone
Bus-Métro (subway): for full details see the Michelin Plan de Paris n⁰ 11. The metro is quicker but the bus is good for sightseeing and practical for short distances.

POSTAL SERVICES

Local post offices: open Mondays to Fridays 8am to 7pm; Saturdays 8am to noon
General Post Office: 52 rue du Louvre, 1st: open 24 hours

SHOPPING IN PARIS

Department stores: Boulevard Haussmann, Rue de Rivoli and Rue de Sèvres
Exclusive shops and boutiques: Faubourg St-Honoré, Rue de la Paix and Rue Royale, Avenue Montaigne.
Antiques and second-hand goods: Swiss Village (Avenue de la Motte Picquet), Louvre des Antiquaires (Place du Palais Royal), Flea Market (Porte Clignancourt).

TIPPING

Service is generally included in hotel and restaurants bills. But you may choose to leave more than the expected tip to the staff. Taxi-drivers, porters, barbers and theatre or cinema attendants also expect a small gratuity.

BREAKDOWN SERVICE

Certain garages in central and outer Paris operate a 24 hour breakdown service. If you breakdown the police are usually able to help by indicating the nearest one.

SPEED LIMITS

The maximum permitted speed in built up areas is 50 km/h - 31 mph; on motorways the speed limit is 130 km/h - 80 mph and 110 km/h - 68 mph on dual carriageways. On all other roads 90 km/h - 56 mph.

SEAT BELTS

The wearing of seat belts is compulsory for drivers and passengers.

Paris and environs

75 Maps : 10, 11, 12 G. Paris – ⊛ 1.

Population : Paris 2 152 333 ; Ile-de-France region : 10 651 000.
Altitude : Observatory : 60 m ; Place Concorde : 34 m
Air Terminals : Esplanade des Invalides, 7th, ☎ 43 23 97 10 – Palais des Congrès, Porte Maillot, 17th, ☎ 42 99 20 18
Paris'Airports : see Orly and Charles de Gaulle (Roissy)
Railways, motorail : information ☎ 45 82 50 50.

ARRONDISSEMENTS

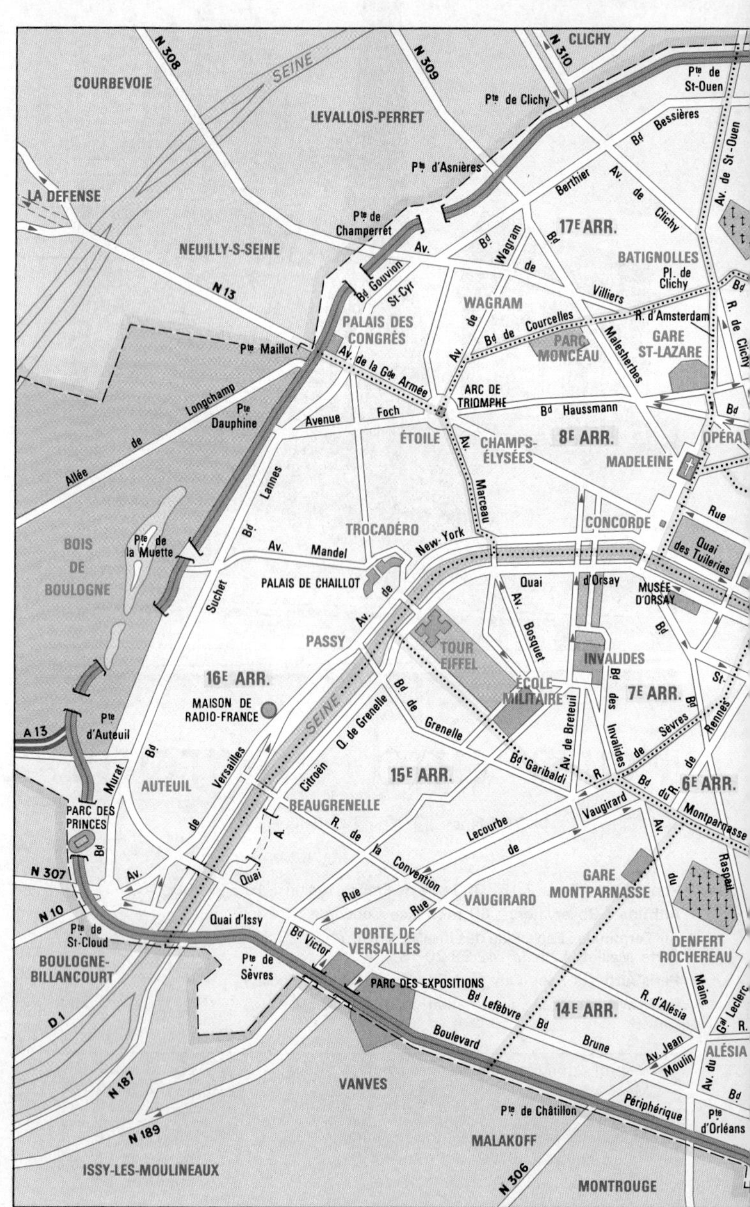

AND DISTRICTS

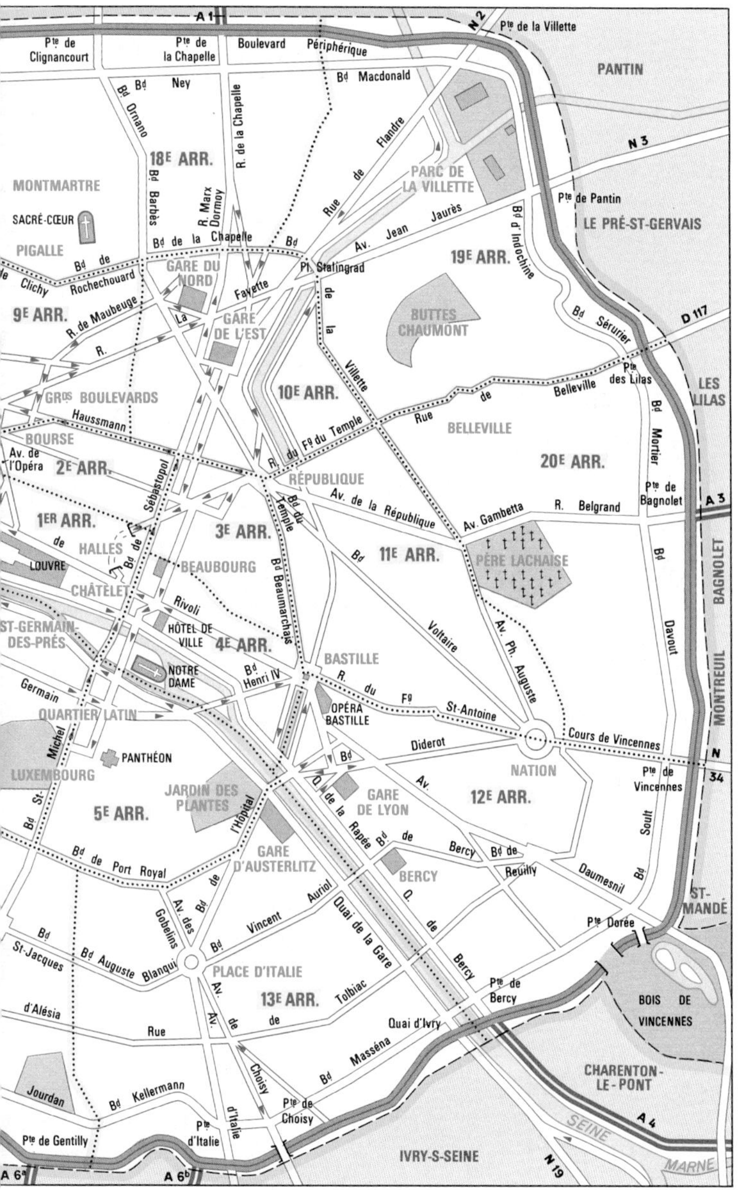

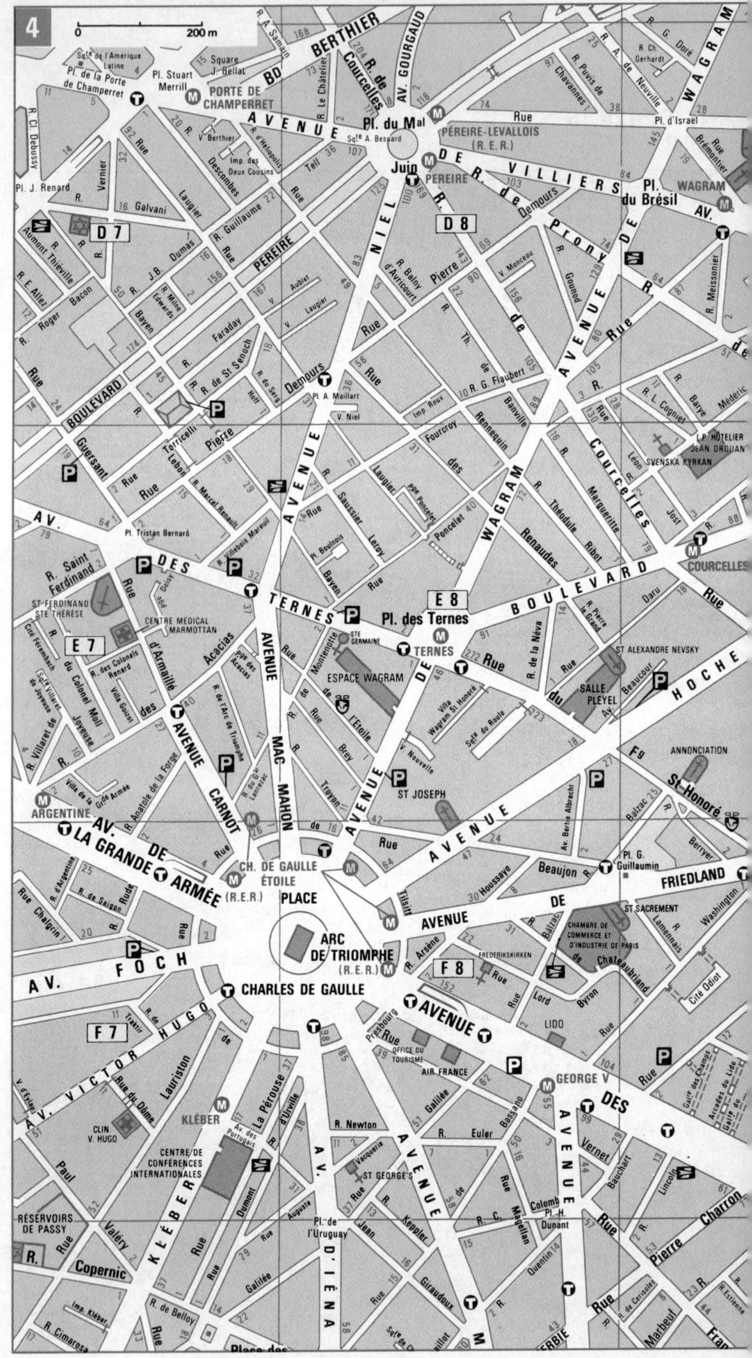
4
0
200 m
Sq^re de l'Amerique Latine
Pl. de la Porte de Champerret
Square J. Bellat
Pl. Stuart Merrill
PORTE DE CHAMPERRET
BD BERTHIER
R. de Courcelles
AV. GOURGAUD
R. Le Châtelier
R. A. Samain
R. Cl. Debussy
Pl. J. Renard
Vernier
Galvani
R. V. Berthier
R. d'Héliopolis
Imp. des Deux Cousins
Descombes
Laugier
R. Guillaume Tell
AVENUE
Pl. du M^al Juin
Sq^re A. Besnard
PEREIRE-LEVALLOIS (R.E.R.)
PEREIRE
DE VILLIERS
R. de Demours
Pl. du Brésil
WAGRAM
R. G. Doré
R. Ch. Gerhardt
R. A. de Neuville
R. Puvis de Chavannes
Pl. d'Israël
R. Brémontier
D 7
D 8
R. Aumont Thiéville
R. E. Allez
Bacon
Roger
R. J.B. Dumas
R. Milne Edwards
Bayen
PEREIRE
V. Aublet
V. Laugier
Faraday
R. de St Senoch
R. du Sergt Hoff
NIEL
R. Balny d'Avricourt
Pierre Demours
V. Monceau
Gounod
R. Prony
R. Meissonier
Rue de Prony
R. Th. de Banville
R. G. Flaubert
Pl. A. Maillart
V. Niel
Imp. Roux
Fourcroy
Rennequin
BOULEVARD
Torricelli
Lebon
Pierre
Guersant
Rue
R. Marcel Renault
R. L. Cogniet
Barye
Médéric
L.P. HÔTELIER JEAN DROUANT
SVENSKA KYRKAN
Léon Jost
Courcelles
Marguerite
Théodule Ribot
Renaudes
Saussier Leroy
Laugier
P^ge Poncelet
Poncelet
AV. DES TERNES
Pl. Tristan Bernard
R. Villebois Mareuil
Pl. Boulnois
Bayen
R. Saint Ferdinand
R. Doisy
ST FERDINAND STE THÉRÈSE
CENTRE MÉDICAL MARMOTTAN
E 7
E 8
Pl. des Ternes
TERNES
BOULEVARD
COURCELLES
R. Daru
R. Pierre le Grand
R. de la Néva
ST ALEXANDRE NEVSKY
SALLE PLEYEL
Av. Beaucour
HOCHE
Cité Férembach
Sq^re Villaret de Joyeuse
R. du Colonel Moll
R. des Colonels Renard
Villa Gauzet
d'Armaillé
Acacias
P^ge des Acacias
R. de l'Arc de Triomphe
AVENUE MAC MAHON
STE GERMAINE
ESPACE WAGRAM
R. Montenotte
R. de l'Étoile
Brey
Troyon
Villa Wagram St Honoré
Sq^re du Roule
V. Nouvelle
ST JOSEPH
ANNONCIATION
Fg St Honoré
R. Villaret de Joyeuse
Joyeuse
AVENUE CARNOT
Villa de la G^de Armée
R. Anatole de la Forge
R. du Gal Lanrezac
ARGENTINE
AV. DE LA GRANDE ARMÉE
CH. DE GAULLE ÉTOILE (R.E.R.)
PLACE
ARC DE TRIOMPHE (R.E.R.)
Rue de Tilsitt
AVENUE DE FRIEDLAND
Beaujon
Houssaye
R. Arsène
Av. Bertie Albrecht
Balzac
Pl. G. Guillaumin
Berryer
ST SACREMENT
CHAMBRE DE COMMERCE ET D'INDUSTRIE DE PARIS
Lamennais
Washington
Chateaubriand
Cité Odiot
R. d'Argentine
R. de Saïgon
Rude
Rue Chalgrin
Rue de Presbourg
AV. FOCH
CHARLES DE GAULLE
F 7
F 8
FREDERIKSKIRKEN
Lord Byron
LIDO
R. de Tilsitt
R. Traktir
AV. VICTOR HUGO
Lauriston
Rue du Dôme
V. d'Eylau
CLIN V. HUGO
KLÉBER
OFFICE DU TOURISME
AIR FRANCE
GEORGE V
AVENUE DES
Galerie des Champs
Arcades du Lido
Galerie du Claridge
Av. des Portugais
La Pérouse
R. Newton
R. Euler
Bassano
Vernet
Bauchart
Lincoln
CENTRE DE CONFÉRENCES INTERNATIONALES
R. Vacquerie
ST GEORGE'S
Rue de Bassano
Magellan
R. C. Colomb
Pl. H. Dunant
Pierre Charron
Paul Valéry
RÉSERVOIRS DE PASSY
Copernic
KLÉBER
Dumont d'Urville
Auguste Vacquerie
Pl. de l'Uruguay
Jean
Keppler
AV. D'IÉNA
Galilée
Quentin Bauchart
Giraudoux
R. de Cerisoles
Marbeuf
R. Cimarosa
Imp. Kléber
R. de Belloy
Sq^re de Chaillot
R. Estienne
AVENUE

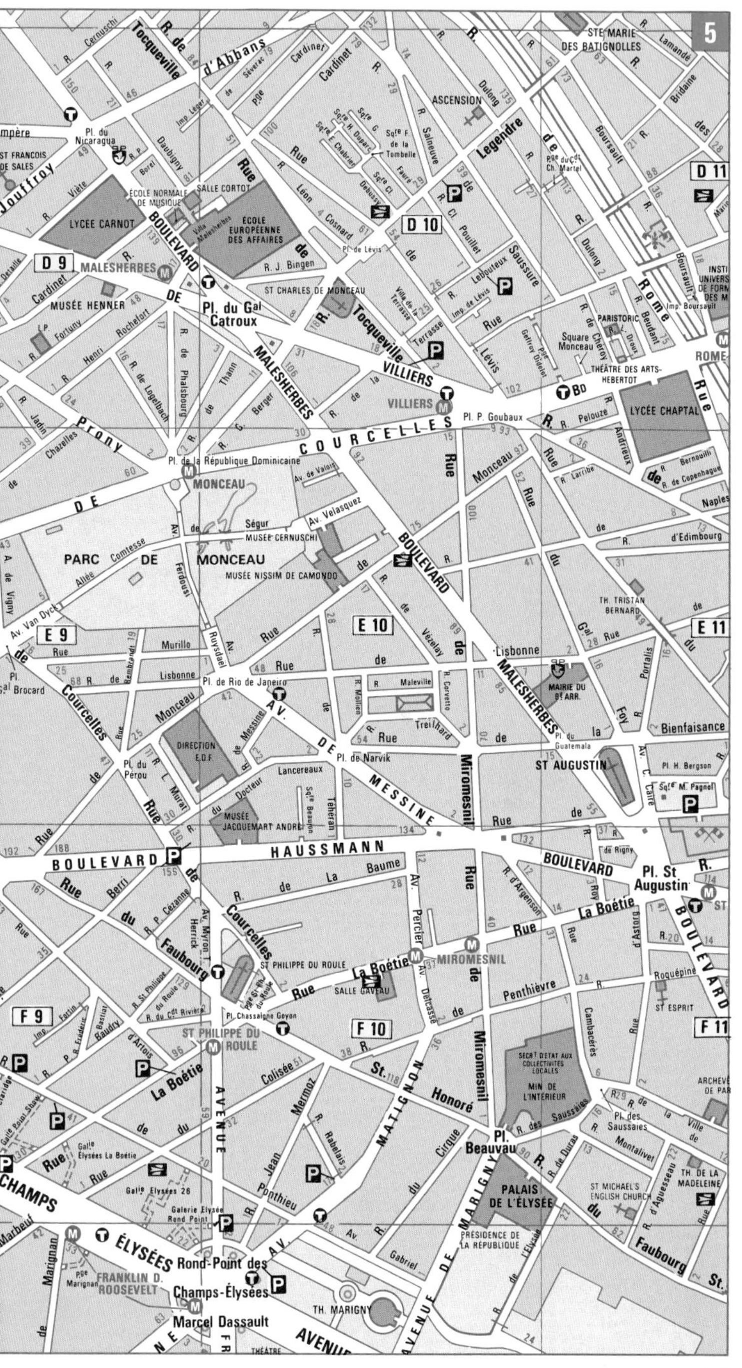
5
D 9
D 10
D 11
E 9
E 10
E 11
F 9
F 10
F 11
STE MARIE DES BATIGNOLLES
ASCENSION
LYCEE CARNOT
ÉCOLE NORMALE DE MUSIQUE
SALLE CORTOT
ÉCOLE EUROPÉENNE DES AFFAIRES
MALESHERBES
MUSÉE HENNER
ST FRANCOIS DE SALES
Pl. du Nicaragua
ST CHARLES DE MONCEAU
Pl. du Gal Catroux
Pl. de Lévis
PARISTORIC
Square Monceau
THÉATRE DES ARTS-HEBERTOT
LYCÉE CHAPTAL
VILLIERS
Pl. P. Goubaux
Pl. de la République Dominicaine
MONCEAU
PARC DE MONCEAU
MUSÉE CERNUSCHI
MUSÉE NISSIM DE CAMONDO
TH. TRISTAN BERNARD
MAIRIE DU 8E ARR.
Pl. de Rio de Janeiro
DIRECTION E.D.F.
Pl. du Pérou
Pl. de Narvik
MUSÉE JACQUEMART ANDRÉ
ST AUGUSTIN
Pl. du Guatemala
Pl. H. Bergson
Pl. St Augustin
BOULEVARD HAUSSMANN
ST PHILIPPE DU ROULE
SALLE GAVEAU
MIROMESNIL
Pl. Chassaigne Goyon
ST ESPRIT
SECRT D'ETAT AUX COLLECTIVITES LOCALES
MIN DE L'INTÉRIEUR
Pl. des Saussaies
Pl. Beauvau
PALAIS DE L'ÉLYSÉE
PRÉSIDENCE DE LA RÉPUBLIQUE
ST MICHAEL'S ENGLISH CHURCH
TH. DE LA MADELEINE
Galerie Elysée Rond Point
CHAMPS ÉLYSÉES
Rond-Point des Champs-Élysées
FRANKLIN D. ROOSEVELT
Marcel Dassault
TH. MARIGNY
AVENUE DE MARIGNY
Faubourg St.

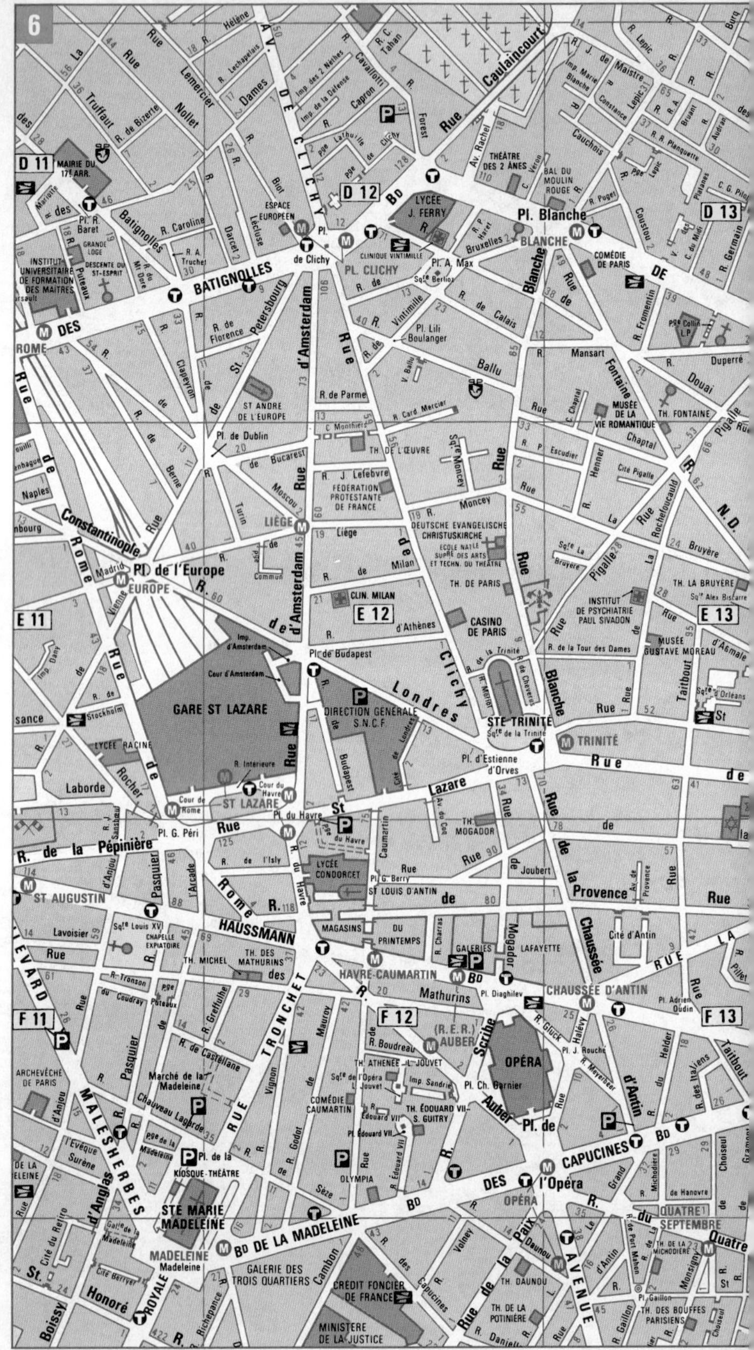
6
D 11
D 12
D 13
E 11
E 12
E 13
F 11
F 12
F 13
Rue Caulaincourt
Pl. Blanche
BLANCHE
BATIGNOLLES
PL. CLICHY
Rue d'Amsterdam
Constantinople
Pl. de l'Europe
EUROPE
LIÈGE
GARE ST LAZARE
ST LAZARE
STE TRINITÉ
TRINITÉ
R. de la Pépinière
ST AUGUSTIN
HAUSSMANN
HAVRE-CAUMARTIN
CHAUSSÉE D'ANTIN
OPÉRA
MALESHERBES
STE MARIE MADELEINE
MADELEINE
BD DE LA MADELEINE
BD DES CAPUCINES
RUE TRONCHET
LYCÉE CONDORCET
MAGASINS DU PRINTEMPS
GALERIES LAFAYETTE
DIRECTION GÉNÉRALE S.N.C.F.
CASINO DE PARIS
CRÉDIT FONCIER DE FRANCE
MINISTERE DE LA JUSTICE

7
BASILIQUE DU SACRÉ CŒUR
Pl. du Parvis du Sacré Cœur
ST PIERRE DE MONTMARTRE
R. du Card. Dubois
Funiculaire
Sq re Willette
Pl. S. Valadon
MUSÉE D'ART NAIF MAX FOURNY
R. Ronsard
R. A. del Sarte
R. P. Picard
STE ANNE
R. Feutrier
Rue Myrha
R. Richomme
R. Polonceau
R. de la Goutte d'Or
R. Christiani
R. de Sofia
BOULEVARD BARBÈS
R. des Islettes
R. Caplat
D 15
ABBESSES
ST JEAN DE MONTMARTRE
R. Ravignan
R. Berthe
R. Gabrielle
R. A. Barsacq
R. des Trois Frères
R. Yvonne Le Tac
R. Tardieu
R. d'Orsel
R. Houdon
R. Foyatier
D 14
ÉLYSÉE MONTMARTRE
BOULEVARD DE ROCHECHOUART
ANVERS
BARBÈS ROCHECHOUART
LARIBOISIÈRE
R. A. Paré
PIGALLE
Pl. Pigalle
CLICHY
LYCÉE J. DECOUR
AVENUE TRUDAINE
R. du Delta
R. de Dunkerque
Rue du Fg Poissonnière
BD DE MAGENTA
LYCÉE E. QUINET
R. Victor Massé
Rue Condorcet
R. Rodier
Rue Turgot
R. Pétrelle
Pl. De Roubaix
R. de Navarin
R. des Martyrs
Rue Clauzel
R. Milton
R. de la Tour d'Auvergne
Rue de Maubeuge
R. Laferrière
ST GEORGES
ST CONSTANTIN STE HÉLÈNE
E 14
LYCÉE LAMARTINE
LYCÉE TECHN. JULES SIEGFRIED
ST VINCENT DE PAUL
E 15
Pl. Franz Liszt
R. Rochambeau
Sq re de Montholon
RUE LA FAYETTE
POISSONNIÈRE
R. de Chabrol
Rue N.-D. de Lorette
R. Lamartine
Pl. Kossuth
Rue de Châteaudun
N.-D. DE LORETTE
CADET
R. des Messageries
MUSÉE DES CRISTALLERIES DE BACCARAT
Cité Paradis
R. de Paradis
MUSÉE DU GRAND ORIENT DE FRANCE
FOLIES BERGÈRE
Rue Richer
R. des Petites Écuries
LE PELETIER
R. Drouot
Rue du Fg Montmartre
Rue de Provence
LYCÉE CH. DE GAULLE
SECRÉT. D'ÉTAT AUX DROITS DES FEMMES
RÉDEMPTION
HÔTEL DES VENTES DROUOT-RICHELIEU
R. de la Grange Batelière
ST-EUGÈNE-STE CÉCILE
Rue Ste Cécile
CONSERVATOIRE NAT. SUP. D'ART DRAMATIQUE
F 14
F 15
R. de Montyon
MAIRIE DU 9e ARR.
Musée Grévin
HAUSSMANN
RICHELIEU DROUOT
BD DES ITALIENS
BD MONTMARTRE
RUE MONTMARTRE
TH. DES NOUVEAUTÉS
TH. DES VARIÉTÉS
BD POISSONNIÈRE
BONNE NOUVELLE
TH. DU GYMNASE-MARIE BELL
BD DE BONNE NOUVELLE
STRASBOURG ST DENIS
OPÉRA COMIQUE
Galie Vivienne
Rue Richelieu
Rue Réaumur
BOURSE DES VALEURS
BOURSE
Place de la Bourse
Rue du 4 Septembre
Rue des Jeûneurs
R. du Croissant
R. St Joseph
LA PENTECÔTE
Rue d'Uzès
R. du Sentier
R. de Cléry
R. d'Aboukir
R. Ste Foy
Rue St Denis
Rue de l'Échiquier
R. d'Enghien
R. de Mazagran
R. de la Lune
R. Beauregard
PHONOTHÈQUE NAT LE
R. L. Cladel
R. des Filles St Thomas

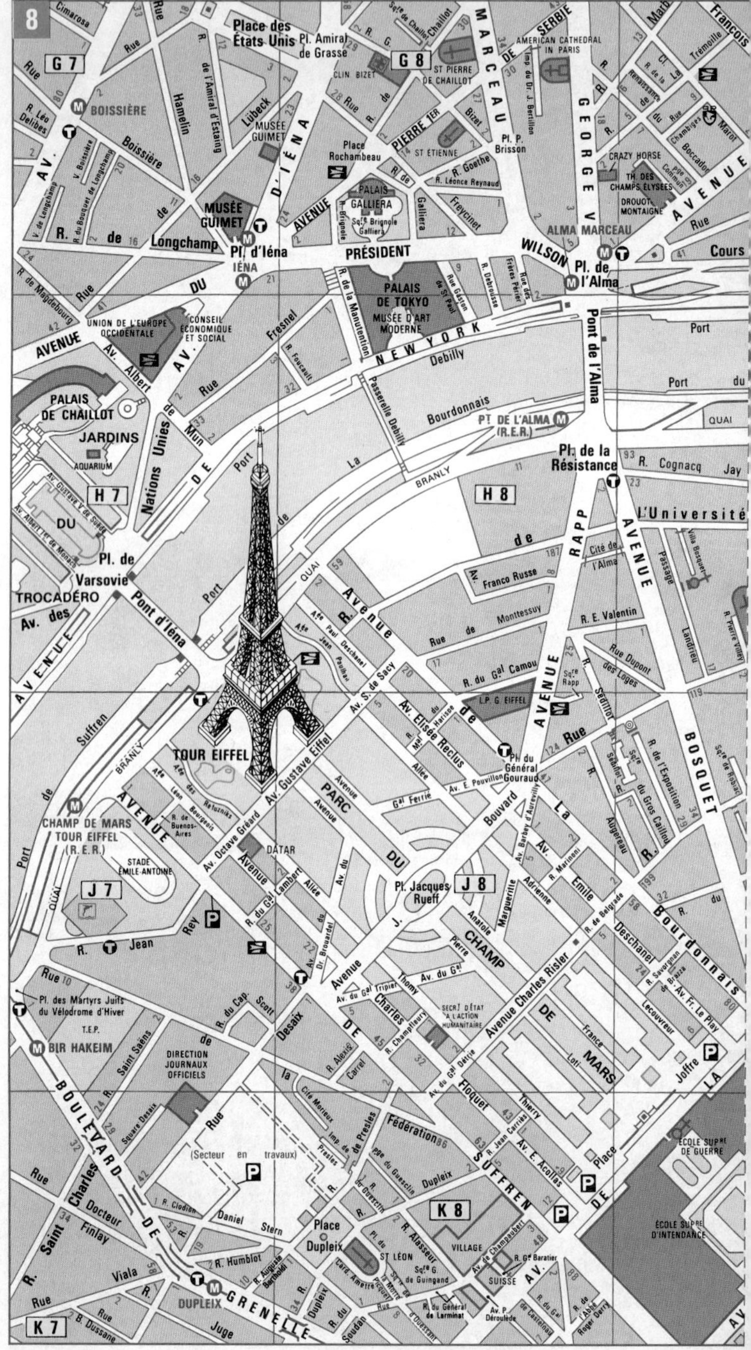
8
Place des États Unis
Pl. Amiral de Grasse
G 7
G 8
BOISSIÈRE
MUSÉE GUIMET
ST PIERRE DE CHAILLOT
AMERICAN CATHEDRAL IN PARIS
Place Rochambeau
PALAIS GALLIERA
ST ETIENNE
Pl. P. Brisson
CRAZY HORSE
TH. DES CHAMPS ELYSÉES
ALMA MARCEAU
Pl. d'Iéna
IÉNA
PRÉSIDENT
WILSON
Pl. de l'Alma
PALAIS DE TOKYO
MUSÉE D'ART MODERNE
UNION DE L'EUROPE OCCIDENTALE
CONSEIL ÉCONOMIQUE ET SOCIAL
NEW YORK
Pont de l'Alma
PALAIS DE CHAILLOT
JARDINS
AQUARIUM
PT DE L'ALMA (R.E.R.)
Pl. de la Résistance
H 7
H 8
Pl. de Varsovie
TROCADÉRO
Pont d'Iéna
L'Université
AVENUE RAPP
AVENUE BOSQUET
L.P. G. EIFFEL
TOUR EIFFEL
Pl. du Général Gouraud
CHAMP DE MARS TOUR EIFFEL (R.E.R.)
STADE ÉMILE-ANTOINE
DATAR
Pl. Jacques Rueff
J 7
J 8
Bourdonnais
Pl. des Martyrs Juifs du Vélodrome d'Hiver
T.E.P.
BIR HAKEIM
DIRECTION JOURNAUX OFFICIELS
SECRT D'ÉTAT A L'ACTION HUMANITAIRE
Avenue Charles Risler
CHAMP DE MARS
ÉCOLE SUPRE DE GUERRE
ÉCOLE SUPRE D'INTENDANCE
(Secteur en travaux)
BOULEVARD DE GRENELLE
Place Dupleix
ST LÉON
VILLAGE SUISSE
K 7
K 8
DUPLEIX
AVENUE DE SUFFREN

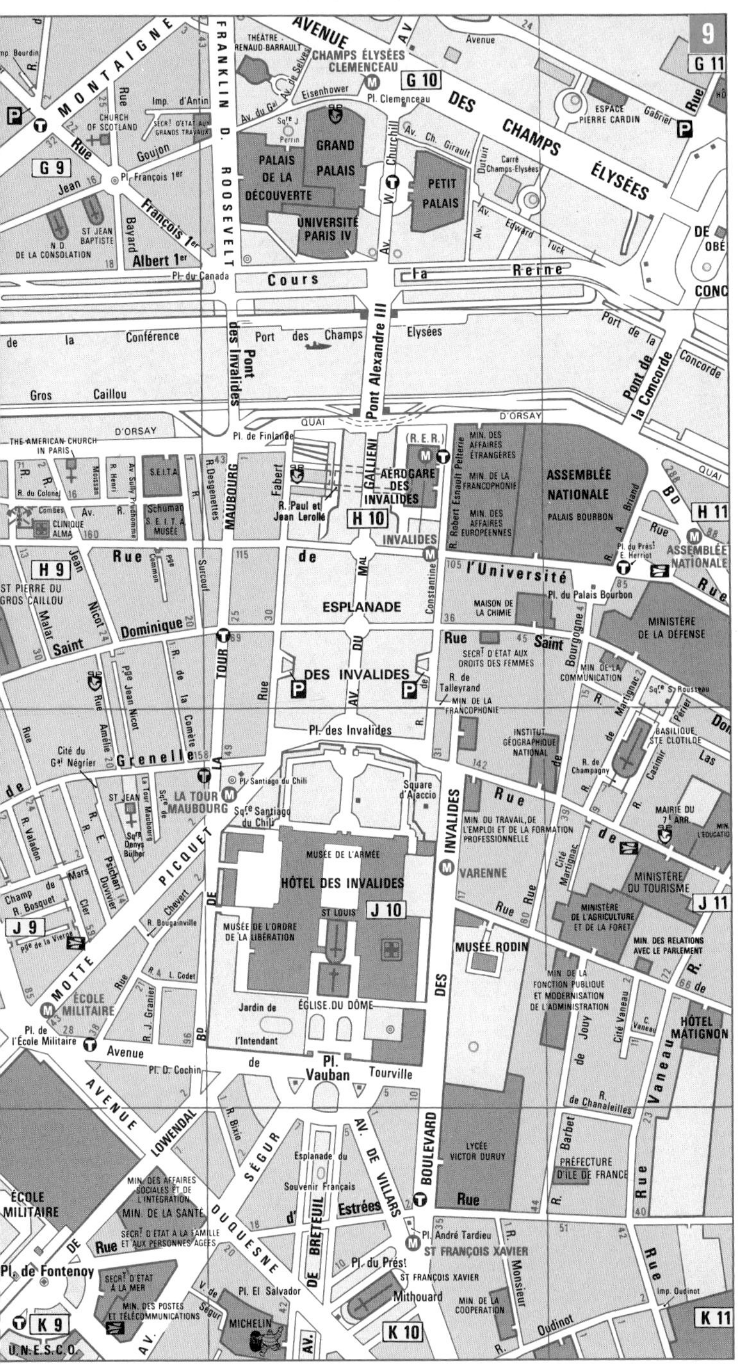

9
G 9
G 10
G 11
H 9
H 10
H 11
J 9
J 10
J 11
K 9
K 10
K 11
AVENUE DES CHAMPS ÉLYSÉES
CHAMPS ÉLYSÉES CLEMENCEAU
Pl. Clemenceau
THÉATRE RENAUD-BARRAULT
ESPACE PIERRE CARDIN
GRAND PALAIS
PALAIS DE LA DÉCOUVERTE
PETIT PALAIS
UNIVERSITÉ PARIS IV
CHURCH OF SCOTLAND
Pl. François 1er
ST JEAN BAPTISTE
N.D. DE LA CONSOLATION
Albert 1er
Pl. du Canada
Cours la Reine
Port de la Conférence
Port des Champs Elysées
Pont des Invalides
Pont Alexandre III
Pont de la Concorde
Port de la Concorde
Gros Caillou
QUAI D'ORSAY
THE AMERICAN CHURCH IN PARIS
Pl. de Finlande
AÉROGARE DES INVALIDES
INVALIDES
MIN. DES AFFAIRES ÉTRANGÈRES
MIN. DE LA FRANCOPHONIE
MIN. DES AFFAIRES EUROPÉENNES
ASSEMBLÉE NATIONALE
PALAIS BOURBON
CLINIQUE ALMA
S.E.I.T.A. MUSÉE
Rue de l'Université
ESPLANADE DES INVALIDES
ST PIERRE DU GROS CAILLOU
Rue Saint Dominique
MAISON DE LA CHIMIE
Pl. du Palais Bourbon
MINISTÈRE DE LA DÉFENSE
SECRT D'ÉTAT AUX DROITS DES FEMMES
MIN. DE LA COMMUNICATION
Sq.re S. Rousseau
Pl. des Invalides
Rue de Grenelle
INSTITUT GÉOGRAPHIQUE NATIONAL
BASILIQUE STE CLOTILDE
LA TOUR MAUBOURG
Pl. Santiago du Chili
Square d'Ajaccio
MAIRIE DU 7E ARR.
MIN. DU TRAVAIL, DE L'EMPLOI ET DE LA FORMATION PROFESSIONNELLE
MUSÉE DE L'ARMÉE
HÔTEL DES INVALIDES
VARENNE
MINISTÈRE DU TOURISME
MINISTÈRE DE L'AGRICULTURE ET DE LA FORET
MUSÉE DE L'ORDRE DE LA LIBÉRATION
ST LOUIS
MUSÉE RODIN
MIN. DES RELATIONS AVEC LE PARLEMENT
MIN. DE LA FONCTION PUBLIQUE ET MODERNISATION DE L'ADMINISTRATION
ÉCOLE MILITAIRE
ÉGLISE DU DÔME
Jardin de l'Intendant
HÔTEL MATIGNON
Pl. de l'École Militaire
Avenue de Tourville
Pl. D. Cochin
Pl. Vauban
Boulevard des Invalides
Avenue de Ségur
Avenue de Lowendal
Esplanade du Souvenir Français
LYCÉE VICTOR DURUY
PRÉFECTURE D'ILE DE FRANCE
MIN. DES AFFAIRES SOCIALES ET DE L'INTÉGRATION
MIN. DE LA SANTÉ
SECRT D'ÉTAT A LA FAMILLE ET AUX PERSONNES AGÉES
Rue d'Estrées
Pl. André Tardieu
ST FRANÇOIS XAVIER
Pl. de Fontenoy
SECRT D'ÉTAT A LA MER
MIN. DES POSTES ET TÉLÉCOMMUNICATIONS
Pl. El Salvador
Pl. du Prés! Mithouard
MIN. DE LA COOPERATION
MICHELIN
U.N.E.S.C.O.

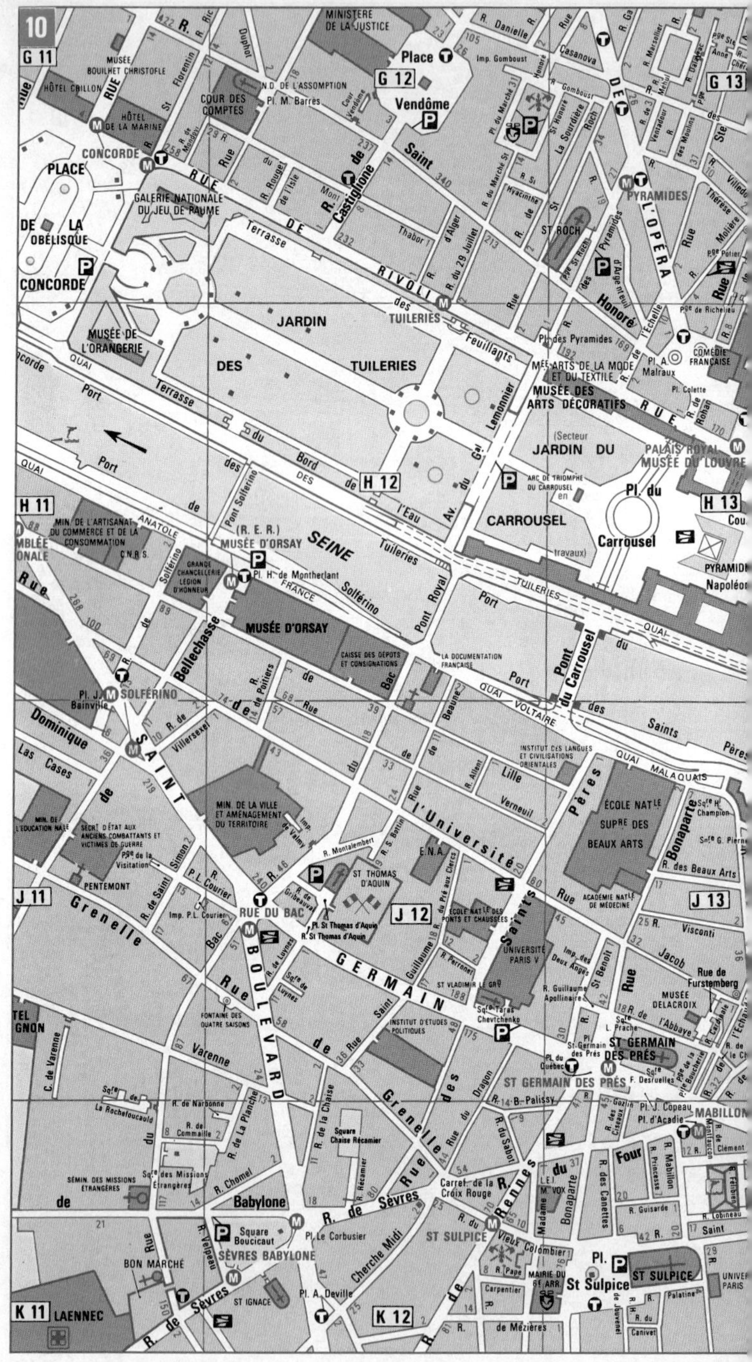
10
G 11
G 12
G 13
H 11
H 12
H 13
J 11
J 12
J 13
K 11
K 12
MINISTERE DE LA JUSTICE
Place Vendôme
MUSÉE BOUILHET CHRISTOFLE
HÔTEL CRILLON
HÔTEL DE LA MARINE
CONCORDE
PLACE DE LA CONCORDE
OBÉLISQUE
COUR DES COMPTES
N.D. DE L'ASSOMPTION
Pl. M. Barrès
GALERIE NATIONALE DU JEU DE PAUME
RUE DE RIVOLI
R. de Castiglione
Saint Honoré
ST ROCH
PYRAMIDES
DE L'OPÉRA
JARDIN DES TUILERIES
TUILERIES
MUSÉE DE L'ORANGERIE
Pl. des Pyramides
Mée ARTS DE LA MODE ET DU TEXTILE
MUSÉE DES ARTS DÉCORATIFS
COMÉDIE FRANÇAISE
Pl. A. Malraux
Pl. Colette
PALAIS ROYAL MUSÉE DU LOUVRE
JARDIN DU CARROUSEL
ARC DE TRIOMPHE DU CARROUSEL
Pl. du Carrousel
PYRAMIDE Napoléon
SEINE
Pont Royal
Pont du Carrousel
Pont Solferino
QUAI ANATOLE FRANCE
QUAI VOLTAIRE
QUAI MALAQUAIS
MIN. DE L'ARTISANAT DU COMMERCE ET DE LA CONSOMMATION
C.N.R.S.
GRANDE CHANCELLERIE LEGION D'HONNEUR
(R.E.R.) MUSÉE D'ORSAY
Pl. H. de Montherlant
MUSÉE D'ORSAY
CAISSE DES DÉPOTS ET CONSIGNATIONS
LA DOCUMENTATION FRANÇAISE
Pl. J. Bainville
SOLFÉRINO
Rue de Bellechasse
Rue de Lille
Rue de l'Université
Rue de Verneuil
Rue des Saints Pères
INSTITUT DES LANGUES ET CIVILISATIONS ORIENTALES
ÉCOLE NATLE SUPRE DES BEAUX ARTS
R. des Beaux Arts
Rue Bonaparte
MIN. DE LA VILLE ET AMÉNAGEMENT DU TERRITOIRE
MIN. DE L'EDUCATION NALE
SECRT D'ÉTAT AUX ANCIENS COMBATTANTS ET VICTIMES DE GUERRE
PENTEMONT
Rue Saint Dominique
Las Cases
R. Montalembert
ST THOMAS D'AQUIN
E.N.A.
RUE DU BAC
Pl. St Thomas d'Aquin
R. St Thomas d'Aquin
ÉCOLE NATLE DES PONTS ET CHAUSSÉES
ACADÉMIE NATLE DE MÉDECINE
UNIVERSITÉ PARIS V
Rue Jacob
Rue de Furstemberg
MUSÉE DELACROIX
Rue de Grenelle
BOULEVARD SAINT GERMAIN
FONTAINE DES QUATRE SAISONS
INSTITUT D'ÉTUDES POLITIQUES
Sqre Taras Chevtchenko
ST GERMAIN DES PRÉS
Pl. du Québec
Rue de Varenne
Square Chaise Récamier
Rue du Dragon
R. B. Palissy
Pl. J. Copeau
Pl. d'Acadie
MABILLON
SÉMIN. DES MISSIONS ÉTRANGÈRES
Rue de Babylone
R. de Sèvres
Carref. de la Croix Rouge
Rue de Rennes
Rue du Four
Square Boucicaut
Pl. Le Corbusier
SÈVRES BABYLONE
ST SULPICE
BON MARCHÉ
ST IGNACE
Pl. A. Deville
Cherche Midi
MAIRIE DU 6e ARR.
Pl. St Sulpice
LAENNEC
de Mézières

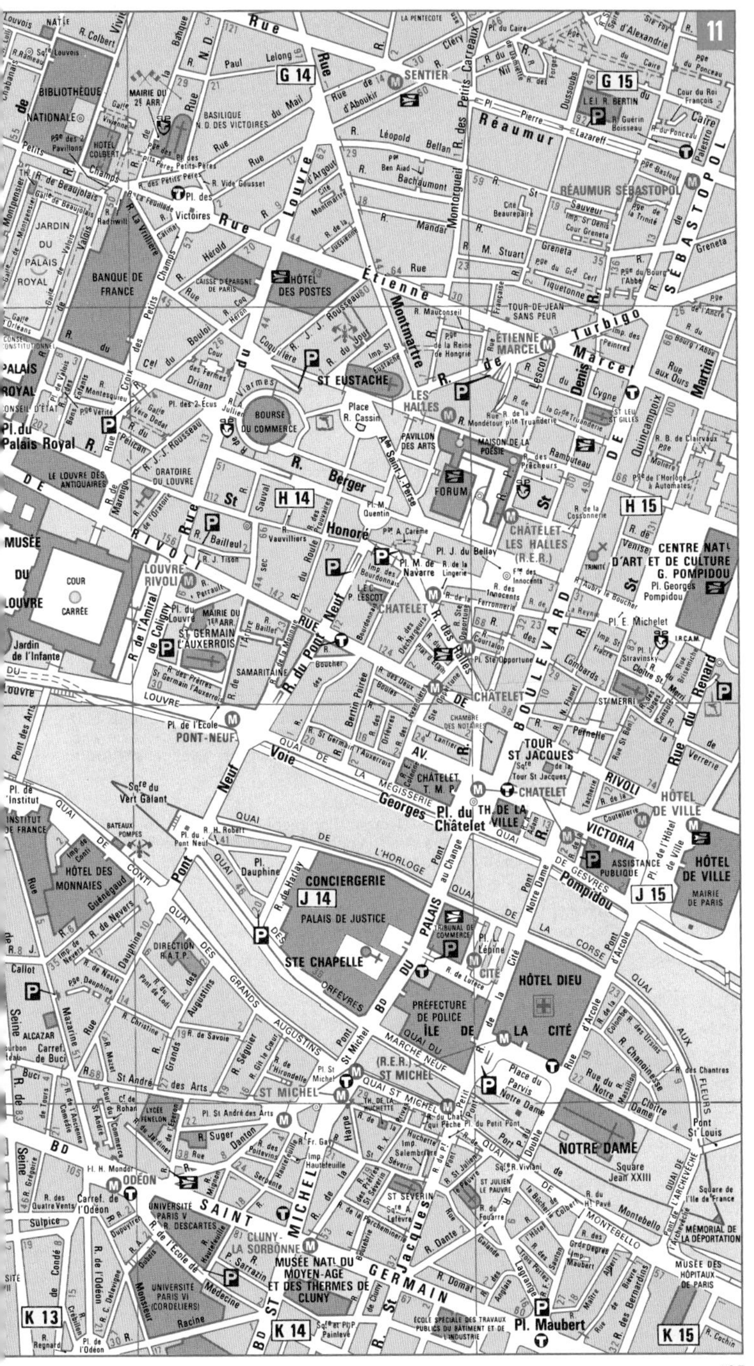
G 14
G 15
H 14
H 15
J 14
J 15
K 13
K 14
K 15
BIBLIOTHÈQUE NATIONALE
MAIRIE DU 2e ARR.
BASILIQUE N.D. DES VICTOIRES
SENTIER
Rue Réaumur
RÉAUMUR SÉBASTOPOL
BOULEVARD DE SÉBASTOPOL
Pl. des Victoires
JARDIN DU PALAIS ROYAL
BANQUE DE FRANCE
CAISSE D'EPARGNE DE PARIS
HÔTEL DES POSTES
Rue Étienne Marcel
TOUR DE JEAN SANS PEUR
ÉTIENNE MARCEL
Rue de Turbigo
PALAIS ROYAL
ST EUSTACHE
BOURSE DU COMMERCE
Place R. Cassin
LES HALLES
PAVILLON DES ARTS
MAISON DE LA POÉSIE
FORUM
Pl. du Palais Royal
LE LOUVRE DES ANTIQUAIRES
ORATOIRE DU LOUVRE
R. St Honoré
R. Berger
CHÂTELET LES HALLES (R.E.R.)
CENTRE NATL D'ART ET DE CULTURE G. POMPIDOU
Pl. Georges Pompidou
MUSÉE DU LOUVRE
COUR CARRÉE
Jardin de l'Infante
RUE DE RIVOLI
LOUVRE RIVOLI
MAIRIE DU 1ER ARR.
ST GERMAIN L'AUXERROIS
SAMARITAINE
CHATELET
PL. E. Michelet
I.R.C.A.M.
Pl. I. Stravinsky
ST MERRI
Pl. de l'Ecole
PONT-NEUF
TOUR ST JACQUES
Sq. de la Tour St Jacques
CHÂTELET T.M.P.
TH. DE LA VILLE
Pl. du Châtelet
Quai de la Mégisserie
HÔTEL DE VILLE
AV. VICTORIA
ASSISTANCE PUBLIQUE
MAIRIE DE PARIS
Pl. de l'Institut
INSTITUT DE FRANCE
Sqre du Vert Galant
HÔTEL DES MONNAIES
Pl. Dauphine
Quai de l'Horloge
CONCIERGERIE
PALAIS DE JUSTICE
STE CHAPELLE
TRIBUNAL DE COMMERCE
DIRECTION R.A.T.P.
Quai des Grands Augustins
PRÉFECTURE DE POLICE
ÎLE DE LA CITÉ
HÔTEL DIEU
Quai aux Fleurs
ST MICHEL
(R.E.R.) ST MICHEL
Place du Parvis Notre Dame
NOTRE DAME
Square Jean XXIII
Pont St Louis
Square de l'Ile de France
MÉMORIAL DE LA DÉPORTATION
Carref. de Buci
LYCÉE FENELON
Pl. St André des Arts
ODÉON
Carref. de l'Odéon
UNIVERSITÉ PARIS V R. DESCARTES
CLUNY-LA SORBONNE
MUSÉE NATL DU MOYEN-AGE ET DES THERMES DE CLUNY
UNIVERSITÉ PARIS VI (CORDELIERS)
BD SAINT GERMAIN
BD ST MICHEL
Sq. St Julien le Pauvre
Sqre R. Viviani
Quai de Montebello
MUSÉE DES HÔPITAUX DE PARIS
ÉCOLE SPÉCIALE DES TRAVAUX PUBLICS DU BÂTIMENT ET DE L'INDUSTRIE
Pl. Maubert
Sqre et PI P Painlevé

Sights

How to make the most of a trip to Paris – some ideas :

A BIRD'S-EYE VIEW OF PARIS

★★★Eiffel Tower J 7 – ★★★Montparnasse Tower LM 11 – ★★★Notre-Dame Tower K 15 – ★★★Sacré Cœur Dome D 14 – ★★★Arc de Triomphe platform F 8.

FAMOUS PARISIAN VISTAS

★★★Arc de Triomphe – Champs-Elysées – Place de la Concorde : ≤ from the Rond Point on the Champs-Élysées G 10.

★★★The Madeleine – Place de la Concorde – Palais Bourbon (National Assembly) : ≤ from the Obelisk in the middle of Place de la Concorde G 11.

★★★The Trocadéro – Eiffel Tower – Ecole Militaire : ≤ from the terrace of Chaillot Palace H 7.

★★★The Invalides – Grand and Petit Palais : ≤ from Alexandre III bridge H 10.

MAIN MONUMENTS

The Louvre★★★ (Square Court, Perrault's Colonnade, Pyramid) H 13 – Eiffel Tower★★★ J 7 – Notre-Dame Cathedral★★★ K 15 – Sainte-Chapelle★★★ J 14 – Arc de Triomphe★★★ F 8 – The Invalides★★★ (Napoleon's Tomb) J 10 – Palais-Royal★★ H 13 – The Opera★★ F 12 – The Conciergerie★★ J 14 – The Pantheon★★ L 14 – Luxembourg★★ (Palace and Gardens) KL 13.

Churches : The Madeleine★★ G 11 – Sacré Cœur★★ D 14 – St-Germain-des-Prés★★ J 13 – St-Etienne-du-Mont★★ – St-Germain-l'Auxerrois★★ H 14.

In the Marais : Place des Vosges★★ – Hôtel Lamoignon★★ – Hôtel Guénégaud★★ (Museum of the Chase and of Nature) – Hôtel de Soubise★★ (Historical Museum of France) by HJ 15.

MAIN MUSEUMS

The Louvre★★★ H 13 – Orsay★★★ (mid-19C to early 20C) H 12 – National Museum of Modern Art★★★ (Georges Pompidou Centre) H 15 – Army Museum★★★ (Invalides) J 10 – Museum of Decorative Arts★★ (107 rue de Rivoli) H 13 – Hôtel de Cluny Museum★★ (Middle Ages and Baths) K 14 – Rodin★★ (Hôtel de Biron) J 10 – Carnavalet★★ (History of Paris) J 17 – Picasso★★ H 17 – City of Science and Industry★★★ (La Villette) – Marmottan★★ (Impressionist artists) – Orangerie★★ (from the Impressionists until 1930) H 11.

MODERN MONUMENTS

La Défense★★ (CNIT, Great Arch) – Georges Pompidou Centre★★ H 15 – Forum des Halles H 14 – Institute of the Arab World★ – Opéra de la Bastille – Bercy (Palais Omnisports, Ministry of Finance).

PRETTY AREAS

Montmartre★★★ D 14 – Ile St-Louis★★ J 14 J 15 – the Quays★★ (between Pont des Arts and Pont de Sully) J 14 J 15 – St Séverin district★★ K 14.

K 14, G 10 : *Reference letters and numbers on the town plans.*

*Use MICHELIN Green Guide **Paris** for a well-informed visit.*

Alphabetical list
(Hotels and Restaurants)

D

E

F

G

S

T

U - V

HOTELS, RESTAURANTS

Listed by districts and arrondissements

(List of Hotels and Restaurants in alphabetical order, see pp 5 to 8)

G 12: These reference letters and numbers correspond to the squares on the Michelin Map of Paris no 10, Paris Atlas no 11, Map with street index no 12 and Map of Paris no 14.

Consult any of the above publications when looking for a car park nearest to a listed establishment.

Opéra, Palais-Royal, Halles, Bourse.

1st and 2nd arrondissements - 1st: ✉ 75001 - 2nd: ✉ 75002

Ritz, 15 pl. Vendôme (1st) ✆ 42 60 38 30, Telex 220262, Fax 42 60 23 71, « Attractive pool and luxurious fitness centre » - 🛗 ▤ TV ☎ ♿ - 🏛 30 - 80. AE ⓓ GB JCB. ✻ rest **M** see **Espadon** below - ☕ 170 - **142 rm** 2850/4150, 45 suites. G 12

Meurice, 228 r. Rivoli (1st) ✆ 44 58 10 10, Telex 220256, Fax 44 58 10 15 - 🛗 ▤ rm TV ☎ ♿ - 🏛 40 - 100. AE ⓓ GB JCB. ✻ rest G 12 **M** see **Le Meurice** below - ☕ 130 - **138 rm** 2200/2900, 42 suites.

Inter-Continental, 3 r. Castiglione (1st) ✆ 44 77 11 11, Telex 220114, Fax 44 77 14 60, 🍽 - 🛗 ▤ TV ☎ ♿ - 🏛 500. AE ⓓ GB JCB. ✻ rest G 12 **Café Tuileries** (coffee shop) **M** 115 and a la carte 200/300 - **La Terrasse Fleurie** *(closed 18 December-3 January)* **M** a la carte 330/520 - ☕ 120 - **450 rm** 2200/2750, 20 suites.

Lotti, 7 r. Castiglione (1st) ✆ 42 60 37 34, Telex 240066, Fax 40 15 93 56 - 🛗 ⇔ rm ▤ TV ☎ - 🏛 25. AE ⓓ GB JCB G 12 **M** 240 and a la carte 280/450 🍷 - ☕ 120 - **129 rm** 1700/3300.

Westminster, 13 r. Paix (2nd) ✆ 42 61 57 46, Telex 680035, Fax 42 60 30 66 - 🛗 ⇔ rm ▤ rm TV ☎ - 🏛 40. AE ⓓ GB JCB G 12 **M** see **Le Céladon** below - ☕ 110 - **84 rm** 1950/2500, 18 suites.

du Louvre, pl. A. Malraux (1st) ✆ 44 58 38 38, Telex 240412, Fax 44 58 38 01 - 🛗 ▤ TV ☎ ♿ - 🏛 100. AE ⓓ GB JCB H 13 **Brasserie Le Louvre M** 160 and a la carte 170/260 🍷 - ☕ 90 - **178 rm** 1500/2000, 22 suites.

Edouard VII and rest. Le Delmonico, 39 av. Opéra (2nd) ✆ 42 61 56 90, Telex 680217, Fax 42 61 47 73 - 🛗 ▤ TV ☎ - 🏛 40. AE ⓓ GB G 13 **M** *(closed 31 July-31 August, Saturday and Sunday)* 148/450 - ☕ 60 - **68 rm** 1000/1130, 4 suites.

Normandy, 7 r. Échelle (1st) ✆ 42 60 30 21, Telex 670250, Fax 42 60 45 81 - 🛗 TV ☎ - 🏛 50. AE ⓓ GB JCB H 13 **L'Échelle** *(closed Saturday and Sunday)* **M** 155 and a la carte 180/300 - ☕ 68 - **123 rm** 1065/1875, 7 suites.

Mayfair without rest, 3 r. Rouget-de-Lisle (1st) ✆ 42 60 38 14, Telex 240037, Fax 40 15 04 78 - 🛗 ▤ TV ☎. AE ⓓ GB JCB. ✻ G 12 ☕ 75 - **53 rm** 900/1630.

Régina, 2 pl. Pyramides (1st) ✆ 42 60 31 10, Telex 670834, Fax 40 15 95 16, 🍽 - 🛗 ⇔ rm ▤ rest TV ☎ - 🏛 25 - 30. AE ⓓ GB JCB. ✻ rest H 13 **M** 210/520 - ☕ 85 - **117 rm** 1450/1850, 13 suites.

Cambon without rest, 3 r. Cambon (1st) ✆ 42 60 38 09, Telex 240814, Fax 42 60 30 59 - 🛗 ▤ TV ☎. AE ⓓ GB JCB G 12 ☕ 70 - **43 rm** 930/1480.

L'Horset Opéra M without rest, 18 r. d'Antin (2nd) ✆ 44 71 87 00, Telex 282676, Fax 42 66 55 54 - 🛗 ▤ TV ☎ ♿. AE ⓓ GB G 13 ☕ 80 - **54 rm** 1100/1250.

Stendhal without rest, 22 r. D. Casanova (2nd) ✉ 75002 ☎ 44 58 52 52, Fax 44 58 52 00 - AE ① GB G 12
☕ 80 - **20 rm** 1400/1800.

Novotel Paris Halles M, 8 pl. M.-de-Navarre (1st) ☎ 42 21 31 31, Telex 216389, Fax 40 26 05 79, 余 - 🛗 ⇔ rm ▤ TV ☎ ♿ - 🏛 40 - 100. AE ① GB H 14
M a la carte approx. 160 - ☕ 58 - **280 rm** 830/900, 5 suites.

de Noailles M without rest, 9 r. Michodière (2nd) ☎ 47 42 92 90, Telex 290644, Fax 49 24 92 71 - 🛗 TV ☎. AE GB G 13
☕ 40 - **58 rm** 650/800.

Favart without rest, 5 r. Marivaux (2nd) ☎ 42 97 59 83, Telex 213126, Fax 40 15 95 58 - 🛗 TV ☎ ♿. AE GB F 13
37 rm ☕ 510/620.

Montana Tuileries without rest, 12 r. St-Roch (1st) ☎ 42 60 35 10, Telex 214404, Fax 42 61 12 28 - 🛗 TV ☎. AE ① GB JCB G 12
☕ 50 - **25 rm** 690/1050.

Louvre St-Honoré M without rest, 141 r. St-Honoré (1st) ☎ 42 96 23 23, Telex 215044, Fax 42 96 21 61 - 🛗 TV ☎ ♿. AE ① GB H 14
☕ 45 - **40 rm** 735/945.

Duminy Vendôme without rest, 3 r. Mont-Thabor (1st) ☎ 42 60 32 80, Telex 213492, Fax 42 96 07 83 - 🛗 TV ☎ - 🏛 30. AE ① GB JCB G 12
79 rm ☕ 700/935.

Molière without rest, 21 r. Molière (1st) ☎ 42 96 22 01, Telex 213292, Fax 42 60 48 68 - 🛗 TV ☎. AE ① GB. ✻ G 13
☕ 50 - **33 rm** 450/700, 3 suites.

Lautrec Opéra M without rest, 8 r. Ambroise (2nd) ☎ 42 96 67 90, Telex 216502, Fax 42 96 06 83 - 🛗 TV ☎. AE GB JCB. ✻ F 13
30 rm ☕ 600/900.

Baudelaire Opéra without rest, 61 r. Ste-Anne (2nd) ☎ 42 97 50 62, Telex 216116, Fax 42 86 85 85 - 🛗 TV ☎. AE ① GB JCB G 13
☕ 33 - **24 rm** 450/600, 5 duplex.

Marsollier Opéra without rest, 13 r. Marsollier (2nd) ☎ 42 96 68 14, Telex 217801, Fax 42 60 53 84 - 🛗 TV ☎. AE ① GB JCB G 13
☕ 30 - **29 rm** 480/620.

Ducs d'Anjou without rest, 1 r. Ste-Opportune (1st) ☎ 42 36 92 24, Telex 218681, Fax 42 36 16 63 - 🛗 TV ☎. AE ① GB JCB H 14
☕ 42 - **38 rm** 432/614.

Vivienne without rest, 40 r. Vivienne (2nd) ☎ 42 33 13 26, Fax 40 41 98 19 - 🛗 ⇔ rm TV ☎. GB F 14
☕ 40 - **44 rm** 340/430.

XXXXX ✿✿ **Espadon** - Hôtel Ritz, 15 pl. Vendôme (1st) ☎ 42 60 38 30, Telex 220262, Fax 42 60 23 71, 余 - ▤. AE ① GB JCB. ✻ G 12
M 330 (lunch)/550 and a la carte 420/660
Spec. Homard. Agneau des Causses Lozériens (November-May). Chariot de desserts.

XXXX ✿✿ **Grand Vefour,** 17 r. Beaujolais (1st) ☎ 42 96 56 27, Fax 42 86 80 71, « Pre-Revolutionary (late 18C) Café Style » - ▤. AE ① GB JCB. ✻ G 13
closed August, Saturday and Sunday - **M** 305 (lunch) and a la carte 500/720
Spec. Langue de boeuf et salade de céleri. Ravioles de foie gras et crème truffée. Millefeuille au moka et poire caramélisée.

XXXX ✿ **Le Meurice** - Hôtel Meurice, 228 r. Rivoli (1st) ☎ 44 58 10 50, Telex 220256, Fax 44 58 10 15 - ▤. AE ① GB JCB. ✻ G 12
M 300 and a la carte 325/500
Spec. Ravioles de homard et petite salade d'herbes. Blanc de turbot au cresson et jus de carotte. Palette de saveurs au caramel.

XXXX ✿✿ **Carré des Feuillants** (Dutournier), 14 r. Castiglione (1st) ☎ 42 86 82 82, Fax 42 86 07 71 - ▤. AE ① GB JCB G 12
closed 1 to 30 August, Saturday lunch and Sunday - **M** 260 (lunch) and a la carte 450/580
Spec. Emincé de Saint-Jacques en "chaud-froid" de céleri truffé (October-March). Rouget rôti aux pommes de terre à la moelle (spring-autumn). Lièvre à la royale "façon Aquitaine" (October-December).

XXXX ✿ **Drouant,** pl. Gaillon (2nd) ☎ 42 65 15 16, Fax 49 24 02 15 - ▤. AE ① GB G 13
M 340 (lunch) and a la carte 450/550 - **Café Drouant M** 230 (dinner and Sunday) and a la carte 250/330
Spec. Charlotte de langoustines aux aubergines confites. Rouget rôti à la tapenade et au safran. Pigeonneau rôti en croûte de pommes de terre.

XXXX ⊛⊛ **Goumard-Prunier,** 9 r. Duphot (1st) ✆ 42 60 36 07, Fax 42 60 04 54 – ▤. AE ⓓ GB JCB G 12
closed Sunday and Monday – **M** Seafood - a la carte 400/580
Spec. Coquilles Saint-Jacques caramélisées et sauté de cardons aux truffes (October-May). Turbot de ligne rôti au cidre, crêpes de sarrazin aux pommes. Homard breton sauce Cayenne.

XXXX ⊛⊛ **Gérard Besson,** 5 r. Coq Héron (1st) ✆ 42 33 14 74, Fax 42 33 85 71 – ▤. AE ⓓ GB
closed Saturday February-August and Sunday – **M** 260 (lunch) and a la carte 400/550 H 14
Spec. Homard et poissons de la baie d'Erquy. Champignons, truffes (season). Gibier.

XXX ⊛ **Mercure Galant,** 15 r. Petits-Champs (1st) ✆ 42 96 98 89, Fax 42 96 08 89 – GB G 13
closed Saturday lunch, Sunday and Bank Holidays – **M** 250 (lunch)/400 and a la carte 320/450
Spec. Filets de rougets poêlés, lentilles vertes et pied de cochon. Saint-Jacques panées, beurre de saumon et choux croquants (October-March). Cœur de Charolais à la moelle en papillote.

XXX ⊛ **Le Céladon** - Hôtel Westminster, 15 r. Daunou (2nd) ✆ 47 03 40 42, Telex 680035, Fax 42 60 30 66 – ▤. AE ⓓ GB JCB G 12
closed 30 July-29 August, Saturday, Sunday and Bank Holidays – **M** 250/450 and a la carte 370/500
Spec. Oeufs brouillés aux oursins (winter). Effeuillée de raie aux herbes en papillote de choux. Corolle de pommes sautées au beurre, jus de cidre (winter).

XXX **Pierre " A la Fontaine Gaillon ",** pl. Gaillon (2nd) ✆ 42 65 87 04, 余 – ▤. AE ⓓ GB
closed August, Saturday lunch and Sunday – **M** a la carte 195/405. G 13

XXX **Serge Granger,** 36 pl. Marché St-Honoré (1st) ✆ 42 60 03 00, Fax 42 60 00 89, 余 – ▤. AE ⓓ GB G 13
closed Saturday lunch and Sunday – **M** 170/250.

XXX **La Corbeille,** 154 r. Montmartre (2nd) ✆ 40 26 30 87 – GB. ✻ G 14
closed Saturday lunch and Sunday – **M** 150/295.

XXX **Chez Vong,** 10 r. Grande-Truanderie (1st) ✆ 40 39 99 89 – ▤. AE ⓓ GB H 15
closed Sunday – **M** Chinese and Vietnamese rest. - a la carte 180/330.

XX **Au Pied de Cochon,** 6 r. Coquillière (1st) ✆ 42 36 11 75, Fax 45 08 48 90 – ▤. AE ⓓ GB
M a la carte 200/300. H 14

XX **Gaya,** 17 r. Duphot (1st) ✆ 42 60 43 03, Fax 42 60 04 54, « Attractive glazed file panels » – ▤. AE GB G 12
closed Sunday and Monday – **M** Seafood - a la carte 200/330.

XX ⊛ **Chez Pauline** (Génin), 5 r. Villédo (1st) ✆ 42 96 20 70, Fax 49 27 99 89 – AE GB
closed 24 July-16 August, Saturday (except lunch from October-March) and Sunday – **M** (▤ 1st floor) 220 (lunch) and a la carte 300/450 G 13
Spec. Jambon persillé. Salade tiède de tête de veau. Ris de veau en croûte.

XX ⊛ **Pierre Au Palais Royal,** 10 r. Richelieu (1st) ✆ 42 96 09 17 – ⓓ GB. ✻ H 13
closed August, Saturday, Sunday and Bank Holidays – **M** 270 and a la carte 240/390
Spec. Escalopes de foie gras de canard chaud. Lotte en papillote à la tomate fraiche. Bœuf à la ficelle.

XX **Saudade,** 34 r. Bourdonnais (1st) ✆ 42 36 30 71 – ▤. AE ⓓ GB. ✻ H 14
closed Sunday – **M** Portugese rest. - a la carte 170/270.

XX **Kinugawa,** 9 r. Mont-Thabor (1st) ✆ 42 60 65 07, Fax 42 60 45 21 – ▤. AE GB JCB. ✻ G 12
M Japanese rest. 145 (lunch)/545.

XX ⊛ **Pharamond,** 24 r. Grande-Truanderie (1st) ✆ 42 33 06 72, Fax 40 28 01 81 – AE ⓓ GB JCB H 15
closed Monday lunch and Sunday – **M** a la carte 230/380
Spec. Tripes à la mode de Caen. Coquilles Saint-Jacques au cidre (15 October-30 April). Poêlée de langoustines au beurre d'estragon.

XX **Le Poquelin,** 17 r. Molière (1st) ✆ 42 96 22 19, Fax 42 96 05 72 – ▤. AE ⓓ GB JCB
closed 1 to 20 August, Saturday lunch and Sunday – **M** a la carte 240/360. G 13

XX **Palais Cardinal,** 43 r. Montpensier (1st) ✆ 42 61 20 23 – GB G 13
closed 8 to 29 August, Saturday lunch and Sunday – **M** 100/148.

XX ⊛ **Pile ou Face,** 52bis r. N.-D.-des-Victoires (2nd) ✆ 42 33 64 33, Fax 42 36 61 09 – ▤. GB
closed 31 July-30 August, 24 to 31 Décember, Saturday, Sunday and Bank holidays – **M** 235 (lunch) and a la carte 300/450 G 14
Spec. Escalope de foie gras de canard poêlée au pain d'épices. Pigeonneau rôti à l'huile de truffe. Fagilité "Bernard Paget".

XX **Bernard Chirent,** 28 r. Mont-Thabor (1st) ✆ 42 86 80 05 – AE GB G 12
closed Saturday lunch and Sunday – **M** 170 b.i./250 b.i..

XX **Velloni,** 22 r. des Halles (1st) ✆ 42 21 12 50 – AE ⓓ GB JCB. ✻ H 14
closed Sunday – **M** Italian rest. - a la carte 190/300.

XX **A la Grille St-Honoré,** 15 pl. Marché St-Honoré (1st) ✆ 42 61 00 93, Fax 47 03 31 64 – ▤. AE GB G 12
closed 1 to 17 August, 25 December-3 January and Sunday – **M** 180/230 ♁.

XX **Le Petit Bourbon,** 15 r. Roule (1st) ✆ 40 26 08 93 – AE ⓓ GB H 14
closed 15 to 31 August, Sunday dinner and Monday – **M** 95/230.

XX **La Passion,** 41 r. Petits Champs (1st) ✆ 42 97 53 41 – ▤. GB. ✻ G 13
closed 25 July-15 August, Saturday lunch andSunday – **M** 170/360.

XX **Vaudeville,** 29 r. Vivienne (2nd) ✆ 40 20 04 62, Fax 49 27 08 78, brasserie – AE ⓓ GB
M 159 b.i. and a la carte 160/270 ♁. G 14

XX **Chatelet Gourmand,** 13 r. Lavandières Ste-Opportune (1st) ✆ 40 26 45 00 – AE ⓓ GB J 14
closed 9 to 22 August, Saturday lunch and Sunday – **M** 160 and a la carte 230/350.

XX **Le Grand Colbert,** 2 r. Vivienne (2nd) ✆ 42 86 87 88, brasserie – ▤. AE GB G 13
closed August – **M** 155 b.i. and a la carte 150/300 ♁.

XX **Coup de Cœur,** 19 r. St-Augustin (2nd) ✆ 47 03 45 70 – ▤. AE GB G 13
closed Saturday lunch and Sunday – **M** 140/180.

XX **Le Soufflé,** 36 r. Mont-Thabor (1st) ✆ 42 60 27 19, Fax 42 60 54 98 – ▤. AE ⓓ GB JCB
closed Sunday and Bank Holidays – **M** 180/210. G 12

XX **Les Cartes Postales,** 7 r. Gomboust (1st) ✆ 42 61 02 93 – GB G 13
closed Saturday lunch and Sunday – **M** (booking essential) 135 (lunch)/350.

XX **Chez Gabriel,** 123 r. St-Honoré (1st) ✆ 42 33 02 99 – ▤. AE ⓓ GB JCB. ✻ H 14
closed 29 July-26 August, 24 December-3 January, Sunday and Bank Holidays – **M** 150/240.

XX **Le Saint Amour,** 8 r. Port Mahon (2nd) ✆ 47 42 63 82 – ▤. AE ⓓ GB G 13
closed 1 to 22 July, Saturday (except dinner from 1 September-15 June), Sunday and Bank Holidays – **M** 165 and a la carte 210/360.

XX **Escargot Montorgueil,** 38 r. Montorgueil (1st) ✆ 42 36 83 51, Fax 42 36 35 05, « Bistro with 1830 decor » – AE ⓓ GB – **M** 180/290. H 14

XX **Caveau du Palais,** 19 pl. Dauphine (1st) ✆ 43 26 04 28, Fax 43 26 81 84 – AE GB J 14
closed Saturday October-May and Sunday – **M** a la carte 210/330.

XX **Bonne Fourchette,** 320 r. St-Honoré, in the backyard (1st) ✆ 42 60 45 27 – ▤. ⓓ GB.
✻ – *closed August, Sunday lunch and Saturday* – **M** 108/148 ♁. G 12

X **La Main à la Pâte,** 35 r. St-Honoré (1st) ✆ 45 08 85 73 – AE ⓓ GB H 14
closed Sunday – **M** Italian rest. - a la carte 210/330.

X **Aux Petits Pères " Chez Yvonne ",** 8 r. N.-D.-des-Victoires (2nd) ✆ 42 60 91 73 – ▤. AE GB G 14
closed August, Saturday, Sunday and Bank Holidays – **M** 165 and a la carte 200/285.

X **Chez Georges,** 1 r. Mail (2nd) ✆ 42 60 07 11 – ▤. AE GB G 14
closed Sunday and Bank Holidays – **M** a la carte 200/330.

X **La Clef du Périgord,** 38 r. Croix des Petits Champs (1st) ✆ 40 20 06 46 – GB G 14
closed 1 to 15 May, 15 to 31 August, Saturday lunch and Sunday – **M** 155/210 b.i..

X **Cochon Doré,** 16 r. Thorel (2nd) ✆ 42 33 29 70 – ▤. GB F 15
closed Monday – **M** 150 ♁.

X **Paul,** 15 pl. Dauphine (1st) ✆ 43 54 21 48 – GB. ✻ J 14
closed August and Monday – **M** a la carte 180/250.

X **La Poule au Pot,** 9 r. Vauvilliers (1st) ✆ 42 36 32 96 – GB JCB. ✻ H 14
M (dinner only) a la carte 220/350.

Bastille, République, Hôtel de Ville.

3rd, 4th and 11th arrondissements.
3rd: ✉ 75003
4th: ✉ 75004
11th: ✉ 75011

Pavillon de la Reine Ⓜ ⛰ without rest, 28 pl. Vosges (3rd) ✆ 42 77 96 40, Telex 216160, Fax 42 77 63 06 – 🛗 ▤ TV ☎ ♿ 🚗. AE ⓓ GB J 17
☕ 85 – **32 rm** 1250/1650, 23 suites.

Holiday Inn Ⓜ, 10 pl. République (11th) ✆ 43 55 44 34, Telex 210651, Fax 47 00 32 34, 🌂 – 🛗 ⚟ rm ▤ TV ☎ ♿ Ⓟ – 🏛 200. AE ⓓ GB JCB. ✻ rest G 17
Belle Époque *(closed 31 July-31 August, Saturday lunch and Sunday)* **M** 245 (lunch)/410 b.i. – **304 rm** ☕ 1800/3900, 7 suites.

Jeu de Paume Ⓜ without rest, 54 r. St-Louis-en-l'Ile (4th) ✆ 43 26 14 18, Telex 205160, Fax 40 46 02 76, « 17C tennis court » – 🛗 TV ☎ – 🏛 30. AE ⓓ GB JCB K 16
☕ 75 – **32 rm** 870/1130, 8 duplex.

Atlantide République [M] without rest, 114 bd Richard-Lenoir (11th) ✆ 43 38 29 29, Telex 216907, Fax 43 38 03 18 – ▮ TV ☎. AE ⓓ GB — H 18
☕ 35 – **27 rm** 440/660.

Beaubourg [M] without rest, 11 r. S. Le Franc (4th) ✆ 42 74 34 24, Fax 42 78 68 11 – ▮ TV ☎. AE ⓓ GB. ✕ — H 15
☕ 35 – **28 rm** 480/560.

Bretonnerie [M] without rest, 22 r. Ste-Croix-de-la-Bretonnerie (4th) ✆ 48 87 77 63, Fax 42 77 26 78 – ▮ TV ☎. GB. ✕ — J 16
☕ 42 – **30 rm** 620/730.

Méridional [M] without rest, 36 bd Richard-Lenoir (11th) ✆ 48 05 75 00, Fax 43 57 42 85 – ▮ TV ☎. AE ⓓ GB JCB — J 18
☕ 40 – **36 rm** 600.

Lutèce without rest, 65 r. St-Louis-en-l'Ile (4th) ✆ 43 26 23 52, Fax 43 29 60 25 – ▮ TV ☎ — K 16
☕ 40 – **23 rm** 620/770.

Bastille Spéria [M] without rest, 1 r. Bastille (4th) ✆ 42 72 04 01, Telex 214327, Fax 42 72 56 38 – ▮ TV ☎. AE ⓓ GB. ✕ — J 17
☕ 40 – **42 rm** 500/580.

Rivoli Notre Dame without rest, 19 r. Bourg Tibourg (4th) ✆ 42 78 47 39, Telex 215314, Fax 40 29 07 00 – ▮ TV ☎. AE ⓓ GB — J 16
☕ 38 – **31 rm** 480/640.

Bel Air [M] without rest, 5/7 r. Rampon (11th) ✆ 47 00 41 57, Fax 47 00 21 56 – ▮ TV ☎ ♿. AE GB. ✕ — G 17
☕ 40 – **48 rm** 490/640.

Paris Voltaire [M] without rest, 79 r. Sedaine (11th) ✆ 48 05 44 66, Telex 215401, Fax 48 07 87 96 – ▮ TV ☎. AE GB JCB. ✕ — J 9
closed 15 to 31 August and 20 to 26 December – ☕ 35 – **28 rm** 380/500.

Mondia without rest, 22 r. Gd Prieuré (11th) ✆ 47 00 93 44, Fax 43 38 66 14 – ▮ TV ☎. AE ⓓ GB — G 17
☕ 35 – **23 rm** 320/370.

Place des Vosges without rest, 12 r. Birague (4th) ✆ 42 72 60 46, Fax 42 72 02 64 – ▮ ☎. AE ⓓ GB — J 17
☕ 40 – **16 rm** 290/415.

XXXX ✿✿✿ **L'Ambroisie** (Pacaud), 9 pl. des Vosges (4th) ✆ 42 78 51 45 – GB. ✕ — J 17
closed 1 to 23 August, February Holidays, Sunday and Monday – **M** a la carte 580/830
Spec. Blanc de turbot poêlé aux épices. Croquant d'oreille de veau farcie aux rillons de ris de veau. Tarte fine sablée au cacao amer et glace vanille.

XXX ✿ **Miravile** (Epié), 72 quai Hôtel de Ville (4th) ✆ 42 74 72 22, Fax 42 74 67 55 – ▤. AE GB — J 15
closed Saturday lunch and Sunday – **M** 175 (lunch) and a la carte 340/530
Spec. Beignet de foie gras au Porto. Saint-Jacques à la moelle et aux truffes (15 November-15 April). Mokafeuilles au chocolat.

XXX **Ambassade d'Auvergne,** 22 r. Grenier St-Lazare (3rd) ✆ 42 72 31 22, Fax 42 78 85 47 – ▤. AE GB — H 15
closed late July-mid August – **M** a la carte 170/230.

XX **Bofinger,** 5 r. Bastille (4th) ✆ 42 72 87 82, Fax 42 72 97 68, brasserie, « Belle Epoque decor » – AE ⓓ GB — J 17
M 166 b.i. and a la carte 170/260 ♁.

XX ✿ **Benoît,** 20 r. St-Martin (4th) ✆ 42 72 25 76 — J 15
closed August, Saturday and Sunday – **M** a la carte 350/450
Spec. Compotiers de bœuf et museau. Cassoulet. Bœuf mode à l'ancienne.

XX ✿ **A Sousceyrac** (Asfaux), 35 r. Faidherbe (11th) ✆ 43 71 65 30, Fax 40 09 79 75 – ▤. AE GB — J 19
closed August, Saturday lunch and Sunday – **M** 175 (dinner) and a la carte 230/350
Spec. Foie gras en terrine. Ris de veau étuvé entier. Cassoulet comme à Sousceyrac.

XX **Blue Elephant,** 43 r. Roquette (11th) ✆ 47 00 42 00, Fax 47 00 45 44, « Thaï decor » – AE ⓓ GB — J 18
closed Saturday lunch – **M** 150 (lunch)/285 ♁.

XX **Repaire de Cartouche,** 8 bd Filles-du-Calvaire (11th) ✆ 47 00 25 86 – AE ⓓ GB — H 17
closed 27 July-24 August, Saturday lunch and Sunday – **M** 150/350.

XX **L'Aiguière,** 37bis r. Montreuil (11th) ✆ 43 72 42 32 – ▤. AE ◑ GB K 20
closed Saturday lunch and Sunday – **M** 120 (lunch) and a la carte 270/370.

XX **Coconnas,** 2bis pl. Vosges (4th) ✆ 42 78 58 16, 🏖 – GB J 17
closed mid January-mid February, Monday and Tuesday – **M** a la carte 215/300 🍷.

XX **L'Alisier,** 26 r. Montmorency (3rd) ✆ 42 72 31 04, Fax 42 72 74 83 – AE GB. ✈ H 16
closed August, Saturday lunch and Sunday – **M** 149 and a la carte 180/290.

XX **La Table Richelieu,** 276 bd Voltaire (11th) ✆ 43 72 31 23 – ▤. AE GB K 21
closed Saturday lunch – **M** 145 b.i. (lunch) and a la carte 200/345.

XX **Wally,** 16 r. Le Regrattier (4th) ✆ 43 25 01 39, Fax 45 86 08 35 – ◑ GB. ✈ K 15
closed Monday lunch and Sunday – **M** North African rest. 300 b.i..

XX **Les Amognes,** 243 r. Fg St-Antoine (11th) ✆ 43 72 73 05 – GB K 20
closed 1 to 21 August, Sunday and Monday – **M** 160 and a la carte 190/275.

XX **Pyrénées Cévennes,** 106 r. Folie-Méricourt (11th) ✆ 43 57 33 78 – AE GB G 17
closed August, Saturday and Sunday – **M** a la carte 205/320.

XX **Guirlande de Julie,** 25 pl. des Vosges (3rd) ✆ 48 87 94 07, 🏖 – ▤. GB J 17
closed January – **M** a la carte 170/250 🍷.

X **Le Navarin,** 3 av. Philippe Auguste (11th) ✆ 43 67 17 49 – GB JCB K 21
closed Saturday lunch and Sunday – **M** 125 b.i. (lunch) and a la carte 190/350.

X **Le Monde des Chimères,** 69 r. St-Louis-en-l'Ile (4th) ✆ 43 54 45 27 – GB K 16
closed February Holidays, Sunday and Monday – **M** 155 and a la carte 230/310.

X **Le Grizzli,** 7 r. St-Martin (4th) ✆ 48 87 77 56 – AE GB J 15
closed 24 December-3 January, Monday lunch and Sunday – **M** 110 (lunch)/145.

X **Astier,** 44 r. J.-P. Timbaud (11th) ✆ 43 57 16 35 – ▤. GB G 18
closed 24 April-9 May, 31 July-5 September, Christmas Holidays, Saturday, Sunday and Bank Holidays – **M** 135.

X **Le Maraîcher,** 5 r. Beautreillis (4th) ✆ 42 71 42 49 – GB K 17
closed 1 August-3 September, 20 to 26 December, Monday lunch and Sunday – **M** 120 (lunch)/450.

X **Chez Fernand,** 17 r. Fontaine au Roi (11th) ✆ 43 57 46 25 – GB G 18
closed 2 to 23 August, Sunday and Monday – **M** 130 (lunch) and a la carte 160/280 - **Les Fernandises** ✆ 48 06 16 96 **M** 100/130 🍷.

Quartier Latin, Luxembourg, Jardin des Plantes.

5th and 6th arrondissements.
5th: ✉ 75005
6th: ✉ 75006

🏨 **Lutétia,** 45 bd Raspail (6th) ✆ 49 54 46 46, Telex 270424, Fax 49 54 46 00 – 🛗 ▤ TV ☎ – 🏛 400. AE ◑ GB JCB K 12
M see **Le Paris** below - **Brasserie Lutétia** ✆ 49 54 46 76 **M** 150/175 🍷 – ☕ 105 – **252 rm** 1500/2050, 28 suites.

🏨 **Relais Christine** M 🌿 without rest, 3 r. Christine (6th) ✆ 43 26 71 80, Telex 202606, Fax 43 26 89 38, « Attractive installation » – 🛗 TV ☎ 🚗. AE ◑ GB J 14
☕ 85 – **38 rm** 1450, 13 suites.

🏨 **Quality Inn** M without rest, 92 r. Vaugirard (6th) ✆ 42 22 00 56, Telex 206900, Fax 42 22 05 39 – 🛗 🚭 rm ▤ TV ☎ ♿ 🚗. AE ◑ GB JCB L 12
☕ 62 – **134 rm** 785/870.

🏨 **Latitudes St Germain** M without rest, 7-11 r. St-Benoit (6th) ✆ 42 61 53 53, Telex 213531, Fax 49 27 09 33 – 🛗 ▤ TV ☎ ♿. AE ◑ GB J 13
☕ 60 – **117 rm** 930.

🏨 **Victoria Palace** 🌿 without rest, 6 r. Blaise-Desgoffe (6th) ✆ 45 44 38 16, Telex 270557, Fax 45 49 23 75 – 🛗 TV ☎. AE ◑ GB. ✈ L 11
☕ 50 – **110 rm** 820/1300.

🏨 **Littré** 🌿 without rest, 9 r. Littré (6th) ✆ 45 44 38 68, Telex 203852, Fax 45 44 88 13 – 🛗 TV ☎ – 🏛 25. AE ◑ GB JCB. ✈ L 11
☕ 50 – **93 rm** 685/910, 4 suites.

🏨 **Madison H.** without rest, 143 bd St-Germain (6th) ✆ 40 51 60 00, Telex 201628, Fax 40 51 60 01 – 🛗 ▤ TV ☎. AE ◑ GB J 13
55 rm ☕ 680/1220.

🏨 **St-Grégoire** M without rest, 43 r. Abbé Grégoire (6th) ✆ 45 48 23 23, Telex 205343, Fax 45 48 33 95 – 🛗 TV ☎. AE ◑ GB JCB. ✈ L 12
☕ 60 – **20 rm** 720/1200.

Abbaye St-Germain without rest, 10 r. Cassette (6th) 45 44 38 11, Fax 45 48 07 86 - AE GB. K 12
46 rm 800/1500, 4 duplex.

Relais Médicis [M] without rest, 23 r. Racine (6th) 43 26 00 60, Fax 40 46 83 39, « Tasteful decor » - AE GB K 13
16 rm 1130/1480.

Relais St Germain [M] without rest, 9 carrefour de l'Odéon (6th) 43 29 12 05, Telex 201889, Fax 46 33 45 30, « Attractive installation » - AE GB K 13
60 - **10 rm** 1230/1430.

Sainte Beuve [M] without rest, 9 r. Ste Beuve (6th) 45 48 20 07, Telex 270182, Fax 45 48 67 52 - AE GB JCB. L 12
80 - **23 rm** 650/1250.

Left Bank H. [M] without rest, 11 r. Ancienne Comédie (6th) 43 54 01 70, Telex 200502, Fax 43 26 17 14 - AE GB JCB K 13
30 - **30 rm** 895/990.

La Villa [M] without rest, 29 r. Jacob (6th) 43 26 60 00, Telex 202437, Fax 46 34 63 63, « Contemporary decor » - AE GB J 13
80 - **29 rm** 1100/1950, 3 suites.

Angleterre without rest, 44 r. Jacob (6th) 42 60 34 72, Fax 42 60 16 93 - AE GB. J 13
45 - **29 rm** 800/1200.

St-Germain-des-Prés without rest, 36 r. Bonaparte (6th) 43 26 00 19, Telex 200409, Fax 40 46 83 63, « Attractive installation » - GB. J 13
30 rm 800/1200.

Villa des Artistes [M] without rest, 9 r. Grande Chaumière (6th) 43 26 60 86, Telex 204080, Fax 43 54 73 70 - AE GB. L 12
59 rm 600/800.

Ferrandi without rest, 92 r. Cherche-Midi (6th) 42 22 97 40, Fax 45 44 89 97 - AE GB JCB. L 11
60 - **41 rm** 440/900.

Panthéon [M] without rest, 19 pl. Panthéon (5th) 43 54 32 95, Telex 206435, Fax 43 26 64 65, ← - AE GB. L 14
35 - **34 rm** 615/730.

Grands Hommes [M] without rest, 17 pl. Panthéon (5th) 46 34 19 60, Telex 200185, Fax 43 26 67 32, ← - AE GB. L 14
35 - **32 rm** 615/730.

Résidence Henri IV [M] without rest, 50 r. Bernardins (5th) 44 41 31 81, Fax 46 33 93 22 - kitchenette AE GB. K 15
40 - **9 rm** 900, 5 suites.

des Saints-Pères without rest, 65 r. Sts-Pères (6th) 45 44 50 00, Fax 45 44 90 83 - GB. J 12
50 - **34 rm** 450/1500, 3 suites.

Odéon H., [M] without rest, 3 r. Odéon (6th) 43 25 90 67, Telex 202943, Fax 43 25 55 98 - AE GB. K 13
55 - **34 rm** 700/1100.

de Fleurie without rest, 32 r. Grégoire de Tours (6th) 43 29 59 81, Telex 206153, Fax 43 29 68 44 - AE GB. K 13
50 - **29 rm** 580/1100.

Le Régent [M] without rest, 61 r. Dauphine (6th) 46 34 59 80, Telex 206257, Fax 40 51 05 07 - AE GB JCB J 13
50 - **25 rm** 750/900.

Parc St-Séverin [M] without rest, 22 r. Parcheminerie (5th) 43 54 32 17, Fax 43 54 70 71 - AE GB. K 14
50 - **27 rm** 450/1500.

St Christophe [M] without rest, 17 r. Lacépède (5th) 43 31 81 54, Fax 43 31 12 54 - AE GB JCB L 15
40 - **31 rm** 650.

Select [M] without rest, 1 pl. Sorbonne (5th) 46 34 14 80, Telex 201207, Fax 46 34 51 79 - AE GB K 14
30 - **67 rm** 650/780.

Belloy St-Germain [M] without rest, 2 r. Racine (6th) 46 34 26 50, Telex 206234, Fax 46 34 66 18 - AE GB JCB K 14
40 - **50 rm** 860.

Elysa Luxembourg [M] without rest, 6 r. Gay-Lussac (5th) 43 25 31 74, Telex 206881, Fax 46 34 56 27 - AE GB. L 14
35 - **30 rm** 595/695.

Aramis St Germain without rest, 124 r. Rennes (6th) 45 48 03 75, Telex 205098, Fax 45 44 99 29 - - 30. AE GB JCB. L 12
45 - **42 rm** 650/850.

de l'Odéon without rest, 13 r. St-Sulpice (6th) ✆ 43 25 70 11, Telex 206731, Fax 43 29 97 34, « 16C setting » – |‡| ▤ TV ☎. AE ⓓ GB K 13
☕ 42 – **29 rm** 580/830.

Jardin des Plantes M without rest, 5 r. Linné (5th) ✆ 47 07 06 20, Telex 203684, Fax 47 07 62 74 – |‡| TV ☎. AE ⓓ GB L 15
☕ 40 – **33 rm** 390/640.

Jardin de Cluny without rest, 9 r. Sommerard (5th) ✆ 43 54 22 66, Telex 206975, Fax 40 51 03 36 – |‡| TV ☎. AE ⓓ GB JCB. ✻ K 14
☕ 45 – **40 rm** 530/700.

Notre Dame M without rest, 1 quai St-Michel (5th) ✆ 43 54 20 43, Telex 206650, Fax 43 26 61 75, ← – |‡| TV ☎. AE ⓓ GB JCB K 14
☕ 37 – **23 rm** 490/790, 3 duplex.

Albe M without rest, 1 r. Harpe (5th) ✆ 46 34 09 70, Telex 203328, Fax 40 46 85 70 – |‡| TV ☎. AE ⓓ GB JCB. ✻ K 14
☕ 35 – **45 rm** 478/554.

Louis II without rest, 2 r. St-Sulpice (6th) ✆ 46 33 13 80, Fax 46 33 17 29 – |‡| TV ☎. AE ⓓ GB K 13
☕ 38 – **22 rm** 460/680.

Marronniers ⛰ without rest, 21 r. Jacob (6th) ✆ 43 25 30 60, Fax 40 46 83 56 – |‡| ☎. ✻
☕ 45 – **37 rm** 620/680. J 13

Nations without rest, 54 r. Monge (5th) ✆ 43 26 45 24, Telex 200397, Fax 46 34 00 13 – |‡| TV ☎. AE ⓓ GB JCB L 15
☕ 55 – **38 rm** 550/600.

La Sorbonne without rest, 6 r. Victor Cousin (5th) ✆ 43 54 58 08, Telex 206373, Fax 40 51 05 18 – |‡| TV ☎. GB K 14
☕ 35 – **37 rm** 400/500.

Gd H. Suez without rest, 31 bd St-Michel (5th) ✆ 46 34 08 02, Telex 202019, Fax 40 51 79 44 – |‡| TV ☎. AE ⓓ GB JCB. ✻ K 14
49 rm ☕ 360/495.

XXXXX ✿✿✿ **Tour d'Argent** (Terrail), 15 quai Tournelle (5th) ✆ 43 54 23 31, Fax 44 07 12 04, « ← Notre-Dame, small museum showing the development of eating utensils. In the cellar : an illustrated history of wine » – AE ⓓ GB K 16
closed Monday – **M** 375 (lunch) and a la carte 680/990
Spec. Quenelles de brochet André Terrail. Caneton Tour d'Argent. Flambée de pêches.

XXX ✿✿ **Jacques Cagna,** 14 r. Gds Augustins (6th) ✆ 43 26 49 39, Fax 43 54 54 48, « Old Parisian house » – ▤. AE ⓓ GB JCB J 14
closed 1 to 23 August, Saturday lunch and Sunday – **M** 260 (lunch) and a la carte 500/630
Spec. Beignets de langoustines aux chips d'artichaut. Filet de barbue farci d'huîtres, sauce cresson. Poularde de Houdan en deux services.

XXX ✿ **Paris** - Hôtel Lutétia, 45 bd Raspail (6th) ✆ 49 54 46 90, Telex 270424, Fax 49 54 46 00, « Transatlantic liner theme in Art Deco style » – ▤. AE ⓓ GB JCB K 12
closed August, February Holidays, Saturday, Sunday and Bank Holidays – **M** 250 (lunch) and a la carte 380/470
Spec. Ravioles de tourteau au chou vert. Tronçon de turbot rôti au lard et rattes du Touquet. Carré de porc braisé, pommes fondantes aux champignons des bois.

XXX ✿ **Relais Louis XIII,** 1 r. Pont de Lodi (6th) ✆ 43 26 75 96, Fax 44 07 07 80, « 16C cellar, fine furniture » – ▤. AE ⓓ GB JCB J 14
closed 19 July-22 August, Monday lunch and Sunday – **M** a la carte 430/570
Spec. Ravioli de langoustines à l'estragon. Saint-Jacques en feuilles croustillantes à l'étuvée de légumes (October-April). Filet de bœuf aux truffes.

XXX **Lapérouse,** 51 quai Gds Augustins (6th) ✆ 43 26 68 04, Fax 43 26 99 39, « Belle Epoque decor » – ▤. AE ⓓ GB. ✻ J 14
closed 8 to 24 août, Monday lunch and Sunday – **M** 390/540.

XXX **Le Procope,** 13 r. Ancienne Comédie (6th) ✆ 43 26 99 20, Fax 43 54 16 86, « Former 18C literary café » – AE ⓓ GB K 13
M 289 b.i. and a la carte 170/310 ♨.

XX **Aub. des Deux Signes,** 46 r. Galande (5th) ✆ 43 25 46 56, Fax 46 33 20 49, « Medieval decor » – AE ⓓ GB JCB K 14
closed August, Saturday lunch and Sunday – **M** 140 (lunch) and a la carte 300/500.

XX **Au Pactole,** 44 bd St-Germain (5th) ✆ 46 33 31 31, Fax 46 33 07 60 – AE GB JCB K 15
closed Saturday lunch and Sunday – **M** 149/279.

XX ✿ **Dodin-Bouffant,** 25 r. F.-Sauton (5th) ☎ 43 25 25 14, Fax 43 29 52 61, ☂ - ▤. AE ⓓ GB JCB K 15
closed 8 to 22 August, Christmas-New Year and Sunday - **M** 195 and a la carte 350/400
Spec. Foie gras. Daube d'huîtres et pied de porc. Soufflé chaud aux fruits de saison.

XX **Calvet,** 165 bd St-Germain (6th) ☎ 45 48 93 51 - ▤. AE ⓓ GB JCB J 12
closed August - **M** 139/195.

XX **Campagne et Provence,** 25 quai Tournelle (5th) ☎ 43 54 05 17, Fax 42 74 67 55 - ▤. GB
closed Saturday lunch and Sunday - **M** a la carte approx. 190. K 15

XX **Yugaraj,** 14 r. Dauphine (6th) ☎ 43 26 44 91 - ▤. AE ⓓ JCB. ✗ J 14
closed Monday lunch - **M** Indian rest. 130 (lunch) and a la carte 190/260.

XX **L'Arrosée,** 12 r. Guisarde (6th) ☎ 43 54 66 59 - ▤. AE ⓓ GB JCB. ✗ K 13
closed 2 to 9 January, lunch Saturday and Sunday - **M** 145/350.

XX **La Truffière,** 4 r. Blainville (5th) ☎ 46 33 29 82 - ▤. AE ⓓ GB L 15
closed Sunday and Monday - **M** 105/180 ♁.

XX **La Petite Cour,** 8 r. Mabillon (6th) ☎ 43 26 52 26, ☂ - GB K 13
M 165 (lunch)/185.

XX **Marty,** 20 av. Gobelins (5th) ☎ 43 31 39 51, Fax 43 37 63 70 - AE ⓓ GB M 15
M 159 b.i. and a la carte 170/330.

XX ✿ **La Timonerie** (de Givenchy), 35 quai Tournelle (5th) ☎ 43 25 44 42 - ▤. GB K 15
closed 22 to 28 February, Sunday and Monday - **M** 195 (lunch) and a la carte 280/400
Spec. Fleurs de courgettes aux aubergines (June-September). Foie gras rôti sur pomme de terre (October-February). Tarte fine au chocolat.

XX **L'Arbuci,** 25 r. Buci (6th) ☎ 44 41 14 14, Fax 44 41 14 10 - ▤. GB J 13
M a la carte 150/300.

XX **La Marlotte,** 55 r. Cherche Midi (6th) ☎ 45 48 86 79 - AE ⓓ GB JCB. ✗ K 12
closed August and Sunday - **M** a la carte 190/300.

XX **Bistrot d'Alex,** 2 r. Clément (6th) ☎ 43 54 09 53 - ▤. AE GB JCB K 13
closed 24 December-2 January and Sunday - **M** 140/190 ♁.

XX **Au Régent,** 97 r. Cherche Midi (6th) ☎ 42 22 32 44 - AE ⓓ GB L 11
closed 26 July-23 August, Sunday and Monday - **M** 170 and a la carte 210/350 ♁.

XX **Petit Germain,** 11 r. Dupin (6th) ☎ 42 22 64 56 - AE GB K 12
closed 10 to 19 April, 7 to 30 August, Saturday and Sunday - **M** a la carte 180/270.

XX **Le Sybarite,** 6 r. Sabot (6th) ☎ 42 22 21 56, Fax 42 22 26 21 - ▤. AE ⓓ GB K 12
closed 2 to 29 August, Saturday lunch and Sunday - **M** 78 (lunch)/170.

XX **Joséphine** "Chez Dumonet", 117 r. Cherche Midi (6th) ☎ 45 48 52 40, Fax 42 84 06 83 - GB L 11
closed July, Saturday and Sunday - **M** 170 b.i. (lunch) and a la carte 230/370 - **La Rôtisserie** ☎ 42 22 81 19 *(closed August, Monday and Tuesday)* **M** 140 b.i. (lunch) and a la carte 170/290.

XX **Chez Maître Paul,** 12 r. Monsieur-le-Prince (6th) ☎ 43 54 74 59 - AE ⓓ GB K 13
closed Saturday lunch and Sunday - **M** 180 b.i. and a la carte 160/300.

XX **Au Grilladin,** 13 r. Mézières (6th) ☎ 45 48 30 38 - AE GB K 12
closed August, 23 December-4 January, Monday lunch and Sunday - **M** 154 and a la carte 190/280.

XX **Chez Toutoune,** 5 r. Pontoise (5th) ☎ 43 26 56 81 - AE GB K 15
closed Monday lunch and Sunday - **M** 179.

X **Allard,** 41 r. St-André-des-Arts (6th) ☎ 43 26 48 23 - AE ⓓ GB K 14
closed 31 July-1 September, 23 December-3 January, Saturday and Sunday - **M** brasserie a la carte 280/400.

X **Moissonnier,** 28 r. Fossés-St-Bernard (5th) ☎ 43 29 87 65 - GB K 15
closed 31 July-7 September, Sunday dinner and Monday - **M** a la carte 150/220.

X **Moulin à Vent "Chez Henri",** 20 r. Fossés-St-Bernard (5th) ☎ 43 54 99 37 - GB. ✗
closed 1 August-1 September, Sunday and Monday - **M** a la carte 240/470. K 15

X **Rôtisserie du Beaujolais,** 19 quai Tournelle (5th) ☎ 43 54 17 47, Fax 44 07 12 04 - GB K 15
closed Monday - **M** 160 b.i./230 b.i.

X **Rôtisserie d'en Face,** 2 r. Christine (6th) ☎ 43 26 40 98 - ▤. GB J 14
closed Saturday lunch and Sunday - **M** 180.

X **Le Palanquin,** 12 r. Princesse (6th) ☎ 43 29 77 66 - GB K 13
closed 8 to 22 August and Sunday - **M** Vietnamese rest. 118/149.

X **Balzar,** 49 r. Écoles (5th) ☎ 43 54 13 67, ☂ - AE ⓓ GB K 14
closed August and 24 December-1 January - **M** brasserie a la carte 140/270.

X **Valérie Tortu,** 11 r. Grande Chaumière (6th) ☎ 46 34 07 58 - GB L 12
closed August, Saturday lunch and Sunday - **M** 78/145.

X **La Vigneraie,** 16 r. Dragon (6th) ☎ 45 48 57 04 - AE ⓓ GB J 12
closed August, Sunday lunch and Monday - **M** 168 and a la carte 210/310.

Faubourg-St-Germain, Invalides, École Militaire.

7th arrondissement.
7th: ✉ 75007

Pont Royal and rest. Les Antiquaires, 7 r. Montalembert ✆ 45 44 38 27, Fax 45 44 92 07 - |‡| ▤ TV ☎ - 30. AE ⓓ GB J 12
M *(closed 31 July-1 September, 23 December-4 January, Saturday and Sunday)* 160 - **74 rm** ☕ 1000/1600, 4 suites.

Montalembert M, 3 r. Montalembert ✆ 45 48 68 11, Telex 200132, Fax 42 22 58 19, « Original decor » - |‡| ▤ TV ☎ - 25. AE ⓓ GB J 12
M 170 and a la carte 230/340 - ☕ 95 - **51 rm** 1525/1950, 5 suites.

Duc de Saint-Simon without rest, 14 r. St-Simon ✆ 45 48 35 66, Telex 203277, Fax 45 48 68 25, « Tastefully furnished interior » - |‡| TV ☎. J 11
☕ 70 - **29 rm** 1000/1500, 5 suites.

Cayré M without rest, 4 bd Raspail ✆ 45 44 38 88, Telex 270577, Fax 45 44 98 13 - |‡| ▤ TV ☎. AE ⓓ GB JCB J 12
126 rm ☕ 1250/1600.

La Bourdonnais, 111 av. La Bourdonnais ✆ 47 05 45 42, Telex 201416, Fax 45 55 75 54 - |‡| TV ☎ ♿. ⓓ GB JCB J 9
M see rest. **La Cantine des Gourmets** below - **60 rm** ☕ 465/650.

Eiffel Park H. M without rest, 17 bis r. Amélie ✆ 45 55 10 01, Telex 202950, Fax 47 05 28 68 - |‡| TV ☎ ♿ - 40. AE ⓓ GB JCB. J 9
☕ 49 - **36 rm** 735/930.

Les Jardins d'Eiffel M without rest, 8 r. Amélie ✆ 47 05 46 21, Telex 206582, Fax 45 55 28 08 - |‡| rm ▤ TV ☎. AE ⓓ GB JCB H 9
44 rm ☕ 690/850.

Bellechasse M without rest, 8 r. Bellechasse ✆ 45 50 22 31, Fax 45 51 52 36 - |‡| rm TV ☎ ♿. AE ⓓ GB H 11
☕ 60 - **43 rm** 650/720.

Bersoly's without rest, 28 r. Lille ✆ 42 60 73 79, Fax 49 27 05 55 - |‡| TV ☎. GB J 13
closed August - ☕ 50 - **16 rm** 580/680.

Sèvres Vaneau M without rest, 86 r. Vaneau ✆ 45 48 73 11, Fax 45 49 27 74 - |‡| rm TV ☎. AE ⓓ GB K 11
☕ 60 - **39 rm** 650/720.

Splendid M without rest, 29 av. Tourville ✆ 45 51 24 77, Telex 206879, Fax 44 18 94 60 - |‡| TV ☎ ♿. AE ⓓ GB. J 9
☕ 42 - **45 rm** 560/760.

Londres M without rest, 1 r. Augereau ✆ 45 51 63 02, Telex 206398, Fax 47 05 28 96 - |‡| TV ☎. AE ⓓ GB JCB J 8
☕ 40 - **30 rm** 470/590.

Lenox Saint-Germain without rest, 9 r. Université ✆ 42 96 10 95, Fax 42 61 52 83 - |‡| TV ☎. AE ⓓ GB. J 12
☕ 45 - **32 rm** 530/870.

Suède without rest, 31 r. Vaneau ✆ 47 05 00 08, Telex 200596, Fax 47 05 69 27 - |‡| ☎. AE GB. K 11
40 rm ☕ 560/880.

Bourgogne et Montana, 3 r. Bourgogne ✆ 45 51 20 22, Telex 270854, Fax 45 56 11 98 - |‡| ▤ rest TV ☎. AE ⓓ GB H 11
M *(closed 1 to 21 August, Saturday and Sunday)* a la carte approx. 160 - ☕ 60 - **28 rm** 770/1080, 5 suites.

St-Germain without rest, 88 r. Bac ✆ 45 48 62 92, Fax 45 48 26 89 - |‡| TV ☎. AE GB. J 11
☕ 39 - **29 rm** 350/680.

Beaugency M without rest, 21 r. Duvivier ✆ 47 05 01 63, Telex 201494, Fax 45 51 04 96 - |‡| TV ☎. AE ⓓ GB J 9
☕ 30 - **30 rm** 500/600.

Élysées Maubourg M without rest, 35 bd La Tour-Maubourg ✆ 45 56 10 78, Telex 206227, Fax 47 05 65 08 - |‡| TV ☎. AE ⓓ GB JCB H 10
☕ 40 - **29 rm** 540/1000.

De Varenne without rest, 44 r. Bourgogne 45 51 45 55, Telex 205329, Fax 45 51 86 63 – AE GB J 10
40 – **24 rm** 470/630.

France without rest, 102 bd La Tour-Maubourg 47 05 40 49, Telex 205020, Fax 45 56 96 78 – AE GB. J 9
35 – **60 rm** 330/450.

Solférino without rest, 91 r. Lille 47 05 85 54, Telex 203865, Fax 45 55 51 16 – GB. H 11
closed 22 December-3 January – 35 – **32 rm** 245/598.

L'Empereur without rest, 2 r. Chevert 45 55 88 02, Fax 45 51 88 54 – GB
36 – **34 rm** 420/460. J 9

Mars H. without rest, 117 av. La Bourdonnais 47 05 42 30, Fax 47 05 45 91, « Collection of tobacco jars » – GB. J 9
40 – **24 rm** 330/400.

Champ de Mars without rest, 7 r. Champ de Mars 45 51 52 30 – GB J 9
closed 12 to 29 August – 35 – **25 rm** 340/400.

Résidence Orsay without rest, 93 r. Lille 47 05 05 27, Fax 47 05 29 48 – GB.
closed August – 30 – **32 rm** 200/440. H 11

XXXX **Jules Verne,** Eiffel Tower : 2nd platform, lift in south leg 45 55 61 44, Telex 205789, Fax 47 05 94 40, ≤ Paris – AE GB. J 7
M 290 (lunch) and a la carte 430/660.

XXXX ✿✿ **Le Divellec,** 107 r. Université 45 51 91 96, Fax 45 51 31 75 – AE GB JCB.
closed August, 24 December-3 January, Sunday and Monday – **M** Seafood 270/370 (lunch) and a la carte 400/680 H 10
Spec. Homard à la presse avec son corail. Filet de barbue au vin de Champagne et salpicon d'huîtres. Marinière de langues de morue aux coquillages.

XXXX ✿✿ **Arpège** (Passard), 84 r. Varenne 45 51 47 33, Fax 44 18 98 39 – AE GB
closed Sunday lunch and Saturday – **M** 290/790 and a la carte 460/750 J 10
Spec. Homard et navet en vinaigrette aigre-douce. Canard "Louise Passard". Feuilletage au chocolat.

XXXX ✿✿ **Duquesnoy,** 6 av. Bosquet 47 05 96 78, Fax 44 18 90 57 – AE GB H 9
closed 1 to 14 August, Saturday lunch and Sunday – **M** 250 (lunch)/520 and a la carte 420/640
Spec. Ballotines de Saint-Jacques et saumon fumé (October-May). Rouelles d'abats de la "saint cochon". Dessert au chocolat.

XXX ✿ **La Cantine des Gourmets,** 113 av. La Bourdonnais 47 05 47 96, Fax 45 51 09 29 – AE GB JCB J 9
M 220 b.i. (lunch)/380 and a la carte 300/450
Spec. Soufflé de homard, soupe de crustacés. Meunière de turbot, tourte de pommes de terre. Millefeuille de veau fermier et lasagnes à l'estragon.

XXX **La Flamberge,** 12 av. Rapp 47 05 91 37, Fax 47 23 60 98 – AE GB. H 8
closed 14 to 21 August, Saturday lunch and Sunday – **M** 230 and a la carte 260/400.

XXX **Chez les Anges,** 54 bd La Tour-Maubourg 47 05 89 86, Fax 45 56 03 83 – AE GB JCB J 9
closed Sunday dinner and Bank Holidays – **M** 230/320 b.i.

XXX ✿ **La Boule d'Or,** 13 bd La Tour-Maubourg 47 05 50 18 – AE GB JCB H 10
closed Saturday lunch and Monday – **M** 195/360 and a la carte 250/370
Spec. Foie gras de canard. Tourte de langoustines aux poireaux. Soufflé chaud au citron.

XXX **Beato,** 8 r. Malar 47 05 94 27 – AE GB. H 9
closed 1 to 22 August, 25 December-2 January, Sunday and Monday – **M** Italian rest. 145 (lunch) and a la carte 230/320.

XXX **Foc Ly,** 71 av. Suffren 47 83 27 12 – AE GB K 8
M Chinese and Thai rest. 100 (lunch)/160 b.i.

XX ✿ **Ferme St-Simon** (Vandenhende), 6 r. St-Simon 45 48 35 74, Fax 40 49 07 31 – AE GB J 11
closed 1 to 21 August, Saturday lunch and Sunday – **M** 160 (lunch) and a la carte 260/360
Spec. Mesclum de coquillages et crustacés à l'huile de homard (January-September). Ballotine de lièvre en feuilleté (October-December). Millefeuille aux fruits rouges (April-September).

XX ✿ **Récamier** (Cantegrit), 4 r. Récamier 45 48 86 58, Fax 42 22 84 76, – AE GB JCB K 12
closed Sunday – **M** a la carte 280/440
Spec. Œufs en meurette. Mousse de brochet sauce Nantua. Sauté de bœuf bourguignon.

XX **Au Quai d'Orsay,** 49 quai d'Orsay ✆ 45 51 58 58 – AE GB H 9
M 180 and a la carte 250/360.

XX **Chez Marius,** 5 r. Bourgogne ✆ 45 51 79 42 – ▤. AE ⓓ GB H 11
closed 1 to 30 August, Saturday lunch and Sunday – **M** 180/450.

XX ✿ **Le Bellecour** (Goutagny), 22 r. Surcouf ✆ 45 51 46 93, Fax 45 50 30 11 – AE ⓓ GB H 9
closed 1 to 21 August, Saturday (except dinner 1 October-1 July) and Sunday – **M** 160 (lunch)/380 and a la carte 285/425
Spec. Langoustines rôties aux cheveux de poireaux frits (March-October). Turbot rôti à la crème de carotte et cumin. Lièvre à la cuillère (October-January).

XX **Le Petit Laurent,** 38 r. Varenne ✆ 45 48 79 64, Fax 45 44 15 95 – AE ⓓ GB J 11
closed 1 to 23 August, Saturday lunch and Sunday – **M** 175/240.

XX **Giulio Rebellato,** 20 r. Monttessuy ✆ 45 55 79 01 – ▤. AE GB. ✖ H 8
closed August, Saturday lunch and Sunday – **M** Italian rest. 180 b.i. and a la carte 230/350.

XX **D'Chez Eux,** 2 av. Lowendal ✆ 47 05 52 55 – AE ⓓ GB J 9
closed August and Sunday – **M** a la carte 240/400.

XX **Les Glénan,** 54 r. Bourgogne ✆ 47 05 96 65 – ▤. AE GB J 10
closed August, 1 to 7 January, Saturday and Sunday – **M** Seafood 240 (dinner)/350 ♁.

XX **Aux Délices de Szechuen,** 40 av. Duquesne ✆ 43 06 22 55, ☂ – ▤. AE GB K 10
closed 27 July-24 August and Monday – **M** Chinese rest. 96 (except Sunday) and a la carte 155/260 ♁.

XX **Le Club,** (Au Bon Marché) 38 r. Sèvres - 1st floor magasin 2 ✆ 45 48 95 25, Fax 45 49 27 99 – ▤. AE ⓓ GB K 11
closed August and Sunday – **M** (lunch only) 149 and a la carte 180/275.

XX **Chez Ribe,** 15 av. Suffren ✆ 45 66 53 79 – AE ⓓ GB J 7
closed 15 to 31 August, Saturday lunch and Sunday – **M** 168 ♁.

XX **Tan Dinh,** 60 r. Verneuil ✆ 45 44 04 84, Fax 45 44 36 93 J 12
closed August and Sunday – **M** Vietnamese rest. - a la carte 230/270.

XX **Gildo,** 153 r. Grenelle ✆ 45 51 54 12, Fax 45 51 57 42 – ▤. GB J 9
closed 25 July-25 August, 23 December-3 January, Monday lunch and Sunday. – **M** Italian rest. 160 (lunch) and a la carte 230/340.

XX **Le Champ de Mars,** 17 av. La Motte-Picquet ✆ 47 05 57 99 – AE ⓓ GB J 9
closed 18 July-25 August, Tuesday dinner and Monday – **M** 118/159.

XX **Clémentine,** 62 av. Bosquet ✆ 45 51 41 16 – GB J 9
closed 15 to 31 August, 24 December-1 January, Saturday lunch and Sunday – **M** 168.

X **Le Maupertu,** 94 bd La Tour Maubourg ✆ 45 51 37 96 – GB. ✖ J 10
closed 7 to 29 August, 13 to 20 February, Saturday lunch and Sunday – **M** 130 and a la carte 200/300.

X **Vin sur Vin,** 20 r. Monttessuy ✆ 47 05 14 20 – GB H 8
closed 1 to 7 May, 12 to 31 August, 22 December-3 January, Monday lunch, Saturday lunch and Sunday – **M** a la carte 250/350.

X **L'Oeillade,** 10 r. St-Simon ✆ 42 22 01 60 – ▤. GB J 11
closed 15 to 31 August, Saturday lunch and Sunday – **M** 155.

X **Chez Collinot,** 1 r. P. Leroux ✆ 45 67 66 42 – GB K 11
closed August, Saturday and Sunday – **M** 130 and a la carte 170/290.

X **Bistrot de Breteuil,** 3 pl. Breteuil ✆ 45 67 07 27, Fax 42 73 11 08, ☂ – GB L 10
M 172 b.i.

X **Nuit de St-Jean,** 29 r. Surcouf ✆ 45 51 61 49, Fax 47 05 36 40 – AE ⓓ GB. ✖ H 9
closed 17 to 26 April, 1 to 15 August, 24 December-3 January, Saturday lunch and Sunday – **M** 120 and a la carte 140/210.

X **La Calèche,** 8 r. Lille ✆ 42 60 24 76 – AE ⓓ GB J 12
closed 11 to 31 August, Christmas-New Year, Saturday and Sunday – **M** 130/170.

X **Le Sédillot,** 2 r. Sédillot ✆ 45 51 95 82, « New Art decor » – AE GB H 8
closed Saturday lunch and Sunday – **M** 120.

X **Le P'tit Troquet,** 28 r. Exposition ✆ 47 05 80 39 – GB J 9
M 115/135 ♁.

X **Thoumieux,** 79 r. St Dominique ✆ 47 05 49 75, Fax 47 05 36 96 – ▤. GB H 9
M a la carte 100/200.

X **La Fontaine de Mars,** 129 r. St-Dominique ✆ 47 05 46 44 – GB J 9
closed Sunday – **M** a la carte 150/230.

X **Du Côté 7ème,** 29 r. Surcouf ✆ 47 05 81 65 – AE GB H 9-10
M 175 b.i.

X **La Ferronnerie,** 18 r. Chaise ✆ 45 49 22 43 – GB K 12
closed 8 to 22 August, Monday lunch and Sunday – **M** 150 (lunch) and a la carte 180/270 ♁.

Champs-Élysées, St-Lazare, Madeleine.

8th arrondissement.
8th: ✉ 75008

Plaza-Athénée, 25 av. Montaigne ✆ 47 23 78 33, Telex 650092, Fax 47 20 20 70 – rm – 30 - 100. AE GB JCB G 9
M see rest. **Régence and Relais Plaza** below – ☕ 120 – **211 rm** 2660/4160, 42 suites.

Crillon, 10 pl. Concorde ✆ 44 71 15 00, Telex 290204, Fax 44 71 15 02 – – 30 - 60. AE GB JCB. rest G 11
M see **Les Ambassadeurs** below - **L'Obélisque** ✆ 44 71 15 15 *(closed August and Bank Holidays)* **M** 250 – ☕ 140 – **122 rm** 2600/3900, 41 suites.

Bristol, 112 r. Fg St-Honoré ✆ 42 66 91 45, Telex 280961, Fax 42 66 68 68, , – rm – 30 - 60. AE GB JCB. F 10
M see **Bristol** below – ☕ 140 – **152 rm** 2450/3500, 45 suites.

George V, 31 av. George-V ✆ 47 23 54 00, Telex 650082, Fax 47 20 40 00, – rm – 350 - 600. AE GB JCB G 8
M see **Les Princes** and **Le Grill** below – ☕ 115 – **298 rm** 1930/3850, 53 suites.

Royal Monceau, 37 av. Hoche ✆ 45 61 98 00, Telex 650361, Fax 45 63 28 93, , « Pool and fitness centre » – – 30 - 300. AE GB JCB. E 8
Le Jardin M 280 (lunch) and a la carte 330/490 – **Carpaccio** Italian rest. *(closed August)* **M** 280 (lunch) and a la carte 300/440 – ☕ 135 – **180 rm** 1950/2950, 39 suites.

Prince de Galles, 33 av. George-V ✆ 47 23 55 11, Telex 651627, Fax 47 20 96 92, – rm – 40 - 110. AE GB JCB G 8
M (Sunday Brunch only 250) 235/600 – ☕ 110 – **141 rm** 2600/2800, 30 suites.

Vernet, 25 r. Vernet ✆ 47 23 43 10, Telex 651357, Fax 40 70 10 14 – . AE GB. rest F 8
M see **Les Élysées** below – ☕ 100 – **60 rm** 1450/2200, 3 suites.

De Vigny M without rest, 9 r. Balzac ✆ 40 75 04 39, Telex 651822, Fax 40 75 05 81, « Tasteful decor » – rm . AE GB F 8
☕ 90 – **25 rm** 1700/2200, 12 suites.

San Régis, 12 r. J. Goujon ✆ 43 59 41 90, Telex 643637, Fax 45 61 05 48, « Tasteful decor » – rm . AE GB. G 9
M a la carte 275/415 – ☕ 100 – **34 rm** 1400/2625, 10 suites.

La Trémoille, 14 r. La Trémoille ✆ 47 23 34 20, Telex 640344, Fax 40 70 01 08 – – 35. AE GB JCB G 9
M 195 and a la carte 260/400 – ☕ 100 – **94 rm** 1910/2870, 14 suites.

Lancaster, 7 r. Berri ✆ 43 59 90 43, Telex 640991, Fax 42 89 22 71, – rm . AE GB JCB F 9
M 230 and a la carte 300/470 – ☕ 110 – **52 rm** 1950/2550, 7 suites.

Élysées Star M without rest, 19 r. Vernet ✆ 47 20 41 73, Telex 651153, Fax 47 23 32 15 – rm – 30. AE GB F 8
☕ 90 – **38 rm** 1700/1900, 4 suites.

Warwick M, 5 r. Berri ✆ 45 63 14 11, Telex 642295, Fax 42 56 77 59 – rm – 30 - 110. AE GB. rest F 9
M see **La Couronne** below – ☕ 105 – **142 rm** 2030/2560, 5 suites.

Balzac M, 6 r. Balzac ✆ 45 61 97 22, Telex 651298, Fax 42 25 24 82 – . AE GB F 8
Bice ✆ 42 89 86 34 - Italian rest. *(closed 8 to 30 August, 22 December-3 January, Saturday lunch and Sunday)* **M** a la carte 280/380 – ☕ 90 – **56 rm** 1550/2100, 14 suites.

Golden Tulip St-Honoré M, 220 r. Fg St-Honoré ✆ 49 53 03 03, Telex 650657, Fax 40 75 02 00, , – kitchenette rm – 120. AE GB JCB. E 8
Relais Vermeer M 210 and a la carte 275/420 – ☕ 110 – **52 rm** 1550/1850, 20 suites.

Relais Carré d'Or M, 46 av. George V ✆ 40 70 05 05, Telex 640561, Fax 47 23 30 90, , – kitchenette . AE GB JCB. F 8
M *(closed Saturday, Sunday and Bank Holidays)* 215 (lunch)/315, 18 suites, 5 duplex.

Pullman Windsor, 14 r. Beaujon ✆ 45 63 04 04, Telex 650902, Fax 42 25 36 81 – rm – 120. AE GB JCB F 8
M see **Le Clovis** below – ☕ 90 – **135 rm** 1250/1500, 6 suites.

Château Frontenac, 54 r. P.-Charron ✆ 47 23 55 85, Telex 644994, Fax 47 23 03 32 – – 30. GB. G 9
Pavillon Frontenac ✆ 47 20 60 69 *(closed Saturday lunch and Sunday)* **M** 140 (lunch) and a la carte 140/270 – ☕ 75 – **99 rm** 880/1350, 4 suites.

Bedford, 17 r. Arcade ✆ 42 66 22 32, Telex 290506, Fax 42 66 51 56 - |$| ▤ TV ☎ - 🚶 80. GB. ✻ rest F 11
M *(closed 1 to 29 August, Saturday and Sunday)* (lunch only) a la carte 230/370 - **137 rm** ☕ 720/1050, 10 suites.

Napoléon, 40 av. Friedland ✆ 47 66 02 02, Telex 640609, Fax 47 66 82 33 - |$| TV ☎ - 🚶 100. AE ⓓ GB JCB F 8
Le Napoléon ✆ 42 27 99 50 *(closed 1 to 21 August, 23 December-3 January, Saturday and Sunday)* **M** 240/420 - ☕ 70 - **70 rm** 1150/1650, 32 suites.

Résidence du Roy without rest, 8 r. François 1er ✆ 42 89 59 59, Telex 648452, Fax 40 74 07 92 - |$| kitchenette ▤ TV ☎ ♿ 🚗 - 🚶 25. AE ⓓ GB JCB G 9
☕ 80, 28 suites1980/2980, 5 studios 1180, 3 duplex.

California, 16 r. Berri ✆ 43 59 93 00, Telex 644634, Fax 45 61 03 62 - |$| ⊭ rm ▤ TV ☎ - 🚶 90. AE ⓓ GB JCB F 9
M *(closed 14 July-15 August, Saturday, Sunday and Bank Holidays)* (lunch only) a la carte 190/240 - ☕ 120 - **160 rm** 2200.

Queen Elizabeth, 41 av. Pierre-1er-de-Serbie ✆ 47 20 80 56, Telex 641179, Fax 47 20 89 19 - |$| ⊭ rm ▤ TV ☎ - 🚶 25 - 30. AE ⓓ GB JCB G 8
M *(closed August and Sunday)* (lunch only) 160 b.i./210 🍷 - ☕ 85 - **54 rm** 1100/1850, 12 suites.

Claridge Bellman, 37 r. François 1er ✆ 47 23 54 42, Telex 641150, Fax 47 23 08 84 - |$| ▤ TV ☎. AE ⓓ GB. ✻ G 9
M *(closed 2 to 31 August, 24 December-3 January, Saturday and Sunday)* 160/220 and a la carte 230/380 🍷 - ☕ 70 - **42 rm** 950/1350.

Concorde-St-Lazare, 108 r. St-Lazare ✆ 40 08 44 44, Fax 42 93 01 20 - |$| ▤ TV ☎ - 🚶 150. AE ⓓ GB JCB. ✻ rest E 12
Café Terminus ✆ 40 08 43 30 - **M** 98/250 🍷 - ☕ 90 - **295 rm** 1350/1950, 5 suites.

Beau Manoir without rest, 6 r. Arcade ✆ 42 66 03 07, Fax 42 68 03 00, « Attractive installation » - |$| ▤ TV ☎ ♿. AE ⓓ GB JCB F 11
☕ 30 - **29 rm** 920/1040, 3 suites.

Sofitel-Paris-Élysées [M], 8 r. J. Goujon ✆ 43 59 52 41, Telex 651838, Fax 49 53 08 42 - |$| ⊭ rm ▤ TV ☎ ♿ 🚗 - 🚶 150. AE ⓓ GB JCB G 9
Les Saveurs ✆ 45 63 17 44 *(closed 1 to 22 August, Saturday and Sunday)* **M** 220 and a la carte 210/350 - ☕ 100 - **40 rm** 1250.

Chateaubriand [M] without rest, 6 r. Chateaubriand ✆ 40 76 00 50, Telex 641012, Fax 40 76 09 22 - |$| ⊭ rm ▤ TV ☎ ♿. AE ⓓ GB F 9
☕ 70 - **28 rm** 1500/1700.

Montaigne [M] without rest, 6 av. Montaigne ✆ 47 20 30 50, Telex 648051, Fax 47 20 94 12 - |$| ▤ TV ☎ ♿. AE ⓓ GB G 9
☕ 90 - **29 rm** 950/1750.

Royal Alma [M] without rest, 35 r. J. Goujon ✆ 42 25 83 30, Telex 641428, Fax 45 63 68 64 - |$| TV ☎. AE ⓓ GB JCB. ✻ G 9
☕ 90 - **57 rm** 1365/1600, 7 suites.

François 1er [M], 7 r. Magellan ✆ 47 23 44 04, Telex 648880, Fax 47 23 93 43 - |$| ⊭ rm ▤ TV ☎ - 🚶 30. AE ⓓ GB JCB F 8
M 175/400 - ☕ 95 - **38 rm** 1350/1480.

Marignan, 12 r. Marignan ✆ 40 76 34 56, Fax 40 76 34 34 - |$| ⊭ rm ▤ TV ☎ - 🚶 50. AE ⓓ GB JCB G 9
M a la carte 220/420 - ☕ 115 - **59 rm** 1900/2200.

Sofitel St-Honoré without rest, 15 r. Boissy d'Anglas ✆ 42 66 93 62, Telex 240366, Fax 42 66 14 98 - |$| ⊭ rm ▤ TV ☎. AE ⓓ GB G 11
☕ 85 - **104 rm** 760/995, 8 suites.

de l'Élysée without rest, 12 r. Saussaies ✆ 42 65 29 25, Fax 42 65 64 28 - |$| TV ☎. AE ⓓ GB JCB. ✻ F 11
☕ 60 - **32 rm** 560/950.

Élysées Ponthieu and Résidence Le Cid without rest, 24 r. Ponthieu ✆ 42 25 68 70, Telex 640053, Fax 42 25 80 82 - |$| kitchenette ⊭ rm ▤ TV ☎ ♿. AE ⓓ GB JCB F 9
☕ 75 - **92 rm** 780/1600, 6 suites.

Concortel without rest, 19 r. Pasquier ✆ 42 65 45 44, Telex 660228, Fax 42 65 18 33 - |$| TV ☎. AE ⓓ GB F 11
☕ 35 - **46 rm** 570/700.

Royal H. without rest, 33 av. Friedland ✆ 43 59 08 14, Telex 651465, Fax 45 63 69 92 - |$| TV ☎. AE ⓓ GB JCB F 8
☕ 65 - **57 rm** 1050/1250.

Résidence Champs-Elysées without rest, 92 r. La Boétie ✆ 43 59 96 15, Telex 650695, Fax 42 56 01 38 - |$| TV ☎. ⓓ GB. ✻ F 9
☕ 70 - **83 rm** 750/1240.

Résidence Monceau without rest, 85 r. Rocher ✆ 45 22 75 11, Fax 45 22 30 88 - |$| TV ☎ ♿. AE ⓓ GB. ✻ E 11
☕ 44 - **51 rm** 610.

Résidence St-Honoré without rest, 214 r. Fg-St-Honoré ☎ 42 25 26 27, Telex 640524, Fax 45 63 30 67 – ▮ ▤ TV ☎. AE ⓓ GB JCB E 9
☕ 60 – **91 rm** 850/1050.

Powers without rest, 52 r. François-1er ☎ 47 23 91 05, Telex 642051, Fax 49 52 04 63 – ▮ TV ☎. AE ⓓ GB G 9
☕ 60 – **48 rm** 800/1100.

Castiglione, 40 r. Fg-St-Honoré ☎ 42 65 07 50, Telex 240362, Fax 42 65 12 27 – ▮ ⇔ rm ▤ TV ☎ – 🏠 80. AE ⓓ GB G 11
M 160 and a la carte 200/380 – **107 rm** ☕ 1760/1800, 14 suites.

New Roblin and rest. Le Mazagran, 6 r. Chauveau-Lagarde ☎ 44 71 20 80, Telex 285154, Fax 42 65 19 49 – ▮ ▤ TV ☎ – 🏠 25. AE ⓓ GB JCB. ✻ rest F 11
M *(closed Saturday, Sunday and Bank Holidays)* 145 and a la carte 220/320 ♨ – ☕ 55 – **74 rm** 675/875, 3 suites.

West End without rest, 7 r. Clément-Marot ☎ 47 20 30 78, Telex 645434, Fax 47 20 34 42 – ▮ TV ☎. AE ⓓ GB JCB G 9
☕ 45 – **54 rm** 650/1250.

Lido M without rest, 4 passage Madeleine ☎ 42 66 27 37, Telex 281039, Fax 42 66 61 23 – ▮ TV ☎. AE ⓓ GB JCB F 11
☕ 30 – **32 rm** 740/820.

Cordélia without rest, 11 r. Greffulhe ☎ 42 65 42 40, Telex 281760, Fax 42 65 11 81 – ▮ TV ☎. AE ⓓ GB F 11
☕ 45 – **30 rm** 710/730.

Newton Opéra without rest, 11 bis r. Arcade ☎ 42 65 32 13, Telex 280340, Fax 42 65 30 90 – ▮ ▤ TV ☎. AE ⓓ GB. ✻ F 11
☕ 50 – **31 rm** 690/850.

Galiléo M without rest, 54 r. Galilée ☎ 47 20 66 06, Fax 47 20 67 17 – ▮ ▤ TV ☎ ♿. AE GB. ✻ F 8
☕ 50 – **27 rm** 800/980.

Franklin Roosevelt without rest, 18 r. Clément-Marot ☎ 47 23 61 66, Telex 643665, Fax 47 20 44 30 – ▮ TV ☎. AE GB. ✻ G 9
45 rm ☕ 700/900.

Atlantic without rest, 44 r. Londres ☎ 43 87 45 40, Telex 285477, Fax 42 93 06 26 – ▮ TV ☎. AE GB JCB. ✻ E 12
☕ 48 – **93 rm** 452/774.

Rochambeau without rest, 4 r. La Boétie ☎ 42 65 27 54, Telex 285030, Fax 42 66 03 81 – ▮ ⇔ rm TV ☎. AE ⓓ GB JCB F 11
☕ 50 – **50 rm** 1050/1200.

Waldorf Madeleine without rest, 12 bd Malesherbes ☎ 42 65 72 06, Telex 285557, Fax 40 07 10 45 – ▮ ⇔ rm TV ☎. AE ⓓ GB JCB F 11
☕ 50 – **44 rm** 950/1050.

Mayflower without rest, 3 r. Chateaubriand ☎ 45 62 57 46, Telex 640727, Fax 42 56 32 38 – ▮ TV ☎. GB F 9
☕ 50 – **24 rm** 650/950.

L'Orangerie without rest, 9 r. Constantinople ☎ 45 22 07 51, Telex 285294, Fax 45 22 16 49 – ▮ TV ☎. AE ⓓ GB. ✻ E 11
☕ 35 – **29 rm** 565/665.

Fortuny without rest, 35 r. Arcade ☎ 42 66 42 08, Telex 280656, Fax 42 66 00 32 – ▮ TV ☎. AE ⓓ GB F 11
☕ 45 – **30 rm** 650/750.

Plaza Haussmann without rest, 177 bd Haussmann ☎ 45 63 93 83, Telex 643716, Fax 45 61 14 30 – ▮ TV ☎. AE ⓓ GB JCB F 9
☕ 30 – **41 rm** 620/710.

Élysées without rest, 100 r. La Boétie ☎ 43 59 23 46, Telex 648572, Fax 42 56 33 80 – ▮ ▤ TV ☎. AE ⓓ GB. ✻ F 9
☕ 25 – **29 rm** 560/640.

Angleterre-Champs-Élysées without rest, 91 r. La Boétie ☎ 43 59 35 45, Telex 640317, Fax 45 63 22 22 – ▮ TV ☎. AE ⓓ GB F 9
☕ 31 – **40 rm** 480/605.

Charing Cross without rest, 39 r. Pasquier ☎ 43 87 41 04, Telex 290681, Fax 42 93 70 45 – ▮ TV ☎. AE ⓓ GB JCB F 11
☕ 35 – **31 rm** 370/435.

In this Guide,
a symbol or a character, printed in red or black,
does not have the same meaning.
Please read the explanatory pages carefully.

XXXXX ✿✿✿ **Lucas-Carton** (Senderens), 9 pl. Madeleine ☎ 42 65 22 90, Telex 281088, Fax 42 65 06 23, « Authentic 1900 decor » – ▤. GB. ✗ G 11
closed 31 July-25 August, 23 December-2 January, Saturday lunch and Sunday – **M** 375 (lunch)/780 and a la carte 600/940
Spec. Foie gras au chou. Homard à la vanille. Canard Apicius.

XXXXX ✿✿ **Lasserre,** 17 av. F.-D.-Roosevelt ☎ 43 59 53 43, Fax 45 63 72 23, Open roof in fine weather – ▤. AE GB. ✗ G 10
closed 1 to 30 August, Monday lunch and Sunday – **M** a la carte 540/750
Spec. Rouget poêlé aux herbes et jus de crustacés. Sauvageon grillé aux épices et pommes craquantes. Truffier "Marco Polo".

XXXXX ✿✿✿ **Taillevent** (Vrinat), 15 r. Lamennais ☎ 45 61 12 90, Fax 42 25 95 18 – ▤. GB. ✗ F 9
closed 24 July-23 August, Saturday, Sunday and Bank Holidays – **M** (booking essential) a la carte 550/700
Spec. Escargots "petit gris" en hochepot. Andouillette de pied de porc truffé. Soufflé chaud à l'orange amère.

XXXXX ✿✿ **Les Ambassadeurs** - Hôtel Crillon, 10 pl. Concorde ☎ 44 71 16 16, Telex 290204, Fax 44 71 15 02, « 18C decor » – ▤. AE ① GB JCB. ✗ G 11
M 320 (lunch)/570 and a la carte 400/670
Spec. Foie gras poêlé aux épices et miel d'acacia. Bar croustillant aux poivrons doux et graines de sésame. Quasi de veau de lait en cocotte, jus corsé au goût d'herbes.

XXXXX ✿✿ **Laurent,** 41 av. Gabriel ☎ 42 25 00 39, Fax 45 62 45 21, « Pleasant summer terrace » – AE ① GB. ✗ G 10
closed Saturday lunch, Sunday and Bank Holidays – **M** 380 (lunch)/880 and a la carte 600/900
Spec. "Mille-chou" aux champignons des bois (September-April). Quasi de veau de lait en cocotte. Friand de framboises à l'orgeat.

XXXXX ✿ **Bristol** - Hôtel Bristol, 112 r. Fg St-Honoré ☎ 42 66 91 45, Telex 280961, Fax 42 66 68 68 – ▤. AE ① GB JCB. ✗ F 10
M 440/590 and a la carte 460/730
Spec. Foie gras de canard poêlé et galette de pommes de terre. Médaillons de Saint-Pierre rôti. Coffret brioché de langoustines, ris de veau et champignons.

XXXXX ✿ **Régence** - Hôtel Plaza Athénée, 25 av. Montaigne ☎ 47 23 78 33, Telex 650092, Fax 47 20 20 70, 余 – ▤. AE ① GB JCB G 9
M 330 and a la carte 450/700
Spec. Soufflé de homard "Plaza Athénée". Noix de Saint-Jacques à la nage (October-April). Filet d'agneau rôti parfumé à l'origan.

XXXXX ✿ **Ledoyen,** carré Champs-Élysées ☎ 47 42 23 23, Telex 282358, Fax 47 42 55 01, 余 – ▤ Ⓟ. AE ① GB. ✗ G 10
M (1st floor) *(closed August, Saturday and Sunday)* 290 (lunch)/480 and a la carte 400/610 - **Le Carré** ☎ 47 42 76 02 *(closed Sunday)* **M** a la carte 250/370
Spec. Langoustines sautées, pommes de terre à la truffe. Saint-Jacques à la nage parfumées à la bière et fritot de houblon (October-March). Pigeonneau aux deux cuissons aux girolles, pommes "Alex Imbert".

XXXX ✿ **Élysée Lenôtre,** 10 av. Champs-Élysées ☎ 42 65 85 10, Fax 42 65 76 23, 余 – |‡| ▤ Ⓟ. AE ① GB G 10
closed Saturday lunch – **Rez-de-Chaussée M** (lunch only) 300 bi/340 – **1er étage M** (dinner only) 340/580 and a la carte 370/580
Spec. Foie gras de canard poêlé. Blanc de turbot dans une courte nage. Chiboust au fromage blanc et citron vert.

XXXX ✿ **Les Princes** - Hôtel George V, 31 av. George V ☎ 47 23 54 00, Telex 650082, Fax 47 20 40 00, 余 – ▤. AE ① GB JCB G 8
M 350 b.i./450 and a la carte 310/630
Spec. Croustillant de rouget au confit de légumes de Provence. Noisettes d'empereur rôties aux épices. Côtelettes de caille des Dombes poêlées en persillade d'amandes.

XXXX ✿✿ **Chiberta,** 3 r. Arsène-Houssaye ☎ 45 63 77 90, Fax 45 62 85 08 – ▤. AE ① GB JCB
closed 1 to 29 August, 24 December-3 January, Saturday, Sunday and Bank Holidays – **M** a la carte 420/580 F 8
Spec. Salade de St-Jacques aux truffes fraîches (December-March). Saint-Pierre rôti aux oignons rouges confits. Côte de veau poêlée aux pommes confites.

XXXX ✿ **Les Élysées** - Hôtel Vernet, 25 r. Vernet ☎ 47 23 43 10 – ▤. AE ① GB F 8
closed 23 July-24 August, Saturday and Sunday – **M** 270 (lunch)/420 and a la carte 335/480
Spec. Bar de ligne rôti et brandade de petits piments. Papeton de pigeonneau croustillé aux olives et cèpes. Damier au chocolat "Guanaja" et aux pistaches caramélisées.

XXXX ✿ **La Marée,** 1 r. Daru ☎ 43 80 20 00, Fax 48 88 04 04 – ▤. ① GB E 8
closed August, Saturday and Sunday – **M** Seafood - a la carte 360/565
Spec. Salade de homard aux pêches de vigne. Cabillaud à la vanille. Gigotin de lotte rôti à l'ananas.

XXXX **Fouquet's,** 99 av. Champs-Élysées ☎ 47 23 70 60, Telex 648227, Fax 47 20 08 69 – AE ① GB F 8
Rez-de-Chaussée (grill) **M** a la carte 265/400 – **1er étage M** a la carte 310/420.

XXXX **Richemond Trémoille,** 7 r. Trémoille ☎ 47 23 88 18 – AE ① GB G 9
closed August, Saturday and Sunday – **M** 250 b.i./300 and a la carte 230/300.

XXX ✿ **15 Montaigne Maison Blanche,** 15 av. Montaigne (6th floor) ☎ 47 23 55 99, Fax 47 20 09 56, ≤, 🏠, « Contemporary decor » – |‡| ▤. AE GB G 9
closed Saturday lunch and Sunday – **M** a la carte 380/520
Spec. Ravioli de tomates confites. Saint-Jacques poêlées aux cèpes (25 September-15 December). Sablé de pommes, cannelle et romarin.

XXX ✿ **Le Clovis** - Hôtel Pullman Windsor, 4 r. B.-Albrecht ☎ 45 61 15 32, Telex 650902, Fax 42 25 36 81 – ▤. AE ① GB F 8
closed 2 to 29 August, 27 December-2 January, Saturday, Sunday and Bank Holidays – **M** 190 and a la carte 340/450
Spec. Mimosa de légumes à la vinaigrette de truffes. Carré d'agneau rôti, lait d'amandes et pommes soufflées. Assiette de quatre douceurs.

XXX ✿ **La Couronne** - Hôtel Warwick, 5 r. Berri ☎ 45 63 78 49, Telex 642295, Fax 42 56 77 59 – ▤. AE ① GB. ✻ F 9
closed August and Sunday – **M** 220 (lunch)/500 and a la carte 350/480
Spec. Mosaïque de homard et de St-Jacques aux pois gourmands (season). Filet de bœuf à la moelle et au vin rouge. Dominance de chocolat à la glace de pain d'épices.

XXX **Le 30 - Fauchon,** pl. Madeleine ☎ 47 42 56 58, Fax 42 66 38 95, 🏠 – ▤. AE ① GB JCB
closed Sunday – **M** 250 and a la carte 270/400. F 12

XXX ✿ **Copenhague,** 142 av. Champs-Élysées (1st floor) ☎ 44 13 86 26, Fax 42 25 83 10, 🏠 – ▤. AE ① GB. ✻ F 8
closed 2 to 29 August, 1 to 7 January, Saturday lunch in summer, Sunday and Bank Holidays – **M** Danish rest. 285 and a la carte 280/450 - **Flora Danica M** a la carte 250/340
Spec. Saumon mariné à l'aneth. Mignons de renne aux épices. Mandelrand avec sorbets et fruits.

XXX **Relais-Plaza** - Hôtel Plaza Athénée, 21 av. Montaigne ☎ 47 23 46 36, Telex 650092, Fax 47 20 20 70 – ▤. AE ① GB JCB G 9
M 285 and a la carte 310/535.

XXX **Le Grill** - Hôtel George V, 31 av. George V ☎ 47 23 60 80, Telex 650082, Fax 47 20 40 00 – ▤. AE ① GB JCB G 8
closed 24 July to 24 August – **M** 198/250.

XXX **Yvan,** 1bis r. J. Mermoz ☎ 43 59 18 40, Fax 45 63 78 69 – ▤. AE ① GB JCB F-G 10
closed Saturday lunch and Sunday – **M** 168/298.

XXX **Les Géorgiques,** 36 av. George V ☎ 40 70 10 49 – ▤. AE ① GB JCB. ✻ G 8
closed Saturday lunch and Sunday – **M** 180 (lunch)/360.

XXX ✿ **Vancouver** (Decout), 4 r. Arsène Houssaye ☎ 42 56 77 77, Fax 42 56 50 52 – ▤. AE GB
closed 1 to 30 August, 25 December-1 January, Saturday, Sunday and Bank Holidays – **M** Seafood 190 and a la carte 260/390 F 8
Spec. Cassolette de homard et champignons. Bouillabaisse "Parisienne". Paris-Brest au craquelin.

XXX **Indra,** 10 r. Cdt-Rivière ☎ 43 59 46 40 – ▤. AE ① GB F 9
closed Saturday lunch – **M** Indian rest. 220/300.

XX **Baumann Marbeuf,** 15 r. Marbeuf ☎ 47 20 11 11, Fax 47 23 69 65 – AE ① GB G 9
closed 9 to 15 August – **M** a la carte 195/300 🍷.

XX **Fermette Marbeuf,** 5 r. Marbeuf ☎ 47 23 31 31, Fax 40 70 02 11, « 1900 decor with genuine ceramics and leaded glass windows » – ▤. AE ① GB G 9
M 160 and a la carte 210/300 🍷.

XX **La Luna,** 69 r. Rocher ☎ 42 93 77 61, Fax 40 08 02 44 – ▤. AE GB. ✻ E 11
closed Sunday – **M** Seafood - a la carte 270/410.

XX **Chez Tante Louise,** 41 r. Boissy d'Anglas ☎ 42 65 06 85, Fax 42 65 28 19 – ▤. AE ① GB JCB F 11
closed August, Saturday and Sunday – **M** 200 and a la carte 250/400.

XX **Kinugawa,** 4 r. St-Philippe du Roule ☎ 45 63 08 07 – ▤. AE GB JCB. ✻ F 9
M Japanese rest. - a la carte 170/350.

XX **Le Bœuf sur le Toit,** 34 r. Colisée ☎ 43 59 83 80, Fax 45 63 45 40 – AE ① GB F 10
M brasserie 159 b.i. and a la carte 160/270 🍷.

XX **Le Grenadin,** 46 r. Naples ☎ 45 63 28 92 – ▤. AE GB E 11
closed Christmas-New Year, Saturday (except dinner October-April) and Sunday – **M** 200/370.

XX **Le Sarladais,** 2 r. Vienne ☎ 45 22 23 62 – ▤. AE GB E 11
closed August, Saturday (except dinner September-June) and Sunday – **M** 145 (dinner) and a la carte 230/335.

XX **Androuët,** 41 r. Amsterdam ☎ 48 74 26 93, Telex 280466, Fax 49 95 02 54 – ▤. AE ① GB JCB E 12
closed Sunday and Bank Holidays – **M** Cheese specialities 175 (lunch)/250.

XX **Marius et Janette,** 4 av. George V ☎ 47 23 41 88, Fax 47 23 07 19, 🏠 – ▤. AE GB
closed 21 to 27 December – **M** Seafood 320/450. G 8

XX **Finzi,** 24 av. George V ☎ 47 20 14 78, Fax 47 20 10 08 – ▤. AE ① GB. ✻ G 8
closed 8 to 15 August and Sunday lunch – **M** Italian rest. - a la carte 225/300 🍷.

XX **Le Pichet,** 68 r. P. Charron ☎ 43 59 50 34, Fax 45 63 07 81 – ▤. AE ① GB GF 9
closed 10 to 31 August, 19 December-2 January, Saturday lunch and Sunday – **M** a la carte 260/360.

XX **Le Lloyd's,** 23 r. Treilhard ☎ 45 63 21 23 - AE GB E 10
closed 24 December-2 January, Saturday and Sunday - **M** 200 b.i./300.

XX **Artois,** 13 r. Artois ☎ 42 25 01 10 - GB F 9
closed Saturday lunch and Sunday - **M** (booking essential) 170 (dinner) and a la carte 230/350.

XX **Village d'Ung et Li Lam,** 10 r. J. Mermoz ☎ 42 25 99 79 - ▤. AE ⓓ GB F 10
M Chinese and Thai rest. 89/119.

XX **Stresa,** 7 r. Chambiges ☎ 47 23 51 62 - AE ⓓ G 9
closed August and 22 December-3 January - **M** Italian rest. - a la carte 260/400.

XX **L'Étoile Marocaine,** 56 r. Galilée ☎ 47 20 54 45 - ▤. AE ⓓ GB. ✗ F 8
M Morrocan rest. 161/243.

XX **Tong Yen,** 1bis r. J. Mermoz ☎ 42 25 04 23, Fax 45 63 51 57 - ▤. AE ⓓ GB F 10
closed 1 to 25 August - **M** Chinese rest. - a la carte 170/250.

XX **Chez Bosc,** 7 r. Richepanse ☎ 42 60 10 27 - ⓓ GB G 12
closed August, Saturday lunch and Sunday - **M** 135/190.

XX **Suntory,** 13 r. Lincoln ☎ 42 25 40 27, Fax 45 63 25 86 - ▤. AE ⓓ GB JCB. ✗ F 9
closed Saturday lunch, Sunday and Bank Holidays - **M** Japan rest. 400/600.

X **Bistrot du Sommelier,** 97 bd Haussmann ☎ 42 65 24 85, Fax 42 94 03 26 - ▤. AE ⓓ GB JCB F 11
closed 24 July-22 August, 25 December-2 January, Saturday and Sunday - **M** a la carte 250/370.

X **Le Bouchon Gourmand,** 25 r. Colisée ☎ 43 59 25 29, Fax 42 56 33 97 - AE ⓓ GB F 9
closed 2 to 22 August, Saturday lunch and Sunday - **M** 130.

X **Bistrot de Marius,** 6 av. George V ☎ 40 70 11 76, ☂ - AE GB G 8
M Seafood 200 b.i./320 b.i.

X **La Petite Auberge,** 48 r. Moscou ☎ 43 87 91 84 - GB D 11
closed Saturday, Sunday and Bank Holidays - **M** 135 and a la carte 200/280.

X **Ferme des Mathurins,** 17 r. Vignon ☎ 42 66 46 39 - GB F 12
closed August, Sunday and Bank Holidays - **M** 150/200.

X **Finzi,** 182 bd Haussmann ☎ 45 62 88 68 - ▤. AE GB F 8
closed Sunday lunch - **M** Italian rest. - a la carte 160/310.

Opéra, Gare du Nord, Gare de l'Est, Grands Boulevards.

9th and 10th arrondissements.
9th: ✉ 75009
10th: ✉ 75010

🏨 **Grand Hôtel Inter-Continental,** 2 r. Scribe (9th) ☎ 40 07 32 32, Telex 220875, Fax 42 66 12 51, ℱ₆ - |♦| ⇔ rm ▤ TV ☎ ♿ - 🏛 350. AE ⓓ GB JCB. ✗ rest F 12
M see **Opéra and Brasserie Café de la Paix** below - rest. **La Verrière** ☎ 40 07 31 00 *(closed dinner in August, Sunday dinner and Monday dinner)* **M** 285 (lunch)/375 - ☐ 150 - **490 rm** 2300/2900, 23 suites.

🏨 **Scribe** Ⓜ, 1 r. Scribe (9th) ☎ 44 71 24 24, Telex 214653, Fax 42 65 39 97 - |♦| ⇔ rm ▤ TV ☎ ♿ - 🏛 80. AE ⓓ GB JCB. ✗ rest F 12
Le Jardin des Muses M 140 and a la carte approx 210 ♁ - **Les Muses** - ☎ **44 71 24 26** *(closed 31 July-29 August, Saturday, Sunday and Bank Holidays)* **M** 190 and a la carte approx. 300 - ☐ 125 - **206 rm** 1450/1950, 11 suites.

🏨 **Ambassador,** 16 bd Haussmann (9th) ☎ 42 46 92 63, Telex 285912, Fax 42 46 19 84 - |♦| ⇔ rm ▤ TV ☎ - 🏛 110. AE ⓓ GB JCB F 13
Le Venantius ☎ 48 00 06 38 *(closed August, 12 to 20/02, Saturday except dinner from 09-06 and Sunday)* **M** 250 and a la carte 320/540 - ☐ 100 - **298 rm** 1600/2500.

🏨 **Commodore,** 12 bd Haussmann (9th) ☎ 42 46 72 82, Telex 280601, Fax 47 70 23 81 - |♦| TV ☎ - 🏛 25. AE ⓓ GB JCB F 13
- **Cancans** (coffee shop) **M** a la carte 150/240 ♁ - **Le Carvery** - (lunch only) *(closed July-August and weekends)* **M** 250 - ☐ 90 - **151 rm** 1950/2050, 11 suites.

🏨 **L'Horset Pavillon** Ⓜ, 38 r. Échiquier (10th) ☎ 42 46 92 75, Telex 283905, Fax 42 47 03 97 - |♦| ▤ TV ☎. AE ⓓ GB JCB F 15
M *(closed Saturday and Sunday)* 160 b.i. and a la carte 180/300 - ☐ 75 - **92 rm** 790/890.

🏨 **Blanche Fontaine** Ⓜ ⛭ without rest, 34 r. Fontaine (9th) ☎ 45 26 72 32, Telex 660311, Fax 42 81 05 52 - |♦| TV ☎ 🚗. AE GB. ✗ D 13
☐ 38 - **45 rm** 445/575.

Cidotel Lafayette M without rest, 49 r. Lafayette (9th) ☎ 42 85 05 44, Telex 283025, Fax 49 95 06 60 – |♦| ⇔ rm TV ☎. AE ⓓ GB JCB F 14
☐ 75 – **75 rm** 780/840.

Brébant, 32 bd Poissonnière (9th) ☎ 47 70 25 55, Telex 280127, Fax 42 46 65 70 – |♦| ▤ rest TV ☎ – 🏛 60. AE ⓓ GB JCB F 14
M 89/198 – **122 rm** ☐ 750/890.

St-Pétersbourg without rest, 33 r. Caumartin (9th) ☎ 42 66 60 38, Telex 680001, Fax 42 66 53 54 – |♦| TV ☎ – 🏛 100. AE ⓓ GB F 12
100 rm ☐ 505/960.

Opéra Cadet M without rest, 24 r. Cadet (9th) ☎ 48 24 05 26, Telex 282287, Fax 42 46 68 09 – |♦| ▤ TV ☎ ♿ 🚗. AE ⓓ GB F 14
☐ 48 – **85 rm** 660/710.

Bergère without rest, 34 r. Bergère (9th) ☎ 47 70 34 34, Telex 290668, Fax 47 70 36 36 – |♦| TV ☎. AE ⓓ GB JCB F 14
☐ 50 – **131 rm** 950/990.

Mercure-Altéa Ronceray M without rest, 10 bd Montmartre (9th) ☎ 42 47 13 45, Telex 283906, Fax 42 47 13 63 – |♦| ⇔ rm TV ☎ – 🏛 65. AE ⓓ GB F 14
☐ 65 – **117 rm** 730/1070.

Trinité Plaza M without rest, 41 r. Pigalle (9th) ☎ 42 85 57 00, Telex 280110, Fax 45 26 41 20 – |♦| TV ☎. AE ⓓ GB JCB E 13
42 rm ☐ 550/660.

Paix République without rest, 2bis bd St Martin (10th) ☎ 42 08 96 95, Telex 680632, Fax 42 06 36 30 – |♦| TV ☎. AE ⓓ GB. ⚘ G 16
☐ 40 – **45 rm** 560/950.

Anjou-Lafayette M without rest, 4 r. Riboutté (9th) ☎ 42 46 83 44, Fax 48 00 08 97 – |♦| TV ☎. AE ⓓ GB JCB E 14
☐ 35 – **39 rm** 460/660.

Carlton's H. without rest, 55 bd Rochechouart (9th) ☎ 42 81 91 00, Telex 285649, Fax 42 81 97 04 – |♦| TV ☎. AE ⓓ GB D 14
☐ 46 – **94 rm** 614/668.

Frantour Paris Est M, cour d'Honneur (10th) ☎ 44 89 27 00, Telex 217916, Fax 44 89 27 49 – |♦| ▤ rm TV ☎. AE GB E 16
M 125 b.i./300 b.i. – ☐ 70 – **44 rm** 490/950.

Mercure Monty M, 5 r. Monthyon (9th) ☎ 47 70 26 10, Telex 660677, Fax 42 46 55 10 – |♦| TV ☎ – 🏛 50. AE ⓓ GB F 14
M *(closed Saturday and Sunday)* 95/160 – ☐ 58 – **71 rm** 520/770.

Printania without rest, 19 r. Château d'Eau (10th) ☎ 42 01 84 20, Telex 215425, Fax 42 39 55 12 – |♦| TV ☎. AE ⓓ GB. ⚘ F 16
☐ 41 – **51 rm** 490/580.

Caumartin M without rest, 27 r. Caumartin (9th) ☎ 47 42 95 95, Telex 680702, Fax 47 42 88 19 – |♦| TV ☎. AE ⓓ GB JCB F 12
☐ 75 – **40 rm** 770/860.

Albert 1er M without rest, 162 r. La Fayette (10th) ☎ 40 36 82 40, Telex 212887, Fax 40 35 72 52 – |♦| ▤ TV ☎. AE ⓓ GB. ⚘ E 16
☐ 35 – **59 rm** 500/645.

La Tour d'Auvergne without rest, 10 r. La Tour d'Auvergne (9th) ☎ 48 78 61 60, Telex 281604, Fax 49 95 99 00 – |♦| ⇔ rm TV ☎. AE ⓓ GB JCB. ⚘ E 14
☐ 40 – **25 rm** 550/650.

Celte La Fayette M without rest, 25 r. Buffault (9th) ☎ 49 95 09 49, Telex 280554, Fax 49 95 01 88 – |♦| TV ☎. AE ⓓ GB. ⚘ E 14
☐ 40 – **50 rm** 495/680.

Corona ⛰ without rest, 8 cité Bergère (9th) ☎ 47 70 52 96, Telex 281081, Fax 42 46 83 49 – |♦| TV ☎. AE ⓓ GB JCB F 14
☐ 40 – **56 rm** 540/680, 4 suites.

Résidence du Pré without rest, 15 r. P. Sémard (9th) ☎ 48 78 26 72, Fax 42 80 64 83 – |♦| TV ☎. AE GB E 15
☐ 40 – **40 rm** 395/450.

du Pré without rest, 10 r. P. Sémard (9th) ☎ 42 81 37 11, Fax 40 23 98 28 – |♦| TV ☎. AE GB E 15
☐ 40 – **41 rm** 395/510.

Gd H. Montmartre M without rest, 2 r. Calais (9th) ☎ 48 74 87 76, Telex 649906, Fax 42 81 31 31 – |♦| ⇔ rm TV ☎. AE ⓓ GB D 12
☐ 60 – **40 rm** 580/750.

Libertel du Moulin M without rest, 39 r. Fontaine (9th) ☎ 42 81 93 25, Telex 660055, Fax 40 16 09 90 – |♦| ⇔ rm TV ☎. AE ⓓ GB JCB. ⚘ D 13
☐ 60 – **50 rm** 650/720.

Monterosa M without rest, 30 r. La Bruyère (9th) ☎ 48 74 87 90, Telex 281154, Fax 42 81 01 12 – |♦| TV ☎. AE ⓓ GB JCB. ⚘ E 13
☐ 32 – **36 rm** 380/600.

🏨 **Montréal** without rest, 23 r. Godot-de-Mauroy (9th) ✆ 42 65 99 54, Fax 49 24 07 33 – |⇕| TV ☎. AE ⓓ GB F 12
closed August – ☕ 35 – **14 rm** 285/600, 5 suites.

🏨 **Modern' Est** without rest, 91 bd Strasbourg (10th) ✆ 40 37 77 20, Fax 40 37 17 55 – |⇕| TV ☎. GB. ✻ E 16
☕ 28 – **30 rm** 350/430.

🏨 **Capucines** without rest, 6 r. Godot de Mauroy (9th) ✆ 47 42 06 37, Fax 42 68 05 05 – |⇕| ☎. AE ⓓ GB JCB F 12
☕ 32 – **46 rm** 290/580.

🏨 **D'Estrées** M without rest, 2bis cité Pigalle (9th) ✆ 48 74 39 22, Telex 290609, Fax 45 96 04 09 – |⇕| TV ☎. AE ⓓ GB E 13
☕ 40 – **23 rm** 560/590.

🏨 **Ibis Lafayette** without rest, 122 r. Lafayette (10th) ✆ 45 23 27 27, Telex 290272, Fax 42 46 73 79 – |⇕| ⇹ rm TV ☎ ♿. AE GB E 16
☕ 36 – **70 rm** 390/440.

XXXX ✿ **Rest. Opéra-Café de la Paix** - Le Grand Hôtel, pl. Opéra (9th) ✆ 40 07 30 10, Telex 220875, Fax 42 66 12 51, « Second Empire decor » – ▤. AE ⓓ GB JCB. ✻ F 12
closed August, Saturday and Sunday – **M** 285 b.i./450 and a la carte 370/630
Spec. Fricassée de chapon aux morilles, pommes aux artichauts (autumn-winter). Subric de Saint-Pierre en homardine. Boudin blanc au foie gras, mousseline de pommes de terre (Winter).

XXX ✿ **La Table d'Anvers** (Conticini), 2 pl. Anvers (9th) ✆ 48 78 35 21, Fax 45 26 66 67 – ▤. AE GB D 14
closed 1 to 15 August, Saturday lunch and Sunday – **M** 190/550 and a la carte 385/465
Spec. Croustillant poivré de langoustines et tourteau. Selle d'agneau rôtie, oignons et aubergines confits au citron. Croquettes au chocolat fondant.

XXX **Charlot "Roi des Coquillages",** 81 bd Clichy (9th) ✆ 48 74 49 64, Fax 40 16 11 00 – ▤. AE ⓓ GB D 12
M Seafood 196 and a la carte 240/410.

XXX **Le Louis XIV,** 8 bd St-Denis (10th) ✆ 42 08 56 56, Fax 42 08 23 50 – AE ⓓ GB JCB G 15
closed May-August – **M** a la carte 230/420.

XX **Au Chateaubriant,** 23 r. Chabrol (10th) ✆ 48 24 58 94, Paintings Collection – ▤. AE GB. ✻ E 15
closed August, Sunday and Monday – **M** Italian rest. 150 and a la carte 210/390.

XX **Chez Michel,** 10 r. Belzunce (10th) ✆ 48 78 44 14 – ▤. AE ⓓ GB JCB E 15
closed 7 to 29 August, Christmas-New Year, Saturday and Sunday – **M** (booking essential) 175 (lunch) and a la carte 280/420.

XX **Brasserie Flo Printemps,** (Printemps de la Mode - 6th floor) 64 bd Haussman (9th) ✆ 42 82 58 81, Fax 45 26 31 24 – ▤. AE ⓓ GB F 12
closed Sunday and Bank Holidays – **M** (lunch only) 159 b.i./245 b.i.

XX **Brasserie Café de la Paix** - Le Grand Hôtel, 12 bd Capucines (9th) ✆ 40 07 30 20, Telex 220875, Fax 42 66 12 51 – AE ⓓ GB JCB. ✻ F 12
M 192 and a la carte 190/320 🍷.

XX **Grand Café Capucines** (24 hr service), 4 bd Capucines (9th) ✆ 47 42 19 00, Fax 47 42 74 22, « Belle Epoque decor » – AE ⓓ GB F 13
M 185 (lunch) and a la carte 200/320 🍷.

XX **Le Quercy,** 36 r. Condorcet (9th) ✆ 48 78 30 61 – AE ⓓ GB E 14
closed August, Sunday and Bank Holidays – **M** 148 and a la carte 180/300.

XX **Comme Chez Soi,** 20 r. Lamartine (9th) ✆ 48 78 00 02 – ▤. AE ⓓ GB JCB E 14
closed August, Saturday and Sunday – **M** 140/300.

XX **Le Saintongeais,** 62 r. Fg Montmartre (9th) ✆ 42 80 39 92 – AE ⓓ GB E 14
closed 5 to 25 August, Saturday and Sunday – **M** a la carte 180/270.

XX **Julien,** 16 r. Fg St-Denis (10th) ✆ 47 70 12 06, Fax 42 47 00 65, « Belle Epoque brasserie » – ▤. AE ⓓ GB F 15
M 99 b.i./159 b.i.

XX **Le Franche-Comté,** 2 bd Madeleine (Maison de la Franche-Comté) (9th) ✆ 49 24 99 09, Fax 49 24 01 63 – AE GB JCB F 12
closed Sunday and Bank Holidays – **M** 110/175 🍷.

XX **Petit Riche,** 25 r. Le Peletier (9th) ✆ 47 70 68 68, Fax 48 24 10 79, « Late 19C decor » – AE ⓓ GB JCB F 13
closed Sunday – **M** 180 b.i. and a la carte 170/320.

XX **Bistrot Papillon,** 6 r. Papillon (9th) ✆ 47 70 90 03 - AE ⓓ GB E 15
closed Easter Holidays, 7 to 29 August, Saturday and Sunday - **M** 135 and a la carte 200/300 ♁.

XX **Aux Deux Canards,** 8 r. Fg Poissonnière (10th) ✆ 47 70 03 23, restaurant for no-smokers only - ▤. AE ⓓ GB JCB F 15
closed 30 July-24 August, Saturday lunch and Sunday - **M** 150/200 b.i. ♁.

XX **Grange Batelière,** 16 r. Grange Batelière (9th) ✆ 47 70 85 15 - GB G 10
closed 2 to 30 August, Monday dinner, Sunday and Bank Holidays - **M** 198 and a la carte 220/300.

XX **Brasserie Flo,** 7 cour Petites-Écuries (10th) ✆ 47 70 13 59, Fax 42 47 00 80, « 1900 decor » - ▤. AE ⓓ GB F 15
M 99 b.i./159 b.i.

XX **Gokado,** 18 r. Caumartin (9th) ✆ 47 42 08 82, Fax 47 42 76 19 - ▤. AE ⓓ GB JCB
closed Saturday dinner and Sunday - **M** Japanese rest. 120 (lunch)/700. F 12

XX **Terminus Nord,** 23 r. Dunkerque (10th) ✆ 42 85 05 15, Fax 40 16 13 98, brasserie - AE ⓓ GB E 16
M 159 b.i. and a la carte 160/270 ♁.

XX **La P'tite Tonkinoise,** 56 r. Fg Poissonnière (10th) ✆ 42 46 85 98 - GB F 15
closed 1 August-15 September, 2 December-5 January, Sunday and Monday - **M** Vietnamese rest. - a la carte 140/250.

X **Relais Beaujolais,** 3 r. Milton (9th) ✆ 48 78 77 91 - GB E 14
closed Saturday and Sunday - **M** 130 (lunch) and a la carte 180/290.

X **Petit Batailley,** 26 r. Bergère (9th) ✆ 47 70 85 81 - AE ⓓ GB F 14
closed 1 to 30 August, 1 to 10 January, Saturday lunch, Sunday and Bank Holidays - **M** 139/205.

X **La Grille,** 80 r. Fg Poissonnière (10th) ✆ 47 70 89 73 - ▤. AE ⓓ GB E 15
closed 15 to 31 August, February Holidays, Friday dinner, Saturday and Sunday - **M** a la carte 200/280.

X **Chez Jean l'Auvergnat,** 52 r. Lamartine (9th) ✆ 48 78 62 73, Fax 48 78 39 29 - GB
closed 13 to 23 August, Saturday lunch and Sunday - **M** 130. E 14

X **Bistro des Deux Théâtres,** 18 r. Blanche (9th) ✆ 45 26 41 43 - ▤. GB E 12
M 165 b.i.

Bastille, Gare de Lyon, Place d'Italie, Bois de Vincennes.

12th and 13th arrondissements.
12th: ✉ 75012
13th: ✉ 75013

Pavillon Bastille M without rest, 65 r. Lyon (12th) ✆ 43 43 65 65, Fax 43 43 96 52 - ▤ ▤ TV ☎ ♿. AE ⓓ GB JCB K 18
☕ 75 - **25 rm** 890.

Novotel Paris Bercy M, 86 r. Bercy (12th) ✆ 43 42 30 00, Telex 218332, Fax 43 45 30 60, 🍴 - ▤ ⇆ rm ▤ TV ☎ ♿ - 🎤 30 - 100. AE ⓓ GB M 19
M a la carte approx. 170 - ☕ 58 - **129 rm** 730/760.

Mercure-Altéa Place d'Italie M without rest, 178 bd Vincent Auriol (13th) ✆ 44 24 01 01, Telex 203424, Fax 44 24 07 07 - ▤ TV ☎ - 🎤 25. AE ⓓ GB N 16
☕ 62 - **70 rm** 650/900.

Mercure Pont de Bercy M, 6 bd Vincent Auriol (13th) ✆ 45 82 48 00, Telex 205010, Fax 45 82 19 16 - ▤ ⇆ rm ▤ rest TV ☎ ♿ - 🎤 40. AE ⓓ GB M 18
M *(closed 31 July-31 August, 24 December-3 January, Saturday, Sunday and Bank Holidays)* a la carte 170/230 - ☕ 60 - **89 rm** 680/800.

Mercure Paris Tolbiac M without rest, 21 r. Tolbiac (13th) ✆ 45 84 61 61, Telex 250822, Fax 45 84 43 38 - ▤ ⇆ rm TV ☎ ♿ P - 🎤 25. AE ⓓ GB P 18
☕ 60 - **71 rm** 520/750.

Équinoxe without rest, 40 r. Le Brun (13th) ✆ 43 37 56 56, Telex 201476, Fax 45 35 52 42 - ▤ TV ☎ 🚗. AE ⓓ GB JCB N 15
☕ 30 - **49 rm** 450/590.

Relais de Lyon without rest, 64 r. Crozatier (12th) ✆ 43 44 22 50, Telex 216690, Fax 43 41 55 12 - ▤ TV ☎ 🚗. AE ⓓ GB. ✂ K 19
☕ 33 - **34 rm** 415/515.

Quatre Saisons Bastille M without rest, 67 r. Lyon (12th) 40 01 07 17, Telex 214223, Fax 40 01 07 27 – 25. AE GB K 18
45 – **36 rm** 760/950.

Modern H. Lyon without rest, 3 r. Parrot (12th) 43 43 41 52, Telex 220083, Fax 43 43 81 16 – . AE GB. L 18
37 – **48 rm** 495/640.

Média M without rest, 22 r. Reine Blanche (13th) 45 35 72 72, Telex 206702, Fax 43 31 43 31 – rm – 25. AE GB JCB M 15
30 – **19 rm** 450/560.

de Weha M without rest, 205 av. Choisy (13th) 45 86 06 06, Telex 206898, Fax 43 31 42 06 – rm . AE GB P 16
40 – **34 rm** 539/660.

Belle Époque without rest, 66 r. Charenton (12th) 43 44 06 66, Telex 211551, Fax 43 44 10 25 – – 25. AE GB JCB K 18
50 – **30 rm** 530/670.

Terminus-Lyon without rest, 19 bd Diderot (12th) 43 43 24 03, Telex 220117, Fax 43 44 09 00 – . AE GB JCB. L 18
38 – **61 rm** 520.

Slavia without rest, 51 bd St-Marcel (13th) 43 37 81 25, Fax 45 87 05 03 – . AE GB. M 16
30 – **37 rm** 310/350, 6 suites.

Midi without rest, 114 av. Daumesnil (12th) 43 07 72 03, Telex 215917, Fax 43 43 21 75 – . AE GB JCB L 20
35 – **36 rm** 375/450.

Résidence Vert Galant M, 43 r. Croulebarbe (13th) 44 08 83 50, Telex 202371, Fax 44 08 83 69 – . AE GB. rm N 15
M see rest. **Etchegory** below – 35 – **15 rm** 400/500.

Ibis Paris Bercy M, 77 r. Bercy (12th) 43 42 91 91, Telex 216391, Fax 43 42 34 79, – rm rest – 25 - 180. AE GB M 19
M 98 – 35 – **368 rm** 465.

Corail without rest, 23 r. Lyon (12th) 43 43 23 54, Telex 212002, Fax 43 43 82 55 – . AE GB JCB L 18
35 – **50 rm** 340/410.

Marceau without rest, 13 r. J. César (12th) 43 43 11 65, Telex 214006, Fax 43 41 67 70 – . GB. K 17
closed 15 July-15 August – 35 – **53 rm** 340/390.

Campanile without rest, 15 bis av. Italie (13th) 45 84 95 95, Telex 205256, Fax 45 70 73 06 – . AE GB. P 16
30 – **122 rm** 365/410.

Nouvel H. without rest, 24 av. Bel Air (12th) 43 43 01 81, Telex 240139, Fax 43 44 64 13, – . AE GB L 21
40 – **28 rm** 395/575.

Gd H. Gobelins without rest, 57 bd St-Marcel (13th) 43 31 79 89, Fax 45 35 43 56 – . AE GB M 16
30 – **45 rm** 400/450.

des Trois Gares without rest, 1 r. J. César (12th) 43 43 01 70, Fax 43 41 36 58 – . GB. K 17
35 – **36 rm** 230/420.

Viator without rest, 1 r. Parrot (12th) 43 43 11 00, Telex 216236, Fax 43 43 10 89 – . GB. L 18
35 – **45 rm** 320/370.

Palym H. without rest, 4 r. E.-Gilbert (12th) 43 43 24 48, Fax 43 41 69 47 – . GB
35 – **51 rm** 320/380. L 18

Ibis without rest, 177 r. Tolbiac (13th) 45 80 16 60, Telex 200821, Fax 45 80 95 80 – rm . AE GB P 15
35 – **60 rm** 370/400.

Résidence Les Gobelins without rest, 9 r. Gobelins (13th) 47 07 26 90, Telex 206566, Fax 43 31 44 05 – . AE GB. N 15
34 – **32 rm** 340/420.

Timhôtel without rest, 22 r. Barrault (13th) 45 80 67 67, Telex 205461, Fax 45 89 36 93 – . AE GB JCB P 15
47 – **73 rm** 425.

If you would like a more complete selection of hotels and restaurants, consult the Michelin Red Guides for the following countries : Benelux, Deutschland, España Portugal, France, Great Britain and Ireland, Italia.

XXX ✿ **Au Pressoir** (Séguin), 257 av. Daumesnil (12th) ✆ 43 44 38 21, Fax 43 43 81 77 - ▤. GB — M 22
closed August, February Holidays, Saturday and Sunday - **M** 370 and a la carte 320/480
Spec. Terrine de lièvre au foie gras (October-December). Sandre au vin rouge, mousseline de céleri. Ravioli de homard en cassolette.

XXX **Train Bleu,** Gare de Lyon (12th) ✆ 43 43 09 06, Fax 43 43 97 96, « Murals evoking the journey from Paris to the Mediterranean » - AE ⓓ GB — L 18
M (1st floor) 280 and a la carte 220/350.

XX ✿ **Au Trou Gascon,** 40 r. Taine (12th) ✆ 43 44 34 26, Fax 43 07 80 55 - ▤. AE ⓓ GB JCB — M 21
closed August, Christmas-New Year, Saturday and Sunday - **M** (booking essential) 200 and a la carte 300/440
Spec. Demi-homard en gaspacho blanc (June-October). Petit pâté chaud de cèpes. Perdreau sauvage rôti en cocotte (October-December).

XX **La Gourmandise,** 271 av. Daumesnil (12th) ✆ 43 43 94 41 - AE GB — M 22
closed 8 to 22 August, Sunday and Monday - **M** 190/350.

XX **Café Fouquet's Bastille,** 130 r. Lyon (12th) ✆ 43 42 18 18, Fax 43 42 08 20 - ▤. AE ⓓ GB JCB — K 18
closed August, Saturday lunch and Sunday - **M** 165 and a la carte 170/300.

XX **Les Vieux Métiers de France,** 13 bd A. Blanqui (13th) ✆ 45 88 90 03 - ▤. AE ⓓ GB JCB — P 15
closed Sunday and Monday - **M** 165/290.

XX **L'Oulette,** 15 pl. Lachambeaudie (12th) ✆ 40 02 02 12, 🏛 - ▤. AE GB — N 20
closed 1 to 15 August, Saturday lunch and Sunday - **M** 130 (lunch) and a la carte 220/320.

XX **Au Petit Marguery,** 9 bd Port-Royal (13th) ✆ 43 31 58 59 - AE ⓓ GB — M 15
closed August, 25 December-2 January, Sunday and Monday - **M** 160 (lunch)/400.

XX **Le Luneau,** 5 r. Lyon (12th) ✆ 43 43 90 85 - AE ⓓ GB — L 18
M 143 and a la carte 210/320 ♁.

XX **La Frégate,** 30 av. Ledru-Rollin (12th) ✆ 43 43 90 32 - ▤. AE GB — L 18
closed August, Saturday and Sunday - **M** Seafood 200/300.

XX **La Flambée,** 4 r. Taine (12th) ✆ 43 43 21 80 - AE GB JCB — M 20
closed 2 to 23 August, 20 to 27 December, Sunday dinner and Monday - **M** 129/175.

XX **Le Traversière,** 40 r. Traversière (12th) ✆ 43 44 02 10 - AE ⓓ GB JCB — K 18
closed August, Sunday dinner and Bank Holidays - **M** 160 and a la carte 200/350.

XX **La Sologne,** 164 av. Daumesnil (12th) ✆ 43 07 68 97 - GB JCB — M 21
closed Saturday lunch, Sunday and Bank Holidays - **M** 175/250.

XX **L'Escapade en Touraine,** 24 r. Traversière (12th) ✆ 43 43 14 96 - GB JCB — L 18
closed 31 July-30 August, Saturday, Sunday and Bank Holidays - **M** 100 (dinner)/140.

X **Mange Tout,** 24 bd Bastille (12th) ✆ 43 43 95 15 - AE GB — K 17
closed 15 to 30 August and Sunday - **M** 98 b.i./190.

X **Le Quincy,** 28 av. Ledru-Rollin (12th) ✆ 46 28 46 76 - ▤ — L 17
closed 10 August-10 September, Saturday, Sunday and Monday - **M** a la carte 210/360.

X **Etchegorry,** 41 r. Croulebarbe (13th) ✆ 44 08 83 51, Fax 44 08 83 69 - ▤. AE ⓓ GB — N 15
closed Sunday - **M** 140 b.i./190 b.i.

X **Chez Françoise,** 12 r. Butte aux Cailles (13th) ✆ 45 80 12 02, Fax 45 65 13 67 - AE ⓓ GB. ✂ — P 15
closed 28 July-1 September, Saturday lunch and Sunday - **M** 66 b.i. (lunch)/134.

X **Le Temps des Cerises,** 216 fg St-Antoine (12th) ✆ 43 67 52 08 - ▤. AE GB — K 20
M 90/200 ♁.

X **A la Biche au Bois,** 45 av. Ledru-Rollin (12th) ✆ 43 43 34 38 - AE ⓓ GB — K 18
closed 15 July-15 August, Christmas-New Year, Saturday and Sunday - **M** 95/108 ♁.

X **Le Rhône,** 40 bd Arago (13th) ✆ 47 07 33 57, 🏛 - GB — N 14
closed August, Saturday, Sunday and Bank Holidays - **M** 80/160 ♁.

Vaugirard, Gare Montparnasse, Grenelle, Denfert-Rochereau.

14th and 15th arrondissements.
14th: ✉ 75014
15th: ✉ 75015

Hilton M, 18 av. Suffren (15th) ✆ 42 73 92 00, Telex 200955, Fax 47 83 62 66, – rm rest TV – 100. AE GB J 7
Western M 170 and a la carte 245/340 – **La Terrasse M** 140/170 – 120 – **436 rm** 1850/2300, 20 suites.

Nikko M, 61 quai Grenelle (15th) ✆ 40 58 20 00, Telex 205811, Fax 45 75 42 35, <, – rm TV – 800. AE GB JCB K 6
M see **Les Célébrités** below - **Brasserie Pont Mirabeau M** 175 and a la carte 190/400 – **Rest. japonais Benkay** *(closed Monday)* **M** a la carte 280/450 – 80 – **761 rm** 1660/2460, 7 suites.

Méridien Montparnasse M, 19 r. Cdt-Mouchotte (14th) ✆ 44 36 44 36, Telex 200135, Fax 44 36 49 00, < – rm TV – 1 400. AE GB JCB. rest M 11
M see **Montparnasse 25** below - **Justine** ✆ 44 36 44 00 **M** a la carte 175/230 – 115 – **918 rm** 1250/1950, 35 suites.

Sofitel Paris Porte de Sèvres M, 8 r. L.-Armand (15th) ✆ 40 60 30 30, Telex 200484, Fax 45 57 04 22, <, indoor pool overlooking Paris, – rm TV – 1 200. AE GB JCB N 5
M see **Le Relais de Sèvres** below - **La Tonnelle** (brasserie) **M** 105 b.i./180 b.i. – 85 – **601 rm** 750/980, 14 suites.

Pullman St-Jacques M, 17 bd St-Jacques (14th) ✆ 40 78 79 80, Telex 270740, Fax 45 88 43 93 – rm TV – 40 - 1 200. AE GB JCB N 13-14
Brasserie Le Français M 179 b.i. – 110 – **783 rm** 1230/1360, 14 suites.

Mercure Paris Vaugirard M, porte de Versailles (15th) ✆ 44 19 03 03, Telex 205628, Fax 48 28 22 11 – rm TV – 120. AE GB N 7
M 150 – 70 – **91 rm** 790/1400.

Mercure Paris Montparnasse M, 20 r. Gaîté (14th) ✆ 43 35 28 28, Telex 201532, Fax 43 27 98 64 – TV – 100. AE GB JCB M 11
Bistrot de la Gaîté M 120/180 – 68 – **178 rm** 790/930, 7 suites.

L'Aiglon without rest, 232 bd Raspail (14th) ✆ 43 20 82 42, Telex 206038, Fax 43 20 98 72 – kitchenette . AE GB JCB M 12
35 – **38 rm** 470/690, 9 suites.

Lenox Montparnasse M without rest, 15 r. Delambre (14th) ✆ 43 35 34 50, Telex 205937, Fax 43 20 46 64 – TV . AE GB JCB M 12
45 – **52 rm** 510/950.

Orléans Palace H. without rest, 185 bd Brune (14th) ✆ 45 39 68 50, Telex 205490, Fax 45 43 65 64 – TV – 35. AE GB R 11
45 – **92 rm** 470/540.

Mercure Paris XV M without rest, 6 r. St-Lambert (15th) ✆ 45 58 61 00, Telex 206936, Fax 45 54 10 43 – TV . AE GB M 7
50 – **56 rm** 580/680.

Messidor without rest, 330 r. Vaugirard (15th) ✆ 48 28 03 74, Telex 204606, Fax 48 28 75 17, – TV . AE GB JCB M 8
50 – **72 rm** 480/940.

Waldorf M without rest, 17 r. Départ (14th) ✆ 43 20 64 79, Telex 201677, Fax 43 35 17 52 – TV . AE GB JCB. L 11
42 – **30 rm** 600/780.

Raspail M without rest, 203 bd Raspail (14th) ✆ 43 20 62 86, Fax 43 20 50 79 – TV . AE GB. M 12
40 – **36 rm** 550/850.

Alizé Grenelle M without rest, 87 av. É. Zola (15th) ✆ 45 78 08 22, Telex 250095, Fax 40 59 03 06 – TV . AE GB JCB L 7
32 – **50 rm** 380/420.

Beaugrenelle St-Charles M without rest, 82 r. St-Charles (15th) ✆ 45 78 61 63, Telex 270263, Fax 45 79 04 38 – TV . AE GB JCB K 7
32 – **51 rm** 350/420.

Renoir M without rest, 39 r. Montparnasse (14th) ✆ 43 21 72 50, Telex 205436, Fax 43 21 68 72 – TV . AE GB. L 12
35 – **29 rm** 500/630.

🏨 **Versailles** M without rest, 213 r. Croix Nivert (15th) ☏ 48 28 48 66, Telex 200473, Fax 45 30 16 22 – lift TV ☎. AE ① GB N 7
☕ 40 – **41 rm** 470/690.

🏨 **Châtillon H.** without rest, 11 square Châtillon (14th) ☏ 45 42 31 17, Fax 45 42 72 09 – lift TV ☎. GB. ✻ P 11
☕ 28 – **31 rm** 300/330.

🏨 **Terminus Vaugirard** without rest, 403 r. Vaugirard (15th) ☏ 48 28 18 72, Telex 206562, Fax 48 28 56 34 – lift ⇔ rm TV ☎. GB. ✻ N 7
closed 20 to 26 December – ☕ 45 – **89 rm** 480/600.

🏨 **Wallace** without rest, 89 r. Fondary (15th) ☏ 45 78 83 30, Telex 205277, Fax 40 58 19 43 – lift TV ☎. AE ① GB JCB. ✻ L 8
☕ 40 – **35 rm** 530/550.

🏨 **Acropole** without rest, 199 bd Brune (14th) ☏ 45 39 64 17, Telex 203131, Fax 45 42 18 21 – lift TV ☎. AE ① GB. ✻ R 12
☕ 30 – **41 rm** 350/460.

🏨 **L'Alligator** without rest, 39 r. Delambre (14th) ☏ 43 35 18 40, Telex 270545, Fax 43 35 30 71 – lift TV ☎. AE ① GB M 12
☕ 45 – **35 rm** 430/650.

🏨 **Résidence St-Lambert** without rest, 5 r. E. Gibez (15th) ☏ 48 28 63 14, Telex 205459, Fax 45 33 45 50 – lift TV ☎. AE ① GB JCB N 8
☕ 38 – **48 rm** 490/550.

🏨 **Alésia Montparnasse** without rest, 84 r. R. Losserand (14th) ☏ 45 42 16 03, Fax 45 42 11 60 – lift ⇔ rm TV ☎. AE ① GB JCB N 10
☕ 40 – **45 rm** 490/520.

🏠 **Carladez Cambronne** without rest, 3 pl. Gén. Beuret (15th) ☏ 47 34 07 12, Telex 206823, Fax 40 65 95 68 – lift TV ☎. AE GB M 9
☕ 30 – **27 rm** 370/415.

🏠 **Apollon Montparnasse** M without rest, 91 r. Ouest (14th) ☏ 43 95 62 00, Fax 43 95 62 10 – lift TV ☎. AE ① GB. ✻ N 10-11
☕ 35 – **32 rm** 380/450.

🏠 **Lion** M without rest, 1 av. Gén. Leclerc (14th) ☏ 40 47 04 00, Fax 43 20 38 18 – lift ⇔ rm TV ☎. AE GB N 12
☕ 40 – **33 rm** 370/570.

🏠 **Lilas Blanc** M without rest, 5 r. Avre (15th) ☏ 45 75 30 07, Fax 45 78 66 65 – lift TV ☎. AE ① GB JCB K 8
☕ 30 – **32 rm** 375/435.

🏠 **Ariane Montparnasse** without rest, 35 r. Sablière (14th) ☏ 45 45 67 13, Telex 203554, Fax 45 45 39 49 – lift TV ☎. AE GB N 11
☕ 35 – **30 rm** 390/500.

🏠 **Fondary** without rest, 30 r. Fondary (15th) ☏ 45 75 14 75, Fax 45 75 84 42 – lift TV ☎. AE GB L 8
☕ 38 – **20 rm** 375/405.

🏠 **Istria** without rest, 29 r. Campagne Première (14th) ☏ 43 20 91 82, Telex 203618, Fax 43 22 48 45 – lift TV ☎. AE GB JCB M 12
☕ 40 – **26 rm** 510/560.

🏠 **Modern H. Val Girard** without rest, 14 r. Pétel (15th) ☏ 48 28 53 96, Fax 48 28 69 94 – lift TV ☎. AE GB M 8
☕ 35 – **39 rm** 360/440.

🏠 **Pasteur** without rest, 33 r. Dr.-Roux (15th) ☏ 47 83 53 17, Fax 45 66 62 39 – lift TV ☎. GB M 10
closed August – ☕ 38 – **19 rm** 310/450.

🏠 **des Bains** without rest, 33 r. Delambre (14th) ☏ 43 20 85 27, Fax 42 79 82 78 – lift TV ☎ M 12
☕ 40 – **41 rm** 340/410.

XXXX ✿ **Les Célébrités** - Hôtel Nikko, 61 quai Grenelle (15th) ✆ 40 58 20 00, Telex 205811, Fax 45 75 42 35, ← - ▤. AE ⓓ GB JCB K 6
closed 8 to 22 August - **M** 280/680 and a la carte 450/700
Spec. Salade tiéde de langoustines aux cèpes (season). Tronçon de turbot à la tomate et basilic. Lièvre à la royale (10 October-31 December).

XXXX ✿ **Montparnasse 25** - Hôtel Méridien Montparnasse, 19 r. Cdt Mouchotte (14th) ✆ 44 36 44 25, Telex 200135, Fax 44 36 49 00 - ▤ Ⓟ. AE ⓓ GB. ✻ M 11
closed 31 July-29 August, 21 to 27 December, Saturday and Sunday - **M** 230 (lunch)/450 and a la carte 270/400
Spec. Grosses langoustines et ris de veau poêlé (March-July). Saumon sauvage rôti et navets confits à la poitrine de porc fumée (May-October). Carré d'agneau de Pauillac en croûte d'épices..

XXXX ✿ **Relais de Sèvres** - Hôtel Sofitel Paris, 8 r. L.-Armand (15th) ✆ 40 60 33 66, Telex 200484, Fax 45 57 04 22 - ▤. AE ⓓ GB JCB N 5
closed August, Christmas-New Year and weekends - **M** 320 (lunch)/430 and a la carte 300/400
Spec. Minute de haddock en salade de pommes aux truffes. Fricassée de sole à l'aigre-doux. Cœur de filet de bœuf à la mitonnée de pleurotes.

XXX ✿ **Morot Gaudry,** 6 r. Cavalerie (15th) (8th floor) ✆ 45 67 06 85, Fax 45 67 55 72, 🏛 - ▤. AE GB JCB K 8
closed Saturday and Sunday - **M** 220 b.i. (lunch)/550 b.i. and a la carte 340/450
Spec. Blanc de turbot à l'huile vierge et coulis de tomate. Côte de veau de lait aux champignons sauvages. Grouse rôtie, gratin de navet et topinambour (15 September-28 February).

XXX **Pavillon Montsouris,** 20 r. Gazan (14th) ✆ 45 88 38 52, Fax 45 88 63 40, ←, 🏛, « 1900 pavilion beside the park » - Ⓟ. AE ⓓ GB. ✻ R 14
M 185/255.

XXX **Armes de Bretagne,** 108 av. Maine (14th) ✆ 43 20 29 50 - ▤. AE ⓓ GB N 11
closed August - **M** 200 and a la carte 245/440.

XXX **Moniage Guillaume** with rm, 88 r. Tombe-Issoire (14th) ✆ 43 22 96 15, Fax 43 27 11 79 - TV ☎. AE ⓓ GB JCB P 12
closed 10 to 31 August and Sunday - **M** 195 b.i. (lunch)/260 and a la carte 260/460 - ☕ 30 - **5 rm** 280/350.

XXX **Lous Landès,** 157 av. Maine (14th) ✆ 45 43 08 04 - ▤. AE ⓓ GB N 11
closed 1 to 25 August, Saturday lunch and Sunday - **M** 295 and a la carte 275/400.

XXX **Olympe,** 8 r. Nicolas Charlet (15th) ✆ 47 34 86 08, Fax 44 49 05 04 - ▤. AE ⓓ GB JCB
closed Monday and lunch Saturday and Sunday - **M** 160 b.i./285 b.i. L 10

XX **Lal Qila,** 88 av. É. Zola (15th) ✆ 45 75 68 40, « Unusual decor » - ▤. AE GB. ✻ L 7
closed Saturday lunch - **M** Indian rest. 105 (lunch)/185.

XX **Jacques Hébert,** 38 r. Sébastien Mercier (15th) ✆ 45 57 77 88 - GB. ✻ L 5
closed 1 to 16 August, Sunday and Monday - **M** 185/260 and a la carte 250/400.

XX **L'Aubergade,** 53 av. La Motte-Picquet (15th) ✆ 47 83 23 85 - AE GB J 9
closed 5 to 15 April, 1 to 26 August, Sunday dinner and Monday - **M** 150 b.i. (lunch) and a la carte 250/380.

XX **La Chaumière des Gourmets,** 22 pl. Denfert-Rochereau (14th) ✆ 43 21 22 59 - AE GB
closed August, Saturday lunch and Sunday - **M** 165/240. N 12

XX **Le Dôme,** 108 bd Montparnasse (14th) ✆ 43 35 25 81, Fax 42 79 01 19 - ▤. AE ⓓ GB
closed Monday - **M** Seafood - a la carte 300/400. LM 12

XX **Bistro 121,** 121 r. Convention (15th) ✆ 45 57 52 90 - AE ⓓ GB JCB M 7
M 200 b.i. and a la carte 210/360.

XX **La Coupole,** 102 bd Montparnasse (14th) ✆ 43 20 14 20, Fax 43 35 46 14, « 1920 Parisian brasserie » - AE ⓓ GB L 12
M 159 b.i. and a la carte 180/280 🍷.

XX ✿ **Petite Bretonnière** (Lamaison), 2 r. Cadix (15th) ✆ 48 28 34 39 - GB N 7
closed August, Saturday lunch and Sunday - **M** a la carte 280/400
Spec. Salade de langoustines rôties. Cœur de rumsteack de boeuf de Chalosse au vin de Madiran. Consommé de cèpes au foie gras chaud (October-December).

XX **Yves Quintard,** 99 r. Blomet (15th) ✆ 42 50 22 27 - GB M 8
closed August - **M** 160 and a la carte 250/350.

XX **Didier Délu,** 85 r. Leblanc (15th) ✆ 45 54 20 49, Fax 40 60 74 88 - AE ⓓ GB M 5
closed 1 to 22 August, 23 December-1 January, Saturday and Sunday - **M** 180 (lunch)/300.

XX **L'Entre Siècle,** 29 av. Lowendal (15th) ✆ 47 83 51 22 - AE GB K 9
closed August, Saturday lunch and Sunday - **M** Belgium rest. 160 (lunch) and a la carte 240/330.

XX **Aux Senteurs de Provence,** 295 r. Lecourbe (15th) ✆ 45 57 11 98 - AE ⓓ GB M 6
closed 3 to 23 August, Sunday and Monday - **M** Seafood 158 (lunch)/198.

XX **Napoléon et Chaix,** 46 r. Balard (15th) ✆ 45 54 09 00 - ▤. GB M 5
closed August, Saturday lunch and Sunday - **M** a la carte 210/310.

XX **Monsieur Lapin,** 11 r. R. Losserand (14th) ✆ 43 20 21 39 – AE GB N 11
closed August, Saturday lunch and Monday – **M** 120 (lunch) and a la carte 210/330.

XX **Le Caroubier,** 122 av. Maine (14th) ✆ 43 20 41 49 – ▤. GB N 11
closed August, Sunday dinner and Monday – **M** North African rest. 130 ♁.

XX **Le Copreaux,** 15 r. Copreaux (15th) ✆ 43 06 83 35 – GB M 9
closed Saturday except dinner September-July and Sunday – **M** 145/255.

XX **L'Étape,** 89 r. Convention (15th) ✆ 45 54 73 49 – ▤. GB M 6
closed 24 December-2 January – **M** 150 b.i./190 b.i.

XX **Le Clos Morillons,** 50 r. Morillons (15th) ✆ 48 28 04 37 – GB N 8
closed 1 to 22 August, February Holidays, Saturday lunch and Sunday – **M** 160/285.

XX **Filoche,** 34 r. Laos (15th) ✆ 45 66 44 60 – GB. ✻ K 8
closed 14 July-20 August, 20 December-3 January, Saturday and Sunday – **M** a la carte 200/280.

XX **La Giberne,** 42bis av. Suffren (15th) ✆ 47 34 82 18 – AE ⓓ GB JCB J 8
closed 25 July-21 August, Saturday lunch and Sunday – **M** 165 b.i./350 ♁.

XX **Les Vendanges,** 40 r. Friant (14th) ✆ 45 39 59 98 – GB R 11
closed August, Saturday lunch, Sunday and Bank Holidays – **M** 155 and a la carte 215/340.

XX **Pierre Vedel,** 19 r. Duranton (15th) ✆ 45 58 43 17, Fax 45 58 42 65 – GB. ✻ M 6
closed Christmas-New Year, Saturday and Sunday – **M** a la carte 210/290.

XX **Mina Mahal,** 25 r. Cambronne (15th) ✆ 47 34 19 88 – ▤. AE ⓓ GB. ✻ L 8
closed Saturday lunch – **M** Indian rest. 230/350.

XX **La Roseraie,** 15 r. Ferdinand Fabre (15th) ✆ 48 28 60 24 – AE GB M 8
closed August, Saturday lunch and Sunday – **M** 160 and a la carte 200/320.

XX **La Chaumière,** 54 av. F.-Faure (15th) ✆ 45 54 13 91 – AE ⓓ GB M 7
closed August, Monday dinner and Tuesday – **M** 150 and a la carte 180/300.

XX **de la Tour,** 6 r. Desaix (15th) ✆ 43 06 04 24 – AE GB J 8
closed 1 to 25 August, Saturday lunch and Sunday – **M** 118 b.i. (lunch)/168 ♁.

X ✿ **La Cagouille** (Allemandou), 10 pl. Constantin Brancusi (14th) ✆ 43 22 09 01, Fax 45 38 57 29, ☂ – AE GB M 11
closed 1 to 10 May, 8 to 30 August and 24 December-3 January – **M** Seafood 150/250 b.i. and a la carte 260/400
Spec. Chaudrée charentaise (winter). Pétoncles noirs au four (October-November). Céteaux à la poêle.

X **L'Épopée,** 89 av. É. Zola (15th) ✆ 45 77 71 37 – GB L 7
closed Saturday lunch and Sunday dinner – **M** 165.

X **Bistrot du Dôme,** 1 r. Delambre (14th) ✆ 43 35 32 00 – AE ⓓ GB M 12
M Seafood - a la carte approx. 175.

X **Oh ! Duo,** 54 av. E. Zola (15th) ✆ 45 77 28 82 – GB L 6
closed 14 July-15 August, Saturday and Sunday – **M** 133/140 ♁.

X **Le Gastroquet,** 10 r. Desnouettes (15th) ✆ 48 28 60 91 – GB N 7
closed late July-early August, Sunday except dinner in winter and Saturday – **M** 140 and a la carte 170/260.

X **La Bonne Table,** 42 r. Friant (14th) ✆ 45 39 74 91 – GB R 11
closed July, 25 December-4 January, Saturday and Sunday – **M** a la carte 200/350.

X **La Datcha Lydie,** 7 r. Dupleix (15th) ✆ 45 66 67 77 – GB K 8
closed 12 July-31 August and Wednesday – **M** Russian rest. 125 b.i. and a la carte 130/280.

X **Chez Pierre,** 117 r. Vaugirard (15th) ✆ 47 34 96 12 – ▤. AE GB L 11
closed August, Saturday lunch, Sunday and Bank Holidays – **M** 145 b.i./210 b.i. and a la carte 185/265.

X **L'Armoise,** 67 r. Entrepreneurs (15th) ✆ 45 79 03 31 – GB L 7
closed 1 to 22 August, February Holidays, Saturday lunch and Sunday – **M** 125 and a la carte 130/150 ♁.

X **Les Cévennes,** 55 r. Cévennes (15th) ✆ 45 54 33 76 – AE GB. ✻ L 6
closed 15 to 31 August, Saturday lunch and Sunday – **M** 110 and a la carte 115/290.

X **Chez Yvette,** 46bis bd Montparnasse (15th) ✆ 42 22 45 54 – GB L 11
closed August, Saturday and Sunday – **M** a la carte 150/250.

X **L'Amuse Bouche,** 186 r. Château (14th) ✆ 43 35 31 61 – AE GB N 11
closed 2 to 16 August, Saturday lunch and Sunday – **M** (booking essential) 145 (lunch) and a la carte 210/360.

X **La Gitane,** 53bis av. La Motte-Picquet (15th) ✆ 47 34 62 92, ☂ – GB K 8
closed Saturday and Sunday – **M** a la carte 130/210.

X **La Régalade,** 49 av. J. Moulin (14th) ✆ 45 45 68 58 – GB. ✻ R 11
closed Saturday lunch, Sunday and Monday – **M** (booking essential) 150.

X **Fellini,** 58 r. Croix-Nivert (15th) ✆ 45 77 40 77 – ▤. GB. ✻ L 8
closed August, Saturday lunch and Sunday – **M** Italian rest. - a la carte 200/300.

X **St-Vincent,** 26 r. Croix-Nivert (15th) ✆ 47 34 14 94 – ▤. GB. ✻ L 8
closed 15 to 22 August, Saturday and Sunday – **M** a la carte 170/220.

Passy, Auteuil, Bois de Boulogne, Chaillot, Porte Maillot.

16th arrondissement.
16th: ✉ 75016

Le Parc Victor Hugo M, 55 av. Poincaré ✉ 75116 ☎ 44 05 66 66, Telex 643862, Fax 44 05 66 00, « Fine English furniture » – rm – 30 - 250. AE GB JCB G 6
Le Relais du Parc ☎ 44 05 66 10 **M** a la carte 175/260 – ☕ 115 – **111 rm** 1600/2200.

Raphaël, 17 av. Kléber ✉ 75116 ☎ 44 28 00 28, Telex 645356, Fax 45 01 21 50, « Elegant decor » – rm rest – 50. AE GB JCB F 7
M 225 and a la carte 270/450 – ☕ 95 – **64 rm** 1600/2700, 23 suites.

St-James Paris, 5 pl. Chancelier Adenauer ✉ 75116 ☎ 47 04 29 29, Telex 643850, Fax 45 53 00 61, « Elegant neo classic style », – – 25. AE GB JCB. rest F 5
M *(closed Saturday and Sunday)* (residents only) a la carte 310/480 – ☕ 110 – **20 rm** 1400/1900, 20 suites, 8 duplex.

Baltimore M, 88bis av. Kléber ✉ 75116 ☎ 44 34 54 54, Telex 645284, Fax 44 34 54 44 – rm rest – 30 - 100. AE GB JCB. rest G 7
L'Estournel *(closed August, Saturday and Sunday)* **M** 210 and a la carte 260/400 – ☕ 115 – **104 rm** 1900/2500.

Garden Elysée M, 12 r. St-Didier ✉ 75116 ☎ 47 55 01 11, Telex 648157, Fax 47 27 79 24, – . AE GB JCB. G 7
M *(closed August, Saturday and Sunday)* 160/250 and a la carte 210/305 – ☕ 80 – **48 rm** 1450/1600.

Villa Maillot M without rest, 143 av. Malakoff ✉ 75116 ☎ 45 01 25 22, Telex 649808, Fax 45 00 60 61 – – 30. AE GB JCB F 6
☕ 110 – **39 rm** 1550/2300, 3 suites.

Pergolèse M without rest, 3 r. Pergolèse ✉ 75116 ☎ 40 67 96 77, Telex 651618, Fax 45 00 12 11 – . AE GB E 6
☕ 70 – **40 rm** 1200/1500.

Majestic without rest, 29 r. Dumont d'Urville ✉ 75116 ☎ 45 00 83 70, Telex 640034, Fax 45 00 29 48 – rm . AE GB JCB F 7
☕ 55 – **27 rm** 900/1400, 3 suites.

Floride Etoile M, 14 r. St-Didier ✉ 75116 ☎ 47 27 23 36, Telex 643715, Fax 47 27 82 87 – rest – 40. AE GB JCB. G 7
closed August, Saturday and Sunday – **M** coffee shop - a la carte approx. 190 – ☕ 45 – **60 rm** 810/860.

Alexander without rest, 102 av. V. Hugo ✉ 75116 ☎ 45 53 64 65, Telex 645373, Fax 45 53 12 51 – . AE GB JCB. G 6
☕ 65 – **59 rm** 830/1300, 3 suites.

Frémiet without rest, 6 av. Frémiet ✉ 75016 ☎ 45 24 52 06, Telex 645329, Fax 42 88 77 46 – . AE GB JCB J 6
☕ 40 – **34 rm** 775/915.

Victor Hugo without rest, 19 r. Copernic ✉ 75116 ☎ 45 53 76 01, Telex 645939, Fax 45 53 69 93 – . AE GB. G 7
☕ 50 – **76 rm** 630/765.

Union H. Étoile without rest, 44 r. Hamelin ✉ 75116 ☎ 45 53 14 95, Telex 645217, Fax 47 55 94 79 – kitchenette . AE GB JCB G 7
☕ 40 – **28 rm** 680/790, 13 suites.

Rond-Point de Longchamp M, 86 r. Longchamp ✉ 75116 ☎ 45 05 13 63, Telex 640883, Fax 47 55 12 80 – – 40. AE GB G 6
M (snack) a la carte approx. 180 – ☕ 65 – **57 rm** 780/870.

Massenet without rest, 5bis r. Massenet ✉ 75116 ☎ 45 24 43 03, Telex 640196, Fax 45 24 41 39 – . AE GB JCB. J 6
☕ 40 – **41 rm** 525/820.

Sévigné without rest, 6 r. Belloy ✉ 75116 ☎ 47 20 88 90, Telex 645219, Fax 40 70 98 73 – . AE GB JCB G 7
☕ 45 – **30 rm** 620/740.

Résidence Bassano M without rest, 15 r. Bassano ✉ 75116 ☎ 47 23 78 23, Telex 649872, Fax 47 20 41 22 – kitchenette TV ☎. AE ① GB G 8
☕ 70 – **27 rm** 850/1300, 3 suites.

Élysées Régencia M without rest, 41 av. Marceau ✉ 75016 ☎ 47 20 42 65, Telex 644965, Fax 49 52 03 42, « Attractive decor » – TV ☎. AE ① GB G 8
☕ 80 – **35 rm** 1200/1500.

Elysées Bassano without rest, 24 r. Bassano ✉ 75116 ☎ 47 20 49 03, Telex 645280, Fax 47 23 06 72 – rm TV ☎. AE ① GB JCB G 8
☕ 75 – **40 rm** 790/820.

Résidence Impériale M without rest, 155 av. Malakoff ✉ 75116 ☎ 45 00 23 45, Telex 651158, Fax 45 01 88 82 – TV ☎. AE ① GB JCB E 6
☕ 45 – **37 rm** 740/890.

Kléber without rest, 7 r. Belloy ✉ 75116 ☎ 47 23 80 22, Telex 642478, Fax 49 52 07 20 – rm TV ☎. AE ① GB – ☕ 45 – **21 rm** 780. G 7

Résidence Kléber M without rest, 97 r. Lauriston ✉ 75116 ☎ 45 53 83 30, Telex 642707, Fax 47 55 92 52 – TV ☎. AE ① GB JCB G 7
☕ 40 – **51 rm** 780.

Résidence Foch without rest, 10 r. Marbeau ✉ 75116 ☎ 45 00 46 50, Telex 645886, Fax 45 01 98 68 – TV ☎. AE ① GB F 6
☕ 40 – **21 rm** 650/740, 4 suites.

Murat M without rest, 119bis bd Murat ✉ 75016 ☎ 46 51 12 32, Telex 648963, Fax 46 51 70 01 – TV ☎. AE ① GB. M 3
☕ 35 – **28 rm** 525/575.

Ambassade without rest, 79 r. Lauriston ✉ 75116 ☎ 45 53 41 15, Telex 613643, Fax 45 53 30 80 – TV ☎. AE ① GB. G 7
☕ 40 – **38 rm** 458/560.

Longchamp without rest, 68 r. Longchamp ✉ 75116 ☎ 47 27 13 48, Fax 47 55 68 26 – TV ☎. AE ① GB – ☕ 50 – **23 rm** 640/780. G 6

Résidence Chambellan Morgane M without rest, 6 r. Keppler ✉ 75116 ☎ 47 20 35 72, Telex 643166, Fax 47 20 95 69 – TV ☎. AE ① GB. GF 8
☕ 50 – **20 rm** 600/900.

Étoile Maillot without rest, 10 r. Bois de Boulogne (angle r. Duret) ✉ 75116 ☎ 45 00 42 60, Fax 45 00 55 89 – TV ☎. AE ① GB – **27 rm** ☕ 560/720. F 6

Passy Eiffel without rest, 10 r. Passy ✉ 75016 ☎ 45 25 55 66, Telex 643753, Fax 42 88 89 88 – TV ☎. AE ① GB JCB – ☕ 30 – **50 rm** 560/620. J 6

Résidence Marceau without rest, 37 av. Marceau ✉ 75116 ☎ 47 20 43 37, Telex 648509, Fax 47 20 14 76 – TV ☎. AE ① GB JCB. G 8
closed 1 to 21 August – ☕ 35 – **30 rm** 530/620.

Beauséjour Ranelagh without rest, 99 r. Ranelagh ✉ 75016 ☎ 42 88 14 39, Fax 40 50 81 21 – TV ☎. AE GB – ☕ 35 – **30 rm** 400/650. J 4

Hameau de Passy M without rest, 48 r. Passy ✉ 75016 ☎ 42 88 47 55, Telex 651469, Fax 42 30 83 72 – TV ☎. AE GB – **32 rm** ☕ 500/560. J 5-6

Eiffel Kennedy M without rest, 12 r. Boulainvilliers ✉ 75016 ☎ 45 24 45 75, Telex 643679, Fax 42 30 83 32 – TV ☎. AE ① GB. – ☕ 40 – **30 rm** 450/600. K 5

Keppler without rest, 12 r. Keppler ✉ 75116 ☎ 47 20 65 05, Fax 47 23 02 29 – TV ☎. AE GB. – ☕ 26 – **49 rm** 400/410. F 8

XXXX ✿✿✿ **Jamin** (Robuchon), 32 r. Longchamp (moving next autumn to : 59 av. R. Poincaré) ✉ 75116 ☎ 47 27 12 27 – . GB G 7
closed July, Saturday and Sunday – **M** (booking essential) 890 and a la carte 550/950
Spec. Petite crème aux oursins et fenouil (October-April). Tarte friande de truffes aux oignons et lard fumé (December-March). Lièvre à la Royale du sénateur Couteaux (October-December).

XXXX ✿✿ **Vivarois** (Peyrot), 192 av. V.-Hugo ✉ 75116 ☎ 45 04 04 31, Fax 45 03 09 84 – . AE ① GB JCB G 5
closed August, Saturday and Sunday – **M** 345 (lunch) and a la carte 385/650
Spec. Fondant de légumes et sa purée d'olive. Ravioli Rastellini. Rissolettes de pieds d'agneau et ses artichauts à la provençale.

XXXX ✿✿ **Faugeron,** 52 r. Longchamp ✉ 75116 ☎ 47 04 24 53, Fax 47 55 62 90 – . GB. G 7
closed August, 23 December-2 January, Saturday (except dinner October-April) and Sunday – **M** 340 (lunch) and a la carte 450/600
Spec. Parmentier de truffes aux fines épices (January-March). Croustillant de ris de veau aux asperges et jus de truffes (May-July). Millefeuille "Amadeus" en duo de chocolat.

XXX ⚙ **Toit de Passy** (Jacquot), 94 av. P. Doumer (6th floor) ✉ 75016 ☎ 45 24 55 37, Fax 45 20 94 57, ☂ - ▤ Ⓟ. AE GB HJ 5
closed Saturday lunch, Sunday and Bank Holidays - **M** 295/495 and a la carte 370/530
Spec. Foie gras froid de canard, poché au vin de Graves. Pigeonneau en croûte de sel. Tarte au chocolat sans sucre (15 October-15 April).

XXX **Pavillon Noura,** 21 av. Marceau ✉ 75116 ☎ 47 20 33 33, Fax 47 20 60 31, ☂ - ▤. AE ⓓ GB G 8
M Lebanese rest. 280/320.

XXX **Sully d'Auteuil,** 78 r. Auteuil ✉ 75016 ☎ 46 51 71 18, Fax 46 51 70 60, ☂ - ▤. AE GB K 3
closed August, 25 December-2 January, Saturday lunch and Sunday - **M** a la carte 320/420.

XXX **Tsé-Yang,** 25 av. Pierre 1er de Serbie ✉ 75016 ☎ 47 20 68 02, « Tasteful decor » - ▤. AE ⓓ GB G 8
M Chinese rest. - a la carte 150/235.

XXX ⚙ **Port Alma,** 10 av. New-York ✉ 75116 ☎ 47 23 75 11 - ▤. AE ⓓ GB H 8
closed August and Sunday - **M** Seafood 200 (lunch) and a la carte 300/420
Spec. Langoustines poêlées aux beignets de courgettes-fleurs. Bar en croûte de sel de Guérande. Macaronade au citron et coulis de coings (season).

XXX ⚙ **Relais d'Auteuil** (Pignol), 31 bd Murat ✉ 75016 ☎ 46 51 09 54, Fax 40 71 05 03 - ▤. AE GB L 3
closed 1 to 15 August, Saturday lunch and Sunday - **M** 200 (lunch)/440 and a la carte 400/500
Spec. Amandine de foie gras. Dos de bar grillé au poivre. Madeleines au miel, glace miel et noix.

XXX **Le Pergolèse,** 40 r. Pergolèse ✉ 75016 ☎ 45 00 21 40, Fax 45 00 81 31 - AE GB F 6
closed 1 to 23 August, Saturday and Sunday - **M** 230 and a la carte 265/405.

XXX **Chez Ngo,** 70 r. Longchamp ✉ 75116 ☎ 47 04 53 20 - ▤. AE GB JCB. ✗ G 6
M Chinese and Thai rest. a la carte 150/220.

XX **Al Mounia,** 16 r. Magdebourg ✉ 75116 ☎ 47 27 57 28 - ▤. AE GB. ✗ G 7
closed 10 July-31 August and Sunday - **M** Morrocan rest. - (dinner : booking essential) a la carte 200/260.

XX ⚙ **Conti,** 72 r. Lauriston ✉ 75116 ☎ 47 27 74 67 - ▤. AE ⓓ GB G 7
closed 9 to 30 August, 24 December-2 January, Saturday and Sunday - **M** 265 b.i. (lunch) and a la carte 300/450
Spec. Turbot rôti au jus de viande et petits farcis. Rognon de veau confit à l'huile d'olive (spring). Figues rôties au Vino Santo (August-October).

XX **Giulio Rebellato,** 136 r. Pompe ✉ 75116 ☎ 47 27 50 26 - ▤. AE GB. ✗ G 6
closed August - **M** Italian rest. 230 b.i./300 b.i..

XX ⚙ **Fontaine d'Auteuil** (Grégoire), 35bis r. La Fontaine ☎ 42 88 04 47 - AE ⓓ GB K 5
closed August, February Holidays, Saturday lunch and Sunday - **M** 170 (lunch) and a la carte 280/420
Spec. Salade de homard, vinaigrette de Sauternes et gingembre. Millefeuille de crabe, crème cocktail au curry (May-September). Pâté chaud de pigeon sauce salmis.

XX **Villa Vinci,** 23 r. P. Valéry ✉ 75116 ☎ 45 01 68 18 - ▤. GB. ✗ F 7
closed August, Saturday and Sunday - **M** Italian rest. 175 (lunch) and a la carte 220/360.

XX **Paul Chêne,** 123 r. Lauriston ✉ 75116 ☎ 47 27 63 17 - ▤. AE ⓓ GB G 6
closed 31July-30 August, 24 December-3 January, Saturday and Sunday - **M** 250 and a la carte 225/445.

XX **Sous l'Olivier,** 15 r. Goethe ✉ 75116 ☎ 47 20 84 81, Fax 47 20 73 75 - AE GB. ✗ G 8
closed 8 to 22 August, Saturday, Sunday and Bank Holidays - **M** 175 and a la carte 210/345.

XX **Palais du Trocadéro,** 7 av. Eylau ✉ 75016 ☎ 47 27 05 02 - ▤. AE GB H 6
M Chinese rest. - a la carte 150/200.

XX ⚙ **La Petite Tour** (Israël), 11 r. Tour ✉ 75116 ☎ 45 20 09 31 - AE ⓓ GB JCB H 6
closed August and Sunday - **M** a la carte 260/410
Spec. Foie de canard chaud aux myrtilles. Fleurs de courgettes soufflées (May-October). Homard breton à la nage.

XX **Marius,** 82 bd Murat ✉ 75016 ☎ 46 51 67 80, ☂ - GB M 2
closed August, 20 December-3 January, Saturday lunch and Sunday - **M** a la carte 200/280.

X **La Butte Chaillot,** 112 av. Kléber ✉ 75016 ☎ 47 27 88 88, Fax 47 04 85 70 - ▤. AE GB JCB G 7
M 110 b.i. (lunch) and a la carte 210/300.

X **Chez Géraud,** 31 r. Vital ✉ 75016 ☎ 45 20 33 00, « Attractive Longwy porcelain mural » - GB H 5
closed August, Saturday (except dinner from October-February) and Sunday - **M** 200 and a la carte 220/370.

𝕏 **Bistrot de l'Étoile,** 19 r. Lauriston ✉ 75016 ✆ 40 67 11 16 – ▤. AE F 7
closed Saturday lunch and Sunday – **M** a la carte 190/250.

𝕏 **Brasserie de la Poste,** 54 r. Longchamp ✉ 75116 ✆ 47 55 01 31 – AE GB G 7
M a la carte 130/290.

𝕏 **Beaujolais d'Auteuil,** 99 bd Montmorency ✉ 75016 ✆ 47 43 03 56, Fax 46 51 27 31 – AE GB K 3
closed Saturday lunch and Sunday – **M** 119 b.i./200 and a la carte 170/240.

𝕏 **Noura,** 27 av. Marceau ✉ 75016 ✆ 47 23 02 20, Fax 49 52 01 26 – ▤. AE ① GB. ✻
M lebanese rest. - a la carte 110/170. G 8

in the Bois de Boulogne :

𝕏𝕏𝕏𝕏 ✿✿ **Pré Catelan,** rte de Suresnes ✉ 75016 ✆ 45 24 55 58, Telex 643692, Fax 45 24 43 25, ☂, ☂ – P. AE ① GB JCB H 2
closed February Holidays, Sunday dinner and Monday – **M** 350 (lunch)/690 and a la carte 440/600
Spec. Risotto de langoustines. Pied de cochon aux champignons. Gâteau moelleux chocolat pistache.

𝕏𝕏𝕏𝕏 ✿ **Grande Cascade,** allée de Longchamp (opposite the hippodrome) ✉ 75016 ✆ 45 27 33 51, Fax 42 88 99 06, ☂ – P. AE ① GB
closed 20 December-20 January and dinner 1 November-15 April – **M** 285 (lunch) and a la carte 380/550
Spec. Filet de turbotin poêlé et effeuillé d'endives caramélisées à l'orange. Noisettes de filet de biche sauce Grand Veneur (season). Tarte fine aux pommes vertes et sa crème glacée.

Clichy, Ternes, Wagram.

17th arrondissement.
17th: ✉ 75017

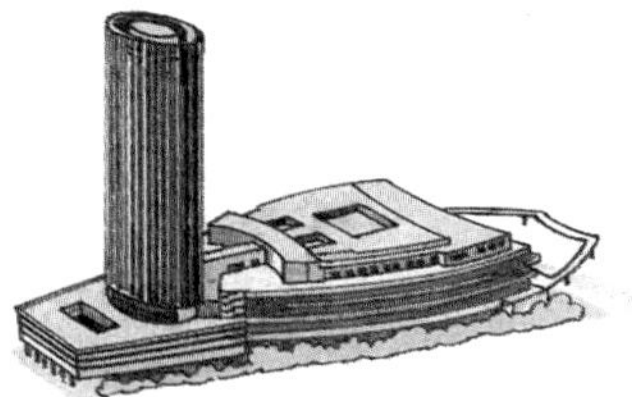

🏨 **Concorde La Fayette** M, 3 pl. Gén.-Koenig ✆ 40 68 50 68, Telex 650892, Fax 40 68 50 43, « Bar with ≤ Paris on 34th floor » – ▮ ⇔ rm ▤ TV ☎ – 🏛 40 - 2 000. AE ① GB JCB E 6
M see **Etoile d'Or** below - **L'Arc-en-Ciel** ✆ 40 68 51 25 **M** 185/215 ₰ – **Les Saisons** (coffee shop) ✆ **40 68 51 19 M** 89 (dinner) and a la carte 175/250 ₰ – ☕ 95 – **973 rm** 1800/2100, 27 suites.

🏨 **Méridien** M, 81 bd Gouvion St Cyr ✆ 40 68 34 34, Telex 651952, Fax 40 68 31 31 – ▮ ⇔ rm ▤ TV ☎ – 🏛 50 - 800. AE ① GB JCB E 6
M see **Clos de Longchamp** below - **Café l'Arlequin M** 148/156 – **Le Yamato** (Japanese rest.) *(closed August, 1 to 7 January, Sunday and Monday)* **M** 135/165 (lunch) and a la carte 170/280 – **La Maison Beaujolaise** *(closed August, 25 to 31 December and Sunday)* **M** 152/190 – ☕ 95 – **989 rm** 1650/1950, 17 suites.

🏨 **Splendid Etoile** without rest, 1bis av. Carnot ✆ 45 72 72 00, Telex 651773, Fax 45 72 72 01 – ▮ ▤ TV ☎. ① GB. ✻ F 7
☕ 70 – **50 rm** 880/1450, 7 suites.

🏨 **Regent's Garden** ⛰ without rest, 6 r. P.-Demours ✆ 45 74 07 30, Telex 640127, Fax 40 55 01 42, « Garden » – ▮ TV ☎. AE ① GB JCB E 7
☕ 36 – **39 rm** 620/920.

🏨 **Quality Inn Pierre** M without rest, 25 r. Th.-de-Banville ✆ 47 63 76 69, Telex 643003, Fax 43 80 63 96 – ▮ ⇔ rm TV ☎ ♿ – 🏛 30. AE ① GB JCB. ✻ D 8
☕ 63 – **50 rm** 780/840.

🏨 **Balmoral** without rest, 6 r. Gén.-Lanrezac ✆ 43 80 30 50, Telex 642435, Fax 43 80 51 56 – ▮ ⇔ rm TV ☎. AE ① GB E 7
☕ 38 – **57 rm** 500/700.

🏨 **Mercure Paris Etoile** M without rest, 27 av. Ternes ✆ 47 66 49 18, Telex 650679, Fax 47 63 77 91 – ▮ ▤ TV ☎. AE ① GB E 8
☕ 60 – **56 rm** 730/980.

🏨 **Résidence St-Ferdinand** M without rest, 36 r. St-Ferdinand ✆ 45 72 66 66, Telex 649565, Fax 45 74 12 92 – ▮ ▤ TV ☎. AE ① GB JCB E 6-7
☕ 60 – **42 rm** 720/880.

🏨 **Magellan** ⛰ without rest, 17 r. J.B.-Dumas ✆ 45 72 44 51, Telex 644728, Fax 40 68 90 36, ☂ – ▮ TV ☎. AE ① GB. ✻ D 7
☕ 35 – **75 rm** 530/560.

Banville without rest, 166 bd Berthier ☏ 42 67 70 16, Telex 643025, Fax 44 40 42 77 – 🛗 📺 ☎. AE GB D 8
☕ 40 – **39 rm** 600/700.

Tilsitt Étoile M without rest, 23 r. Brey ☏ 43 80 39 71, Telex 640629, Fax 47 66 37 63 – 🛗 📺 ☎. AE ⓓ GB. ✂ E 8
☕ 45 – **39 rm** 570/920.

Cheverny M without rest, 7 villa Berthier ☏ 43 80 46 42, Telex 648848, Fax 47 63 26 62 – 🛗 📺 ☎. AE ⓓ GB JCB D 7
☕ 35 – **46 rm** 520/760.

De Neuville, 3 r. Verniquet ☏ 43 80 26 30, Fax 43 80 38 55 – 🛗 📺 ☎. AE ⓓ GB JCB C 8
M *(closed August and weekends)* 100/170 – ☕ 45 – **28 rm** 680.

Mercédès M without rest, 128 av. Wagram ☏ 42 27 77 82, Telex 644751, Fax 40 53 09 89 – 🛗 ▤ 📺 ☎. AE GB. ✂ D 9
☕ 50 – **35 rm** 540/680.

Étoile Pereire ⛵ without rest, 146 bd Péreire ☏ 42 67 60 00, Fax 42 67 02 90 – 🛗 📺 ☎. AE ⓓ GB. ✂ D 7
☕ 50 – **21 rm** 500/700, 5 duplex.

Abrial M without rest, 176 r. Cardinet ☏ 42 63 50 00, Fax 42 63 50 03 – 🛗 📺 ☎ ♿. AE GB JCB C 11
☕ 39 – **80 rm** 630/680.

Monceau without rest, 7 r. Rennequin ☏ 47 63 07 52, Fax 47 66 84 44 – 🛗 ⇔ rm 📺 ☎. AE ⓓ GB E 8
25 rm ☕ 620/690.

Étoile Park H. without rest, 10 av. Mac Mahon ☏ 42 67 69 63, Telex 649266, Fax 43 80 18 99 – 🛗 ⇔ rm 📺 ☎. AE ⓓ GB E 8
closed 24 December-2 January – ☕ 49 – **28 rm** 490/770.

Harvey without rest, 7bis r. Débarcadère ☏ 45 74 27 19, Telex 650855, Fax 40 68 03 56 – 🛗 📺 ☎. AE ⓓ GB JCB E 6
☕ 35 – **32 rm** 480/680.

Star H. Étoile without rest, 18 r. Arc de Triomphe ☏ 43 80 27 69, Telex 643569, Fax 40 54 94 84 – 🛗 📺 ☎. AE ⓓ GB JCB E 7
☕ 39 – **62 rm** 440/690.

Monceau Étoile without rest, 64 r. Levis ☏ 42 27 33 10, Telex 643170, Fax 42 27 59 58 – 🛗 📺 ☎. GB. ✂ D 10
26 rm ☕ 500/590.

Royal Magda without rest, 7 r. Troyon ☏ 47 64 10 19, Telex 641068, Fax 47 64 02 12 – 🛗 📺 ☎. AE ⓓ GB E 8
☕ 35 – **26 rm** 590/660, 11 suites.

Acacias Étoile without rest, 11 r. Acacias ☏ 43 80 60 22, Telex 643551, Fax 48 88 96 40 – 🛗 📺 ☎. AE ⓓ GB JCB E 7
☕ 37 – **37 rm** 500/630.

Campanile M, 4 bd Berthier ☏ 46 27 10 00, Telex 282920, Fax 46 27 00 57, 🏖 – 🛗 ▤ 📺 ☎ ♿ 🚗 – 🏛 40. AE GB B 10
M 88 b.i./118 b.i. – ☕ 30 – **247 rm** 395.

XXXX ✿✿ **Guy Savoy,** 18 r. Troyon ☏ 43 80 40 61, Fax 46 22 43 09 – ▤. AE GB E 8
closed Saturday except dinner October-Easter and Sunday – **M** 680 and a la carte 570/700
Spec. Foie gras de canard au sel gris et gelée de canard. Bar en écailles grillées aux épices douces. "Craquant-moelleux" vanille et pomme.

XXXX ✿✿ **Michel Rostang,** 20 r. Rennequin ☏ 47 63 40 77, Fax 47 63 82 75 – ▤. AE GB D 8
closed 1 to 21 August, Saturday (except dinner September-June) and Sunday – **M** 285 (lunch)/680 and a la carte 490/650
Spec. Galette d'artichaut au foie gras de canard (December-March). Grosse sole de ligne et sa compotée d'échalote. Tarte chaude au chocolat amer.

XXXX ✿✿ **Le Clos Longchamp** - Hôtel Méridien, 81 bd Gouvion-St-Cyr (Pte Maillot) ☏ 40 68 00 70, Telex 651952, Fax 40 68 30 81 – ▤. AE ⓓ GB JCB E 6
closed 7 to 16 August, Saturday and Sunday – **M** 250 (lunch)/470 and a la carte 420/570
Spec. Marbré de foie de canard au Beaumes de Venise. Blanc de turbot aux girolles (May-October). Rognon de veau entier à la moutarde violette.

XXXX ✿ **Étoile d'Or** - Hôtel Concorde La Fayette, 3 pl. Gén.-Koenig ✆ 40 68 51 28, Fax 40 68 50 43 – ▤. AE ⓓ GB JCB E 6
closed August, Saturday lunch and Sunday – **M** 250/600 and a la carte 340/550
Spec. Maraîchère de homard au miel de romarin. La "fameuse" joue de bœuf en ravigotte. Soufflé chaud au chocolat.

XXXX ✿ **Manoir de Paris,** 6 r. P. Demours ✆ 45 72 25 25, Fax 45 74 80 98 – ▤. AE ⓓ GB JCB
closed Saturday (except dinner from September-May) and Sunday – **M** 295 (lunch)/460 and a la carte 370/530 E 7
Spec. Effeuillée de morue fraîche aux œufs de caille et chorizo (January-July). Carré de cochon de lait rôti à la sauge (October-March). Merveille à la fleur d'oranger.

XXXX ✿✿ **Apicius** (Vigato), 122 av. Villiers ✆ 43 80 19 66, Fax 44 40 09 57 – ▤. AE GB D 8
closed August, Saturday and Sunday – **M** a la carte 460/600
Spec. Poêlée de foie gras chaud aux radis noirs confits. Gelée de crustacés à l'eau de mer. Grand dessert au chocolat.

O XXX ✿✿ **Amphyclès** (Groult), 78 av. Ternes ✆ 40 68 01 01, Fax 40 68 91 88 – ▤. AE ⓓ GB
closed Saturday lunch and Sunday – **M** 260/680 (lunch) and a la carte 550/750 E 7
Spec. Gelée de pied de veau au fumet de truffes. Risotto à l'étuvée de homard aux girolles. Joue de bœuf braisée aux carottes confites.

XXX ✿ **Le Sormani** (Fayet), 4 r. Gén.-Lanrezac ✆ 43 80 13 91 – ▤. GB E 7
closed 12 to 18 April, 1 to 22 August, 23 December-4 January, Saturday, Sunday and Bank Holidays – **M** Italian rest. 300/400 and a la carte 300/420
Spec. Risotto au beure de truffes blanches et calamars (October-January). Soupe de pâtes aux haricots blancs (October-March). Polenta gratinée à la morue et au mascarpone.

XXX ✿ **Faucher,** 123 av. Wagram ✆ 42 27 61 50, Fax 46 22 25 72, 斎 – AE GB D 8
closed 8 to 16 August, Saturday lunch and Sunday – **M** 180 (lunch)/390 and a la carte 280/430
Spec. Millefeuille de bœuf cru, sauce digoinaise. Filets de rougets à l'huile d'olive et macaroni farcis. Ris de veau croustillant et réduction de Porto.

XXX **Pétrus,** 12 pl. Mar. Juin ✆ 43 80 15 95 – ▤. AE ⓓ GB D 8
closed 10 to 25 August – **M** 250 and a la carte 300/400.

XXX ✿ **Timgad** (Laasri), 21 r. Brunel ✆ 45 74 23 70, Telex 649239, Fax 40 68 76 46, « Moorish decor » – ▤. AE ⓓ GB. ✻ E 7
M North African rest. - a la carte 250/550
Spec. Couscous princier. Tagine d'agneau aux pruneaux. Tagine de poulet au citron confit.

XXX **Paul et France,** 27 av. Niel ✆ 47 63 04 24, Fax 44 15 92 20 – ▤. AE ⓓ GB D 8
closed August, Saturday lunch and Sunday – **M** 230 and a la carte 250/480.

XXX **Augusta,** 98 r. Tocqueville ✆ 47 63 39 97, Fax 42 27 21 71 – ▤. GB C 9
closed 7 to 23 August, Saturday (except dinner October-April) and Sunday – **M** Seafood - a la carte 370/500.

XXX **La Table de Pierre,** 116 bd Péreire ✆ 43 80 88 68, 斎 – AE GB D 8
closed Sunday dinner – **M** 210 and a la carte 210/325.

XXX **Il Ristorante,** 22 r. Fourcroy ✆ 47 63 34 00 – ▤. AE GB D 8
closed 8 to 18 August and Sunday – **M** Italian rest. 165 (lunch) and a la carte 220/360.

XX **Le Madigan,** 22 r. Terrasse ✆ 42 27 31 51, Fax 42 67 70 29, 斎 – ▤. AE ⓓ GB. ✻
closed 9 August-4 September, Saturday lunch and Sunday – **M** 150 (lunch)/280 ♁. D 10

XX ✿ **Le Petit Colombier** (Fournier), 42 r. Acacias ✆ 43 80 28 54, Fax 44 40 04 29 – AE GB
closed 1 to 18 August, Sunday lunch, Saturday and Bank Holidays – **M** 200 (lunch) and a la carte 310/440 E 7
Spec. Oeufs rôtis à la broche aux truffes fraîches (November-February). Filet de bœuf "Blonde d'Aquitaine" en feuilletage, sauce Périgueux. Pigeonneau rôti à la "croque au sel" et jus de truffe.

XX **Billy Gourmand,** 20 r. Tocqueville ✆ 42 27 03 71 – GB D 10
closed 9 to 18 April, 5 to 23 August, Saturday except dinner in winter, Sunday and Bank Holidays – **M** 155 (dinner) and a la carte 240/370.

XX **Graindorge,** 15 r. Arc de Triomphe ✆ 47 54 00 28 – AE GB E 7
closed Saturday lunch and Sunday – **M** 160 (lunch) and a la carte 185/250.

XX **Le Beudant,** 97 r. Dames ✆ 43 87 11 20 – ▤. AE ⓓ GB JCB D 11
closed Saturday lunch and Sunday – **M** 150/285.

XX **La Truite Vagabonde,** 17 r. Batignolles ✆ 43 87 77 80, 斎 – AE GB JCB D 11
closed Sunday dinner – **M** 160 and a la carte 230/380.

XX **Le Cougar,** 10 r. Acacias ✆ 47 66 74 14, Fax 47 66 74 14 – ▤. AE ⓓ GB E 7
closed 9 to 15 August, Saturday lunch and Sunday – **M** 150/320.

XX **La Coquille,** 6 r. Débarcadère ✆ 45 74 25 95 – ▤. AE GB E 7
closed 28 July-1 September, 24 December-4 January, Sunday, Monday and Bank Holidays – **M** a la carte 250/410.

XX **Baumann Ternes,** 64 av. Ternes ✆ 45 74 16 66, Fax 45 72 44 32 – ▤. AE ⓓ GB E 7
M a la carte 190/350 ♁.

XX **La Soupière,** 154 av. Wagram ✆ 42 27 00 73 – ▤. AE GB D 9
closed 7 to 15 August, Saturday lunch and Sunday – **M** 160/270.

XX **La Braisière,** 54 r. Cardinet ✆ 47 63 40 37, Fax 47 63 04 76 – AE GB D 9
closed 1 to 7 May, August, Saturday and Sunday – **M** 175/320.

XX **La Niçoise,** 4 r. P. Demours ✆ 45 74 42 41, Fax 45 74 80 98 - ▤. AE ⓓ GB JCB E 7
closed Saturday (ecxept dinner September-June) and Sunday - **M** 145 (lunch) and a la carte 180/250.

XX **Epicure 108,** 108 r. Cardinet ✆ 47 63 50 91 - GB D 10
closed Saturday lunch and Sunday - **M** 170/230.

XX **L'Écailler du Palais,** 101 av. Ternes ✆ 45 74 87 07, Fax 40 68 75 37 - ▤. AE ⓓ GB JCB
M Seafood 175 b.i. and a la carte 230/380. E 6

XX **Chez Léon,** 32 r. Legendre ✆ 42 27 06 82 - ⓓ GB D 10
closed August, February Holidays, Saturday, Sunday and Bank Holidays - **M** 150/230.

XX **La Petite Auberge,** 38 r. Laugier ✆ 47 63 85 51 - GB D 7-8
closed 1 to 16 August, Sunday dinner and Monday - **M** (booking essential) 160 and a la carte 235/350.

XX **Ballon des Ternes,** 103 av. Ternes ✆ 45 74 17 98, Fax 45 72 18 84 - AE GB E 6
closed 30 July-30 August - **M** a la carte 170/300.

XX **Chez Georges,** 273 bd Péreire ✆ 45 74 31 00, Fax 45 74 02 56 - GB. ⚘ E 6
closed August - **M** a la carte 180/340.

XX **Chez Laudrin,** 154 bd Péreire ✆ 43 80 87 40 - ▤. AE GB D 7
closed Saturday (except dinner September-May) and Sunday - **M** a la carte 270/390.

XX **Chez Guyvonne,** 14 r. Thann ✆ 42 27 25 43 - AE GB D 10
closed 6 to 30 August, 24 December-31 January, Saturday and Sunday - **M** 200/230 ♁.

XX **Aub. des Dolomites,** 38 r. Poncelet ✆ 42 27 94 56 - AE GB E 8
closed August, Saturday lunch and Sunday - **M** 165.

X **Bistrot de l'Étoile,** 75 av. Niel ✆ 42 27 88 44 - ▤. AE GB D 8
closed Sunday - **M** a la carte 190/270.

X **Les Béatilles,** 127 r. Cardinet ✆ 42 27 95 64 - GB D 10
closed 1 to 7 May, 1 to 21 August, Saturday, Sunday and Bank Holidays - **M** 130 (lunch)/290.

X **La Rôtisserie d'Armaillé,** 6 r. Armaillé ✆ 42 27 19 20 - ▤. GB E 7
closed Saturday lunch and Sunday - **M** 185.

X **Mère Michel,** 5 r. Rennequin ✆ 47 63 59 80 - AE GB E 8
closed August, Saturday lunch and Sunday - **M** (booking essential) 195 and a la carte 210/390.

X **Bistro du 17e,** 108 av. Villiers ✆ 47 63 32 77 - GB D 8
M 165 b.i..

X **Caves Petrissans,** 30 bis av. Niel ✆ 42 27 83 84, Fax 40 54 87 56, 斎 - AE GB D 8
closed 1 to 22 August, Saturday, Sunday and Bank Holidays - **M** a la carte 180/270.

X **Bistrot d'à Côté Flaubert,** 10 r. G. Flaubert ✆ 42 67 05 81, Fax 47 63 82 75 - AE GB
M a la carte 180/270. D 8

X **Bistrot de l'Étoile,** 13 r. Troyon ✆ 42 67 25 95 - ▤. AE GB E 8
closed Saturday and Sunday - **M** a la carte approx. 200.

Montmartre, La Villette, Belleville.

18th, 19th and 20th arrondissements.
18th: ✉ 75018
19th: ✉ 75019
20th: ✉ 75020

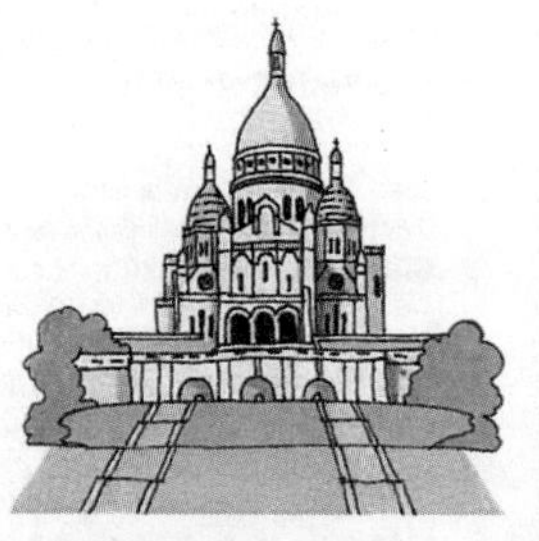

Terrass'H. Ⓜ, 12 r. J. de Maistre (18th) ✆ 46 06 72 85, Telex 280830, Fax 42 52 29 11 - |♦| ⇔ rm ▤ rest ▣ ☎ Ⓟ - ♣ 120. AE ⓓ GB JCB C 13
La Terrasse **M** 160 ♁ - ☐ 70 - **88 rm** 880/1160, 13 suites.

Mercure Paris Montmartre Ⓜ without rest, 1 r. Caulaincourt (18th) ✆ 42 94 17 17, Telex 285605, Fax 42 93 66 14 - |♦| ▤ ▣ ☎ ♿ - ♣ 120. AE ⓓ GB JCB D 12
☐ 68 - **308 rm** 760/940.

Belgrand Ⓜ without rest, 60 r. Belgrand (20th) ✆ 43 61 28 38, Telex 233620, Fax 40 30 03 50 - |♦| ▣ ☎. AE ⓓ GB G 22
☐ 35 - **27 rm** 370/420.

Roma Sacré Cœur Ⓜ without rest, 101 r. Caulaincourt (18th) ✆ 42 62 02 02, Telex 281671, Fax 42 54 34 92 - |♦| ▣ ☎. AE ⓓ GB JCB C 14
☐ 37 - **57 rm** 410/430.

H. Le Laumière without rest, 4 r. Petit (19th) ✆ 42 06 10 77, Fax 42 06 72 50 – GB D 19
33 – **54 rm** 250/360.

Palma without rest, 77 av. Gambetta (20th) ✆ 46 36 13 65, Telex 216056, Fax 46 36 03 27 – AE GB. G 21
30 – **32 rm** 330/380.

Regyn's Montmartre without rest, 18 pl. Abbesses (18th) ✆ 42 54 45 21, Fax 42 54 45 21 – GB D 13
40 – **22 rm** 360/470.

Eden H. without rest, 90 r. Ordener (18th) ✆ 42 64 61 63, Fax 42 64 11 43 – AE GB B 14
30 – **35 rm** 340/370.

des Arts without rest, 5 r. Tholozé (18th) ✆ 46 06 30 52, Fax 46 06 10 83 – AE GB. D 13
30 – **50 rm** 390/440.

Super H. without rest, 208 r. Pyrénées (20th) ✆ 46 36 97 48, Fax 46 36 26 10 – GB G 21
closed August – 30 – **28 rm** 280/450.

Pyrénées Gambetta without rest, 12 av. Père Lachaise (20th) ✆ 47 97 76 57, Fax 47 97 17 61 – AE GB H 21
28 – **32 rm** 170/420.

Climat de France M, 2 av. Prof. A. Lemierre (20th) ✆ 40 31 08 80, Telex 232711, Fax 40 31 09 66 – rm – 100. AE GB. rm J 23
M 95/130 – 38 – **325 rm** 430.

Prima-Lepic without rest, 29 r. Lepic (18th) ✆ 46 06 44 64, Telex 281162, Fax 46 06 66 11 – GB. D 13
35 – **38 rm** 320/380.

Capucines Montmartre without rest, 5 r. A.-Bruant (18th) ✆ 42 52 89 80, Telex 281648, Fax 42 52 29 57 – AE GB D 13
29 rm 305/420.

City H. M without rest, 11 r. Boucry (18th) ✆ 42 09 30 62, Telex 213417, Fax 42 09 02 49 – AE GB B 16-17
35 – **46 rm** 350/390.

XXX ✿ **Beauvilliers** (Carlier), 52 r. Lamarck (18th) ✆ 42 54 54 42, Fax 42 62 70 30, « 1900 decor, terrace » – AE GB JCB. C 14
closed 30 August-6 September, Monday lunch and Sunday – **M** 180 b.i. (lunch)/700 b.i. and a la carte 350/440
Spec. Ris de veau en aspic de Sauternes au foie gras. Turbot rôti au jarret de veau. Grande assiette aux trois chocolats.

XXX **Pavillon Puebla,** Parc Buttes-Chaumont, entrance : av. Bolivar, r. Botzaris (19th) ✆ 42 08 92 62, Fax 42 39 83 16, « Pleasant parkland setting » – GB E 19
closed Sunday and Monday – **M** 230 and a la carte 300/450.

XXX ✿ **Cochon d'Or,** 192 av. J.-Jaurès (19th) ✆ 42 45 46 46, Fax 42 40 43 90 – AE GB
M 240 and a la carte 270/500 C 20
Spec. Salade de tête de veau sauce moutarde. Ris et rognon de veau aux girolles. Grillades.

XXX **Charlot 1er "Merveilles des Mers",** 128bis bd Clichy (18th) ✆ 45 22 47 08, Fax 44 70 07 50 – AE GB D 12
closed Monday in July-August – **M** Seafood - a la carte 250/400.

XX **La Chaumière,** 46 av. Secrétan (19th) ✆ 42 06 54 69 – AE GB E 18
closed August and Sunday – **M** 143/198 b.i.

XX **Cottage Marcadet,** 151 bis r. Marcadet (18th) ✆ 42 57 71 22 – GB. C 13
closed 30 April-11 May, 14 to 31 August and Sunday – **M** 200 b.i. and a la carte 200/370.

XX **Au Clair de la Lune,** 9 r. Poulbot (18th) ✆ 42 58 97 03 – AE GB D 14
closed 1 to 15 February – **M** 170 and a la carte 210/300.

XX **Poulbot Gourmet,** 39 r. Lamarck (18th) ✆ 46 06 86 00 – GB C 14
closed Sunday – **M** a la carte 190/290.

XX **Au Boeuf Couronné,** 188 av. J. Jaurès (19th) ✆ 42 39 44 44, Fax 42 39 17 30 – AE GB
closed Sunday – **M** 140 and a la carte 180/380. C 20

XX **Grandgousier,** 17 av. Rachel (18th) ✆ 43 87 66 12 – AE GB D 12
closed 8 to 22 August, Bank Holidays lunch, Saturday lunch and Sunday – **M** 145 and a la carte 170/240.

X **Marie-Louise,** 52 r. Championnet (18th) ✆ 46 06 86 55 – GB B 15
closed late July-early September, Sunday, Monday and Bank Holidays – **M** 120 and a la carte 140/210.

X **Le Sancerre,** 13 av. Corentin Cariou (19th) ✆ 40 36 80 44 – AE GB B 19
closed August, Saturday and Sunday – **M** 120 and a la carte 180/230.

X **Aucune Idée,** 2 pl. St-Blaise (20th) ✆ 40 09 70 67 – AE GB H 22
closed 1 to 21 August, Sunday dinner and Monday – **M** 110/215.

X **L'Oriental,** 76 r. Martyrs (18th) ✆ 42 64 39 80 – AE GB. D 14
closed 1 to 25 August and Monday – **M** North African rest. - 70 a la carte Sunday.

ENVIRONS

The outskirts of Paris up to 25Km

When calling the following places from the provinces dial 1 + eight-digit number.

K 11: These reference letters and numbers correspond to the squares on the **Michelin plans of Parisian suburbs** nos 18, 20, 22, 24.

La Défense 92 Hauts-de-Seine 101 ⑭, 18 – ✉ 92400 Courbevoie.

See : Quarter★★ : perspective★ from the parvis.

Paris 8,5.

Sofitel Paris CNIT M ⛺, 2 pl. Défense ☎ 46 92 10 10, Telex 613782, Fax 46 92 10 50 – |♦| ⅍ rm ▤ rm TV ☎ ♿. AE ⓓ GB JCB. ⚔ rest U-V 19
M see **Les Communautés** below – ☕ 90 – **141 rm** 1280/1600, 6 suites.

Sofitel Paris La Défense M ⛺, 34 cours Michelet by ring road, exit La Défense 4 ☎ 47 76 44 43, Telex 612189, Fax 47 73 72 74 – |♦| ⅍ rm ▤ TV ☎ ♿ 🚗 – 🏫 50. AE ⓓ GB JCB V 20
Les 2 Arcs *(closed Sunday lunch and Saturday)* **M** 325 (lunch) and a la carte 260/380 – ☕ 90 – **149 rm** 1150.

Novotel Paris La Défense M, 2 bd Neuilly ☎ 47 78 16 68, Telex 630288, Fax 47 78 84 71, ← – |♦| ⅍ rm ▤ TV ☎ ♿ – 🏫 25 - 150. AE ⓓ GB JCB V 21
M a la carte approx. 160 – ☕ 58 – **278 rm** 750/790.

Ibis Paris La Défense M, 4 bd Neuilly ☎ 47 78 15 60, Telex 611555, Fax 47 78 94 16, 🍽 – |♦| ⅍ rm ▤ TV ☎ ♿ – 🏫 120. AE GB – **M** 100 🍷 – ☕ 36 – **284 rm** 495. V 21

XXXX ✿ **Fouquet's Europe,** au CNIT, 2 pl. Défense, (5th floor) ☎ 46 92 28 04, Fax 46 92 28 16 – ▤. AE ⓓ GB JCB. ⚔ V 19
closed Saturday and Sunday – **M** a la carte 270/400
Spec. Tarte de poivrons doux sur émincé d'encornets. Rouget rôti au romarin croustillant. Feuilletage à la vanille.

XXX ✿ **Les Communautés** - Hôtel Sofitel Paris CNIT, 2 pl. Défense ☎ 46 92 10 10, Fax 46 92 10 50 – ▤. AE ⓓ GB JCB. ⚔ U-V 19
closed Saturday, Sunday and Bank Holidays – **M** 285 (lunch) and a la carte 280/390
Spec. Chartreuse de champignons sauvages au foie gras (autumn-winter). Morue fraîche à la chair de tourteau, lentilles vertes du Puy. Queue de bœuf mijotée à l'ancienne.

Enghien-les-Bains 95880 Val-d'Oise 101 ⑤, 18 – pop. 10 077 alt. 50 – Spa (closed January) – Casino.

See : Lake★ – Deuil-la-Barre : historiated capitals★ in Notre-Dame Church, NE : 2 km.

⛳18 of Domont Montmorency ☎ 39 91 07 50, N : 8 km.

🅘 fice de Tourisme 2 bd Cotte ☎ 34 12 41 15.

Paris 19.

Grand Hôtel M ⛺, 85 r. Gén.-de-Gaulle ☎ 34 12 80 00, Telex 607842, Fax 34 12 73 81, 🍽, 🌳 – |♦| ▤ rm TV ☎ Ⓟ – 🏫 25. AE ⓓ GB K 25
M 165/450 – ☕ 70 – **48 rm** 980/1100, 3 suites.

XXXX ✿✿ **Duc d'Enghien,** au Casino ☎ 34 12 90 00, Fax 34 12 41 70, ← lake, 🍽 – ▤. AE ⓓ GB
closed 2 August-2 September, 3 to 13 January, Sunday dinner and Monday – **M** 340/460 and a la carte 450/640 J 25
Spec. Filets de rouget et leur nage d'artichaut à l'anis étoilé. Turbot rôti aux oignons frits et tomates confites. Aiguillettes de canette rôtie et la cuisse en Parmentier.

XX **Aub. Landaise,** 32 bd d'Ormesson ☎ 34 12 78 36 – ▤. AE GB JCB J 26
closed August, 17 to 23 February, Sunday dinner and Wednesday – **M** a la carte 155/280.

Maisons-Laffitte 78600 Yvelines 101 ⑬, 18 – pop. 22 173 alt. 40.

See : Château★.

Paris 21.

XXX ✿✿ **Le Tastevin** (Blanchet), 9 av. Eglé ☎ 39 62 11 67, Fax 39 62 73 09, 🍽, 🌳 – AE ⓓ GB JCB M 11
closed 7 to 17 August, February Holidays, Monday dinner and Tuesday – **M** 230 and a la carte 350/500
Spec. Escalope de foie gras poêlée aux deux pommes. Fricassée de queues de langoustines et de pommes de terre. Millefeuille au caramel et aux noix (autumn).

XX **Le Laffitte,** 5 av. St-Germain ☎ 39 62 01 53 – AE GB M 11
closed 26 July-1 September, Sunday dinner and Monday – **M** 220/320.

Marne-la-Vallée **77206** S.-et-M. 101 ⑲.

Paris 28.

at Collégien - pop. 2 331 - ✉ 77080 :

Novotel M, à l'échangeur de Lagny A 4 ☎ 64 80 53 53, Telex 691990, Fax 64 80 48 37, - rm - 130. AE GB JCB
M a la carte approx. 160 - ☕ 55 - **203 rm** 490/570.

at Euro Disney access by Highway A 4 and Euro Disney exit

Disneyland M, ☎ 60 45 65 00, Fax 60 45 65 33, ≤, « Victorian style architecture, at the entrance to the Euro Disney Resort », - rm TV. AE GB.
California Grill M a la carte 250/400 - **Inventions M** 220 - ☕ 75 - **479 rm** 1950/2300, 21 suites.

New-York M, ☎ 60 45 73 00, Fax 60 45 73 33, ≤, « Evokes the architecture of Manhattan », - rm TV - 1 500. AE GB.
Club Manhattan (dinner and dancing) *(closed Sunday and Monday)* **M** a la carte 250/400 - **Parkside Diner M** a la carte 150/200 - ☕ 75 - **537 rm** 1600/2100, 36 suites.

Newport Bay Club M, ☎ 60 45 55 00, Fax 60 45 55 33, ≤, « In the style of a New England seaside resort », - rm rest TV - 30. AE GB.
Cape Cod M 225 - **Yacht Club M** a la carte 150/300 - ☕ 65 - **1 083 rm** 950/1700, 15 suites.

Séquoia Lodge M, ☎ 60 45 51 00, Fax 60 45 51 33, ≤, « The atmosphere of an American mountain lodge », - rm rest TV - 80. AE GB.
Hunter's Grill M a la carte 200/300 - ☕ 65 - **997 rm** 900/1550, 14 suites.

Cheyenne M, ☎ 60 45 62 00, Fax 60 45 62 33, « Resembles a frontier town of The American Wild West » - rm rest TV. AE GB.
Chuck Wagon Café self **M** a la carte 150/200 - ☕ 60 - **1 000 rm** 750.

Santa Fé M, ☎ 60 45 78 00, Fax 60 45 78 33, « Evokes a New Mexican pueblo » - rm rest TV. AE GB.
La Cantina self **M** a la carte 100/150 - ☕ 60 - **1 000 rm** 550.

Neuilly-sur-Seine **92200** Hauts-de-Seine 101 ⑮, 18 - pop. 61 768 alt. 36.

See : Bois de Boulogne★★ : Jardin d'acclimatation★, (Children's Amusement Park, Miniature Railway and Zoo in the Bois de Boulogne), Bagatelle★ (Park and - Garden) National Museum of Popular Art and Traditions★★ - Palais des Congrès★ : main conference hall★★, ≤★ from hotel Concorde-Lafayette.

Paris 7,5.

L'Hôtel International de Paris, 58 bd V.-Hugo ☎ 47 58 11 00, Telex 610971, Fax 47 58 75 52, - TV - 120. AE GB — V 23
M 160/175 - ☕ 75 - **318 rm** 950/1300, 3 suites.

Jardin de Neuilly without rest, 5 r. P. Déroulède ☎ 46 24 51 62, Telex 612004, Fax 46 37 14 60 - TV. AE GB JCB. — W 23
☕ 50 - **30 rm** 900/1200.

Paris Neuilly M without rest, 1 av. Madrid ☎ 47 47 14 67, Telex 613170, Fax 47 47 97 42 - TV. AE GB JCB — W 21
☕ 53 - **74 rm** 780/850, 6 suites.

Parc without rest, 4 bd Parc ☎ 46 24 32 62, Fax 46 40 77 31 - TV. GB — U 22
☕ 28 - **71 rm** 295/450.

XXX ✿ **Jacqueline Fénix,** 42 av. Ch. de Gaulle ☎ 46 24 42 61 - . AE GB — W 23
closed August, 25 December-2 January, Saturday and Sunday - **M** (booking essential) 290/400 and a la carte 320/400
Spec. Tarte croustillante de rougets au basilic. Poitrine de canette caramélisée aux graines de sésame. Fondant de chocolat, salade d'agrumes.

XXX ✿ **Truffe Noire** (Jacquet), 2 pl. Parmentier ☎ 46 24 94 14, Fax 46 37 27 02 - AE GB.
closed August, Saturday and Sunday - **M** 230/400 and a la carte 270/370 — W 23
Spec. Mitonnée potagère de poulet et foie gras (September-December). Salade de truffes aux pommes de terre crémées (10 January-30 March). Mousseline de brochet au beurre blanc.

XXX **Foc Ly,** 79 av. Ch. de Gaulle ☎ 46 24 43 36, Fax 46 24 48 46 - . AE GB — V 21
closed Sunday in August - **M** Chinese rest. - a la carte 160/270.

XX **San Valero,** 209 ter av. Ch. de Gaulle ☎ 46 24 07 87 - AE GB. — V 21
closed 24 December-2 January, Saturday lunch, Sunday and Bank Holidays - **M** Spanish rest. 150/190.

XX **Jarrasse,** 4 av. Madrid ☎ 46 24 07 56, Fax 40 88 35 60 - AE GB — W 21
closed 26 July-31 August and Sunday dinner - **M** 220 and a la carte 270/515.

X **Bistrot d'à Côté Neuilly,** 4 r. Boutard ☎ 47 45 34 55, Fax 47 63 82 75 - AE GB — W 21
closed 1 to 21 August, Saturday (except dinner September-June) and Sunday - **M** 175.

X **La Catounière,** 4 r. Poissonniers ☎ 47 47 14 33 - . GB — V 22
closed 1 to 16 May, August, Saturday lunch and Sunday - **M** 173 b.i.

Orly (Paris Airports) 94396 Val-de-Marne 101 ㉖, 24 – pop. 21 646 alt. 89.

✈ ☎ 49 75 15 15.

Paris 15.

Hilton Orly M, near airport station ✉ 94544 ☎ 46 87 33 88, Telex 265971, Fax 49 78 06 75 – ▮ ⇔ rm ▤ TV ☎ ♿ P – 🏛 300. AE ⓓ GB JCB AR 31
M 185 ♁ – ☕ 80 – **359 rm** 1000/1500.

Mercure Paris Orly M, N 7, Z.I. Nord ✉ 94547 ☎ 46 87 23 37, Telex 265665, Fax 46 87 71 92 – ▮ ⇔ rm ▤ TV ☎ ♿ P – 🏛 30. AE ⓓ GB
M a la carte 155/250 – ☕ 57 – **193 rm** 630/870.

Orly Airport South :

XX Le Grillardin, 3rd floor ✉ 94542 ☎ 49 75 78 23, Fax 49 75 36 69, ← – ▤ – **M** (lunch only).

Orly Airport West :

XXXX **Maxim's,** 2nd floor ✉ 94546 ☎ 46 86 87 84, Telex 265247, Fax 46 87 05 39, ← – ▤. AE ⓓ GB
closed August, Saturday, Sunday and Bank Holidays – **M** a la carte 400/540.

XXX **Le Grill,** 2nd floor ✉ 94546 ☎ 46 87 16 16, Telex 265247, Fax 46 87 05 39, ← – ▤. AE ⓓ GB. ✗ – **M** 260 b.i. and a la carte 250/330.

See also ***Rungis***

Roissy-en-France (Paris Airports) 95700 Val-d'Oise 101 ⑧ – pop. 2 054 alt. 85.

✈ ☎ 48 62 22 80.

Paris 26.

at Roissy-Town :

Copthorne M, allée Verger ☎ 34 29 33 33, Telex 606055, Fax 34 29 03 05, Fб, ⛶ – ▮ ⇔ rm ▤ rm TV ☎ ♿ 🚗 P – 🏛 200. AE ⓓ GB JCB
Brasserie l'Europe *(closed Saturday lunch)* **M** a la carte 250/300 – ☕ 75 – **238 rm** 1050/1250.

Holiday Inn M, allée Verger ☎ 34 29 30 00, Telex 605143, Fax 34 29 90 52, Fб – ▮ ⇔ rm ▤ TV ☎ P – 🏛 25 - 200. AE ⓓ GB JCB – **M** 145/240 – ☕ 75 – **240 rm** 760/980.

Mercure, allée Verger ☎ 34 29 40 00, Telex 605205, Fax 34 29 00 18 – ▮ ⇔ rm ▤ TV ☎ ♿ P – 🏛 30 - 160. AE ⓓ GB JCB
Brasserie M 90/160 ♁ – ☕ 65 – **198 rm** 660/910, 4 suites.

Ibis M, av. Raperie ☎ 34 29 34 34, Telex 688413, Fax 34 29 34 19 – ▮ ▤ TV ☎ ♿ P – 🏛 25 - 80. AE ⓓ GB – **M** 105 ♁ – ☕ 37 – **200 rm** 445/495.

in the airport area :

Sofitel M, ☎ 48 62 23 23, Telex 230166, Fax 48 62 78 49, ⛶, ⚔ – ▮ ⇔ rm ▤ TV ☎ ♿ P – 🏛 25 - 180. AE ⓓ GB
Les Valois panoramic rest. *(closed lunch Saturday, Sunday and Bank Holidays)* **M** a la carte 260/370 – **Le Jardin** – **brasserie** (ground floor) **M** a la carte 140/230 ♁ – ☕ 80 – **344 rm** 1050, 8 suites.

Novotel M, ☎ 48 62 00 53, Telex 232397, Fax 48 62 00 11 – ▮ ⇔ rm ▤ TV ☎ ♿ P – 🏛 25 - 70. AE ⓓ GB JCB – **M** a la carte approx. 150 – ☕ 52 – **201 rm** 660/695.

in the airport nr. 1 :

XXX **Maxim's,** ☎ 48 62 16 16, Telex 236356, Fax 48 62 45 96 – ▤. AE ⓓ GB
M (lunch only) 250 and a la carte 280/490.

XX **Grill Maxim's,** ☎ 48 62 16 16, Telex 236356, Fax 48 62 45 96 – ▤. AE ⓓ GB
M 220 b.i. and a la carte 200/310.

Z.I. Paris Nord II – ✉ 95912 :

Hyatt Regency M, av. Bois de la Pie ☎ 48 17 12 34, Fax 48 17 17 17, « Original contemporary decor », Fб, ⛶ – ▮ ⇔ rm ▤ rm TV ☎ ♿ P – 🏛 250. AE ⓓ GB JCB
Brasserie Espace M 170 ♁ – **Le Mirage M** a la carte 150/240 – ☕ 75 – **383 rm** 1050/1650, 5 suites.

Rungis 94150 Val-de-Marne 101 ㉖, 24 – pop. 2 939 alt. 80.

Paris 14.

at Pondorly : Access : from Paris, Highway A 6 and take Orly Airport exit ; from outside of Paris, A 6 and Rungis exit :

Pullman Orly M, 20 av. Ch. Lindbergh ✉ 94656 ☎ 46 87 36 36, Telex 260738, Fax 46 87 08 48, ⛶ – ▮ ⇔ rm ▤ TV ☎ 🚗 P – 🏛 25 - 250. AE ⓓ GB AM 29
La Rungisserie M 150/185 – ☕ 75 – **196 rm** 600/750.

Holiday Inn M, 4 av. Ch. Lindbergh ✉ 94656 ☎ 46 87 26 66, Telex 265803, Fax 45 60 91 25, ⚔ – ▮ ⇔ rm ▤ TV ☎ ♿ P – 🏛 50 - 200. AE ⓓ GB JCB AM 29
M 130/180 – ☕ 70 – **172 rm** 950.

Ibis M, 1 r. Mondétour ✉ 94656 ☎ 46 87 22 45, Telex 261173, Fax 46 87 84 72, 🏕 – ▮ ⇔ rm TV ☎ ♿ P – 🏛 80. AE GB – **M** 91 ♁ – ☕ 36 – **119 rm** 340/370. AM 29

St-Germain-en-Laye 78100 Yvelines **101** ⑫, **18** – pop. 39 926 alt. 78.

See : Terrace★★ BY – English Garden★ BY – Castel★ BZ : Museum of National Antiquities★★ – Priory Museum★ AZ.

9 18 (private) ℘ 34 51 75 90 by ④ : 3 km ; 9 9 9 of Fourqueux (private) ℘ 34 51 41 47 by r. de Mareil AZ.

fice Municipal de Tourisme 38 r. au Pain ℘ 34 51 05 12.

Paris 23 ③.

ST-GERMAIN EN-LAYE

Street	Grid
Bonnenfant (R. A.)	AZ 3
Marché-Neuf (Pl. du)	AZ
Pain (R. au)	AZ 20
Paris (R. de)	AZ
Poissy (R. de)	AZ 22
Vieux-Marché (R. du)	AZ 33
Coches (R. des)	AZ 4
Denis (R. M.)	AZ 5
Detaille (Pl.)	AY 6
Giraud-Teulon (R.)	BZ 9
Gde-Fontaine (R.)	AZ 10
Loges (Av. des)	AY 14
Malraux (Pl. A.)	BZ 16
Mareil (Pl.)	AZ 19
Pologne (R. de)	AY 23
Surintendance (R. de la)	AY 28
Victoire (Pl. de la)	AY 30
Vieil-Abreuvoir (R. du)	AZ 32

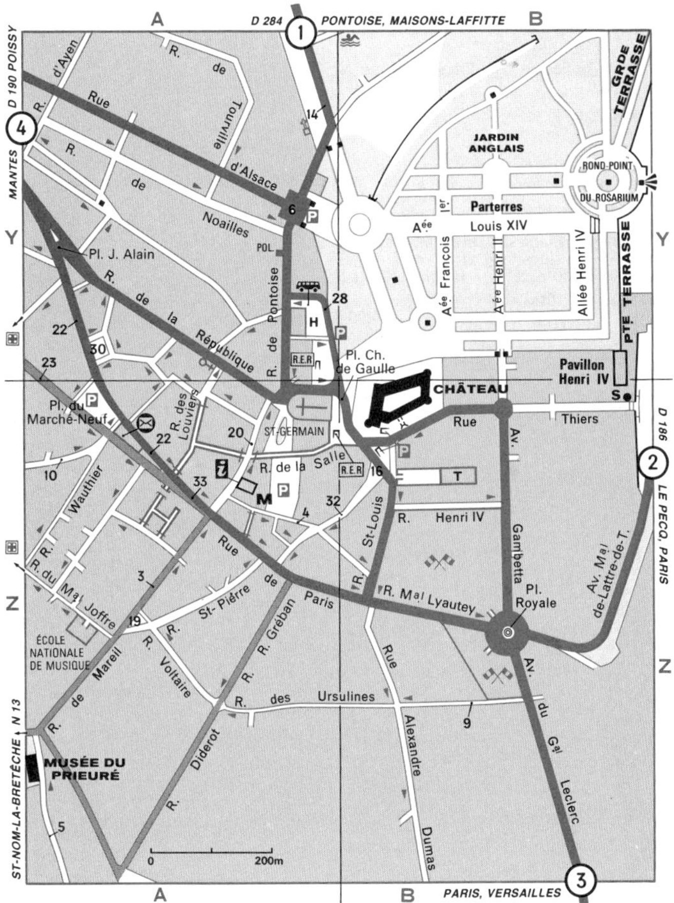

Pavillon Henri IV, 21 r. Thiers ℘ 39 10 15 15, Telex 695822, Fax 39 73 93 73, ≤ Paris and the River Seine, – rest – 200. AE GB BZ **s**

M 240/700 – 50 – **42 rm** 500/1300, 3 suites.

to the NW by ① : 2,5 km on N 284 and rte des Mares – ✉ 78100 St-Germain-en-Laye :

La Forestière M, 1 av. Prés.-Kennedy ✆ 39 73 36 60, Telex 696055, Fax 39 73 73 88, – TV – 30. GB JCB
M see **Cazaudehore** below – ☕ 65 – **25 rm** 680/830, 5 suites.

Cazaudehore, 1 av. Prés.-Kennedy ✆ 34 51 93 80, Telex 696055, Fax 39 73 73 88, « Flowered garden in woods » – . GB JCB
closed Monday except Bank Holidays – **M** 240 (lunch) and a la carte 300/465.

*If you would like a more complete selection of hotels and restaurants, consult the **MICHELIN** Red Guides for the following countries :*
Benelux, Deutschland, España Portugal, France,
Great Britain and Ireland,** and **Italia,
all in annual editions.

Versailles P **78000** Yvelines 101 ㉒, 22 – pop. 87 789 alt. 132.

See : Castel★★★ Y – Gardens★★★ (fountain display★★★ (grandes eaux) and illuminated night performances★★★ (fêtes de nuit) in summer) – Ecuries Royales★ Y – The Trianons★★ – Lambinet Museum★ Y **M**.

Racing Club France (private) ✆ 39 50 59 41 by ③ : 2,5 km.

Office de Tourisme 7 r. Réservoirs ✆ 39 50 36 22.

Paris 20 ①.

Plan opposite

Trianon Palace M, 1 bd Reine ✆ 30 84 38 00, Telex 698863, Fax 39 49 00 77, ≤, park, « Tasteful early 20C decor », – rm TV . AE GB JCB. rest X **r**
M see **Les Trois Marches** below – ☕ 95 – **69 rm** 1500/3500, 25 suites.

Pullman Place d'Armes M, 2 av. Paris ✆ 39 53 30 31, Telex 697042, Fax 39 53 87 20 – rm rest TV – 150. AE GB JCB Y **a**
M 135/180 – ☕ 65 – **146 rm** 690, 6 suites.

Trianon Hôtel M, 1 bd Reine ✆ 30 84 38 00, Telex 699210, Fax 39 51 57 79, – TV – 400. AE GB JCB X **r**
M 165 – ☕ 85 – **96 rm** 990/1370.

Novotel M, 4 bd St-Antoine at Le Chesnay ✉ 78150 ✆ 39 54 96 96, Telex 689624, Fax 39 54 94 40 – rm TV – 25 - 150. AE GB X **z**
M a la carte approx. 160 – ☕ 52 – **102 rm** 520/550.

Mercure M without rest, r. Marly-le-Roi at Le Chesnay, in front of Commercial Centre Parly II ✉ 78150 ✆ 39 55 11 41, Telex 695205, Fax 39 55 06 22 – rm TV . AE GB
☕ 49 – **78 rm** 510/550.

Résidence du Berry M without rest, 14 r. Anjou ✆ 39 49 07 07, Telex 689058, Fax 39 50 59 40 – TV . AE GB Z **s**
☕ 40 – **38 rm** 370/440.

Arcade M without rest, 4 av. Gén. de Gaulle ✆ 39 53 03 30, Telex 695652, Fax 39 50 06 31 – TV – 25. AE GB Y **u**
☕ 42 – **85 rm** 370/490.

Ibis M without rest, av. Dutartre at Le Chesnay, Commercial Centre Parly II ✉ 78150 ✆ 39 63 37 93, Telex 689188, Fax 39 55 18 66 – rm TV . AE GB
☕ 36 – **72 rm** 350/380.

Les Trois Marches (Vié), 1 bd Reine ✆ 39 50 13 21, Fax 30 21 01 25, ≤, – . AE GB JCB. X **r**
closed 29 August-7 September, Sunday dinner and Monday – **M** 260 (lunch except Saturday)/595 and a la carte 400/650
Spec. Foie gras de canard cuit entier au poivre. Canette mijotée au Madère, flambée au lard de jambon. Côte de veau au jus truffé.

La Grande Sirène, 25 r. Mar. Foch ✆ 39 53 08 08, Fax 39 53 37 15 – . AE GB. Y **v**
closed 2 to 10 May, August, Sunday and Monday – **M** 175 (lunch)/240 and a la carte 310/420
Spec. Trilogie de canard. Saint-Pierre rôti au jus de veau. Pyramide de chocolat fondant.

Rescatore, 27 av. St-Cloud ✆ 39 50 23 60, Fax 30 21 96 57 – . AE GB Y **s**
closed Saturday lunch and Sunday – **M** Seafood 145/200.

Le Chesnoy, 24 r. Pottier at Le Chesnay ✉ 78150 ✆ 39 54 01 01 – . AE GB
closed 1 to 21 August, Sunday dinner and Monday – **M** a la carte 200/300.

Marée de Versailles, 22 r. au Pain ✆ 30 21 73 73, Fax 39 50 55 87 – . GB Y **t**
closed August, 23 December-2 January, Monday dinner and Sunday – **M** Seafood 240 .

Potager du Roy, 1 r. Mar.-Joffre ✆ 39 50 35 34, Fax 30 21 69 30 – . GB Z **r**
closed Sunday and Monday except Bank Holidays – **M** 120/169.

VERSAILLES

Carnot (R.) . . . . Y
Clemenceau
(R. Georges) . . . . Y 7
États-Généraux (R. des) . . Z
Foch (R. du Mar.) . . . . Y
Hoche (R.) . . . . Y

Leclerc (R. du Gén.) . . . . Z 24
Orangerie (R. de l') . . . . YZ
Paroisse (R. de la) . . . . Y
Royale (R.) . . . . Z
Satory (R. de) . . . . YZ 42
Vieux-Versailles (R. du) . YZ 47

Chancellerie (R. de la) . Y 3
Chantiers (R. des) . . . . . Z 5

Cotte (R. Robert-de) . . . Y 10
Europe (Av. de l') . . . . . Y 14
Gambetta (Pl.) . . . . Y 17
Gaulle (Av. Gén.-de) . . . YZ 19
Indép. Américaine (R.) . Y 20
Mermoz (R. Jean) . . . . . Z 27
Nolhac (R. Pierre-de) . . Y 30
Porte de Buc (R.) . . . . . Z 34
Rockefeller (Av.) . . . . . . Y 37

AND BEYOND...

Joigny 89300 Yonne 65 ④ - pop. 9 697 alt. 101.
See : Vierge au Sourire★ in St-Thibault's Church - Côte St-Jacques ≤★ 1,5 km by D 20.
Office de Tourisme quai H.-Ragobert ✆ 86 62 11 05.
Paris 147 - Auxerre 27 - Gien 75 - Montargis 59 - Sens 30 - Troyes 76.

✿✿✿ **A la Côte St-Jacques** (Lorain) M ⛫, 14 fg Paris ✆ 86 62 09 70, Telex 801458, Fax 86 91 49 70, ≤, « Tasteful decor », ⛫, - ⛫ ▤ rm TV ☎ ♿ ⛫ P - ⛫ 30. AE ⓓ GB
closed 3 January-3 February - **M** (Sunday booking essential) 300 (lunch)/640 and a la carte 500/750 - ⛫ 100 - **25 rm** 690/1650, 4 suites
Spec. Huîtres arcachonnaises en petite terrine océane. Bar légèrement fumé à la crème de caviar. Filet de canard rôti et endives braisées, sauce à l'infusion d'arabica. Wines Chablis, Irancy.

Pontoise SP 95300 Val d'Oise 196 ⑤ - pop. 27 150 alt. 27.
Office de Tourisme 6 pl. Petit-Martroy ✆ (1) 30 38 24 45.
Paris 36 - Beauvais 50 - Dieppe 135 - Mantes-la-Jolie 39 - Rouen 91.

at Cormeilles-en-Vexin NW by D 915 - ✉ 95830 :

✿✿ **Relais Ste-Jeanne** (Cagna), on D 915 ✆ (1) 34 66 61 56, Fax (1) 34 66 40 31, ⛫, « Garden » - P. AE GB
closed 27 July-26 August, 23 to 28 December, February Holidays, Monday, dinner Tuesday and Sunday - **M** 260 (lunch)/600 and a la carte 390/620
Spec. Suprême de pigeon aux navets acidulés. Turbot rôti au thym sauce moutarde. Homard breton "Maître Pierre" en deux services.

Rheims SP 51100 Marne 56 ⑥ ⑯ - pop. 180 620 alt. 83.
See : Cathedral★★★ : tapestries★★ - St-Remi Basilica★★ : interior★★★ - Palais du Tau★★ - Champagne cellars★ - Place Royale★ - Porte Mars★ - Hôtel de la Salle★ - Foujita Chapel★ - Library★ of Ancient College des Jésuites - St-Remi Museum★★ - Hôtel le Vergeur Museum★ - St-Denis Museum★ - Historical centre of the French motor industry★.
Envir. : Fort de la Pompelle : German helmets★ 9 km to the SE by N 44.
18 Rheims-Champagne ✆ 26 03 60 14 at Gueux ; to the NW by N 31-E 46 : 9,5 km.
⛫ ✆ 26 88 50 50.
Office de Tourisme and Accueil de France (Informations facilities and hotel reservations - not more than 5 days in advance) 2 r. Guillaume-de-Machault ✆ 26 47 25 69 Telex 8408 - A.C. 7 bd Lundy ✆ 26 47 34 76.
Paris 144 - Brussels 214 - Châlons-sur-Marne 48 - Lille 199 - Luxembourg 232.

✿✿✿ **Boyer "Les Crayères"** M ⛫, 64 bd Vasnier ✆ 26 82 80 80, Telex 830959, Fax 26 82 65 52, ≤, ⛫, « Elegant mansion in park », ⛫ - ⛫ ▤ TV ☎ P. AE GB
closed 23 December-13 January - **M** *(closed Tuesday lunch and Monday)* (booking essential) a la carte 480/650 - ⛫ 89 - **16 rm** 990/1760, 3 suites
Spec. Pied de porc farci au foie gras et aux cèpes. Filet de Saint-Pierre au poivre blanc. Pigeonneau en habit vert et fumet de truffes. Wines Champagne.

Saulieu 21210 Côte-d'Or 65 ⑰ - pop. 2 917 alt. 514.
Paris 249 - Autun 41 - Avallon 38 - Beaune 64 - Clamecy 76 - Dijon 73.

✿✿✿ **Côte d'Or** (Loiseau) M ⛫, 2 r. Argentine ✆ 80 64 07 66, Fax 80 64 08 92, « Tasteful inn with flowered garden » - TV ☎ ⛫ - ⛫ 25. AE ⓓ GB JCB
closed 28 November-29 December, Tuesday lunch and Monday January-March (except Bank Holidays) - **M** 290 (lunch)/690 and a la carte 580/900 - ⛫ 95 - **15 rm** 310/980, 4 suites, 3 duplex
Spec. Jambonnettes de grenouilles à la purée d'ail. Sandre à la fondue d'échalotes sauce au vin rouge. Blanc de volaille au foie gras chaud et aux truffes. Wines Chablis, Savigny-lès-Beaune.

When driving through towns
use the plans in the Michelin *Red Guide.*
Features indicated include :
throughroutes and by-passes,
traffic junctions and major squares,
new streets, car parks, pedestrian streets...
All this information is revised annually.

Vézelay **89450** Yonne 65 ⑮ – pop. 571 alt. 302 pilgrimage (22 July).
See : Ste-Madeleine Basilica★★★ : tower ※★.
Envir. : Site★ of Pierre-Perthuis SE : 6 km.
Syndicat d'Initiative r. St-Pierre (April-October) ℘ 86 33 23 69.
Paris 223 – Auxerre 51 – Avallon 15 – Château-Chinon 60 – Clamecy 22.

at St-Père : SE : 3 km by D 957 – alt. 148 – ✉ 89450.
See : Church of N.-Dame★

L'Espérance (Meneau) ⑤, ℘ 86 33 20 45, Telex 800005, Fax 86 33 26 15, ≤, « Country garden », ⛳, ⛱, ✂ – ▤ TV ☎ P. AE ① GB
closed mid January-mid February – **M** *(closed Wednesday except dinner from May-November and Tuesday)* (booking essential) 330 (lunch)/790 and a la carte 480/850 – ☐ 100 – **34 rm** 400/1300, 6 suites
Spec. Chaud-froid de homard en gelée. Tourte d'asperges au foie gras (season). Pillette rôtie aux truffes. Wines Irancy, Vézelay.

☞ *To go a long way quickly, use* ***Michelin maps*** *at a scale of 1:1 000 000.*

BORDEAUX P **33000** Gironde 71 ⑨ – pop. 210 336 Greater Bordeaux 624 286 alt. 5.
See : Old Bordeaux★★ DXY – Grand Théâtre★★ DX – Cathedral★ and Pey Berland Belfry★ DY **E** – Place de la Bourse★★ EX – St Michael's Basilica★ EY **F** – Place du Parlement★ EX **66** – Church of Notre-Dame★ DX **D** – Fountains★ of the Monument to the Girondins DX **R** – Great Bell★ (Grosse Cloche) EY **D** – Façade★ of Ste-Croix Church FZ – Main courtyard★ of the Town Hall (Hôtel de Ville) DY **H** – Balconies★ along the Cours Xavier-Arnozan AU **5** – Museums : Fine Arts★★ (Beaux Arts) CDY **M**[1], Decorative Arts★ DY **M**[2], Aquitaine★★ DY **M**[3], Entrepôt Lainé★★ : Museum of Modern Art★ (Nw.).
Envir. : Pessac Mint★ (Sw.).
18 Golf Bordelais ℘ 56 28 56 04, to the NW D109 : 4 km ; 18 18 de Bordeaux Lac ℘ 56 50 92 72, to the N by D 2 : 10 km ; 9 18 of Cameyrac ℘ 56 72 96 79, to the NE by N 89 : 18 km ; 9 9 9 9 Internat. of Bordeaux-Pessac ℘ 56 36 24 47 to the SW N 150 ; 9 of Artigues ℘ 56 86 49 26, E by D 241 : 8 km.
✈ of Bordeaux-Mérignac : ℘ 56 34 50 00 to the W : 11 km.
🚗 ℘ 56 92 50 50.
Office de Tourisme and Accueil de France, (Information, exchange facilities and hotel reservations - not more than 5 days in advance) 12 cours 30-Juillet ℘ 56 44 28 41, Telex 570362 at the Gare St-Jean ℘ 56 91 64 70 and the airport, Arrivals Hall ℘ 52 34 39 39 - A.C. du Sud-Ouest 8 pl. Quinconces ℘ 56 44 22 92 – Bordeaux wine Exhibition (Maison du vin de Bordeaux), 3 cours 30-Juillet (Information, wine-tasting - closed weekends from 16 Oct.-14 May) – ℘ 56 00 22 66 DX **z**.
Paris 579 – Lyons 531 – Nantes 324 – Strasbourg 919 – Toulouse 245.

Plans on following pages

Château Chartron M, 81 cours St-Louis ✉ 33300 ℘ 56 43 15 00, Telex 573938, Fax 56 69 15 21, ⛱, 🚗 – 🛗 ▤ TV ☎ ♿ 🚗 – 🎤 30 - 200. AE ① GB
Novamagus *(closed August, Saturday and Sunday)* **M** 180 – **Le Cabernet M** a la carte approx. 150 – ☐ 65 – **144 rm** 690/1200, 6 suites.

Burdigala M, 115 r. G. Bonnac ℘ 56 90 16 16, Telex 572981, Fax 56 93 15 06 – 🛗 ▤ TV ☎ ♿ 🚗 – 🎤 100. AE ① GB JCB CX **r**
M 140/340 – ☐ 75 – **68 rm** 760/1350, 8 suites, 7 duplex.

Pullman Mériadeck M, 5 r. R. Lateulade ℘ 56 56 43 43, Telex 540565, Fax 56 96 50 59 – 🛗 ⊁ rm ▤ TV ☎ – 🎤 350. AE ① GB JCB. ⊁ rest CY **w**
Le Mériadeck ℘ 56 56 43 60 **M** 130/185 b.i. – ☐ 65 – **192 rm** 510/950.

Holiday Inn M, 30 r. de Tauzia ✉ 33800 ℘ 56 92 21 21, Telex 573848, Fax 56 91 08 06, ⛱ – 🛗 ⊁ rm ▤ TV ☎ ♿ 🚗 – 🎤 80. AE GB FZ **v**
M *(closed Sunday lunch and Saturday)* 90 – ☐ 55 – **90 rm** 474/527.

Novotel Bordeaux-Centre M, 45 cours Maréchal Juin ℘ 56 51 46 46, Telex 573749, Fax 56 98 25 56, ⛱ – 🛗 ⊁ rm ▤ TV ☎ ♿ 🚗 – 🎤 80. AE ① GB JCB CY **m**
M a la carte approx. 160 – ☐ 50 – **138 rm** 480/530.

Claret M ⑤, Cité Mondiale du Vin, 18 parvis des Chartrons ℘ 56 01 79 79, Fax 56 01 79 00, ⛱ – 🛗 ▤ TV ☎ ♿. AE ① GB
M a la carte 175/260 – ☐ 60 – **97 rm** 510/570.

Sainte-Catherine M without rest, 27 r. Parlement Ste-Catherine ℘ 56 81 95 12, Telex 573215, Fax 56 44 50 51 – 🛗 ▤ TV ☎ – 🎤 45. AE ① GB JCB DX **m**
☐ 70 – **82 rm** 550/870.

Normandie without rest, 7 cours 30-Juillet ℘ 56 52 16 80, Telex 570481, Fax 56 51 68 91 – 🛗 TV ☎. AE ① GB JCB DX **z**
☐ 39 – **100 rm** 300/550.

Majestic without rest, 2 r. Condé ℘ 56 52 60 44, Telex 572938, Fax 56 79 26 70 – 🛗 ▤ TV ☎. AE ① GB JCB DX **a**
☐ 36 – **49 rm** 360/500.

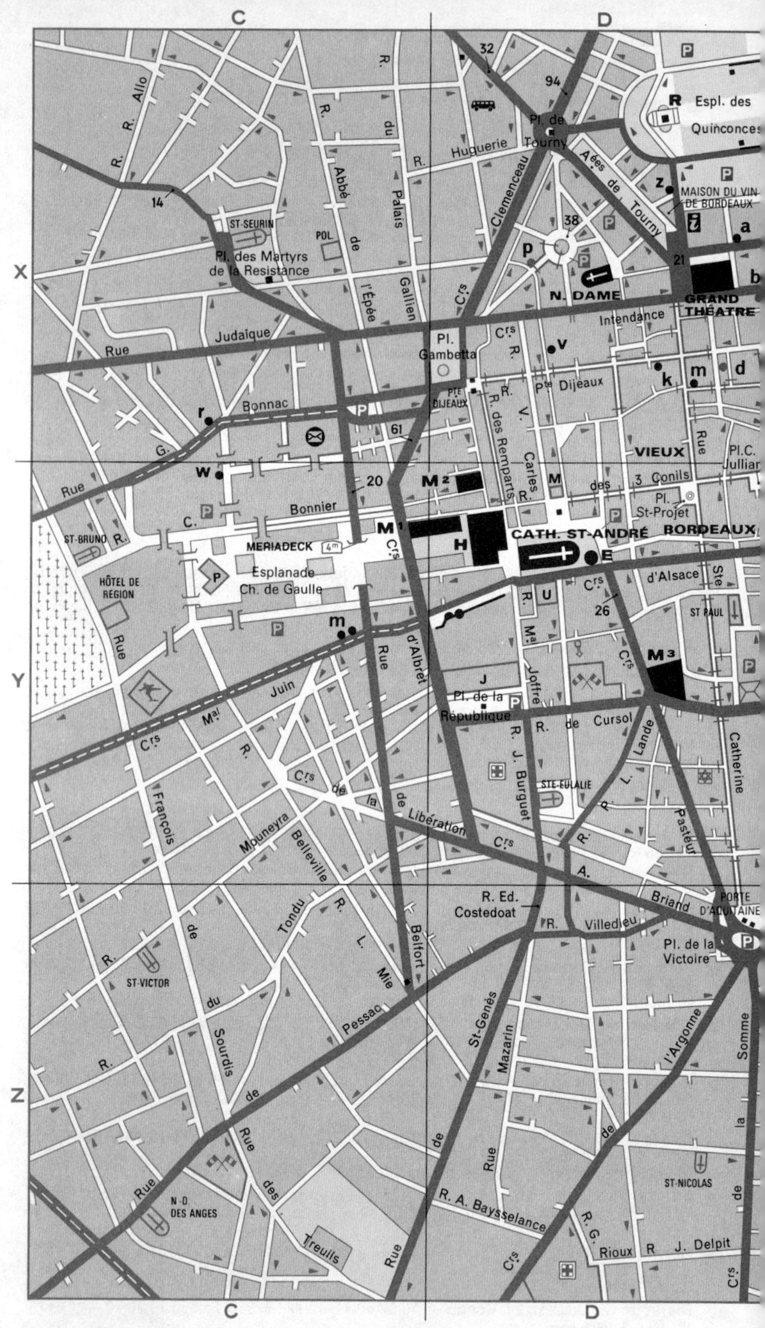

To go a long way quickly, use ***Michelin Maps*** *at scale of 1: 1 000 000.*

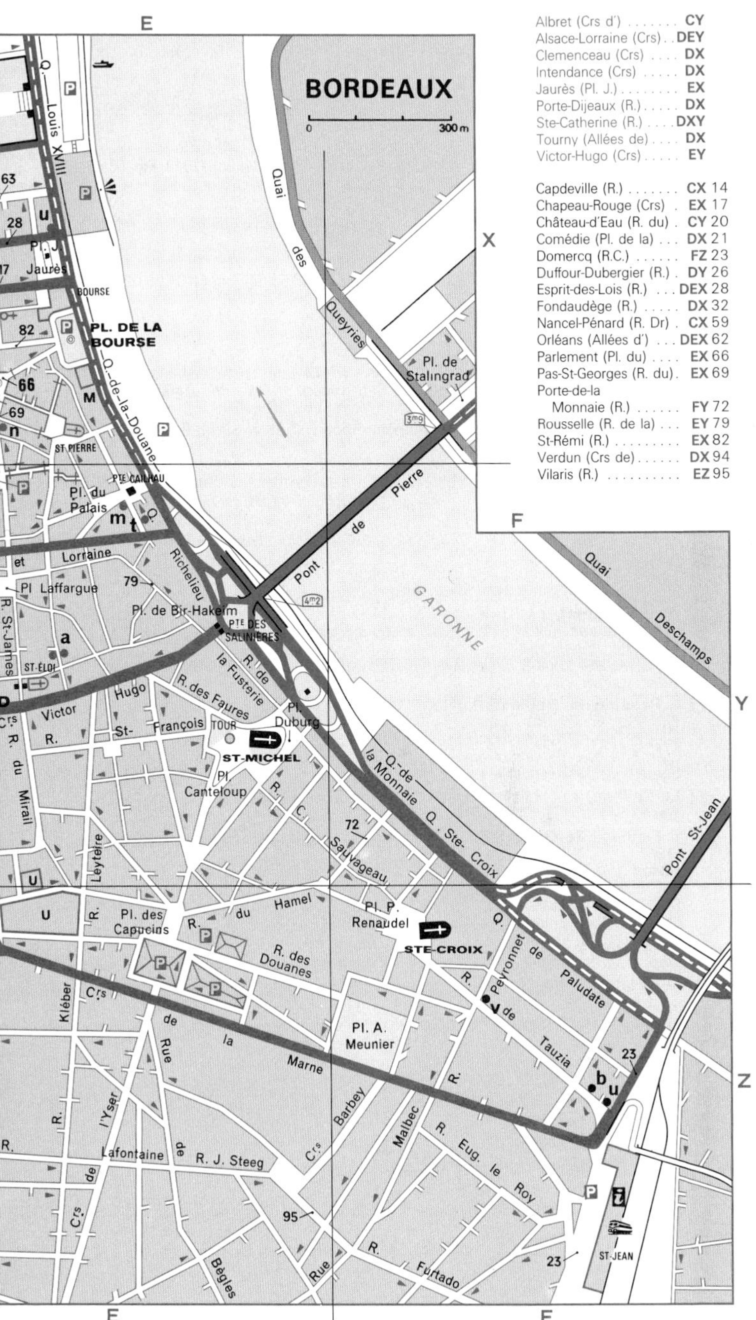

Ensure that you have up to date Michelin maps *in your car.*

Gd H. Français M without rest, 12 r. Temple ☎ 56 48 10 35, Telex 550587, Fax 56 81 76 18 – AE GB DX **v**
45 – **35 rm** 340/590.

Royal St Jean M without rest, 15 r. Ch. Domercq ✉ 33800 ☎ 56 91 72 16, Telex 570468, Fax 56 94 08 32 – AE GB JCB FZ **u**
45 – **37 rm** 330/470.

Ibis Mériadeck M, 35 cours Mar. Juin ☎ 56 90 10 33, Telex 572918, Fax 56 96 33 15 – rm – 250. AE GB CY **m**
M 80/155 – 34 – **210 rm** 315/380.

Relais Bleus M, 68 r. Tauzia ✉ 33800 ☎ 56 91 55 50, Fax 56 91 08 41 – rest – 60. AE GB. FZ **b**
M 88 b.i./120 b.i. – 32 – **88 rm** 280/350.

Presse M without rest, 6 r. Porte Dijeaux ☎ 56 48 53 88, Fax 56 01 05 82 – AE GB DX **k**
30 – **29 rm** 270/350.

XXXX ✿ **Le Chapon Fin** (Garcia), 5 r. Montesquieu ☎ 56 79 10 10, Fax 56 79 09 10, « Authentic 1900 Rococo decor » – AE GB JCB DX **p**
closed 17 to 24 August, Sunday and Monday – **M** 150 (lunch)/420 and a la carte 370/480
Spec. Gaspacho de homard (15 May-15 September). Ravioles de langoustines au citron vert. Noisettes d'agneau aux parfums du midi. Wines Entre-Deux-Mers.

XXX ✿ **Le Rouzic** (Gautier), 34 cours Chapeau Rouge ☎ 56 44 39 11, Fax 56 40 55 10 – AE GB JCB DX **b**
closed Saturday lunch and Sunday – **M** 160/420 and a la carte 260/470
Spec. Lamproie à la bordelaise. Huîtres en geleé d'eau de mer. Agneau de Pauillac. Wines St-Julien.

XXX ✿ **La Chamade** (Carrère), 20 r. Piliers de Tutelle ☎ 56 48 13 74, Fax 56 79 29 67 – AE GB DX **d**
closed Saturday and Sunday 17 July-16 Agust and Saturday lunch – **M** 180/280 and a la carte 240/370
Spec. Terrine de foie gras de canard. Turbotin au beurre nantais. Noix de ris de veau piquée au foie gras. Wines Saint-Julien, Saint-Emilion.

XXX ✿ **Jean Ramet,** 7 pl. J. Jaurès ☎ 56 44 12 51 – AE GB EX **u**
closed Saturday (except dinner in Winter) and Sunday – **M** 150 (lunch)/320 and a la carte 260/430
Spec. Feuilleté d'huîtres tièdes à la nage. Gibier (season). Champignons (season). Wines Graves blanc, Listrac.

XXX ✿ **Pavillon des Boulevards** (Franc), 120 r. Croix de Seguey ☎ 56 81 51 02, Fax 56 51 14 58, – AE GB JCB
closed 15 to 22 August, Saturday lunch and Sunday – **M** 290/390
Spec. Foie gras de canard aux épices douces. Poêlée de homard bardé de choux au vin de Sauternes. Chinoiseries de pigeonneau.

XXX **Le Cailhau,** 3 pl. Palais ☎ 56 81 79 91, Fax 56 44 86 58 – AE GB JCB. EY **m**
closed Saturday lunch and Sunday – **M** 160/220.

XXX ✿ **Le Vieux Bordeaux** (Bordage), 27 r. Buhan ☎ 56 52 94 36, Fax 56 44 25 11, – AE GB EY **a**
closed 1 to 23 August, February Holidays, Saturday lunch, Sunday and Bank Holidays – **M** 155/260 and a la carte 210/360
Spec. Foie gras de canard. Filets d'anguilles sautés aux champignons. Tranche de cerises au chocolat. Wines Entre-Deux-Mers.

XXX **Villa Carnot,** 335 bd Wilson ✉ 33200 ☎ 56 08 04 21, – AE GB.
closed 1 to 15 September, Sunday and Monday – **M** 158/320.

XX **Les Plaisirs d'Ausone,** 10 r. Ausone ☎ 56 79 30 30, Fax 56 51 38 16 – AE GB EY **t**
closed 1 to 10 May, 13 to 22 August, Monday lunch, Saturday lunch and Sunday – **M** 150/280.

XX **Le Buhan,** 28 r. Buhan ☎ 56 52 80 86 – AE GB EY **a**
closed 30 August-5 September, February Holidays, Sunday dinner and Monday lunch – **M** 130/250.

XX **Didier Gélineau,** 26 r. Pas St Georges ☎ 56 52 84 25, Fax 56 51 93 25 – AE GB
closed Sunday (except lunch 15 October-15 April) – **M** 99/320. EX **n**

at Parc des Expositions : North of the town – ✉ 33300 Bordeaux :

Sofitel Aquitania M, ☎ 56 50 83 80, Telex 570557, Fax 56 39 73 75, ←, – rm – 25 - 600. AE GB
Le Flore **M** a la carte 160/220 – 70 – **211 rm** 580/1300.

Mercure Pont d'Aquitaine M, ☎ 56 43 36 72, Telex 540097, Fax 56 50 23 95, – rm – 80 - 120. AE GB. rest
M a la carte 150/240 – 48 – **100 rm** 460/580.

Novotel-Bordeaux le Lac M, ☎ 56 50 99 70, Telex 570274, Fax 56 43 00 66, ←, – rm rest AE GB
M a la carte approx. 180 – 50 – **176 rm** 440.

Mercure Bordeaux le Lac M, ☎ 56 11 71 11, Telex 540077, Fax 56 43 07 55, – rm – 250. AE GB
M *(closed Saturday, Sunday and Bank Holidays)* 95 b.i./140 – 50 – **108 rm** 420/580.

at Carbon-Blanc NE : 8 km – pop. 5 842 – ✉ 33560 :

XXX **Marc Demund,** av. Gardette ☎ 56 74 72 28, Fax 56 06 55 40, park – P. AE ① GB
closed 15 to 31 August, Sunday dinner and Monday – **M** 240/345.

at Bouliac – ✉ 33270 :

⚜ **Le St-James** (Amat) M, pl. C. Hosteins, near church ☎ 56 20 52 19, Telex 573001, Fax 56 20 92 58, ≤ Bordeaux, « Original contemporary decor », – TV ☎ P. AE ① GB JCB.
M 250 (lunch)/400 and a la carte 355/620 - **Le Bistroy** *(closed Monday November-March and Sunday)* **M** a la carte approx. 160 – ☕ 70 – **17 rm** 800/1350
Spec. Homard rôti aux pommes de terre et gousses d'ail. Pigeon grillé aux épices et sa pastilla. Civet et canard compoté, désossé et dégraissé. Wines Premières Côtes de Bordeaux-Cadillac, Médoc.

to the W :

at Pessac : 9 km - pop. 51 055 – ✉ 33600 :

La Réserve M, av. Bourgailh ☎ 56 07 13 28, Fax 56 36 31 02, « Park », – TV ☎ P – 60. AE ① GB
closed December and January – **M** 150/350 – ☕ 60 – **20 rm** 600/900.

Royal Brion without rest, 10 r. Pin Vert ☎ 56 45 07 72, Fax 56 46 13 75 – TV ☎ P. AE ① GB
closed 20 December-5 January – ☕ 35 – **25 rm** 280/340.

at the airport : 11 km by D 106E – ✉ 33700 Mérignac :

Novotel-Mérignac M, av. Kennedy ☎ 56 34 10 25, Telex 540320, Fax 56 55 99 64, – rm TV ☎ P – 25 - 100. AE ① GB JCB
M a la carte approx. 180 – ☕ 50 – **137 rm** 450.

Mercure Aéroport M, 1 av. Ch. Lindbergh ☎ 56 34 74 74, Telex 573953, Fax 56 34 30 84, – rm TV ☎ P – 200. AE ① GB
M 98 – ☕ 48 – **105 rm** 440/550.

Le Patio M, av. J.-F. Kennedy at Mérignac ☎ 56 55 93 42, Telex 540183, Fax 56 47 64 94, – rm TV ☎ P – 60. AE ① GB
M 135/180 – ☕ 48 – **80 rm** 415/470.

Fimotel M, 97 av. J.-F. Kennedy ☎ 56 34 33 08, Fax 56 34 01 90, – TV ☎ P – 35. AE ① GB
M 80/280 – ☕ 35 – **60 rm** 295/315.

Eugénie-les-Bains

40320 Landes 82 ① – pop. 467 alt. 90 – Spa (15 February-November).
Bordeaux 151.

⚜⚜⚜ **Les Prés d'Eugénie** (Guérard) M, ☎ 58 05 06 07, Telex 540470, Fax 58 51 13 59, ≤, « Elegantly decorated 19C mansion, park », – TV ☎ P. AE ① GB.
closed 1 December-24 February – **M** (low-calorie menu for residents only) 310/350 and a la carte - **rest. Michel Guérard** (booking essential) *(closed Thursday lunch and Wednesday 10/9-12/7 except Bank Holidays)* **M** 360/580 and a la carte 380/510 – ☕ 95 – **28 rm** 1250/1450, 7 suites
Spec. Rillettes de lapereau en venaison. Pigeonneau "à la soie", cuit au bois fruitier. Gâteau mollet du Marquis de Béchamel. Wines Côtes de Gascogne, Tursan blanc.
Le Couvent des Herbes M, « 18C convent », – TV ☎ P. AE ① GB. rest
closed 1 December-24 February – **M** see **Les Prés d'Eugénie** and **Michel Guérard** – ☕ 95 – **5 rm** 1450/1650, 3 suites.
Maison Rose M, ☎ 58 05 05 05, « Guesthouse ambiance », – kitchenette TV ☎ P
27 rm.

Grenade-sur-l'Adour

40270 Landes 82 ① – pop. 2 187 alt. 55.
Bordeaux 140.

⚜⚜ **Pain Adour et Fantaisie** (Oudill) M, 7 pl. Tilleuls ☎ 58 45 18 80, Fax 58 45 16 57, « Riverside terrace » – rm TV ☎. AE ① GB
closed Sunday dinner and Monday (except July-August and Bank Holidays) – **M** 180/450 and a la carte 330/450 – ☕ 85 – **10 rm** 600/900
Spec. Foie gras de canard rôti au laurier. Marmite de cèpes au vieux jambon (autum). Vacherin glacé au romarin et coulis de nectarine. Wines Jurançon, Madiran.

Langon

SP 33210 Gironde 79 ② – pop. 5 842 alt. 22.
Bordeaux 48.

⚜⚜ **Claude Darroze** M, 95 cours Gén. Leclerc ☎ 56 63 00 48, Fax 56 63 41 15, – TV ☎ P – 25. AE ① GB. rm
closed 15 October-5 November and 5 to 25 January – **M** 210/520 and a la carte 320/480 – ☕ 70 – **16 rm** 320/430
Spec. Foie gras de canard. Feuilleté de fruits de mer et crustcés (March to November). Gibier (season). Wines Entre-Deux-Mers, Graves rouge.

Pons **17800** Char.-Mar. 71 ⑤ – pop. 4 412 alt. 20.
Bordeaux 95.

at Mosnac S : 11 km by Bordeaux road and D 134 – ✉ 17240 :

Moulin de Marcouze (Bouchet) M, ✆ 46 70 46 16, Fax 46 70 48 14, park, « Elegant inn on the banks of the River Seugne », – ▤ TV ☎ ♿ P. GB JCB
closed 15 to 30 November, February, Wednesday lunch and Tuesday 15 September-15 June except Bank Holidays – **M** 195/420 and a la carte 340/460 – ☐ 75 – **10 rm** 530/1100
Spec. Tarte aux pommes de terre, saumon fumé et crème au caviar. Gigot d'agneau de sept heures à la cuillère. Pêche glacée sur granité de Champagne.

CANNES **06400** Alpes-Mar. 84 ⑨, 115 ㉟ ㊳ – pop. 68 676 alt. 2 – Casinos Carlton Casino BYZ, Palm Beach (temp. closed) X, Municipal BZ.

See : Site★★ - Sea-Front★★ : Boulevard★★ BCDZ – and Pointe de la Croisette★ X – ≤★ from the Mount Chevalier Tower AZ **V** – The Castre Museum★ (Musée de la Castre) AZ **M** – Tour into the Hills★ (Chemin des Collines) NE : 4 km V – The Croix des Gardes X **E** ≤★ W : 5 km then 15 mn.

18 Country-Club of Cannes-Mougins ✆ 93 75 79 13 by ⑤ : 9 km ; 9 18 Golf-Club of Cannes-Mandelieu ✆ 93 49 55 39 by ② : 6,5 km ; 18 Biot ✆ 93 65 08 48 by ⑤ : 14 km ; 18 Riviera Golf Club at Mandelieu ✆ 93 38 32 55 by ② : 8 km.

🅸 Direction Générale du Tourisme et des Congrès and Accueil de France, Information, exchange facilities and hotel reservations not more than 5 days in advan, espl. Prés. Georges-Pompidou ✆ 93 39 01 01, Telex 470749 (Welcome Office ✆ 93 39 24 53) and Railway Station ✆ 93 99 19 77, Telex 470795 – A.C. 12bis r. L. Blanc ✆ 93 39 38 94.

Paris 903 ⑤ – Aix-en-Provence 146 ⑤ – Grenoble 312 ⑤ – Marseilles 159 ⑤ – Nice 32 ⑤ – Toulon 121 ⑤.

Plans on following pages

Carlton Inter-Continental, 58 bd Croisette ✆ 93 68 91 68, Telex 470720, Fax 93 38 20 90, ≤, Fб, – |♯| ▤ rest TV ☎ ♿ – 30 - 250. AE ⓓ GB JCB CZ **e**
M see **La Côte** below- **Café Carlton M** a la carte 260/500 – ☐ 145 – **326 rm** 2000/3350, 28 suites.

Martinez, 73 bd Croisette ✆ 92 98 73 00, Telex 470708, Fax 93 39 67 82, ≤, – |♯| ▤ TV ☎ P – 60 - 700. AE ⓓ GB JCB DZ **n**
closed mid-November-mid-January – **M** see **La Palme d'Or** below - **L'Orangeraie** ✆ 92 98 74 12 *(dinner only in July-August)* **M** 195 – ☐ 100 – **418 rm** 1300/3250, 12 suites.

Majestic, 14 bd Croisette ✆ 92 98 77 00, Telex 470787, Fax 93 38 97 90, ≤, – |♯| ▤ TV ☎ ♿ – 400. AE ⓓ GB BZ **n**
closed 10 November-20 December – **Le Sunset M** 240 – ☐ 110 – **263 rm** 1150/3500, 24 suites.

Noga Hilton M, 50 bd Croisette ✆ 92 99 70 00, Telex 470013, Fax 92 99 70 11, Fб, – |♯| rm ▤ TV ☎ ♿ – 25 - 600. AE ⓓ GB. rest CZ **b**
La Scala *(closed Monday and Tuesday November-March)* **M** (dinner only in July-August) 350/490 – **Le Grand Bleu - (brasserie) M** 165/320 – ☐ 110 – **192 rm** 1790/3190, 33 suites.

Gray d'Albion M, 38 r. Serbes ✆ 92 99 79 79, Telex 470744, Fax 93 99 26 10, – |♯| rm ▤ TV ☎ ♿ – 30 - 200. AE ⓓ GB JCB BZ **d**
M see **Royal Gray** below - **Les 4 Saisons M** carte 160 à 260 – ☐ 85 – **172 rm** 1200/1550, 14 suites.

L'Horset-Savoy M, 5 r. F. Einessy ✆ 92 99 72 00, Telex 461873, Fax 93 68 25 59, – |♯| rm ▤ TV ☎ ♿ – 120. AE ⓓ GB CZ **u**
M 130/180 – ☐ 85 – **101 rm** 860/1200, 5 suites.

Pullman Beach M without rest, 13 r. Canada ✆ 93 94 50 50, Telex 470034, Fax 93 68 35 38, – |♯| rm ▤ TV ☎ – 40. AE ⓓ GB JCB DZ **y**
closed 20 November-26 December and 28 January-1 March – ☐ 85 – **93 rm** 990/1650.

Sofitel Méditerranée M, 2 bd J. Hibert ✆ 92 99 73 00, Telex 470728, Fax 92 99 73 29, « Roof-top swimming pool and terrace ≤ bay of Cannes » – |♯| rm ▤ TV ☎ – 150. AE ⓓ GB AZ **n**
closed 21 November-22 December – **Le Palmyre** ✆ 92 99 73 10 **M** a la carte 230/350 – ☐ 90 – **145 rm** 875/1290, 5 suites.

Grand Hôtel, 45 bd Croisette ✆ 93 38 15 45, Telex 470727, Fax 93 68 97 45, ≤, – |♯| ▤ rm TV ☎ P – 30. AE ⓓ GB. rest CZ **q**
M 140/190 – ☐ 60 – **74 rm** 730/1460.

Cristal M, 15 rd-pt Duboys d'Angers ✆ 93 39 45 45, Telex 470844, Fax 93 38 64 66, – |♯| ▤ TV ☎. AE ⓓ GB CZ **s**
M *(closed 15 November-18 December)* 135/250 – **47 rm** ☐ 765/1070, 4 suites.

Novotel M, 25 av. Beauséjour ✆ 93 68 91 50, Telex 470039, Fax 93 38 37 08, ≤, « Garden », Fб, – |♯| rm ▤ rest TV ☎ – 400. AE ⓓ GB JCB DY **r**
M a la carte approx. 180 – ☐ 60 – **181 rm** 650/950.

Splendid without rest, 4 r. F. Faure ✆ 93 99 53 11, Telex 470990, Fax 93 99 55 02, ≤ – |♯| kitchenette ▤ TV ☎. AE ⓓ GB BZ **a**
☐ 50 – **63 rm** 570/870.

Victoria M without rest, rd-pt Duboys d'Angers ✆ 93 99 36 36, Fax 93 38 03 91, – |♯| ▤ TV ☎. AE ⓓ GB JCB. CZ **x**
closed 10 November-20 December – ☐ 50 – **25 rm** 710/1100.

Canberra without rest, rd-pt Duboys d'Angers ✆ 93 38 20 70, Telex 470817, Fax 92 98 03 47 – 🛗 ▤ 📺 ☎ 🅿. AE ⓓ GB – ☕ 40 – **45 rm** 470/735. CZ **h**

Fouquet's Ⓜ without rest, 2 rd-pt Duboys d'Angers ✆ 93 38 75 81, Fax 92 98 03 39 – ▤ 📺 ☎ 🚗. AE ⓓ GB JCB CZ **y**
closed 1 November-26 December – ☕ 60 – **10 rm** 1100/1300.

Paris without rest, 34 bd Alsace ✆ 93 38 30 89, Telex 470995, Fax 93 39 04 61, 🏊, 🌳 – 🛗 ▤ 📺 ☎ 🚗 – 🏛 40. AE ⓓ GB JCB. ✻ CY **a**
closed 15 November-27 December and 3 to 20 January – ☕ 50 – **45 rm** 750/980, 5 suites.

Embassy, 6 r. Bône ✆ 93 38 79 02, Telex 470081, Fax 93 99 07 98 – 🛗 ▤ 📺 ☎. AE ⓓ GB – **M** 115/200 – **60 rm** ☕ 680/800. DY **j**

Mondial Ⓜ without rest, 77 r. d'Antibes ✆ 93 68 70 00, Telex 462918, Fax 93 99 39 11 – 🛗 ⇔ rm ▤ 📺 ☎ ♿. AE ⓓ GB CY **e**
☕ 40 – **56 rm** 530/740.

Abrial without rest, 24 bd Lorraine ✆ 93 38 78 82, Telex 470761, Fax 92 98 67 41 – 🛗 ▤ 📺 ☎ 🚗 – 🏛 30. AE ⓓ GB JCB CY **s**
☕ 53 – **50 rm** 392/640.

Ligure without rest, 5 pl. Gare ✆ 93 39 03 11, Telex 970275, Fax 93 39 19 48 – 🛗 ▤ 📺 ☎. AE ⓓ GB – ☕ 35 – **36 rm** 610/710. BY **n**

Beau Séjour, 5 r. Fauvettes ✆ 93 39 63 00, Telex 470975, Fax 92 98 64 66, 🍽, 🏊, 🌳 – 🛗 ▤ rm 📺 ☎ 🚗 – 🏛 30. AE ⓓ GB JCB. ✻ rest AZ **d**
closed 1 November-14 December – **M** 120/140 🍷 – **46 rm** ☕ 690/790.

La Madone 🐦 without rest, 5 av. Justinia ✆ 93 43 57 87, Fax 93 43 22 79, 🏊, 🌳 – kitchenette ⇔ rm 📺 ☎. AE ⓓ GB – ☕ 50 – **31 rm** 450/760. X **y**

Château de la Tour 🐦, 10 av. Font-de-Veyre by ③ ✉ 06150 Cannes-La-Bocca ✆ 93 47 34 64, Telex 470906, Fax 93 47 86 61, 🏊 – 🛗 📺 ☎ 🅿. AE ⓓ GB. ✻ rest
M *(closed 20 November-10 December)* 85/110 – ☕ 35 – **42 rm** 520/680.

America Ⓜ without rest, 13 r. St-Honoré ✆ 93 68 36 36, Fax 93 68 04 58 – 🛗 ⇔ rm ▤ 📺 ☎. AE ⓓ GB JCB. ✻ – ☕ 50 – **30 rm** 500/770. BZ **r**

Host. de l'Olivier without rest, 5 r. Tambourinaires ✆ 93 39 53 28, Fax 93 39 55 85, 🏊 – 📺 ☎ 🅿. AE GB. ✻ AZ **e**
closed 23 November-28 December – ☕ 35 – **23 rm** 480/570.

Des Congrès et Festivals without rest, 12 r. Teisseire ✆ 93 39 13 81, Fax 93 39 56 28 – 🛗 ▤ 📺 ☎. AE ⓓ GB JCB – ☕ 35 – **20 rm** 350/550. CY **p**

Albert 1er Ⓜ without rest, 68 av. Grasse ✆ 93 39 24 04, Fax 93 38 83 75 – 📺 ☎ 🅿. GB
closed November – ☕ 27 – **11 rm** 280/320. AY **d**

Cheval Blanc without rest, 3 r. Maupassant ✆ 93 39 88 60, Fax 93 38 01 50 – 📺 ☎. GB
closed November – ☕ 27 – **16 rm** 220/320. AY **a**

Modern without rest, 11 r. Serbes ✆ 93 39 09 87 – 🛗 📺 ☎ BZ **b**
closed 1 November to 23 December – ☕ 30 – **19 rm** 295/470.

XXXXX ✿✿ **La Belle Otéro,** 58 bd Croisette, on the 7th floor of the Carlton hotel ✆ 93 68 00 33, Fax 93 39 09 06, 🍽 – ▤. AE ⓓ GB CZ **e**
closed 1 to 15 November, 1 to 22 February, Sunday and Monday 15 September-15 June – **M** 250 b.i./550 (lunch) and a la carte 470/650
Spec. Minestrone de homard bleu en bouillon de crustacés. Tian de Saint-Pierre aux artichauts violets. Filet mignon de veau en jus d'osso-bucco. Wines Muscat des coteaux varois, Côtes de Provence.

XXXXX ✿ **La Côte** - Hôtel Carlton Intercontinental, 58 bd Croisette ✆ 93 68 91 68, Telex 470720, Fax 93 38 20 90 – ▤. AE ⓓ GB JCB. ✻ – *closed 12 November-16 December, Tuesday and Wednesday* – **M** 210 (lunch)/470 and a la carte 360/530 CZ **e**
Spec. Petits poivrons farcis et grillade de bonite en marinade de citron vert. Chapon rôti aux gousses d'ail. Tagliatelles et pieds d'agneau mijotés aux morilles. Wines Bandol.

XXXXX ✿✿ **La Palme d'Or** - Hôtel Martinez, 73 bd Croisette ✆ 92 98 74 14, Telex 470708, Fax 93 39 67 82, ≤, 🍽 – ▤ 🅿. AE ⓓ GB JCB DZ **n**
closed mid-November-mid-January, Tuesday (except dinner 15 May-15 September) and Monday – **M** 290 (lunch)/540 and a la carte 410/580
Spec. Saint-Pierre "poire et thym" à la concassée d'olives. Pigeonneau de ferme en crépinette de laitue, crème de févettes à la sarriette. Fraises des bois, jus tiède au Grand-Marnier et crème de lait glacée. Wines Côtes de Provence.

XXXX ✿✿ **Royal Gray** - Hôtel Gray d'Albion, 6 r. Etats-Unis ✆ 92 99 79 60, Telex 470744, Fax 93 99 26 10, 🍽, « Tasteful, contemporary decor » – ▤. AE ⓓ GB JCB CYZ **m**
closed February, Monday except dinner in July-August and Sunday – **M** 550/580 and a la carte 410/540
Spec. Papillon de langoustines à la chiffonnade de basilic. Saint Pierre rôti au fumet de fenouil sec. Palmier de pamplemousse rôti au miel et sorbet coco. Wines Côtes de Provence.

XXX **Poêle d'Or,** 23 r. États-Unis ✆ 93 39 77 65, Fax 93 40 45 59 – AE GB CZ **v**
closed 22 to 30/3, 28/6-5/7, 22/11-13/12, Tuesday lunch 1/4-15/11, Sunday dinner 15/11-31/3 and Monday – **M** (weekends : booking essential) 170/195 and a la carte 340/480.

XXX **Gaston et Gastounette,** 7 quai St-Pierre ✆ 93 39 47 92, 🍽 – AE ⓓ GB AZ **v**
closed 5 to 20 January – **M** 195.

CANNES

André (R. du Cdt) . . . . . **CZ**
Antibes (R. d') . . . . **BCZ**
Belges (R. des) . . . . **BZ** 12
Chabaud (R.) . . . . **CY** 22
Croisette (Bd de la) . . . **BDZ**
Félix-Faure (R.) . . . . **ABZ**
Foch (R. du Mar.) . . . . . **BY** 44
Joffre (R. du Mar.) . . . . . **BY** 60
Riouffe (R. Jean de) . . . **BY** 98

Albert-Édouard (Jetée) . **BZ**
Alexandre-III (Bd) . . . . . . **X** 2
Alsace (Bd) . . . . **BDY**
Amouretti (R. F.) . . . . . . **CZ** 3
Anc. Combattants d'Afrique du Nord (Av.) . . . . . **AYZ** 4
Beauséjour (Av.) . . . . . **DYZ**
Beau-Soleil (Bd) . . . . **X** 10
Blanc (R. Louis) . . . . . . **AYZ**
Broussailles (Av. des) . . **V** 16
Buttura (R.) . . . . **BZ** 17
Canada (R. du) . . . . **DZ**
Carnot (Bd) . . . . **X**
Carnot (Square) . . . . **V** 20
Castre (Pl. de la) . . . . . . **AZ** 21
Clemenceau (R. G.) . . . . **AZ**
Coteaux (Av. des) . . . . . **V**
Croix-des-Gardes (Bd) . . **VX** 29
Delaup (Bd) . . . . **AY** 30
Dr-Pierre Gazagnaire (R.) . **AZ** 32
Dr-R. Picaud (Av.) . . . . . **X**
Dollfus (R. Jean) . . . . . . **AZ** 33
Faure (R. Félix) . . . . **ABZ**
Favorite (Av. de la) . . . . **X** 38
Ferrage (Bd de la) . . . . **ABY** 40
Fiesole (Av.) . . . . **X** 43
Gallieni (R. du Mar.) . . . **BY** 48
Gaulle (Pl. Gén.-de) . . . . **BZ** 51
Gazagnaire (Bd Eugène) . **X**
Grasse (Av. de) . . . . **VX** 53
Guynemer (Bd) . . . . **AY**
Haddad-Simon (R. Jean) . **CY** 54
Hespérides (Av. des) . . . **X** 55
Hibert (Bd Jean) . . . . . . **AZ**
Hibert (R.) . . . . **AZ**
Isola-Bella (Av. d') . . . . . **X**
Jaurès (R. Jean) . . . . . **BCY**
Juin (Av. Mar.) . . . . **DZ**
Koenig (Av. Gén.) . . . . . **DY**
Lacour (Bd Alexandre) . . **X** 62
Latour-Maubourg (R.) . . **DZ**
Lattre-de-T. (Av. de) . . . **AY** 63
Laubeuf (Quai Max) . . . **AZ**
Leader (Bd) . . . . **VX** 64
Lérins (Av. de) . . . . **X** 65
Lorraine (Bd. de) . . . . . **CDY**
Macé (R.) . . . . **CZ** 66
Madrid (Av. de) . . . . **DZ**
Meynadier (R.) . . . . **ABY**
Midi (BD. du) . . . . **X**
Mimont (R. de) . . . . **BY**
Mont-Chevalier (R. du) . **AZ** 72
Montfleury (Bd) . . . . . . **CDY** 74
Monti (R. Marius) . . . . . **AY** 75
Moulin (Bd du) . . . . **AY** 76
Noailles (Av. J.-de) . . . . . **X**
Observatoire (Bd de l') . . **X** 84
Oxford (Bd d') . . . . **V** 87
Pantiero (la) . . . . **ABZ**
Paradis-Terrestre (Corniches du) . . . . . **V** 88
Pasteur (R.) . . . . **DZ**
Pastour (R. Louis) . . . . . **AY** 90
Perier (Bd du) . . . . **V** 92
Perrissol (R. Louis) . . . . **AZ** 93
Petit-Juas (Av. du) . . . . **VX**
Pins (Bd des) . . . . **X** 95
Pompidou (Espl. G.) . . . **BZ**
Prince-de-Galles (Av. du) **X** 96
République (Bd de la) . . **X**
Riou (Bd du) . . . . **VX**
Roi-Albert (Av.) . . . . **X**
Rouguière (R.) . . . . **BYZ** 100
St-Nicolas (Av.) . . . . . . **BY** 105
St-Pierre (Quai) . . . . . . **AZ**
Sardou (R. Léandre) . . . **X** 108
Serbes (R. des) . . . . . . **BZ** 110
Source (Bd de la) . . . . . **X** 112
Stanislas (Pl.) . . . . **AY**
Strasbourg (Bd de) . . . **CDY**
Teisseire (R.) . . . . **CY** 114
Tuby (Bd Victor) . . . . . **AYZ** 115
Vallauris (Av. de) . . . . . **VX** 116
Vallombrosa (Bd) . . . . . **AY** 118
Vautrin (Bd Gén.) . . . . . **DZ**
Vidal (R. du Cdt) . . . . . **CY** 120
Wemyss (Av. Amiral Wester) . **X** 122

LE CANNET

Aubarède (Ch. de l') . . **V** 8
Bellevue (Pl.) . . . . **V** 13
Bréguières (Ch. de) . . . **V** 14
Cannes (R. des) . . . . . . **V** 19
Carnot (. de) . . . . **V**
Cheval (Av. Maurice) . . **V** 23
Collines (Ch. des) . . . . **V**
Doumer (Bd Paul) . . . . **V**
Écoles (Av. des) . . . . . . **V** 34
Four-à-Chaux (Bd du) . **V** 45
Gambetta (Bd) . . . . **V** 50
Gaulle (Av. Gén.-de) . . . **V**
Jeanpierre (Av. Maurice) . **V** 58
Mermoz (Av. Jean) . . . **V** 67
Monod (Bd Jacques . . . **V** 68
Mont-Joli (Av. du) . . . . **V** 73
N.-D.-des-Anges (Av.) . . **V** 79
Olivet (Ch. de l') . . . . . **V** 85
Olivetum (Bd) . . . . **V** 86
Paris (R. de) . . . . **V** 89
Pinède (Av. de la) . . . . . **V** 94
Pompidou (Av. de la) . . **V**
République (Bd de la) . **V**
Roosevelt (Av. Franklin) . **V**
St-Sauveur (R.) . . . . . . **V** 106
Victor-Hugo (R.) . . . . . . **V** 119
Victoria (Av.) . . . . **V**

VALLAURIS

Cannes (Av. de) . . . . . . **V** 18
Clemenceau (Av. G.) . . **V** 25
Fournas (Av. de) . . . . . **V** 46
Golfe (Av. du) . . . . **V** 52
Isnard (Pl. Paul) . . . . . . **V** 56
Rouvier (Bd Maurice) . . **V** 102
Tapis-Vert (Av. du) . . . . **V** 113

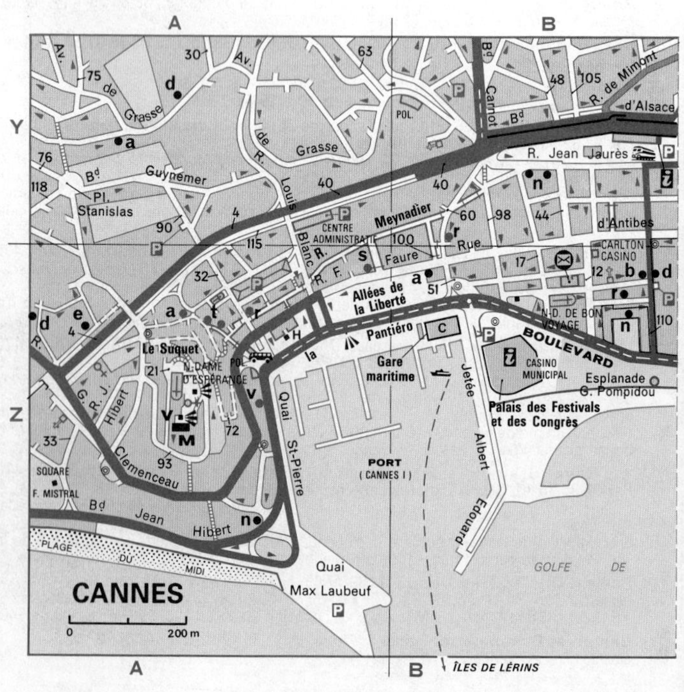

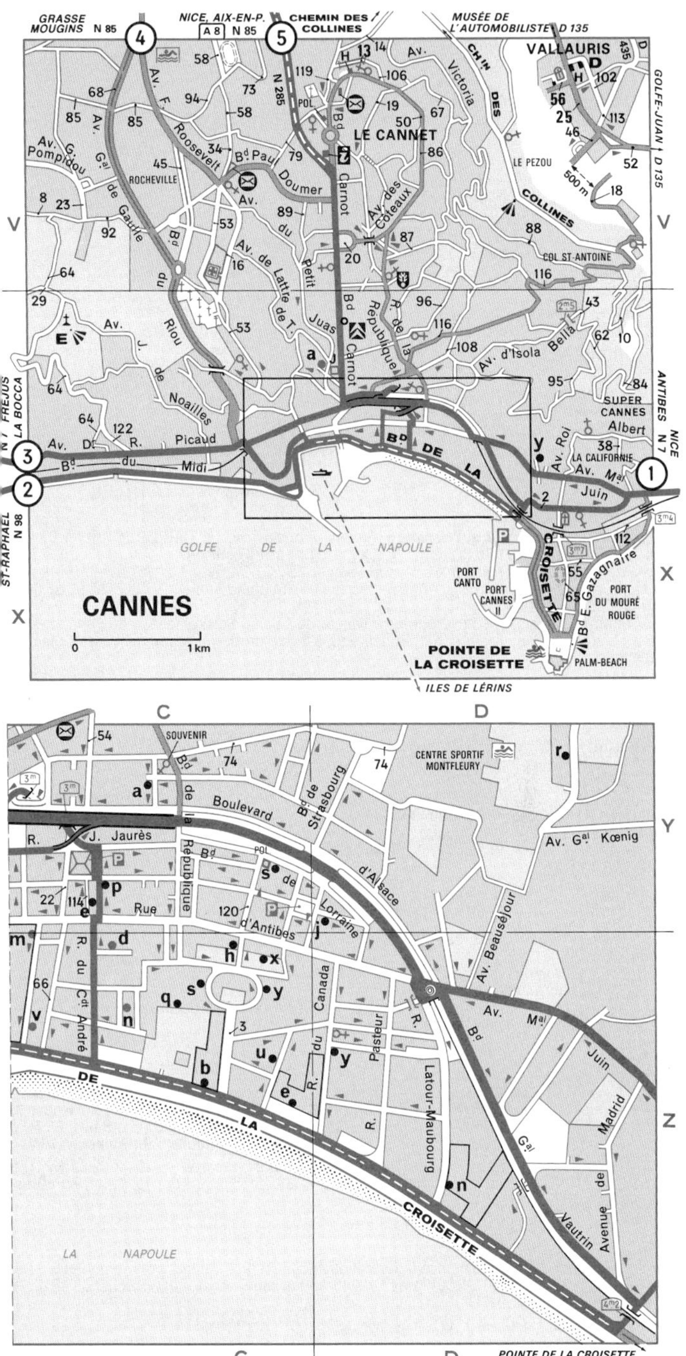
GRASSE MOUGINS N 85
NICE, AIX-EN-P. A 8 N 85
CHEMIN DES COLLINES
MUSÉE DE L'AUTOMOBILISTE D 135
VALLAURIS
GOLFE-JUAN D 135
LE CANNET
ROCHEVILLE
LE PEZOU
COLLINES
COL ST-ANTOINE
SUPER CANNES
LA CALIFORNIE
ANTIBES NICE N 7
N 7 FRÉJUS LA BOCCA
ST-RAPHAËL N 98
GOLFE DE LA NAPOULE
PORT CANTO
PORT CANNES II
PORT DU MOURÉ ROUGE
CROISETTE
POINTE DE LA CROISETTE
PALM-BEACH
ILES DE LÉRINS
CANNES
0 1 km
Bd DE LA CROISETTE
Bd du Midi
Av. Dr R. Picaud
Av. du Roi Albert
Av. Mal Juin
Bd E. Gazagnaire
Av. d'Isola Bella
Bd Carnot
R. de la République
Av. des Coteaux
Bd Paul Doumer
Av. F. Roosevelt
Av. Gal de Gaulle
Av. G. Pompidou
Bd du Riou
Av. de Lattre de T.
Av. du Petit Juas
Av. J. de Noailles
Av. Victoria
CH. DES COLLINES
SOUVENIR
CENTRE SPORTIF MONTFLEURY
Boulevard d'Alsace
Bd de Strasbourg
Bd de la République
R. J. Jaurès
Bd de Lorraine
Rue d'Antibes
R. du Cdt André
R. du Canada
R. Pasteur
R. Latour-Maubourg
Av. Gal Kœnig
Av. Beauséjour
Av. Mal Juin
Bd Gal Vautrin
Avenue de Madrid
DE LA CROISETTE
LA NAPOULE
POINTE DE LA CROISETTE

XX **La Mirabelle,** 24 r. St Antoine ✆ 93 38 72 75 – ▤. AE ⓓ GB JCB AZ **a**
closed 15 November-15 December, 15 February-1 March and Tuesday – **M** (dinner only) 175/255.

XX **Le Mesclun,** 16 r. St Antoine ✆ 93 99 45 19, Fax 93 47 68 29 – ▤. AE GB JCB AZ **t**
closed 15 November-15 December and Wednesday out of season – **M** (dinner only) 165/235.

XX **Relais des Semailles,** 9 r. St Antoine ✆ 93 39 22 32, Fax 93 94 45 00 – ▤. AE GB
closed November, February and Sunday out of season – **M** (dinner only) 135/280. AZ **t**

XX **Maître-Pierre,** 6 r. Mar. Joffre ✆ 93 99 36 30 – ▤. AE GB BY **r**
closed July, Wednesday dinner and Sunday except Bank Holidays – **M** (dinner only in season) 95/145.

XX **St-Benoit,** 9 r. Bateguier ✆ 93 39 04 17 – AE GB CZ **n**
closed 25 November-15 December and Monday except July-August – **M** (dinner only in July-August) 95/200.

XX **La Cigale,** 1 r. Florian ✆ 93 39 65 79 – ▤. AE ⓓ GB CZ **d**
closed 15 to 30 November, Sunday dinner and Monday – **M** 105/148 ♁.

X **Côté Jardin,** 12 av. St Louis ✆ 93 38 60 28, 斎 – ▤. AE GB X **a**
closed February-mid-March, Monday (except dinner May-September) and Sunday – **M** 155.

X **Chez Astoux,** 43 r. F. Faure ✆ 93 39 06 22, Fax 93 99 45 47, 斎 – AE ⓓ GB AZ **s**
M Seafood 92/148.

X **Aux Bons Enfants,** 80 r. Meynadier – ⌘ AZ **r**
closed August, 20 December-5 January, Saturday dinner out of season and Sunday – **M** 88.

Juan-les-Pins 06160 Alpes-Mar. 84 ⑨, 115 ㉟ ㊴ – alt. 2.

Cannes 8,5.

✿✿ **Juana and rest. La Terrasse** ⛱, la Pinède, av. G. Gallice ✆ 93 61 08 70, Telex 470778, Fax 93 61 76 60, 斎, ⛱, ♠ – |‡| ▤ rm TV ☎ P
6 April-late October – **M** *(closed Wednesday except 13 to 24 May, 21 to 26 June, July-August and October)* (dinner only in July-August) 250 (lunch)/590 and a la carte 490/780 – ☕ 90 – **45 rm** 900/2100, 5 suites
Spec. Cannelloni de supions et palourdes à l'encre de seiche. Selle d'agneau de Pauillac cuite en terre d'argile. Millefeuille aux fraises des bois à la crème de mascarpone. Wines Côtes de Provence.

Mougins 06250 Alpes-Mar. 84 ⑨, 115 ㉔ ㊳ – pop. 13 014 alt. 260.

Cannes 7.

XXXX ✿✿ **Moulin de Mougins** (Vergé) with rm, at Notre-Dame-de-Vie SE : 2,5 km by D 3 ✆ 93 75 78 24, Telex 970732, Fax 93 90 18 55, 斎, « Converted 16C oil mill », 🐕 – ▤ TV ☎ P. AE ⓓ GB
closed 31 January-2 April – **M** *(closed Monday (except dinner 15 July-31 August) and Thursday lunch)* 550/700 and a la carte 600/800 – ☕ 75 – **5 rm** 800/1300
Spec. Poupeton de fleur de courgette aux truffes du Vaucluse. Fricassée des viviers d'Audierne en crème de Sauternes. Wines Cassis, Côtes de Provence.

La Napoule 06210 Alpes-Mar. 84 ⑧, 115 ㉞ – alt. 18.

Cannes 9,5.

XXXX ✿✿ **L'Oasis,** ✆ 93 49 95 52, Fax 93 49 64 13, 斎, « Shaded and flowered patio » – ▤. AE ⓓ GB JCB
closed lunch 15 July-7 September (except Sunday), Sunday dinner and Monday out of season – **M** 450/600 and a la carte 430/560
Spec. Foie gras chaud en verdure de blettes. Turbot en meunière de betteraves aux câpres. Langouste aux herbes thaïes. Wines Côtes de Provence.

LILLE P 59000 Nord 51 ⑯ – pop. 172 142 Greater Lille 1 081 479 alt. 21.

See : Old Lille★ (Vieux Lille) EFY : Old Stock Exchange★★ (Vieille Bourse) FY, Comtesse Hospice★ (keel-shaped timber ceiling★★) FY **B**, rue de la Monnaie★ FY 142, Gilles de la Boé's House★ FY **E** – St-Maurice Church★ FY **K** – Citadel★ BUV – Paris Gate★ FZ – View★ from Belfry FZ **H** – Fine Arts Museum★★ (Musée des Beaux Arts) FZ **M¹** – General de Gaulle's Birthplace CU **W**.

⛳9 of Flandres (private) ✆ 20 72 20 74 by ② : 4,5 km ; ⛳18 of Sart (private) ✆ 20 72 02 51 by ② : 7 km ; ⛳18 of Brigode at Villeneuve d'Ascq ✆ 20 91 17 86 by ③ : 9 km ; ⛳18 ⛳18 of Bondues ✆ 20 23 20 62 by ① : 9,5 km.

✈ of Lille-Lesquin : ✆ 20 49 68 68 by ④ : 8 km.

🚗 ✆ 20 74 50 50.

ℹ Office de Tourisme and Accueil de France (Information and hotel reservations, not more than 5 days in advance) Palais Rihour ✆ 20 30 81 00, Telex 110213 and at the Railway station ✆ 20 06 40 65 – A.C. 8 r. Quennette ✆ 20 55 29 44.

Paris 221 ④ – Brussels 116 ② – Ghent 71 ② – Luxembourg 312 ④ – Strasbourg 525 ④.

Plans on following pages

Holiday Inn M, quai du Wault ☎ 20 30 62 62, Fax 20 42 94 25, « Former 17C convent » – rm TV ☎ – 150. AE GB JCB EY **d**
M 160 b.i./245 – 70 – **75 rm** 610/730, 10 suites.

Novotel Lille Centre M, 116 r. Hôpital Militaire ✉ 59800 ☎ 20 30 65 26, Telex 160859, Fax 20 30 04 04 – rm TV ☎ – 30. AE GB JCB EY **s**
M a la carte approx. 150 – 55 – **102 rm** 560/600.

Carlton, 3 r. Paris ✉ 59800 ☎ 20 13 33 13, Telex 110400, Fax 20 51 48 17 – rm rm TV ☎ – 30 - 100. AE GB JCB. rest FY **n**
Bistrot Opéra M a la carte 140/210 – **Brasserie Jean** – ☎ 20 55 75 72 **M** a la carte 150/220 – 65 – **57 rm** 690/790, 3 suites.

Gd H. Bellevue without rest, 5 r. J. Roisin ✉ 59800 ☎ 20 57 45 64, Telex 120790, Fax 20 40 07 93 – rm TV ☎ – 100. AE GB FY **z**
50 – **61 rm** 375/760.

Mercure Royal Lille Centre without rest, 2 bd Carnot ✉ 59800 ☎ 20 51 05 11, Telex 820575, Fax 20 74 01 65 – rm TV ☎ – 30. AE GB JCB FY **h**
57 – **102 rm** 580.

Treille M without rest, 7 pl. L. de Bettignies ✉ 59800 ☎ 20 55 45 46, Telex 136761, Fax 20 51 51 69 – TV ☎ – 50. AE GB FY **d**
41 – **40 rm** 330/360.

Paix without rest, 46 bis r. Paris ✉ 59800 ☎ 20 54 63 93, Fax 20 63 98 97 – TV ☎. AE GB FY **r**
32 – **35 rm** 300/370.

Fimotel M, 75 bis r. Gambetta ☎ 20 42 90 90, Fax 20 57 14 24 – TV ☎ – 30 - 180. AE GB EZ **e**
M 105 – 45 – **98 rm** 370/390.

Ibis M, av. Ch. St-Venant ✉ 59800 ☎ 20 55 44 44, Telex 136950, Fax 20 31 06 25, – rm TV ☎ – 25 - 80. AE GB FY **a**
M 83 – 33 – **151 rm** 340/360.

Cottage H. M, 1 r. C. Colomb ✉ 59800 ☎ 20 55 21 55, Fax 20 55 87 49 – TV ☎ – 60 DV **e**
61 rm.

Nord H., 46 r. Fg d'Arras ☎ 20 53 53 40, Telex 136589, Fax 20 53 20 95 – TV ☎ – 40. AE GB
M *(closed Sunday)* 79/130 – 30 – **80 rm** 200/250.

Ibis M without rest, 21 r. Lepelletier ✉ 59800 ☎ 20 06 21 95, Telex 136846, Fax 20 74 91 30 – rm TV ☎. AE GB FY **s**
32 – **60 rm** 340/360.

XXXX ✿✿ **Le Flambard** (Bardot), 79 r. Angleterre ✉ 59800 ☎ 20 51 00 06, Fax 20 55 09 17, « 17C houses in the old part of Lille » – AE GB EY **r**
closed Sunday dinner and Monday – **M** 280/580 and a la carte 330/550
Spec. Œuf mollet à la crème de poireaux et jus de truffes. Langoustines entourées de gnocchi au cumin. Rognon de veau aux échalotes grillées.

XXX ✿ **A L'Huîtrière,** 3 r. Chats Bossus ✉ 59800 ☎ 20 55 43 41, Fax 20 55 23 10, « Decorated with the original fish shop ceramics » – AE GB FY **g**
closed 22 July-1 September, dinner Sunday and Bank Holidays – **M** 600 and a la carte 280/450
Spec. Produits de la mer. Galette de pommes de terre à l'anguille fumée et aux poireaux. Turbotin rôti au thym.

XXX ✿ **Le Paris,** 52 bis r. Esquermoise ✉ 59800 ☎ 20 55 29 41 – AE GB EY **f**
closed early August-early September and Sunday (except Bank Holidays) – **M** 196/300 and a la carte 250/400
Spec. Noix de Saint-Jacques sauce Véronique (October-March). Etuvée de queues de langoustines en salade. Gibier (season).

XXX **La Laiterie,** 138 av. Hippodrome at Lambersart NW : 2 km ✉ 59130 Lambersart ☎ 20 92 79 73, Fax 20 22 16 19, – . AE GB AV **s**
closed Monday dinner and Sunday – **M** 230 b.i./360.

XXX **Le Varbet,** 2 r. Pas ✉ 59800 ☎ 20 54 81 40 – AE GB EFY **t**
closed 13 July-17 August, 23 December-4 January, Sunday, Monday and Bank Holidays – **M** 150/320.

XXX **Le Club,** 16 r. Pas ✉ 59800 ☎ 20 57 01 10, Fax 20 57 39 69 – AE GB EY **n**
closed August, Easter Holidays, Monday dinner, Saturday lunch and Sunday – **M** 135/200.

XX **Le Queen, l'Écume des Mers,** 10 r. Pas ✉ 59800 ☎ 20 54 95 40 – . AE GB EY **n**
closed Sunday dinner – **M** Seafood - a la carte 150/210 .

XX **Le Bistrot Tourangeau,** 61 bd Louis XIV ✉ 59800 ☎ 20 52 74 64, Fax 20 85 06 39 – AE GB DV **t**
closed 1 to 15 August and Sunday – **M** (booking essential) 95/195.

XX **Le Cardinal,** 84 façade Esplanade ✉ 59800 ☎ 20 06 58 58 – GB EY **x**
closed 9 to 15 August and Sunday – **M** 230.

XX **La Fringale,** 141 r. Solférino ☎ 20 42 02 80 – AE GB EZ **f**
closed 15 July-15 August, 14 to 21 February, Saturday lunch and Sunday – **M** (booking essential) 160/320.

LILLE

Alsace (Bd) .... CDX
Arras (R. d') CX
Artois (R. d') CX
Ballon (R. du) .... DU
Bapaume (R. de) .... CX 12
Bassée (R. de la) ...... AVX
Bateliers (R. des) ...... CU 13
Becquart (Av.) .... ABU
Beethoven (Av.) .... AX 14
Belfort (Bd de) .... DX
Bernos (R.) .... DV 18
Béthune
(R. du Fg de) .... AX 19
Bigo-Danel (Bd) .... BV 21
Blanqui (R.) .... DV 22
Boilly (R.) .... DV 25
Bois (Av. du) .... ABU
Bonte (R. Auguste) ..... AU
Buisson (R. du) .... DU
Cambrai (R. de) ...... CDX
Carnot (Bd) CV
Carrel (R. Armand) ..... DX 38
Churchill (Av. W.) ...... CU
Colbert (R.) .... BV
Colpin (R. du Lt) ...... BUV 45
Cordonnier (R. Denis) ... DX 51
Coubertin (Bd P. de) .. CDU
Courmont (R.) .... CX 53
Cuvier (Av.) .... BV 57
Debierre (R. Ch.) .... DV 58
Défenseurs de Lille
(Bd) .... CDX 60
Delescaux (Av. H.) ..... AU
Destrée (Av. Julien) .... DV 65
Dr-Calmette (Bd) .... DV 67
Dorez (Pl. B.) .... BX 68
Douai (R. de) .... CDX
Dubuisson
(Bd Emile) .... DV 69
Dunkerque (Av. de) .... AV
Esquermes (R. d') ...... BX
Fébvrier (Pl. J.) .... CX 78
Fives (Bd des) .... DV
Gambetta (R. Léon) .... BV
Gand (R. de) .... CU
Gaulle (R. du Gén.-de) .. CU 85
Guérin (R. Camille) ..... DV 90
Guesde (R. Jules) ...... BX
Halle (R. de la) .... CU 93
Hippodrome (Av. de l'). AUV
Isly (R. d') .... ABX

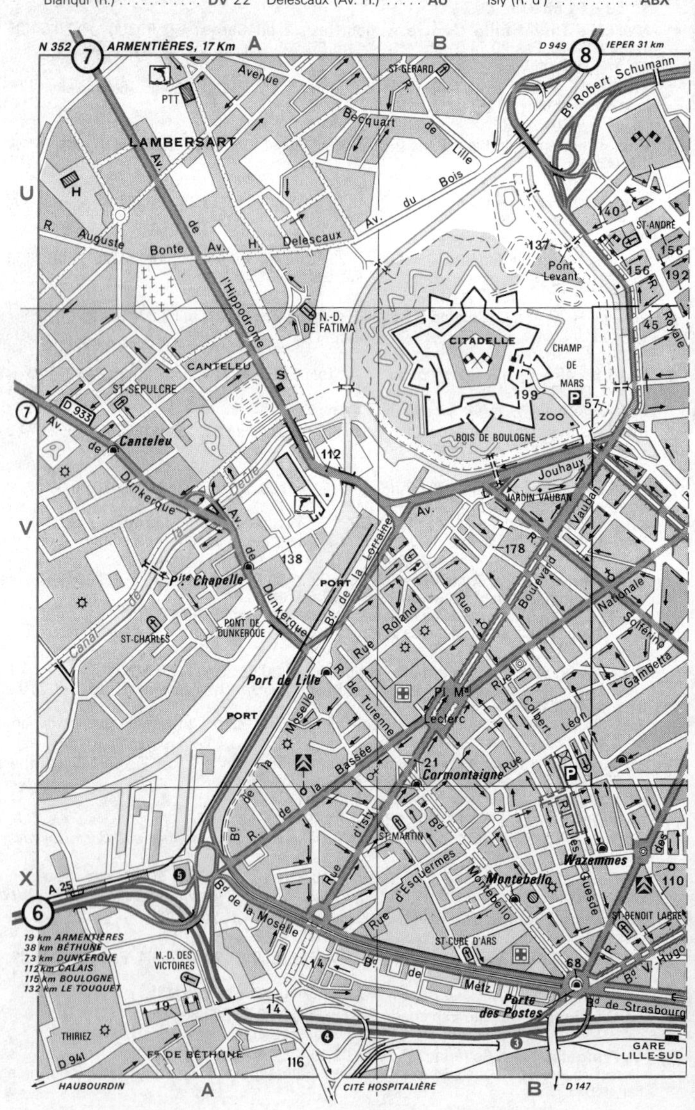

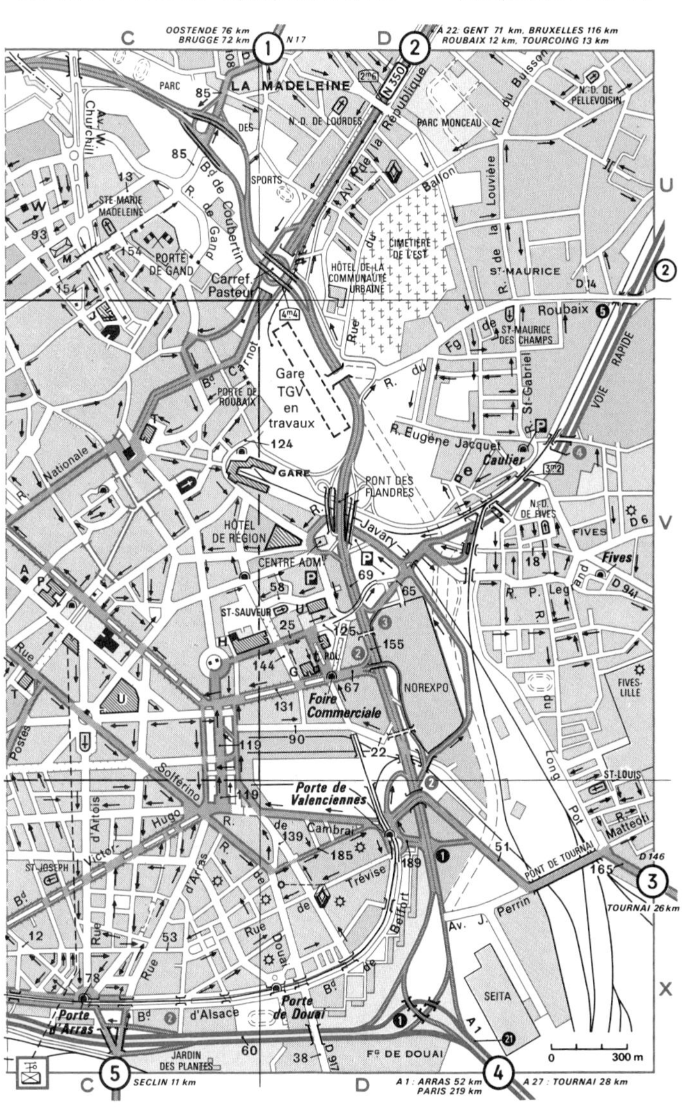

OOSTENDE 76 km
BRUGGE 72 km
N 17
A 22: GENT 71 km, BRUXELLES 116 km
ROUBAIX 12 km, TOURCOING 13 km
LA MADELEINE
PARC
N.-D. DE LOURDES
PARC MONCEAU
N.-D. DE PELLEVOISIN
Av. de la République
R. du Buisson
Bd de Coubertin
R. de Gand
SPORTS
Av. W. Churchill
STE-MARIE MADELEINE
PORTE DE GAND
Carref. Pasteur
CIMETIÈRE DE L'EST
HÔTEL DE LA COMMUNAUTÉ URBAINE
R. du Ballon
R. de la Louvière
ST-MAURICE
Roubaix
ST-MAURICE DES CHAMPS
Fg de
VOIE RAPIDE
R. St-Gabriel
Bd Carnot
PORTE DE ROUBAIX
Gare TGV en travaux
R. du
R. Eugène Jacquet
Caulier
R. Nationale
GARE
PONT DES FLANDRES
N.-D. DE FIVES
FIVES
Fives
R. Javary
HÔTEL DE RÉGION
CENTRE ADM.
R. P. Legrand
ST-SAUVEUR
NOREXPO
Foire Commerciale
FIVES-LILLE
Rue des Postes
Solférino
R. du Long Pot
ST-LOUIS
Porte de Valenciennes
R. de Cambrai
R. Matteoti
Bd Victor Hugo
R. d'Artois
R. d'Arras
R. de Trévise
PONT DE TOURNAI
TOURNAI 26 km
ST-JOSEPH
R. de Douai
Bd de Belfort
Av. J. Perrin
SEITA
Porte d'Arras
Bd d'Alsace
Porte de Douai
JARDIN DES PLANTES
Fg DE DOUAI
D 917
A 1
SECLIN 11 km
A 1 : ARRAS 52 km
PARIS 219 km
A 27 : TOURNAI 28 km
300 m

LILLE

Béthune (R. de) .... FYZ
Esquermoise (R.) .... EFY
Faidherbe (R.) ...... FY 74
Gambetta (R. Léon) . EZ
Gaulle (Pl. Gén.-de)
(Grand Place) ..... FY 84
Grande Chaussée
(R. de la) .... FY 88
Monnaie (R. de la) .. FY 142
Nationale (R.) ..... EYZ
Neuve (R.) .... FY 148

Amiens (R. d') ..... FZ 6
Anatole-France (R.) .. FY 7
Angleterre (R. d') ... EY
Arts (R. des) .... FY
Baignerie (R. de la) . EY 10
Barre (R. de la) ..... EY
Basse (R.) .... EFY
Bettignies (Pl. L. de) . FY 20
Bourse (R. de la) .... FY 28
Brûle-Maison (R.) ... EFZ
Buisses (Pl. des) .... FY 33
Carnot (Bd) .... FY
Chats-Bossus (R. des) FY 41
Colbrant (R.) .... EZ
Collégiale (R. de la) . EY 43
Comédie (R. de la) .. FY 47
Comtesse (R.) ...... FY 49
Courtrai (R. de) ..... FY
Cuvier (Av.) .... EY
Danel (R. L.) .... EY
Delory (R. G.) ...... FZ
Esplanade
(Façade de l') .... EY
Flandre (R. de) ..... EZ
Foch (Av.) .... EY
Fosses (R. des) ..... FY 81
Gosselet (R.) .... FZ
Guérin (R. Camille) .. FZ 90
Halloterie (R. de la) .. EY 95
Hôpital-Militaire (R.) . EY 98
Inkermann (R.) ...... EZ
Jacquart (Pl.) .... FZ 103
Jacquemars-
Giélée (R.) ...... EYZ
Jardins (R. des) ..... FY 104
Jean-Bart (R.) ...... FZ
Jeanne-d'Arc (Pl.) ... FZ 107
Jeanne-d'Arc (R.) .... FZ
Jean-sans-Peur (R.) .. EZ
Lebas (Bd J.-B.) ..... FZ 119
Leblanc (R. Nicolas) . EZ 121
Liberté (Bd de la) .. EYZ
Lion d'Or (Pl. du) .... FY 130
Louis XIV (Bd) ...... FZ 131
Maillotte (R.) .... FZ 132
Manneliers (R. des) .. FY 134
Marronniers (Av. des) EY
Masséna (R.) .... EZ
Mendès-France (Pl.) . EY 137
Molinel (R. du) ..... FYZ
Paris (R. de) .... FYZ
Philippe-le-Bon (Pl.) ... EZ 153
Postes (R. des) ...... EZ
Président-Kennedy
(Av. du) .... FZ
Pyramides (R. des) ... EZ 157
Réduit (R. du) .... FZ 158
République
(Pl. de la) .... EFZ 159
Richebé (Pl.) .... EFZ 160
Rihour (Pl.) .... FY 161
Roisin (R. Jean) ..... EFY 162
Roubaix (R. de) ..... FY
Royale (R.) .... EY
St-Génois (R.) .... FY 168
St-Jacques (R.) ...... FY
St-Sauveur (R.) ...... FZ 170
St-Venant (Av. Ch.) .. FYZ 172
Ste-Catherine (R.) .... EY 173
Sec-Arembault
(R. du) .... FY 175
Solférino (R.) .... EZ
Tanneurs (R. des) ... FYZ 176
Tenremonde (R.) .... EY
Théâtre (Pl. du) ..... FY 177
Thiers (R.) .... EY
Tournai (R. de) ...... FY 180
Trois-Mollettes (R.) ... EY 182
Urbanistes (R. des) ... FY
Valmy (R. de) .... FZ
Vauban (Bd) .... EY 188

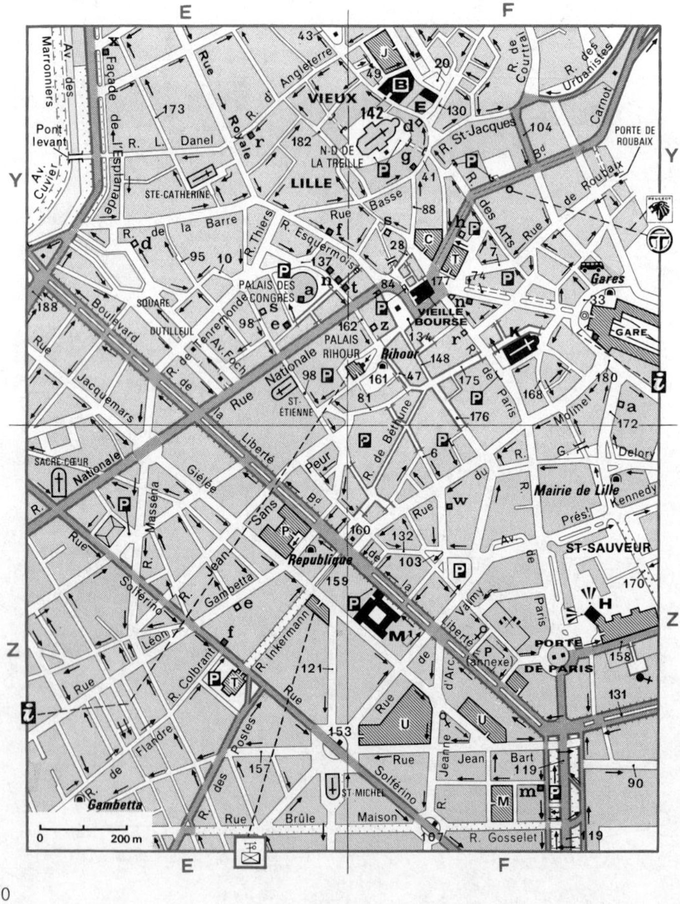

XX **Charlot II,** 26 bd J.-B. Lebas ℘ 20 52 53 38 – AE ⓓ GB JCB — FZ **m**
closed Saturday lunch and Sunday – **M** Seafood - a la carte 260/340.

XX **Lutterbach,** 10 r. Faidherbe ✉ 59800 ℘ 20 55 13 74 – AE ⓓ GB — FY **n**
closed 25 July-8 August – **M** 105/130 ♁.

XX **Le Féguide** (Buffet Gare), pl. Gare ✉ 59800 ℘ 20 06 15 50, Fax 20 06 10 40 – AE ⓓ GB
M *(closed August and Saturday)* 122/198 ♁ - **Le P'tit Féguide M** 75/80 ♁, enf. 45. — FY

XX **La Petite Taverne,** 9 r. Plat ✉ 59800 ℘ 20 54 79 36 – AE GB — FZ **w**
closed August, Tuesday dinner and Sunday – **M** 99/230 ♁.

XX **La Coquille,** 60 r. St-Étienne ✉ 59800 ℘ 20 54 29 82, 17C house – GB — EY **e**
closed 31 July-22 August, 26 February-6 March, Saturday lunch and Sunday – **M** 130/235.

X **Le Hochepot,** 6 r. Nouveau Siècle ℘ 20 54 17 59, Fax 20 42 92 43 – GB — EY **a**
closed Saturday lunch and Sunday – **M** 130/180.

at Marcq-en-Baroeul by ② and N 350 : 5 km – pop. 36 601 – ✉ 59700 :

Sofitel M, av. Marne ℘ 20 72 17 30, Telex 132785, Fax 20 89 92 34 – rm rm TV ☎ ♿ P – 200. AE ⓓ GB JCB
L'Europe **M** 120/170 – 65 – **125 rm** 600.

XXX **Septentrion,** parc du château Vert Bois N : 2 km ℘ 20 46 26 98, Fax 20 46 38 33, « In a park with lake » – P. AE ⓓ GB
closed 1 to 21 August, February Holidays, Sunday dinner and Monday – **M** 180/290.

at Villeneuve-d'Ascq by ②, N 356 and Highway of Roubaix (exit Recueil-La Cousinerie) : 7 km – pop. 65 320 – ✉ 59650 :

Relais d'Hermès M, 13 av. Créativité, Parc des Moulins ℘ 20 47 46 46, Telex 130060, Fax 20 91 36 55, – rm TV ☎ ♿ P – 50 - 180. AE ⓓ GB JCB
M 80/158 – 45 – **84 rm** 310/380.

Campanile, av. Canteleu, La Cousinerie ℘ 20 91 83 10, Telex 133335, Fax 20 67 21 18 – TV ☎ ♿ P. AE GB
M 80 b.i./102 b.i. – 29 – **46 rm** 268.

XX **Vieille Forge,** 160 r. Lannoy at Le Recueil ℘ 20 05 50 75, Fax 20 91 28 24, – P. AE ⓓ GB JCB
closed Sunday dinner June-August and dinner out of season (except Saturday) – **M** 110 b.i./250 ♁.

at Lille-Lesquin Airport by ④ and A 1 : 8 km – ✉ 59810 Lesquin :

Mercure Lille Aéroport M, ℘ 20 87 46 46, Telex 132051, Fax 20 87 46 47, – rm TV ☎ ♿ P – 25 - 1 000. AE ⓓ GB JCB
Grill La Flamme M 95 b.i./170 b.i. - **Snack Angus M** 72/90 ♁ – 56 – **213 rm** 540/590.

Novotel Lille Aéroport M, ℘ 20 62 53 53, Telex 820519, Fax 20 97 36 12, – rm rest TV ☎ P – 25 - 200. AE ⓓ GB JCB
M a la carte approx. 170 – 55 – **92 rm** 520/550.

Agena without rest, ✉ 59155 Faches-Thumesnil ℘ 20 60 13 14, Fax 20 97 31 79 – TV ☎ ♿ P. AE GB
46 – **40 rm** 340/370.

Climat de France, ✉ 59155 Faches-Thumesnil ℘ 20 97 00 24, Fax 20 97 00 67 – TV ☎ ♿ P. AE GB
M 60/110 ♁ – 30 – **42 rm** 280/320.

at Loos SW : 4 km by D 941 – pop. 20 657 – ✉ 59120 :

XX ✿ **L'Enfant Terrible** (Desplanques), 25 r. Mar. Foch ℘ 20 07 22 11, – GB
closed Sunday dinner and Monday – **M** (booking essential) 100/400 and a la carte 220/360
Spec. Foie gras en terrine au vin de pêche. Pigeon à la vapeur d'ail. Millefeuille de crêpes à la chicorée.

at Englos by ⑥ and A 25 : 10 km (exit Lomme) – ✉ 59320 :

Novotel Lille Lomme M, ℘ 20 07 09 99, Telex 132120, Fax 20 44 74 58, – rm TV ☎ ♿ P – 25 - 300. AE ⓓ GB
M a la carte approx. 160 – 52 – **124 rm** 420/460.

Mercure Lille Lomme M, ℘ 20 92 30 15, Telex 820302, Fax 20 93 75 66, – rest TV ☎ P – 200. AE ⓓ GB
M 99 b.i./145 ♁ – 50 – **87 rm** 380/430.

Pleasant hotels and restaurants
are shown in the Guide by a red sign.
Please send us the names
of any where you have enjoyed your stay.
Your **Michelin Guide** will be even better.

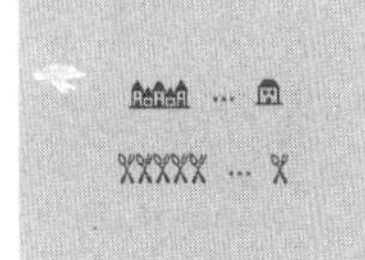

LYONS P 69000 Rhône 74 ⑪ ⑫ - pop. 415 487 Greater Lyons 1 200 000 alt. 169.

See : Site★★★ - Old Lyons★★ (Vieux Lyon) BX : Hôtel Bullioud loggia★★ B, St John's★ : Chancel★★ - rue St-Jean★ 92, Hôtel de Gadagne★ M1, Maison du Crible★ D, Lantern-tower★ of St Paul's Church BV - Basilica of Notre-Dame-de-Fourvière ※★★ from the observatory, ≤★ from the esplanade BX - Capitals★ in St-Martin-d'Ainay Basilica BYZ - Garillan Hill★ BX - Virgin and the Infant Jesus★ in St-Nizier Church CX - Tête d'Or Park★ HRS : rose garden★ (roseraie) R - Place des Terreaux : fountain★ CV - Chaponost arches★ FT - Underground passageways (Traboules) CUV - Punch and Judy show (Théâtre de Guignol) BX N - Museums : Textile★★★ CZ M2, Gallo-Roman Civilisation★★ (Claudian table★★★) BX M3, Fine Arts★★★ CV M4, Decorative Arts★★ CZ M5, Printing and Banking★★ CX M6, Guimet Natural History★★ DU M7, Puppet★ BX M1, Historical★ : lapidary BX M1, Pharmacy★ (Hospital Museum) CY M8.

Envir. : Rochetaillée : Museum Henri Malartre★★ : 12 km.

9 18 Villette d'Anthon ☏ 78 31 11 33 to the E : 21 km ; 18 Verger-Lyon at St-Symphorien-d'Ozon ☏ 78 02 24 20, to the S : 14 km ; 9 18 Lyon-Chassieu at Chassieu ☏ 78 90 84 77, E : 12 km by D 29 ; 18 Salvagny (private) at the Tour of Salvagny ☏ 78 48 83 60 ; jonction Lyon-Ouest : 8 km.

✈ of Lyon-Satolas ☏ 72 22 76 20 to the E : 27 km. - ☏ 78 92 50 50.

Office de Tourisme and Accueil de France (Information, exchange facilities, hotel reservations - not more than 5 days in advance), pl. Bellecour ☏ 78 42 25 75, Telex 330032 and Centre d'Echange de Perrache ☏ 78 42 22 07 - A.C. du Rhône 7 r. Grolée ☏ 78 42 51 01.

Paris 462 - Geneva 151 - Grenoble 105 - Marseilles 313 - St-Étienne 60 - Turin 300.

Plans on following pages

Hotels

Town Centre (Bellecour-Terreaux) :

Sofitel M, 20 quai Gailleton ✉ 69002 ☏ 72 41 20 20, Telex 330225, Fax 72 40 05 50, ≤ - rm TV ☎ - 250. AE GB — CY **k**
Les Trois Dômes (8th floor) ☏ 72 41 20 97 *(closed 1 to 29 August)* **M** 200/245 - **Sofi Shop** - (ground floor) ☏ 72 41 20 80 **M** carte 150 à 220 - 75 - **167 rm** 770/850, 29 suites.

Gd Hôtel Concorde M, 11 r. Grolée ✉ 69002 ☏ 72 40 45 45, Telex 330244, Fax 78 37 52 55 - rm TV ☎ - 80. AE GB JCB. — DX **e**
Le Fiorelle *(closed Sunday lunch)* **M** 79/160 - 60 - **140 rm** 595/890, 3 suites.

Royal, 20 pl. Bellecour ✉ 69002 ☏ 78 37 57 31, Telex 310785, Fax 78 37 01 36 - rm rm TV ☎. AE GB JCB — CY **d**
M grill 97/145 - 63 - **80 rm** 510/890.

Carlton without rest, 4 r. Jussieu ✉ 69002 ☏ 78 42 56 51, Telex 310787, Fax 78 42 10 71 - TV ☎. AE GB — DX **f**
50 - **83 rm** 440/700.

Gd H. des Beaux-Arts without rest, 75 r. Prés. E. Herriot ✉ 69002 ☏ 78 38 09 50, Telex 330442, Fax 78 42 19 19 - rm TV ☎ - 30. AE GB — CX **t**
52 - **79 rm** 350/600.

La Résidence without rest, 18 r. V. Hugo ✉ 69002 ☏ 78 42 63 28, Telex 900950, Fax 78 42 85 76 - TV ☎. AE GB — CY **s**
32 - **65 rm** 280/310.

Globe et Cécil without rest, 21 r. Gasparin ✉ 69002 ☏ 78 42 58 95, Telex 305184, Fax 72 41 99 06 - TV ☎. AE GB — CY **b**
45 - **65 rm** 360/500.

Bellecordière without rest, 18 r. Bellecordière ✉ 69002 ☏ 78 42 27 78, Fax 72 40 92 27 - TV ☎ &. AE GB - 34 - **45 rm** 260/320. — CY **a**

Perrache :

Pullman Perrache, 12 cours Verdun ✉ 69002 ☏ 78 37 58 11, Telex 330500, Fax 78 37 06 56, « New Art decor » - rm TV ☎ & P - 250. AE GB
Les Belles Saisons M 135/250 - 62 - **122 rm** 610/790. — BZ **a**

Charlemagne M, 23 cours Charlemagne ✉ 69002 ☏ 78 92 81 61, Telex 380401, Fax 78 42 94 84, - TV ☎ P - 120. AE GB
M *(closed Saturday and Sunday)* 85/180 - 50 - **116 rm** 395/545.

Vieux-Lyon :

Cour des Loges M, 6 r. Boeuf ✉ 69005 ☏ 78 42 75 75, Telex 330831, Fax 72 40 93 61, « Contemporary decor in houses of Old Lyons » - rm TV ☎ & - 45. AE GB JCB — BX **n**
Tapas des Loges M a la carte approx. 160 - 105 - **53 rm** 1200/1700, 10 suites.

✿ **Tour Rose** (Chavent) M, 22 r. Boeuf ✉ 69005 ☏ 78 37 25 90, Fax 78 42 26 02, « 17C house, tasteful decor depicting the story of silk », - TV ☎ - 25. AE GB JCB — BX **e**
M *(closed Sunday)* 395/625 and a la carte 450/600 - 95 - **6 rm** 1050/1650, 6 suites, 4 duplex
Spec. Salade de pommes de terre à la crème de caviar pressé. Saumon mi-cuit au fumoir, au naturel. Foie chaud de canard et filet de rouget barbet poêlés aux lentilles. Wines Brouilly, Viognier.

Phénix H. M without rest, 7 quai Bondy ✉ 69005 ☏ 78 28 24 24, Telex 310291, Fax 78 28 62 86 - TV ☎ & - 35. AE GB — BV **k**
36 rm 600/1220.

La Croix-Rousse (Bord de Saône) :

Lyon Métropole M, 85 quai J. Gillet ✉ 69004 ☎ 78 29 20 20, Telex 380198, Fax 78 39 99 20, ☂, ⛱, ✂ – |‡| ▤ TV ☎ ♿ 🚗 P – 🏃 350. AE ⓓ GB
Grill M 85/120 🍷 – **Les Eaux Vives** – ☎ **78 29 36 36** *(closed Christmas-1 January and Sunday in July-August)* **M** 145 b.i. – ☕ 50 – **119 rm** 455/550.

Les Brotteaux :

Roosevelt without rest, 25 r. Bossuet ✉ 69006 ☎ 78 52 35 67, Telex 300295, Fax 78 52 39 82 – |‡| ▤ TV ☎ 🚗 P – 🏃 40. AE ⓓ GB
☕ 50 – **87 rm** 420/570.

Olympique without rest, 62 r. Garibaldi ✉ 69006 ☎ 78 89 48 04, Fax 78 89 49 97 – |‡| TV ☎. AE GB
☕ 30 – **23 rm** 250/285.

La Part-Dieu :

Holiday Inn Crowne Plaza M, 29 r. Bonnel ✉ 69003 ☎ 72 61 90 90, Telex 330703, Fax 72 61 17 54, Fᵴ – |‡| ⇆ rm ▤ TV ☎ ♿ 🚗 – 🏃 200. AE ⓓ GB JCB
M 135/175 🍷 – ☕ 72 – **155 rm** 830/1350.

Pullman Part-Dieu M, 129 r. Servient (32nd floor) ✉ 69003 ☎ 78 63 55 00, Telex 380088, Fax 78 60 41 77, ≤ Lyons and Valley of the Rhône – |‡| ⇆ rm ▤ TV ☎ 🚗 – 🏃 300. AE ⓓ GB JCB
L'Arc-en-Ciel *(closed 15 July-24 August and Sunday dinner)* **M** 205/295 and a la carte 320/440 – **La Ripaille** – **grill** (ground floor) **M** a la carte 120/190 🍷 – ☕ 58 – **245 rm** 590/890
Spec. Andouillette beaujolaise à la moutarde. Foie de veau à la lyonnaise. Blanquette de veau à l'ancienne et riz pilaf. Wines Beaujolais, Côtes-du-Rhône.

Mercure M, 47 bd Vivier-Merle ✉ 69003 ☎ 72 34 18 12, Telex 306469, Fax 78 53 40 69 – |‡| ▤ TV ☎ ♿ P – 🏃 100. AE ⓓ GB JCB
M 95/160 🍷 – ☕ 50 – **124 rm** 550/610.

Créqui M without rest, 158 r. Créqui ✉ 69003 ☎ 78 60 20 47, Fax 78 62 21 12 – |‡| TV ☎. GB
☕ 43 – **28 rm** 330/360.

Ibis M, pl. Renaudel ✉ 69003 ☎ 78 95 42 11, Telex 310847, Fax 78 60 42 85, ☂ – |‡| ⇆ rm ▤ TV ☎ ♿ 🚗 – 🏃 30. AE GB
M 83 🍷 – ☕ 33 – **144 rm** 335/355.

La Guillotière :

Gd H. Helder et Institut without rest, 38 r. Marseille ✉ 69007 ☎ 78 61 61 61, Telex 306411, Fax 78 61 61 00 – |‡| TV ☎. AE ⓓ GB
98 rm ☕ 350/430.

Columbia without rest, 8 pl. A. Briand ✉ 69003 ☎ 78 60 54 65, Telex 305551, Fax 78 62 04 88 – |‡| TV ☎. AE ⓓ GB JCB
☕ 31 – **66 rm** 240/275.

Ibis Université M without rest, 51 r. Université ✉ 69007 ☎ 78 72 78 42, Telex 340455, Fax 78 69 24 36 – |‡| ⇆ rm ▤ TV ☎ 🚗. AE GB
☕ 34 – **53 rm** 295/345.

Gerland :

Mercure M, 70 av. Leclerc ✉ 69007 ☎ 72 71 11 11, Telex 305484, Fax 72 71 11 00, ☂, ⛱ – |‡| ▤ TV ☎ ♿ 🚗 – 🏃 450. AE ⓓ GB JCB
M 125/145 🍷 – ☕ 50 – **194 rm** 550/610.

Ibis M, 68 av. Leclerc ✉ 69007 ☎ 78 58 30 70, Telex 305483, Fax 78 72 28 61 – |‡| TV ☎ ♿ 🚗 – 🏃 30. AE GB
M 83 🍷 – ☕ 33 – **129 rm** 310/330.

Montchat-Monplaisir :

Mercure Lyon Lumière M, 71 cours A. Thomas ✉ 69003 ☎ 78 53 76 76, Telex 301928, Fax 72 36 97 65 – |‡| ⇆ rm ▤ TV ☎ ♿ 🚗 – 🏃 25 - 70. AE ⓓ GB
M 140 🍷 – ☕ 50 – **79 rm** 490/570.

Mercure-Altea Park, 4 r. Prof. Calmette ✉ 69008 ☎ 78 74 11 20, Telex 380230, Fax 78 01 43 38, ☂ – |‡| ⇆ rm TV ☎ 🚗 – 🏃 25. AE ⓓ GB JCB
le Patio *(closed Sunday lunch and Saturday)* **M** 110 🍷 – ☕ 50 – **72 rm** 430/500.

Lacassagne without rest, 245 av. Lacassagne ✉ 69003 ☎ 78 54 09 12, Fax 72 36 99 23 – |‡| ▤ TV ☎. AE ⓓ GB
☕ 29 – **40 rm** 190/280.

at Bron – pop. 39 683 – ✉ 69500 :

Novotel M, av. J. Monnet ☎ 78 26 97 48, Telex 340781, Fax 78 26 45 12, ☂, ⛱, 🌳 – |‡| ⇆ rm ▤ TV ☎ ♿ P – 🏃 25 - 800. AE ⓓ GB JCB
M a la carte approx. 160 🍷 – ☕ 48 – **189 rm** 430/445.

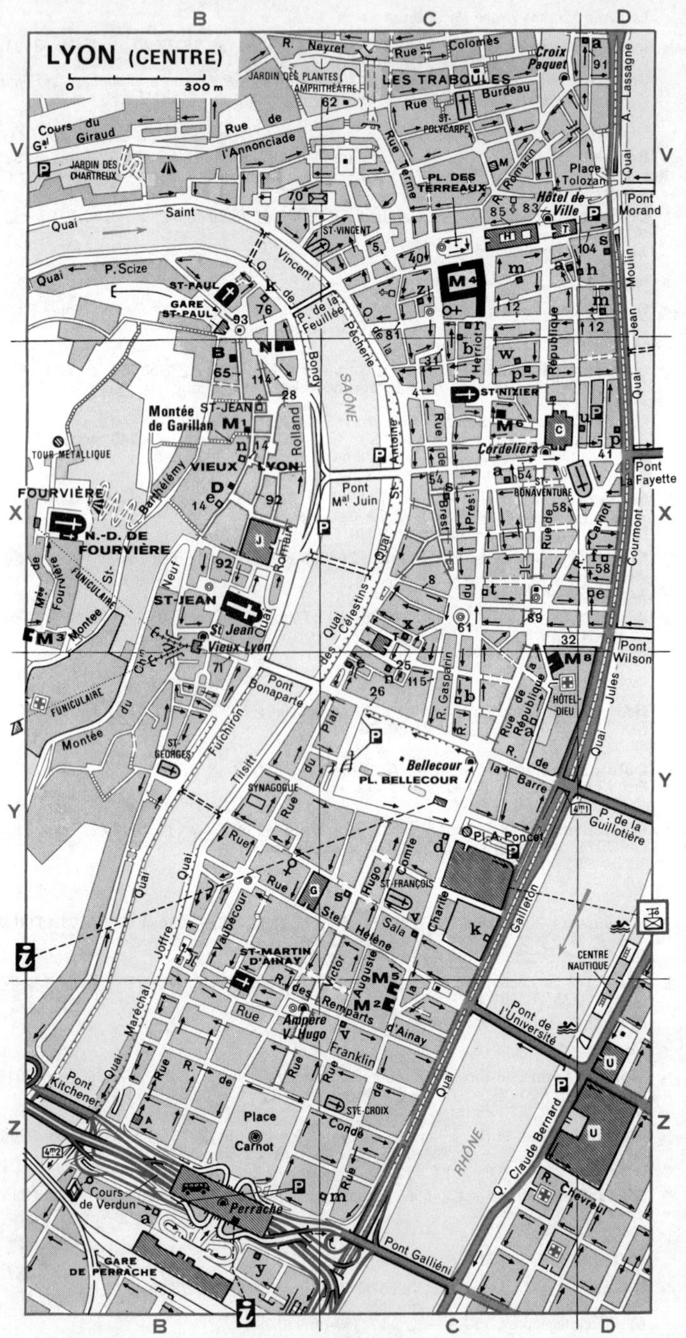
LYON (CENTRE)
0
300 m
LES TRABOULES
PL. DES TERREAUX
Hôtel de Ville
FOURVIÈRE
N.-D. DE FOURVIÈRE
VIEUX LYON
ST-JEAN
PL. BELLECOUR
Perrache
GARE DE PERRACHE
SAÔNE
RHÔNE
Pont Morand
Pont La Fayette
Pont Wilson
Pont Bonaparte
Pont de l'Université
Pont Gallièni
Pont Kitchener
Cordeliers
St Jean Vieux Lyon
Ampère V. Hugo
CENTRE NAUTIQUE
HÔTEL-DIEU

STREET INDEX TO LYON TOWN PLAN

République (R.) CX
Terme (R.) CV
Victor-Hugo (R.) . . . . CY

Ainay (Remp. d') . . . . CZ
Albon (Pl.) . . . . CX 4
Algérie (R. d') . . . . CV 5
Anc.-Préfect. (R.) . . . . CX 8
Annonciade (R.) . . . . BV
Barre (R. de la) . . . . CY
Bât-d'Argent (R.) . . . . CV 12
Bellecour (Pl.) . . . . CY
Bœuf (R. du) . . . . BX 14
Bonaparte (Pont) . . . . BY
Bondy (Quai de) . . . . BX
Brest (R. de) CX
Burdeau (R.) CV
Carnot (Pl.) . . . . BZ
Carnot (R.) . . . . DX
Célestins (Pl. des) . . . . CY 25
Célestins (Q. des) CX
Chambonnet (R.) . . . . CY 26
Change (Pl. du) . . . . BX 28
Charité (R. de la) . . . . CY
Ch.-Neuf (Montée) . . . . BX
Chenevard (R. P.) . . . . CX 31
Chevreul (R.) . . . . DZ
Childebert (R.) . . . . CX 32
Cl.-Bernard (Quai) . . . . CZ
Colomès (R.) CV

Comte (R. A.) . . . . CY
Condé (R. de) . . . . CZ
Constantine (R.) . . . . CV 40
Cordeliers (Pl.) . . . . DX 41
Courmont (Quai J.) . . . . DX
Feuillée (Pl. de la) . . . . BV
Fourvière (Mtée de) . . . . . . BX
Franklin (R.) . . . . CZ
Fulchiron (Quai) . . . . BY
Gailleton (Quai) . . . . CY
Gallieni (Pont) . . . . CZ
Gasparin (R.) . . . . CY
Giraud (Crs Gén.) . . . . BV
Grenette (R.) . . . . CX 54
Grolée (R.) . . . . DX 58
Guillotière (Pl. de la) . . . . . DY
Jacobins (Pl. des) . . . . CX 61
Jardin-Plantes (R.) . . . . CV 62
Joffre (Quai Mar.) . . . . BZ
Juin (Pont Mar.) CX
Juiverie (R.) . . . . BX 65
Kitchener (Pont) . . . . BZ
La Fayette (Pont) . . . . DX
Lassagne (Quai A.) . . . . DV
Martinière (R.) . . . . BV 70
Max (Av. Adolphe) . . . . BY 71
Morand (Pont) . . . . DV
Moulin (Quai J.) . . . . DV
Neyret (R.) . . . . BV
Octavio-Mey (R.) . . . . BV 76

Pêcherie (Quai) CX
Plat (R. du) . . . . BY
Platière (R. de la) . . . . CV 81
Poncet (Pl. A.) . . . . CY
Pradel (Pl. Louis) . . . . CV 83
Prés.-Herriot (R.) CX
Puits-Gaillot (R.) . . . . CV 85
République (Pl.) . . . . CX 89
Rom.-Rolland (Quai) . . . . . . BX
Romarin (R.) CV
Royale (R.) . . . . DV 91
St-Antoine (Quai) CX
St-Barthélemy
(Montée) . . . . BX
St-Jean (R.) . . . . BX 92
St-Paul (Pl.) . . . . BV 93
St-Vincent (Quai) . . . . BV
Ste-Hélène (R.) . . . . CY
Sala (Rue) . . . . CY
Scize (Quai Pierre) . . . . BV
Serlin (R. J.) . . . . DV 104
Terreaux (Pl. des) CV
Tilsitt (Quai) . . . . BY
Tolozan (Pl.) . . . . DV
Université (Pl. de l') . . . . . . CZ
Vaubécour (R.) . . . . BY
Verdun (Cours de) . . . . BZ
Vernay (R. Fr.) . . . . BX 114
Wilson (Pont) . . . . DX
Zola (R. Emile) . . . . CY 115

Restaurants

XXXXX ✿✿✿ **Paul Bocuse,** bridge of Collonges N : 12 km by the banks of River Saône (D 433, D 51 ✉ 69660 Collonges-au-Mont-d'Or ✆ 72 27 85 85, Fax 72 27 85 87, « Tasteful decor » – ▤ Ⓟ. AE ① GB
M 290 (lunch)/710 and a la carte 470/700
Spec. Soupe aux truffes noires. Filets de sole "Fernand Point". Volaille de Bresse. Wines Saint-Véran, Brouilly.

XXXX ✿ **Orsi,** 3 pl. Kléber ✉ 69006 ✆ 78 89 57 68, Fax 72 44 93 34, ☂, « Elegant decor » – ▤. AE ① GB JCB
closed Saturday in July-August and Sunday (except lunch from September-June) – **M** 240 (lunch)/500 and a la carte 390/570
Spec. Raviole de foie gras au jus de Porto. Gratin de homard "Acadien". Pigeonneau de Bresse aux gousses d'ail confites.

XXXX **Roger Roucou "Mère Guy",** 35 quai J. J. Rousseau ✉ 69350 La Mulatière ✆ 78 51 65 37, Fax 78 51 99 47 – ▤ Ⓟ. AE ① GB
closed August, Sunday dinner and Monday – **M** 250/450.

XXXX **Le Gourmandin,** 14 pl. J. Ferry (Brotteaux Railway station) ✉ 69006 ✆ 78 52 02 52, Fax 78 52 33 05, ☂, « Original contemporary decor in a former railway station » – ▤ Ⓟ. AE ① GB
closed Saturday lunch and Sunday – **M** 135/395 🍷.

XXX ✿ **Léon de Lyon** (Lacombe), 1 r. Pleney ✉ 69001 ✆ 78 28 11 33, Fax 78 39 89 05, « Lyonnaise atmosphere » – ▤. AE GB CVX **b**
closed 8 to 23 August, Monday lunch and Sunday – **M** 300/470 and a la carte 340/450
Spec. Pâté en croûte à l'ancienne. Volaille de Bresse et anguille sautées au Beaujolais. Six desserts à la praline. Wines Coteaux du Lyonnais, Régnié.

XXX **Christian Têtedoie,** 54 quai Pierre Scize ✉ 69005 ✆ 78 29 40 10, Fax 72 07 05 65 – ▤ Ⓟ. AE GB
closed Saturday lunch and Sunday except Bank Holidays September-June – **M** 180/260.

XXX ✿ **Aub. de Fond-Rose** (Brunet), 23 quai Clemenceau ✉ 69300 Caluire-et-Cuire ✆ 78 29 34 61, Fax 72 00 28 67, ☂, « Shaded and flowered garden, aviary » – Ⓟ. AE ① GB JCB
closed Monday from 15 October-Easter, dinner Sunday and Bank Holidays – **M** 200/450 and a la carte 350/500
Spec. Suprême de daurade au vin rouge (October-April). Filet de bar, sauce aux huîtres (October-April). Grenadin d'agneau en croûte à la fleur de thym. Wines Saint-Véran, Côtes de Brouilly.

XXX ✿ **Bourillot,** 8 pl. Célestins ✉ 69002 ✆ 78 37 38 64 – ▤. AE ① GB JCB CY **n**
closed 4 July-4 August, 23 December-2 January, Monday lunch, Sunday and Bank Holidays – **M** 225/430 and a la carte 300/450
Spec. Quenelle de brochet au fumet de homard. Volaille de Bresse "Marie", pommes aux truffes. Soufflé glacé au chocolat. Wines Coteaux du Lyonnais, Mâcon Villages.

XXX ✿ **Nandron,** 26 quai J. Moulin ✉ 69002 ✆ 78 42 10 26, Fax 78 37 69 88 – ▤. AE ① GB JCB DX **p**
closed 24 July-22 August and Saturday – **M** 300/450 and a la carte 320/460
Spec. Terrine tiède de champignons des bois. Quenelle de brochet à la Nantua. Volaille de Bresse rôtie "Grand-Mère". Wines Mâcon, Saint-Joseph.

XXX ✿ **Mère Brazier,** 12 r. Royale ✉ 69001 ☎ 78 28 15 49, « Lyonnaise atmosphere » – AE ⓓ GB JCB DV **a**
closed August, Saturday (except dinner 1 August-15 June) and Sunday – **M** 340/390 and a la carte 235/430
Spec. Fond d'artichaut au foie gras. Quenelle au gratin. Volaille de Bresse "demi-deuil". Wines Chiroubles, Saint-Joseph.

XXX ✿ **Fédora** (Judéaux), 249 r. M. Merieux ✉ 69007 ☎ 78 69 46 26, Fax 72 73 38 80, 余 – AE ⓓ GB JCB
closed 22 December-3 January, Saturday lunch, Sunday and Bank Holidays – **M** 160/290 and a la carte 250/350 ♁
Spec. Saint-Jacques en coquille au beurre demi-sel (October-April). Homard en os à moëlle. Ragoût d'encornets au poivre, riz sauvage des Amériques. Wines Mâcon-Cruzille.

XXX **Quatre Saisons,** 15 r. Sully ✉ 69006 ☎ 78 93 76 07, Fax 78 94 39 98 – ▤. AE ⓓ GB
closed 14 July-15 August, Saturday lunch, Sunday and Bank Holidays – **M** 120/300.

XXX **Le Saint Alban,** 2 quai J. Moulin ✉ 69001 ☎ 78 30 14 89 – ▤. AE GB DV **s**
closed 2 to 22 August, February Holidays, Saturday (except dinner from August-June), Sunday and Bank Holidays – **M** 145/280.

XXX **Les Fantasques,** 47 r. Bourse ✉ 69002 ☎ 78 37 36 58 – ▤. AE ⓓ GB JCB DX **u**
closed 7 to 23 August and Sunday – **M** 245/280.

XX **La Mère Vittet** (24 hr service), 26 cours Verdun ✉ 69002 ☎ 78 37 20 17, Fax 78 42 40 70 – ▤. AE ⓓ GB JCB BZ **y**
M 140/220 ♁.

XX **Le Nord,** 18 r. Neuve ✉ 69002 ☎ 78 28 24 54, Fax 78 28 76 58 – ▤. AE GB JCB CX **p**
closed 9 to 21 August and Saturday – **M** 90/230.

XX ✿ **L'Alexandrin** (Alexanian), 83 r. Moncey ✉ 69003 ☎ 72 61 15 69, Fax 78 62 75 57 – ▤. AE GB. ✗
closed 20 to 24 May, 11 to 14 July, 8 to 23 August, 24/12-3/1, 16 to 27 January, Sunday, Monday and Bank Holidays – **M** 200 and a la carte 230/330
Spec. Terrine de foie gras aux champignons des bois. Filet de Charolais grillé, sauce au jus de truffes et paillasson lyonnais. Entremets au chocolat amer. Wines Côte Rôtie, Condrieu.

XX ✿ **Aub. de l'Ile** (Ansanay), quartier St-Rambert, Ile Barbe ✉ 69009 ☎ 78 83 99 49, Fax 78 47 80 46 – Ⓟ. GB. ✗
closed 8 to 22 August, February Holidays, Sunday dinner and Monday – **M** 160/280 and a la carte 300/410
Spec. Tempuras de grenouilles et salade de fèves. Selle de lapereau en rognonade et galette de maïs au parmesan. Feuillantine aux abricots.

XX **Le Passage,** 8 r. Plâtre ✉ 69001 ☎ 78 28 11 16, Fax 72 00 84 34 – ▤. AE ⓓ GB
closed Saturday lunch, Sunday and Bank Holidays – **M** 275/340. CV **r**

XX **Gervais,** 42 r. P. Corneille ✉ 69006 ☎ 78 52 19 13 – AE ⓓ GB
closed 1 July-1 August, Saturday except dinner October-April and Sunday – **M** 145/185.

XX **Gourmet de Sèze,** 129 r. Sèze ✉ 69006 ☎ 78 24 23 42 – ▤. AE GB
closed 14 July-15 August, Saturday lunch, Sunday and Bank Holidays – **M** (booking essential) 100/300.

XX **La Tassée,** 20 r. Charité ✉ 69002 ☎ 78 37 02 35, Fax 72 40 05 91 – ▤. AE ⓓ GB
closed 24 December-2 January, Saturday in July-August and Sunday – **M** 125/290. CY **v**

XX **Thierry Gache,** 37 r. Thibaudière ✉ 69007 ☎ 78 72 81 77, Fax 78 72 01 75 – ▤. AE GB
closed Sunday dinner – **M** 108/248.

XX **Tante Alice,** 22 r. Remparts d'Ainay ✉ 69002 ☎ 78 37 49 83 – ▤. AE GB CZ **v**
closed August, Friday dinner and Saturday – **M** 90/194.

XX **La Voûte,** 11 pl. A. Gourju ✉ 69002 ☎ 78 42 01 33, Fax 78 37 36 41 – ▤. AE ⓓ GB
closed Sunday – **M** 118/220. CY **e**

XX **La Pinte à Gones,** 59 r. Ney ✉ 69006 ☎ 78 24 81 75 – ▤. GB
closed August, 24 December-1 January, Saturday lunch, Sunday and Bank Holidays – **M** 98/198.

XX **L'Italien de Lyon,** 25 r. Bât d'Argent ✉ 69001 ☎ 78 39 58 58, Fax 72 07 98 96 – AE GB
closed Sunday – **M** Italian rest 140/200 ♁. DV **m**

X **Chez Jean-François,** 2 pl. Célestins ✉ 69002 ☎ 78 42 08 26 – ▤. GB CX **x**
closed Easter Holidays and 24 July-16 August – **M** 80/115 ♁.

Bouchons : Regional specialities and wine tasting in a Lyonnaise atmosphere

X **Le Garet,** 7 r. Garet ✉ 69001 ☎ 78 28 16 94, Fax 72 00 06 84 – GB CDV **h**
closed 16 July-16 August, Saturday Sunday and Bank Holidays – **M** (booking essential) a la carte 110/160 ♁.

X **Chez Sylvain,** 4 r. Tupin ✉ 69002 ☎ 78 42 11 98 CX **s**
closed 15 July-9 August, February Holidays, Saturday and Sunday – **M** (booking essential) 83/95 and dinner a la carte.

X **La Meunière,** 11 r. Neuve ✉ 69002 ☎ 78 28 62 91 – AE ⓓ GB JCB CX **w**
closed 15 July-15 August, Sunday and Monday – **M** (booking essential) 85/140.

X **Café des Fédérations,** 8 r. Major Martin ✉ 69001 ☎ 78 28 26 00 – AE GB CV **z**
closed August, Saturday and Sunday – **M** (booking essential) 140.

Café du Jura, 25 r. Tupin ✉ 69002 ☎ 78 42 20 57 - AE GB CX **a**
closed 1 to 21 August, Christmas-New Year, Saturday (except dinner in winter) and Sunday - **M** (booking essential) a la carte 115/165 ♁.

Chez Hugon, 12 rue Pizay ✉ 69001 ☎ 78 28 10 94 - GB CV **m**
closed August, Saturday and Sunday - **M** (booking essential)(lunch only) a la carte 120/150.

Au Petit Bouchon "chez Georges", 8 r. Garet ✉ 69001 ☎ 78 28 30 46 - GB CV **a**
closed Saturday and Sunday - **M** 76/99 and dinner a la carte.

Environs

to the NE :

at Rillieux-la-Pape : 7 km by N 83 and N 84 - pop. 30 791 - ✉ 69140 :

✿ **Larivoire** (Constantin), chemin des Iles ☎ 78 88 50 92, Fax 78 88 35 22, ←, - P. GB
closed 26 August-2 September, 1 to 20 February, Monday dinner and Tuesday - **M** 190/390 and a la carte 285/365
Spec. Foie gras poêlé à la rhubarbe. Coquilles Saint-Jacques à la crème de céleri (October to April). Fricassée de volaille de Bresse au vinaigre. Wines Pouilly-Loché, Morgon.

at Neyron-le-Haut (01 Ain) 14 km by A 42 and A 46 - ✉ 01700 :

✿ **Le Saint Didier** (Champin), ☎ 78 55 28 72, Fax 78 55 01 55, - P. GB
closed 9 to 23 August, 27 December-11 January, Sunday lunch and Monday - **M** (booking essential) 175/400 and a la carte 260/380
Spec. Foie gras de canard, gelée au Jurançon. Gougeonnettes de carpe royale à la Roussette. Blancs de volaille farcis aux morilles, sauce estragon. Wines Roussette de Seyssel, Montagnieu.

to the E :

at the airport of Satolas : 27 km by A 43 - ✉ 69125 Lyon Satolas Airport :

Sofitel M without rest, 3rd floor ☎ 72 23 38 00, Telex 380480, Fax 72 23 98 00, ← - rm TV ☎ ♿. AE GB - 65 - **120 rm** 630.

La Gde Corbeille, 1st floor ☎ 72 22 71 76, Telex 306723, Fax 72 22 71 72, ← - .

Le Bouchon, 1st floor ☎ 72 22 71 99, Telex 306723, Fax 72 22 71 72 - .

to the NW :

Porte de Lyon - motorway junction A 6 N 6 Exit road signposted Limonest N : 10 km - ✉ 69570 Dardilly :

Novotel Lyon-Nord M, ☎ 72 17 29 29, Telex 330962, Fax 78 35 08 45, - rm TV ☎ P - 150. AE GB JCB
M a la carte approx. 160 - 48 - **107 rm** 400/445.

Mercure M, ☎ 78 35 28 05, Telex 330045, Fax 78 47 47 15, - rm rest TV ☎ P - 30 - 250. AE GB JCB
M 120/160 b.i. - 52 - **172 rm** 370/496.

Ibis Lyon Nord M, ☎ 78 66 02 20, Telex 305250, Fax 78 47 47 93, - rm TV ☎ ♿ P - 30. AE GB
M 88/120 ♁ - 35 - **69 rm** 310/340.

Chagny 71150 S.-et-L. 69 ⑨ - pop. 5 346 alt. 216.
Lyons 145.

✿✿✿ **Lameloise** M, pl. d'Armes ☎ 85 87 08 85, Telex 801086, Fax 85 87 03 57, « Old Burgundian house, tasteful decor » - TV ☎ . AE GB
closed 22 December-27 January, Thursday lunch and Wednesday - **M** (booking essential) 360/550 and a la carte 360/500 - 80 - **19 rm** 600/1300
Spec. Embeurrée d'escargots aux herbes fraîches. Pigeonneau en vessie et pâtes fraîches au foie gras. Feuillantine au chocolat et marmelade d'oranges. Wines Rully blanc, Chassagne-Montrachet rouge.

Fleurie 69820 Rhône 74 ① - pop. 1 105 alt. 295.
Lyons 59.

✿✿ **Aub. du Cep,** pl. Église ☎ 74 04 10 77, Fax 74 04 10 28 - . AE GB
closed mid December-mid January, Sunday dinner and Monday - **M** (booking essential) 290/550 and a la carte 310/450 ♁
Spec. Cuisses de grenouilles rôties. Queues d'écrevisses en petit ragoût. Volaille fermière au vin de Fleurie. Wines Fleurie, Beaujolais blanc.

Mionnay 01390 Ain 74 ② - pop. 1 103 alt. 288.
Lyons 23.

✿✿ **Alain Chapel** with rm, ☎ 78 91 82 02, Fax 78 91 82 37, , « Flowered garden » - TV ☎ P. AE GB - *closed January, Tuesday lunch and Monday* - **M** 320 (lunch)/780 and a la carte 475/725 - 77 - **13 rm** 700/825
Spec. Crème de primeurs à l'estragon, en gelée de crustacés (April-June). Pommes de terre farcies aux truffes blanches et cuisses de grenouilles à la ciboulette. Rognon de veau rôti dans sa graisse. Wines Mâcon Villages, Bourgogne.

Montrond-les-Bains 42210 Loire 73 ⑱ - pop. 3 627 alt. 356.
Lyons 62.

🏨 ✿✿ **Host. La Poularde** (Etéocle), ✆ 77 54 40 06, Telex 307002, Fax 77 54 53 14, - rm ▤ rest TV ☎ - 40. AE ⓓ GB JCB
closed 2 to 15 January, Tuesday lunch and Monday - **M** (Sunday : booking essential) 180/490 and a la carte 380/550 - ☕ 60 - **11 rm** 300/480
Spec. Filet de bar étuvé aux ravioles d'écrevisses. Suprême de poulette fermière cuit à l'os. Charolais en papillote au jus de viande. Wines Condrieu, Saint-Joseph.

Roanne ⟨SP⟩ 42300 Loire 73 ⑦ - pop. 41 756 alt. 279.
Lyons 87.

🏨 ✿✿✿ **Troisgros** M, pl. Gare ✆ 77 71 66 97, Fax 77 70 39 77, « Tasteful contemporary decor », - ▤ TV ☎ P. AE ⓓ GB JCB
closed February Holidays, Tuesday dinner and Wednesday - **M** (booking essential) 490/610 and a la carte 420/650 - ☕ 100 - **14 rm** 700/1400, 3 suites, 3 duplex
Spec. Effiloché de crabe dormeur à la gelée de tomate. Saumon à l'oseille "Version 1993". Fleur de tournesol (dessert). Wines Bourgogne blanc, Côte Roannaise rouge.

St-Etienne P 42000 Loire 73 ⑲, 76 ⑨ - pop. 199 396 alt. 517.
Lyons 60.

XXXX ✿✿✿ **Pierre Gagnaire,** 7 r. Richelandière ✆ 77 42 30 90, Fax 77 42 30 91, « Elegantly installed in a 1930 style house » - ▤. AE ⓓ GB
closed 15 to 22 August, 14 to 22 February, Sunday dinner and Wednesday - **M** 280 (lunch)/635 and a la carte 350/560
Spec. Attereaux de crêtes de coq et jus de cuisson au miel. Fricassée de lapin frotté de cannelle et de genièvre frais. Le grand dessert Pierre Gagnaire. Wines Crozes-Hermitage, Saint-Joseph.

Valence P 26000 Drôme 77 ⑫ - pop. 63 437 alt. 123.
Lyons 101.

XXXXX ✿✿✿ **Pic** with rm, 285 av. V. Hugo, Motorway exit sign-posted Valence-Sud ✆ 75 44 15 32, Fax 75 40 96 03, « Shaded garden » - ▤ TV ☎ P. AE ⓓ GB.
closed 2 to 26 August, Sunday dinner and Wednesday - **M** (Sunday : booking essential) 250 (lunch)/600 and a la carte 560/700 - ☕ 80 - **5 rm** 650/1000
Spec. Galette de truffes et céleri au foie de canard. Filet de loup au caviar. Strate de bœuf au Cornas. Wines Condrieu, Hermitage.

at Pont-de-l'Isère to the N by N 7 : 9 km - ✉ 26600 :

XXXX ✿✿ **Chabran** M with rm, N 7 ✆ 75 84 60 09, Fax 75 84 59 65, - ▤ TV ☎. AE ⓓ GB
closed Sunday dinner (except Bank Holidays and School Holidays) - **M** 255/525 and a la carte 380/550 - ☕ 70 - **12 rm** 350/660
Spec. Millefeuille de foie gras aux artichauts et aux courgettes. Nage de sole et langoustines aux "Creuses" de Bretagne. Dos d'agneau cuit à l'os, aux gousses d'ail. Wines Crozes-Hermitage, Hermitage.

Vienne ⟨SP⟩ 38200 Isère 74 ⑪ ⑫ - pop. 29 449 alt. 158.
Lyons 31.

🏨 ✿✿ **La Pyramide** M, 14 bd F. Point par ④ ✆ 74 53 01 96, Telex 308058, Fax 74 85 69 73, , - ▤ TV ☎ ♿ P - 25. AE ⓓ GB
closed 1 to 7 March and February - **M** *(closed Thursday lunch and Wednesday)* 270 and a la carte 550/650 - ☕ 80 - **22 rm** 750/850, 4 suites
Spec. Gratin de queues d'écrevisses (15 June-15 October). Poularde truffée en vessie. Les trois gourmandises de la Pyramide. Wines Condrieu, Côtes du Rhône rouge.

Vonnas 01540 Ain 74 ② - pop. 2 381 alt. 189.
Lyons 63.

🏨 ✿✿✿ **Georges Blanc** M, ✆ 74 50 00 10, Telex 380776, Fax 74 50 08 80, « Elegant inn on the banks of the Veyle, flowered garden », - ▤ TV ☎ P. AE ⓓ GB
closed 3 January-11 February - **M** *(closed Thursday except dinner 15 June-15 September and Wednesday except Bank Holidays)* (booking essential) 440/650 and a la carte 500/650 - ☕ 85 - **34 rm** 800/1700, 7 suites
Spec. Crêpe parmentière au saumon et caviar. Saint-Jacques rôties aux cèpes (October-April). Pigeon de Bresse au foie gras. Wines Mâcon-Azé, Chiroubles.

Do not mix up :

Comfort of hotels	: 🏨 ... 🏠
Comfort of restaurants	: XXXXX ... X
Quality of the cuisine	: ✿✿✿, ✿✿, ✿

MARSEILLES P 13000 B.-du-R. 84 ⑬ – pop. 800 550.

See : N.-D.-de-la-Garde Basilica ※*** EV – Old Port** DETU – Corniche Président-J.-F.-Kennedy** – Modern Port** – Palais Longchamp* GS – St-Victor Basilica* : crypt** DU – Old Major Cathedral* DS N – Pharo Parc ≤* DU – St-Laurent Belvedere ≤* DT E – Museum : Grobet-labadié** GS M7, Cantini* : Marseilles and Moustiers pottery** (galerie de la Faïence de Marseille et de Moustiers) FU – M5, Fine Arts* GS M8, Natural History Museum* GS M9 – Mediterranean Archaeology* : collection of Egyptian antiquities** (Old Charity*) DS M6, Roman Docks DET M2 – Old Marseilles* DT M3.

Envir. : Corniche road** of Callelongue S : 13 km along the sea front.

Exc. : – Château d'If** (※***) 1 h 30.

18 of Marseilles-Aix ☎ 42 24 20 41 to the N : 22 km ; 18 of Allauch-Marseilles (private) ☎ 91 05 20 60 ; junction Marseilles-East : 15 km, by D 2 and D 4=A ; 9 18 Country Club of la Salette ☎ 91 27 12 16 by A 50.

✈ Marseilles-Marignane : ☎ 42 78 21 00 to the N : 28 km. – ☎ 91 08 50 50.

ℹ Office de Tourisme 4 Canebière, 13001 ☎ 91 54 91 11, Telex 430402 and St-Charles railway station ☎ 91 50 59 18 – A.C. 149 bd Rabatau, 13010 ☎ 91 78 83 00.

Paris 772 – Lyons 312 – Nice 188 – Turin 407 – Toulon 64 – Toulouse 401.

Plans on following pages

Sofitel Vieux Port M, 36 bd Ch. Livon ✉ 13007 ☎ 91 52 90 19, Telex 401270, Fax 91 31 46 52, « Panoramic restaurant ≤ old port », – rm – 180. AE GB DU **n**
les Trois Forts M 145/195 – ☕ 70 – **127 rm** 700/960, 3 suites.

Mercure-Centre M, r. Neuve St-Martin ✉ 13001 ☎ 91 39 20 00, Telex 401886, Fax 91 56 24 57, ≤ – rm – 200. AE GB EST **g**
Oursinade *(closed August)* **M** 150/220 – **Oliveraie** *(closed Sunday)(lunch only)* **M** 75/120 – ☕ 60 – **198 rm** 575/750.

Pullman Beauvau without rest, 4 r. Beauvau ✉ 13001 ☎ 91 54 91 00, Telex 401778, Fax 91 54 15 76, « Antiques » – rm – 30. AE GB ET **r**
☕ 65 – **71 rm** 600/800.

Holiday Inn M, 103 av. Prado ✉ 13008 ☎ 91 83 10 10, Fax 91 79 84 12 – rm – 60 - 200. AE GB
M 155 – ☕ 55 – **116 rm** 580/640, 4 suites.

Concorde Prado M, 11 av. Mazargues ✉ 13008 ☎ 91 76 51 11, Telex 420209, Fax 91 77 95 10 – – 180. AE GB JCB. rest
M a la carte 160/220 – ☕ 60 – **100 rm** 480/730.

New H. Bompard without rest, 2 r. Flots Bleus ✉ 13007 ☎ 91 52 10 93, Telex 400430, Fax 91 31 02 14, – – 40. AE GB JCB
☕ 48 – **46 rm** 395/450.

Novotel Marseille Centre M, 36 bd Ch. Livon ✉ 13007 ☎ 91 59 22 22, Telex 402937, Fax 91 31 15 48, ≤, – rm – 350. AE GB JCB
M a la carte approx. 160 – ☕ 48 – **90 rm** 500/560. DU **n**

St-Ferréol's M without rest, 19 r. Pisançon ✉ 13001 ☎ 91 33 12 21, Fax 91 54 29 97 – . AE GB FU **h**
closed 25 July-21 August – ☕ 38 – **19 rm** 276/432.

Alizé M without rest, 35 quai Belges ✉ 13001 ☎ 91 33 66 97, Fax 91 54 80 06, ≤ – . AE GB ETU **b**
☕ 35 – **35 rm** 275/425.

New H. Astoria without rest, 10 bd Garibaldi ✉ 13001 ☎ 91 33 33 50, Fax 91 54 80 75 – . AE GB JCB. FT **f**
☕ 48 – **58 rm** 325/440.

New H. Sélect without rest, 4 allée Gambetta ✉ 13001 ☎ 91 50 65 50, Telex 402175, Fax 91 50 45 56 – – 25. AE GB JCB. FS **k**
☕ 48 – **60 rm** 325/440.

Castellane M without rest, 31 r. Rouet ✉ 13006 ☎ 91 79 27 54, Telex 402326, Fax 91 25 44 07 – . AE GB GV **f**
☕ 43 – **55 rm** 310/437.

XXX **Jambon de Parme,** 67 r. La Palud ✉ 13006 ☎ 91 54 37 98 – . AE GB JCB FU **s**
closed 11 July-24 August, Sunday dinner and Monday – **M** a la carte 210/330.

XXX **Patalain,** 49 r. Sainte ✉ 13001 ☎ 91 55 02 78, Fax 91 54 15 29, « Elegant decor » – . AE GB EU **f**
closed 14 July-2 September, Saturday lunch, Sunday and Bank Holidays – **M** 195/350.

XXX **La Ferme,** 23 r. Sainte ✉ 13001 ☎ 91 33 21 12 – . AE GB EU **m**
closed August, Saturday lunch and Sunday – **M** 180/250.

XXX **Les Échevins,** 44 r. Sainte ✉ 13001 ☎ 91 33 08 08 – . AE GB JCB EU **x**
closed 14 July-15 August, Saturday lunch and Sunday – **M** 150/210.

XXX ✿ **Miramar** (Minguella), 12 quai Port ✉ 13002 ☎ 91 91 10 40, Fax 91 56 64 31, ≤, – . AE GB ET **v**
closed 31 July-23 August, 23 December-6 January and Sunday – **M** a la carte 265/430
Spec. Sar grillé au beurre de Pisala et olives noires. Bouillabaisse. Bourride.

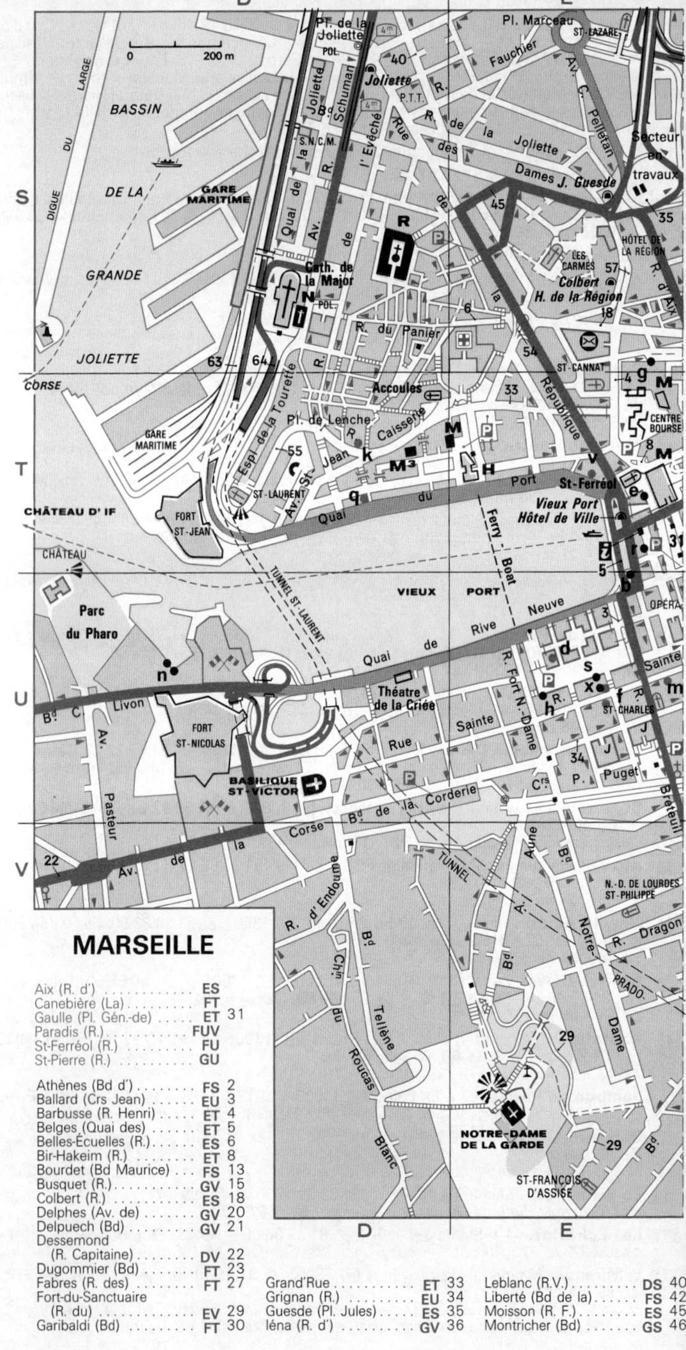

MARSEILLE

Aix (R. d') . . . . ES
Canebière (La) . . . . FT
Gaulle (Pl. Gén.-de) . . . . . ET 31
Paradis (R.) . . . . FUV
St-Ferréol (R.) . . . . FU
St-Pierre (R.) . . . . GU

Athènes (Bd d') . . . . FS 2
Ballard (Crs Jean) . . . . . . EU 3
Barbusse (R. Henri) . . . . . ET 4
Belges (Quai des) . . . . . . ET 5
Belles-Écuelles (R.) . . . . . . ES 6
Bir-Hakeim (R.) . . . . ET 8
Bourdet (Bd Maurice) . . . FS 13
Busquet (R.) . . . . GV 15
Colbert (R.) . . . . ES 18
Delphes (Av. de) . . . . GV 20
Delpuech (Bd) . . . . GV 21
Dessemond
(R. Capitaine) . . . . DV 22
Dugommier (Bd) . . . . FT 23
Fabres (R. des) . . . . FT 27
Fort-du-Sanctuaire
(R. du) . . . . EV 29
Garibaldi (Bd) . . . . FT 30

Grand'Rue . . . . ET 33
Grignan (R.) . . . . EU 34
Guesde (Pl. Jules) . . . . . ES 35
Iéna (R. d') . . . . GV 36

Leblanc (R.V.) . . . . DS 40
Liberté (Bd de la) . . . . . . FS 42
Moisson (R. F.) . . . . ES 45
Montricher (Bd) . . . . GS 46

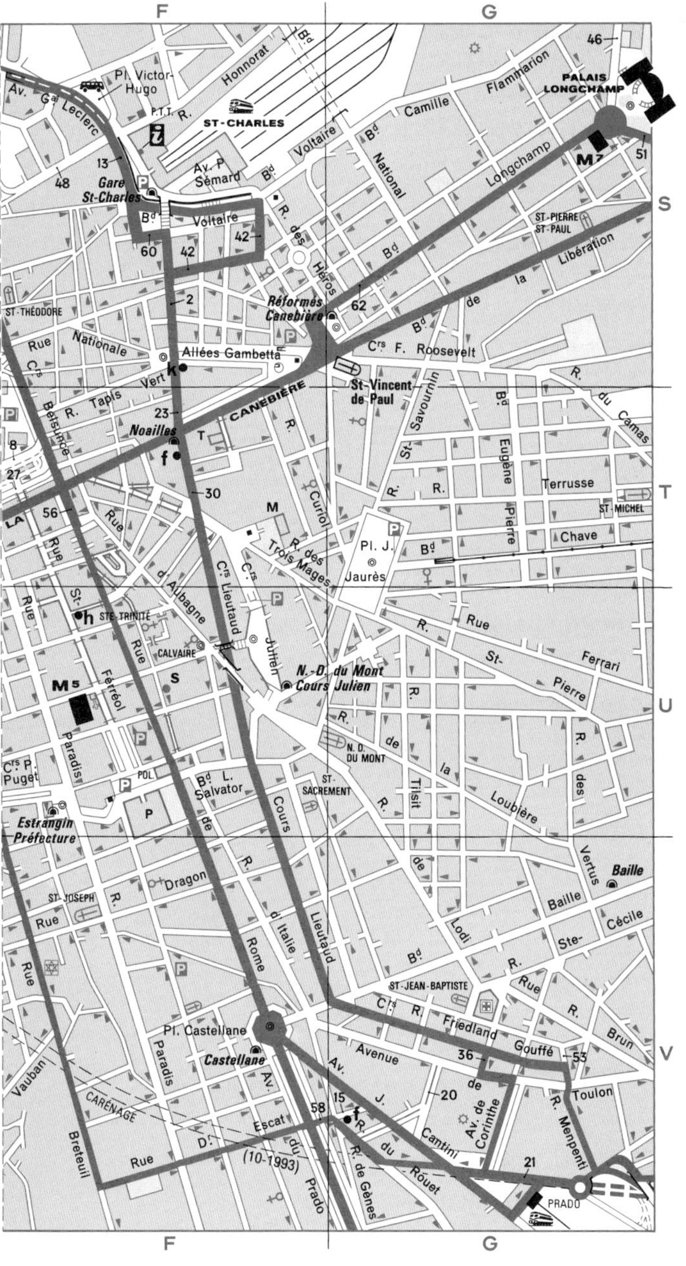

Nedelec (Bd Ch.) . . . . . . FS 48	St-Laurent (R.) . . . . DT 55	Sembat (R. Marcel) . . . . . FS 60
Philipon (Bd) . . . . GS 51	St-Louis (Crs) . . . . FT 56	Thierry (Crs J.) . . . . GS 62
Raynouard (Traverse) . . . GV 53	Ste-Barbe (R.) . . . . ES 57	Tourette (Quai) . . . . DS 63
Sadi-Carnot (Pl.) . . . . ES 54	Ste-Philomène (R.) . . . . FV 58	Vaudoyer (Av.) . . . . DS 64

XX **Michel-Brasserie des Catalans,** 6 r. Catalans ✉ 13007 ☎ 91 52 30 63, Fax 91 59 23 05 – ▤. AE GB JCB
M Seafood - a la carte 260/370.

XX **Calypso,** 3 r. Catalans ✉ 13007 ☎ 91 52 40 60, ← – AE GB
M Seafood 230.

XX **L'Ambassade des Vignobles,** 42 pl. aux Huiles ✉ 13001 ☎ 91 33 00 25, Fax 91 54 25 60 – ▤. AE GB EU **h**
closed August, Saturday lunch and Sunday – **M** 140 b.i./280 b.i..

XX **Les Arcenaulx,** 25 cours d'Estienne d'Orves ☎ 91 54 77 06, Fax 91 54 76 33, 🏖, « Bookseller and restaurant in original decor » – ▤. AE ⓪ GB JCB EU **s**
closed Sunday except lunch in Winter – **M** 180/225.

XX **Brasserie New-York Vieux Port,** 7 quai Belges ✉ 13001 ☎ 91 33 60 98, Fax 91 33 29 46, 🏖 – ▤. AE ⓪ GB JCB ETU **e**
M a la carte 180/260 ♂.

X **La Charpenterie,** 22 r. Paix ✉ 13001 ☎ 91 54 22 89, Fax 91 55 51 41, 🏖 – AE ⓪ GB
closed 1 to 15 August and 24 to 29 December – **M** 99/160. EU **d**

at the Corniche :

🏨 **Concorde-Palm Beach** M 🐌, 2 promenade Plage ✉ 13008 ☎ 91 16 19 00, Telex 401894, Fax 91 16 19 39, ←, 🏖, 🏊, 🏖 – |‡| ▤ TV ☎ 🚗 P – 🏛 450. AE ⓪ GB JCB. ✗ rest
La Réserve M 205 – **Les Voiliers M** a la carte 140/200 ♂ – ☕ 60 – **145 rm** 515/803.

🏨 ✿✿ **Le Petit Nice** (Passédat) M 🐌, anse de Maldormé (turn off when level with no 160 Corniche Kennedy) ✉ 13007 ☎ 91 59 25 92, Telex 401565, Fax 91 59 28 08, 🏖, « Villas overlooking the sea, elegant decor, ← », 🏊 – |‡| ▤ TV ☎ P. AE GB
M *(closed Saturday lunch and Sunday from November-March except Bank Holidays)* 300 b.i. (lunch)/650 and a la carte 450/650 – ☕ 100 – **13 rm** 1000/1900, 3 suites
Spec. Gâteau de grenouilles aux pieds de porc. Loup de palangre. Grosse tomate aux supions et crème de sarriette (summer). Wines Bandol, Palette.

XX **Peron,** 56 corniche Prés. Kennedy ✉ 13007 ☎ 91 52 43 70, Fax 91 59 16 40, ← harbour entrance and château d'If – AE ⓪ GB
closed 1 to 9 May, January, Sunday dinner and Monday – **M** a la carte 200/375.

Les Baux-de-Provence 13520 B.-du-R. 84 ① – pop. 457 alt. 280.

Marseilles 83.

in the Vallon :

XXXXX ✿✿ **Oustaù de Baumanière** (Thuilier) 🐌 with rm, ☎ 90 54 33 07, Telex 420203, Fax 90 54 40 46, ←, « Period houses, floral terraces, 🏖, 🏊, riding club », 🌳 – ▤ rm TV ☎ P. AE ⓪ GB
closed 15 January-1 March, Thursday lunch and Wednesday November-March – **M** 400/700 and a la carte 335/575 – ☕ 95 – **11 rm** 900/1050, 13 suites
Spec. Ravioli de truffes. Filets de rougets au basilic. Gigot d'agneau en croûte. Wines Coteaux des Baux, Gigondas.

to the SW on D 78 F :

🏨 ✿ **La Cabro d'Or** M 🐌, à 1 km ☎ 90 54 33 21, Telex 401810, Fax 90 54 45 98, ←, 🏖, « Shaded terraces, floral garden, lake », 🏊, 🎾 – ▤ rm TV ☎ P – 🏛 80. AE ⓪ GB
closed 15 November-19 December, Tuesday lunch and Monday 31 October-31 March – **M** 180 (lunch)/370 and a la carte 220/315 – ☕ 65 – **22 rm** 575/850
Spec. Salade "Cabro d'Or". Pageot grillé au pistou. Noisettes d'agneau "Cabro d'Or". Wines Coteaux des Baux.

Carry-le-Rouet 13620 B.-du-R. 84 ⑩ – pop. 5 224 alt. 4.

Marseilles 27.

XXXX ✿✿ **L'Escale** (Clor), ☎ 42 45 00 47, Fax 42 44 72 69, 🏖, « Terraces overlooking the Harbour, pleasant view », 🌳 – GB
2 February-1 November and closed Monday except dinner in July-August and Sunday dinner September-June – **M** (Sunday : booking essential) 310/450 and a la carte 380/500
Spec. Coquilles Saint-Jacques poêlées aux truffes (October to April). Turbotin rôti en civet de Châteauneuf. Homard rôti au beurre de corail. Wines Coteaux d'Aix en Provence, Cassis.

MONACO (Principality of) 84 ⑩, 115 ㉗ ㉘ – pop. 29 972 alt. 65 – Casino.

Monaco Capital of the Principality – ✉ 98000.

See : Tropical Garden★★ (Jardin exotique) : ←★ – Observatory Caves★ (Grotte de l'Observatoire) – St-Martin Gardens★ – Early paintings of the Nice School★★ in Cathedral – Recumbent Christ★ in the Misericord Chapel – Place du Palais★ – Prince's Palace★ – Museums : oceanographic★★ (aquarium★★, ←★★ from the terrace), Prehistoric Anthropology★, Napoleon and Monaco History★.

Urban racing circuit – A.C.M. 23 bd Albert-1er ☎ 93 15 26 00, Telex 469003, Fax 93 25 80 08.

Paris 956 – ♦ Nice 21 – San Remo 44.

Monte-Carlo Fashionable resort of the Principality - Casinos Grand Casino, Monte-Carlo Sporting Club, Sun Casino - ✉ 98000.

See : Terrace★★ of the Grand casino - Museum of Dolls and Automata★.

Monte-Carlo Golf Club ☏ 93 41 09 11 to the S by N 7 : 11 km.

Direction Tourisme et Congrès, 2A bd Moulins ☏ 93 30 87 01, Telex 469760.

Paris, pl. Casino ☏ 92 16 30 00, Telex 469925, Fax 93 15 90 03, ≤, - 25 - 70. AE GB JCB. rest
M see **Louis XV** and **Le Grill** below - **Salle Empire** *(24 June-3 October) (dinner only)* **M** a la carte 515/810 - 140 - **164 rm** 2600/2900, 41 suites.

Hermitage, square Beaumarchais ☏ 92 16 40 00, Telex 479432, Fax 93 50 47 12, ≤, « Dining room in Baroque style », - 25 - 80. AE GB. rest
M 320/450 - 140 - **215 rm** 1700/2700, 25 suites.

Loews M, 12 av. Spélugues ☏ 93 50 65 00, Telex 479435, Fax 93 30 01 57, ≤, Casino and cabaret, - 30 - 2 000. AE GB JCB. rest
Le Foie Gras (dinner only) **M** a la carte 365/480 - **L'Argentin** - (dinner only) **M** a la carte 260/410 - **Le Pistou** (dinner only 30 Sept.-1 May) **M** 200/330 - **Café de la mer M** a la carte 150/270 - 115 - **600 rm** 1700/2000, 35 suites.

Métropole Palace M, 4 av. Madone ☏ 93 15 15 15, Telex 489836, Fax 93 25 24 44, - - 50 - 150. AE GB JCB
Les Ambassadeurs M 250 - 100 - **98 rm** 1400/1950, 30 suites.

Beach Plaza M, av. Princesse Grace, à la Plage du Larvotto ☏ 93 30 98 80, Telex 479617, Fax 93 50 23 14, ≤, « Attractive resort » - - 50 - 300. AE GB JCB. rest
La Terrasse M 185/220 - 115 - **304 rm** 1680/2150, 9 suites.

Mirabeau M, 1 av. Princesse Grace ☏ 92 16 65 65, Telex 479413, Fax 93 50 84 85, ≤, - - 25 - 100. AE GB JCB. rest
M see **La Coupole** below - 135 - **99 rm** 1500/2000, 4 suites.

Alexandra without rest, 35 bd Princesse Charlotte ☏ 93 50 63 13, Telex 489286, Fax 92 16 06 48 - . AE GB.
50 - **56 rm** 650/780.

Balmoral, 12 av. Costa ☏ 93 50 62 37, Telex 479436, Fax 93 15 08 69, ≤ - rm . AE GB JCB.
M snack *(closed November, Sunday dinner, Monday and Bank Holidays)* a la carte 130/180 - 55 - **77 rm** 500/850.

✿✿✿ **Le Louis XV** - Hôtel de Paris, pl. Casino ☏ 92 16 30 01, Telex 469925, Fax 92 16 30 04, - . AE GB JCB.
closed 30 November-29 December, 15 February-2 March, Tuesday and Wednesday (except dinner 23 June-25 August) - **M** 680/790 and a la carte 620/800
Spec. Légumes des jardins de Provence mijotés à la truffe noire. Pigeonneau cuit sur la braise, cèpes piqués d'ail confit. Baba au rhum. Wines Côtes de Provence.

✿ **Grill de l'Hôtel de Paris,** pl. Casino ☏ 92 16 30 02, Telex 469925, Fax 92 16 30 04, « Roof-top restaurant with sliding roof and ≤ the Principality » - . AE GB JCB.
closed 10 January-9 February - **M** a la carte 460/600
Spec. Risotto à la fleur de courgette et copeaux de pancetta. Rougets de roche en filets poêlés "niçoise". Chaud-froid vanille-chocolat au caramel d'oranges. Wines Côtes de Provence rosé et rouge.

✿ **La Coupole** - Hôtel Mirabeau, 1 av. Princesse Grace ☏ 92 16 66 99, Telex 479413, Fax 93 50 84 85, - . AE GB JCB.
closed lunch in July and August - **M** 280/410 and a la carte 380/520
Spec. Noix de St-Jacques rôties, fondue de mâche et flan de langues d'oursins (season). Trilogie de poissons au beurre de crustacés. Ravioli de chocolat, crémeux tiède à la pistache.

Le Saint Benoit, 10 ter av. Costa ☏ 93 25 02 34, Fax 93 30 52 64, ≤ port and Monaco, - . AE GB JCB
closed 13 December-6 January and Monday - **M** 165/230.

Polpetta, 6 av. Roqueville ☏ 93 50 67 84 - GB
closed 15 to 31 October, 1 to 21 February, Saturday lunch and Tuesday - **M** Italian rest. 150.

at Monte-Carlo-Beach (06 Alpes-Mar.) at 2,5 km - ✉ 06190 Roquebrune-Cap-Martin :

Monte-Carlo Beach H. M, ☏ 93 28 66 66, Telex 462010, Fax 93 78 14 18, ≤ sea and Monaco, « Fashionable resort with bathing facilities », - rm . AE GB JCB. rest
19 May-10 October - **M** a la carte 260/420 - 140 - **44 rm** 2300/2500.

Send us your comments on the restaurants we recommend
and your opinion on the specialities
and local wines they offer.

NICE P 06000 Alpes-Mar. 84 ⑨ ⑩ 115 ㉖ ㉗ – pop. 342 439 alt. 5 – Casino Ruhl FZ.

See : Site★★ – Promenade des Anglais★★ EFZ – Old Nice★ : Château ≤★★ JZ, Interior★ of church of St-Martin-St-Augustin HY **D** – Balustraded staircase★ of the Palais Lascaris HZ **K**, Interior★ of Ste-Reparate Cathedral – HZ **L**, St-Jacques Church★ HZ **N**, Decoration★ of St-Giaume's Chapel HZ **R** – Mosaic★ by Chagall in Law Faculty DZ **U** – Cimiez : Monastery★ (Masterpieces★★ of the early Nice School in the church) HV **Q**, Roman Ruins★ HV – Museums : Marc Chagall★★ GX, Matisse★ HV **M2**, Fine Arts Museum★★ DZ **M**, Masséna★ FZ **M1** – International Naive Style Museum★ – Carnival★★★ (before Shrove Tuesday) – Mount Alban ≤★★ 5 km – Mount Boron ≤★ 3 km – St-Pons Church★ : 3 km.

Envir. : St-Michel Plateau ≤★★ 9,5 km.

18 Biot ☎ 93 65 08 48 : 22 km.

✈ of Nice-Côte d'Azur ☎ 93 21 30 12 : 7 km.

☎ 93 87 50 50.

Office de Tourisme and Accueil de France (hotel reservations - not more than 7 days in advance) av. Thiers ☎ 93 87 07 07, Telex 460042 ; 5 av. Gustave-V ☎ 93 87 60 60 and Nice-Ferber near the Airport ☎ 93 83 32 64 – A.C. 9 r. Massenet ☎ 93 87 18 17.

Paris 932 – Cannes 32 – Genova 194 – Lyons 472 – Marseilles 188 – Turin 220.

Plans on following pages

Négresco, 37 promenade des Anglais ☎ 93 88 39 51, Telex 460040, Fax 93 88 35 68, ≤, « Empire and Napoléon III furniture » – rest – 50 - 400. AE GB JCB FZ **k**
M see **Chantecler** below - **La Rotonde M** a la carte 190/330 – 110 – **132 rm** 1550/2250, 18 suites.

Palais Maeterlinck M, 6 km by Inferior Corniche ✉ 06300 ☎ 92 00 72 00, Fax 92 00 72 10, ≤ sea, kitchenette rm – 25. AE GB.
closed 3 January-16 February – **M** *(closed Sunday dinner and Monday)* 220/370 – 80 – **22 rm** 1800/3500, 6 suites.

Sofitel M, 2-4 parvis de l'Europe ✉ 06300 ☎ 92 00 80 00, Fax 93 26 27 00, « Roof-top swimming pool, ≤ Nice » – rm – 60. AE GB JX **t**
M 120 b.i./350 b.i. – 75 – **152 rm** 830.

Sofitel Splendid, 50 bd V. Hugo ☎ 93 16 41 00, Telex 460938, Fax 93 87 02 46, « Roof-top swimming pool ≤ Nice » – rm – 30 - 100. AE GB JCB. rest FYZ **g**
M 140 – 75 – **113 rm** 790/1060, 14 suites.

Abela H. M, 223 promenade des Anglais ☎ 93 37 17 17, Telex 461635, Fax 93 71 21 71, « Roof-top swimming pool ≤ bay », – rm – 400. AE GB JCB DZ **a**
Les Mosaïques M 165/175 – **La Piscine** – **grill** *(open 15 June-15 September)* **M** 148/188 – 85 – **320 rm** 1095/1395, 12 suites.

Élysée Palace M, 59 promenade des Anglais ☎ 93 86 06 06, Telex 970336, Fax 93 44 50 40, « Roof-top swimming pool ≤ Nice », – – 45. AE GB. rest EZ **d**
M 180/270 – 95 – **143 rm** 1000/1950, 4 suites.

Holiday Inn M, 20 bd V. Hugo ☎ 93 16 55 00, Telex 461630, Fax 93 16 55 55, – rm – 100. AE GB JCB. FY **a**
M *(closed Sunday)* 170 – 80 – **129 rm** 810/960.

Méridien M, 1 promenade des Anglais ☎ 93 82 25 25, Telex 470361, Fax 93 16 08 90, « Roof-top swimming pool, ≤ bay » – – 400. AE GB FZ **d**
L'Habit Blanc *(closed Sunday and Monday in July-August)* **M** 180/240 – **La Terrasse** *(May-September)* **M** a la carte 180/380 – 95 – **314 rm** 1130/3300.

Plaza Concorde, 12 av. Verdun ☎ 93 87 80 41, Telex 461443, Fax 93 82 50 70, ≤, « Roof-top terrace » – – 30 - 400. AE GB JCB GZ **f**
M 100/130 – 80 – **183 rm** 800/1500, 10 suites.

Beau Rivage M, 24 r. St-François-de-Paule ✉ 06300 ☎ 93 80 80 70, Telex 462708, Fax 93 80 55 77, – rm – 40. AE GB JCB. rest GZ **y**
M *(closed dinner Saturday and Sunday)* a la carte 200/300 – 89 – **98 rm** 850/1050, 10 suites.

Westminster Concorde, 27 promenade des Anglais ☎ 93 88 29 44, Telex 460872, Fax 93 82 45 35, ≤, – – 40 - 350. AE GB JCB. FZ **m**
Le Farniente *(closed Sunday November-March) (dinner only in July and August)* **M** a la carte 210/400 – 75 – **105 rm** 700/1200.

West End, 31 promenade des Anglais ☎ 93 88 79 91, Telex 460879, Fax 93 88 85 07, ≤, – – 150. AE GB JCB FZ **p**
M 165/290 – 80 – **130 rm** 500/1300, 5 suites.

Pullman Nice without rest, 28 av. Notre-Dame ✆ 93 13 36 36, Telex 470662, Fax 93 62 61 69, « Hanging garden on 2nd floor, on 8th floor, ≤ » – 25 - 120. AE GB FXY **q**
70 – **200 rm** 590/930.

La Pérouse, 11 quai Rauba-Capéu ✉ 06300 ✆ 93 62 34 63, Telex 461411, Fax 93 62 59 41, « ≤ Nice and Baie des Anges », – rm – 25. AE GB JCB. rest HZ **k**
M grill *(15 May-16 September)* a la carte 190/230 – 75 – **62 rm** 460/1150, 3 suites.

Park, 6 av. de Suède ✆ 93 87 80 25, Telex 970176, Fax 93 82 29 27, ≤ – – 100. AE GB JCB FZ **x**
Le Passage *(closed Sunday)* **M** 120/160 – 75 – **131 rm** 650/1250.

Atlantic, 12 bd V. Hugo ✆ 93 88 40 15, Telex 460840, Fax 93 88 68 60, – – 30 - 80. AE GB JCB FY **d**
M 130/150 – 65 – **123 rm** 600/850.

Novotel M, 8-10 Parvis de l'Europe ✉ 06300 ✆ 93 13 30 93, Telex 460243, Fax 93 13 09 04, – rm – 90. AE GB JX **v**
M a la carte approx. 160 – 50 – **173 rm** 510/575.

Mercure-Altea Masséna M without rest, 58 r. Gioffredo ✆ 93 85 49 25, Telex 470192, Fax 93 62 43 27 – rm . AE GB GZ **k**
60 – **116 rm** 520/830.

Grand H. Aston, 12 av. F. Faure ✆ 93 80 62 52, Telex 470290, Fax 93 80 40 02, « Roof-top terrace » – – 80. AE GB HZ **u**
Le Café de l'Horloge **M** 99/250 – 70 – **156 rm** 600/900.

La Malmaison, 48 bd V. Hugo ✆ 93 87 62 56, Telex 470410, Fax 93 16 17 99 – rm . AE GB JCB FYZ **e**
M *(closed November, Sunday dinner and Monday)* 120/230 – 35 – **50 rm** 540/950.

Ambassador without rest, 8 av. Suède ✆ 93 87 90 19, Telex 460025, Fax 93 82 14 90 – . AE GB JCB FZ **x**
closed December and January – 50 – **45 rm** 570/850.

Frantour Napoléon without rest, 6 r. Grimaldi ✆ 93 87 70 07, Telex 460949, Fax 93 16 17 80, – . AE GB FZ **r**
55 – **83 rm** 500/800.

Petit Palais without rest, 10 av. E. Bieckert ✆ 93 62 19 11, Telex 462233, Fax 93 62 53 60, ≤ Nice and sea – . AE GB HX **p**
50 – **25 rm** 480/680.

Victoria without rest, 33 bd V. Hugo ✆ 93 88 39 60, Telex 461337, Fax 93 88 39 60, – . AE GB JCB FYZ **z**
39 rm 570/660.

Lausanne without rest, 36 r. Rossini ✆ 93 88 85 94, Telex 461269, Fax 93 88 15 88 – FY **t**
36 rm.

Windsor, 11 r. Dalpozzo ✆ 93 88 59 35, Telex 970072, Fax 93 88 94 57, – rm . AE GB. rest FZ **f**
M coffee shop *(closed Sunday)* a la carte 175/195 – 40 – **60 rm** 405/650.

Apogia M without rest, 26 r. Smolett ✉ 06300 ✆ 93 89 18 88, Telex 461118, Fax 93 89 16 06 – . AE GB JY **e**
50 – **101 rm** 650.

Gounod without rest, 3 r. Gounod ✆ 93 88 26 20, Telex 461705, Fax 93 88 23 84 – . AE GB JCB FYZ **g**
30 – **44 rm** 490/580, 6 suites.

Vendôme M without rest, 26 r. Pastorelli ✆ 93 62 00 77, Telex 461762, Fax 93 13 40 78 – . AE GB GY **f**
40 – **56 rm** 495/560.

Alexandra without rest, 41 r. Lamartine ✆ 93 62 14 43, Telex 461802, Fax 93 62 30 34 – . AE GB. GX **u**
45 – **53 rm** 435/515.

Agata without rest, 46 bd Carnot ✉ 06300 ✆ 93 55 97 13, Telex 462426, Fax 93 55 67 38, ≤ – rm . AE GB JZ **s**
40 – **45 rm** 400/550.

Oasis without rest, 23 r. Gounod ✆ 93 88 12 29, Fax 93 16 14 40, – . AE GB JCB FY **r**
38 – **37 rm** 340/420.

Trianon without rest, 15 av. Auber ✆ 93 88 30 69, Telex 970984, Fax 93 88 11 35 – . AE GB FY **u**
28 – **32 rm** 260/320.

Marbella without rest, 120 bd Carnot ✉ 06300 ✆ 93 89 39 35, Fax 92 04 22 56, ≤ – . AE GB.
28 – **17 rm** 230/430.

NICE

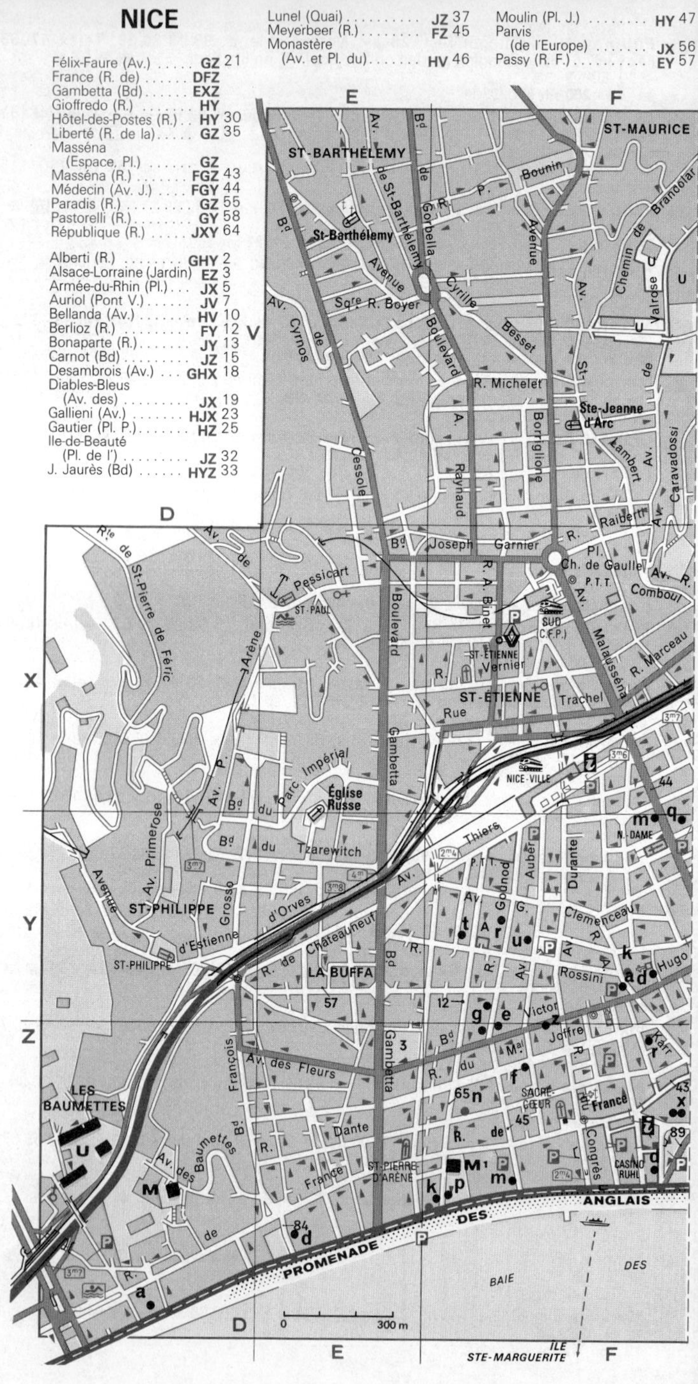

E
F
D
V
X
Y
Z
ST-BARTHÉLEMY
St-Barthélemy
ST-MAURICE
Av. de St-Barthélemy
Bd de Gorbella
R. P. Bounin
Avenue Cyrille Besset
Chemin de Brancolar
Valrose
Sq^re R. Boyer
Av. de Cyrnos
Boulevard
R. Michelet
Ste-Jeanne d'Arc
Av. Borriglione
A. Raynaud
Cessole
Lambert
Av. Caravadossi
Bd Joseph Garnier
R. Raiberti
Pl. Ch. de Gaulle
P.T.T.
Av. R. Comboul
Rte de St-Pierre de Féric
Av. de Pessicart
ST-PAUL
Arène
Boulevard Gambetta
R. A. Binet
SUD C.F.P.
ST-ÉTIENNE
R. Vernier
Rue Trachel
Av. Malaussena
R. Marceau
NICE-VILLE
Av. P.
Bd du Parc Impérial
Église Russe
Bd du Tzarewitch
Av. Thiers
N.-DAME
Av. Primerose
Avenue
ST-PHILIPPE
Grosso
d'Estienne d'Orves
Av. G. Gounod
Auber
Durante
Clemenceau
R. de Châteauneuf
LA BUFFA
57
R. Rossini
Hugo
Victor
Bd Joffre
Bd Mal
François
Av. des Fleurs
Bd Gambetta
R. du
Karr
SACRÉ-CŒUR
R. de France
R. Dante
Congrès
CASINO RUHL
LES BAUMETTES
Av. des Baumettes
ST-PIERRE D'ARÈNE
PROMENADE DES ANGLAIS
BAIE DES
ÎLE STE-MARGUERITE
0
300 m

hocéens (Av. des) . . . . GZ 59
ivoli (R. de) . . . . FZ 65
t-François
de Paule (R.) . . . . . . GHZ 72

St-Jean
Baptiste (Av.) . . . . HY 73
Saleya (Cours) . . . . HZ 82
Sauvan (R. H.) . . . . EZ 84

Verdun (Av. de) . . . . . . FGZ 89
Walesa
(Bd Lech) . . . . JYZ 91
Wilson (Pl.) . . . . HY 92

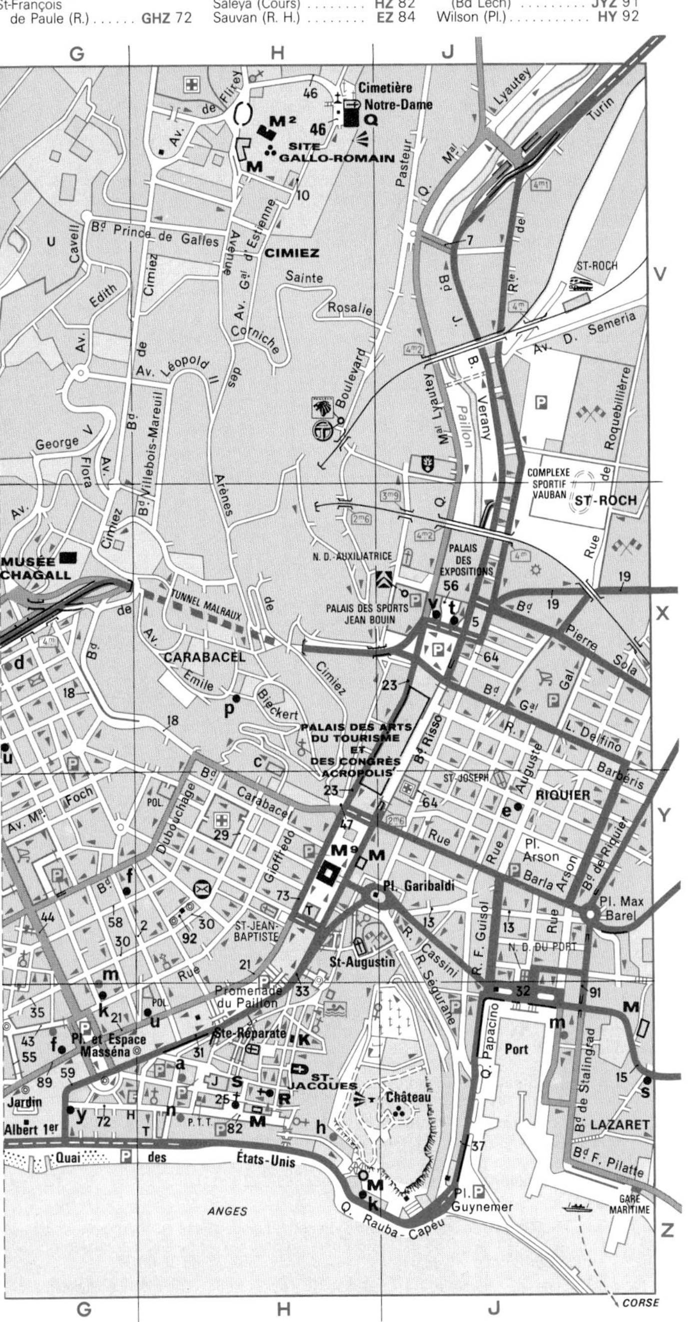

XXXXX ✿✿ **Chantecler** - Hôtel Négresco, 37 promenade des Anglais ✆ 93 88 39 51, Telex 460040, Fax 93 88 35 68 – ▤. AE ⓓ GB JCB FZ **k**
closed mid November-mid December – **M** 250 b.i./550 and a la carte 400/600
Spec. Ravioli ouvert aux artichauts et langoustines à l'huile d'olive (1 January-15 May). Filet de Saint-Pierre au jus de ratatouille et palets d'aubergines. Filets de rouget en aïoli. Wines Côtes de Provence.

XXX ✿ **Florian** (Gillon), 22 r. A. Karr ✆ 93 88 86 60, Fax 93 87 31 98 – ▤. GB FY **k**
closed 13 July-1 September, Saturday lunch and Sunday – **M** 250/350 and a la carte 270/350
Spec. Pastilla de pied de porc aux truffes. Ravioles de daube niçoise. Pigeon de Bresse confit. Wines Bellet, Côtes de Provence.

XXX **L'Ane Rouge,** 7 quai Deux-Emmanuel ✉ 06300 ✆ 93 89 49 63 – AE ⓓ GB JCB JZ **m**
closed 20 July-1 September, Saturday, Sunday and Bank Holidays – **M** a la carte 370/520.

XXX **La Toque Blanche,** 40 r. Buffa ✆ 93 88 38 18 – ▤. AE ⓓ GB FZ **n**
closed Sunday dinner and Monday – **M** (booking essential) 140/160.

XX **Les Dents de la Mer,** 2 r. St-François-de-Paule ✉ 06300 ✆ 93 80 99 16, Fax 93 85 05 78, ☂, « Unusual decor depicting a submerged galleon » – ▤. AE ⓓ GB JCB HZ **n**
M Seafood 145/255.

XX **Boccaccio,** 7 r. Masséna ✆ 93 87 71 76, Fax 93 82 09 06, « Carvel decor » – ▤. AE ⓓ GB
M Seafood - a la carte 260/360. GZ **f**

XX **Flo,** 4 r. S. Guitry ✆ 93 80 70 10, Fax 93 62 37 79, brasserie – ▤. AE ⓓ GB GYZ **m**
M 99 b.i./145 b.i..

XX **Don Camillo,** 5 r. Ponchettes ✉ 06300 ✆ 93 85 67 95 – ▤. GB HZ **h**
closed Sunday and Monday – **M** 180.

X **Mireille,** 19 bd Raimbaldi ✆ 93 85 27 23 – ▤. GB GX **d**
closed 7 June-9 July, Monday and Tuesday except Bank Holidays – **M** One dish only : paella a la carte approx. 140.

X **La Merenda,** 4 r. Terrasse ✉ 06300 HZ **a**
closed August, February, Saturday, Sunday and Monday – **M** Specialities of Nice - a la carte 150/180.

at the airport : 7 km - ✉ 06200 Nice :

Holiday Inn M, 179 bd R. Cassin ✆ 93 83 91 92, Telex 970202, Fax 93 21 69 57, ☂, ⛱ – |‡| ⇸ rm ▤ TV ☎ ♿ ⇔ – 🏛 150. AE ⓓ GB JCB
M 95/150 ♁ – ☕ 78 – **150 rm** 850/950.

Nice Arenas M, 455 promenade des Anglais ✆ 93 21 22 50, Telex 461660, Fax 93 21 63 50 – |‡| ⇸ rm ▤ TV ☎ ♿ P – 🏛 200. AE ⓓ GB
M 90/225 – ☕ 47 – **130 rm** 480/580.

Campanile M, 459 promenade des Anglais ✆ 93 21 20 20, Telex 461640, Fax 93 83 83 96 – |‡| ▤ TV ☎ ♿ ⇔ – 🏛 25 - 80. AE GB
M 88 b.i./115 b.i. – ☕ 30 – **170 rm** 370.

St-Martin-du-Var

06670 Alpes-Mar. 84 ⑨, 195 ⑯ – pop. 1 869 alt. 122 – Nice 26.

XXXX ✿✿ **Jean-François Issautier,** to the S : 3 km on N 202 ✆ 93 08 10 65, Fax 93 29 19 73 – ▤ P. AE ⓓ GB
closed 2 to 10 November, mid February-mid March, Sunday (except lunch September-June) and Monday – **M** (booking essential) 260/465 and a la carte 450/600
Spec. Courgette de Gattières avec sa fleur farcie. Marinière de poissons de roche aux aromates. Rognon de veau rôti entier en casserole. Wines Bellet, Côtes de Provence.

STRASBOURG

P **67000** B.-Rhin 62 ⑩ – pop. 252 338 Greater Strasbourg 429 880 alt. 140.

See : Cathedral★★★ : Astronomical clock★, ≤★ of rue Mercière CX **53** – Old City★★★ BCX : la Petite France★★ BX, Rue du Bain-aux-Plantes★★ BX **7**, Place de la Cathédrale★ CX **17**, – Maison Kammerzell★ CX **e**, Château des Rohan★ CX, Cour du Corbeau★ CX **18**, – Ponts couverts★ BX **B**, Place Kléber★ CV **53** – Barrage Vauban ✳★★ BX **D** – Mausoleum★★ in St-Thomas Church CX **E** – Hôtel de Ville★ CV **H** – Orangery★ – St-Pierre-le-Vieux Church : painted panels★, scenes of the Passion of Christ★ BV – Boat trips on the Ill river and the canals★ CX – Museums : Oeuvre N.-Dame★★★ CX **M1**, Château des Rohan (Museums★★) CX, Alsatian★ CX **M2** – Historical★ CX **M3** – Guided tours of the Port★ by boat – Palais de l'Europe★.

⛳9 ⛳9 ⛳9 at Illkirch-Graffenstaden (private) ✆ 88 66 17 22 ; ⛳18 of the Wantzenau at Wantzenau (private) ✆ 88 96 37 73 ; N by D 468 : 12 km ; ⛳18 of Kempferhof at Plobsheim ✆ 88 98 72 72, S by D 468 : 15 km.

✈ of Strasbourg International : ✆ 88 64 67 67 by D 392 : 12 km FR.

🚗 ✆ 88 22 50 50.

ℹ Office de Tourisme and Accueil de France (Information and hotel reservations, not more than 5 days in advance), 17, pl. de la Cathédrale ✆ 88 52 28 28, Telex 870860, Fax 88 52 28 29 annexes : pl. Gare ✆ 88 32 51 49 - and Pont Europe ✆ 88 61 39 23 – A.C. 5 av. Paix ✆ 88 36 04 34.

Paris 490 – Basle 145 – Bonn 360 – Bordeaux 915 – Frankfurt 218 – Karlsruhe 81 – Lille 545 – Luxembourg 223 – Lyons 485 – Stuttgart 157.

STRASBOURG

Street	Square	No.
Division Leclerc (R.)	CX	
Gdes Arcades (R. des)	CV	
Kléber (Pl.)	CV	
Maire Kuss (R. du)	BV	48
Mésange (R. de la)	CV	54
Nuée-Bleue (R. de la)	CV	
Vieux-Marché-aux-Poissons (R. du)	CX	94
22-Novembre (R. du)	BV	

Street	Square	No.
Arc-en-ciel (R. de l')	CV	3
Austerlitz (R. d')	CX	4
Bains-aux-Plantes (R.)	BX	7
Castelnau (R. Gén. de)	CV	16
Cathédrale (Pl. de la)	CX	17
Course (Pte R. de la)	BV	19
Desaix (Q.)	BV	21
Douane (R. de la)	CX	23
Finkmatt (Q.)	CV	24
Finkwiller (Q. et R.)	BX	25
Fossé-des-Tanneurs (R. du)	BX	27
Francs-Bourgeois (R. des)	CX	30
Frères Matthis (R. des)	BX	31
Frey (Q. Ch.)	CX	32
Haute-Montée (R.)	CV	40
Homme de fer (Pl.)	CV	41
Kellermann (Q.)	CV	43
Kuss (Pont)	BV	46
Mercière (R.)	CX	53
Noyer (R. du)	BV	55
Parchemin (R. du)	CV	60
Paris (Q. de)	BV	61
Pierre (R. du Fg de)	CV	62
Recollets (R. des)	CV	70
St-Jean (Quai)	BV	76
St-Michel (R.)	BX	77
Sébastopol (R. de)	BV	83
Serruriers (R. des)	CX	84
Temple Neuf (Pl. et R.)	CV	89
Turckheim (Q.)	BX	91
Vieux-Marché-aux Vins (R. du)	CX	94
1re Armée (R.)	CX	99

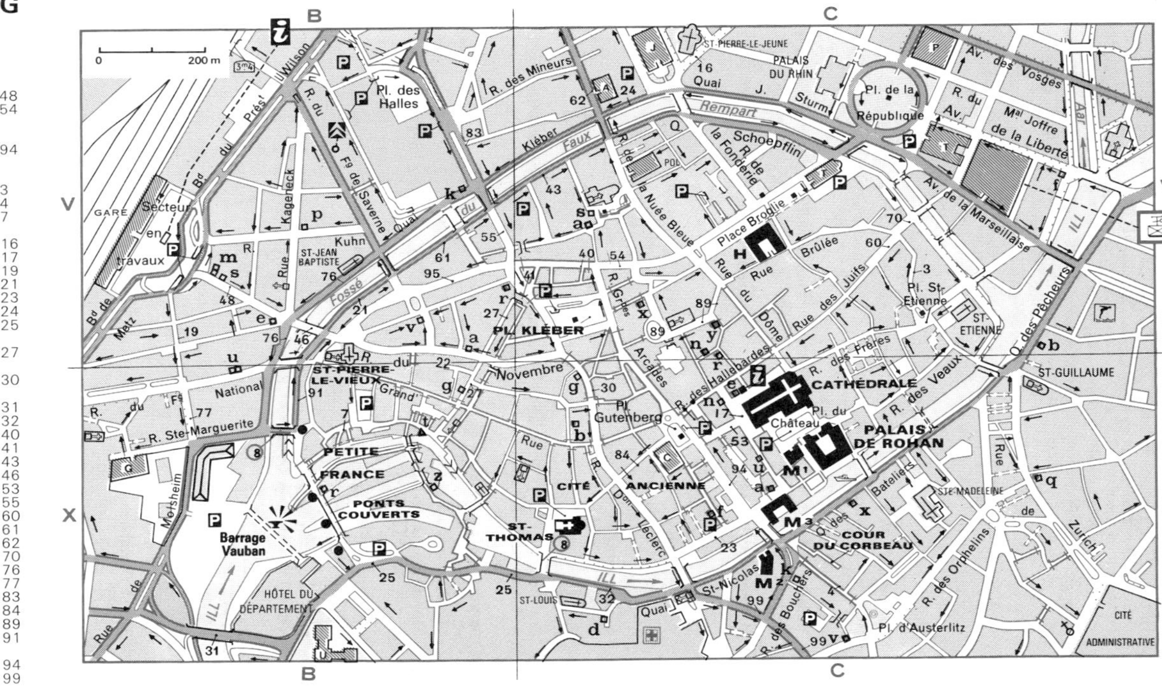

Hilton [M], av. Herrenschmidt ✆ 88 37 10 10, Telex 890363, Fax 88 36 83 27, – kitchenette rm – 30 - 350. AE GB. rest
La Maison du Bœuf ✆ 88 37 10 06 *closed August, Saturday lunch and Sunday)* **M** 165/280 – **Le Jardin** – ✆ **88 37 10 05 M** 149/162 – 90 – **241 rm** 990/1090, 5 suites.

Régent Petite France [M], 5 r. Moulins ✆ 88 76 43 43, Telex 880418, Fax 88 76 43 76, ←, , « Former ice-factory on the banks of River Ill » – rm – 60. AE GB BX **z**
M a la carte 250/330 – 80 – **61 rm** 800/1200, 7 suites, 4 duplex.

Sofitel [M], pl. St-Pierre-le-Jeune ✆ 88 32 99 30, Telex 870894, Fax 88 32 60 67, , patio – rm rest – 120. AE GB CV **s**
L'Alsace Gourmande ✆ 88 75 11 10 **M** a la carte 130/210 – 75 – **155 rm** 650/750, 3 suites.

Holiday Inn [M], 20 pl. Bordeaux ✆ 88 37 80 00, Telex 890515, Fax 88 37 07 04, , – rm – 50 - 600. AE GB JCB
La Louisiane M 170 – 75 – **170 rm** 850.

Régent Contades [M] without rest, 8 av. Liberté ✆ 88 36 26 26, Telex 890641, Fax 88 37 13 70, – rm . AE GB CV **f**
80 – **36 rm** 750/1200, 8 suites.

Beaucour [M] without rest, 5 r. Bouchers ✆ 88 76 72 00, Fax 88 76 72 60, « Tasteful decor » – – 40. AE GB CX **k**
60 – **49 rm** 550/750.

H. Maison Rouge without rest, 4 r. Francs-Bourgeois ✆ 88 32 08 60, Telex 880130, Fax 88 22 43 73, « Tasteful decor, antique furniture » – – 40. AE GB CX **g**
55 – **140 rm** 540/580.

Terminus-Plaza, 10 pl. Gare ✆ 88 32 87 00, Telex 870998, Fax 88 32 16 46 – – 60. AE GB JCB BV **m**
M 160 - **La Brasserie M** 90 – 58 – **66 rm** 250/580, 12 suites.

Monopole-Métropole without rest, 16 r. Kuhn ✆ 88 32 11 94, Telex 890366, Fax 88 32 82 55, « Alsatian and contemporary decor » – . AE GB JCB BV **p**
closed Christmas-New Year – 60 – **94 rm** 360/580.

Europe without rest, 38 r. Fossé des Tanneurs ✆ 88 32 17 88, Telex 890220, Fax 88 75 65 45, « Half timbered Alsatian house » – rm . GB JCB BX **g**
30 – **60 rm** 310/480.

Novotel [M], quai Kléber ✆ 88 22 10 99, Telex 880700, Fax 88 22 20 92, – rm rest – 30 - 200. AE GB BV **k**
M a la carte approx. 150 – 50 – **97 rm** 530/550.

Mercure [M] without rest, 25 r. Thomann ✆ 88 75 77 88, Telex 880955, Fax 88 32 08 66 – rm . AE GB CV **a**
55 – **98 rm** 530/650.

Gd Hôtel without rest, 12 pl. Gare ✆ 88 32 46 90, Telex 870011, Fax 88 32 16 50 – rm – 25. AE GB BV **m**
65 – **80 rm** 380/560.

France [M] without rest, 20 r. Jeu des Enfants ✆ 88 32 37 12, Telex 890084, Fax 88 22 48 08 – – 30. AE GB JCB BV **v**
50 – **66 rm** 390/595.

des Rohan without rest, 17 r. Maroquin ✆ 88 32 85 11, Telex 870047, Fax 88 75 65 37 – rm . AE GB CX **u**
52 – **36 rm** 350/595.

Cathédrale [M] without rest, 12 pl. Cathédrale ✆ 88 22 12 12, Telex 871054, Fax 88 23 28 00 – – 25. AE GB JCB CX **n**
48 – **32 rm** 420/750.

Royal [M] without rest, 3 r. Maire Kuss ✆ 88 32 28 71, Telex 871067, Fax 88 23 05 39, – – 40. AE GB JCB. BV **e**
59 – **52 rm** 370/505.

Dragon [M] without rest, 2 r. Ecarlate ✆ 88 35 79 80, Telex 871102, Fax 88 25 78 95 – rm . GB. CX **d**
52 – **30 rm** 420/590.

La Dauphine without rest, 30 r. 1e Armée ✆ 88 36 26 61, Telex 880766, Fax 88 35 50 07 – . GB – *closed 23 December-2 January* – 50 – **45 rm** 415/475.

Pax, 24 r. Fg National ✆ 88 32 14 54, Telex 880506, Fax 88 32 01 16, – – 25 - 100. AE GB JCB BVX **u**
accommodation : closed Christmas-New Year ; rest. : closed Sunday November-March – **M** 90/190 – 34 – **106 rm** 315/335.

Continental without rest, 14 r. Maire Kuss ✆ 88 22 28 07, Fax 88 32 22 25 – . AE GB JCB BV **s**
38 – **48 rm** 307/350.

XXXXX ✿✿✿ **Le Crocodile** (Jung), 10 r. Outre ☏ 88 32 13 02, Fax 88 75 72 01 – ▤. AE ⓓ GB. ✈
closed 11 July-2 August, 24 December-3 January, Sunday and Monday – **M** 380 and a la carte 450/560 CV **x**
Spec. Flan de cresson aux cuisses de grenouilles. Sandre rôti à l'anguille fumée et laitance de carpe. Streusel aux Granny Smith et fruits épicés. Wines Riesling, Tokay-Pinot gris.

XXXX ✿✿ **Buerehiesel** (Westermann), set in the Orangery Park ☏ 88 61 62 24, Fax 88 61 32 00, « Attractive Alsatian mansion in a park » – ▤ ⓟ. AE ⓓ GB JCB
closed 11 to 26/08, 23/12-5/01, February Holidays, Tuesday (except lunch May-October) and Wednesday – **M** 280 (lunch)/530 and a la carte 380/550
Spec. Langue, cervelle et fritot de tête de veau en vinaigrette. Schniederspäetle et cuisses de grenouilles poêlées au cerfeuil. Noisettes de chevreuil au jus de vin rouge et späetzle (June-late January). Wines Pinot Auxerrois, Riesling.

XXX **Maison Kammerzell and H. Baumann** Ⓜ with rm, 16 pl. Cathédrale ☏ 88 32 42 14, Telex 891012, Fax 88 23 03 92, « Attractive 16C Alsatian house » – |‡| ▤ rm TV ☎ – 🏛 120. AE ⓓ GB – **M** 190/260 – ☐ 55 – **9 rm** 420/630. CX **e**

XXX **Valentin Sorg,** 6 pl. Homme de Fer (14th floor) ☏ 88 32 12 16, Fax 88 32 40 62, ≤ Strasbourg – ▤. AE GB – *closed Saturday lunch and Sunday* – **M** 170/380. BV **r**

XXX **Maison des Tanneurs dite "Gerwerstub",** 42 r. Bain aux Plantes ☏ 88 32 79 70, « Old Alsatian house on the banks of the River Ill » – AE ⓓ GB BX **t**
closed 18 July-August, 24 December-25 January, Sunday and Monday – **M** a la carte 200/290.

XXX **Zimmer,** 8 r. Temple Neuf ☏ 88 32 35 01, Fax 88 32 42 28, 余 – AE ⓓ GB CV **y**
closed 1 to 22 August, 1 to 8 January, Saturday lunch and Sunday – **M** 135/390.

XXX **Estaminet Schloegel,** 19 r. Krutenau ☏ 88 36 21 98 – ▤. AE GB CX **q**
closed 10 to 24 July, Sunday and Monday – **M** 190/280.

XX ✿ **Julien,** 22 quai Bateliers ☏ 88 36 01 54, Fax 88 35 40 14 – ▤. AE ⓓ GB CX **x**
closed 1 to 22 August, 24 December-2 January, Saturday lunch and Sunday – **M** 190 (lunch)/420 and a la carte 290/400
Spec. Foie de canard gras d'Alsace poêlé à la rhubarbe (April-October). Croustillant de saumon au beurre rouge. Lotte en croûte de saumon fumé au jus de viande. Wines Tokay-Pinot gris.

XX **Au Gourmet Sans Chiqué,** 15 r. Ste Barbe ☏ 88 32 04 07, Fax 88 22 42 40 – ▤. AE ⓓ GB – *closed 1 to 18 August, Monday lunch and Sunday* – **M** 240/350. CX **b**

XX **Buffet Gare,** pl. Gare ☏ 88 32 68 28, Fax 88 32 88 34 – AE ⓓ GB BV
L'Argentoratum M 90/150 – **L'Assiette M** 66.

XX **Bec Doré,** 8 quai Pêcheurs ☏ 88 35 39 57 – ▤. AE ⓓ GB CV **b**
closed Monday and Tuesday – **M** 150.

X **Ami Schutz,** 1 r. Ponts Couverts ☏ 88 32 76 98, Fax 88 32 38 40, 余 – AE GB BX **r**
M 155/179 b.i..

Winstubs : Regional specialities and wine tasting in a typical Alsatian atmosphere :

X **Zum Strissel,** 5 pl. Gde Boucherie ☏ 88 32 14 73, Fax 88 32 70 24, rustic decor – ▤. GB CX **a**
closed 8 July-2 August, 25 February-8 March, Sunday and Monday – **M** 56/130.

X **S'Burjerstuewel (Chez Yvonne),** 10 r. Sanglier ☏ 88 32 84 15 – GB CVX **r**
closed 11 July-8 August – **M** (booking essential) a la carte 145/190.

X **Le Clou,** 3 r. Chaudron ☏ 88 32 11 67 – ▤. GB CV **n**
closed 15 to 31 August, 1 December-7 January and Sunday – **M** (dinner only) a la carte 160/260.

at La Wantzenau : NE by D 468 : 12 km – pop. 4 394 – ✉ 67610 :

🏨 **Hôtel Le Moulin** Ⓜ 🦢, S : 1,5 km by D 468 ☏ 88 96 27 83, Fax 88 96 68 32, ≤, « Old watermill on a branch of the River Ill », 🌳 – |‡| TV ☎ ⓟ. AE GB
closed 24 December-2 January – **M** see **Au Moulin** below – ☐ 42 – **19 rm** 290/390.

🏨 **A la Gare** without rest, 32 r. Gare ☏ 88 96 63 44 – TV ☎ ⓟ. GB
closed 8 to 22 August – ☐ 28 – **18 rm** 200/260.

XXX **Relais de la Poste** Ⓜ with rm, 21 r. Gén. de Gaulle ☏ 88 96 20 64, Fax 88 96 36 84, 余, 🌳 – |‡| ▤ TV ☎ ♿ ⓟ. AE ⓓ GB
closed 23 December-15January – **M** *(closed 31 July-12 August, lunch Saturday and Monday and Sunday dinner* 215/380 – ☐ 50 – **17 rm** 250/400.

XXX **A la Barrière,** 3 rte Strasbourg ☏ 88 96 20 23, Fax 88 96 25 59, 余 – ⓟ. AE ⓓ GB
closed 11 August-3 September, 23 February-10 March, Tuesday dinner and Wednesday – **M** (Sunday : booking essential) 175/250.

XXX **Zimmer,** 23 r. Héros ☏ 88 96 62 08 – AE ⓓ GB
closed 18 July-11 August, 17 January-3 February, Sunday dinner and Monday – **M** 135/330.

XX **Rest. Au Moulin** - Hôtel Au Moulin, S : 1,5 km by D 468 ☏ 88 96 20 01, Fax 88 96 68 32, 余, « Floral garden » – ▤ ⓟ. AE ⓓ GB
closed 26 June-20 July, 15 to 30 January, Wednesday, dinner Sunday and Bank Holidays – **M** 140/345.

XX **Schaeffer,** 1 quai Bateliers ☏ 88 96 20 29, 余 – ⓟ. AE ⓓ GB
closed 12 to 27 July, 23 December-11 January, Sunday dinner and Monday – **M** 135/260.

Colmar 🅿 68000 H.-Rhin 62 ⑲ – pop. 63 498 alt. 193.
Strasbourg 70.

XXXX ✿✿ **Schillinger,** 16 r. Stanislas ✆ 89 41 43 17, Fax 89 24 28 87, « Fine decor » – ▤. AE ⓓ GB
closed 5 to 26 July, Sunday dinner and Monday except Bank Holidays – **M** 270/500 and a la carte 270/410 ♁
Spec. Foie gras truffé. Ravioles de foie de canard fumé. Caneton au citron. Wines Pinot blanc, Riesling.

Colroy-la-Roche 67420 B.-Rhin 62 ⑧ – pop. 435 alt. 424.
Strasbourg 62.

✿✿ **Host. La Cheneaudière** Ⓜ, ✆ 88 97 61 64, Telex 870438, Fax 88 47 21 73, ≤, « Elegant country inn, garden », – ▤ rest TV ☎ Ⓟ. AE ⓓ GB JCB
closed January and February – **M** 280 (lunch)/550 and a la carte 360/520 – ☐ 120 – **25 rm** 880/1100, 7 suites
Spec. Foie gras fumé au bois et aux fruits du genévrier. Ravioles de Munster au persil frit. Carte de venaison (season). Wines Tokay-Pinot gris, Riesling.

Illhaeusern 68 H.-Rhin 62 ⑲ – pop. 578 alt. 176 – ✉ 68150 Ribeauvillé.
Strasbourg 60.

La Clairière Ⓜ without rest, rte Guémar ✆ 89 71 80 80, Fax 89 71 86 22, – TV ☎ Ⓟ. GB – *closed January and February* – ☐ 60 – **26 rm** 420/1150.

XXXXX ✿✿✿ **Aub. de l'Ill** (Haeberlin), ✆ 89 71 83 23, Telex 871289, Fax 89 71 82 83, « Tasteful decor, on the banks of the River Ill, ≤ over floral gardens » – ▤. AE ⓓ GB
closed February, Monday (except lunch in summer) and Tuesday – **M** (booking essential) 460 (lunch)/660 and a la carte 450/600
Spec. Salade de tripes aux fèves et au foie d'oie. Ragoût de homard et tête de veau à l'orge perlé. Grande assiette d'oie "non grasse" sous toutes ses façons. Wines Sylvaner, Riesling.
H. des Berges Ⓜ, ✆ 89 71 87 87, Telex 871289, Fax 89 71 87 88, ≤, « Evocatio Resembling a tobacco shed in the Ried country », – ▤ rm TV ☎ ♿. AE ⓓ GB
closed February and Tuesday – **M** see **Aub. de l'Ill** – ☐ 90 – **11 rm** 1250/2000.

Lembach 67510 B.-Rhin 57 ⑲ – pop. 1 710 alt. 190.
Strasbourg 55.

XXXX ✿✿ **Aub. Cheval Blanc** (Mischler), ✆ 88 94 41 86, Fax 88 94 20 74, « Old coaching inn », – Ⓟ. AE GB.
closed 5 to 23 July, 31 January-18 February, Monday and Tuesday – **M** 170/390 and a la carte 270/450
Spec. Farandole de quatre foies d'oie chauds. Suprême de sandre au fumet de truffe. Médaillons de chevreuil à la moutarde et aux fruits rouges (1 June-15 February). Wines Pinot blanc.

Marlenheim 67520 B.-Rhin 62 ⑨ – pop. 2 956 alt. 184.
Strasbourg 20.

XXX ✿✿ **Le Cerf** (Husser) with rm, ✆ 88 87 73 73, Fax 88 87 68 08, – TV ☎ Ⓟ – 25. AE ⓓ GB
closed late February-early March, Tuesday and Wednesday – **M** 310/550 and a la carte 330/580 ♁ – ☐ 65 – **15 rm** 500/650
Spec. Presskopf de tête de veau poêlé, sauce gribiche. Choucroute au cochon de lait et foie gras fumé. Aumonière aux griottines et glace au fromage blanc. Wines Sylvaner.

Tours P 37000 I.-et-L. 64 ⑮ – pop. 129 509 alt. 48.

See : Cathedral quarter★★ : Cathedral★★ CY, Fine Arts Museum★★ CY **M2**, – Historial de Touraine★ (château) CY, The Psalette★ CY **F**, Place Grégoire de Tours★ CY 20 – Old Tours★★ : Place Plumereau★ AY , hôtel Gouin★ AY **M4**, rue Briçonnet★ AY 3 – St-Julien quarter★ : Craft Guilds Museum★★ (Musée du Compagnonnage) BY **M5**, Beaune-Semblançay Garden★ BY **B**, – St-Cosme Priory★ W : 3 km – Meslay Tithe Barn★ (Grange de Meslay) NE : 10 km.

18 of Touraine ✆ 47 53 20 28 ; domaine de la Touche at Ballan-Miré : 14 km ; 18 of Ardrée ✆ 47 56 77 38 : 14 km.

✈ of Tours-St-Symphorien : T.A.T ✆ 47 54 19 46, NE : 7 km.

ℹ Office de Tourisme and Accueil de France (Informations, exchange facilities and hotel reservations - not more than 5 days in advance) bd Heurteloup ✆ 47 05 58 08, Telex 750008 – Automobile Club de l'Ouest 4 pl. J. Jaurès ✆ 47 05 50 19.

Paris 234 – Angers 109 – Bordeaux 346 – Chartres 140 – Clermont-Ferrand 335 – Limoges 220 – Le Mans 80 – Orléans 115 – Rennes 219 – St-Étienne 474.

Plans on following pages

✿✿ **Jean Bardet** M, 57 r. Groison ✉ 37100 ✆ 47 41 41 11, Telex 752463, Fax 47 51 68 72, ≤, « Park », – AE GB JCB.
closed 20 February-9 March – **M** *(closed Monday except dinner April-October and Sunday dinner November-March except Bank Holidays)* 300/850 and a la carte 500/800 – ☕ 110 – **16 rm** 700/1300, 5 suites
Spec. Symphonie de champignons au sot-l'y-laisse. Pintadeau fermier truffé et Parmentier de charlotte. Gésier de canard et homard rôti au vin de Graves. Wines Vouvray moelleux, Saint Nicolas de Bourgueil.

Univers and rest. La Touraine, 5 bd Heurteloup ✆ 47 05 37 12, Telex 751460, Fax 47 61 51 80, « Murals depicting past famous visitors » – rm – 70. AE GB — BZ **u**
M *(closed Saturday)* 180/220 – ☕ 60 – **84 rm** 650/750, 8 suites.

H. de Groison and rest. Jardin du Castel, 16 r. Groison ✉ 37100 ✆ 47 41 94 40, Fax 47 51 50 28, « Former 18C mansion », – AE GB JCB
closed 21 November-5 December and 10 to 30 January – **M** *(closed Monday lunch and Sunday 15/11-15/4 and Tuesday lunch and Monday 15/4-15/11* 235/450 – ☕ 85 – **10 rm** 490/910.

Alliance, 292 av. Grammont ✉ 37200 ✆ 47 28 00 80, Telex 750922, Fax 47 27 77 61, – rm – 200. AE GB JCB
M a la carte 170/320 – ☕ 60 – **119 rm** 440/515, 6 suites.

Harmonie M, 15 r. F. Joliot-Curie ✆ 47 66 01 48, Telex 752587, Fax 47 61 66 38 – – 40. AE GB JCB — CZ **b**
closed mid December-mid January, Saturday and Sunday except accomodation late February-15 November) – **M** (dinner only) 110 – ☕ 50 – **48 rm** 400/450, 6 suites.

Royal M without rest, 65 av. Grammont ✆ 47 64 71 78, Telex 752006, Fax 47 05 84 62 – – 60. AE GB
☕ 38 – **50 rm** 322/382.

Holiday Inn M, 15 r. Ed. Vaillant ✆ 47 31 12 12, Fax 47 38 53 35 – rm – 30. AE GB. rest — CZ **m**
M 75/180 – ☕ 50 – **104 rm** 460/515.

Bordeaux, 3 pl. Mar. Leclerc ✆ 47 05 40 32, Telex 750414, Fax 47 64 05 72 – – 35. AE GB — BZ **t**
M 140/162 – ☕ 39 – **55 rm** 310/485.

Mercure M, 4 pl. Thiers ✆ 47 05 50 05, Telex 752740, Fax 47 20 22 07 – rm – 70. AE GB
M a la carte 185/305 – ☕ 50 – **120 rm** 430/600.

Le Francillon M, 9 r. Bons Enfants ✆ 47 66 44 66, Fax 47 66 17 18, – . AE GB
M *(closed Saturday lunch)* 190/390 – ☕ 45 – **10 rm** 380/440. — AY **s**

Mirabeau without rest, 89 bis bd Heurteloup ✆ 47 05 24 60, Fax 47 05 31 09 – . AE GB JCB — CZ **e**
☕ 30 – **25 rm** 250/310.

Le Manoir without rest, 2 r. Traversière ✆ 47 05 37 37, Fax 47 20 10 42 – . AE GB — CY **h**
☕ 30 – **20 rm** 240/320.

Central H. without rest, 21 r. Berthelot ✆ 47 05 46 44, Telex 751173, Fax 47 66 10 26 – . AE GB – ☕ 40 – **41 rm** 300/400. — BY **k**

Criden without rest, 65 bd Heurteloup ✆ 47 20 81 14, Fax 47 39 05 12 – . AE GB JCB – ☕ 33 – **33 rm** 273/337. — CZ **g**

Fimotel M, 247 r. Giraudeau ✆ 47 37 00 36, Fax 47 38 50 91 – – 40. AE GB
M 75/105 – ☕ 34 – **47 rm** 280/350.

TOURS

Bordeaux (R. de)	BZ	
Commerce (R. du)	AY	22
Grammont (Av. de)	BZ	
Halles (Pl. et R.)	AY	
Marceau (R.)	ABYZ	
Nationale (R.)	BYZ	
Scellerie (R. de la)	BY	
Bretonneau (R.)	AY	10
Briçonnet (R.)	AY	12
Carmes (Pl. des)	AY	16
Châteauneuf (R. de)	AY	18
Constantine (R. de)	AY	23
Courrier (R. L.)	AY	25
Courteline (R. G.)	AY	27
Cygne (R. du)	BY	28
Descartes (R.)	AZ	32
Grand-Marché (Pl. du)	AY	43
Grand-Marché (R. du)	AY	44
Grégoire-de-Tours (Pl.)	CY	46
Grosse-Tour (R. de la)	AY	49
Lavoisier (R.)	BY	57
Manceau (R.)	CY	59
Merville (R. du Prés.)	AY	65
Meunier (R. Gén.)	CY	66
Monnaie (R. de la)	AY	68
Paix (R. de la)	AY	73
Petit Cupidon (R. du)	CY	77
Picou (Pl. R.)	AY	78
Racine (R.)	CY	82
Rapin (R.)	AZ	83
Victoire (Pl. de la)	AY	102

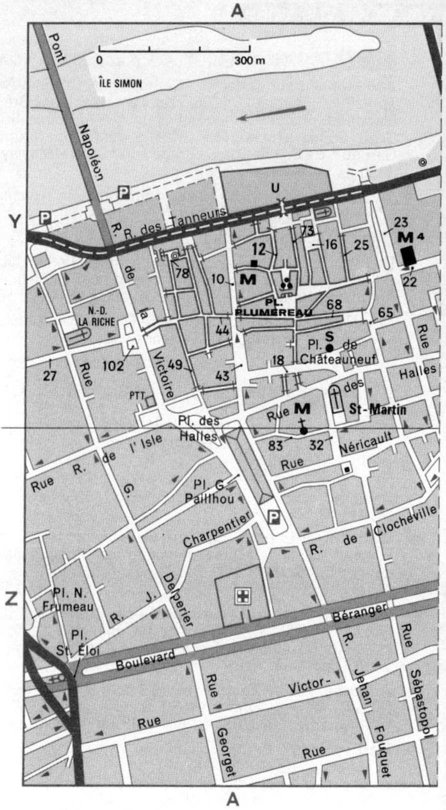

The names of main shopping streets are indicated in red at the beginning of the list of streets,

Do not lose your way in Europe. use the Michelin Main Road maps. scale: 1 inch: 16 miles.

XXXX ✿✿ **Charles Barrier,** 101 av. Tranchée ✉ 37100 ✆ 47 54 20 39, Fax 47 41 80 95 – ▤ Ⓟ. GB
closed Sunday dinner – **M** 230/560 and a la carte 360/530
Spec. Matelote d'anguille de Loire au Chinon. Canette rôtie au miel. Pied de cochon farci au ris d'agneau et truffes. Wines Vouvray, Bourgueil.

XXX ✿ **La Roche Le Roy** (Couturier), 55 rte St Avertin ✉ 37200 ✆ 47 27 22 00, Fax 47 28 08 39, 龠 – Ⓟ. AE GB
closed 29 July-23 August, February Holidays, Saturday lunch and Sunday – **M** 150/285 (lunch) and a la carte 230/340
Spec. Homard breton à la vinaigrette de corail (season). Pied de porc farci. Soufflé chaud aux fruits et liqueurs. Wines Montlouis, Chinon.

XX **Les Tuffeaux,** 19 r. Lavoisier ✆ 47 47 19 89 – ▤. GB — BY r
closed Monday lunch and Sunday – **M** 110/200.

XX **La Ruche,** 105 r. Colbert ✆ 47 66 69 83 – GB JCB — BY a
closed 24 December-15 January, Monday lunch and Sunday – **M** 80/135 ♁.

at Rochecorbon NE : by N 152 – ✉ 37210 :

🏨 ✿ **Les Hautes Roches** Ⓜ ⛟, 86 quai Loire ✆ 47 52 88 88, Telex 300121, Fax 47 52 81 30, ←, 龠, « Elegantly furnished former troglodyte dwellings » – 🛗 TV ☎ Ⓟ. AE GB
closed late January-mid March – **M** *(closed Sunday dinner and Monday from November-March)* 220/300 and a la carte 250/350 – ☕ 70 – **8 rm** 580/1100, 3 suites
Spec. Vapeur de sandre au beurre blanc nantais. Dos de rouget à la lie de vin. Mousse au caramel de vieux Vouvray en croustilles de pomme. Wines Chinon, Vouvray.

All this Guide's information can also be found on the small laser disk « Electronic Book – Michelin's EUROPE Guide » (access by portable laser disk drive, EBG standard).

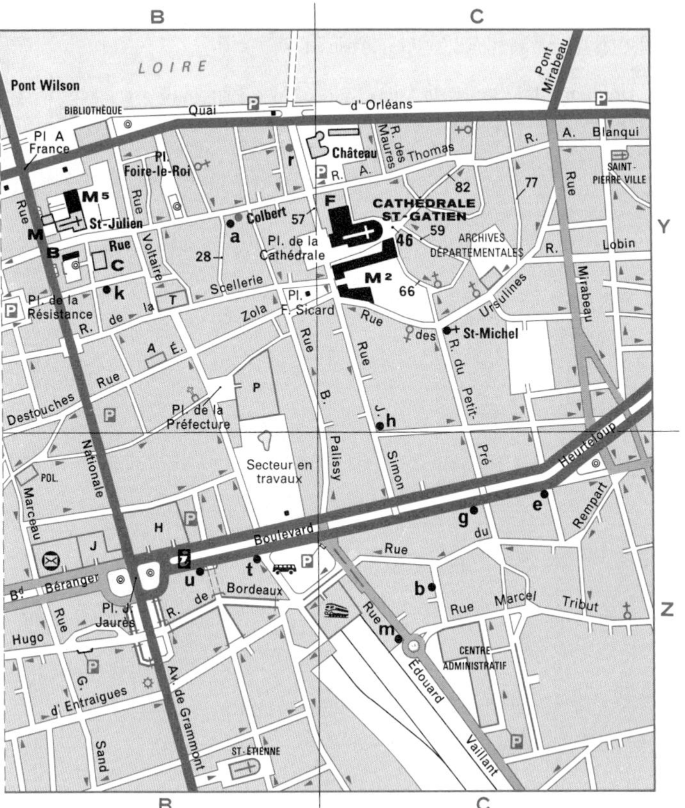

Bracieux 41250 L.-et-Ch. 64 ⑱ - pop. 1 157 alt. 81.

Tours 82.

XXXX ✿✿ **Bernard Robin,** ✆ 54 46 41 22, Fax 54 46 03 69, ⛱, 🌳 - AE GB
closed 15 December-19 January, Tuesday dinner and Wednesday - **M** (booking essential) 205 (lunch)/535 and a la carte 400/500
Spec. Salade de homard breton. Queue de bœuf en hachis parmentier. Gibier (season). Wines Vouvray, Chinon.

Montbazon 37250 I.-et-L. 64 ⑮ - pop. 3 354 alt. 71.

Tours 15.

Château d'Artigny ⛰, SW : 2 km by D 17 ✆ 47 26 24 24, Telex 750900, Fax 47 65 92 79, « Park, ≤ River Indre, riverside alodge with 8 rm », 🏋, 🏊, 🎾 - 🛗 TV ☎ P - 🏛 60. GB
closed 28 November-8 January - **M** 280/440 and a la carte 300/470 - ☕ 85 - **51 rm** 600/1575.

XXX ✿✿ **La Chancelière,** 1 pl. Marronniers ✆ 47 26 00 67, Fax 47 73 14 82, « Tasteful decor » - ▤. GB
closed 5 to 15/10, 8/2-6/3, Sunday (except lunch September-June) and Monday except Bank Holidays - **M** 350 and a la carte 310/470 - **Le Jeu de Cartes M** 230 b.i. (lunch)/250
Spec. Ravioles d'huîtres au Champagne (September-June). Sauté de homard au lard et champignon (season). Colvert aux figues fraîches (late August-October). Wines Touraine-Mesland, Vouvray.

to the W : 5 km by N 10, D 287 and D 87 - ✉ 37250 Montbazon :

XX **Moulin Fleuri** ⛰ with rm, ✆ 47 26 01 12, ≤, « Terrace overlooking the River Indre », 🌳 - TV ☎ P. AE GB
closed 1 to 9 March, February and Monday except Bank Holidays - **M** 150 - ☕ 46 - **12 rm** 170/310.

Onzain **41150** L.-et-Ch. 64 ⑯ – pop. 3 080 alt. 67.

Tours 47.

Domaine des Hauts de Loire M, NW : 3 km by D 1 and private lane ✆ 54 20 72 57, Telex 751547, Fax 54 20 77 32, « Elegant hunting lodge in a park », – 80. AE GB.
1 March-1 December – **M** *(closed Tuesday lunch and Monday in March and November)* 280/300 and a la carte 300/450 – 75 – **25 rm** 900/1300, 9 suites
Spec. Salade d'anguilles croustillantes à la vinaigrette d'échalotes (season). Mousse tiède de persil à l'huile de noisettes (season). Filet de bœuf poché au vin de Montlouis. Wines Touraine blanc, Mesland rouge.

Romorantin-Lanthenay **41200** L.-et-Ch. 64 ⑱ – pop. 17 865 alt. 88.

Tours 91.

Gd H. Lion d'Or M, 69 r. Clemenceau ✆ 54 76 00 28, Telex 750990, Fax 54 88 24 87, « Tasteful decor, floral patio » – rest – 50. AE GB JCB
closed early January-mid February – **M** (booking essential) 400 (lunch)/630 and a la carte 475/590 – 110 – **13 rm** 600/1800, 3 suites
Spec. Cuisses de grenouilles à la rocambole. Langoustines rôties à la poudre d'épices douces. Flan de poires au curry et au caramel de lait. Wines Bourgueil, Vouvray.

Germany

Deutschland

BERLIN - COLOGNE - DRESDEN
DÜSSELDORF - FRANKFURT ON MAIN
HAMBURG - HANOVER - LEIPZIG
MUNICH - STUTTGART

PRACTICAL INFORMATION

LOCAL CURRENCY

Deutsche Mark: 100 DM = 61.10 US $ = 51.28 Ecus (Jan. 93)

TOURIST INFORMATION

Deutsche Zentrale für Tourismus (DZT) :
Beethovenstr. 69, 6000 Frankfurt 1, ✆ 069/7 57 20, Fax 069/75 19 03
Hotel booking service :
Allgemeine Deutsche Zimmerreservierung (ADZ)
Corneliusstr. 34, 6000 Frankfurt 1, ✆ 069/74 07 67
Telex 416666, Fax 069/75 10 56

AIRLINES

DEUTSCHE LUFTHANSA AG: Von-Gablenz-Str. 2, 5000 Köln 21, ✆ 0221/82 60, Fax 826 38 18

AIR CANADA: 6000 Frankfurt, Friedensstr. 7, ✆ 069/23 40 32, Fax 23 61 03

AIR FRANCE: 6000 Frankfurt, Friedensstr. 11, ✆ 069/2 56 63 20, Fax 23 60 80

AMERICAN AIRLINES: 6000 Frankfurt, Wiesenhüttenplatz 26, ✆ 069/2 56 01 72, Fax 23 04 61

BRITISH AIRWAYS: 1000 Berlin 15, Kurfürstendamm 178, ✆ 030/8 800 01 10, Fax 882 41 35

JAPAN AIRLINES: 6000 Frankfurt, Roßmarkt 15, ✆ 069/1 36 00, Fax 29 57 84

SABENA: 6000 Frankfurt, Roßmarkt 10, ✆069/29 90 06 94

SAS: 6000 Frankfurt, Saonestr. 3, ✆ 069/66 44 61 50, Fax 666 83 79

TWA: 6000 Frankfurt 90, Hamburger Allee 2, ✆ 069/77 06 01, Fax 77 41 23

FOREIGN EXCHANGE

Is possible in banks, savings banks and at exchange offices.
Hours of opening from Monday to Friday 8.30am to 12.30pm and 2.30pm to 4pm except Thursday 2.30pm to 6pm.

SHOPPING

In the index of street names, those printed in red are where the principal shops are found.

BREAKDOWN SERVICE

ADAC: for the addresses see text of the towns mentioned

AvD: Lyoner Str. 16, 6000 Frankfurt 71-Niederrad, ✆ 069/6 60 60, Telex 41 12 37, Fax 069/660 62 10

In Germany the ADAC (emergency number 01308/19211), and the AvD (emergency number 0130/99 09), make a special point of assisting foreign motorists. They have motor patrols covering main roads.

TIPPING

In Germany, prices include service and taxes. You may choose to leave a tip if you wish but there is no obligation to do so.

SPEED LIMITS

The speed limit, generally, in built up areas is 50 km/h - 31 mph and on all other roads it is 100 km/h - 62mph. On motorways and dual carriageways, the recommanded speed limit is 130 km/h - 80 mph.

SEAT BELTS

The wearing of seat belts is compulsory for drivers and passengers.

Berlin

1 000. Berlin 987 ⑰ ⑱, 984 ⑮ ⑯ - Pop. 3 210 000 - alt. 40 m. - ☎ 030 (00372 fur den Ostteil).

MUSEUMS, GALLERYS

Pergamon Museum★★★ PY - Old National Gallery★ (Alte Nationalgalerie) PY **M 1** - Bode-Museum★★ PY **M 2** - Altes Museum★ PY **M3** - Museum of Decorativ Arts★ (Kunstgewerbemuseum) NZ **M 4** - New National Gallery★ (Neue Nationalgalerie) NZ **M 5** - Schoß Charlottenburg★★ (Equestrian Statue of the Great Elector★★, Historical Rooms★, Porcelain Room★★) - National Gallery★★ White Hall★ (Nationalgalerie, Weißer Saal) - Golden Gallery★★ (Goldene Galerie) EY - Antique Museum★ (Antikenmuseum) (Ancient Treasure★★★) EY **M 6** - Egyptian Museum★ (Ägyptisches Museum) (Bust of Queen Nefrititi★★) EY **M 6** - Dahlem Museums★★★ (Museum Dahlem) (Painting Gallery★★, Sculpture Department★★, Drawing and Prints Department★, Ethnographic Museum★★) by Rheinbabenallee EZ - Museum of Transport and Technology★ (Museum für Verkehr und Technik) GZ **M 8** - Käthe-Kollwitz-Museum★ LXY **M 9** - Berlin Museum★ GY - Museum of Decorative Arts★ (at Schloß Köpenick) (Kunstgewerbemuseum) by Stralauer Allee HY.

HISTORIC BUILDINGS AND MONUMENTS, STREETS, SQUARES

Brandenburg Gate★★ (Brandenburger Tor) NZ - Unter den Linden★ NPZ - Gendarmenmarkt★ PZ - State Opera House★ (Deutsche Staatsoper) PZ - Neue Wache★ PY - Arsenal★★ (Zeughaus) PY - Nikolaiviertel★ RZ - Victory Column ⋞ (Siegessäule) MX - Philharmonie★★★ NZ - Kurfürstendamm★ JLY - Martin-Gropius-Building★ NZ - Soviet Memorial★ (Sowjetisches Ehrenmal) by Köpenicker Straße HYZ - Radio Tower ⋞★ (Funkturm) EY - Olympic Stadium★ (Olympia Stadion) by Kaiserdamm EY - Nikolai Church★ (Nikolaikirche) RZ - Memorial Church (Kaiser-Wilhelm-Gedächtniskirche) (Ceilling-and Wallmosaic★ of the former Entrancehall) MX.

PARKS, GARDENS, LAKES

Zoological Park★★ (Zoologischer Garten) MX - Castle Park of Charlottenburg★ (Schloßpark Charlottenburg) (at Belvedere Historical Porcelain Exhibition★) EY - Botanical Gardens★ (Botanischer Garten) by Rheinbabenallee EZ - Grunewald Forest★ (at Grunewald Lake : Hunting Lodge) by Rheinbabenallee EZ - Havel★ and Peacook Island★ by Clay-Allee EZ - Wannsee★★ by Clay-Allee EZ.

⛳9 Berlin-Wannsee, Am Stölpchenweg, ☎ 8 05 50 75.

✈ Tegel, ☎ 4 11 01 - ✈ Schönefeld (S : 25 km), Stadtbüro, Alexanderplatz 5, ☎ 210 91 81.

🚘 Berlin - Wannsee, ☎ 8 03 20 81.

Exhibition Grounds (Messegelände), ☎ 3 03 81, Telex 182908.

ℹ Berlin Tourist-Information, Europa-Center (Budapester Straße), ☎ 2 62 60 31, Telex 183356, Fax 21 23 25 20.

ℹ Berlin Information, at Television Tower (Fernsehturm) 1020 Berlin ☎ 2 42 46 75.

ℹ Verkehrsamt at Airport Tegel ☎ 41 01 31 45

ADAC, Berlin-Wilmersdorf, Bundesallee 29 (B 31), ☎ 8 68 61, Telex 183513.

Frankfurt/Oder 105 - Hamburg 289 - Hannover 288 - Leipzig 183 - Rostock 222.

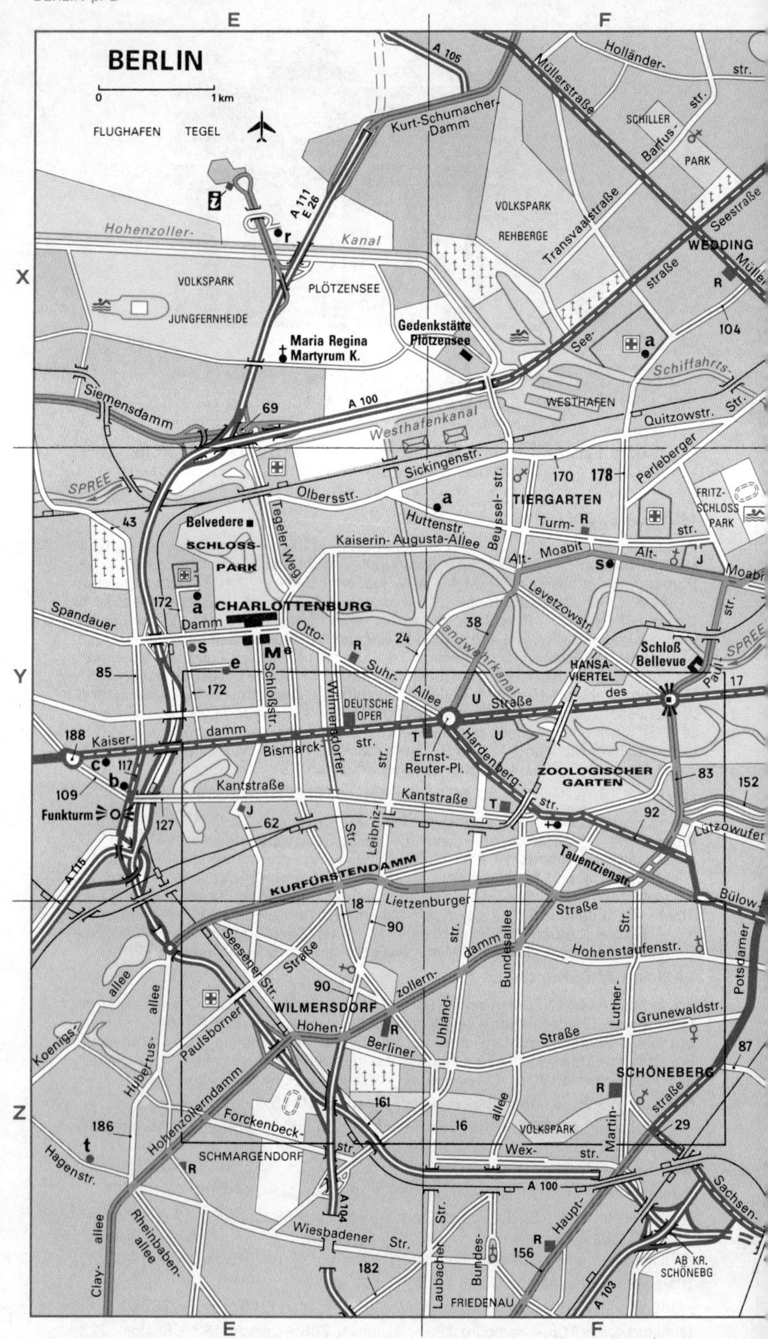
BERLIN
0
1 km
FLUGHAFEN TEGEL
E
F
X
Y
Z
A 105
Holländer-
str.
Müllerstraße
Kurt-Schumacher-Damm
SCHILLER PARK
Barfus-
str.
A 111
E 26
VOLKSPARK
REHBERGE
Transvaalstraße
Seestraße
Hohenzoller-
Kanal
WEDDING
VOLKSPARK
JUNGFERNHEIDE
PLÖTZENSEE
straße
Gedenkstätte Plötzensee
Maria Regina Martyrum K.
See-
104
Schiffahrts-
Siemensdamm
A 100
WESTHAFEN
69
Westhafenkanal
Quitzowstr.
Str.
Sickingenstr.
Perleberger
170
178
SPREE
Olbersstr.
Beussel-
str.
TIERGARTEN
FRITZ-SCHLOSS PARK
43
Belvedere
SCHLOSS-PARK
Tegeler Weg
Huttenstr.
Turm-
str.
Kaiserin-Augusta-Allee
Alt-Moabit
Alt-
Moabit
172
CHARLOTTENBURG
Levetzowstr.
Spandauer
Damm
Otto-
Suhr-
Allee
38
Landwehrkanal
str.
Schloß Bellevue
SPREE
24
HANSA-VIERTEL
Y
85
Schloßstr.
Wilmersdorfer
str.
DEUTSCHE OPER
Paul-
des
17
172
Straße
188
Kaiser-
damm
Bismarck-
str.
Ernst-Reuter-Pl.
Hardenberg-
ZOOLOGISCHER GARTEN
117
109
Funkturm
Kantstraße
Kantstraße
str.
83
152
127
62
Leibniz-
Str.
92
Lützowufer
A 115
KURFÜRSTENDAMM
Tauentzienstr.
18
Lietzenburger
Straße
Bülow-
90
Seesener Str.
Straße
Bundesallee
Str.
Hohenstaufenstr.
Potsdamer
allee
allee
90
zollern-
damm
WILMERSDORF
Uhland-
str.
Luther-
Grunewaldstr.
Koenigs-
Hubertus-
Paulsborner
Hohen-
Berliner
Straße
87
SCHÖNEBERG
Hohenzollerndamm
161
allee
Martin-
straße
29
186
Forckenbeck-
str.
16
VOLKSPARK
Hagenstr.
SCHMARGENDORF
Wex-
str.
A 100
A 104
Laubacher
Str.
Haupt-
Sachsen-
Clay-allee
Rheinbaben-allee
Wiesbadener Str.
Bundes-
156
AB KR. SCHÖNEBG
182
FRIEDENAU
A 103

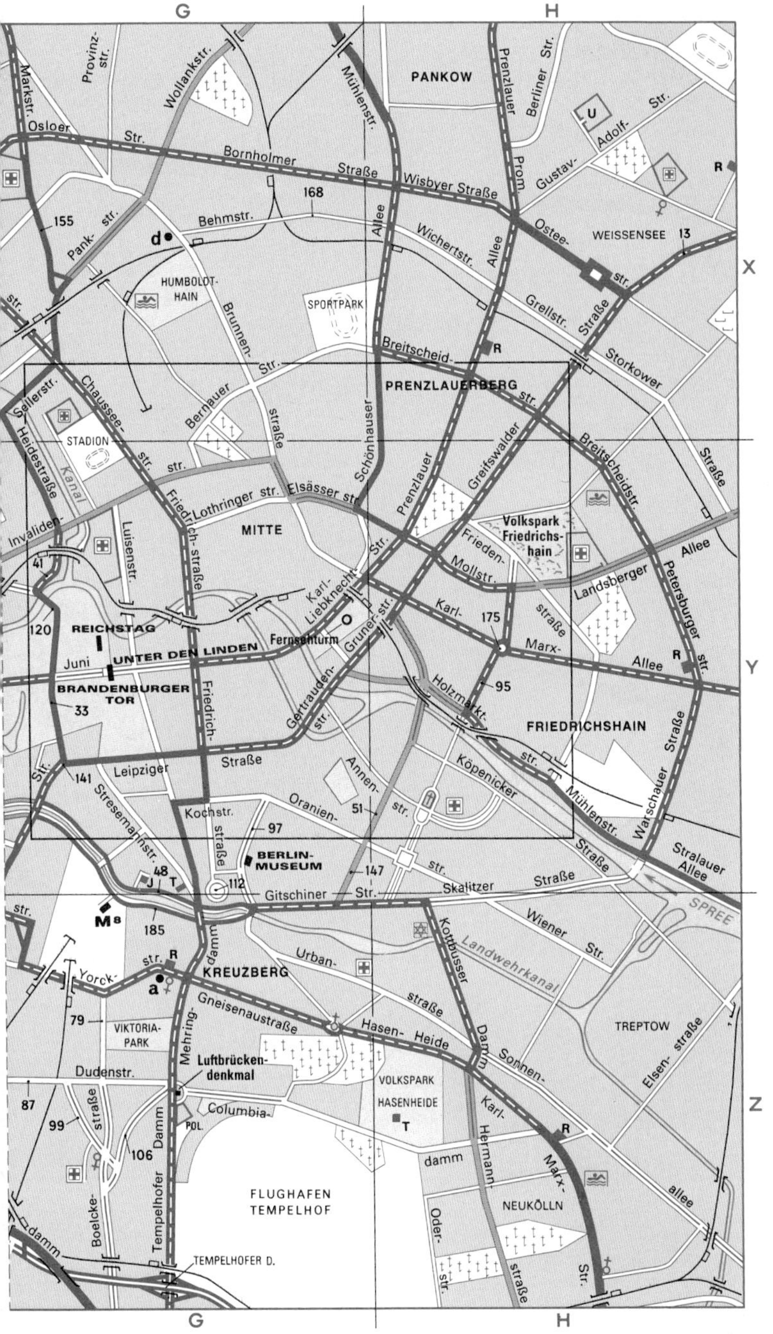
G
H
X
Y
Z
PANKOW
WEISSENSEE
PRENZLAUERBERG
MITTE
FRIEDRICHSHAIN
KREUZBERG
TREPTOW
NEUKÖLLN
HUMBOLDT-HAIN
SPORTPARK
STADION
Volkspark Friedrichshain
REICHSTAG
UNTER DEN LINDEN
BRANDENBURGER TOR
Fernsehturm
BERLIN-MUSEUM
VIKTORIA-PARK
Luftbrücken-denkmal
VOLKSPARK HASENHEIDE
FLUGHAFEN TEMPELHOF
TEMPELHOFER D.
SPREE
Landwehrkanal
Kanal
Bornholmer Straße
Wisbyer Straße
Ostee-str.
Breitscheid-str.
Breitscheidstr.
Storkower
Grellstr.
Wichertstr.
Behmstr.
Osloer Str.
Markstr.
Provinz-str.
Wollankstr.
Mühlenstr.
Schönhauser Allee
Prenzlauer Allee
Prenzlauer Prom.
Berliner Str.
Gustav-Adolf-Str.
Pank-str.
Brunnen-straße
Bernauer Str.
Chaussee-str.
Sellerstr.
Heidestraße
Invaliden-str.
Lothringer str.
Elsässer str.
Friedrich-straße
Luisenstr.
Karl-Liebknecht-Str.
Gruner-str.
Gertrauden-str.
Greifswalder Straße
Frieden-straße
Mollstr.
Landsberger Allee
Petersburger Str.
Karl-Marx-Allee
Holzmarkt-str.
Köpenicker Str.
Mühlenstr.
Warschauer Straße
Stralauer Allee
Juni
Leipziger Straße
Stresemannstr.
Kochstr.
Oranien-str.
Annen-str.
Skalitzer Straße
Gitschiner Str.
Wiener Str.
Urban-straße
Kottbusser Damm
Yorck-str.
Gneisenaustraße
Hasen-Heide
Sonnen-allee
Elsen-straße
Mehring-damm
Dudenstr.
Columbia-damm
Karl-Marx-Str.
Hermann-straße
Oder-str.
Boelcke-straße
Tempelhofer Damm
POL.
155
168
13
41
120
33
141
175
95
97
48
112
185
51
147
79
87
99
106
d
a
O
U
R
T
J
M8

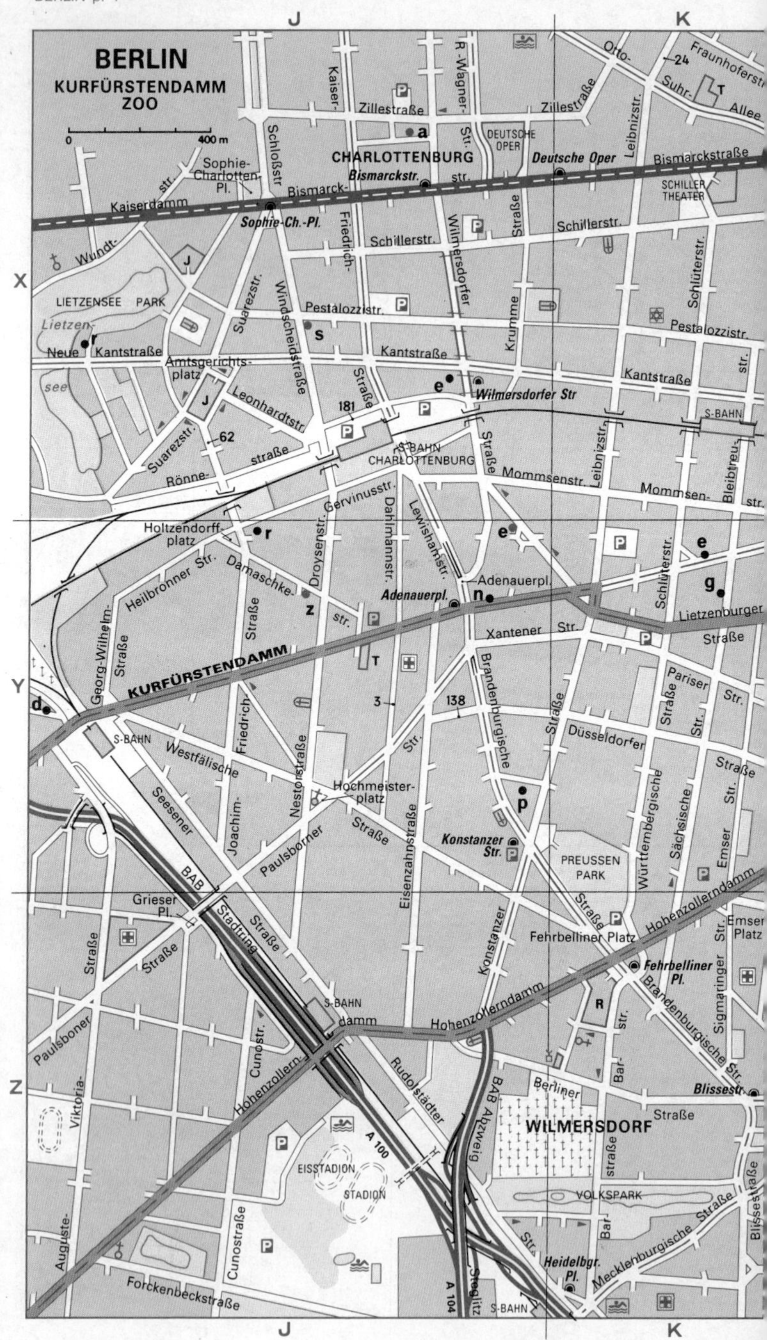
BERLIN
KURFÜRSTENDAMM
ZOO
0
400 m
CHARLOTTENBURG
WILMERSDORF
KURFÜRSTENDAMM
Kaiserdamm
Bismarckstraße
Deutsche Oper
Bismarckstr.
Sophie-Ch.-Pl.
Wilmersdorfer Str
Adenauerpl.
Konstanzer Str.
Fehrbelliner Pl.
Heidelbgr. Pl.
Blissestr.
S-BAHN CHARLOTTENBURG
DEUTSCHE OPER
SCHILLER THEATER
LIETZENSEE PARK
PREUSSEN PARK
VOLKSPARK
EISSTADION
STADION
Kantstraße
Pestalozzistr.
Schillerstr.
Zillestraße
Mommsenstr.
Lietzenburger Straße
Hohenzollerndamm
Fehrbelliner Platz
Berliner Straße
Forckenbeckstraße
A 100
A 104
BAB Abzweig
Stadtring

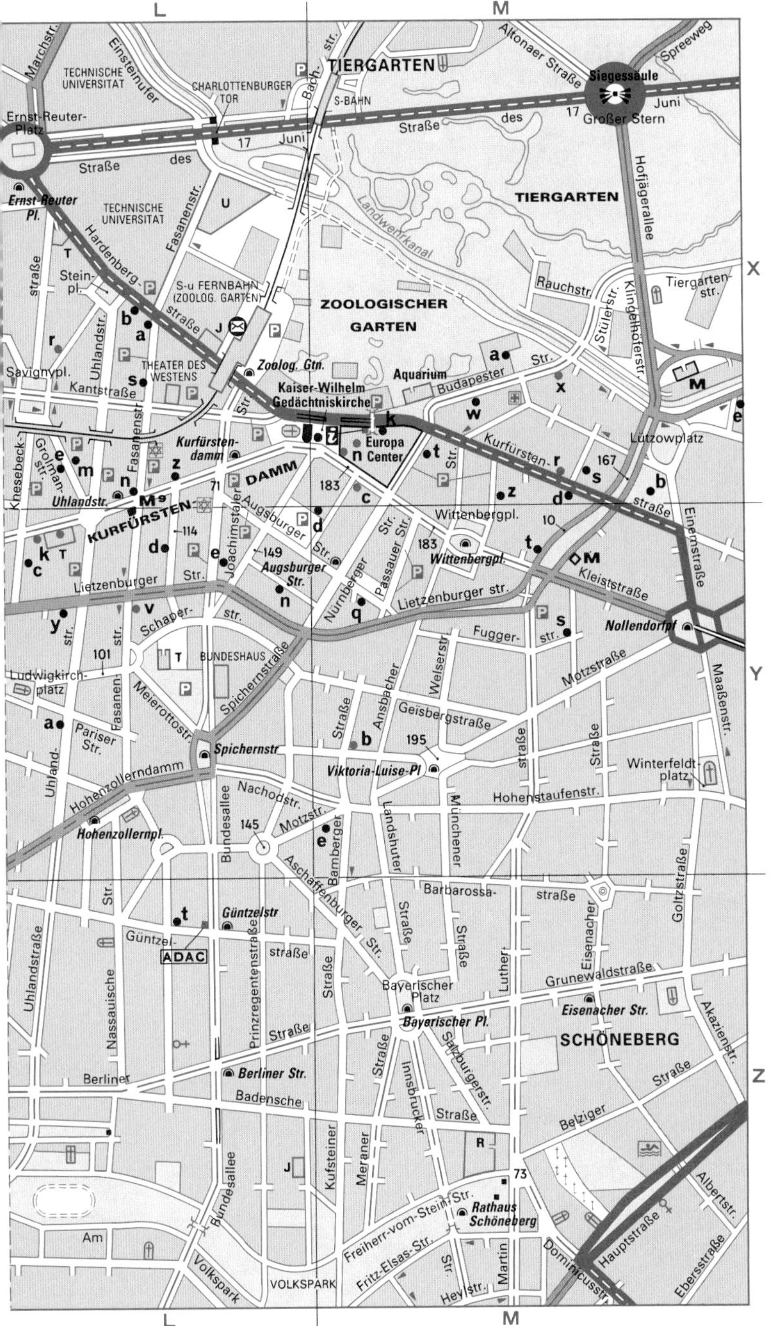
L
M
X
Y
Z
TIERGARTEN
Siegessäule
Großer Stern
Straße des 17. Juni
Ernst-Reuter-Platz
Ernst-Reuter Pl.
TECHNISCHE UNIVERSITÄT
CHARLOTTENBURGER TOR
S-BAHN
Landwehrkanal
ZOOLOGISCHER GARTEN
S-u FERNBAHN (ZOOLOG. GARTEN)
Zoolog. Gtn.
Aquarium
Budapester Str.
Kaiser-Wilhelm Gedächtniskirche
Europa Center
Kurfürstendamm
KURFÜRSTENDAMM
THEATER DES WESTENS
Hardenbergstraße
Kantstraße
Savignypl.
Steinpl.
Uhlandstr.
Fasanenstr.
Joachimstaler Str.
Augsburger Str.
Nürnberger Str.
Passauer Str.
Wittenbergpl.
Kurfürstenstraße
Lützowplatz
Einemstraße
Kleiststraße
Nollendorfpl.
Lietzenburger Str.
Schaperstr.
BUNDESHAUS
Spichernstraße
Spichernstr.
Ludwigkirchplatz
Pariser Str.
Meierottostr.
Hohenzollerndamm
Hohenzollernpl.
Nachodstr.
Motzstr.
Viktoria-Luise-Pl.
Geisbergstraße
Ansbacher Str.
Welserstr.
Fuggerstr.
Maaßenstr.
Winterfeldtplatz
Hohenstaufenstr.
Münchener Str.
Landshuter Str.
Bamberger Str.
Aschaffenburger Str.
Barbarossastraße
Goltzstraße
Eisenacher Str.
Grunewaldstraße
Bayerischer Platz
Bayerischer Pl.
Salzburgerstr.
Innsbrucker Str.
SCHÖNEBERG
Akazienstr.
Belziger Straße
Hauptstraße
Albertstr.
Ebersstraße
Dominicusstr.
Rathaus Schöneberg
Freiherr-vom-Stein-Str.
Fritz-Elsas-Str.
Martin Luther Str.
Heylstr.
VOLKSPARK
Volkspark
Bundesallee
Prinzregentenstraße
Güntzelstraße
Güntzelstr
ADAC
Berliner Str.
Badensche Straße
Nassauische Straße
Uhlandstraße
Kufsteiner Str.
Meraner Str.
Am
Altonaer Straße
Spreeweg
Hofjägerallee
Klingelhöferstr.
Stülerstr.
Tiergartenstr.
Rauchstr.
Bachstr.
Einsteinufer
Marchstr.
Knesebeckstr.
Grolmanstr.
Uhlandstr.
Wittenbergpl.
167
183
114
149
71
101
195
145
73
10
17

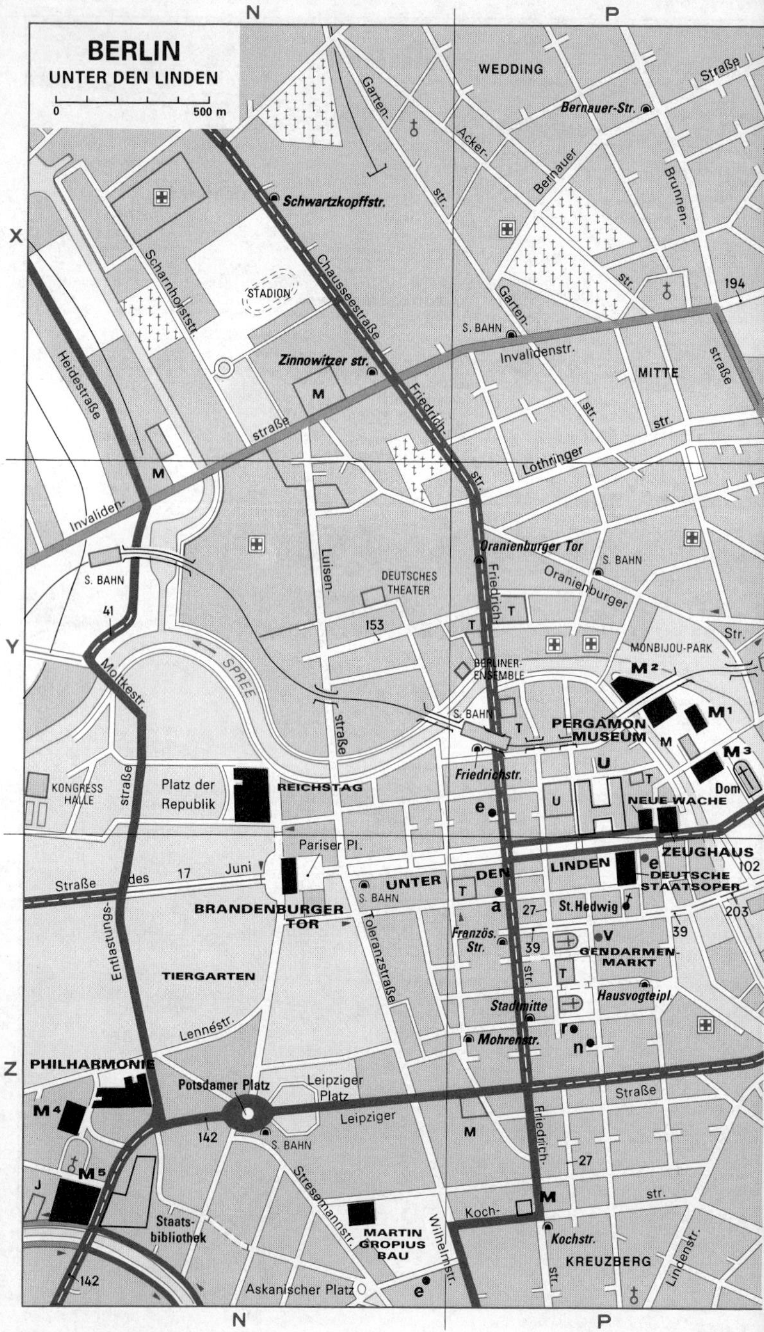
BERLIN
UNTER DEN LINDEN
0
500 m
N
P
X
Y
Z
WEDDING
MITTE
KREUZBERG
TIERGARTEN
Bernauer-Str.
Schwartzkopffstr.
Zinnowitzer str.
Oranienburger Tor
Friedrichstr.
Französ. Str.
Stadtmitte
Mohrenstr.
Hausvogteipl.
Kochstr.
STADION
SPREE
S. BAHN
REICHSTAG
KONGRESS HALLE
Platz der Republik
Pariser Pl.
BRANDENBURGER TOR
UNTER DEN LINDEN
DEUTSCHES THEATER
BERLINER-ENSEMBLE
MONBIJOU-PARK
PERGAMON MUSEUM
NEUE WACHE
ZEUGHAUS
DEUTSCHE STAATSOPER
St. Hedwig
GENDARMEN-MARKT
Dom
PHILHARMONIE
Potsdamer Platz
Leipziger Platz
Staats-bibliothek
MARTIN GROPIUS BAU
Askanischer Platz
Heidestraße
Scharnhorststr.
Chausseestraße
Garten-str.
Acker-str.
Bernauer
Brunnen-str.
Invaliden-straße
Invalidenstr.
Lothringer str.
Oranienburger Str.
Friedrich-str.
Luisen-straße
Moltkestr.
Entlastungs-straße
Straße des 17 Juni
Toleranzstraße
Lennéstr.
Leipziger Straße
Stresemannstr.
Wilhelmstr.
Koch-str.
Lindenstr.
194
41
153
102
203
27
39
142

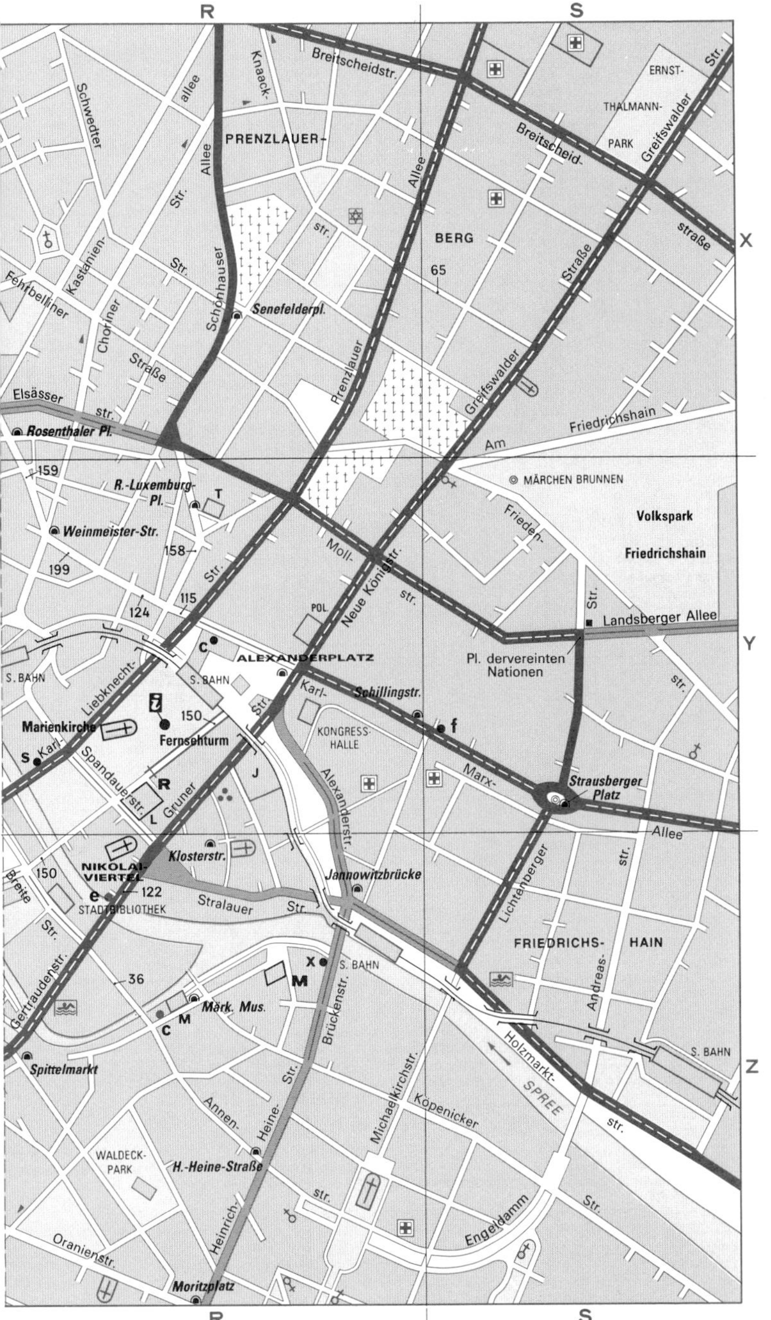
R
S
X
Y
Z
Breitscheidstr.
Knaack-
Schwedter
allee
PRENZLAUER-
Allee
Str.
ERNST-
THÄLMANN-
PARK
Breitscheid-
Greifswalder
straße
BERG
Str.
65
Kastanien-
Fehrbelliner
Choriner
Straße
Schönhauser
Senefelderpl.
Prenzlauer
Greifswalder
Friedrichshain
Am
Elsässer
str.
Rosenthaler Pl.
159
R.-Luxemburg-
Pl.
T
Weinmeister-Str.
MÄRCHEN BRUNNEN
Frieden-
Volkspark
Friedrichshain
158
199
Moll-
Neue Königstr.
str.
115
124
POL.
Landsberger Allee
Pl. dervereinten
Nationen
ALEXANDERPLATZ
Liebknecht-
S. BAHN
Karl-
Schillingstr.
150
Marienkirche
Fernsehturm
KONGRESS-
HALLE
Alexanderstr.
Marx-
Strausberger
Platz
Spandauerstr.
Gruner
Allee
Klosterstr.
NIKOLAI-
VIERTEL
Breite
Jannowitzbrücke
Lichtenberger
122
STADTBIBLIOTHEK
Stralauer
FRIEDRICHS-
HAIN
Andreas-
36
Gertraudenstr.
Märk. Mus.
Brückenstr.
Spittelmarkt
Holzmarkt-
SPREE
Annen-
Heine-
Michaelkirchstr.
Köpenicker
WALDECK-
PARK
H.-Heine-Straße
Heinrich-
Engeldamm
Oranienstr.
Moritzplatz

Continued p. 9

STREET INDEX TO BERLIN TOWN PLANS (Concluded)

Town Centre (Berlin - City, -Schöneberg and - Tiergarten) :

Bristol-Hotel Kempinski, Kurfürstendamm 27 (B 15), ☎ 88 43 40, Telex 185651, Fax 8836075, Massage, ⇌s, ⊡ - |♦| ⇆ rm ▤ TV ⇌ - 🏛 300. AE ⓓ E VISA. ✗ LX **n**
Kempinski-Grill *(dinner only)* **M** a la carte 71/105 - **Kempinski-Restaurant M** a la carte 65/95 - **Kempinski-Eck M** 30(lunch) and a la carte 50/70 - **315 rm** ☐ 447/664, 32 suites.

Maritim Grand Hotel, Friedrichstr. 158, ✉ O-1080, ☎ 2 32 70, Telex 304076, Fax 23273362, Massage, ⇌s - |♦| ⇆ rm TV ♿ ⇌ - 🏛 100. AE ⓓ E VISA PZ **a**
- **Coelln** *(remarkable wine list)* **M** a la carte 47/88 - **Le Grand Silhouette** *(dinner only) (closed Sunday and 20 July - 20 August)* **M** a la carte 79/98 - **Goldene Gans M** a la carte 41/59 - **350 rm** ☐ 423/636, 35 suites.

Inter-Continental, Budapester Str. 2 (B 30), ☎ 2 60 20, Telex 184380, Fax 260280760, Massage, ⇌s, ⊡ - |♦| ⇆ rm ▤ TV ♿ ⇌ Ⓟ - 🏛 800. AE ⓓ E VISA. ✗ rest MX **a**
- **Zum Hugenotten** *(remarkable wine list)* **M** a la carte 80/100 - **Buffet-Restaurant Brasserie M** a la carte 50/70 - **580 rm** ☐ 404/604, 70 suites.

Grand Hotel Esplanade (modern hotel featuring contemporary art), Lützowufer 15 (B 30), ☎ 26 10 11, Telex 185986, Fax 2629121, Massage, ⇌s, ⊡ - |♦| ⇆ rm ▤ TV ⇌ - 🏛 300. AE ⓓ E VISA. ✗ rest - **M** *(closed Saturday lunch and Sunday)* a la carte 70/94 - **402 rm** ☐ 439/578, 17 suites. MX **e**

Metropol, Friedrichstr. 150, ✉ O-1086, ☎ 2 38 75, Telex 114141, Fax 23874209, Massage, Fø, ⇌s, ⊡ - |♦| ⇆ rm TV ♿ ⇌ - 🏛 150. AE ⓓ E VISA. ✗ rest PY **e**
M a la carte 50/100 - **340 rm** ☐ 305/490, 34 suites.

Schweizerhof, Budapester Str. 21 (B 30), ☎ 2 69 60, Telex 185501, Fax 2696900, Massage, Fø, ⇌s, ⊡ - |♦| ⇆ rm ▤ TV ⇌ Ⓟ - 🏛 400. AE ⓓ E VISA. ✗ rest MX **w**
M a la carte 50/100 - **430 rm** ☐ 397/554, 10 suites.

Palace, Budapester Str. 42 (Europa-Centre) (B 30), ☎ 2 50 20, Telex 184825, Fax 2626577, free entrance to the thermal recreation centre - |♦| ⇆ rm TV - 🏛 25/260. AE ⓓ E VISA. ✗ rest MX **k**
M *(lunch only)* a la carte 48/85 - **La Réserve** *(dinner only)* **M** a la carte 65/95 - **322 rm** ☐ 336/552, 10 suites.

Berlin Hilton, Mohrenstr. 30, O-1080, 2 38 20, Telex 113401, Fax 2384269, Massage, - rm rest - 400 PZ **r**
La Coupole *(dinner only) (closed Sunday and Monday)* **M** a la carte 78/164 - **Mark Brandenburg M** a la carte 40/62 - **357 rm** 344/578, 12 suites.

Berlin, Lützowplatz 17 (B 30), 2 60 50, Telex 184332, Fax 26052715, Massage, - rm rest - 500. MX **b**
M 28 buffet (lunch) and a la carte 50/86 - **490 rm** 330/625, 6 suites.

Steigenberger Berlin, Los-Angeles-Platz 1 (B 30), 2 10 80, Telex 181444, Fax 2108117, Massage, - rm - 600. MY **d**
- **Park-Restaurant** *(dinner only) (closed Sunday and Monday)* **M** a la carte 62/105 - **Berliner Stube M** a la carte 33/59 - **397 rm** 371/572, 11 suites.

Savoy, Fasanenstr. 9 (B 12), 31 10 30, Telex 184292, Fax 31103333, - rm - 30. rest LX **s**
M a la carte 46/70 - **130 rm** 340/530 - 6 suites 570/950.

Brandenburger Hof, Eislebener Str. 14 (B 30), 21 40 50, Fax 21405100 - - 40. LY **n**
M a la carte 35/70 - **87 rm** 280/415.

Mondial, Kurfürstendamm 47 (B 15), 88 41 10, Telex 182839, Fax 88411150, - - 50. rest KY **e**
M a la carte 52/77 - **75 rm** 220/420.

Palasthotel, Karl-Liebknecht-Str. 5, O-1020, 2 38 28, Telex 304754, Fax 23827590, Massage, - - 420. RY **s**
- **Märkisches Restaurant M** a la carte 38/65 - **Rôti d'or** *(closed Sunday and Monday)* **M** a la carte 57/83 - **Domklause M** a la carte 25/48 - **600 rm** 300/490, 40 suites.

Berlin Penta Hotel, Nürnberger Str. 65 (B 30), 21 00 70, Telex 182877, Fax 2132009, Massage, - rm - 120. rest MX **t**
M a la carte 59/94 - **425 rm** 318/436.

Forum-Hotel Berlin, Alexanderplatz, O-1020, 2 38 90, Telex 114113, Fax 23894305, - rm - 400. RY **c**
- **Esprit M** a la carte 31/72 - **Panorama M** *(dinner only)* a la carte 56/84 - **1006 rm** 241/455.

Ambassador, Bayreuther Str. 42 (B 30), 21 90 20, Telex 184259, Fax 21902380, Massage, - rm rest - 70. rest MX **z**
M a la carte 34/65 - **199 rm** 290/440.

Alsterhof, Augsburger Str. 5 (B 30), 21 24 20, Telex 183484, Fax 2183949, Massage, - rm . rest MY **q**
M a la carte 47/68 - **144 rm** 197/460, 4 suites.

President, An der Urania 16 (B 30), 21 90 30, Telex 184018, Fax 2141200, - - 40. rest MY **t**
M *(closed Sunday dinner)* a la carte 43/68 - **132 rm** 255/375 - 6 suites 400/450.

Art-Hotel Sorat without rest (modern hotel with exhibition of contemporary art), Joachimstalerstr. 28 (B 15), 88 44 70, Fax 88447700 - . LY **e**
75 rm 243/326.

Am Zoo without rest, Kurfürstendamm 25 (B 15), 88 43 70, Telex 183835, Fax 88437714 - - 30. LX **z**
136 rm 225/370.

Berliner Congress Center, Märkisches Ufer 54, O-1026, 2 70 05 31, Telex 304501, Fax 27822165, - - 350. rm RZ **x**
M a la carte 32/49 - **110 rm** 175/300, 12 suites.

Berlin Excelsior Hotel, Hardenbergstr. 14 (B 12), 3 15 50, Telex 184781, Fax 31551002 - rm rest - 100. rest LX **b**
- **Peacock M** a la carte 46/80 - **Store House Grill M** a la carte 33/60 - **320 rm** 325/525.

Residenz -Restaurant Grand Cru, Meinekestr. 9 (B 15), 88 44 30, Telex 18 30 82, Fax 8824726 - . rest LY **d**
M a la carte 69/88 - **92 rm** 225/440, 6 suites.

Hecker's Deele, Grolmanstr. 35 (B 12), 8 89 00, Telex 184954, Fax 8890260 - rm rest . LX **e**
M a la carte 33/65 - **52 rm** 295/380.

Sylter Hof, Kurfürstenstr. 116 (B 30), 2 12 00, Telex 183317, Fax 2142826 - - 80. rest MX **d**
M a la carte 46/73 - **154 rm** 250/416, 16 suites.

Bremen without rest, Bleibtreustr. 25 (B 15), 8 81 40 76, Telex 184892, Fax 8824685 - . KY **g**
53 rm 275/420.

Curator without rest, Grolmanstr. 41 (B 12), 88 42 60, Telex 183389, Fax 88426500, - . LX **m**
100 rm 240/350, 3 suites.

Kronprinz without rest (restored 1894 house), Kronprinzendamm 1 (B 31), ✆ 89 60 30, Telex 181459, Fax 8931215 – |♦| TV ☎ – 25. AE ① E VISA JY **d**
66 rm ☐ 190/315.

Park Consul without rest, Alt-Moabit 86a (B 21), ✆ 39 07 80, Fax 39078900 – |♦| TV ☎. AE ① E VISA FY **s**
52 rm ☐ 255/325.

Domus without rest, Uhlandstr. 49 (B 15), ✆ 88 20 41, Telex 185975, Fax 8820410 – |♦| ☎. AE ① E VISA LY **a**
closed 24 December - 2 January – **73 rm** ☐ 140/245.

Hamburg, Landgrafenstr. 4 (B 30), ✆ 26 47 70, Telex 184974, Fax 2629394 – |♦| rm TV ☎ Ⓟ – 80. AE ① E VISA. rest MX **s**
M a la carte 40/63 – **240 rm** ☐ 225/298.

Berlin-Plaza, Knesebeckstr. 63 (B 15), ✆ 88 41 30, Telex 184181, Fax 88413754, – |♦| rm TV ☎ Ⓟ – 30. AE ① E VISA. LY **c**
M a la carte 35/50 – **131 rm** ☐ 225/335.

Berlin Hilton Kroneflügel without rest, Kronenstr. 48, ✉ O-1080, ✆ 2 38 20, Fax 23824269 – TV ☎. AE ① E VISA PZ **n**
148 rm ☐ 223/395.

Arosa Parkschloß - Hotel, Lietzenburger Str. 79 (B 15), ✆ 88 00 50, Telex 183397, Fax 8824579, , – |♦| rm TV ☎ – 40. AE ① E VISA LY **y**
M *(closed Sunday)* a la carte 41/71 – **90 rm** ☐ 225/480.

Scandotel Castor without rest, Fuggerstr. 8 (B 30), ✆ 21 30 30, Fax 21303160 – |♦| TV ☎. AE ① E VISA. MY **s**
78 rm ☐ 210/295.

Astoria without rest, Fasanenstr. 2 (B 12), ✆ 3 12 40 67, Telex 181745, Fax 3125027 – |♦| TV ☎. AE ① E VISA LX **a**
32 rm ☐ 208/380.

Kurfürstendamm without rest, Kurfürstendamm 68 (B 15), ✆ 88 46 30, Telex 184630, Fax 8825528 – |♦| TV ☎ Ⓟ – 35. AE ① E VISA JY **n**
34 rm ☐ 160/255, 4 suites.

Atrium-Hotel without rest, Motzstr. 87 (B 30), ✆ 2 18 40 57, Fax 2117563 – |♦| TV ☎. E MY **e**
22 rm ☐ 95/150.

Berolina, Karl-Marx-Allee 31, ✉ O-1026, ✆ 23 81 30, Telex 114331, Fax 2423409 – |♦| TV ☎ Ⓟ – 50. AE ① E VISA SY **f**
M a la carte 26/42 – **344 rm** ☐ 185/275, 11 suites.

XXX **Opernpalais-Königin Luise**, Unter den Linden 5, ✉ -1080, ✆ 2 00 22 69, Fax 2004438 – 50. AE E VISA. PZ **e**
closed Monday – **M** *(dinner only)* a la carte 66/81 – **Fridericus M** a la carte 40/60.

XXX **Ristorante Anselmo**, Damaschkestr. 17 (B 31), ✆ 3 23 30 94, Fax 3246228, « Modern Italian rest. » – AE. JY **z**
closed Monday – **M** a la carte 60/100.

XX ✿ **Bamberger Reiter**, Regensburger Str. 7 (B 30), ✆ 2 18 42 82, Fax 2142348, – AE ① VISA. MY **b**
closed Sunday and Monday, 1 to 13 January and 2 to 24 August – **M** (dinner only) (booking essential) 145/175 and a la carte 92/115 – **Bistro** *(lunch and dinner)* **M** a la carte 53/64
Spec. Marinierte Gänsestopfleber in Trüffelgelee, Bretonischer Hummer in Sauternes, Feigenstrudel mit Buttermilcheis.

XX **Mövenpick**, Europa-Centre (1st floor) (B 30), ✆ 2 62 70 77, Fax 2629486, ← – AE ① E VISA
M a la carte 32/65. MX **n**

XX Ephraim - Palais, Poststr. 16, ✉ O-1020, ✆ 21 71 31 64 RZ **e**

XX **Französischer Hof**, Otto-Nuschke-Str. 56, ✉ O-1086, ✆ 2 29 39 69, Fax 2293152 – ♿. AE ① E VISA PZ **v**
M a la carte 38/70.

XX **Du Pont**, Budapester Str. 1 (B 30), ✆ 2 61 88 11, – AE ① E VISA MX **x**
closed Saturday lunch, Sunday, Bank Holidays and 24 December - 2 January – **M** a la carte 65/85.

XX **Ermeler Haus** (reconstructed 18 C Patrician house), Märkisches Ufer 10 (1st floor), ✉ O-1026, ✆ 2 79 40 28 – RZ **c**
M a la carte 40/80.

XX **Daitokai** (Japanese rest.), Tauentzienstr. 9 (Europa Centre, 1st floor) (B 30), ✆ 2 61 80 99, Fax 2616036 – AE ① E VISA. MX **n**
closed Monday – **M** a la carte 49/68.

XX Ming's Garden (Chinese rest.), Tauentzienstr. 16 (entrance Marburger Str.) (B 30), ✆ 2 11 87 28, Fax 2118914 – MX **c**

XX **Ristorante Il Sorriso** (Italian rest.), Kurfürstenstr. 76 (B 30), ✆ 2 62 13 13, Fax 2650277, – AE E VISA. MX **r**
closed Sunday – **M** *(booking essential for dinner)* a la carte 49/73.

XX **Peppino** (Italian rest.), Fasanenstr. 65 (B 15), ✆ 8 83 67 22 – AE LY **v**
closed Monday and 4 weeks July - August – **M** a la carte 53/70.

Stachel (Bistro style), Giesebrechtstr. 3 (B 12), 8 82 36 29, – AE E VISA JY e
closed Bank Holidays – **M** (dinner only) a la carte 48/75.

Kopenhagen (Danish Smørrebrød), Kurfürstendamm 203 (B 15), 8 81 62 19 – . AE E VISA LY k
M a la carte 32/62.

Hongkong (Chinese rest.), Kurfürstendamm 210 (2nd floor, |‡|) (B 15), 8 81 57 56 – AE ◑ E VISA LY T
M a la carte 26/70.

at Berlin-Britz by Karl-Marx-Allee HZ :

Britzer Hof without rest, Jahnstr. 13 (B 47), 6 85 00 80, Fax 68500868 – |‡| TV ☎ . AE ◑ E VISA
30 rm 120/250.

at Berlin-Charlottenburg :

Seehof, Lietzensee-Ufer 11 (B 19), 32 00 20, Telex 182943, Fax 32002251, <, « Garden terrace », , – |‡| rest TV – 50. AE ◑ E VISA JX r
M a la carte 52/74 – **77 rm** 219/468.

Kanthotel without rest, Kantstr. 111 (B 12), 32 30 26, Telex 183330, Fax 3240952 – |‡| TV ☎ . AE ◑ E VISA. JX e
55 rm 209/249.

Schloßparkhotel, Heubnerweg 2a (B 19), 3 22 40 61, Telex 183462, Fax 3258861, , – |‡| TV ☎ – 50. AE ◑ E VISA EY a
M a la carte 40/63 – **39 rm** 189/285.

Kardell, Gervinusstr. 24 (B 12), 3 24 10 66, Fax 3249710 – |‡| TV ☎ . AE ◑ E VISA JY r
M *(closed Saturday lunch)* a la carte 49/69 – **33 rm** 125/220.

Am Studio without rest, Kaiserdamm 80 (B 19), 30 20 81, Telex 182825, Fax 3019578 – |‡| TV ☎ . AE ◑ E VISA EY c
80 rm 155/255.

Ibis without rest, Messedamm 10 (B 19), 30 39 30, Telex 182882, Fax 3019536 – |‡| TV ☎ – 40 EY b
191 rm 155/199.

Ponte Vecchio (Tuscan rest.), Spielhagenstr. 3 (B 10), 3 42 19 99 – ◑ JX a
closed Tuesday and 4 weeks July - August – **M** (dinner only) (booking essential) a la carte 58/86.

✲ **Alt Luxemburg**, Windscheidtstr. 31 (B 12), 3 23 87 30 – ◑ VISA JX s
closed Saturday lunch, Sunday, Monday, 3 weeks January and 3 weeks June - July – **M** (booking essential) 98/135 and a la carte 71/95
Spec. Hummerlasagne, Entenbrust mit Honig-Ingwer-Sauce, Krokantblätterteig mit Früchten.

Fioretto, Carmerstr. 2 (B 12), 3 12 31 15 – AE E VISA LX r
closed Sunday – **M** *(June - August dinner only)* a la carte 59/81.

Ana e Bruno (Italian rest.), Sophie-Charlotten-Str. 101 (B 19), 3 25 71 10 – AE E
closed Sunday and Monday, 1 to 13 January and 3 weeks June - July – **M** (dinner only) a la carte 67/84. EY s

Trio, Klausenerplatz 14 (B 19), 3 21 77 82 EY e
closed Wednesday and Thursday – **M** (dinner only) (booking essential) a la carte 47/65.

Funkturm - Restaurant (|‡|, DM 3), Messedamm 22 (B 19), 30 38 29 96, Fax 30383915, < Berlin – . AE ◑ E VISA. EY
M (booking essential) a la carte 54/84.

at Berlin-Dahlem by Clayallee EZ :

Forsthaus Paulsborn, Am Grunewaldsee (B 33), 8 14 11 56, – TV ☎ . AE ◑ E VISA
M *(closed Monday)* 28/35 (lunch) and a la carte 47/72 – **11 rm** 110/200.

Alter Krug, Königin-Luise-Str. 52 (B 33), 8 32 50 89, « Terrace » – . ◑ E VISA
closed Thursday – **M** a la carte 41/81.

at Berlin-Grunewald :

Hemingway's, Hagenstr. 18 (B 33), 8 25 45 71, Fax 82600270 – AE ◑ E VISA EZ t
closed Saturday lunch – **M** (booking essential for dinner) a la carte 65/83.

Grand Slam, Gottfried-von-Cramm-Weg 47 (B 33), 8 25 38 10, Fax 8266300, – AE ◑ E VISA.
closed Sunday, Monday and July – **M** (dinner only) (booking essential) a la carte 87/102.

at Berlin-Kreuzberg :

Stuttgarter Hof, Anhalter Str. 9 (B 61), 26 48 30, Telex 183966, Fax 26483900, – |‡| rm TV ☎ – 30. AE ◑ E VISA NZ e
M a la carte 46/70 – **110 rm** 275/440.

Riehmers Hofgarten, Yorckstr. 83 (B 61), 78 10 11, Fax 7866059 – |‡| TV ☎. AE ◑ E VISA GZ a
M *(closed Sunday)* (dinner only) a la carte 45/61 – **21 rm** 186/270.

at Berlin-Lichterfelde by Boelcke Straße GZ :

Villa Toscana without rest, Bahnhofstr. 19 (B 45), ☎ 7 72 39 61, Fax 7734488, « Villa with elegant installation » – AE VISA
15 rm 178/276.

at Berlin-Reinickendorf by Sellerstr. GX :

Rheinsberg am See, Finsterwalder Str. 64 (B 26), ☎ 4 02 10 02, Telex 185972, Fax 4035057, « Lakeside garden terrace », – E VISA
M a la carte 40/78 – **80 rm** 166/300.

at Berlin-Siemensstadt by Siemensdamm EX :

Novotel, Ohmstr. 4 (B 13), ☎ 38 10 61, Telex 181415, Fax 3819403, – rm rm – 200. AE E VISA
M a la carte 31/61 – **119 rm** 189/260.

at Berlin-Steglitz by Hauptstr. FZ :

Steglitz International, Albrechtstr. 2 (B 41), ☎ 79 00 50, Telex 183545, Fax 79005550, Massage, – rm – 400. AE E VISA. rest
M a la carte 43/65 – **212 rm** 260/480, 3 suites.

Ravenna Hotel without rest, Grunewaldstr. 8 (B 41), ☎ 7 92 80 31, Fax 7924412 – – 25. AE E VISA
48 rm 125/190, 3 suites.

at Berlin-Tegel :

Sorat-Hotel Humboldt-Mühle, An der Mühle 5 (B 27), ☎ 4 39 04, Fax 439004, – rm – 50. AE E VISA by Müllerstraße FX
M a la carte 59/72 – **107 rm** 243/326.

Novotel Berlin Airport, Kurt-Schumacher-Damm 202 (by airport approach) (B 51), ☎ 4 10 60, Telex 181605, Fax 4106700, , , (heated) – rm – 150. AE E VISA EX **r**
M a la carte 36/57 – **185 rm** 194/248.

at Berlin-Tiergarten :

Alfa-Hotel, Ufnaustr. 1 (B 21), ☎ 34 40 31, Fax 3452111 – . AE E VISA.
M (residents only) (dinner only) – **33 rm** 205/287. FY **a**

at Berlin-Waidmannslust by Sellerstr. GX :

XXX ✿✿ **Rockendorf's Restaurant**, Düsterhauptstr. 1 (B 28), ☎ 4 02 30 99, Fax 4022742, « Elegant installation » – . AE E VISA.
closed Sunday, Monday, 28 June - 21 July and 22 December - 6 January – **M** *(booking essential)* 98/165 (lunch) 165/210 (dinner)
Spec. Zander in der Kartoffelkruste, Rehrücken mit Teltower Rübchen, Mascarponetorte mit weißem Schokoladeneis.

at Berlin-Wilmersdorf :

Queens Hotel without rest, Güntzelstr. 14 (B 31), ☎ 87 02 41, Telex 182948, Fax 8619326 – . AE E VISA LZ **t**
110 rm 195/290.

Pension Wittelsbach without rest, Wittelsbacher Str. 22 (B 31), ☎ 87 63 45, Fax 8621532, « Tasteful decor » – . AE E VISA JY **p**
37 rm 120/320.

at Großer Müggelsee SE : 15 km by Holzmarktstr. SZ :

Müggelsee , Am Müggelsee (southern bank), ✉ O-1170 Berlin-Köpenick, ☎ (030) 65 88 20, Fax 65882263, , Massage, , – – 200. AE E VISA
M a la carte 34/54 – **175 rm** 200/330, 6 suites.

Seehotel Belvedere, Müggelseedamm 288 (northern bank), ✉ O-1162 Berlin-Köpenick-Friedrichshagen, ☎ (030) 6 45 56 82, ←, « Lakeside terrace », – – 100.
32 rm, 8 suites.

at Peetzsee SE : 31 km by Köpenicker Landstraße SZ :

Seegarten Grünheide , Am Schlangenbuch 12, ✉ O-1252 Grünheide, ☎ (03362) 61 80, Fax 6129, , , – – 40. AE E VISA
M a la carte 34/45 – **22 rm** 80/205, 14 suites.

In addition to establishments indicated by
XXXXX ... X ,
many hotels possess
good class restaurants.

COLOGNE (KÖLN) 5000. Nordrhein-Westfalen 987 ㉓ ㉔, 412 D 14 – pop. 992 000 – alt. 65 m – ☎ 0221.

See : Cathedral (Dom)★★ (Magi's Shrine★★★, gothic stained glass windows★, Cross of Gero (Gerokreuz)★, south chapel (Marienkapelle) : altarpiece★★★, stalls★, treasury★) GY – Roman-Germanic Museum (Römisch-Germanisches Museum)★★★ (Dionysos Mosaic) GY **M1** – Wallraf-Richartz-Museum and Museum Ludwig★★★ (Photo-Historama Agfa★) GY **M2** – Diocesan Museum (Diözesan-Museum)★ GY **M3** – Schnütgen-Museum★★ GZ **M4** – Museum of East-Asian Art (Museum für Ostasiatische Kunst)★★ S **M 5** – Museum for Applied Art (Museum für Angewandte Kunst)★ GYZ **M 6** – St. Maria Lyskirchen (frescoes★★) FX – St. Severin (inside★) FX – St. Pantaleon (rood screen★) EX – St. Aposteln (apse★) EV – St. Ursula : treasure★ (Goldene Kammer) FU – St. Kunibert (chancel : stained glass windows★) FU – St. Mary the Queen (St. Maria Königin) : wall of glass★ by BonnerstraßeFX – Old Town Hall (Altes Rathaus)★ GZ – Botanical garden Flora★ by Konrad-Adenauer-UferFU.

9 Köln-Marienburg, Schillingsrotter Weg, ☎ 38 40 53 ; 18 Bergisch Gladbach-Refrath (E : 17 km), ☎ (02204) 6 31 14.

✈ Köln-Bonn at Wahn (SE : 17 km), ☎ (02203) 4 01.

☎ 1 41 56 66.

Exhibition Centre (Messegelände) by Deutzer Brücke FV, ☎ 82 11, Telex 8873426.

ℹ Tourist office (Verkehrsamt), Am Dom, ☎ 2 21 33 40, Telex 8883421, Fax 2213320.

ADAC, Luxemburger Str. 169, ☎ 47 27 47.

Düsseldorf 40 – Aachen 69 – Bonn 28 – Essen 68.

The reference (K 15) at the end of the address is the postal district : Köln 15

Plans on following pages

Excelsior Hotel Ernst - Restaurant Hanse Stube, Trankgasse 1 (K 1), ☎ 27 01, Telex 8882645, Fax 135150 – 80. AE E VISA. rest GY **a**
M a la carte 69/106 – **160 rm** 325/610, 20 suites.

Maritim, Heumarkt 20 (K 1), ☎ 2 02 70, Telex 8886667, Fax 2027826, Massage, – rm – 1300. AE E VISA GZ **m**
La Galérie *(closed Sunday and Monday and July to August)* **M** *(dinner only)* a la carte 65/115 – **Bellevue** « Terrace with ≤ Cologne » *(closed Sunday lunch)* **M** a la carte 51/89 – **Rôtisserie M** 39/45 (buffet lunch) and a la carte 44/71 – **450 rm** 239/484, 28 suites.

Hotel im Wasserturm (former 19C water tower, elegant modern installation), Kaygasse 2 (K 1), ☎ 2 00 80, Telex 8881109, Fax 2008888, roof garden terrace with ≤ Cologne, – rm rest – 20. AE E VISA. rest FX **c**
M a la carte 69/96 – **90 rm** 399/536, 42 suites.

Dom-Hotel , Domkloster 2a (K 1), ☎ 2 02 40, Telex 8882919, Fax 2024444, « Terrace with ≤ » – rm – 70. AE E VISA GY **d**
M a la carte 57/94 – **126 rm** 355/710.

Ramada Renaissance Hotel, Magnusstr. 20 (K 1), ☎ 2 03 40, Fax 2034777, , Massage, , – rm – 200. AE E VISA. rest EV **b**
M a la carte 54/78 – **240 rm** 279/594.

SAS Royal Hotel, Helenenstr. 14 (K 1), ☎ 22 80, Telex 8882162, Fax 2281301, Massage, , – rm – 800. AE E VISA. rest EV **p**
M 45/buffet lunch and a la carte 56/92 – **290 rm** 301/1076, 12 suites.

Holiday Inn Crowne Plaza, Habsburger Ring 9 (K 1), ☎ 2 09 50, Telex 8886618, Fax 251206, Massage, , – rm – 250. AE E VISA
La Cave *(closed Sunday and Bank Holidays)* **M** *(dinner only)* a la carte 65/100 – **Le Bouquet M** a la carte 54/85 – **300 rm** 330/592. by Hahnenstraße EV

Consul, Belfortstr. 9 (K 1), ☎ 7 72 10, Telex 8885242, Fax 7721259, Massage, , – rm – 200. AE E VISA. rest FU **v**
– **Quirinal** **M** a la carte 55/70 – **Consülchen Pub M** a la carte 38/48 – **120 rm** 190/630.

Senats Hotel, Unter Goldschmied 9 (K 1), ☎ 2 06 20, Fax 2062200 – – 200. rest GZ **b**
60 rm.

Pullman-Hotel Mondial, Kurt-Hackenberg-Platz 1 (K 1), ☎ 2 06 30, Telex 8881932, Fax 2063522, – rm – 180. AE E VISA. rest GY **f**
M 28/38 (lunch) and a la carte 47/80 – **204 rm** 210/385.

Dorint Hotel, Friesenstr. 44 (K 1), ☎ 1 61 40, Telex 8881483, Fax 1614100 – rm – 100. AE E VISA. rest EV **n**
M a la carte 46/78 – **103 rm** 250/620.

Haus Lyskirchen, Filzengraben 28 (K 1), ☎ 2 09 70, Telex 8885449, Fax 2097718, , – rm rest – 60. AE E VISA FX **u**
closed 23 December - 2 January – **M** *(closed Saturday lunch, Sunday and Bank Holidays)* a la carte 48/70 – **94 rm** 170/340.

Altea Hotel Severinshof, Severinstr. 199 (K 1), ☎ 2 01 30, Telex 8881852, Fax 2013666, , – – 140. AE E VISA. rest FX **a**
M a la carte 44/71 – **253 rm** 170/350, 15 suites.

Viktoria without rest, Worringer Str. 23 (K 1), ☎ 72 04 76, Telex 8881979, Fax 727067 – 🛗 📺 ☎ 🅿. AE ⓓ E VISA — by Konrad-Adenauer-Ufer FU
closed 24 December - 1 January – **47 rm** ☐ 165/460.

Bristol without rest (antique furniture), Kaiser-Wilhelm-Ring 48 (K 1), ☎ 12 01 95, Telex 8881146, Fax 131495 – 🛗 📺 ☎. AE ⓓ E VISA — EU **m**
closed 22 December - 2 January – **44 rm** ☐ 165/360.

Savoy without rest, Turiner Str. 9 (K 1), ☎ 1 62 30, Telex 8886360, Fax 1623200, ≘s – 🛗 ⇔ rm 📺 ☎ 🅿. AE ⓓ E VISA — FU **s**
closed 24 to 31 December – **100 rm** ☐ 175/475.

Ascot-Hotel without rest, Hohenzollernring 95 (K 1), ☎ 52 10 76, Telex 8883018, Fax 521070, 🏋, ≘s – 🛗 📺 ☎. AE ⓓ E VISA. ✻ — EV **a**
closed 23 December - 2 January – **46 rm** ☐ 248/409.

REMA-Hotel Europa am Dom, Am Hof 38 (K 1), ☎ 2 05 80, Telex 8881728, Fax 211021 – 🛗 ⇔ rm 📺 ☎ – 🎤 25. AE ⓓ E VISA — GYZ **z**
M see **Ambiance am Dom** below – **90 rm** ☐ 290/390.

Coellner Hof, Hansaring 100 (K 1), ☎ 12 20 75, Telex 8885264, Fax 135235 – 🛗 📺 ☎ 🚗 – 🎤 30. AE ⓓ E VISA — FU **k**
M *(closed Friday dinner and Saturday)* a la carte 38/67 – **70 rm** ☐ 140/360.

Königshof without rest, Richartzstr. 14 (K 1), ☎ 23 45 83, Telex 8881318, Fax 238642 – 🛗 📺 ☎. AE ⓓ E VISA — GY **n**
85 rm ☐ 135/395.

Kommerzhotel without rest, Breslauer Platz (K 1), ☎ 1 61 00, Fax 1610122, ≘s – 🛗 📺 ☎. AE ⓓ E VISA — GY **r**
77 rm ☐ 165/285.

Lasthaus am Ring - Restaurant Charrue d'or, Hohenzollernring 20 (K 1), ☎ 2 57 00 85 (hotel) 25 46 10 (rest.), Telex 8882856, Fax 253714 – 🛗 📺 ☎ 🅿 — EV **u**
52 rm.

Rema-Hotel Residence without rest, Alter Markt 55 (K 1), ☎ 23 57 81, Telex 8885344, Fax 234140 – 🛗 📺 ☎. AE ⓓ E VISA — GZ **c**
60 rm ☐ 170/380.

Central Hotel without rest, An den Dominikanern 3 (K 1), ☎ 13 50 88, Telex 8881807, Fax 135080 – 🛗 📺 ☎. AE ⓓ E VISA — GY **b**
closed 20 December - 6 January – **62 rm** ☐ 115/340.

Esplanade without rest, Hohenstaufenring 56 (K 1), ☎ 21 03 11, Telex 8881029, Fax 216822 – 🛗 📺 ☎ 🚗. AE ⓓ E VISA — EX **a**
closed 24 December - 2 January – **33 rm** ☐ 165/385.

Eden-Hotel without rest, Am Hof 18 (K 1), ☎ 2 58 04 91, Telex 8882889, Fax 2580495 – 🛗 📺 ☎. AE ⓓ E VISA — GY **w**
closed 24 December - 3 January – **33 rm** ☐ 185/355.

Astor und Aparthotel without rest, Friesenwall 68 (K 1), ☎ 25 31 01, Telex 8886367, Fax 253106 – 🛗 📺 ☎ 🅿. AE ⓓ E VISA — EV **y**
52 rm ☐ 144/304.

Merian-Hotel without rest, Allerheiligenstr. 1 (K 1), ☎ 1 66 50, Telex 8883305, Fax 1665200 – 🛗 📺 ☎ 🚗 — FU **c**
closed 22 December - 4 January – **32 rm** ☐ 110/350.

Leonet without rest, Rubensstr. 33 (K 1), ☎ 23 60 16, Telex 8883506, Fax 210893, ≘s, 🏊 – 🛗 📺 ☎ 🅿. AE ⓓ E VISA — EX **e**
closed 20 December - 5 January – **78 rm** ☐ 120/280.

Kolpinghaus International, St.-Apern-Str. 32 (K 1), ☎ 2 09 30, Fax 246518 – 🛗 ☎ 🅿 – 🎤 110. AE ⓓ E VISA — EV **q**
M a la carte 28/62 – **48 rm** ☐ 100/155.

XXXX ✿ **Chez Alex**, Mühlengasse 1 (K 1), ☎ 2 58 10 69 – AE ⓓ E VISA — GZ **k**
closed Saturday lunch and Sunday and Bank Holidays (except exhibitions) – **M** *(booking essential)* 40/60 (lunch) and a la carte 83/113
Spec. Carpaccio von Jacobsmuscheln mit Trüffel, Steinpilzravioli mit Langustinen, Milchlamm mit Artischocken.

XXXX ✿ **Rino Casati**, Ebertplatz 3 (K 1), ☎ 72 11 08, Fax 728097 – AE ⓓ E VISA. ✻ — FU **t**
closed 4 weeks July - August and Sunday (except exhibitions) – **M** (dinner only, booking essential) a la carte 75/107
Spec. Hausgemachte Nudelgerichte, Wachtel auf Linsencrème, Hohe Rippe mit Rindermark und Schalotten.

XXX ✿ **Ambiance am Dom** (at Europa-Hotel am Dom), Am Hof 38 (K 1), ☎ 24 91 27 – AE ⓓ E VISA. ✻ — GYZ **z**
closed Saturday lunch, Sunday, Monday, Bank Holidays and 3 weeks August – **M** 53 (lunch) and a la carte 74/92
Spec. Hummergratin mit Nudeln, Gefüllter Ochsenschwanz in Burgunder, Nougatparfait mit weißer Schokoladensauce.

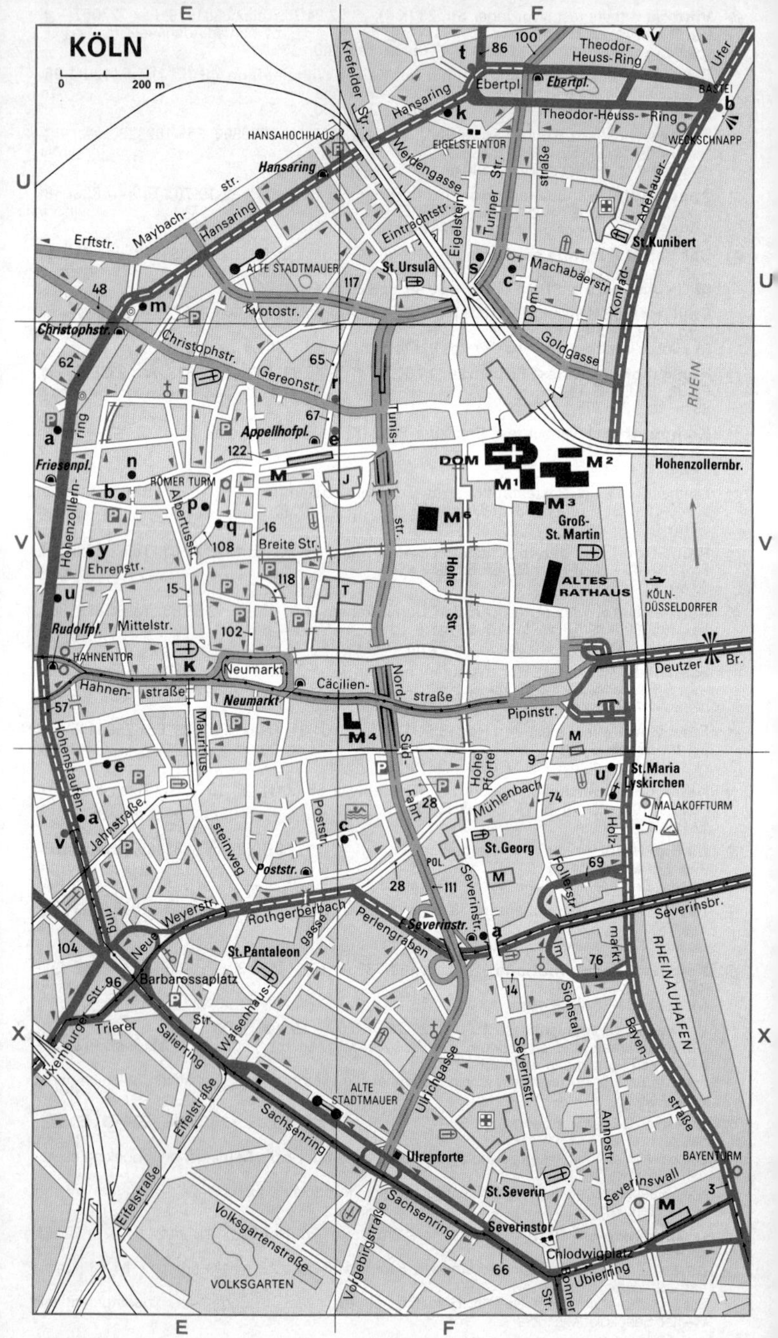
KÖLN
0
200 m
E
F
U
V
X
Theodor-Heuss-Ring
Ebertpl.
Hansaring
Krefelder Str.
HANSAHOCHHAUS
EIGELSTEINTOR
Weidengasse
Turiner Str.
WECKSCHNAPP
BASTEI
Ufer
Konrad-Adenauer-
Eintrachtstr.
Eigelstein
St.Kunibert
Machabäerstr.
St.Ursula
ALTE STADTMAUER
Maybach-str.
Erftstr.
Kyotostr.
Christophstr.
Goldgasse
Dom-
Gereonstr.
Tunis-str.
RHEIN
Appellhofpl.
Friesenpl.
Hohenzollern-ring
RÖMER TURM
Albertusstr.
DOM
Hohenzollernbr.
Groß-St. Martin
Breite Str.
Ehrenstr.
Hohe Str.
ALTES RATHAUS
KÖLN-DÜSSELDORFER
Rudolfpl.
Mittelstr.
HAHNENTOR
Neumarkt
Cäcilien-
Nord-
straße
Deutzer Br.
Hahnen-straße
Pipinstr.
Hohenstaufen-ring
Mauritius
Süd-Fahrt
Hohe Pforte
St.Maria Lyskirchen
MALAKOFFTURM
Mühlenbach
Holz-markt
Jahnstraße
steinweg
Poststr.
St.Georg
Follerstr.
Severinstr.
Severinsbr.
Weyerstr.
Rothgerberbach
Perlengraben
Severinstr.
St.Pantaleon
Neue
Barbarossaplatz
Im Sionstal
RHEINAUHAFEN
Waisenhaus-gasse
Luxemburger Str.
Trierer Str.
Salierring
Bayen-straße
Eifelstraße
ALTE STADTMAUER
Ulrichgasse
Sachsenring
Annostr.
Ulrepforte
BAYENTURM
St.Severin
Severinswall
Volksgartenstraße
Vorgebirgstraße
Severinstor
Chlodwigplatz
VOLKSGARTEN
Ubierring
Bonner Str.

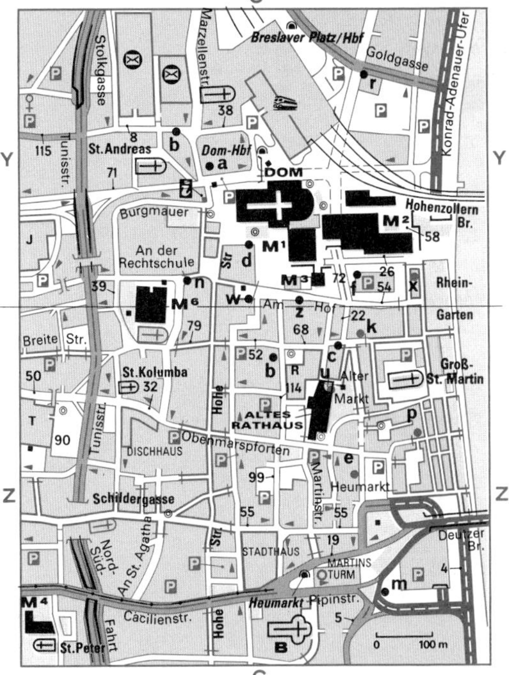

Breite Straße . . . . GZ
Ehrenstraße . . . . EV
Eigelstein . . . . FU
Gürzenichstraße . . . . GZ 55
Habsburgerring . . . . EV 57
Hahnenstraße . . . . EV
Hohenstaufenring . . . . . . EX
Hohenzollernring . . . . . . EV
Hohe Straße . . . . GYZ
Mittelstraße . . . . EV
Neumarkt . . . . EV
Richmodstraße . . . . EV 102
Schildergasse . . . . GZ
Severinstraße . . . . FX
Zeppelinstraße . . . . EV 118

Am Bayenturm . . . . FX 3
Am Leystapel . . . . GZ 4
Am Malzbüchel . . . . GZ 5
An den Dominikanern . . GY 8
An der Malzmühle . . . . . FX 9
An St-Katharinen . . . . . . FX 14
Apostelnstraße . . . . EV 15
Auf dem Berlich . . . . EV 16
Augustinerstraße . . . . . . GZ 19
Bechergasse . . . . GZ 22
Bischofsgarten-Straße . . GY 26
Blaubach . . . . FX 28
Brückenstraße . . . . GZ 32
Dompropst-Ketzer-Straße . . . . GY 38
Drususgasse . . . . GY 39
Gladbacher Straße . . . . . EU 48
Glockengasse . . . . GZ 50
Große Budengasse . . . . . GZ 52
Große Neugasse . . . . GY 54
Heinrich-Böll-Platz . . . . . GY 58
Kaiser-Wilhelm-Ring . . . . EV 62
Kardinal-Frings-Straße . . . . EV 65
Karolingerring . . . . FX 66
Kattenbug . . . . EV 67
Kleine Budengasse . . . . . GZ 68
Kleine Witschgasse . . . . FX 69
Komödienstraße . . . . GY 71
Kurt-Hackenberg-Platz . . GY 72
Mathiasstraße . . . . FX 74
Mechtildisstraße . . . . FX 76
Minoritenstraße . . . . GZ 79
Neusser Straße . . . . FU 86
Offenbachplatz . . . . GZ 90
Pfälzer Straße . . . . EX 96
Quatermarkt . . . . GZ 99

Riehler Straße . . . . FU 100
Roonstraße . . . . EX 104
Sankt-Apern-Straße . . . . EV 108
Tel-Aviv-Straße . . . . FX 111

Unter Goldschmied . . . . . . GZ 114
Unter Sachsenhausen . . . . GY 115
Victoriastraße . . . . FU 117
Zeughausstraße . . . . EV 122

XXX **Börsen-Restaurant Maître**, Unter Sachsenhausen 10 (K 1), ☎ 13 30 21, Fax 133040 – ▤. AE ⓘ E VISA. ✻ EV **r**
closed Sunday, Bank Holidays and 4 weeks July - August – **M** a la carte 69/95 – **Börsenstube M** a la carte 44/74.

XXX **Die Bastei**, Konrad-Adenauer-Ufer 80 (K 1), ☎ 12 28 25, Fax 1390187, ≤ Rhein – AE ⓘ E VISA. ✻ FU **b**
closed Saturday lunch – **M** a la carte 70/115.

XX **Em Krützche**, Am Frankenturm 1 (K 1), ☎ 2 58 08 39, Fax 253417, 斎 – ⓘ E VISA GY **x**
closed Monday – **M** *(booking essential)* a la carte 47/73.

XX **Weinhaus im Walfisch** (17C timber framed house), Salzgasse 13 (K 1), ☎ 2 57 78 79, Fax 235681 – AE ⓘ E VISA GZ **p**
closed Saturday lunch, Sunday, Bank Holidays and 22 December - 6 January – **M** a la carte 64/96.

XX **Soufflé**, Hohenstaufenring 53 (K 1), ☎ 21 20 22, Fax 247059, 斎 – AE ⓘ E VISA EX **v**
closed 1 to 6 January, Saturday lunch, Sunday and Bank Holidays (except exhibitions) – **M** a la carte 62/75.

XX **Ratskeller**, Rathausplatz 1 (entrance Alter Markt) (K 1), ☎ 21 83 01, Fax 246942, « Courtyard » – ▤ ♿ – 🏛 80. AE ⓘ E VISA – **M** a la carte 38/68. GZ **u**

XX **Daitokai** (Japanese rest.), Kattenbug 2 (K 1), ☎ 12 00 48, Fax 137503 – ▤. AE ⓘ E VISA. ✻ EV **e**
closed Sunday – **M** a la carte 43/74.

X **Ristorante Pan e vin**, Heumarkt 75 (K 1), ☎ 24 84 10, Fax 728097 – AE E. ✻ GZ **e**
closed Monday (except exhibitions) – **M** a la carte 54/82.

at Cologne 41-Braunsfeld by Rudolfplatz EV :

🏨 **Regent**, Melatengürtel 15, ☎ 5 49 90, Telex 8881824, Fax 5499998, ≘s – |‡| ⇔ rm 📺 🅟 – 🏛 80. AE ⓘ E VISA
M *(closed 24 December - 7 January)* a la carte 47/70 – **168 rm** ⊒ 215/451, 3 suites.

at Cologne 21-Deutz by Deutzer Brücke FV :

Hyatt Regency, Kennedy-Ufer 2a, 8 28 12 34, Telex 887525, Fax 8281370, <, beer-garden, Massage, – rm – 400. rest
– **Graugans** *(closed Saturday lunch and Sunday)* **M** 45 (lunch) and a la carte 72/87 – **Glashaus** **M** a la carte 55/65 – **307 rm** 320/695 – 5 suites 950/2600.

XX **Der Messeturm**, Kennedy-Ufer (18th floor,), 88 10 08, Fax 818575, < Cologne – – 25.
closed Saturday lunch – **M** a la carte 55/86.

at Cologne 30-Ehrenfeld by Rudolfplatz EV :

Imperial, Barthelstr. 93, 51 70 57, Telex 8883452, Fax 520993, – .
M (dinner only) a la carte 38/64 – **35 rm** 170/330.

XXX ✿ **Zum offenen Kamin**, Eichendorffstr. 25, 55 68 78 –
closed Saturday lunch, Sunday and Bank Holidays (except exhibitions) – **M** 55 (lunch) and a la carte 68/91 *(vegetarian menu available)* by Erftstraße EU
Spec. Mille-feuille von Poularde, Ente und Gänseleber, Steinbutt in der Kartoffelkruste, Kalbsbries und Krebse mit Gänseleberschaum.

at Cologne 80-Holweide by Konrad-Adenauer-Ufer FU :

XXX **Isenburg**, Johann-Bensberg-Str. 49, 69 59 09, Fax 698703, « Garden terrace » – .
closed Saturday lunch, Sunday, Monday, carnival, mid July - mid August and Christmas – **M** *(booking essential)* a la carte 68/85.

at Cologne 40-Junkersdorf by Rudolfplatz EV :

Brenner'scher Hof, Wilhelm-von-Capitaine-Str. 15, 94 86 00 67, Fax 94860010, – – 50. .
M *(closed Monday)* a la carte 50/88 – **40 rm** 190/365, 7 suite.

at Cologne 41-Lindenthal by Rudolfplatz EV and B 264 :

Queens Hotel, Dürener Str. 287, 4 67 60, Telex 8882516, Fax 433765, « Garden terrace » – rm rest – 350. . rest
M a la carte 52/88 – **147 rm** 260/518.

at Cologne 51-Marienburg by Bonner Straße FX :

Marienburger Bonotel, Bonner Str. 478, 3 70 20, Telex 8881515, Fax 3702132, , – – 70. . rest
M a la carte 46/68 – **93 rm** 180/365, 4 suites.

at Cologne 40-Marsdorf by Rudolfplatz EV and B 264 :

Novotel Köln-West, Horbeller Str. 1, (02234) 51 40, Telex 8886355, Fax 514106, , , (heated), – rest – 300
199 rm.

at Cologne 41-Müngersdorf by Rudolfplatz EV and B 55 :

XXX **Landhaus Kuckuck**, Olympiaweg 2, 49 23 23, Fax 4972847, – 120.
closed Monday and 22 February - 4 March – **M** 45 (lunch) and a la carte 62/85.

XX **Remise**, Wendelinstr. 48, 49 18 81, « Historic farmhouse » – .
closed Saturday lunch and Sunday – **M** *(booking essential)* a la carte 70/90.

at Cologne 90-Porz-Wahnheide SE : 17 km by A 59 :

Holiday Inn, Waldstr. 255, (02203) 56 10, Telex 8874665, Fax 5619, , , – rm – 90.
M a la carte 48/79 – **177 rm** 260/455.

Quelle without rest, Heidestr. 246, (02203) 60 81, Fax 608317 – – 30
95 rm.

Laasphe, Bad

5928 Nordrhein-Westfalen 412 I14, 987 ㉔ – pop. 16 000 – alt. 335 m – 02752.

Köln 144.

at Bad Laasphe 9-Hesselbach SW : 10 km :

XXX ✿✿ **L'ecole**, Hesselbacher Str. 23, 53 42, « Elegant installation » – .
closed Saturday lunch, Monday, Tuesday and January – **M** (booking essential) 65/120 and a la carte
Spec. Gebratene Gänseleber in Trüffeljus, Rehrücken mit Pinienkruste und Tannenhonigsauce, Pumpernickel-Steinhägercreme mit Birnensülze und Mandeleis.

Wittlich **5560.** Rheinland - Pfalz 987 ㉓ ㉔, 412 D 17 - pop. 17 000 - alt. 155 m - ☎ 06571.

Köln 130.

at Dreis **5561** SW : 8 km :

XXXX ✿✿ **Waldhotel Sonnora** with rm, Auf dem Eichelfeld, ☎ (06578) 4 06, Fax 1402, ≤, « Garden » - TV ☎ P. E.
closed 6 January - 6 February - **M** *(closed Monday and Tuesday)* (booking essential) 105/145 and a la carte 85/115 - **18 rm** 65/120
Spec. Ravioli von Langustinen im Minestronefond, Steinbutt mit Kaisergranat im Maisstrudelblatt, Taubenbrustroulade im Wirsingmantel mit Trüffeljus.

DRESDEN **O-8010.** Sachsen 984 ㉔, 987 ⑱ - pop. 500 000 - alt. 105 m - ☎ 003751.

See : Zwinger★★★ (Wall Pavilion★★, Nymphs' Bath★★, Porcelain Collection★★, National Mathematical-Physical Salon★★) AY - Semper Opera★★ AY - Former court church★★ (Hofkirche) BY - Palace (Schloß) : royal houses★ (Fürstenzug-Mosaik), Long Passage★ (Langer Gang) BY - Albertinum : Picture Gallery Old Masters★★★ (Gemäldegalerie Alte Meister), Picture Gallery New Masters★★★ (Gemäldegalerie Neue Meister), Green Vault★★★ (Grünes Gewölbe) BY - Prager Straße★ ABZ - Museum of History of the town Dresden★ (Museum für Geschichte der Stadt Dresden) BY **L** - Church of the Cross★ (Kreuzkirche) BY - Japanese Palace★ (Japanisches Palais) ABX - Museum of Folk Art★ (Museum für Volkskunst) BX **M 2** - Great Garden★ (Großer Garten) CDZ - Russian-Orthodox Church★ (Russisch-orthodoxe Kirche) (by Leningrader Str. BZ) - Brühl's Terrace ≤★ (Brühlsche Terrasse) BY **6** - Equestrian statue of Augustus the Strong ★ (Reiterstandbild Augusts des Starken) BX **E**.

Envir. : Schloß (palace) Moritzburg★ (NW : 14 km by Hansastr. BX) - Schloß (palace) Pillnitz★ (SE : 15 km by Bautzener Str. CX) - Saxon Swiss★★★ (Sächsische Schweiz) : Bastei★★★, Festung (fortress) Königstein★★ ≤★★, Großsedlitz : Baroque Garden★.

✈ Dresden-Klotzsche (N : 13 km), ☎ 58 31 41. City Office, Rampische Str. 2, ☎ 4 95 60 13.

ℹ Dresden-Information, Prager Str. 10, ☎ 4 95 50 25, Telex 26198, Fax 4951276.

Berlin 198 - Chemnitz 70 - Görlitz 98 - Leipzig 111 - Praha 152.

Plans on following pages

Maritim Hotel Bellevue, Große Meißner Str. 15, ✉ O-8060, ☎ 5 66 20, Telex 329330, Fax 55997, ≤, « Courtyard terraces », Massage, ♨, ☎, 🏊 - 🛗 ⇔ rm ▤ TV ♿ 🚗 P - 🏛 250. rest — BX **a**
M a la carte 53/75 - **328 rm** 449/538, 16 suites.

Dresdner Hilton, An der Frauenkirche 5, ✉ O-8012, ☎ 4 84 10, Telex 2488, Fax 4841700, ♨, ☎, 🏊 - 🛗 ⇔ rm ▤ TV ♿ 🚗 - 🏛 320. AE ⓓ E VISA — BY **e**
M a la carte 44/71 - **333 rm** 355/510, 12 suites.

Martha Hospiz without rest, Nieritzstr. 11, ✉ O-8060, ☎ 5 24 25, Fax 53218 - 🛗 TV ☎ ♿. E VISA. — BX **s**
36 rm 130/230.

Alpha without rest, Fritz-Reuter-Str. 21, ✉ O-8060, ☎ 5 02 24 41, Fax 571390 - 🛗 TV ☎ P. AE E VISA — by Hansastraße BX
75 rm 230/330, 4 suites.

Bastei, Prager Straße, ✉ O-8012, ☎ 4 85 63 85, Fax 4954076 - 🛗 ⇔ rm TV ☎ - 🏛 30. AE ⓓ E VISA. — BZ **e**
M a la carte 23/46 - **300 rm** 210/250, 9 suites.

Mercure Newa, Prager Straße, ✉ O-8012, ☎ 4 81 40, Telex 329409, Fax 4955137, ☎ - 🛗 TV ☎ 🚗 - 🏛 30. AE ⓓ E VISA. rest — BZ **n**
M a la carte 31/62 - **310 rm** 230/330, 8 suites.

Lilienstein, Prager Str. 15, ✉ O-8012, ☎ 4 85 63 72, Fax 4952506, - 🛗 TV ☎ - 🏛 30. AE ⓓ E VISA. rest — BZ **b**
M a la carte 26/41 - **303 rm** 210/250, 12 suites.

Königstein, Prager Str. 9, ✉ O-8012, ☎ 4 85 63 62, Fax 4954054 - 🛗 TV ☎ - 🏛 30. AE ⓓ E VISA. rest — BZ **d**
M a la carte 24/43 - **306 rm** 210/250, 9 suites.

Astoria, Strehlener Platz 1, ✉ O-8020, ☎ 4 71 51 71, Fax 4718872 - 🛗 TV ☎ P
82 rm - 3 suites. — by Parkstr. BZ

XX **Opernrestaurant**, Theaterplatz 2 (1st floor), ☎ 4 84 25 00, - AE ⓓ E VISA — AY **r**
M a la carte 31/56.

at Dresden-Loschwitz **O-8060** by Bautzner Straße CDX :

Schloß Eckberg, Bautzner Str. 134, ☎ 5 25 71, Fax 55379, ≤, « Park », ♨, ☎, - ⇔ rm TV ☎ P - 🏛 90. E VISA. rest - **Schloßrestaurant M** a la carte 44/76 - **Remise** *(closed Saturday-Sunday)* **M** (dinner only) a la carte 27/60 - **83 rm** 160/260, 4 suites.

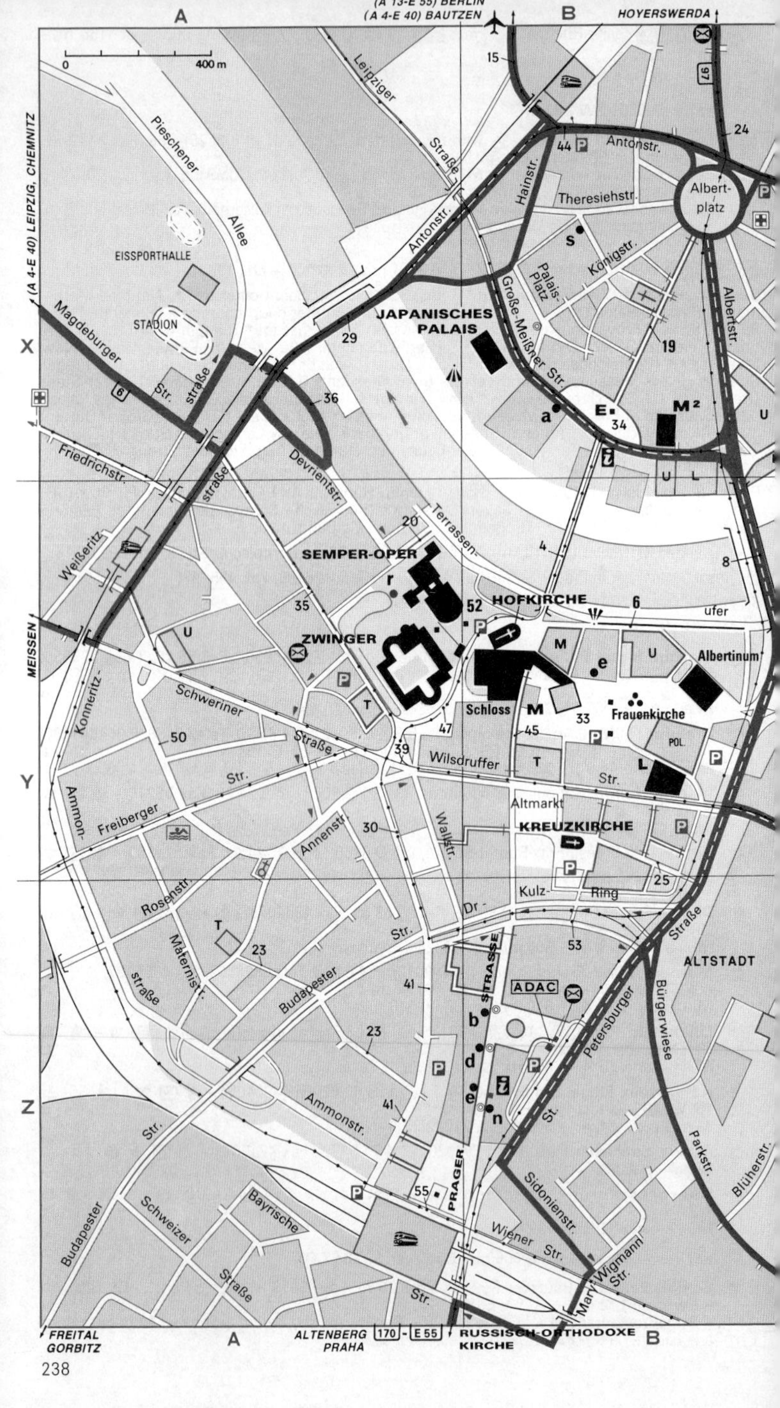

(A 13-E 55) BERLIN
(A 4-E 40) BAUTZEN
HOYERSWERDA
A
B
X
Y
Z
0
400 m
(A 4-E 40) LEIPZIG, CHEMNITZ
MEISSEN
FREITAL
GORBITZ
ALTENBERG
PRAHA
170
E 55
RUSSISCH-ORTHODOXE
KIRCHE
Leipziger
Straße
Pieschener
Allee
EISSPORTHALLE
STADION
Magdeburger
Str.
straße
Antonstr.
Antonstr.
Hainstr.
Theresiehstr.
Albert-
platz
Königstr.
Palais-
Platz
Große-Meißner Str.
Albertstr.
JAPANISCHES
PALAIS
Friedrichstr.
Devrientstr.
Terrassen-
ufer
Weißeritz
SEMPER-OPER
HOFKIRCHE
ZWINGER
Schloss
Albertinum
Frauenkirche
POL.
Schweriner
Straße
Wilsdruffer
Str.
Altmarkt
KREUZKIRCHE
Konneritz-
Ammon-
Freiberger
Str.
Annenstr.
Wallstr.
Rosenstr.
Maternistr.
straße
Kulz-
Ring
Dr.-
Str.
Budapester
Ammonstr.
PRAGER
STRASSE
ADAC
Petersburger
St.
Straße
ALTSTADT
Bürgerwiese
Parkstr.
Blüherstr.
Sidonienstr.
Wiener
Str.
Mary-Wigmann
Str.
Bayrische
Schweizer
Straße
Budapester
Str.
Str.
15
24
44
29
19
36
34
20
4
8
6
52
35
50
33
45
47
39
30
25
53
23
23
41
41
55

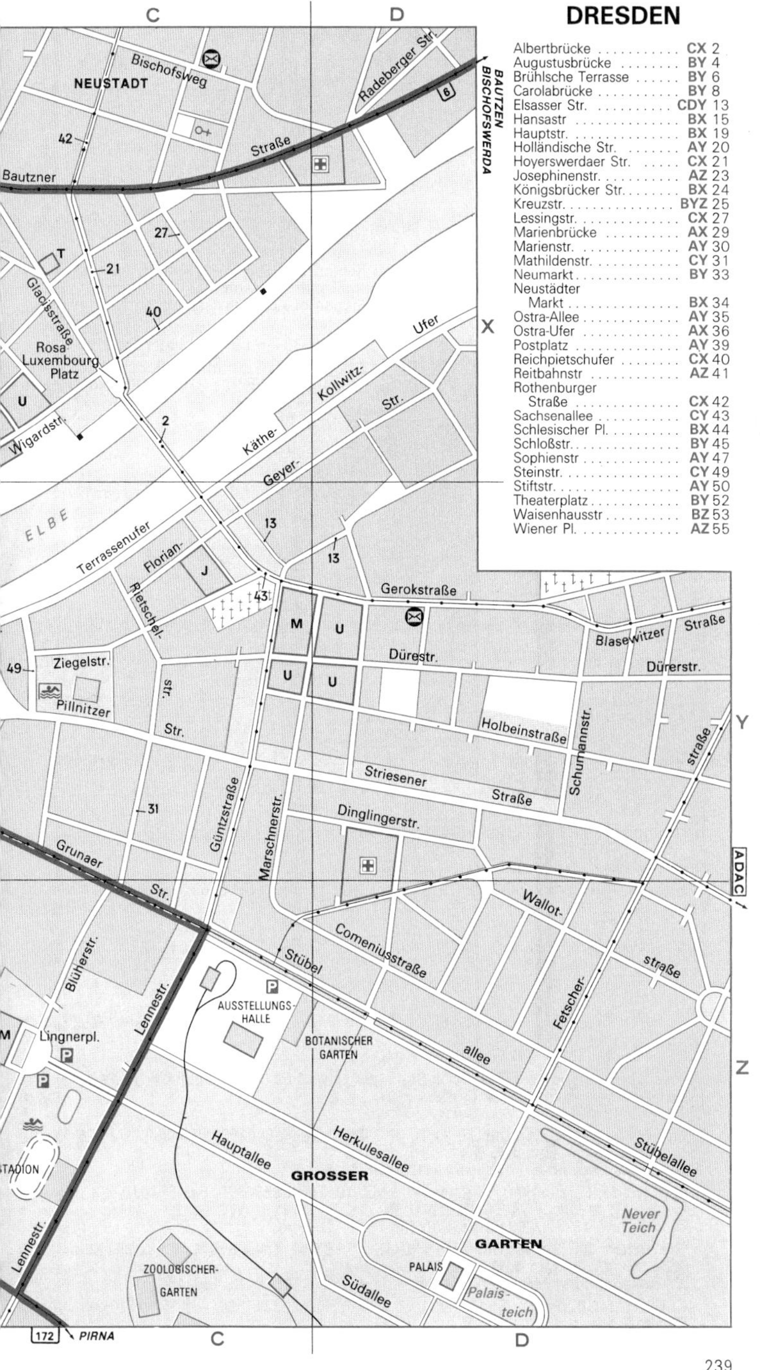
DRESDEN
Albertbrücke CX 2
Augustusbrücke BY 4
Brühlsche Terrasse BY 6
Carolabrücke BY 8
Elsasser Str. CDY 13
Hansastr BX 15
Hauptstr. BX 19
Holländische Str. AY 20
Hoyerswerdaer Str. CX 21
Josephinenstr. AZ 23
Königsbrücker Str. BX 24
Kreuzstr. BYZ 25
Lessingstr. CX 27
Marienbrücke AX 29
Marienstr. AY 30
Mathildenstr. CY 31
Neumarkt BY 33
Neustädter Markt BX 34
Ostra-Allee AY 35
Ostra-Ufer AX 36
Postplatz AY 39
Reichpietschufer CX 40
Reitbahnstr AZ 41
Rothenburger Straße CX 42
Sachsenallee CY 43
Schlesischer Pl. BX 44
Schloßstr. BY 45
Sophienstr AY 47
Steinstr. CY 49
Stiftstr. AY 50
Theaterplatz BY 52
Waisenhausstr BZ 53
Wiener Pl. AZ 55
C
D
X
Y
Z
NEUSTADT
Bischofsweg
Radeberger Str.
Bautzner Straße
BAUTZEN BISCHOFSWERDA
Glacisstraße
Rosa Luxembourg Platz
Wigardstr.
ELBE
Terrassenufer
Käthe-Kollwitz-Ufer
Geyer-Str.
Florian-
Rietschel-str.
Gerokstraße
Blasewitzer Straße
Dürestr.
Dürerstr.
Ziegelstr.
Pillnitzer Str.
Holbeinstraße
Schumannstr.
Striesener Straße
Dinglingerstr.
Güntzstraße
Marschnerstr.
Grunaer Str.
Wallot-straße
Comeniusstraße
Stübel allee
Fetscher-straße
ADAC
Blüherstr.
Lennestr.
Lingnerpl.
AUSSTELLUNGS-HALLE
BOTANISCHER GARTEN
STADION
Hauptallee
Herkulesallee
GROSSER GARTEN
Stübelallee
Never Teich
PALAIS
Palais-teich
Südallee
ZOOLOGISCHER-GARTEN
172
PIRNA

at Dresden-Zschernitz **O-8020** by St. Petersburger Straße BZ :

Am Bismarck Turm (Motel), Münzmeisterstr. 10, O-8020, 4 93 36 45, Fax 4933648, , - . rest
M a la carte 32/44 - **93 rm** 185/240 - 4 suites 400.

at Freital-Wurgwitz **O-8225** SW : 12 km by Freiberger Straße AY :

Solar Parkhotel, Ernst-Thälmann-Straße, (0351) 4 60 17 00, Fax 641276, , - rm - 100. rest
M a la carte 38/73 - **79 rm** 198/258.

DÜSSELDORF **4000.** L Nordrhein-Westfalen 411 412 D 13, 987 ㉓ ㉔ - pop. 570 000 - alt. 40 m - 0211.

See : Königsallee★ EZ - Hofgarten★ DEY und Schloß Jägerhof (Goethemuseum★ EY **M1**) - Hetjensmuseum★ DZ **M4** - Land Economic Museum (Landesmuseum Volk u. Wirtschaft)★ DY **M5** - Museum of Art (Kunstmuseum)★ DY **M2** - Collection of Art (Kunstsammlung NRW)★ DY **M3** - Löbbecke-Museum und Aquazoo★ by Kaiserswerther Str. AU.

Envir. : Chateau of Benrath (Schloß Benrath) (Park★) S : 10 km by Siegburger Str. CX.

18 Ratingen-Hösel, NE : 16 km, (02102) 6 86 29 ; 18 Gut Rommeljans, NE : 12 km, (02102) 8 10 92 ; 18 Düsseldorf-Hubbelrath, E : 12 km, (02104) 7 21 78 ; 9 Düsseldorf-Hafen, Auf der Lausward, (0211) 39 65 98

18 Düsseldorf-Schmidtberg, NE : 2 km, (02104) 7 70 60.

Düsseldorf-Lohausen (N : 8 km), 42 10 - 3 68 04 68.

Exhibition Centre (Messegelände), 4 56 01, Telex 8584853.

Tourist office, Konrad-Adenauer-Platz and Heinrich-Heine-Allee 24, 35 05 05, Telex 8587785, Fax 161071.

ADAC, Himmelgeister Str. 63, 3 10 93 33.

Amsterdam 225 - Essen 31 - Köln 40 - Rotterdam 237.

The reference (D 15) at the end of the address is the postal district : Düsseldorf 15

Plans on following pages

Breidenbacher Hof, Heinrich-Heine-Allee 36 (D 1), 1 30 30, Telex 8582630, Fax 1303830, - rm - 100. EY **a**
Grill Royal M a la carte 64/112 - **Breidenbacher Eck M** a la carte 48/76 - **Trader Vic's M** (dinner only) a la carte 56/97 - **132 rm** 290/610, 31 suites.

Steigenberger Parkhotel, Corneliusplatz 1 (D 1), 1 38 10, Telex 8582331, Fax 131679 - rm - 200. rest EY **p**
M a la carte 67/101 - **160 rm** 315/570, 12 suites.

Nikko, Immermannstr. 41 (D 1), 83 40, Telex 8582080, Fax 161216, , Massage, , - rm - 500. rest BV **g**
- **Benkay** (japanese rest.) **M** a la carte 85/135 - **Traveller's M** a la carte 53/88 - **301 rm** 323/531, 16 suites.

Queens Hotel, Ludwig-Erhard-Allee 3, 7 77 10, Fax 7771777, - rm . BV **s**
M a la carte 43/71 - **120 rm** 270/510, 5 suites.

Holiday Inn, Graf-Adolf-Platz 10 (D 1), 3 87 30, Telex 8586359, Fax 3873390, , - rm - 80. rest EZ **t**
M a la carte 63/86 *(vegetarian menu available)* - **177 rm** 422/554.

Majestic - Restaurant La Grappa (Italian rest.), Cantadorstr. 4 (D 1), 36 70 30 (hotel) 35 72 92 (rest.), Telex 8584649, Fax 3670399, - - 30. BV **a**
closed 24 December - 4 January - **M** *(closed Sunday and Bank Holidays except exhibitions)* a la carte 59/82 - **52 rm** 217/410.

Savoy, Oststr. 128 (D 1), 36 03 36, Telex 8584215, Fax 356642, Massage, , - - 100. EZ **w**
M a la carte 42/70 - **123 rm** 215/380.

Madison I without rest, Graf-Adolf-Str. 94 (D 1), 1 68 50, Fax 1685328, , , - - 60. BV **n**
95 rm 150/390.

Eden without rest, Adersstr. 29 (D 1), 3 89 70, Telex 8582530, Fax 3897777 - - 90. EZ **m**
closed 22 December - 2 January - **130 rm** 193/424.

Esplanade, Fürstenplatz 17 (D 1), 37 50 10, Telex 8582970, Fax 374032, , - rm - 60. BX **s**
M a la carte 48/75 - **80 rm** 179/468.

Graf Adolf, Stresemannplatz 1 (D 1), 3 55 40, Telex 8587844, Fax 354120 - - 50. rest EZ **j**
M *(closed Saturday and Sunday)* a la carte 46/69 - **151 rm** 190/430.

Carat Hotel, Benrather Str. 7a (D 1), 1 30 50, Fax 322214, - rm - 30. DZ **r**
M (dinner only) (residents only) - **73 rm** 205/395.

Madison II without rest, Graf-Adolf-Str. 47 (D 1), ☎ 37 02 96, Fax 1685328 – closed August and 20 December - 8 January – **24 rm** 130/245. EZ e

Astoria without rest, Jahnstr. 72 (D 1), ☎ 38 20 88, Fax 372089 – closed 22 December - 7 January – **27 rm** 140/290, 4 suites. BX b

Rema-Hotel Concorde without rest, Graf-Adolf-Str. 60 (D 1), ☎ 36 98 25, Telex 8588008, Fax 354604 – **83 rm** 170/330. EZ f

Uebachs, Leopoldstr. 5 (D 1), ☎ 36 05 66, Telex 8587620, Fax 358064 – rm – 30. rest BV r
M *(closed Sunday except exhibitions)* a la carte 47/80 – **82 rm** 179/380.

Hotel An der Kö without rest, Talstr. 9 (D 1), ☎ 37 10 48, Fax 370835 – **44 rm** 158/320. EZ n

Rema-Hotel Monopol without rest, Oststr. 135 (D 1), ☎ 8 42 08, Telex 8587770, Fax 328843 – **50 rm** 170/330. EZ d

Rema-Hotel Central without rest, Luisenstr. 42 (D 1), ☎ 37 90 01, Telex 8582145, Fax 379094 – *closed 20 December - 1 January* – **72 rm** 155/310. EZ y

Bellevue without rest, Luisenstr. 98 (D 1), ☎ 37 70 71, Fax 377076 – *closed 23 December - 2 January* – **52 rm** 205/295. EZ z

Terminus without rest, Am Wehrhahn 81 (D 1), ☎ 35 05 91, Fax 358350, – *closed 23 December - 4 January* – **44 rm** 160/370. BV f

Fürstenhof without rest, Fürstenplatz 3 (D 1), ☎ 37 05 45, Telex 8586540, Fax 379062, – *closed 24 December - 2 January* – **43 rm** 210/305. BX e

City without rest, Bismarckstr. 73 (D 1), ☎ 36 50 23, Telex 8587362, Fax 365343 – *closed 23 December - 2 January* – **54 rm** 130/320. EZ k

Cornelius without rest, Corneliusstr. 82 (D 1), ☎ 38 20 55, Telex 8587385, Fax 382050, – 25. *closed 20 December - 7 January* – **48 rm** 130/280. BX s

Prinz Anton without rest, Karl-Anton-Str. 11 (D 1), ☎ 35 20 00, Fax 362010 – *closed 25 December - 3 January* – **40 rm** 135/295. BV k

Residenz without rest, Worringer Str. 88 (D 1), ☎ 36 08 54, Telex 8587897, Fax 364676 – **34 rm** 135/320. BV z

Schumacher without rest, Worringer Str. 55 (D 1), ☎ 36 78 50, Fax 3678570, – **30 rm** 150/350. BV d

Lancaster without rest, Oststr. 166 (D 1), ☎ 35 10 66, Fax 162884 – **40 rm** 145/195. EZ f

Minerva without rest, Cantadorstr. 13a (D 1), ☎ 35 09 61, Fax 356398 – **15 rm** 110/245. BV a

Astor without rest, Kurfürstenstr. 23 (D 1), ☎ 36 06 61, Telex 8586201, Fax 162597, – *closed 22 December - 5 January* – **16 rm** 105/220. BV k

Großer Kurfürst without rest, Kurfürstenstr. 18 (D 1), ☎ 35 76 47, Telex 8586201, Fax 162597 – *closed 22 December - 4 January* **22 rm** 105/220. BV k

✻ **Victorian**, Königstr. 3a (1st floor) (D 1), ☎ 32 02 22, Fax 131013 – *closed Sunday and Bank Holidays* – **M** (booking essential) a la carte 75/115 – **Lounge** *(closed Sunday and Bank Holidays mid July - August)* **M** a la carte 41/77 EZ c
Spec. Hummer à la nage, Gedämpfter Steinbutt mit Champagnersauce, Kalbsbries mit Rosmarinkruste.

La Scala (Italian rest.), Königsallee 14 (1st floor) (D 1), ☎ 32 68 32 – *closed Sunday during exhibitions* – **M** (dinner only Sunday) a la carte 68/96. EY y

La Terrazza (Italian rest.), Königsallee 30 (Kö-Centre, 2nd floor,) (D 1), ☎ 32 75 40, Fax 320975 – *closed Sunday and Bank Holidays (except exhibitions)* – **M** (booking essential) a la carte 77/89. EZ v

Mövenpick -Kö-Stübli, Königsallee 60 (Kö-Galerie) (D 1), ☎ 32 03 14, Fax 328058 – *closed Sunday* – **M** a la carte 48/77. EZ h

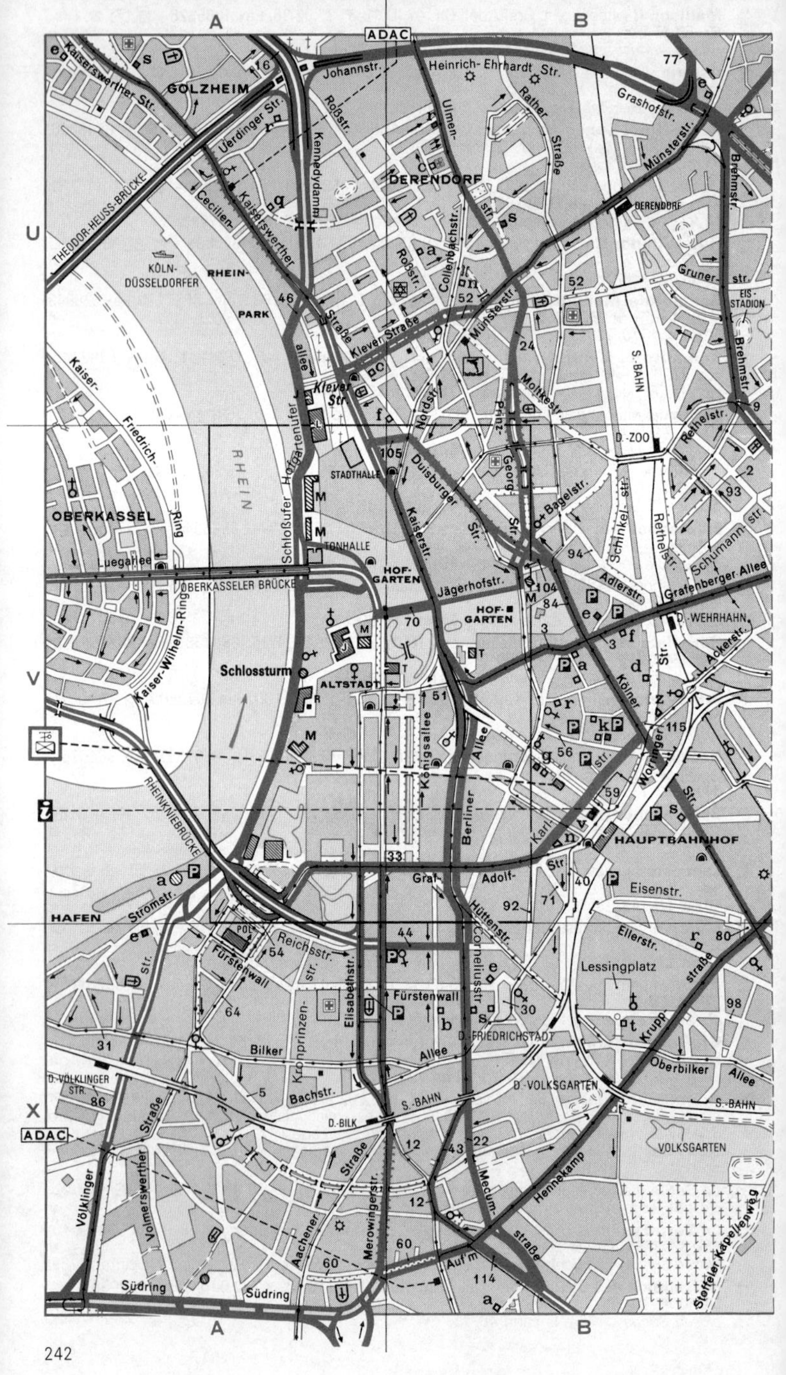
A
B
ADAC
GOLZHEIM
DERENDORF
Johannstr.
Heinrich-Ehrhardt Str.
Kaiserswerther Str.
Uerdinger Str.
Roßstr.
Kennedydamm
Ulmen-
Rather Straße
Grashofstr.
Münsterstr.
Brehmstr.
THEODOR-HEUSS-BRÜCKE
Cecilien-
Kaiserswerther Straße
KÖLN-DÜSSELDORFER
RHEIN-PARK
Collenbachstr.
Gruner-str.
EIS-STADION
Klever Straße
Klever Str.
Prinz-Georg-Str.
Moltkestr.
S.-BAHN
Nordstr.
Kaiser-Friedrich-Ring
Hofgartenufer
Schloßufer
RHEIN
STADTHALLE
Duisburger Str.
D.-ZOO
Rethelstr.
Schinkel-str.
Schumann-str.
OBERKASSEL
TONHALLE
Kaiserstr.
Bagelstr.
Luegallee
OBERKASSELER BRÜCKE
HOF-GARTEN
Jägerhofstr.
Adlerstr.
Grafenberger Allee
D.-WEHRHAHN
Kaiser-Wilhelm-Ring
Schlossturm
ALTSTADT
Kölner Str.
Ackerstr.
Königsallee
Berliner Allee
Worringer Str.
RHEINKNIEBRÜCKE
Karl-Str.
HAUPTBAHNHOF
Graf-Adolf-Str.
Eisenstr.
HAFEN
Stromstr.
Reichsstr.
Hüttenstr.
Corneliusstr.
Ellerstr.
Lessingplatz
Fürstenwall
Elisabethstr.
Kronprinzen-str.
Bilker Allee
D.-FRIEDRICHSTADT
Kruppstraße
Oberbilker Allee
D.-VÖLKLINGER STR.
Bachstr.
D.-VOLKSGARTEN
S.-BAHN
D.-BILK
VOLKSGARTEN
Völklinger Straße
Volmerswerther Straße
Aachener Straße
Merowingerstr.
Mecumstraße
Hennekamp
Stoffeler Kapellenweg
Auf'm
Südring
U
V
X

DÜSSELDORF

DÜSSELDORF

Am Wehrhahn .... EY 3
Berliner Allee .... EZ
Flinger Str. .... DY 28
Graf-Adolf-Str. .... EZ
Königsallee .... EZ
Schadowstraße .... EY 91

Blumenstraße .... EZ 7
Bolkerstraße .... DY 8
Citadellstraße .... DZ 13
Corneliusstraße .... EZ 15
Elberfelder Str. .... EY 21
Ernst-Reuter-Platz .... EZ 23
Fischerstraße .... EY 27
Friedrich-Ebert-Straße .... EZ 29
Grabbeplatz .... DY 32
Graf-Adolf-Platz .... EZ 33
Heinrich-Heine-Allee .... EY 42
Hofgartenrampe .... DY 45
Jan-Wellem-Platz .... EY 51
Marktplatz .... DY 68
Martin-Luther-Platz .... EZ 69
Maximilian-Weyhe-Allee .... EY 70
Mühlenstraße .... DY 73
Ratinger Str. .... DY 88
Schadowplatz .... EY 90
Schneider-Wibbel-Gasse .... DY 95
Schwanenmarkt .... DZ 96
Tonhallenstraße .... EY 101
Vagedesstraße .... EY 104
Venloer Str. .... EY 105

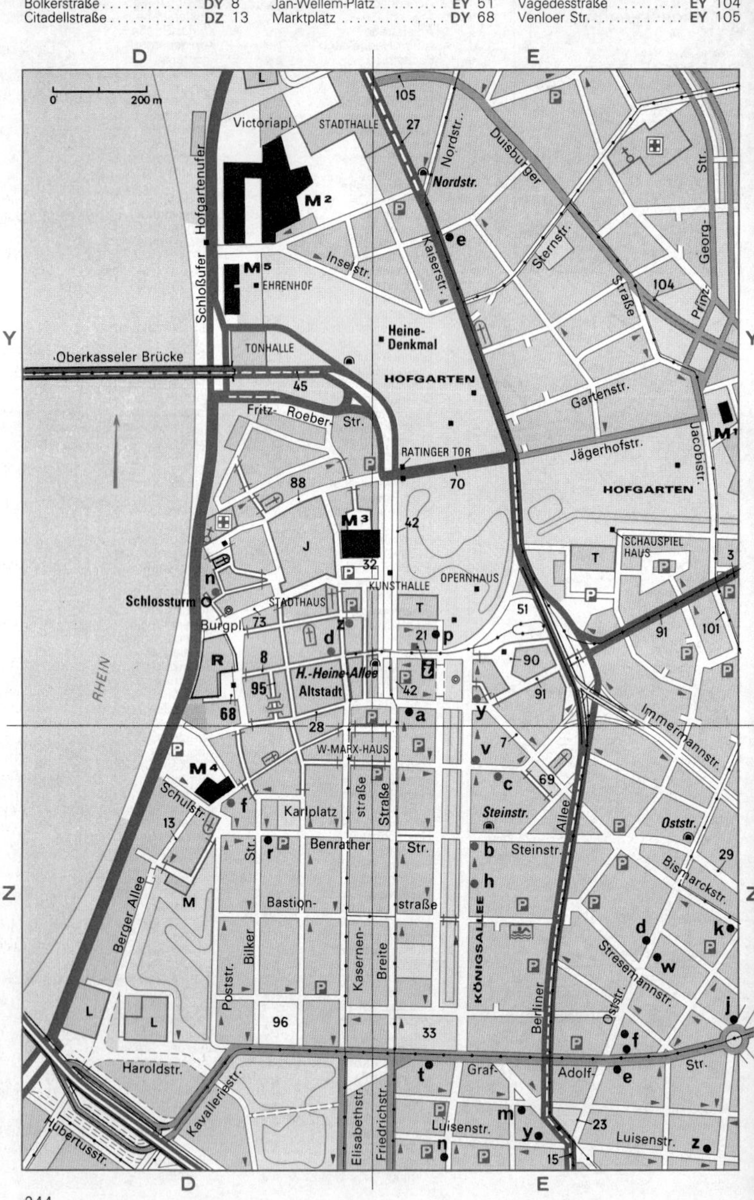

XX **Tse Yang** (Chinese rest.), Immermannstr. 65 (Immermannhof, entrance Konrad-Adenauer-Platz) (D 1), ☎ 36 90 20, Fax 1649423 – AE ⓓ E VISA BV **v**
M a la carte 42/65.

XX Nippon Kan (Japanese rest.), Immermannstr. 35 (D 1), ☎ 35 31 35, Fax 3613625 – ✻ BV **g**
M (booking essential).

XX **Daitokai** (Japanese rest.), Mutter-Ey-Str. 1 (D 1), ☎ 32 50 54, Fax 325056 – ▤. AE ⓓ E VISA. ✻ DY **z**
closed Sunday (except exhibitions) – **M** a la carte 52/87.

Brewery-inns :

X **Zum Schiffchen**, Hafenstr. 5 (D 1), ☎ 13 24 22, Fax 134596 – AE ⓓ E VISA DZ **f**
closed Christmas - New Year, Sunday and Bank Holidays – **M** a la carte 35/66.

X Frankenheim, Wielandstr. 14 (D 1), ☎ 35 14 47, beer garden BV **e**

X **Im Goldenen Ring**, Burgplatz 21 (D 1), ☎ 13 31 61, Fax 324780, beer garden – AE ⓓ E VISA DY **n**
M a la carte 28/54.

X **Benrather Hof**, Steinstr. 1 (D 1), ☎ 32 52 18, Fax 132957, ☂ EZ **b**
closed Christmas and New Year – **M** a la carte 27/59.

X Im Goldenen Kessel, Bolker Str. 44 (D 1), ☎ 32 60 07 DY **d**

at Düsseldorf 13-Benrath by Siegburger Str. CX :

Rheinterrasse, Benrather Schloßufer 39, ☎ 99 69 90, Telex 8582459, Fax 9969999, « Terrace with ≤ » – TV ☎ P – 25. AE E VISA
M a la carte 42/69 – **42 rm** ☐ 145/265.

XX **Lignano** (Italian rest.), Hildener Str. 43, ☎ 7 11 89 36 – AE ⓓ E VISA. ✻
closed Saturday and Bank Holidays lunch, Sunday and 3 weeks July - August – **M** a la carte 57/74.

XX **Giuseppe Verdi** (Italian rest.), Paulistr. 5, ☎ 7 18 49 44 – AE ⓓ E VISA
closed Monday – **M** a la carte 50/80.

at Düsseldorf 1-Bilk :

Grand Hotel without rest, Varnhagenstr. 37 (D 1), ☎ 31 08 00, Telex 8584072, Fax 316667, ≘s – |‡| ⇔ TV ☎ ♿ ⇔ – 30. AE ⓓ E VISA BX **a**
70 rm 215/395.

Aida without rest, Ubierstr. 36, ☎ 1 59 90, Fax 1599103, ≘s – |‡| TV ☎ ♿ P – 30. AE ⓓ E VISA. ✻ by Aachener Str. AX
93 rm ☐ 148/350.

at Düsseldorf 30-Derendorf by Prinz-Georg-Str. BU :

Villa Viktoria without rest, Blumenthalstr. 12, ☎ 46 90 00, Fax 46900601, ≘s, ☘ – |‡| ⇔ TV ⇔. AE ⓓ E VISA. ✻ BU **c**
40 suites 315/1140.

Lindner Hotel Rhein Residence, Kaiserswerther Str. 20, ☎ 4 99 90, Fax 4999499, Massage, ≘s – |‡| ⇔ rm TV – 30. AE ⓓ E VISA ABU **f**
M *(closed Saturday)* a la carte 41/69 – **126 rm** ☐ 270/450.

Saga Excelsior without rest, Kapellstr. 1, ☎ 4 95 90, Telex 8584737, Fax 4959200 – |‡| TV. AE ⓓ E VISA. ✻ EY **e**
65 rm ☐ 220/350.

Michelangelo without rest, Roßstr. 61, ☎ 48 01 01, Telex 8588649, Fax 467742 – |‡| TV ☎ ⇔. AE ⓓ E VISA BU **a**
closed 21 December - 1 January – **70 rm** 130/260.

Consul without rest, Kaiserswerther Str. 59, ☎ 4 92 00 78, Telex 8584624, Fax 4982577 – |‡| TV ☎ ⇔. AE ⓓ E VISA AU **c**
29 rm ☐ 145/260.

Gildors Hotel without rest (with guest house), Collenbachstr. 51, ☎ 48 80 05, Telex 8584418, Fax 444844 – |‡| TV ☎ ⇔ BU **n**
50 rm ☐ 155/295.

XX **Amalfi** (Italian rest.), Ulmenstr. 122, ☎ 43 38 09 – AE ⓓ E BU **r**
closed Sunday and 3 weeks August – **M** (dinner only) a la carte 54/75.

XX **Gatto Verde** (Italian rest.), Rheinbabenstr. 5, ☎ 46 18 17, ☂ – AE ⓓ E VISA BU **s**
closed Saturday lunch, Sunday, Monday and 4 weeks July - August – **M** a la carte 50/82.

at Düsseldorf 13-Eller by Karl-Geusen-Str. CX :

Novotel Düsseldorf Süd, Am Schönenkamp 9, ☎ 74 10 92, Telex 8584374, Fax 745512, ☂, ⛱ (heated), ☘ – |‡| ⇔ rm ▤ TV ☎ ♿ P – 270. AE ⓓ E VISA
M a la carte 36/66 – **120 rm** ☐ 184/216.

at Düsseldorf 30-Golzheim by Fischerstr. BV :

SAS Royal Scandinavia Hotel, Karl-Arnold-Platz 5, ✆ 4 55 30, Telex 8584601, Fax 4553110, Massage, ≘s, ☒ - |♯| ▤ TV ♿ ⇔ P - 🎓 400. AE ⓓ E VISA. ✻ rest AU **q**
- **Les Continents** *(closed Saturday lunch, Sunday and 4 weeks July - August)* **M** a la carte 72/94 - **Café de la Paix M** a la carte 47/71 - **310 rm** ☐ 304/682, 20 suites.

Düsseldorf Hilton, Georg-Glock-Str. 20, ✆ 4 37 70, Telex 8584376, Fax 4377791, ☂, Massage, ♀, Fб, ≘s, ☒, ☒ - |♯| ✂ rm ▤ TV ♿ ⇔ P - 🎓 1000. AE ⓓ E VISA. ✻ rest - **San Francisco** *(closed Monday and July)* **M** (dinner only) a la carte 67/98 - **Hofgarten M** a la carte 48/70 - **374 rm** ☐ 320/564, 8 suites. AU **r**

Golzheimer Krug ⛢, Karl-Kleppe-Str. 20, ✆ 43 44 53, Telex 8588919, Fax 453299, ☂ - TV ☎ P - 🎓 40. AE ⓓ E VISA AU **e**
M *(closed Monday)* a la carte 45/71 - **33 rm** ☐ 170/320.

XX **Rosati** (Italian rest.), Felix-Klein-Str. 1, ✆ 4 36 05 03, Fax 452963, ☂ - P. AE ⓓ E VISA. ✻ AU **s**
closed Saturday lunch and Sunday - **M** (booking essential) a la carte 62/85 - **Rosati due M** a la carte 47/65.

at Düsseldorf 12-Grafenberg by Grafenberger Allee CU :

Rolandsburg ⛢, Rennbahnstr. 2, ✆ 61 00 90, Fax 6100943, ☂, ≘s, ☒ - |♯| TV ☎ P - 🎓 50. AE ⓓ E VISA
M a la carte 50/74 - **59 rm** ☐ 210/490.

at Düsseldorf 31-Kaiserswerth by Kaiserswerther Str. AU :

XXXX ✿✿✿ **Im Schiffchen** (French rest.), Kaiserswerther Markt 9 (1st floor), ✆ 40 10 50, Fax 403667 - ⓓ E VISA. ✻
closed Sunday, Monday and Bank Holidays - **M** (dinner only) (booking essential) 166/186 and a la carte 115/192
Spec. Bretonischer Hummer in Kamillenblüten gedämpft, Kalbsbries-Canelloni in Trüffelbuttersauce, Plinsen mit Quarkschaum.

XX ✿ **Aalschokker**, Kaiserswerther Markt 9 (ground floor), ✆ 40 39 48, Fax 403667 - ⓓ E VISA. ✻
closed Sunday, Monday and Bank Holidays - **M** (dinner only) (booking essential) a la carte 72/137
Spec. Sülze von Schweinebacke mit grünen Linsen, "Himmel und Erde" mit Gänseleber, Schwarzwälder Kirschtorte "eigene Art".

at Düsseldorf 11-Lörick by Luegallee AV :

Fischerhaus ⛢, Bonifatiusstr. 35, ✆ 59 20 07, Telex 8584449, Fax 593989 - TV ☎ P. AE ⓓ E VISA
M (see **Hummerstübchen** below) - **35 rm** ☐ 229/318.

XXX ✿✿ **Hummerstübchen**, Bonifatiusstr. 35 (at Fischerhaus H.), ✆ 59 44 02 - P. AE ⓓ E VISA
closed Sunday, Monday and 3 weeks July - August - **M** (dinner only) (booking essential) 125/159 and a la carte 86/121
Spec. Hummersuppe, Gratin von Hummer mit Gemüseravioli, Gefüllter Steinbutt mit Langustinen.

at Düsseldorf 30-Lohausen by Danziger Str. AU :

Arabella Airport Hotel ⛢, am Flughafen, ✆ 4 17 30, Telex 8584612, Fax 4173707 - |♯| ✂ rm ▤ TV ♿ - 🎓 180. AE ⓓ E VISA
M a la carte 42/67 - **200 rm** ☐ 187/450.

at Düsseldorf 30-Mörsenbroich by Rethelstr. DV :

Ramada-Renaissance-Hotel, Nördlicher Zubringer 6, ✆ 6 21 60, Telex 172114001, Fax 6216666, Massage, ≘s, ☒ - |♯| ✂ rm ▤ TV ♿ ⇔ - 🎓 400. AE ⓓ E VISA. ✻ rest
M a la carte 47/84 - **245 rm** ☐ 295/560, 8 suites. BU **e**

Merkur without rest, Mörsenbroicher Weg 49, ✆ 63 40 31, Fax 622525 - TV ☎ P. AE ⓓ E VISA CU **a**
closed 1 to 5 January - **28 rm** 95/290.

at Düsseldorf 11-Oberkassel by Luegallee AV :

Ramada, Am Seestern 16, ✆ 59 10 47, Telex 8585575, Fax 593569, ≘s, ☒ - |♯| ✂ rm ▤ TV P - 🎓 150. AE ⓓ E VISA
M a la carte 52/80 - **222 rm** ☐ 235/555, 6 suites.

Hanseat without rest, Belsenstr. 6, ✆ 57 50 69, Telex 8581997, Fax 589662, « Elegant furnishings » - TV ☎. AE ⓓ E VISA
37 rm ☐ 160/280.

XXX **De' Medici** (Italian rest.), Amboßstr. 3, ✆ 59 41 51 - AE ⓓ E VISA
closed Saturday lunch, Sunday and Bank Holidays except exhibitions - **M** (booking essential for dinner) a la carte 50/77.

XX **Edo** (Japanese restaurants : Teppan, Robata and Tatami), Am Seestern 3, ✆ 59 10 82, Fax 591394, « Japanese garden » - ▤ P. AE ⓓ E VISA. ✻
closed Saturday lunch, Sunday, Easter and 25 December - 1 January - **M** a la carte 50/90.

at Düsseldorf 12-Unterbach SE : 11 km by Grafenberger Allee BV :

Landhotel Am Zault - Residenz, Gerresheimer Landstr. 40, ✆ 25 10 81, Telex 8581872, Fax 254718, ≘s – TV ☎ P – 🏔 80. AE ⓓ E VISA
M *(closed Saturday lunch)* 30/59 (lunch) and a la carte 58/89 – **61 rm** ☐ 180/520.

at Düsseldorf 1-Unterbilk :

XXX **Savini**, Stromstr. 47, ✆ 39 39 31, Fax 391719 – ⓓ E VISA AX **e**
closed Sunday, Monday and 2 weeks Easter and 2 weeks July - August – **M** (booking essential) a la carte 88/112.

XX **Rheinturm Top 180** (revolving restaurant at 172 m), Stromstr. 20, ✆ 84 85 80, Fax 325619, ✳ Düsseldorf and Rhein (|$|, DM 5,00) – ▤ ♿ – 🏔 60. AE ⓓ E VISA. ⛌ AV **a**
M a la carte 48/78.

at Meerbusch 1-Büderich **4005** by Luegallee AV – ☎ 02132 :

XXX **Landhaus Mönchenwerth**, Niederlöricker Str. 56 (at the boat landing stage), ✆ 7 79 31, Fax 71899, ≤, « Garden terrace » – P. AE ⓓ E VISA. ⛌
closed Saturday – **M** a la carte 57/102.

XXX **Landsknecht** with rm, Poststr. 70, ✆ 59 47, Fax 10978, 🌂 – TV ☎ P. AE ⓓ E. ⛌
M *(closed Saturday lunch and Monday)* a la carte 57/91 – **8 rm** ☐ 160/280.

X **Lindenhof**, Dorfstr. 48, ✆ 26 64
closed Monday, 3 weeks in August and 1 to 15 January – **M** (dinner only, booking essential) a la carte 39/70.

Essen **4300.** Nordrhein-Westfalen 411 412 E 12, 987 ⑭ – pop. 620 000 – alt. 120 m – ☎ 0201.

Düsseldorf 31.

at Essen 18-Kettwig S : 11 km :

XXXX ✿✿ **Résidence** 🐎 with rm, Auf der Forst 1, ✆ (02054) 89 11, Fax 82501, 🌂 – ⇔ rest TV ☎ P. ⓓ E VISA
closed 1 to 8 January and 3 weeks July - August – **M** *(closed Sunday and Monday)* (dinner only) (booking essential) (remarkable wine list) a la carte 97/125 – **18 rm** ☐ 210/550
Spec. Sülze von Gänsestopfleber und Ochsenschwanz mit Trüffelremoulade, Hummer auf Dicken Bohnen in Thymianrahm, Quarkauflauf mit Sherryeis.

Grevenbroich **4048.** Nordrhein-Westfalen 412 C 13, 987 ㉓ – pop. 57 000 – alt. 60 m – ☎ 02181.

Düsseldorf 28.

XXXXX ✿✿ **Zur Traube** with rm, Bahnstr. 47, ✆ 6 87 67, Telex 8517193, Fax 61122 – TV ☎ P. ⓓ E VISA. ⛌
closed 6 to 12 April, 20 July - 3 August and 18 December - 18 January – **M** *(closed Sunday and Monday)* (booking essential) (remarkable wine list) 146/178 and a la carte 92/132 – **6 rm** ☐ 190/490
Spec. Parfait vom Stör mit Kaviar, Taubenbrüstchen in Blätterteig mit Gänseleberschaum, Gratinierter Limonenflan mit Mangosalat und Vanillesauce.

☞ *Inclusion in the **Michelin Guide** cannot be achieved by pulling strings or by offering favours.*

FRANCFURT ON MAIN (FRANKFURT AM MAIN) **6000.** Hessen 412 413 IJ 16, 987 ㉕ – pop. 627 500 – alt. 91 m – ☎ 069.

See : Zoo★★★ FV – Goethe's House (Goethehaus)★ GZ – Cathedral (Dom)★ (Gothic Tower★★, Choir-stalls★, Museum★) HZ – Tropical Garden (Palmengarten)★ CV – Senckenberg-Museum★ (Palaeontology department★★) CV **M9** – Städel Museum (Städelsches Museum and Städtische Galerie) ★★ GZ – Museum of Applied Arts (Museum für Kunsthandwerk)★ HZ – German Cinema Museum★ GZ **M7** – Henninger Turm ✳★ FX.

⛳18 Frankfurt-Niederrad, by Kennedy-Allee CDX, ✆ 6 66 23 17.

✈ Rhein-Main (SW : 12 km), ✆ 6 90 25 95.

🚗 at Neu-Isenburg (S : 7 km) ✆ (06102) 85 75.

Exhibition Centre (Messegelände) (CX), ✆ 7 57 50, Telex 411558.

ℹ Tourist Information, Main Station (Hauptbahnhof), ✆ 21 23 88 49.

ℹ Tourist Information, im Römer, ✆ 21 23 87 08.

ADAC, Schumannstr. 4, ✆ 7 43 00.

Wiesbaden 41 – Bonn 178 – Nürnberg 226 – Stuttgart 204.

The reference (F 15) at the end of the address is the postal district : Frankfurt 15

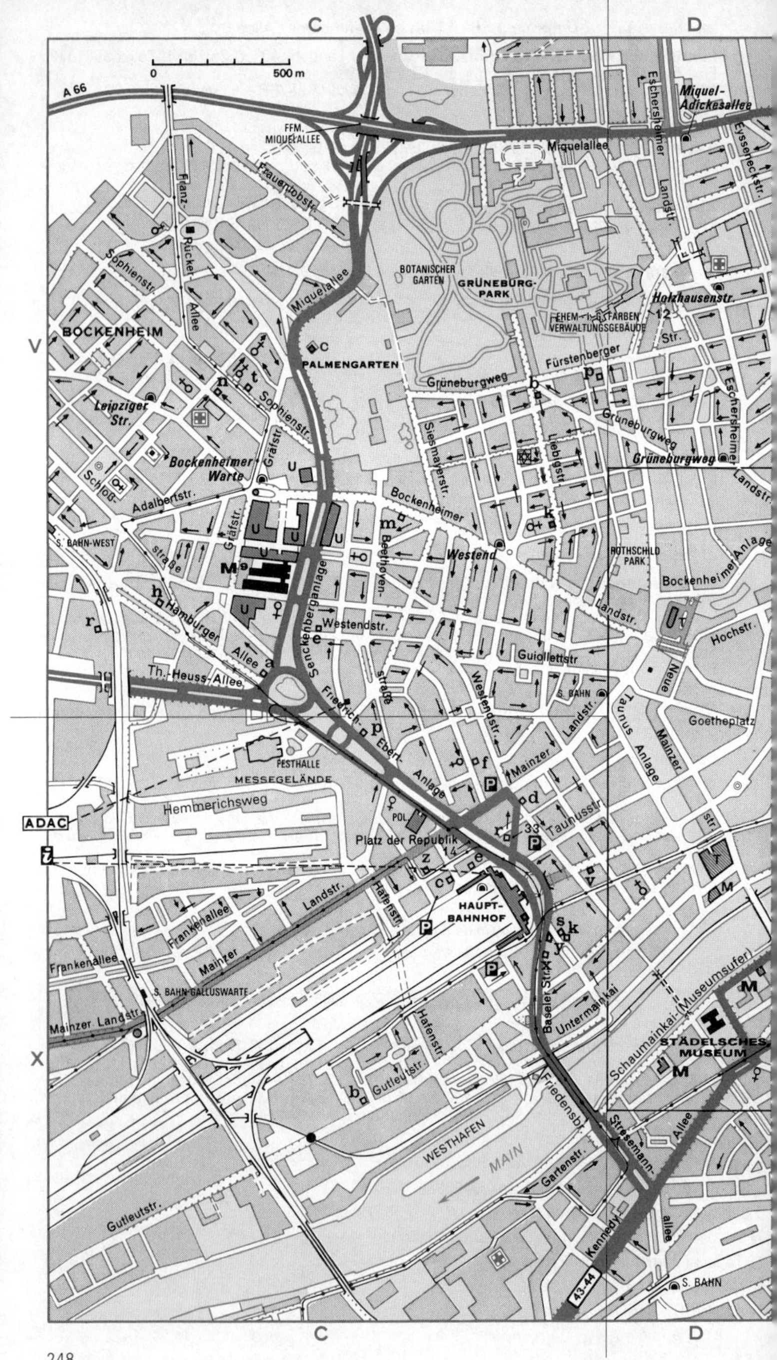
C
D
A 66
500 m
FFM. MIQUELALLEE
Miquelallee
Miquel-Adickesallee
Eschersheimer Landstr.
Eysseneckstr.
Frauenlobstr.
Franz-Rücker-Allee
Sophienstr.
BOTANISCHER GARTEN
GRÜNEBURG-PARK
EHEM. I.G. FARBEN VERWALTUNGSGEBÄUDE
Holzhausenstr.
BOCKENHEIM
PALMENGARTEN
Fürstenberger Str.
Grüneburgweg
Leipziger Str.
Bockenheimer Warte
Siesmayerstr.
Liebigstr.
Schloß-
Adalbertstr.
Gräfstr.
Bockenheimer Landstr.
S. BAHN-WEST
Westend
ROTHSCHILD PARK
Bockenheimer Anlage
Beethovenstr.
Senckenberganlage
Hamburger Allee
Westendstr.
Hochstr.
Guiollettstr.
Th.-Heuss-Allee
S. BAHN
Neue Mainzer Str.
Taunus Anlage
Goetheplatz
Friedrich-Ebert-Anlage
PESTHALLE
MESSEGELÄNDE
Mainzer Landstr.
Hemmerichsweg
ADAC
POL.
Taunusstr.
Platz der Republik
HAUPT-BAHNHOF
Frankenallee
Hafenstr.
S. BAHN-GALLUSWARTE
Baseler Str.
Untermainkai
Schaumainkai (Museumsufer)
STÄDELSCHES MUSEUM
Gutleutstr.
Friedensbr.
Stresemann-allee
WESTHAFEN
MAIN
Gartenstr.
Kennedy-Allee
43-44
V
X

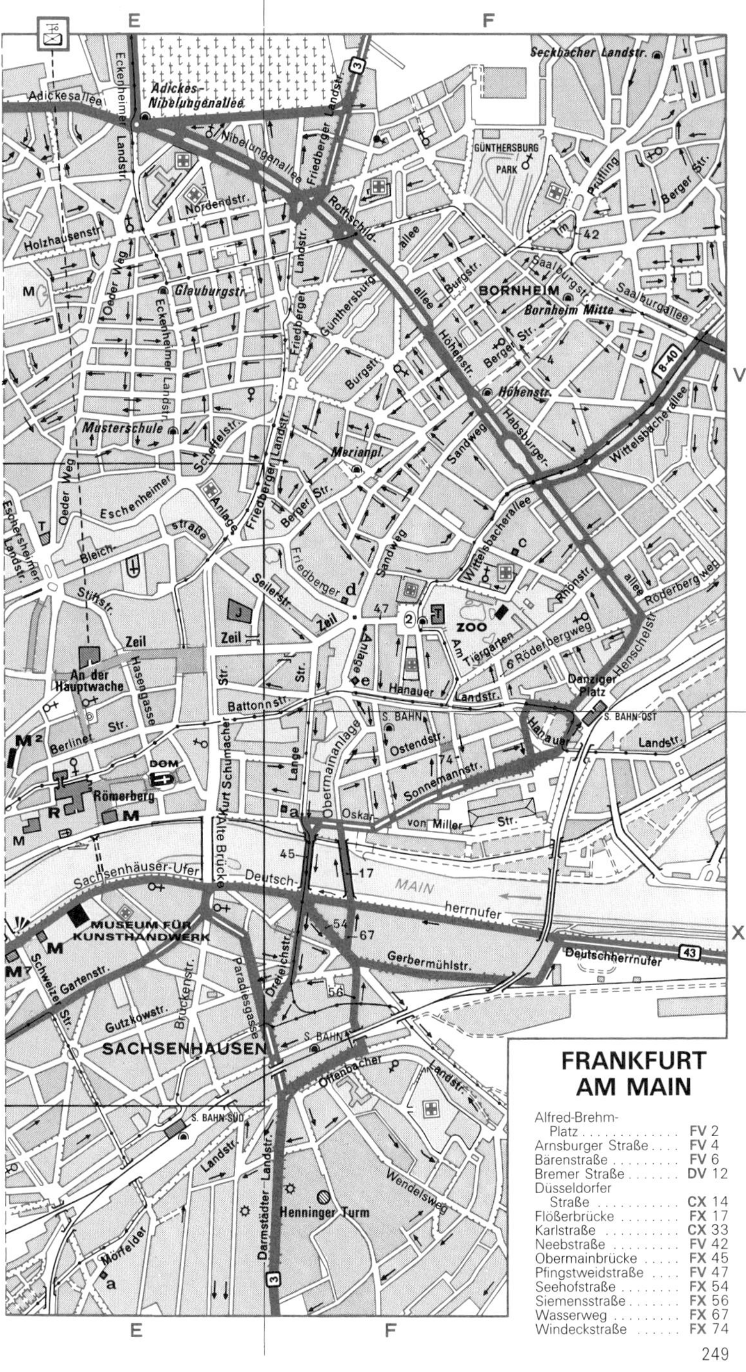

FRANKFURT AM MAIN

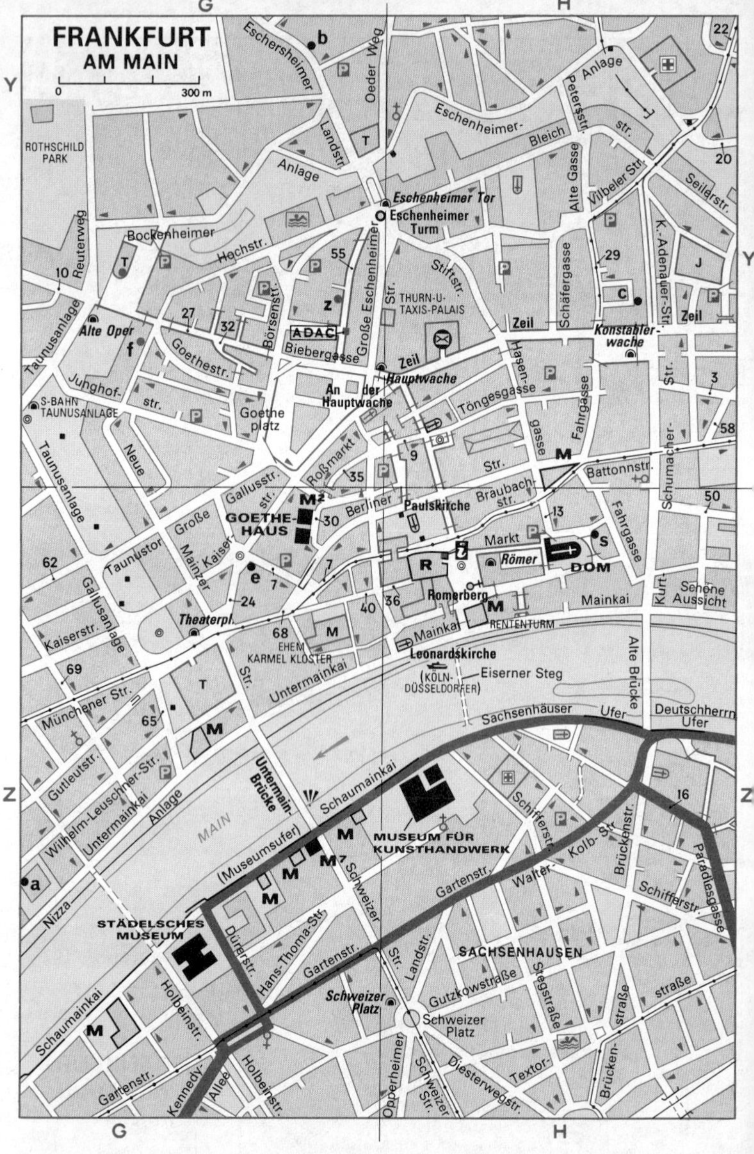

An der Hauptwache . . . GHY
Goethestraße . . . . GY
Gr. Bockenheimer Straße . . . . GY 27
Kaiserstraße . . . . GZ
Münchener Straße . . . . GZ
Roßmarkt . . . . GY
Schillerstraße . . . . GY 55
Zeil . . . . HY

Allerheiligenstraße . . . . HY 3

Bethmannstraße . . . . GZ 7
Bleidenstraße . . . . HY 9
Bockenheimer Landstr. . . . . GY 10
Domstraße . . . . HZ 13
Elisabethenstraße . . . . HZ 16
Friedberger Anlage . . . . HY 20
Friedberger Landstr. . . . . HY 22
Friedensstraße . . . . GZ 24
Große Friedberger Str. . . . . HY 29

Großer Hirschgraben . . . . . GZ 30
Kalbächer Gasse . . . . GY 32
Kleiner Hirchgraben . . . . . . GY 35
Limpurgergasse . . . . HZ 36
Münzgasse . . . . GZ 40
Rechneigrabenstr. . . . . HZ 50
Stoltzestraße . . . . HY 58
Taunusstraße . . . . GZ 62
Untermainanlage . . . . GZ 65
Weißfrauenstraße . . . . GZ 68
Weserstraße . . . . GZ 69

Steigenberger Frankfurter Hof, Bethmannstr. 33 (F 1), 2 15 02, Telex 411806, Fax 215900, – rm – 250. AE E VISA. rest GZ **e**
M see **Restaurant francais** below – **Hofgarten** *(closed Saturday)* **M** a la carte 62/85 – **Frankfurter Stubb** (booking essential) *(closed Sunday and Bank Holidays and 4 weeks July - August)* **M** a la carte 42/73 – **Kaiserbrunnen M** a la carte 38/56 – **350 rm** 322/684, 30 suites.

Hessischer Hof, Friedrich-Ebert-Anlage 40 (F 1), 7 54 00, Telex 411776, Fax 7540924, « Rest. with collection of Sèvres porcelain » – rm – 120. AE E VISA. rest CX **p**
M 40 lunch and a la carte 65/100 – **114 rm** 301/685, 11 suites.

Arabella Grand Hotel, Konrad-Adenauer-Str. 7 (F 1), 2 98 10, Telex 4175926, Fax 2981810, Massage, – rm – 300. AE E VISA. rest HY **c**
Premiere *(closed Sunday and Bank Holidays)* **M** (dinner only) a la carte 72/106 – **Brasserie M** a la carte 42/66 – **Dynasty** (Chinese rest.) **M** 25 (lunch) and a la carte 45/80 – **378 rm** 370/610, 11 suites.

Frankfurt Intercontinental, Wilhelm-Leuschner-Str. 43 (F 1), 2 60 50, Telex 413639, Fax 252467, Massage, – rm – 800. AE E VISA. rest GZ **a**
M *(closed Saturday lunch, Sunday - Monday)* a la carte 53/85 – **800 rm** 362/609, 45 suites.

Mövenpick Parkhotel Frankfurt, Wiesenhüttenplatz 28 (F 1), 2 69 70, Telex 412808, Fax 26978849, – rm – 160. AE E VISA CX **k**
La Truffe *(closed Saturday, Sunday, Bank Holidays and 4 weeks June - July)* **M** a la carte 70/100 – **Mövenpick-Restaurants M** a la carte 35/68 – **300 rm** 317/616, 4 suites.

Frankfurt Marriott Hotel, Hamburger Allee 2 (F 90), 7 95 50, Telex 412573, Fax 79552432, Frankfurt – rm – 600. AE E VISA. rest CV **a**
M a la carte 46/80 – **585 rm** 383/704, 17 suites.

Altea Hotel, Voltastr. 29 (F 90), 7 92 60, Telex 413791, Fax 79261606, – rm . AE E VISA by Th.-Heuss-Allee CV
M a la carte 43/80 – **426 rm** 190/400, 12 suites.

Scandic Crown Hotel, Wiesenhüttenstr. 42 (F 16), 27 39 60, Telex 416394, Fax 27396795, – rm – 100. AE E VISA CX **s**
closed 23 December - 3 January – **M** a la carte 50/80 – **144 rm** 250/650.

Palmenhof - Restaurant Bastei, Bockenheimer Landstr. 89 (F 1), 7 53 00 60, Fax 75300666 – . AE E VISA CV **m**
closed 20 December - 6 January – **M** *(closed Saturday, Sunday and Bank Holidays)* a la carte 64/88 – **47 rm** 170/350.

Pullman Hotel Savigny, Savignystr. 14 (F 1), 7 53 30, Telex 412061, Fax 7533175 – – 80. AE E VISA CX **f**
M a la carte 43/75 – **124 rm** 225/460.

National, Baseler Str. 50 (F 1), 27 39 40, Telex 412570, Fax 234460 – – 60. AE E VISA CX **x**
M a la carte 43/75 *(vegetarian menu available)* – **70 rm** 176/384.

An der Messe without rest, Westendstr. 104 (F 1), 74 79 79, Telex 4189009, Fax 748349 – . AE E VISA CV **e**
46 rm 200/430.

Imperial, Sophienstr. 40 (F 90), 7 93 00 30, Telex 4189636, Fax 79300388 – . AE E VISA CV **t**
M *(dinner only)* a la carte 44/78 – **60 rm** 290/410.

Novotel Frankfurt-Messe, Voltastr. 1 b (F 90), 79 30 30, Telex 412054, Fax 79303930, – rm – 140. AE E VISA CV **r**
M a la carte 36/68 – **235 rm** 210/270.

Rhein-Main without rest, Heidelberger Str. 3 (F 1), 25 00 35, Telex 413434, Fax 252518 – . AE E VISA. CX **b**
50 rm 180/350.

Mozart without rest, Parkstr. 17 (F 1), 55 08 31 – . AE E VISA CV **p**
closed 24 December - 1 January – **35 rm** 145/210.

Bauer Hotel Domicil without rest, Karlstr. 14 (F 1), 27 11 10, Fax 253266 – rm . AE E VISA CX **d**
70 rm 179/269.

Turm-Hotel without rest, Eschersheimer Landstr. 20 (F 1), 15 40 50, Fax 553578 – . AE E VISA GY **b**
closed 21 December - 6 January – **75 rm** 130/195.

Continental, Baseler Str. 56 (F 1), 23 03 41, Telex 412502, Fax 232914 – – 20. AE E VISA. CX **y**
M *(closed Sunday and Bank Holidays)* a la carte 34/61 – **80 rm** 155/325.

Intercity, Poststr. 8 (F 1), 27 39 10, Telex 414709, Fax 27391999 – rm – 35. AE E VISA CX **e**
M a la carte 38/64 – **227 rm** 182/286.

Concorde without rest, Karlstr. 9 (F 1), 23 32 30, Fax 237828 – . CX **r**
closed 20 December - 2 January – **45 rm** 140/300.

Topas without rest, Niddastr. 88 (F 1), 23 08 52, Fax 237228 – . CX **z**
31 rm 120/310.

Cristall without rest, Ottostr. 3 (F 1), 23 03 51, Telex 4170654, Fax 253368 – . . CX **c**
30 rm 120/310.

Am Dom without rest, Kannengießergasse 3 (F 1), 28 21 41, Fax 283237 – . HZ **s**
30 rm 140/300.

Falk without rest, Falkstr. 38a (F 90), 70 80 94, Fax 708017 – CV **n**
closed 2 weeks July - August and Christmas - early January – **32 rm** 135/235.

XXXX ✿ **Restaurant Français** (at Steigenberger Frankfurter Hof H.), Bethmannstr. 33 (F 1), 2 15 02 – . . GZ **e**
closed Monday, Sunday, Bank Holidays, (except exhibitions) and 4 weeks June - July – **M** (booking essential) a la carte 86/120
Spec. Salat von Hummer und Zwergorangen, Lachsschnitte mit Beluga Kaviar, Überbackenes Rinderfilet mit Portweinsauce.

XXXX ✿ **Zauberflöte**, Opernplatz 1 (F 1), 1 34 03 86, Fax 1340391, – . GY **T**
closed Sunday, Monday, Bank Holidays and 6 July - 16 August – **M** (dinner only) (booking essential) a la carte 79/96 – **Bistro M** a la carte 36/49
Spec. Gegrillte Jakobsmuscheln mit Apfelvinaigrette, Wolfsbarsch in Blätterteig, Mousse von Trockenpflaumen mit Honigeis.

XXXX ✿✿ **Weinhaus Brückenkeller**, Schützenstr. 6 (F 1), 28 42 38, « Old vaulted cellar with precious antiques » – . . FX **a**
closed Sunday and Bank Holidays (except exhibitions) and Christmas - early January – **M** (dinner only) (booking essential) a la carte 80/117
Spec. Carpaccio von Langustinen mit Kaviar Crème, Geschmorte Ochsenbäckchen in Rotweinsauce, Kokos-Soufflé mit Passionsfrucht-Sabayon.

XXX ✿ **Humperdinck**, Grüneburgweg 95 (F 1), 72 21 22 – CV **b**
closed Saturday lunch, Sunday, 3 weeks June - July and Christmas - early January – **M** a la carte 82/120
Spec. Scampi im Reisblatt mit Sojacrème, Nantaiser Ente mit Kartoffelmaultaschen (2 pers.), Variation von Schokolade.

XXX Mövenpick - Baron de la Mouette, Opernplatz 2 (F 1), 2 06 80, Fax 296135, – GY **f**

XXX **Villa Leonhardi**, Zeppelinallee 18 (F 1), 74 25 35, Fax 740476, « Terrace in park » – . CV **c**
closed Saturday, Sunday, Bank Holidays and 23 December - 7 January – **M** a la carte 68/86.

XXX **Tse-Yang** (Chinese rest.), Kaiserstr. 67 (F 1), 23 25 41, Fax 237825 – . CX **v**
M a la carte 44/81.

XX **Kikkoman** (Japanese rest.), Friedberger Anlage 1 (Zoo-Passage) (F 1), 4 99 00 21, Fax 447032 – . FV **e**
closed Sunday – **M** 23/50 (lunch) and a la carte 44/98.

XX **Casa Toscana** (Italian rest.), Friedberger Anlage 14 (F 1), 44 98 44, « Courtyard terrace » – FV **d**
closed Monday – **M** a la carte 52/87.

XX **Börsenkeller**, Schillerstr. 11 (F 1), 28 11 15, Fax 294551, – . GY **z**
closed Sunday and Bank Holidays (except exhibitions) – **M** a la carte 32/75 *(vegetarian menu available).*

XX **Intercity-Restaurant**, im Hauptbahnhof (1 st floor) (F 1), 27 39 50, Fax 27395168 – – 80. CX
M a la carte 27/60.

X **Gasthof im Elsass**, Waldschmidtstr. 59 (F 1), 44 38 39 FV **c**
closed 22 December - 4 January – **M** (dinner only) a la carte 35/76.

X **Ernos Bistro** (French rest.), Liebigstr. 15 (F 1), 72 19 97, – CV **k**
closed Saturday and Sunday (except exhibitions) and mid June - mid July – **M** (booking essential) a la carte 75/100.

at Francfurt 80-Griesheim by Th.-Heuss-Allee CV :

Ramada, Oeserstr. 180, 3 90 50, Telex 416812, Fax 3808218, , – rm rest – 300.
M a la carte 60/85 – **236 rm** 285/475.

at Francfurt 71-Niederrad by Kennedy-Allee CDX :

Queens Hotel International, Isenburger Schneise 40, ✆ 6 78 40, Telex 416717, Fax 6702634, – rm TV P – 400. rest
264 rm, 3 suites.

Arabella Congress Hotel, Lyoner Str. 44, ✆ 6 63 30, Telex 416760, Fax 6633666, – rm TV P – 330. AE E VISA
M a la carte 38/73 – **400 rm** 261/444, 8 suites.

Dorint, Hahnstr. 9, ✆ 66 30 60, Telex 4032180, Fax 66306600, – rm TV P – 180. AE E VISA
M a la carte 49/75 – **191 rm** 270/690.

Weidemann, Kelsterbacher Str. 66, ✆ 67 59 96, Fax 673928 – P
closed Saturday lunch, Sunday and Bank Holidays – **M** (booking essential) a la carte 66/98.

at Francfurt 80-Nordweststadt by Miquelallee C :

Ramada Hotel Nordwest Zentrum without rest, Walter-Möller-Platz, ✆ 58 09 30, Fax 582447 – TV – 20. AE E VISA by Miquelallee C
93 rm 168/210.

at Francfurt 70 - Sachsenhausen :

Holiday Inn Crowne Plaza, Mailänder Str. 1, ✆ 6 80 20, Telex 411805, Fax 6802333, – rm TV P – 400. AE E VISA. rest
M (dinner only) a la carte 62/97 – **404 rm** 314/610.
by Darmstädter Landstr. (B 3) FX

Bistrot 77, Ziegelhüttenweg 1, ✆ 61 40 40, – AE E VISA EX **a**
closed Saturday lunch, Sunday, 15 June - 8 July and 23 December - 6 January – **M** (remarkable wine list) a la carte 92/110.

at Eschborn **6236** NW : 12 km :

Novotel, Philipp-Helfmann-Str. 10, ✆ (06196) 90 10, Telex 4072842, Fax 482114, (heated), – rm TV P – 200. AE E VISA by A 66 CV
M a la carte 34/65 – **227 rm** 228/360.

at Neu-Isenburg 2-Gravenbruch **6078** SE : 11 km by Darmstädter Landstr. FX and B 459 :

Gravenbruch-Kempinski-Frankfurt, ✆ (06102) 50 50, Telex 417673, Fax 505445, « Park », (heated), – rm TV P – 350. AE E VISA. rest
M a la carte 67/135 – **289 rm** 343/571, 29 suites.

near Rhein-Main airport SW : 12 km by Kennedy-Allee CX – ✉ **6000** Francfurt 75 – ☎ 069 :

Sheraton, at the airport (Central Terminal), ✆ 6 97 70, Telex 4189294, Fax 69772209, – rm TV P – 900. AE E VISA. rest
– **Papillon** *(closed Sunday and Bank Holidays)* (remarkable wine list) **M** a la carte 98/135 – **Maxwell's Bistro M** a la carte 51/81 – **Taverne** *(closed Saturday and Sunday lunch only)* **M** a la carte 43/75 – **1050 rm** 364/642, 30 suites.

Steigenberger Avance Frankfurt Airport, Unterschweinstiege 16, ✆ 6 97 50, Telex 413112, Fax 69752505, Massage, – rm TV – 500. AE E VISA
M a la carte 54/77 – **430 rm** 352/554, 9 suites.

5 Continents, in the Airport, Ankunft Ausland B (Besucherhalle, Ebene 3), ✆ 6 90 34 44, Fax 694730, ≤ – – 30. AE E VISA.
M a la carte 57/95.

Waldrestaurant Unterschweinstiege, Unterschweinstiege 16, ✆ 69 75 25 00, « Country house atmosphere, terrace » – P. AE E VISA
M (booking essential) 39 buffet and a la carte 46/79.

on the road from Neu-Isenburg to Götzenhain S : 13 km by Darmstädter Landstr. FX :

Gutsschänke Neuhof, ✉ 6072 Dreieich-Götzenhain, ✆ (06102) 32 00 14, Fax 31710, « Country house atmosphere, terrace » – P. AE E VISA
M a la carte 48/91.

Maintal 6457. Hessen 412 413 J 16 – pop. 40 000 – alt. 95 m – ☎ 06109.

Frankfurt am Main 13.

at Maintal-Dörnigheim **6457** :

✿ **Hessler** with rm, Am Bootshafen 4 (Dörnigheim), ✆ (06181) 49 29 51, Fax 45029 – TV P. AE E. rest
closed Sunday, Monday and 3 weeks July – **M** (booking essential) (remarkable wine list) 61/74 (lunch) and a la carte 85/128 – **4 rm** 180/380
Spec. Lasagne in Steinpilzsauce, Gebratene Rotbarbe in Tomaten-Basilikum-Vinaigrette, Taube in Piroggenteig.

Guldental **6531.** Rheinland-Pfalz 412 G 17 – pop. 2 600 – alt. 150 m – ☎ 06707.
Frankfurt am Main 75.

XXX ✿✿ **Le Val d'Or**, Hauptstr. 3, ✆ 17 07, Fax 8489, ☂ – ◑ E
closed lunch Tuesday to Friday, Monday, 3 weeks January and 2 weeks August – **M** (booking essential) (remarkable wine list) 125/154 and a la carte 92/123
Spec. Räucherlachs und Lachstatar im Kartoffelrösti, Lammkarree mit Pesto, Dessert-Impressionen.

Mannheim **6800** Baden-Württemberg 987 ㉕, 412 413 I 18 – pop. 310 000 – alt. 95 m – ☎ 0621.
Frankfurt am Main 79.

XXX ✿✿ **Da Gianni** (elegant Italian rest.), R 7, 34 (Friedrichsring), ✆ 2 03 26 – AE E
closed Monday, Bank Holidays and 3 weeks July – **M** (booking essential) a la carte 87/117
Spec. Variation von Vorspeisen, Steinbutt mit Basilikumkruste, Zicklein mit geschmorten Artischocken.

Wertheim **6980.** Baden-Württemberg 987 ㉕, 412 413 L 17 – pop. 21 700 – alt. 142 m – ☎ 09342.
Frankfurt am Main 87.

at Wertheim-Bettingen E : 10 km :

✿✿ **Schweizer Stuben** 🐎, Geiselbrunnweg 11, ✆ 30 70, Telex 689190, Fax 307155, ☂, « Hotel in a park », ≘s, ⛱ (heated), 🌳, 🎾 (indoor) – TV P – 🏛 30. AE ◑ E VISA
M *(closed Monday, Tuesday and January)* (dinner only) (booking essential) 168/198 and a la carte 110/160 – **Taverna La vigna** (Italian rest.) *(closed Sunday, Monday and February)* **M** a la carte 71/86 – **Schober** *(closed Wednesday, Thursday and January)* **M** a la carte 47/65 – **33 rm** ☕ 255/495 – 3 suites 990
Spec. Confit vom Kaninchen mit Ratatouille, Scampi in der Zucchiniblüte mit Rotwein-Kapernsauce, Zicklein in Sarriette geschmort mit Olivensauce und Artischocken.

HAMBURG **2000.** L Stadtstaat Hamburg 411 N 6, 987 ⑤ – pop. 1 650 000 – alt. 10 m – ☎ 040.

See : Jungfernstieg★ GY – Außenalster★★★ (trip by boat★★★) GHXY – Hagenbeck Zoo (Tierpark Hagenbeck)★★ by Schröderstiftstr. EX – Television Tower (Fernsehturm)★ (❋★★) EX – Fine Arts Museum (Kunsthalle)★★ HY **M1** – St. Michael's church (St. Michaelis)★ (tower ❋★) EFZ – Stintfang (≤★) EZ – Port (Hafen)★★ EZ – Decorative Arts and Crafts Museum (Museum für Kunst und Gewerbe)★ HY **M2** – Historical Museum (Museum für Hamburgische Geschichte)★ EYZ **M3** – Post-Museum★ FY **M4** – Planten un Blomen Park★ EFX – Museum of Ethnography (Hamburgisches Museum für Völkerkunde)★ by Rothenbaumchaussee FX.

Envir. : Altona and Northern Germany Museum (Norddeutsches Landesmuseum)★★ by Reeperbahn EZ – Altona Balcony (Altonaer Balkon) ≤★ by Reeperbahn EZ – Elbchaussee★ by Reeperbahn EZ.

⛳18 Hamburg-Blankenese, In de Bargen 59 (W : 17 km), ✆ 81 21 77 ; ⛳18 Ammersbek (NE : 15 km), ✆ (040) 6 05 13 37 ; ⛳18 Hamburg-Wendlohe (N : 14 km), ✆ 5 50 50 14 ; ⛳18 Wentorf, Golfstr. 2 (SE : 21 km), ✆ (040) 7 20 26 10.

✈ Hamburg-Fuhlsbüttel (N : 15 km), ✆ 50 80.

🚗 ✆ 39 18 45 56.

Exhibition Centre (Messegelände) (EFX), ✆ 3 56 91, Telex 212609.

ℹ Tourismus-Zentrale Hamburg, Burchardstr. 14, ✆ 30 05 10, Telex 2163036, Fax 30051253.

ℹ Tourist-Information im Bieberhaus, Hachmannplatz, ✆ 30 05 12 45.

ℹ Tourist-Information im Hauptbahnhof (main station), ✆ 30 05 12 30.

ℹ Tourist-Information im Flughafen (airport, terminal 3 - arrivals), ✆ 30 05 12 40.

ADAC, Amsinckstr. 39 (H 1), ✆ 2 39 90.

Berlin 289 – Bremen 120 – Hannover 151.

The reference (H 15) at the end of the address is the postal district : Hamburg 15

Plans on following pages

near Hauptbahnhof, at St. Georg, east of the Außenalster :

Atlantic-Hotel Kempinski 🐎, An der Alster 72 (H 1), ✆ 2 88 80, Telex 2163297, Fax 247129, ≤ Außenalster, Massage, ≘s, ⛱ – 🛗 TV 🚗 – 🏛 250. AE ◑ E VISA. ✂ rest
M a la carte 76/106 – **256 rm** ☕ 320/480, 13 suites. HY **a**

Maritim Hotel Reichshof, Kirchenallee 34 (H 1), ✆ 24 83 30, Telex 2163396, Fax 24833588, ≘s, ⛱ – 🛗 ⇔ rm TV 🚗 – 🏛 200. AE ◑ E VISA. ✂ rest HY **d**
M a la carte 45/86 – **303 rm** ☕ 239/448, 6 suites.

Holiday Inn Crowne Plaza, Graumannsweg 10 (H 76), ✆ 22 80 60, Telex 2165287, Fax 2208704, Massage, ≘s, ⛱ – 🛗 ⇔ rm ▤ TV ♿ 🚗 – 🏛 120. AE ◑ E VISA
M a la carte 68/92 – **290 rm** ☕ 316/482. by Lange Reihe HX

Europäischer Hof, Kirchenallee 45 (H 1), ☎ 24 82 48, Telex 2162493, Fax 24824799, Massage, – rest – 120. AE ⓓ E VISA HY e
M a la carte 42/71 – **320 rm** 200/460.

Prem-Restaurant La mer, An der Alster 9 (H 1), ☎ 24 17 26, Telex 2163115, Fax 2803851, « Antique furnishings, garden », – rest HX c
59 rm, 3 suites.

Berlin, Borgfelder Str. 1 (H 26), ☎ 25 16 40, Telex 213939, Fax 25164413 – rest – 30. AE ⓓ E VISA. rest by Kurt-Schumacher-Allee HY
M a la carte 53/70 – **93 rm** 160/215.

St. Raphael, Adenauerallee 41 (H 1), ☎ 24 82 00, Telex 2174733, Fax 24820333, – rm – 70. AE ⓓ E VISA. rest by Adenauerallee HY
M *(closed Saturday, Sunday and Bank Holidays)* a la carte 46/71 – **135 rm** 180/280, 3 suites

Senator without rest, Lange Reihe 18 (H 1), ☎ 24 12 03, Telex 2174002, Fax 2803717 – . AE ⓓ E VISA HY u
56 rm 165/260.

Novotel City Süd, Amsinckstr. 53 (H 1), ☎ 23 63 80, Telex 211001, Fax 234230, – rm – 50. AE ⓓ E VISA by Amsinckstraße HZ
M a la carte 29/64 – **185 rm** 190/300.

Bellevue, An der Alster 14 (H 1), ☎ 24 80 11, Telex 2162929, Fax 2803380 – – 60. AE ⓓ E VISA – **M** a la carte 44/64 – **78 rm** 155/250. HX d

Aussen-Alster-Hotel, Schmilinskystr. 11 (H 1), ☎ 24 15 57, Telex 211278, Fax 2803231, – . AE ⓓ E VISA HX e
closed 24 to 27 December – **M** *(closed Saturday lunch and Sunday)* a la carte 49/78 – **27 rm** 190/360.

Ambassador, Heidenkampsweg 34 (H 1), ☎ 23 00 02, Telex 2166100, Fax 230009, – – 120. AE ⓓ E VISA. rest by Amsinckstr. HZ
M a la carte 41/75 – **124 rm** 175/330.

Eden without rest, Ellmenreichstr. 20 (H 1), ☎ 24 84 80, Telex 2174350, Fax 241521 – . AE ⓓ E VISA HY r
63 rm 130/200.

Alte Wache without rest, Adenauerallee 25 (H 1), ☎ 24 12 91, Fax 2801754 – – 40. AE ⓓ E VISA HY s
closed 22 December - 2 January - **85 rm** 145/215.

Peter Lembcke, Holzdamm 49 (H 1), ☎ 24 32 90 – AE ⓓ E VISA HY t
closed Saturday lunch, Sunday and Bank Holidays – **M** (booking essential) a la carte 55/102.

at Binnenalster, Altstadt, Neustadt :

Vier Jahreszeiten, Neuer Jungfernstieg 9 (H 36), ☎ 3 49 40, Telex 211629, Fax 3494602, ≤ Binnenalster – rm – 70. AE ⓓ E VISA. GY v
M a la carte 84/118 – **172 rm** 355/770, 11 suites.

Ramada Renaissance Hotel, Große Bleichen (H 36), ☎ 34 91 80, Fax 34918431, Massage, – rm – 130. AE ⓓ E VISA. rest FY e
M a la carte 54/92 – **211 rm** 302/634, 3 suites.

Marriott Hotel, ABC-Str. 52 (H 36), ☎ 3 50 50, Telex 2165871, Fax 35051777, Massage, – rm – 160. AE ⓓ E VISA. rest FY b
M (mainly Seafood) 35/(buffet lunch) and a la carte 60/95 – **278 rm** 383/461, 6 suites.

SAS Plaza Hotel, Marseiller Str. 2 (H 36), ☎ 3 50 20, Telex 214400, Fax 35023333, ≤ Hamburg, – rm – 600. rm FX a
562 rm, 7 suites.

Steigenberger Hamburg, Heiligengeistbrücke 4 (H 11), ☎ 36 80 60, Fax 36806777 – rm – 200. AE ⓓ E VISA. rest FZ s
– **Fleetrestaurant M** a la carte 56/103 – **Wintergarten M** a la carte 38/58 – **234 rm** 300/475, 6 suites.

Hafen Hamburg, Seewartenstr. 9 (H 11), ☎ 31 11 30, Telex 2161319, Fax 3192736, ≤ – – 80. AE ⓓ E VISA EZ y
M a la carte 47/90 – **250 rm** 160/205.

Alster-Hof without rest, Esplanade 12 (H 36), ☎ 35 00 70, Fax 35007514 – . AE ⓓ E VISA GY x
closed 23 December - 1 January – **117 rm** 140/290, 3 suites.

Baseler Hof, Esplanade 11 (H 36), ☎ 35 90 60, Fax 35906918 – – 40. AE ⓓ E VISA. – **M** a la carte 32/60 – **153 rm** 135/330. GY x

Zum alten Rathaus, Börsenbrücke 10 (H 11), ☎ 36 75 70, Fax 373093 – AE ⓓ E VISA
closed Sunday, Bank Holidays and Saturday June - September – **M** (booking essential) a la carte 52/90. GZ n

✿ **Cölln's Austernstuben** (private dining rooms), Brodschrangen 1 (H 11), ☎ 32 60 59 – AE ⓓ E VISA GZ v
closed Saturday lunch, Sunday, Saturday January - August Bank Holidays – **M** (booking essential) (mainly Seafood) a la carte 82/114
Spec. Krusten- und Schalentiere, "Feines vom Fischmarkt", Karamelisierter Apfelpfannkuchen.

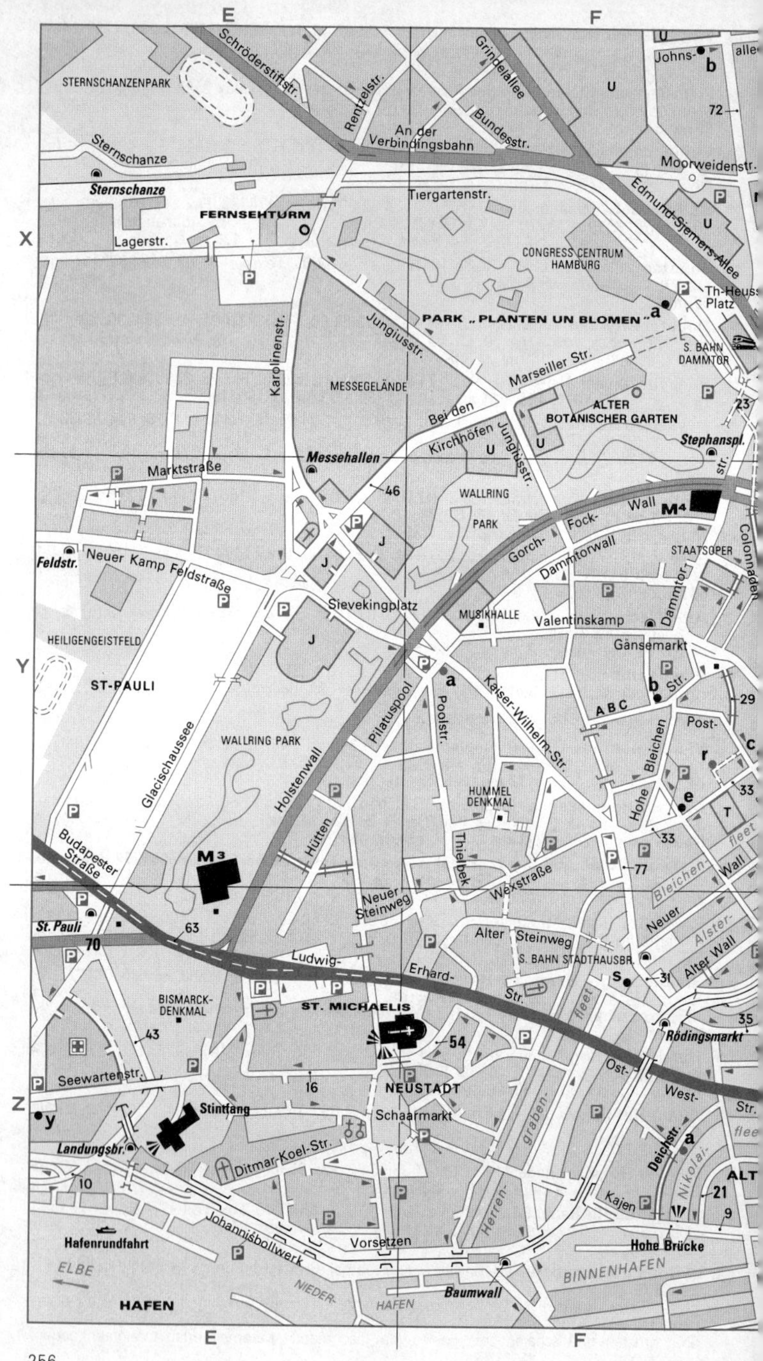

E
F
STERNSCHANZENPARK
Schröderstiftstr.
Rentzelstr.
Grindelallee
Bundesstr.
An der Verbindungsbahn
Sternschanze
Sternschanze
Tiergartenstr.
Moorweidenstr.
Edmund-Siemers-Allee
Johns-
FERNSEHTURM
Lagerstr.
CONGRESS CENTRUM HAMBURG
Th.-Heuss Platz
PARK „PLANTEN UN BLOMEN"
Jungiusstr.
Karolinenstr.
MESSEGELÄNDE
Marseiller Str.
S. BAHN DAMMTOR
Bei den Kirchhöfen
Jungiusstr.
ALTER BOTANISCHER GARTEN
Stephanspl.
Messehallen
Marktstraße
WALLRING PARK
Gorch-Fock-Wall
Feldstr.
Neuer Kamp
Feldstraße
Dammtorwall
STAATSOPER
Colonnaden
Sievekingplatz
MUSIKHALLE
Valentinskamp
Dammtor
HEILIGENGEISTFELD
Gänsemarkt
ST-PAULI
Poolstr.
Kaiser-Wilhelm-Str.
ABC
Post-
Pilatuspool
Glacischaussee
WALLRING PARK
Holstenwall
HUMMEL DENKMAL
Bleichen
Hohe
Hütten
Thielbek
Budapester Straße
Wexstraße
Bleichenfleet
Neuer Wall
Neuer Steinweg
Alsterfleet
St. Pauli
Alter Steinweg
S. BAHN STADTHAUSBR.
Alter Wall
Ludwig-Erhard-Str.
BISMARCK-DENKMAL
ST. MICHAELIS
Rödingsmarkt
Seewartenstr.
NEUSTADT
Ost-West-Str.
Stintfang
Schaarmarkt
Herrengraben-fleet
Landungsbr.
Ditmar-Koel-Str.
Deichstr.
Nikolai-
Kajen
Johannisbollwerk
Vorsetzen
Hafenrundfahrt
Hohe Brücke
ELBE
NIEDER-HAFEN
BINNENHAFEN
Baumwall
HAFEN
X
Y
Z

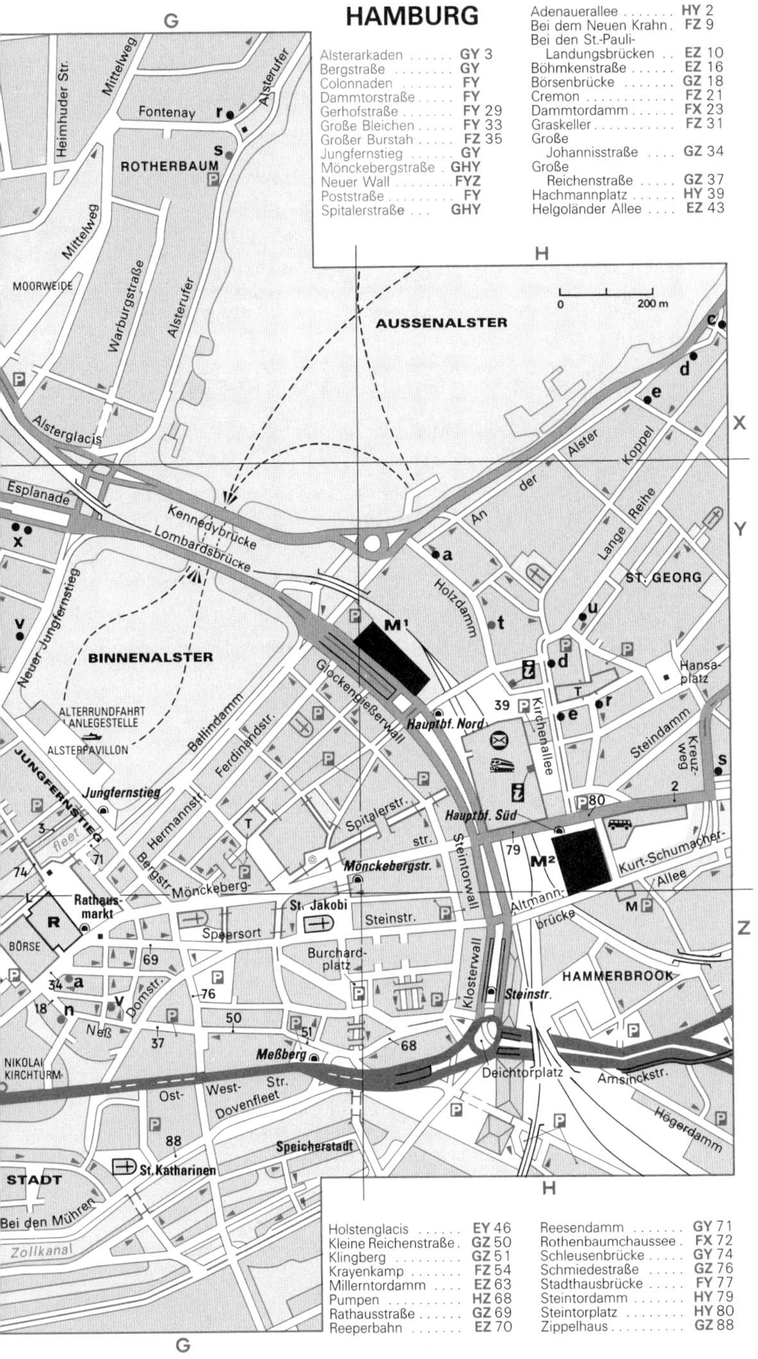
HAMBURG
Alsterarkaden . . . . . . GY 3
Bergstraße . . . . GY
Colonnaden . . . . FY
Dammtorstraße . . . . . FY
Gerhofstraße . . . . FY 29
Große Bleichen . . . . . FY 33
Großer Burstah . . . . . FZ 35
Jungfernstieg . . . . . . GY
Mönckebergstraße . GHY
Neuer Wall . . . . FYZ
Poststraße . . . . FY
Spitalerstraße . . . GHY
Adenauerallee . . . . HY 2
Bei dem Neuen Krahn . FZ 9
Bei den St.-Pauli-Landungsbrücken . . EZ 10
Böhmkenstraße . . . . . . EZ 16
Börsenbrücke . . . . GZ 18
Cremon . . . . FZ 21
Dammtordamm . . . . . . FX 23
Graskeller . . . . FZ 31
Große Johannisstraße . . . . GZ 34
Große Reichenstraße . . . . . GZ 37
Hachmannplatz . . . . . . HY 39
Helgoländer Allee . . . . EZ 43
Holstenglacis . . . . . . EY 46
Kleine Reichenstraße . GZ 50
Klingberg . . . . GZ 51
Krayenkamp . . . . FZ 54
Millerntordamm . . . . EZ 63
Pumpen . . . . HZ 68
Rathausstraße . . . . . . GZ 69
Reeperbahn . . . . EZ 70
Reesendamm . . . . GY 71
Rothenbaumchaussee . FX 72
Schleusenbrücke . . . . . GY 74
Schmiedestraße . . . . . GZ 76
Stadthausbrücke . . . . . FY 77
Steintordamm . . . . HY 79
Steintorplatz . . . . HY 80
Zippelhaus . . . . GZ 88
G
H
X
Y
Z
0
200 m
ROTHERBAUM
Heimhuder Str.
Mittelweg
Fontenay
Alsterufer
MOORWEIDE
Warburgstraße
AUSSENALSTER
Alsterglacis
Esplanade
Kennedybrücke
Lombardsbrücke
Neuer Jungfernstieg
BINNENALSTER
ALTERRUNDFAHRT ANLEGESTELLE
ALSTERPAVILLON
JUNGFERNSTIEG
Jungfernstieg
Ballindamm
Ferdinandstr.
Hermannstr.
Bergstr.
Glockengießerwall
Hauptbf. Nord
Hauptbf. Süd
Holzdamm
An der Alster
Koppel
Lange Reihe
ST. GEORG
Hansaplatz
Kirchenallee
Steindamm
Kreuzweg
Spitalerstr.
Mönckebergstr.
Mönckeberg-
Steintorwall
Kurt-Schumacher-Allee
Altmannbrücke
Rathausmarkt
BÖRSE
St. Jakobi
Steinstr.
Speersort
Burchardplatz
Klosterwall
Steinstr.
HAMMERBROOK
Domstr.
Neß
Meßberg
Deichtorplatz
Amsinckstr.
Högerdamm
NIKOLAI KIRCHTURM
Ost-West-Str.
Dovenfleet
Speicherstadt
St. Katharinen
STADT
Bei den Mühren
Zollkanal

XX **Ratsweinkeller**, Große Johannisstr. 2 (H 11), ✆ 36 41 53, Fax 372201, « 1896 Hanseatic rest. » - 400. AE E VISA GZ **R**
closed Sunday and Bank Holidays - **M** a la carte 36/76.

XX **Deichgraf**, Deichstr. 23 (H 11), ✆ 36 42 08, Fax 373055 - AE E VISA FZ **a**
closed Saturday lunch, Sunday and Bank Holidays - **M** (booking essential) a la carte 49/109.

XX **il Ristorante** (Italian rest.), Große Bleichen 16 (1st floor) (H 36), ✆ 34 33 35, Fax 481719 - AE E - **M** a la carte 66/88. FY **c**

XX **Mövenpick - Café des Artistes**, Große Bleichen 36 (ground-floor,) (H 36), ✆ 3 41 00 32, Fax 3410042 - AE E VISA FY **r**
closed Sunday - **M** a la carte 48/77 - **Mövenpick-Restaurant M** a la carte 32/63.

XX **al Pincio** (Italian rest.), Schauenburger Str. 59 (1st floor,) (H 1), ✆ 36 52 55 - AE E. GZ **a**
closed Saturday lunch, Sunday and Bank Holidays - **M** (booking essential) a la carte 40/69.

X **Dominique**, Karl-Muck-Platz 11 (H 36), ✆ 34 45 11 - . FY **a**
closed Saturday lunch, Sunday and 3 weeks May - June - **M** a la carte 60/77.

at Hamburg-Alsterdorf by Grindelallee FX :

Alsterkrug-Hotel, Alsterkrugchaussee 277 (H 60), ✆ 51 30 30, Telex 2173828, Fax 51303403, - rm - 50. AE E VISA. rest
M a la carte 53/71 - **80 rm** 191/283.

at Hamburg-Altona by Reeperbahn EZ :

Raphael Hotel Altona, Präsident-Krahn-Str. 13 (H 50), ✆ 38 02 40, Fax 38024444, - . AE E VISA
closed 23 December - 2 January - **M** (dinner only) (residents only) - **45 rm** 135/250.

Rema-Hotel Domicil without rest, Stresemannstr. 62 (H 50), ✆ 4 31 60 26, Telex 2164614, Fax 4397579 - . AE E VISA by Budapester Straße EY
75 rm 250/360.

XXXXX ✿✿ **Landhaus Scherrer**, Elbchaussee 130 (H 50), ✆ 8 80 13 25, Fax 8806260 - . AE E VISA
closed Sunday and Bank Holidays - **M** (remarkable wine-list) a la carte 75/159 - **Bistro M** (lunch only) a la carte 60/85
Spec. Gedämpfter Schellfisch mit Pommery-Senfsauce, Kalbskopf in Burgundersauce, Ente mit Wirsinggemüse (2 pers.).

XXX ✿ **Le canard**, Elbchaussee 139 (H 50), ✆ 8 80 50 57, Fax 472413, <, - . AE E VISA.
closed Sunday - **M** (booking essential) (remarkable wine-list) 85 (lunch) and a la carte 91/125
Spec. Hamburger Aalsuppe "Andere Art", Borschtschsülze mit Kaviarschmand und Blinis, Kasseler vom Lammrücken mit Thymianjus.

XXX **Fischereihafen-Restaurant Hamburg** (Seafood), Große Elbstr. 143 (H 50), ✆ 38 18 16, Fax 3893021, < - . AE E VISA - **M** a la carte 62/111.

at Hamburg-Bahrenfeld by Budapester Str. EY :

X ✿ **Tafelhaus**, Holstenkamp 71 (H 54), ✆ 89 27 60, Fax 8993324, -
closed Saturday lunch, Sunday, Monday 22 December - 19 January and 3 weeks July - **M** (booking essential) 54 (lunch) and a la carte 71/82
Spec. Spießchen von Steinpilzen und Kaisergranat, Taube mit Senfkörnersauce, Ananaskrapfen mit Kokoseis.

at Hamburg-Billstedt by Kurt Schumacher-Allee and B 5 HY :

Panorama without rest, Billstedter Hauptstr. 44 (H 74), ✆ 73 35 90, Telex 212162, Fax 73359950, - - 200. AE E VISA
closed 24 December - 2 January - **111 rm** 198/265, 7 suites.

at Hamburg-Blankenese W : 16 km by Reeperbahn EZ :

Strandhotel , Strandweg 13 (H 55), ✆ 86 13 44, Fax 864936, <, , « Villa with elegant installation », - . AE E VISA
M *(closed Sunday dinner and Monday)* a la carte 53/86 - **16 rm** 150/470.

XXX Sagebiels Fährhaus, Blankeneser Hauptstr. 107 (H 55), ✆ 86 15 14, « Terrace with < » - .

XX **Strandhof**, Strandweg 27 (H 55), ✆ 86 52 36, Fax 863353, <, - . AE E VISA
closed Monday and Tuesday - **M** a la carte 45/81.

at Hamburg-City Nord by Grindelallee FX :

Queens Hotel, Mexicoring 1 (H 60), ✆ 63 29 40, Telex 2174155, Fax 6322472 - rm - 150. AE E VISA. rest - **M** a la carte 52/76 - **183 rm** 225/315.

at Hamburg-Duvenstedt by Grindelallee FX :

XXX **Le Relais de France**, Poppenbütteler Chaussee 3 (H 65), ✆ 6 07 07 50, Fax 6072673 - .
closed Sunday and Monday - **M** (dinner only) (booking essential) a la carte 74/98 - **Bistro M** a la carte 39/50.

at Hamburg-Eppendorf by Grindelallee FX :

XX ✿ **Anna e Sebastiano** (Italian rest.), Lehmweg 30 (H 20), ✆ 4 22 25 95, Fax 4208008 – Ⓓ E VISA. ✻
closed Sunday and Monday, 24 December - 19 January and 3 weeks June - July – **M** (dinner only) (booking essential) 100/120 and a la carte 74/85
Spec. Warmer Salat von Hummer und weißen Bohnen, Milchlamm mit Artischocken in Balsamicoessigsauce, Feige in Barolo mit Mandelmousse.

XX **Il Gabbiano** (Italian rest.), Eppendorfer Landstr. 145 (H 20), ✆ 4 80 21 59, Fax 4807921 – AE Ⓓ E VISA
closed Sunday and 3 weeks July – **M** (booking essential) a la carte 56/79.

XX **Sellmer** (mainly Seafood), Ludolfstr. 50 (H 20), ✆ 47 30 57, Fax 4601569 – Ⓟ. AE Ⓓ E VISA
M a la carte 50/98.

at Hamburg-Fuhlsbüttel by Grindelallee FX :

Airport Hotel Hamburg, Flughafenstr. 47 (H 62), ✆ 53 10 20, Telex 2166399, Fax 53102222, Massage, ≘s, ⊡ – |‡| ⇔ rm ▤ rest TV ⇔ Ⓟ – 🏛 170. AE Ⓓ E VISA
M a la carte 40/67 – **158 rm** ⊏ 231/382, 12 suites.

at Hamburg-Hamm by Kurt-Schumacher-Allee HY :

Hamburg International, Hammer Landstr. 200 (H 26), ✆ 21 14 01, Telex 2164349, Fax 211409 – |‡| TV ☎ ⇔ Ⓟ – 🏛 30. AE E VISA
M *(closed Sunday)* a la carte 68/107 – **112 rm** ⊏ 170/275.

at Hamburg-Harburg 2100 S : 15 km by Amsinckstr. HZ :

Panorama, Harburger Ring 8 (H 90), ✆ 76 69 50, Telex 2164824, Fax 76695183 – |‡| TV ⇔ – 🏛 110. AE Ⓓ E VISA
M a la carte 38/73 – **98 rm** ⊏ 198/340.

at Hamburg-Harvestehude :

Inter-Continental, Fontenay 10 (H 36), ✆ 41 41 50, Telex 211099, Fax 41415186, ≤ Hamburg and Alster, ⛱, Massage, ≘s, ⊡ – |‡| ⇔ rm ▤ TV ⇔ Ⓟ – 🏛 240. AE Ⓓ E VISA. ✻ rest GX **r**
– **Fontenay-Grill M** (dinner only) a la carte 74/109 – **Orangerie M** a la carte 53/75 – **270 rm** ⊏ 306/712, 14 suites.

Garden Hotels Pöseldorf ⑤ without rest, Magdalenenstr. 60 (H 13), ✆ 41 40 40, Telex 212621, Fax 4140420, « Elegant modern installation » – |‡| TV. AE Ⓓ E VISA
61 rm ⊏ 240/570. by Mittelweg GX

Smolka, Isestr. 98 (H 13), ✆ 47 50 57, Fax 473008 – |‡| TV ☎ ⇔. AE Ⓓ E VISA. ✻ rest
M *(closed Saturday dinner, Sunday and Bank Holidays)* a la carte 42/67 – **38 rm** ⊏ 155/300. by Rothenbaumchaussee FX

Abtei ⑤, Abteistr. 14 (H 13), ✆ 45 75 65, Fax 449820, ⛱ – TV ☎. AE Ⓓ E VISA. ✻ by Rothenbaumchaussee FX
M *(closed Sunday and Monday)* (dinner only) a la carte 66/101 – **12 rm** ⊏ 230/550.

X **Daitokai** (Japanese rest.), Milchstr. 1 (H 13), ✆ 4 10 10 61, Fax 4102296 – ▤. AE Ⓓ E VISA. ✻ by Mittelweg GX
closed Sunday – **M** (booking essential) a la carte 49/78.

at Hamburg-Langenhorn N : 8 km by B 433 :

Dorint-Hotel-Airport, Langenhorner Chaussee 183 (H 62), ✆ 53 20 90, Telex 213599, Fax 53209600, ≘s, ⊡ – |‡| ⇔ rm ▤ TV ♿ ⇔ – 🏛 100. AE Ⓓ E VISA. ✻ rest
M a la carte 42/76 – **147 rm** ⊏ 215/460.

at Hamburg-Lemsahl-Mellingstedt by An der Alster NE : 16 km :

Treudelberg ⑤, Lemsahler Landstr. 45 (H 65), ✆ 60 82 20, Fax 60822444, ≤, ⛱, Lб, ≘s, ⊡, ✂, 18 – |‡| ⇔ rm Ⓟ – 🏛 125. AE Ⓓ E VISA
Szenario M a la carte 49/75 – **Club Restaurant M** a la carte 38/52 – **135 rm** ⊏ 259/498.

at Hamburg-Rotherbaum :

Elysee ⑤, Rothenbaumchaussee 10 (H 13), ✆ 41 41 20, Telex 212455, Fax 41412733, Massage, ≘s, ⊡ – |‡| ⇔ rm ▤ TV ♿ ⇔ – 🏛 350. AE Ⓓ E VISA FX **m**
Piazza Romana M a la carte 51/66 – **Brasserie M** a la carte 40/55 – **305 rm** ⊏ 249/420.

Vorbach without rest, Johnsallee 63 (H 13), ✆ 44 18 20, Telex 213054, Fax 44182888 – |‡| TV ☎ ⇔. AE E VISA FX **b**
106 rm ⊏ 145/280.

XX **Ventana** (European-Asiatic cooking), Grindelhof 77 (H 13), ✆ 45 65 88 – AE Ⓓ
closed Saturday lunch and Sunday – **M** (booking essential for dinner) a la carte 60/88. by Grindelallee FX

XX ✿ **L'auberge française** (French rest.), Rutschbahn 34 (H 13), ✆ 4 10 25 32, Fax 4105857 – AE Ⓓ E VISA. ✻ by Grindelallee FX
closed Saturday lunch, Sunday and Saturday June - August – **M** (booking essential) a la carte 60/88
Spec. Gebratene Gänsestopfleber in Trüffelsauce, Seeteufel mit Safransauce, Gratinierte Früchte mit Kirschwassercreme.

at Hamburg-Schnelsen by Grindelallee FX :

Novotel-Nord, Oldesloer Str. 166 (H 61), ☎ 5 50 20 73, Telex 212923, Fax 5502020, (heated) – rm – 200. rest
M a la carte 34/66 – **122 rm** 179/218.

at Hamburg-Stellingen by Grindelallee FX :

Helgoland without rest, Kieler Str. 177 (H 54), ☎ 85 70 01, Fax 8511445 – – 25.
110 rm 160/240.

at Hamburg-Stillhorn by Amsinckstr. HZ :

Forte Hotel, Stillhorner Weg 40 (H 93), ☎ 7 52 50, Telex 217940, Fax 7525444, – rest – 160. rest
M a la carte 47/72 – **148 rm** 208/486.

at Hamburg-Uhlenhorst by An der Alster HX :

Parkhotel Alster-Ruh without rest, Am Langenzug 6 (H 76), ☎ 22 45 77, Fax 2278966 –
24 rm 140/330.

Nippon (Japanese installation and rest.), Hofweg 75 (H 76), ☎ 2 27 11 40, Telex 211081, Fax 22711490 –
M *(closed Monday)* (dinner only) a la carte 46/73 – **42 rm** 177/349.

Ristorante Roma (Italian rest.), Hofweg 7 (H 76), ☎ 2 20 25 54, –
closed Saturday lunch and Sunday – **M** a la carte 63/79.

at Hamburg-Veddel by Amsinckstr. HZ :

Carat-Hotel, Sieldeich 9 (H 26), ☎ 78 96 60, Telex 2163354, Fax 786196, – rm – 30.
closed 23 to 27 December – **M** *(closed Sunday lunch)* a la carte 38/63 – **91 rm** 190/250.

HANOVER (HANNOVER) 3000. Niedersachsen 411 412 LM 9, 987 ⑮ – pop. 510 000 – alt. 55 m – ☎ 0511.

See : Herrenhausen Gardens (Herrenhäuser Gärten)★★ (Großer Garten★★, Berggarten★) CV – Kestner-Museum★ DY **M1** – Market Church (Marktkirche) (Altarpiece★★) DY – Museum of Lower Saxony (Niedersächsisches Landesmuseum) (Prehistorical department★) EZ **M2** – Museum of Arts (Kunstmuseum) (Collection Sprengel★) EZ.

Garbsen, Am Blauen See (⑥ : 14 km), ☎ (05137) 7 30 68 ; Isernhagen FB, Gut Lohne, ☎ (05139) 29 98.

Hanover-Langenhagen (① : 11 km), ☎ 7 30 51.

☎ 1 28 54 65.

Exhibition Center (Messegelände) (by ② and B 6), ☎ 8 90, Telex 922728.

Tourist office, Ernst-August-Platz 8, ☎ 1 68 23 19, Fax 1685072.

ADAC, Hindenburgstr. 37, ☎ 8 50 00.

Berlin 288 ② (über Helmstedt) – Bremen 123 ① – Hamburg 151 ①.

Plans on following pages

Kastens Hotel Luisenhof, Luisenstr. 1, ☎ 3 04 40, Telex 922325, Fax 3044807 – rm rest – 100. rest EX **b**
M *(closed Sunday July - August)* a la carte 60/93 – **160 rm** 199/558, 5 suites.

Inter-Continental, Friedrichswall 11, ☎ 3 67 70, Telex 923656, Fax 325195 – rm rest – 300. rest DY **a**
– **L'Adresse** *(closed 15 July - 11 August)* **M** a la carte 62/92 – **Wilhelm-Busch-Stube M** a la carte 26/42 – **285 rm** 300/640, 14 suites.

Maritim Stadthotel, Hildesheimer Str. 34, ☎ 1 65 31, Telex 9230268, Fax 884846, – rm – 400. rest EZ **b**
M a la carte 60/94 – **293 rm** 239/588.

❀ **Schweizerhof Hannover - Schu's Restaurant**, Hinüberstr. 6, ☎ 3 49 50 (hotel) 3 49 52 52 (rest.), Telex 923359, Fax 3495123 – rest – 250. EX **d**
M *(closed Saturday lunch and Sunday)* a la carte 57/104 – **200 rm** 248/690, 3 suites
Spec. Terrine von Büsumer Krabben, Pot au feu vom Hummer, Geschmorte Heidschnucke.

Grand Hotel Mussmann without rest, Ernst-August-Platz 7, ☎ 32 79 71, Telex 922859, Fax 324325 – – 50. EX **v**
100 rm 168/498.

Congress-Hotel am Stadtpark, Clausewitzstr. 6, ☎ 2 80 50, Telex 921263, Fax 814652, Massage, – rm – 1800. by ②
M a la carte 46/79 *(diet menu available)* – **252 rm** 170/455, 4 suites.

Königshof without rest, Königstr. 12, ✆ 31 20 71, Fax 312079 – 🛗 TV ☎ – 🚗 – 🅰 30. AE ⓓ E VISA. ✗ EX c
84 rm ☐ 178/410.

Plaza, Fernroder Str. 9, ✆ 3 38 80, Telex 921513, Fax 3388488, – 🛗 rm TV ☎ – 200. AE ⓓ E VISA EX e
M a la carte 39/65 – **102 rm** ☐ 168/456.

Mercure, Am Maschpark 3, ✆ 8 00 80, Telex 921575, Fax 8093704, – 🛗 rm rest TV ☎ – 130. AE ⓓ E VISA EZ n
M a la carte 45/77 – **144 rm** ☐ 209/598.

Central-Hotel Kaiserhof, Ernst-August-Platz 4, ✆ 3 68 30, Telex 922810, Fax 3683114 – 🛗 TV ☎ – 100. AE ⓓ E VISA EX a
M a la carte 28/50 – **81 rm** ☐ 136/356.

Am Funkturm - Ristorante Milano, Hallerstr. 34, ✆ 3 39 80 (hotel) 33 23 09 (rest.), Fax 3398111 – 🛗 TV ☎ P EV s
accommodation closed mid July - mid August – **M** a la carte 34/60 – **46 rm** ☐ 98/298.

Intercity-Hotel, Ernst-August-Platz 1, ✆ 32 74 61, Telex 921171, Fax 324119 – 🛗 rest TV ☎ – 100. AE ⓓ E VISA EX r
M a la carte 23/54 – **57 rm** ☐ 115/310.

Am Leineschloß without rest, Am Markte 12, ✆ 32 71 45, Telex 922010, Fax 325502 – 🛗 TV ☎. AE ⓓ E VISA DY z
81 rm ☐ 190/349.

Loccumer Hof, Kurt-Schumacher-Str. 16, ✆ 1 26 40, Fax 131192 – 🛗 TV ☎ – 50. AE ⓓ E VISA DX s
M a la carte 41/70 – **75 rm** ☐ 140/240.

Körner, Körnerstr. 24, ✆ 1 63 60, Telex 921313, Fax 18048, – 🛗 rm TV ☎ – 60. AE ⓓ E VISA DX e
M *(closed Christmas - New Year)* a la carte 42/62 – **75 rm** ☐ 138/210.

Am Rathaus, Friedrichswall 21, ✆ 32 62 68, Fax 328868, – 🛗 TV ☎. ⓓ E VISA EY y
M *(closed Saturday and Sunday)* a la carte 33/61 – **47 rm** ☐ 135/340.

Vahrenwalder Hotel 181 without rest, Vahrenwalder Str. 181, ✆ 35 80 60, Fax 3505250, – 🛗 TV ☎ P. ⓓ E VISA by ①
34 rm ☐ 125/190.

Vahrenwald without rest, Vahrenwalder Str. 205, ✆ 63 30 77, Fax 673163 – 🛗 TV ☎ P. ⓓ E VISA by ①
26 rm ☐ 125/190.

Thüringer Hof without rest, Osterstr. 37, ✆ 3 60 60, Telex 923994, Fax 3606277 – 🛗 TV ☎. ⓓ E VISA EY e
closed 23 December - 2 January – **52 rm** ☐ 98/300.

Atlanta without rest, Hinüberstr. 1, ✆ 3 38 60, Telex 924603, Fax 345928 – 🛗 TV ☎. E VISA EX t
closed 22 December - 1 January – **38 rm** ☐ 160/290.

Alpha - Tirol without rest, Lange Laube 20, ✆ 13 10 66, Fax 341535 – TV ☎ DX f
15 rm ☐ 118/238.

XXXX ✿ **Landhaus Ammann** with rm, Hildesheimer Str. 185, ✆ 83 08 18, Fax 8437749, « Elegant installation, patio with terrace », – 🛗 TV ☎ P – 100. AE ⓓ E VISA. ✗ rest
M (remarkable wine-list) 120/160 and a la carte 92/115 – **14 rm** ☐ 260/680 by ③
Spec. Salat vom Ochsenschwanz in Kartoffel-Vinaigrette, Langustinen und Hummer mit Tomatenschaum, Reh- und Wildschweingerichte.

XXX **Lila Kranz**, Kirchwender Str. 23, ✆ 85 89 21, Fax 854383, – ⓓ E VISA FX b
closed Saturday and Sunday lunch – **M** 52 (lunch) and a la carte 80/94.

XXX ✿ **Romantik Hotel Georgenhof - Stern's Restaurant** with rm, Herrenhäuser Kirchweg 20, ✆ 70 22 44, Fax 708559, « Lower Saxony country house in a park, terrace » – TV ☎ P. AE ⓓ E VISA by Engelbosteler Damm CV
M (remarkable wine list) a la carte 75/120 – **14 rm** ☐ 140/360
Spec. Trüffel-Gerichte (mid November - mid March), Hummerfrikassee in Champagner, Heidschnucken-Rücken.

XXX **Bakkarat im Casino am Maschsee**, Arthur-Menge-Ufer 3 (1st floor), ✆ 88 40 57, Fax 885733, ≤, – AE ⓓ E VISA. ✗ DZ a
closed Sunday - Monday and 2 weeks January – **M** (dinner only) a la carte 68/90.

XXX **Mövenpick - Baron de la Mouette**, Georgstr. 35 (1st floor), ✆ 32 43 43, Fax 3632539 – . AE ⓓ E VISA EX x
M a la carte 46/69.

XX **Seerestaurant im Maritim am Maschsee**, Arthur-Menge-Ufer 3, ✆ 88 40 57, Fax 887533, ≤, – AE ⓓ E VISA DZ a
M a la carte 39/59.

XX **Gattopardo** (Italian rest.), Hainhölzer Str. 1 (Am Klagesmarkt), ✆ 1 43 75, Fax 318283 – AE DV f
M (dinner only) a la carte 43/60.

XX **Clichy**, Weißekreuzstr. 31, ✆ 31 24 47, Fax 318283 – AE EV d
closed Saturday lunch and Sunday – **M** a la carte 68/96.

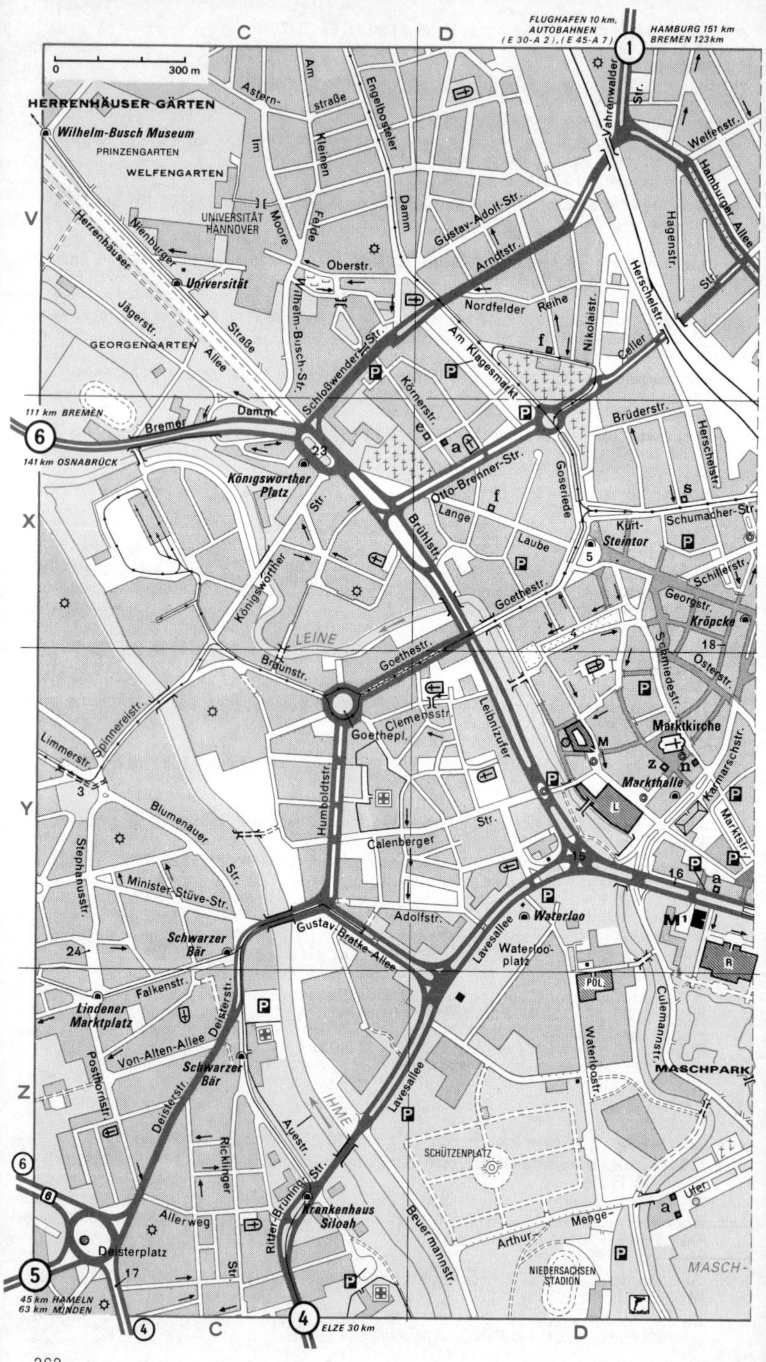
FLUGHAFEN 10 km, AUTOBAHNEN (E 30-A 2), (E 45-A 7)
HAMBURG 151 km
BREMEN 123 km
HERRENHÄUSER GÄRTEN
Wilhelm-Busch Museum
PRINZENGARTEN
WELFENGARTEN
UNIVERSITÄT HANNOVER
Universität
GEORGENGARTEN
111 km BREMEN
141 km OSNABRÜCK
Königsworther Platz
LEINE
Steintor
Kröpcke
Marktkirche
Markthalle
Goethepl.
Schwarzer Bär
Lindener Marktplatz
Waterloo
Waterlooplatz
MASCHPARK
IHME
SCHÜTZENPLATZ
NIEDERSACHSEN STADION
Krankenhaus Siloah
Deisterplatz
45 km HAMELN
63 km MINDEN
ELZE 30 km
MASCH-

HANNOVER

Bahnhofstraße ..... EX 7
Georgstraße ..... DEX
Große Packhofstraße DX 18
Karmarschstraße ... DY

Aegidientorplatz ... EY 2
Am Küchengarten .. CY 3
Am Marstall .... DX 4
Am Steintor .... DX 5
Bischofsholer Damm FY 8
Braunschweiger Platz FY 9
Emmichplatz ...... FX 12
Ernst-August-Platz .. EX 13
Friederikenplatz .... DY 15
Friedrichswall ..... DEY 16
Göttinger Straße ... CZ 17
Hans-Böckler-Allee .. FY 19
Hartmannstraße .... FZ 20
Joachimstraße ..... EX 21
Königsworther Platz . CX 23
Lindener Marktplatz . CY 24
Opernplatz .... EY 25
Scharnhorststraße .. FX 28
Thielenplatz .... EX 29
Volgersweg .... EX 30

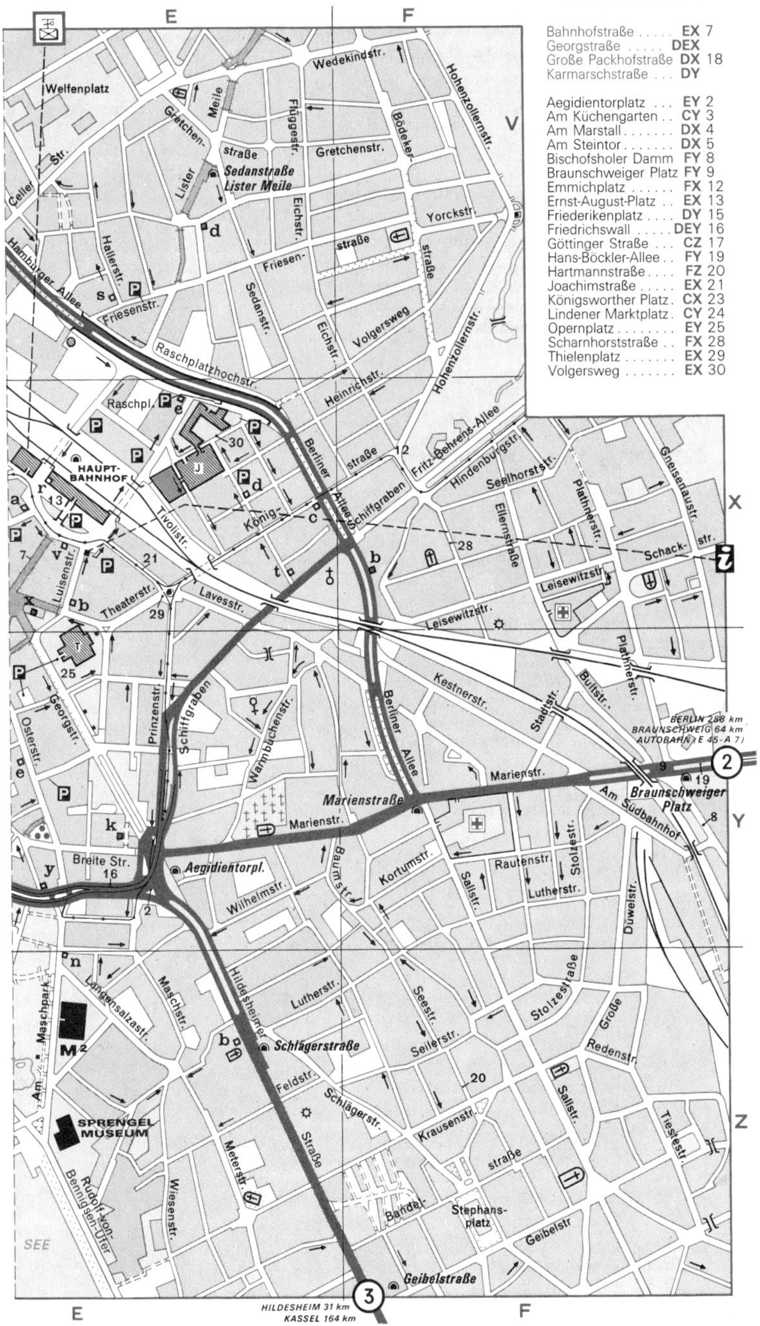

XX **Das Körbchen**, Körnerstr. 3, ✆ 1 31 82 96 - E. ✻ DX **a**
closed Sunday and Bank Holidays - **M** (dinner only) 68/105.

XX **Ratskeller**, Köbelinger Str. 60 (entrance Schmiedestraße), ✆ 36 36 44, Fax 3631351 - AE E VISA DY **n**
closed Sunday and Bank Holidays - **M** a la carte 34/76.

X **Rôtisserie Helvetia**, Georgsplatz 11, ✆ 30 10 00, Fax 3010046, ☂ - ◑ E VISA EY **k**
M a la carte 32/57.

at Hanover 51-Bothfeld by Bödekerstr. FV :

Residenz Hotel Halberstadt without rest, Im Heidkampe 80, ✆ 64 01 18, Fax 6478988, ✿ - TV ☎ P. AE E VISA
closed 20 December - 3 January - **40 rm** ☐ 150/220.

at Hanover 51-Buchholz by Bödekerstr. FV :

Pannonia Atrium Hotel, Karl-Wiechert-Allee 68, ✆ 5 40 70, Fax 572878, ☂, Massage, ≘s - |‡| ⇆ rm TV ☎ ♿ ⇔ P - 🎙 150. AE ◑ E VISA
M a la carte 35/70 - **223 rm** ☐ 220/480, 7 suites.

XX **Buchholzer Windmühle**, Pasteurallee 30, ✆ 64 91 38, Fax 6478930, ☂ - P. ✻
closed Sunday, Monday, Bank Holidays and 22 December - 5 January - **M** (dinner only) a la carte 45/80.

at Hanover 81-Döhren by ③ :

XXX **Wichmann**, Hildesheimer Str. 230, ✆ 83 16 71, Fax 8379811, « Courtyard » - E VISA
M a la carte 67/97.

XX ✿ **Joachim Stern Restaurant**, Wiehbergstr. 98, ✆ 83 55 24, Fax 8386538 - AE ◑ E VISA
closed Sunday, Monday and 3 weeks July - August - **M** (dinner only) (booking essential) a la carte 59/94
Spec. Rote Bete-Apfel-Suppe, Lammrücken aus dem Kräutersud, Dessertteller.

at Hanover 42-Flughafen (Airport) by ① : 11 km :

Holiday Inn Crowne Plaza, Am Flughafen, ✆ 7 70 70, Telex 924030, Fax 737781, ≘s, ⊠ - |‡| ⇆ rm ▤ TV ♿ P - 🎙 150. AE ◑ E VISA
M a la carte 55/87 - **210 rm** ☐ 320/550.

X **Mövenpick- Restaurant**, Abflugebene (departure), ✆ 9 77 25 09, Fax 9772709 - ▤ - 🎙 300. AE ◑ E VISA
M a la carte 30/56.

at Hanover 71-Kirchrode by ② and B 65 :

Queens Hotel am Tiergarten ⑤, Tiergartenstr. 117, ✆ 5 10 30, Telex 922748, Fax 526924, ☂, Fб, ≘s - |‡| ⇆ rm TV ☎ P - 🎙 200. AE ◑ E VISA
M a la carte 52/76 - **176 rm** ☐ 230/390, 3 suites.

at Hanover 61-Kleefeld by ② and B 65 :

Kleefelder Hof without rest, Kleestr. 3a, ✆ 5 30 80, Telex 922474, Fax 5308333 - |‡| TV ☎ ♿ ⇔ P. AE ◑ E VISA
90 rm ☐ 175/250.

XX **Alte Mühle** (lower Saxony farmhouse), Hermann-Löns-Park 3, ✆ 55 94 80, Fax 552680, « Terrace » - ♿ P. AE E
closed Tuesday, 11 to 28 January and 3 weeks July - **M** a la carte 50/79.

at Hanover 51-Lahe by Hohenzollernstraße FV :

Holiday Inn Garden Court, Oldenburger Allee 1, ✆ 6 15 50, Fax 6155555 - |‡| ⇆ rm TV ☎ ♿ ⇔ P - 🎙 300. AE ◑ E VISA. ✻ rest
M a la carte 45/70 - **150 rm** ☐ 198/490.

Föhrenhof, Kirchhorster Str. 22, ✆ 6 17 21, Fax 619719, ☂ - |‡| ⇆ rm TV ☎ P - 🎙 90. AE ◑ E VISA
M a la carte 40/69 - **78 rm** ☐ 145/420.

at Hanover 72-Messe (near Exhibition Centre) by ② :

Parkhotel Kronsberg, Laatzener Str. 18 (at Exhibition Centre), ✆ 86 10 86, Telex 923448, Fax 867112, ☂, ≘s, ⊠ - |‡| ▤ rest TV ⇔ P - 🎙 200. AE ◑ E VISA
M a la carte 42/75 - **144 rm** ☐ 140/400.

at Laatzen **3014** by ③ : 9 km :

Treff-Hotel Britannia Hannover, Karlsruher Str. 26, ✆ (0511) 8 78 20, Telex 9230392, Fax 863466, ≘s ✂ (covered court) - |‡| ⇆ rm TV ☎ ♿ P - 🎙 180. AE ◑ E VISA. ✻ rest
M a la carte 47/73 - **100 rm** ☐ 180/595.

at Langenhagen **3012** by ① : 10 km :

Grethe, Walsroder Str. 151, ✆ (0511) 73 80 11, Fax 772418, ☂, ≘s, ⊠ - |‡| TV ☎ P - 🎙 40. AE E
closed 28 July - 18 August and 22 December - 10 January - **M** *(closed Saturday and Sunday)* a la carte 33/57 - **51 rm** ☐ 110/180.

at Langenhagen 6-Krähenwinkel 3012 by ① : 11 km :

Jägerhof, Walsroder Str. 251, ✆ (0511) 7 79 60, Fax 7796111, ☂, ♨ - TV ☎ P - 🏔 70. AE ⓪ E VISA
closed 21 December - 4 January - **M** *(closed Saturday lunch and Sunday)* a la carte 42/69 - **77 rm** ☐ 90/220.

at Ronnenberg-Benthe 3003 ⑤ : 10 km by B 65 :

Benther Berg ⛰, Vogelsangstr. 18, ✆ (05108) 6 40 60, Fax 640650, ☂, ♨, ☐, 🌳 - |♦| ▤ rest TV P - 🏔 60. AE ⓪ E VISA. ✗
M *(closed Sunday dinner and Bank Holidays)* a la carte 65/95 - **70 rm** ☐ 145/250.

at Garbsen 4-Berenbostel 3008 ⑥ : 13 km by B 6 :

Landhaus Köhne am See ⛰, Seeweg 27, ✆ (05131) 9 10 85, Fax 8367, ≤, « Garden terrace », ♨, ☐ (heated), 🌳, ✗ - TV ☎ P. ⓪ VISA
M *(closed Saturday dinner and Sunday lunch)* a la carte 41/65 - **26 rm** ☐ 95/210.

LEIPZIG O-7010. Sachsen 984 ⑲, 987 ⑰ - pop. 530 000 - alt. 88 m - ✆ 003741.
See : Old Town Hall★ (Altes Rathaus) BY - Old Stock Exchange★ (Naschmarkt) BY - Museum of Fine Arts★ (Museum der Bildenden Künste) BZ.

✈ Leipzig-Schkeuditz (NW : 15 km), ✆ 39 13 65.

Exhibition Grounds (Messegelände), Universitätsstr. 5 (Information Centre), ✆ 29 53 36. Messeamt (Fair Office), Markt 11, ✆ 7 18 10, Telex 512294, Fax 7181575.

ℹ Leipzig-Information, Sachsenplatz 1, ✆ 7 95 90, Fax 281854.

ADAC, Georg-Schumann-Str. 134, ✉ O-7022, ✆ 41 58 42 81.

Berlin 165 - Dresden 109 - Erfurt 126.

Plans on following pages

Merkur, Gerberstr. 15, ✆ 79 90, Telex 311245, Fax 7991229, ☂, Massage, ♨, ☐ - |♦| ✗ rm ▤ TV ♿ 🚗 - 🏔 220. AE ⓪ E BY **a**
M a la carte 38/82 - **440 rm** ☐ 325/445, 16 suites.

Gästehaus am Park, Schwägrichenstr. 14, ✆ 3 93 90, Fax 326098, ☂, « Park » - |♦| TV ♿ 🚗 P - 🏔 120. AE E VISA by Wächterstraße AZ
M *(closed Sunday)* a la carte 29/50 - **38 rm** ☐ 250/370, 5 suites.

Stadt Leipzig, Richard-Wagner-Str. 1, ✆ 2 14 50, Telex 51426, Fax 2145600, ☂, ♨ - |♦| ✗ rm TV ☎ P - 🏔 120. AE ⓪ E VISA CY **d**
M a la carte 33/61 - **348 rm** ☐ 230/330.

Maritim Hotel Astoria, Platz der Republik 2, ✆ 7 22 20, Fax 7224747, ♨ - |♦| ✗ rm ▤ rest TV ☎ - 🏔 100. AE ⓪ E VISA CY **b**
M a la carte 39/65 - **323 rm** ☐ 290/456, 5 suites.

Deutschland, Augustusplatz 5, ✆ 2 14 60, Telex 311468, Fax 289165 - |♦| TV ☎ - 🏔 40. AE ⓪ E VISA. ✗ rest CZ **f**
M a la carte 35/64 - **283 rm** ☐ 230/340, 10 suites.

Adagio without rest, Seeburgerstr. 96, ✆ 21 66 99, Fax 216699 - |♦|. E DZ **a**
27 rm ☐ 160/300.

Leipziger Vereinshaus, Seeburgstr. 5, ✆ 28 75 13, Telex 311496, Fax 292125 - TV ☎ - 🏔 350. AE E VISA. ✗ CZ **d**
M *(closed Sunday)* a la carte 21/32 - **24 rm** ☐ 125/210.

Zum Löwen, Rudolf-Breitscheid-Str. 1, ✆ 7 22 30, Fax 7224140 - |♦| ▤ rest TV ☎. AE ⓪ E VISA CY **g**
M (dinner only) a la carte 26/48 - **110 rm** ☐ 170/250, 6 suites.

Continental, Georgiring 13, ✆ 75 66, Fax 7566 - |♦| TV ☎. AE ⓪ E VISA CY **e**
M a la carte 26/48 - **52 rm** ☐ 159/239.

Auerbachs Keller (16 C. wine tavern), Grimmaische Str. 2 (Mädler-Passage), ✆ 2 11 60 34, Fax 292302 - AE ⓪ E VISA BYZ
M a la carte 30/48.

Stadtpfeiffer, Augustusplatz 8 (Neues Gewandhaus), ✆ 28 64 94, ☂ - AE E VISA CZ
closed Sunday lunch, June - August - **M** (remarkable wine-list) a la carte 35/60.

Falstaff, Georgiring 9, ✆ 28 64 03, Fax 286425 - AE E VISA CY **m**
M a la carte 32/65.

Plovdiv (Bulgarian rest.), Katharinenstr. 17, ✆ 29 17 67, Fax 2115816, ☂ - AE ⓪ E VISA
M a la carte 30/54 *(vegetarian dishes available)*. BY **p**

Apels Garten Kolonnadenstr. 2, ✆ 28 50 93, Fax 285093, ☂ - ♿. AE E VISA AZ **q**
closed Sunday - **M** a la carte 23/44.

Ratskeller, Lotter Str. 1 ((Neues Rathaus), ✆ 7 91 62 02 BZ **n**
closed Sunday dinner - **M** a la carte 21/40 🍷.

Thüringer Hof, Burgstr. 19, ✆ 20 98 84, Fax 287093, ☂ - AE E VISA BZ **r**
closed Friday and Saturday dinner - **M** a la carte 20/38.

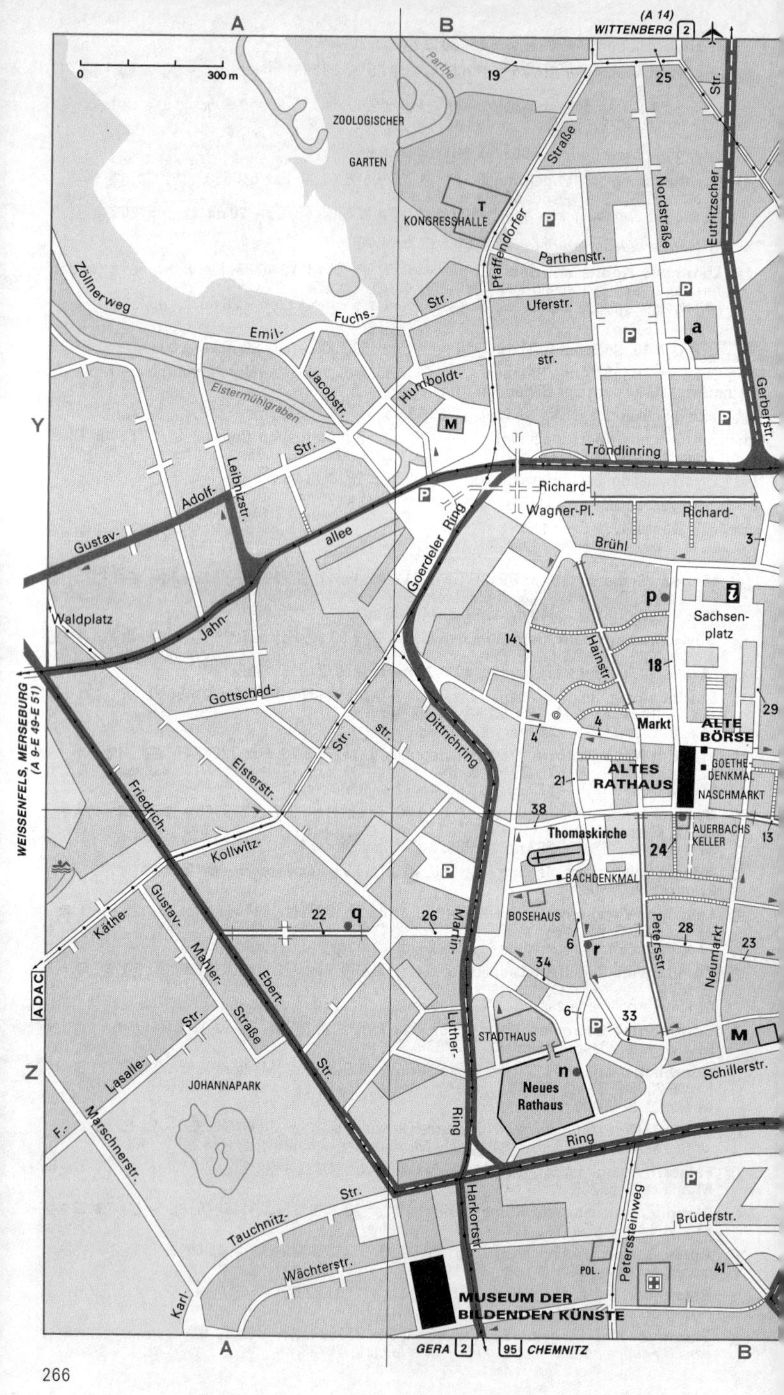

(A 14)
WITTENBERG 2
A
B
Y
Z
0
300 m
Parthe
ZOOLOGISCHER
GARTEN
KONGRESSHALLE
Pfaffendorfer
Straße
Nordstraße
Eutritzscher
Str.
Parthenstr.
Uferstr.
Zöllnerweg
Emil-
Fuchs-
Str.
str.
Humboldt-
Jacobstr.
Elstermühlgraben
Gerberstr.
Tröndlinring
Leibnizstr.
Str.
Adolf-
Gustav-
allee
Richard-
Wagner-Pl.
Richard-
Brühl
Goerdeler Ring
Waldplatz
Jahn-
Sachsen-
platz
Hainstr.
Gottsched-
str.
Str.
Dittrichring
Markt
ALTE
BÖRSE
GOETHE-
DENKMAL
NASCHMARKT
ALTES
RATHAUS
WEISSENFELS, MERSEBURG
(A 9-E 49-E 51)
Elsterstr.
Friedrich-
Kollwitz-
Thomaskirche
AUERBACHS
KELLER
BACHDENKMAL
BOSEHAUS
Gustav-
Mahler-
Straße
Käthe-
Ebert-
Str.
Martin-
Luther-
Ring
Petersstr.
Neumarkt
ADAC
STADTHAUS
Schillerstr.
Neues
Rathaus
Ring
Lasalle-
Str.
JOHANNAPARK
F.-
Marschnerstr.
Harkortstr.
Peterssteinweg
Brüderstr.
Tauchnitz-
Str.
Wächterstr.
POL.
Karl-
MUSEUM DER
BILDENDEN KÜNSTE
GERA 2
95 CHEMNITZ

LEIPZIG

Althner Straße	DY 2
Am Hallischen Tor	BY 3
Barfußgäßchen	BY 4
Burgstraße	BZ 6
Dörrienstraße	DY 8
Grimmaischer Steinweg	CZ 12
Grimmaische Str.	BCYZ 13
Große Fleischergasse	BY 14
Katharinenstraße	BY 18
Kickerlingsberg	BY 19
Klostergasse	BY 21
Kolonnadenstr.	AZ 22
Kupfergasse	BZ 23
Mädlerpassage	BZ 24
Nordplatz	BY 25
Otto-Schill-Str.	BZ 26
Preußergäßchen	BZ 28
Reichsstraße	BY 29
Reudnitzer Str.	DY 32
Schloßgasse	BZ 33
Schulstraße	BZ 34
Schützenstraße	DY 37
Thomaskirchhof	BYZ 38
Universitätsstr.	CZ 39
Windmühlenstr.	BCZ 41
Wintergartenstr.	CY 42

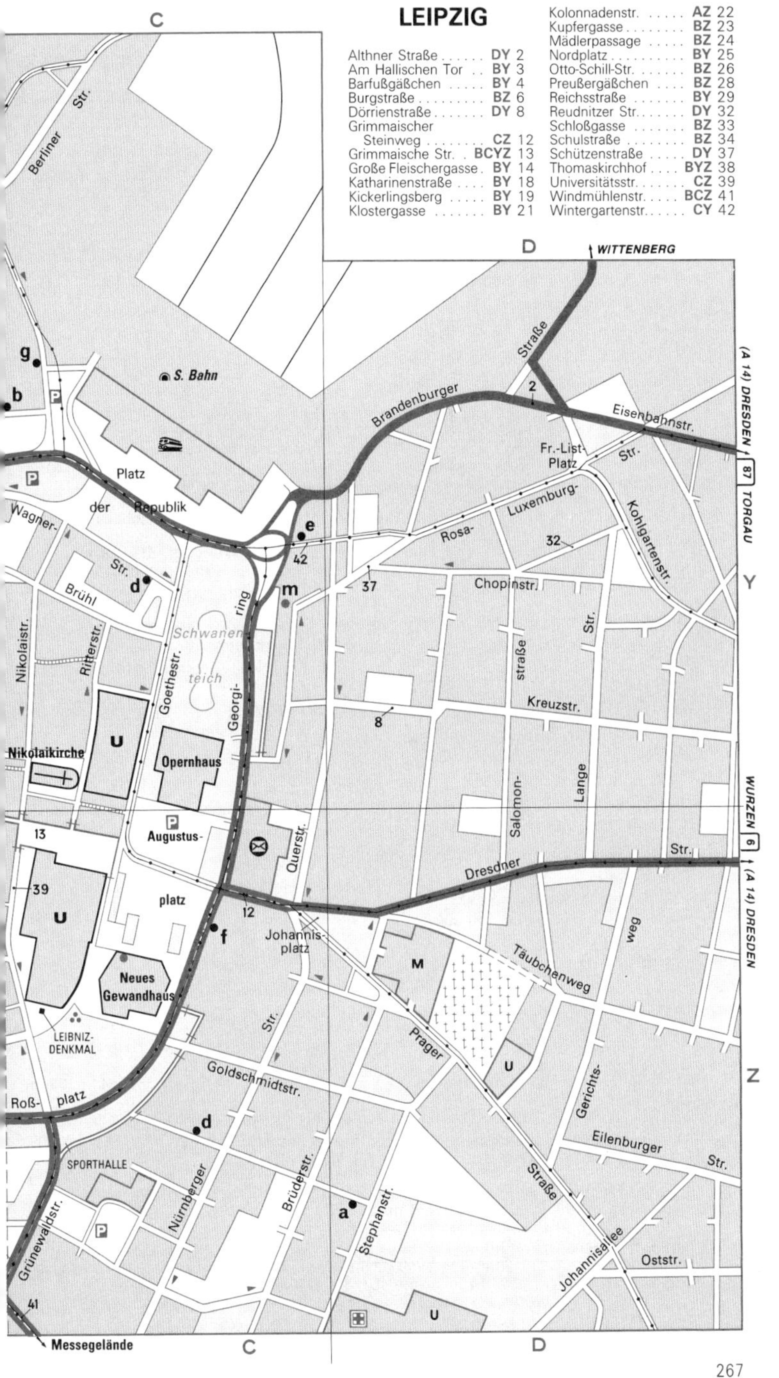

at Leipzig-Connewitz **O-7030** by Peterssteinweg BZ :

Schilling, Meusdorfer Str. 47a, ☎ 31 23 64, Fax 312364, – TV ☎ P. AE O E VISA
closed 1 to 15 January – **M** (Monday to Friday dinner only) a la carte 19/43 – **33 rm** 150/300.

at Leipzig-Eutritzsch **O-7021** by Eutritzscher Str. BY :

Nestor, Gräfestr. 15a (near Eutritzscher Markt), ☎ 5 96 30 – rm TV ☎ P – 60. AE O E VISA
M (residents only) – **81 rm** 172/284.

at Leipzig-Gohlis **O-7022** by Pfaffendorfer Str. BY :

Schaarschmidt's, Coppistr. 32, ☎ 58 48 28, beer garden
closed Sunday – **M** (dinner only) a la carte 24/48.

at Leipzig-Wahren **O-7026** by Kickerlingsberg BY :

Garni, Stahmelner Str. 30, ☎ 2 12 33 17, Fax 2123317 – TV ☎. E.
closed Christmas - New Year – **20 rm** 110/230.

MUNICH (MÜNCHEN) **8000.** L Bayern 413 R 22, 987 37, 426 G 4 – pop. 1 300 000 – alt. 520 m – ☎ 089.

See : Marienplatz★ KZ – Church of Our Lady (Frauenkirche)★ (tower ★) KZ – Old Pinakothek (Alte Pinakothek)★★★ KY – German Museum (Deutsches Museum)★★★ LZ – The Palace (Residenz)★ (Treasury★★ Palace Theatre★) KY – Church of Asam Brothers (Asamkirche)★ KZ – Nymphenburg★★ (Castle★, Park★, Amalienburg★★, Botanical Garden (Botanischer Garten)★★, Carriage Museum (Marstallmuseum) and China-Collection (Porzellansammlung★) by Arnulfstr. EV – New Pinakothek (Neue Pinakothek)★ KY – City Historical Museum (Münchener Stadtmuseum)★ (Moorish Dancers★★) KZ **M7** – Villa Lenbach Collections (Städt. Galerie im Lenbachhaus) (Portraits by Lenbach★) JY **M4** – Antique Collections (Staatliche Antikensammlungen)★ JY **M3** – Glyptothek★ JY **M2** – German Hunting Museum (Deutsches Jagdmuseum)★ KZ **M1** – Olympic Park (Olympia-Park) (Olympic Tower ★★★) by Schleißheimer Str. FU – Hellabrunn Zoo (Tierpark Hellabrunn)★ by Lindwurmstr. (B 11) EX – English garden (Englischer Garten)★ (view from Monopteros Temple ★) LY.

18 Straßlach, Tölzer Straße (S : 17 km), ☎ (08170) 4 50 ; 9 München-Thalkirchen, Zentralländstr. 40 (by Lindwurmstr. (B 11) EX ; 18 Eichenried (NE : 24 km), Münchener Str. 55, ☎ (08123) 10 05.

München (NE : 29 km) by Ungererstraße HU, City Air Terminal, Arnulfstraße (Main Station).

☎ 12 88 44 25.

Exhibition Centre (Messegelände) (EX), ☎ 5 10 70, Telex 5212086, Fax 5107506.

Tourist office in the Main Station, (opposite plattform 11), ☎ 2 39 12 56.

Tourist-Information, Pettenbeckstr. 3, ☎ 2 39 12 72, Fax 2391313.

Tourist-office, airport München-Riem, ☎ 2 39 12 66.

ADAC, Sendlinger-Tor-Platz 9, ☎ 59 39 79.

Innsbruck 162 – Nürnberg 165 – Salzburg 140 – Stuttgart 222.

The reference (M 15) at the end of the address is the postal district : Munich 15

Plans on following pages

Vier Jahreszeiten Kempinski, Maximilianstr. 17 (M 22), ☎ 23 03 90, Telex 523859, Fax 23039693, Massage, – rm TV – 350. AE O E VISA. rest — LZ **a**
M *(closed August)* (dinner only) a la carte 76/105 – **Bistro Eck** (vegetarian dishes available) **M** a la carte 46/74 – **322 rm** 395/753, 45 suites.

Rafael, Neuturmstr. 1 (M 2), ☎ 29 09 80, Telex 5213666, Fax 222539, « Roof garden with terrace and » – TV – 45. AE O E VISA. rest — KZ **s**
M 45 (lunch) and a la carte 67/107 – **74 rm** 420/820, 7 suites.

Königshof, Karlsplatz 25 (M 2), ☎ 55 13 60, Telex 523616, Fax 55136113 – TV – 85. AE O E VISA. rest — JY **s**
M (booking essential) (remarkable wine list) 112/138 and a la carte 76/144 – **103 rm** 298/451, 9 suites
Spec. Hummerterrine, Steinbutt mit Safransauce, Gefüllter Kaninchenrücken in Blätterteig.

Bayerischer Hof-Palais Montgelas, Promenadeplatz 6 (M 2), ☎ 2 12 00, Telex 523409, Fax 2120906, , Massage, , – rm TV – 1500. AE O E VISA — KY **y**
– **Garden-Restaurant M** a la carte 61/102 – **Trader Vic's M** (dinner only) a la carte 46/77 – **Palais Keller M** a la carte 28/50 – **428 rm** 287/543, 45 suites.

Park Hilton, Am Tucherpark 7 (M 22), ☎ 3 84 50, Telex 5215740, Fax 38451845, , beer-garden, Massage, , – rm TV – 750. AE O E VISA — HU **n**
M see also **Hilton Grill below - Tse Yang** (Chinese rest.) **M** a la carte 46/80 – **Isar Terrassen** *(vegetarian dishes available)* **M** a la carte 45/78 – **477 rm** 322/594, 21 suites.

Grand Hotel Continental, Max-Joseph-Str. 5 (M 2), ☎ 55 15 70, Telex 522603, Fax 55157500, – rm TV – 110. AE O E VISA. rest — KY **f**
M a la carte 62/94 – **149 rm** 325/620, 12 suites.

Excelsior, Schützenstr. 11 (M 2), 55 13 70, Telex 522419, Fax 55137121 – 30. rest JY **z**
M *(closed 1 to 10 January and 26 July - 29 August)* a la carte 64/90 – **Vinothek** *(closed Sunday and Bank Holidays)* **M** a la carte 37/57 – **114 rm** 245/375 – 4 suites 530.

Maritim, Goethestr. 7 (M 2), 55 23 50, Fax 55235900, rm – 600. JZ **j**
Rôtisserie **M** a la carte 53/87 – **Bistro M** a la carte 38/58 – **352 rm** 239/478, 5 suites.

Eden-Hotel-Wolff, Arnulfstr. 4 (M 2), 55 11 50, Telex 523564, Fax 55115555 – rm – 250 JY **p**
M a la carte 38/72 – **214 rm** 170/450, 4 suites.

Arabella-Westpark-Hotel, Garmischer Str. 2 (M 2), 5 19 60, Telex 523680, Fax 5196100, – rm rest – 80. by Leopoldstr. GU
closed 20 December - 10 January – **M** 37 (buffet lunch) and a la carte 44/67 – **258 rm** 238/418, 5 suites.

King's Hotel without rest, Dachauer Str. 13 (M 2), 55 18 70, Fax 5232667 – – 30. JY **f**
closed 23 December - 6 January – **96 rm** 180/240, 7 suites.

Trustee Parkhotel without rest, Parkstr. 31 (approach Gollierstraße) (M 2), 51 99 50, Fax 51995420 – – 25. EX **r**
closed 20 December - 6 January – **36 rm** 217/454, 7 suites.

Drei Löwen without rest, Schillerstr. 8 (M 2), 55 10 40, Telex 523867, Fax 55104905 – rm – 20. JZ **m**
130 rm 175/250.

Exquisit without rest, Pettenkoferstr. 3 (M 2), 5 51 99 00, Telex 529863, Fax 55199499, – – 30. JZ **s**
50 rm 195/280, 5 suites.

Platzl-Restaurant Pfistermühle, Platzl 1 (Entrance Sparkassenstraße) (M 2), 23 70 30, Telex 522910, Fax 23703800, – rm – 70. rest
M *(closed Sunday and mid July - mid August)* 35 (lunch) and a la carte 54/80 – **167 rm** 198/394. KZ **z**

Krone without rest, Theresienhöhe 8 (M 2), 50 40 52, Fax 506706 – . EX **a**
30 rm 170/280.

Arabella-Central-Hotel without rest, Schwanthalerstr. 111 (M 2), 51 08 30, Telex 5216031, Fax 51083249, – rm – 30. EX **s**
closed 22 December - 6 January – **103 rm** 205/405.

Erzgießerei-Europe, Erzgießereistr. 15 (M 2), 12 68 20, Telex 5214977, Fax 1236198 – – 70. JY **a**
M *(closed Sunday lunch and Saturday)* a la carte 31/62 – **106 rm** 165/270.

Germania without rest, Schwanthalerstr. 28 (M 2), 5 16 80, Telex 523790, Fax 598491, – – 40. JZ **z**
100 rm 215/355.

Concorde without rest, Herrnstr. 38 (M 22), 22 45 15, Telex 522002, Fax 2283282 – . LZ **q**
closed 23 December - 6 January – **71 rm** 190/370.

Domus without rest, St.-Anna-Str. 31 (M 22), 22 17 04, Telex 529835, Fax 2285359 – . LY **b**
closed 23 to 26 December – **45 rm** 190/300.

Austrotel München, Arnulfstr. 2 (M 2), 5 38 60, Telex 522650, Fax 53862255, 15th floor rest. with ≤ Munich – – 150. JY **r**
M a la carte 35/69 – **174 rm** 205/370.

Intercity-Hotel, Bayerstr. 10 (M 2), 55 85 71, Telex 523174, Fax 596229 – – 150. – **M** a la carte 37/62 – **203 rm** 175/305, 4 suites. JY **u**

Admiral without rest, Kohlstr. 9 (M 5), 22 66 41, Telex 529111, Fax 293674 – . LZ **r**
33 rm 180/295.

Torbräu without rest, Tal 37 (M 2), 22 50 16, Telex 522212, Fax 225019 – LZ **g**
88 rm, 3 suites.

Mercure without rest, Senefelder Str. 9 (M 2), 55 13 20, Telex 5218428, Fax 596444 – – 100. JZ **r**
164 rm 205/362.

Kraft without rest, Schillerstr. 49 (M 2), 59 48 23, Fax 5232856 – . JZ **y**
closed 23 to 26 December – **39 rm** 140/195.

Metropol, Bayerstr. 43, (Entrance Goethestr.) (M 2), 53 07 64, Telex 522816, Fax 5328134 – – 60. JZ **k**
M a la carte 29/65 – **260 rm** 150/230.

Hungar-Hotel, Paul-Heyse-Str. 24 (M 2), 51 49 00, Telex 522395, Fax 51490701, – – 120. rest JZ **c**
M a la carte 35/66 – **182 rm** 199/410.

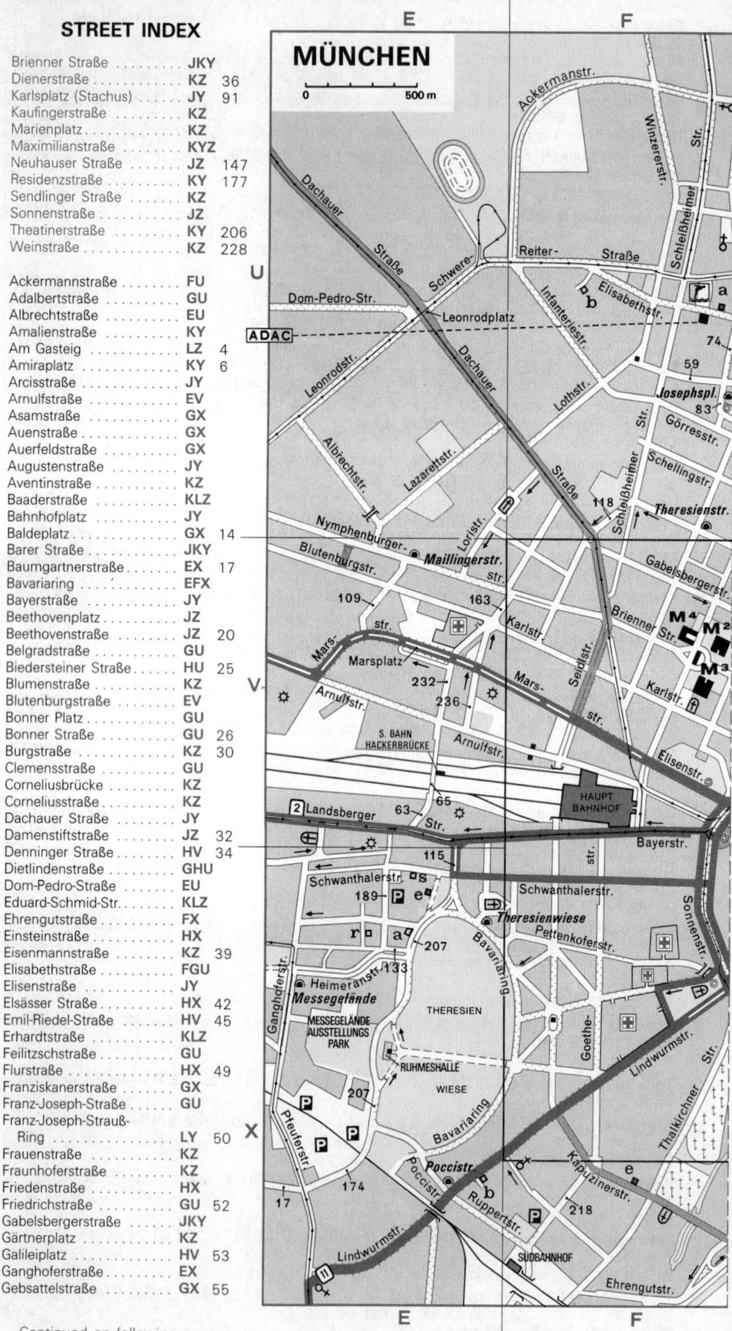

STREET INDEX

Continued on following pages

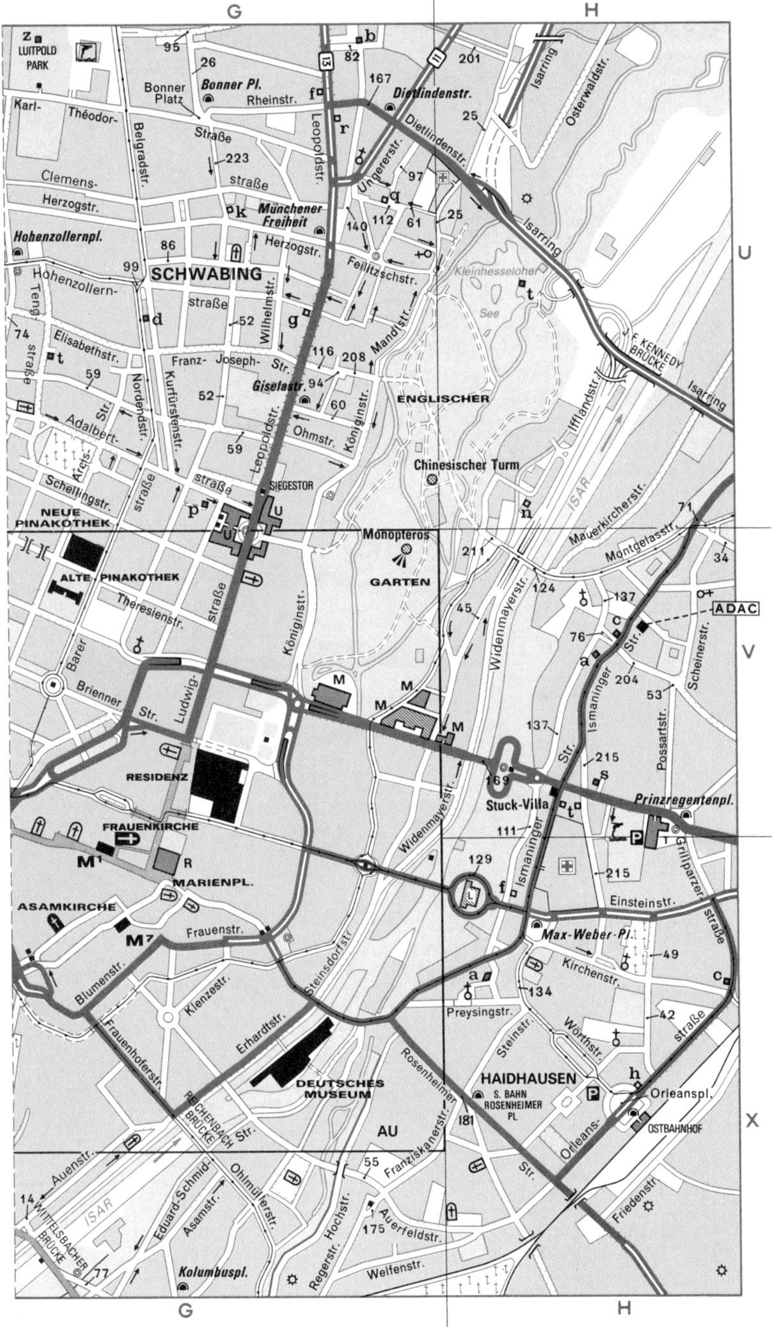

G
H
U
V
X
LUITPOLD PARK
SCHWABING
Bonner Platz
Bonner Pl.
Rheinstr.
Leopoldstr.
Dietlindenstr.
Isarring
Osterwaldstr.
Karl-Theodor-Straße
Belgradstr.
Clemens-straße
Herzogstr.
Münchener Freiheit
Hohenzollernpl.
Hohenzollern-straße
Ungererstr.
Feilitzschstr.
Kleinhesseloher See
F. KENNEDY BRÜCKE
Wilhelmstr.
Mandlstr.
Tengstraße
Elisabethstr.
Franz-Joseph-Str.
Giselastr.
Nordendstr.
Kurfürstenstr.
Adalbert-Str.
Ohmstr.
Königinstr.
ENGLISCHER GARTEN
Chinesischer Turm
Ifflandstr.
ISAR
Schellingstr.
SIEGESTOR
NEUE PINAKOTHEK
ALTE PINAKOTHEK
Monopteros
Mauerkircherstr.
Montgelasstr.
Theresienstr.
Ludwigstraße
Widenmayerstr.
ADAC
Ismaninger Str.
Possartstr.
Scheinerstr.
Barer
Brienner Str.
RESIDENZ
Stuck-Villa
Prinzregentenpl.
FRAUENKIRCHE
MARIENPL.
Grillparzerstraße
Einsteinstr.
ASAMKIRCHE
Frauenstr.
Max-Weber-Pl.
Kirchenstr.
Blumenstr.
Klenzestr.
Steinsdorfstr.
Preysingstr.
Steinstr.
Wörthstr.
Erhardtstr.
Frauenhoferstr.
DEUTSCHES MUSEUM
Rosenheimer Str.
HAIDHAUSEN
S. BAHN ROSENHEIMER PL.
Orleanspl.
OSTBAHNHOF
Orleans-
REICHENBACH BRÜCKE
AU
Auenstr.
Franziskanerstr.
Eduard-Schmid-
Ohlmüllerstr.
Asamstr.
Regerstr.
Hochstr.
Auerfeldstr.
Friedenstr.
WITTELSBACHER BRÜCKE
Kolumbuspl.
Welfenstr.

STREET INDEX

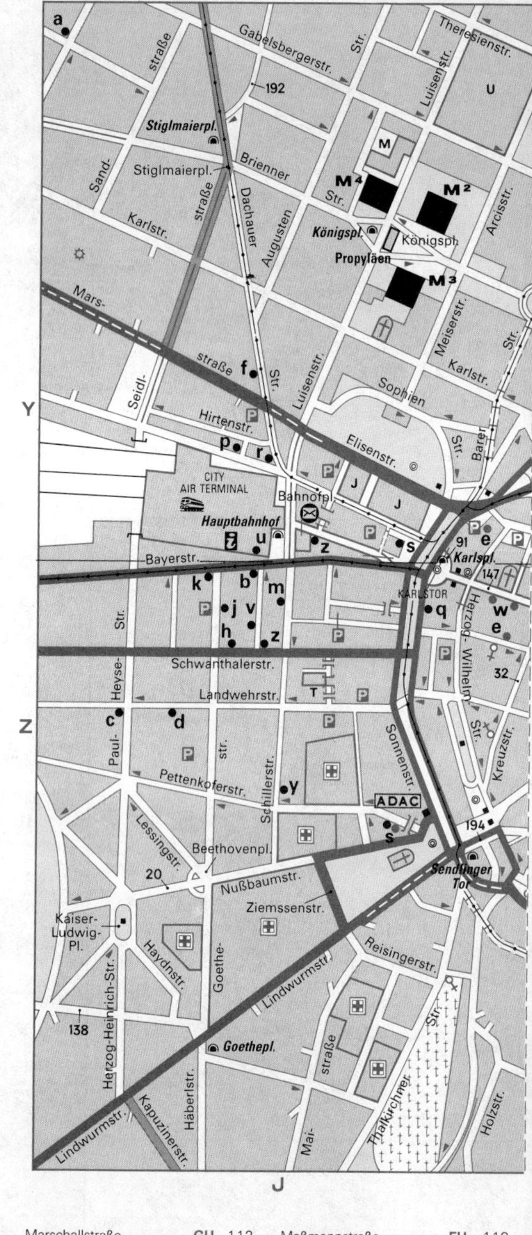

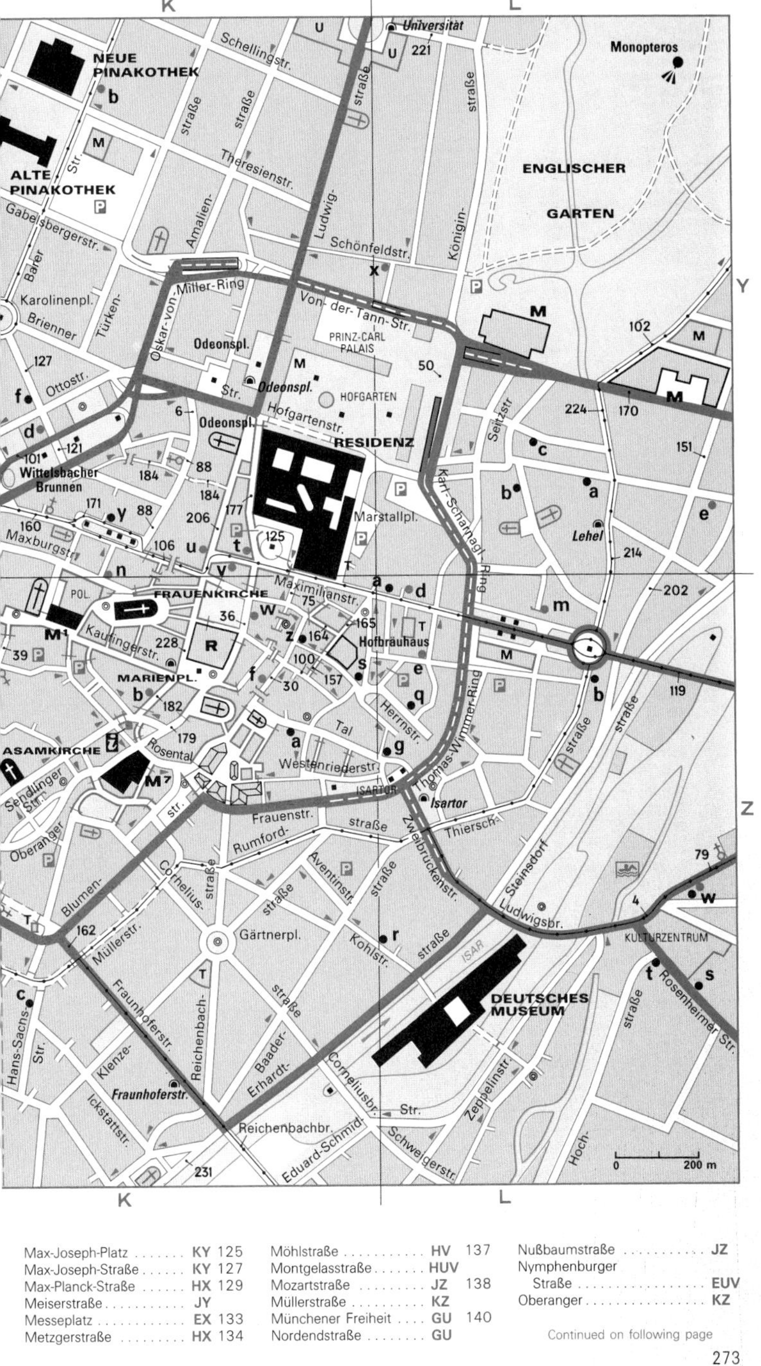

Continued on following page

STREET INDEX TO MÜNCHEN TOWN PLANS (Concluded)

Street	Grid	No.
Odeonsplatz	KY	
Oettingenstraße	LY	151
Ohlmüllerstraße	GX	
Ohmstraße	GU	
Orlandostraße	KZ	157
Orleansplatz	HX	
Orleansstraße	HX	
Oskar-von-Miller-Ring	KY	
Osterwaldstraße	HU	
Ottostraße	KY	
Pacellistraße	KY	160
Papa-Schmid-Straße	KZ	162
Pappenheimstraße	EV	163
Paul-Heyse-Straße	JZ	
Pettenkoferstraße	JZ	
Pfeuferstraße	EX	
Pfisterstraße	KZ	164
Platzl	KZ	165
Poccistraße	EX	
Possartstraße	HV	
Potsdamer Straße	GU	167
Preysingstraße	HX	
Prinzregentenbrücke	HV	169
Prinzregentenstraße	LY	170
Promenadeplatz	KY	171
Radlkoferstraße	EX	174
Regerplatz	GX	175
Regerstraße	GX	
Reichenbachbrücke	KZ	
Reichenbachstraße	KZ	
Reisingerstraße	JZ	
Rheinstraße	GU	
Rindermarkt	KZ	179
Rosenheimer Platz	HX	181
Rosenheimer Straße	LZ	
Rosenstraße	KZ	182
Rosental	KZ	
Rumfordstraße	KZ	
Ruppertstraße	EFX	
Salvatorstraße	KY	184
Sandstraße	JY	
Scheinerstraße	HV	
Schellingstraße	KY	
Schießstättstraße	EX	189
Schillerstraße	JZ	
Schleißheimer Str.	JY	192
Schönfeldstraße	KLY	
Schwanthalerstraße	JZ	
Schweigerstraße	LZ	
Schwere-Reiter-Straße	EFU	
Seidlstraße	JY	
Seitzstraße	LY	
Sendlinger-Tor-Platz	JZ	194
Sophienstraße	JY	
Steinsdorfstraße	LZ	
Steinstraße	HX	
Stengelstraße	HU	201
Sternstraße	LZ	202
Sternwartstraße	HV	204
Stiglmaierplatz	JY	
Tal	KZ	
Tengstraße	GU	
Thalkirchner Straße	JZ	
Theresienhöhe	EX	207
Theresienstraße	JK	
Thiemestraße	GU	208
Thierschstraße	LZ	
Thomas-Wimmer-Ring	LZ	
Tivolistraße	HV	211
Triftstraße	LY	214
Trogerstraße	HVX	215
Türkenstraße	KY	
Tumblingerstraße	FX	218
Ungererstraße	GU	
Veterinärstraße	LY	221
Viktoriastraße	GU	223
Von-der-Tann-Straße	KLY	
Wagmüllerstraße	LY	224
Welfenstraße	GX	
Westenriederstraße	KZ	
Widenmayerstraße	GHV	
Wilhelmstraße	GU	
Winzererstraße	FU	
Wittelsbacherbrücke	GX	
Wittelsbacherstraße	KZ	231
Wörthstraße	HX	
Wredestraße	EV	232
Zeppelinstraße	LZ	
Ziemssenstraße	JZ	
Zirkus-Krone-Straße	EV	236
Zweibrückenstraße	LZ	

Budapest, Schwanthalerstr. 36 (M 2), ☎ 55 11 10, Telex 522395, Fax 51490701 – rest – 150. AE VISA. rest — JZ **h**
M a la carte 35/66 – **100 rm** 199/410.

Atrium without rest, Landwehrstr. 59 (M 2), ☎ 51 41 90, Telex 5212162, Fax 598491, – rm – 50. AE VISA — JZ **d**
163 rm 215/355.

Splendid without rest, Maximilianstr. 54 (M 22), ☎ 29 66 06, Telex 522427, Fax 2913176 – . AE VISA — LZ **b**
40 rm 145/390.

Brack without rest, Lindwurmstr. 153 (M 2), ☎ 77 10 52, Fax 7250615 – . AE VISA — EX **b**
50 rm 135/225.

Europäischer Hof without rest, Bayerstr. 31 (M 2), ☎ 55 15 10, Telex 522642, Fax 55151222 – . AE VISA — JZ **b**
160 rm 140/280, 7 suites.

Ariston without rest, Unsöldstr. 10 (M 22), ☎ 22 26 91, Telex 522437, Fax 2913595 – . AE VISA — LY **c**
closed Christmas - 7 January – **61 rm** 120/210.

Schlicker without rest, Tal 74 (M 2), ☎ 22 79 41, Fax 296059 – . AE VISA — KZ **a**
closed 20 December - 7 January – **70 rm** 125/240.

Olympic without rest, Hans-Sachs-Str. 4 (M 5), ☎ 23 18 90, Fax 23189199 – — KZ **c**
32 rm 145/240.

Daniel without rest, Sonnenstr. 5 (M 2), ☎ 55 49 45, Telex 523863, Fax 553420 – . AE VISA — JZ **q**
76 rm 116/290.

Adria without rest, Liebigstr. 8a (M 22), ☎ 29 30 81, Telex 5214111, Fax 227015 – . AE VISA — LY **a**
closed 22 to 25 December – **47 rm** 135/220.

XXXX ✿✿✿ **Aubergine**, Maximiliansplatz 5 (M 2), ☎ 59 81 71, Fax 5236753/5504353 – . AE VISA — KY **d**
closed Sunday, Monday, Bank Holidays and 23 December - 7 January – **M** (booking essential) 165/225 and a la carte 98/154
Spec. Délice von Bresse-Taube mit getrüffelter Gänsestopfleber, Zander mit kroß gebratener Haut, Pralinenparfait mit glasierten Babybananen.

XXXX ✿ **Le Gourmet Schwarzwälder**, Hartmannstr. 8 (1st floor) (M 2), ☎ 2 12 09 58, Fax 2904172 – AE VISA — KYZ **n**
closed Sunday, Monday and 23 December - 7 January – **M** (booking essential) (remarkable wine list) 170 and a la carte 90/130
Spec. Falsche Prinzregententorte, Weißwurst von Meeresfrüchten, Soufflierte Wachtelbrüstchen mit Trüffelsauce.

XXXX ✿ **Hilton Grill** (Hotel Park Hilton), Am Tucherpark 7 (M 22), ☎ 3 84 52 61, Fax 38451845 – . AE VISA. – **M** 49 (lunch) and a la carte 66/93 — HU **n**
Spec. Seezungenroulade mit Hummer gefüllt, Wachtelkotelett in der Kartoffelkruste, Marzipan-lasagne mit Eierliköreis.

XXX **Weinhaus Schwarzwälder** (Old Munich wine restaurant), Hartmannstr. 8 (M 2), ✆ 2 12 09 79, Fax 2904172 – AE ⓓ E VISA KYZ **n**
closed Sunday – **M** a la carte 49/88 *(vegetarian dishes available).*

XXX **El Toula**, Sparkassenstr. 5 (M 2), ✆ 29 28 69, Fax 298043 – ▤. AE ⓓ E VISA KZ **f**
closed Sunday, Monday, and 3 weeks July - August – **M** (booking essential for dinner) a la carte 68/95.

XXX ✿ **Sabitzer**, Reitmorstr. 21 (M 22), ✆ 29 85 84, Fax 3003304 – AE E VISA. ✻ LY **e**
closed Sunday, 7 to 24 January and 10 to 22 August – **M** (dinner only) (booking essential) a la carte 89/119
Spec. Lasagne von Lachs und Steinbutt in Schnittlauchsauce, Lamm- und Wildgerichte, Topfenschaum mit Früchten.

XX ✿ **Boettner** (small Old Munich rest.), Theatinerstr. 8 (M 2), ✆ 22 12 10, ☂ – AE ⓓ E VISA KY **u**
closed Saturday dinner, Sunday and Bank Holidays – **M** (booking essential) a la carte 67/130
Spec. Hechtsoufflé mit Sauce Nantua, Hummereintopf "Hartung", Rote Grütze.

XX **Zum Bürgerhaus**, Pettenkoferstr. 1 (M 2), ✆ 59 79 09, Fax 595657, « Bavarian farmhouse furniture, court terrace » – ⓓ E VISA JZ **s**
closed Saturday lunch, Sunday and Bank Holidays – **M** (booking essential) a la carte 47/79.

XX **Gasthaus Glockenbach** (former old Bavarian pub), Kapuzinerstr. 29 (M 2), ✆ 53 40 43 – E VISA FX **e**
closed Sunday, Monday, Bank Holidays and 24 December - 2 January – **M** (booking essential) a la carte 64/93.

XX **Halali**, Schönfeldstr. 22 (M 22), ✆ 28 59 09, Fax 282786 – AE E LY **x**
closed Sunday and Bank Holidays and 2 weeks August – **M** (booking essential) a la carte 48/76.

XX **Weinhaus Neuner** (19C wine restaurant), Herzogspitalstr. 8 (M 2), ✆ 2 60 39 54 – AE E
closed Sunday, Bank Holidays and 2 weeks August – **M** a la carte 43/65. JZ **e**

XX **Chesa**, Wurzerstr. 18 (M 22), ✆ 29 71 14, Fax 2285698, ☂ – ▤. AE ⓓ E VISA LZ **d**
closed Sunday and Bank Holidays – **M** (booking essential) a la carte 51/76.

XX **Austernkeller**, Stollbergstr. 11 (M 22), ✆ 29 87 87 – AE ⓓ E VISA. ✻ LZ **e**
closed Monday and 23 to 26 December – **M** (dinner only, booking essential) a la carte 47/83.

XX **Mövenpick**, Lenbachplatz 8 (M 2), ✆ 55 78 65, Fax 5236538, ☂ – 🏛 180. AE ⓓ E VISA
M a la carte 30/69. JY **e**

XX **Dallmayr**, Dienerstr. 14 (1st floor) (M 2), ✆ 2 13 51 00, Fax 2135167 – AE ⓓ E VISA
closed Saturday dinner and Sunday, dinner August – **M** a la carte 55/82. KZ **w**

X **Goldene Stadt** (Bohemian specialities), Oberanger 44 (M 2), ✆ 26 43 82 – AE ⓓ E JZ **f**
M (booking essential for dinner) a la carte 28/60.

X **Straubinger Hof** (bavarian rest.), Blumenstr. 5 (M 2), ✆ 2 60 84 44, beer garden – AE E. ✻ – **M** a la carte 22/43. KZ **c**

Brewery - inns :

X **Spatenhaus-Bräustuben**, Residenzstr. 12 (M 2), ✆ 2 90 70 60, Fax 2913054, ☂, « Furnished in traditional alpine style » – AE ⓓ E VISA KY **t**
M a la carte 45/74.

X **Augustiner Gaststätten**, Neuhauser Str. 16 (M 2), ✆ 55 19 92 57, Fax 2605379, « Beer garden » – AE ⓓ E VISA JZ **w**
M a la carte 29/64.

X **Franziskaner Fuchsenstuben**, Perusastr. 5 (M 2), ✆ 2 31 81 20, Fax 23181244, ☂ – AE ⓓ E VISA – **M** a la carte 31/58. KY **v**

X **Zum Spöckmeier**, Rosenstr. 9 (M 2), ✆ 26 80 88, Fax 2605509, ☂ – ⓓ E VISA KZ **b**
closed Sunday June - August – **M** a la carte 31/56.

X **Spatenhofkeller**, Neuhauser Str. 26 (M 2), ✆ 26 40 10, Fax 685586 – AE E VISA JZ **w**
M a la carte 24/47.

X **Hackerkeller und Schäfflerstuben**, Theresienhöhe 4 (M 2), ✆ 50 70 04, Fax 501721, beer garden – AE ⓓ E VISA – **M** a la carte 33/69. EX **e**

at Munich 50-Allach by Arnulfstr. EV :

🏨 **Lutter** without rest, Eversbuschstr. 109, ✆ 8 12 70 04, Fax 8129584 – TV ☎ P. E VISA. ✻
26 rm ☕ 110/160.

at Munich-Bogenhausen :

🏨 **Sheraton**, Arabellastr. 6 (M 81), ✆ 9 26 40, Fax 916877, ≤ Munich, beer garden, Massage, ≘s, 🏊 – 🛗 ⅹ rm ▤ TV ♿ 🚗 – 🏛 650. AE ⓓ E VISA. ✻ rest by Isarring HU
M a la carte 49/88 – **637 rm** ☕ 282/492, 16 suites.

🏨 **Palace**, Trogerstr. 21 (M 80), ✆ 4 70 50 91, Telex 528256, Fax 4705090, « Elegant installation with period furniture », ≘s, 🌳 – 🛗 ⅹ TV 🚗 – 🏛 40. AE ⓓ E VISA. ✻ rest
M a la carte 48/72 – **71 rm** ☕ 259/568, 6 suites. HV **t**

🏨 **Arabella-Hotel**, Arabellastr. 5 (M 81), ✆ 9 23 20, Telex 529987, Fax 92324447, ≤, ☂, Massage, 🏋, ≘s, 🏊 – 🛗 ⅹ rm ▤ rest TV ♿ 🚗 – 🏛 320. AE ⓓ E VISA
M a la carte 41/69 – **467 rm** ☕ 303/476, 32 suites. by Isarring HU

Rothof without rest, Denniger Str. 114 (M 81), 91 50 61, Fax 915066, – by Einsteinstr. HX
closed 24 December - 6 January – **37 rm** 198/460.

Prinzregent without rest, Ismaninger Str. 42 (M 80), 41 60 50, Telex 524403, Fax 41605466, – – 40. HV **t**
closed 24 December - 11 January – **68 rm** 270/480.

Queens Hotel München, Effnerstr. 99 (M 81), 92 79 80, Telex 524757, Fax 983813 – rm rest – 220. by Ismaninger Str. HV
M a la carte 49/72 – **152 rm** 262/434.

da Pippo (Italian rest.), Mühlbaurstr. 36 (M 80), 4 70 48 48, Fax 476464, – by Mühlbaurstr. HV
closed Saturday lunch, Sunday and Bank Holidays – **M** a la carte 55/78.

Käfer-Schänke, Schumannstr. 1 (M 80), 4 16 82 47, Fax 4703658, « Several rooms with elegant rustic decor » – HV **s**
closed Sunday and Bank Holidays – **M** (booking essential) a la carte 58/105.

Bogenhauser Hof (1825 former hunting lodge), Ismaninger Str. 85 (M 80), 98 55 86, Fax 9810221, « Garden terrace » – HV **c**
closed Sunday, Bank Holidays and Christmas - 6 January – **M** (booking essential) a la carte 61/99.

Louis XIII, Ismaninger Str. 71a (M 80), 98 92 00, – HV **a**
closed Sunday and Bank Holidays – **M** a la carte 58/86.

Prielhof, Oberföhringer Str. 44 (M 81), 98 53 53, –
closed Saturday lunch, Sunday, Bank Holidays and 23 December - 6 January – **M** (booking essential) a la carte 52/84. by Ismaninger Str. HV

at Munich 80-Haidhausen :

City Hilton, Rosenheimer Str. 15, 4 80 40, Telex 529437, Fax 48044804, – rm – 180. LZ **s**
Zum Gasteig M a la carte 49/87 – **Löwenschänke M** a la carte 44/59 – **483 rm** 279/508, 4 suites.

Preysing, Preysingstr. 1, 48 10 11, Telex 529044, Fax 4470998, – rm – 50 LZ **w**
closed 23 December - 6 January – **M** (see **Preysing-Keller** below) – **76 rm** 160/289, 5 suites.

München Penta Hotel, Hochstr. 3, 4 80 30, Telex 529046, Fax 4488277, Massage, – rm – 360. LZ **t**
M a la carte 51/83 – **583 rm** 310/471, 12 suites.

Habis, Maria-Theresia-Str. 2a, 4 70 50 71, Fax 4705101 – . HX **f**
M (dinner only) a la carte 38/60 – **26 rm** 135/190.

Stadt Rosenheim without rest, Orleansplatz 6a, 4 48 24 24, Fax 485987 – . HX **h**
58 rm 104/184.

Preysing-Keller, Innere-Wiener-Str. 6, 48 10 15, Fax 4470998, « Vaulted cellar, country house furniture » – LZ **w**
closed Sunday, Bank Holidays and 23 December - 6 January – **M** (dinner only) (remarkable wine list) 125 and a la carte 52/87
Spec. Jacobsmuscheln mit Limonenbutter, Gefüllte Wachtel im Kartoffelmantel, Aprikosenkrapfen mit Weinschaum.

Balance, Grillparzerstr. 1, 4 70 54 72, – HX **c**
closed Saturday lunch, Sunday and Bank Holidays – **M** a la carte 45/64.

Rue Des Halles (Bistro), Steinstr. 18, 48 56 75 – HX **a**
M (dinner only) (booking essential) a la carte 60/75.

at Munich 90-Harlaching by Regerstr. GX :

Hunsinger, Braunstr. 6, 6 42 27 78, –
closed Monday lunch and Sunday – **M** (mainly Seafood) a la carte 58/95.

at Munich 21-Laim by Landsberger Str. (B 2) EV :

Transmar-Park-Hotel without rest, Zschokkestr. 55, 57 93 60, Telex 5218609, Fax 57936100, – – 30.
68 rm 230/260.

at Munich 60 - Langwied NW : 13 km by Arnulfstr. EV

Das kleine Restaurant im Gasthof Böswirth, Waidachanger 9, 8 64 41 63, Fax 8643857 –
closed Sunday, Monday, Bank Holidays, 3 weeks January and 2 weeks June – **M** (remarkable wine list) 48 (lunch) and a la carte 70/95
Spec. Kalbskopf in Kerbeldressing, Steinbutt mit Olivenpüree, Mango-Joghurtparfait mit Früchten.

at Munich 83-Neu Perlach by Rosenheimer Str. HX

Mercure, Karl-Marx-Ring 87, 6 32 70, Telex 5213357, Fax 6327407, beer garden, – rm rest – 130. AE E VISA – **Perlacher Bürgerstuben M** a la carte 46/76 – **Hubertuskeller M** (dinner only) a la carte 37/56 – **185 rm** 185/285, 4 suites.

at Munich 40-Schwabing :

Marriott-Hotel, Berliner Str. 93, 36 00 20, Telex 5216641, Fax 36002200, – rm – 350. AE E VISA. rest by Ungererstr. (B 11) HU
M a la carte 48/81 – **350 rm** 406/532, 14 suites.

Ramada Parkhotel, Theodor-Dombart-Str. 4 (corner Berliner Straße), 36 09 90, Telex 5218720, Fax 36099684, – rm – 45. AE E VISA. rest by Ungererstr. (B 11) HU
M a la carte 51/75 – **260 rm** 257/484, 80 suites.

Holiday Inn Crowne Plaza, Leopoldstr. 194, 38 17 90, Fax 38179888, Massage, – rm – 320. AE E VISA by Leopoldstr. GU
M 39/buffet (lunch) and a la carte 50/78 – **363 rm** 278/506, 3 suites.

Residence, Artur-Kutscher-Platz 4, 38 17 80, Telex 529788, Fax 38178951, – rm – 60. AE E VISA. rest GU **q**
M (dinner only) a la carte 44/72 – **165 rm** 193/350.

König Ludwig without rest, Hohenzollernstr. 3, 33 59 95, Telex 5216607, Fax 394658 – AE E VISA GU **g**
46 rm 205/330.

Arabella - Olympiapark-Hotel, Helene-Mayer-Ring 12, 3 51 60 71, Fax 3543730, – – 30. AE E VISA by Schleißheimer Str. FU
closed 23 December - 8 January – **M** *(Saturday and Sunday dinner only)* a la carte 39/80 – **106 rm** 194/288.

Mercure without rest, Leopoldstr. 120, 39 05 50, Fax 349344 – AE E VISA GU **r**
67 rm 190/320.

Vitalis, Kathi-Kobus-Str. 24, 12 00 80, Telex 5215161, Fax 1298382 – rm – 80. AE E VISA. rest FU **b**
M *(closed Saturday, Sunday and Bank Holidays)* (dinner only) a la carte 37/65 – **100 rm** 190/265.

Consul without rest, Viktoriastr. 10, 33 40 35, Fax 399266 – AE E GU **k**
31 rm 130/200.

Leopold, Leopoldstr. 119, 36 70 61, Telex 5215160, Fax 367061, – AE E VISA GU **f**
closed 23 December - 3 January – **M** *(closed Saturday and 4 to 10 January)* a la carte 30/61 – **75 rm** 145/195.

Ibis, Ungererstr. 139, 36 08 30, Telex 5215080, Fax 363793, – – 35. AE E VISA by Ungererstraße GHU
M a la carte 30/44 – **138 rm** 154/198.

Tantris, Johann-Fichte-Str. 7, 36 20 61, Fax 3618469, – AE E VISA.
closed lunch Monday and Saturday Sunday, Bank Holidays, and 1 week January – **M** (booking essential) a la carte 93/145 GU **b**
Spec. Salat von Edelfischen mit Hummer und marinierten Artischocken, Geschmorte Rinderbacke mit Gemüse und Marknockerl, Topfen-Soufflé mit eingelegten Zwetschgen.

Seehaus, Kleinhesselohe 3, 3 81 61 30, Fax 341803, « Lakeside setting, terrace » – AE E VISA HU **t**
M a la carte 45/70.

Savoy (Italian rest.), Tengstr. 20, 2 71 14 45 – AE E VISA GU **t**
closed Sunday – **M** (booking essential for dinner) a la carte 42/73.

Bistro Terrine, Amalienstr. 89 (Amalien-Passage), 28 17 80, – AE E GU **p**
closed Saturday and Monday lunch, Sunday, Bank Holidays and 2 weeks January – **M** (booking essential for dinner) a la carte 60/80.

Romagna Antica (Italian rest.), Elisabethstr. 52, 2 71 63 55, Fax 2711364, – AE E VISA. FU **a**
closed Sunday and Bank Holidays – **M** (booking essential for dinner) a la carte 47/70.

Vis à vis, Barerstr. 42, 28 34 07 – AE E KY **b**
closed Sunday and Bank Holidays – **M** (dinner only) a la carte 55/75.

Daitokai (Japanese rest), Nordendstr. 64 (entrance Kurfürstenstr.), 2 71 14 21, Fax 2718392 – AE E VISA. GU **d**
closed Sunday – **M** (booking essential) a la carte 51/78.

Bei Grazia (Italian rest.), Ungererstr. 161, 36 69 31 – AE E by Ungererstr. HU
closed Saturday and Sunday – **M** (booking essential) a la carte 48/72.

Bamberger Haus, Brunnenstr. 2 (at Luitpoldpark), 3 08 89 66, Fax 3003304, « 18C palace with brewery and terrace » – AE E VISA GU **z**
closed Monday and June - September – **M** a la carte 43/71.

at Munich 70 - Sendling by Lindwurmstr. (B 11) EX

Holiday Inn München - Süd, Kistlerhofstr. 142, 78 00 20, Telex 5218645, Fax 78002672, beer garden, Massage, , - rm - 100.
M a la carte 53/75 - **320 rm** 268/500, 8 suites.

Ambassador Parkhotel, Plinganserstr. 102, 72 48 90, Telex 524444, Fax 72489100, beer garden - .
closed 20 December - 6 January - **M** *(Saturday dinner only)* (Italian rest.) a la carte 35/67 - **42 rm** 170/230.

K u. K Hotel am Harras, Albert-Rosshaupter-Str. 4, 77 00 51, Telex 5213167, Fax 7212820 - .
M residents only (dinner only) - **129 rm** 190/345.

at Munich 50-Untermenzing by Arnulfstr. EV

Romantik-Hotel Insel Mühle, von-Kahr-Str. 87, 8 10 10, Fax 8120571, , beer garden, « Converted 16C riverside mill » - .
M *(closed Sunday and Bank Holidays)* a la carte 46/80 - **37 rm** 180/410.

at Unterhaching **8025** by Kapuzinerstr. GX

Schrenkhof without rest, Leonhardsweg 6, 6 10 09 10, Fax 61009150, « Bavarian farm-house furniture », - - 40.
closed 20 December - 8 January - **26 rm** 200/250.

at Aschheim **8011** NE : 13 km by Riem :

Schreiberhof, Erdinger Str. 2, (089) 90 00 60, Fax 90006459, , - rm - 90.
M a la carte 44/77 - **86 rm** 195/265.

Zur Post, Ismaninger Str. 11 (B 471), (089) 9 03 20 27, Fax 9044669, - . - **M** a la carte 24/50 - **55 rm** 85/170.

at Grünwald **8022** S : 13 km by Wittelsbacher Brücke GX - 089 :

Tannenhof without rest, Marktplatz 3, 6 41 70 74, Fax 6415608, « Period house with elegant interior » - .
closed 20 December - 6 January - **21 rm** 140/200, 3 suites.

Alter Wirt, Marktplatz 1, 6 41 78 55, Fax 6414266, , « Traditional Bavarian inn » - - 70.
M a la carte 34/68 - **49 rm** 160/210.

Schloß-Hotel Grünwald, Zeillerstr.1, 6 41 79 35, Fax 6414771, <, « Terrace » - .
closed 27 December - 15 January - **M** *(closed November - Easter Monday and Tuesday)* a la carte 42/74 - **16 rm** 150/320.

Aschau im Chiemgau

8213. Bayern 413 TU 23, 987 ㊲, 426 I 5 - pop. 5 200 - alt. 615 m - 08052 - München 82.

Residenz Heinz Winkler, Kirchplatz 1, 1 79 90, Fax 179966, < Kampenwand, « Elegant hotel with carefully renovated coaching inn », - . rest
M (closed Monday) 155/186 and a la carte 90/142 - **32 rm** 210/580
Spec. Emincé vom Lachs mit Kaviar-Schnittlauchsauce, Taubenbrust im Kartoffelmantel mit Senf-körnersauce, Quarksoufflé mit Birnensauce.

STUTTGART

7000. L Baden-Württemberg 413 KL 20, 987 ㉟ - pop. 559 000 - alt. 245 m - 0711.

See : Linden Museum ★★ KY **M1** - Park Wilhelma★ HT and Killesberg-Park★ GT - Television Tower (Fernsehturm) ★★ HX - Stuttgart Gallery (Otto-Dix-Collection★) LY **M4** - Swabian Brewerymuseum (Schwäb. Brauereimuseum)★ by Böblinger Straße FX - Old Castle (Altes Schloß) (Renaissance courtyard★) - Württemberg Regional Museum★ (Sacred Statuary★★) LY **M3** - State Gallery★ (Old Masters Collection★★) LY **M2** - Collegiate church (Stiftskirche) (Commemorative monuments of dukes★) KY **A** - State Musem of Natural History (Staatl. Museum für Naturkunde)★ HT **M5** - Daimler-Benz Museum★ JV **M6** - Porsche Museum★ by Heilbronner Straße GT - Schloß Solitude★ by Rotenwaldstraße FX.

Envir. : Bad Cannstatt Spa Park (Kurpark)★ E : 4 km JT.

18 Kornwestheim, Aldinger Str. (N : 11 km), (07141) 87 13 19 ; 18 Mönsheim (NW : 30 km by A 8), (07044) 69 09.

Stuttgart-Echterdingen, by Obere Weinsteige (B 27) GX, 7 90 11, City Air Terminal, Stuttgart, Lautenschlagerstr. 14, 20 12 68.

Exhibition Centre (Messegelände Killesberg) (GT), 2 58 91, Telex 722584.

Amt für Touristik - Tourist-Info, Königstr. 1a, 2 22 82 40, Fax 2228251.

ADAC, Am Neckartor 2, 2 80 00.

Frankfurt am Main 204 - Karlsruhe 88 - München 222 - Strasbourg 156.

Plans on following pages

Steigenberger-Hotel Graf Zeppelin, Arnulf-Klett-Platz 7, ✆ 2 04 80, Telex 722418, Fax 2048542, Massage, ≘s, ⛆ - |‡| ⇆ rm ▤ TV ♿ - 🏛 300. AE ⓞ E VISA LY **s**
M a la carte 34/90 - **280 rm** ☕ 295/485, 20 suites.

Am Schloßgarten, Schillerstr. 23, ✆ 2 02 60, Telex 722936, Fax 2026888, « Terrace with ≤ » - |‡| ⇆ rm TV 🚗 - 🏛 120. AE ⓞ E VISA. ✻ rest LY **u**
M a la carte 67/104 - **121 rm** ☕ 255/490, 2 suites.

Inter-Continental, Neckarstr. 60, ✆ 2 02 00, Telex 721996, Fax 202012, Massage, Fó, ≘s, ⛆ - |‡| ⇆ rm ▤ TV ♿ 🚗 - 🏛 500. AE ⓞ E VISA. ✻ rest HV **t**
- **Les Continents** *(closed Saturday lunch)* **M** a la carte 70/100 - **Neckarstube** *(closed Sunday)* **M** a la carte 38/60 - **277 rm** ☕ 361/552, 24 suites.

Royal, Sophienstr. 35, ✆ 62 50 50, Telex 722449, Fax 628809 - |‡| ▤ rest TV 🚗 Ⓟ - 🏛 70. AE ⓞ E VISA KZ **b**
M *(closed Sunday and Bank Holidays)* a la carte 45/79 - **94 rm** ☕ 208/420, 3 suites.

Parkhotel, Villastr. 21, ✆ 2 80 10, Telex 723405, Fax 2864353, 🍽 - |‡| TV 🚗 - 🏛 80. AE ⓞ E VISA HU **r**
M a la carte 57/79 - **Radio Stüble M** (dinner only) a la carte 37/68 - **75 rm** ☕ 200/320.

Ruff, Friedhofstr. 21, ✆ 2 58 70, Telex 721645, Fax 2587404, ≘s, ⛆ - |‡| TV ☎ 🚗 Ⓟ. AE ⓞ E VISA GU **a**
closed 22 December - 2 January and 8 to 12 April - **M** *(closed Sunday lunch and Saturday and 17 July - 1 August)* a la carte 36/62 - **85 rm** ☕ 135/198.

Rega Hotel, Ludwigstr. 18, ✆ 61 93 40, Telex 722701, Fax 6193477 - |‡| TV ☎ 🚗 - 🏛 30. AE ⓞ E VISA FV **a**
M a la carte 36/59 - **60 rm** ☕ 175/235.

Intercity-Hotel without rest, Arnulf-Klett-Platz 2, ✆ 2 23 98 01, Telex 723543, Fax 2261899 - |‡| TV ☎ - 🏛 30. AE ⓞ E VISA. ✻ LY **p**
130 rm ☕ 180/240.

Unger without rest, Kronenstr. 17, ✆ 2 09 90, Telex 723995, Fax 2099100 - |‡| ⇆ TV ☎ 🚗. AE ⓞ E VISA LY **a**
closed 24 December - 9 January - **80 rm** ☕ 149/299.

Bergmeister without rest, Rotenbergstr. 16, ✆ 28 33 63, Fax 283719, ≘s - |‡| TV ☎ 🚗. AE ⓞ E VISA HV **r**
45 rm ☕ 148/330.

Kronen-Hotel without rest, Kronenstr. 48, ✆ 29 96 61, Telex 723632, Fax 296940, ≘s - |‡| TV ☎ 🚗 - 🏛 20. AE ⓞ E VISA KY **m**
closed for reconstruction until April 1993 - **85 rm** ☕ 160/300.

Wörtz zur Weinsteige, Hohenheimer Str. 30, ✆ 24 53 96, Telex 723821, Fax 6407279, « Terrace » - TV ☎ Ⓟ. AE ⓞ E VISA LZ **p**
closed 20 December - 10 January - **M** *(closed Saturday, Sunday and Bank Holidays)* a la carte 27/74 - **25 rm** ☕ 135/280.

Azenberg, Seestr. 114, ✆ 22 10 51, Fax 297426, ≘s, ⛆ - |‡| ⇆ rm TV ☎ 🚗 Ⓟ. AE ⓞ E VISA FU **e**
M (residents only) (dinner only) - **55 rm** ☕ 140/250.

Wartburg, Lange Str. 49, ✆ 2 04 50, Telex 721587, Fax 2045450 - |‡| ▤ rest TV ☎ Ⓟ - 🏛 45 KY **g**
closed Easter and 21 December - 2 January - **M** *(closed Sunday and Bank Holidays)* a la carte 26/51 - **81 rm** ☕ 139/265.

Ketterer, Marienstr. 3, ✆ 2 03 90, Telex 722340, Fax 2039600 - |‡| TV ☎ 🚗. AE ⓞ E VISA KZ **y**
closed 21 December - 7 January - **M** *(closed Friday, Saturday and 24 July - 22 August)* a la carte 36/67 - **100 rm** ☕ 139/320.

Rieker without rest, Friedrichstr. 3, ✆ 22 13 11, Fax 293894 - |‡| TV ☎ LY **d**
63 rm.

Rema-Hotel Astoria without rest, Hospitalstr. 29, ✆ 29 93 01, Telex 722783, Fax 299307 - |‡| ⇆ TV ☎ Ⓟ. AE ⓞ E VISA KY **r**
closed 22 December - 2 January - **50 rm** ☕ 165/340.

City-Hotel without rest, Uhlandstr. 18, ✆ 21 08 10, Fax 2369772 - TV ☎ Ⓟ. AE ⓞ E VISA LZ **a**
31 rm ☕ 140/195.

Am Feuersee, Johannesstr. 2, ✆ 62 61 03, Fax 627804 - |‡| TV ☎. AE ⓞ E VISA FV **t**
closed 20 to 31 December - **M** *(closed Saturday, Sunday and Bank Holidays)* (dinner only) a la carte 28/52 - **38 rm** ☕ 135/180.

XXX ✿ **Alte Post**, Friedrichstr. 43, ✆ 29 30 79 - AE ⓞ E VISA KY **e**
closed lunch Saturday and Monday Sunday, Bank Holidays and 3 weeks July - August - **M** (booking essential) 46 (lunch) and a la carte 69/100
Spec. Hausgemachte Gänseleberterrine, Seezungenfilet in vin jaune, Kalbsniere mit Rosmarinsauce.

XX **Da Franco** (Italian rest.), Calwer Str. 23, ✆ 29 15 81, Fax 294549 - ▤. AE ⓞ E VISA KYZ **c**
closed Monday - **M** a la carte 47/71.

XX **Mövenpick-La Pêcherie** (mainly Seafood), Kleiner Schloßplatz 11 (entrance Theodor-Heuss-Str.), ✆ 2 26 89 34, Fax 2991610, 🍽 - ▤. AE ⓞ E VISA KY **a**
M a la carte 43/83.

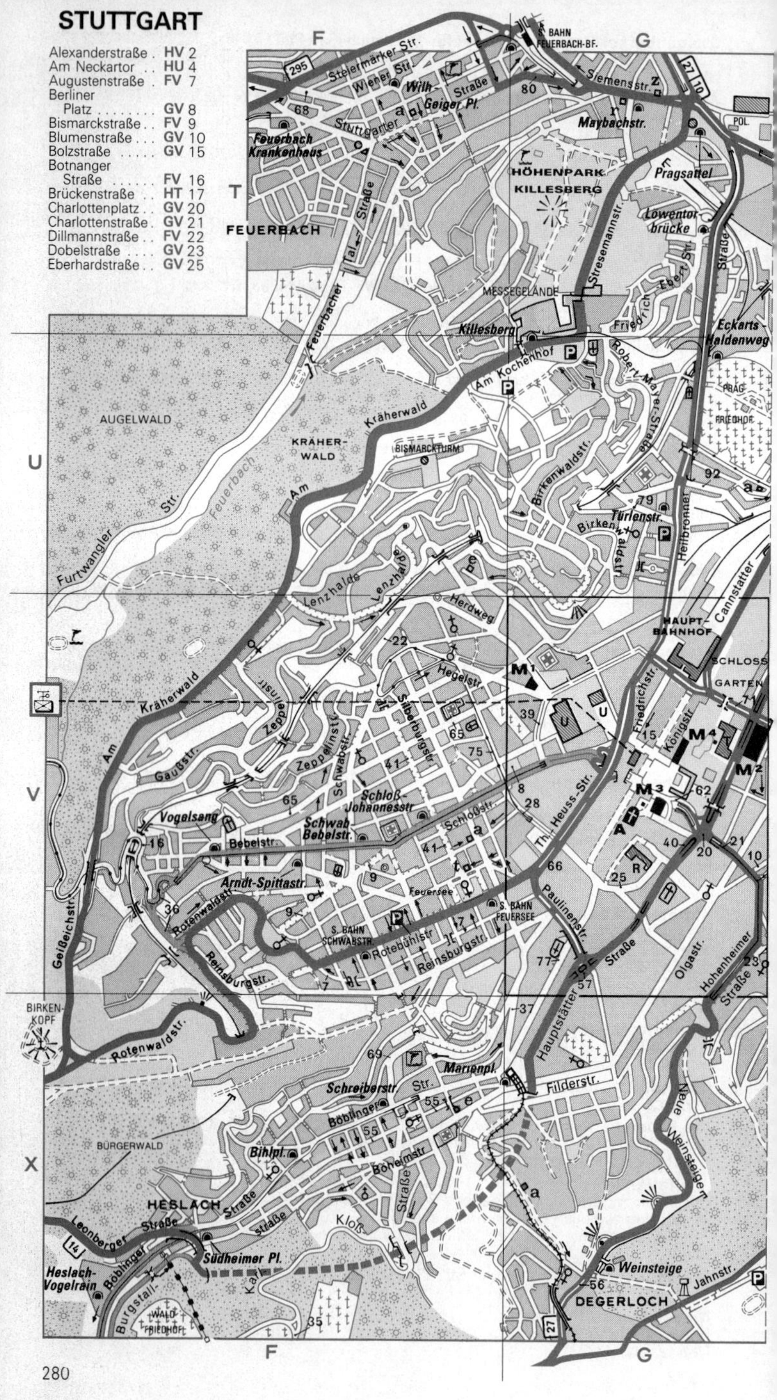
STUTTGART
Alexanderstraße . HV 2
Am Neckartor . . HU 4
Augustenstraße . FV 7
Berliner Platz . . . . GV 8
Bismarckstraße . . FV 9
Blumenstraße . . . GV 10
Bolzstraße . . . . . GV 15
Botnanger Straße . . . . . . FV 16
Brückenstraße . . HT 17
Charlottenplatz . . GV 20
Charlottenstraße . GV 21
Dillmannstraße . . FV 22
Dobelstraße . . . . GV 23
Eberhardstraße . . GV 25
F
G
T
U
V
X
S. BAHN FEUERBACH-BF.
Steiermärker Str.
Wiener Str.
Wilh.-Geiger Pl.
Straße
Siemensstr.
Maybachstr.
POL.
Stuttgarter
Feuerbach Krankenhaus
HÖHENPARK KILLESBERG
Pragsattel
Löwentor-brücke
FEUERBACH
Tal-Straße
Feuerbacher
MESSEGELÄNDE
Stresemannstr.
Friedrich-Ebert-Str.
Killesberg
Eckarts-Haldenweg
Am Kochenhof
Robert-Mayer-Straße
PRAG FRIEDHOF
AUGELWALD
KRÄHER-WALD
Kräherwald
BISMARCKTURM
Birkenwaldstr.
Türlenstr.
Heilbronner
Feuerbach
Furtwangler Str.
Am
Lenzhalde
Herdweg
Cannstatter
HAUPT-BAHNHOF
SCHLOSS GARTEN
Hegelstr.
Friedrichstr.
Königstr.
Am Kräherwald
Zeppelinstr.
Silberburgstr.
Gaußstr.
Schwabstr.
Schloß-Johannesstr.
Th.-Heuss-Str.
Vogelsang
Bebelstr.
Schwab-Bebelstr.
Schloßstr.
Arndt-Spittastr.
Feuersee
S. BAHN FEUERSEE
Rotenwaldstr.
S. BAHN SCHWABSTR.
Rotebühlstr.
Reinsburgstr.
Paulinenstr.
Straße
Olgastr.
Hohenheimer Straße
Geißeichstr.
BIRKENKOPF
Hauptstätter
Marienpl.
Filderstr.
Schreiberstr.
Böblinger
BÜRGERWALD
Bihlpl.
Böheimstr.
Neue Weinsteige
HESLACH
Leonberger Straße
Kloß
Südheimer Pl.
Weinsteige
Jahnstr.
Heslach-Vogelrain
Burgstall-
WALD FRIEDHOF
DEGERLOCH

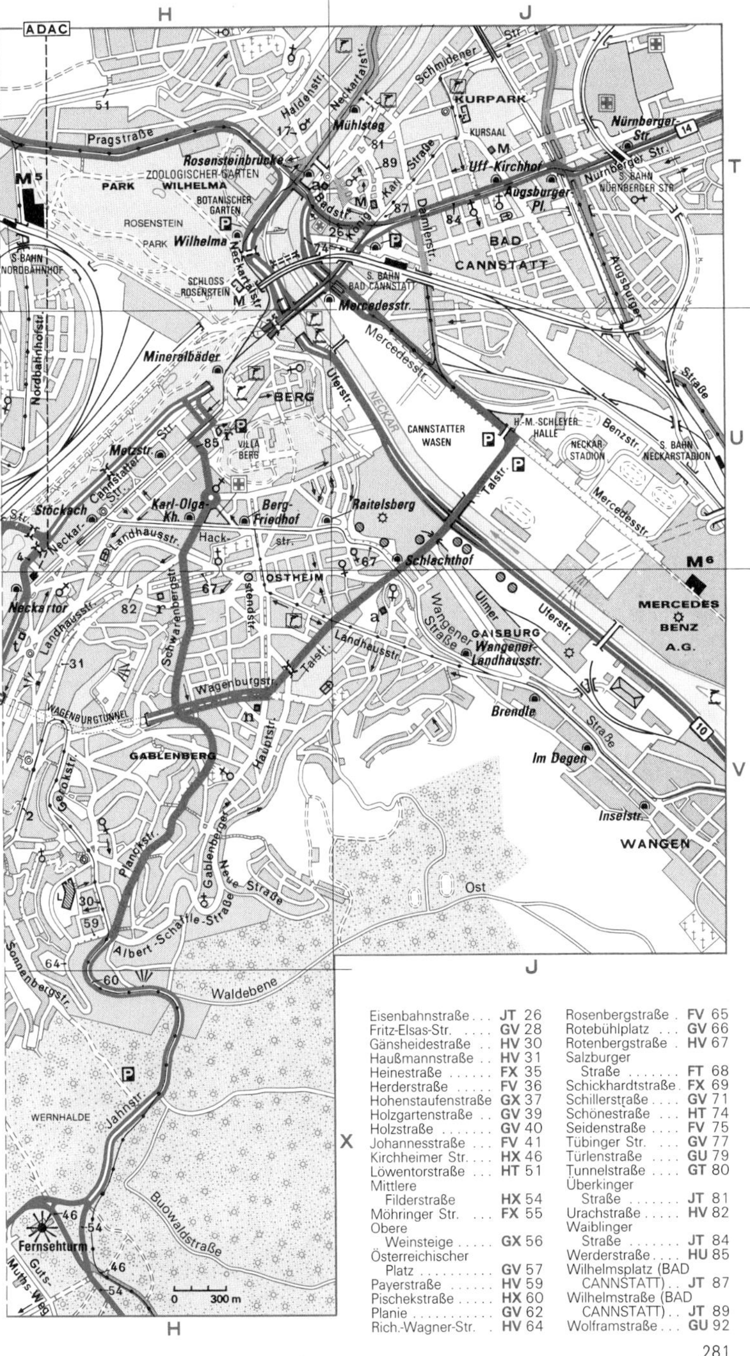
ADAC
H
J
T
U
V
X
PARK WILHELMA
ZOOLOGISCHER GARTEN
BOTANISCHER GARTEN
ROSENSTEIN PARK
Wilhelma
SCHLOSS ROSENSTEIN
S-BAHN NORDBAHNHOF
Pragstraße
Rosensteinbrücke
Mühlsteg
Neckartalstr.
Haldenstr.
Schmidener Str.
KURPARK
KURSAAL
Uff-Kirchhof
Augsburger Pl.
Nürnberger Str.
S. BAHN NÜRNBERGER STR.
BAD CANNSTATT
S. BAHN BAD CANNSTATT
Mercedesstr.
Badstr.
König Karl Straße
Daimlerstr.
Augsburger Straße
Mineralbäder
BERG
VILLA BERG
Uferstr.
NECKAR
CANNSTATTER WASEN
H.-M.-SCHLEYER-HALLE
NECKAR STADION
Benzstr.
S. BAHN NECKARSTADION
Talstr.
Metzstr.
Cannstatter Str.
Stöckach
Neckar-Str.
Karl-Olga-Kh.
Berg-Friedhof
Raitelsberg
Hackstr.
Landhausstr.
Schlachthof
OSTHEIM
Ostendstr.
Neckartor
Schwarenbergstr.
Wangener Straße
Ulmer Str.
GAISBURG
Wangener-Landhausstr.
MERCEDES BENZ A.G.
Wagenburgstr.
WAGENBURGTUNNEL
Brendle
Hauptstr.
GABLENBERG
Im Degen
Inselstr.
WANGEN
Gerokstr.
Planckstr.
Gablenberger
Neue Straße
Albert-Schäffle-Straße
Ost
Sonnenbergstr.
Waldebene
WERNHALDE
Jahnstr.
Buowaldstraße
Fernsehturm
Guts-Muths-Weg
0 300 m

STUTTGART

Charlottenplatz	LZ	20
Eberhardstraße	KLZ	25
Königstraße	KLYZ	
Schulstraße	KZ	75
Theodor- Heuss- Str.	KYZ	80
Arnulf-Klett-Platz	LY	6
Augustenstraße	KZ	7
Blumenstraße	LZ	10
Bolzstraße	LY	15
Calwer Str.	KYZ	18
Dorotheenstraße	LZ	24
Friedrichsplatz	KY	27
Hauptstätter Str.	KZ	30
Hegelplatz	KY	32
Heilbronner Str.	LY	34
Holzstraße	LZ	40
Karlsplatz	LY	43
Karlstraße	LZ	44
Katharinenplatz	LZ	45
Kirchstraße	LZ	46
Konrad- Adenauer- Str.	LY	47
Kronenstraße	KLY	48
Kronprinzstraße	KYZ	49
Leonhardsplatz	LZ	50
Marktplatz	KLZ	52
Marktstraße	LZ	53
Österreichischer Platz	KZ	57
Pfarrstraße	LZ	61
Rotebühlplatz	KZ	66
Rotebühlstraße	KZ	70
Schloßplatz	LY	72
Silberburgstraße	KZ	76
Sophienstraße	KZ	78
Torstraße	KZ	82
Ulrichstraße	LY	83
Wilhelmsplatz	LZ	86
Wilhelmstraße	LZ	88
Willi- Bleicher- Str.	KY	91

XX **La nuova Trattoria da Franco**, Calwer Str. 32 (1st floor), ✆ 29 47 44, Fax 294549 - AE ① E VISA - **M** a la carte 40/70. KYZ **c**

XX **Delice**, Hauptstätter Str. 61, ✆ 6 40 32 22 - ✱ KZ **a**
closed Saturday, Sunday and Bank Holidays - **M** (dinner only) (booking essential) a la carte 87/106.

XX **Der Goldene Adler**, Böheimstr. 38, ✆ 6 40 17 62 - P. AE ① E VISA FX **e**
closed Monday and August - **M** a la carte 46/78.

XX **Gaisburger Pastetchen**, Hornbergstr. 24, ✆ 48 48 55, Fax 487565 JV **a**
closed Sunday and Bank Holidays - **M** (dinner only) a la carte 65/84.

XX Intercity-Restaurant, Arnulf-Klett-Platz 2, ✆ 29 49 46, Fax 2268256 LY **v**

XX **Krämer's Bürgerstuben**, Gablenberger Hauptstr. 4, ✆ 46 54 81, Fax 486508 - AE ① E VISA
closed Sunday dinner, Monday and 3 weeks July - August - **M** (booking essential) a la carte 53/88. HV **n**

X **Brauereigasthof Ketterer**, Marienstr. 3b, ✆ 29 75 51, Fax 297065 - AE E KZ **y**
closed Sunday - **M** a la carte 34/55.

Swabian wine taverns (Weinstuben) (mainly light meals only) :

X **Kachelofen**, Eberhardstr. 10 (entrance Töpferstraße), ✆ 24 23 78, 🌳 KZ **x**
closed Sunday and Bank Holidays and 22 December - 2 January - **M** (dinner only) a la carte 30/46.

X Weinstube Schellenturm, Weberstr. 72, ✆ 2 36 48 88, 🌳 - ✱ LZ **u**

X **Weinstube Klösterle** (part of former monastery), Marktstr. 71 (S 50-Bad Cannstatt), ✆ 56 89 62, 🌳 - E VISA HT **a**
closed Sunday and Bank Holidays - **M** (dinner only) a la carte 32/53.

X **Weinhaus Stetter**, Rosenstr. 32, ✆ 24 01 63 LZ **e**
closed Monday to Friday until 3 p.m., Saturday dinner, Sunday and Bank Holidays - **M** *(mainly cold dishes)* a la carte 12/17.

at Botnang by Botnanger Str. FV :

Hirsch, Eltinger Str. 2, ✆ 69 29 17, Fax 6990788 - |♦| ☎ 🚗 P - 🏛 140. ① E VISA. ✱ rm
M *(closed Sunday dinner and Monday)* a la carte 36/72 - **44 rm** ☐ 96/150.

XX **La Fenice**, Beethovenstr. 9, ✆ 6 99 07 03, Fax 6990703, 🌳 - AE ① E VISA. ✱
closed Tuesday lunch and Monday - **M** (booking essential for dinner) a la carte 57/78.

at Stuttgart 80-Büsnau by Rotenwaldstraße FX :

Relexa Hotel Stuttgart, Am Solitudering, ✆ 6 86 70, Telex 7255557, Fax 6867999, 🌳, ≘s - |♦| ⇔ rm TV ♿ 🚗 P - 🏛 80. AE ① E VISA. ✱ rest
La Fenêtre *(closed Saturday, Sunday and 4 weeks July - August)* **M** (dinner only) a la carte 78/100 - **Kaminrestaurant M** a la carte 48/74 - **144 rm** ☐ 240/330, 7 suites.

at Stuttgart 70 - Degerloch :

Waldhotel Degerloch 🐦, Guts-Muths-Weg 18, ✆ 76 50 17, Telex 7255728, Fax 7653762, 🌳, ≘s, 🎾 - |♦| TV ☎ ♿ P - 🏛 100. AE ① E VISA by Guts-Muths-Weg HX
M a la carte 38/70 - **50 rm** ☐ 150/280.

XXXX ✿ **Wielandshöhe**, Alte Weinsteige 71, ✆ 6 40 88 48, Fax 6409408, ≤ Stuttgart, 🌳 - AE ① E VISA GX **a**
closed Sunday, Monday and Bank Holidays - **M** (booking essential) a la carte 80/130
Spec. Salat von Kalbskopf mit Koriander, Lachs mit Kaviar und Champagnersauce, Lammrücken mit Rosmarinjus.

at Stuttgart 30 - Feuerbach :

Messehotel Europe, Siemensstr. 33, ✆ 81 48 30, Telex 7252132, Fax 8148348 - |♦| ⇔ rm ▤ TV 🚗. AE ① E VISA GT **r**
M *(closed Saturday and Sunday)* (dinner only) a la carte 57/81 - **110 rm** ☐ 250/400.

Kongresshotel Europe, Siemensstr. 26, ✆ 81 00 40, Telex 723650, Fax 854082, ≘s - |♦| ⇔ rm ▤ TV 🚗 - 🏛 130. AE ① E VISA GT **z**
M a la carte 51/81 - **150 rm** ☐ 150/310.

Weinsberg (Bistro style rest.), Grazer Str. 32, ✆ 13 54 60, Fax 1354666 - |♦| ⇔ rm TV ☎ 🚗 - 🏛 30. AE ① E VISA FT **a**
M a la carte 20/40 - **37 rm** ☐ 215/285.

Feuerbach without rest, Feuerbacher Talstr. 4, ✆ 13 55 90, Fax 1355959 - |♦| TV ☎ 🚗. AE ① E VISA FT **c**
36 rm ☐ 165/275.

at Stuttgart 23 - Flughafen (Airport) S : 15 km by Obere Weinsteige (B 27) GX :

Airport Mövenpick-Hotel, Randstraße, ✆ 7 90 70, Telex 7245677, Fax 793585, 🌳, ≘s - |♦| ⇔ rm ▤ rest TV ♿ P - 🏛 45. AE ① E VISA - **M** a la carte 38/75 - **230 rm** ☐ 272/435.

XXX ✿ **Top air**, Randstraße (in the airport) Terminal 1, ✆ 9 48 21 37, Fax 7979210 - ▤ - 🏛 170. AE ① E VISA - **M** a la carte 74/104
Spec. Charlotte von Meeresfrüchten, Gefüllte Seezungenfilets mit Kaviarsauce, Beerengratin mit Champagnereis.

at Stuttgart 80 - Möhringen SW : 7 km by Obere Weinsteige GX :

Fora Hotel, Vor dem Lauch 20 (Businesspark Fasanenhof), 7 25 50, Fax 7255666, - rm rest - 80. AE E VISA
M 37 buffet (lunch) and a la carte 55/70 - **101 rm** 217/304.

Gloria - Restaurant Möhringer Hexle, Sigmaringer Str. 59, 7 18 50 (hotel) 7 18 51 17 (rest.), Fax 7185121, - - 50
M a la carte 28/61 - **70 rm** 129/194.

Möhringen without rest, Filderbahnstr. 43, 71 60 80, Fax 7160850 - . AE E VISA
39 rm 175/210.

Neotel without rest, Vaihinger Str. 151, 7 80 06 35, Telex 7255179, Fax 7804314 - . AE E VISA
71 rm 152/214.

Hirsch-Weinstuben, Maierstr. 3, 71 13 75, Fax 71700620, - . AE E VISA.
closed Monday and Saturday lunch, Sunday, Bank Holidays and Easter 1 week - **M** (booking essential) (remarkable wine list) a la carte 57/95.

at Stuttgart 61 - Obertürkheim by Augsburger Straße JU :

Brita Hotel - Restaurant Post, Augsburger Str. 671, 32 02 30, Fax 32023400 - rm rest - 80. AE E VISA
closed 24 December - 6 January - **M** *(closed Sunday and Bank Holidays)* a la carte 41/66 - **70 rm** 122/352.

at Stuttgart 70 - Plieningen S : 14 km by Mittlere Filderstraße HX :

Fissler-Post, Filderhauptstr. 2, 4 58 40, Fax 4584333, - - 80. AE E VISA.
M (booking essential) a la carte 49/74 *(vegetarian menu available)* - **60 rm** 95/210.

Traube, Brabandtgasse 2, 45 89 20, Fax 4589220, -
closed 23 December - 6 January - **M** *(closed Saturday and Sunday)* (booking essential) a la carte 49/97 - **23 rm** 135/250.

Apartment Hotel without rest, Scharnhauser Str. 4, 4 50 10, Fax 4501100 - . AE E VISA
56 rm 155/329.

Recknagel's Nagelschmiede, Brabandtgasse 1, 4 58 92 50 -
closed Sunday and lunch Monday - Friday - **M** a la carte 47/75.

at Stuttgart 40 - Stammheim by Heilbronner Straße GT :

Novotel, Korntaler Str. 207, 98 06 20, Telex 7252137, Fax 803673, , (heated) - rm - 150. AE E VISA
M a la carte 35/62 - **117 rm** 165/215.

at Stuttgart 80-Vaihingen by Böblinger Str. FX :

Fontana Stuttgart, Vollmöllerstr. 5, 73 00, Telex 7255763, Fax 7302525, Massage, , , , , - rm - 250. AE E VISA. rest
- **Fontana** *(closed lunch Saturday, 4 weeks July - August)* **M** a la carte 62/90 - **Bräustube** **M** a la carte 35/70 - **250 rm** 250/360, 5 suites.

near Schloß Solitude by Rotenwaldstr. FX :

Herzog Carl Eugen, 7000 Stuttgart, (0711) 6 99 07 45, Fax 6990771 - . AE E VISA
closed Sunday, Monday, Bank Holidays and 27 July - 9 August - **M** a la carte 70/100 - **Schloß - Restaurant** (vegetarian dishes available) *(closed Monday)* **M** a la carte 43/65
Spec. Marinierter Seeteufel mit Kaviar und Schnittlauch, Taube mit Petersilienpüree, Topfennocken mit Kirschragout und Portweinsauce.

at Stuttgart 40-Zuffenhausen by Heilbronner Straße GT :

Residence, Schützenbühlstr. 16, 8 20 01 00, Fax 8200101, - rm rest - 60. AE E VISA
M a la carte 39/63 - **120 rm** 195/220.

at Fellbach 7012 NE : 8 km by Nürnberger Straße (B 14) JT - 0711 :

Classic Congress Hotel, Tainer Str. 7, 5 85 90, Telex 7254900, Fax 5859304, - - 70. AE E VISA
closed 23 December - 6 January - **M** (see **Alt Württemberg** below) - **150 rm** 195/350.

Alt Württemberg, Tainer Str. 7 (Schwabenlandhalle), 58 00 88 - . AE E VISA
M a la carte 43/83.

Weinstube Germania with rm, Schmerstr. 6, 58 20 37 - .
closed 3 weeks July - August and 2 weeks December - January - **M** *(closed Sunday, Monday and Bank Holidays)* a la carte 44/68 - **8 rm** 75/140.

Weinkeller Häussermann (18C vaulted cellar), Kappelbergstr. 1, 58 77 75 - . E
closed lunch Saturday, Sunday, Bank Holidays and 2 weeks July - August - **M** a la carte 36/64.

at Fellbach-Schmiden **7012** NE : 8,5 km by Nürnberger Straße (B 14) JT :

Hirsch, Fellbacher Str. 2, (0711) 9 51 30, Fax 5181065, - TV - 25. AE E VISA
M *(closed Friday and Sunday)* a la carte 38/59 - **114 rm** 90/200.

at Gerlingen **7016** W : 10 km by Rotenwaldstraße FX - 07156 :

Carlston Hotel, Dieselstr. 2, 43 13 00, Fax 431343, - rm TV - 150. AE E VISA
M 35 buffet (lunch) and a la carte 38/65 - **97 rm** 160/245.

Krone, Hauptstr. 28, 2 10 04, Fax 21009 - TV - 80. AE E VISA
M *(closed Monday, Sunday, Bank Holidays, Easter, Christmas and 2 weeks July - August)* (booking essential) a la carte 43/80 *(vegetarian dishes available)* - **50 rm** 128/240.

Domicil, Weilimdorfer Str. 70, 4 31 80, Fax 4318400, - rm TV - 100. AE E VISA
M a la carte 36/66 - **120 rm** 135/195.

at Korntal-Münchingen 2 **7015** NW : 9 km, by Heilbronner Str. GT :

Mercure, Siemensstr. 50, (07150) 1 30, Telex 723589, Fax 13266, beer garden, , - TV - 160. AE E VISA
M a la carte 45/76 - **209 rm** 210/265, 6 suites.

at Leinfelden-Echterdingen 1 **7022** S : 10 km by Obere Weinsteige GX :

Drei Morgen without rest, Bahnhofstr. 39, (0711) 16 05 60, Fax 1605646 - TV . AE E VISA - **25 rm** 95/150.

Stadt Leinfelden without rest, Lessingstr. 4, (0711) 75 25 10, Fax 755649 - **20 rm** 90/130.

at Leinfelden-Echterdingen 2 **7022** S : 11 km by Obere Weinsteige (B 27) GX - 0711 :

Filderland without rest, Tübinger Str. 16, 7 97 89 13, Telex 7255972, Fax 7977576 - TV - 20. AE E VISA
closed 24 December - 2 January - **48 rm** 135/220.

Lamm, Hauptstr. 98, 79 90 65, Fax 795275 - TV . AE E VISA
M *(closed 3 weeks July - August)* a la carte 26/52 - **26 rm** 99/138.

Adler, Obergasse 18, 79 35 90, Fax 7977476, , - TV - 20
closed 24 December - 6 January - **M** *(closed Saturday, Sunday and 3 weeks July - August)* a la carte 31/57 - **18 rm** 105/170.

Baiersbronn

7292. Baden-Württemberg 413 HI 21, 987 ㉟ - pop. 14 000 - alt. 550 m - 07442.

Stuttgart 100.

XXXXX ✿✿✿ **Schwarzwaldstube** (French rest.), Tonbachstr. 237 (at Kur- and Sporthotel Traube Tonbach), 49 26 65, ≤ - . AE E VISA.
closed Monday, Tuesday, 11 January - 2 February and 5 to 27 July - **M** (booking essential) 135/175 and a la carte 96/128
Spec. Seeigelgratin mit Kamm-Muscheln (October - January), Blätterteigschnitte mit Taubenbrustscheiben, Gänseleber und Trüffelsauce, Gefüllte Lachsröllchen mit Störmousse und Kaviar.

XXXX ✿✿ **Restaurant Bareiss**, Gärtenbühlweg 14 (at Hotel Bareiss), 4 70, Fax 47320, ≤ - . AE E VISA
closed Monday, Tuesday, June - 2 July and 22 November - 24 December - **M** (booking essential) (remarkable wine list) 140/180 and a la carte 100/120
Spec. Salat von bretonischem Hummer in schwarzer Olivenvinaigrette, Nantaiser Ente aus dem Rohr (2 pers.), Feuilleté von Mandelblättern und Babyananas mit weißem Schokoladeneis.

Öhringen

7110. Baden-Württemberg 413 L 19, 987 ㉕ - pop. 18 000 - alt. 230 m - 07941.

Stuttgart 68.

at Friedrichsruhe **7111** N : 6 km :

✿✿ **Wald- und Schloßhotel Friedrichsruhe** , (07941) 6 08 70, Telex 74498, Fax 61468, , « Garden, park », , , , , 18 - - 60. AE E VISA
M *(closed Monday und Tuesday)* (remarkable wine list) 125/195 and a la carte 85/130 - **49 rm** 165/395, 11 suites
Spec. Bretonischer Hummer mit Lauch und Tomaten, Steinbuttfilet in der Haut gebraten mit geschmorten Artischockenböden, Glasiertes Kalbsbriesnüßchen mit Trüffel und Gemüsen.

Greece

Hellás

ATHENS

PRACTICAL INFORMATION

LOCAL CURRENCY

Greek Drachma: 100 Drs = 0.45 US $ = 0.38 Ecu (Jan. 93)

TOURIST INFORMATION

National Tourist Organisation (EOT): 2 Kar. Servias, ✆ 322 25 45 (information) and 1 Ermou, 323 41 30. Hotel reservation: Hellenic Chamber of Hotels, 24 Stadiou, ✆ 323 71 93, Telex: 214 269. Fax 332 54 49, Also at East Airport ✆ 961 27 22 - Tourist Police: 7 Singrou ✆ 171.

FOREIGN EXCHANGE

Banks are usually open on weekdays from 8am to 2pm. A branch of the National Bank of Greece is open daily from 8am to 2pm (from 9am to 1pm at weekends) at 2 Karageorgi Servias (Sindagma).

AIRLINES

OLYMPIC AIRWAYS: 96 Leoforos Singrou 117 41 Athens, ✆ 926 72 51 and 6 Othonos (Sindagma) 105 57 Athens, reservations only ✆ 966 66 66.
All following Companies are located near Sindagma Square:
AIR FRANCE: 4 Karageorgi Servias 105 62 Athens, ✆ 323 85 07.
BRITISH AIRWAYS: 10 Othonos 105 57 Athens, ✆ 325 06 01.
JAPAN AIRLINES: 17 Filellinon 105 57 Athens, ✆ 324 82 11.
LUFTHANSA: 11 Vasilissis Sophias 106 71 Athens, ✆ 771 60 02.
SABENA: 8 Othonos 105 57 Athens, ✆ 323 68 21.
SWISSAIR: 4 Othonos 105 57 Athens, ✆ 323 75 81.
TWA: 8 Xenofondos 105 57 Athens, ✆ 322 64 51.

TRANSPORT IN ATHENS

Taxis: may be hailed in the street even when already engaged: it is advised to always pay by the meter.
Bus: good for sightseeing and practical for short distances: 75 Drs.
Metro: one single line crossing the city from North (Kifissia) to South (Pireas) : 100 Drs.

POSTAL SERVICES

General Post Office: 100 Eolou (Omonia) with poste restante, and also at Sindagma.
Telephone (OTE): 15 Stadiou, and 85 Patission (all services), 65 Stadiou and 50 Athinas (only for telephone calls).

SHOPPING IN ATHENS

In summer, shops are usually open from 8am to 1.30pm, and 5.30 to 8.30pm. They close on Sunday, and at 2.30pm on Monday, Wednesday and Saturday. In winter they open from 9am to 5pm on Monday and Wednesday, from 10am to 7pm on Tuesday, Thursday and Friday, from 8.30am to 3.30pm on Saturday. Department Stores in Patission and Eolou are open fron 8.30 am to 8 pm on weekdays and 3 pm on Saturdays. The main shopping streets are to be found in Sindagma, Kolonaki, Monastiraki and Omonia areas. Flea Market (generally open on Sunday) and Greek Handicraft in Plaka and Monastiraki.

TIPPING

Service is generally included in the bills but it is usual to tip employees.

SPEED LIMITS

The speed limit in built up areas is 50 km/h (31 mph); on motorways the maximum permitted speed is 100 km/h (62 mph) and 80 km/h (50 mph) on others roads.

SEAT BELTS

The wearing of seat belts is compulsory for drivers and front seat passengers.

BREAKDOWN SERVICE

The ELPA (Automobile and Touring Club of Greece) operate a 24 hour breakdown service: phone 104.

Athens

(ATHÍNA) Atikí 980 ㉚ – Pop. 3 076 786 (Athens and Piraeus area) – ☎ 01.

SIGHTS :

Views of Athens : Lycabettos (Likavitós) ☼*** DX – Philopappos Hill (Lófos Filopápou) ≤*** AY.

ANCIENT ATHENS

Acropolis*** (Akrópoli) ABY – Theseion** (Thissío) AY and Agora* (Arhéa Agorá) AY – Theatre of Dionysos** (Théatro Dionissou) BY and Odeon of Herod Atticus* (Odío Iródou Atikóu) AY – Olympieion** (Naós Olimbíou Diós) BY and Hadrian's Arch* (Píli Adrianóu) BY – Tower of the Winds* BY **G** in the Roman Forum (Romaïkí Agorá).

OLD ATHENS AND THE TURKISH PERIOD

Pláka** : Old Metropolitan** BY **A2** – Monastiráki* (Old Bazaar) : Kapnikaréa (Church) BY **A6**, Odós Pandróssou* BY **29**, Monastiráki Square* BY.

MODERN ATHENS

Sindagma Square* CY : Greek guard on sentry duty – Academy, University and Library Buildings* (Akadimía CX, Panepistímio CX, Ethnikí Vivliothíki BX) – National Garden* (Ethnikós Kípos) CY.

MUSEUMS

National Archaelogical Museum*** (Ethnikó Arheologikó Moussío) BX – Acropolis Museum*** BY **M** – Museum of Cycladic and Ancient Greek Art** DY **M15** – Byzantine Museum** (Vizandinó Moussío) DY – Benaki Museum** (private collection of antiquities and traditional art) CDY – Museum of Traditional Greek Art* BY **M2** – National Historical Museum* BY **M7** – Jewish Museum of Greece* BY **M16** – National Gallery and Soutzos Museum* (painting and sculpture) DY **M8**.

EXCURSIONS

Cape Sounion*** (Soúnio) SE : 71 km BY – Kessariani Monastery**, E : 9 km DY – Daphne Monastery** (Dafní) NW : 10 km AX – Aigina Island* (Égina) : Temple of Aphaia**, 3 hours Return.

18 Glifáda (near airport) ☎ 894 68 20.

✈ S : 15 km, East Airport ☎ 969 91 11 (International Airport – All companies except Olympic Airways), West Airport ☎ 936 33 63 (Elinikó Airport – Olympic Airways only).

🚗 1 Karolou ☎ 524 06 01.

ℹ Tourist Information (EOT), 26 Amerikis ☎ 322 31 11 and East Airport ☎ 961 27 22.

ELPA (Automobile and Touring Club of Greece), 2 Messogion ☎ 779 16 15.

Igoumenítsa 581 – Pátra 215 – Thessaloníki 479.

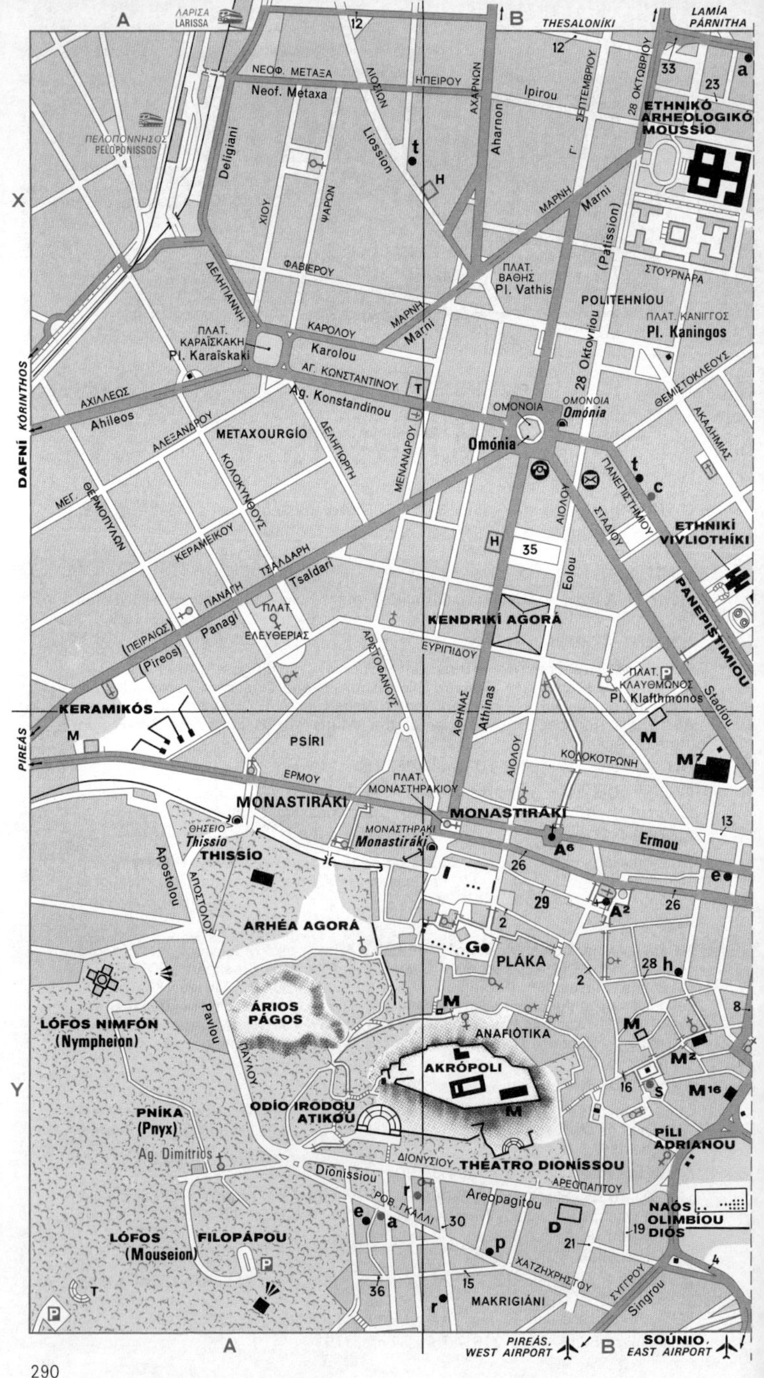

ΛΑΡΙΣΑ
LARISSA
THESALONÍKI
LAMÍA
PÁRNITHA
ΠΕΛΟΠΟΝΝΗΣΟΣ
PELOPONISSOS
ΝΕΟΦ. ΜΕΤΑΞΑ
Neof. Metaxa
Deligiani
Liossion
Aharnon
Ipirou
28 Oktovriou
ETHNIKÓ ARHEOLOGIKÓ MOUSSÍO
Marni
(Patission)
ΠΛΑΤ. ΒΑΘΗΣ
Pl. Vathis
POLITEHNÍOU
ΠΛΑΤ. ΚΑΝΙΓΓΟΣ
Pl. Kaningos
ΠΛΑΤ. ΚΑΡΑΪΣΚΑΚΗ
Pl. Karaïskaki
Karolou
Ag. Konstandinou
Ahileos
METAXOURGÍO
ΟΜΟΝΟΙΑ
Omónia
ETHNIKÍ VIVLIOTHÍKI
PANEPISTIMIOU
Tsaldari
Panagi
(Pireos)
Eolou
KENDRIKÍ AGORÁ
Athinas
ΠΛΑΤ. ΚΛΑΥΘΜΩΝΟΣ
Pl. Klafthmonos
Stadiou
DAFNÍ KÓRINTHOS
KERAMIKÓS
PIREÁS
PSÍRI
MONASTIRÁKI
Ermou
Thissio
THISSÍO
Apostolou
ARHÉA AGORÁ
PLÁKA
ÁRIOS PÁGOS
ANAFIÓTIKA
LÓFOS NIMFÓN (Nympheion)
Pavlou
AKRÓPOLI
ODÍO IRODOU ATIKOÚ
PNÍKA (Pnyx)
Ag. Dimitrios
THEATRO DIONÍSSOU
Dionissiou
Areopagitou
PÍLI ADRIANOU
NAÓS OLIMBÍOU DIÓS
LÓFOS FILOPÁPOU (Mouseion)
MAKRIGIÁNI
Singrou
PIREÁS, WEST AIRPORT
SOÚNIO, EAST AIRPORT

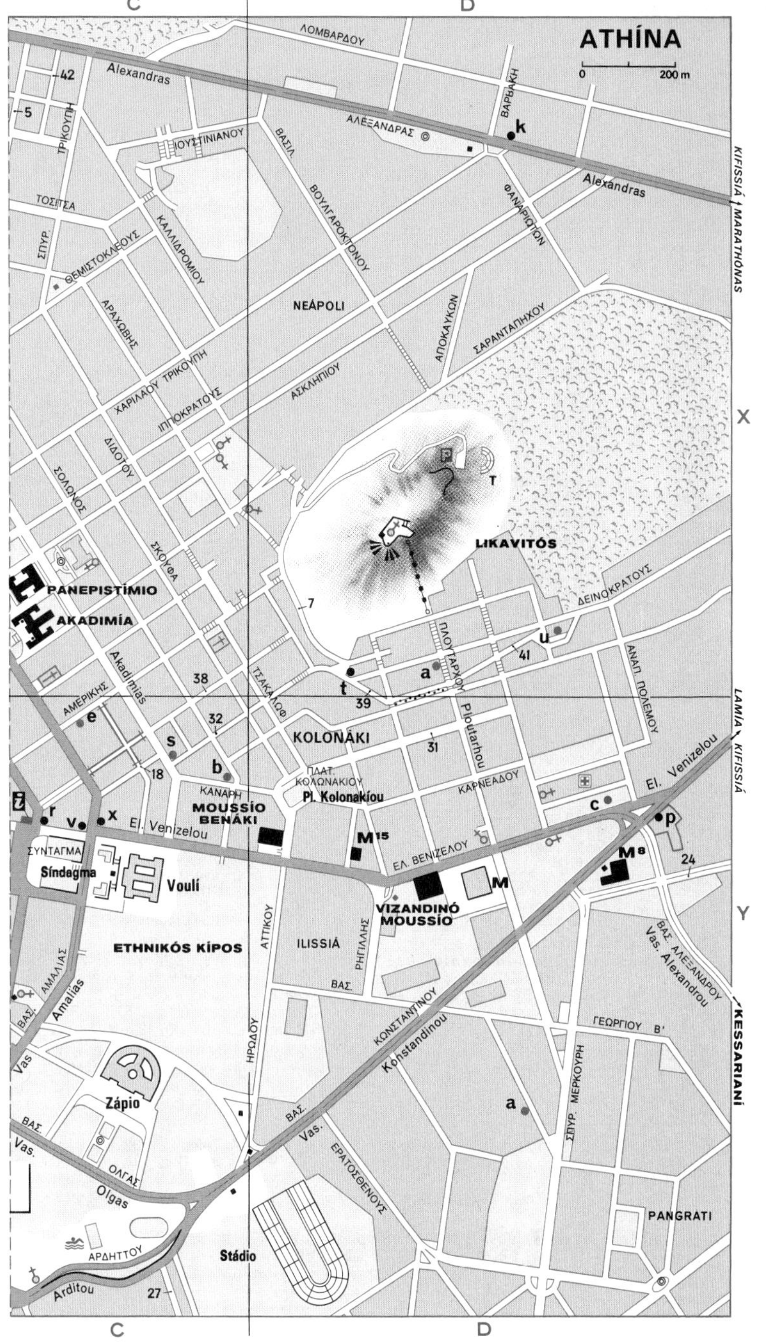

ATHÍNA
0
200 m
C
D
Alexandras
ΑΛΕΞΑΝΔΡΑΣ
ΛΟΜΒΑΡΔΟΥ
ΒΑΡΒΑΚΗ
KIFISSIÁ MARATHÓNAS
NEÁPOLI
LIKAVITÓS
PANEPISTÍMIO
AKADIMÍA
KOLONÁKI
Pl. Kolonakíou
MOUSSÍO BENÁKI
VIZANDINÓ MOUSSÍO
Síndagma
Voulí
ETHNIKÓS KÍPOS
ILISSIÁ
Zápio
Stádio
PANGRATI
LAMÍA KIFISSIÁ
KESSARIANÍ
El. Venizelou
Vas. Konstandinou
Vas. Alexandrou
Vas. Amalias
Vas. Olgas
Arditou
Akadimias
Ploutarhou
X
Y

STREET INDEX TO ATHÍNA TOWN PLAN

Street	Greek	Grid	No.
Adrianou	ΑΔΡΙΑΝΟΥ	BY	2
Ag. Konstandinou	ΑΓ. ΚΩΝΣΤΑΝΤΙΝΟΥ	AX	
Aharnon	ΑΧΑΡΝΩΝ	BX	
Ahilleos	ΑΧΙΛΛΕΩΣ	AX	
Akadimias	ΑΚΑΔΗΜΙΑΣ	BCX	
Alexandras	ΑΛΕΞΑΝΔΡΑΣ	CDX	
Amerikis	ΑΜΕΡΙΚΗΣ	CXY	
Anapiron Polemou	ΑΝΑΠΗΡΩΝ ΠΟΛΕΜΟΥ	DXY	
Apokafkon	ΑΠΟΚΑΥΚΩΝ	DX	
Apostolou Pavlou	ΑΠΟΣΤΟΛΟΥ ΠΑΥΛΟΥ	AY	
Arahovis	ΑΡΑΧΩΒΗΣ	CX	
Arditou	ΑΡΔΗΤΤΟΥ	CY	
Aristofanous	ΑΡΙΣΤΟΦΑΝΟΥΣ	AX	
Asklipiou	ΑΣΚΛΗΠΙΟΥ	DX	
Ath. Diakou	ΑΘ. ΔΙΑΚΟΥ	BY	4
Athinas	ΑΘΗΝΑΣ	BXY	
Bouboulinas	ΜΠΟΥΜΠΟΥΛΙΝΑΣ	CX	5
Deligiani	ΔΕΛΗΓΙΑΝΝΗ	AX	
Deligiorgi	ΔΕΛΗΓΙΩΡΓΗ	AX	
Didotou	ΔΙΔΟΤΟΥ	CX	
Dionissiou Areopagitou	ΔΙΟΝΥΣΙΟΥ ΑΡΕΟΠΑΓΙΤΟΥ	ABY	
El. Venizelou	ΕΛ ΒΕΝΙΖΕΛΟΥ	CDY	
Eolou	ΑΙΟΛΟΥ	BXY	
Eratosthenous	ΕΡΑΤΟΣΘΕΝΟΥΣ	DY	
Ermou	ΕΡΜΟΥ	ABY	
Evelpidos Rongakou	ΕΥΕΛΠΙΔΟΣ ΡΟΓΚΑΚΟΥ	DX	7
Fanarioton	ΦΑΝΑΡΙΩΤΩΝ	DX	
Favierou	ΦΑΒΙΕΡΟΥ	AX	
Filelinon	ΦΙΛΕΛΛΗΝΩΝ	BY	8
Hadzihristou	ΧΑΤΖΗΧΡΗΣΤΟΥ	BY	
Harilaou Trikoupi	ΧΑΡΙΛΑΟΥ ΤΡΙΚΟΥΠΗ	CX	
Hiou	ΧΙΟΥ	AX	
Ioulianou	ΙΟΥΛΙΑΝΟΥ	AX	12
Ioustinianou	ΙΟΥΣΤΙΝΙΑΝΟΥ	CX	
Ipirou	ΗΠΕΙΡΟΥ	ABX	
Ipokratous	ΙΠΠΟΚΡΑΤΟΥΣ	CX	
Irodou Atikou	ΗΡΩΔΟΥ ΑΤΤΙΚΟΥ	DY	
Kalidromiou	ΚΑΛΛΙΔΡΟΜΙΟΥ	CX	
Kanari	ΚΑΝΑΡΗ	CY	
Kar. Servias	ΚΑΡ. ΣΕΡΒΙΑΣ	BY	13
Karneadou	ΚΑΡΝΕΑΔΟΥ	DY	
Karolou	ΚΑΡΟΛΟΥ	AX	
Kavaloti	ΚΑΒΑΛΛΟΤΙ	BY	15
Keramikou	ΚΕΡΑΜΕΙΚΟΥ	AX	
Kidathineon	ΚΥΔΑΘΗΝΑΙΩΝ	BY	16
Kolokinthous	ΚΟΛΟΚΥΝΘΟΥΣ	AX	
Kolokotroni	ΚΟΛΟΚΟΤΡΩΝΗ	BY	
Kriezotou	ΚΡΙΕΖΩΤΟΥ	CY	18
Liossion	ΛΙΟΣΙΩΝ	AX	
Lomvardou	ΛΟΜΒΑΡΔΟΥ	DX	
Makri	ΜΑΚΡΗ	BY	19
Makrigiani	ΜΑΚΡΥΓΙΑΝΝΗ	BY	21
Marni	ΜΑΡΝΗ	ABX	
Meg. Alexandrou	ΜΕΓ. ΑΛΕΞΑΝΔΡΟΥ	AX	
Menandrou	ΜΕΝΑΝΔΡΟΥ	AX	
Metsovou	ΜΕΤΣΟΒΟΥ	BX	23
Mihalakopoulou	ΜΙΧΑΛΑΚΟΠΟΥΛΟΥ	DY	24
Mitropoleos	ΜΗΤΡΟΠΟΛΕΩΣ	BY	26
N. Theotoki	Ν. ΘΕΟΤΟΚΗ	CY	27
Navarhou Nikodimou	ΝΑΥΑΡΧΟΥ ΝΙΚΟΔΗΜΟΥ	BY	28
Neof. Metaxa	ΝΕΟΦ. ΜΕΤΑΞΑ	AX	
Omonia	ΟΜΟΝΟΙΑ	BX	
Pandrossou	ΠΑΝΔΡΟΣΟΥ	BY	29
Panepistimiou	ΠΑΝΕΜΙΣΤΗΜΙΟΥ	BCX	
Parthenonos	ΠΑΡΘΕΝΩΝΟΣ	BY	30
Patission (28 Oktovriou)	ΠΑΤΗΣΙΩΝ (28 ΟΚΤΩΒΡΙΟΥ)	BX	
Patr. Ioakim	ΠΑΤΡ. ΙΩΑΚΕΙΜ	DY	31
Pindarou	ΠΙΝΔΑΡΟΥ	CY	32
Pireos (Panagi Tsaldari)	ΠΕΙΡΑΙΩΣ (ΠΑΝΑΓΗ ΤΣΑΛΔΑΡΗ)	AX	
Pl. Anexartissias (Vathis)	ΠΛΑΤ. ΑΝΕΞΑΡΤΗΣΙΑΣ (ΒΑΘΗΣ)	BX	
Pl. Egiptou	ΠΛΑΤ. ΑΙΓΥΠΤΟΥ	BX	33
Pl. Eleftherias	ΠΛΑΤ. ΕΛΕΥΘΕΡΙΑΣ	AX	
Pl. Eth. Andistasseos (Kodzia)	ΠΛΑΤ. ΕΘΝ. ΑΝΤΙΣΤΑΣΕΩΣ ΚΟΤΖΙΑ)	BX	35
Pl. Kaningos	ΠΛΑΤ. ΚΑΝΙΓΓΟΣ	BX	
Pl. Karaïskaki	ΠΛΑΤ. ΚΑΡΑΙΣΚΑΚΗ	AX	
Pl. Klafthmonos	ΠΛΑΤ. ΚΛΑΥΘΜΩΝΟΣ	BX	
Pl. Kolonakiou	ΠΛΑΤ. ΚΟΛΩΝΑΚΙΟΥ	DY	
Pl. Monastirakiou	ΠΛΑΤ. ΜΟΝΑΣΤΗΡΑΚΙΟΥ	ABY	
Ploutarhou	ΠΛΟΥΤΑΡΧΟΥ	DX	
Psaron	ΨΑΡΩΝ	AX	
Radzieri	ΡΑΤΖΙΕΡΗ	AY	36
Rigilis	ΡΗΓΙΛΛΗΣ	DY	
Rovertou Gali	ΡΟΒΕΡΤΟΥ ΓΚΑΛΛΙ	AY	
Sarandapihou	ΣΑΡΑΝΤΑΠΗΧΟΥ	DX	
Sindagma	ΣΥΝΤΑΓΜΑ	CY	
Singrou	ΣΥΓΓΡΟΥ	BY	
Skoufa	ΣΚΟΥΦΑ	CX	
Solonos	ΣΟΛΩΝΟΣ	CX	
Spir. Merkouri	ΣΠΥΡ. ΜΕΡΚΟΥΡΗ	DY	
Spir. Trikoupi	ΣΠΥΡ. ΤΡΙΚΟΥΠΗ	CX	
Stadiou	ΣΤΑΔΙΟΥ	BXY	
Stournara	ΣΤΟΥΡΝΑΡΑ	BX	
Themistokleous	ΘΕΜΙΣΤΟΚΛΕΟΥΣ	BCX	
Thermopilon	ΘΕΡΜΟΠΥΛΩΝ	AX	
Tossitsa	ΤΟΣΙΤΣΑ	CX	
Tsakalof	ΤΣΑΚΑΛΩΦ	DXY	
Varvaki	ΒΑΡΒΑΚΗ	DX	
Vas. Alexandrou	ΒΑΣ. ΑΛΕΞΑΝΔΡΟΥ	DY	
Vas. Amalias	ΒΑΣ. ΑΜΑΛΙΑΣ	CY	
Vas. Georgiou B'	ΒΑΣ. ΓΕΩΡΓΙΟΥ Β	DY	
Vas. Konstandinou	ΒΑΣ. ΚΩΝΣΤΑΝΤΙΝΟΥ	DY	
Vas. Olgas	ΒΑΣ. ΟΛΓΑΣ	CY	
Vassiliou Voulgaroktonou	ΒΑΣΙΛΕΙΟΥ ΒΟΥΛΓΑΡΟΚΤΟΝΟΥ	DX	
Voukourestiou	ΒΟΥΚΟΥΡΕΣΤΙΟΥ	CX	38
Xanthipou	ΞΑΝΘΙΠΠΟΥ	DXY	39
Xenokratous	ΞΕΝΟΚΡΑΤΟΥΣ	DX	41
Zaïmi	ΖΑΙΜΗ	CX	42
3 Septemvriou	Γ'ΣΕΠΤΕΜΒΡΙΟΥ	BX	

Athenaeum Inter-Continental, 89-93 Singrou, 117 45, SW : 2 ¾ km ✆ 9023 666, Telex 221554, Fax 9243 000, ≤, « Première rooftop restaurant with ≤ Athens », - 2 000. AE ① E VISA. BY
M - **Kublai Khan** *(closed Sunday)* (dinner only) 7500 and a la carte 6900/12050 - **Première** (dinner only) a la carte 6000/10600 - ☐ 3800 - **511 rm** 42000/58000, 49 suites.

Athens Hilton, 46 El Venizelou, 115 28, ✆ 7250 201, Telex 215808, Fax 7253 110, ≤, « Roof terrace with ≤ Athens », heated - rm - 600. AE ① E VISA DY **p**
M Ta Nissia *(closed June-August)* (dinner only) 7900 and a la carte - **Byzantine** *(closed June-August)* 5700 and a la carte - ☐ 4430 - **434 rm** 41800/63600, 19 suites.

Ledra Marriott, 115 Singrou, 117 45, SW : 3 km ✆ 9347 711, Telex 221833, Fax 935 9153, « Rooftop terrace with and Athens » - rm - 500. AE ① E VISA. BY
M - (see also **Kona Kai** below) - **Zephyros** 3700/6900 and a la carte - ☐ 3200 - **242 rm** 39000, 16 suites.

Grande Bretagne, Vas. Georgiou, Sindagma, 105 63, ✆ 3230 251, Telex 219615, Fax 3228 034 - - 500. AE ① E VISA CY **v**
M G B Corner a la carte 6200/10500 - ☐ 3800 - **338 rm** 42500/63000, 24 suites.

Astir Palace, Panepistimiou and El Venizelou, 106 71, ✆ 3643 112, Telex 222380, Fax 3642 825, ≤ - - 200. AE ① E VISA. CY **x**
M 6000 and a la carte 4300/7650 - ☐ 3200 - **59 rm** 29000/39000, 18 suites.

Divani Palace Acropolis, 19-25 Parthenonos, 117 42, ✆ 9222 945, Telex 218306, Fax 9214 993, « Ancient ruins of Themistocles wall in basement », – 🛗 ▤ TV ☎ – 400. AE ⓓ E VISA. BY r
M – **Aspassia** 5100 and a la carte – **Roof Garden** *(closed Tuesday) (summer only)* (dinner only) (live music) 5700 – **247 rm** ☐ 40000/44500, 6 suites.

Le NJV Meridien, 2 Vas. Georgiou, Sindagma, 105 64, ✆ 3255 301, Telex 210568, Fax 3235 856 – rm ▤ TV ☎ – 75. AE ⓓ E VISA. CY r
☐ 3200 – **163 rm** 40000/63500, 14 suites.

Novotel Mirayia, 4-6 Mihail Voda, 104 39, ✆ 8627 053, Telex 226264, Fax 8837 816, « Roof garden with and Athens » – 🛗 ▤ TV ☎ – 520. AE ⓓ E VISA AX t
M (Italian rest.) (summer only) (dinner only) 3000/3600 and a la carte – ☐ 2000 – **190 rm** 17200/20000, 5 suites.

Park, 10 Alexandras, 106 82, ✆ 8832 712, Telex 214748, Fax 8238 420, « Roof garden with and Athens » – 🛗 ▤ TV ☎ – 700. AE ⓓ E VISA. BX a
M 4000 and a la carte – **126 rm** ☐ 18600/24800, 19 suites.

St. George Lycabettus, 2 Kleomenous, 106 75, ✆ 7290 711, Telex 214253, Fax 7290 439, ←, « ← Athens from rooftop restaurant », – 🛗 ▤ TV ☎ – 120. AE ⓓ E VISA DX t
M – **Grand Balcon** a la carte 6100/12500 – **Coffee Shop** 3500 – **157 rm** ☐ 21450/37750, **5 suites.**

Chandris, 385 Singrou, 175 64, SW : 7 km ✆ 9414 824, Telex 218112, Fax 9425 082, « Summer rooftop restaurant with and Athens » – 🛗 ▤ TV ☎ – 450. AE ⓓ E VISA. BY
M – **Four Seasons** *(October-May) (closed Sunday and Monday)* a la carte 6000/11000 – **364 rm** ☐ 20400/28800, 6 suites.

Holiday Inn, 50 Mihalakopoulou, 115 28, ✆ 7248 322, Telex 218870, Fax 7248 187, – 🛗 ▤ TV ☎ – 800. AE ⓓ E VISA. DY
M 4400 and a la carte – ☐ 2700 – **185 rm** 28500/38000, 4 suites.

Zafolia, 87-89 Alexandras, 114 74, ✆ 6449 002, Telex 214468, Fax 6442 042, « Rooftop terrace with and ← Athens » – 🛗 ▤ TV ☎ – 200. AE ⓓ E VISA. DX k
M 3400 and a la carte – **183 rm** ☐ 15950/19900, 8 suites.

Electra, 5 Ermou, 105 63, ✆ 3223 222, Group Telex 216896, Fax 3220 310 – 🛗 ▤ TV ☎. AE ⓓ E VISA. BY e
M 3900 – **110 rm** ☐ 18900/23900.

Herodion, 4 Rov. Gali, 117 42, ✆ 9236 832, Telex 219423, Fax 9235 851, « Roof garden with ← Acropolis » – 🛗 ▤ TV ☎ – 50. AE ⓓ E VISA. BY p
M 2500/2800 and a la carte – **86 rm** ☐ 18800/23870, 4 suites.

Electra Palace, 18 Nikodimou, 105 57, ✆ 3241 401, Group Telex 216896, Fax 3241 875, « Roof garden with and ← Athens », – 🛗 ▤ TV ☎ – 50. AE ⓓ E VISA. BY h
M 3900 and a la carte – **106 rm** ☐ 18900/23900, 5 suites.

Titania, 52 Panepistimiou Av., 106 78, ✆ 3609 611, Telex 214673, Fax 3630 497, « Roof garden with ← Athens » – 🛗 ▤ TV ☎ – 700. AE ⓓ E VISA. rest BX t
M 3500 and a la carte – **379 rm** ☐ 12980/17350, 21 suites.

Acropolis View without rest., 10 Wemster, off Rov. Gali, 117 42, ✆ 9217 303, Telex 219936, Fax 9230 705, ← – 🛗 ▤ ☎. AE E AY e
32 rm ☐ 9800/13100.

Precieux Gastronomie, 14 Akadimias (1st floor), 106 71, ✆ 3608 616, Fax 3608 619, French rest., « Skyscape mural by Italian artist » – 🛗 ▤ – 50. AE ⓓ E VISA CY s
closed Sunday, Easter, 25 December and 1 January – **M** a la carte 10000/15000.

Athenaeum, 8 Amerikis, International Cultural Centre, 106 71, ✆ 3631 125 – ▤. AE ⓓ E VISA CY e
closed Sunday, July-August and Bank Holidays – **M** a la carte 10000/20000.

Boschetto, Evangelismos Park, off El Venizelou, 106 75, ✆ 7210 893, Fax 7223 598, , Italian rest., « Summerhouse in small park » – ▤. AE ⓓ VISA DY c
closed lunch November-March, Sunday and 2 weeks August – **M** a la carte 8000/10000.

Kona Kai (at Ledra Marriott H.), 115 Singrou, 117 45, ✆ 9347 711, Telex 223465, Fax 9358 603, Polynesian and Japanese, (Teppan-Yaki) rest., « Pacific islands style decor » – ▤ . AE ⓓ E VISA BY
closed Sunday – **M** (dinner only) a la carte 7000/15000.

Symbosium, 46 Erehthiou, 117 42, ✆ 9225 321, « Conservatory in winter, in summer » – AE E VISA AY r
closed Sunday – **M** (dinner only) 9600/18200 and a la carte.

Bajazzo, 35 Ploutarhou St., 106 75, ✆ 7291420 – ▤. AE ⓓ VISA DX a
closed Sunday, 4 days at Easter, August, 25-26 December and 1 January – **M** (booking essential) (dinner only) a la carte 9800/15000.

Dolce Vita, 26b Dinokratous, 106 75, ✆ 7291258, Fax 7261258, Italian rest. – ▤. AE ⓓ E VISA DX a
closed Sunday, 4 days at Easter, 25 December and 1 January – **M** (dinner only) a la carte 6750/8300.

XX **Ideal,** 46 Panepistimiou Av., 106 78, ✆ 3614 604, Fax 3631 000 – ▤. AE ⓓ E VISA BX c
closed Sunday – **M** a la carte 3300/5500.

XX **La Brasserie,** 292 Kifissias (3rd floor), N. Psihiko, 154 51, NE : 7 ½ km on Kifissia Rd ✆ 6716 572, Fax 6417 940, ☂ – |‡| ▤ ⇔. AE ⓓ E VISA DY
closed Sunday – **M** a la carte 6150/10000.

XX **Dioscuri,** 16 Dimitriou Vassiliou, N. Psihiko, 154 51, NE : 7 km by Kifissia Rd turning at A.B. supermarket ✆ 6713 997, ☂ – ▤. AE ⓓ E VISA DY
closed lunch July and August, Sunday and Bank Holidays – **M** (booking essential) a la carte approx. 5000.

XX **L'Abreuvoir,** 51 Xenokratous, Kolonaki, 106 76, ✆ 7229 106, ☂, French rest. – ▤. AE ⓓ E VISA DX u
M a la carte 5000/10000.

XX **Spiros Vasilis,** 5 Lahitos, 115 21 off El Venizelou, turn left at second set of traffic lights after Hilton H. ✆ 7237 575, Steak rest. – AE ⓓ by El Venizelou DY
closed Sunday, 3 days at Easter, June-September and 25 to 27 December – **M** (booking essential) (dinner only) a la carte 5200/9200.

X **Dodeka Apostoloi,** Kanari 17, Kolonaki, 106 71, ✆ 3619 358 – ▤ CY b
closed Sunday and August – **M** a la carte 11000/16000.

X **Strofi,** 25 Rov. Gali, 117 42, ✆ 9214 130, ☂, « ≤ Acropolis from rooftop terrace » – AE ⓓ E VISA AY a
closed Sunday, 4 days at Easter and Christmas – **M** (dinner only) a la carte 2500/3000.

"The Tavernas"

Typical little Greek restaurants, generally very modest, where it is pleasant to spend the evening, surrounded with noisy but friendly locals, sometimes with guitar or bouzouki entertainment. These particular restaurants are usually open for dinner only.

XX **Myrtia,** 32 Trivonianou, 116 36, ✆ 7012 276 – ▤. AE ⓓ E VISA
closed Sunday and August – **M** (music) (booking essential) (dinner only) 6500/9000. by Anapafseos Rd CY

X **O Anthropos,** 13 Arhelaou, Pangrati, ✆ 7235 914, Seafood – E DY a
closed Sunday and June-early October – **M** (dinner only) a la carte 3500/11000.

X **Kidathineon,** 3 Filomoussou Eterias Sq., 105 58, ✆ 3234 281, ☂ – AE ⓓ E VISA BY s
M (dinner only) 2900/3300 and a la carte.

At Kifissia NE : 15 km by El Venizelou DY

Pentelikon, 66 Diligianni St., 145 62 (Kifissia), off Harilaou Trikoupi follow signs to Politia ✆ 8080 311, Telex 224649, Fax 8010 314, ☂, ⛱, ⛱ – |‡| ▤ TV ☎ – 🏛 150. AE ⓓ E VISA. ✂
M – **Vardis** (dinner only) 11500/15000 and a la carte – **La Terrasse** a la carte 6000/8000 – ☕ 3200 – **32 rm** 42000/48100, 11 suites.

at Pireas SW : 10 km by Singrou BY

Mistral [M], 105 Vas. Pavlou, Kastella, 185 33, ✆ 4117 150, Telex 212811, Fax 4122 096 – |‡| ▤ ☎ ⇔ – 🏛 200. AE E VISA. ✂
M 3000 – **71 rm** ☕ 12900/16900, 3 suites.

XX **Aglamer,** 54-56 Akti Koumoundourou, Mikrolimano, 185 33, ✆ 4115 511, ≤ Harbour, ☂, Seafood – ▤. AE ⓓ E VISA
closed 25 December – **M** a la carte approx. 6000.

X **Durambeis,** 29 Athinas Dilaveri, 185 33, ✆ 4122 092, ☂, Seafood
closed 4 days at Easter, August and 25 December – **M** a la carte 4000/10000.

Hungary

Magyarország

BUDAPEST

PRACTICAL INFORMATION

LOCAL CURRENCY

Forint : 100 Forints = 1.27 US $ = 1.06 Ecu (Jan. 93)

PRICES

Prices may change if goods and service costs in Hungary are revised and it is therefore always advisable to confirm rates with the hotelier when making a reservation.

FOREIGN EXCHANGE

It is strongly advised against changing money other than in banks, exchange offices or authorised offices such as large hotels, tourist offices, etc... Banks are usually open on weekdays from 8.30 to 11.30 am.

HOTEL RESERVATIONS

In case of difficulties in finding a room through our hotel selection, it is always possible to apply to IBUSZ Hotel Service, Petőfi tér 3, Budapest 5th ☏ (1) 118 57 07 and 118 39 25, Fax 117 90 99. This office offer a 24 hour assistance to the visitor.

POSTAL SERVICES

Post offices are open from 8am to 6pm on weekdays and 2pm on Saturdays.
General Post Office : Varoshaz u. 19, Budapest 5th, ☏ (1) 17 01 11.

SHOPPING IN BUDAPEST

In the index of street names, those printed in red are where the principal shops are found. Typical goods to be bought include embroidery, lace, china, leather goods, paprika, salami, Tokay, palinka, foie-gras... Shops are generally open from 10am to 6pm on weekdays (8pm on Thursday) and 9am to 1pm on Saturday.

TIPPING

Hotel, restaurant and café bills include service in the total charge but it is usual to leave the staff a gratuity which will vary depending upon the service given.

CAR HIRE

The international car hire companies have branches in Budapest. Your hotel porter should be able to give details and help you with your arrangements.

BREAKDOWN SERVICE

A breakdown service is operated by SARGA ANGYAL (Yellow Angel), ☏ (02) 52 80 00.

SPEED LIMIT

On motorways, the maximum permitted speed is 120 km/h – 74 mph, 100 km/h – 62 mph on other roads and 60 km/h – 37 mph in built up areas.

SEAT BELTS

In Hungary, the wearing of seat belts is compulsory for drivers and front seat passengers.

Budapest

Hungary 970 N 6 – Pop. 2 172 000 – ☎ 1.

Views of Budapest

St. Gellert Monument and Citadel (Szt. Gellért-szobor, Citadella) ≤★★★ EX – Fishermen's Bastion (Halászbástya) ≤★★ DU.

BUDA

Matthias Church★★ (Mátyás-templom) DU – Attractive Streets★★ (Tancsics Mihaly utca – Fortuna utca – Uri utca) CDU – Royal Palace★★ (Budavári palota) DV – Hungarian National Gallery★★ (Magyar Nemzeti Galéria) DV **M1** – Budapest Historical Museum★ (Budapesti Történeti Múzeum) DV **M1** – Vienna Gate★ (Bécsi kapu) CU **D** – War History Museum★ (Hadtörténety Múzeum) CU **M2**.

PEST

Parliament Building★★★ (Országház) EU – Museum of Fine Arts★★★ (Szepmüveszeti Múzeum) BY **M3** – Hungarian National Museum★★ (Magyar Nemzeti Múzeum) FVX **M4** – Museum of Applied Arts★★ (Iparmüvészeti Múzeum) BZ **M5** – Szechenyi Thermal Baths★★ (Széchenyi Gyógyés Strandfürdö) BY **D** – Hungarian State Opera House★ (Magyar Állami Operaház) FU **B** – Liszt Conservatory : foyer★ (Liszt Ferenc Zenemüvészeti Föiskola) FU **D** – Chinese Art Museum★ (Kína Muzéum) BYZ **M6** – St. Stephen's Basilica★ (Szt. István-bazilika) EU **E** – City Parish Church★ (Belvárosi plébániatemplom) EV **K** – University Church★ (Egyetemi Templom) FX **R** – Franciscan Church★ (Ferences templom) FV **L** – Municipal Concert Hall★ (Vigadó) EV **F** – Town Hall★ (Fövárosi Tanács) EFV **H** – Paris Arcade★ (Párizsi udvar) EV **P** – Vaci Street★ (Váci utca) EV – Hungaria Restaurant★ (Hungaria Ettermek) BZ **N** – Budapest West Station★ (Nyugati pályaudvar) AY – Millenary Monument★ (Millenniumi emlékmu) BY **F** – City Park★ (Városliget) BYZ – Vajdahunyad Castle★ (Vajdahunyad vára) BY **B** – Hungarian Transport Museum★ (Magyar Közlekedesi Múzeum) BY **M7**.

ADDITIONAL SIGHTS

Chain Bridge★★ (Széchenyi Lánchíd) DEV – Margaret Island★ (Margitsziget) AY – Aquincum Museum★ (Aquincumi Muzéum) N : 12 km by Szentendrei út AY – Gellert Thermal Baths★ (Gellért gyógyfürdö) EX – St. Ann's Church★ (Szent Anna templom) DU.

Envir.

Szentendre★ N : 20 km – Visegrad N : 42 km : Citadel, view★★

✈ Ferihegy SE : 16 km by Üllői FX, ☎ 57 22 24 (information) and 57 00 86 (passenger service), Bus to airport : Volán, from International Bus station, Engels tér, Station 6 Budapest 5th and Express Bus Airport, Erzsebet Place – MALEV, Roosevelt tér 2, Budapest 5th ☎ 18 90 33

ℹ Tourinform, Sütő u. 2, ✉ H 1052 ☎ 17 98 00 – IBUSZ Head Office, Felszabadulas tér 5, Budapest 5th ☎ 18 49 83 – Documentation : IPV, Angol u. 22 ✉ H 1149.

München 678 – Praha 533 – Venezia 740 – Wien 243 – Zagreb 350

Grand H. Corvinus Kempinski, Erzsébet Tér 7, 1051, ✆ 266 1000, Fax 266 1000, – AE VISA EV **a**
M – **Bistro Jardin** a la carte 1890/2220 – **Gourmet** *(closed Saturday lunch, Sunday and Bank Holidays)* a la carte 2660/3980 – 1445 – **341 rm** 16585/25145, 28 suites.

Hilton, Hess András tér 1-3, 1014, ✆ 1751000, Telex 225984, Fax 1560285, ≤ Danube and Buda, « Remains of a 13C Dominican church » – rm – 600. AE VISA DU **a**
M Dominican 2500/6000 and a la carte – **Kolocsa** – 1337 – **295 rm** 13375/24075, 28 suites.

Forum, Apáczai Csere J. utca 12-14, 1052, ✆ 117 80 88, Telex 224178, Fax 117 98 08, ≤ Danube and Buda, – rm – 200. AE VISA EV **n**
M 5350 and a la carte – **Silhouette** 4710/6280 and a la carte – **384 rm** 16050/22470, 16 suites.

Atrium Hyatt, Roosevelt tér 2, 1051, ✆ 266 1234, Telex 225485, Fax 266 9101, ≤, – rm – 350. AE VISA EV **k**
M – **Old Timer** 3210/4280 and a la carte – **Tokaj** – **331 rm** 20865/25145, 22 suites.

Thermal H. Aquincum , Arpád Fejedelem Îtja 94, 1036, ✆ 188 93 40, Telex 222160, Fax 168 88 72, ≤, Therapy centre, – rm – 250. AE VISA AY **d**
M – **Ambrosia** (dinner only) a la carte 920/2934 – **Apicius** a la carte 955/2213 – **304 rm** 13375/16050, 8 suites.

Radisson Béke, Teréz Krt. 43, 1067, ✆ 132 33 00, Telex 22 57 48, Fax 153 33 80, – rm – 120. AE VISA FU **a**
M 2675/3210 and a la carte – **238 rm** 13107/15782, 8 suites.

Thermal Helia, Kárpát Utca 62-64, 1133, ✆ 129 86 50, Telex 202539, Fax 120 14 29, ≤, Therapy centre, – rm rest – 400. AE VISA AY **c**
M 2500/3000 and dinner a la carte – **254 rm** 14445/17120, 8 suites.

Gellert, Gellert tér 1, 1111, ✆ 185 22 00, Telex 224363, Fax 166 66 31, Direct entrance to the Therapic bath, heated, – – 500. AE VISA. rest EX **n**
M 2355/6280 and a la carte – **221 rm** 9897/16799, 14 suites.

Korona, Kecskeméti Utca 14, 1053, ✆ 117 91 17, Telex 223622, Fax 118 38 67, – rm – 80. AE VISA FX **s**
M 1605/1875 and a la carte - **422 rm**, 13375/16585, 11 suites.

Ramada , Margitsziget, 1138, ✆ 132 11 00, Telex 226682, Fax 153 30 29, – rm – 85. AE VISA AY **b**
M 3000/4500 and a la carte – **152 rm** 11235/16585, 10 suites.

Astoria, Kossuth Lajos Utca 19, 1053, ✆ 117 34 11, Telex 224205, Fax 118 67 98 – – 30. AE VISA. rest FV **q**
M 856/1337 and a la carte – **123 rm** 9362/12572, 6 suites.

Grand Hotel Hungaria, Rákóczí Utca 90, 1074, ✆ 122 90 50, Fax 122 80 29, – – 500. AE VISA BZ **f**
M approx. 1380 – **521 rm** 10700/14445, 8 suites.

Flamenco, Tas Vezér Utca 7, 1113, ✆ 161 22 50, Telex 224647, Fax 165 80 07, – – 200. AE VISA. rest AZ **p**
M 1178/1962 – **336 rm** 10205/12560, 12 suites.

Buda Penta, Krisztina Krt. 41-43, 1013, ✆ 156 63 33, Telex 223444, Fax 155 69 64, – rm – 60. AE VISA CV **f**
M 1498 and a la carte – **389 rm** 10860/13214, 7 suites.

Alba without rest., Apor Péter Utca 3, 1011, ✆ 175 86 58, Telex 225671, Fax 175 98 99 – – 25. AE VISA DV **e**
95 rm 8025/10700.

Novotel, Alkotás Utca 63-67, 1444, ✆ 186 95 88, Telex 225496, Fax 166 56 36, ≤, – rm – 1 750. AE VISA CX **h**
M 2800/4000 and a la carte – 600 – **318 rm** 11770/14445, 6 suites.

Taverna, Váci Utca 20, ✆ 138 49 99, Telex 227707, Fax 118 71 88, – rest – 100. AE VISA. rest EV **h**
M a la carte 1605/4280 – **196 rm** 8185/10486, 28 suites.

Victoria without rest., Bem Rakpart 11, 1011, ✆ 201 86 44, Telex 202650, Fax 201 58 16, ≤, – . AE VISA DU **d**
23 rm 8025/12305, 1 suite.

Liget without rest., Dozsa György utca 106, 1068, ✆ 111 32 00, Telex 223648, Fax 131 71 53, – BY **e**
140 rm.

Nemzeti, József krt. 4, 1088, ✆ 133 91 60, Telex 227710, Fax 114 00 19 – – 25. AE VISA BZ **k**
M 1500 and a la carte – **75 rm** 6420/9897 Bb, 1 suite.

BUDAPEST

Bécsi u. EV
Deák Ferenc u. EV 8
Haris Köz EV 21
Párizsi u. EV 53
Petőfi Sándor u. EV 55
Régi posta u. EV 58
Váci u. EFV
Vörösmarty Tér EV

Apáczai Csere János u. EV 2
Árpád Fejedelem útja AY 3
Erzsébet Krt BZ 4
Bárczy István u. EV 5
Batthyány u. CDU 6
Fehérvári út. AZ 11
Felszabadulás Tér EFV 12
Ferenc Krt. BZ 14
Fortuna u. CDU 15
Fö u. DUV 17
Gerlóczy u. FV 19
Groza Péter Rakpart EVX 20
Hattyú u. CU 22
Hunfalvy u. CDU 24
Irányi u. EX 26
Irinyi József u. AZ 27
Kálmán Imre u. EU 29
Karinthy Frigyes út. AZ 31
Karolina út. AZ 32
Károlyi Mihály u. FVX 33
Kecskeméti u. FX 35
Kosciuszko Tádé u. CV 37
Kuny Domokos u. CV 39
Lajos u. AY 40
Logodi u. CU 42
Magyar u. FVX 44
Nagyenyed u. CV 46
Nagyszőlős u. AZ 47
Naphegy u. CDV 48
Országház u. CDU 50
Pacsirtamező u. AY 52
Reáltanoda u. FV 57
Rumbach Sebestyén u. FV 60
Schönherz Zoltán u. AZ 62
Szabó Ilonka u. CDU 64
Szentendrei út. AY 65
Szerb u. FX 66
Szt. István Krt. AY 67
Tábor u. CDV 70
Táncsics Mihály u. CDV 71
Városház u. EFV 73
Vörösvári út. AY 75

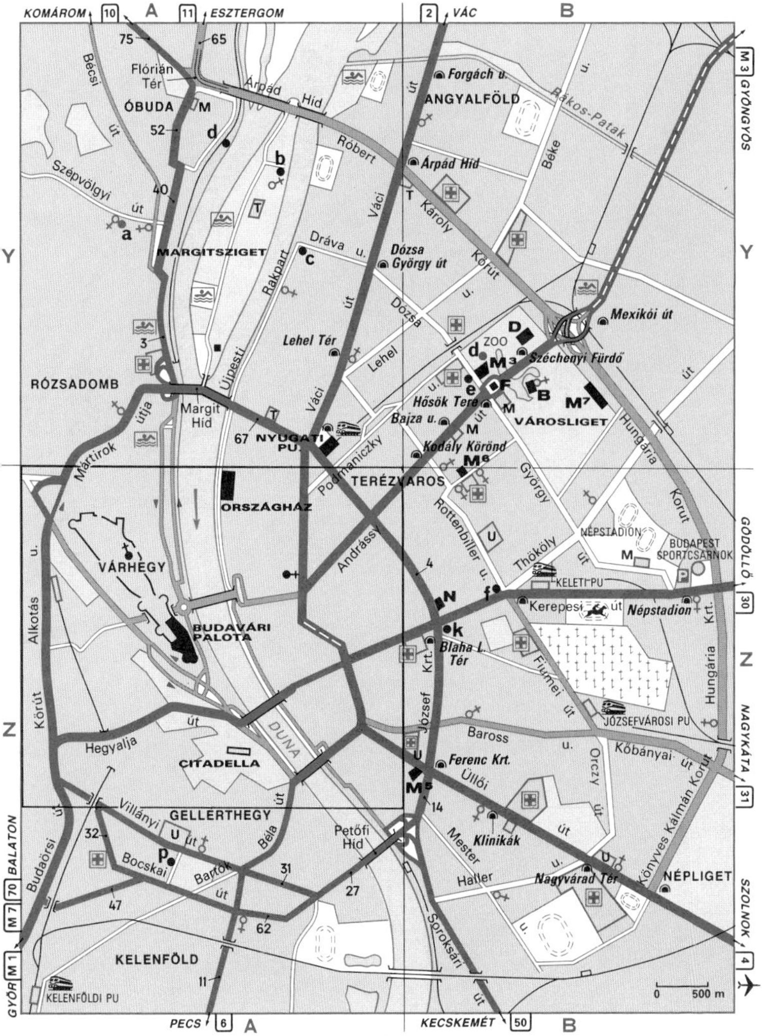

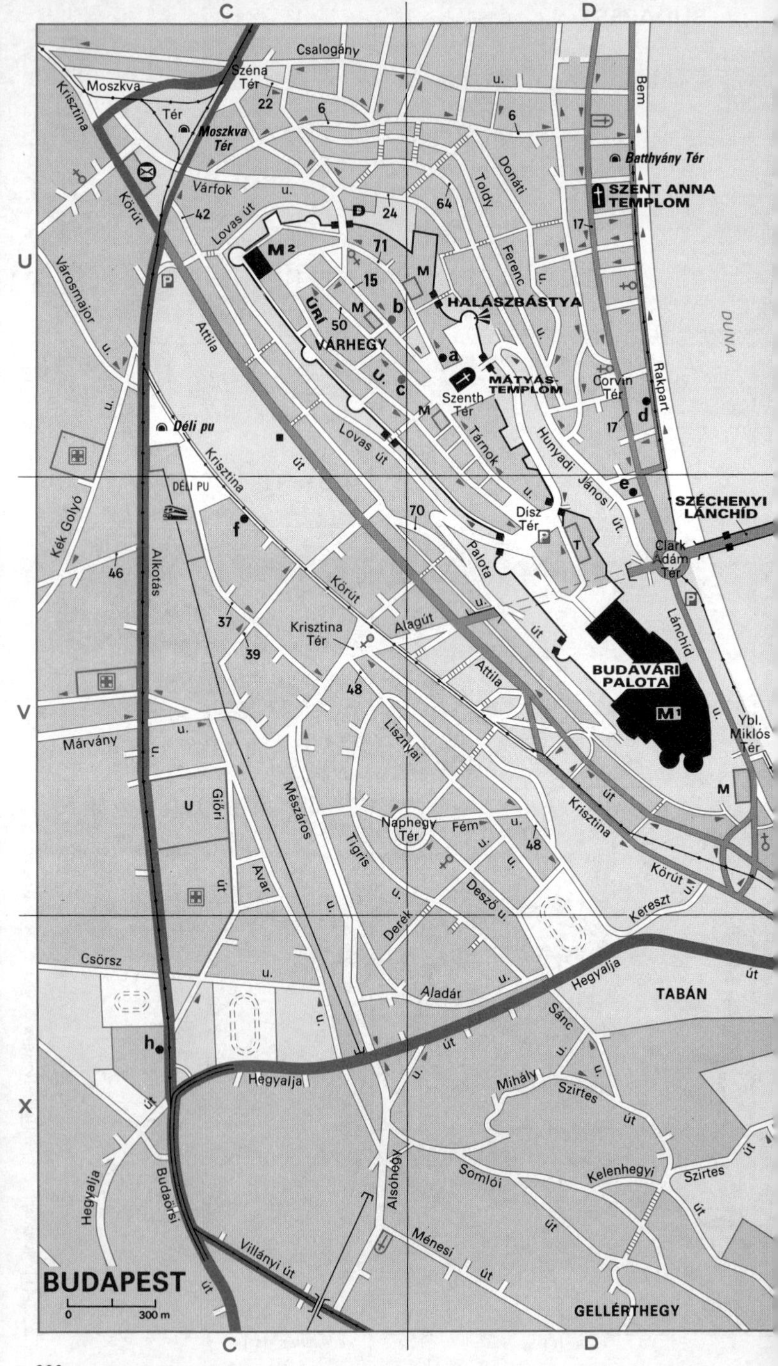
BUDAPEST
0
300 m
C
D
U
V
X
Csalogány
Széna Tér
Moszkva Tér
Moszkva
Krisztina
Várfok
Lovas út
M²
D
71
15
50
M
b
ÚRI
VÁRHEGY
HALÁSZBÁSTYA
MÁTYÁS-TEMPLOM
Szenth Tér
Tárnok
Hunyadi János út
Toldy
Donáti
Ferenc
Bem
Batthyány Tér
SZENT ANNA TEMPLOM
Corvin Tér
Rakpart
DUNA
Déli pu
DÉLI PU
Krisztina Körút
Attila
Városmajor u.
Kék Golyó
Alkotás
Dísz Tér
SZÉCHENYI LÁNCHÍD
Clark Ádám Tér
Palota út
Alagút
Krisztina Tér
BUDAVÁRI PALOTA
M¹
Lánchíd u.
Ybl. Miklós Tér
Márvány u.
Győri út
Mészáros u.
Lisznyai
Naphegy Tér
Fém u.
Tigris u.
Desző u.
Derék u.
Avar
Kereszt
Csörsz u.
Aladár u.
Hegyalja út
TABÁN
Sánc u.
Mihály
Szirtes út
Kelenhegyi
Somlói út
Alsóhegy
Ménesi út
Villányi út
Budaörsi út
Hegyalja
GELLÉRTHEGY

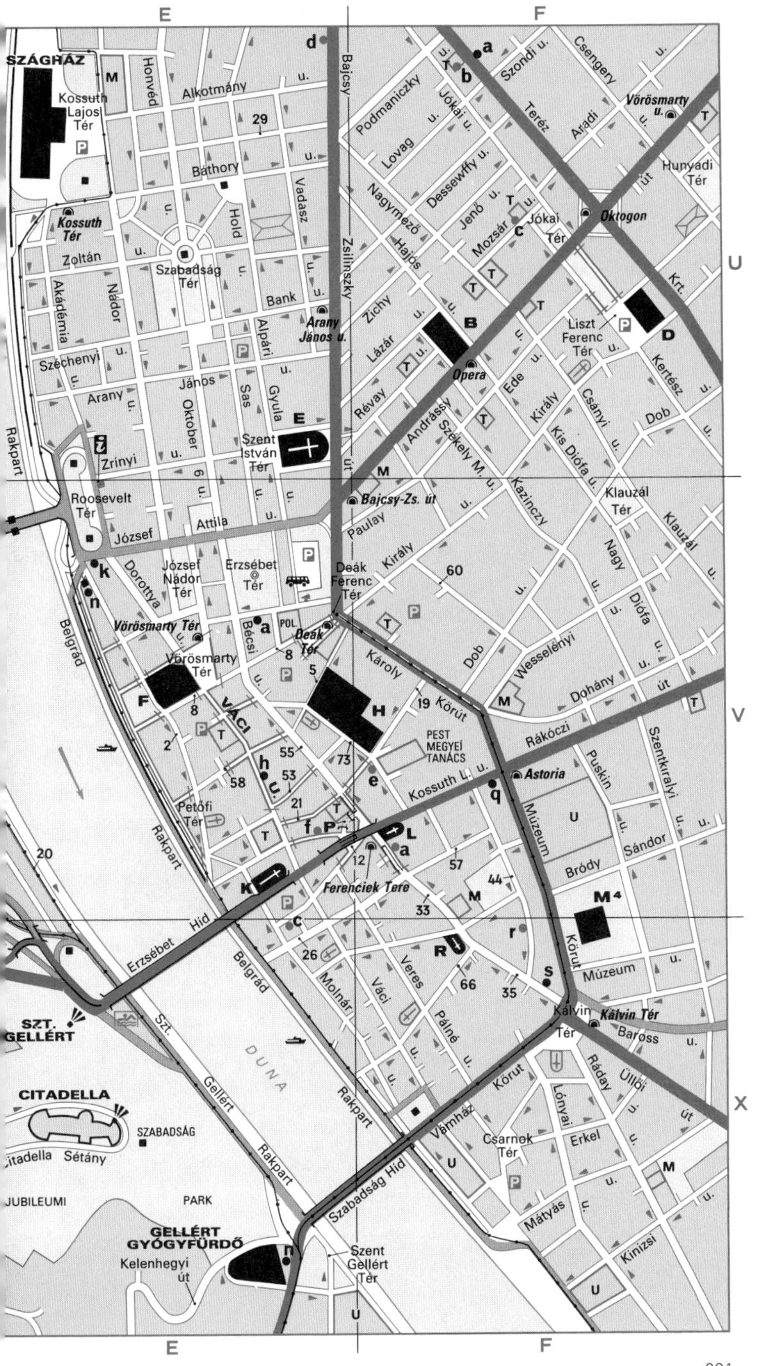
E
F
U
V
X
SZÁGHÁZ
Kossuth Lajos Tér
Kossuth Tér
Alkotmány u.
Honvéd
Báthory u.
Vadasz
Hold
Szabadság Tér
Zoltán u.
Akadémia
Nádor
Bank u.
Arany János u.
Alpári
Széchenyi u.
Arany u.
János
Október
Sas
Gyula u.
Szent István Tér
Zrínyi u.
Roosevelt Tér
József
Attila u.
József Nádor Tér
Erzsébet Tér
Deák Ferenc Tér
Dorottya
Vörösmarty Tér
Bécsi u.
Deák Tér
Váci
Petőfi Tér
Belgrád
Rakpart
Erzsébet Híd
Bajcsy-Zsilinszky út
Bajcsy-Zs. út
Podmaniczky
Lovag
Jókai u.
Nagymező
Hajós
Dessewffy u.
Zichy
Lázár
Révay
Andrássy
Opera
Mozsár
Jenő u.
Jókai Tér
Oktogon
Teréz
Aradi
Szondi u.
Csengery u.
Vörösmarty u.
Hunyadi Tér
Liszt Ferenc Tér
Krt.
Kertész u.
Ede u.
Király u.
Csányi u.
Dob u.
Székely M. u.
Kazinczy
Kis Diófa u.
Klauzál Tér
Klauzál u.
Paulay
Király
Nagy Diófa u.
Wesselényi
Dohány u.
Károly Körút
PEST MEGYEI TANÁCS
Rákóczi út
Astoria
Kossuth L. u.
Puskin
Múzeum Körút
Szentkirályi u.
Sándor u.
Bródy
Ferenciek Tere
Múzeum u.
Kálvin Tér
Baross u.
Ráday u.
Üllői út
Lónyai
Erkel u.
Csarnok Tér
Vámház Körút
Mátyás u.
Kinizsi
Molnár
Váci u.
Veres Pálné u.
Szabadság Híd
Szt. Gellért Rakpart
DUNA
SZT. GELLÉRT
CITADELLA
Citadella Sétány
SZABADSÁG
JUBILEUMI PARK
GELLÉRT GYÓGYFÜRDŐ
Kelenhegyi út
Szent Gellért Tér
POL.

XXXX **Gundel,** Állatkertí Körut 2, ✆ 121 35 50, Fax 142 29 17, ☂ - Ⓟ. AE ⓞ E VISA BY **d**
M (booking essential) 3135/4389 and a la carte.

XXX Alabardos, Orszaghaz utca 2, 1014, ✆ 156 02 51, ☂, Vaulted, Gothic interior, covered courtyard ☂ CU **c**
M (booking essential) (dinner only).

XXX **Legradí Testverek,** Magyar Utca 23, 1053, ✆ 118 68 04, Vaulted cellar - AE FX **r**
closed Saturday and Sunday - **M** (booking essential) (dinner only) a la carte 1750/2500.

XXX **Barokk,** Mozsar Utca 12, 1066, ✆ 131 89 42, cellar - AE FU **c**
M (booking essential) 2800/4500 and a la carte.

XX Szindbád, Bajcsy-Zsilinszky Utca 74, 1055, ✆ 132 27 49, Fax 112 38 36, Vaulted cellar
M (booking essential). EU **d**

XX **Garvics,** Urömí Köz 2, 1025, ✆ 168 32 54, Vaulted converted chapel - AE E AY **a**
closed Sunday and Bank Holidays - **M** (booking essential) (dinner only) a la carte 1800/3500.

XX **Karpatia,** Ferenciek tere 4-8, 1366, ✆ 173596, Fax 180591, ☂, « Part of former Franciscan monastry » - AE ⓞ E VISA FV **a**
M 1000/5000 and a la carte.

XX **Mátyás Pince,** Március 15 tér, n° 7, 1056, ✆ 181693, Fax 384622, Hungarian cuisine, « Vaulted cellar, murals » - AE ⓞ E VISA EX **c**
M 1200/3500 and a la carte.

XX Pilvax, Pitvax Köz 1, 1052, ✆ 117 63 96 FV **e**

XX Margitkert, Márgit Utca 15, 1205, ✆ 354791, ☂.

XX **Gambrinus,** Teréz Körut 46, 1066, ✆ 112 76 31, Fax 112 32 51 - AE ⓞ E VISA. ✂
M 2500/3500 and a la carte. FU **b**

X Pest-Buda, Fortuna Utca 3, 1014, ✆ 156 98 49, Vaulted restaurant, antiques CU **b**
M (booking essential).

X Apostolok, Kigyo Utca 4, 1052, ✆ 118 37 04, « Old chapel decor, wood carving » EV **f**

X **Golden Squirrel,** Istenhegyi Utca 25, 1126, ✆ 155 67 28, Fax 155 95 94, ☂ - AE ⓞ E VISA by CV
M a la carte 910/2070.

Republic of

Ireland

DUBLIN

The town plans in the Republic of Ireland Section of this Guide are based upon the Ordnance Survey of Ireland by permission of the Government of the Republic, Permit number 5647.

PRACTICAL INFORMATION

LOCAL CURRENCY

Punt (Irish Pound): 1 punt = 1.60 US $ = 1.35 Ecu (Jan. 93)

TOURIST INFORMATION

The telephone number and address of the Tourist Information office is given in the text under ℹ.

FOREIGN EXCHANGE

Banks are open 10am to 12.30pm and 1.30pm to 3pm on weekdays only. Banks in Dublin stay open to 5pm on Thursdays and banks at Dublin and Shannon airports are open on Saturdays and Sundays.

SHOPPING IN DUBLIN

In the index of street names those printed in red are where the principal shops are found.

CAR HIRE

The international car hire companies have branches in each major city. Your hotel porter should be able to give details and help you with your arrangements.

TIPPING

Many hotels and restaurants include a service charge but where this is not the case an amount equivalent to between 10 and 15 per cent of the bill is customary. Additionally doormen, baggage porters and cloakroom attendants are generally give a gratuity.

Taxi drivers are customarily tipped between 10 and 15 per cent of the amount shown on the meter in addition to the fare.

SPEED LIMITS

The maximum permitted speed in the Republic is 55 mph (88 km/h) except where a lower speed limit is signposted.

SEAT BELTS

The wearing of seat belts is compulsory if fitted for drivers and front seat passengers. Additionaly, children under 12 are not allowed in front seats unless in a suitable safety restraint.

ANIMALS

It is forbildden to bring domestic animals (dogs, cats...) into the Republic of Ireland.

Dublin

(Baile Átha Cliath) Dublin 405 N 7 - pop. 528 882 - ☎ 01.

See : City★★★ - Trinity College★★★ (Library★★★) EY - Chester Beatty Library★★★ - Phoenix Park★★★ - Dublin Castle★★ DY - Christ Church Cathedral★★ DY - St. Patrick's Cathedral★★ DZ - March's Library★★ DZ - National Museum★★ (Treasury★★), FZ - National Gallery★★ FZ - Merrion Square★★ FZ - Rotunda Hospital Chapel★★ EX - Kilmainham Hospital★★ - Kilmainham Gaol Museum★★ - National Botanic Gardens★★ - Nº 29★ FZ **D** - Liffey Bridge★ EY - Taylors' Hall★ DY - City Hall★ DY **H** - Viking Adventure★ DY **K** - St. Audoen's Gate★ DY **B** - St. Stephen's Green★ EZ - Grafton Street★ EYZ - Powerscourt Centre★ EY - Civic Museum★ EY **M1** - Bank of Ireland★ EY - O'Connel Street★ (Anna Livia Fountain★), EX - St. Michan's Church★ DY **E** - Hush Lane Municipal Gallery of Modern Art★ EX **M4** - Pro-Cathedral★ EX - Garden of remembrance★ EX - Custom House★ FX - Bluecoat school★ - Guiness Museum★ - Marino Casino★ - Zoological Gardens★ - Newman House EZ.

Envir. : Powerscourt★★ (Waterfall★★★) S : 14 m by N 11 and R 117 Russborough House★★★, SW : 22 m by N 81.

18 Edmondstown, Rathfarnham ☎ 932461, S : 3 m by N 81 - 18 Elm Park, Nutley House, Donnybrook ☎ 693438, SE : 3 m by N 11 - 18 Lower Churchtown Rd, Milltown ☎ 977060, S : by R 117 - 18 Royal Dublin, Bull Island ☎ 336346 NE : by R 105 - 18 Clontarf, Donnycarney House, Malahide Rd ☎ 331520, NE : 2 m by R 107.

✈ ☎ 379900, Telex 31266, Fax 425 138, N : 5 ½ m. by N 1 - Terminal : Busaras (Central Bus Station) Store St.

⛴ to Holyhead (B & I Line) 2 daily - to the Isle of Man : Douglas (Isle of Man Steam Packet Co.) (Summer only) (4 h 45 mn).

ℹ 14 Upper O'Connell St. ☎ 747733, Fax 743660 - College Green, Foster Place ☎ 711488 (March-September) - Dublin Airport ☎ 376387, Fax 425886 North Wall Ferryport (end June-early September) - Baggot St. Bridge ☎ 747733.

Belfast 103 - Cork 154 - Londonderry 146.

DUBLIN
CENTRE

Street	Grid	No.
Anne Street South	EYZ	3
Dawson Street	EYZ	
Duke Street	EY	29
Grafton Street	EYZ	
Henry Street	EX	
Ilac Centre	DEX	
Irish Life Mall Centre	EFX	
O'Connell Street	EX	
Brunswick Street North	DX	10
Buckingham Street	FY	12
Bull Alley	DZ	13
Chancery Street	DY	16
Clanbrassil Street	DZ	17
College Green	EY	18
College Street	EY	19
Cornmarket	DY	21
D'Olier Street	EY	25
Earlsfort Terrace	EZ	32
Essex Quay	DY	34
Fishamble Street	DY	36
George's Quay	FY	38
Golden Lane	DZ	39
Henrietta Street	DX	42
High Street	DY	43
Kevin Street Upper	DZ	50
Kildare Street	EFZ	51
King Street South	EZ	52
Mariborough Street	EX	57
Merchants Quay	DY	58
Montague Street	EZ	59
Mont Street Upper	FZ	61
Nicholas Street	DY	64
Parnell Square East	EX	67
Parnell Square North	EX	68
Parnell Square West	DEX	69
St. Mary's Abbey St.	DY	79
St. Patrick Close	DZ	80
Stephen Street	DEY	85
Tara Street	FY	89
Wellington Quay	DEY	95
Werburgh Street	DY	96
Westland Row	FY	98
Westmoreland Street	EY	99
Wexford Street	DEZ	100
Winetavern Street	DY	101
Wolfe Tone Quay	DX	103
Wood Quay	DY	104

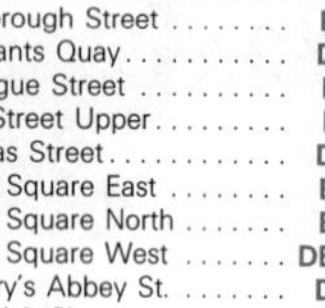

Town plans: roads most used by traffic and those on which guide-listed hotels and restaurants stand are fully drawn; the beginning only of lesser roads is indicated.

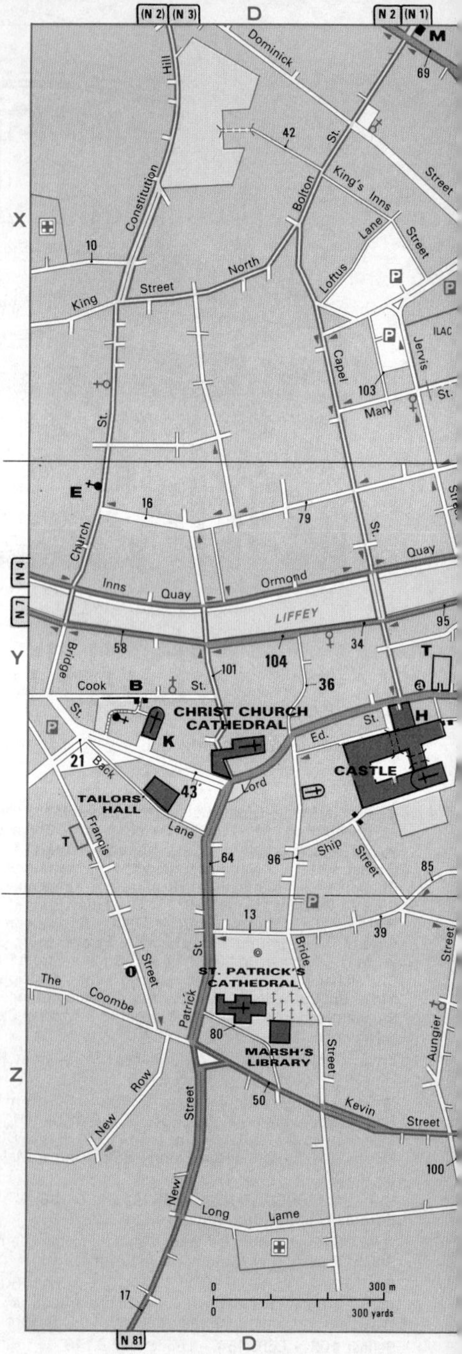

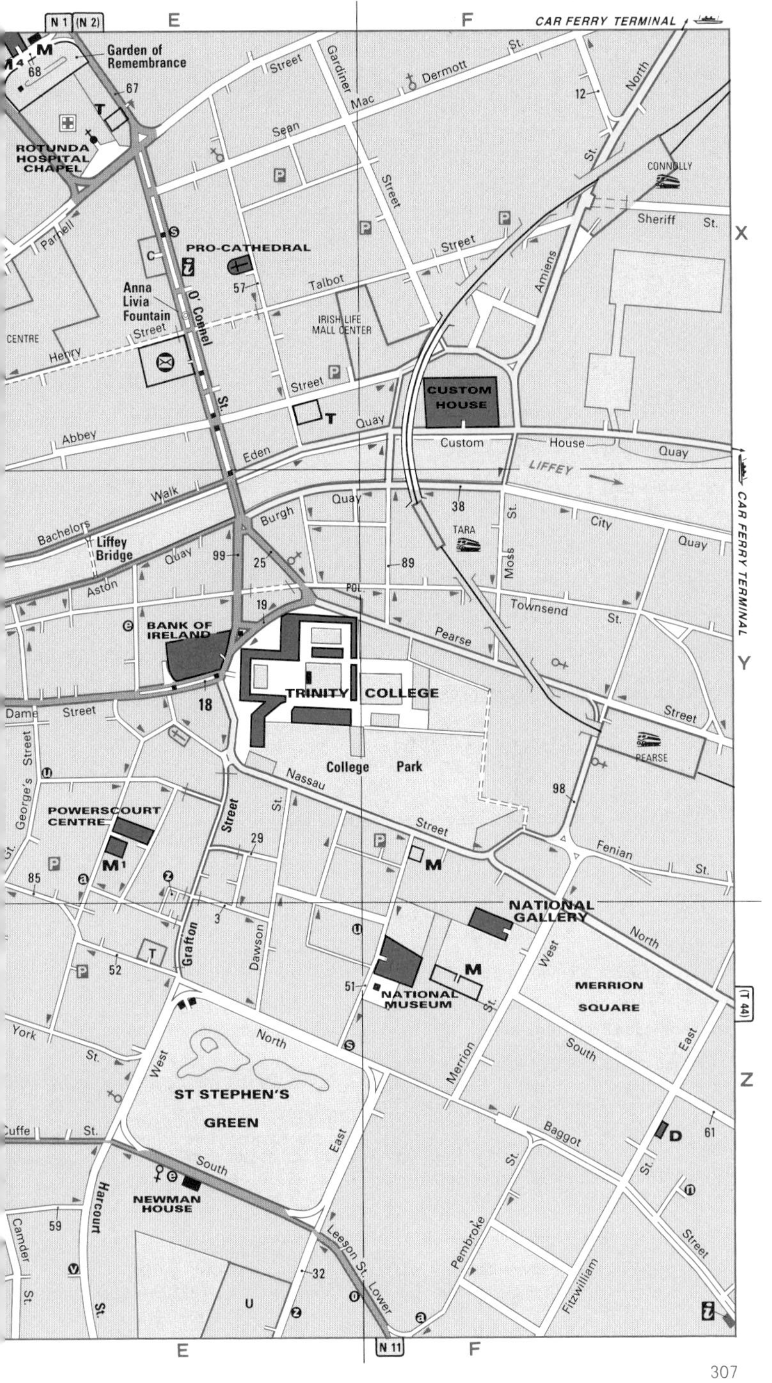

E
F
CAR FERRY TERMINAL
N 1
(N 2)
Garden of Remembrance
ROTUNDA HOSPITAL CHAPEL
PRO-CATHEDRAL
Anna Livia Fountain
O' Connell St.
IRISH LIFE MALL CENTER
CUSTOM HOUSE
CONNOLLY
Sheriff St.
Amiens
Talbot Street
Henry Street
Abbey Street
Eden Quay
Custom House Quay
LIFFEY
Bachelors Walk
Liffey Bridge
Aston Quay
Burgh Quay
City Quay
TARA
Moss St.
Townsend St.
Pearse Street
PEARSE
BANK OF IRELAND
TRINITY COLLEGE
College Park
Dame Street
Nassau Street
Fenian St.
POWERSCOURT CENTRE
George's Street
Grafton Street
Dawson St.
NATIONAL GALLERY
NATIONAL MUSEUM
MERRION SQUARE
Merrion St.
North
South
East
West
ST STEPHEN'S GREEN
York St.
Cuffe St.
NEWMAN HOUSE
Harcourt St.
Camden St.
Leeson St. Lower
Pembroke St.
Baggot Street
Fitzwilliam
Sean Mac Dermott St.
Gardiner Street
Parnell
CENTRE
N 11
T 44
X
Y
Z

Conrad, Earlsfort Terr., 765555, Telex 91872, Fax 765424 – rm – 300. VISA. EZ z
M 16.50/22.50 **t.** and a la carte 7.00 – 10.00 – **181 rm** 130.00/160.00 **t.**, **9 suites.**

Berkeley Court, Lansdowne Rd, Ballsbridge, 601711, Telex 30554, Fax 617238, – rest – 250. VISA.
M 16.00/20.50 **t.** and a la carte 4.95 – 8.00 – **196 rm** 120.00/140.00 **t.**, **9 suites.**

Westbury, Grafton St., 6791122, Telex 91091, Fax 6797078 – rest – 200. VISA. EY z
M 16.00/20.50 **t.** and a la carte 4.95 – 7.50 – **195 rm** 120.00/140.00 **t.**, **8 suites.**

Shelbourne (Forte), 27 St. Stephen's Green, 766471, Telex 93653, Fax 616006 – – 350. VISA EZ s
M 14.50/20.00 **t.** and a la carte 5.50 – 9.75 – **159 rm** 125.00/150.00 **t.**, **5 suites.**

Gresham, O'Connell St., 746881, Telex 32473, Fax 787175 – rest – 300. VISA. EX s
closed 1 week Christmas – **M** 15.75 **st.** (dinner) and a la carte 14.70/17.70 **t.** 5.35 – 8.00 **180 rm** 90.00/140.00 **t.**, **6 suites.**

Jurys, Pembroke Rd, Ballsbridge, 605000, Telex 93723, Fax 605540, heated – rm rest – 400. VISA.
M 15.50/19.95 **t.** and a la carte 5.75 – 9.00 – **282 rm** 101.00/175.00 **t.**, **2 suites** – SB (weekends only) 96.90/146.90 **st.**

Annex : **Towers at Jurys,** Pembroke Rd, Ballsbridge, 605000, Telex 93723, Fax 605540 – rm . VISA.
M (see **Jurys H.** above) – 9.00 – **98 rm** 145.00/175.00 **t.**, **2 suites** – SB (weekends only) 126.90/176.90 **st.**

Burlington, Upper Leeson St., 605222, Telex 93815, Fax 608496 – – 1 000. VISA
M 12.00/16.00 **t.** 4.50 **478 rm** 92.00/115.00 **t.**, **4 suites.**

Buswells, 25-26 Molesworth St., 764013, Fax 762090 – – 100. VISA. EZ u
M *(closed lunch Saturday, Sunday and Bank Holidays)* 11.95/19.50 **t.** and dinner a la carte 5.50 – **67 rm** 57.00/90.00 **t.**

Central, 1-5 Exchequer St., 6797302, Fax 6797303 – rm – 70. VISA. EY u
M 10.50/18.50 **t.** and dinner a la carte 4.50 – 7.50 – **69 rm** 69.00/95.00 **t.**, **1 suite** – SB (weekends only) 98.00/156.00 **st.**

Stephens Hall, 14-17 Lower Leeson St., 610585, Fax 610606 – . VISA. EZ o
M *(closed lunch Saturday and Sunday)* a la carte 15.45/21.65 **st.** 5.00 – 6.00 – **3 rm** 90.00/130.00 **st.**, **?P6734 suites** 130.00 **st.** – SB (weekends only) 170.00/260.00 **st.**

Blooms, Anglesea St., 715622, Telex 31688, Fax 715997 – – 30. VISA. EY e
closed 24 to 26 December – **M** *(closed lunch Saturday, Sunday and Bank Holidays)* a la carte 10.40/18.40 **st.** 5.50 – 6.90 – **86 rm** 90.00/130.00 **t.** – SB (weekends only) 69.00/100.00 **st.**

Russell Court, 21-23 Harcourt St., 784066, Fax 781576 – – 100. VISA. EZ v
M 9.95/16.00 **t.** and a la carte 6.00 – 5.25 – **41 rm** 49.00/77.00 **t.**, **1 suite.**

Skylon, Upper Drumcondra Rd, N : 2 ½ m. on N 1 379121, Fax 372778 – rest – 35. VISA.
M 9.30/11.30 **t.** and a la carte 3.90 – 6.25 – **92 rm** 54.00/80.00 **t.**

Tara Tower, Merrion Rd, SE : 4 m. on T 44 2694666, Fax 2691027 – – 180. VISA.
M 9.30/13.25 **t.** and a la carte 4.20 – 6.25 – **82 rm** 54.00/80.00 **t.**

Anglesea Town House without rest., 63 Anglesea Rd, Ballsbridge, 683877, Fax 683461 – . VISA.
7 rm 40.00/60.00 **t.**

XXX ✿ **Patrick Guilbaud,** 46 James' Pl., James' St., off Lower Baggot St., 764192, Fax 601546, French rest. – . VISA FZ n
closed Sunday and Monday – **M** 18.50/25.00 **t.** and a la carte 28.00/36.00 **t.** 10.00
Spec. Fillet of lamb with aubergines and red pepper sauce (spring), Fillet of Turbot topped with a spicy bread and herb butter, Cheesecake with red berries (summer).

XXX **Le Coq Hardi,** 35 Pembroke Rd, 689070, Fax 689887 – . VISA
closed Saturday lunch, Sunday, 2 weeks August and Bank Holidays – **M** 17.00/30.00 **t.** and a la carte 8.00.

XXX **The Commons,** Newman House, 85-86 St. Stephen's Green, 780539, Fax 780551 – VISA EZ c
closed Saturday lunch and Sunday – **M** 17.00/27.50 **t.** and a la carte 6.00.

XXX **Ernie's,** Mulberry Gdns, off Morehampton Rd, Donnybrook, 2693300, « Contemporary Irish Art collection » – VISA
closed Saturday lunch, Sunday, Monday and 1 week Christmas – **M** 13.95/25.00 **t.** and a la carte 6.25.

XX **Locks,** 1 Windsor Terr., Portobello, ✆ 543391, Fax 538352 – AE VISA
closed Saturday lunch, Sunday, 1 week Christmas and Bank Holidays – **M** 12.95/18.95 **t.** and a la carte 5.15.

XX **Old Dublin,** 90-91 Francis St., ✆ 542028, Fax 541406, Russian-Scandinavian rest. – AE VISA DZ **i**
closed Saturday lunch, Sunday and Bank Holidays – **M** 11.50/22.00 **t.** 4.75.

XX **Grey Door** with rm, 22/23 Upper Pembroke St., ✆ 763286, Fax 763287 – TV ☎. AE VISA. FZ **a**
M *(closed Saturday lunch, Sunday and Bank Holidays)* 16.00/22.50 **t.** and dinner a la carte 5.00 – 6.95 – **7 rm** 70.00/105.00 **t.** – SB 110.00/160.00 **st.**

XX **Les Frères Jacques,** 74 Dame St., ✆ 6794555, Fax 6794725, French rest. – AE VISA
closed Saturday lunch, Sunday and Bank Holidays – **M** 13.00/20.00 **t.** and dinner a la carte 5.10. DY **a**

XX **Chandni,** 174 Pembroke Rd, Ballsbridge, ✆ 681458, Indian rest. – . AE VISA
closed 9 April and 25-26 December – **M** 15.95/18.95 **t.** and a la carte.

XX **Kapriol,** 45 Lower Camden St., ✆ 751235, Italian rest. – AE VISA
M (dinner only) a la carte 17.50/36.30 **t.** 5.20.

XX **Zen,** 89 Upper Rathmines Rd, ✆ 979428, Chinese (Szechuan) rest. – . AE VISA
closed lunch Saturday, Sunday and Bank Holidays – **M** 8.00/16.00 **st.** and a la carte 6.00.

XX Puerto Bella, 1 Portobello Rd, ✆ 720851.

XX **Eastern Tandoori,** 34-35 South William St., ✆ 710428, Fax 779232, Indian rest. – . AE VISA EY **a**
closed lunch Sunday and Bank Holidays, 9 April and 25-26 December – **M** a la carte 12.25/18.55 **st.**

at Dublin Airport N : 6 ½ m. by N 1 – ✉ 01 Dublin :

Forte Crest Dublin, ✆ 8444211, Telex 32849, Fax 8425874 – TV ☎ & P – 120. AE VISA
closed 25 December – **M** 10.95/17.95 **t.** and a la carte – 7.95 – **188 rm** 85.00/95.00 **t.**

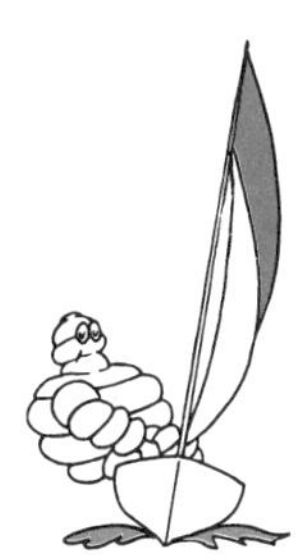

Italia

ROME - FLORENCE - MILAN - NAPLES
PALERMO - TAORMINA - TURIN - VENICE

PRACTICAL INFORMATION

LOCAL CURRENCY

Italian Lire: 1000 lire = 0.66 US $ = 0.55 Ecu (Jan. 93)

TOURIST INFORMATION

Welcome Office (Ente Provinciale per il Turismo), closed Saturday and Sunday:
– Via Parigi 5 - 00185 ROMA, ✆ 06/4883748, Fax 481 93 16
– Via Marconi 1 - 20123 MILANO, ✆ 02/809662, Fax 720 22 432
See also telephone number and address of other Tourist Information offices in the text of the towns under 🅸.
American Express:
– Piazza di Spagna 38 - 00187 ROMA, ✆ 06/72282, Fax 722 23 03
– Via Brera 3 - 20121 MILANO, ✆ 02/87 66 74, Fax 86 46 34 78

AIRLINES

ALITALIA: Via Bissolati 13 - 00187 ROMA, ✆ 06/46881
Piazzale Pastore (EUR) - 00144 ROMA, ✆ 06/54441
Via Albricci 5 - 20122 MILANO, ✆ 02/62817
AIR FRANCE: Via Vittorio Veneto 93 - 00187 ROMA, ✆ 06/4818741
Piazza Cavour 2 - 20121 MILANO, ✆ 02/77381
DELTA AIRLINES: Via Bissolati 46 - 00187 ROMA, ✆ 06/4773
Via Melchiorre Gioia 66 - 20125 MILANO, ✆ 02/66 80 35 00
TWA: Via Barberini 59 - 00187 ROMA, ✆ 06/4721
Corso Europa 11 - 20122 MILANO, ✆ 02/77961

FOREIGN EXCHANGE

Money can be changed at the Banca d'Italia, other banks and authorised exchange offices (Banks close at 1.15pm and at weekends).

POSTAL SERVICES

Local post offices: open Monday to Saturday 8.00am to 2.00pm
General Post Office (open 24 hours only for telegrams):
– Piazza San Silvestro 00187 ROMA – Piazza Cordusio 20123 MILANO

SHOPPING

In the index of street names those printed in red are where the principal shops are found. In Rome, the main shopping streets are: Via del Babuino, Via Condotti, Via Frattina, Via Vittorio Veneto; in Milan: Via Dante, Via Manzoni, Via Monte Napoleone, Corso Vittorio Emanuele.

BREAKDOWN SERVICE

Certain garages in the centre and outskirts of towns operate a 24 hour breakdown service. If you break down the police are usually able to help by indicating the nearest one.
A free car breakdown service (a tax is levied) is operated by the A.C.I. for foreign motorists carrying the fuel card (Carta Carburante). The A.C.I. also offerts telephone information in English (8am to 5pm) for road and weather conditions and tourist events: 06/4212.

TIPPING

As well as the service charge, it is the custom to tip employees. The amount can vary with the region and the service given.

SPEED LIMITS

On motorways, the maximum permitted speed is 130 km/h - 80 mph for vehicles over 1000 cc, 110 km/h - 68 mph for all other vehicles. On other roads, the speed limit is 90 km/h - 56 mph.

Rome

(ROMA) 00100 988 ㉖ 430 Q 19 - Pop. 2 791 351 - alt. 20 - ☎ 06.

⛳9 ⛳18 Parco de' Medici (closed Tuesday) ✉ 00148 Roma SW : 4,5 km ☎ 655 34 77 - Fax 655 33 44.

⛳18 (closed Monday) at Acquasanta ✉ 00178 Roma SE : 12 km. ☎ 780 34 07.

⛳9 Fioranello (closed Wednesday) at Santa Maria delle Mole ✉ 00040 Roma SE : 19 km ☎ 713 82 91 - Fax 713 82 12.

⛳9 and ⛳18 (closed Monday) at Olgiata ✉ 00123 Roma NW : 19 km ☎ 3789141, Fax 378 99 68.

✈ Ciampino SE : 15 km ☎ 794941, Telex 611168 and Leonardo da Vinci di Fiumicino ☎ 60121, Telex 620511 - Alitalia, via Bissolati 13 ✉ 00187 ☎ 46881 and piazzale Pastore (EUR) ✉ 00144 ☎ 65643.

🚗 Termini ☎ 464923 - Tiburtina ☎ 4956626.

ℹ via Parigi 5 ✉ 00185 ☎ 4883748, Telex 624 682, Fax 481 93 16 ; at Termini station ☎ 4871270 ; at Fiumicino Airport ☎ 6011255.

A.C.I. via Cristoforo Colombo 261 ✉ 00147 ☎ 514 971 and via Marsala 8 ✉ 00185 ☎ 49981, Telex 610686, Fax 499 82 34.
Distances from Rome are indicated in the text of the other towns listed in this Guide.

SIGHTS

Rome's most famous sights are indicated on the town plans pp. 2 to 5.
For a more complete visit use the Michelin Green Guide to Rome.

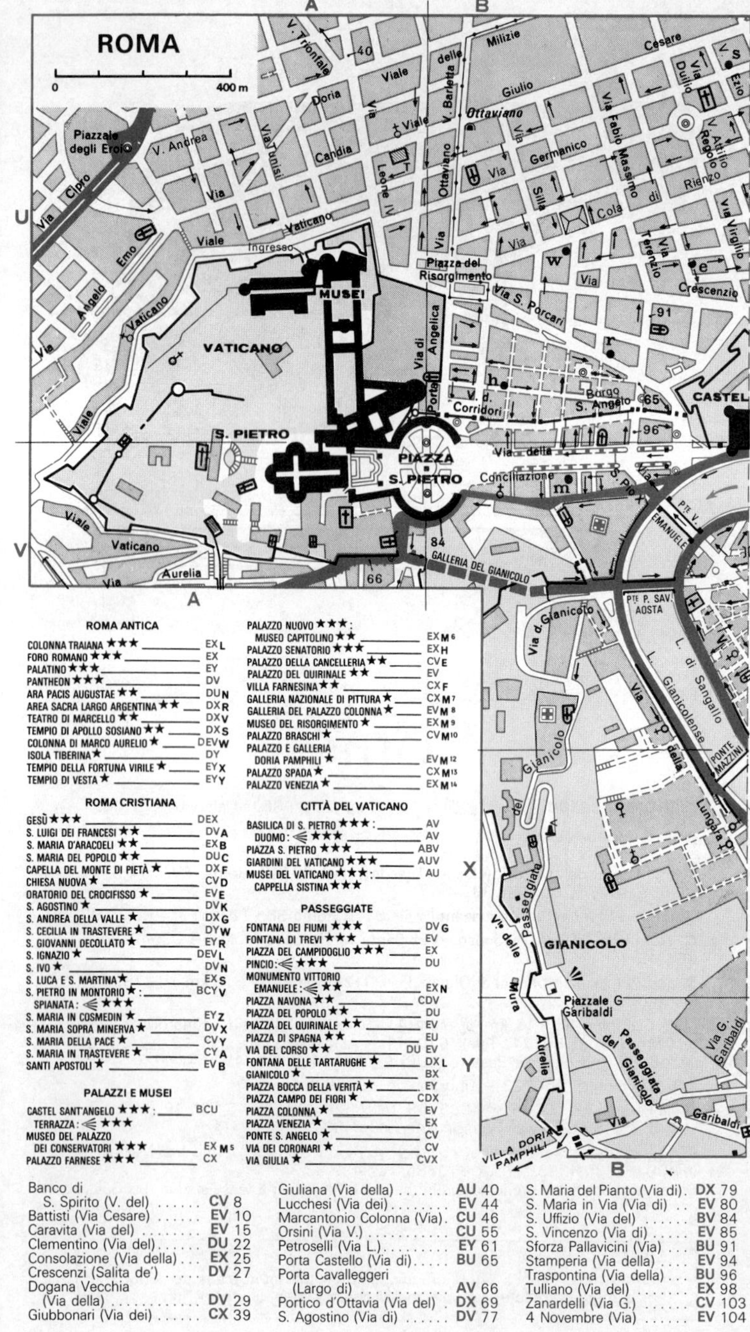

ROMA ANTICA

COLONNA TRAIANA ★★★ ______ EX L
FORO ROMANO ★★★ ______ EX
PALATINO ★★★ ______ EY
PANTHEON ★★★ ______ DV
ARA PACIS AUGUSTAE ★★ ______ DU N
AREA SACRA LARGO ARGENTINA ★★ ______ DX R
TEATRO DI MARCELLO ★★ ______ DX V
TEMPIO DI APOLLO SOSIANO ★★ ______ DX S
COLONNA DI MARCO AURELIO ★ ______ DEV W
ISOLA TIBERINA ★ ______ DY
TEMPIO DELLA FORTUNA VIRILE ★ ______ EY X
TEMPIO DI VESTA ★ ______ EY Y

ROMA CRISTIANA

GESÙ ★★★ ______ DEX
S. LUIGI DEI FRANCESI ★★ ______ DV A
S. MARIA D'ARACOELI ★★ ______ EX B
S. MARIA DEL POPOLO ★★ ______ DU C
CAPELLA DEL MONTE DI PIETÀ ★ ______ DX F
CHIESA NUOVA ★ ______ CV D
ORATORIO DEL CROCIFISSO ★ ______ EV E
S. AGOSTINO ★ ______ DV K
S. ANDREA DELLA VALLE ★ ______ DX G
S. CECILIA IN TRASTEVERE ★ ______ DY W
S. GIOVANNI DECOLLATO ★ ______ EY R
S. IGNAZIO ★ ______ DEV L
S. IVO ★ ______ DV N
S. LUCA E S. MARTINA ★ ______ EX S
S. PIETRO IN MONTORIO ★ : ______ BCY V
SPIANATA : ⋞ ★★★
S. MARIA IN COSMEDIN ★ ______ EY Z
S. MARIA SOPRA MINERVA ★ ______ DV X
S. MARIA DELLA PACE ★ ______ CV Y
S. MARIA IN TRASTEVERE ★ ______ CY A
SANTI APOSTOLI ★ ______ EV B

PALAZZI E MUSEI

CASTEL SANT'ANGELO ★★★ : ______ BCU
TERRAZZA : ⋞ ★★★
MUSEO DEL PALAZZO DEI CONSERVATORI ★★★ ______ EX M5
PALAZZO FARNESE ★★★ ______ CX
PALAZZO NUOVO ★★★ : MUSEO CAPITOLINO ★★ ______ EX M6
PALAZZO SENATORIO ★★★ ______ EX H
PALAZZO DELLA CANCELLERIA ★★ ______ CV E
PALAZZO DEL QUIRINALE ★★ ______ EV
VILLA FARNESINA ★★ ______ CX F
GALLERIA NAZIONALE DI PITTURA ★ ______ CX M7
GALLERIA DEL PALAZZO COLONNA ★ ______ EV M8
MUSEO DEL RISORGIMENTO ★ ______ EX M9
PALAZZO BRASCHI ★ ______ CV M10
PALAZZO E GALLERIA DORIA PAMPHILI ★ ______ EV M12
PALAZZO SPADA ★ ______ CX M13
PALAZZO VENEZIA ★ ______ EX M14

CITTÀ DEL VATICANO

BASILICA DI S. PIETRO ★★★ : ______ AV
DUOMO : ⋞ ★★★ ______ AV
PIAZZA S. PIETRO ★★★ ______ ABV
GIARDINI DEL VATICANO ★★★ ______ AUV
MUSEI DEL VATICANO ★★★ : ______ AU
CAPPELLA SISTINA ★★★

PASSEGGIATE

FONTANA DEI FIUMI ★★★ ______ DV G
FONTANA DI TREVI ★★★ ______ EV
PIAZZA DEL CAMPIDOGLIO ★★★ ______ EX
PINCIO : ⋞ ★★★ ______ DU
MONUMENTO VITTORIO EMANUELE : ⋞ ★★ ______ EX N
PIAZZA NAVONA ★★ ______ CDV
PIAZZA DEL POPOLO ★★ ______ DU
PIAZZA DEL QUIRINALE ★★ ______ EV
PIAZZA DI SPAGNA ★★ ______ EU
VIA DEL CORSO ★★ ______ DU EV
FONTANA DELLE TARTARUGHE ★ ______ DX L
GIANICOLO ★ ______ BX
PIAZZA BOCCA DELLA VERITÀ ★ ______ EY
PIAZZA CAMPO DEI FIORI ★ ______ CDX
PIAZZA COLONNA ★ ______ EV
PIAZZA VENEZIA ★ ______ EX
PONTE S. ANGELO ★ ______ CV
VIA DEI CORONARI ★ ______ CV
VIA GIULIA ★ ______ CVX

Banco di S. Spirito (V. del) ...... **CV** 8
Battisti (Via Cesare) ...... **EV** 10
Caravita (Via del) .... **EV** 15
Clementino (Via del) ...... **DU** 22
Consolazione (Via della) ... **EX** 25
Crescenzi (Salita de') ..... **DV** 27
Dogana Vecchia (Via della) .... **DV** 29
Giubbonari (Via dei) ...... **CX** 39
Giuliana (Via della) .... **AU** 40
Lucchesi (Via dei) .... **EV** 44
Marcantonio Colonna (Via). **CU** 46
Orsini (Via V.) .... **CU** 55
Petroselli (Via L.) .... **EY** 61
Porta Castello (Via di) ..... **BU** 65
Porta Cavalleggeri (Largo di) .... **AV** 66
Portico d'Ottavia (Via del) . **DX** 69
S. Agostino (Via di) .... **DV** 77
S. Maria del Pianto (Via di) . **DX** 79
S. Maria in Via (Via di) .. **EV** 80
S. Uffizio (Via del) ...... **BV** 84
S. Vincenzo (Via di) ..... **EV** 85
Sforza Pallavicini (Via) ... **BU** 91
Stamperia (Via della) .... **EV** 94
Traspontina (Via della) ... **BU** 96
Tulliano (Via del) .... **EX** 98
Zanardelli (Via G.) ...... **CV** 103
4 Novembre (Via) ...... **EV** 104

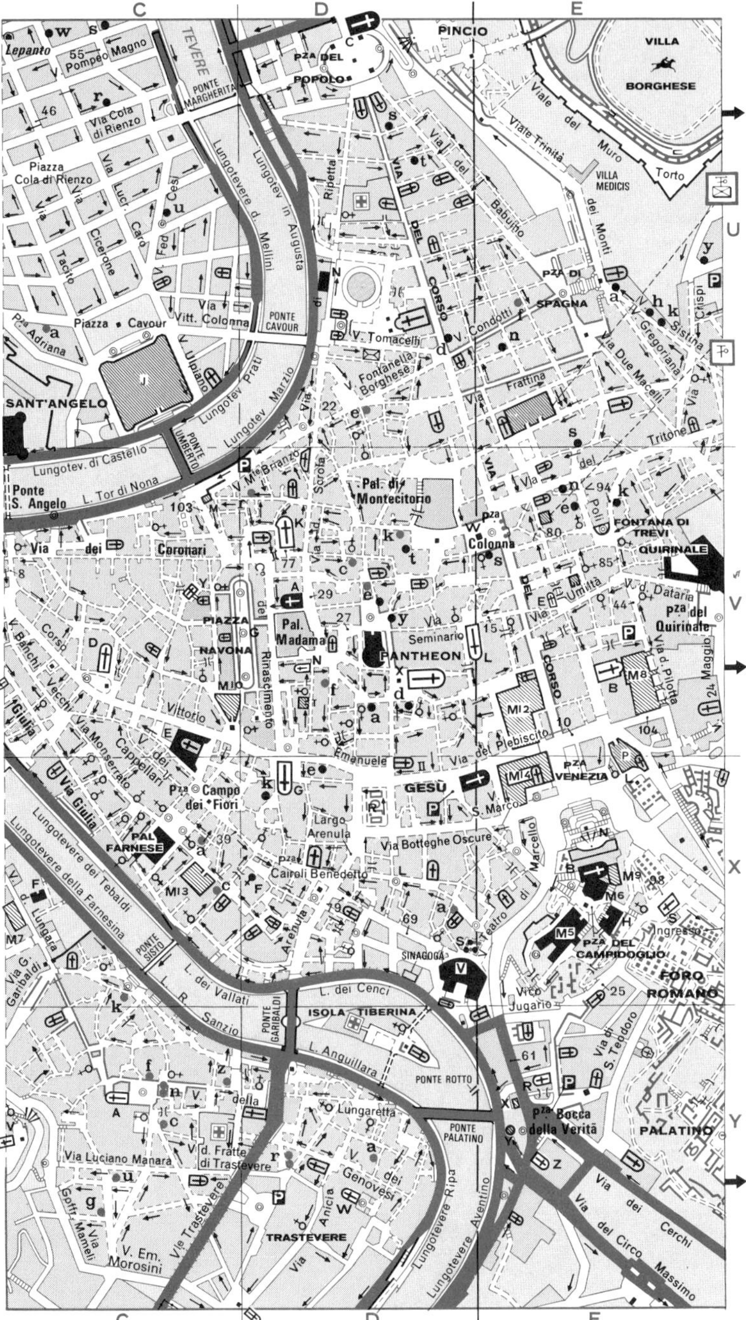
C
D
E
Lepanto
Pompeo Magno
TEVERE
PONTE MARGHERITA
PZA DEL POPOLO
PINCIO
VILLA BORGHESE
Viale del Muro Torto
Viale Trinità
VILLA MEDICIS
Via Cola di Rienzo
Piazza Cola di Rienzo
Lungotevere d. Mellini
Lungotev in Augusta
Ripetta
VIA DEL CORSO
Via del Babuino
dei Monti
U
PZA DI SPAGNA
Via Sistina
Crispi
V. Gregoriana
Via Due Macelli
Piazza Cavour
Vitt. Colonna
PONTE CAVOUR
V. Tomacelli
V. Condotti
Fontanella Borghese
Via Frattina
Tritone
P^za Adriana
SANT'ANGELO
Lungotev Prati
Lungotev Marzio
PONTE UMBERTO
Lungotev. di Castello
Ponte S. Angelo
L. Tor di Nona
Scrofa
Pal. di Montecitorio
P^za Colonna
FONTANA DI TREVI
QUIRINALE
Via dei Coronari
PIAZZA NAVONA
Pal. Madama
PANTHEON
Seminario
V. d. Dataria
P^za del Quirinale
V
Rinascimento
Corso Vittorio Emanuele II
V. Banchi Vecchi
Via Monserrato
V. dei Cappellari
P^za Campo dei Fiori
PAL. FARNESE
Via Giulia
Via del Plebiscito
P^ZA VENEZIA
GESÙ
S. Marco
Largo Arenula
Via Botteghe Oscure
P^za Cairoli Benedetto
Teatro di Marcello
X
PZA DEL CAMPIDOGLIO
FORO ROMANO
Ingresso
SINAGOGA
Lungotevere dei Tebaldi
Lungotevere della Farnesina
PONTE SISTO
L. dei Vallati
L. R. Sanzio
PONTE GARIBALDI
L. dei Cenci
ISOLA TIBERINA
L. Anguillara
PONTE ROTTO
Vico Jugario
Via di S. Teodoro
V. d. Lungara
Via G. Garibaldi
V. della Lungaretta
Via Luciano Manara
V. d. Fratte di Trastevere
PONTE PALATINO
P^za Bocca della Verità
PALATINO
Y
V. dei Genovesi
Anicia
TRASTEVERE
Via Goffr. Mameli
V. Em. Morosini
V^le Trastevere
Lungotevere Ripa
Lungotevere Aventino
Via dei Cerchi
Via del Circo Massimo

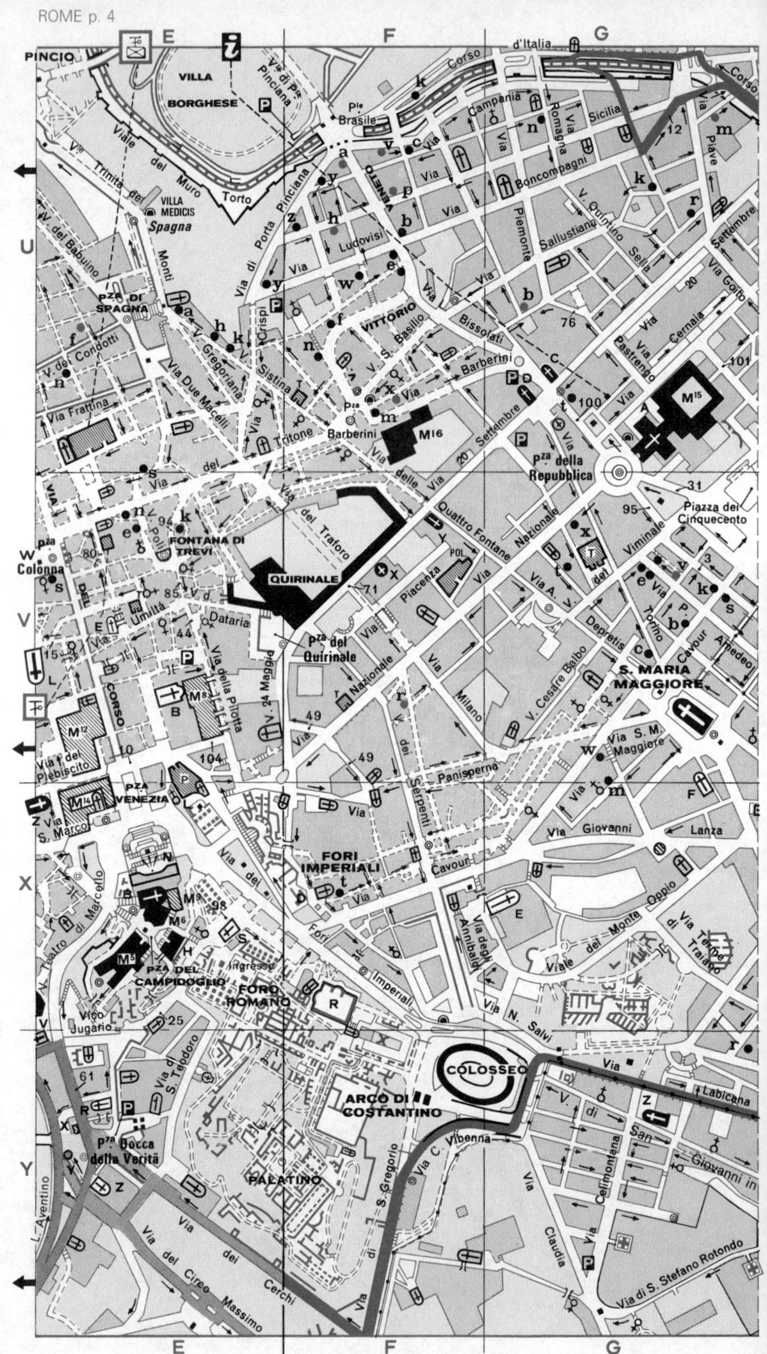

E
F
G
U
V
X
Y
PINCIO
VILLA BORGHESE
VILLA MEDICIS
Spagna
Pza DI SPAGNA
FONTANA DI TREVI
QUIRINALE
Pza del Quirinale
Pza della Repubblica
Piazza dei Cinquecento
S. MARIA MAGGIORE
Pza VENEZIA
FORI IMPERIALI
Pza DEL CAMPIDOGLIO
FORO ROMANO
COLOSSEO
ARCO DI COSTANTINO
PALATINO
Pza Bocca della Verità
Barberini
Colonna
Via del Corso
Via Nazionale
Via Cavour
Via dei Fori Imperiali
Via del Circo Massimo
Via di S. Gregorio
Via di S. Stefano Rotondo

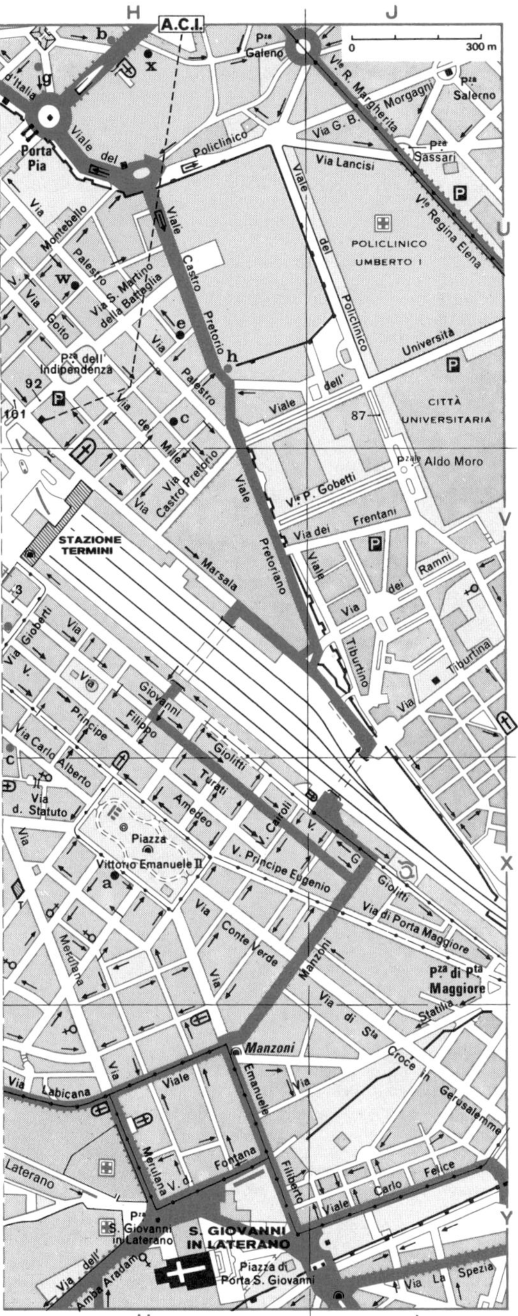

ROMA

ROMA ANTICA

ARCO DI COSTANTINO ★★★ ______ FY
BASILICA DI MASSENZIO ★★★ ____ FX R
COLONNA TRAIANA ★★★ ________ EX L
COLOSSEO ★★★ ______________ FGY
FORI IMPERIALI ★★★ ___________ FX
FORO ROMANO ★★★ ___________ EX
PALATINO ★★★ ______________ EFY
TEATRO DI MARCELLO ★★ ________ EX V
COLONNA DI MARCO AURELIO ★ ____ EV W
TEMPIO DELLA FORTUNA VIRILE ★ ___ EY X
TEMPIO DI VESTA ★ ______________ EY Y

ROMA CRISTIANA

GESÙ ★★★ ___________________ EX Z
S. GIOVANNI IN LATERANO ★★★ __ HY
S. MARIA MAGGIORE ★★★ _______ GV
S. ANDREA AL QUIRINALE ★★ _____ FV X
S. CARLO
ALLE QUATTRO FONTANE ★★ _____ FV Y
S. CLEMENTE ★★ ______________ GY Z
S. MARIA DEGLI ANGELI ★★ _______ GU A
S. MARIA D'ARACOELI ★★ _________ EX B
S. MARIA DELLA VITTORIA ★★ _____ GU C
S. SUSANNA ★★ _______________ GU D
ORATORIO DEL CROCIFISSO ★ ______ EV E
S. IGNAZIO ★ __________________ EV L
S. GIOVANNI DECOLLATO ★ ________ EY R
S. LUCA E S. MARTINA ★ _________ EX S
S. MARIA IN COSMEDIN ★ _________ EY Z
S. PIETRO IN VINCOLI ★ __________ GX E
S. PRASSEDE ★ ________________ GVX F
SANTI APOSTOLI ★ ______________ EV B

PALAZZI E MUSEI

MUSEO NAZIONALE ROMANO ★★★ _ GU M^{15}
MUSEO DEL PALAZZO
DEI CONSERVATORI ★★★ _______ EX M^{5}
PALAZZO NUOVO ★★★ :
MUSEO CAPITOLINO ★★ ________ EX M^{6}
PALAZZO SENATORIO ★★★ _______ EX H
PALAZZO BARBERINI ★★ _________ FU M^{16}
PALAZZO DEL QUIRINALE ★★ _____ EV
GALLERIA DEL PALAZZO COLONNA ★ _ EV M^{8}
MUSEO DEL RISORGIMENTO ★ ______ EX M^{9}
PALAZZO E GALLERIA
DORIA PAMPHILI ★ ______________ EV M^{12}
PALAZZO VENEZIA ★ _____________ EX M^{14}

PASSEGGIATE

FONTANA DI TREVI ★★★ _________ EV
PIAZZA DEL CAMPIDOGLIO ★★★ ___ EX
MONUMENTO VITTORIO
EMANUELE : ⋞ ★★ ____________ EX N
PIAZZA DEL QUIRINALE ★★ _______ FV
PIAZZA DI SPAGNA ★★ __________ EU
VIA VITTORIO VENETO ★★ _______ FU
PIAZZA BOCCA DELLA VERITÀ ★ _____ EY
PIAZZA COLONNA ★ _____________ EV
PIAZZA DI PORTA MAGGIORE ★ ____ JX
PIAZZA VENEZIA ★ ______________ EX
PORTA PIA ★ ___________________ HU

North area - Monte Mario, Stadio Olimpico, via Flaminia-Parioli, Villa Borghese, via Salaria, via Nomentana (Plans : Rome pp. 2 to 5) :

Cavalieri Hilton, via Cadlolo 101 ⊠ 00136 ℘ 31511, Telex 625337, Fax 31512241, ≤ City, « Terraces and park », – 25-2500. AE E VISA. rest — by via Trionfale AU
M a la carte 68/105000 – 31000 – **374 rm** 570000, 13 suites.

Lord Byron, via De Notaris 5 ⊠ 00197 ℘ 3220404, Telex 611217, Fax 3220405, – AE E VISA — by lungotevere in Augusta DU
M (see rest. **Relais le Jardin** below) – 25000 – **42 rm** 350/500000, 3 suites.

Aldrovandi Palace Hotel, via Aldrovandi 15 ⊠ 00197 ℘ 3223993, Telex 616141, Fax 3221435, – – 50-350. AE E VISA.
M Grill Le Relais Rest. *(dinner only)* a la carte 84/148000 – **140 rm** 380/400000 10 suites. — by viale Trinità EU

Albani, via Adda 45 ⊠ 00198 ℘ 84991, Telex 625594, Fax 8499399 – rm – 80. AE E VISA. — by via Piave GU
M a la carte 36/58000 – **157 rm** 270/375000, 15 suites.

Polo without rest., piazza Gastaldi 4 ⊠ 00197 ℘ 3221041, Telex 623107, Fax 3221359 – – 80. AE E VISA. — by lungotevere in Augusta DU
66 rm 320/360000.

Borromini, without rest., via Lisbona 7 ⊠ 00198 ℘ 8841321, Telex 621625, Fax 8417550 – – 50-100 — by viale Regina Margherita JU
75 rm.

Rivoli, via Torquato Taramelli 7 ⊠ 00197 ℘ 3224042, Telex 614615, Fax 3227373 – – 40. AE E VISA. — by lungotevere in Augusta DU
M *(closed August)* 38000 – **54 rm** 249000.

Degli Aranci, via Oriani 11 ⊠ 00197 ℘ 8070202, Fax 8085250, – – 50. AE E VISA. — by lungotevere in Augusta DU
M 35/45000 – **40 rm** 206/286000.

Clodio without rest., via di Santa Lucia 10 ⊠ 00195 ℘ 317541, Telex 625050, Fax 3250745 – AE E VISA. — by via Ottaviano Barletta BU
114 rm 165/220000.

XXXX ✿✿ **Relais le Jardin,** via De Notaris 5 ⊠ 00197 ℘ 3220404, Fax 3220405, Elegant rest. – AE E VISA. — by lungotevere in Augusta DU
closed Sunday and August – **M** (booking essential) a la carte 105/170000
Spec. Zuppa tiepida di fave cicoria e polipetti (spring), Cavatelli al nero di seppia con baccalà, totani e pecorino, Sautè di crostacei e ortica con animelle in pasta all'olio (spring). Wines Colle Picchioni, Torre Ercolana.

XXX **Relais la Piscine,** via Mangili 6 ⊠ 00197 ℘ 3216126, – AE E VISA.
closed Sunday dinner and August – **M** a la carte 84/148000. — by lungotevere in Augusta DU

XXX **Il Peristilio,** via Monte Zebio 10/d ⊠ 00195 ℘ 3223623, Fax 3223639 – AE E VISA.
closed Monday and 2 to 23 August – **M** a la carte 50/85000. — by via Marcantonio Colonna CU

XX **Al Fogher,** via Tevere 13/b ⊠ 00198 ℘ 8417032, Typical Venetian rest. – AE.
closed Saturday lunch, Sunday and August – **M** a la carte 57/86000. — by via Piave GU

XX **Al Ceppo,** via Panama 2 ⊠ 00198 ℘ 8419696 – AE E VISA – *closed Monday and 8 to 30 August* – **M** a la carte 46/83000. — by viale Regina Margherita JU

XX **Il Caminetto,** viale dei Parioli 89 ⊠ 00197 ℘ 8083946, – AE E VISA.
closed Thursday and 10 to 23 August – **M** a la carte 44/63000. — by lungotevere in Augusta DU

X **Delle Vittorie,** via Monte Santo 62/64 ⊠ 00195 ℘ 386847 – AE E VISA.
closed Sunday, 1 to 20 August and 23 December-3 January – **M** a la carte 40/62000. — by via Marcantonio Colonna CU

Middle-western area - San Pietro (Vatican City), Gianicolo, corso Vittorio Emanuele, piazza Venezia, Pantheon and Quirinale, Pincio and Villa Medici, piazza di Spagna, Palatino and Fori (Plans : Rome pp. 2 and 3) :

Hassler, piazza Trinità dei Monti 6 ⊠ 00187 ℘ 6792651, Telex 610208, Fax 6789991, ≤ City from roof-garden rest. – – 70. AE E VISA. — EU **a**
M *(closed Sunday dinner)* a la carte 96/151000 – 40000 – **100 rm** 400/600000, 15 suites.

Eden, via Ludovisi 49 ⊠ 00187 ℘ 4743551, Telex 610567, Fax 4821584, « Roof-garden rest. with ≤ City » – – 50-100 — EU **y**
119 rm.

Holiday Inn Minerva, piazza della Minerva 69 ⊠ 00186 ℘ 6841888, Telex 620091, Fax 6794165 – rm – 80. AE E VISA — DV **d**
M a la carte 85/136000 – 27000 – **133 rm** 365/520000, 3 suites.

De la Ville Inter-Continental, via Sistina 69 ⊠ 00187 ℘ 67331, Telex 620836, Fax 6784213 – – 40-120 — EU **h**
193 rm.

D'Inghilterra, via Bocca di Leone 14 ⊠ 00187 ℘ 672161, Telex 614552, Fax 6840828, « Stylishly furnished period hotel » – AE E VISA. — EU **n**
M (residents only) a la carte 66/102000 – 23000 – **97 rm** 311/436000, 20 suites.

Jolly Leonardo da Vinci, via dei Gracchi 324 ✉ 00192 ✆ 32499, Telex 611182, Fax 3610138 – rm – 30-220. AE VISA. rest CU **r**
M 60/80000 – **256 rm** 270/380000.

Dei Borgognoni without rest., via del Bufalo 126 ✉ 00187 ✆ 6780041, Telex 623074, Fax 6841501 – – 25-70. AE VISA. EUV **s**
50 rm 330/390000, 1 suite.

Visconti Palace without rest., via Cesi 37 ✉ 00193 ✆ 3684, Telex 622489, Fax 3200551 – – 25-150. AE VISA. CU **u**
247 rm 260/360000, 13 suites.

Plaza, via del Corso 126 ✉ 00186 ✆ 672101, Telex 624669, Fax 6841575 – – 60. AE VISA. DU **d**
M a la carte 63/100000 – 18000 – **207 rm** 260/339000, 5 suites.

Atlante Star, via Vitelleschi 34 ✉ 00193 ✆ 6873233, Telex 622355, Fax 6872300, « Roof-garden rest. and terrace summer service with ≤ St. Peter's Basilica » – – 50. AE VISA. rest BU **r**
M Les Etoiles Rest. a la carte 90/120000 – **61 rm** 412/430000, 3 suites.

Valadier without rest., via della Fontanella 15 ✉ 00187 ✆ 3611998, Telex 620873, Fax 3201558 – – 35. AE VISA DU **s**
38 rm 270/405000.

Delle Nazioni without rest., via Poli 7 ✉ 00187 ✆ 6792441, Telex 614193, Fax 6782400 – . AE VISA. EV **e**
81 rm 305/385000, 4 suites.

Colonna Palace without rest., piazza Montecitorio 12 ✉ 00186 ✆ 6781341, Telex 621467, Fax 6794496 – . AE VISA. EV **s**
105 rm 355/490000, 1 suite.

Giulio Cesare without rest., via degli Scipioni 287 ✉ 00192 ✆ 3210751, Telex 613010, Fax 3211736, – – 40. AE VISA. CU **s**
90 rm 280/380000.

Farnese without rest., via Alessandro Farnese 30 ✉ 00192 ✆ 3212553, Fax 3215129 – . AE VISA. CU **w**
22 rm 260/360000.

Nazionale without rest., piazza Montecitorio 131 ✉ 00186 ✆ 6789251, Telex 621427, Fax 6786677, – . AE VISA DV **t**
86 rm 260/390000, 10 suites.

Del Sole al Pantheon without rest., piazza della Rotonda 63 ✉ 00186 ✆ 6780441, Fax 6840689, « Renovated 14C building » – . AE VISA. DV **u**
26 rm 320/400000.

Santa Chiara without rest., via Santa Chiara 21 ✉ 00186 ✆ 6540142, Fax 6873144 – – 40. AE VISA. DV **a**
83 rm 195/275000, 3 suites.

Internazionale without rest., via Sistina 79 ✉ 00187 ✆ 6841823, Telex 614333, Fax 6784764 – . AE VISA. EU **k**
42 rm 180/240000, 2 suites.

Arcangelo without rest., via Boezio 15 ✉ 00192 ✆ 6896459, Fax 6893050 – . AE VISA. BU **e**
33 rm 160/240000.

Della Torre Argentina without rest., corso Vittorio Emanuele 102 ✉ 00186 ✆ 6833886, Telex 623281, Fax 6541641 – . AE VISA. DX **e**
32 rm 165/230000.

Tritone without rest., via del Tritone 210 ✉ 00187 ✆ 6782624, Telex 614254 – . AE VISA EV **n**
43 rm 180/220000.

Olympic without rest., via Properzio 2/a ✉ 00193 ✆ 6896650, Telex 623368, Fax 6548255 – . AE VISA. BU **w**
52 rm 165/220000.

Gerber without rest., via degli Scipioni 241 ✉ 00192 ✆ 3216485, Fax 3217048 – . AE VISA. BU **s**
27 rm 132/180000.

Columbus, via della Conciliazione 33 ✉ 00193 ✆ 6865435, Telex 620096, Fax 6864874, « 15 C building, period decor », – – 30-200. AE VISA. rest
M a la carte 58/80000 – **105 rm** 185/245000. BV **m**

Sant'Anna without rest., borgo Pio 134 ✉ 00193 ✆ 6541602, Fax 68308717 – . AE VISA BU **h**
20 rm 165/230000.

Accademia without rest., piazza Accademia di San Luca 75 ✉ 00187 ✆ 6786705, Fax 6785897 – . AE VISA. EV **k**
58 rm 180/230000.

Teatro di Pompeo without rest., largo del Pallaro 8 ✉ 00186 ✆ 6872812, Fax 6545531, « Vaults of Pompeius' theatre » – – 30. AE VISA. DX **k**
12 rm 210000.

Senato without rest., piazza della Rotonda 73 ✉ 00186 ☎ 6793231, Fax 6840297, ≤ Pantheon – ♦ ▤ TV ☎. AE ◉ VISA. ✂ DV **y**
51 rm ☐ 145/200000, ▤ 22000.

Margutta without rest., via Laurina 34 ✉ 00187 ☎ 3223674 – ♦ ☎. AE ⓢ ◉ E VISA. ✂
21 rm ☐ 122000. DU **t**

XXX **El Toulà,** via della Lupa 29/b ✉ 00186 ☎ 6873498, Fax 6871115, Elegant rest. – ▤. AE ⓢ ◉ E VISA. ✂ – *closed Saturday lunch, Sunday, August and 24 to 26 December* – **M** (booking essential) a la carte 73/103000 (15 %). DU **e**

XXX ✿ **Patrizia e Roberto del Pianeta Terra,** via dell'Arco del Monte 95 (via dei Pettinari) ✉ 00186 ☎ 6869893 – ▤. AE ⓢ ◉ E VISA CX **c**
closed Monday and August – **M** (dinner only) (booking essential) a la carte 100/150000 (10 %)
Spec. Zuppetta agli ortaggi zafferano e scampi, Rotolo di coniglio e agnello in salsa di aceto balsamico, Faraona e gamberi in salsa di scampi. Wines Fontarca, Monsecco.

XXX **Camponeschi,** piazza Farnese 50 ✉ 00186 ☎ 6874927, Fax 6865244, « Summer service with ≤ Farnese palace » – ▤. AE ⓢ ◉ E VISA. ✂ – *closed Sunday and 13 to 22 August* – **M** (dinner only) (booking essential) a la carte 67/100000 (13 %). CX **a**

XX ✿ **Quinzi Gabrieli,** via delle Coppelle 6 ✉ 00186 ☎ 6879389 – AE ◉ VISA. ✂ DV **c**
closed lunch, Sunday and August – **M** (booking essential) (fish only) a la carte 110/155000
Spec. Carpaccio di pesce, Spaghetti con crostacei, Pesce al sale. Wines Riesling.

XX ✿ **Rosetta,** via della Rosetta 9 ✉ 00187 ☎ 6861002, Fax 6872852, Seafood – ▤. AE ◉ VISA
closed Sunday and August – **M** (booking essential) a la carte 71/109000 DV **e**
Spec. Insalata di merluzzo con pomodorini, Linguine ai fiori di zucca, scampi e pecorino romano, Brodetto di scorfano. Wines Chardonnay, Freisa.

XX **Vecchia Roma,** piazza Campitelli 18 ✉ 00186 ☎ 6864604, 🏖, Typical roman rest. with local and seafood specialities – ▤. AE ◉ DX **a**
closed Wednesday and 10 to 25 August – **M** a la carte 47/77000 (12 %).

XX **Ranieri,** via Mario de' Fiori 26 ✉ 00187 ☎ 6786505 – ▤. AE ⓢ ◉ E VISA EU **f**
closed Sunday – **M** (booking essential) a la carte 49/91000.

XX **Piccola Roma,** via Uffici del Vicario 36 ✉ 00186 ☎ 6798606 – ▤. AE ◉. ✂ DV **k**
closed Sunday and August – **M** a la carte 36/51000.

XX **Eau Vive,** via Monterone 85 ✉ 00186 ☎ 6541095, Catholic missionaries ; international cuisine, « 16C building » – ▤. AE ⓢ E VISA. ✂ DV **f**
closed Sunday and 10 to 20 August – **M** (booking essential for dinner) a la carte 39/69000.

X **Hostaria da Cesare,** via Crescenzio 13 ✉ 00193 ☎ 6861227, Trattoria-pizzeria, Seafood – ▤. AE ⓢ ◉ E VISA. ✂ CU **a**
closed Sunday dinner, Monday, Easter, August and Christmas – **M** a la carte 45/63000.

X **L'Orso 80,** via dell'Orso 33 ✉ 00186 ☎ 6864904 – ▤. AE ⓢ ◉ E VISA. ✂ CDV **r**
closed Monday and 2 to 28 August – **M** a la carte 45/73000.

Central eastern area - via Vittorio Veneto, via Nazionale, Viminale, Santa Maria Maggiore, Colosseum, Porta Pia, via Nomentana, Stazione Termini, Porta San Giovanni (Plans : Rome pp. 4 and 5) :

Excelsior, via Vittorio Veneto 125 ✉ 00187 ☎ 4708, Telex 610232, Fax 4826205 – ♦ ▤ TV ☎ – 🏛 25-600. AE ⓢ ◉ E VISA. ✂ FU **b**
M a la carte 85/124000 – ☐ 29000 – **327 rm** 381/584000, 45 suites.

Le Grand Hotel, via Vittorio Emanuele Orlando 3 ✉ 00185 ☎ 4709, Telex 610210, Fax 4747307 – ♦ ▤ TV ☎ – 🏛 25-500 – **168 rm**. GU **t**

Majestic, via Vittorio Veneto 50 ✉ 00187 ☎ 486841, Telex 622262, Fax 4880984 – ♦ ▤ TV ☎ ♿ – 🏛 150. AE ⓢ ◉ E VISA. ✂ FU **f**
M a la carte 105/155000 – **95 rm** ☐ 400/540000, 7 suites.

Bernini Bristol, piazza Barberini 23 ✉ 00187 ☎ 4883051, Telex 610554, Fax 4824266 – ♦ ⇔ rm ▤ TV ☎ – 🏛 40-120. AE ⓢ ◉ E VISA. ✂ rest FU **m**
M a la carte 66/110000 – ☐ 22000 – **124 rm** 340/470000, 14 suites.

Quirinale, via Nazionale 7 ✉ 00184 ☎ 4707, Telex 610332, Fax 4820099, « Summer service in garden » – ♦ ▤ TV ☎ ♿ – 🏛 25-250. AE ⓢ ◉ E VISA. ✂ rest GV **x**
M 55000 – **186 rm** ☐ 265/350000, 3 suites.

Jolly Vittorio Veneto, corso d'Italia 1 ✉ 00198 ☎ 8495, Telex 612293, Fax 8841104 – ♦ ⇔ rm ▤ TV ☎ 🚗 – 🏛 35-450. AE ⓢ ◉ E VISA. ✂ rest FU **k**
M a la carte 65/93000 – **200 rm** ☐ 270/405000.

Regina Baglioni, via Vittorio Veneto 72 ✉ 00187 ☎ 476851, Telex 620863, Fax 485483 – ♦ ⇔ rm ▤ TV ☎ – 🏛 60. AE ⓢ ◉ E VISA. ✂ FU **e**
M a la carte 65/100000 – **130 rm** ☐ 350/490000, 7 suites.

Ambasciatori Palace, via Vittorio Veneto 70 ✉ 00187 ☎ 47493, Telex 610241, Fax 4743601, ≘ – ♦ ▤ TV ☎ ♿ – 🏛 50-200. AE ⓢ ◉ E VISA. ✂ rest FU **e**
M Grill Bar ABC Rest. a la carte 73/120000 – **149 rm** ☐ 330/460000, 11 suites.

Starhotel Metropol, via Principe Amedeo 3 ✉ 00185 ☎ 4774, Telex 611061, Fax 4740413 – ♦ ▤ TV ☎ ♿ 🚗 – 🏛 200 GV **e**
268 rm.

Imperiale, via Vittorio Veneto 24 ✉ 00187 ☎ 4826351, Telex 621071, Fax 4826351 – ♦ ▤ TV ☎ – **73 rm**. FU **n**

Forum, via Tor de' Conti 25 ✉ 00184 ℰ 6792446, Telex 622549, Fax 6786479, « Roof-garden rest. with ≤ Imperial Forums » – |♦| ▤ TV ☎ – 🚗 – 🎤 100. AE ⑤ ⓓ E VISA. ✂ FX t
M *(closed Sunday)* a la carte 78/142000 – **81 rm** ☕ 335/495, 6 suites.

Victoria, via Campania 41 ✉ 00187 ℰ 473931, Telex 610212, Fax 4871890 – |♦| ▤ TV ☎. AE ⑤ ⓓ E VISA. ✂ rest FU c
M 40000 – **110 rm** ☕ 220/320000.

Londra e Cargill, piazza Sallustio 18 ✉ 00187 ℰ 473871, Telex 622227, Fax 4746674 – |♦| ▤ TV ☎ 🚗 – 🎤 25-200. AE ⑤ ⓓ E VISA. ✂ GU k
M *(closed August)* a la carte 51/69000 – **105 rm** ☕ 290/380000.

Genova without rest., via Cavour 33 ✉ 00184 ℰ 476951, Telex 621599, Fax 4827580 – |♦| ▤ TV ☎. AE ⑤ ⓓ E VISA. ✂ GV b
91 rm ☕ 220/346000.

Mediterraneo, via Cavour 15 ✉ 00184 ℰ 4884051, Fax 4744105 – |♦| ▤ TV ☎ – 🎤 25-90. AE ⑤ ⓓ E VISA. ✂ GV k
M *(closed Saturday)* 47000 – **268 rm** ☕ 267/365000, 10 suites.

Pullman Boston, via Lombardia 47 ✉ 00187 ℰ 473951, Telex 622247, Fax 4821019 – |♦| ▤ TV ☎ – 🎤 25-90 FU z
125 rm.

Napoleon, piazza Vittorio Emanuele 105 ✉ 00185 ℰ 4467264, Telex 611069, Fax 4467282 – |♦| ▤ TV ☎ – 🎤 25-60. AE ⑤ ⓓ E VISA. ✂ HX a
M (dinner only) (residents only) a la carte 36/54000 – **80 rm** ☕ 190/290000.

La Residenza without rest., via Emilia 22 ✉ 00187 ℰ 4880789, Fax 485721 – |♦| ▤ TV ☎. AE E VISA. ✂ FU w
27 rm ☕ 120/230000.

Massimo D'Azeglio, via Cavour 18 ✉ 00184 ℰ 4870270, Telex 610556, Fax 4827386 – |♦| ▤ TV ☎ – 🎤 200. AE ⑤ ⓓ E VISA. ✂ GV s
M *(closed Sunday)* 47000 – **210 rm** ☕ 230/315000.

Eliseo without rest., via di Porta Pinciana 30 ✉ 00187 ℰ 4870456, Telex 610693, Fax 4819629 – |♦| ▤ TV ☎ – 🎤 50. AE ⑤ ⓓ E VISA. ✂ FU y
58 rm ☕ 250/380000, 7 suites.

Universo, via Principe Amedeo 5 ✉ 00185 ℰ 476811, Telex 610342, Fax 4745125 – |♦| ▤ TV ☎ ♿ – 🎤 25-300 GV e
199 rm.

Britannia without rest., via Napoli 64 ✉ 00184 ℰ 4883153, Telex 611292, Fax 4882343 – |♦| ▤ TV ☎ 🅟. AE ⑤ ⓓ E VISA GV t
32 rm ☕ 250000.

Commodore without rest., via Torino 1 ✉ 00184 ℰ 485656, Telex 612170, Fax 4747562 – |♦| ▤ TV ☎. AE ⑤ ⓓ E VISA. ✂ GV c
☕ 30000 – **60 rm** 210/320000.

Canada without rest., via Vicenza 58 ✉ 00185 ℰ 4457770, Telex 613037, Fax 4450749 – |♦| ▤ TV ☎. AE ⑤ ⓓ E VISA. ✂ HU e
74 rm ☕ 135/184000.

Marcella without rest., via Flavia 106 ✉ 00187 ℰ 4746451, Telex 621351, Fax 4815832 – |♦| ▤ TV ☎. AE ⑤ ⓓ E VISA. ✂ GU r
68 rm ☕ 170/250000.

Regency without rest., via Romagna 42 ✉ 00187 ℰ 4819281, Telex 622321, Fax 4746850 – |♦| ▤ TV ☎. AE ⑤ ⓓ E VISA. ✂ GU n
51 rm ☕ 220/330000.

Venezia without rest., via Varese 18 ✉ 00185 ℰ 4457101, Telex 616038, Fax 4457687 – |♦| ▤ TV ☎. AE ⑤ ⓓ E VISA. ✂ HU c
61 rm ☕ 145/200000, ▤ 25000.

Turner without rest., via Nomentana 27 ✉ 00161 ℰ 8541716, Fax 8543107 – |♦| ▤ TV ☎. AE ⑤ ⓓ E VISA. ✂ HU x
☕ 15000 – **38 rm** 140/179000, 1 suite.

Edera 🕊 without rest., via Poliziano 75 ✉ 00184 ℰ 7316341, Fax 738275, 🌳 – |♦| TV ☎ 🅟. AE ⑤ ⓓ E VISA GY r
53 rm ☕ 160/220000.

Colosseum without rest., via Sforza 10 ✉ 00184 ℰ 4827228, Fax 4827285 – |♦| ☎. AE ⑤ ⓓ E VISA GVX m
48 rm ☕ 137/190000.

Diana, via Principe Amedeo 4 ✉ 00185 ℰ 4827541, Telex 611198, Fax 486998 – |♦| ▤ TV ☎ – 🎤 25. AE ⑤ E VISA. ✂ GV e
M (residents only) 38000 – **187 rm** ☕ 135/194000.

Siviglia without rest., via Gaeta 12 ✉ 00185 ℰ 4441195, Fax 4441195 – |♦| TV ☎. AE ⑤ ⓓ E VISA HU w
41 rm ☕ 160/220000.

Valle without rest., via Cavour 134 ✉ 00184 ℰ 4815736, Fax 4885837 – |♦| ▤ TV ☎. AE ⑤ ⓓ E VISA. ✂ GV w
28 rm ☕ 190/260000.

XXXX **Sans Souci,** via Sicilia 20/24 ✉ 00187 ☏ 4821814, Fax 4821771, Elegant tavern-late night dinners – ▤. AE ⓢ ⓓ E VISA. ✻ – *closed Monday and 13 August-4 September* – **M** (dinner only) (booking essential) a la carte 78/135000 (15 %). FU **p**

XXX Harry's Bar, via Vittorio Veneto 150 ✉ 00187 ☏ 4745832, Fax 484643, (booking essential) – ▤ FU **a**

XX **Coriolano,** via Ancona 14 ✉ 00198 ☏ 8551122 – ▤. AE ⓢ ⓓ E VISA HU **g**
closed Sunday and 3 to 24 July – **M** (booking essential) a la carte 59/114000 (15 %).

XX **Agata e Romeo,** via Carlo Alberto 45 ✉ 00185 ☏ 4465842 (will change to 4466115), Fax 4465842 – ▤. AE ⓢ ⓓ E VISA. ✻ – *closed Sunday, Monday lunch, 10 to 23 August and Christmas* – **M** (booking essential) a la carte 68/103000. HV **c**

XX **Loreto,** via Valenziani 19 ✉ 00187 ☏ 4742454, Seafood – ▤. E. ✻ GU **m**
closed Sunday and 10 to 28 August – **M** a la carte 46/82000.

XX L'Idea, viale Castro Pretorio 70 ✉ 00185 ☏ 4457722 HU **h**

XX **Edoardo,** via Lucullo 2 ✉ 00187 ☏ 486428, Fax 486428 – ▤. AE ⓢ ⓓ E VISA. ✻
closed Sunday and August – **M** a la carte 50/86000 (15 %). GU **b**

XX **Girarrosto Toscano,** via Campania 29 ✉ 00187 ☏ 4821899, Fax 4821899 – ▤. AE ⓢ ⓓ E VISA. ✻ – *closed Wednesday* – **M** a la carte 47/78000. FU **v**

X **La Taverna,** via Massimo d'Azeglio 3/f ✉ 00184 ☏ 4744305 – ▤. AE ⓢ ⓓ E VISA
closed Saturday and 25 July-25 August – **M** a la carte 32/53000. GV **v**

X **Tullio,** via San Nicola da Tolentino 26 ✉ 4818564, Tuscan trattoria – ▤. AE ⓢ ⓓ E VISA. ✻ – *closed Sunday and August* – **M** a la carte 47/70000. FU **x**

X **Hostaria Costa Balena,** via Messina 5/7 ✉ 00198 ☏ 8417686, Seafood trattoria – ▤. AE ⓢ ⓓ E VISA. ✻ HU **b**
closed Saturday lunch, Sunday and 10 to 29 August – **M** a la carte 41/67000.

X **Crisciotti-al Boschetto,** via del Boschetto 30 ✉ 00184 ☏ 4744770, ⛱, Rustic trattoria – ⓢ E VISA FV **r**
closed Saturday and August – **M** a la carte 27/41000 (10 %).

X **Tempio di Bacco,** via Lombardia 36/38 ✉ 00187 ☏ 4814625, « Fresco mural in small hall » – ▤. AE ⓢ ⓓ E VISA. ✻ FU **h**
closed Saturday and August Holidays – **M** a la carte 35/46000 (16 %).

Southern area - Aventino, Porta San Paolo, Terme di Caracalla, via Appia Nuova (Plans : Rome pp. 2 to 5) :

🏨 **Domus Aventina** ⚘ without rest., via Santa Prisca 11/b ✉ 00153 ☏ 5746135, Fax 57300044 – TV ☎. AE ⓢ ⓓ E VISA. ✻ by via del Circo Massimo EY
26 rm ☕ 165/240000.

🏨 **Sant'Anselmo** ⚘ without rest., piazza Sant'Anselmo 2 ✉ 00153 ☏ 5743547, Telex 622812, Fax 5783604, ⛱ – ⇆ ☎. AE ⓢ VISA. ✻ by lungotevere Aventino DY
45 rm ☕ 130/190000.

🏨 **Villa San Pio** ⚘ without rest., via di Sant'Anselmo 19 ✉ 00153 ☏ 5743547, Fax 5783604, ⛱ – |‡| ☎. AE ⓢ VISA. ✻ by lungotevere Aventino DY
59 rm ☕ 130/190000.

XX ✿ **Checchino dal 1887,** via Monte Testaccio 30 ✉ 00153 ☏ 5746318, Fax 5743816, ⛱, Period building, typical roman food – AE ⓢ ⓓ VISA. ✻ by lungotevere Aventino DY
closed August, 23 to 30 December, Sunday dinner and Monday, Sunday lunch June-September – **M** (booking essential) a la carte 49/81000 (15 %)
Spec. Bucatini alla gricia, Coda alla vaccinara, Trippa alla romana. Wines Colle Picchioni, Le Vignole.

XX **Da Severino,** piazza Zama 5/c ✉ 00183 ☏ 7000872 – ▤. AE ⓢ ⓓ E VISA. ✻
closed Monday and 1 to 28 August – **M** a la carte 44/66000.
by via dell'Amba Aradam HY

XX **Apuleius,** via Tempio di Diana 15 ✉ 00153 ☏ 5742160, « Tavern in ancient roman style » – AE ⓢ E VISA by lungotevere Aventino DY
closed Saturday lunch and Sunday – **M** a la carte 47/77000.

Trastevere area (typical district) (Plan : Rome p. 3) : :

XXX **Alberto Ciarla,** piazza San Cosimato 40 ✉ 00153 ☏ 5818668, Fax 5884377, ⛱ – ▤. AE ⓢ ⓓ E VISA. ✻ CY **u**
closed lunch (except October-May), Sunday, 12 to 28 August and 1 to 13 January – **M** (booking essential) a la carte 60/110000.

XXX **Cul de Sac 2,** vicolo dell'Atleta 21 ✉ 00153 ☏ 5813324 – ▤. AE ⓢ ⓓ E VISA DY **a**
closed Sunday dinner, Monday and August – **M** (booking essential) a la carte 73/90000.

XX **Tentativo,** via della Luce 5 ✉ 00153 ☏ 5895234 – ▤. ⓢ ⓓ E VISA DY **r**
closed lunch, Sunday and August – **M** (fixed menu) (booking essential) 70/95000 b.i. (10 %).

XX **Corsetti-il Galeone,** piazza San Cosimato 27 ✉ 00153 ☏ 5816311, Fax 5896255, Seafood, « local atmosphere » – ▤. AE ⓢ ⓓ E VISA. ✻ CY **g**
closed Wednesday and 17 to 25 July – **M** a la carte 37/70000.

XX **Carlo Menta,** via della Lungaretta 101 ✉ 00153 ☏ 5884450, ⛱, Seafood – ▤. AE ⓢ ⓓ E VISA. ✻ – *closed Monday and 16 July-10 August* – **M** (dinner only) (booking essential) a la carte 53/78000 (15 %). CY **z**

XX **Galeassi,** piazza di Santa Maria in Trastevere 3 ✉ 00153 ✆ 5803775, Roman Seafood rest. – CY **f**
closed Monday and 20 December-20 January – **M** a la carte 44/74000.

XX **Paris,** piazza San Callisto 7/a ✉ 00153 ✆ 5815378, – . AE E VISA. CY **c**
closed Sunday dinner, Monday and August – **M** a la carte 53/80000.

XX **Sabatini,** vicolo Santa Maria in Trastevere 18 ✉ 00153 ✆ 5818307, Fax 5898386, Roman Seafood rest. – . AE E VISA. CY **n**
M a la carte 60/100000.

XX **Checco er Carettiere,** via Benedetta 10 ✉ 00153 ✆ 5817018, Roman Seafood rest. – . AE E VISA CX **k**
closed Sunday dinner, Monday and 10 August-10 September – **M** a la carte 52/78000.

XX **Pastarellaro,** via di San Crisogono 33 ✉ 00153 ✆ 5810871, Roman Seafood rest. – . AE E VISA – *closed Tuesday and August* – **M** a la carte 45/67000 (10 %). DY **r**

Outskirts of Rome

on national road 1 - Aurelia :

Jolly Hotel Midas, via Aurelia al 8 km ✉ 00165 ✆ 66396, Telex 622821, Fax 66418457, – 650. AE E VISA. rest by via Aurelia AV
M a la carte 52/83000 – **347 rm** 330000, 5 suites.

Villa Pamphili, via della Nocetta 105 ✉ 00164 ✆ 5862, Telex 626539, Fax 66157747, (covered in winter), – 25-500. AE E VISA. rest by via Garibaldi BY
M a la carte 50/85000 – **254 rm** 309000.

Holiday Inn St. Peter's, via Aurelia Antica 415 ✉ 00165 ✆ 6642, Telex 625434, Fax 6637190, – rm – 25-300. AE E VISA. by via Garibaldi BY
M a la carte 48/74000 – 24000 – **321 rm** 396000.

AgipHotel, via Aurelia al 8 km ✉ 00165 ✆ 6379001, Telex 613699, Fax 66414437, – – 25-150. AE VISA. by via Aurelia AV
M 35/50000 – 22000 – **213 rm** 165/235000.

XX La Maielletta, via Aurelia Antica 270 ✉ 00165 ✆ 6374957, Fax 6374957, Typical Abruzzi rest. – by via Aurelia AV

XX **13 da Checco,** via Aurelia al 13 km ✉ 00165 ✆ 66180040, – . AE E VISA
closed Sunday dinner, Monday and August – **M** a la carte 49/64000. by via Aurelia AV

on national road 4 - Salaria :

Hotel la Giocca, via Salaria 1223 ✉ 00138 ✆ 8804365, Fax 8804495, – – 40. AE VISA. by via Piave AV
M (see **L'Elite** below) – 20000 – **62 rm** 135/169000, 3 suites, 16000.

Eurogarden without rest., raccordo anulare Salaria Flaminia ✉ 00138 ✆ 8804507, Fax 8804417, – . AE E VISA. by via Piave AV
15000 – **40 rm** 160000.

XXX **L'Elite,** via Salaria 1223 ✉ 00138 ✆ 8804503 – . AE VISA. by via Piave AV
closed Sunday, 8 to 28 August and 23 December-6 January – **M** a la carte 60/86000.

on the Ancient Appian way :

XX **Cecilia Metella,** via Appia Antica 125/127/129 ✉ 00179 ✆ 5136743, « Shaded garden » – . AE E VISA by via Claudia GY
closed Monday and 12 to 30 August – **M** a la carte 46/70000.

to E.U.R. Garden City :

Sheraton, viale del Pattinaggio ✉ 00144 ✆ 5453, Telex 626073, Fax 5940689, – – 25-1800. AE E VISA.
M a la carte 66/131000 – **609 rm** 450000, 22 suites. by via di San Gregorio FY

Shangri Là-Corsetti, viale Algeria 141 ✉ 00144 ✆ 5916441, Telex 614664, Fax 5413813, heated, – – 25-80. AE E VISA. by via di San Gregorio FY
M *(closed 5 to 24 August)* a la carte 42/76000 – **52 rm** 218/297000.

Dei Congressi without rest., viale Shakespeare 29 ✉ 00144 ✆ 5926021, Fax 5911903 – – 25-300. AE E VISA. by via di San Gregorio FY
96 rm 170/250000.

XX **Vecchia America-Corsetti,** piazza Marconi 32 ✉ 00144 ✆ 5926601, Fax 5922284, Typical rest. and ale house – AE E VISA by via di San Gregorio FY
closed Tuesday – **M** a la carte 45/76000.

on the motorway to Fiumicino close to the ring-road :

Holiday Inn-Eur Parco dei Medici, viale Castello della Magliana 65 ✉ 00148 ✆ 65581, Telex 613302, Fax 6557005, – – 650. AE E VISA.
M 68000 – 17000 – **316 rm** 250/360000. by viale Trastevere CY

close to exit 32 of the ring-road :

Pisana Palace, via della Pisana 374 ✉ 00163 ✆ 66690, Telex 620062, Fax 66161190, – – 25-250. AE E VISA. by via Gregorio VII CY
M (residents only) 38/40000 – **210 rm** 360000.

FLORENCE (FIRENZE) 50100 P 988 ⑮, 429 430 K 15 – pop. 408 403 alt. 49 – ☎ 055.

See : Cathedral★★★ (Duomo) : east end★★★, dome★★★ (✻★★) Campanile★★ : ✻★★ Baptistry★★★ : doors★★★, mosaics★★★ Cathedral Museum★★ – Piazza della Signoria★★ Loggia della Signoria★★ : Perseus★★★ by B. Cellini Palazzo Vecchio★★★ Uffizi Gallery★★★ – Bargello Palace and Museum★★★ San Lorenzo★★★ : Church★★, Laurentian Library★★, Medici tombs★★★ in Medici Chapels★★ – Medici-Riccardi Palace★★ : Chapel★★★, Luca Giordano Gallery★★ – Church of Santa Maria Novella★★ : frescoes by Ghirlandaio★★★ – Ponte Vecchio★ Pitti Palace★★ : Palatine Gallery★★★, Silver Museum★★, Works by Macchiaioli★★ in Modern Art Gallery★ – Boboli Garden★ ABZ : ✻★★ from the Citadel Belvedere Monastery and Museum of St. Mark★★ : works★★★ by Beato Angelico – Academy Gallery★★ : main gallery★★★ Piazza della Santissima Annunziata★ CX : frescoes★ in the church **E**, portico★ with corners decorated with terracotta Mediallons★★ in the Foundling Hospital **M3** – Church of Santa Croce★★ : Pazzi Chapel★★ Excursion to the hills★★ : ←★★ from Michelangelo Square, Church of San Miniato al Monte★★ Strozzi Palace★ BY **F** – Rucellai Palace★ BYZ Frescoes★★ by Masaccio in the Church of Santa Maria del Carmine AY **G** Last Supper of San Salvi★★ Orsanmichele★ : tabernacle★★ by Orcagna BCY **L** – La Badia CY **S** : campanile★, delicate relief sculpture in marble★★, tombs★, Virgin appearing to St. Bernard★ by Filippino Lippi – Sassetti Chapel★★ and the Chapel of the Annunciation★ in the Holy Trinity Church BY **N** Church of the Holy Spirit★ ABY **R** – Last Supper★ of Sant'Apollonia CVX **V** Last Supper★ by Ghirlandaio AX **X** Davanzanti Palace★ BY **M5** New Market Loggia★ BY **Y** – Museums : Archaeological★ (Chimera from Arezzo★★) CX **M4**, Science★ CY **M6**, Semi-precious Stone Workshop★ CX **M7**.

Envir. : Medici Villas★★ : garden★ of the Villa della Petraia, Villa di Poggio a Caiano★ by via P. Toselli AV : 17 km – Cloister★ in the Galluzzo Carthusian Monastery S : 6 km.

18 Dell'Ugolino (closed Monday), to Grassina ⊠ 50015 ℘ 2301009, S : 12 km.

✈ of Peretola NW : 4 km ℘ 373498 – Alitalia, lungarno Acciaiuoli 10/12 r, ⊠ 50123 ℘ 27888.

i via Manzoni 16 ⊠ 50121 ℘ 2346284.

A.C.I. viale Amendola 36 ⊠ 50121 ℘ 24861.

Roma 277 – Bologna 105 – Milano 298.

Plans on following pages

Excelsior, piazza Ognissanti 3 ⊠ 50123 ℘ 264201, Telex 570022, Fax 210278, « Rest. with summer service on terrace with ← » – 50-350. AE VISA. rest AY **g**
M a la carte 88/133000 – 28500 – **192 rm** 368/536000, 10 suites.

Grand Hotel Ciga, piazza Ognissanti 1 ⊠ 50123 ℘ 288781, Telex 570055, Fax 217400 – 25-220. AE VISA. rest AXY **a**
M a la carte 65/134000 – 29000 – **107 rm** 405/595000, 17 suites.

Savoy, piazza della Repubblica 7 ⊠ 50123 ℘ 283313, Telex 570220, Fax 284840 – 150. AE VISA. rest BY **e**
M a la carte 75/120000 – **101 rm** 350/530000, 5 suites.

Villa Medici and Rest. Lorenzo de' Medici, via Il Prato 42 ⊠ 50123 ℘ 2381331, Telex 570179, Fax 2381336, – 30-90. AE VISA AX **g**
M a la carte 60/96000 – 28000 – **103 rm** 322/500000, 14 suites.

Regency and Rest. Relais le Jardin, piazza Massimo D'Azeglio 3 ⊠ 50121 ℘ 245247, Telex 571058, Fax 2342938, –. AE VISA. rest DX **c**
M *(closed Sunday)* (booking essential) a la carte 70/110000 – 25000 – **35 rm** 350/500000, 5 suites.

Helvetia e Bristol, via dei Pescioni 2 ⊠ 50123 ℘ 287814, Telex 572696, Fax 288353 – . AE VISA. BY **f**
M a la carte 68/106000 – 28000 – **52 rm** 352/524000, 15 suites.

Brunelleschi, piazza Santa Elisabetta 3 ⊠ 50122 ℘ 562068, Telex 575805, Fax 219653 – rm – 100. AE VISA. rest CY **p**
M a la carte 54/79000 – **94 rm** 275/375000, 7 suites.

Plaza Hotel Lucchesi, lungarno della Zecca Vecchia 38 ⊠ 50122 ℘ 264141, Telex 570302, Fax 2480921, ← – rm – 70-160. AE VISA. rest DY **f**
M (residents only) *(closed Sunday)* a la carte 54/87000 – **97 rm** 270/385000, 10 suites.

Grand Hotel Baglioni, piazza Unità Italiana 6 ⊠ 50123 ℘ 218441, Telex 570225, Fax 215695, « Roof-garden rest. with ← » – 25-200. AE VISA. rest BX **e**
M a la carte 48/63000 – **195 rm** 260/360000, 5 suites.

Jolly, piazza Vittorio Veneto 4/a ⊠ 50123 ℘ 2770, Telex 570191, Fax 294794, « on panoramic terrace » – rm – 30-100. AE VISA. rest AX **u**
M 40/52000 – **167 rm** 240/350000.

Majestic, via del Melarancio 1 ⊠ 50123 ℘ 264021, Telex 570628, Fax 268428 – 80. AE VISA. rest BX **u**
M a la carte 44/68000 – 27000 – **103 rm** 231/310000, 1 suite.

De la Ville, piazza Antinori 1 ⊠ 50123 ℘ 2381805, Telex 570518, Fax 2381809 – 60. AE VISA. BX **n**
M (residents only) a la carte 48/58000 – **75 rm** 254/361000, 4 suites.

Berchielli without rest., piazza del Limbo 6 r ⊠ 50123 ℘ 264061, Telex 575582, Fax 218636, ← – 100. AE VISA. BY **b**
74 rm 320/350000, 3 suites.

Bernini Palace without rest., piazza San Firenze 29 ✉ 50122 ℘ 288621, Telex 573616, Fax 268272 – |‡| ▤ TV ☎ – 🏛 40. AE ⓢ ⓞ E VISA CY **x**
86 rm ☐ 268/385000, 5 suites.

Montebello Splendid, via Montebello 60 ✉ 50123 ℘ 2398051, Telex 574009, Fax 211867, – |‡| ▤ TV ☎ – 🏛 100. AE ⓢ ⓞ E VISA. ✗ rest AX **e**
M *(closed Sunday)* a la carte 48/94000 – **53 rm** ☐ 240/345000, 1 suite.

Anglo American, via Garibaldi 9 ✉ 50123 ℘ 282114, Telex 570289, Fax 268513 – |‡| ▤ TV ☎ – 🏛 50-150. AE ⓢ ⓞ E VISA. ✗ rest AX **d**
M *(closed Sunday)* a la carte 65/90000 – **107 rm** ☐ 250/350000, 4 suites.

Gd H. Minerva, piazza Santa Maria Novella 16 ✉ 50123 ℘ 284555, Telex 570414, Fax 268281, – |‡| ▤ TV ☎ – 🏛 30-90. AE ⓢ ⓞ E VISA. ✗ rest BX **s**
M a la carte 42/69000 – ☐ 20000 – **96 rm** 235/310000, 3 suites.

Kraft, via Solferino 2 ✉ 50123 ℘ 284273, Telex 571523, Fax 2398267, « Roof-garden rest. with ≤ », – |‡| ▤ TV ☎ – 🏛 40-50. AE ⓢ ⓞ E VISA. ✗ rest AX **c**
M 45000 – **78 rm** ☐ 255/365000.

Londra, via Jacopo da Diacceto 18 ✉ 50123 ℘ 2382791, Telex 571152, Fax 210682, – |‡| ▤ TV ☎ ♿ – 🏛 200. AE ⓢ ⓞ E VISA. ✗ rest AX **n**
M a la carte 50/77000 – **158 rm** ☐ 255/350000.

Alexander, viale Guidoni 101 ✉ 50127 ℘ 4378951, Telex 574026, Fax 416818 – |‡| ▤ TV ☎ ♿ P – 🏛 50-300. AE ⓢ ⓞ E VISA by viale F. Redi AV
M a la carte 48/78000 – ☐ 28000 – **88 rm** 178/222000.

Augustus without rest., piazzetta dell'Oro 5 ✉ 50123 ℘ 283054, Telex 570110, Fax 268557 – |‡| ▤ TV ☎ – 🏛 70. AE ⓢ ⓞ E VISA BY **a**
☐ 20000 – **62 rm** 260/290000.

Pullman Astoria Palazzo Gaddi, via del Giglio 9 ✉ 50123 ℘ 2398095, Telex 571070, Fax 214632 – |‡| ▤ TV ☎ ♿ – 🏛 50-130. AE ⓢ ⓞ E VISA. ✗ rest BX **f**
M *(closed Sunday)* a la carte 51/79000 – **88 rm** ☐ 240/320000, 3 suites.

Sofitel, via de' Cerretani 10 ✉ 50123 ℘ 2381301, Telex 580515, Fax 2381312 – |‡| ⇔ rm ▤ TV ☎. AE ⓢ ⓞ E VISA. ✗ BX **h**
M a la carte 35/67000 – **84 rm** ☐ 280000.

Holiday Inn and Rest. la Tegolaia, viale Europa 205 ✉ 50126 ℘ 6531841, Telex 570376, Fax 6531806, – |‡| ⇔ rm ▤ TV ☎ ♿ P – 🏛 50-120. AE ⓢ ⓞ VISA. ✗ rest by via Orsini DZ
M a la carte 50/76000 – **92 rm** ☐ 225000.

Rivoli without rest., via della Scala 33 ✉ 50123 ℘ 282853, Telex 571004, Fax 294041, – |‡| ▤ TV ☎ ♿ – 🏛 100. AE ⓢ ⓞ E VISA. ✗ AX **f**
☐ 20000 – **62 rm** 230/300000.

Lungarno without rest., borgo Sant'Jacopo 14 ✉ 50125 ℘ 264211, Telex 570129, Fax 268437, ≤, « Collection of modern pictures » – |‡| ▤ TV ☎ – 🏛 30. AE ⓢ ⓞ E VISA BY **d**
☐ 20000 – **66 rm** 210/295000, 6 suites.

Pierre without rest., via de' Lamberti 5 ✉ 50123 ℘ 217512, Telex 573175, Fax 2396573 – |‡| ▤ TV ☎. AE ⓢ ⓞ E VISA BY **k**
☐ 25000 – **39 rm** 273000.

Raffaello, viale Morgagni 19 ✉ 50134 ℘ 4224141, Telex 580035, Fax 434374 – |‡| ▤ TV ☎ – 🏛 110. AE ⓢ ⓞ E VISA. ✗ rest by via del Romito AV
M a la carte 35/62000 – **141 rm** ☐ 290/315000, 4 suites.

Cavour without rest., via del Proconsolo 3 ✉ 50122 ℘ 282461, Telex 580318, Fax 218955, « Panoramic terrace with ≤ city » – |‡| ▤ TV ☎. AE ⓢ ⓞ E VISA. ✗ CY **c**
89 rm ☐ 130/210000.

Croce di Malta and Rest. il Coccodrillo, via della Scala 7 ✉ 50123 ℘ 218351, Telex 570540, Fax 287121, – |‡| ▤ TV ☎ ♿ – 🏛 50. AE ⓢ ⓞ E VISA. ✗ rest BX **d**
M *(closed Sunday and Monday lunch)* a la carte 40/65000 – **83 rm** ☐ 255/340000, 15 suites.

Principe without rest., lungarno Vespucci 34 ✉ 50123 ℘ 284848, Telex 571400, Fax 283458, ≤, – |‡| ▤ TV ☎. AE ⓢ ⓞ E VISA AX **b**
27 rm ☐ 265/365000.

J and J without rest., via di Mezzo 20 ✉ 50121 ℘ 240951, Telex 570554, Fax 240282 – ▤ TV ☎. AE ⓢ ⓞ E VISA. ✗ DY **c**
19 rm ☐ 320000, 2 suites.

Continental without rest., lungarno Acciaiuoli 2 ✉ 50123 ℘ 282392, Telex 580525, Fax 283139, « Floral terrace with ≤ » – |‡| ▤ TV ☎. AE ⓢ ⓞ E VISA BY **a**
☐ 20000 – **61 rm** 220/290000, 9 suites.

Calzaiuoli without rest., via Calzaiuoli 6 ✉ 50122 ℘ 212456, Telex 580589, Fax 268310 – |‡| ▤ TV ☎. AE ⓢ ⓞ E VISA CY **s**
☐ 12000 – **41 rm** 142000.

Loggiato dei Serviti without rest., piazza SS. Annunziata 3 ✉ 50122 ℘ 289592, Telex 575808, Fax 289595 – |‡| ▤ TV ☎. AE ⓢ ⓞ E VISA CX **d**
29 rm ☐ 140/210000, 4 suites.

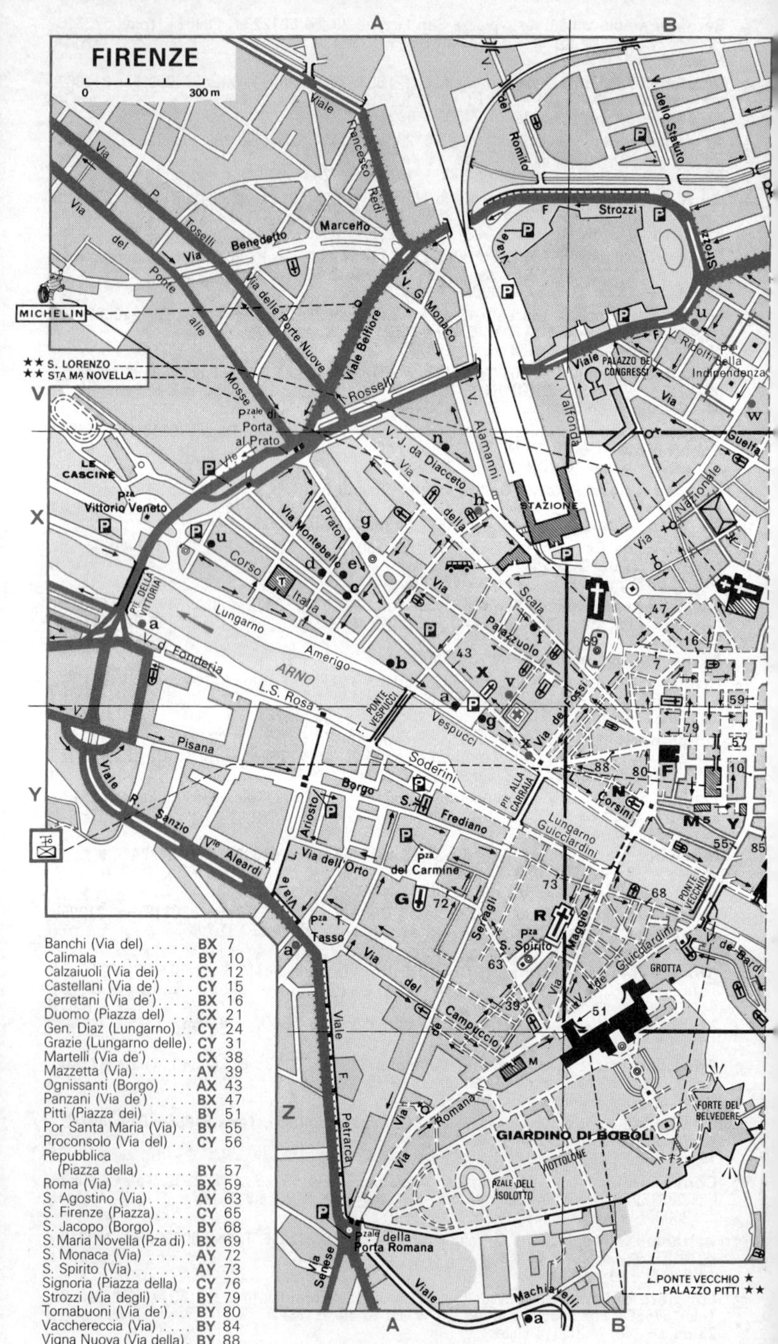

Banchi (Via del) . . . . . . **BX** 7
Calimala . . . . **BY** 10
Calzaiuoli (Via dei) . . . . **CY** 12
Castellani (Via de') . . . . **CY** 15
Cerretani (Via de') . . . . . **BX** 16
Duomo (Piazza del) . . . **CX** 21
Gen. Diaz (Lungarno) . . **CY** 24
Grazie (Lungarno delle) . **CY** 31
Martelli (Via de') . . . . . . **CX** 38
Mazzetta (Via) . . . . **AY** 39
Ognissanti (Borgo) . . . . **AX** 43
Panzani (Via de') . . . . . . **BX** 47
Pitti (Piazza dei) . . . . . . **BY** 51
Por Santa Maria (Via) . . **BY** 55
Proconsolo (Via del) . . . **CY** 56
Repubblica
(Piazza della) . . . . **BY** 57
Roma (Via) . . . . **BX** 59
S. Agostino (Via) . . . . . . **AY** 63
S. Firenze (Piazza) . . . . . **CY** 65
S. Jacopo (Borgo) . . . . . **BY** 68
S. Maria Novella (Pza di) . **BX** 69
S. Monaca (Via) . . . . **AY** 72
S. Spirito (Via) . . . . **AY** 73
Signoria (Piazza della) . **CY** 76
Strozzi (Via degli) . . . . . **BY** 79
Tornabuoni (Via de') . . . **BY** 80
Vaccchereccia (Via) . . . . **BY** 84
Vigna Nuova (Via della) . **BY** 88

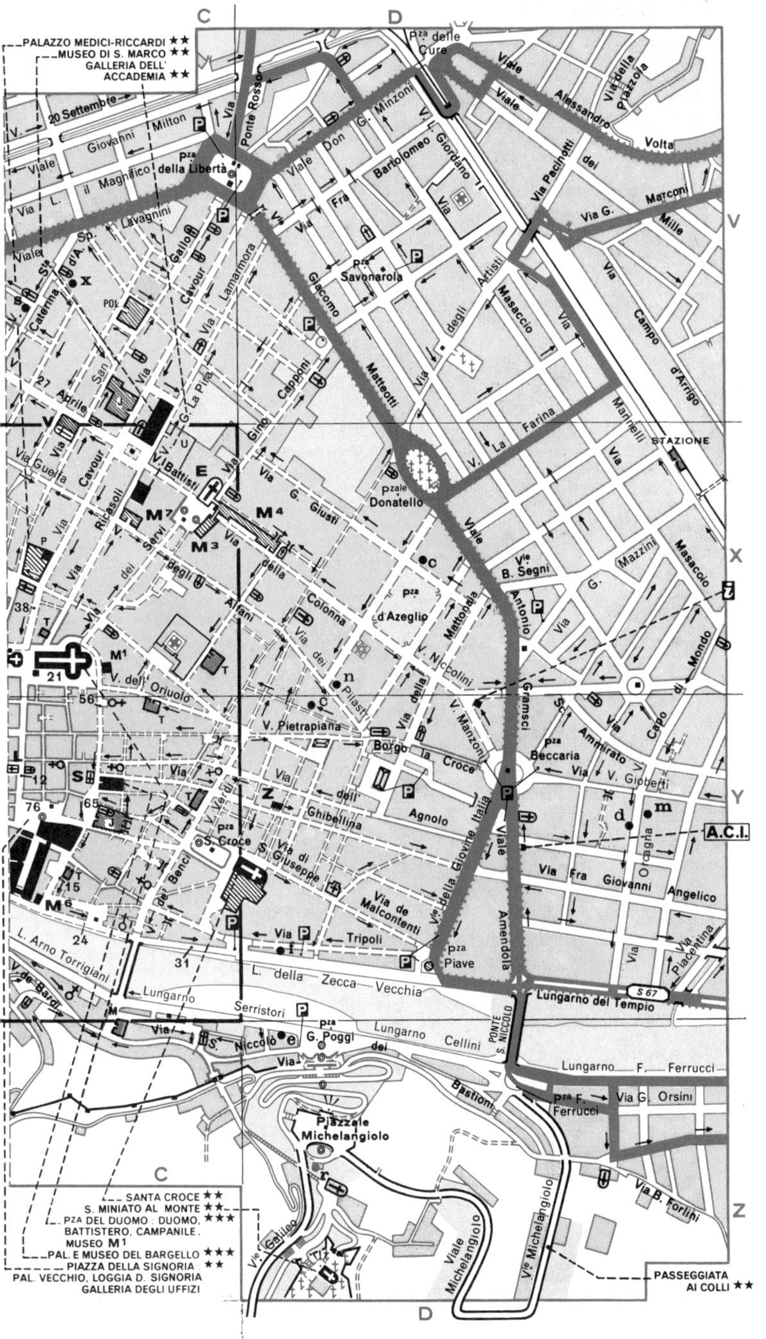
PALAZZO MEDICI-RICCARDI ★★
MUSEO DI S. MARCO ★★
GALLERIA DELL' ACCADEMIA ★★
SANTA CROCE ★★
S. MINIATO AL MONTE ★★
Pza DEL DUOMO : DUOMO, BATTISTERO, CAMPANILE, MUSEO M1 ★★★
PAL. E MUSEO DEL BARGELLO ★★★
PIAZZA DELLA SIGNORIA ★★
PAL. VECCHIO, LOGGIA D. SIGNORIA
GALLERIA DEGLI UFFIZI
PASSEGGIATA AI COLLI ★★
STAZIONE
A.C.I.
Pza della Libertà
Ponte Rosso
Pza delle Cure
Pza Savonarola
Pzale Donatello
Pza d'Azeglio
Pza Beccaria
Pza S. Croce
Pza Piave
Pza G. Poggi
Pza F. Ferrucci
Piazzale Michelangiolo
PONTE S. NICCOLÒ
Lungarno del Tempio
Lungarno Serristori
Lungarno Cellini
Lungarno F. Ferrucci
L. della Zecca Vecchia
L. Arno Torrigiani
Viale Matteotti
Viale Antonio Gramsci
Viale Amendola
Viale Michelangiolo
Vle Galileo
Via G. Orsini
Via B. Forlini
Via Fra Giovanni Angelico
Via Ghibellina
Borgo la Croce
Via dell' Agnolo
Via Pietrapiana
Via dei Pilastri
Via della Colonna
Via Giusti
Via Gino Capponi
Via Cavour
Via Ricasoli
Via dei Servi
Via degli Alfani
V. dell' Oriuolo
Via Tripoli
Via de Malcontenti
Via di S. Giuseppe
Via Verdi
Via de' Benci
V. de Bardi
Via S. Niccolò
Via dei Bastioni
Via Lamarmora
Via La Pira
Via Guelfa
Via San Gallo
Via 27 Aprile
Via Sta Caterina d'A.
Viale Giovanni Milton
Via XX Settembre
Viale Lavagnini
Viale Don G. Minzoni
Via Bartolomeo Giordano
Viale Fra Giacomo
Via degli Artisti
Via Masaccio
Via Mannelli
Via Campo d'Arrigo
Via Pacinotti
Viale Alessandro Volta
Via della Piazzola
Viale dei Mille
Via G. Marconi
Via La Farina
Via Mazzini
Via Capo di Mondo
Via V. Gioberti
Via Orcagna
Via Piacentina
V. Manzoni
Via della Mattonaia
V. Niccolini
Vle della Giovine Italia
Vle B. Segni
Sc. Ammirato
S 67
M1 M3 M4 M6 M7
C D V X Y Z

FIRENZE

Calimala . . . . BY 10
Calzaiuoli (Via dei) . . . . CY
Guicciardini (Via) . . . . BY
Ponte Vecchio . . . . BY
Por Santa Maria (Via) . . . . BY 55
Porta Rossa (Via) . . . . BY
Roma (Via) . . . . BXY
S. Jacopo (Borgo) . . . . BY
Strozzi (Via degli) . . . . BY
Tornabuoni (Via de) . . . . . BXY

Archibusieri (Lungarno degli) . . . . . . BY 4
Avelli (Via degli) . . . . BX 6
Baroncelli (Chiasso dei) . . . . BCY 8
Canto de' Nelli (Via) . . . . . BX 13
Castellani (Via de') . . . . . . CY 15
Duomo (Piazza del) . . . . . . CX 21
Leoni (Via dei) . . . . CY 33
Medici (Lungarno A.M.Luisa de') . . . . CY 40
Pellicceria (Via) . . . . BY 49
Repubblica (Piazza della) . BY 57
Rondinelli (Via de') . . . . . . BX 60
S. Firenze (Piazza) . . . . CY 65
S. Giovanni (Piazza) . . . . . . BX 67
S. Maria Nuova (Piazza di) . . . . CX 69
Sassetti (Via de') . . . . BY 73
Signoria (Piazza della) . . . . CY 76
Speziali (Via degli) . . . . BCY 77
Trebbio (Via del) . . . . BX 81
Uffizi (Piazzale degli) . . . . . CY 83
Unità Italiana (Piazza) . . . . BX 84
Vaccchereccia (Via) . . . . BY 85
Vecchietti (Via de') . . . . . . BXY 86

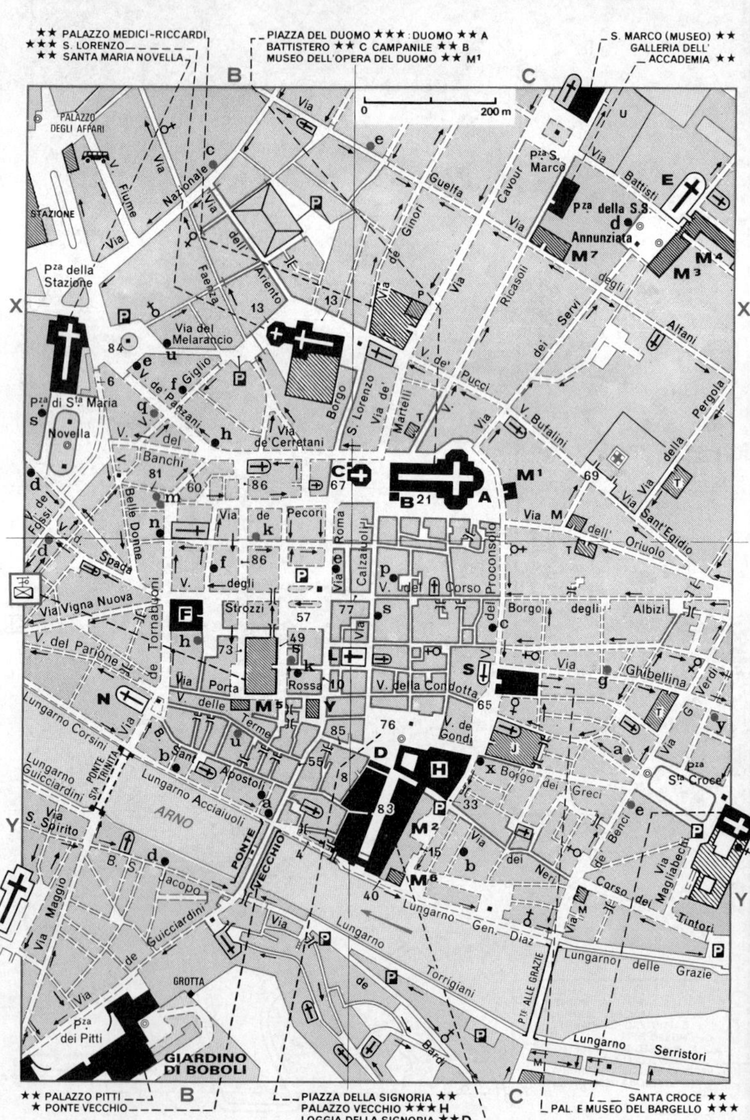

Grifone without rest., via Pilati 22 ✉ 50136 ☎ 661367, Telex 570624, Fax 677628 – |♦| ▤ TV ☎ P – 🏃 50-200. AE ⑤ ⊙ E VISA. ✂ by Lungarno del Tempio DY
62 rm ☕ 168/186000, 8 suites.

Royal without rest., via delle Ruote 52 ✉ 50129 ☎ 483287, Fax 490976, « Garden » – |♦| ▤ TV ☎ P. AE ⑤ E VISA CV **x**
39 rm ☕ 131/202000.

Rapallo, via di Santa Caterina d'Alessandria 7 ✉ 50129 ☎ 472412, Telex 574251, Fax 470385 – |♦| ▤ TV ☎ 🚗. AE ⑤ ⊙ E VISA. ✂ CV **s**
M (residents only) 32000 – ☕ 13000 – **30 rm** 89/132000.

Franchi without rest., via Sgambati 28 ✉ 50127 ☎ 315425, Telex 580425, Fax 315563 – |♦| TV ☎ P. AE ⑤ ⊙ E VISA by via P. Toselli AV
☕ 14000 – **35 rm** 86/127000.

Arizona without rest., via Farini 2 ✉ 50121 ☎ 245321, Telex 575572 – |♦| TV ☎. AE ⑤ ⊙ E VISA. ✂ DX **n**
21 rm ☕ 110/158000.

Fiorino without rest., via Osteria del Guanto 6 ✉ 50122 ☎ 210579, Fax 210579 – ▤ ☎
☕ 14000 – **21 rm** 65/95000, ▤ 8000. CY **b**

Jane without rest., via Orcagna 56 ✉ 50121 ☎ 677382, Fax 677383 – |♦| ▤ TV ☎. ✂
☕ 10000 – **24 rm** 80/105000, ▤ 7000. DY **m**

Orcagna without rest., via Orcagna 57 ✉ 50121 ☎ 669959 – |♦| ☎. ⑤ ⊙ E VISA DY **d**
18 rm ☕ 110/130000.

San Remo without rest., lungarno Serristori 13 ✉ 50125 ☎ 2342823, Fax 2342269 – |♦| ▤ TV ☎. AE ⑤ ⊙ E VISA DZ **e**
☕ 9000 – **20 rm** 90/127000.

XXXX ✿✿✿ **Enoteca Pinchiorri,** via Ghibellina 87 ✉ 50122 ☎ 242777, Fax 244983, « Summer service in a cool courtyard » – ▤. AE – *closed Sunday, Monday lunch, August and 24 to 28 December* – **M** (booking essential) a la carte 115/185000 CY **y**
Spec. Lamelle di branzino e vitello con verdure, Gnocchetti di patate ripieni di pesto al brodetto di calamaretti, Costolette di agnello con timballo di melanzane e pomodori verdi. Wines Cervaro della Sala, Cannaio di Monte Vertine.

XXXX **Sabatini,** via de' Panzani 9/a ✉ 50123 ☎ 211559, Fax 210293, Elegant traditional decor – ▤. AE ⑤ ⊙ E VISA. ✂ BX **q**
closed Monday – **M** a la carte 61/100000 (13 %).

XXX Doney, piazza Strozzi 18 r ✉ 50123 ☎ 239806, Fax 2398182, 🏠 BY **h**

XXX **Harry's Bar,** lungarno Vespucci 22 r ✉ 50123 ☎ 2396700 – ▤. AE ⑤ E VISA AY **x**
closed Sunday and 15 December-5 January – **M** (booking essential) a la carte 51/74000 (16 %).

XXX **La Loggia,** piazzale Michelangiolo 1 ✉ 50125 ☎ 2342832, Fax 2345288, « Outdoor summer service with ⩽ » – ▤ P – 🏃 50. AE ⑤ ⊙ E VISA DZ **r**
closed Wednesday and 4 to 19 August – **M** a la carte 49/74000 (13 %).

XXX **Al Lume di Candela,** via delle Terme 23 r ✉ 50123 ☎ 294566 – ▤. AE ⑤ ⊙ E VISA. ✂
closed Sunday and 10 to 25 August – **M** (dinner only) (booking essential) a la carte 53/86000 (14 %). BY **u**

XXX ✿ **Don Chisciotte,** via Ridolfi 4 r ✉ 50129 ☎ 475430 – ▤. AE ⑤ ⊙ E VISA BV **u**
closed Sunday, Monday lunch and August – **M** (booking essential) a la carte 50/74000
Spec. Panzanella di mare, Tagliatelle agli scampi, Rombo ai porcini. Wines Verdicchio, Chianti.

XX **Al Campidoglio,** via del Campidoglio 8 r ✉ 50123 ☎ 287770, Fax 287770 – ▤. AE ⑤ ⊙ E VISA. ✂ BXY **k**
closed Tuesday – **M** a la carte 30/40000 (10 %).

XX **I 4 Amici,** via degli Orti Oricellari 29 ✉ 50123 ☎ 215413 – ▤. AE ⑤ ⊙ E VISA. ✂
closed Wednesday and 7 to 25 August – **M** (fish only) a la carte 50/63000 (12 %). AX **h**

XX **La Posta,** via de' Lamberti 20 r ✉ 50123 ☎ 212701 – ▤. AE ⑤ E VISA BY **s**
closed Tuesday – **M** a la carte 40/67000 (13 %).

XX **i' Toscano,** via Guelfa 70/r ✉ 50129 ☎ 215475 – ▤. AE ⑤ ⊙ E VISA. ✂ CX **e**
closed Tuesday and August – **M** a la carte 29/53000.

XX **Leo in Santa Croce,** via Torta 7 r ✉ 50122 ☎ 210829, Fax 2396705 – ▤. AE ⑤ ⊙ E VISA. ✂ CY **a**
closed Monday and 23 July-7 August – **M** a la carte 41/65000 (12 %).

XX **13 Gobbi,** via del Porcellana 9 r ✉ 50123 ☎ 2398769, Tuscan rest. – ▤. ⑤ ⊙ E VISA
closed Sunday, Monday and 31 July-30 August – **M** a la carte 41/62000 (12 %). AX **v**

XX **Buca Mario,** piazza Ottaviani 16 r ✉ 50123 ☎ 214179, Fax 214179, Typical trattoria – ▤. AE ⑤ ⊙ E VISA. ✂ BXY **d**
closed Wednesday, Thursday lunch and August – **M** a la carte 44/64000 (12 %).

XX **Acquerello,** via Ghibellina 156 r ✉ 50122 ☎ 2340554 – ▤. AE ⑤ ⊙ E VISA CY **g**
closed Thursday – **M** a la carte 35/52000 (12 %).

XX **Cantinetta Antinori,** piazza Antinori 3 ✉ 50123 ☎ 292234, Tuscan rest. – ▤. AE ⑤ ⊙ E VISA. ✂ BX **m**
closed Saturday, Sunday, August and Christmas – **M** a la carte 49/70000 (10 %).

XX **Le Fonticine,** via Nazionale 79 r ✉ 50123 ☎ 282106 – AE ⑤ ⊙ E VISA. ✂ BX **c**
closed Monday and 22 July-22 August – **M** a la carte 39/59000 (12 %).

La Capannina di Sante, piazza Ravenna ang. Ponte da Verrazzano ✉ 50126 ℘ 688345, ≤, – ▤. AE Ⓢ ⓞ E VISA. ✗ by Lungarno F. Ferrucci DZ
closed Sunday, Monday lunch, 10 to 20 August and 24 to 31 December – **M** (fish only) a la carte 53/83000.

Trattoria Vittoria, via della Fonderia 52 r ✉ 50142 ℘ 225657 – ▤. AE Ⓢ ⓞ E VISA
closed Wednesday and 15 to 30 August – **M** (fish only) a la carte 68/80000 (12 %). AX **a**

Il Giardino di Barbano, piazza Indipendenza 3 r ✉ 50129 ℘ 486752, « Summer service in garden » – AE Ⓢ ⓞ E VISA BV **w**
closed Wednesday – **M** a la carte 25/39000.

Buca Lapi, via del Trebbio 1 r ✉ 50123 ℘ 213768, Typical tavern – ▤. AE Ⓢ ⓞ E VISA BX **m**
closed Sunday and Monday lunch – **M** a la carte 39/53000 (12 %).

Alla Vecchia Bettola, viale Ludovico Ariosto 32 r ✉ 50124 ℘ 224158, « Local atmosphere » – ✗ AY **a**
closed Sunday, Monday, August and 23 December-2 January – **M** a la carte 28/47000.

on the hills S : 3 km :

Gd H. Villa Cora and Rest. Taverna Machiavelli ♨, viale Machiavelli 18 ✉ 50125 ℘ 2298451, Telex 570604, Fax 229086, , « Floral park with ⛱ » – |♦| ▤ TV ☎ Ⓟ – 🏛 50-150. AE Ⓢ ⓞ E VISA. ✗ rest by viale Machiavelli ABZ
M a la carte 52/76000 (15 %) – ☕ 24000 – **48 rm** 464/539000, 16 suites.

Torre di Bellosguardo ♨ without rest., via Roti Michelozzi 2 ✉ 50124 ℘ 2298145, Fax 229008, ✳ town and hills, « Park and terrace with ⛱ » – |♦| ☎ Ⓟ. AE Ⓢ ⓞ E VISA by via Senese AZ
☕ 22000 – **10 rm** 230/300000, 6 suites.

Villa Carlotta ♨, via Michele di Lando 3 ✉ 50125 ℘ 2336134, Telex 573485, Fax 2336147, – |♦| ▤ TV ☎ Ⓟ. AE Ⓢ ⓞ E VISA. ✗ rest AZ **a**
M (resident only) a la carte 46/74000 – **27 rm** ☕ 240/340000.

Villa Belvedere ♨ without rest., via Benedetto Castelli 3 ✉ 50124 ℘ 222501, Telex 575648, Fax 223163, ≤ town and hills, « Garden-Park with ⛱ », ✂ – |♦| ▤ TV ☎ ♿ Ⓟ. AE Ⓢ ⓞ E VISA. ✗ by via Senese AZ
March-November – **27 rm** ☕ 180/280000.

Antico Crespino, largo Enrico Fermi 15 ✉ 50125 ℘ 221155, Fax 221155, ≤ – AE Ⓢ ⓞ E VISA by via Senese AZ
closed Wednesday and 25 July-20 August – **M** a la carte 41/77000 (13 %).

at Arcetri S : 5 km – ✉ **50125** Firenze :

Omero, via Pian de' Giullari 11 r ℘ 220053, Country trattoria with ≤, « Summer service on terrace » – AE Ⓢ ⓞ E VISA. ✗ by viale Galileo DZ
closed Tuesday and August – **M** a la carte 39/45000 (13 %).

at Galluzzo S : 6,5 km – ✉ **50124** Firenze :

Relais Certosa, via Colle Ramole 2 ℘ 2047171, Telex 574332, Fax 268575, ≤, « Garden-Park », ✂ – |♦| ▤ TV ☎ Ⓟ – 🏛 35-70. AE Ⓢ ⓞ E VISA. ✗ rest
M a la carte 47/77000 – **69 rm** ☕ 258/295000, 6 suites. by via Senese AZ

at Candeli E : 7 km – ✉ **50010** :

Villa La Massa and Rest. Il Verrocchio ♨, via La Massa 6 ℘ 666141, Telex 573555, Fax 632579, ≤, , « 18C house and furnishings », ⛱, , ✂ – |♦| ▤ TV ☎ ♿ Ⓟ – 🏛 120. AE Ⓢ ⓞ E VISA. ✗ rest
M *(closed Monday and Tuesday lunch November-March)* a la carte 55/70000 – **39 rm** ☕ 290/490000, 5 suites.

towards Trespiano N : 7 km :

Villa le Rondini ♨, via Bolognese Vecchia 224 ✉ 50139 Firenze ℘ 400081, Telex 575679, Fax 268212, ≤ town, « Among the olive trees », ⛱, , ✂ – ☎ Ⓟ – 🏛 80-200. AE Ⓢ ⓞ E VISA. ✗ rest
M 45/90000 – **33 rm** ☕ 160/250000, 2 suites.

on the motorway at ring-road A1-A11 NW : 10 km

MotelAgip, ✉ 50013 Campi Bisenzio ℘ 4211881, Telex 570263, Fax 4219015 – |♦| ▤ TV ☎ ♿ Ⓟ – 🏛 40-200. AE Ⓢ ⓞ E VISA. ✗ rest
M *(closed Sunday)* 50000 – **163 rm** ☕ 165/250000.

close to motorway station A1 Florence South SE : 6 km :

Sheraton Firenze Hotel, ✉ 50126 ℘ 64901, Telex 575860, Fax 680747, ⛱, ✂ – |♦| ⇔ rm ▤ TV ☎ ♿ 🚗 Ⓟ – 🏛 30-1500. AE Ⓢ ⓞ E VISA. ✗
M a la carte 58/92000 – **301 rm** ☕ 332000, 20 suites.

MILAN (MILANO) 20100 P 988 ③ 428 F 9 – pop. 1 423 184 alt. 122 – ☎ 02.

See: Cathedral*** (Duomo) MZ – Cathedral Museum** MZ **M1** – Via and Piazza Mercanti* MZ **155** – La Scala Opera House* MZ – Brera Art Gallery*** KV - Castle of the Sforzas*** JV : Municipal Art Collection*** Sempione Park* HJUV – Ambrosian Library** MZ : portraits*** of Gaffurio and Isabella d'Este, Raphael's cartoons*** – Poldi-Pezzoli Museum** KV **M2** : portrait of a woman*** (in profile) by Pollaiolo – Leonardo da Vinci Museum of Science and Technology* HX **M4** : Leonardo da Vinci Gallery** – Church of St. Mary of Grace* HX : Leonardo da Vinci's Last Supper*** – Basilica of St. Ambrose* HJX : altar front** – Church of St. Eustorgius* JY : Portinari Chapel** General Hospital* KXY **U** – Church of St. Maurice* JX – Church of St. Lawrence Major* JY – Dome* of the Church of St. Satiro MZ **E.**

Envir.: Chiaravalle Abbey* SE : 7 km.

18, 9 (closed Monday) at Monza Park ✉ 20052 Monza ☎ (039) 303081, Fax 304427 by N : 20 km;

18 Molinetto (closed Monday) at Cernusco sul Naviglio ✉ 20063 ☎ (02) 92105128, Fax 92106635 by NE : 14 km;

18 Barlassina (closed Monday) at Birago di Camnago ✉ 20030 ☎ (0362) 560621, Fax 560934 by N : 26 km;

18 (closed Monday) at Zoate di Tribiano ✉ 20067 ☎ (02) 90632183, Fax 90631861 SE : 20 km;

9 Le Rovedine (closed Monday) at Noverasco di Opera ✉ 20090 Opera ☎ (02) 57602730, Fax 57606405 by via Ripamonti KY.

Motor-Racing circuit at Monza Park by N : 20 km, ☎ (039) 22366.

✈ Forlanini of Linate E : 8 km ☎ 74852200 and Malpensa by NW : 45 km ☎ 74852200 – Alitalia, corso Como 15 ✉ 20154 ☎ 62818 and via Albricci 5 ✉ 20122 ☎ 62817.

☎ 6690734.

i via Marconi 1 ✉ 20123 ☎ 809662, Fax 72022432 – Central Station ✉ 20124 ☎ 6690532.

A.C.I. corso Venezia 43 ✉ 20121 ☎ 77451.

Roma 572 ⑦ – Genève 323 ⑫ – Genova 142 ⑨ – Torino 140 ⑫.

Plans on following pages

Historical centre - Duomo, Scala, Sforza Castle, corso Magenta, via Torino, corso Vittorio Emanuele, via Manzoni :

Jolly Hotel President, largo Augusto 10 ✉ 20122 ☎ 7746, Telex 312054, Fax 783449 – rm ☎ – 30-100. AE VISA. rest NZ **q**
M a la carte 69/106000 – **220 rm** 390/460000.

Brunelleschi, via Baracchini 12 ✉ 20123 ☎ 8843, Telex 312256, Fax 870144 – TV ☎ – 40. AE VISA. MZ **z**
M (residents only) *(closed Saturday and August)* a la carte 57/80000 – **128 rm** 330/500000 5 suites.

Dei Cavalieri, piazza Missori 1 ✉ 20123 ☎ 8857, Telex 312040, Fax 72021683 – TV ☎ – 40-60. AE VISA. rest MZ **m**
M *(dinner only)* 70/136000 – **177 rm** 265/313000, 7 suites.

Pierre Milano, via Edmondo de Amicis 32 ✉ 20123 ☎ 72000581, Telex 333303, Fax 8052157 – TV ☎. AE VISA. JY **b**
M *(closed August)* a la carte 65/108000 – **47 rm** 230/570000, 6 suites.

Gd H. Duomo, via San Raffaele 1 ✉ 20121 ☎ 8833, Telex 312086, Fax 86462027 – TV ☎. AE VISA. MZ **u**
M 48/81000 – 20000 – **160 rm** 290/380000, 18 suites.

Galileo without rest., corso Europa 9 ✉ 20122 ☎ 7743, Telex 322095, Fax 76020584 – TV ☎. AE VISA. NZ **x**
76 rm 330/440000, 6 suites.

Carlton Hotel Senato, via Senato 5 ✉ 20121 ☎ 76015535, Telex 331306, Fax 783300 – TV ☎. AE VISA. rest KV **b**
closed August – **M** *(closed Saturday, Sunday and 20 December-7 January)* a la carte 54/76000 – 18000 – **79 rm** 220/280000.

Bonaparte Hotel, via Cusani 13 ✉ 20121 ☎ 8560, Fax 8693601 – TV ☎ – 25. AE VISA. rest JV **a**
M a la carte 55/89000 – **56 rm** 420000, 13 suites.

Cavour, via Fatebenefratelli 21 ✉ 20121 ☎ 6572051, Telex 320498, Fax 6592263 – TV ☎. AE VISA. rest KV **r**
M *(closed Friday dinner, Saturday and Sunday lunch)* 55000 – 16000 – **113 rm** 225/250000 2 suites.

Spadari al Duomo, via Spadari 11 ✉ 20123 ☎ 72002371, Fax 861184, « Collection of modern art » – TV ☎. AE VISA. MZ **f**
closed August – **M** (residents only) a la carte 42/66000 – **38 rm** 330/450000.

Rosa, without rest., via Pattari 5 ✉ 20122 ☎ 8831, Telex 316067, Fax 8057964 – TV ☎ – 30-120 – **184 rm**. NZ **v**

De la Ville without rest., via Hoepli 6 ✉ 20121 ☎ 867651, Telex 312642, Fax 866609 – TV ☎ – 60. AE VISA NZ **h**
104 rm 330/400000, 2 suites.

MILANO

Street	Ref.
Augusto (Largo)	KX 12
Aurispa (V.)	JY 14
Battisti (V. C.)	KLX 20
Bocchetto (V.)	JX 30
Borgogna (V.)	KX 36
Borgonuovo (V.)	KV 38
Calatafimi (V.)	JY 45
Castelbarco	KY 56
Cerano (V.)	HY 57
Ceresio (V.)	JU 59
Circo (V.)	JX 63
Col di Lana (Vie)	JY 65
Col Moschin (V.)	JY 66
Conça del Naviglio (V.)	JY 69
Cordusio (Pza)	KX 72
Cune (Vie P.M.)	HV 77
Dugnani (V.)	HY 80
Edison (Pza)	JX 83
Fatebenefratelli (V.)	KV 92
Gangliano (V.)	KT 98
Ghislen (V. A.)	HY 101
Giardini (V. dei)	KV 102
Guastalla (V.)	KX 110
Induno (V. Flli)	HT 116
Lambertenghi (V.P.)	KT 122
Lepetit (V.)	LTU 128
Maffei (V. A.)	LY 135

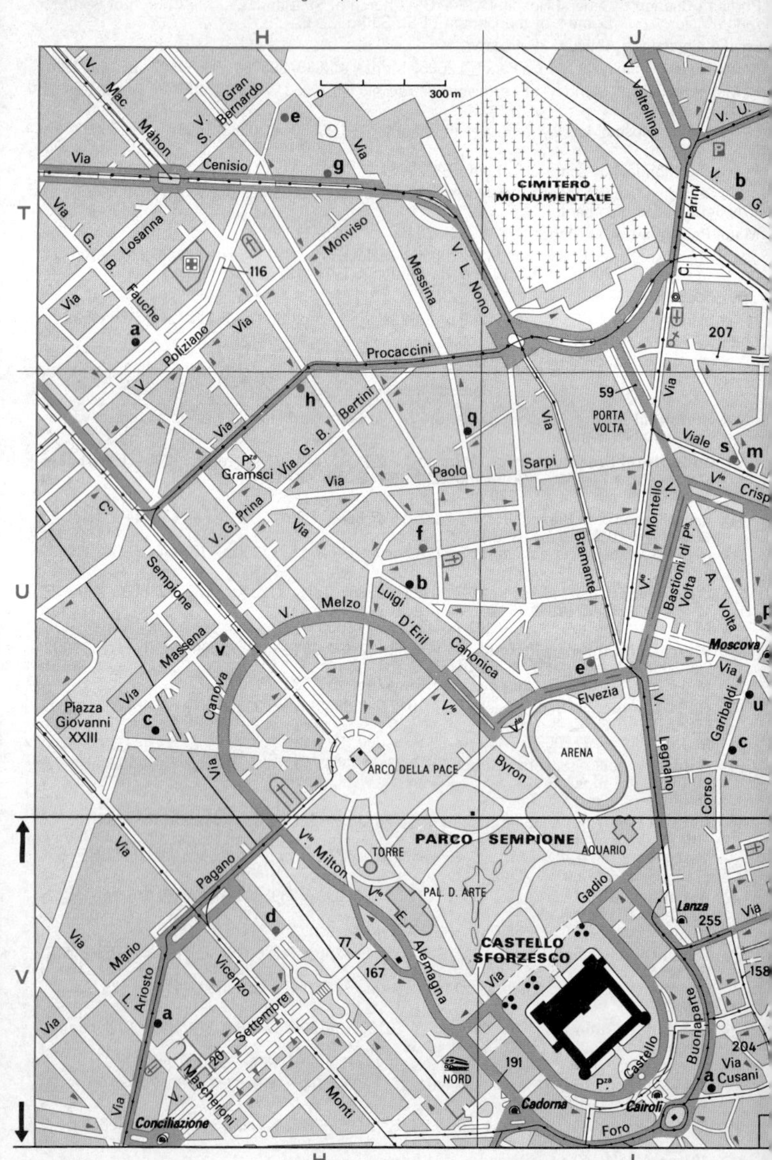

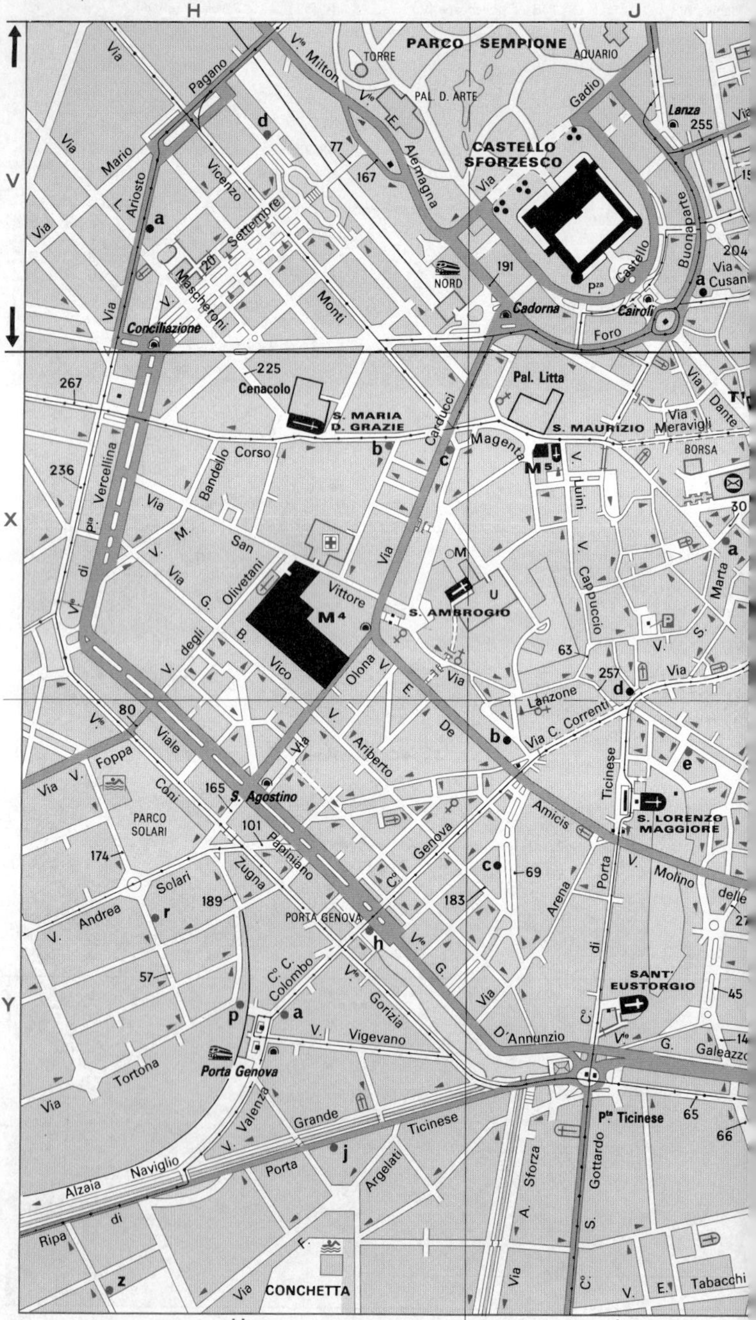

H J

V X Y

PARCO SEMPIONE
TORRE
AQUARIO
PAL. D. ARTE
CASTELLO SFORZESCO
Vle Milton
Vle E. Alemagna
Via Pagano
Via Mario
L. Ariosto
Via Vicenzo
20 Settembre
Mascheroni
Monti
Conciliazione
NORD
Cadorna
Cairoli
Lanza
Foro
Pza Castello
Via Gadio
Buonaparte
Via Cusani
Via Dante
Via Meravigli
BORSA
Pal. Litta
S. MAURIZIO
Magenta
M5
V. Luini
V. Cappuccio
Cenacolo
S. MARIA D. GRAZIE
Corso
Bandello
Carducci
Via Vercellina
Pta
V. M. San Vittore
Via G. Olivetani
V. degli
B. Vico
M4
S. AMBROGIO
Via Lanzone
Via C. Correnti
V. Olona
V. E. De Amicis
V. Ariberto
Via Marta
Ticinese
S. LORENZO MAGGIORE
V. Molino delle
Vle Foppa
Viale Coni
Via V.
PARCO SOLARI
S. Agostino
Papiniano
Zugna
Solari
V. Andrea
Cso Genova
PORTA GENOVA
Vle G. D'Annunzio
Arena
Porta di
SANT' EUSTORGIO
Vle G. Galeazzo
Cso C. Colombo
Vle Gorizia
V. Vigevano
Porta Genova
Via Tortona
V. Valenza
Grande
Ticinese
Porta
Argelati
Pta Ticinese
Alzaia Naviglio
Ripa di
A. Sforza
Cso S. Gottardo
Via
V. E. Tabacchi
CONCHETTA
Via

a b c d e h j p r z
225 267 236 77 167 191 255 204 30 63 257 80 165 101 174 189 183 69 57 45 14 65 66 27

H J

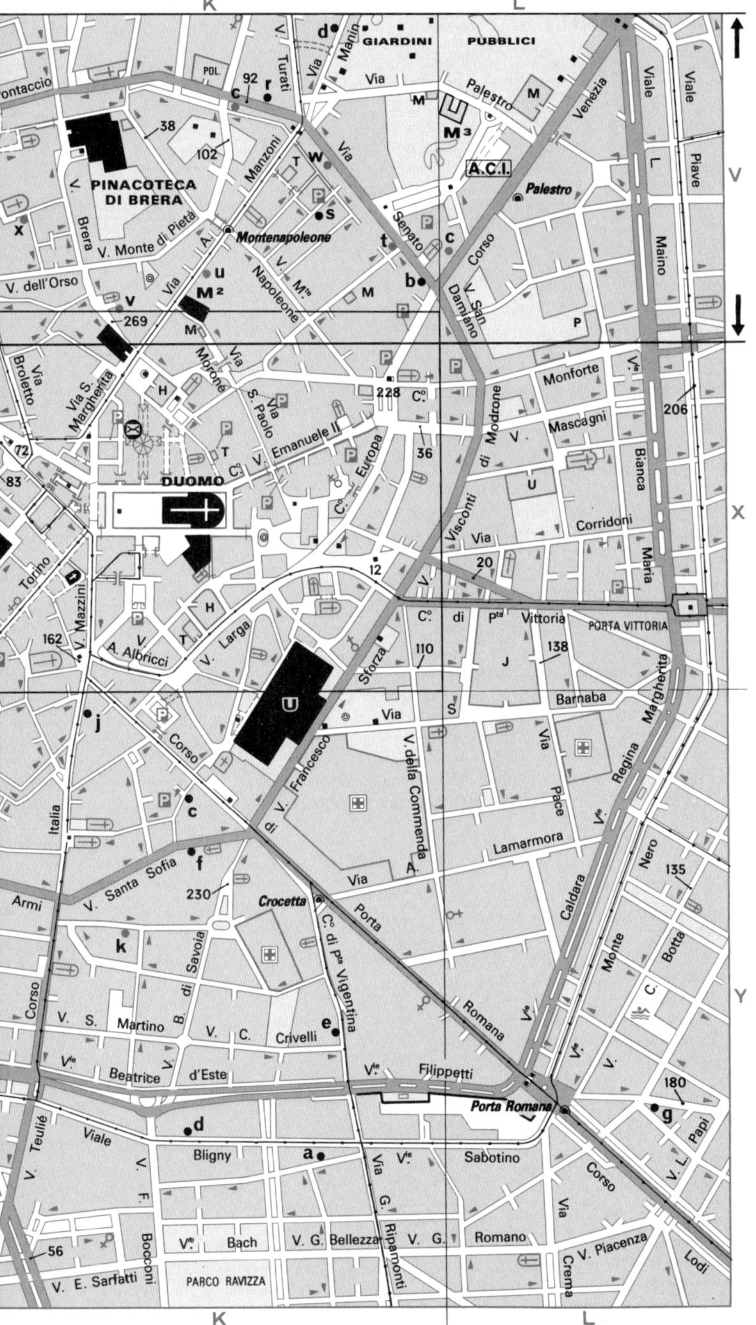

K
L
GIARDINI PUBBLICI
PINACOTECA DI BRERA
Montenapoleone
Palestro
A.C.I.
DUOMO
Crocetta
Porta Romana
PORTA VITTORIA
PARCO RAVIZZA
V. Turati
Via Manin
Via Palestro
Via Manzoni
Via Senato
Corso Venezia
Viale Piave
Viale L. Maino
V. Monte di Pietà
V. dell'Orso
Brera
V. Napoleone
Via Morone
Via S. Paolo
C. V. Emanuele II
C. Europa
V. San Damiano
Via Visconti di Modrone
V. Monforte
V. Mascagni
Via Corridoni
Viale Bianca Maria
Via S. Margherita
Via Broletto
Torino
V. Mazzini
V. A. Albricci
V. Larga
Via Sforza
Via Francesco
C. di Pta Vittoria
Via Barnaba
Via Pace
V. della Commenda
Via Lamarmora
Viale Regina Margherita
Corso Italia
V. Santa Sofia
Armi
Corso di Porta Romana
C. di Pta Vigentina
V. di Savoia
V. S. Martino
V. C. Crivelli
Vle Beatrice d'Este
Vle Filippetti
Viale Bligny
Vle Sabotino
Via G. Ripamonti
V. G. Bellezza
V. G. Romano
Via Crema
V. Piacenza
Corso Lodi
V. L. Papi
V. Teulié
V. F. Bocconi
Vle Bach
V. E. Sarfatti
C. Monte Nero
C. Botta
Vle Caldara
V. Morone
V. Mte Napoleone
V
X
Y

MILANO

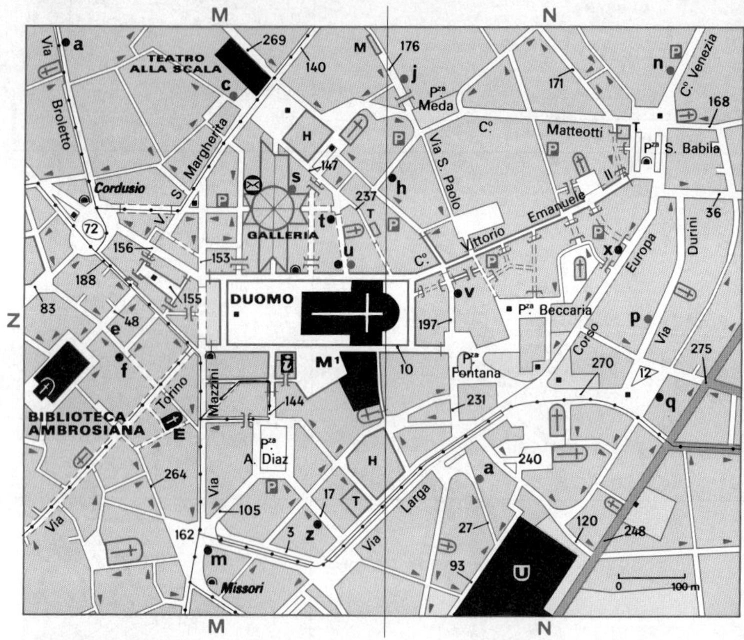

Ascot without rest., via Lentasio 3/5 ⊠ 20122 ℘ 58303300, Telex 311303, Fax 58303203 – . AE E VISA. KY **c**
closed August – **63 rm** 215/310000.

Manzoni without rest., via Santo Spirito 20 ⊠ 20121 ℘ 76005700, Fax 784212 – . AE E VISA. KV **s**
16000 – **52 rm** 140/192000, 3 suites.

Ambrosiano without rest., via Santa Sofia 9 ⊠ 20122 ℘ 58306044, Telex 333872, Fax 58305067 – . AE E VISA. KY **f**
closed 23 December-2 January and August – **79 rm** 137/205000.

Carrobbio without rest., via Medici 3 ⊠ 20123 ℘ 89010740, Fax 8053334 – . AE E VISA JX **d**
closed August and 22 December-6 January – **35 rm** 210/290000, 1 suite.

Zurigo without rest., corso Italia 11/a ⊠ 20122 ℘ 72022260, Telex 353091, Fax 72000013 – . AE E VISA KY **j**
closed 24 December-7 January – **41 rm** 160/250000.

Casa Svizzera without rest., via San Raffaele 3 ⊠ 20121 ℘ 8692246, Telex 316064, Fax 72004690 – . AE E VISA MZ **t**
closed 28 July-24 August – **45 rm** 150/210000.

Savini, galleria Vittorio Emanuele II ⊠ 20121 ℘ 72003433, Fax 86461060, Elegant traditional decor, « Winter garden » – . AE E VISA MZ **s**
closed Sunday, 10 to 19 August and 23 December-3 January – **M** (booking essential) a la carte 88/166000 (15 %).

St. Andrews, via Sant'Andrea 23 ⊠ 20121 ℘ 76023132, Fax 798565, Elegant installation, late night dinners – . AE E VISA. KV **t**
closed Sunday and August – **M** (booking essential) a la carte 71/145000 (15 %).

XXX **Biffi Scala,** piazza della Scala ✉ 20121 ☎ 866651, Fax 86461060, Late night dinners – ▤. AE ⓢ ⓞ E VISA MZ **c**
closed Sunday, 10 to 20 August and 25 December-6 January – **M** a la carte 82/126000 (15 %).

XXX ✿ **Peck,** via Victor Hugo 4 ✉ 20123 ☎ 876774, Fax 860408 – ▤. AE ⓢ ⓞ E VISA. ✻
closed Sunday, Bank Holidays and 2 to 23 July – **M** a la carte 62/105000 MZ **e**
Spec. Insalata di medaglioni d' astice calda, Filetto di San Pietro all'aceto balsamico, Ossobuco alla milanese. Wines Arneis, Borgo di Peuma.

XXX **Santini,** corso Venezia 3 ✉ 20121 ☎ 782010, Fax 76014691, ☂ – ▤. AE ⓢ ⓞ E VISA. ✻ NZ **n**
closed Sunday and 2 to 26 August – **M** a la carte 75/115000.

XXX **Don Lisander,** via Manzoni 12/a ✉ 20121 ☎ 76020130, Fax 784573, « Outdoor summer service » – ▤. AE ⓢ ⓞ E VISA KV **u**
closed Saturday, Sunday, 14 to 29 August and 24 December-13 January – **M** (booking essential) a la carte 62/100000.

XXX **Suntory,** via Verdi 6 ✉ 20121 ☎ 8693022, Fax 72023282, Japanese rest. – ▤. AE ⓢ ⓞ E VISA. ✻ KV **v**
closed Sunday, 11 to 16 August and Christmas – **M** a la carte 74/126000.

XXX **Boeucc,** piazza Belgioioso 2 ✉ 20121 ☎ 76020224, Fax 796173, ☂ – ▤. AE. ✻ NZ **j**
closed Saturday, Sunday lunch, August and 24 December-2 January – **M** (booking essential) a la carte 63/91000.

XXX **Alfio,** via Senato 31 ✉ 20121 ☎ 780731, Fax 783446 – ▤. AE ⓢ ⓞ E VISA KV **w**
closed Saturday, Sunday lunch, August and 23 December-3 January – **M** a la carte 58/105000.

XXX **L'Ulmet,** via Disciplini ang. via Olmetto ✉ 20123 ☎ 86452718 – ▤. AE ⓢ E VISA JY **d**
closed Sunday and Monday lunch – **M** (booking essential) a la carte 63/87000.

XXX **San Vito da Nino,** via San Vito 5 ✉ 20123 ☎ 8377029 – ▤. ⓢ VISA. ✻ JY **e**
closed Monday, August and Christmas – **M** (booking essential) a la carte 60/70000 (13 %).

XXX **Peppino,** via Durini 7 ✉ 20122 ☎ 781729 – ▤. AE ⓞ VISA. ✻ NZ **p**
closed Friday dinner, Saturday and 24 July-15 August – **M** a la carte 53/81000.

XXX Royal Dynasty, via Bocchetto 15/a ✉ 20123 ☎ 86450905, Chinese rest. – ▤ JX **a**

XX **Bistrot di Gualtiero Marchesi,** via San Raffaele 2 ✉ 20121 ☎ 877120, Fax 877035, ← Cathedral, Rest. and piano bar – ▤. AE ⓢ ⓞ E VISA MZ **u**
closed Sunday and 8 to 29 August – **M** a la carte 46/78000.

XX **Odeon,** via Bergamini 11 ✉ 20122 ☎ 58307418 – ▤. AE ⓢ ⓞ E VISA NZ **a**
closed Saturday lunch, Sunday and August – **M** a la carte 45/55000.

XX **La Bitta,** via del Carmine 3 ✉ 20121 ☎ 879159 – ▤. AE ⓢ ⓞ E VISA KV **x**
closed Saturday lunch, Sunday, August and Christmas – **M** (fish only) a la carte 51/80000.

XX Boccondivino, via Carducci 17 ✉ 20123 ☎ 866040, Specialities salumi, cheese and regional wines, (booking essential) – ▤ HX **c**
M *(dinner only)*.

X **La Tavernetta-da Elio,** via Fatebenefratelli 30 ✉ 20121 ☎ 653441, Tuscan rest. – ▤. AE VISA KV **c**
closed Sunday and August – **M** a la carte 47/65000.

Directional centre - via della Moscova, via Solferino, via Melchiorre Gioia, viale Zara, via Carlo Farini :

Executive, viale Luigi Sturzo 45 ✉ 20154 ☎ 6294, Telex 310191, Fax 29010238 – |‡| ▤ TV ☎ ♿ 🚗 – 🎤 25-800. AE ⓢ ⓞ E VISA. ✻ rest KTU **e**
M *(closed Friday)* a la carte 66/102000 – **414 rm** ☕ 400000, 6 suites.

Carlyle Brera Hotel without rest., corso Garibaldi 84 ✉ 20121 ☎ 29003888, Telex 323357, Fax 29003993 – |‡| ⚡ ▤ TV ☎ ♿ 🚗. AE ⓢ ⓞ E VISA. ✻ JU **u**
98 rm ☕ 320/360000.

Royal without rest., via Cardano 1 ✉ 20124 ☎ 6709151, Telex 333167, Fax 6703024 – |‡| ⚡ ▤ TV ☎ ♿ 🚗 – 🎤 60-200. AE ⓢ ⓞ E VISA KT **b**
closed August – **205 rm** ☕ 290/390000, 10 suites.

Ritter without rest., corso Garibaldi 68 ✉ 20121 ☎ 29006860, Telex 326863, Fax 6571512 – |‡| ▤ TV ☎. AE ⓢ ⓞ E VISA JU **c**
88 rm ☕ 131/195000.

XX Gianni e Dorina, via Pepe 38 ✉ 20159 ☎ 606340, ☂, (booking essential) – ▤ JT **b**

XX ✿ **A Riccione,** via Taramelli 70 ✉ 20124 ☎ 6686807, Seafood – ▤. AE ⓢ ⓞ E VISA
closed Monday and August – **M** (booking essential) a la carte 80/113000
by via Melchiorre Gioia KLT
Spec. Pasta fresca con sugo di pesce, Paella, Grigliata mista alla brace. Wines del Collio.

XX **Piccolo Teatro-Fuori Porta,** viale Pasubio 8 ✉ 20154 ☎ 6572105 – ▤. AE ⓢ ⓞ VISA
closed Sunday and 5 to 26 August – **M** (booking essential) a la carte 51/81000. JU **m**

XX **San Fermo,** via San Fermo della Battaglia 1 ✉ 20121 ☎ 29000901 – AE ⓢ ⓞ E VISA KU **h**
closed 1 to 20 August, 1 to 7 January, Saturday dinner in June-July, Sunday and Monday dinner August to May – **M** a la carte 37/59000.

XX **Alla Cucina delle Langhe,** corso Como 6 ✉ 20154 ☎ 6554279, Piedmontese rest. – AE $ ⓞ E VISA KU **d**
closed Sunday and August – **M** a la carte 47/68000.

XX **Il Verdi,** piazza Mirabello 5 ✉ 20121 ☎ 6590797 – ▤ KU **k**
closed Saturday lunch, Sunday, 11 to 31 August and 23 December-1 January – **M** a la carte 41/65000 (13 %).

XX **Casa Fontana,** piazza Carbonari 5 ✉ 20125 ☎ 6892684 – ▤. AE $ E VISA. ※
closed 5 to 27 August, Monday, Saturday lunch, and Saturday dinner and Sunday in July – **M** (booking essential) a la carte 44/74000. by via Melchiorre Gioia KLT

XX **Al Garibaldi,** viale Monte Grappa 7 ✉ 20124 ☎ 6598006 – ▤. AE $ ⓞ VISA. ※
closed Friday and August – **M** a la carte 46/83000. KU **m**

XX **Le Colline Pisane,** largo La Foppa 5 ✉ 20121 ☎ 6599136, Tuscan rest. – AE $ ⓞ E VISA JU **p**
closed Sunday and August – **M** a la carte 35/54000.

X **Trattoria della Pesa,** viale Pasubio 10 ✉ 20154 ☎ 6555741, Typical old Milanese trattoria with Lombardy specialities – ▤ JU **s**
closed Sunday and August – **M** a la carte 40/63000.

Central Station - corso Buenos Aires, via Vittor Pisani, piazza della Repubblica :

Principe di Savoia, piazza della Repubblica 17 ✉ 20124 ☎ 6230, Telex 310052, Fax 6595838, – ▤ TV ☎ ♿ Ⓟ – 🏛 700. AE $ ⓞ E VISA. ※ rest KU **a**
M a la carte 85/120000 – ☕ 45000 – **235 rm** 459/655000, 49 suites.

Palace and Rest. Casanova Grill, piazza della Repubblica 20 ✉ 20124 ☎ 6336 and rest ☎ 29000803, Telex 311026, Fax 654485 – ▤ TV ☎ ♿ – 🏛 25-250. AE $ ⓞ E VISA. ※ rest LU **b**
M (booking essential) a la carte 85/100000 – ☕ 30000 – **216 rm** 417/595000, 8 suites.

Excelsior Gallia, piazza Duca d'Aosta 9 ✉ 20124 ☎ 6785, Telex 311160, Fax 66713239, – ▤ TV ☎ – 🏛 40-500. AE $ ⓞ E VISA. ※ LT **a**
M a la carte 86/134000 – ☕ 24000 – **252 rm** 405/560000, 10 suites.

Milano Hilton, via Galvani 12 ✉ 20124 ☎ 69831, Telex 330433, Fax 66710810 – ▤ TV ☎ ♿ – 🏛 30-250. AE $ ⓞ E VISA. ※ rest LT **c**
M a la carte 46/89000 – ☕ 29500 – **321 rm** 295/360000, 2 suites.

Duca di Milano, piazza della Repubblica 13 ✉ 20124 ☎ 6284, Telex 325026, Fax 655966 – ▤ TV ☎ – 🏛 40-60. AE $ ⓞ E VISA. ※ rest KU **c**
M a la carte 60/80000 – ☕ 29000 – **99 suites** 453/631000.

Michelangelo, piazza Luigi di Savoia ang. via Scarlatti ✉ 20124 ☎ 6755, Telex 340330, Fax 6694232 – rm ▤ TV ☎ ♿ – 🏛 25-450. AE $ ⓞ E VISA. ※ rest LTU **d**
M a la carte 85/115000 – **300 rm** ☕ 360/500000, 7 suites.

Century Tower Hotel, via Fabio Filzi 25/b ✉ 20124 ☎ 67504, Telex 330557, Fax 66980602 – ▤ TV ☎ ♿ – 🏛 40-60. AE $ ⓞ E VISA. ※ LT **f**
M a la carte 50/77000 – **148 suites** ☕ 360000.

Jolly Hotel Touring and Rest. Amadeus, via Tarchetti 2 ✉ 20121 ☎ 6335, Telex 320118, Fax 6592209 – ▤ TV ☎ ♿ – 🏛 25-120. AE $ ⓞ E VISA. ※ rest KU **f**
M a la carte 65/84000 – **317 rm** ☕ 290/350000.

Starhotel Ritz, via Spallanzani 40 ✉ 20129 ☎ 2055, Telex 333116, Fax 29518679 – ▤ TV ☎ – 🏛 25-160 by corso Buenos Aires LU
207 rm.

Splendido, viale Andrea Doria 4 ✉ 20124 ☎ 6789, Telex 321413, Fax 66713369 – ▤ TV ☎ – 🏛 25-100 LT **g**
166 rm.

Atlantic without rest., via Napo Torriani 24 ✉ 20124 ☎ 6691941, Telex 321451, Fax 6706533 – ▤ TV ☎ – 🏛 25. AE $ E VISA LU **h**
62 rm ☕ 200/300000.

Madison without rest., via Gasparotto 8 ✉ 20124 ☎ 6085991, Telex 326543, Fax 6887821 – ▤ TV ☎ – 🏛 100. AE $ ⓞ E VISA LT **j**
92 rm ☕ 215/305000 8 suites.

Mediolanum without rest., via Mauro Macchi 1 ✉ 20124 ☎ 6705312, Telex 310448, Fax 66981921 – ▤ TV ☎ ♿. AE $ E VISA LU **n**
52 rm ☕ 182/276000, 1 suite.

Sanpi without rest., via Lazzaro Palazzi 18 ✉ 20124 ☎ 29513341, Fax 29402451 – ▤ TV ☎ – 🏛 30. AE $ ⓞ E VISA. ※ LU **e**
closed August – **63 rm** ☕ 220/280000, 2 suites.

Manin, via Manin 7 ✉ 20121 ☎ 6596511, Telex 320385, Fax 6552160, – ▤ TV ☎ – 🏛 25-100. AE $ ⓞ E VISA. ※ rest KV **d**
closed 6 to 24 August and 24 December-7 January – **M** *(closed Sunday)* a la carte 52/91000 – ☕ 22000 – **112 rm** 218/276000, 6 suites.

Berna without rest., via Napo Torriani 18 ✉ 20124 ☎ 6691441, Telex 334695, Fax 6693892 – ▤ TV ☎ – 🏛 30-60. AE $ ⓞ E VISA. ※ LU **h**
115 rm ☕ 200/280000.

Auriga without rest., via Pirelli 7 ✉ 20124 ✆ 66985851, Fax 66980698 – |‡| ▤ TV ☎ – 🏛 25. AE ⑤ ⓞ E VISA. ⚘ LTU **k**
closed August – ☐ 18000 – **65 rm** 200/245000.

Windsor, via Galilei 2 ✉ 20124 ✆ 6346, Telex 330562, Fax 6590663 – |‡| ▤ TV ☎ 🚗 – 🏛 40-60. AE ⑤ ⓞ E VISA. ⚘ rest KU **g**
M *(closed lunch and Saturday)* a la carte 40/70000 – **118 rm** ☐ 205/260000 7 suites.

Augustus without rest., via Napo Torriani 29 ✉ 20124 ✆ 66988271, Fax 6703096 – |‡| ▤ TV ☎. AE ⑤ ⓞ E VISA LU **q**
closed 25 July-25 August and 23 December-5 January – **56 rm** ☐ 160/200000.

Galles without rest., via Ozanam 1 ✉ 20129 ✆ 29404250, Telex 322091, Fax 29404872 – |‡| ▤ TV ☎ – 🏛 25-150. AE ⑤ ⓞ E VISA. ⚘ by corso Buenos Aires LU
105 rm ☐ 240/340000.

Doria Hotel Baglioni without rest., viale Andrea Doria 22 ✉ 20124 ✆ 6696696, Telex 360173, Fax 6696669 – |‡| ⚟ ▤ TV ☎ ♿ 🚗 – 🏛 25-100. AE ⑤ ⓞ E VISA. ⚘
118 rm ☐ 320/390000 2 suites. by corso Buenos Aires LU

New York without rest., via Pirelli 5 ✉ 20124 ✆ 66985551, Telex 325057, Fax 6697267 – |‡| ▤ TV ☎. AE ⑤ ⓞ E VISA. ⚘ LTU **k**
closed 1 to 28 August and 24 December-5 January – **70 rm** ☐ 133/197000.

City without rest., corso Buenos Aires 42/5 ✉ 20124 ✆ 29523382, Telex 312150, Fax 2046957 – ▤ TV ☎. AE ⑤ E VISA. ⚘ by corso Buenos Aires LU
closed August and 23 December-2 January – **55 rm** ☐ 150/220000.

XXX **Nino Arnaldo,** via Poerio 3 ✉ 20129 ✆ 76005981 – ▤. AE ⑤ E VISA
closed Saturday lunch, Sunday, August and 23 December-7 January – **M** (booking essential) a la carte 70/83000. by via Mascagni LX

XX **Joia,** via Panfilo Castaldi 18 ✉ 20124 ✆ 29522124, Vegetarian cuisine – ⚟ ▤. AE ⑤ ⓞ E VISA LU **c**
closed Saturday lunch, Sunday and 1 to 21 August – **M** (booking essential) a la carte 46/67000.

XX **Cavallini,** via Mauro Macchi 2 ✉ 20124 ✆ 6693771, Fax 6693174, « Outdoor summer service » – AE ⑤ ⓞ E VISA LU **y**
closed Saturday, Sunday, 3 to 23 August and 22 December-4 January – **M** a la carte 41/72000 (12 %).

XX ✿ **Calajunco,** via Stoppani 5 ✉ 20129 ✆ 2046003, Aeolian rest. – ▤. ⑤ ⓞ E VISA. ⚘
closed Saturday lunch, Sunday, 10 to 31 August and 23 December-4 January – **M** (booking essential) a la carte 76/110000 by corso Buenos Aires LU
Spec. Risotto con scampi e asparagi, Filetti di San Pietro al rosmarino, Crostata ai fichi d'India (September-February). Wines Terre di Ginestra, Pinot nero.

XX **Buriassi-da Lino,** via Lecco 15 ✉ 20124 ✆ 29523227 – ▤ – 🏛 35. AE VISA LU **a**
closed Saturday lunch, Sunday and 7 to 24 August – **M** (booking essential for dinner) a la carte 37/73000.

XX **Al Girarrosto da Cesarina,** corso Venezia 31 ✉ 20121 ✆ 76000481 – ▤. AE ⑤ E VISA LV **c**
closed Saturday, Sunday lunch, August and 25 December-10 January – **M** a la carte 50/77000.

XX **La Buca,** via Antonio da Recanate ang. via Napo Torriani ✉ 20124 ✆ 6693774 – ▤. AE ⑤ ⓞ E VISA LU **z**
closed Friday dinner, Saturday, August and 25 December-6 January – **M** a la carte 42/70000.

XX **Le 5 Terre,** via Appiani 9 ✉ 20121 ✆ 653034, Seafood – ▤. AE ⑤ ⓞ E VISA KU **j**
closed Saturday lunch, Sunday and 8 to 22 August – **M** a la carte 60/86000.

XX **13 Giugno,** via Goldoni 44 ✉ 20129 ✆ 719654, ☂, Sicilian rest. – ▤. AE ⑤ E VISA
closed Saturday lunch, Sunday and 10 to 30 August – **M** (booking essential) 35000 (lunch) and dinner a la carte 60/80000. by via Mascagni LX

XX **Olivo 2,** via Monte Santo 2 ✉ 20124 ✆ 653846 – ▤. AE ⑤ ⓞ E VISA KU **g**
closed Saturday, Sunday and 10 to 22 August – **M** a la carte 58/80000.

Romana-Vittoria - corso Porta Romana, corso Lodi, viale XXII Marzo, corso Porta Vittoria :

Mediterraneo without rest., via Muratori 14 ✉ 20135 ✆ 55019151, Telex 335812, Fax 55019151 – |‡| ▤ TV ☎ – 🏛 30-70. AE ⑤ ⓞ E VISA LY **g**
closed 1 to 21 August – **93 rm** ☐ 280/370000.

XXXX ✿✿✿ **Gualtiero Marchesi,** (Transfer estimated at Erbusco/Bs ✆ 030-7267003) via Bonvesin de la Riva 9 ✉ 20129 ✆ 741246, Fax 7384079, Elegant installation – ▤. AE ⑤ ⓞ E VISA. ⚘
closed Bank Holidays, Sunday, Monday lunch, July, August and 23 December-7 January – **M** (booking essential) a la carte 90/150000 by corso di Porta Vittoria LX
Spec. Raviolo aperto, Rombo in crosta, Costoletta di vitello alla milanese. Wines Gualtiero Marchesi bianco e rosso.

XXXX **Giannino,** via Amatore Sciesa 8 ✉ 20135 ✆ 55195025, Fax 5452765, Traditional style, « Original decor, winter garden » – Ⓟ. AE ⑤ ⓞ E VISA. ⚘
closed Sunday and August – **M** a la carte 87/145000. by corso di Porta Vittoria

XXXX **Soti's,** via Pietro Calvi 2 ✉ 20129 ✆ 796838, Fax 796838, Elegant installation – ▤. AE ⑤ ⓞ E VISA. ⚘ by via Mascagni LX
closed Saturday lunch, Sunday and 10 to 24 August – **M** (booking essential) 80000 b.i. (lunch only) and dinner a la carte 90/115000.

XXX **La Zelata,** via Anfossi 10 ✉ 20135 ℘ 59902115, Fax 5483612 – ▤. AE ⓓ E VISA. ✻ by corso di Porta Vittoria LX
closed Saturday lunch, Sunday and August – **M** (booking essential) a la carte 42/72000.

XX **La Risacca 6,** via Marcona 6 ✉ 20129 ℘ 5400029, 余 – ▤. AE Ⓢ E VISA
closed Sunday, Monday lunch, August and Christmas – **M** (fish only) a la carte 60/84000. by corso di Porta Vittoria LX

Navigli : via Solari, Ripa di Porta Ticinese, viale Bligny, piazza XXIV Maggio :

D'Este without rest., viale Bligny 23 ✉ 20136 ℘ 5461041, Telex 324216, Fax 5454330 – |‡| ▤ TV ☎ – 🔔 40-80. AE Ⓢ ⓓ E VISA. ✻ KY **d**
☕ 24000 – **54 rm** 195/280000.

Crivi's without rest., corso Porta Vigentina 46 ✉ 20122 ℘ 58302000, Telex 313255, Fax 58318182 – |‡| ▤ TV ☎ 🚗 – 🔔 30-120. AE Ⓢ ⓓ E VISA KY **e**
closed August – **86 rm** ☕ 200/280000, 3 suites.

Liberty without rest., viale Bligny 56 ✉ 20136 ℘ 58318562, Fax 58319061 – |‡| ▤ TV ☎ 🚗. AE Ⓢ E VISA. ✻ KY **a**
closed 10 to 25 August – ☕ 20000 – **52 rm** 160/260000.

Adriatico without rest., via Conca del Naviglio 20 ✉ 20123 ℘ 58104141, Fax 58104145 – |‡| ▤ TV ☎. AE Ⓢ ⓓ E VISA JY **c**
closed 1 to 21 August – **105 rm** ☕ 170/240000.

XXX ✿ **Scaletta,** piazzale Stazione Genova 3 ✉ 20144 ℘ 58100290 – ▤. ✻ HY **a**
closed Sunday, Monday, Easter, August and 24 December-6 January – **M** (booking essential) a la carte 80/90000
Spec. Insalata di seppioline e porcini, Risotto Pollock, Coniglio farcito alla trippa. Wines Villa Bucci, Chianti.

XXX ✿ **Al Genovese,** via Ettore Troilo 14 ang. via Conchetta ✉ 20136 ℘ 8373180, 余, Ligurian rest. – ▤. AE Ⓢ ⓓ E VISA. ✻ by corso San Gottardo JY
closed Sunday, Monday lunch, 10 to 30 August and 1 to 7 January – **M** (booking essential) a la carte 55/91000
Spec. Insalatina di calamaretti novelli, Trofie di farina di castagne al pesto, Cappon magro. Wines Vermentino, Rossese.

XX **Yar,** via Mercalli 22 ✉ 20122 ℘ 58305234, Typical Russian cuisine – ▤. AE Ⓢ E VISA. ✻ KY **k**
closed Sunday, Monday and August – **M** (dinner only) (booking essential) a la carte 56/80000.

XX ✿ **Al Porto,** piazzale Generale Cantore ✉ 20123 ℘ 8321481, Fax 8321481, Seafood – ▤. AE Ⓢ ⓓ E VISA HY **h**
closed Sunday, Monday lunch, August and 24 December-3 January – **M** (booking essential) a la carte 55/85000
Spec. Zuppa di fagioli e scampi, Bavette al nero di seppia con pecorino, Branzino al Pigato e olive nere. Wines Pigato, Franciacorta rosso.

XX ✿ **Sadler-Osteria di Porta Cicca,** ripa di Porta Ticinese 51 ✉ 20143 ℘ 58104451 – ▤. Ⓢ ⓓ E VISA HY **j**
closed Sunday, 5 to 30 August and 1 to 10 January – **M** (dinner only) (booking essential) a la carte 68/103000
Spec. Carpaccio di tonno al pesto di ortaggi (spring-summer), Ravioli ai funghi misti, Crostatina di lamponi gratinata con zabaione al Moscato. Wines Chardonnay, Bonarda.

XX **Osteria del Binari,** via Tortona 1 ✉ 20144 ℘ 89409428, 余, Old Milan atmosphere – AE VISA
closed Sunday, and 10 to 17 August – **M** (dinner only) (booking essential) 52000. HY **p**

X **Trattoria all'Antica,** via Montevideo 4 ✉ 20144 ℘ 58104860, Lombard cuisine – ▤. VISA. ✻ HY **r**
closed Saturday lunch, Sunday, August and 26 December-7 January – **M** a la carte 31/53000 (lunch) and dinner 45000.

Fiera-Sempione : corso Sempione, piazzale Carlo Magno, via Monte Rosa, via Washington :

Hermitage, via Messina 10 ✉ 20154 ℘ 33107700, Fax 33107399 – |‡| ▤ TV ☎ 🚗 – 🔔 30-240. AE Ⓢ ⓓ E VISA. ✻ HJU **q**
M a la carte 64/80000 – **131 rm** ☕ 235/330000, 12 suites.

Gd H. Fieramilano, viale Boezio 20 ✉ 20145 ℘ 336221, Telex 331426, Fax 314119, 🌳 – |‡| ▤ TV ☎ ♿ 🚗 – 🔔 60. AE Ⓢ ⓓ E VISA. ✻ rest by via Vincenzo Monti HV
M a la carte 38/62000 – **238 rm** ☕ 280/330000.

Poliziano without rest., via Poliziano 11 ✉ 20154 ℘ 33602494, Fax 33106410 – |‡| ▤ TV ☎ 🚗 – 🔔 70. AE Ⓢ ⓓ E VISA. ✻ HT **a**
98 rm ☕ 250000, 2 suites.

Washington, without rest., via Washington 23 ✉ 20146 ℘ 4813216, Fax 4814761 – |‡| ▤ TV ☎ by corso Magenta HX
34 rm.

Capitol, via Cimarosa 6 ✉ 20144 ℘ 4988851, Telex 316150, Fax 4694724 – |‡| ▤ TV ☎ – 🔔 60. AE Ⓢ ⓓ E VISA. ✻ rest by corso Magenta HX
M *(closed lunch and August)* a la carte 52/83000 – **96 rm** ☕ 225/295000.

Ariosto without rest., via Ariosto 22 ✉ 20145 ℘ 4817844, Fax 4980516 – |‡| ▤ TV ☎ ♿ – 🔔 40. AE Ⓢ ⓓ E VISA HV **a**
☕ 12000 – **53 rm** 120/162000.

Domenichino without rest., via Domenichino 41 ✉ 20149 ✆ 48009692, Fax 48003953 – 50. by corso Sempione HU
67 rm 138/198000, 4 suites.

Europeo without rest., via Canonica 38 ✉ 20154 ✆ 3314751, Fax 33105410, – 25. HU **b**
closed August – **45 rm** 145/210000.

Wagner without rest., via Buonarroti 13 ✉ 20149 ✆ 4696051, Telex 353121, Fax 48020948 – by corso Magenta HX
closed August and 23 December-7 January – **49 rm** 136/199000.

Lancaster without rest., via Abbondio Sangiorgio 16 ✉ 20145 ✆ 315602, Fax 344649 – HU **c**
closed August – **30 rm** 145/210000.

Mini Hotel Portello without rest., via Guglielmo Silva 12 ✉ 20152 ✆ 4814944, Fax 4819243 – – 50-100. by corso Sempione HU
96 rm 130/195000.

Mini Hotel Tiziano without rest., via Tiziano 6 ✉ 20145 ✆ 4988921, Telex 325420, Fax 4812153, « Small park » – – 30.
54 rm 130/195000. by via Vincenzo Monti HV

Orti di Leonardo, via Aristide de' Togni 6/8 ✉ 20123 ✆ 4983197, Fax 4983476 – . HX **b**
closed Sunday and 1 to 26 August – **M** a la carte 74/104000.

Alfredo-Gran San Bernardo, via Borgese 14 ✉ 20154 ✆ 3319000, Fax 6555413, Milanese rest. – . HT **e**
closed August, 24 December-2 January, Sunday and Saturday in June-July – **M** (booking essential) a la carte 63/93000
Spec. Risotto alla milanese ed al salto, Stracotto al Barbaresco, Costoletta alla milanese. Wines Sauvignon, Dolcetto.

Trattoria del Ruzante, via Massena 1 ✉ 20145 ✆ 316102, (booking essential) – HU **v**

Raffaello, via Monte Amiata 4 ✉ 20149 ✆ 4814227 – .
closed Wednesday and 1 to 24 August – **M** a la carte 45/69000. by via Vincenzo Monti HV

China Club, via Giusti 34 ✉ 20154 ✆ 33104309 – . HU **f**
closed Tuesday and August – **M** (booking essential) a la carte 49/64000 (15 %).

Dall'Antonio, via Cenisio 8 ✉ 20154 ✆ 33101511 – . HT **g**
closed Sunday and August – **M** (booking essential) a la carte 60/103000.

Gocce di Mare, via Petrarca 4 ✉ 20123 ✆ 4692487, Fax 433854 – .
close Saturday lunch, Sunday and 9 to 31 August – **M** a la carte 44/66000. HV **d**

La Torre del Mangia, via Procaccini 37 ✉ 20154 ✆ 33105587 – . HU **h**
closed Sunday dinner, Monday, August and Christmas – **M** (booking essential) a la carte 41/75000.

Trattoria Vecchia Arena, piazza Lega Lombarda 1 ✉ 20154 ✆ 3315538 – . JU **e**
closed Sunday, Monday lunch and 1 to 21 August – **M** (booking essential) a la carte 58/77000.

North-Western area - viale Fulvio Testi, Niguarda, viale Fermi, viale Certosa, San Siro, via Novara :

Gd H. Brun and Rest. Ascot, via Caldera 21 ✉ 20153 ✆ 45271 and rest. ✆ 4526279, Telex 315370, Fax 48204746 – – 500. rest by corso Sempione HU
M *(closed August)* a la carte 85/110000 – **324 rm** 420000, 16 suites.

Leonardo da Vinci, via Senigallia 6 ✉ 20161 ✆ 64031, Telex 331552, Fax 64074839, – rm – 60-1200.
M 52000 – **290 rm** 240/320000, 26 suites. by via Mac Mahon HT

Blaise e Francis without rest., via Butti 9 ✉ 20158 ✆ 66802366, Fax 66802909 – – 40-200. by via Valtellina JT
closed 2 to 23 August and 24 December-2 January – **110 rm** 320000.

Novotel Milano Nord, viale Suzzani 13 ✉ 20162 ✆ 66101861, Telex 331292, Fax 66101961, – – 25-500.
M a la carte 44/69000 – **172 rm** 270000. by via Valtellina JT

Accademia without rest., viale Certosa 68 ✉ 20155 ✆ 39211122, Telex 315550, Fax 33103878, « Rooms with fresco murals » – .
67 rm 250/340000. by corso Sempione HU

Raffaello without rest., viale Certosa 108 ✉ 20156 ✆ 3270146, Telex 315499, Fax 3270440 – – 180. by corso Sempione HU
149 rm 180/250000, 2 suites

Rubens without rest., via Rubens 21 ✉ 20148 ✆ 40302, Telex 353617, Fax 48193114 – – 25. by corso Magenta HX
closed 1 to 21 August – **87 rm** 235/340000.

Ibis Ca' Granda, viale Suzzani 13/15 ✉ 20162 ✆ 66103000, Telex 360141, Fax 66102797 – |♦| ▤ TV ☎ ♿ 🚗 P – 🏛 50. AE ⓢ ⓞ E VISA by via Valtellina JT
M (residents only) a la carte 30/45000 – **132 rm** ☐ 155000.

Mirage without rest., via Casella 61 angolo viale Certosa ✉ 20156 ✆ 39210471, Fax 39210589 – |♦| ▤ TV ☎ ♿ – 🏛 30-60. AE ⓢ ⓞ E VISA by corso Sempione HU
☐ 20000 – **50 rm** 200/270000.

La Pobbia, via Gallarate 92 ✉ 20151 ✆ 38006641, Modern rustic rest., « Outdoor summer service » – 🏛 40. AE ⓢ E VISA. ✈ by corso Sempione HU
closed Sunday and August – **M** a la carte 48/75000 (12 %).

Ribot, via Cremosano 41 ✉ 20148 ✆ 33001646, « Summer service in garden » – P. AE. ✈ by corso Sempione HU
closed Monday and 10 to 25 August – **M** a la carte 49/60000.

Al Bimbo, via Marcantonio dal Re 38 ✉ 20156 ✆ 3272290, Fax 39216365 – ▤. AE ⓢ ⓞ E VISA by corso Sempione HU
closed Saturday lunch, Sunday and August – **M** a la carte 37/58000.

Northern-Eastern area - viale Monza, via Padova, via Porpora, viale Romagna, viale Argonne, viale Forlanini :

Concorde without rest., via Petrocchi 1 ang. viale Monza ✉ 20125 ✆ 26112020, Telex 315805, Fax 26147879 – |♦| ▤ TV ☎ 🚗. AE ⓢ ⓞ E VISA. ✈
closed 1 to 24 August – **120 rm** ☐ 235/350000. by corso Buenos Aires LU

Lombardia, viale Lombardia 74 ✉ 20131 ✆ 2824938, Telex 315327, Fax 2893430 – |♦| ▤ TV ☎ 🚗 – 🏛 30-100. AE ⓢ ⓞ E VISA. ✈ by corso Buenos Aires LU
closed 7 to 21 August – **M** *(closed Saturday dinner and Sunday)* a la carte 35/60000 – **72 rm** ☐ 137/201000.

Zefiro without rest., via Gallina 12 ✉ 20129 ✆ 7384253, Fax 713811 – |♦| ▤ TV ☎ – 🏛 30. ⓢ E VISA. ✈ by via Mascagni LX
closed August and 23 December-3 January – **55 rm** ☐ 132/195000.

✿ **L'Ami Berton,** via Nullo 14 angolo via Goldoni ✉ 20129 ✆ 713669 – ▤. AE ⓢ E VISA. ✈ by via Mascagni LX
closed Saturday lunch, Sunday, August and Christmas – **M** (booking essential) a la carte 100/130000
Spec. Sfogliatina di salmone e caviale, Cestino di mare con riso indiano, Filetti di triglia ai ricci di mare con purea di rape. Wines Sauvignon.

3 Pini, via Tullo Morgagni 19 angolo via Arbe ✉ 20125 ✆ 68805413, « Summer service under the pergola » – AE ⓢ ⓞ E VISA by via Valtellina JT
closed Saturday, Sunday dinner, 5 to 31 August and 25 December-4 January – **M** (booking essential) a la carte 47/76000.

Hostaria Mamma Lina, viale Monza 256 ✉ 20128 ✆ 2574770, ☂, Rest. and piano-bar with Apulian specialities – AE ⓢ ⓞ E VISA by corso Buenos Aires LU
closed Monday, Easter and Christmas – **M** a la carte 51/77000.

Montecatini Alto, viale Monza 7 ✉ 20125 ✆ 2846773 – ▤. AE ⓢ E VISA
closed Saturday lunch, Sunday and August – **M** a la carte 39/59000 (10 %).
by Corso Buenos Aires LU

Antica Osteria la Gobba, via Padova 395 ✉ 20132 ✆ 26300255, Milanese rest. – P. AE ⓢ ⓞ E VISA. ✈ by corso Buenos Aires LU
closed Saturday lunch, Sunday, 5 to 25 August and 23 December-2 January – **M** a la carte 45/71000.

Osteria Corte Regina, via Rottole 60 ✉ 20132 ✆ 2593377, ☂, Rustic modern rest. – AE ⓢ ⓞ E VISA by corso Buenos Aires LU
closed Saturday lunch, Sunday and August – **M** (booking essential) a la carte 56/78000.

Da Renzo, piazza Sire Raul ang. via Teodosio ✉ 20131 ✆ 2846261, ☂ – ▤. AE ⓢ ⓞ E VISA by corso Buenos Aires LU
closed Monday dinner, Tuesday, August and 26 December-2 January – **M** a la carte 38/61000.

L'Altra Scaletta, viale Zara 116 ✉ 20125 ✆ 6888093 – ▤. AE ⓢ ⓞ E VISA. ✈
closed Saturday lunch, Sunday and August – **M** a la carte 45/68000.
by via Valtellina JT

Southern-Eastern area - viale Molise, corso Lodi, via Ripamonti, corso San Gottardo :

Quark, via Lampedusa 11/a ✉ 20141 ✆ 84431, Telex 353448, Fax 8464190, ☂, ⛱ – |♦| ⊁ rm ▤ TV ☎ 🚗 P – 🏛 25-1100. AE ⓢ ⓞ E VISA. ✈ rest by corso Italia KY
M *(closed 31 July-22 August)* a la carte 53/80000 – **285 rm** ☐ 300000, 92 suites.

Novotel Milano Est Aeroporto, via Mecenate 121 ✉ 20138 ✆ 58011085, Telex 331237, Fax 58011086, ⛱ – |♦| ▤ TV ☎ ♿ P – 🏛 25-350. AE ⓢ ⓞ E VISA. ✈ rest by corso di Porta Vittoria LX
M a la carte 41/64000 – **206 rm** ☐ 225/290000.

La Plancia, via Cassinis 13 ✉ 20139 ✆ 5390558, Seafood pizzeria – ▤. AE ⓢ ⓞ E VISA. ✈ by corso Lodi LY
closed Sunday and August – **M** a la carte 30/60000.

Southern-Western area - viale Famagosta, viale Liguria, via Lorenteggio, viale Forze Armate, via Novara

Holiday Inn and Rest. l'Univers Gourmand, via Lorenteggio 278 ✉ 20152 ☎ 410014, Fax 48304729, – rm 70. AE VISA. rest
M a la carte 37/62000 – 28000 – **119 rm** 289/357000. by via Foppa HY

Green House without rest., viale Famagosta 50 ✉ 20142 ☎ 8132451, Fax 816624 – AE VISA. by Ripa di Porta Ticinese HY
12000 – **45 rm** 130000.

XXX ✿✿ **Aimo e Nadia,** via Montecuccoli 6 ✉ 20147 ☎ 416886 – AE VISA.
closed Saturday lunch, Sunday and August – **M** (booking essential) a la carte 84/120000 by via Foppa HY
Spec. Zuppa di lenticchie e vongole veraci, Risotto con gallina fegatini e porcini (summer-autumn), Pesche allo sciroppo con gelato all'amaretto. Wines Tocai, Marzemino.

XX **La Corba,** via dei Gigli 14 ✉ 20147 ☎ 4158977, « Summer service in garden » – AE VISA by via Foppa HY
closed Sunday dinner, Monday and 7 to 30 August – **M** a la carte 51/76000.

on national road 35-Milanofiori by via Francesco Sforza JY : 10 km :

Jolly Hotel Milanofiori, Strada 2 ✉ 20090 Assago ☎ 82221, Telex 325314, Fax 89200946, – 120. AE VISA. rest
M 50/80000 – **255 rm** 340/380000.

at Forlanini Park (West) E : 10 km :

XX **Osteria I Valtellina,** via Taverna 34 ✉ 20134 Milan ☎ 7561139, , Valtellinese Rest. – AE VISA
closed Friday, Saturday lunch and 7 to 25 August – **M** a la carte 54/87000.

on road New Vigevanese-Zingone by via Foppa HY : 11 km :

Eur without rest., ✉ 20090 Zingone di Trezzano ☎ 4451951, Fax 4451075 – – 70. AE VISA
41 rm 149/195000.

on national road West-Assago by via Foppa HY : 11 km :

MotelAgip, ✉ 20094 Assago ☎ 4880441, Telex 325191, Fax 48843958, – – 300. AE VISA. rest
M 40/60000 – **219 rm** 240000.

Abbiategrasso 20081 Milano 988 ③, 428 F 8 – pop. 27 787 alt. 120 – 02.
Roma 590 – Alessandria 74 – Milano 23 – Novara 29 – Pavia 33.

at Cassinetta di Lugagnano N : 3 km – ✉ **20080** :

XXXX ✿✿✿ **Antica Osteria del Ponte,** ☎ 9420034, Fax 9420610, – AE VISA.
closed Sunday, Monday, August and 25 December-12 January – **M** (booking essential) a la carte 94/152000
Spec. Lasagnetta alla fonduta di porri e cipollotti con tartufo nero (January-April), foie gras d'anitra caldo alla crema di borlotti (July-November), Buridda di rombo branzino e gamberi (April-September). Wines Franciacorta bianco, Barolo.

Malgrate 22040 Como 428 E 10, 219 ⑨ ⑩ – pop. 4 203 alt. 224 – 0341.
Roma 623 – Bellagio 20 – Como 27 – Lecco 2 – Milano 54.

✿✿ **Il Griso,** ☎ 202040, Fax 202248, ≤ lake and mountains, , « Small park », , – – 30. AE VISA
closed 20 December-6 January – **M** a la carte 70/125000 – 20000 – **41 rm** 150/180000
Spec. Ravioli di rane con salsa allo scalogno e basilico, Suprema di lucioperca al vino rosso, Filetti di coniglio con vinaigrette al tartufo. Wines Franciacorta bianco, Sassella superiore.

Ranco 21020 Varese 428 E 7, 219 ⑦ – pop. 996 alt. 214 – 0331.
Roma 644 – Laveno Mombello 21 – Milano 67 – Novara 51 – Sesto Calende 12 – Varese 27.

XXX ✿✿ **Il Sole** with rm, ☎ 976507, Fax 976620, ≤, « Summer service under the pergola », , – AE VISA.
closed January-14 February – **M** (booking essential) (closed Monday dinner except June-September and Tuesday) a la carte 78/123000 (10 %) – 7 suites 255000
Spec. Uova di quaglia in brioche ai quattro caviali, Lavarello affumicato su insalata di patate tiepide, Agnello in padella al rosmarino. Wines Ribolla, Barbaresco.

Soriso 28018 Novara 428 E 7, 219 ⑯ – pop. 769 alt. 452 – 0322.
Roma 654 – Arona 20 – Milano 78 – Novara 40 – Torino 114 – Varese 46.

XXXX ✿✿ **Al Sorriso** with rm, ☎ 983228, Fax 983328 – rest . AE VISA.
closed 7 to 21 August and 25 December-15 January – **M** (booking essential) (closed Monday and Tuesday lunch) a la carte 91/144000 – **8 rm** 130/190000
Spec. Frittelle di mele con fegato d'oca in salsa di ribes, Zuppa di porri e patate con calamaretti polipetti e scampi, Piccione novello all'aceto balsamico. Wines Monteriolo, Boca.

NAPLES (NAPOLI) 80100 P 988 ㉗, 431 E 24 – pop. 1 206 013 – Hight Season : April-October – ☎ 081.

See : National Archaeological Museum★★★ KY – New Castle★★ KZ – Port of Santa Lucia★★ : ≤★★ of Vesuvius and bay – ≤★★★ at night from via Partenope of the Vomero and Posillipo FX – San Carlo Theatre★ KZ **T** – Piazza del Plebiscito★ JKZ – Royal Palace★ KZ – Carthusian Monastery of St. Martin★★ JZ : ≤★★★ of the Bay of Naples from gallery 25.

Spacca-Napoli quarter★★ KY – Tomb★★ of King Robert the wise in Church of Santa Chiara★ KY **C** – Caryatids★ by Tino da Camaino in Church of St. Dominic Major KY **L** – Sculptures★ in Chapel of St. Severo KY **V** – Arch★, Tomb★ of Catherine of Austria, apse★ in Church of St. Lawrence Major LY **K** – Capodimonte Palace and National Gallery★★.

Mergellina★ : ≤★★ of the bay – Villa Floridiana★ EVX : ≤★ – Catacombs of St. Gennaro★ – Church of Santa Maria Donnaregina★ LY **B** – Church of St. Giovanni Carbonara★ LY **G** – Capuan Gate★ LMY **D** – Cuomo Palace★ LY **Q** – Sculptures★ in the Church of St. Anne of the Lombards KYZ **R** – Posillipo★ – Marechiaro★ – ≤★★ of the Bay from Virgiliano Park (or Rimembranza Park).

Exc. : Bay of Naples★★★ by the coast road to Campi Flegrei★★ by ⑧, to Sorrento Peninsula by ⑦ Island of Capri★★★ Island of Ischia★★★.

(closed Monday) at Arco Felice ✉ 80072 ☎ 5264296, by ⑧ : 19 km.

Ugo Niutta of Capodichino NE : 6 km (except Saturday and Sunday) ☎ 5425333 – Alitalia, via Medina 41 ✉ 80133 ☎ 5425222 helicopter pad from Napoli-Capodichino to Capri-Anacapri and Ischia-Casamicciola (16 April-4 October) (10 mn) - Eliambassador, Capodichino airport ☎ 7896273, Telex 710593, Fax 7803006.

to Capri daily (1 h 15 mn) – Navigazione Libera del Golfo, molo Beverello ✉ 80133 ☎ 5520763, Telex 722661, Fax 5525589; to Capri (1 h 15 mn), Ischia (1 h 15 mn) and Procida (1 h), daily – Caremar-Centro Servizi Beverello, molo Beverello ✉ 80133 ☎ 5513882, Fax 5522011; to Cagliari June-September Tuesday, Friday and Sunday, Friday and Sunday in other months (15 h 45 mn) and Palermo daily (10 h 30 mn) – Tirrenia Navigazione, Stazione Marittima, molo Angioino ✉ 80133 ☎ 5512181, Telex 710030, Fax 7201441 ; to Ischia daily (1 h 15 mn) – Linee Lauro, piazza Municipio 88 ✉ 80133 ☎ 5513352, Fax 5524329; to Aeolian Island Tuesday, Thursady and Saturday, 15 June-15 September Monday and Friday too (13 h 30 mn) – Siremar-Genovese Agency, via De Petris 78 ✉ 80133 ☎ 5512112, Telex 710196, Fax 5512114.

to Capri (45 mn), Ischia (45 mn) and Procida (35 mn), daily – Caremar-Centro Servizi Beverello, molo Beverello ✉ 80133 ☎ 5513882, Fax 5522011; to Ischia daily (40 mn) – Alilauro, via Caracciolo 11 ✉ 80122 ☎ 7611004, Fax 7614250; to Capri daily (30 mn), Aeolian Island 15 May-15 October daily (4 h) and Procida-Ischia daily (35 mn) – Aliscafi SNAV, via Caracciolo 10 ✉ 80122 ☎ 7612348, Telex 720446, Fax 7612141.

via Partenope 10/a ✉ 80121 ☎ 7644871 – piazza del Plebiscito (Royal Palace) ✉ 80132 ☎ 418744 – Central Station ✉ 80142 ☎ 268779 - Capodichino Airport ✉ 80133 ☎ 7805761 – piazza del Gesú Nuovo 7 ✉ 80135 ☎ 5523328 - Passaggio Castel dell'Ovo ✉ 80132 ☎ 7646414.

A.C.I. piazzale Tecchio 49/d ✉ 80125 ☎ 614511.

Roma 219 ③ – Bari 261 ⑤

Plans on following pages

Grande Albergo Vesuvio, via Partenope 45 ✉ 80121 ☎ 7640044, Telex 710127, Fax 7640044, « Roof-garden rest. with ≤ gulf and Castel dell'Ovo » – rm – 40-400. AE E VISA. FX **n**
M Caruso Rest. *(closed Monday)* a la carte 56/82000 – **170 rm** 250/370000, 20 suites.

Gd H. Parker's, corso Vittorio Emanuele 135 ✉ 80121 ☎ 7612474, Telex 710578, Fax 663527, « Roof-garden rest. with ≤ City and gulf » – – 50-250. AE E VISA. EX **r**
M *(closed Sunday)* a la carte 60/85000 – **83 rm** 210/310000, 10 suites.

Santa Lucia without rest., via Partenope 46 ✉ 80121 ☎ 7640666, Telex 710595, Fax 7648580, ≤ gulf and Castel dell'Ovo – – 140. AE E VISA. GX **w**
107 rm 204/296000, 3 suites.

Jolly, via Medina 70 ✉ 80133 ☎ 416000, Telex 720335, Fax 5518010, « Roof-garden rest. with ≤ City, gulf and Vesuvius » – – 250. AE E VISA. rest KZ **s**
M a la carte 58/99000 – **251 rm** 210/270000.

Britannique, corso Vittorio Emanuele 133 ✉ 80121 ☎ 7614145, Telex 722281, Fax 669760, ≤, « Garden » – – 25-100. AE E VISA. rest EX **r**
M (residents only) 40000 – 11000 – **88 rm** 180/240000, 8 suites.

Royal, via Partenope 38 ✉ 80121 ☎ 7644800, Telex 710167, Fax 7645707, ≤ gulf, Posillipo and Castel dell'Ovo, – – 25-200. AE E VISA. rest FX **n**
M a la carte 65/108000 – **273 rm** 259/347000, 14 suites, 40000.

Paradiso, via Catullo 11 ✉ 80122 ☎ 7614161, Telex 722049, Fax 7613449, ≤ gulf, City and Vesuvius, – – 40-50. AE E VISA.
M *(closed 8 to 27 August)* a la carte 45/67000 – **71 rm** 158/260000.
by Riviera di Chiaia EFX

San Germano, via Beccadelli 41 ✉ 80125 ☎ 5705422, Telex 720080, Fax 5701546, « Attractive garden-park », – P – 300. AE E VISA. rest
M (resident only) *(closed August)* 43000 – **104 rm** 140/230000. by ⑧

Continental without rest., via Partenope 44 ✉ 80121 ☎ 7644636, Fax 7644661, ≤ gulf and Castel dell'Ovo – rm – 600. AE E VISA. FX **n**
166 rm 265/352000 19 suites, 40000.

Majestic, largo Vasto a Chiaia 68 ✉ 80121 ✆ 416500, Telex 720408, Fax 416500 – ▤ ☎ – 25-100. AE ⓢ ⓞ E VISA. ✻ FX **b**
M a la carte 35/50000 – **132 rm** ☐ 170/270000.

Miramare, via Nazario Sauro 24 ✉ 80132 ✆ 7647589, Fax 7640775, ← gulf and Vesuvius – ▤ TV ☎. AE ⓢ ⓞ E VISA. ✻ GX **e**
M *(closed 16 to 31 August)* a la carte 50/75000 – **30 rm** ☐ 220/320000.

Rex without rest., via Palepoli 12 ✉ 80132 ✆ 7649389, Fax 7649227 – ▤ TV ☎. AE ⓢ ⓞ E VISA
40 rm ☐ 103/160000. GX **r**

Serius, viale Augusto 74 ✉ 80125 ✆ 614844, Fax 614844 – ▤ TV ☎. AE ⓢ E VISA. ✻ rest by ⑧
M 40000 – **69 rm** ☐ 110/165000, ▤ 10000.

Nuovo Rebecchino without rest., corso Garibaldi 356 ✉ 80142 ✆ 5535327, Fax 268026 – ▤ TV ☎. AE ⓢ ⓞ E VISA MY **b**
58 rm ☐ 120/152000.

Cavour, piazza Garibaldi 32 ✉ 80142 ✆ 283122, Fax 287488 – TV ☎. AE ⓢ ⓞ E VISA
M (see **rest. Cavour** below) – **94 rm** ☐ 98/150000. MY **b**

Palace Hotel, piazza Garibaldi 9 ✉ 80142 ✆ 5535978, Telex 720262, Fax 264306 – TV ☎ – 30-80. AE ⓢ ⓞ E VISA MY **s**
M (see **rest. Cavour** below) – **102 rm** ☐ 98/150000.

Executive without rest., via del Cerriglio 10 ✉ 80134 ✆ 5520611, Fax 5520611, ≘s – ▤ TV ☎. AE ⓢ ⓞ E VISA KZ **c**
18 rm ☐ 140/180000, 1 suite.

XXX **La Sacrestia,** via Orazio 116 ✉ 80122 ✆ 7611051, Elegant rest., « Summer service in garden terrace with ← » – ▤. AE ⓞ VISA. ✻ by Riviera di Chiaia EFX
closed August, Sunday in July and Monday in other months – **M** a la carte 80/100000.

XXX ✿ **La Cantinella,** via Cuma 42 ✉ 80132 ✆ 7648684, Fax 7648769 – ▤. AE ⓢ ⓞ E VISA. ✻ GX **v**
closed Sunday, August, Christmas and New Year's Day – **M** a la carte 51/88000 (12 %)
Spec. Pilaf di gamberi, Linguine Santa Lucia, Pesce "all'acqua pazza". Wines Fiano, Taurasi.

XXX **Rosolino,** via Nazario Sauro 5/7 ✉ 80132 ✆ 415873, Fax 405457, Rest. and piano bar – ▤ – 70. AE ⓢ ⓞ E VISA. ✻ GX **a**
closed Sunday and 11 to 31 August – **M** a la carte 45/80000.

XX **San Carlo,** via Cesario Console 18/19 ✉ 80132 ✆ 7649757 – AE ⓢ ⓞ E VISA. ✻ KZ **a**
closed Sunday and 3 August-3 September – **M** (booking essential) a la carte 45/69000.

XX ✿ **Giuseppone a Mare,** via Ferdinando Russo 13-Capo Posillipo ✉ 80123 ✆ 7696002, Seaside rest. with ← – Ⓟ. AE ⓞ E VISA. ✻ by Riviera di Chiaia EFX
closed Sunday and 23 to 31 December – **M** a la carte 37/62000 (12 %)
Spec. Linguine con gamberoni e frutti di mare, Polipetti al pignatiello, Spigola "all'acqua pazza". Wines Biancolella, Per'e Palummo.

XX Ciro a Santa Brigida, via Santa Brigida 73 ✉ 80132 ✆ 5524072, Fax 5528992, Rest. and pizzeria – ▤ JZ **w**

XX **Cavour,** piazza Garibaldi 34 ✉ 80142 ✆ 264730 – ▤. AE ⓢ ⓞ E VISA. ✻ MY **b**
closed Sunday – **M** a la carte 36/60000.

XX **Ciro a Mergellina,** via Mergellina 18/23 ✉ 80122 ✆ 681780 – AE ⓢ ⓞ E VISA
closed Friday and 14 July-25 August – **M** a la carte 37/73000 (12 %).
by Riviera di Chiaia EFX

X **Sbrescia,** rampe Sant'Antonio a Posillipo 109 ✉ 80122 ✆ 669140, Typical Neapolitan rest. with ← City and gulf – AE VISA. ✻ by Riviera di Chiaia EFX
closed Monday and 15 to 28 August – **M** a la carte 30/56000 (12 %).

Island of Capri 80073 Napoli 988 ㉗, 431 F 24 – pop. 12 761 alt. 0 to 589 – High Season : Easter and June-September – ☎ 081.
The limitation of motor-vehicles' access is regulated by legislative rules.

Gd H. Quisisana and Rest. La Colombaia, via Camerelle 2 ✆ 8370788, Telex 710520, Fax 8376080, ← sea and Certosa, ⛱, « Garden with ⛱ », Fš, ≘s, ⛱, ✻ – ▤ TV ☎ – 25-400. AE ⓢ ⓞ E VISA. ✻
Easter-October – **M** 65000 – **150 rm** ☐ 380/580000, 15 suites.

Scalinatella ⛱ without rest., via Tragara 8 ✆ 8370633, Fax 8378291, ← sea and Certosa, ⛱ heated – ▤ TV ☎. VISA
15 March-5 November – **28 rm** ☐ 550000.

Europa Palace, via Capodimonte 2 ✆ 8370955, Telex 710397, Fax 8373191, ←, ⛱, « Floral terraces with ⛱ », Fš, ≘s – ▤ TV ☎ – 30-200. AE ⓢ ⓞ E VISA. ✻
April-October – **M** a la carte 53/86000 – **90 rm** ☐ 240/350000, 1 suite.

Luna ⛱, viale Matteotti 3 ✆ 8370433, Telex 721247, Fax 8377459, ← sea, Faraglioni and Certosa, ⛱, « Terraces and garden with ⛱ » – ▤ rm TV ☎. AE ⓢ ⓞ E VISA. ✻ rest
April-October – **M** a la carte 56/84000 – **48 rm** ☐ 240/410000, 4 suites.

La Palma and Rest. Relais la Palma, via Vittorio Emanuele 39 ✆ 8370133, Telex 722015, Fax 8376966, ⛱, ≘s – ▤ TV ☎ – 25-200. AE ⓢ ⓞ E VISA. ✻
M a la carte 45/68000 – **80 rm** ☐ 230/380000.

NAPOLI

Giordano (Via L.) .... **EV** 64
Scarlatti
(Via Alessandro) ...... **EV** 153

Arcoleo (Via G.) .... **FX** 5
Arena della Sanità (Via) ... **GU** 6
Artisti (Piazza degli) ...... **EV** 9
Bernini (Via G. L.) .... **EV** 12
Bonito (Via G.) .... **FV** 13
Carducci (Via G.) .... **FX** 20
Chiatamone (Via) .... **FX** 25

Cirillo (Via D.) .... **GU** 27
Colonna (Via Vittoria) ..... **FX** 29
Crocelle (Via) .... **GU** 35
D'Auria (Via G.) .... **FV** 40
Ferraris (Via Galileo) ...... **HV** 54
Fontana (Via Domenico) .. **EU** 58
Gen. Pignatelli (Via) ...... **HU** 62

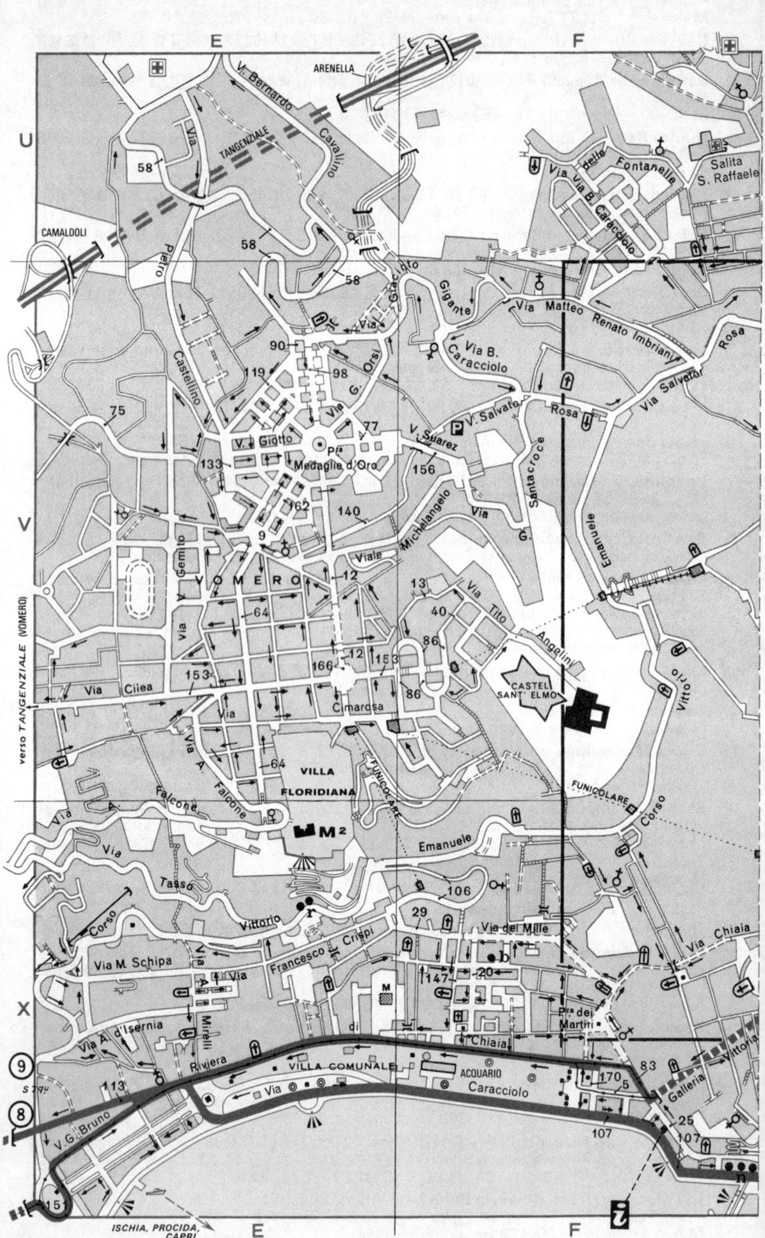

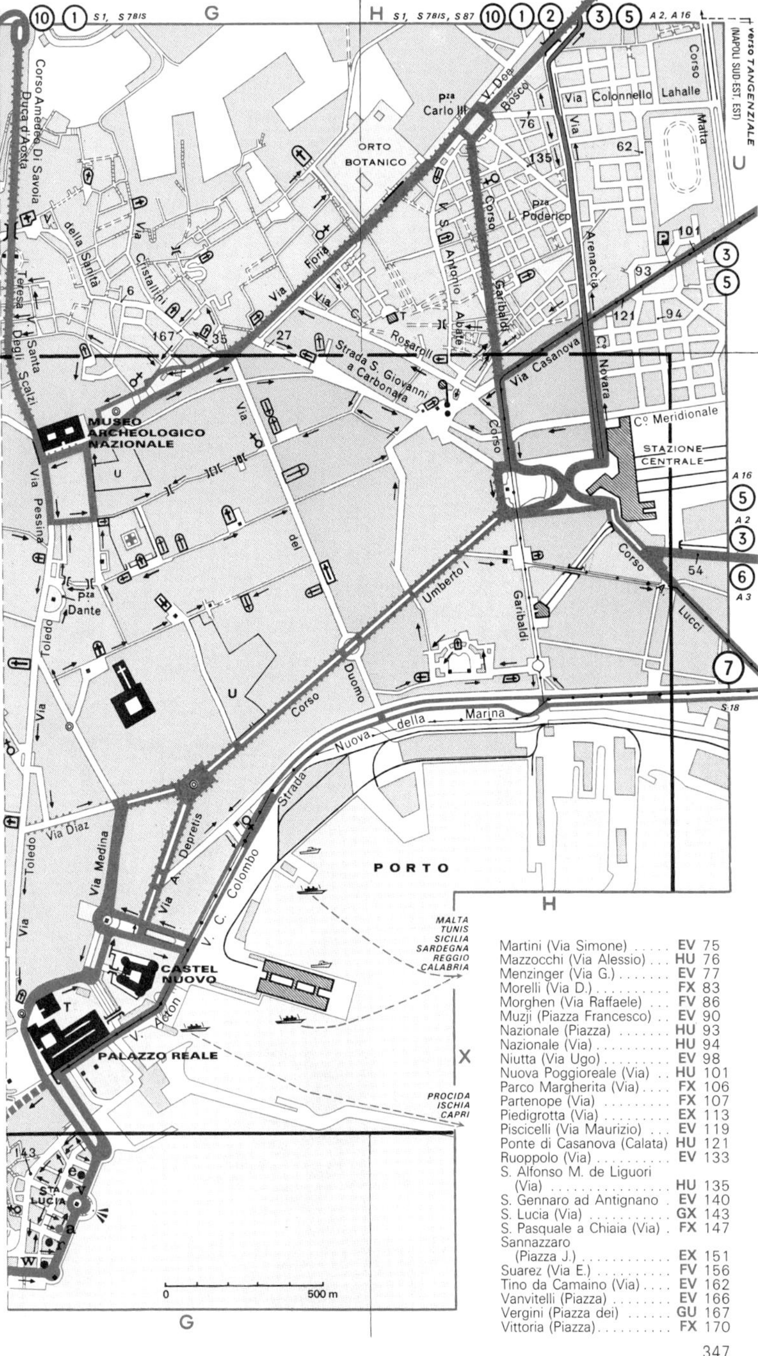
G
H
S 1, S 7BIS
S 1, S 7BIS, S 87
A 2, A 16
verso TANGENZIALE
(NAPOLI SUD-EST, EST)
Corso Amedeo Di Savoia Duca d'Aosta
Pza Carlo III
V. Don Bosco
Via Colonnello Lahalle
Corso Malta
ORTO BOTANICO
Pza L. Poderico
Corso Garibaldi
V. S. Antonio Abate
Via Arenaccia
Via della Sanità
Via Cristallini
Via Foria
Via C. Rosaroll
Strada S. Giovanni a Carbonara
Via Casanova
Co Novara
V. Santa Teresa Degli Scalzi
MUSEO ARCHEOLOGICO NAZIONALE
Co Meridionale
STAZIONE CENTRALE
A 16
A 2
A 3
S 18
Via Pessina
Via del Duomo
Corso Umberto I
Corso A. Lucci
Pza Dante
Toledo
Via Toledo
Corso Garibaldi
Via Nuova della Marina
Strada
Via Diaz
Via Medina
Via A. Depretis
V. C. Colombo
PORTO
MALTA
TUNIS
SICILIA
SARDEGNA
REGGIO CALABRIA
CASTEL NUOVO
V. Acton
PALAZZO REALE
PROCIDA
ISCHIA
CAPRI
Sta LUCIA
X
U
0
500 m

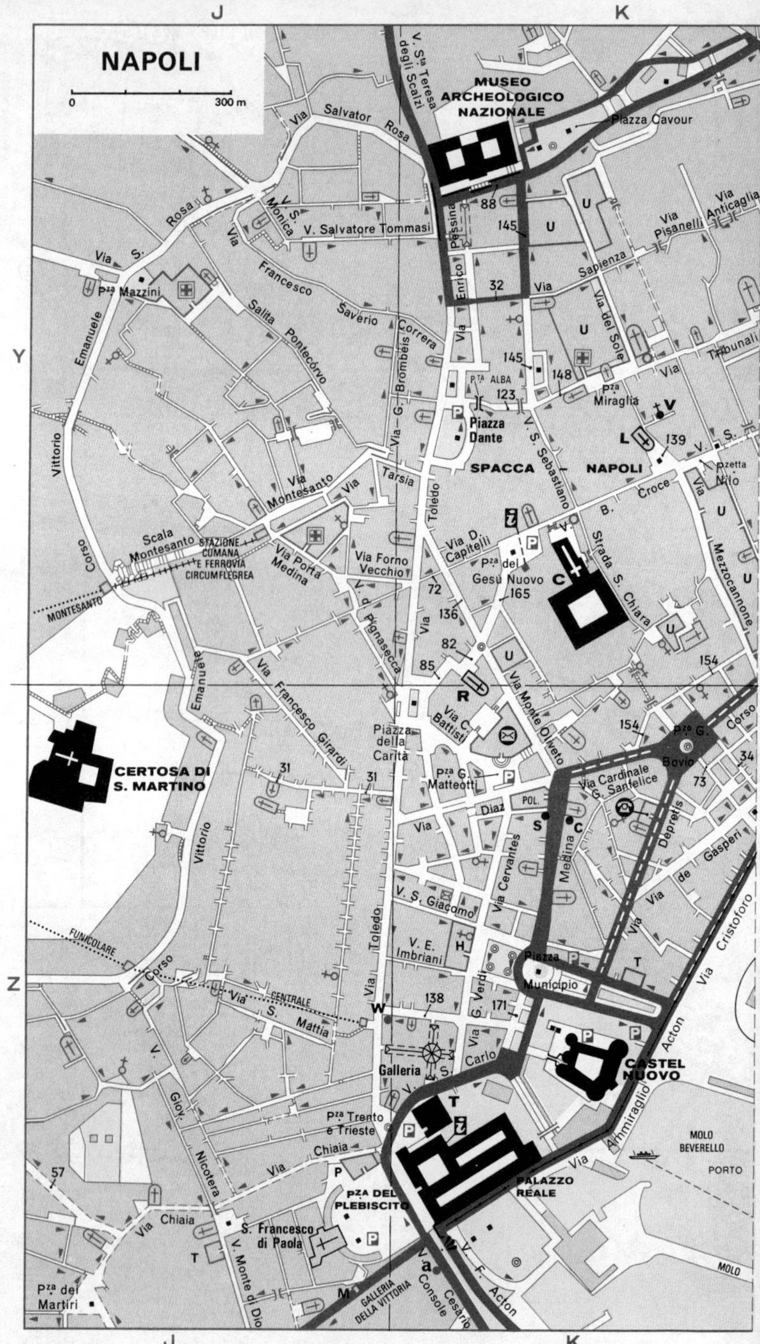

J
K
NAPOLI
0
300 m
V. Sta Teresa degli Scalzi
MUSEO ARCHEOLOGICO NAZIONALE
Piazza Cavour
Via Salvator Rosa
Via S. Rosa
V. S. Monica
V. Salvatore Tommasi
Pessina
88
145
U
Via Anticaglia
Via Pisanelli
Via Sapienza
Via Francesco Saverio Correra
Enrico
32
Via
P^za Mazzini
Salita Pontecorvo
Emanuele
Vittorio
Corso
Y
Via G. Brombeis
Via del Sole
Tribunali
145
148
P^ta ALBA
123
P^za Miraglia
V
L
139
Piazza Dante
V. S. Sebastiano
SPACCA NAPOLI
V. S.
P^zetta Nilo
Via Montesanto
Via Tarsia
Toledo
Croce
B.
Via Mezzocannone
Scala Montesanto
STAZIONE CUMANA E FERROVIA CIRCUMFLEGREA
Via Porta Medina
Via Forno Vecchio
Via D. Capitelli
P^za del Gesù Nuovo
C
Strada S. Chiara
MONTESANTO
72
165
V. d. Pignasecca
136
82
85
R
Via Monte Oliveto
154
Via Francesco Girardi
Via C. Battisti
Piazza della Carità
P^za G. Bovio
Corso
34
CERTOSA DI S. MARTINO
31
P^za G. Matteotti
Via Cardinale G. Sanfelice
73
Via Diaz
POL.
S
C
Medina
Depretis
Via de Gasperi
Via Cervantes
V. S. Giacomo
Via Cristoforo
FUNICOLARE
V. E. Imbriani
H
Piazza Municipio
T
Via Acton
Z
Corso
Via S. Mattia
CENTRALE
W
138
Via G. Verdi
171
Via Carlo
CASTEL NUOVO
Galleria
V. S.
V. Gioy. Nicotera
P^za Trento e Trieste
Via Chiaia
P
P^ZA DEL PLEBISCITO
PALAZZO REALE
Via Ammiraglio
MOLO BEVERELLO
PORTO
57
Via Chiaia
S. Francesco di Paola
T
V. Monte di Dio
a
V. F. Acton
Console
Cesario
MOLO
M
GALLERIA DELLA VITTORIA
P^za dei Martiri

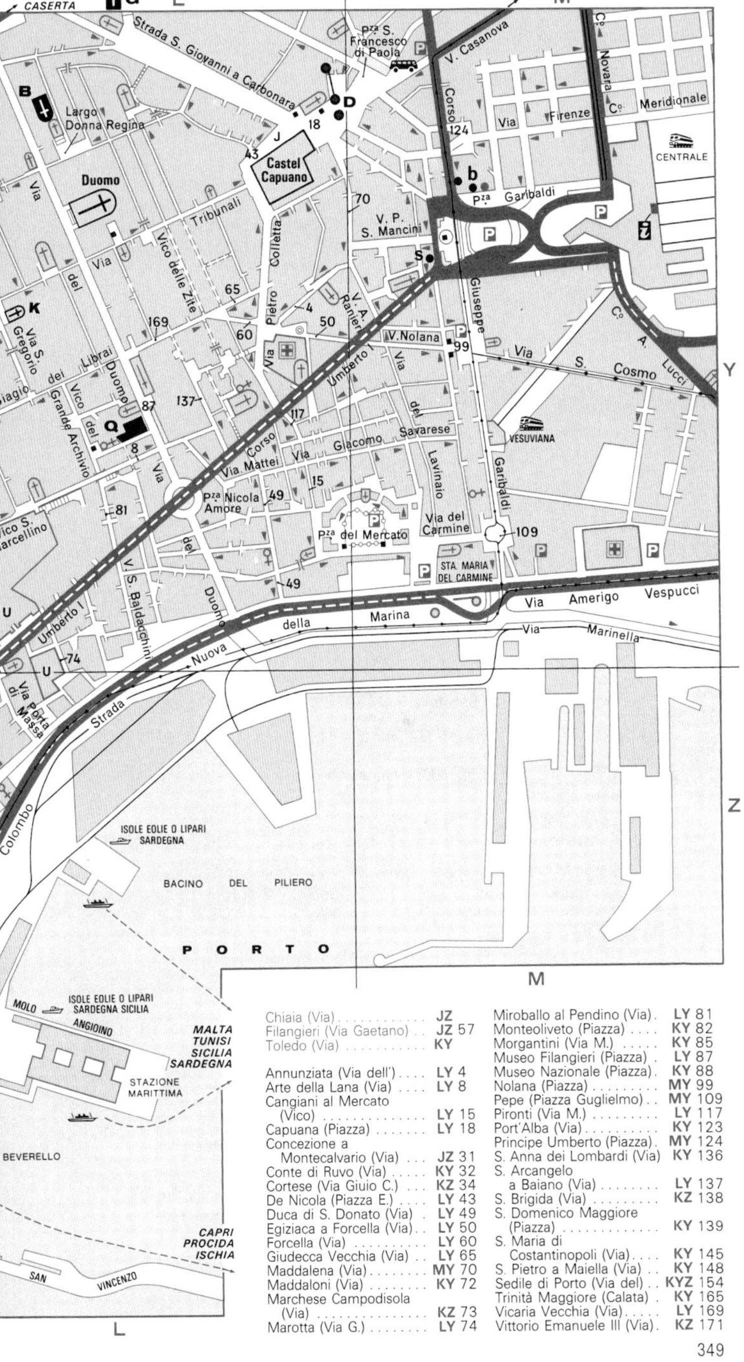

Chiaia (Via) . . . . JZ
Filangieri (Via Gaetano) . . JZ 57
Toledo (Via) . . . . KY

Annunziata (Via dell') . . . . LY 4
Arte della Lana (Via) . . . . LY 8
Cangiani al Mercato (Vico) . . . . LY 15
Capuana (Piazza) . . . . LY 18
Concezione a Montecalvario (Via) . . . JZ 31
Conte di Ruvo (Via) . . . . . KY 32
Cortese (Via Giuio C.) . . . KZ 34
De Nicola (Piazza E.) . . . . LY 43
Duca di S. Donato (Via) . . LY 49
Egiziaca a Forcella (Via) . . LY 50
Forcella (Via) . . . . LY 60
Giudecca Vecchia (Via) . . . LY 65
Maddalena (Via) . . . . MY 70
Maddaloni (Via) . . . . KY 72
Marchese Campodisola (Via) . . . . KZ 73
Marotta (Via G.) . . . . LY 74
Miroballo al Pendino (Via) . LY 81
Monteoliveto (Piazza) . . . . KY 82
Morgantini (Via M.) . . . . . KY 85
Museo Filangieri (Piazza) . LY 87
Museo Nazionale (Piazza) . KY 88
Nolana (Piazza) . . . . MY 99
Pepe (Piazza Guglielmo) . . MY 109
Pironti (Via M.) . . . . LY 117
Port'Alba (Via) . . . . KY 123
Principe Umberto (Piazza) . MY 124
S. Anna dei Lombardi (Via) KY 136
S. Arcangelo a Baiano (Via) . . . . LY 137
S. Brigida (Via) . . . . KZ 138
S. Domenico Maggiore (Piazza) . . . . KY 139
S. Maria di Costantinopoli (Via) . . . . KY 145
S. Pietro a Maiella (Via) . . KY 148
Sedile di Porto (Via del) . . KYZ 154
Trinità Maggiore (Calata) . KY 165
Vicaria Vecchia (Via) . . . . . LY 169
Vittorio Emanuele III (Via) . KZ 171

La Pazziella without rest., via Fuorlovado 36 8370044, Fax 8370085, « Floral garden » – AE VISA.
19 rm 220/330000 suite.

Punta Tragara , via Tragara 57 8370844, Telex 710261, Fax 8377790, Faraglioni and coast, , « Panoramic terrace with heated » – AE VISA.
7 April-October – **M** a la carte 57/87000 – 33 suites 250/650000.

Flora , via Serena 26 8370211, Fax 8378949, sea and Certosa, « Floral terrace », heated – AE VISA. rest
closed 9 January-14 March – **M** a la carte 60/80000 – **24 rm** 350000.

La Pineta , via Tragara 6 8370644, Telex 710011, Fax 8376445, sea and Certosa, « Pine terraces, flowers », , , – – 30. AE VISA.
M a la carte 40/64000 – **52 rm** 200/300000 4 suites.

Villa delle Sirene, via Camerelle 51 8370102, Fax 8370957, , , « Lemon-grove with » – AE VISA
April-October – **M** *(closed Tuesday)* a la carte 39/51000 – **35 rm** 240/300000.

La Brunella , via Tragara 24 8370122, Fax 8370430, sea and coast, , « Floral terraces », heated – rm AE VISA.
19 March-5 November – **M** a la carte 31/60000 (12 %) – **18 rm** 280000.

Gatto Bianco, via Vittorio Emanuele 32 8370446, Fax 8378060, « Summer service under the pergola » – rm AE VISA.
March-October and 27 December-6 January – **M** 30/45000 – **34 rm** 140/250000, 20000.

Villa Sarah without rest., via Tiberio 3/a 8377817, , « Shaded garden » – AE VISA.
Easter-October – **20 rm** 110/180000.

La Capannina, via Le Botteghe 14 8370732, Fax 8376990, (booking essential for dinner) –
season.

Casanova, via Le Botteghe 46 8377642 – AE VISA
closed 3 January-March and Thursday (except July-September) – **M** a la carte 37/60000 (15 %).

La Sceriffa, via Provinciale Marina Grande 86 A 8377953, ,
April-October ; closed Tuesday and 15 July-15 September also lunch – **M** a la carte 40/55000 (12 %).

La Tavernetta, via Lo Palazzo 23/a 8376864 – AE VISA
closed Monday and 15 January-February – **M** a la carte 33/65000 (15 %).

Da Gemma, via Madre Serafina 6 8377113, Fax 8378947, sea – AE VISA
closed Monday and November-5 December – **M** a la carte 31/60000 (15 %).

Sant'Agata sui due Golfi 80064 Napoli 431 F 25 – alt. 391 – High Season : April-September – 081.
Roma 266 – Castellammare di Stabia 28 – Napoli 57 – Salerno 56 – Sorrento 9.

Don Alfonso 1890 with rm, 8780026, Fax 5330226, – . AE VISA.
closed 10 January-25 February – **M** *(closed Monday and Sunday dinner except June-September)* (booking essential) a la carte 69/106000 – **2 suites** 180/200000
Spec. Astice e aragosta agli agrumi, Linguine alle vongole e zucchine, Costolette di agnello alle erbe mediterranee. Wines Biancolella, Aglianico.

PALERMO (PALERMO) 90100 P 988 ㉟, 432 M 22 – pop. 734 238 – ☎ 091.

See : Palace of the Normans★★ : the palatine Chapel★★★, mosaics★★★ AZ – Regional Gallery of Sicily★★ in Abbatellis Palace★ : Death Triumphant★★★ CY **M1** – Piazza Bellini★★ BY : Martorana Church★★, Church of St. Cataldo★★ – Church of St. John of the Hermits★★ AZ – Capuchin Catacombs★★ AZ – Piazza Pretoria★ BY : fountain★★ **B** – Archaeological Museum★ : metopes from the temples at Selinus★★, the Ram★★ BY **M** – Chiaramonte Palace★ : magnolia fig trees★★ in Garibaldi Gardens CY – St. Lawrence Oratory★ CY **N** Quattro Canti★ BY – Cathedral★ AYZ Villa Bonanno★ AZ – Zisa Palace★ AY – Botanical garden★ CDZ – Sicilian carts★ in Ethnographic Museum.

Envir. : Monreale★★★ AZ by ② : 8 km – Monte Pellegrino★★ BX by ③ : 14 km.

✈ Punta Raisi by ③ : 30 km ✆ 6019333 – Alitalia, via della Libertà 29 ✉ 90139 ✆ 6019111.

⛴ to Genova Tuesday, Friday and Sunday, (22 h) and to Livorno Monday, Wednesday and Friday (19 h) – Grandi Traghetti, via Mariano Stabile 53 ✉ 90141 ✆ 587939, Telex 910098, Fax 589629; to Napoli daily (10 h 30 mn), to Genova June-September, Monday, Wednesday, Friday and Saturday, Monday, Wednesday and Friday in other months (23 h) and to Cagliari June-September Sunday and Friday in other months (12 h 30 mn) – Tirrenia Navigazione, via Roma 385 ✉ 90133 ✆ 333300, Telex 910020, Fax 6021221; to Ustica daily (2 h 20 mn) – Siremar Prestifilippo Agency, via Crispi 118 ✉ 90133 ✆ 582403.

⛴ to Ustica daily (1 h 15 mn) – Siremar Prestifilippo Agency, via Crispi 118 ✉ 90133 ✆ 582403; to Aeolian Island June-September daily (2 h 30 mn) – SNAV Barbaro Agency, piazza Principe di Belmonte 51/55 ✉ 90139 ✆ 586533, Telex 910093, Fax 584830.

ℹ piazza Castelnuovo 34 ✉ 90141 ✆ 583847, Telex 910179, Fax 331854 – Punta Raisi Airport ✆ 591698 – Central Station ✉ 90127 ✆ 6165914, Fax 331854.

A.C.I. via delle Alpi 6 ✉ 90144 ✆ 300471.

Messina 235 ①.

Plans on following pages

Villa Igiea Gd H. ⛭, salita Belmonte 43 ✉ 90142 ✆ 543744, Telex 910092, Fax 547654, ≤, « Floral terraces overlooking the sea », ⛱, 🌳, 🎾 – 🛗 ▤ TV ☎ ♿ P – 🅰 50-500. AE ⓢ ⓓ E VISA. ✗ rest — by ③
M 80000 – **117 rm** ☕ 290/450000, 6 suites.

Astoria Palace, via Monte Pellegrino 62 ✉ 90142 ✆ 6371820, Telex 911045, Fax 6372178 – 🛗 ▤ TV ☎ P – 🅰 30-1000. AE ⓢ ⓓ VISA. ✗ — by via Crispi BX
M 50/70000 – **325 rm** ☕ 154/213000.

Jolly, Foro Italico 22 ✉ 90133 ✆ 6165090, Telex 910076, Fax 6161441, ⛱, 🌳 – 🛗 ⚡ rm ▤ TV ☎ P – 🅰 50-500. AE ⓢ ⓓ E. ✗ rest — DY **s**
M 50000 – **273 rm** ☕ 160/210000.

President, via Crispi 230 ✉ 90139 ✆ 580733, Telex 910359, Fax 6111588, ≤, « Roof-garden rest. » – 🛗 ▤ TV ☎ P – 🅰 30-150. AE ⓢ ⓓ E VISA. ✗ — BX **e**
M a la carte 36/52000 – **129 rm** ☕ 140/180000.

Excelsior Palace, via Marchese Ugo 3 ✉ 90141 ✆ 6256176, Telex 911149, Fax 342139 – 🛗 ⚡ rest ▤ TV ☎ – 🅰 50-100. AE ⓢ ⓓ E VISA. ✗ rest — AX **c**
M 45000 – **128 rm** ☕ 160/210000, 7 suites.

MotelAgip, viale della Regione Siciliana 2620 ✉ 90145 ✆ 552033, Telex 911196, Fax 408198 – 🛗 ▤ TV ☎ P – 🅰 90. AE ⓢ ⓓ E VISA. ✗ rest — by ③
M 36000 – **105 rm** ☕ 126/174000.

Politeama Palace, piazza Ruggero Settimo 15 ✉ 90139 ✆ 322777, Telex 911053, Fax 6111589 – 🛗 ▤ TV ☎ – 🅰 50-130. AE ⓢ ⓓ E VISA. ✗ — AX **s**
M a la carte 50/75000 – **102 rm** ☕ 175/250000.

Europa, via Agrigento 3 ✉ 90141 ✆ 6256323, Fax 6256323 – 🛗 ▤ TV ☎ — AX **r**
73 rm.

Mediterraneo, via Rosolino Pilo 43 ✉ 90139 ✆ 581133, Fax 586974 – 🛗 ▤ TV ☎ – 🅰 50. AE ⓢ ⓓ E VISA. ✗ — BX **k**
M (residents only) 33000 – **104 rm** ☕ 100/150000.

Cristal Palace, via Roma 477/d ✉ 90139 ✆ 6112580, Telex 911205, Fax 6112589 – 🛗 ▤ TV ☎ – 🅰 80. AE ⓢ ⓓ E VISA. ✗ — BX **m**
M a la carte 53/89000 – **90 rm** ☕ 115/190000.

Ponte, via Crispi 99 ✉ 90139 ✆ 583744, Telex 910492, Fax 581845 – 🛗 ▤ TV ☎. AE ⓢ ⓓ VISA. ✗ — BX **a**
M a la carte 30/43000 – **137 rm** ☕ 80/110000.

Sausele without rest., via Vincenzo Errante 12 ✉ 90127 ✆ 6161308 – 🛗 ☎ 🚗. AE ⓢ ⓓ E VISA — BZ **u**
☕ 9000 – **37 rm** 50/75000.

Touring without rest., via Mariano Stabile 136 ✉ 90139 ✆ 584444 – 🛗 ▤ ☎. AE ⓢ ⓓ E VISA. ✗ — BX **h**
☕ 12000 – **22 rm** 65/90000, ▤ 20000.

Villa Archirafi without rest., via Lincoln 30 ✉ 90133 ✆ 6168827 – 🛗 ☎ P. ⓢ E VISA — CZ **m**
☕ 10000 – **30 rm** 70/100000.

Moderno without rest., via Roma 276 angolo via Napoli ✉ 90133 ✆ 588683 – TV ☎. AE ⓢ ⓓ E VISA — BY **a**
☕ 3000 – **38 rm** 50/75000.

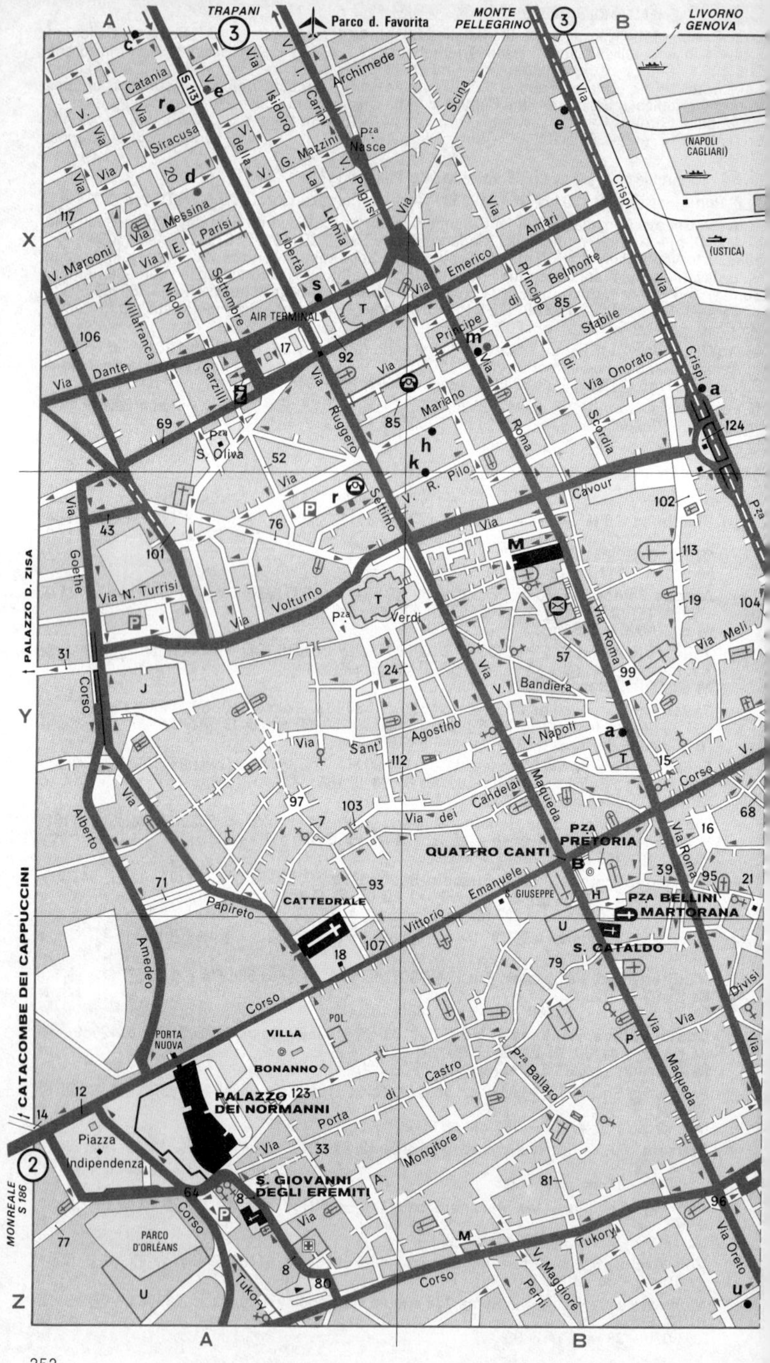
TRAPANI
Parco d. Favorita
MONTE PELLEGRINO
LIVORNO GENOVA
(NAPOLI CAGLIARI)
(USTICA)
AIR TERMINAL
QUATTRO CANTI
Pza PRETORIA
CATTEDRALE
S. GIUSEPPE
Pza BELLINI
MARTORANA
S. CATALDO
VILLA BONANNO
PORTA NUOVA
PALAZZO DEI NORMANNI
S. GIOVANNI DEGLI EREMITI
Piazza Indipendenza
PARCO D'ORLÉANS
PALAZZO D. ZISA
CATACOMBE DEI CAPPUCCINI
MONREALE S 186
Via Dante
Via Volturno
Via Maqueda
Via Roma
Corso Vittorio Emanuele
Via Crispi
Via Cavour
Via Libertà
Via Ruggero Settimo
Corso Tukory
Corso Alberto Amedeo
Via Papireto
Pza Verdi
Pza Ballarò
Pza S. Oliva

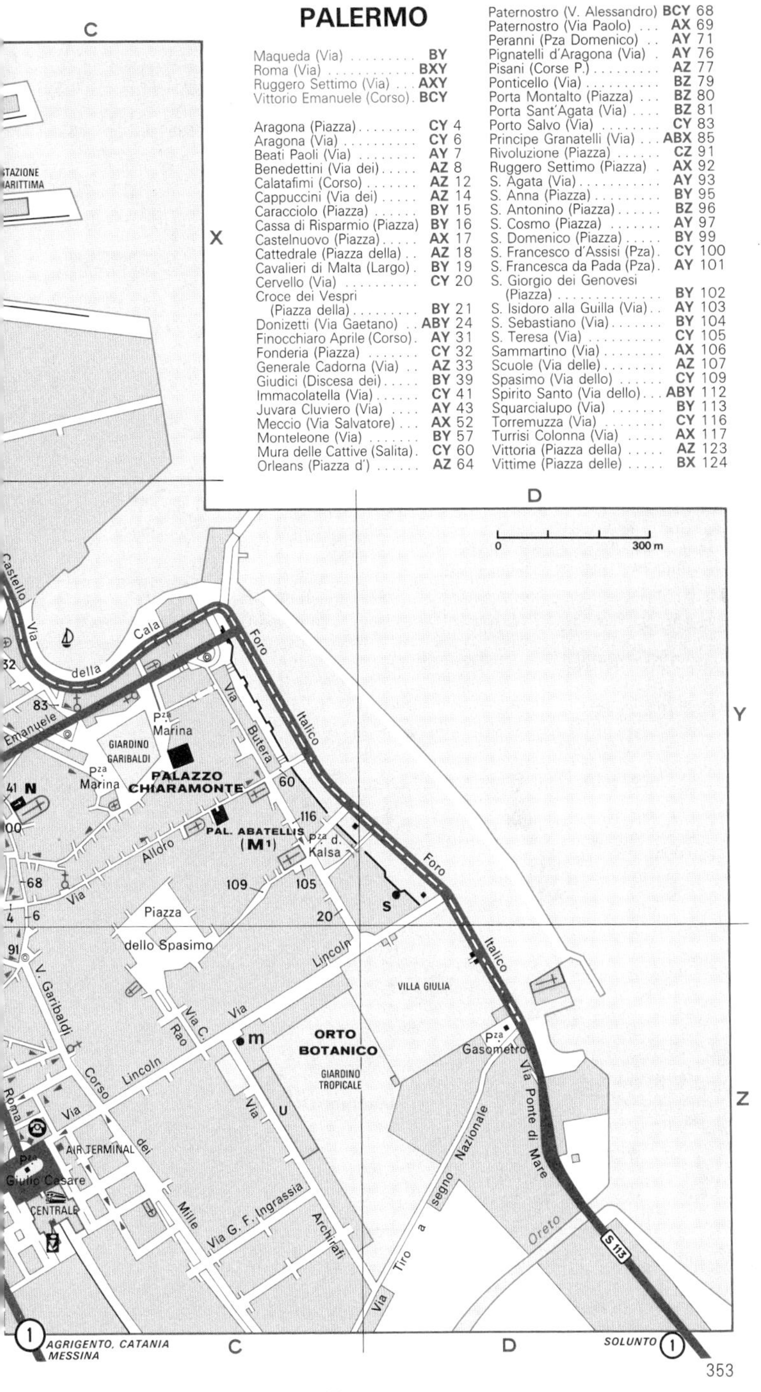
PALERMO
Maqueda (Via) BY
Roma (Via) BXY
Ruggero Settimo (Via) AXY
Vittorio Emanuele (Corso) BCY
Aragona (Piazza) CY 4
Aragona (Via) CY 6
Beati Paoli (Via) AY 7
Benedettini (Via dei) AZ 8
Calatafimi (Corso) AZ 12
Cappuccini (Via dei) AZ 14
Caracciolo (Piazza) BY 15
Cassa di Risparmio (Piazza) BY 16
Castelnuovo (Piazza) AX 17
Cattedrale (Piazza della) AZ 18
Cavalieri di Malta (Largo) BY 19
Cervello (Via) CY 20
Croce dei Vespri (Piazza della) BY 21
Donizetti (Via Gaetano) ABY 24
Finocchiaro Aprile (Corso) AY 31
Fonderia (Piazza) CY 32
Generale Cadorna (Via) AZ 33
Giudici (Discesa dei) BY 39
Immacolatella (Via) CY 41
Juvara Cluviero (Via) AY 43
Meccio (Via Salvatore) AX 52
Monteleone (Via) BY 57
Mura delle Cattive (Salita) CY 60
Orleans (Piazza d') AZ 64
Paternostro (V. Alessandro) BCY 68
Paternostro (Via Paolo) AX 69
Peranni (Pza Domenico) AY 71
Pignatelli d'Aragona (Via) AY 76
Pisani (Corse P.) AZ 77
Ponticello (Via) BZ 79
Porta Montalto (Piazza) BZ 80
Porta Sant'Agata (Via) BZ 81
Porto Salvo (Via) CY 83
Principe Granatelli (Via) ABX 85
Rivoluzione (Piazza) CZ 91
Ruggero Settimo (Piazza) AX 92
S. Agata (Via) AY 93
S. Anna (Piazza) BY 95
S. Antonino (Piazza) BZ 96
S. Cosmo (Piazza) AY 97
S. Domenico (Piazza) BY 99
S. Francesco d'Assisi (Pza) CY 100
S. Francesca da Pada (Pza) AY 101
S. Giorgio dei Genovesi (Piazza) BY 102
S. Isidoro alla Guilla (Via) AY 103
S. Sebastiano (Via) BY 104
S. Teresa (Via) CY 105
Sammartino (Via) AX 106
Scuole (Via delle) AZ 107
Spasimo (Via dello) CY 109
Spirito Santo (Via dello) ABY 112
Squarcialupo (Via) BY 113
Torremuzza (Via) CY 116
Turrisi Colonna (Via) AX 117
Vittoria (Piazza della) AZ 123
Vittime (Piazza delle) BX 124
STAZIONE MARITTIMA
0 300 m
Via Castello
Cala
Via della Cala
Foro Italico
Via Butera
Emanuele
Pza Marina
GIARDINO GARIBALDI
PALAZZO CHIARAMONTE
PAL. ABATELLIS (M1)
Pza d. Kalsa
Via Alloro
Piazza dello Spasimo
Via Lincoln
VILLA GIULIA
ORTO BOTANICO
GIARDINO TROPICALE
Pza Gasometro
Via Ponte di Mare
Via Tiro a segno Nazionale
Oreto
S 113
V. Garibaldi
Via C. Rao
Corso Lincoln
Via Roma
Pza Giulio Cesare
AIR TERMINAL
CENTRALE
Via dei Mille
Via G. F. Ingrassia
Archirafi
1 AGRIGENTO, CATANIA MESSINA
SOLUNTO 1

XXXX ✿ **Charleston,** piazzale Ungheria 30 ✉ 90141 ✆ 321366, Fax 321347 – ▤. AE ⑤ ⓞ E VISA. ✗ AY **r**
closed Sunday and June-September – **M** a la carte 70/100000
Spec. Risotto "delizie dell'orto", Spiedino di pesce, Cassata siciliana. Wines Rapitalà, Rosso del Conte.

XXX ✿ **L'Approdo da Renato,** via Messina Marine 224 ✉ 90123 ✆ 6302881, ☂ – AE ⑤ ⓞ VISA. ✗ by ① DZ
closed Wednesday and 10 to 25 August – **M** (booking essential) a la carte 52/84000 (10 %)
Spec. Pesce azzurro saradìsu (in agrodolce), Gnocchetti in salsa di gamberoni, Trancio di cernia ripiena alla siciliana. Wines Chardonnay, Duca Enrico.

XXX **Gourmand's,** via della Libertà 37/e ✉ 90139 ✆ 323431, Fax 322507 – ▤. AE ⑤ ⓞ E VISA. ✗ AX **e**
closed Sunday and 5 to 25 August – **M** a la carte 47/75000.

XXX **Friend's Bar,** via Brunelleschi 138 ✉ 90145 ✆ 201066, ☂ – ▤. AE ⓞ by ③
closed Monday and 16 to 31 August – **M** (booking essential) a la carte 35/50000.

XXX **La Scuderia,** viale del Fante 9 ✉ 90146 ✆ 520323, Fax 520467 – ▤ Ⓟ. AE ⑤ ⓞ E VISA. ✗ by via C.A. Dalla Chiesa AX
closed Sunday and 15 to 31 August – **M** a la carte 48/93000.

XX **Regine,** via Trapani 4/a ✉ 90141 ✆ 586566 – ▤. AE ⑤ ⓞ E VISA. ✗ AX **d**
closed Sunday and August – **M** a la carte 40/55000.

XX **A Cuccagna,** via Principe Granatelli 21/a ✉ 90139 ✆ 587267 – ▤. AE ⑤ ⓞ E VISA. ✗ BX **m**
closed Friday and 7 to 24 August – **M** a la carte 33/55000.

TAORMINA (TAORMINA) **98039** Messina 988 ㊲, 432 N 27 – pop. 10 905 alt. 250 – ☎ 0942.
See : Site★★★ – Greek Theatre★★ : ≤★★★ B – Public garden★★ B – ✳★★ from the Square 9 Aprile A **12** – Corso Umberto★ A – Belvedere★ B – Castle★ : ≤★ A.
Exc. : Etna★★★, SW : for Linguaglossa.
ℹ largo Santa Caterina (Corvaja palace) ✆ 23243, Telex 981167, Fax 24941.
Catania 52 ② – Enna 135 ② – Messina 52 ① – Palermo 255 ② – Siracusa 111 ② – Trapani 359 ②.

TAORMINA

Umberto (Corso) . . . . A
Cappuccini (Via) . . . . A 2
Crocifisso (Via) . . . . A 3
Dionisio (Via) . . . . A 5
Duomo (Piazza) . . . . A 6
Rotabile Castelmola . . . . . . A 8
S. Antonio (Piazza) . . . . A 9
Vittorio Emanuele (Pza) . . . B 10
9 Aprile (Piazza) . . . . A 13

Traffic restricted in the town centre from June to September

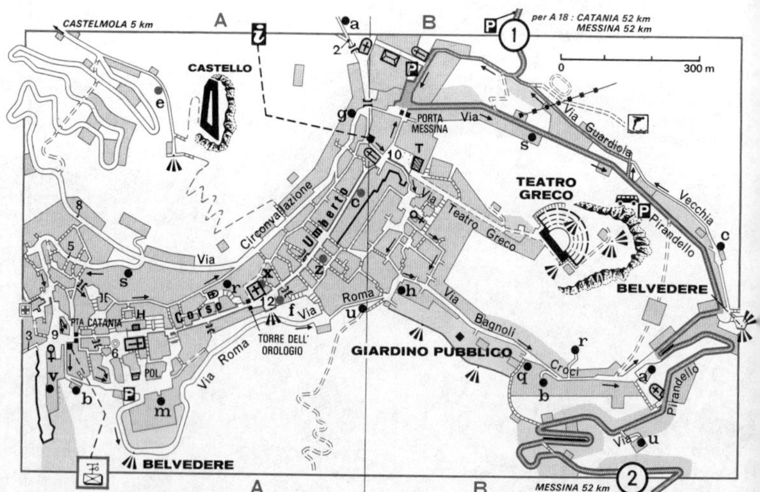

🏨 **San Domenico Palace** ⚘, piazza San Domenico 5 ✆ 23701, Telex 980013, Fax 625506, ☂, « 15C monastery with floral garden, ≤ sea, coast and Etna », ♨ heated – |‡| ▤ TV ☎ – 🚶 400. AE ⑤ ⓞ E VISA. ✗ rest A **m**
M 95/120000 – **101 rm** ☕ 350/620000, 8 suites.

Excelsior Palace ⑤, via Toselli 8 ☎ 23975, Telex 980185, Fax 23978, ≤ sea, coast and Etna, « Small park, heated ⛱ on terrace with panoramic view » – |‡| ▤ TV ☎ P – 🅰 100. AE 🅂 ⊙ E VISA. ✻ rest A v
M 65000 – **89 rm** ☐ 160/230000.

Jolly Diodoro, via Bagnoli Croci 75 ☎ 23312, Telex 980028, Fax 23391, ≤ sea, coast and Etna, « ⛱ on terrace with panoramic view », ⌂s, ⚘ – |‡| ▤ TV ☎ P – 🅰 250. AE 🅂 ⊙ E VISA. ✻ rest B q
M 35/60000 – **102 rm** ☐ 210/240000.

Bristol Park Hotel, via Bagnoli Croci 92 ☎ 23006, Telex 980005, Fax 24519, ≤ sea, coast and Etna, ⛱ – |‡| ▤ TV ☎ 🚗. AE 🅂 ⊙ E VISA. ✻ rest B r
closed 1 to 20 December and 10 January-February – **M** 40/60000 – **50 rm** ☐ 125/200000 3 suites.

Monte Tauro ⑤, via Madonna delle Grazie 3 ☎ 24402, Telex 980048, Fax 24403, ≤ sea and coast, ⛱ – |‡| ▤ TV ☎ P – 🅰 100. AE 🅂 ⊙ E VISA. ✻ AB u
M 50000 – **70 rm** ☐ 230000.

Gd H. Miramare, via Guardiola Vecchia 27 ☎ 23401, Fax 23978, ≤ sea and coast, ⛱ heated, ⚘, ✂ – |‡| ▤ TV ☎ P. AE 🅂 ⊙ VISA. ✻ rest B c
M 65000 – **68 rm** ☐ 180/250000, 1 suite.

Villa Paradiso without rest., via Roma 2 ☎ 23922, Fax 625800, ≤ sea, coast and Etna – |‡| ▤ TV ☎. AE 🅂 ⊙ E VISA. ✻ B h
April-October – **33 rm** ☐ 145/230000.

Villa Fiorita without rest., via Pirandello 39 ☎ 24122, Fax 625967, ≤ sea and coast, ⛱, ⚘ – |‡| ▤ TV ☎ 🚗. AE 🅂 E VISA. ✻ B s
24 rm ☐ 125000.

Vello d'Oro, via Fazzello 2 ☎ 23788, Telex 980186, Fax 626117, « Sun bathing terrace with ≤ sea and coast » – |‡| ▤ ☎. AE 🅂 ⊙ E VISA. ✻ A r
15 March-October – **M** *(dinner only)* 30000 – ☐ 15000 – **57 rm** 75/140000.

Villa Belvedere without rest., via Bagnoli Croci 79 ☎ 23791, Fax 625830, ≤ gardens, sea and Etna, « ⛱ on terrace with panoramic view », ⚘ – |‡| ☎ P. 🅂 E VISA B b
16 March-October – **43 rm** ☐ 93/168000.

Villa Sirina, contrada Sirina ☎ 51776, Fax 51671, ⛱, ⚘ – ▤ ☎ P. AE 🅂 ⊙ E VISA. ✻ rest
closed November-20 December – **M** *(dinner only)* 30/38000 – **15 rm** ☐ 159000.
2 km by via Crocifisso A

Villa Riis ⑤ without rest., via Rizzo 13 ☎ 24874, Fax 626254, ≤ sea, coast and Etna, 🍽, ⛱, ⚘ – |‡| ▤ ☎ ♿ P. AE 🅂 E VISA A b
April-October – **30 rm** ☐ 120/180000.

Continental, via Dionisio I 2/a ☎ 23805, Telex 981144, 🍽, « Panoramic terrace with ≤ sea and coast », ⚘ – |‡| ▤ ☎. AE 🅂 ⊙ E VISA. ✻ rest A s
M *(closed lunch May-September)* 35/45000 – ☐ 15000 – **43 rm** 85/130000.

Andromaco without rest., via Fontana Vecchia ☎ 23436, Fax 24985, ≤, ⛱ – ▤ ☎. AE 🅂 ⊙ E VISA. ✻ by via Cappuccini A
16 rm ☐ 65/115000.

La Campanella without rest., via Circonvallazione 3 ☎ 23381, ≤ – ✻ A g
12 rm ☐ 70/100000.

Villa Carlotta without rest., via Pirandello 81 ☎ 23732, Fax 23732, ≤ sea and coast, ⚘ – ☎ B a
15 March-October – ☐ 13000 – **21 rm** 55/86000.

Condor, via Cappuccini 25 ☎ 23124, Fax 24559, ≤ – ☎. 🅂 ⊙ E VISA. ✻ rest A a
Easter-15 October and 23 December-2 January – **M** (residents only) (dinner only) a la carte 20/35000 – ☐ 8000 – **12 rm** 60/80000.

Belsoggiorno, via Pirandello 60 ☎ 23342, ≤ sea and coast, ⚘ – ☎ P. AE 🅂 ⊙ E VISA. ✻ rest B u
M *(dinner only)* 25/30000 – ☐ 5000 – **19 rm** 70/110000.

XXXX **La Giara,** vico La Floresta 1 ☎ 23360, Fax 23233, 🍽 – ▤. AE 🅂 ⊙ E VISA. ✻ A f
closed Monday (except June-September) – **M** (dinner only) a la carte 51/79000.

XX **Al Castello da Ciccio,** via Madonna della Rocca ☎ 28158, « Outdoor summer service with ≤ Giardini Naxos, sea and Etna » – ✻ A e
closed January, Sunday in July-August and Wednesday in other months – **M** a la carte 50/75000.

XX **La Griglia,** corso Umberto 54 ☎ 23980, Fax 626047 – ▤. AE 🅂 ⊙ E VISA. ✻ A c
closed Tuesday and 20 November-20 December – **M** a la carte 36/59000.

XX **Quattropini,** contrada Sant'Antonio ☎ 24832, Fax 24832, ≤, 🍽 – P. AE 🅂 ⊙ E VISA
closed Monday and 26 November-26 December – **M** a la carte 42/69000. 1 km by ①

X **A' Zammara,** via Fratelli Bandiera 15 ☎ 24408, 🍽 – AE 🅂 ⊙ E VISA A z
closed Wednesday and 5 to 20 January – **M** a la carte 33/52000.

X **Vicolo Stretto,** via Vicolo Stretto ☎ 29849, 🍽 – ▤. AE 🅂 E VISA A x
closed Monday and 15 November-15 December – **M** a la carte 31/60000.

at Capo Taormina by ② : 3 km – ✉ **98030** Mazzarò :

Grande Alb. Capotaormina, ✆ 24000, Telex 980147, Fax 625467, ≤ sea and coast, ⛱, ⛵, – |‡| ▤ TV ☎ ⇔ Ⓟ – ⚐ 150-350. AE Ⓢ ⓞ E VISA. ✻ rest
20 March-December – **M** 80000 – **207 rm** ☐ 323000.

at Castelmola NO : 5 km A – alt. 550 – ✉ **98030** :

Il Faro, contrada Petralia ✆ 28193, ≤ sea and coast, ⛱ – Ⓟ
closed Wednesday – **M** (booking essential) a la carte 26/35000.

at Mazzarò by ② : 5,5 km – ✉ **98030** :

Mazzarò Sea Palace, ✆ 24004, Telex 980041, Fax 626237, ≤ small bay, ⛱, ⛵ heated, ⛵ – |‡| ▤ TV ☎ ⇔. AE Ⓢ ⓞ E VISA. ✻ rest
April-October – **M** a la carte 75/114000 – **87 rm** ☐ 245/490000, 3 suites.

Villa Sant'Andrea, ✆ 23125, Telex 980077, Fax 24838, ≤ small bay, ⛱, « Shaded terraces », ⛵, ⛱ – ▤ ☎ Ⓟ. AE Ⓢ ⓞ E VISA. ✻
closed 10 January-18 March – **M** 55/70000 – **Oliviero Rest.** (dinner only) (booking essential) a la carte 54/95000 – **67 rm** ☐ 380000.

Il Pescatore, ✆ 23460, ≤ sea, cliffs and Isolabella – Ⓟ. E VISA
3 March-October – **M** *(closed Monday)* a la carte 34/62000.

Il Delfino-da Angelo, ✆ 23004, ≤ small bay, ⛱ – AE Ⓢ ⓞ E VISA
15 March-October – **M** a la carte 29/45000.

Da Giovanni, ✆ 23531, ≤ sea and Isolabella – AE Ⓢ ⓞ VISA. ✻
closed Monday and 7 January-7 February – **M** a la carte 41/73000.

at Lido di Spisone by ① : 7 km – ✉ **98030** Mazzarò :

Lido Mediterranée, ✆ 24422, Telex 980175, Fax 24774, ≤, ⛵ – ▤ TV ☎ Ⓟ – ⚐ 100. AE Ⓢ ⓞ E VISA. ✻ rest
April-October – **M** a la carte 57/80000 – **72 rm** ☐ 300000.

TURIN (TORINO) 10100 Ⓟ 988 ⑫, 428 G 5 – pop. 991 870 alt. 239 – ✆ 011.

See : Piazza San Carlo★★ CXY – Egyptian Museum★★, Sabauda Gallery★★ in Academy of Science CX **M** – Cathedral★ CX : relic of the Holy Shroud★★★ – Mole Antonelliana★ : ✻★★ DX – Madama Palace★ : museum of Ancient Art★ CX **A** – Royal Palace★ : Royal Armoury★ CDVX – Risorgimento Museum★ in Carignano Palace CX **M2** – Carlo Biscaretti di Ruffia Motor Museum★ – Model medieval village★ in the Valentino Park CDZ.

Envir. : Basilica of Superga★ : ≤★★★, royal tombs★ – Tour to the pass, Colle della Maddalena★ : ≤★★ of the city from the route Superga-Pino Torinese, ≤★ of the city from the route Colle della Maddalena-Cavoretto.

⛳18, ⛳9 I Roveri (March-November ; closed Monday) at La Mandria ✉ 10070 Fiano ✆ 9235719, Fax 9235669, by ① : 18 km;

⛳18, ⛳18 (closed January, February and Monday), at Fiano ✉ 10070 ✆9235440, Fax 9235886, by ① : 20 km;

⛳18 Le Fronde (closed Monday and January) at Avigliana ✉ 10051 ✆ 938053, Fax 938053, W : 24 km;

⛳9 (closed Monday and August), at Stupinigi ✉ 10135 Torino, ✆ 3472640, Fax 3978038;

⛳9 (closed Monday and 24 December-7 January) at Vinovo ✉ 10048 ✆ 9653880, Fax 9623748.

✈ Turin Airport of Caselle by ① : 15 km ✆ 5778361, Fax 5778420 – Alitalia, via Lagrange 35 ✉ 10123 ✆ 57697.

🚗 ✆ 6651111-int. 2611.

🛈 via Roma 226 (piazza C.L.N.) ✉ 10121 ✆ 535901, Fax 530070 – Porta Nuova Railway station ✉ 10125 ✆ 531327.

A.C.I. via Giovanni Giolitti 15 ✉ 10123 ✆ 57791.

Roma 669 ⑦ – Briançon 108 ⑪ – Chambéry 209 ⑪ – Genève 252 ③ – Genova 170 ⑦ – Grenoble 224 ⑪ – Milano 140 ③ – Nice 220 ⑨.

Plans on following pages

Turin Palace Hotel, via Sacchi 8 ✉ 10128 ✆ 5625511, Telex 221411, Fax 5612187 – |‡| ▤ TV ☎ ♿ ⇔ – ⚐ 30-200. AE Ⓢ ⓞ E VISA. ✻ rest CY **u**
M *(closed 1 to 22 August)* a la carte 60/112000 – ☐ 28000 – **123 rm** 280/330000, 2 suites.

Jolly Principi di Piemonte, via Gobetti 15 ✉ 10123 ✆ 5629693, Telex 221120, Fax 5620270 – |‡| ▤ TV ☎ – ⚐ 100. AE Ⓢ ⓞ E VISA. ✻ CY **z**
M *(closed August)* 60/80000 – **107 rm** ☐ 340/390000 8 suites.

Gd H. Sitea, via Carlo Alberto 35 ✉ 10123 ✆ 5570171, Telex 220229, Fax 548090 – |‡| ▤ TV ☎ – ⚐ 30-100. AE Ⓢ ⓞ E VISA. ✻ rest CY **t**
M a la carte 60/95000 – **117 rm** ☐ 250/350000.

Jolly Ambasciatori, corso Vittorio Emanuele 104 ✉ 10121 ✆ 5752, Telex 221296, Fax 544978 – rm – 25-400. AE E VISA. rest BX **a**
M 45/85000 – **199 rm** 245/315000, 4 suites.

Diplomatic, via Cernaia 42 ✉ 10122 ✆ 5612444, Telex 225445, Fax 540472 – – 50-200. AE E VISA BX **g**
M (residents only) *(closed Saturday and Sunday)* 40/45000 – **129 rm** 220/295000.

Jolly Hotel Ligure, piazza Carlo Felice 85 ✉ 10123 ✆ 55641, Telex 220167, Fax 535438 – – 30-250. AE E VISA. rest CY **b**
M 50/60000 – **156 rm** 265/340000, 2 suites.

City without rest., via Juvarra 25 ✉ 10122 ✆ 540546, Telex 216228, Fax 548188 – . AE E VISA BV **e**
closed August, Christmas and New Year's Day – **44 rm** 260/350000.

Concord, via Lagrange 47 ✉ 10123 ✆ 5576756, Telex 221323, Fax 5576305 – – 180. AE E VISA. rest CY **s**
M 55000 – **139 rm** 245/330000, 3 suites.

Majestic, without rest., corso Vittorio Emanuele II 54 ✉ 10123 ✆ 539153, Telex 216260, Fax 534963 – – 30-40 CY **e**
159 rm.

Genio without rest., corso Vittorio Emanuele II 47 ✉ 10125 ✆ 6505771, Telex 220308, Fax 6508264 – – 35. AE E VISA CYZ **w**
75 rm 125/175000, 12000.

Royal, corso Regina Margherita 249 ✉ 10144 ✆ 4376777, Telex 220259, Fax 4376393, – – 25-600. AE E VISA BV **u**
closed 1 to 28 August – **M** (see **Vecchio Mulino** below) – 17000 – **73 rm** 180/250000.

Boston without rest., via Massena 70 ✉ 10128 ✆ 500359, Fax 599358, – . AE E VISA BZ **c**
50 rm 125/175000, 12000.

Victoria without rest., via Nino Costa 4 ✉ 10123 ✆ 5611909, Telex 212580, Fax 5611806 – . AE E VISA. CY **v**
70 rm 135/180000.

Luxor without rest., corso Stati Uniti 7 ✉ 10128 ✆ 5620777, Telex 225549, Fax 5628324 – . AE E VISA CZ **s**
closed August – **70 rm** 115/150000, 2 suites, 12000.

Stazione e Genova without rest., via Sacchi 14 ✉ 10128 ✆ 5629400, Telex 224242, Fax 5629896 – – 40. AE E VISA. CZ **b**
closed 1 to 18 August – **60 rm** 125/175000.

President without rest., via Cecchi 67 ✉ 10152 ✆ 859555, Telex 220417, Fax 2480465 – . AE E VISA CV **s**
72 rm 160000.

Giada without rest., via Gasparo Barbera 6 ✉ 10135 ✆ 3489383, Fax 3489383 – . E VISA by corso Unione Sovietica BZ
closed August – **28 rm** 95/115000, 12000.

Smeraldo without rest., piazza Carducci 169/b ✉ 10126 ✆ 634577 – . E VISA. 15000 – **12 rm** 99000. CZ **q**

Villa Sassi-El Toulà with rm, strada al Traforo del Pino 47 ✉ 10132 ✆ 890556, Telex 225437, Fax 890095, , « 18C country house in extensive parkland » – rm – 200. AE E VISA. by ⑤
closed August – **M** *(closed Sunday)* a la carte 70/102000 – 20000 – **15 rm** 250/380000 suite.

Vecchia Lanterna, corso Re Umberto 21 ✉ 10128 ✆ 537047, Elegant installation – . E VISA. CY **x**
closed Saturday lunch, Sunday and 10 to 20 August – **M** (booking essential) a la carte 78/118000
Spec. Scaloppa di fegato d'oca e gamberi al Porto, Zuppa di tartufi in crosta (autumn-winter), Scaloppa d'anitra in salsa peverada. Wines Moscato giallo, Solaia.

Del Cambio, piazza Carignano 2 ✉ 10123 ✆ 546690, Fax 543760, Elegant traditional decor, « 19C decor » – . AE E VISA. CX **a**
closed Sunday and 27 July-27 August – **M** (booking essential) a la carte 68/119000 (15 %).

Balbo, via Andrea Doria 11 ✉ 10123 ✆ 832274 – . AE VISA. CY **n**
closed Monday and 18 July-18 August – **M** (booking essential) a la carte 75/102000.

Due Lampioni da Carlo, via Carlo Alberto 45 ✉ 10123 ✆ 8397409, Fax 831970 – . AE E VISA. CY **n**
closed Sunday and August – **M** a la carte 65/90000
Spec. Timballo di verdure con fonduta leggera, Ravioli di funghi porcini e patate al sugo tartufato (autumn-winter), Filetto di sanato alla finanziera in crosta. Wines Vinnae, Freisa.

TORINO

Street	Grid	No.
Carlo Felice (Piazza)	CY	16
Roma (Via)	CXY	
S. Carlo (Piazza)	CXY	
Alfieri (Via)	CY	5
Cadorna (Lungo Po L.)	DY	12
Carignano (Piazza)	CX	13
Carlo Emanuele II (Pza)	DY	15
Casale (Corso)	DY	17
Castello (Piazza)	CX	19
Cesare Augusto (Piazza)	CV	23
Consolata (Via della)	CV	25
Diaz (Lungo Po A.)	DY	29
Gran Madre di Dio (Piazza)	DY	33
Milano (Via)	CV	40
Ponte Vittorio Emanuele I	DY	48
Repubblica (Piazza della)	CV	53
S. Francesco d'Assisi (Via)	CX	55
Solferino (Piazza)	CX	64
Vitt. Emanuele II (Lgo)	BCY	75
4 Marzo (Via)	CX	77
20 Settembre (Via)	CXY	78

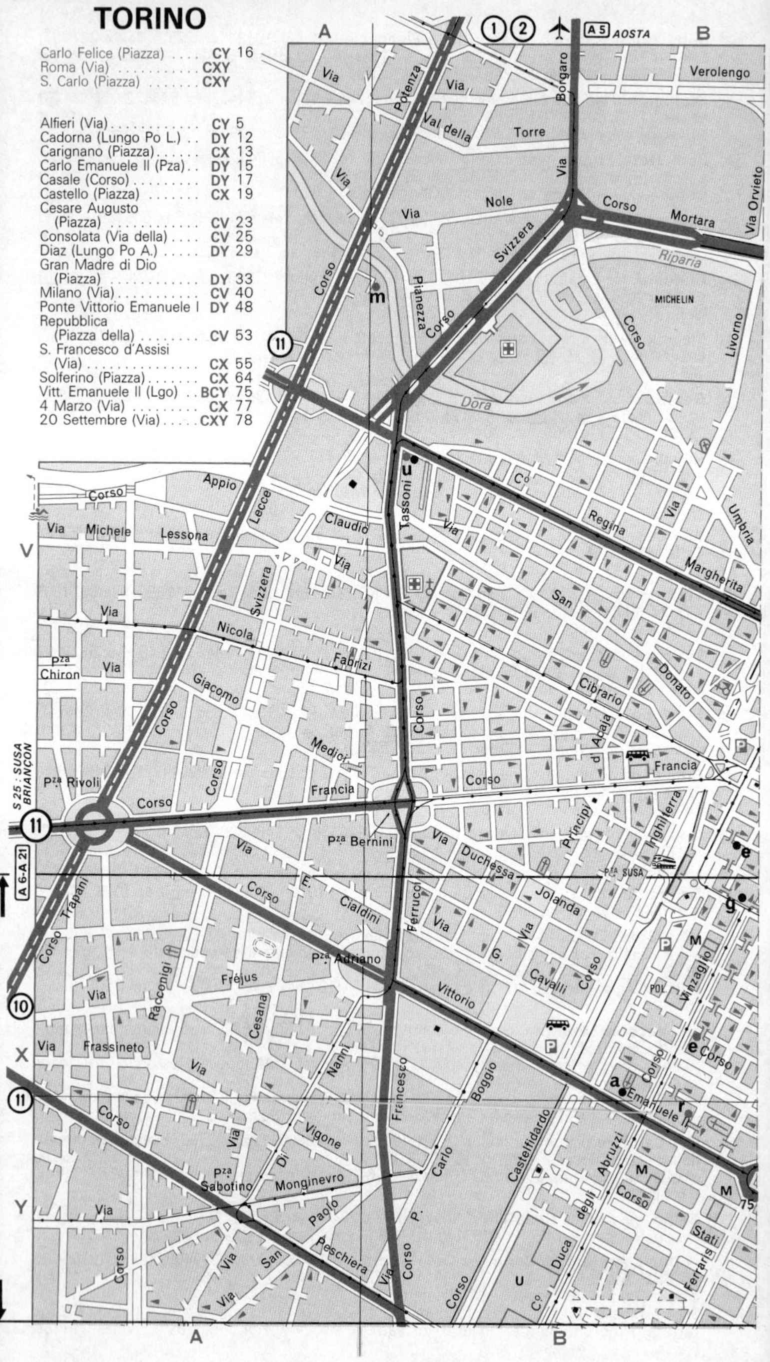

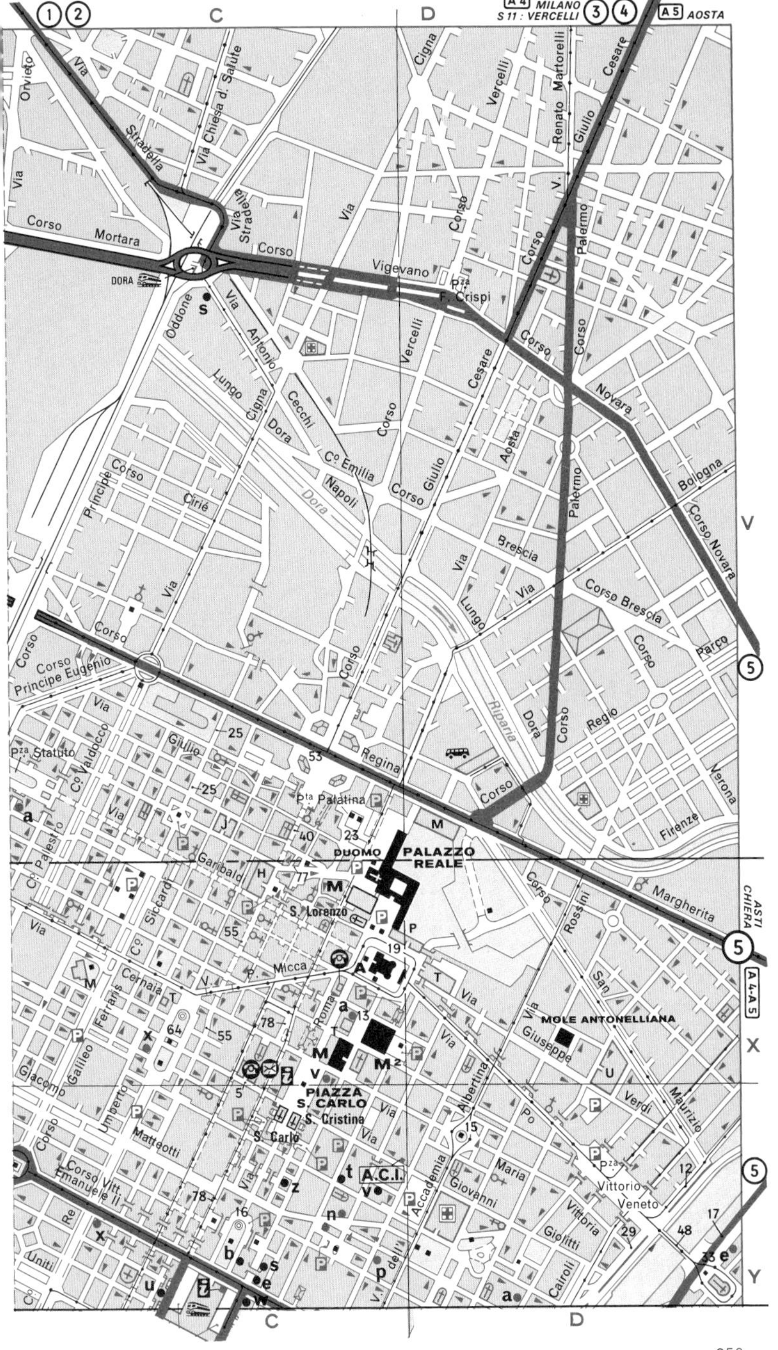

A 4 MILANO
S 11 : VERCELLI
A 5 AOSTA
PALAZZO REALE
DUOMO
MOLE ANTONELLIANA
PIAZZA S. CARLO
A.C.I.
Corso Vigevano
Corso Novara
Corso Regina
Corso Vitt. Emanuele II
Via Garibaldi
Via Roma
Via Po
Corso Principe Eugenio
P.za Statuto
P.ta Palatina
P.za Vittorio Veneto
ASTI CHIERI
A 4-A 5

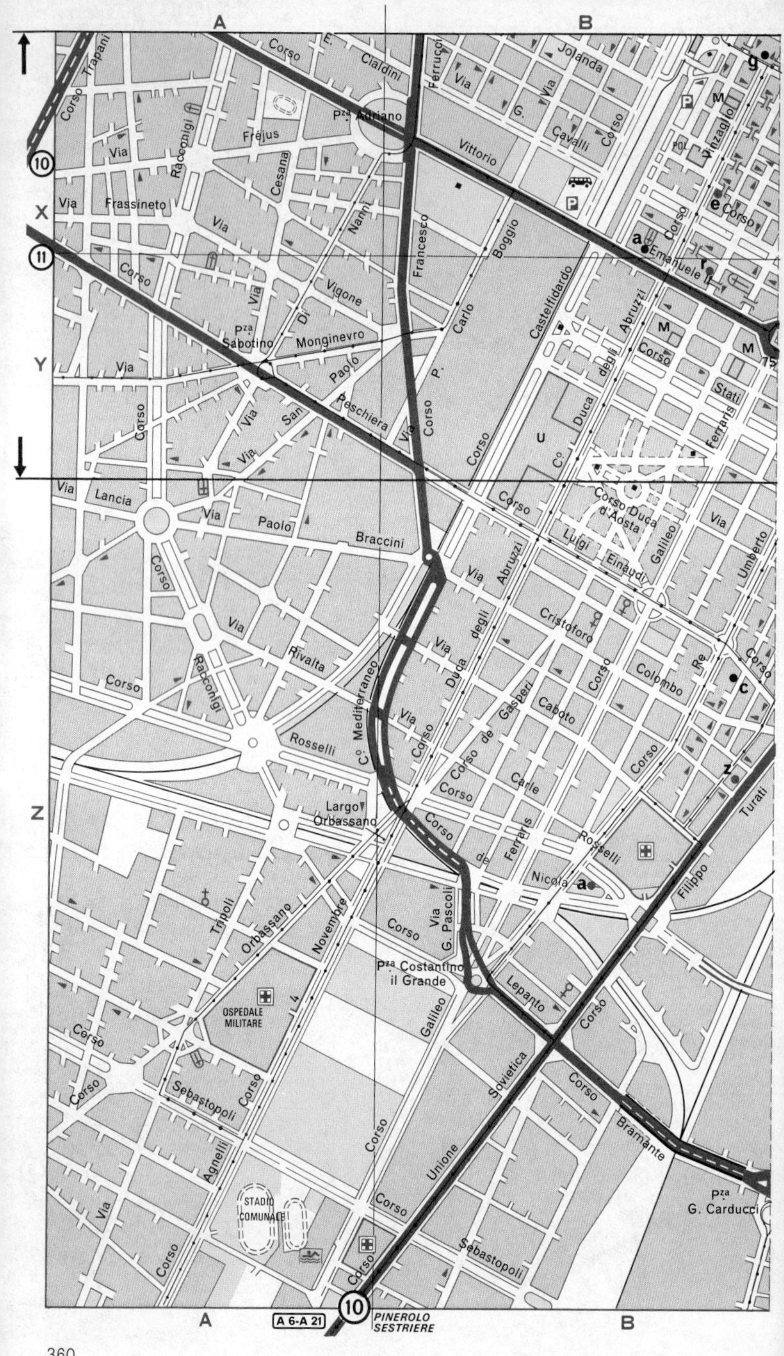

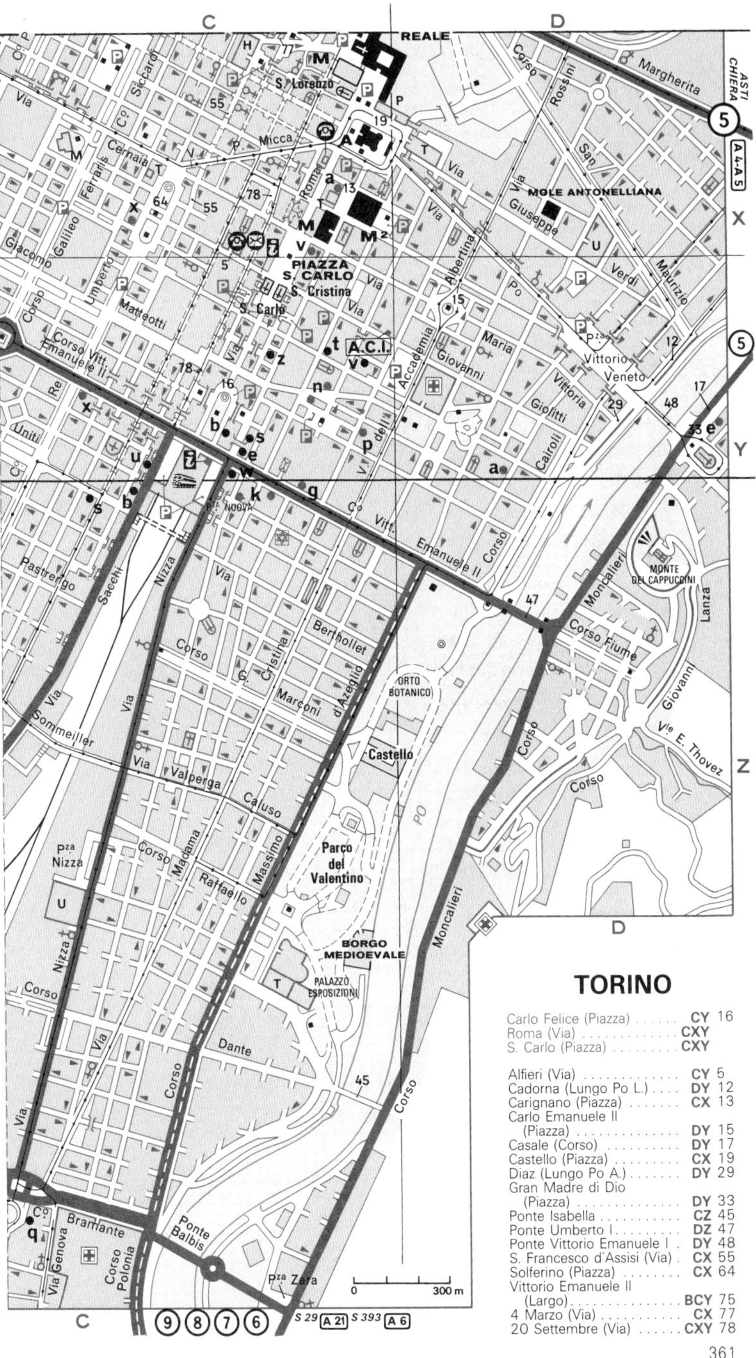

TORINO

Carlo Felice (Piazza) . . . . . . CY 16
Roma (Via) . . . . CXY
S. Carlo (Piazza) . . . . CXY

Alfieri (Via) . . . . CY 5
Cadorna (Lungo Po L.) . . . . DY 12
Carignano (Piazza) . . . . CX 13
Carlo Emanuele II (Piazza) . . . . DY 15
Casale (Corso) . . . . DY 17
Castello (Piazza) . . . . CX 19
Diaz (Lungo Po A.) . . . . DY 29
Gran Madre di Dio (Piazza) . . . . DY 33
Ponte Isabella . . . . CZ 45
Ponte Umberto I . . . . DZ 47
Ponte Vittorio Emanuele I . DY 48
S. Francesco d'Assisi (Via) . CX 55
Solferino (Piazza) . . . . CX 64
Vittorio Emanuele II (Largo) . . . . BCY 75
4 Marzo (Via) . . . . CX 77
20 Settembre (Via) . . . . . . CXY 78

XXX ✿ **Neuv Caval 'd Brôns,** piazza San Carlo 157 ✉ 10123 ✆ 5627483 – ▤. AE ⓢ ⓞ E VISA CXY **v**
closed Saturday lunch, Sunday, July or August – **M** (booking essential) a la carte 65/130000
Spec. Flan di Castelmagno, Ravioli del plin in salsa di arrosto profumata al rosmarino, Manzo di Carrì al midollo in salsa al vino rosso. Wines Favorita, Brachetto secco.

XXX **Rendez Vous,** corso Vittorio Emanuele 38 ✉ 10123 ✆ 830215, Fax 8396961 – ▤. AE ⓢ ⓞ E VISA. ✻ CZ **g**
closed Saturday lunch and Sunday – **M** a la carte 40/76000.

XXX **Villa Somis,** strada Val Pattonera 138 ✉ 10133 ✆ 6613086, « In a 18C house with park ; summer service under a pergola » – Ⓟ. AE ⓢ ⓞ E VISA by viale E. Thovez DZ
closed Monday – **M** (booking essential) a la carte 60/90000.

XXX ✿ **La Prima Smarrita,** corso Unione Sovietica 244 ✉ 10134 ✆ 3179657 – ▤. AE ⓢ ⓞ E VISA. ✻ by ⑩
closed Monday and 3 to 27 August – **M** (booking essential) a la carte 57/82000
Spec. Moscardini al pomodoro, Spaghetti alle vongole e porcini, Filetto di sanato alla casalese. Wines Gavi, Barbera.

XXX Tiffany, piazza Solferino 16/h ✉ 10121 ✆ 540538 – ▤ CX **x**

XXX **3 Colonne,** corso Rosselli 1 ✉ 10128 ✆ 3185220, ⛱, Locals rest. – AE ⓢ ⓞ E VISA BZ **a**
closed Monday, Saturday lunch and 3 to 24 August – **M** a la carte 43/75000.

XXX **La Cloche,** strada al Traforo del Pino 106 ✉ 10132 ✆ 8999462, Fax 8981522, Typical atmosphere – ▤ Ⓟ – 🏟 100. AE ⓢ ⓞ E VISA. ✻ by corso Moncalieri CDZ
closed Sunday dinner, Monday, 17 to 31 August and 7 to 15 January – **M** (surprise menu) 60/123000.

XXX **Al Gatto Nero,** corso Filippo Turati 14 ✉ 10128 ✆ 590414 – ▤. AE ⓢ ⓞ E VISA. ✻ BZ **z**
closed Sunday and August – **M** a la carte 60/80000.

XX **Al Bue Rosso,** corso Casale 10 ✉ 10131 ✆ 8191393 – ▤. AE ⓞ VISA DY **e**
closed Monday, Saturday lunch and August – **M** a la carte 58/78000 (10 %).

XX **Della Rocca,** via della Rocca 22/b ✉ 10123 ✆ 835861 – ▤. AE ⓢ ⓞ E VISA. ✻ DY **a**
closed Sunday and August – **M** (booking essential) a la carte 36/55000.

XX **Vecchio Mulino,** corso Regina Margherita 251 ✉ 10144 ✆ 740357 – ▤. AE ⓢ ⓞ E VISA. ✻ BV **u**
closed Saturday and August – **M** a la carte 39/65000.

XX **Due Mondi-da Ilio,** via San Pio V 3 ang. via Saluzzo ✉ 10125 ✆ 6692056 – AE ⓢ E VISA CZ **k**
closed Sunday and 1 to 15 August – **M** a la carte 38/84000.

XX **Porta Rossa,** via Passalacqua 3/b ✉ 10122 ✆ 530816 – AE ⓢ ⓞ VISA CV **a**
closed Sunday and August – **M** a la carte 34/68000.

X **La Capannina,** via Donati ✉ 10121 ✆ 545405, Piedmontese rest. – ▤. VISA BY **r**
closed Sunday and August – **M** a la carte 40/66000.

X **C'era una volta,** corso Vittorio Emanuele II 41 ✉ 10125 ✆ 655498, Piedmontese rest. – ▤. AE ⓢ ⓞ E VISA CZ **k**
closed Sunday and August – **M** (dinner only) (booking essential) 45000.

X **Anaconda,** via Angiolino 16 (corso Potenza) ✉ 10143 ✆ 752903, Rustic trattoria, « Outdoor summer service » – Ⓟ. AE ⓢ ⓞ E VISA BV **m**
closed Friday dinner, Saturday and August – **M** 50000 b.i..

Costigliole d'Asti 14055 Asti 988 ⑫, 428 H 6 – pop. 5 960 alt. 242 – ☎ 0141.

Roma 629 – Acqui Terme 34 – Alessandria 51 – Asti 15 – Genova 108 – Milano 141 – Torino 70.

XXX ✿✿ **Guido,** piazza Umberto I 27 ✆ 966012, Fax 966012 – ⓢ E VISA
closed Sunday, Bank Holidays, 1 to 20 August and 23 December-10 January – **M** (dinner only) (booking essential) 100/120000
Spec. Agnolotti di Costigliole, Stracotto di bue al vino rosso (winter), Capretto di Roccaverano al forno con olio e acciughe (spring). Wines Arneis, Barolo.

Pleasant hotels and restaurants
are shown in the Guide by a red sign.
Please send us the names
of any where you have enjoyed your stay.
Your Michelin Guide will be even better.

🏨🏨🏨 ... 🏠
XXXXX ... X

VENICE (VENEZIA) 30100 P 988 ⑤, 429 F 19 - pop. 317 837 - ☎ 041.

See : St. Marks Square*** FGZ :.
St. Mark's Basilica*** GZ - Doges Palace*** GZ - Campanile** : ※** FGZ **F** - Procuratie** FZ - Libreria Vecchia* GZ - Correr Museum* FZ **M** - Clock Tower* FZ **K** - Bridge of Sighs* GZ.
Grand Canal*** :.
Rialto Bridge* FY - Right bank : Cà d'Oro*** : Franchetti Gallery** EX - Vendramin-Calergi Palace** BT **R** - Cà Loredan** EY **H** - Grimani Palace** EY **Q** Corner-Spinelli Palace** BTU **D** Grassi Palace** BU **M5** - Left bank : Academy of Fine Arts*** BV Dario Palace** BV **S** - Peggy Guggenheim Collection** in Palazzo Venier dei Leoni BV **M2** - Rezzonico Palace** : museum on 18C Venice AU **M3** - Giustinian Palace** AU **X** - Cà Foscari** AU **Y** Bernardo Palace** BT **Z** - Palazzo dei Camerlenghi** FX **A** - Pesaro Palace** : Museum of Modern Art* EX.
Churches :.
Santa Maria della Salute** : Marriage at Cana*** by Tintoretto BV - St. Giorgio Maggiore** : ※*** from campanile** CV - St. Zanipolo** : polyptych*** of St. Vincenzo Ferrari, ceiling*** of the Rosary Chapel GX - Santa Maria Gloriosa dei Frari** : works by Titian*** AT - St. Zaccaria* : altarpiece*** by Bellini, altarpieces** by Vivarini and by Ludovico da Forlì GZ - Interior decoration** by Veronese in the Church of St. Sebastiano AU - Paintings* by Guardi in the Church of Angelo Raffaele AU - Ceiling* of the Church of St. Pantaleone AT - Santa Maria dei Miracoli* GX - Madonna and Child* in the Church of St. Francesco della Vigna DT - Madonna and Child* in the Church of Redentore (Giudecca Island) AV.
Scuola di St. Rocco*** AT - Scuola di St. Giorgio degli Schiavoni* : paintings** by Carpaccio DT - Scuola dei Carmini : paintings** by Tiepolo AU - Querini-Stampalia Palace* GY - Rio dei Mendicanti* GX - Facade* of the Scuola di St. Marco GX - Frescoes* by Tiepolo in Palazzo Labia AT.
The Lido** - Murano** : Glass Museum***, Church of Santi Maria e Donato** - Burano** - Torcello** : mosaics*** in the Cathedral of Santa Maria Assunta**, peristyle** and columns** inside the Church of Santa Fosca*.

18 (closed Monday) at Lido Alberoni ✉ 30011 ☎ 731333, Fax 731339, 15 mn by boat and 9 km;

18, 9 Cà della Nave (closed Tuesday), at Martellago ✉ 30030 ☎ 5401555, Fax 5401926, NW : 12 km;

18, 9 Villa Condulmer (closed Monday), at Zerman ✉ 21021 ☎ 457062, Fax 457202, N : 17 km.

✈ Marco Polo di Tessera, NE : 13 km ☎ 661262 - Alitalia, San Marco-Bacino Orseolo 1166 ✉ 30124 ☎ 5216333.

⛴ to Lido - San Nicolò from piazzale Roma (Tronchetto) daily (35 mn) ; to Punta Sabbioni from Riva degli Schiavoni daily (40 mn); to island of Pellestrina-Santa Maria del Mare from Lido Alberoni daily (1 h 15 mn); to islands of Murano (10 mn), Burano (40 mn) and Torcello (45 mn) daily, from Fondamenta Nuove ; to Treporti-Cavallino from Fondamenta Nuove daily (1 h 10 mn) - Information : ACTV - Venetian Transport Union, piazzale Roma ✉ 30135 ☎ 5287886, Fax 5207135.

ℹ San Marco Ascensione 71/c ✉ 30124 ☎ 5226356 - Santa Lucia Railway station ✉ 30121 ☎ 719078.

A.C.I. fondamenta Santa Chiara 518/a ✉ 30125 ☎ 5200300.

Roma 528 ① - Bologna 152 ① - Milano 267 ① - Trieste 158 ①

Plans on following pages

Cipriani ⛵, isola della Giudecca 10 ✉ 30133 ☎ 5207744, Telex 410162, Fax 5203930, ≤, « Floral garden with heated ⛱ », ≘s, 🎾 - |‡| ▤ TV ☎ - 🏛 100. AE 🄱 ⊙ E VISA. ✕
M *(March-November)* a la carte 110/160000 - **98 rm** ☐ 679/881000, 7 suites. CV **h**

Gritti Palace, campo Santa Maria del Giglio 2467 ✉ 30124 ☎ 794611, Telex 410125, Fax 5200942, ≤ Grand Canal, « Outdoor summer service on the Grand Canal » - |‡| ▤ TV ☎ ♿ - 🏛 50. AE 🄱 ⊙ E VISA. ✕ EZ **a**
M a la carte 120/170000 - ☐ 31000 - **88 rm** 476/667000, 2 suites.

Danieli, riva degli Schiavoni 4196 ✉ 30122 ☎ 5226480, Telex 410077, Fax 5200208, ≤ San Marco Canal, « Hall in a small Venetian style courtyard and terrace summer service with panoramic view » - |‡| ▤ TV ☎ - 🏛 70-150. AE 🄱 ⊙ E VISA. ✕ GZ **a**
M a la carte 112/177000 - ☐ 29000 - **222 rm** 417/619000, 6 suites.

Bauer Grünwald, campo San Moisè 1459 ✉ 30124 ☎ 5231520, Telex 410075, Fax 5207557, ≤ Grand Canal, ⛱ - |‡| ▤ TV ☎ - 🏛 25-180. AE 🄱 ⊙ E VISA. ✕ rest
M a la carte 100/130000 - **214 rm** ☐ 340/540000, 3 suites. FZ **h**

Londra Palace, riva degli Schiavoni 4171 ✉ 30122 ☎ 5200533, Telex 420681, Fax 5225032, ≤ San Marco Canal - |‡| ▤ TV ☎ - 🏛 100. AE 🄱 ⊙ E VISA GZ **t**
M (see **Les Deux Lions** below) - ☐ 18000 - **69 rm** 241/385000.

Europa e Regina, calle larga 22 Marzo 2159 ✉ 30124 ☎ 5200477, Telex 410123, Fax 5231533, ≤ Grand Canal, « Outdoor rest. summer service on the Grand Canal » - |‡| ▤ TV ☎ ♿ - 🏛 30-140. AE 🄱 ⊙ E VISA. ✕ rest FZ **d**
M 85/90000 - ☐ 26500 - **192 rm** 322/536000, 13 suites.

Monaco e Grand Canal, calle Vallaresso 1325 ✉ 30124 ☎ 5200211, Telex 410450, Fax 5200501, ≤ Grand Canal and Santa Maria della Salute Church, « Outdoor rest. summer service on the Grand Canal » - |‡| ▤ TV ☎ ♿ - 🏛 40. AE 🄱 ⊙ E VISA. ✕ rest FZ **e**
M Grand Canal Rest. a la carte 85/130000 - **70 rm** ☐ 280/420000, 2 suites.

Metropole, riva degli Schiavoni 4149 ✉ 30122 ☎ 5205044, Telex 410340, Fax 5223679, ≤ San Marco canal, « Collection of period bric-a-brac » - |‡| ▤ TV ☎ - 🏛 40. AE 🄱 ⊙ E VISA DU **t**
M 42000 - **74 rm** ☐ 350/398000.

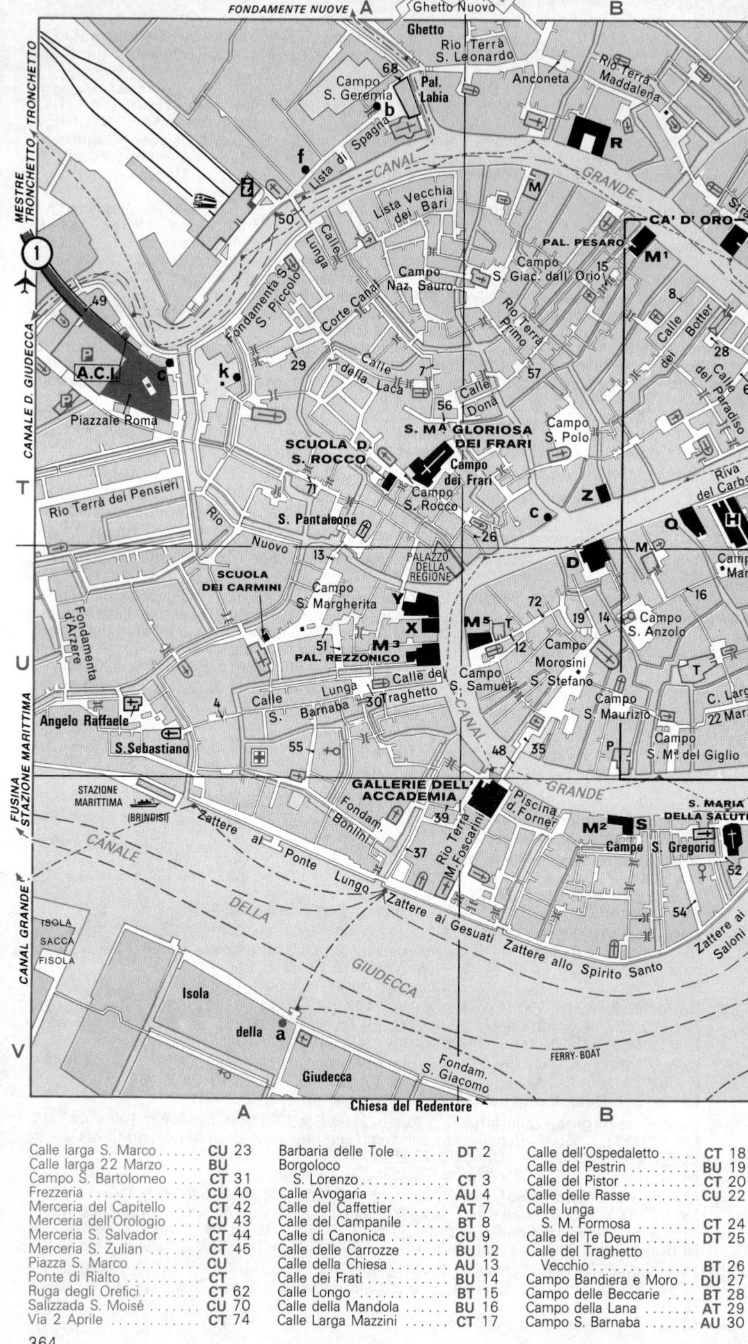

Calle larga S. Marco	**CU**	23
Calle larga 22 Marzo	**BU**	
Campo S. Bartolomeo	**CT**	31
Frezzeria	**CU**	40
Merceria del Capitello	**CT**	42
Merceria dell'Orologio	**CU**	43
Merceria S. Salvador	**CT**	44
Merceria S. Zulian	**CT**	45
Piazza S. Marco	**CU**	
Ponte di Rialto	**CT**	
Ruga degli Orefici	**CT**	62
Salizzada S. Moisé	**CU**	70
Via 2 Aprile	**CT**	74
Barbaria delle Tole	**DT**	2
Borgoloco S. Lorenzo	**CT**	3
Calle Avogaria	**AU**	4
Calle del Caffettier	**AT**	7
Calle del Campanile	**BT**	8
Calle di Canonica	**CU**	9
Calle delle Carrozze	**BU**	12
Calle della Chiesa	**AU**	13
Calle dei Frati	**BU**	14
Calle Longo	**BT**	15
Calle della Mandola	**BU**	16
Calle Larga Mazzini	**CT**	17
Calle dell'Ospedaletto	**CT**	18
Calle del Pestrin	**BU**	19
Calle del Pistor	**CT**	20
Calle delle Rasse	**CU**	22
Calle lunga S. M. Formosa	**CT**	24
Calle del Te Deum	**DT**	25
Calle del Traghetto Vecchio	**BT**	26
Campo Bandiera e Moro	**DU**	27
Campo delle Beccarie	**BT**	28
Campo della Lana	**AT**	29
Campo S. Barnaba	**AU**	30

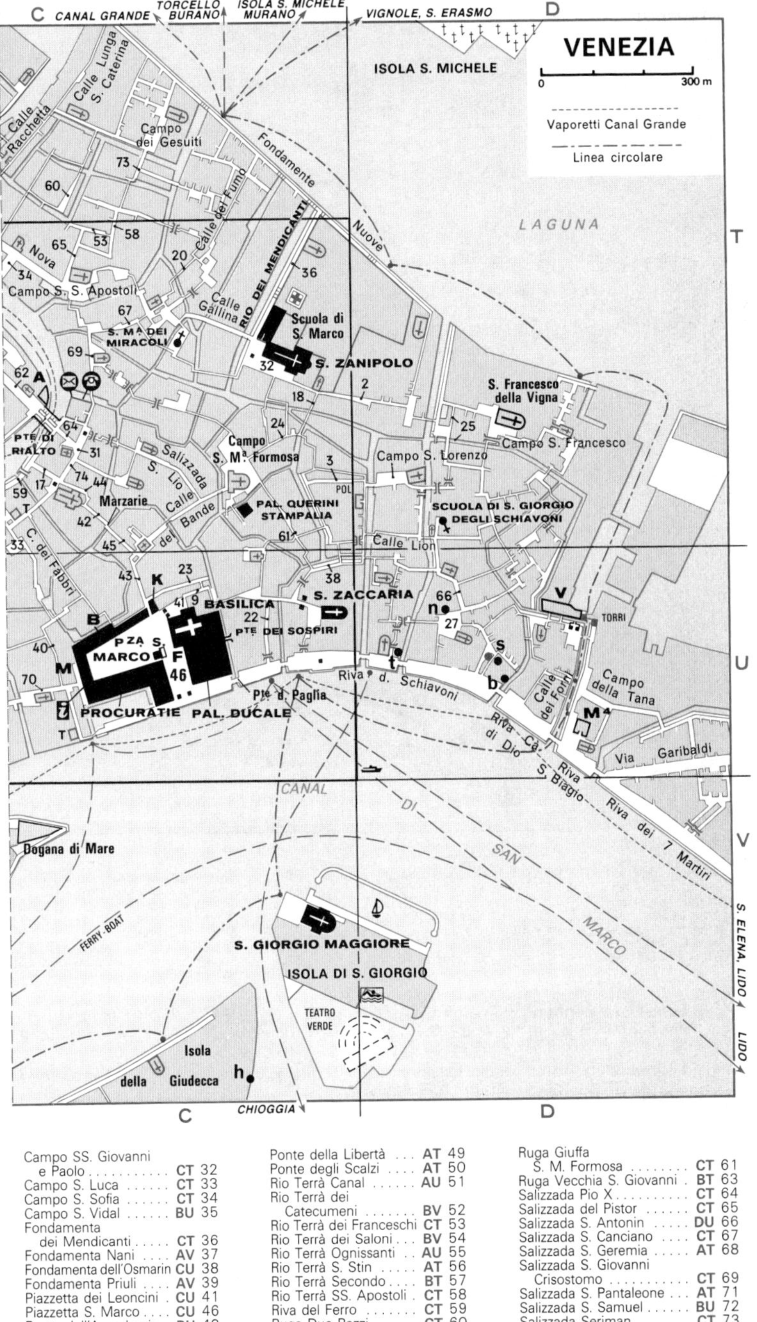

Campo SS. Giovanni e Paolo	CT	32
Campo S. Luca	CT	33
Campo S. Sofia	CT	34
Campo S. Vidal	BU	35
Fondamenta dei Mendicanti	CT	36
Fondamenta Nani	AV	37
Fondamenta dell'Osmarin	CU	38
Fondamenta Priuli	AV	39
Piazzetta dei Leoncini	CU	41
Piazzetta S. Marco	CU	46
Ponte dell'Accademia	BU	48
Ponte della Libertà	AT	49
Ponte degli Scalzi	AT	50
Rio Terrà Canal	AU	51
Rio Terrà dei Catecumeni	BV	52
Rio Terrà dei Franceschi	CT	53
Rio Terrà dei Saloni	BV	54
Rio Terrà Ognissanti	AU	55
Rio Terrà S. Stin	AT	56
Rio Terrà Secondo	BT	57
Rio Terrà SS. Apostoli	CT	58
Riva del Ferro	CT	59
Ruga Due Pozzi	CT	60
Ruga Giuffa S. M. Formosa	CT	61
Ruga Vecchia S. Giovanni	BT	63
Salizzada Pio X	CT	64
Salizzada del Pistor	CT	65
Salizzada S. Antonin	DU	66
Salizzada S. Canciano	CT	67
Salizzada S. Geremia	AT	68
Salizzada S. Giovanni Crisostomo	CT	69
Salizzada S. Pantaleone	AT	71
Salizzada S. Samuel	BU	72
Salizzada Seriman	CT	73

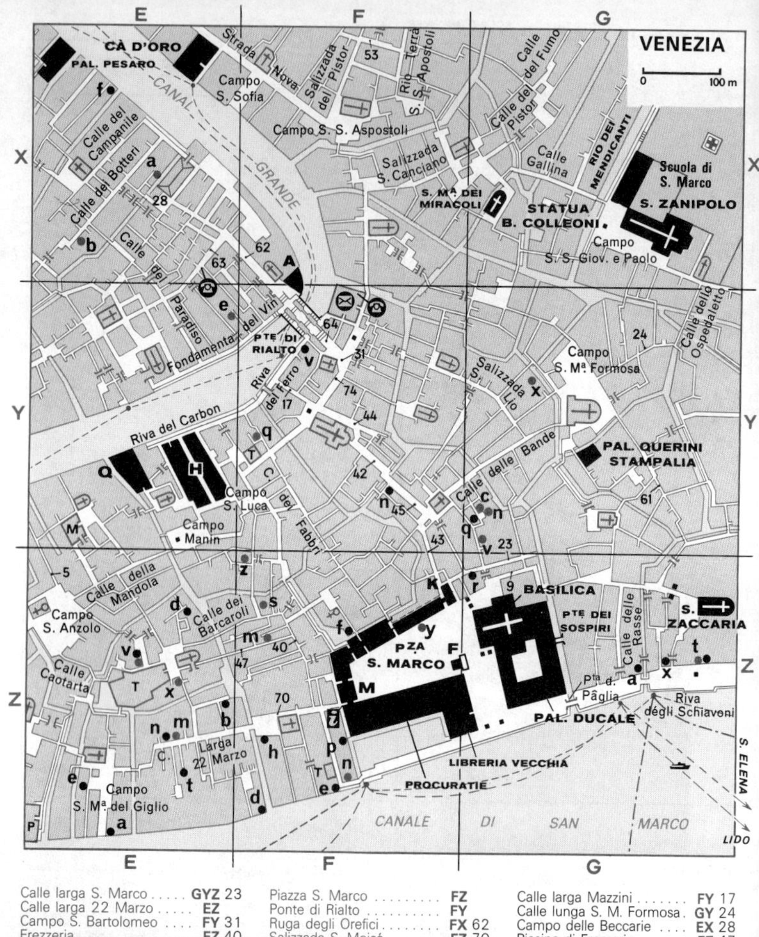

- Calle larga S. Marco . . . . . **GYZ** 23
- Calle larga 22 Marzo . . . . . **EZ**
- Campo S. Bartolomeo . . . . **FY** 31
- Frezzeria . . . . **FZ** 40
- Merceria del Capitello . . . . **FY** 42
- Merceria dell Orologio . . . . **FY** 43
- Merceria S. Salvador . . . . . **FY** 44
- Merceria S. Zulian . . . . **FY** 45
- Piazza S. Marco . . . . **FZ**
- Ponte di Rialto . . . . **FY**
- Ruga degli Orefici . . . . **FX** 62
- Salizzada S. Moisé . . . . **FZ** 70
- Via 2 Aprile . . . . **FY** 74
- Calle degli Avvocati . . . . . . **EZ** 5
- Calle di Canonica . . . . **GZ** 9
- Calle larga Mazzini . . . . **FY** 17
- Calle lunga S. M. Formosa . **GY** 24
- Campo delle Beccarie . . . . **EX** 28
- Piscina di Frezzeria . . . . **FZ** 47
- Rio Terrà dei Franceschi . . **FX** 53
- Ruga Giuffa S. M. Formosa . **GY** 61
- Ruga Vecchia S. Giovanni . . **EX** 63
- Salizzada Pio X . . . . **FY** 64

Luna Hotel Baglioni, calle larga dell'Ascensione 1243 ✉ 30124 ☎ 5289840, Telex 410236, Fax 5287160 – |‡| ⅔ rm ▤ TV ☎ – 🏛 30-150. AE ⓢ ⓞ E VISA. ✻ rest FZ **p**
M a la carte 68/99000 – **109 rm** ☕ 290/510000, 6 suites.

Pullman Park Hotel, giardini Papadopoli ✉ 30125 ☎ 5285394, Telex 410310, Fax 5230043 – |‡| ▤ TV ☎ – 🏛 60. AE ⓢ ⓞ E VISA. ✻ AT **k**
M a la carte 71/118000 – **100 rm** ☕ 210/320000.

Starhotel Splendid-Suisse, San Marco-Mercerie 760 ✉ 30124 ☎ 5200755, Telex 410590, Fax 5286498 – |‡| ▤ TV ☎ – 🏛 80 – **157 rm**. FY **n**

Bellini without rest., Cannaregio 116-Lista di Spagna ✉ 30121 ☎ 5242488, Fax 715193 – |‡| ▤ TV ☎. AE ⓢ E VISA. ✻ – **65 rm** ☕ 205/300000, 3 suites. AT **f**

Amadeus, Lista di Spagna 227 ✉ 30121 ☎ 715300, Telex 420811, Fax 5240841, « Garden » – |‡| ▤ TV ☎ – 🏛 40-150. AE ⓢ ⓞ E VISA. ✻ AT **b**
M *(closed Wednesday)* 50/70000 – ☕ 18000 – **63 rm** 240/340000, 3 suites.

Saturnia-International and Rest. Il Cortile, calle larga 22 Marzo 2398 ✉ 30124 ☎ 5208377, Telex 410355, Fax 5207131, 🏛, « 14C patrician building » – |‡| ▤ TV ☎ – 🏛 60. AE ⓢ ⓞ E VISA. ✻ rest EZ **n**
M *(closed Wednesday)* a la carte 67/102000 – **95 rm** ☕ 250/380000.

Gabrielli Sandwirth, riva degli Schiavoni 4110 ✉ 30122 ☎ 5231580, Telex 410228, Fax 5209455, ≤ San Marco Canal, « Small courtyard and garden » – |♦| ▤ TV ☎. AE $ ◑ E VISA. ✻ rest DU **b**
closed 23 November-10 February – **M** 40/60000 – **100 rm** ☕ 250/395000.

La Fenice et des Artistes without rest., campiello de la Fenice 1936 ✉ 30124 ☎ 5232333, Telex 411150, Fax 5203721 – |♦| ▤ TV ☎. $ E VISA EZ **v**
65 rm ☕ 160/230000, 3 suites.

Cavalletto e Doge Orseolo, calle del Cavalletto 1107 ✉ 30124 ☎ 5200955, Telex 410684, Fax 5238184, ≤ – |♦| ▤ TV ☎. AE $ ◑ E VISA. ✻ rest FZ **f**
M a la carte 60/97000 – **79 rm** ☕ 250/350000.

Rialto, riva del Ferro 5149 ✉ 30124 ☎ 5209166, Telex 420809, Fax 5238958 – ▤ TV ☎. AE $ ◑ E VISA. ✻ FY **v**
M *(closed Thursday and November-15 March)* a la carte 35/72000 (12 %) – **71 rm** ☕ 210/294000.

Concordia without rest., calle larga San Marco 367 ✉ 30124 ☎ 5206866, Telex 411069, Fax 5206775 – |♦| ▤ TV ☎. AE $ ◑ E VISA GZ **r**
55 rm ☕ 220/330000.

Flora ⛳ without rest., calle larga 22 Marzo 2283/a ✉ 30124 ☎ 5205844, Telex 410401, Fax 5228217, « Small flower garden » – |♦| ▤ ☎. AE $ ◑ E VISA EZ **t**
44 rm ☕ 165/220000, ▤ 18000.

Santa Chiara without rest., Santa Croce 548 ✉ 30125 ☎ 5206955, Telex 420690, Fax 5228799 – |♦| ▤ TV ☎. AE $ ◑ E VISA. ✻ AT **c**
28 rm ☕ 160/220000.

San Cassiano without rest., Santa Croce 2232 ✉ 30125 ☎ 5241768, Telex 420810, Fax 721033, ≤ – ▤ TV ☎. AE $ E VISA EX **f**
35 rm ☕ 165/252000.

Ala without rest., campo Santa Maria del Giglio 2494 ✉ 30124 ☎ 5208333, Telex 410275, Fax 5206390 – |♦| ▤ TV ☎. AE $ ◑ E VISA. ✻ EZ **e**
85 rm ☕ 150/212000.

San Moisè without rest., San Marco 2058 ✉ 30124 ☎ 5203755, Telex 420655 – ▤ TV ☎. AE $ ◑ E VISA EZ **b**
16 rm ☕ 165/230000.

Ateneo without rest., San Marco 1876, calle Minelli ✉ 30124 ☎ 5200777, Fax 5228550 – ▤ TV ☎. AE $ E VISA EZ **d**
20 rm ☕ 164/222000.

Nuovo Teson without rest., calle de la Pescaria 3980 ✉ 30122 ☎ 5205555, Fax 5285335 – ☎. AE $ E VISA DU **s**
30 rm ☕ 140000.

Carpaccio without rest., San Polo-calle Corner 2765 ✉ 30125 ☎ 5235946, Fax 5242134, ≤ Grand Canal – ☎. $ E VISA BT **c**
19 March-15 November – **17 rm** ☕ 130/198000.

La Residenza without rest., campo Bandiera e Moro 3608 ✉ 30122 ☎ 5285315, Fax 5238859, « 14C building » – ▤ TV ☎. AE $ ◑ E VISA. ✻ DU **n**
closed 10 November-7 December and 8 January-20 February – **15 rm** ☕ 95/145000, ▤ 10000.

XXXX **Caffè Quadri,** piazza San Marco 120 ✉ 30124 ☎ 5289299, Fax 5208041 – AE $ ◑ E VISA. ✻ FZ **y**
closed Monday and 3 to 20 August – **M** a la carte 84/108000.

XXXX **Antico Martini,** campo San Fantin 1983 ✉ 30124 ☎ 5224121, Fax 5289857, 🏛 – ▤. AE $ ◑ E VISA. ✻ EZ **x**
closed lunch 24 November-March – **M** a la carte 68/111000 (15 %).

XXX ✿ **Harry's Bar,** calle Vallaresso 1323 ✉ 30124 ☎ 5285777, Fax 5208822, American bar rest. – ▤. AE $ ◑ E VISA FZ **n**
closed Monday – **M** a la carte 80/140000 (20 %)
Spec. Tagliolini agli scampi e zucchine, Sogliola Casanova con riso pilaf, Pasticceria della Casa. Wines Tocai, Cabernet.

XXX **Les Deux Lions,** riva degli Schiavoni 4175 ✉ 30122 ☎ 5200533, Fax 5225032, Elegant rest., « Summer service on the canal bank » – ▤. AE $ ◑ E VISA. ✻ GZ **t**
closed Tuesday – **M** (dinner only) (booking essential) a la carte 80/129000.

XXX ✿ **La Caravella,** calle larga 22 Marzo 2397 ✉ 30124 ☎ 5208901, Typical rest. – ▤. AE $ ◑ E VISA. ✻ EZ **m**
closed Wednesday – **M** (booking essential) a la carte 80/117000
Spec. Bigoli in salsa, Scampi allo Champagne, Filetto di bue "Caravella". Wines Sauvignon, Cabernet-Sauvignon.

XXX **Taverna la Fenice,** campiello de la Fenice ✉ 30124 ☎ 5223856, « Outdoor summer service » – AE $ ◑ E VISA. ✻ EZ **v**
closed Sunday, Monday lunch, 2 to 22 August and 11 to 27 January – **M** a la carte 62/112000 (12 %).

XXX **Al Campiello,** calle dei Fuseri 4346 ✉ 30124 ✆ 5206396, American Bar rest., late night dinners – ▤. AE ⓢ ⓓ E VISA FZ **z**
closed Monday – **M** (booking essential) a la carte 61/98000 (13 %).

XXX **La Colomba,** piscina di Frezzeria 1665 ✉ 30124 ✆ 5221175, Fax 5221468, ⛱, « Collection of contemporary art » – ▤ – 🏛 60. AE ⓢ ⓓ E VISA. ✻ FZ **m**
closed Wednesday except September-October – **M** a la carte 74/130000 (15 %).

XX **Do Forni,** calle dei Specchieri 457/468 ✉ 30124 ✆ 5237729, Telex 420832, Fax 5288132 – ▤. AE ⓢ ⓓ E VISA GY **c**
closed 22 November-5 December and Thursday (except June-October) – **M** a la carte 57/78000 (12 %).

XX **Antico Pignolo,** calle dei Specchieri 451 ✉ 30124 ✆ 5228123, Fax 5209007 – AE ⓢ ⓓ E VISA. ✻ GY **v**
closed Tuesday except September-October – **M** a la carte 78/125000 (12 %).

XX **Harry's Dolci,** Giudecca 773 ✉ 30133 ✆ 5224844, Fax 5222322, « Outdoor summer service on the Giudecca canal » – ▤. AE ⓓ E VISA AV **a**
closed 7 November-7 March and Tuesday (except July-September) – **M** a la carte 42/86000 (15 %).

X **Madonna,** calle della Madonna 594 ✉ 30125 ✆ 5223824, Venetian trattoria – ▤. AE ⓢ E VISA. ✻ EY **e**
closed Wednesday, 4 to 17 August and 24 December-January – **M** a la carte 34/53000 (12 %).

X **Antica Carbonera,** calle Bembo 4648 ✉ 30124 ✆ 5225479, Venetian trattoria – ▤. AE ⓢ ⓓ E VISA FY **q**
closed 20 July-10 August, 8 January-2 February, Sunday July-August and Tuesday in other months – **M** a la carte 37/59000 (12 %).

X **Antica Trattoria Poste Vecie,** Pescheria 1608 ✉ 30125 ✆ 721822, ⛱, Typical venetian trattoria – ▤. AE ⓢ ⓓ E VISA EX **a**
closed Tuesday except September-October – **M** a la carte 49/81000.

in Lido : 15 mn by boat from San Marco FZ – ✉ **30126** Venezia Lido.
ℹ Gran Viale S. M. Elisabetta 6 ✆ 5265721 :

🏨🏨🏨🏨 **Excelsior,** lungomare Marconi 41 ✆ 5260201, Telex 410023, Fax 5267276, ≤, 🏊, 🏖, 🎾, ⛳18 – 🛗 ▤ 📺 ☎ ♿ 🚗 🅟 – 🏛 40-600. AE ⓢ ⓓ E VISA. ✻ rest
April-October – **M** a la carte 88/125000 – ☕ 30000 – **194 rm** 560000 15 suites.

🏨🏨🏨🏨 **Des Bains,** lungomare Marconi 17 ✆ 5265921, Telex 410142, Fax 5260113, ≤, ⛱, « Floral park with heated 🏊 and 🎾 », 🏊, 🏖 – 🛗 ▤ 📺 ☎ 🅟 – 🏛 90-380. AE ⓢ ⓓ E VISA. ✻ rest
April-October – **M** 85/110000 – **191 rm** ☕ 450/475000 suite.

🏨🏨 **Quattro Fontane** 🐚, via 4 Fontane 16 ✆ 5260227, Telex 411006, Fax 5260726, ⛱, 🌳, 🎾 – ▤ 📺 ☎ 🅟 – 🏛 40. AE ⓢ ⓓ E VISA. ✻ rest
21 April-October – **M** a la carte 68/108000 – **64 rm** ☕ 220/330000.

🏨🏨 **Le Boulevard** without rest., Gran Viale S. M. Elisabetta 41 ✆ 5261990, Telex 410185, Fax 5261917, ⛱ – 🛗 ▤ 📺 ☎ 🅟 – 🏛 60. AE ⓢ ⓓ E VISA
45 rm ☕ 272/355000.

🏨🏨 **Villa Mabapa,** riviera San Nicolò 16 ✆ 5260590, Telex 410357, Fax 5269441, « Summer rest. in garden » – 🛗 ▤ rm 📺 ☎ ♿ – 🏛 60. AE ⓢ ⓓ E VISA. ✻ rest
M *(closed 3 November-15 March)* a la carte 44/60000 – **62 rm** ☕ 180/290000.

🏨 **Rigel** without rest., viale Dandolo 13 ✆ 5268810, Fax 2760077 – 🛗 ▤ ☎. AE ⓢ ⓓ E VISA
February-October – **42 rm** ☕ 124/183000.

🏨 **Vianello,** località Alberoni ✉ 30011 Alberoni ✆ 731072, 🌳 – ✻ rm
15 March-15 October – **M** *(closed September-June)* 25000 – ☕ 10000 – **20 rm** 75/90000.

XX **Ai Murazzi,** località Cà Bianca ✆ 5267278, ≤ – ▤ 🅟. AE
April-October – **M** *(closed Tuesday)* a la carte 40/77000 (12 %).

X **Trattoria da Ciccio,** via S. Gallo 241-in direction of Malamocco ✆ 5265489, ⛱ – 🅟. ⓢ E VISA
closed Tuesday and 15 to 30 November – **M** a la carte 26/42000 (12 %).

in Torcello 45 mn by boat from fondamenta Nuove CT – ✉ **30012** Burano :

XX **Locanda Cipriani,** ✆ 730150, Fax 735433, « Summer service in garden » – ▤. AE ⓢ E VISA
19 March-10 November – **M** *(closed Tuesday)* a la carte 80/113000 (15 %).

XX **Ostaria al Ponte del Diavolo,** ✆ 730401, Fax 730250, ⛱, 🌳 – AE ⓢ E VISA
closed January, February, Thursday and dinner (except Saturday) – **M** a la carte 52/78000 (10 %).

Norway

Norge

OSLO

PRATICAL INFORMATION

LOCAL CURRENCY

Norwegian Kroner: 100 N-Kr = 14.30 US $ = 12 Ecus (Jan. 93)

TOURIST INFORMATION

The telephone number and address of the Tourist Information office is given in the text under ▮.

FOREIGN EXCHANGE

In the Oslo area banks are usually open between 8.15am and 3.30pm, but in summertime, 15.5 - 31/8, they close at 3pm. Thursdays they are open till 5pm. Saturdays and Sundays closed.
Most large hotels, main airports and railway stations have exchange facilities. At Fornebu Airport the bank is open from 6.30am to 10.30pm on weekdays and 7.00am to 10pm on Sundays, all the year round.

MEALS

At lunchtime, follow the custom of the country and try the typical buffets of Scandinavian specialities.
At dinner, the a la carte and the menus will offer you more conventional cooking.

SHOPPING IN OSLO

(Knitted ware - Silver ware)

Your hotel porter should be able to help you and give you information.

CAR HIRE

The international car hire companies have branches in each major city. Your hotel porter should be able to give details and help you with your arrangements.

TIPPING IN NORWAY

A service charge is included in hotel and restaurant bills and it is up to the customer to give something in addition if he wants to.
The cloakroom is sometimes included in the bill, sometimes you pay a certain amount.
Taxi drivers and baggage porters have no claim to be tipped. It is up to you if you want to give a gratuity.

SPEED LIMITS

The maximum permitted speed within congested areas is 50 km/h - 31mph. Outside congested areas it is 80 km/h - 50mph. Where there are other speed limits (lower or higher) they are signposted.

SEAT BELTS

The wearing of seat belts in Norway is compulsory for drivers and passengers. All cars registered in Norway after 1/1-84 must have seat belts in the back seat too, and it is compulsory to use them.

ANIMALS

Very strict quarantine regulations for animals from all countries except Sweden. NO dispensations.

Oslo

Norge 985 M 7 – pop. 458 364.

See : Bygdøy AZ : Viking Ships★★★ (Vikingeskipene), Folk Museum (Norsk Folkemuseum), Kon-Tiki and RA Museum★ (Kon-Tiki Museet), Polarship Fram★ (Fram Museet), Maritime Museum★ (Norsk Sjøfartsmuseum) – Frognerparken★ (Vigeland Sculptures★★) AX – City-Hall★ (Rådhuset) BY **H** – Munch Museum★ (Munchmuseet) CY – National Gallery★ (Nasjonalgalleriet) BY **M1** – Akershus Castle★ (Akershus Festning) BZ – Historical Museum★ (Historisk Museum) BY **M2**.

Outskirts : Holmenkollen★★ (NW : 10 km) : Ski Jump★, Ski Museum★ AX – Tryvann Tower★★ (Tryvannstårnet) (NW : 14 km) : ☀★★ AX – Sonja Henie-Onstad Art Centre★ (Henie-Onstads Kultursenter) (W : 12 km) AY.

18 Oslo Golfklubb ✆ 22 50 44 02.

✈ Fornebu SW : 8 km ✆ 67 59 67 16 – SAS : Oslo City, Stenersg. 1 a ✆ Business travel : 22 17 00 10 (Europe and Overseas) 22 17 00 20 (Domestics and Scandinavia), Vacation travel : 22 42 77 60 – Air Terminal : Havnegata, main railway station, seaside.

⛴ Copenhagen, Frederikshavn, Kiel : contact tourist information centre (see below).

ℹ Norwegian Information Centre Vestbaneplassen 1 ✆ 22 83 00 50, Fax 22 83 91 50, Telex 71969 and main railway station ✆ 22 17 11 24 – KNA (Kongelig Norsk Automobilklub) Royal Norwegian Automobile Club, Drammensveien 20C ✆ 22 56 19 00 – NAF (Norges Automobil Forbund), Storg. 2 ✆ 22 34 14 00.

Hamburg 888 – København 583 – Stockholm 522.

OSLO

Street	Grid	No.
Karl Johans gate	BCY	
Grensen	CY	
Lille Grensen	CY	37
Torggata	CY	
Apotekergata	CY	2
Biskop Gunnerus' gate	CY	8
Bygdøy kappellvei	AZ	9
Christian Frederiks plass	CY	10
Christiania torv	CY	13
Dronningens gate	CYZ	14
Dronning Mauds gate	BY	16
Edvard Storms gate	BX	17
Elisenbergveien	AX	19
Fredriksborgveien	AZ	20
Fridtjof Nansens plass	BY	21
Frimanns gate	CX	23
Gimleveien	AX	24
Grubbegata	CY	27
Haakon VII's gate	BY	28
Hammersborgtunnelen	CY	30
Jernbanetorget	CY	31
Josefines gate	ABX	32
Kristian Augusts gate	BCY	33
Langés gate	CX	34
Lapsetorvet	AY	35
Lassons gate	AY	36
Løchenveien	AZ	38
Løkkeveien	ABY	39
Munchs gate	CY	41
Munkedamsveien	ABY	42
Nedre Slottsgate	CYZ	44
Nedre Vollgate	BY	45
Nygata	CY	47
Pløens gate	CY	48
Professor Aschehougs pl.	CY	49
Professor Dahls gate	AX	51
Riddervolds gate	AX	52
Roald Amundsens gate	BY	53
Rosteds gate	CX	54
Ruseløkkveien	ABY	55
Rådhusplassen	BY	56
Schives gate	AX	57
Skillebekk	AY	59
Skovveien	AXY	60
Stortingsgata	BY	62
Stortorvet	CY	63
Strandgata	CZ	64
Sven Bruns gate	BX	65
Thor Olsens gate	CX	67
Tullins gate	BX	68
Uelands gate	CX	69
Vaterlandtunnelen	CY	71
Youngstorget	CY	72
Øvre Slottsgate	CY	73

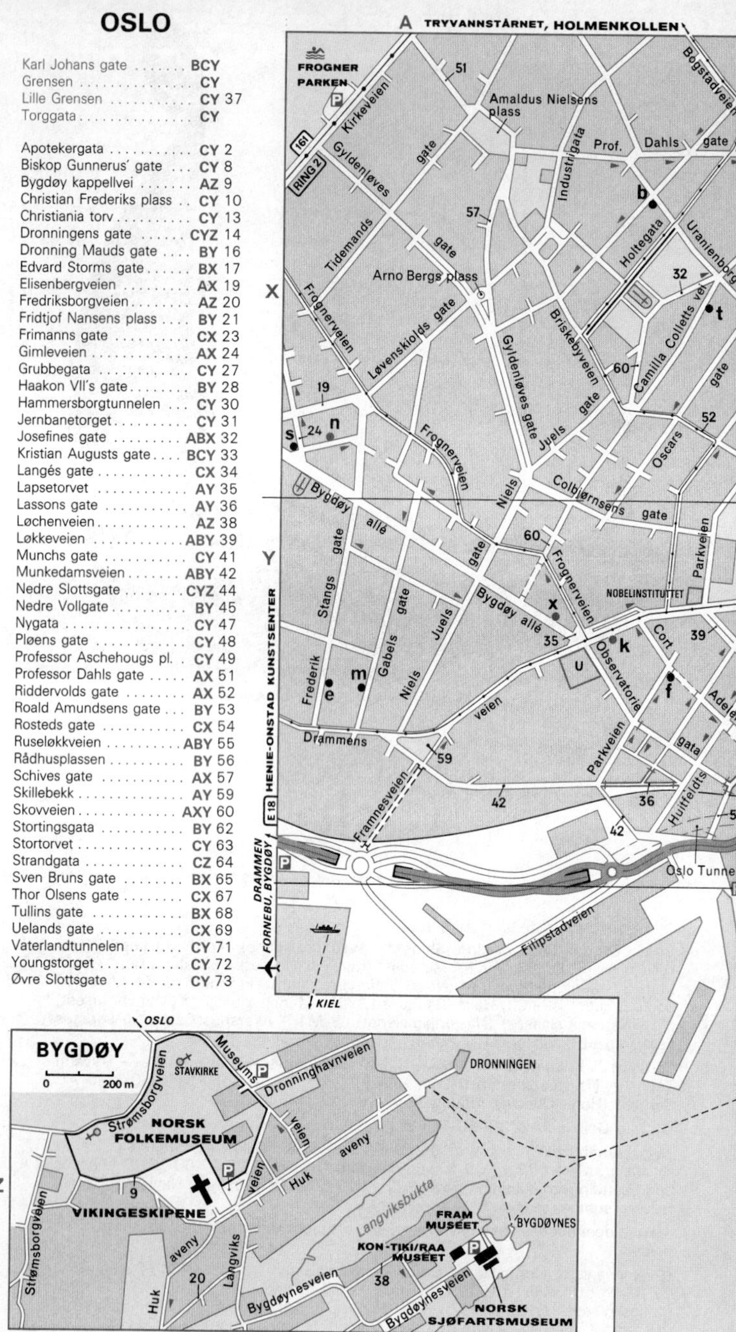

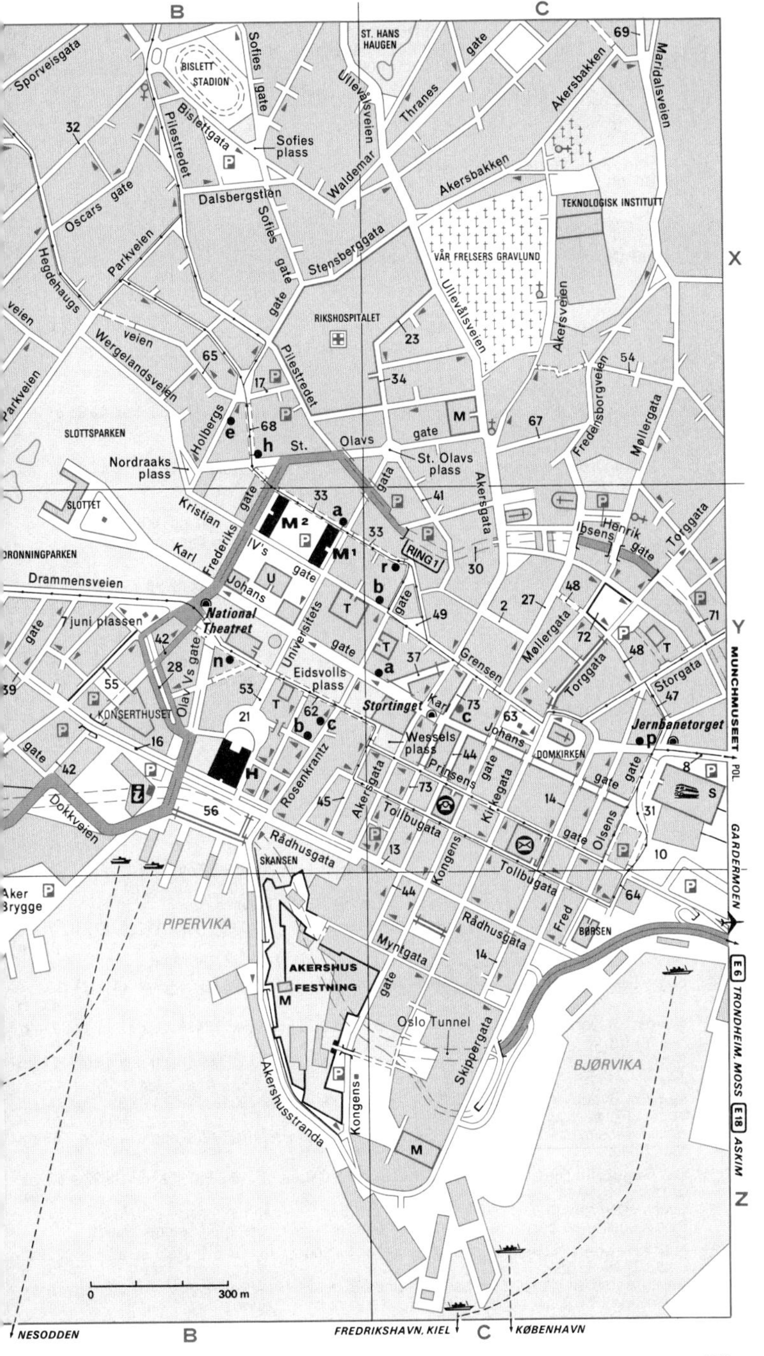

B
C
X
Y
Z
ST. HANS HAUGEN
BISLETT STADION
Sofies gate
Sofies plass
Bislettgata
Pilestredet
Sporveisgata
Oscars gate
Parkveien
Hegdehaugsveien
Dalsbergstien
Stensberggata
Waldemar Thranes gate
Ullevålsveien
Akersbakken
Maridalsveien
TEKNOLOGISK INSTITUTT
VÅR FRELSERS GRAVLUND
RIKSHOSPITALET
Akersveien
Fredensborgveien
Møllergata
Wergelandsveien
SLOTTSPARKEN
Nordraaks plass
Holbergs
St. Olavs gate
St. Olavs plass
Akersgata
SLOTTET
DRONNINGPARKEN
Kristian IV's gate
Frederiks gate
Karl Johans gate
Drammensveien
RING 1
Henrik Ibsens gate
Torggata
National Theatret
7 juni plassen
Universitets gata
Eidsvolls plass
Grensen
KONSERTHUSET
Olav Vs gate
Stortinget
Wessels plass
Rosenkrantz gate
DOMKIRKEN
Jernbanetorget
Storgata
Prinsens gate
Kirkegata
Tollbugata
Rådhusgata
Dokkveien
SKANSEN
Kongens gate
Olsens gate
Fred
BØRSEN
Myntgata
Aker Brygge
PIPERVIKA
AKERSHUS FESTNING
Oslo Tunnel
Skippergata
BJØRVIKA
Akershusstranda
MUNCHMUSEET
POL.
GARDERMOEN
E 6 TRONDHEIM, MOSS
E 18 ASKIM
NESODDEN
FREDRIKSHAVN, KIEL
KØBENHAVN
0
300 m

Grand, Karl Johansgate 31, 0159 Oslo 1, ✆ 42 93 90, Telex 71683, Fax 42 12 25, – rm – 300. AE E VISA. CY **a**
M (see **Grand Café** below) – **Etoile** 260/300 and a la carte – **269 rm** 1450/2150, **6 suites.**

Oslo Plaza, Sonja Henies Plass 3, 0134 Oslo 1, ✆ 17 10 00, Telex 11241, Fax 17 73 00, City and Fjord, – rm – 900. AE E VISA
M 205 (dinner) and a la carte 221/352 – **644 rm** 1195/1845, **18 suites.**
by Biskop Gunnerus' Gate CY

Continental, Stortingsgaten 24-26, 0161 Oslo 1, ✆ 41 90 60, Telex 71012, Fax 42 96 89 – rm – 300. AE E VISA. BY **n**
closed Christmas – **M** (see also **Theatercaféen** below) – **Annen Etage** *(closed Saturday, Sunday, Easter, July, Christmas and Bank Holidays)* (dinner only) a la carte 425/587 – **155 rm** 1450/2200, **8 suites.**

Royal Christiana, Biskop Gunnerus gate 3, 0106 Oslo 1, ✆ 42 94 10, Fax 42 46 22, – rm – 400. AE E VISA. CY **p**
closed Christmas – **M** *(closed Sunday lunch)* 195/250 and a la carte **383 rm** 1245/1445, **73 suites.**

SAS Scandinavia, Holbergsgate 30, 0166 Oslo 1, ✆ 11 30 00, Telex 79090, Fax 11 30 17, City and Fjord, – rm – 800. AE E VISA
M Holberg *(closed Sunday and Monday)* (dinner only) a la carte approx. 305/466 – **487 rm** 1345/1545, **4 suites.** BX **e**

Bristol, Kristian IV's des gate 7, 0130 Oslo 1, ✆ 41 58 40, Telex 71668, Fax 42 86 51 – rm rest – 200. CY **b**
138 rm, 3 suites.

Scandic Crown, Parkveien 68, 0254 Oslo 2, ✆ 44 69 70, Telex 71763, Fax 44 26 01, – rm rest – 100. AE E VISA AY **f**
M 195/205 and dinner a la carte – **185 rm** 765/1395.

Ambassadeur, Camilla Colletts vei 15, 0258 Oslo 2, ✆ 44 18 35, Fax 44 47 91, « Distinctively themed bedrooms », – rest. AE E VISA AX **t**
M (see below) – **34 rm** 1195/1445, **8 suites.**

Rica Victoria, Rosenkrantzgate 13, 0160, Oslo 1 ✆ 42 99 40, Fax 42 99 43 – rm. AE E VISA. BY **b**
closed 25 and 26 December – **M** *(closed Sunday lunch)* a la carte 258/405 – **153 rm** 795/1100, **3 suites.**

Gabelshus, Gabelsgate 16, 0272 Oslo 2, ✆ 55 22 60, Telex 74073, Fax 44 27 30, « Antique furniture, paintings » – rm – 60. AE E VISA. AY **m**
closed 1 week Easter and 23 December-4 January – **M** a la carte – **45 rm** 770/1000.

Stefan, Rosenkrantzgate 1, 0158 Oslo 1, ✆ 42 92 50, Telex 19809, Fax 33 70 22 – rm – 70. AE E VISA. CY **r**
closed Christmas and Easter – **M** *(closed Sunday)* (unlicensed) (buffet lunch)/dinner 155 and a la carte – **130 rm** 825/945.

Ritz without rest., Frederik Stangs Gate 3, 0272 Oslo 2, ✆ 44 39 60, Fax 44 67 13 – – 60. AE E VISA AY **e**
closed 23 December-4 January – **50 rm** 770/970.

Europa without rest., St. Olavsgate 31, 0166 Oslo 1, ✆ 20 99 90, Telex 71512, Fax 11 27 27 – . AE E VISA. BX **h**
closed 23 December-2 January – **156 rm** 585/1045, **2 suites.**

Cecil without rest., Stortingsgatan 8, 0161 Oslo 1, ✆ 42 70 00, Telex 11228, Fax 42 26 70 – . AE E VISA. BY **c**
closed 7 to 12 April and 23 December-3 January – **112 rm** 765/995.

Saga, Eilert Sundtsgt. 39, 0259, Oslo 2 ✆ 43 04 85, Fax 44 08 63 – – 30
37 rm. AX **b**

Savoy, Universitetsgt. 11, 0164 Oslo 1, ✆ 22 20 26 55, Telex 76418, Fax 22 11 24 80 – rm – 80. AE E VISA. rest BY **a**
closed 23 December-3 January – **M** *(closed Sunday dinner)* 200/350 and a la carte – **77 rm** 1050/1540.

Norum, Bygdøy Allé 53, 0265 Oslo 2, ✆ 44 79 90, Telex 79315, Fax 44 92 39 – rm rest – 60. AE E VISA. AX **s**
closed Christmas – **M** *(closed Sunday, Christmas and Easter)* 76/210 and a la carte – **55 rm** 720/850.

XXX **Bagatelle** (Hellstrøm), Bygdøy Allé 3, 0257 Oslo 2, ✆ 44 63 97, Fax 55 35 92 – AE E VISA AY **x**
closed Easter and Christmas – **M** (dinner only) 350/650 and a la carte 395/525
Spec. Coquillages, crustacés et poissons, Gibier en saison, Gratin aux mûres jaunes.

XXX **D'Artagnan** (Nielsen), Øvre Slottsgate 16 (1st floor), 0157 Oslo 1, ✆ 41 50 62, Fax 427741 – . AE E VISA CY **c**
closed Saturday except October-December, Sunday, 12 July-9 August and 22 December-4 January – **M** (dinner only) 490/575 and a la carte 470/545
Spec. Salade de crabe et émince d'avocat, Roulade de sole et saumon, Confit de cuisses de canard.

XXX **Ambassadeur** Camilla Colletts vei 15, 0208 Oslo 2, ✆ 44 18 35, Fax 44 47 91, « Elegant decor, paintings » – ▤. AE ⓓ E VISA. ✻ AX **t**
closed Sunday, Easter and Christmas – **M** (dinner only) 365/495.

XX ✿ **Feinschmecker,** Balchensgate 5, Box 3165, 0265 Oslo 2, ✆ 44 17 77 – ▤. AE ⓓ E VISA
closed Sunday, Easter, 5-25 July and Christmas – **M** (dinner only) 325/395 and a la carte 300/440 AX **n**
Spec. Fresh marinated salmon with a caviar sauce and avocado salad, Grilled monkfish with creamed morels, wild mushrooms and a red wine sauce, Herb and mustard coated rack of lamb with tarragon glazed root vegetables.

XX **Det Blå Kjøkken,** Drammensveien 30, 0255 Oslo 2, ✆ 44 26 50, Fax 55 71 56 – ▤ AY **k**
closed Sunday, 23 December-5 January and Easter – **M** (dinner only) 375/520 and a la carte.

XX **Theatercaféen** (at Continental H.), Stortingsgaten 24-26, 0161 Oslo 1, ✆ 33 32 00, Telex 71012, Fax 41 20 94 – AE ⓓ E VISA BY **n**
M (buffet lunch) 75 and a la carte 192/435.

X **A Touch of France,** Øvre Slottsgate 16, 0157, Oslo 1 ✆ 42 56 97, Fax 42 77 41, (French style Brasserie) – ▤. AE ⓓ E VISA CY **c**
closed Sunday lunch and 22 December-2 January – **M** 145/315 and a la carte.

X Grand Café (at Grand H.), Karl Johansgt. 31, 0159 Oslo 1, ✆ 42 93 90, Telex 71683, Fax 42 12 25 – ▤ CY **a**

at Fornebu Airport SW : 8 km by E 18 AY and Snarøyveien – ✉ ⚙ 02 Oslo :

SAS Park Royal, Fornebuparken, 1324 Lysaker/Oslo ✆ 12 02 20, Telex 78745, Fax 12 00 11, « Private beach and park », 🏋, ≘s, 🎾 – |‡| ⇆ rm ▤ 📺 ☎ ♿ 🅟 – 🏛 170. AE ⓓ E VISA. ✻
M 110/205 and a la carte – **254 rm** ☕ 1345/1695.

at Sandvika SW : 14 km by E 18 Exit E 68 – ✉ ⚙ 02 Oslo :

Rica H.Oslofjord, Sandviksveien 184, 1301 Sandvika, ✆ 54 57 00, Telex 74345, Fax 54 27 33, 🏋, ≘s – |‡| ⇆ rm ▤ 📺 ☎ ♿ 🚗 🅟 – 🏛 500. AE ⓓ E VISA
M Orchidee 175 (buffet lunch) and a la carte 290/420 – **239 rm** ☕ 1210/1330, **3 suites.**

at Holmenkollen NW : 10 km by Bogstadveien, Sørkedalsveien and Holmenkollveien – ✉⚙ 02 Oslo :

Holmenkollen Park H. Rica 🐦, Kongeveien 26, 0390 Oslo, ✆ 14 60 90, Telex 72094, Fax 14 61 92, ≤ Oslo city and Fjord, ≘s, 🏊 – |‡| ⇆ rm ▤ 📺 ☎ ♿ 🚗 🅟 – 🏛 400. AE ⓓ E VISA
M De Fem Stuer *(closed Sunday)* (buffet lunch) 245/295 and a la carte 315/530 – **183 rm** ☕ 1145/1245, **8 suites.**

Portugal

LISBON

PRATICAL INFORMATION

LOCAL CURRENCY

Escudo: 100 Esc. = 0.68 US $ = 0.57 Ecu (Jan. 93).

FOREIGN EXCHANGE

Hotels, restaurants and shops do not always accept foreign currencies and the tourist is therefore advised to change cheques and currency at banks, saving banks and exchange offices - The general opening times are as follows: banks 8.30am to noon and 1 to 2.45pm (closed on Saturdays), money changers 9.30am to 6pm (usually closed on Saturday afternoons and Sundays).

TRANSPORT

Taxis may be hailed when showing the green light or sign "Livre" on the windscreen.

Metro (subway) network. In each station complete information and plans will be found.

SHOPPING IN LISBON

Shops and boutiques are generally open from 9am to 1pm and 3 to 7pm - In Lisbon, the main shopping streets are: Rua Augusta, Rua do Carmo, Rua Garrett (Chiado), Rua do Ouro, Rua da Prata, Av. da Roma.

TIPPING

A service charge is added to all bills in hotels, restaurants and cafés; it is usual, however, to give an additional tip for personal service; 10 % of the fare or ticket price is also the usual amount given to taxi drivers and cinema and theatre usherettes.

SPEED LIMITS

The speed limit on motorways is 120 km/h - 74 mph, on other roads 90 km/h - 56 mph and in built up areas 60 km/h - 37 mph.

SEAT BELTS

Out of cities, it is compulsory for drivers and front seat passengers to wear seat belts.

THE FADO

The Lisbon Fado (songs) can be heard in restaurants in old parts of the town such as the Alfama, the Bairro Alto and the Mouraria. A selection of fado cabarets will be found at the end of the Lisbon restaurant list.

Lisbon

(LISBOA) 1100 440 P 2 - Pop. 826 140 - alt. 111 m - ☎ 01.

SEE :

View : ★★ from the Suspension Bridge (Ponte de 25 Abril), ★★ from Christ in Majesty (Cristo-Rei) S : 3,5 km.

CENTRE : POMBALINE LISBON

See : Rossio★ (square) GY - Avenida da Liberdade★ FX - Edward VII Park★ (Cold Greenhouse★) EX - St. Rock Church★ (Igreja São Roque) FY **M**[1] - Terreiro do Paço★ (square) GZ - São Pedro de Alcantara Belvedere★ FY **A**.

MEDIEVAL LISBON

See : St. George's Castle★★ (Castelo de São Jorge) GY - Cathedral★ (Sé) GZ - Santa Luzia Belvedere★ (Miradouro de Santa Luzia) - Alfama★★ (Beco do Carmeiro★ and Rua de São Pedro★) HYZ.

MANUELINE LISBON

See : Hieronymite Monastery★★ (Mosteiro dos Jerónimos : church★★, cloister★★★) - Belém Tower★★ (Torre de Belém) - Monument to the Discoveries★ (Padrão dos Descobrimentos).

MUSEUMS

Museum of Ancient Art★★ (Museu Nacional de Arte Antiga : polyptych by Nuno Gonçalves★★★, Portuguese Primitive paintings★★) - Calouste Gulbenkian Museum★★★ (Art collection) - Azulejo Museum★ - Coach Museum★★ (Museu Nacional dos Coches) - Maritime Museum★★ (Museu de Marinha) - Popular Art★.

OTHER CURIOSITIES

Church of the Mother of God★★ (Igreja da Madre de Deus : ínterior★★, altar★, chapter house★★, paintings★) - Modern Art Center★ - Zoologic Garden and climatizated★★ - Botanic Garden★ EX - Monsanto Park★ - Fronteira Palace Garden★ - Free waters aqueduct★ (Aqueduto das Águas Livres) EX.

9, 18 Estoril Golf Club W : 25 km ☎ 468 01 76 Estoril - 18 Lisbon Sports Club NW : 20 km ☎ 431 00 77 - 18 Club de Campo de Lisboa S : 15 km ☎ 226 32 44 Aroeira, Monte da Caparica.

✈ Lisbon Airport N : 8 km from city centre ☎ 848 11 01 - T.A.P., Praça Marquês de Pombal 3, ✉ 1200, ☎ 54 40 80 and airport ☎ 848 91 81.

🚘 ☎ 87 75 09.

⛴ to Madeira : E.N.M., Rua de São Julião 5-1º, ✉ 1100, ☎ 87 01 21 and Cais Rocha Conde de Óbidos, ✉ 1300 ☎ 396 25 47.

ℹ Palácio Foz, Praça dos Restaudores ☎ 346 63 07 and airport ☎ 89 42 48 - **A.C.P.** Rua Rosa Araújo 24, ✉ 1200, ☎ 356 39 31, Telex 12581 - **A.C.P.** Av Barbosa do Bocage 23-1º, ✉ 1000, ☎ 793 61 21, Fax 793 40 26.

Madrid 658 - Bilbao 904 - Paris 1820 - Porto 314 - Sevilla 417.

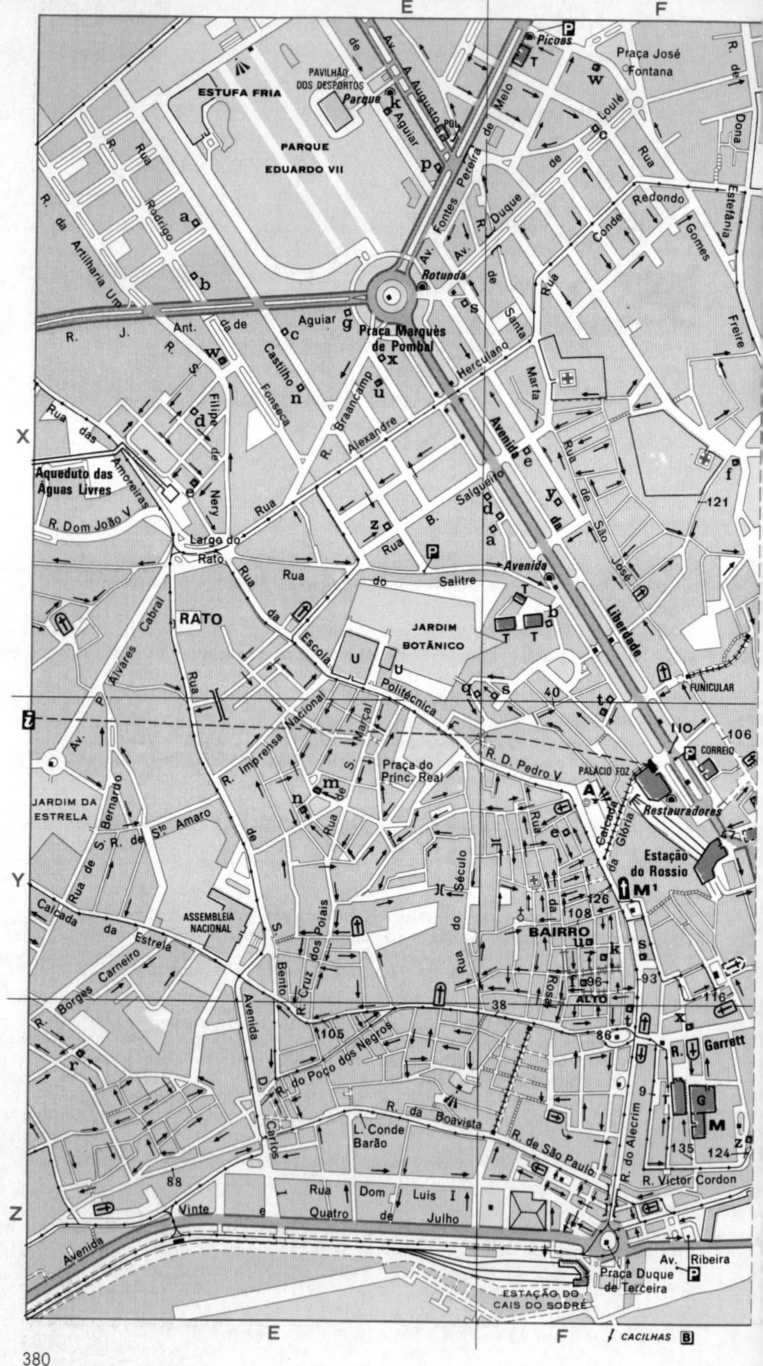
E
F
ESTUFA FRIA
PAVILHÃO DOS DESPORTOS
Parque
PARQUE
EDUARDO VII
Picoas
Praça José Fontana
Rotunda
Praça Marquês de Pombal
Aqueduto das Águas Livres
Largo do Rato
RATO
JARDIM BOTÂNICO
FUNICULAR
CORREIO
PALÁCIO FOZ
Restauradores
Estação do Rossio
Praça do Princ. Real
JARDIM DA ESTRELA
ASSEMBLEIA NACIONAL
BAIRRO ALTO
R. Garrett
L. Conde Barão
R. Victor Cordon
Praça Duque de Terceira
ESTAÇÃO DO CAIS DO SODRÉ
Av. Ribeira
CACILHAS
X
Y
Z

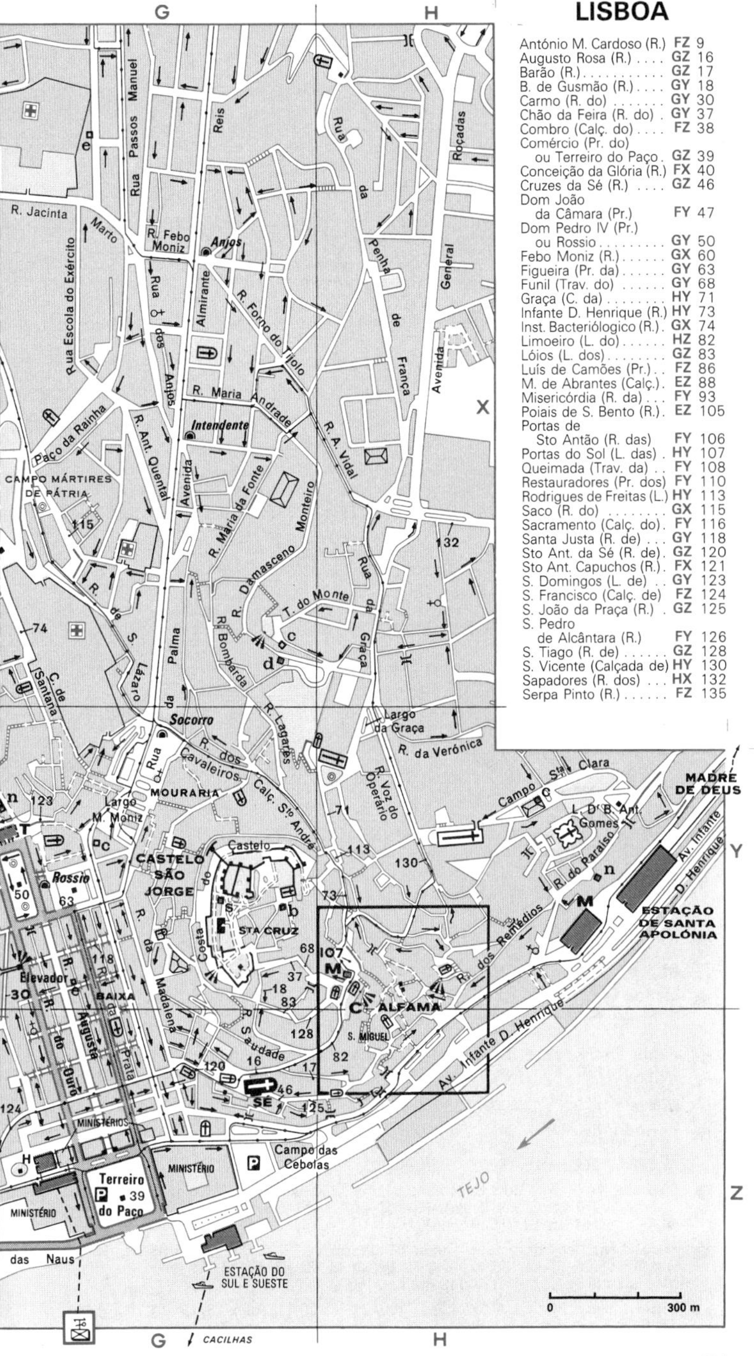

LISBOA

Street	Grid	No.
António M. Cardoso (R.)	FZ	9
Augusto Rosa (R.)	GZ	16
Barão (R.)	GZ	17
B. de Gusmão (R.)	GY	18
Carmo (R. do)	GY	30
Chão da Feira (R. do)	GY	37
Combro (Calç. do)	FZ	38
Comércio (Pr. do) ou Terreiro do Paço	GZ	39
Conceição da Glória (R.)	FX	40
Cruzes da Sé (R.)	GZ	46
Dom João da Câmara (Pr.)	FY	47
Dom Pedro IV (Pr.) ou Rossio	GY	50
Febo Moniz (R.)	GX	60
Figueira (Pr. da)	GY	63
Funil (Trav. do)	GY	68
Graça (C. da)	HY	71
Infante D. Henrique (R.)	HY	73
Inst. Bacteriólogico (R.)	GX	74
Limoeiro (L. do)	HZ	82
Lóios (L. dos)	GZ	83
Luís de Camões (Pr.)	FZ	86
M. de Abrantes (Calç.)	EZ	88
Misericórdia (R. da)	FY	93
Poiais de S. Bento (R.)	EZ	105
Portas de Sto Antão (R. das)	FY	106
Portas do Sol (L. das)	HY	107
Queimada (Trav. da)	FY	108
Restauradores (Pr. dos)	FY	110
Rodrigues de Freitas (L.)	HY	113
Saco (R. do)	GX	115
Sacramento (Calç. do)	FY	116
Santa Justa (R. de)	GY	118
Sto Ant. da Sé (R. de)	GZ	120
Sto Ant. Capuchos (R.)	FX	121
S. Domingos (L. de)	GY	123
S. Francisco (Calç. de)	FZ	124
S. João da Praça (R.)	GZ	125
S. Pedro de Alcântara (R.)	FY	126
S. Tiago (R. de)	GZ	128
S. Vicente (Calçada de)	HY	130
Sapadores (R. dos)	HX	132
Serpa Pinto (R.)	FZ	135

Ritz, Rua Rodrigo da Fonseca 88, ✉ 1093, ✆ 69 20 20, Telex 12589, Fax 69 17 83, – 25/600. AE ① E VISA JCB. rest EX **b**
M Varanda a la carte 4200/5500 - **The Grill** a la carte 6700/8600 - 2000 - **310 rm** 50000/54000.

Sheraton Lisboa H., Rua Latino Coelho 1, ✉ 1097, ✆ 57 57 57, Telex 12774, Fax 54 71 64, heated – – 25/550. AE ① E VISA JCB.
M Alfama Grill *(closed Saturday, and Sunday)* a la carte 5200/10000 - **Caravela** a la carte 3900/5400 - 2750 - **384 rm** 35000/50000. by Av. Fontes Pereira de Melo EFX

Le Meridien Lisboa, Rua Castilho 149, ✉ 1000, ✆ 69 09 00, Telex 64315, Fax 69 32 31, – – 25/480. AE ① E VISA JCB. EX **a**
M Atlantic *(closed Saturday, Sunday and August)* a la carte 5300/7400 - **Brasserie des Amis** a la carte 4050/5200 - 2000 - **331 rm** 38000/41000.

Da Lapa, Rua do Pau de Bandeira, ✉ 1200, ✆ 395 00 05, Fax 395 06 65, « Park with waterfall and », – – 25/226. AE ① E VISA. W by Av. 24 de Julho EZ
M a la carte 6150/9250 - 1800 - **102 rm** 37000/40000.

Tívoli Lisboa, Av. da Liberdade 185, ✉ 1200, ✆ 52 11 01, Telex 12588, Fax 57 94 61, « Terrace with City », heated, – – AE ① E VISA. FX **d**
M Grill Terraço a la carte approx. 7500 - **Zodíaco** a la carte approx. 4800 - **327 rm** 37500/44000.

Alfa Lisboa, Av. Columbano Bordalo Pinheiro, ✉ 1000, ✆ 726 21 21, Telex 18477, Fax 726 30 31, – – 25/250. AE ① E VISA.
M A Aldeia a la carte 3450/4700 - **Grill Pombalino** a la carte 3900/6200 - **350 rm** 27500/33000. NW by Av. A. Augusto de Aguiar EX

Altis, Rua Castilho 11, ✉ 1200, ✆ 52 24 96, Telex 13314, Fax 54 86 96, – – AE ① E VISA JCB. EX **z**
M Girasol (buffet, lunch only) 5000 - **Grill Dom Fernando** *(closed Sunday)* a la carte 4750/7650 - **307 rm** 26000/30000.

Continental, Rua Laura Alves 9, ✉ 1000, ✆ 793 50 05, Telex 65632, Fax 797 36 69 – – 25/180. AE ① E VISA JCB.
M D. Miguel *(closed Sunday)* a la carte approx. 5700 - **Coffee Shop Continental** a la carte approx. 5700 - **220 rm** 25900/ 29200. N by Av. Fontes Pereira de Melo EFX

Lisboa Penta, Av. dos Combatentes, ✉ 1600, ✆ 726 40 54, Telex 18437, Fax 726 42 81, – – 25/600. AE ① E VISA JCB. rest
M 3750 - **Grill Passarola** a la carte 4610/7210 - **Verde Pino** a la carte 2570/3400 - **588 rm** 19400/23600. NW by Av. A. Augusto de Aguiar EX

Holiday Inn Crowne Plaza, Av. Marechal Craveiro Lopes 390, ✉ 1700, ✆ 759 96 39, Telex 61170, Fax 758 66 05, – – 25/200. AE ① E VISA. N by Av. Fontes Pereira de Melo EFX
M 4200 - **221 rm** 31500/38000.

Pullman Lisboa, Av. da Liberdade 125, ✉ 1200, ✆ 342 92 02, Fax 342 92 22 – – 25/300. AE ① E VISA JCB. rest
M 4500 - 1150 - **170 rm** 21500/26000.

Holiday Inn Lisboa, Av. António José de Almeida 28 A, ✉ 1000, ✆ 793 52 22, Telex 60330, Fax 793 66 72 – – AE ① E VISA.
M 3600 - **169 rm** 16500. NW by Av. Fontes Pereira de Melo EFX

Novotel Lisboa, Av. José Malhoa 1642, ✉ 1000, ✆ 726 60 22, Telex 40114, Fax 726 64 96, – – 25/300. AE ① E VISA. rest
M 3850 - 1100 - **246 rm** 13800/15050. NW by Av. A. Augusto de Aguiar EX

Lisboa Plaza, Travessa do Salitre 7, ✉ 1200, ✆ 346 39 22, Telex 16402, Fax 347 16 30 – AE ① E VISA JCB. FX **b**
M 3500 - **112 rm** 24000/29500.

Fénix and Rest. El Bodegón, Praça Marqués de Pombal 8, ✉ 1200, ✆ 386 21 21, Telex 12170, Fax 386 01 31 – – 25/100. AE ① E VISA JCB. EX **g**
M a la carte 3200/5200 - **123 rm** 17500/19500.

Zurique, Rua Ivone Silva, ✉ 1000, ✆ 793 71 11, Fax 793 72 90, – – 25/150. AE ① E VISA. N by Av. Fontes Pereira de Melo EFX
M 3000 - **252 rm** 15000/17000.

Lutécia, Av. Frei Miguel Contreiras 52, ✉ 1700, ✆ 80 31 21, Telex 12457, Fax 80 78 18, – AE ① E VISA JCB. N by Av. Almirante Reis GX
M 4000 - **151 rm** 18000/21500.

Tívoli Jardim, Rua Julio Cesar Machado 7, ✉ 1200, ✆ 53 99 71, Telex 12172, Fax 355 65 66, heated, – AE ① E VISA. FX **a**
M a la carte approx. 4900 - **119 rm** 21500/26500.

Diplomático, Rua Castilho 74, ✉ 1200, ✆ 386 20 41, Telex 13713 – – AE ① E VISA. rest EX **c**
M a la carte 2350/2500 - **90 rm** 17500/20500.

Flórida without rest, Rua Duque de Palmela 32, ✉ 1200, ☎ 57 61 45, Telex 12256, Fax 54 35 84 - |☰| ▤ TV ☎ - 🏛 25/100. AE ⓓ E VISA JCB. ✻ EX **x**
112 rm ☕ 16500/20000.

Mundial, Rua D. Duarte 4, ✉ 1100, ☎ 886 31 01, Telex 12308, Fax 87 91 29, ≤ - |☰| ▤ TV ☎ P - 🏛 25/140. AE ⓓ E VISA. ✻ GY **c**
M 3850 - **147 rm** ☕ 18200/22800.

Barcelona without rest, Rua Laura Alves 10, ✉ 1000, ☎ 795 42 73, Fax 795 42 81 - |☰| ▤ TV ☎ 🚗 - 🏛 25/300. AE ⓓ E VISA. ✻ N by Av. Fontes Pereira de Melo EFX
125 rm ☕ 16300/18500.

Dom Manuel I without rest, Av. Duque d'Avila 189, ✉ 1000, ☎ 57 61 60, Telex 43558, Fax 57 69 85, « Tasteful decor » - |☰| ▤ TV ☎. AE ⓓ E VISA JCB. ✻
64 rm ☕ 12900/14500. N by Av. Fontes Pereira de Melo EFX

Dom Rodrigo Suite H. without rest, Rua Rodrigo da Fonseca 44, ✉ 1200, ☎ 386 38 00, Fax 386 30 00, ⛱ - |☰| ▤ TV ☎ 🚗. AE ⓓ E VISA. ✻
☕ 800 **57 suites** 15500/19000

Lisboa Alif H. without rest, av. João XXI-Campo Pequeno, ✉ 1000, ☎ 795 24 64, Telex 64460, Fax 795 41 16 - |☰| ▤ TV ☎ 🚗 - 🏛 25/40. AE ⓓ VISA. ✻
115 rm ☕ 15000/17500. N by Av. Fontes Pereira de Melo EFX

Lisboa without rest, Rua Barata Salgueiro 5, ✉ 1100, ☎ 355 41 31, Telex 60228, Fax 355 41 39 - |☰| ▤ TV ☎ 🚗. AE ⓓ E VISA JCB. ✻ FX **e**
61 rm ☕ 23000/27000.

Veneza without rest, Av. da Liberdade 189, ✉ 1200, ☎ 352 26 18, Fax 352 66 78, « Old palace » - |☰| ▤ TV ☎ P. AE ⓓ E VISA. ✻ FX **d**
38 rm ☕ 14000/17000.

Lisboa Carlton without rest, Av. Conde Valbon 56, ✉ 1000, ☎ 795 11 57, Telex 65618, Fax 795 11 66 - |☰| ▤ TV ☎ 🚗. AE ⓓ E VISA. ✻
72 rm ☕ 19000/23000. N by Av. Augusto de Aguiar EX

Amazónia H., Travessa Fábrica dos Pentes 12, ✉ 1200, ☎ 387 70 06, Telex 66361, Fax 387 90 90, ⛱ heated - |☰| ▤ TV ☎ 🚗 - 🏛 25/150. AE ⓓ E VISA. ✻ EX **d**
M *(closed Saturday dinner and Sunday)* 3000 - **192 rm** ☕ 12100/15300.

Roma, Av. de Roma 33, ✉ 1700, ☎ 796 77 61, Telex 16586, Fax 793 29 81, ≤, ⛱ - |☰| ▤ TV ☎ - 🏛 25/230. AE ⓓ E VISA JCB. ✻ N by Av. Almirante Reis GX
M 3000 - **265 rm** ☕ 11500/15000.

Eduardo VII, Av. Fontes Pereira de Melo 5, ✉ 1000, ☎ 53 01 41, Telex 18340, Fax 53 38 79, ≤ - |☰| ▤ TV ☎ - 🏛 25/60. AE ⓓ E VISA. ✻ EX **p**
M 3600 - ☕ 1000 - **121 rm** 15300/17500.

Dom Carlos without rest, Av. Duque de Loulé 121, ✉ 1000, ☎ 53 90 71, Telex 16468, Fax 352 07 28 - |☰| ▤ TV ☎. AE ⓓ E VISA. ✻ EX **s**
73 rm ☕ 11500/14500.

Miraparque, Av. Sidónio Pais 12, ✉ 1000, ☎ 57 80 70, Telex 16745, Fax 57 89 20 - |☰| ▤ TV ☎. AE ⓓ E VISA. ✻ EX **k**
M 3000 - **100 rm** ☕ 10500/12500.

Príncipe Real, Rua da Alegria 53, ✉ 1200, ☎ 346 01 16, Telex 44571, Fax 342 21 04 - |☰| ▤ TV ☎. AE ⓓ E VISA JCB. ✻ EX **q**
M 3000 - **24 rm** ☕ 16500/19000.

Britânia without rest, Rua Rodrigues Sampaio 17, ✉ 1100, ☎ 315 50 16, Telex 13733, Fax 315 50 21 - |☰| ▤ TV ☎. AE ⓓ E VISA. ✻ FX **y**
30 rm ☕ 13900/17400.

York House, Rua das Janelas Verdes 32, ✉ 1200, ☎ 396 25 44, Telex 16791, Fax 397 27 93, ☂, « Former 16C convent, Portuguese decor » - ☎. AE ⓓ E VISA JCB. ✻
M a la carte 2700/3800 - **35 rm** ☕ 19000/21000. W by Calçada M. de Abrantes EZ

As Janelas Verdes without rest, Rua das Janelas Verdes 47, ✉ 1200, ☎ 396 81 43, Telex 16791, Fax 397 27 93 - ☎. AE ⓓ E VISA JCB. ✻ W by Av. 24 de Julho EZ
17 rm ☕ 19000/21000.

Botánico without rest, Rua Mãe de Agua 16, ✉ 1200, ☎ 342 03 92, Telex 16174, Fax 342 01 25 - |☰| ▤ TV ☎. AE ⓓ E VISA JCB. ✻ FX **s**
30 rm ☕ 10500/15000.

Da Torre, Rua dos Jerónimos 8, ✉ 1400, ☎ 363 62 62, Fax 364 59 95 - |☰| TV ☎ - 🏛. AE ⓓ E VISA JCB W by Av. 24 de Julho EZ
M (see rest. **São Jerónimo** below) - **50 rm** ☕ 11500/14750.

Flamingo, Rua Castilho 41, ✉ 1200, ☎ 386 21 91, Telex 14736, Fax 386 12 16 - |☰| ▤ TV ☎. AE ⓓ E VISA. ✻ EX **n**
M 3000 - **39 rm** ☕ 13500/16500.

Berna without rest, Av. António Serpa 13, ✉ 1000, ☎ 793 67 67, Telex 62516, Fax 793 62 78 - |☰| ▤ TV ☎ 🚗 - 🏛 25/140. AE ⓓ E VISA. ✻
240 rm ☕ 12000/14000. N by Av. Fontes Pereira de Melo EFX **x**

Albergaria Senhora do Monte without rest, Calçada do Monte 39, ✉ 1100, ☎ 886 60 02, Fax 87 77 83, ≤ São Jorge castle, town and river Tejo - |☰| ▤ TV ☎. AE ⓓ E VISA. ✻ GX **c**
28 rm ☕ 11500/14000.

Fonte Luminosa without rest, Alameda D. Afonso Enriques 70-6°, ✉ 1000, ☎ 80 81 69, Telex 15063, Fax 80 90 03 - |$| TV ☎. E VISA. ✻ N by Av. Almirante Reis GX
37 rm ☐ 6800/9200.

Insulana without rest, Rua da Assunção 52, ✉ 1100, ☎ 342 76 25 - |$| TV ☎. AE ⓓ E VISA. ✻ GY **e**
32 rm ☐ 8500/10500.

Dom João without rest, Rua José Estêvão 43, ✉ 1100, ☎ 54 30 64 - |$| TV ☎. AE ⓓ E VISA. ✻ GX **e**
18 rm ☐ 8500/9500.

Imperador without rest, Av. 5 de Outubro 55, ✉ 1000, ☎ 352 48 84, Fax 352 65 37 - |$| ☎. AE ⓓ E VISA. ✻ N by Av. Fontes Pereira de Melo EFX
43 rm ☐ 7500/9300.

XXXX **Tágide,** Largo da Academia Nacional de Belas Artes 18, ✉ 1200, ☎ 342 07 20, Fax 347 18 80, ≤ - ▤. AE ⓓ E VISA JCB. ✻ FZ **z**
closed Saturday and Sunday - **M** a la carte 6650/10000.

XXXX **Antonio Clara - Clube de Empresários,** Av. da República 38, ✉ 1000, ☎ 796 63 80, Telex 62506, Fax 797 41 44, « Former old palace » - ▤ Ⓟ. AE ⓓ E VISA. ✻
closed Sunday - **M** a la carte 4800/7400. N by Av. Fontes Pereira de Melo EFX

XXXX **Clara,** Campo dos Mártires da Patria 49, ✉ 1100, ☎ 355 73 41, Fax 54 20 82, 🏠 - ▤. AE ⓓ E VISA. ✻ FX **f**
closed Saturday lunch, Sunday and 1 to 15 August - **M** a la carte 5200/7800.

XXXX **Aviz,** Rua Serpa Pinto 12-B, ✉ 1200, ☎ 342 83 91 - ▤. AE ⓓ E VISA. ✻ FZ **x**
closed Saturday lunch, Sunday and August - **M** a la carte 6150/9500.

XXXX **Tavares,** Rua da Misericórdia 37, ✉ 1200, ☎ 32 11 12, Late 19C decor - ▤. AE ⓓ E VISA. ✻ FZ **t**
closed Saturday and Sunday lunch - **M** a la carte 5700/8000.

XXX **Gare Tejo,** Gare Marítima de Alcântara-Alcântara Sul, ✉ 1300, ☎ 397 63 35, Fax 397 85 59, « Beside of the river Tejo with ≤ » - ▤. AE ⓓ E VISA W by Av. 24 de Julho EZ
closed Saturday lunch, Sunday and August - **M** a la carte 4500/6400.

XXX **Gambrinus,** Rua das Portas de Santo Antão 25, ✉ 1100, ☎ 32 14 66, Fax 346 50 32 - ▤. AE VISA. ✻ GY **n**
M a la carte 10000/13000.

XXX **Escorial,** Rua das Portas de Santo Antão 47, ✉ 1100, ☎ 346 44 29, Fax 346 37 58 - ▤. AE ⓓ E VISA JCB. ✻ GY **n**
M a la carte 4930/6000.

XXX ✿ **Casa da Comida,** Travessa das Amoreiras 1, ✉ 1200, ☎ 388 53 76, Fax 387 51 32, « Patio with plants » - ▤. AE ⓓ E VISA. ✻ EX **e**
closed Saturday lunch, Sunday and August - **M** a la carte 6000/10900
Spec. Sopa de crustáceos, Pregado com pimenta verde, Perdiz ou faisão à convento de Alcântara..

XXX **Mister Cook** with coffee shop, Av. Guerra Junqueiro 1, ✉ 1000, ☎ 80 72 37, Fax 793 71 52 - ▤. AE ⓓ E VISA. ✻ N by Av. Fontes Pereira de Melo EFX
closed Saturday lunch and Sunday - **M** a la carte 3600/6000.

XXX **Pabe,** Rua Duque de Palmela 27-A, ✉ 1200, ☎ 53 74 84, Fax 53 64 37, English pub style - ▤. AE ⓓ E VISA JCB. ✻ EX **u**
M a la carte 6200/7100.

XXX **Chester,** Rua Rodrigo da Fonseca 87-D, ✉ 1200, ☎ 65 73 47, Meat specialities - ▤. AE ⓓ E VISA JCB. ✻ EX **w**
closed Sunday - **M** a la carte 5050/6980.

XXX **Braseiro Grande,** av. Elias García 13, ✉ 1000, ☎ 797 70 77 - ▤. AE ⓓ VISA. ✻
closed Saturday lunch, Sunday and August - **M** a la carte 3000/3300.
N by Av. Fontes Pereira de Melo EFX

XXX **Saraiva's,** Rua Eng. Canto Resende 3, ✉ 1000, ☎ 53 19 87, Fax 53 19 87, Modern decor - ▤. AE ⓓ E VISA JCB. ✻ N by Av. Augusto de Aguiar EX
closed Saturday - **M** a la carte 3630/6500.

XXX **Bachus,** Largo da Trindade 9, ✉ 1200, ☎ 342 28 28, Fax 342 12 60 - ▤. AE ⓓ E VISA JCB. ✻ FY **s**
M a la carte 3400/6600.

XXX ✿ **Conventual,** Praça das Flores 45, ✉ 1200, ☎ 60 91 96 - ▤. AE ⓓ E VISA EY **m**
closed Saturday lunch, Sunday and August - **M** a la carte 3950/6500
Spec. Lombo de linguado com molho de marisco, Pato com Champagne e pimenta rosa, Migas e miolos com entrecosto..

XXX **O Faz Figura,** Rua do Paraíso 15 B, ✉ 1100, ☎ 886 89 81, ≤, 🏠 - ▤. AE ⓓ E VISA. ✻
closed Sunday - **M** a la carte 3800/6000. HY **n**

XX **Via Graça,** Rua Damasceno Monteiro 9 B, ✉ 1100, ☎ 87 08 30, ≤ São Jorge castle, city and river Tejo - ▤. AE ⓓ E VISA JCB. ✻ GX **d**
closed Saturday lunch, Sunday and 15 to 31 August - **M** a la carte 3180/5000.

XX **Casa do Leão,** Castelo de São Jorge, ✉ 1100, ☎ 888 01 54, Fax 87 63 29, ≤ - ▤. AE ⓓ VISA. ✻ GY **s**
M a la carte 4600/6550.

XX **Santa Cruz - Michel,** Largo de Santa Cruz do Castelo 5, ✉ 1100, ☎ 86 43 38 - ▤. AE ⓓ E VISA JCB GY **b**
closed Saturday lunch, Sunday and Bank Holidays - **M** a la carte 3500/5000.

XX **São Jerónimo,** Rua dos Jerónimos 12, ✉ 1400, ☎ 64 87 96 - ▤. AE ⓓ E VISA JCB. ✂
closed Sunday - **M** a la carte 2890/4880.

XX **Espelho d'Água,** Av. de Brasilia, ✉ 1400, ☎ 301 73 73, Fax 363 26 92, ←, 🏠, Artificial lake side setting. Modern decor - ▤. AE ⓓ E VISA JCB. ✂
closed Sunday - **M** a la carte 3190/5860.

XX **Sancho,** Travessa da Glória 14, ✉ 1200, ☎ 346 97 80 - ▤. AE ⓓ E VISA JCB. ✂
closed Sunday - **M** a la carte 2060/3980. FXY **t**

XX **Saddle Room,** Praça José Fontana 17C, ✉ 1000, ☎ 352 31 57, Telex 64269, Fax 54 09 61, Rustic English style decor - ▤. AE ⓓ E VISA FX **w**
closed Saturday lunch and Sunday - **M** a la carte 3450/7000.

XX **Adega Tía Matilde,** Rua da Beneficéncia 77, ✉ 1600, ☎ 797 21 72 - ▤. AE ⓓ E VISA. ✂ N by Av. Fontes Pereira de Melo EFX
closed Saturday dinner and Sunday - **M** a la carte 4175/6175.

X **Xêlê Bananas,** Praça das Flores 29, ✉ 1200, ☎ 395 25 15, Tropical style decor - ▤. AE ⓓ E VISA EY **n**
closed Saturday lunch and Sunday - **M** a la carte 2700/4350.

X **Sua Excelencia,** Rua do Conde 42, ✉ 1200, ☎ 60 36 14 - ▤. AE ⓓ E VISA JCB
closed Saturday lunch, Sunday lunch, Monday and September - **M** a la carte 3350/6100.
N by Av. 24 de Julho EZ

X **Chez Armand,** Rua Carlos Mardel 38, ✉ 1900, ☎ 52 07 70, Fax 52 42 57, French rest., Meat specialities - ▤. AE ⓓ E VISA N by Av. Almirante Reis GX
closed Saturday lunch, Sunday and August - **M** a la carte 3830/5150.

X **Porta Branca,** Rua do Teixeira 35, ✉ 1200, ☎ 32 10 24 - ▤. AE ⓓ E VISA. ✂ FY **e**
closed Saturday lunch, Sunday and July - **M** a la carte 4500/5300.

Typical atmosphere :

XX **Sr. Vinho,** Rua do Meio-à-Lapa 18, ✉ 1200, ☎ 397 74 56, Fax 395 20 72, Fado cabaret - ▤. AE ⓓ E VISA JCB. ✂ EZ **r**
closed Sunday - **M** (dinner only) a la carte 3870/6960.

X **Adega Machado,** Rua do Norte 91, ✉ 1200, ☎ 342 87 13, Fax 346 75 07, Fado cabaret - ▤. AE ⓓ E VISA JCB. ✂ FY **k**
closed Monday - **M** (dinner only) a la carte 5600/7300.

Spain

España

MADRID - BARCELONA - MALAGA
MARBELLA - SEVILLA - VALENCIA

PRACTICAL INFORMATION

LOCAL CURRENCY

Peseta: 100 ptas = 0,86 US $ = 0.72 Ecu (Jan. 93)

TOURIST INFORMATION

The telephone number and address of the Tourist Information offices is given in the text of the towns under ℹ.

FOREIGN EXCHANGE

Banks are usually open fron 9am to 2pm (12.30pm on Saturdays).
Exchange offices in Sevilla and Valencia airports open from 9am to 2pm, in Barcelone airport from 9am to 2pm and 7 to 11pm. In Madrid and Málaga airports, offices operate a 24 hour service.

TRANSPORT

Taxis may be hailed when showing the green light or sign "Libre" on the windscreen.
Madrid, Barcelona and Valencia have a Metro (subway) network. In each station complete information and plans will be found.

SHOPPING

In the index of street names, those printed in red are where the principal shops are found.
The big stores are easy to find in town centres; they are open from 10am to 8pm.
Exclusive shops and boutiques are open from 10am to 2pm and 5 to 8pm - In Madrid they will be found in Serrano, Princesa and the Centre; in Barcelona, Passeig de Gracia, Diagonal and the Rambla de Catalunya.
Second-hand goods and antiques: El Rastro (Flea Market), Las Cortes, Serrano in Madrid; in Barcelona, Los Encantes (Flea Market), Barrio Gótico.

TIPPING

Hotel, restaurant and café bills always include service in the total charge. Nevertheless it is usual to leave the staff a small gratuity which may vary with the district and the service given. Doormen, porters and taxi-drivers are used to being tipped.

SPEED LIMITS

The maximum permitted speed on motorways is 120 km/h - 74 mph, and 90 km/h - 56 mph on other roads.

SEAT BELTS

The wearing of seat belts is compulsory for drivers and passengers.

"TAPAS"

Bars serving "tapas" (typical spanish food to be eaten with a glass of wine or an aperitif) will usually be found in central, busy or old quarters of towns. In Madrid, idle your way to the Calle de Cuchilleros (Plaza Mayor) or to the Calle Cardenal Cisnero (Glorieta de Bilbao).

Madrid

Madrid 28000 444 y 447 K 19 - Pop. 3 188 297 - alt. 646 m - ✆ 91.

See : The Prado Museum*** (Museo del Prado) NY - The Old Madrid* : Plaza Mayor** KY, Plaza de la Villa* KY, Bishop Chapel* KZ, Vistillas Gardens KYZ panorama*, San Francisco El Grande Church (chairs*, sacristy chair*) KZ - Oriente Quarter** : Royal Palace (Palacio Real)*** KX (Real Armería**, Royal Carriage Museum* DY **M1**), Descalzas Reales Convent** KLX (Convento de las Descalzas, Reales), Encarnación Royal Monastery* KX (Real Monasterio de la Encarnación), University City* (Ciudad Universitaria) DV, West Park* (Parque del Oeste) DV, Country House* (Casa de Campo) DX, Zoo** - El Madrid de los Borbones** : Plaza de la Cibeles* MNX, Paseo del Prado* MNXZ, Palacio de Villahermosa (colección Thyssen-Bornemisza**) MY **M6**, Casón del Buen Retiro* NY, Reina Sofia Art Center* (El Guernica**) MZ, Puerta de Alcalá* NX, Parque del Buen Retiro** NYZ.

Other Museums : Archeological Museum** (Museo Arqueológico Nacional : Dama de Elche***) NV - Lázaro Galdiano Museum** (enamels and ivories collection***) HV **M4** - Real Academia de Bellas Artes de San Fernando* LX **M2** - San Antonio de la Florida (Frescos**) DX - Wax Museum* (Museo de Cera) NV - Sorolla Museum* GV **M5** - Plaza Monumental de las Ventas* JV **B** - Army Museum* (Museo del Ejército) NY.

Envir. : El Pardo (Palacio*) NW : 13 km by C 601.

Racecourse of the Zarzuela - 18, 18 Puerta de Hierro ✆ 216 17 45 - 9, 18 Club de Campo ✆ 357 21 32 - 18 La Moraleja N : 11 km ✆ 650 07 00 - 9 Club Barberán SW : 10 km ✆ 218 85 05 - 18 Las Lomas, El Bosque SW : 18 km ✆ 616 21 70 - 18 Real Automóvil Club de España N : 28 km ✆ 652 26 00 - 18 Nuevo Club de Madrid, Las Matas W : 26 km ✆ 630 08 20 - 9 Somosaguas W : 10 km by Casa de Campo ✆ 212 16 47.

Madrid-Barajas by ② : 13 km ✆ 305 83 44 - Iberia : Velazquez 130, ✉ 28006, ✆ 587 87 87 HV, and Aviaco, Mandés 51, ✉ 28003, ✉ 534 42 00 FV.

Chamartin ✆ 733 11 22 - Principe Pio ✆ 248 87 16.

Shipping Companies : Cia. Trasmediterránea, Pedro Munõz Seca 2 NX, ✉ 28001, ✆ 431 07 00, Fax 431 08 04.

Princesa 1, ✉ 28008, ✆ 541 23 25, Duque de Medinaceli 2, ✉ 28014, ✆ 429 49 51 pl. Mayor 3, ✉ 28012, ✆ 266 54 77, Chamartin Station, ✉ 28036, ✆ 315 99 76 and Barajas airport ✆ 305 86 56 - R.A.C.E. José Abascal 10, ✉ 28003, ✆ 447 32 00, Fax 447 79 48.

Paris (by Irún) 1310 - Barcelona 627 - Bilbao 397 - La Coruña 603 - Lisboa 653 - Málaga 548 - Porto 599 - Sevilla 550 - Valencia 351 - Zaragoza 322.

Centre : Paseo del Prado, Puerta del Sol, Gran Vía, Alcalá, Paseo de Recoletos, Plaza Mayor, (plan pp. 6 and 7) :

Palace, pl. de las Cortes 7, ✉ 28014, ✆ 429 75 51, Telex 23903, Fax 429 82 66 – 25/500. AE ⓓ E VISA JCB. rest — MY **e**
M 6750 - **Grill Neptuno** *(closed Saturday)* a la carte 5650/7850 – 2325 – **487 rm** 29500/37000.

Princesa, Princesa 40, ✉ 28008, ✆ 542 21 00, Telex 44377, Fax 542 35 01 – 25/750. AE ⓓ E VISA JCB. — plan p. 6 KV **c**
M 3000 – 1950 – **406 rm** 24900/31200.

Villa Real, pl. de las Cortes, 10, ✉ 28014, ✆ 420 37 67, Telex 44600, Fax 420 25 47, « Tasteful decor » – 25/150. AE ⓓ E VISA. — MY **c**
M a la carte 4500/5000 – 1650 – **115 rm** 26400/33000.

Tryp Plaza, pl. de España, ✉ 28013, ✆ 547 12 00, Telex 27383, Fax 548 23 89, ← – 25/300. AE ⓓ VISA. — KV **s**
M 2500 – 1300 – **306 rm** 18325/22950.

Tryp Ambassador, Cuesta de Santo Domingo 5, ✉ 28013, ✆ 541 67 00, Telex 49538, Fax 559 10 40 – 25/280. AE ⓓ E VISA. — KX **k**
M a la carte 4450/5450 – 1300 – **181 rm** 18325/22950.

G.H. Reina Victoria, pl. del Ángel 7, ✉ 28012, ✆ 531 45 00, Telex 47547, Fax 522 03 07 – AE ⓓ E VISA. — LY **s**
M a la carte 4000/6300 – 1300 – **201 rm** 18325/22950.

Liabeny, Salud 3, ✉ 28013, ✆ 532 53 06, Telex 49024, Fax 532 74 21 – AE E VISA. – **M** 2600 – 900 – **219 rm** 9300/14300. — LX **c**

Suecia and Rest. Bellman, Marqués de Casa Riera 4, ✉ 28014, ✆ 531 69 00, Telex 22313, Fax 521 71 41 – 25/150. AE ⓓ E VISA JCB. — MX **r**
M *(closed Saturday lunch, Sunday, Bank Holidays and August)* a la carte 4500/5700 – 1375 – **128 rm** 18900/24675.

Emperador without rest, Gran Vía 53, ✉ 28013, ✆ 547 28 00, Telex 46261, Fax 547 28 17, – 25/300. AE ⓓ E VISA. — KX **n**
1450 – **232 rm** 13400/16800.

Arosa coffee shop only, Salud 21, ✉ 28013, ✆ 532 16 00, Telex 43618, Fax 531 31 27 – AE ⓓ E VISA JCB — LX **q**
1200 – **139 rm** 12700/17500.

Mayorazgo, Flor Baja 3, ✉ 28013, ✆ 547 26 00, Telex 45647, Fax 541 24 85 – 25/250. AE ⓓ E VISA JCB. — KV **c**
M 3500 – 1200 – **200 rm** 10500/14500.

Tryp Menfis, Gran Vía 74, ✉ 28013, ✆ 547 09 00, Telex 48773, Fax 547 51 99 – AE ⓓ E VISA JCB. — KV **u**
M 1975 – 875 – **116 rm** 13500/16900.

Tryp Washington, Gran Vía 72, ✉ 28013, ✆ 541 72 27, Telex 48773, Fax 547 51 99 – AE ⓓ E VISA JCB. — KV **u**
M (at Hotel **Tryp Menfis** above) – 825 – **117 rm** 11600/14500.

El Coloso, Leganitos 13, ✉ 28013, ✆ 559 76 00, Telex 47017, Fax 547 49 68 – 25/175. AE ⓓ E VISA JCB. — KX **y**
M 2750 – 1200 – **84 rm** 15100/18850.

Regina without rest, Alcalá 19, ✉ 28014, ✆ 521 47 25, Telex 27500, Fax 521 47 25 – AE ⓓ E VISA. – 750 – **142 rm** 9050/11900. — LX **v**

Casón del Tormes without rest, Río 7, ✉ 28013, ✆ 541 97 46, Fax 541 18 52 – E VISA. – 570 – **63 rm** 7100/10500. — KV **v**

Mercator coffee shop only, Atocha 123, ✉ 28012, ✆ 429 05 00, Telex 46129, Fax 369 12 52 – AE ⓓ E VISA — NZ **b**
750 – **89 rm** 7800/10800.

Los Condes without rest, Los Libreros 7, ✉ 28004, ✆ 521 54 55, Telex 42730, Fax 521 78 82 – AE E VISA. – 700 – **68 rm** 8000/15000. — KLV **g**

El Prado, Prado 11, ✉ 28014, ✆ 369 02 34, Fax 429 28 29 – AE ⓓ E VISA. rest — LY **a**
M *(closed Sunday dinner)* 1150 – 300 – **47 rm** 10000/15000.

Carlos V without rest, Maestro Vitoria 5, ✉ 28013, ✆ 531 41 00, Telex 48547, Fax 531 37 61 – AE ⓓ E VISA JCB. — LX **f**
650 – **67 rm** 8900/11200.

Atlántico without rest, Gran Vía 38 - 3°, ✉ 28013, ✆ 522 64 80, Telex 43142, Fax 531 02 10 – AE ⓓ E VISA JCB. — LX **e**
500 – **62 rm** 6970/9500.

Anaco coffee shop only, Tres Cruces 3, ✉ 28013, ✆ 522 46 04, Fax 531 64 84 – AE ⓓ E VISA. — LX **a**
655 – **39 rm** 6800/10500.

California without rest, Gran Vía 38, ✉ 28013, ✆ 522 47 03, Fax 531 61 01 – AE ⓓ E VISA. – 350 – **26 rm** 5600/7500. — LX **e**

Alexandra without rest, San Bernardo 29, ✉ 28015, ✆ 542 04 00, Fax 559 28 25 – AE E VISA JCB. – 560 – **79 rm** 6050/8100. — KV **z**

MADRID

Caidos de la División Azul . . . . HS 21
Capitán Haya . . . . GS 25
Comandante Zorita . . . FT 45
Costa Rica (Av. de) . . . HS 55
Cuatro Caminos (Glorieta de) . . . . FU 56
Doctor Arce (Av. del) . HU 62
Doctor Fleming . . . . . . GT 63
Enrique Larreta . . . . . . HS 76
Estébanez Calderón . . . GS 80
Fray Bernardino Sahagún . . . . HS 90
Gen. López Pozas . . . . HS 92
Gen. Moscardó . . . . . . FT 95
Jerez . . . . HS 107
Pedro Teixeira . . . . GT 145
Pinos Alta . . . . FS 146
Pintor Juan Gris . . . . . . FS 148
Presidente Carmona . . FT 157
Raimundo Fernández Villaverde . . . . FU 162
Reina Mercedes . . . . . FT 168
República Dominicana (Pl.) . . . . HS 172
Rosa de Silva . . . . FS 177
Rosario Pino . . . . GS 179
San Amaro (Pl.) . . . . . . FT 183
Segre . . . . HT 206
Sinesio Delgado . . . . . GR 209
Sor Angela de la Cruz . GS
Teruel . . . . FT 210
Victor Andrés Belaunde . . . . HT 229
Victor de la Serna . . . . HT 231

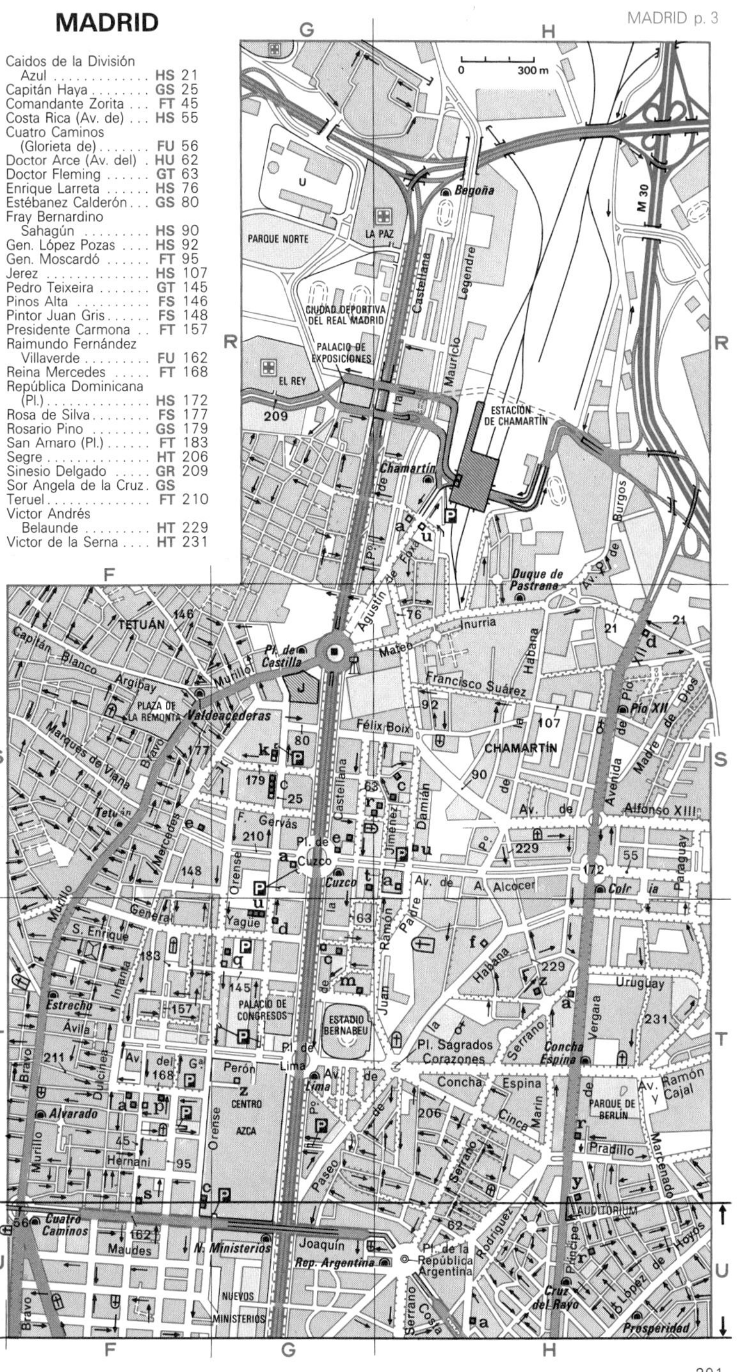

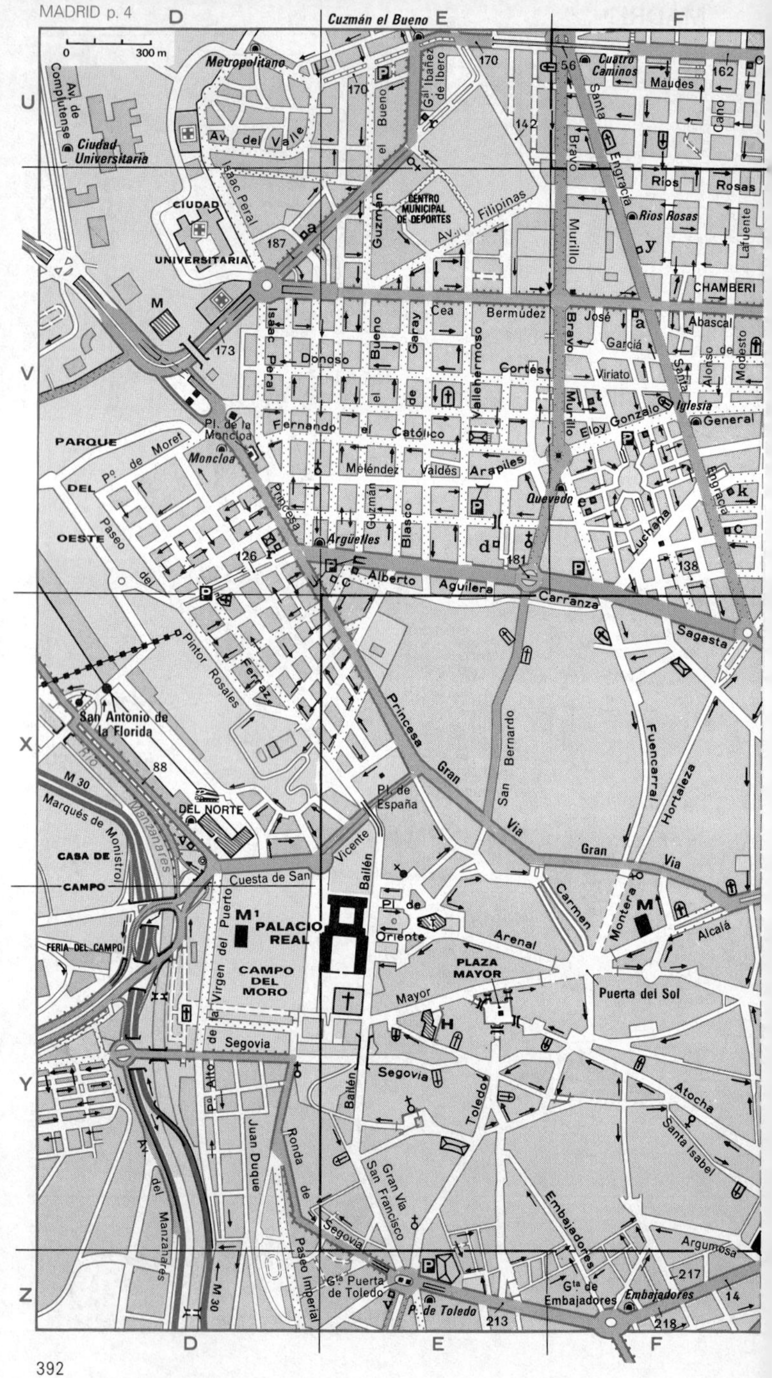
D
E
F
U
V
X
Y
Z
0
300 m
Cuzmán el Bueno
Metropolitano
Cuatro Caminos
Av. de Complutense
Ciudad Universitaria
Av. del Valle
Isaac Peral
Gal Ibañez de Ibero
Bueno
Guzmán el Bueno
Santa Engracia
Bravo Murillo
Maudes
Cano
Ríos Rosas
Lafuente
CIUDAD UNIVERSITARIA
CENTRO MUNICIPAL DE DEPORTES
Av. Filipinas
CHAMBERI
M
José Abascal
Bermúdez
Cea
Garay
Donoso
García
Alonso de
Modesto
Vallehermoso
Cortés
Viriato
Iglesia
General
Eloy Gonzalo
Pl. de la Moncloa
Moncloa
PARQUE DEL OESTE
Fernando el Católico
Po. de Moret
Meléndez Valdés
Arapiles
Quevedo
Luchana
Princesa
Argüelles
Blasco
Paseo del Pintor Rosales
Alberto Aguilera
Carranza
Sagasta
Ferraz
San Antonio de la Florida
Río Manzanares
M 30
Marqués de Monistrol
CASA DE CAMPO
DEL NORTE
Pl. de España
Gran Vía
San Bernardo
Fuencarral
Hortaleza
Cuesta de San Vicente
Bailén
Pl. de Oriente
M¹
PALACIO REAL
CAMPO DEL MORO
Virgen del Puerto
FERIA DEL CAMPO
Carmen
Montera
Alcalá
Arenal
PLAZA MAYOR
Mayor
Puerta del Sol
H
Segovia
Po. Alto de la Virgen del Puerto
Juan Duque
Ronda de Segovia
Toledo
Atocha
Santa Isabel
Gran Vía San Francisco
Embajadores
Argumosa
Av. del Manzanares
Paseo Imperial
Gta Puerta de Toledo
P. de Toledo
Gta de Embajadores
170
142
162
56
187
173
126
181
138
88
213
217
218
14

MADRID

Atocha (Ronda de)	FZ	14
Florida (Paseo de la)	DX	88
Lagasca	HVX	116
Marqués de Salamanca (Pl.)	HV	125
Marqués de Urquijo	DV	126
Miguel Angel	GV	136
Reina Cristina (Paseo)	HZ	166
Reina Victoria (Av.)	EU	170
Reyes Católicos (Av.)	DV	173
Ruiz Jiménez (Glorieta)	EV	181
San Francisco de Sales (Pas.)	DV	187
Toledo (Ronda de)	EZ	213
Valencia	FZ	217
Valencia (Ronda de)	FZ	218

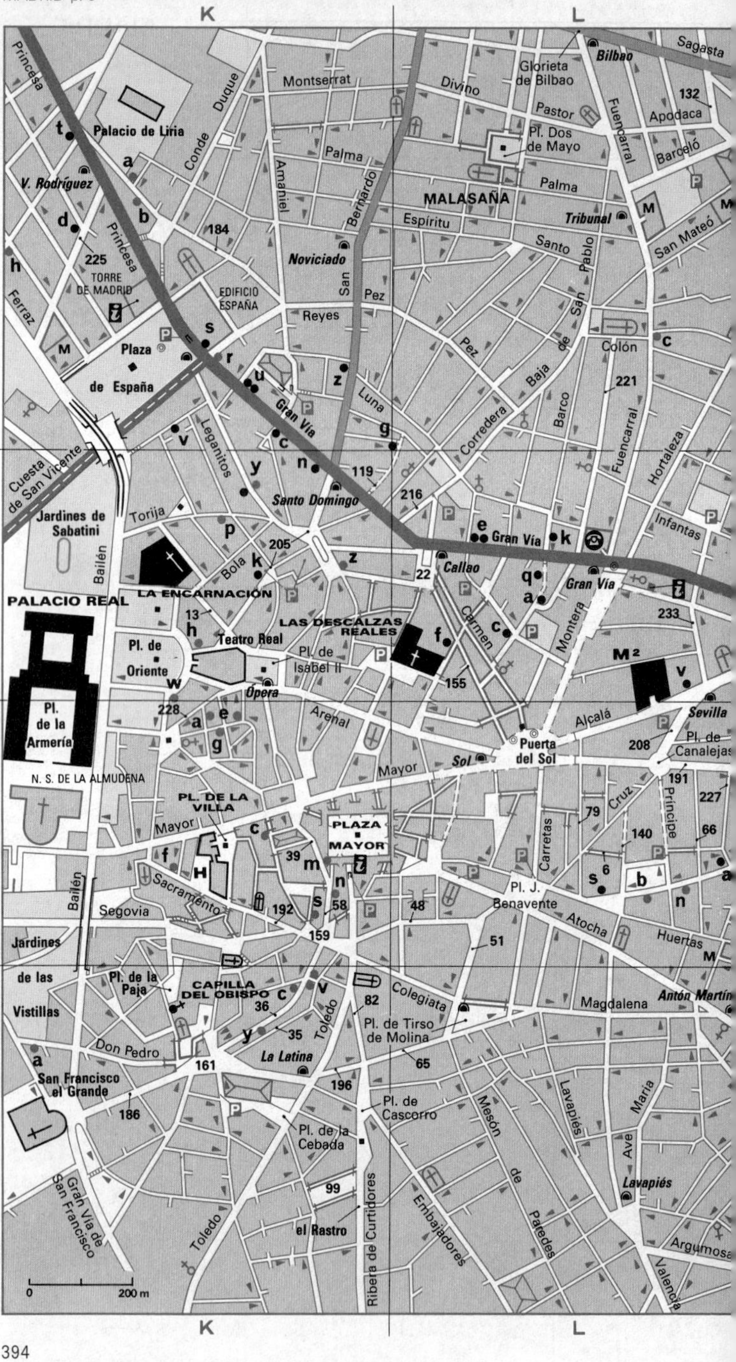

K L

V X Y Z

Princesa
Palacio de Liria
V. Rodríguez
225
TORRE DE MADRID
Ferraz
Plaza de España
Conde Duque
184
EDIFICIO ESPAÑA
Montserrat
Palma
Amaniel
San Bernardo
Noviciado
Reyes
Pez
Divino
Glorieta de Bilbao
Bilbao
Sagasta
Pastor
Pl. Dos de Mayo
Fuencarral
Apodaca
Barceló
132
Palma
MALASAÑA
Espíritu
Tribunal
San Mateo
Santo
San Pablo
Baja de San
Colón
Pez
Barco
221
Luna
Gran Vía
Leganitos
Corredera
Fuencarral
Hortaleza
Cuesta de San Vicente
Jardines de Sabatini
Torija
119
216
Santo Domingo
Infantas
Gran Vía
205
Bola
Bailén
22
Callao
Gran Vía
PALACIO REAL
LA ENCARNACIÓN
13
Teatro Real
LAS DESCALZAS REALES
Carmen
Montera
233
Pl. de Oriente
Pl. de Isabel II
Ópera
155
M^2
Pl. de la Armería
228
Arenal
Alcalá
Sevilla
Puerta del Sol
208
Pl. de Canalejas
Sol
Mayor
N. S. DE LA ALMUDENA
PL. DE LA VILLA
191
227
Príncipe
Mayor
PLAZA MAYOR
79
Cruz
140
66
Carretas
39
6
Sacramento
Bailén
Segovia
192
58
48
Pl. J. Benavente
Atocha
159
51
Huertas
Jardines de las Vistillas
Pl. de la Paja
CAPILLA DEL OBISPO
82
Colegiata
Antón Martín
Magdalena
36
35
Toledo
Pl. de Tirso de Molina
Don Pedro
161
La Latina
65
San Francisco el Grande
196
186
Pl. de Cascorro
Pl. de la Cebada
Mesón de Paredes
Lavapiés
María
Ave
Lavapiés
99
Gran Vía de San Francisco
Toledo
el Rastro
Ribera de Curtidores
Embajadores
Argumosa
Valencia
0 200 m

MADRID

Street	Grid	No.
Alcalá	LMXY	
Arenal	KY	
Carmen	LX	
Fuencarral	LV	
Gran Via	KLX	
Hortaleza	LVX	
Mayor	KLY	
Mayor (Plaza)	KY	
Montera	LX	
Preciados	LX	155
Puerta del Sol (Pl.)	LY	
San Jerónimo (Carrera de)	LMY	191
Alvarez Gato	LY	6
Arrieta	KX	13
Ayala	NV	18
Bárbara de Braganza	NV	19
Callao (Pl. de)	LX	22
Cava Alta	KZ	35
Cava Baja	KZ	36
Cava de San Miguel	KY	39
Ciudad de Barcelona	NZ	41
Colón (Pl.de)	NV	44
Concepción Jerónima	LY	48
Conde de Romanones	LY	51
Cortes (Pl. de las)	MY	53
Cuchilleros	KY	58
Duque de Alba	LZ	65
Echegaray	LY	66
Espoz y Mina	LY	79
Estudios	KZ	82
Fernando el Santo	NV	85
Gen. Vara de Rey (Pl.)	KZ	99
Goya	NV	100
Independencia (Pl. de la)	NX	103
Infanta Isabel (Pas.)	NZ	105
Libreros	KX	119
Madrazo	MY	121
Mejia Lequerica	LMV	132
Núñez de Arce	LY	140
Puerta Cerrada (Pl.)	KY	159
Puerta de Moros (Pl.)	KZ	161
Recoletos	NX	163
San Bernardino	KV	184
San Francisco (Carrera de)	KZ	186
San Justo	KY	192
San Millán	KZ	196
Santa Engracia	MV	203
Santo Domingo (Cuesta, Pl. de)	KX	205
Sevilla	LY	208
Tudescos	LX	216
Valverde	LV	221
Ventura Rodriguez	KV	225
Ventura de la Vega	LY	227
Vergara	KY	228
Villa de Paris (Pl.)	NV	232
Virgen de los Peligros	LX	233

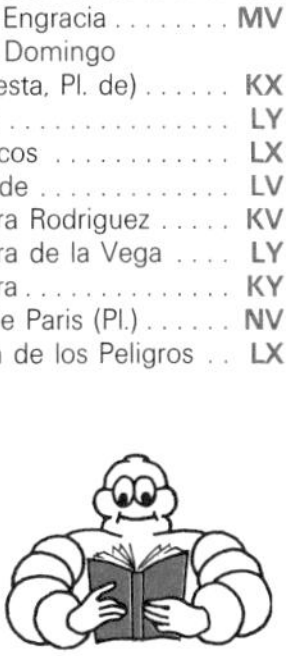

The names of main shopping streets are indicated in red at the beginning of the list of streets.

XXXX ❀ **El Cenador del Prado,** Prado 4, ✉ 28014, ✆ 429 15 61, Fax 369 04 55 – ▤. AE ◑ E VISA JCB. ✗ LY **n**
closed Saturday lunch, Sunday and 15 days in August – **M** a la carte 5300/6800
Spec. Patatas a la importancia con almejas, Solomillo sobre hojaldre a la pera, Helado de plátano.

XXX ❀ **Café de Oriente,** pl. de Oriente 2, ✉ 28013, ✆ 541 39 74, Fax 547 77 07, In a cellar – ▤. AE ◑ E VISA. ✗ KXY **w**
closed Saturday lunch, Sunday and August – **M** a la carte 5000/6700
Spec. Nazarenos de pimientos y chipirones en su tinta, Lomos de merluza con almejas en salsa verde, Medallones de corzo con brik de hongos (season).

XXX **Paradís Madrid,** Marqués de Cubas 14, ✉ 28014, ✆ 429 73 03, Fax 429 32 95 – ▤. AE ◑ VISA. ✗ MY **v**
closed Saturday lunch, Sunday and August – **M** a la carte 3050/5300.

XXX ❀ **Jaun de Alzate,** Princesa 18, ✉ 28008, ✆ 547 00 10, Fax 559 49 39 – ▤. AE ◑ E VISA. ✗ KV **a**
closed Saturday lunch, Sunday and August – **M** a la carte 5450/6300
Spec. Carpaccio de bacalao al vinagre de verduras, Risotto con bogavante, Hojaldre de mango a la crema de limón..

XXX **Bajamar,** Gran Vía 78, ✉ 28013, ✆ 548 48 18, Fax 559 13 26, Seafood – ▤. AE ◑ E VISA JCB. ✗ KV **r**
M a la carte 4050/6100.

XXX **El Landó,** pl. Gabriel Miró 8, ✉ 28005, ✆ 266 76 81, Tasteful decor – ▤. AE ◑ E VISA. ✗
closed Sunday, Bank Holidays and August – **M** a la carte 4200/6000. KZ **a**

XX **El Espejo,** paseo de Recoletos 31, ✉ 28004, ✆ 308 23 47, Fax 593 22 23, « Old Parisian café style » – ▤. AE ◑ E VISA. ✗ NV **a**
M a la carte 4000/4900.

XX **Ainhoa,** Bárbara de Braganza 12, ✉ 28004, ✆ 308 27 26, Basque rest – ▤. VISA. ✗
closed Sunday and August – **M** a la carte 3900/6400. NV **s**

XX **Horno de Santa Teresa,** Santa Teresa 12, ✉ 28004, ✆ 319 10 61 – ▤. AE ◑ E VISA. ✗
closed Saturday, Sunday and August – **M** a la carte 4500/5950. MV **t**

XX **Platerías,** pl. de Santa Ana 11, ✉ 28012, ✆ 429 70 48, Early 20C café style – ▤. AE ◑ E VISA. ✗ LY **b**
closed Saturday lunch, Sunday and August – **M** a la carte approx. 4500.

XX **El Asador de Aranda,** Preciados 44, ✉ 28013, ✆ 547 21 56, Roast lamb, « Castilian decor » – ▤. E VISA. ✗ KX **z**
closed Monday dinner and 19 July-9 August – **M** a la carte 3200/4000.

XX **Arce,** Augusto Figueroa 32, ✉ 28004, ✆ 522 59 13, Fax 522 04 40 – ▤. AE ◑ E VISA JCB. ✗ MV **c**
closed Saturday lunch, Sunday, Holy Week and 15 to 31 August – **M** a la carte 4700/6325.

XX **La Fonte del Cai,** Farmacia 2 - 2° - edificio Asturias, ✉ 28004, ✆ 522 42 18, Asturian rest – ▤. AE ◑ E VISA. ✗ LV **c**
closed Sunday and 30 July-30 August – **M** a la carte 3230/4500.

XX **El Mentidero de la Villa,** Santo Tomé 6, ✉ 28004, ✆ 308 12 85, Fax 319 87 92, « Original decor » – ▤. AE ◑ E VISA JCB. ✗ MV **b**
closed Saturday lunch, Sunday and 15 to 31 August – **M** a la carte 3950/5200.

XX **La Taberna de Liria,** Duque de Liria 9, ✉ 28015, ✆ 541 45 19 – ▤. AE ◑ E VISA. ✗
closed Saturday lunch, Sunday and Bank Holidays – **M** a la carte 3980/5055. KV **b**

XX **Casa Gallega,** pl. de San Miguel 8, ✉ 28005, ✆ 547 30 55, Galician rest – ▤. AE ◑ E VISA JCB. ✗ KY **c**
M a la carte 4000/5400.

XX **La Ópera de Madrid,** Amnistía 5, ✉ 28013, ✆ 559 50 92 – ▤. AE ◑ E VISA. ✗ KY **g**
closed Sunday and 1 to 20 August – **M** a la carte 2800/4100.

X **Casa Paco,** Puerta Cerrada 11, ✉ 28005, ✆ 266 31 66 – ▤. ◑. ✗ KY **s**
closed Sunday and August – **M** a la carte 4400/4500.

X **Taberna Carmencita,** Libertad 16, ✉ 28004, ✆ 531 66 12, Typical tavern – ▤. AE ◑ VISA. ✗ – *closed Sunday and Bank Holidays* – **M** a la carte 2750/4600. MX **u**

X **La Esquina del Real,** Amnistía 2, ✉ 28013, ✆ 559 43 09 – ▤. AE E VISA. ✗ KY **e**
closed Sunday, Holy Week and 15 to 31 August – **M** a la carte 3400/4700.

X **El Ingenio,** Leganitos 10, ✉ 28013, ✆ 541 91 33, Fax 547 35 34 – ▤. AE ◑ E VISA. ✗
M a la carte 2575/2775. KX **y**

Typical atmosphere :

XX **Posada de la Villa,** Cava Baja 9, ✉ 28005, ✆ 266 18 80, Fax 266 18 80, « Castilian decor » – ▤. AE ◑ E VISA. ✗ KZ **v**
closed Sunday dinner and 26 July-25 August – **M** a la carte 3275/5125.

XX **Botín,** Cuchilleros 17, ✉ 28005, ✆ 266 42 17, Fax 266 84 94, Old Madrid decor, typical bodega – ▤. AE ◑ E VISA JCB KY **n**
M a la carte 2775/5050.

XX **Café de Chinitas,** Torija 7, ✉ 28013, ✆ 559 51 35, Fax 547 04 63, Flamenco cabaret – ▤. AE E JCB. ✗ KX **p**
closed Sunday – **M** (dinner only, fee for show) a la carte 6600/7700.

Casa Lucio, Cava Baja 35, ✉ 28005, ☎ 365 32 52, Fax 366 48 66, Castilian decor – ▤. AE ⓓ VISA. ✻ – *closed Saturday lunch and August* – **M** a la carte approx. 5200. KZ **y**

Las Cuevas de Luis Candelas, Cuchilleros 1, ✉ 28005, ☎ 266 54 28, Old Madrid decor-Staff in bandit costume – ▤. AE ⓓ E VISA. ✻ KY **m**
M a la carte 3275/5125.

Taberna del Alabardero, Felipe V - 6, ✉ 28013, ☎ 547 25 77, Fax 547 77 07, Typical tavern – ▤. AE ⓓ E VISA. ✻ KX **h**
M a la carte 3300/4500.

Retiro-Salamanca-Ciudad Lineal : Castellana, Velázquez, Serrano, Goya, Príncipe de Vergara, Narváez, (plan p.5 except where otherwise stated))

Ritz, pl. de la Lealtad 5, ✉ 28014, ☎ 521 28 57, Telex 43986, Fax 532 87 76, 余 – |‡| ▤ TV ☎ – 🔬 25/280. AE ⓓ E VISA JCB. ✻ rest plan p. 7 NY **k**
M 5425 – ☐ 2400 – **158 rm** 37400/49500.

Villa Magna, paseo de la Castellana 22, ✉ 28046, ☎ 578 20 00, Telex 22914, Fax 575 31 58 – |‡| ▤ TV ☎ ♿ 🚗 – 🔬 25/250. AE ⓓ E VISA JCB. ✻ rest GV **y**
M (see rest. **Berceo** below) – ☐ 2750 – **182 rm** 45000/55000.

Wellington, Velázquez 8, ✉ 28001, ☎ 575 44 00, Telex 22700, Fax 576 41 64, 🏊 – |‡| ▤ TV ☎ 🚗 – 🔬 25/300. AE ⓓ E VISA. ✻ HX **t**
M (see rest. **El Fogón** below) – ☐ 2100 – **258 rm** 19520/30500.

Tryp Fénix, Hermosilla 2, ✉ 28001, ☎ 431 67 00, Telex 45639, Fax 576 06 61 – |‡| ▤ TV ☎ – 🔬 25/100. AE ⓓ E VISA. ✻ plan p. 7 NV **c**
M a la carte 3500/5000 – ☐ 1450 – **226 rm** 22000/27700.

Sol Los Galgos and Rest. Diábolo, Claudio Coello 139, ✉ 28006, ☎ 562 42 27, Telex 43957, Fax 561 76 62 – |‡| ▤ TV ☎ 🚗 – 🔬 25/300. AE ⓓ E VISA. ✻ HV **a**
M a la carte 3800/5300 – ☐ 1500 – **358 rm** 14750/22500.

NH Príncipe de Vergara, Príncipe de Vergara 92, ✉ 28006, ☎ 563 26 95, Telex 27064, Fax 563 72 53 – |‡| ▤ TV ☎ 🚗 – 🔬 25/300. AE ⓓ E VISA. ✻ HV **c**
M 3500 – ☐ 1700 – **170 rm** 17000/24400.

NH Sanvy, Goya 3, ✉ 28001, ☎ 576 08 00, Telex 44994, Fax 575 24 43 – |‡| ▤ TV ☎ – 🔬 25/120. AE ⓓ E VISA JCB. ✻ plan p. 7 NV **r**
M a la carte 3400/4900 – ☐ 1700 – **141 rm** 17000/24400.

Tryp G.H. Velázquez, Velázquez 62, ✉ 28001, ☎ 575 28 00, Telex 22779, Fax 575 28 09 – |‡| ▤ TV ☎ 🚗 – 🔬 25/280. AE ⓓ E VISA. ✻ rest HX **s**
M a la carte 3020/4225 – ☐ 1100 – **144 rm** 15000/18800.

Agumar coffee shop only, paseo Reina Cristina 7, ✉ 28014, ☎ 552 69 00, Telex 22814, Fax 433 60 95 – |‡| ▤ TV ☎ 🚗 – 🔬 25/150. AE ⓓ E VISA JCB. ✻ HZ **a**
☐ 1150 – **252 rm** 12800/16000.

Novotel Madrid, Albacete 1, ✉ 28027, ☎ 405 46 00, Telex 41862, Fax 404 11 05, 余, 🏊 – |‡| ▤ TV ☎ ♿ 🚗 Ⓟ – 🔬 25/250. AE ⓓ E VISA E : by M 30 JY
M 3600 – ☐ 1150 – **236 rm** 14900/17900.

Convención coffee shop only, O'Donnell 53, ✉ 28009, ☎ 574 84 00, Telex 23944, Fax 574 56 01 – |‡| ▤ TV ☎ 🚗 – 🔬 25/1000. AE ⓓ E VISA JCB. ✻ JX **a**
☐ 1100 – **790 rm** 12800/16000.

Alcalá and Rest. Basque, Alcalá 66, ✉ 28009, ☎ 435 10 60, Telex 48094, Fax 435 11 05 – |‡| ▤ TV ☎ 🚗 – 🔬 25/60. AE ⓓ E VISA. ✻ HX **w**
M a la carte approx. 4200 – ☐ 950 – **153 rm** 13400/17900.

Pintor, Goya 79, ✉ 28001, ☎ 435 75 45, Telex 23281, Fax 576 81 57 – |‡| ▤ TV ☎ 🚗 – 🔬 25/350. AE E VISA. ✻ HX **c**
M a la carte 1925/3900 – ☐ 1250 – **176 rm** 14720/18400.

Conde de Orgaz, av. Moscatelar 24, ✉ 28043, ☎ 388 40 99, Fax 388 00 09 – |‡| ▤ TV ☎ 🚗 – 🔬 25/100. AE ⓓ E VISA JCB. ✻ NE : by López de Hoyos HU
M 2500 – ☐ 1100 – **91 rm** 14800/18500.

G. H. Colón, Pez Volador 11, ✉ 28007, ☎ 573 59 00, Telex 22984, Fax 573 08 89, 🏊, 🏋 – |‡| ▤ TV ☎ 🚗 – 🔬 25/130. AE ⓓ E VISA JCB. ✻ JY **x**
M 3250 – ☐ 900 – **389 rm** 10500/15500.

Emperatriz, López de Hoyos 4, ✉ 28006, ☎ 563 80 88, Telex 43640, Fax 563 98 04 – |‡| ▤ TV ☎ ♿ – 🔬 25/150. AE ⓓ E VISA JCB. ✻ GV **z**
M 3250 – ☐ 1200 – **170 rm** 11000/17500.

Serrano without rest, Marqués de Villamejor 8, ✉ 28006, ☎ 435 52 00, Fax 435 48 49 – |‡| ▤ TV ☎. AE ⓓ E VISA JCB. ✻ – ☐ 850 – **34 rm** 11500/14770. GHV **k**

NH Balboa, Núñez de Balboa 112, ✉ 28006, ☎ 563 03 24, Telex 27063, Fax 262 69 80 – |‡| ▤ TV ☎ 🚗 – 🔬 25/30. AE ⓓ E VISA JCB. ✻ HV **n**
M 4500 – ☐ 1300 – **122 rm** 15500/21600.

NH Sur, paseo Infanta Isabel 9, ✉ 28014, ☎ 539 94 00, Telex 47494, Fax 467 09 96 – ▤ – 🔬 25/45. AE ⓓ E VISA JCB. ✻ plan p. 7 NZ **a**
M 3000 – ☐ 1050 – **67 rm** 12600/17300.

Abeba without rest, Alcántara 63, ✉ 28006, ☎ 401 16 50, Fax 402 75 91 – |‡| ▤ TV ☎ 🚗. AE ⓓ E VISA. ✻ HV **r**
☐ 600 – **90 rm** 9000/11750.

XXXXX **Berceo,** Ortega y Gasset 2, ✉ 28006, ℘ 575 33 77, 🏨 – ▤ 🚗. AE ⓓ E VISA JCB. ✂
M a la carte 5100/6500. GV **y**

XXX **Club 31,** Alcalá 58, ✉ 28014, ℘ 531 00 92 – ▤. AE ⓓ E VISA JCB. ✂
closed August – **M** a la carte 5500/7800. plan p. 7 NX **e**

XXX ✿ **El Amparo,** Puigcerdá 8, ✉ 28001, ℘ 431 64 56, Fax 575 54 91, « Original decor » – ▤. AE E VISA JCB. ✂ HX **h**
closed Saturday lunch, Sunday and August – **M** a la carte 5350/7275
Spec. Terrina de hígado de pato, Espárragos verdes gratinados con salmón, Rabo de toro con puré de apio..

XXX **Suntory,** Castellana 36, ✉ 28046, ℘ 577 37 34, Fax 577 44 55, Japanese rest. – ▤ 🚗. AE ⓓ E VISA JCB. ✂ GV **d**
closed Sunday and Bank Holidays – **M** a la carte 6000/8000.

XXX **Balzac,** Moreto 7, ✉ 28014, ℘ 420 01 77, 🏨 – ▤. AE ⓓ E VISA. ✂ plan p. 7 NY **a**
closed Sunday, Holy Week and August – **M** a la carte 4600/6450.

XXX **Villa y Corte de Madrid,** Serrano 110, ✉ 28006, ℘ 564 50 19, Fax 564 50 19, Tasteful decor – ▤. AE ⓓ E VISA. ✂ HV **a**
closed Sunday and August – **M** a la carte 3600/4150.

XXX **El Gran Chambelán,** Ayala 46, ✉ 28001, ℘ 431 77 45 – ▤. AE ⓓ E VISA. ✂ HX **r**
closed Sunday, Bank Holidays dinner and August – **M** a la carte 3350/4000.

XXX **Sorolla,** Hermosilla 4, ✉ 28001, ℘ 576 08 00, Telex 44994, Fax 575 24 43 – ▤. AE ⓓ E VISA. ✂ plan p. 7 NV **r**
closed August – **M** a la carte 4800/5400.

XXX **El Fogón,** Villanueva 34, ✉ 28001, ℘ 575 44 00, Telex 22700, Fax 576 41 64 – ▤. AE ⓓ E VISA. ✂ HX **t**
closed August – **M** a la carte 5250/5950.

XXX **El Comedor,** Montalbán 9, ✉ 28014, ℘ 531 69 68, Fax 531 61 91, 🏨 – ▤. AE ⓓ E VISA JCB. ✂ plan p. 7 NX **a**
closed Saturday lunch and Sunday – **M** a la carte 3825/5250.

XXX **Ponteareas,** Claudio Coello 96, ✉ 28006, ℘ 575 58 73, Fax 541 65 98, Galician rest – ▤ 🚗. AE ⓓ E VISA. ✂ HV **w**
closed Sunday, Bank Holidays and August – **M** a la carte 3950/6050.

XX **La Paloma,** Jorge Juan 39, ✉ 28001, ℘ 576 86 92 – ▤. AE E VISA. ✂ HX **g**
closed Saturday lunch, Sunday, Holy Week and August – **M** a la carte 3600/5300.

XX ✿ **Viridiana,** Juan de Mena 14, ✉ 28014, ℘ 523 44 78 – ▤ plan p. 7 NY **r**
closed Sunday and August – **M** a la carte 3550/5250
Spec. Crepes de morcilla en salsa de pimientos, Salteado de buey con hongos (boletus edulis), Hojaldre de membrillo y mango con salsa de regaliz..

XX **Al Mounia,** Recoletos 5, ✉ 28001, ℘ 435 08 28, North African rest., « Oriental atmosphere » – ▤. AE ⓓ E VISA. ✂ plan p. 7 NV **u**
closed Sunday, Monday, Holy Week and August – **M** a la carte 4500/5000.

XX **St.-James,** Juan Bravo 26, ✉ 28006, ℘ 575 00 69, 🏨, Rice dishes – ▤. AE. ✂ HV **t**
closed Sunday – **M** a la carte 3500/5100.

XX **La Fonda,** Lagasca 11, ✉ 28001, ℘ 577 79 24, Catalonian rest. – ▤. AE ⓓ E VISA. ✂ HX **f**
closed Sunday – **M** a la carte 2425/4075.

XX **Rafa,** Narváez 68, ✉ 28009, ℘ 573 10 87, 🏨 – ▤. AE ⓓ E VISA JCB. ✂ HY **a**
M a la carte 4700/6400.

XX ✿ **Casa d'a Troya,** Emiliano Barral 14, ✉ 28043, ℘ 416 44 55 – ▤. VISA. ✂
closed Sunday, Bank Holidays and 15 July-31 August – **M** (booking essential) a la carte 2900/5400 E : by M 30 JY
Spec. Pulpo a la gallega, Merluza a la gallega, Lacón con grelos (15 October-15 May)).

XX **El Chiscón de Castelló,** Castelló 3, ✉ 28001, ℘ 575 56 62 – ▤. AE ⓓ VISA. ✂ HX **e**
closed Sunday, Bank Holidays and August – **M** a la carte 3175/3900.

XX **Castelló 9,** Castelló 9, ✉ 28001, ℘ 435 00 67 – ▤. AE VISA. ✂ HX **e**
closed Sunday, Bank Holidays and August – **M** a la carte 3900/5600.

XX **El Asador de Aranda,** Diego de León 9, ✉ 28006, ℘ 563 02 46, Roast lamb – ▤. E VISA. ✂ HV **s**
closed Sunday dinner – **M** a la carte 3175/4000.

X **Asador Velate,** Jorge Juan 91, ✉ 28009, ℘ 435 10 24, Basque rest. – ▤. AE ⓓ E VISA. ✂ HJX **x**
closed Sunday and August – **M** a la carte 4150/4700.

X ✿ **La Trainera,** Lagasca 60, ✉ 28001, ℘ 576 05 75, Fax 575 47 17, Seafood – ▤. E VISA. ✂ HX **k**
closed Sunday and August – **M** a la carte 3300/5300
Spec. Pescados y mariscos, Rodaballo al horno, Langosta y bogavante americana.

X ✿ **El Pescador,** José Ortega y Gasset 75, ✉ 28006, ℘ 402 12 90, Seafood – ▤. E VISA. ✂
closed Sunday and August – **M** a la carte 4200/5300 JV **t**
Spec. Angulas de Aguinaga, Lenguado "Evaristo", Bogavante a la americana.

Arganzuela, Carabanchel Villaverde : Antonio López, paseo de Las Delicias, paseo de Santa María de la Cabeza (plan p. 2 except where otherwise stated)

Carlton, paseo de las Delicias 26, ✉ 28045, ℘ 539 71 00, Telex 44571, Fax 527 85 10 – AE E VISA JCB. plan p. 5 GZ **n**
M 2750 – 1050 – **112 rm** 16530/20670.

Praga coffee shop only, Antonio López 65, ✉ 28019, ℘ 469 06 00, Telex 22823, Fax 469 83 25 – 25/350. AE E VISA JCB.
725 – **428 rm** 8750/11500. by pl. Emperador Carlos V NZ

Aramo, paseo Santa María de la Cabeza 73, ✉ 28045, ℘ 473 91 11, Telex 45885, Fax 473 92 14 – AE E VISA. rest by pl. Emperador Carlos V NZ
M a la carte approx. 3550 – 900 – **105 rm** 13000/17000.

Puerta de Toledo, glorieta Puerta de Toledo 4, ✉ 28005, ℘ 474 71 00, Telex 22291, Fax 474 07 47 – AE E VISA JCB. EZ **v**
M (see rest. **Puerta de Toledo** below) – 700 – **152 rm** 6450/10800.

Puerta de Toledo, glorieta Puerta de Toledo 4, ✉ 28005, ℘ 474 76 75, Fax 474 30 35 – AE E VISA. – *closed Sunday dinner* – **M** a la carte 3050/3675. EZ **v**

Moncloa : Princesa, paseo del Pintor Rosales, paseo de la Florida, Casa de Campo (plan p. 4 except where otherwise stated)

Meliá Madrid, Princesa 27, ✉ 28008, ℘ 541 82 00, Telex 22537, Fax 541 19 88 – 25/200. AE E VISA. plan p. 6 KV **t**
M a la carte 4600/6100 – 1985 – **266 rm** 24400/30100.

Tryp Monte Real, Arroyofresno 17, ✉ 28035, ℘ 316 21 40, Telex 22089, Fax 316 21 40, « Garden », – 25/200. AE E VISA. NW : 8 km
M a la carte 3200/4400 – 1500 – **80 rm** 22250/27825.

Florida Norte, paseo de la Florida 5, ✉ 28008, ℘ 542 83 00, Telex 23675, Fax 547 78 33 – AE VISA JCB. plan p. 4 DX **v**
M 2300 – 750 – **399 rm** 11500/16000.

Pullman Calatrava without rest, Tutor 1, ✉ 28008, ℘ 541 98 80, Telex 43190, Fax 248 51 26 – AE E VISA JCB. plano p. 6 KV **d**
1250 – **98 rm** 14250/18200.

Tirol coffee shop only, Marqués de Urquijo 4, ✉ 28008, ℘ 548 19 00 – E VISA JCB.
97 rm 6825/9650. DV **r**

Café Viena, Luisa Fernanda 23, ✉ 28008, ℘ 548 15 91, « Old style café » – AE E VISA. – *closed Sunday and August* – **M** a la carte approx. 4500. plan p. 6 KV **h**

Currito, Casa de Campo - Pabellón de Vizcaya, ✉ 28011, ℘ 464 57 04, Fax 479 72 54, Basque rest. – AE E VISA. by Segovia DY
closed Sunday dinner and Monday – **M** a la carte 3800/5100.

Chamberí : San Bernardo, Fuencarral, Alberto Aguilera, Santa Engracia (plan p. 4 to 7)

NH Santo Mauro and Rest. Belagua, Zurbano 36, ✉ 28010, ℘ 319 69 00, Fax 308 54 77, « Elegant palace, garden », – AE VISA. GV **e**
M *(closed Sunday, Bank Holidays and August)* a la carte 6000/8200 – 2500 – **36 rm** 35200/52800.

Miguel Ángel, Miguel Ángel 31, ✉ 28010, ℘ 442 00 22, Telex 44235, Fax 442 53 20, – 25/300. AE E VISA. GV **c**
M 5500 – 1800 – **272 rm** 26000/32500.

Mindanao, San Francisco de Sales 15, ✉ 28003, ℘ 549 55 00, Telex 22631, Fax 544 55 96, – 25/200. AE E VISA JCB. DV **a**
M 5200 – 1750 – **289 rm** 22000/27500.

Castellana Inter-Continental, paseo de la Castellana 49, ✉ 28046, ℘ 310 02 00, Telex 27686, Fax 319 58 53, – 25/550. AE E VISA.
M 5000 – 1900 – **305 rm** 29700/37200. GV **a**

Escultor, Miguel Ángel 3, ✉ 28010, ℘ 310 42 03, Telex 44285, Fax 319 25 84 – AE E VISA. GV **s**
M (see rest. **Señorío de Errazu** below) – 1125 – **82 rm** 11775/19600.

NH Embajada, Santa Engracia 5, ✉ 28010, ℘ 594 02 13, Fax 447 33 12, Spanish style building – 25/30. AE E VISA. MV **r**
M 4000 – 1600 – **101 rm** 17000/24400.

Sol Alondras coffee shop only, José Abascal 8, ✉ 28003, ℘ 447 40 00, Telex 49454, Fax 593 88 00 – AE E VISA. – 950 – **72 rm** 13700/17175. FV **a**

Gran Versalles without rest, Covarrubias 4, ✉ 28010, ℘ 447 57 00, Telex 49150, Fax 446 39 87 – 25/140. AE E VISA. – 975 – **145 rm** 14500/21000. MV **a**

NH Zurbano, Zurbano 79, ✉ 28003, ℘ 441 45 00, Telex 27578, Fax 441 32 24 – 25/100. AE E VISA. – **M** 4500 – 1300 – **269 rm** 17200/21600. GV **x**

NH Suites Prisma, Santa Engracia 120, ✉ 28003, ℘ 441 93 77, Telex 41156, Fax 442 58 51 – 25/70. AE E VISA.
M 4000 – 1700 – **103 suites** 19500/40000.

G.H. Conde Duque without rest, pl. Conde Valle de Suchil 5, ✉ 28015, ℘ 447 70 00, Telex 22058, Fax 448 35 69 – 25/160. AE E VISA JCB. EV **d**
1500 – **136 rm** 22850.

XXXXX ✿✿ **Fortuny,** Fortuny 34, ⊠ 28010, ℘ 308 32 67, Fax 593 22 23, 佘, « Former palace, tastefully decorated-summer terrace » – ▤. AE ⓓ E VISA. ⚡ GV **n**
closed Saturday lunch, Bank Holidays and August – **M** a la carte 6500/8200
Spec. Ensalada de langostinos y fettuchines, Goujons de lenguado envueltos en pasta china con salsa de soja. Hojaldre de frutas rojas.

XXXX ✿ **Jockey,** Amador de los Ríos 6, ⊠ 28010, ℘ 319 24 35, Fax 319 24 35 – ▤. AE ⓓ E VISA JCB. ⚡ NV **k**
closed Saturday, Sunday, Bank Holidays and August – **M** a la carte 5750/9700
Spec. Sopa fria de tomate a la albahaca (May-October), Langostinos fritos con verduras a la japonesa, Pichones de Talavera asados al estilo de Jockey.

XXXX ✿ **Lúculo,** Génova 19, ⊠ 28004, ℘ 319 40 29, 佘 – ▤. AE ⓓ E VISA. ⚡ NV **d**
closed Saturday lunch, Sunday and August – **M** a la carte 6000/8000
Spec. Escabeche de hígado de pato, Cocido de pescados y verduras con codillo rancio, Pechuga de gallo asada en su jugo con trufas..

XXXX ✿ **Las Cuatro Estaciones,** General Ibáñez Íbero 5, ⊠ 28003, ℘ 553 63 05, Telex 43709, Fax 553 32 98, Modern decor – ▤. AE ⓓ E VISA JCB. ⚡ EU **r**
closed Saturday lunch, Sunday and August – **M** a la carte 4550/5525
Spec. Ensalada de jamón de pato y foie-gras al vinagre de Jerez, Lomo de merluza "Las Cuatro Estaciones", Lomo de cordero asado al tomillo con patatas panadera.

XXX **Lur Maitea,** Fernando el Santo 4, ⊠ 28010, ℘ 308 03 50, Basque rest. – ▤. AE ⓓ E VISA. ⚡ MV **u**
closed Saturday lunch, Sunday, Bank Holidays and August – **M** a la carte approx. 5500.

XXX **Annapurna,** Zurbano 5, ⊠ 28010, ℘ 308 32 49, Indian rest. – ▤. AE ⓓ VISA. ⚡ MV **w**
closed Sunday – **M** a la carte 3050/4050.

XXX **Cortegrande,** Sagasta 27, ⊠ 28004, ℘ 445 55 43 – ▤. AE ⓓ E VISA JCB. ⚡ MV **a**
closed Saturday lunch, Sunday, Bank Holidays and August – **M** a la carte 4000/5200.

XXX **Señorío de Errazu,** Miguel Angel 3, ⊠ 28010, ℘ 308 24 25 – ▤. AE ⓓ VISA. ⚡ GV **s**
closed Saturday lunch, Sunday and August – **M** a la carte 3050/4100.

XX **Aymar,** Fuencarral 138, ⊠ 28010, ℘ 445 57 67, Seafood – ▤. AE ⓓ E VISA. ⚡ FV **e**
M a la carte 3600/5700.

XX **La Plaza de Chamberí,** pl. de Chamberí 10, ⊠ 28010, ℘ 446 06 97, 佘 – ▤. AE ⓓ E VISA JCB. ⚡ FV **k**
closed Sunday and Holy Week – **M** a la carte 3375/4000.

XX **O'Xeito,** paseo de la Castellana 47, ⊠ 28046, ℘ 308 17 18, Galician style decor-Seafood – ▤. AE ⓓ E VISA. ⚡ GV **a**
closed Saturday, Sunday and August – **M** a la carte 4050/5600.

X **La Gran Tasca,** Santa Engracia 24, ⊠ 28010, ℘ 448 77 79, Castilian decor – ▤. AE ⓓ E VISA JCB. ⚡ FV **c**
closed Sunday and Holy Week – **M** a la carte 3675/6000.

X **Nicolás,** Cardenal Cisneros 82, ⊠ 28010, ℘ 448 36 64 – ▤. AE ⓓ E VISA. ⚡ FV **t**
closed Sunday, Monday, Holy Week and August – **M** a la carte approx. 3600.

Chamartín, Tetuán : Capitán Haya, Orense, Alberto Alcocer, paseo de la Habana (plan p. 3 except where otherwise stated)

Eurobuilding, Padre Damián 23, ⊠ 28036, ℘ 345 45 00, Telex 22548, Fax 345 45 76, « Garden and terrace with 🏊 » – |‡| ▤ TV ☎ 🚗 – 🎤 25/900. AE ⓓ E VISA JCB. ⚡
M 4500 - **La Taberna** a la carte 4920/5745 - **Le Relais** (buffet) – ☕ 1900 – **520 rm** 23200/29900. HS **a**

Meliá Castilla, Capitán Haya 43, ⊠ 28020, ℘ 571 22 11, Telex 23142, Fax 571 22 10, 🏊 – |‡| ▤ TV ☎ ♿ 🚗 – 🎤 25/800. AE ⓓ E VISA. ⚡ GS **c**
M (see **L'Albufera**, **La Fragata** and **El Hidalgo** below) – ☕ 2050 – **1000 rm** 23250/28600.

Holiday Inn, pl. Carlos Trías Beltrán 4 (entrance by Orense 22-24), ⊠ 28020, ℘ 597 01 02, Telex 44709, Fax 597 02 92, 🏊 – |‡| ▤ TV ☎ ♿ – 🎤 25/400. AE ⓓ E VISA JCB. ⚡
M La Terraza a la carte 5700/6400 – ☕ 1925 – **313 rm** 24900/31200. GT **z**

Cuzco coffee shop only, paseo de la Castellana 133, ⊠ 28046, ℘ 556 06 00, Telex 22464, Fax 556 03 72 – |‡| ▤ TV ☎ 🚗 Ⓟ – 🎤 25/500. AE ⓓ E VISA. ⚡ GS **a**
☕ 1190 – **330 rm** 16200/20550.

Chamartín, Chamartín railway station, ⊠ 28036, ℘ 323 18 33, Telex 49201, Fax 733 02 14 – |‡| ▤ TV ☎ – 🎤 25/500. AE ⓓ E VISA JCB. ⚡ HR
M (see rest. **Cota 13** below) – ☕ 1000 – **378 rm** 13500/17900.

NH La Habana, paseo de la Habana 73, ⊠ 28036, ℘ 345 82 84, Telex 41869, Fax 457 75 79 – |‡| ▤ TV ☎ 🚗 – 🎤 25/250. AE ⓓ E VISA. ⚡ HT **f**
M a la carte 3900/5900 – ☕ 1700 – **157 rm** 17000/24400.

Orense 38 coffee shop only, Pedro Teixeira 5, ⊠ 28020, ℘ 597 15 68, Fax 597 12 95 – |‡| ▤ TV ☎ 🚗. AE ⓓ E VISA. ⚡ GT **q**
☕ 925 – **140 rm** 19400/23400.

Foxá 32 coffee shop only, Agustín de Foxá 32, ⊠ 28036, ℘ 733 10 60, Fax 314 11 65 – |‡| ▤ TV ☎ 🚗 – 🎤 25/250. AE ⓓ E VISA. ⚡ HR **u**
☕ 925 – **161 rm** 15800/18800.

Foxá 25 coffee shop only, Agustín de Foxá 25, ✉ 28036, ☎ 323 11 19, Fax 314 53 11 – AE ⓓ E VISA. HR **a**
925 – **121 rm** 15800/18800.

El Gran Atlanta without rest, Comandante Zorita 34, ✉ 28020, ☎ 553 59 00, Telex 45210, Fax 533 08 58 – 25/120. AE ⓓ E VISA. FT **p**
1025 – **180 rm** 15400.

Apartotel El Jardín without rest, carret. N I : km 5'7 (service lane), ✉ 28050, ☎ 202 83 36, Fax 766 86 91, – AE ⓓ E VISA. N : by M30 HR
850 – **38 suites** 19000

Aitana coffee shop only, paseo de la Castellana 152, ✉ 28046, ☎ 344 11 42, Fax 457 07 81 – AE ⓓ E VISA JCB. GT **c**
800 – **111 rm** 10400/15000.

Aristos and Rest. El Chaflán, av. Pío XII-34, ✉ 28016, ☎ 345 04 50, Fax 345 10 23, – AE ⓓ E VISA. HS **d**
M *(closed Sunday)* a la carte 3400/4600 – 700 – **25 rm** 10800/13500.

XXXXX ✿✿✿ **Zalacaín,** Álvarez de Baena 4, ✉ 28006, ☎ 561 48 40, Fax 561 47 32, – AE ⓓ E VISA JCB. plan p. 5 GV **b**
closed Saturday lunch, Sunday, Holy Week and August – **M** a la carte 7050/9400
Spec. Lasagna de hongos y foie-gras, Pequeño búcaro (May-October), Tournedo de pato con morros de ternera.

XXXXX **Príncipe y Serrano,** Serrano 240, ✉ 28016, ☎ 457 28 52, Fax 457 57 47 – AE ⓓ E VISA. HT **a**
closed Saturday lunch, Sunday and August – **M** a la carte 3700/5850.

XXXX **El Bodegón,** Pinar 15, ✉ 28006, ☎ 562 88 44 – AE ⓓ E VISA JCB. plan p. 5 GV **q**
closed Saturday lunch, Sunday, Bank Holidays and August – **M** a la carte 5400/7050.

XXXX ✿ **Príncipe de Viana,** Manuel de Falla 5, ✉ 28036, ☎ 457 15 49, Fax 457 52 83, – AE ⓓ E VISA JCB. GT **c**
closed Saturday lunch, Sunday, Holy Week and August – **M** a la carte 6000/7200
Spec. Menestra de verduras, Bacalao ajoarriero, Manitas de cerdo asadas.

XXXX **La Máquina,** Sor Ángela de la Cruz 22, ✉ 28020, ☎ 572 33 18, Fax 570 13 04 – AE ⓓ E VISA. FS **e**
closed Sunday, Holy Week and 15 to 31 August – **M** a la carte 3700/4300.

XXXX **Nicolasa,** Velázquez 150, ✉ 28002, ☎ 563 17 35, Fax 564 32 75 – AE ⓓ E VISA.
closed Sunday and August – **M** a la carte 4125/5450. HU **a**

XXX **O'Pazo,** Reina Mercedes 20, ✉ 28020, ☎ 553 23 33, Seafood – E VISA. FT **p**
closed Sunday and August – **M** a la carte 4200/5500.

XXX **L'Albufera,** Capitán Haya 43, ✉ 28020, ☎ 579 63 74, Fax 571 22 10, Rice dishes – AE ⓓ E VISA. – **M** a la carte 4655/5855. GS **c**

XXX **La Fragata,** Capitán Haya 43, ✉ 28020, ☎ 570 98 34 – AE ⓓ E VISA. GS **c**
closed August – **M** a la carte 4150/6190.

XXX **El Hidalgo,** Capitán Haya 45, ✉ 28020, ☎ 570 68 16, Regional rest. – AE ⓓ E VISA. GS **c**
closed August – **M** (lunch only) a la carte 3575/4715.

XXX **José Luis,** Rafael Salgado 11, ✉ 28036, ☎ 250 02 42, Telex 41779, Fax 250 99 11 – AE ⓓ E VISA JCB. GT **m**
closed Sunday and August – **M** a la carte 4000/5000.

XXX ✿ **Señorío de Bertiz,** Comandante Zorita 6, ✉ 28020, ☎ 533 27 57 – AE ⓓ E VISA. FT **s**
closed Saturday lunch, Sunday and August – **M** a la carte 4875/7400
Spec. Verduras del tiempo guisadas con caldo de ave, Lomos de merluza romana con pimientos asados, Muslos de pato guisados con manitas de cerdo.

XXX **La Toc,** Suero de Quiñones 42, ✉ 28002, ☎ 563 02 70 – AE ⓓ E VISA. HT **y**
closed Saturday lunch, Sunday, Holy Week and August – **M** a la carte 5600/6400.

XXX **Cota 13,** Chamartín railway station, ✉ 28036, ☎ 315 10 83, Fax 733 02 14 – AE ⓓ E VISA. HR
closed Saturday, Sunday, Bank Holidays, Holy Week and August – **M** a la carte approx. 4500.

XXX **Bogavante,** Capitán Haya 20, ✉ 28020, ☎ 556 21 14, Fax 597 00 79, Seafood – AE ⓓ E VISA JCB. – *closed Sunday* – **M** a la carte 4300/5950. GT **d**

XXX **Señorío de Alcocer,** Alberto Alcocer 1, ✉ 28036, ☎ 345 16 96 – AE ⓓ E VISA JCB.
closed Sunday, Bank Holidays, Holy Week and August – **M** a la carte approx. 6000. GS **e**

XXX ✿ **El Olivo,** General Gallegos 1, ✉ 28036, ☎ 359 15 35 – AE ⓓ E VISA. HS **c**
closed Sunday, Monday and August – **M** a la carte 4450/5300
Spec. Ensalada de bogavante con su vinagreta templada, Lamprea bordalesa con vino de Toro (spring), Foie-gras caliente con uvas al vino de Pedro Ximénez.

XXX ✿ **Goizeko Kabi,** Comandante Zorita 37, ✉ 28020, ☎ 533 01 85, Fax 533 02 14, Basque rest. – AE ⓓ E VISA. FT **a**
closed Saturday lunch (15 June-15 September) and Sunday – **M** a la carte 5650/7000
Spec. Merluza rellena de carabineros, bacalao al estilo de la casa, Becada asada al brandy viejo (November-March).

XXX ✿ **Cabo Mayor,** Juan Ramón Jiménez 37, ✉ 28036, ✆ 350 87 76, Fax 359 16 21 – ▤. AE ⓓ E VISA JCB. ✻ GHS r
closed Sunday, Holy Week and 15 to 24 August – **M** a la carte 5200/7300
Spec. Tartar de bonito con pistachos (May-September), Merluza a la muselina de albahaca, Pintada rellena con salsa de trufas y pasta fresca (October-May).

XXX **El Foque de Quiñones,** Suero de Quiñones 22, ✉ 28002, ✆ 519 25 72, Cod dishes – ▤. AE ⓓ E VISA. ✻ HU r
closed Sunday – **M** a la carte 4300/5500.

XXX **Blanca de Navarra,** av. de Brasil 13, ✉ 28020, ✆ 555 10 29 – ▤. AE ⓓ E VISA. ✻
closed Sunday and August – **M** a la carte 4600/5800. GT q

XXX **Lutecia,** Corazón de María 78, ✉ 28002, ✆ 519 34 15 – ▤. AE E VISA. ✻
closed Saturday lunch, Sunday and August – **M** a la carte 2650/3575.
by López de Hoyos HU

XX **Rheinfall,** Padre Damián 44, ✉ 28036, ✆ 345 48 88, ☂, German rest., « Regional German decor » – ▤. AE ⓓ E VISA. ✻ HS u
M a la carte 2800/4300.

XX **Combarro,** Reina Mercedes 12, ✉ 28020, ✆ 554 77 84, Fax 534 25 01, Seafood – ▤. AE ⓓ E VISA JCB. ✻ FT a
closed Sunday dinner, Holy Week and August – **M** a la carte approx. 5500.

XX **La Tahona,** Capitán Haya 21 (side), ✉ 28020, ✆ 555 04 41, Roast lamb, « Castilian-medieval decor » – ▤. E VISA. ✻ GT u
closed Sunday dinner and 2 to 30 August – **M** a la carte 3200/4000.

XX **De Funy,** Serrano 213, ✉ 28016, ✆ 458 85 84, Fax 457 95 22, ☂, Lebanese rest. – ▤. AE ⓓ E VISA. ✻ – *closed Monday* – **M** a la carte 3950/5750. HT z

XX **Serramar,** Rosario Pino 12, ✉ 28020, ✆ 570 07 90, Seafood – ▤. AE ⓓ E VISA. ✻
closed Sunday – **M** a la carte 3975/5275. GS k

XX **Sacha,** Juan Hurtado de Mendoza 11 (back), ✉ 28036, ✆ 345 59 52, ☂ – ▤. AE ⓓ E VISA. ✻ – *closed Sunday and August* – **M** a la carte 3850/5050. GHS r

XX **House of Ming,** paseo de la Castellana 74, ✉ 28046, ✆ 561 10 13, Chinese rest. – ▤. AE ⓓ VISA. ✻ plan p. 5 GV f
M a la carte 2390/3560.

X **La Ancha,** Príncipe de Vergara 204, ✉ 28002, ✆ 563 89 77, ☂ – ▤. AE ⓓ E VISA. ✻
closed Sunday, Bank Holidays and Holy Week – **M** a la carte 3050/4500. HT r

Environs

on the road to the Airport E : 12,5 km – ✉ 28042 Madrid – ☎ 91 :

Diana and Rest. Asador Duque de Osuna, Galeón 27 (Alameda de Osuna) ✆ 747 13 55, Telex 45688, Fax 747 97 97, ⛱ – ⇅ ▤ TV ☎ – 🏛 25/220. AE ⓓ E VISA. ✻
M *(closed Sunday)* a la carte 2350/4500 – ☕ 760 – **265 rm** 12800/16000.

by motorway N VI – ✉ 28023 Madrid – ☎ 91 :

XXX **Gaztelubide,** Sopelana 13 - La Florida NW : 12,8 km, ✆ 372 85 44, ☂, Basque rest. – ▤ Ⓟ. AE ⓓ E VISA. ✻
closed Sunday dinner – **M** a la carte approx. 5500.

XX **Los Remos,** NW : 13 km ✆ 307 72 30, ☂, Seafood – ▤ Ⓟ. E VISA. ✻
closed Sunday dinner and 15 to 31 August – **M** a la carte 4000/5000.

at Barajas E : 14 km – ✉ 28042 Madrid – ☎ 91 :

Barajas, av. de Logroño 305 ✆ 747 77 00, Telex 22255, Fax 747 87 17, ☂, Ƒ₆, ⛱, 🌳 – ⇅ ▤ TV ☎ Ⓟ – 🏛 25/675. AE ⓓ E VISA. ✻ rest
M 5150 – ☕ 1850 – **230 rm** 22800/28500.

Alameda, av. de Logroño 100 ✆ 747 48 00, Telex 43809, Fax 747 89 28, ⛱ – ⇅ ▤ TV ☎ Ⓟ – 🏛 25/280. AE ⓓ E VISA JCB.
M 4750 – ☕ 1300 – **145 rm** 18000/22500.

at Alcobendas N : 16 km – ✉ 28100 Alcobendas – ☎ 91 :

La Moraleja without rest, av. de Europa 17 - Parque Empresarial La Moraleja, SW : 3 km ✆ 661 80 55, Fax 661 21 88, Ƒ₆, ⛱ – ⇅ ▤ TV ☎ 🚗 Ⓟ. AE ⓓ E VISA JCB. ✻
☕ 1350 – **37 suites** 32000

at San Sebastián de los Reyes N : 17 km – ✉ 28700 San Sebastián de los Reyes – ☎ 91 :

XXX **Mesón Tejas Verdes,** ✆ 652 73 07 , ☂, Castilian decor, 🌳 – ▤ Ⓟ. AE ⓓ E VISA. ✻
closed Sunday dinner, Bank Holidays dinner and August – **M** a la carte 2900/4700.

Moralzarzal 28411 Madrid 444 J 18 – pop. 1600 – ☎ 91 – ♦Madrid 42.

XXX ✿ **El Cenador de Salvador,** av. de España 30 ✆ 857 77 22, Fax 857 77 80, ☂, « Garden Terrace » – Ⓟ. AE ⓓ E VISA. ✻
closed Sunday dinner, Monday and 15 to 30 October – **M** a la carte 5700/6400
Spec. Alcachofas con berenjenas, Salmonetes a la parrilla con salsa de alcaparras, Tórtola en salmis.

BARCELONA 08000 443 H36 - pop. 1 754 900 - ☎ 93.

See : Gothic Quarter★★ (Barri Gotic) : Cathedral★★ MX, Plaça del Rei★ MX 149, Frederic Marès Museum★★ (Museu F. Marès) MX - La Rambla★ LX, MY : Atarazanas and Maritim Museum★★ MY, Plaça Reial★ MY - Montcada st.★ (carrer de Montcada) NVX : Picasso Museum★ NV, Santa María del Mar Church★ NX - Montjuich★ (Montjuïc) : Museum of Catalonian Art★★★ (romanic and gothic collections★★★), Spanish Village★ (Poble espanyol), Joan Miró Foundation★ - Archeological Museum★ (Museo Arqueológico) - El Eixample : Holy Family★★ (Sagrada Familia) JU, Passeig de Gràcia★ HV, Casa Batlló★ HVB, La Pedrera or Casa Milà★ HVP - Güell Park★★ (Parque Güell) - Catalonian Music Palace★ (Palau de la Música Catalana) MVY, Antoni Tàpies Foundation★ HVS.

Other curiosities : Pedralbes Monastery★ - Zoo★ (Parc zoologic) KX Tibidabo (※★★).

18, 9 of Prat by S : 16 km ☎ 379 02 78 - 18 of Sant Cugat by NW : 20 km ☎ 674 39 58 - 18 of Vallromanas by NW : 25 km ☎ 568 03 62.

✈ Barcelona by S : 12 km ☎ 317 10 11 - Iberia : Passeig de Gràcia 30, ✉ 08007, ☎ 301 68 00 HV - and Aviaco : airport ☎ 379 24 58.

🚘 Sants ☎ 490 75 91.

⛴. to the Balearic islands : Cía. Trasmediterránea, muelle Barcelona-Estación Marítima 1, ✉ 08039, ☎ 317 42 62, Fax 412 28 42.

ℹ Gran Vía de les Corts Catalanes 658, ✉ 08010, ☎ 301 74 43, and at airport ☎ 325 58 29 - R.A.C.C. Santaló 8, ✉ 08021, ☎ 200 33 11, Fax 200 39 64.

Madrid 627 - Bilbao/Bilbo 607 - Lérida/Lleida 169 - Perpignan 187 - Tarragona 109 - Toulouse 388 - Valencia 361 - Zaragoza 307.

Plans on following pages

Old Town and the Gothic Quarter : Ramblas, pl. S. Jaume, via Laietana, passeig Nacional, passeig de Colom

Le Meridien Barcelona, Ramblas 111, ✉ 08002, ☎ 318 62 00, Telex 54634, Fax 301 77 76 - |‡| ▤ TV ☎ ♿ 🚗 - 🏛 25/200. AE ⓓ E VISA JCB. ✂ LX **b**
M *(closed 15 to 31 August)* 2600 - ☕ 2600 - **208 rm** 22500/32000.

Colón, av. de la Catedral 7, ✉ 08002, ☎ 301 14 04, Telex 52654, Fax 317 29 15 - |‡| ▤ TV ☎ - 🏛 25/200. AE ⓓ E VISA JCB. ✂ rest MV **e**
M 3400 - ☕ 1350 - **147 rm** 32500/37000.

Rivoli Rambla, Rambla dels Estudis 128, ✉ 08002, ☎ 302 66 43, Telex 99222, Fax 317 50 53 - |‡| ▤ TV ☎ ♿ - 🏛 25/180. AE ⓓ E VISA JCB. ✂ LX **r**
M a la carte 4500/5500 - ☕ 1900 - **89 rm** 20500/25900.

Royal coffee shop only, Rambla dels Estudis 117, ✉ 08002, ☎ 301 94 00, Telex 97565, Fax 317 31 79 - |‡| ▤ TV ☎ 🚗 - 🏛 25/100. AE ⓓ E VISA JCB. LX **e**
☕ 1550 - **108 rm** 14175/22900.

Ambassador, Pintor Fortuny 13, ✉ 08001, ☎ 412 05 30, Telex 99222, Fax 317 50 53, 🏋, 🏊 - |‡| ▤ TV ☎ ♿ 🚗 - 🏛 25/200. AE ⓓ E VISA. ✂ LX **v**
M 2500 - ☕ 1600 - **105 rm** 18500/25900.

Almirante without rest, Vía Laietana 42, ✉ 08003, ☎ 268 30 20, Fax 268 31 92 - |‡| ▤ TV ☎ 🚗 - 🏛 25/40. AE ⓓ E VISA. ✂ MV **d**
☕ 1500 - **76 rm** 18000/22500.

Gravina coffee shop only, Gravina 12, ✉ 08001, ☎ 301 68 68, Telex 99370, Fax 317 28 38 - |‡| ▤ TV ☎ - 🏛 25/50. AE ⓓ E VISA. ✂ HX **d**
☕ 1000 - **60 rm** 9900/14900.

Montecarlo without rest, Rambla dels Estudis 124, ✉ 08002, ☎ 317 58 00, Telex 93345, Fax 318 73 23 - |‡| ▤ TV ☎ ♿ 🚗. AE ⓓ E VISA JCB. LX **r**
☕ 850 - **75 rm** 10000/15000.

Reding, Gravina 5, ✉ 08001, ☎ 412 10 97, Fax 268 34 82 - |‡| ▤ TV ☎ 🚗. AE ⓓ E VISA. ✂ HX **d**
M 1900 - ☕ 950 - **44 rm** 17500.

Atlantis without rest, Pelai 20, ✉ 08001, ☎ 318 90 12, Fax 412 09 14 - |‡| ▤ TV ☎. AE E VISA. ✂ HX **a**
☕ 850 - **42 rm** 12000/16000.

Metropol without rest, Ample 31, ✉ 08002, ☎ 315 40 11, Fax 319 12 76 - |‡| ▤ TV ☎. AE ⓓ E VISA. ✂ NY **r**
☕ 900 - **68 rm** 13200/17600.

Regencia Colón without rest, Sagristans 13, ✉ 08002, ☎ 318 98 58, Telex 98175, Fax 317 28 22 - |‡| ▤ TV ☎. AE ⓓ E VISA JCB. ✂ MV **r**
☕ 950 - **55 rm** 8700/12700.

Rialto coffee shop only, Ferrán 42, ✉ 08002, ☎ 318 52 12, Telex 97206, Fax 315 38 19 - |‡| ▤ TV ☎ - 🏛 25/50. AE ⓓ E VISA JCB. MX **s**
☕ 975 - **132 rm** 9880/13500.

Lleó without rest, Pelai 24, ✉ 08001, ☎ 318 13 12, Telex 98338, Fax 412 26 57 - |‡| ▤ TV ☎ ♿. ⓓ E VISA JCB. ✂ rest HX **a**
☕ 925 - **75 rm** 9000/12000.

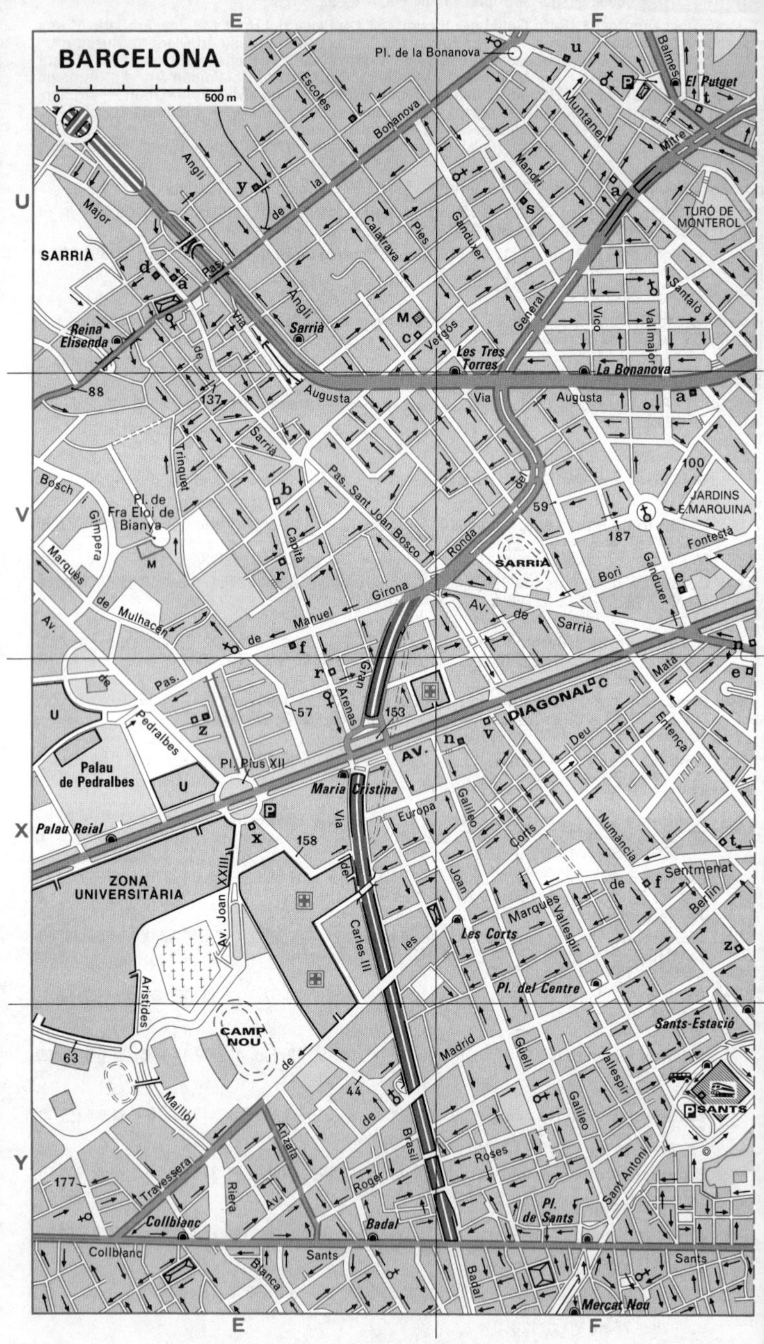
BARCELONA
0
500 m
E
F
U
V
X
Y
SARRIÀ
Reina Elisenda
Sarrià
Les Tres Torres
La Bonanova
El Putget
TURÓ DE MONTEROL
JARDINS E.MARQUINA
Pl. de la Bonanova
Pl. de Fra Eloi de Bianya
Palau de Pedralbes
Palau Reial
ZONA UNIVERSITÀRIA
CAMP NOU
Maria Cristina
Les Corts
Pl. del Centre
Sants-Estació
SANTS
Collblanc
Badal
Pl. de Sants
Mercat Nou
DIAGONAL
AV.
Pl. Pius XII
Augusta
Via Augusta
Ronda del General Mitre
Bonanova
Muntaner
Balmes
Ganduxer
Calatrava
Escoles
Angli
Major
Vergós
Santaló
Vico
Valmajor
Fontestà
Borì
Girona
Av. de Sarrià
Manuel
Gran Via de Carles III
Entença
Numància
Sentmenat
Berlín
Europa
Galileo
Joan
Marquès
Vallespir
Madrid
Guell
Roses
Sant Antoni
Brasil
Roger
Arizala
Travessera
Riera Blanca
Sants
Badal
Maillol
Arístides
Av. Joan XXIII
Pedralbes
Gimpera
Bosch
Marquès de Mulhacèn
Trinquet
Capità
Pas. Sant Joan Bosco
Mata
Deu
Corts
88
137
100
59
187
57
153
158
63
44
177

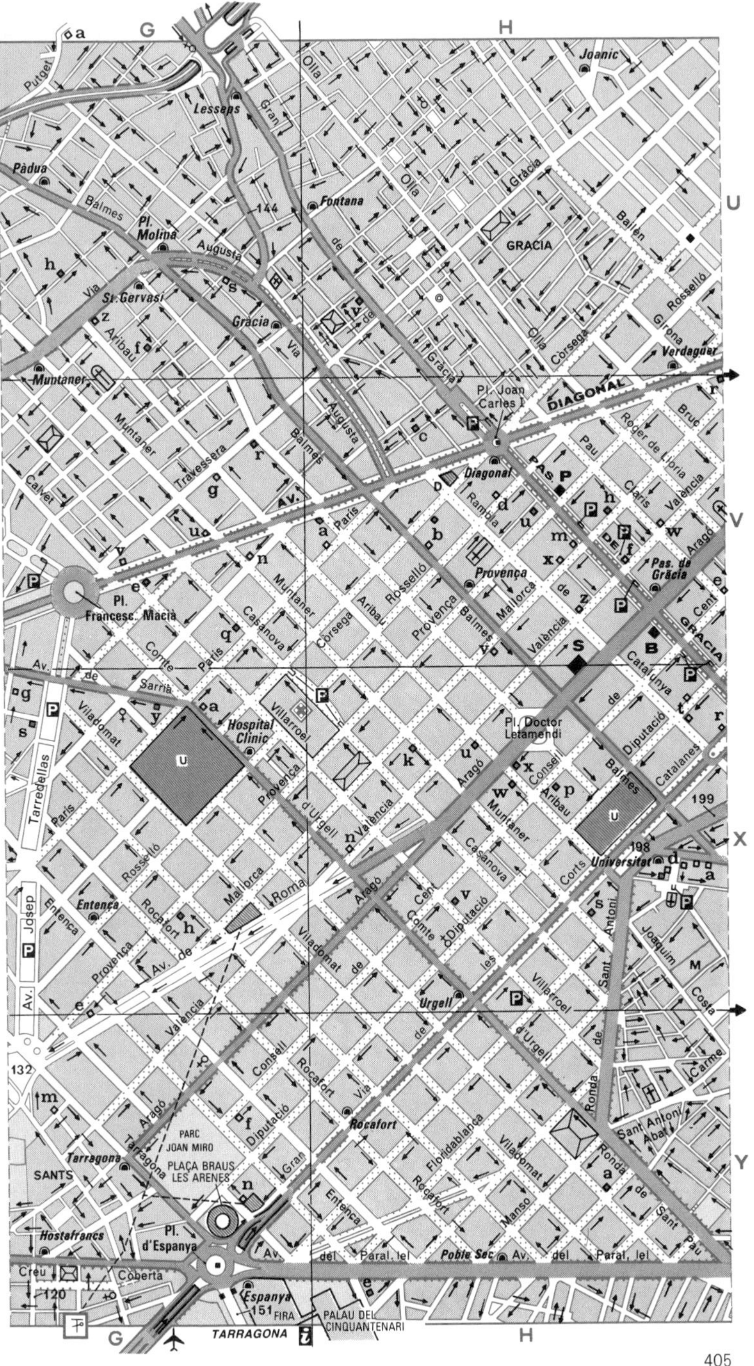
G
H
U
V
X
Y
Joanic
Lesseps
Pàdua
Fontana
Pl. Molina
St. Gervasi
Gràcia
GRACIA
Muntaner
Verdaguer
DIAGONAL
Pl. Joan Carles I
Diagonal
Provença
Pas. de Gràcia
Pl. Francesc. Macià
Hospital Clinic
Pl. Doctor Letamendi
Universitat
Entença
Urgell
Rocafort
PARC JOAN MIRO
PLAÇA BRAUS LES ARENES
Tarragona
SANTS
Hostafrancs
Pl. d'Espanya
Poble Sec
Espanya
FIRA
PALAU DEL CINQUANTENARI
TARRAGONA
144
132
120
151
198
199
Av. de Sarrià
Tarradellas
Av. Josep
Av. del Paral.lel
Creu Coberta
Sant Antoni Abat
Ronda de Sant Antoni
Ronda de Sant Pau
Gran Via
Travessera
Balmes
Aribau
Augusta
Casanova
Villarroel
Comte d'Urgell
Viladomat
Calàbria
Floridablanca
Manso
Consell de Cent
Diputació
Aragó
València
Mallorca
Rosselló
Còrsega
París
Provença
Corts Catalanes
Rambla de Catalunya
Claris
Roger de Llúria
Pau
Bruc
Girona
Bailèn
Olla
Joaquim Costa
Carme
Calvet
Putget
Roma
Rocafort
Entença
Urgell
Muntaner

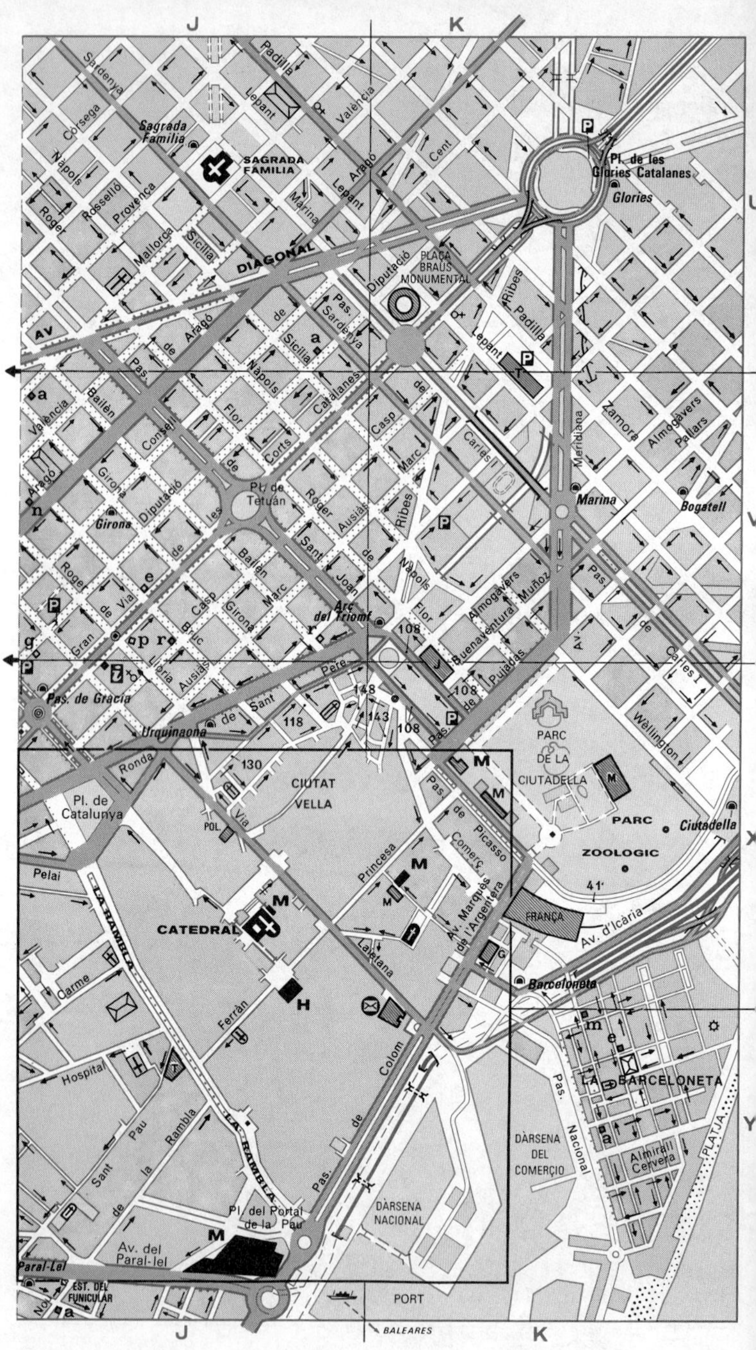
J
K
Sagrada Familia
SAGRADA FAMILIA
Pl. de les Glòries Catalanes
Glories
DIAGONAL
PLAÇA BRAUS MONUMENTAL
Pl. de Tetuán
Marina
Bogatell
Girona
Arc del Triomf
Pas. de Gràcia
Urquinaona
PARC DE LA CIUTADELLA
PARC ZOOLOGIC
Ciutadella
CIUTAT VELLA
Pl. de Catalunya
CATEDRAL
FRANÇA
Av. d'Icària
Barceloneta
LA BARCELONETA
DÀRSENA DEL COMERÇ
DÀRSENA NACIONAL
Pl. del Portal de la Pau
Av. del Paral-lel
Paral-lel
EST. DEL FUNICULAR
PORT
BALEARES
PLATJA
LA RAMBLA

STREET INDEX TO BARCELONA TOWN PLAN

BARCELONA

Capútxins
(Rambla dels) . . . . **MY** 35
Catalunya (Pl. de) . . . . **LV**
Estudis (Rambla dels) . . . . **LX**
Sant Josep (Rambla de) . . **LX** 168
Santa Mònica
(Rambla de) . . . . **MY**
Universitat
(Ronda de la) . . . . **LV** 199

Banys Nous . . . . **MX** 7
Bergara . . . . **LV** 10
Bisbe Irurita . . . . **MX** 15
Bòria . . . . **MV** 18
Born (Pas. del) . . . . **NX** 20
Boters . . . . **MX** 23
Canaletes (Rambla de) . . . . **LV** 27
Canonge Colom (Pl.) . . . . . **LY** 28
Canvis Vells . . . . **NX** 32
Cardenal Casañas . . . . **LX** 36
Catedral (Av.) . . . . **MV** 40
Ciutat . . . . **MX** 43
Comercial (Pl.) . . . . **NV** 45
Cucurella . . . . **LX** 55
Doctor Joaquim Pou . . . . . **MV** 61
Escudellers . . . . **MY** 72
Francesc Cambó
(Av.) . . . . **MV** 79
Isabel II (Pas. d') . . . . **NX** 98
Montcada . . . . **NX** 121
Montjuïc del Bisbe . . . . . . **MX** 123
Nou de Sant Francesc . . . . **MY** 126
Nova (Pl.) . . . . **MX** 128
Paradis . . . . **MX** 135
Pintor Fortuny . . . . **LX** 140
Portal de Santa
Madrona . . . . **MY** 142
Ramón Berenguer
el Gran (Pl.) . . . . **MX** 147
Rei (Plaça del) . . . . **MX** 149
Sant Felip Neri (Pl.) . . . . . . **MX** 163
Sant Miquel (Pl. de) . . . . . . **MX** 173
Sant Sever . . . . **MX** 181
Santa Anna . . . . **LV** 182
Santa Maria (Pl.) . . . . **NX** 189

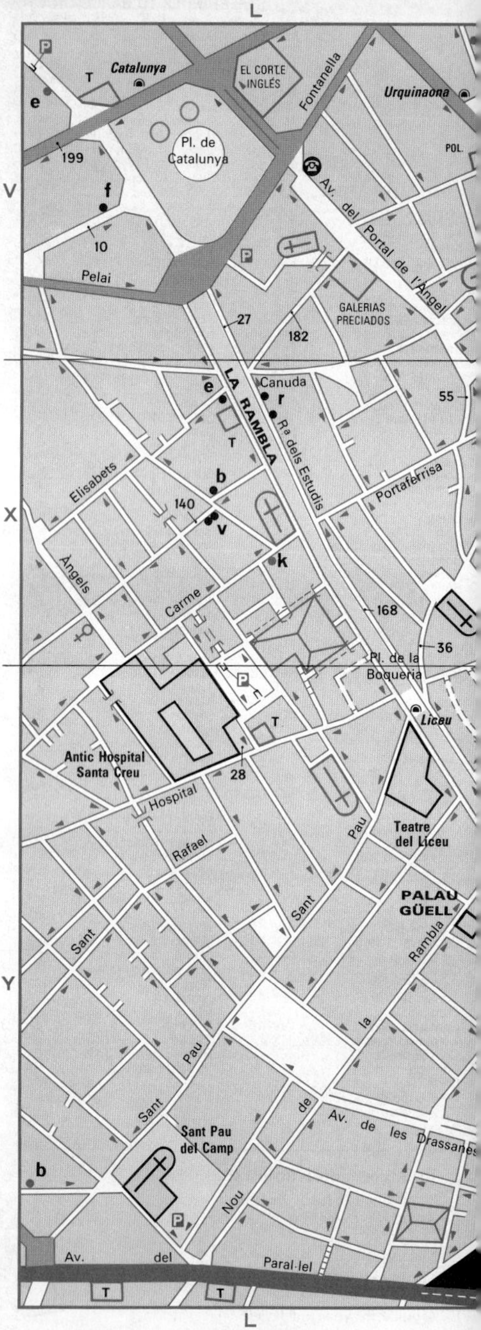

We suggest:

For a successful tour, that you prepare it in advance.
***Michelin maps** and **guides** will give you much useful information on route planning, places of interest, accommodation, prices etc.*

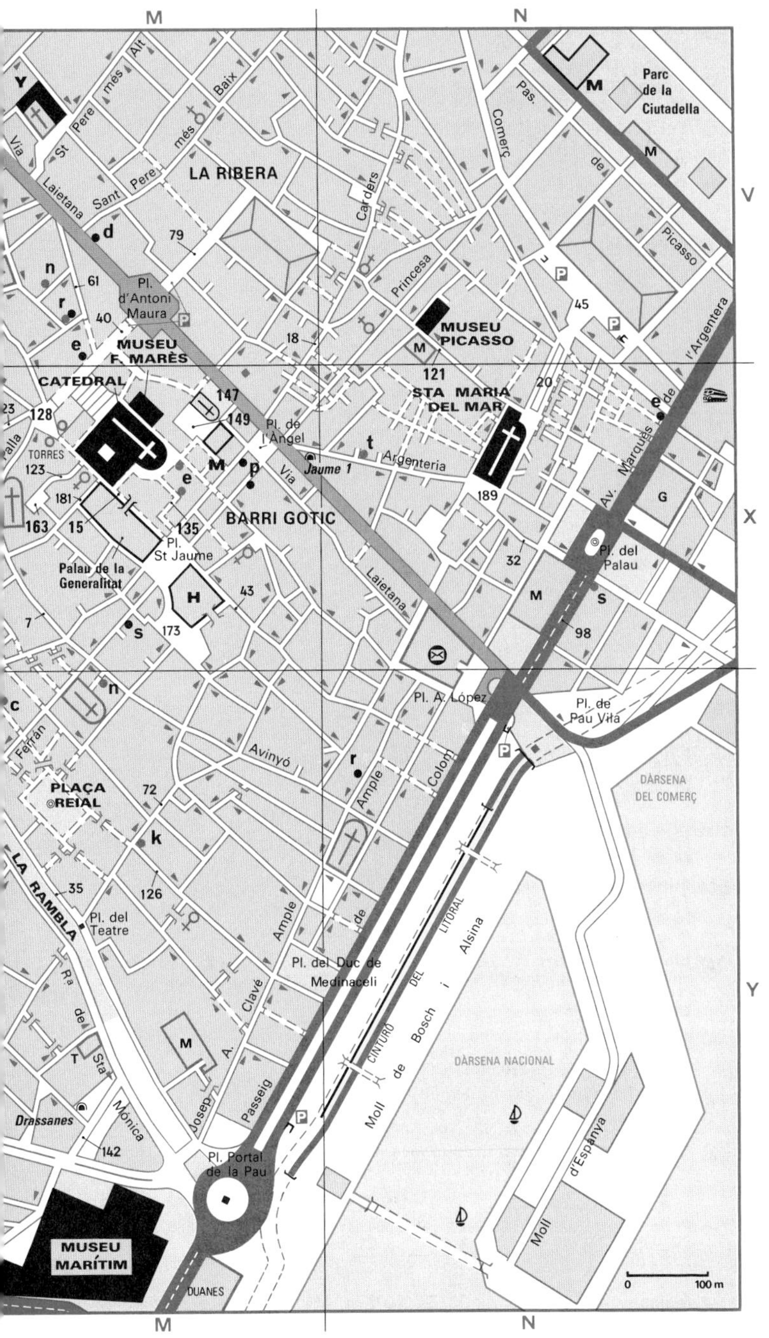
M
N
V
X
Y
LA RIBERA
BARRI GOTIC
MUSEU PICASSO
MUSEU F. MARÈS
CATEDRAL
STA MARIA DEL MAR
Palau de la Generalitat
Pl. St Jaume
Pl. d'Antoni Maura
Pl. de l'Àngel
Jaume 1
Pl. del Palau
Pl. A. López
Pl. de Pau Vila
PLAÇA REIAL
LA RAMBLA
Pl. del Teatre
Pl. del Duc de Medinaceli
Pl. Portal de la Pau
MUSEU MARÍTIM
Drassanes
DUANES
Parc de la Ciutadella
DÀRSENA DEL COMERÇ
DÀRSENA NACIONAL
Moll de Bosch i Alsina
Moll d'Espanya
CINTURÓ DEL LITORAL
Via Laietana
Sant Pere més Alt
Sant Pere més Baix
St Pere
Carders
Princesa
Pas. de Picasso
Comerç
Argenteria
Av. Marquès de l'Argentera
Avinyó
Ample
Colom
Passeig de Colom
Josep A. Clavé
Ferran
Rª de Sta Mònica
TORRES
Muralla
0
100 m

Turín, Pintor Fortuny 9, ✉ 08001, ☎ 302 48 12, Fax 302 10 05 – AE E VISA. rest – **M** 1100 – ☐ 800 – **60 rm** 9900/14000. LX **v**

Park H., av. Marqués de l'Argentera 11, ✉ 08003, ☎ 319 60 00, Telex 99883, Fax 319 45 19 – AE E VISA JCB. NX **e**
M 2500 – ☐ 1150 – **87 rm** 11000/14500.

Suizo, pl. del Àngel 12, ✉ 08002, ☎ 315 41 11, Telex 97206, Fax 315 38 19 – AE E VISA JCB. rest MX **p**
M 2750 – ☐ 975 – **48 rm** 9880/13500.

Gótico without rest, Jaume I-14, ✉ 08002, ☎ 315 22 11, Telex 97206, Fax 315 38 19 – AE E VISA JCB. MX **p**
☐ 975 – **70 rm** 9330/12950.

La Odisea, Copons 7, ✉ 08002, ☎ 302 36 92, Fax 412 32 67 – E VISA MV **n**
closed Saturday, Sunday, Holy Week and August – **M** a la carte 4030/5200.

Agut d'Avignon, Trinitat 3, ✉ 08002, ☎ 302 60 34, Fax 302 53 18 – AE E VISA JCB. MY **n**
M a la carte 3395/5940.

Nostromo, Ripoll 16, ✉ 08002, ☎ 412 24 55 – AE E VISA JCB. MV **r**
closed Saturday lunch, Sunday and Bank Holidays – **M** a la carte 3475/4225.

Quo Vadis, Carme 7, ✉ 08001, ☎ 302 40 72, Fax 301 04 35 – AE E VISA LX **k**
closed Sunday and August – **M** a la carte 4325/5975.

Aitor, Carbonell 5, ✉ 08003, ☎ 319 94 88, Basque rest – E VISA KY **m**
closed Monday and 11 August-11 September – **M** a la carte approx. 4800.

Brasserie Flo, Junqueres 10, ✉ 08003, ☎ 319 31 02, Fax 268 23 95 – AE E VISA
M a la carte 3500/4500. LV **a**

Senyor Parellada, Argentería 37, ✉ 08003, ☎ 315 40 10 – AE E VISA JCB.
closed Sunday and Bank Holidays – **M** a la carte 2800/3500. NX **t**

7 Portes, passeig d'Isabel II - 14, ✉ 08003, ☎ 319 30 33, Fax 319 46 62 – AE E VISA.
– **M** a la carte approx. 3500. NX **s**

Can Ramonet, Maquinista 17, ✉ 08003, ☎ 319 30 64, Fax 319 70 14, Seafood – AE E VISA JCB. KY **e**
closed 9 August-9 September – **M** a la carte 2900/4100.

Can Solé, Sant Carles 4, ✉ 08003, ☎ 319 50 12, Seafood – AE E VISA KY **a**
closed Saturday dinner and Sunday – **M** a la carte 4025/3100.

South of Av. Diagonal pl. de Catalunya, Gran Vía de les Corts Catalanes, Passeig de Gràcia, Balmes, Muntaner, Aragó

Rey Juan Carlos I, av. Diagonal 661, ✉ 08028, ☎ 448 08 08, Fax 448 06 07, ≤ city, « Modern installation-park with lake and » – – 25/1000. AE E VISA JCB. by Av. Diagonal YX
M Chez Vous a la carte 3450/5200 - **Kokoro** *(japanese rest.)* a la carte 4100/5800 - **Café Polo** a la carte 2950/4350 – ☐ 2100 – **412 rm** 27000/36000.

Ritz, Gran Vía de les Corts Catalanes 668, ✉ 08010, ☎ 318 52 00, Telex 52739, Fax 318 01 48 – – 25/350. AE E VISA JCB. rest JV **p**
M 3250 – ☐ 2150 – **158 rm** 32800/43000.

Princesa Sofía, pl. de Pius XII 4, ✉ 08028, ☎ 330 71 11, Telex 51032, Fax 330 76 21, ≤, – – 25/1200. AE E VISA JCB. EX **x**
M 4600 - **Le Gourmet** *(closed Sunday, Monday and August)* a la carte 3750/4650 - **L'Empordá** *(closed Saturday, Sunday and July* a la carte 3000/3300 – ☐ 1800 – **505 rm** 22500/35500.

Claris, Pau Claris 150, ✉ 08009, ☎ 487 62 62, Fax 215 79 70, « Modern installation with antiques-archelogy museum », – – 25/60. AE E VISA JCB. rest HV **w**
M Caviar Caspio *(dinner only)* a la carte approx. 5500 – ☐ 1800 – **124 rm** 20800/26000.

Barcelona Hilton, av. Diagonal 589, ✉ 08014, ☎ 419 22 33, Telex 99623, Fax 405 25 73, – – 25/800. AE E VISA JCB. FX **v**
M 3250 – ☐ 2500 – **290 rm** 35500/44500.

Meliá Barcelona Sarriá, av. de Sarriá 50, ✉ 08029, ☎ 410 60 60, Telex 51638, Fax 321 51 79, ≤ – – . AE E VISA. FV **n**
M a la carte 4000/5150 – ☐ 2200 – **291 rm** 26000/33000.

G.H. Havana and Rest. Grand Place, Gran Vía de les Corts Catalanes 647, ✉ 08010, ☎ 412 11 15, Telex 51531, Fax 412 26 11 – – 25/200. AE E VISA JCB. JV **e**
M a la carte 2600/3250 – ☐ 1700 – **145 rm** 23000/29000.

Feria Palace, av. Rius i Taulet 1, ✉ 08004, ☎ 426 22 23, Telex 97588, Fax 424 86 79, – – 25/1300. AE E VISA JCB. by Lleida HY
M L'Aria *(Italian rest.)* a la carte 2450/2950 - **Ell Mall** a la carte 3100/3850 – ☐ 975 – **276 rm** 18480/23100.

Majestic, passeig de Gràcia 70, ✉ 08008, ☎ 488 17 17, Telex 52211, Fax 488 18 80, – – 25/600. AE E VISA JCB. HV **f**
M 3500 – ☐ 1500 – **335 rm** 15700/24900.

Diplomatic and Rest. La Salsa, Pau Claris 122, ✉ 08009, ☎ 488 02 00, Telex 54701, Fax 488 12 22, – 25/250. *(closed Sunday)* HV **e**
M *(closed Sunday)* a la carte 4050/5000 – ☕ 1750 – **217 rm** 20000/25000.

NH Calderón, Rambla de Catalunya 26, ✉ 08007, ☎ 301 00 00, Telex 99529, Fax 317 31 57, – – 25/200. HX **t**
M a la carte 4000/6000 – ☕ 1500 – **248 rm** 20400/25500.

Barcelona Sants, pl. dels Països Catalans (railway Barcelona Sants), ✉ 08014, ☎ 490 95 95, Telex 97568, Fax 490 60 45 – – 25/1500. FY
M 2500 – ☕ 1250 – **377 rm** 17600/22000.

Avenida Palace, Gran Vía de les Corts Catalanes 605, ✉ 08007, ☎ 301 96 00, Telex 54734, Fax 318 12 34 – – 25/300. rest HX **r**
M 5100 – ☕ 1400 – **211 rm** 21700/27200.

G.H. Catalonia, Balmes 142, ✉ 08008, ☎ 415 90 90, Telex 97532, Fax 415 22 09 – – 48/260. HV **b**
M 3000 – ☕ 1500 – **84 rm** 18500/24900.

Condes de Barcelona and annexe, passeig de Gràcia 75, ✉ 08008, ☎ 484 86 00, Telex 51531, Fax 487 14 42, – – 25/180.
M 3000 – ☕ 1500 – **183 rm** 23000/29000. HV **m**

Gallery H., Roselló 249, ✉ 08008, ☎ 415 99 11, Telex 97518, Fax 415 91 84, – – 25/200. HV **d**
M a la carte 3135/4875 – ☕ 1500 – **115 rm** 27000.

St. Moritz, Diputació 262 bis, ✉ 08007, ☎ 412 15 00, Fax 412 12 36 – – 25/140. rest JV **g**
M 3000 – ☕ 1500 – **92 rm** 18100/25500.

L'Illa without rest, av. Diagonal 555, ✉ 08029, ☎ 410 33 00, Fax 410 88 92 – FX **c**
☕ 1000 – **103 rm** 17600/22000.

Gran Derby without rest, Loreto 28, ✉ 08029, ☎ 322 20 62, Telex 97429, Fax 419 68 20 – – 25/100. GX **g**
☕ 1250 – **40 rm** 20000/23000.

Balmes, Mallorca 216, ✉ 08008, ☎ 451 19 14, Fax 451 00 49, « Terrace with » – – 25/70. rest HV **v**
M 2500 – ☕ 975 – **100 rm** 12000/16500.

City Park H., Nicaragua 47, ✉ 08029, ☎ 419 95 00, Fax 419 71 63 – – 25/40. rest FX **z**
M 2100 – ☕ 1300 – **80 rm** 14500/20500.

NH Podium, Bailén 4, ✉ 08010, ☎ 265 02 02, Telex 97007, Fax 265 05 06, – – 25/240. JV **r**
M 1600 – ☕ 1400 – **145 rm** 16700/23100.

Derby, Loreto 21, ✉ 08029, ☎ 322 32 15, Telex 97429, Fax 410 08 62 – – 25/100. rest FX **e**
M 3500 – ☕ 1250 – **119 rm** 14500/22000.

Alexandra, Mallorca 251, ✉ 08008, ☎ 487 05 05, Telex 81107, Fax 216 06 06 – – 25/100. HV **x**
M 3850 – ☕ 1400 – **75 rm** 19300/24000.

Astoria without rest, Paris 203, ✉ 08036, ☎ 209 83 11, Telex 81129, Fax 202 30 08 – – 25/30. HV **a**
☕ 975 – **114 rm** 11700/15500.

NH Master, Valencia 105, ✉ 08011, ☎ 323 62 15, Telex 81258, Fax 323 43 89 – – 25/170. HX **n**
M 3600 – ☕ 1000 – **81 rm** 12800/17600.

Cristal, Diputació 257, ✉ 08007, ☎ 487 87 78, Telex 54560, Fax 487 90 30 – – 25/70. HX **t**
M 2850 – ☕ 925 – **148 rm** 12500/18000.

NH Numancia, Numancia 74, ✉ 08029, ☎ 322 44 51, Fax 410 76 42 – – 25/70. FX **f**
M a la carte 3100/3800 – ☕ 1000 – **140 rm** 12800/17600.

Sant'Angelo without rest, Consell de Cent 74, ✉ 08015, ☎ 423 46 47, Fax 423 88 40 – GY **f**
☕ 1100 – **51 rm** 12500/19500.

Grand Passage Suites H., Muntaner 212, ✉ 08036, ☎ 201 03 06, Telex 98311, Fax 201 00 04 – – 25/80. GV **n**
M 2500 – ☕ 1350 – **40 rm** 19300/24000.

Núñez Urgel without rest, Comte d'Urgell 232, ✉ 08036, ☎ 322 41 53, Fax 419 01 06 – – 25/100. GX **a**
☕ 1000 – **120 rm** 13500/20000.

Regente, Rambla de Catalunya 76, ✉ 08008, ☎ 215 25 70, Telex 51939, Fax 487 32 27, – – 25/30. HV **z**
M 2650 – ☕ 1300 – **78 rm** 15000/22000.

Expo H., Mallorca 1, 08014, 325 12 12, Telex 54147, Fax 325 11 44, - 25/900. AE E VISA. GY **m**
M 2335 - 1050 - **435 rm** 13230/17325.

Duques de Bergara, Bergara 11, 08002, 301 51 51, Telex 81257, Fax 317 34 42 - 25/80. AE E VISA. LV **f**
M 2500 - 1200 - **56 rm** 17500/21900.

Abbot without rest, av. de Roma 23, 08029, 430 04 05, Fax 419 57 41 - 25/100. AE E VISA. GXY **e**
1000 - **42 rm** 11550/18150.

NH Forum, Ecuador 20, 08029, 419 36 36, Fax 419 89 10 - 25/50. AE E VISA. FX **t**
M a la carte approx. 2500 - 1000 - **48 rm** 12800/17600.

Onix without rest, Llançà 30, 08015, 426 00 87, Fax 426 19 81, - 25/150. AE VISA. GY **n**
900 - **80 rm** 11600/14500.

Beltxenea, Mallorca 275, 08008, 215 30 24, Fax 487 00 81, « Garden-Terrace » - . AE E VISA. HV **h**
closed Saturday lunch and Sunday - **M** a la carte 5300/6700.

La Dama, av. Diagonal 423, 08036, 202 06 86, Fax 200 72 99 - . AE E VISA. HV **a**
M a la carte 4550/6675
Spec. Ensalada tibia de salmonetes con patatas al caviar, Rape estilo Costa Brava, Carro de pastelería y de quesos artesanos.

Finisterre, av. Diagonal 469, 08036, 439 55 76, Fax 439 99 41 - . AE E VISA. - *closed Saturday* - **M** a la carte 5000/7500. GV **e**

Oliver y Hardy, av. Diagonal 593, 08014, 419 31 81, - . AE E VISA.
closed Sunday - **M** a la carte approx. 5500. FX **n**

Jaume de Provença, Provença 88, 08029, 430 00 29, Fax 439 29 50 - . AE E VISA JCB. GX **h**
closed Sunday dinner, Monday, Holy Week, August and Christmas - **M** a la carte 4350/7100
Spec. "Panellets" de foie-gras, Tournedo de bogavante, Manitas de cerdo en hojaldre con foie-gras y trufas.

Bel Air, Córsega 286, 08008, 237 75 88, Fax 237 95 26, Rices dishes - . AE E VISA JCB. HV **b**
closed Sunday and Holy Week - **M** a la carte 3950/6100.

Tikal, Rambla de Catalunya 5, 08007, 302 22 21 - . AE E VISA. LV **e**
closed Saturday, Sunday, Bank Holidays and August - **M** a la carte 4400/5400.

El Tragaluz, passatge de la Concepció 5 - 1º, 08008, 487 01 96, Fax 217 01 19, « Original decor conservatory » - AE E VISA. HV **u**
closed Sunday - **M** a la carte 4250/5600.

Rías de Galicia, Lleida 7, 08004, 424 81 52, Fax 426 13 07, Seafood - . AE E VISA JCB. HY **e**
M a la carte 3100/6000.

Vinya Rosa - Magí, av. de Sarriá 17, 08029, 430 00 03, Fax 430 00 41 - . AE E VISA - *closed Saturday lunch and Sunday* - **M** a la carte 3200/5700. GX **y**

Gorría, Diputació 421, 08013, 245 11 64, Fax 232 78 57, Basque rest. - . AE E VISA JCB. - *closed Sunday and August* - **M** a la carte 4100/4950. JU **a**

La Sopeta, Muntaner 6, 08011, 323 56 32 - . AE E VISA JCB. HX **s**
closed Sunday - **M** a la carte 3480/4900.

Ca l'Isidre, Les Flors 12, 08001, 441 11 39, Fax 442 52 71 - . AE E VISA.
closed Saturday April to September, Sunday, Bank Holidays, Holy Week, August and 1 to 14 February - **M** a la carte 4500/5500 LY **b**
Spec. Ragoût de manitas de cerdo con almejas y espárragos trigueros, Arroz con porchinis y fondos de aves, Gelée de frutas al Sauternes.

Casa Chus, av. Diagonal 339 bis, 08037, 207 02 15 - . AE E VISA HV **r**
closed Sunday dinner and August - **M** a la carte 3450/4450.

Sibarit, Aribau 65, 08011, 453 93 03 - . AE E VISA JCB. HX **u**
closed Saturday lunch, Sunday and 1 to 15 August - **M** a la carte approx. 4800.

L'Aram, Aragó 305 207 01 88 - . AE E VISA. JV **n**
closed Saturday lunch, Sunday, Holy week and August - **M** a la carte 3600/4800.

St. Pauli, Muntaner 101, 08036, 454 75 48 - . AE E VISA. HX **k**
closed Saturday lunch, Sunday, Bank Holidays and August - **M** a la carte approx. 5200.

El Pescador, Mallorca 314, 08037, 207 10 24, Seafood - . AE E VISA.
closed Sunday - **M** a la carte 2650/4900. JV **a**

Els Perols de l'Empordá, Villarroel 88, 08011, 323 10 33, Ampurdan rest - . AE E VISA. HX **v**
closed Sunday dinner, Monday, Holy Week and 1 to 22 August - **M** a la carte 2575/3450.

Azpiolea, Casanova 167, 08036, 430 90 30, Basque rest. - . AE E VISA.
closed Sunday and August - **M** a la carte 3500/4350. GV **q**

North of Av. Diagonal vía Augusta, Capitá Arenas, ronda General Mitre, passeig de la Bonanova, av. de Pedralbes

Presidente, av. Diagonal 570, ⊠ 08021, ℘ 200 21 11, Telex 52180, Fax 209 51 06, – TV – 25/420. AE E VISA. GV **u**
M 3750 – 1500 – **152 rm** 23000/28750.

Hesperia coffee shop only, Vergós 20, ⊠ 08017, ℘ 204 55 51, Telex 98403, Fax 204 43 92 – TV – 25/150. AE E VISA. EU **c**
1250 – **139 rm** 16400/20500.

Suite H., Muntaner 505, ⊠ 08022, ℘ 212 80 12, Telex 99077, Fax 211 23 17 – TV – 25/90. AE E VISA. FU **a**
M 3000 – 1500 – **70 rm** 18500/24900.

Balmoral without rest, vía Augusta 5, ⊠ 08006, ℘ 217 87 00, Telex 54087, Fax 415 14 21 – TV – 25/250. AE E VISA JCB. HV **n**
– **M** *(closed Saturday, July-August and 1 to 22 August* 1600 – 1050 – **94 rm** 15700/24000.

NH Cóndor, via Augusta 127, ⊠ 08006, ℘ 209 45 11, Telex 52925, Fax 202 27 13 – TV – 25/50. AE E VISA. GU **z**
M a la carte 2500/3600 – 1400 – **78 rm** 16800/21000.

Arenas coffee shop dinner only, Capitá Arenas 20, ⊠ 08034, ℘ 280 03 03, Telex 54990, Fax 280 33 92 – TV – 25/50. AE E VISA JCB. EX **r**
925 – **59 rm** 14000/20000.

Victoria, av. de Pedralbes 16 bis, ⊠ 08034, ℘ 280 15 15, Telex 98302, Fax 280 52 67, – TV. AE E VISA. rest EX **z**
M *(closed Saturday, Sunday and August)* 1375 – 1350 - 79 suites 26000/38500

Park Putxet, Putxet 68, ⊠ 08023, ℘ 212 51 58, Telex 98718, Fax 418 58 17 – TV – 25/200. AE E VISA. GU **a**
M 1900 – 950 – **141 rm** 11500/14500.

NH Belagua, vía Augusta 89, ⊠ 08006, ℘ 237 39 40, Telex 99643, Fax 415 30 62 – TV – 25 /90. AE E VISA. rest GU **s**
M 3500 – 1000 – **72 rm** 12800/17600.

Mitre without rest, Bertrán 9, ⊠ 08023, ℘ 212 11 04, Telex 98671, Fax 418 94 81 – TV. AE E VISA FU **t**
725 – **57 rm** 11200/14000.

Condado, Aribau 201, ⊠ 08021, ℘ 200 23 11, Telex 54546, Fax 200 25 86 – TV. AE E VISA. rest GV **g**
M *(closed Saturday and Sunday)* 1850 – 900 – **88 rm** 12800/16000.

NH Pedralbes coffee shop dinner only, Fontcuberta 4, ⊠ 08034, ℘ 203 71 12, Fax 205 70 65 – TV – 25/35. AE E VISA. EV **b**
1000 – **28 rm** 14100/17600.

Covadonga without rest, av. Diagonal 596, ⊠ 08021, ℘ 209 55 11, Telex 93394, Fax 209 58 33 – TV. AE E VISA JCB. GV **v**
550 – **85 rm** 7200/11400.

Bonanova Park without rest, Capitá Arenas 51, ⊠ 08034, ℘ 204 09 00, Telex 98671, Fax 204 50 14 – TV – 25/35. AE E VISA. EV **r**
550 – **60 rm** 10000/12500.

Albéniz without rest, Aragó 591, ⊠ 08026, ℘ 265 26 26, Fax 265 40 07 – TV – 25/50. AE E VISA. NE : by Aragó HV
950 – **47 rm** 9500/11500.

XXXX ✿ **Via Veneto,** Ganduxer 10, ⊠ 08021, ℘ 200 72 44, Fax 201 60 95, « Early 20C style » – . AE E VISA JCB. FV **e**
closed Saturday lunch, Sunday and 1 to 20 August – **M** a la carte 4590/6130
Spec. Ensalada tibia de ternera con tomate confitado, Pollo con bogavante y arroz blanco, Crepes flambeadas tres gustos : helado vainilla, crema y nata.

XXXX **Reno,** Tuset 27, ⊠ 08006, ℘ 200 91 29, Fax 414 41 14 – . AE E VISA JCB.
closed Saturday – **M** a la carte 5500/7000. GV **r**

XXX ✿✿ **Neichel,** av. de Pedralbes 16 bis, ⊠ 08034, ℘ 203 84 08, Fax 205 63 69 – . AE E VISA. EX **z**
closed Sunday, Bank Holidays, Holy Week, August and Christmas – **M** a la carte 5350/6200
Spec. Ensalada de bogavante y cabeza de cerdo con lentejas a la albahaca, "Lluerna" de roca al horno, Tournedos de buey con pure de olivada y piperada.

XXX ✿ **Botafumeiro,** Gran de Gràcia 81, ⊠ 08012, ℘ 218 42 30, Fax 415 58 48, Seafood – . AE E VISA JCB. HU **v**
closed Sunday dinner, Monday, Holy Week and August – **M** a la carte 4300/6800
Spec. Judías con almejas, Fideuá con marisco, Rodaballo a la brasa con salsa de limón.

XXX ✿ **Eldorado Petit,** Dolors Monserdá 51, ⊠ 08017, ℘ 204 51 53, Fax 280 57 02, – . AE E VISA JCB. – *closed Sunday and 15 days in August* – **M** a la carte 4550/6450.
Spec. Foie, bogavante y puerros al vinagre de Módena, Cigalas, gambas, espardenyas y rodaballo en suquet, Galta de ternera braseada con salsafins y setas (season). EU **y**

XXX **Paradis Roncesvalles,** vía Augusta 201, ⊠ 08021, ℘ 209 01 25, Fax 209 12 95 – . AE E VISA. FV **a**
closed Sunday dinner – **M** a la carte 3800/4550.

XX **La Petite Marmite,** Madrazo 68, ✉ 08006, ☎ 201 48 79 – ▤. AE ⓓ E VISA. ⛌ GU **f**
closed Sunday, Bank Holidays, Holy Week and August – **M** a la carte 2425/3450.

XX ❁ **Florián,** Bertrand i Serra 20, ✉ 08022, ☎ 212 46 27, Fax 418 72 30 – ▤. AE ⓓ E VISA. ⛌ FU **s**
closed Sunday and July – **M** a la carte 4700/5250
Spec. Ensalada de trufa fresca con chips y serrano (December-March), Rabo de buey alCabernet Sauvignon, Galleta de chocolate con mousse de Guanaja.

XX **El Trapío,** Esperanza 25, ✉ 08017, ☎ 211 58 17, Fax 417 10 37, ☂, « Terrace » – AE ⓓ E VISA. ⛌ EU **t**
closed Sunday and Monday lunch – **M** a la carte 3810/6400.

XX **El Asador de Aranda,** av. del Tibidabo 31, ✉ 08022, ☎ 417 01 15, ☂, Roast lamb, « Former palace » – AE E VISA. ⛌ by Balmes FU
closed Sunday dinner – **M** a la carte 3000/4950.

XX ❁ **El Racó D'En Freixa,** Sant Elíes 22, ✉ 08006, ☎ 209 75 59 – ▤. AE ⓓ E VISA. ⛌ GU **h**
closed Bank Holidays dinner, Monday, Holy Week and August – **M** a la carte 3550/5775
Spec. Ragout de cigalas, setas y crestas de gallo, Lubina grille con una declinación de tomates, Hojaldre con pies de cerdo y salsa de trufas (December-March).

XX ❁ **Gaig,** passeig de Maragall 402, ✉ 08031, ☎ 429 10 17 – ▤. AE ⓓ E VISA
closed Bank Holidays, Monday, Holy Week and August – **M** a la carte 3455/3850
N : by Travessera de Gràcia HU
Spec. Terrina de foie de pato al natural, Pie de cerdo estofado con rossinyols, Mousse de yogurt con salsa de frambuesas.

XX **Roig Robi,** Séneca 20, ✉ 08006, ☎ 218 92 22, ☂, « Patio-Terrace » – ▤. AE ⓓ E VISA. ⛌ HV **c**
closed Saturday lunch and Sunday – **M** a la carte 3575/5050.

XX **Tram-Tram,** Major de Sarriá 121, ✉ 08017, ☎ 204 85 18, ☂ – ▤. AE E VISA. ⛌ EU **d**
closed Saturday in August, Sunday and 24 December- 8 January – **M** a la carte 4240/4900.

X **Vivanda,** Major de Sarrià 134, ✉ 08017, ☎ 205 47 17, Fax 203 19 18, ☂ – ▤. AE E VISA. ⛌ EU **a**
closed Sunday, Monday lunch and Holy Week – **M** a la carte 3125/4575.

X **Es Plá,** Sant Gervasi de Cassoles 86, ✉ 08022, ☎ 212 65 54, Seafood – ▤. AE ⓓ E VISA. ⛌ FU **u**
closed Sunday dinner – **M** a la carte 3250/7200.

Typical atmosphere :

XX **Font del Gat,** passeig Santa Madrona, Montjuic, ✉ 08004, ☎ 424 02 24, ☂, Regional decor – Ⓟ. AE ⓓ E VISA. ⛌ by Av. Reina María Cristina GY
closed Monday except Bank Holidays – **M** a la carte 3400/4300.

X **La Cuineta,** Paradis, 4, ✉ 08002, ☎ 315 01 11, Fax 315 07 98, « In a 17C cellar » – ▤. AE ⓓ E VISA JCB MX **e**
M a la carte 3250/6575.

X **Can Culleretes,** Quintana 5, ✉ 08002, ☎ 317 64 85 – ▤. AE E VISA MY **c**
closed Sunday dinner, Monday and 5 to 26 July – **M** a la carte 1950/2900.

X **Los Caracoles,** Escudellers 14, ✉ 08002, ☎ 302 31 85, Fax 302 07 43, Rustic regional decor – ▤. AE ⓓ E VISA JCB. ⛌ MY **k**
M a la carte 3100/4650.

X **Pá i Trago,** Parlament 41, ✉ 08015, ☎ 441 13 20, Fax 441 13 20 – ▤. AE. ⛌ HY **a**
closed Monday and 23 Juny- 23 July – **M** a la carte 2900/4900.

X **A la Menta,** passeig Manuel Girona 50, ✉ 08034, ☎ 204 15 49, Tavern – ▤. AE ⓓ E VISA. ⛌ EV **f**
closed Sunday – **M** a la carte 3000/4350.

Environs

at Esplugues de Llobregat W : 5 km – ✉ 08950 Esplugues de Llobregat – ☎ 93 :

XXX **La Masía,** av. Països Catalans 58 ☎ 371 00 09, Fax 372 84 00, ☂, « Terrace under pine trees » – ▤ Ⓟ. AE ⓓ E VISA JCB. ⛌
closed Sunday dinner – **M** a la carte 3575/4850.

X ❁ **Quirze,** Laureá Miró 202 ☎ 371 10 84, Fax 371 65 12, ☂ – ▤ Ⓟ. AE E VISA
closed Sunday dinner, Monday, Bank Holidays and August – **M** a la carte 3800/5100
Spec. Surtido de setas salteadas (September-January), Lubina a la crema de ciboulette, Filete de ternera tres salsas.

at Sant Just Desvern W : 6 km – ✉ 08960 Sant Just Desvern – ☎ 93

🏨 **Sant Just,** Frederic Mompou 1 ☎ 473 25 17, Fax 473 24 50 – |♦| ▤ TV ☎ 🚗 – 🏛 25/450. AE ⓓ E VISA. ⛌
M 2750 – ☕ 1200 – **150 rm** 17900/22400.

at Valldoreix NW : 14,5 km - ✉ 08190 Valldoreix - ☎ 93 :

La Reserva, Rambla Mossèn Jacint Verdaguer 41 ☎ 589 21 21, Fax 674 21 00, « Former manor house », 🏊, 🌳 - 🛗 ▤ 📺 ☎ 🚗. AE ⓓ E VISA. 🚫
M 2500 - ☕ 1250 - **16 rm** 18500/33000.

at Sant Cugat del Vallés NW : 18 km - ✉ 08190 Sant Cugat del Vallés - ☎ 93 :

Novotel Barcelona-Sant Cugat 🐦, pl. Xavier Cugat NW : 3 km, ✉ apartado 122, ☎ 589 41 41, Fax 589 30 31, ⛱, 🏊 - 🛗 ▤ 📺 ☎ ♿ 🚗 🅿 - 🎤 25/300. AE ⓓ E VISA
M 3000 - ☕ 1150 - **150 rm** 14500/17900.

San Celoni 08470 Barcelona 443 G37 - pop. 11929 alt. 152 - ☎ 93.

Barcelona 49.

✕✕✕ ✿✿ **El Racó de Can Fabes,** Sant Joan 6 ☎ 867 28 51, Fax 867 38 61, Rustic decor - ▤ 🚗. AE ⓓ E VISA. 🚫
closed Sunday dinner, Monday, February and 28 Juny- 11 July - **M** a la carte 6400/7500
Spec. Royal a la esencia de trufas, Becada con setas del Montseny (hunting season), Coco con sandia crujiente..

MÁLAGA - MARBELLA

Málaga 29000 446 V16 - pop. 503 251 - ☎ 95 - Seaside resort.

See : Gibralfaro : ≤** DY - Alcazaba* (museum *) DY.

Envir. : Finca de la Concepción* N : 7 km - Road* from Málaga to Antequera ≤**

⛳18 Club de Campo of Málaga S : 9 km ☎ 38 11 20 - ⛳9 of El Candado E : 5 km ☎ 29 46 66.

✈ Málaga S : 9 km ☎ 32 20 00 - Iberia : Molina Larios 13, ✉ 29015, ☎ 21 37 31 and - Aviaco : airport ☎ 31 78 58.

🚆 ☎ 31 62 49.

⛴. to Melilla : Cía Trasmediterránea, Estación Marítima, ✉ 29016 (CZ), ☎ 22 43 93, Fax 22 48 83.

ℹ pasaje de Chinitas 4, ✉ 29015, ☎ 21 34 45 and Císter 11 (first floor), ✉ 29015, ☎ 22 79 07 - R.A.C.E. Calderería 1, ✉ 29008, ☎ 21 42 60, Fax 38 77 42.

Madrid 548 - Algeciras 133 - Córdoba 175 - Sevilla 217 - Valencia 651.

Plan on next page

Centre :

Málaga Palacio without rest, av. Cortina del Muelle 1, ✉ 29015, ☎ 221 51 85, Telex 77021, Fax 221 51 85, ≤, 🏊 - 🛗 ▤ 📺 ☎ - 🎤 25/300. AE ⓓ E VISA. 🚫 CZ **b**
☕ 950 - **223 rm** 11950/15300.

Don Curro coffee shop only, Sancha de Lara 7, ✉ 29015, ☎ 222 72 00, Telex 77366, Fax 221 59 46 - 🛗 ▤ 📺 ☎. AE ⓓ E VISA CZ **e**
☕ 625 - **105 rm** 7500/11000.

Suburbs :

Parador de Málaga-Gibralfaro 🐦, ✉ 29016, ☎ 222 19 03, Fax 222 19 02, « Magnificent setting with ≤ Málaga and sea » - ▤ rm ☎ 🅿. AE ⓓ VISA. 🚫 at Gibralfaro DY
M 3200 - ☕ 1100 - **12 rm** 11500.

✕✕✕ **Café de París,** Vélez Málaga 8, ✉ 29016, ☎ 222 50 43, Fax 222 50 43 - ▤. AE ⓓ VISA JCB. 🚫 by Pas. Cánovas del Castillo DZ
closed Sunday - **M** a la carte 2500/4400.

✕✕ **Antonio Martín,** paseo Marítimo 4, ✉ 29016, ☎ 222 21 13, Fax 221 10 18, ≤, ⛱, Large terrace by the sea - ▤ 🅿. AE ⓓ E VISA. 🚫 by Pas. Cánovas del Castillo DZ
closed Sunday dinner in winter - **M** a la carte 3200/5450.

✕ **La Taberna del Pintor,** Maestranza 6, ✉ 29016, ☎ 221 53 15, Typical decor, - ▤. AE ⓓ E VISA by Pas. Cánovas del Castillo DZ
closed Sunday - **M** (Meat) a la carte 2295/4370.

at Club de Campo E : 9 km - ✉ 29000 Málaga - ☎ 95 :

Parador de Málaga del Golf, junto al golf : 5 km, ✉ 29080 apartado 324 Málaga, ☎ 238 12 55, Fax 238 21 41, ≤, ⛱, « Overlooking the golf course », 🏊, 🎾, ⛳18 - ▤ 📺 ☎ 🅿 - 🎤 25/70. AE ⓓ VISA. 🚫
M 3200 - ☕ 1100 - **60 rm** 14000.

at Urbanización Mijas Golf by N 340 SW : 30 km - ✉ 29640 Fuengirola - ☎ 95 :

Byblos Andaluz 🐦, ☎ 247 30 50, Telex 79713, Fax 247 67 83, ≤ golf course and mountains, ⛱, Thalassotherapy facilities, « Andalusian style, situated between two golf courses », 🏋, 🏊, 🏊, 🌳, 🎾, ⛳18 ⛳18 - 🛗 ▤ 📺 ☎ 🅿 - 🎤 30/200. AE ⓓ E VISA. 🚫 rest
M 5000 - **Le Nailhac** *(dinner only, closed Wednesday)* a la carte 3300/6100 - **El Andaluz** a la carte 3300/6100 - ☕ 1700 - **144 rm** 22000/26000.

MÁLAGA

Constitución .... CY 40
Granada .... CDY
Marqués de Larios ..... CYZ 84
Nueva .... CYZ
Santa Lucía .... CY 123

Aduana (Pl. de la) ...... DY 2
Arriola (Pl. de la) .... CZ 5
Atocha (Pasillo) .... CZ 8
Calderena .... CY 13
Cánovas del Castillo (Pas.) . DZ 18
Cárcer .... CY 27
Casapalma .... CY 30
Colón (Alameda de) ...... CZ 32
Comandante Benítez
(Av. del) .... CZ 35
Compañía .... CY 37
Cortina del Muelle .... CZ 42
Especerías .... CY 56
Frailes .... CDY 61
Huerto del Conde .... DY 67
Mariblanca .... CY 77
Martínez .... CZ 86
Molina Larios .... CYZ 95
Postigo de los Abades . . CDZ 106
Reding (Paseo de) .... DY 110
Santa Isabel (Pasillo de) . . CYZ 120
Santa María .... CY 125
Sebastián Souvirón ...... CZ 130
Strachan .... CZ 133
Teatro (Pl. del) .... CY 135
Tejón y Rodríguez ...... CY 138
Tetuán (Puente de) ..... CZ 140

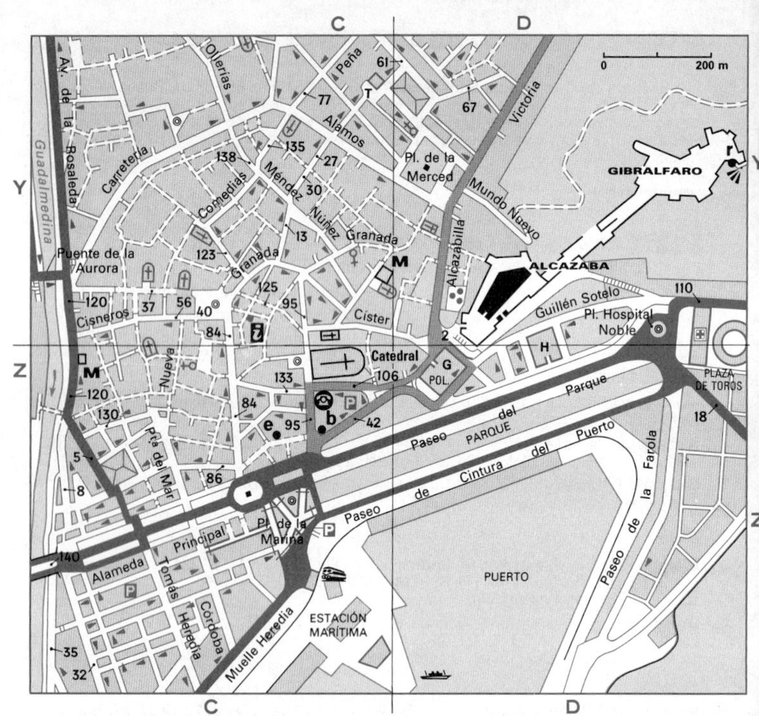

Marbella **29600** Málaga 446 W 15 - pop. 67 882 - 95 - Beach.

Río Real-Los Monteros by ① : 5 km 77 37 76 - Nueva Andalucía by ② : 5 km 78 72 00 - Aloha golf, urbanización Aloha by ② : 8 km 81 23 88 - golf Las Brisas, Nueva Andalucía by ② 81 08 75 - Iberia : paseo Marítimo 77 02 84.

Miguel Cano 1 77 14 42.

Madrid 602 ① - Algeciras 77 ② - Málaga 56 ①.

Plan opposite

Meliá Don Pepe and Grill La Farola, Finca Las Merinas by ② 277 03 00, Telex 77055, Fax 277 03 00, ≤ sea and mountains, « Subtropical plants », - - 25/400. AE E VISA.
M 4950 - 1400 - **204 rm** 21000/31000.

El Fuerte, av. del Fuerte 277 15 00, Telex 77523, Fax 282 44 11, ≤, « Terraces with garden and palm trees », heated, - - 25/600. AE E VISA JCB. rest — AB **e**
M 3100 - 1100 - **263 rm** 8900/14500.

San Cristóbal, Ramón y Cajal 3 277 12 50, Telex 77712, Fax 286 20 44 - . AE E VISA. — A **t**
M 1450 - 425 - **97 rm** 5750/7975.

Lima without rest, av. Antonio Belón 2 277 05 00, Fax 286 30 91 - . AE E VISA. — A **h**
425 - **64 rm** 5600/7000.

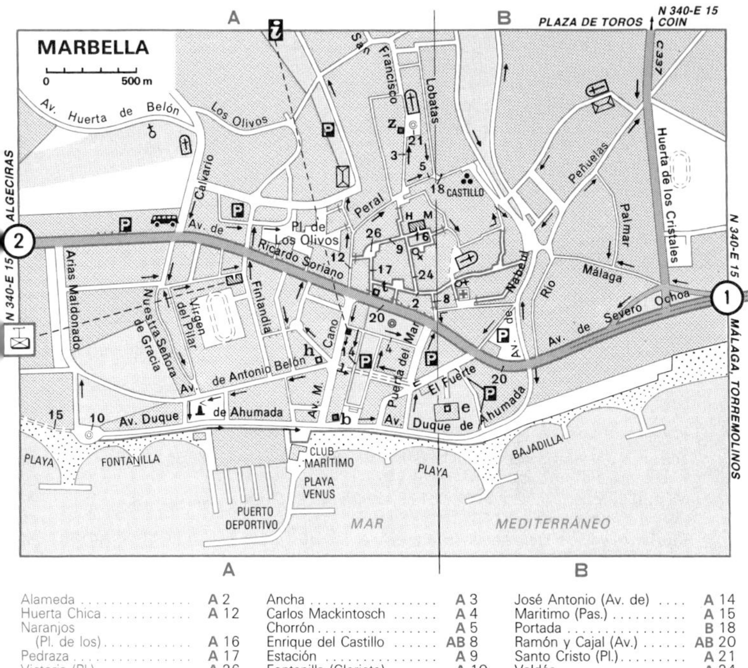

Alameda	A 2	Ancha	A 3	José Antonio (Av. de)	A 14
Huerta Chica	A 12	Carlos Mackintosch	A 4	Maritimo (Pas.)	A 15
Naranjos (Pl. de los)	A 16	Chorrón	A 5	Portada	B 18
Pedraza	A 17	Enrique del Castillo	AB 8	Ramón y Cajal (Av.)	AB 20
Victoria (Pl.)	A 26	Estación	A 9	Santo Cristo (Pl.)	A 21
		Fontanilla (Glorieta)	A 10	Valdés	A 24

XXX ✿ **La Fonda,** pl. Santo Cristo 10 ✆ 277 25 12, ⛱, « Andalusian Patio » – AE ① E VISA. ✂
closed Sunday – **M** (dinner only) a la carte 4525/6275 A **z**
Spec. Ensalada de sardinas marinadas, Dorada al estilo Fonda, Crêpe Sir Holden.

XX **Santiago,** av. Duque de Ahumada 5 ✆ 277 43 39, Fax 282 45 03, ⛱, Seafood – ▤. AE ① E VISA JCB. ✂ A **b**
M a la carte 3100/5100.

XX **Cenicienta,** av. Cánovas del Castillo 52 (by pass) ✆ 277 43 18, ⛱ – AE ① E VISA
M (dinner only) a la carte approx. 3800.

on the road to Cádiz by ② – ✉ 29600 Marbella – ✪ 95 :

Marbella Club ⛻, 3 km ✆ 277 13 00, Telex 77319, Fax 282 98 84, ⛱, « Comfortable installation in a large garden », ⛹, ⛱ heated, ⛱, ✂ – ▤ TV ☎ P – 25/180. AE ① E VISA JCB. ✂ – **M** 5000 – ☐ 2000 – **100 rm** 25500/35500.

Puente Romano ⛻, 3,5 km ✆ 277 01 00, Telex 77399, Fax 277 57 66, ⛱, « Elegant Andalusian complex in attractive garden », ⛱ heated, ⛱, ✂ – ▤ TV ☎ P – 25/170. AE ① E VISA JCB. ✂ rest
M a la carte 3950/5850 – ☐ 2000 – **218 rm** 23000/29500.

Coral Beach and Rest. Florencia, 5 km ✆ 282 45 00, Telex 79816, Fax 282 62 57, ⛹, ⛱, ⛱, ⛱ – ⛰ ▤ TV ☎ ♿ ⛟ P – 25/300. AE ① E VISA. ✂
March-October – **M** a la carte 4450/6750 – ☐ 1500 – **170 rm** 18000/23000.

Andalucía Plaza, urb. Nueva Andalucía - 7,5 km, ✉ 29660 Nueva Andalucía, ✆ 281 20 00, Telex 77086, Fax 281 47 92, ⛱, ⛹, ⛱, ⛱, ⛱, ✂ – ⛰ ▤ TV ☎ P – 25/800. AE ① E VISA JCB. ✂
M 4050 – ☐ 1080 – **415 rm** 10250/15800.

Marbella Dinamar Club 24, 6 km, ✉ 29660 Nueva Andalucía, ✆ 281 05 00, Telex 77656, Fax 281 23 46, ≤, ⛱, « Garden with ⛱ », ⛱, ✂ – ⛰ ▤ TV ☎ P – 25/150. AE ① E VISA. ✂
M 3300 – ☐ 1200 – **117 rm** 14550/18150.

Guadalpín, 1,5 km ✆ 277 11 00, Fax 277 33 34, ⛱, ⛱, ⛱ – ☎ P. AE ① E VISA. ✂ rest
M 1850 – ☐ 450 – **110 rm** 6550/9400.

XXXX **La Meridiana,** camino de la Cruz, urb. Lomas del Virrey - 3,5 km ✆ 277 61 90, Fax 282 60 24, ≤, ⛱, « Garden-Terrace » – ▤ P. AE ① E VISA – *closed Monday lunch, Twesday lunch and 15 January-15 February* – **M** (dinner only in summer) a la carte 5500/7500.

XXX **Villa Tiberio,** 2,5 km ✆ 277 17 99, ⛱, « Garden-Terrace » – P. AE E VISA. ✂
closed Sunday – **M** (dinner only) a la carte 3700/4700.

on the road to Málaga by ① - ✉ 29600 Marbella - ☎ 95 :

Los Monteros ⛰, 5,5 km ☎ 277 17 00, Telex 77059, Fax 282 58 46, ←, terrace, « Subtropical garden », gym, pool, indoor pool, tennis, golf 18 - lift ▤ TV ☎ P - 🏛 25/80. AE ⓓ E VISA. ✗
M (see also rest. **El Corzo** below) 6000 - ▭ 1500 - **170 rm** 21200/27300.

Don Carlos and Rest. Los Naranjos ⛰, 10 km ☎ 283 11 40, Telex 77481, Fax 283 34 29, ←, terrace, « Large garden », gym, pool heatet beach, tennis - lift ▤ TV ☎ P - 🏛 25/1200. AE ⓓ E VISA JCB. ✗
M a la carte 4400/7550 - ▭ 1200 - **238 rm** 19300/24500.

Artola, 12,5 km ☎ 283 13 90, Fax 283 04 50, ←, terrace, « On a golf course », pool, garden, golf 9 - lift ☎ garage P. AE E VISA. ✗ rest
M *(closed Monday in winter)* 1700 - ▭ 600 - **31 rm** 6500/8750.

XXXX ✿ **El Corzo,** Hotel Los Monteros - 5,5 km ☎ 277 17 00, Telex 77059, Fax 282 58 46, terrace - ▤ P. AE ⓓ E VISA. ✗
M a la carte 4650/6550
Spec. Terrina de hígado de pato, Merluza con almejas y angulas en salsa verde, Profiteroles rellenos de helado de vainilla con salsa de chocolate caliente.

XXX **La Hacienda,** 11,5 km and detour 1,5 km ☎ 283 12 67, Fax 283 33 28, terrace, « Rustic decor-Patio » - P. AE ⓓ E VISA JCB
closed Monday (except dinner August), Tuesday and 15 November-20 December - **M** a la carte 5700/5980.

at Puerto Banús W : 8 km - ✉ 29660 Nueva Andalucía - ☎ 95 :

XXX **Taberna del Alabardero,** Muelle Benabola ☎ 281 27 94, Fax 281 86 30, terrace - ▤. AE ⓓ E VISA. ✗ - *closed January-February* - **M** a la carte 4400/5500.

XX **Michel's,** Muelle Ribera 48 ☎ 281 55 19, terrace - ▤. AE ⓓ E VISA JCB. ✗
closed February - **M** a la carte 3450/4700.

XX **Cipriano,** edificio Levante - local 4 and 5 ☎ 281 10 77, Fax 281 10 77, terrace, Seafood - ▤. AE ⓓ E VISA JCB
M a la carte 3600/5650.

SEVILLA 41000 P 446 T 11 12 - pop. 653 833 alt. 12 - ☎ 954.

See : Giralda★★★ BX - Cathedral★★★ (Capilla mayor altarpiece★★, Capilla Real★★) BX - Reales Alcázares★★★ BXY ; (Admiral Apartment : Virgin of the Mareantes altarpiece★ Palacio de Pedro El Cruel★★★ : Ambassadors room - vault★★, - Carlos V Palace : tapices★★, gardens★) - Santa Cruz Quarter BCX - Fine Arts Museum★★ AV - Pilate's House★★ (Azulejos★★, Cupule of the staircase★) CX - María Luisa Park★★ - Archeological Museum (Carambolo tresor★). Charity Hospital★ BY.

Envir. : Itálica ←★ 9 km.

golf 9 and Racecourse Club Pineda : 3 km ☎ 461 14 00.

✈ Sevilla - San Pablo : 14 km ☎ 455 61 11 - Iberia : Almirante Lobo 3, ✉ 41001, ☎ 421 88 00 BX.

🚗 Santa Justa ☎ 453 86 86.

ℹ av. de la Constitución 21 B ✉ 41004, ☎ 422 14 04, and paseo de las Delicias ✉ 41012, ☎ 423 44 65 - R.A.C.E. (R.A.C. de Andalucía) av. Eduardo Dato 22, ✉ 41002, ☎ 463 13 50.

Madrid 550 - La Coruña/A Coruña 950 - Lisboa 417 - Málaga 217 - Valencia 682.

Plans on following pages

Alfonso XIII, San Fernando 2, ✉ 41004, ☎ 422 28 50, Telex 72725, Fax 421 60 33, terrace, « Magnificient Andalusian building », pool, garden - lift ▤ TV ☎ garage P - 🏛 25/500. AE ⓓ E VISA. ✗ BY **c**
M 6800 - ▭ 2150 - **147 rm** 28000/38000.

Radisson Príncipe de Asturias Plaza H. ⛰, Isla de La Cartuja, ✉ 41092, ☎ 446 22 22, Fax 446 04 28, gym, pool - lift ▤ TV ☎ ♿ garage P - 🏛 25/1000. AE ⓓ E VISA. ✗
M 3500 - ▭ 2100 - **295 rm** 24000/30000. N : by Torneo AV

Tryp Colón, Canalejas 1, ✉ 41001, ☎ 422 29 00, Telex 72726, Fax 422 09 38, gym - lift ▤ TV ☎ ♿ garage - 🏛 25/240. AE ⓓ E VISA JCB. ✗ AX **s**
M a la carte 3400/4450 - ▭ 1700 - **218 rm** 24800/31000.

Sol Lebreros, Luis Morales 2, ✉ 41005, ☎ 457 94 00, Telex 72772, Fax 458 27 26, terrace, gym, pool - lift ▤ TV ☎ ♿ garage - 🏛 25/500. AE ⓓ E VISA. ✗ by Luis Montoto CX
M (see rest. **la Dehesa** below) - ▭ 1500 - **439 rm** 27000/31500.

Meliá Sevilla, Doctor Pedro de Castro 1, ✉ 41004, ☎ 442 15 11, Telex 73094, Fax 442 16 08, pool - lift ▤ TV ☎ ♿ garage - 🏛 25/1000. AE ⓓ E VISA. ✗
M a la carte 3250/4050 - ▭ 1500 - **366 rm** 28000/32500. by av. de Portugal CY

Porta Coeli, av. Eduardo Dato 49, ✉ 41018, ☎ 453 35 00, Telex 72913, Fax 453 23 42, indoor pool - lift ▤ TV ☎ - 🏛. AE ⓓ E VISA. ✗ by Dematrio de los Rios CXY
M (see rest. **Florencia** below) - ▭ 950 - **243 rm** 18000/30000.

Sol Macarena, San Juan de Ribera 2, ✉ 41009, ☎ 437 58 00, Telex 72815, Fax 438 18 03, pool - lift ▤ TV ☎ ♿ - 🏛 25/700. AE ⓓ E VISA. ✗ N : barrio La Macarena
M 3500 - ▭ 1500 - **327 rm** 25000/28800.

Occidental Sevilla, av. Kansas City, ✉ 41007, ☎ 458 20 00, Fax 458 46 15, - 25/320. AE E VISA. NE : by Luis Montoto CX
M (see rest. **Florencia Pórtico** below) - 1200 - **242 rm** 16000/20000.

NH Ciudad de Sevilla, av. Manuel Siurot 25, ✉ 41013, ☎ 423 05 05, Fax 423 85 39, - 25/300. AE E VISA. S : by paseo de las Delicias BY
M 4000 - 1400 - **94 rm** 12000/18000.

Al-Andalus Palace, av. de la Palma, ✉ 41012, ☎ 423 06 00, Fax 423 19 12, - 25/800. AE E VISA JCB. S : by paseo de las Delicias BY
M 2000 - **Grill El Patio** a la carte approx. 4000 - 1500 - **678 rm** 18000/22500.

Inglaterra, pl. Nueva 7, ✉ 41001, ☎ 422 49 70, Telex 72244, Fax 456 13 36 - AE E VISA JCB. rest AX **r**
M 3000 - 750 - **116 rm** 16000/23000.

Los Seises, Segovia, ✉ 41004, ☎ 422 94 95, Fax 422 43 34, « On the 3rd patio of the Archbishop's Palace », - 25/100. AE E VISA. BX **f**
M a la carte 2800/4150 - 1500 - **42 rm** 15000/18000.

Sevilla Congresos, av. Montes Sierra, ✉ 41080, ☎ 425 90 00, Telex 73224, Fax 425 95 00, - 25/270. AE E VISA. rest
M 3900 - 1400 - **218 rm** 21600/27000. NE : by Luis Montoto CX

Pasarela without rest, av. de la Borbolla 11, ✉ 41004, ☎ 441 55 11, Telex 72486, Fax 442 07 27, - AE E VISA. by av. de Portugal CY
1200 - **82 rm** 14700/21500.

G. H. Lar, pl. Carmen Benítez 3, ✉ 41003, ☎ 441 03 61, Telex 72816, Fax 441 04 52 - 25/250. AE E VISA. CX **f**
M 2600 - 1000 - **137 rm** 12500/18000.

Husa Sevilla, Pagés del Corro 90, ✉ 41010, ☎ 434 24 12, Fax 434 27 07 - 25/220. AE E VISA. AY **a**
M 3250 - 1100 - **128 rm** 12400/19000.

NH Plaza de Armas, av. Marqués de Paradas, ✉ 41001, ☎ 490 19 92, Fax 490 12 32, heated - 25/150. AE E VISA JCB. AV **c**
M 3500 - 1200 - **262 rm** 10800/16000.

Armendariz, carret. de Su Eminencia 15, ✉ 41013, ☎ 423 29 60, Fax 423 42 30 - 25/150. AE E VISA. S : by paseo de las Delicias BY
M a la carte 3300/5200 - 1300 - **89 suites** 12000/18000

Emperador Trajano, José Laguillo 8, ✉ 41003, ☎ 441 11 11, Fax 453 57 02 - 25/150. AE E VISA. CV **a**
M 2000 - 1000 - **78 rm** 14500/16900.

Giralda, Sierra Nevada 3, ✉ 41003, ☎ 441 66 61, Telex 72417, Fax 441 93 52 - 25/250. AE E VISA. CX **e**
M 2000 - 950 - **90 rm** 13500/15900.

Derby without rest, pl. del Duque 13, ✉ 41002, ☎ 456 10 88, Telex 72709, Fax 421 33 91, Terrace with - AE E VISA. BV **r**
550 - **75 rm** 7000/9500.

Bécquer without rest, Reyes Católicos 4, ✉ 41001, ☎ 422 89 00, Telex 72884, Fax 421 44 00 - 25/45. AE E VISA. AX **v**
700 - **120 rm** 7000/10000.

Doña María without rest, Don Remondo 19, ✉ 41004, ☎ 422 49 90, Fax 421 95 46, « Elegant classic decor, Terrace with and » - 25/40. AE E VISA JCB. BX **u**
1000 - **61 rm** 10000/16000.

Monte Triana without rest, Clara de Jesús Montero 24, ✉ 41010, ☎ 434 31 11, Fax 434 33 28 - 25/50. AE E VISA.
700 - **117 rm** 7000/10000. W : by puente Isabel II AX

Alcázar without rest, Menéndez Pelayo 10, ✉ 41004, ☎ 441 20 11, Telex 72360, Fax 442 16 59 - AE E VISA. CY **u**
700 - **100 rm** 10000/15000.

Fernando III, San José 21, ✉ 41004, ☎ 421 77 08, Telex 72491, Fax 422 02 46, - 25/250. AE E VISA. rest CX **z**
M 2500 - 850 - **157 rm** 11500/16000.

América coffee shop only, Jesús del Gran Poder 2, ✉ 41002, ☎ 422 09 51, Telex 72709, Fax 421 06 26 - AE E VISA. BV **h**
550 - **100 rm** 7000/9500.

Hispalis, av. de Andalucía 52, ✉ 41006, ☎ 452 94 33, Telex 73208, Fax 467 53 13 - 25/40. AE E VISA. E : by Luis Montoto CX
M 2000 - 950 - **68 rm** 8900/11500.

Regina without rest, San Vicente 97, ✉ 41002, ☎ 490 75 75, Fax 490 75 62 - AE E VISA. by María Auxiliadora CV
800 - **72 rm** 7500/11000.

Monte Carmelo without rest, Turia 7, ✉ 41011, ☎ 427 90 00, Telex 73195, Fax 427 10 04 - AE VISA. SW : by pl. de Cuba AY
700 - **68 rm** 7000/10000.

SEVILLA

Francos . . . . BX
Sierpes . . . . BVX
Tetuán . . . . BX

Alemanes . . . . BX 12
Alfaro (Pl.) . . . . CXY 15
Almirante Apodaca . . . . CV 20
Almirante Lobo . . . . BY 22
Álvarez Quintero . . . . . . BX 23
Amparo . . . . BV 25
Aposentadores . . . . BV 28
Argote de Molina . . . . . . BX 30
Armas (Pl. de) . . . . AX 31
Banderas (Patio) . . . . . . BXY 35
Capitán Vigueras . . . . . . CY 42
Cardenal Spinola . . . . . . AV 47
Castelar . . . . AX 55
Chapina (Puente) . . . . . . AX 59
Cruces . . . . CX 75
Doña Elvira . . . . BX 95
Doña Guiomar . . . . AX 97
Escuelas Pías . . . . CV 112
Farmaceútico E.
  Murillo Herrera . . . . . . AY 115
Feria . . . . BV 123
Francisco Carrión
  Mejías . . . . CV 126
Fray Ceferino
  González . . . . BX 127
García de Vinuesa . . . . . BX 130
General Polavieja . . . . . . BX 135
Jesús de la Vera Cruz . . AV 147
José María Martínez
  Sánchez Arjona . . . . . AY 150
Julio César . . . . AX 152
Luis Montoto . . . . CX 160
Marcelino Champagnat . AY 172
Martín Villa . . . . BV 190
Mateos Gago . . . . BX 192
Murillo . . . . AV 202
Museo (Pl.) . . . . AV 205
Navarros . . . . CVX 207
O'Donnell . . . . BV 210
Pasqual de Gayangos . . AV 220
Pastor y Landero . . . . . . AX 222
Pedro del Toro . . . . AV 227
Ponce de León (Pl.) . . . . CV 234
Puente y Pellón . . . . BV 239
Puerta de Jerez . . . . BY 242
República Argentina
  (Av.) . . . . AY 255
Reyes Católicos . . . . AX 260
San Gregorio . . . . BY 272
San Juan
  de la Palma . . . . BV 277
San Pedro (Pl.) . . . . BV 286
San Sebastián (Pl.) . . . . . CY 287
Santa María
  La Blanca . . . . CX 297
Santander . . . . BY 300
Saturno . . . . CV 302
Triunfo (Pl.) . . . . BX 307
Velázquez . . . . BV 310
Venerables (Pl.) . . . . BX 312
Viriato . . . . BV 329

Inclusion in the Michelin Guide cannot be achieved by pulling strings or by offering favours.

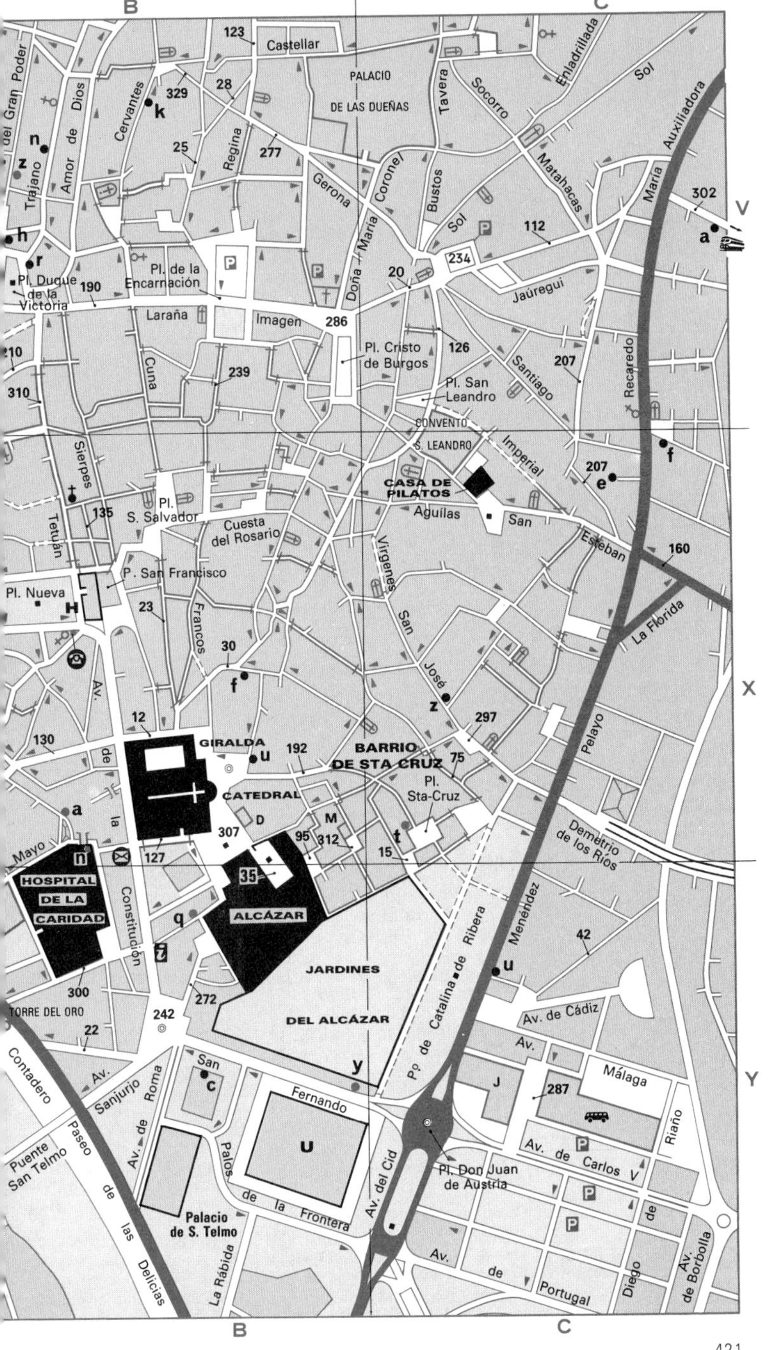

B
C
Castellar
PALACIO DE LAS DUEÑAS
Cervantes
Regina
Gerona
Coronel
Tavera
Socorro
Enladrillada
Sol
Auxiliadora
María
Matahacas
Bustos
Sol
Amor de Dios
Trajano
del Gran Poder
Pl. de la Encarnación
Pl. Duque de la Victoria
Laraña
Imagen
Doña María
Jaúregui
Pl. Cristo de Burgos
Pl. San Leandro
Santiago
Recaredo
Cuna
Sierpes
CONVENTO S. LEANDRO
Imperial
CASA DE PILATOS
Aguílas
San Esteban
Pl. S. Salvador
Cuesta del Rosario
Tetuán
Vírgenes
P. San Francisco
Pl. Nueva
Francos
San José
La Florida
Pelayo
GIRALDA
BARRIO DE STA CRUZ
Pl. Sta-Cruz
CATEDRAL
Av. de la Constitución
Demetrio de los Ríos
Mayo
HOSPITAL DE LA CARIDAD
ALCÁZAR
JARDINES DEL ALCÁZAR
Menéndez
Pelayo
Pº de Catalina de Ribera
Av. de Cádiz
TORRE DEL ORO
Contadero
Paseo de las Delicias
Av. Sanjurjo
Av. de Roma
San
Fernando
Av. del Cid
Av. Málaga
Pl. Don Juan de Austria
Av. de Carlos V
Riaño
Puente San Telmo
Palos de la Frontera
Palacio de S. Telmo
La Rábida
Av. de Portugal
Diego de Riaño
Av. de Borbolla
V
X
Y

Cervantes without rest, Cervantes 10 ✆ 490 05 52, Fax 490 05 36 – |‡| ▤ TV ☎ 🚗. AE ⓓ E VISA. ✗ BV **k**
☕ 800 – **48 rm** 9200/11500.

La Rábida, Castelar 24, ✉ 41001, ✆ 422 09 60, Telex 73062, Fax 422 43 75, 🍽 – |‡| ▤ rm TV ☎. ✗ rest AX **d**
M 1750 – ☕ 350 – **100 rm** 5000/8000.

Venecia without rest, Trajano 31, ✉ 41002, ✆ 438 11 61, Fax 490 19 55 – |‡| ▤ TV ☎ 🚗. AE VISA. ✗ BV **n**
☕ 400 – **24 rm** 12000/20000.

Montecarlo, Gravina 51, ✉ 41001, ✆ 421 75 03, Telex 72729, Fax 421 68 25 – |‡| ▤ rest TV ☎. AE ⓓ E VISA. ✗ AX **e**
M 1800 – ☕ 500 – **51 rm** 9000/14000.

XXX ✿ **Egaña Oriza,** San Fernando 41, ✉ 41004, ✆ 422 72 11, Fax 421 04 29, « Winter garden » – ▤. AE ⓓ E VISA. ✗ BY **y**
closed Saturday lunch, Sunday and August – **M** a la carte 5400/6600
Spec. Marinado de bacalao a la vinagreta de centollo (Spring), Salmorejo con ostras, jamón y huevos de codorniz (Autumn), Tórtolas al vino tinto (September)..

XXX **Florencia,** av. Eduardo Dato 49, ✉ 41018, ✆ 453 35 00, Telex 72913, Fax 453 23 42, Tasteful decor – ▤. AE ⓓ E VISA. ✗ by Demetrio de los Rios CXY
closed August – **M** a la carte 2800/4725.

XXX **El Burladero,** Canalejas 1, ✉ 41001, ✆ 422 29 00, Telex 72726, Fax 422 09 38, Bullfighting theme – ▤. AE ⓓ E VISA. ✗ – *closed August* – **M** a la carte 3500/4150. AX **a**

XXX **Pello Roteta,** Farmacéutico Murillo Herrera 10, ✉ 41010, ✆ 427 84 17, Basque rest – ▤. AE ⓓ E VISA. ✗ AY **y**
closed Sunday and 15 August-15 September – **M** a la carte 2800/4000.

XXX **Florencia Pórtico,** av. Kansas City, ✉ 41007, ✆ 458 20 00, Fax 458 46 15 – ▤. AE ⓓ E VISA. ✗ NE : by Luis Montoto CX
M a la carte 3200/4700.

XXX **La Dehesa,** Luis Morales 2, ✉ 41005, ✆ 457 94 00, Telex 72772, Fax 458 23 09, Typical Andalusian decor-Meat dishes – ▤. AE ⓓ E. ✗ by Luis Montoto CX
M a la carte 3470/4850.

XXX **Rincón de Curro,** Virgen de Luján 45, ✉ 41011, ✆ 445 02 38 – ▤. AE ⓓ E VISA. ✗
closed Sunday and August – **M** a la carte 4100/5000. by pl. de Cuba AY

XX **Ox's,** Betis 61, ✉ 41010, ✆ 427 95 85, Fax 427 84 65, Basque rest – ▤. AE ⓓ E VISA. ✗
closed Sunday in Summer, Sunday dinner in winter and August – **M** a la carte 4600/5500.

XX **La Isla,** Arfe 25, ✉ 41001, ✆ 421 26 31, Fax 456 22 19 – ▤. AE ⓓ E VISA. ✗ BX **a**
closed 15 August-15 September – **M** a la carte 4200/5400.

XX **Río Grande,** Betis, ✉ 41010, ✆ 427 39 56, Fax 427 98 46, ≤, 🍽, « Large terrace on riverside » – ▤. AE ⓓ E VISA JCB AY **r**
M a la carte 3200/4300.

XX **Jamaica,** Jamaica 16, ✉ 41012, ✆ 461 12 44, Fax 461 10 50 – ▤. AE ⓓ VISA. ✗
closed Sunday dinner and August – **M** a la carte 2850/4400.
by paseo de las Delicias BY

XX **La Encina,** Virgen de Aguas Santas 6-access E, ✉ 41011, ✆ 445 93 22 – ▤. AE ⓓ E VISA JCB. ✗ by pl. de Cuba AY
closed Sunday, 1 to 15 January and 1 to 15 August – **M** a la carte approx. 4500.

XX **La Albahaca,** pl. Santa Cruz 12, ✉ 41004, ✆ 422 07 14, Fax 456 12 04, 🍽, « Former manor house » – ▤. AE ⓓ E VISA JCB. ✗ CX **t**
closed Sunday – **M** a la carte 4400/5400.

XX **Rincón de Casana,** Santo Domingo de la Calzada 13, ✉ 41018, ✆ 453 17 10, Fax 464 49 74, Regional decor – ▤. AE ⓓ E VISA. ✗ by Av. E. Dato DX
closed Sunday in July and August – **M** a la carte 3575/4475.

X **El Cantábrico,** Jesús del Gran Poder 20, ✉ 41002, ✆ 438 73 03 – ▤. AE E VISA. ✗
closed Sunday, Bank Holidays dinner and August – **M** a la carte 2650/4050. BV **z**

X **Los Alcázares,** Miguel de Mañara 10, ✉ 41004, ✆ 421 31 03, Fax 456 18 29, 🍽, Regional decor – ▤. AE ⓓ VISA. ✗ BY **q**
closed Sunday – **M** a la carte 2775/3825.

on the road to Utrera – ✉ 41089 sevilla – ☏ 95 :

Palmera Real, ✆ 412 41 11, Fax 412 43 44, 🏊, 🎾 – |‡| ▤ TV ☎ 🅟 – 🏛 25/300. AE VISA. ✗
M 2800 – ☕ 800 – **134 rm** 12000/15000. SE : by av. de Carlos V CY

at San Juan de Aznalfarache W : 4 km – ✉ 41920 San Juan de Aznalfarache – ☏ 95 :

Alcora 🐚, carret. de Tomares ✆ 476 94 00, Fax 476 94 98, ≤, « Patio with plants », 🏋, 🏊 – |‡| ▤ TV ☎ ♿ 🚗 🅟 – 🏛 25/600. AE ⓓ E VISA. ✗
M 3000 – ☕ 1500 – **421 rm** 16000/20000.

Betania, cerro del Sagrado Corazón ✆ 476 80 33, Fax 476 44 99, ≤, Former convent, « Terrace, garden with 🏊 » – |‡| ▤ TV ☎ 🅟 – 🏛 25/120. AE ⓓ E VISA. ✗ rest
closed August – **M** 3000 – ☕ 900 – **97 rm** 14400/18000.

at Benacazón W : 23 km – ✉ 41805 Benacazón – ☎ 95 :

Andalusi Park H., Autopista A 49 salida 6 ☎ 570 56 00, Fax 570 50 79, « Arabian style building-garden », ⛳, 🏊, 🎾 – |‡| ▤ 📺 ☎ 🅿 – 🏛 25/400. AE ⓓ E VISA. ✻
M Los Olivos a la carte 4000/5100 - Al'Mutamid – ☕ 1500 – **200 rm** 16700/20900.

at Sanlúcar la Mayor W : 27 km – ✉ 41800 Sanlúcar la Mayor – ☎ 95 :

Hacienda Benazuza 🐦, carret. de Benacazón ☎ 570 33 44, Fax 570 34 10, « On a 10C arabian farmhouse », 🏊, 🐎, 🎾 – |‡| ▤ 📺 ☎ 🅿 – 🏛 25/300. AE ⓓ E VISA. ✻ rest
M 5000 - **La Alquería** a la carte 3800/6275 - **Patio** *(dinner only)* a la carte 3100/4500 – ☕ 1500 – **50 rm** 29000/37000.

at Carmona E : 33 km – ✉ 41410 Carmona – ☎ 95 :

Parador Alcázar del Rey Don Pedro 🐦, ☎ 414 10 10, Telex 72992, Fax 414 17 12, ≤ Corbones fertile plain, « Mudejar style », 🏊 – |‡| ▤ 📺 ☎ 🅿 – 🏛 25/100. AE ⓓ VISA. ✻
M 3500 – ☕ 1200 – **63 rm** 16000.

Casa de Carmona, pl. de Lasso 1 ☎ 414 33 00, Fax 414 37 52, « 16C palace, antique furnishings » – |‡| ▤ 📺 ☎ 🚗. AE ⓓ E VISA. ✻ rest
M a la carte 4275/5600 – ☕ 1600 – **30 rm** 16000/19000.

Alcázar de la Reina, pl. de Lasso 2 ☎ 419 00 64, Fax 414 28 32, 🏊 – |‡| ▤ 📺 ☎ 🚗 – 🏛 25/230. AE ⓓ VISA. ✻
M 3000 – ☕ 1000 – **68 rm** 11000/14000.

VALENCIA 46000 446 N 28 29 – pop. 751 734 alt. 13 – ☎ 96.

See : The Old town★ : Cathedral★ (El Miguelete★) EX – Palacio de la Generalidad★ (ceilings★) EX – Lonja★ (silkhall★★, Maritime consulate hall : ceiling★) DY – Ceramics Museum★★ (Museo de Cerámica : palacio del Marqués de Dos Aguas★) EY **M1** – San Pío V Museum★ (valencian primitifs★★) FX – Patriarc College or of the Corpus Christi★ (museum : Passion triptych★) EY **N** – Serranos Towers★ EX.

⛳9 of Manises W : 12 km ☎ 379 08 50 – ⛳18 Club Escorpión NW : 19 km by Liria Road ☎ 160 12 11 – ⛳18 El Saler, Parador Luis Vives E : 15 km ☎ 161 11 86.

✈ Valencia - Manises Airport W : 9,5 km ☎ 152 14 51 – Iberia : Paz 14, ✉ 46003, ☎ 351 37 39.

🚘 ☎ 351 00 43.

⛴. To the Balearic and Canary Islands : Cía. Trasmediterránea, av. Manuel Soto Ingeniero 15, ✉ 46024, ☎ 367 07 04, Fax 367 33 45.

ℹ pl. del Ayuntamiento 1, ✉ 46002, ☎ 351 04 17, Paz 48, ✉ 46003, ☎ 352 28 97, and Airport, ☎ 370 95 00 – R.A.C.E. (R.A.C. de Valencia) av. Jacinto Benavente 25, ✉ 46005, ☎ 374 94 05.

Madrid 351 – Albacete 183 – Alicante (by coast) 174 – Barcelona 361 – Bilbao 606 – Castellón de la Plana 75 – Málaga 654 – Sevilla 682 – Zaragoza 330.

Plans on following pages

Meliá Valencia, av. Baleares 2, ✉ 46023, ☎ 360 73 00, Telex 64252, Fax 360 89 21, 🏊 – |‡| ▤ 📺 ☎ 🅿 – 🏛 25/250. AE ⓓ E VISA. ✻ — by Puente de Aragón FZ
M 4400 – ☕ 1400 – **314 rm** 15725/19950.

Astoria Palace and Rest Vinatea, pl. Rodrigo Botet 5, ✉ 46002, ☎ 352 67 37, Telex 62733, Fax 352 80 78 – |‡| ▤ 📺 ☎ – 🏛 25/500. AE ⓓ E VISA. ✻ — EY **p**
M a la carte 2800/4300 – ☕ 1000 – **207 rm** 14800/19200.

Conqueridor, Cervantes 9, ✉ 46007, ☎ 352 29 10, Fax 352 28 83 – |‡| ▤ 📺 ☎ 🚗. AE VISA. ✻ — DZ **b**
M 2500 – ☕ 1000 – **60 rm** 12600/19800.

Reina Victoria, Barcas 4, ✉ 46002, ☎ 352 04 87, Telex 64755, Fax 352 04 87 – |‡| ▤ 📺 ☎ – 🏛 25/50. AE ⓓ E VISA. ✻ — EY **s**
M 3000 – ☕ 950 – **97 rm** 11350/18600.

Dimar coffee shop only, Gran Vía Marqués del Turia 80, ✉ 46005, ☎ 395 10 30, Fax 395 19 26 – |‡| ▤ 📺 ☎ 🚗 – 🏛 25/80. AE ⓓ E VISA. ✻ — FZ **q**
☕ 1100 – **107 rm** 9925/16500.

NH Ciudad de Valencia, av. del Puerto 214, ✉ 46023, ☎ 367 75 00, Telex 63069, Fax 367 98 64 – |‡| ▤ 📺 ☎ 🚗 – 🏛 30/80. AE ⓓ E VISA. ✻
M a la carte 3000/5000 – ☕ 1000 – **149 rm** 10500/16000. — SE by Puente de Aragón FZ

NH Abashiri, av. Ausias March 59, ✉ 46013, ☎ 373 28 52, Telex 63017, Fax 373 49 66 – |‡| ▤ 📺 ☎ 🚗 – 🏛 30/250. AE ⓓ E VISA. ✻ — S by Castellón EZ
M 3000 – ☕ 1000 – **105 rm** 10500/16000.

Expo H. coffee shop only, av. Pío XII-4, ✉ 46009, ☎ 347 09 09, Telex 63212, Fax 348 31 81, 🏊 – |‡| ▤ 📺 ☎ – 🏛 25/500. AE ⓓ E VISA JCB. ✻ — by Cuart DX
☕ 900 – **400 rm** 7900/13500.

Inglés, Marqués de Dos Aguas 6, ✉ 46002, ☎ 351 64 26, Telex 62228, Fax 394 02 51 – |‡| ▤ 📺 ☎. AE ⓓ E VISA JCB. ✻ — EY **m**
M 1700 – ☕ 700 – **62 rm** 7500/13750.

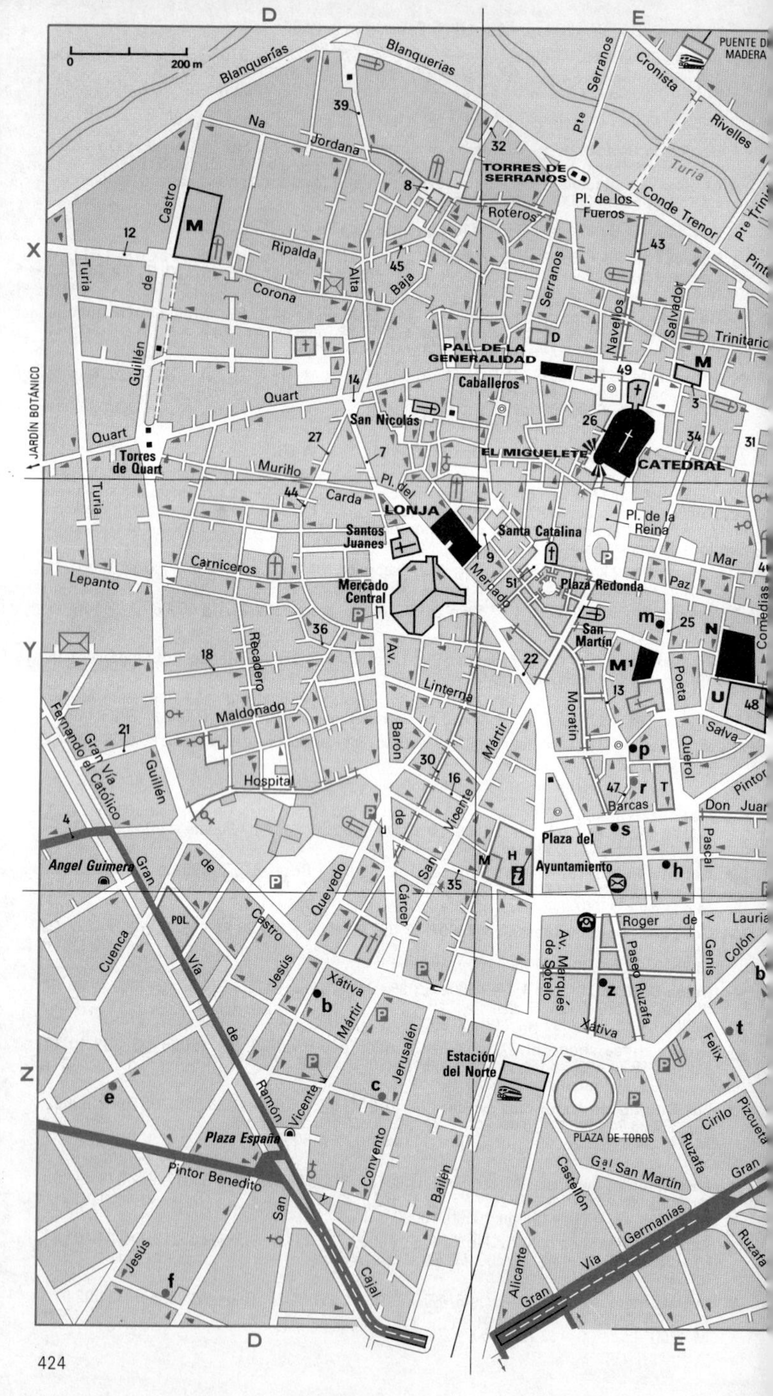

D
E
0
200 m
PUENTE DE MADERA
Blanquerías
Blanquerías
Na Jordana
39
32
TORRES DE SERRANOS
Pte Serranos
Cronista
Rivelles
Turia
Pl. de los Fueros
Conde Trenor
Pte Trinidad
Castro
M
12
X
Turia
de
Ripalda
Roteros
8
45
Baja
Alta
Corona
Serranos
43
Navellos
Salvador
Trinitarios
D
PAL. DE LA GENERALIDAD
Caballeros
49
M
3
Guillén
Quart
14
San Nicolás
26
34
31
JARDÍN BOTÁNICO
Quart
Torres de Quart
27
7
EL MIGUELETE
CATEDRAL
Murillo
Pl. del
Turia
44
Carda
LONJA
Pl. de la Reina
Santos Juanes
Santa Catalina
9
Mar
Carniceros
Lepanto
Mercado Central
Mercado
51
Plaza Redonda
Paz
Comedias
25
N
San Martín
36
Y
18
Av.
Recadero
22
M1
Linterna
Poeta
U
48
13
Maldonado
Salva
Fernando el Católico
Gran Vía
21
Barón
Mártir
Moratín
p
Querol
30
16
Hospital
Guillén
47
r
T
Pintor
Don Juan
Barcas
Vicente
de
4
s
Pascal
Plaza del
Angel Guimera
Gran
de
M
H
San
Ayuntamiento
h
35
Quevedo
Cárcel
POL.
Castro
Roger de Lauria
Cuenca
Vía
Av. Marqués de Sotelo
Paseo Ruzafa
Genís
Colón
Jesús
Xátiva
b
b
Mártir
z
de
Xátiva
Jerusalén
t
Feliz
Estación del Norte
Z
Ramón
c
e
Vicente
Cirilo
Pizcueta
PLAZA DE TOROS
Plaza España
Convento
Gal San Martín
Ruzafa
Pintor Benedito
Castellón
Gran
Bailén
San
y
Germanías
Ruzafa
Jesús
Cajal
Vía
f
Alicante
Gran
D
E

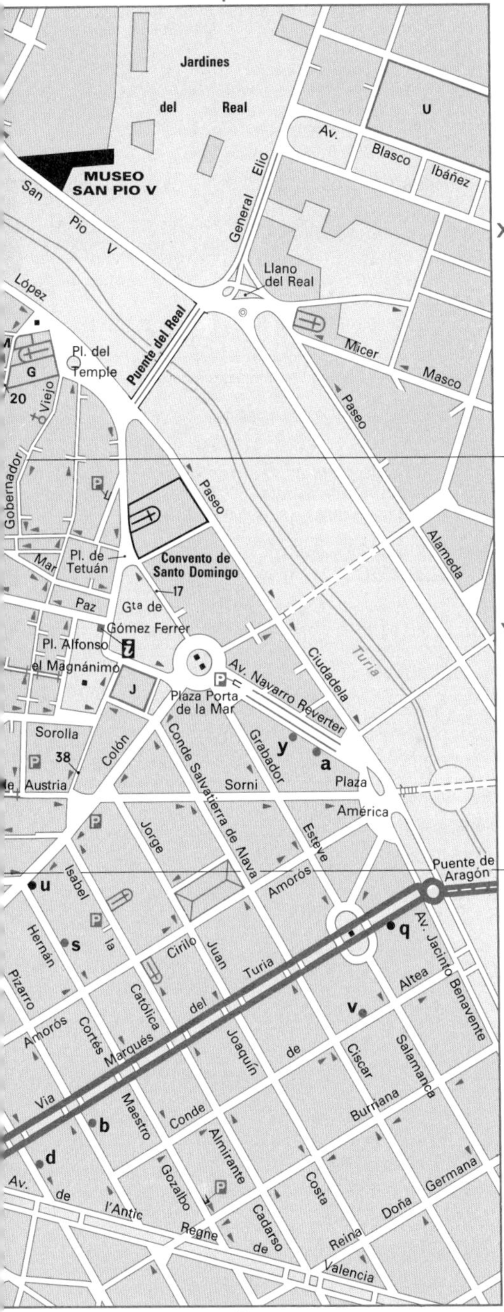

VALENCIA

Street	Grid	No.
Ayuntamiento (Pl. del)	EY	
Marqués de Sotelo (Av.)	EZ	
Pascual y Genís	EYZ	
Paz	EFY	
San Vicente Mártir	DY	
Almirante	EX	2
Almudin	EX	3
Ángel Guimerá	DY	4
Bolsería	DX	7
Carmen (Pl. del)	DX	8
Dr. Collado (Pl.)	EY	9
Dr. Sanchís Bergón	DX	12
Embajador Vich	EY	13
Esparto (Pl. del)	DX	14
Garrigues	DY	16
General Palanca	FY	17
Guillem Sorolla	DY	18
Maestres	FX	20
Maestro Palau	DY	21
María Cristina (Av.)	EY	22
Marqués de Dos Aguas	EY	25
Micalet	EX	26
Moro Zeit	DX	27
Músico Peydro	DY	30
Nápoles y Sicilia (Pl.)	EX	31
Padre Huérfanos	EX	32
Palau	EX	34
Periodista Azzati	DY	35
Píe de la Cruz	DY	36
Poeta Quintana	FY	38
Salvador Giner	DX	39
San Vicente Ferrer (Pl.)	EY	40
Santa Ana (Muro)	EX	43
Santa Teresa	DY	44
Santo Tomás	DX	45
Transits	EY	47
Universidad	EY	48
Virgen (Pl. de la)	EX	49
Virgen de la Paz (Pl.)	EY	51

We suggest:

For a successful tour, that you prepare it in advance.

Michelin maps and guides will give you much useful information on route planning, places of interest, accommodation, prices, etc.

Renasa coffee shop only, av. Cataluña 5, 46010, 369 24 50, Fax 393 18 24 – 25/75. W by Puente del Real FX
550 – **73 rm** 6700/10900.

Llar without rest, Colón 46, 46004, 352 84 60, Fax 351 90 00 – 25/30. FZ **u**
600 – **50 rm** 6750/9350.

Sorolla without rest, no, Convento de Santa Clara 5, 46002, 352 33 92, Fax 352 14 65 – EZ **z**
50 rm 5200/9100.

Continental without rest, Correos 8, 46002, 351 09 26, Fax 351 09 26 – – 400 – **43 rm** 5250/8500. EY **h**

Chambelán, Chile 4, 46021, 393 37 74, Fax 393 37 72 – by Puente de Aragón FZ
closed Saturday lunch, Sunday and Holy Week – **M** a la carte 5300/7000.

Eladio, Chiva 40, 46018, 384 22 44 – by Cuart DX
closed Sunday and August – **M** a la carte 4350/5450.

Oscar Torrijos, Dr. Sumsi 4, 46005, 373 29 49 –
closed Sunday and 15 August-15 September – **M** a la carte 3800/5900
by av. Antic Regne de Valencia EF
Spec. Arroz de langosta, Ensalada tibia de bogavante a la vinagreta de tomate (October-May), Tarta fina de manzana con hojaldre.

La Hacienda, Navarro Reverter 12, 46004, 373 18 59, Fax 138 89 62 – FY **y**
closed Saturday lunch, Sunday and Holy Week – **M** a la carte 5300/6300.

Derby, Navarro Reverter 16, 46004, 334 86 02, Fax 374 20 02 –
close Saturday lunch, Sunday and August – **M** a la carte 3300/4500. FY **a**

Rías Gallegas, Matemático Marzal 11, 46007, 357 20 07, Galician rest – DZ **c**
closed Sunday and August – **M** a la carte 3950/5200.

Versalles, Dolores Alcayde 14, 46007, 342 37 38, Fax 342 18 04, « In a villa » – by San Vicente Mártir DZ
closed Saturday lunch, Sunday, Holy Week and August – **M** a la carte 3650/5075.

Galbìs, Marvá 28, 46007, 380 94 73, Fax 380 06 54 – DZ **f**
closed Saturday lunch, Sunday, and 1 August- 5 September – **M** a la carte 3200/4850.

Comodoro, Transits 3, 46002, 351 38 15 – EY **r**
closed Saturday lunch, Sunday, Bank Holidays and August – **M** a la carte 3200/4400.

Kailuze, Gregorio Mayáns 5, 46005, 374 39 99, Basque rest – FZ **d**
closed Saturday lunch, Sunday, Bank Holidays and August – **M** a la carte 3050/4750.

Lionel, Pizarro 9, 46004, 351 65 66 – EZ **b**
closed Sunday dinner and 15 to 31 August – **M** a la carte 2495/2920.

El Gastrónomo, av. Primado Reig 149, 46020, 369 70 36 – by Puente del Real FX
closed Sunday, Holy Week and August – **M** a la carte 2950/3900.

El Gourmet, Taquígrafo Martí 3, 46005, 395 25 09 – FZ **b**
closed Sunday and August – **M** a la carte 2250/3100.

José Mari, Estación Marítima, 1°, 46024, 367 20 15, Basque rest –
closed Sunday and August – **M** a la carte 2700/4300. by Puente de Aragón FZ

Civera, Lérida 11, 46009, 347 59 17, Seafood –
closed Monday and August – **M** a la carte 2800/4800. by Pl. de Santa Mónica EX

Mey Mey, Historiador Diago 19, 46007, 384 07 47, Chinese rest. –
closed Sunday in summer, Sunday dinner and Monday lunch, Holy Week and 15 to 31 August – **M** carta 1520 a 2285. DZ **e**

Asador de Aranda, Félix Pizcueta 9, 46004, 352 97 91, Roast lamb – EZ **t**
closed Sunday dinner and Holy Week – **M** a la carte 2645/3300.

Eguzki, av. Baleares, 1, 46023, 369 90 60, Basque rest. –
closed Sunday, Bank Holidays and August – **M** a la carte 3400/4600.
by Puente de Aragón FZ

El Plat, Conde de Altea 41, 46005, 395 15 11, Rices dishes – FZ **v**
closed Monday, Bank Holidays dinner and Sunday dinner – **M** a la carte 2450/4050.

Palace Fesol, Hernán Cortés 7, 46004, 352 93 23, Fax 352 93 23, « Regional decor » – FZ **s**
closed Sunday dinner, Monday, Holy Week and 15 to 30 August – **M** a la carte 2900/3800.

by road C 234 NW : 8,5 km – 46035 Valencia – 96 :

Feria, av. de las Ferias, 2 364 44 11, Telex 61079, Fax 364 54 83 – 25/60. rest
M a la carte 3350/4650 – 800 – **136 rm** 10700/25500.

at El Saler SE : 8 km – ✉ 46012 Valencia – ☎ 96

Sidi Saler ⛰, SE : 3 km ✆ 161 04 11, Telex 64208, Fax 161 08 38, ←, 🏊, 🏊, 🌳, 🎾 – 🛗 ≡ TV ☎ P – 🎤 25/300. AE ① E VISA. ✻ rest
M 2950 – ☕ 1400 – **276 rm** 12000/17000.

Parador Luis Vives ⛰, SE : 7 km ✆ 161 11 86, Telex 61069, Fax 162 70 16, ←, « In the middle of the golf course », 🏊, 🎾, 🏌18 – 🛗 ≡ TV ☎ P – 🎤 25/300. AE ① VISA. ✻
M 3500 – ☕ 1200 – **58 rm** 15000.

at Manises – on the Airport road NW : 9,5 km – ✉ 46940 Manises – ☎ 96 :

Sol Azafata, autopista del aeropuerto ✆ 154 61 00, Telex 61451, Fax 153 20 19 – 🛗 ≡ TV ☎ 🚗 P – 🎤 25/300. AE ① E VISA. ✻
M 3100 – ☕ 1000 – **130 rm** 10000/12500.

at Puçol N : 25 km by motorway A 7 – ✉ 46760 Puçol – ☎ 96

Monte Picayo ⛰, urbanización Monte Picayo ✆ 142 01 00, Telex 62087, Fax 142 21 68, 🍽, « On a hillside with ← », 🏊, 🌳, 🎾 – 🛗 ≡ TV ☎ P – 🎤 25/600. AE ① E VISA. ✻
M a la carte 3100/4200 – ☕ 1250 – **82 rm** 15950/19950.

Sweden

Sverige

STOCKHOLM - GOTHENBURG

PRACTICAL INFORMATION

LOCAL CURRENCY

Swedish Kronor: 100 SEK = 13.95 US $ = 11.70 Ecus (Jan. 93).

TOURIST INFORMATION

In Stockholm, the Tourist Centre is situated in the Sweden House, entrance from Kungsträdgården at Hamngatan. Open Mon-Fri 9am-5pm. Sat. and Sun. 9am-2pm. Telephone weekdays 08/789 20 00, weekends to Excursion Shop and Tourist Centre 08/789 24 28 or 789 24 29. For Gothenburg, see information in the text of the town under ℹ.

FOREIGN EXCHANGE

Banks are open between 9.00am and 3.00pm on weekdays only. Some banks in the centre of the city are usually open weekdays 9am to 5.30pm. Most large hotels have exchange facilities, and Arlanda airport has banking facilities between 7am to 10pm seven days a week.

MEALS

At lunchtime, follow the custom of the country and try the typical buffets of Scandinavian specialities.
At dinner, the a la carte and the menus will ofter you more conventional cooking.

SHOPPING

In the index of street names, those printed in red are where the principal shops are found.
The main shopping streets in the centre of Stockholm are: Hamngatan, Biblioteksgatan, Drottninggatan.
In the Old Town mainly Västerlänggatan.

THEATRE BOOKINGS

Your hotel porter will be able to make your arrangements or direct you to Theatre Booking Agents.

CAR HIRE

The international car hire companies have branches in Stockholm, Gothenburg, Arlanda and Landvetter airports. Your hotel porter should be able to give details and help you with your arrangements.

TIPPING

Hotels and restaurants normally include a service charge of 15 per cent.
Doormen, baggage porters etc. are generally given a gratuity.
Taxi included 10 % tip in the amount shown on the meter.

SPEED LIMITS - SEAT BELTS

The maximum permitted speed on motorways and dual carriageways is 110 km/h - 68 mph and 90 km/h - 56 mph on other roads except where a lower speed limit is signposted.
The wearing of seat belts is compulsory for drivers and passengers.

Stockholm

Sverige 985 M 15 - pop. 674 459 Greater Stockholm 1 491 726 - ☎ 08.

See : Old Town★★★ (Gamla Stan) : Stortorget★★, AZ, Köpmangatan★★ AZ **35**, Österlånggatan★★ AZ ; Vasa Museum★★★ (Vasamuseet) DY, Skansen Open-Air Museum★★★ DY.
Royal Palace★★ (Kungliga Slottet) AZ ; Changing of the Guard★★ ; Apartments★★, Royal Armoury★★, Treasury★ ; Museum★ ; Stockholm Cathedral★★ (Storkyrkan) AZ ; Riddarholmen Church★★ (Riddarholmskyrkan) AZ ; City Hall★★ (Stadshuset) BYH : ☼★★★, Djurgården DYZ ; Prins Eugens Waldemarsudde★★ (house and gallery), Rosendal Palace★, Thiel Gallery★ ; Gröna Lunds Tivoli★ DZ.
Kaknäs TV Tower★ (Kaknästornet) ☼★★★ DY ; Gustav Adolf Square★ (Gustav Adolfs Torg) CY **16** ; Kings Gardens★ (Kungsträdgården) CY ; House of the Nobility★ (Riddarhuset) AZ ; German Church★ (Tyska Kyrkan) AZ ; Fjällgatan★ DZ ; Sergels Torg CY **54** - Hötorget★ CY **20**.

Museums : Museum of National Antiquities★★★ (Historiska Museet) DY ; National Art Gallery★★ (Nationalmuseum) DY **M1** ; Nordic Museum★★ (Nordiska Museet) DY **M2** ; Museum of Far Eastern Antiquities★★ (Ostasiatiska Museet) DY **M3** ; Museum of Modern Art (Moderna Museet) DY **M4** ; National Maritime Museum★★ (Sjöhistoriska Museet) DY ; Hallwyl Collection★ (Hallwylska Museet) CY **M5** ; City Museum★ (Stads Museet) CZ **M6** ; Strindberg Museum★ BX **M7** ; Museum of Medieval Stockholm★ (Stockholms Medeltidsmuseum) CY **M8** ; Swedish Museum of Natural History (Naturhistoriska Riksmuseet : Cosmonova★) CX.

Outskirts : Drottningholm Palace★★ (Drottningholms Slott) W : 12 km BY ; Apartments★★, Gardens★★, Court Theatre★, Chinese Pavilion★ ; Tours by boat★★ (in summer) : Under the Bridges★★ ; Archipelago★★ (Vaxholm, Möja, Sandhamn, Utö), Mälarenlake★ (Gripsholm, Skokloster) ; Haga Park and Pavilion of Gustav III★ (N : 4 km) BX ; Millesgården★ (E : 4 km) DX.

18 Svenska Golfförbundet (Swedish Golf Federation) ☎ 622 15 00.

✈ Stockholm-Arlanda N : 41 km ☎ 797 60 00 - SAS : Flygcity, Klarabergsviadukten 72 ☎ 020/797 40 58, Reservations 020/91 01 50 - Air-Terminal : opposite main railway station.

Motorail for Southern Europe : SJ Travel-Agency, Vasagatan 22 ☎ 24 00 90.

To Finland : contact Silja Line ☎ 22 21 40 or Viking Line ☎ 714 56 00 - Excursions by boat : contact Stockholm Information Service (see below).

ℹ Stockholm Information Service, Tourist Centre, Sverigehuset, Hamngatan 27 ☎ 789 20 00 - Motormännens Riksförbund ☎ 782 38 00 - Kungl. Automobilklubben (Royal Automobile Club) Gyllenstiernsgatan 4 ☎ 660 00 55.

Hamburg 935 - København 630 - Oslo 522.

STOCKHOLM

Street	Grid	No.
Biblioteksgatan	CY	2
Drottninggatan	BX, CY	10
Gallerian	CY	14
Grev Turegatan	CY	18
Hamngatan	CY	
Kungsgatan	BCY	
Sergelgatan	CY	52
Vasterlänggatan	AZ	
Osterlänggatan	AZ	
Birger Jarlsgatan	CXY	3
Brunkebergstorg	CY	5
Brunnsgränd	AZ	6
Bryggargatan	BY	8
Djurgårdsbron	DY	9
Erstagatan	DZ	13
Gustav Adolfs Torg	CY	16
Götgatan	CZ	17
Herkulesgatan	CY	19
Hötorget	CY	20
Järntorget	AZ	21
Järntorgsgatan	AZ	23
Kindstugatan	AZ	24
Klarabergsgatan	CY	25
Klarabergsviadukten	BY	27
Kornhamnstorg	AZ	28
Kungsbron	BY	30
Kungsträdgårdsgatan	CY	32
Källargränd	AZ	34
Köpmangatan	AZ	35
Lilla Nygatan	AZ	37
Munkbrogatan	AZ	40
Myntgatan	AZ	41
Norrbro	CY	43
Norrlandsgatan	CY	44
Nybroplan	CY	46
Odenplan	BX	47
Olof Palmes Gata	BY	48
Riddarhusgränd	AZ	49
Riddarhustorget	AZ	50
Rådhusgränd	AZ	51
Sergels Torg	CY	54
Slottskajen	AZ	55
Slussplan	AZ	56
Stadshusbron	BY	57
Stallgatan	CY	59
Storkyrkobrinken	AZ	60
Strömbron	CY	61
Strömgatan	CY	63
Södermalmstorg	CZ	64
Södra Blasieholmshamnen	CY	66
Tegelbacken	CY	67
Tegnérlunden	BX	69
Triewaldsgränd	AZ	70
Tyska Brinken	AZ	73
Vasagatan	BY	75
Östermalmstorg	DY	76
Östra Järnvägsgatan	BY	78

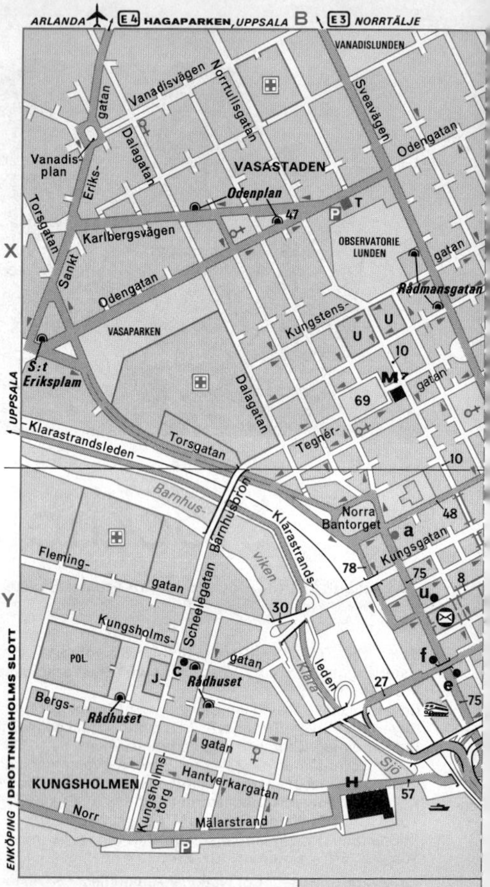

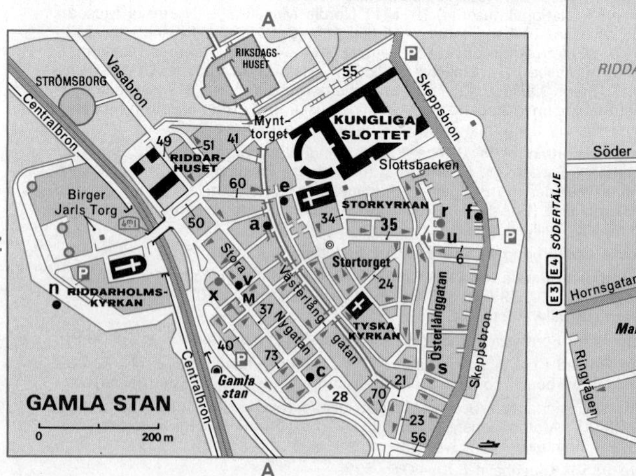

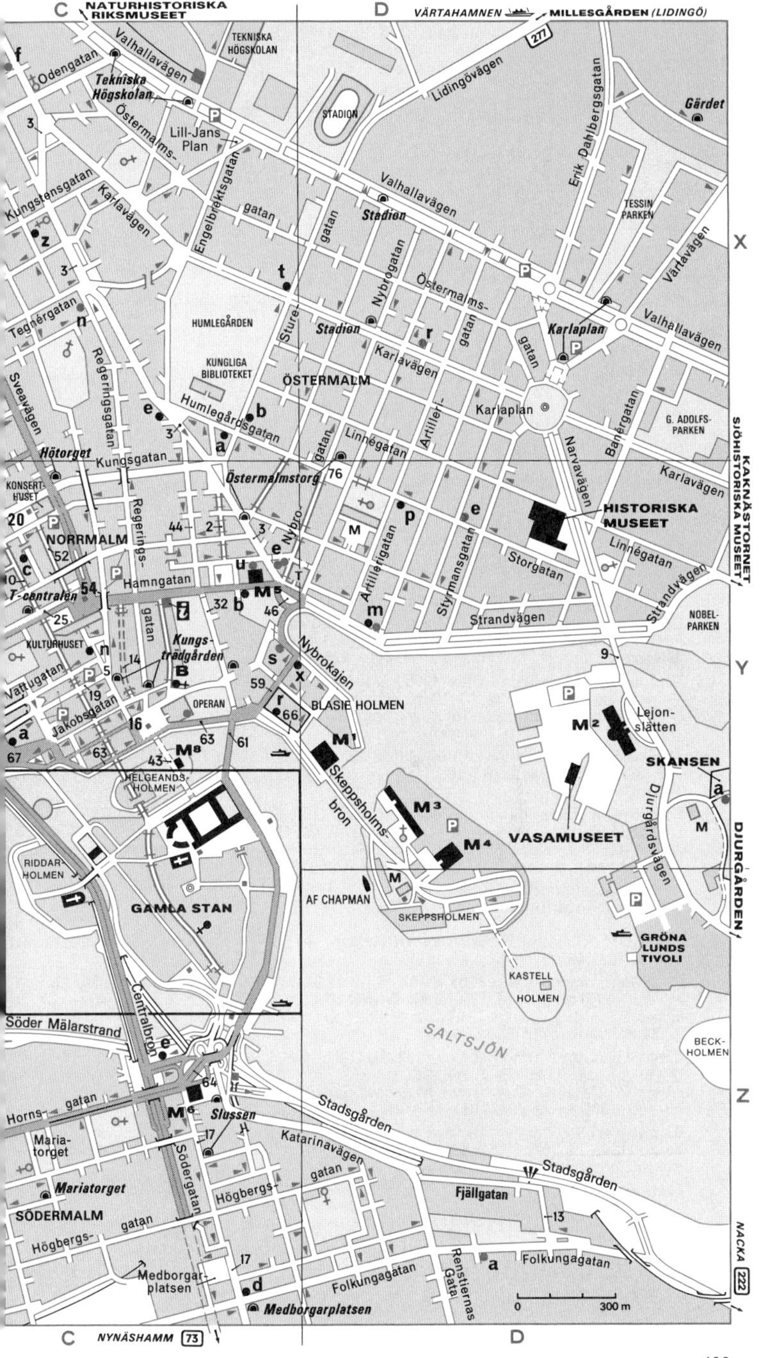
NATURHISTORISKA RIKSMUSEET
VÄRTAHAMNEN
MILLESGÅRDEN (LIDINGÖ)
TEKNISKA HÖGSKOLAN
Tekniska Högskolan
Valhallavägen
Odengatan
STADION
Lidingövägen
Erik Dahlbergsgatan
Gärdet
Lill-Jans Plan
Östermalmsgatan
Kungstensgatan
Karlavägen
Engelbrektsgatan
Stadion
TESSIN PARKEN
Värtavägen
Nybrogatan
Tegnérgatan
HUMLEGÅRDEN
KUNGLIGA BIBLIOTEKET
Sturegatan
ÖSTERMALM
Karlaplan
Regeringsgatan
Sveavägen
Humlegårdsgatan
Linnégatan
Artillerigatan
Narvavägen
Banérgatan
G. ADOLFS-PARKEN
SJÖHISTORISKA MUSEET
KAKNÄSTORNET
Hötorget
Kungsgatan
Östermalmstorg
KONSERT-HUSET
NORRMALM
HISTORISKA MUSEET
Storgatan
Strandvägen
Styrmansgatan
Hamngatan
T-centralen
NOBEL-PARKEN
KULTURHUSET
Kungsträdgården
Nybrokajen
Vattugatan
Jakobsgatan
OPERAN
BLASIEHOLMEN
Lejonslätten
SKANSEN
HELGEANDSHOLMEN
Skeppsholmsbron
VASAMUSEET
Djurgårdsvägen
DJURGÅRDEN
RIDDARHOLMEN
GAMLA STAN
AF CHAPMAN
SKEPPSHOLMEN
GRÖNA LUNDS TIVOLI
KASTELLHOLMEN
SALTSJÖN
BECKHOLMEN
Söder Mälarstrand
Centralbron
Slussen
Hornsgatan
Stadsgården
Mariatorget
Katarinavägen
Södergatan
Högbergsgatan
Fjällgatan
SÖDERMALM
Renstiernas Gata
Folkungagatan
Medborgarplatsen
NACKA
NYNÄSHAMM
0 300 m

Grand H., Södra Blasieholmshamnen 8, Box 16424, S-103 27, ℘ 22 10 20, Telex 19500, Fax 611 86 86, ≤, - rm rest - 400. AE VISA. CY **r**
M - **Verandan** approx. 330 and a la carte - **302 rm** 1590/2660, **19 suites.**

Sheraton-Stockholm, Tegelbacken 6, Box 195, S-101 23, ℘ 14 26 00, Telex 17750, Fax 21 70 26, ≤, - rm - 400. AE VISA. rest.
M - **Premiere** *(Seafood)* - **Bistro** 125 (buffet lunch) and a la carte - **449 rm,** 1280/2280, 10 suites. CY **a**

SAS Royal Viking, Vasagatan 1, Box 234, S-101 24, ℘ 14 10 00, Telex 13900, Fax 14 10 00, - rm - 250. BY **f**
M (Italian rest.) - **315 rm**, 4 suites.

Scandic Crown, Guldgränd 8, Box 15270, S-104 65, ℘ 702 25 00, Telex 11019, Fax 642 83 58, - rm - 285. AE VISA CZ **e**
M La Couronne d'Or *(closed Saturday lunch, Sunday and Bank Holidays)* 200/350 and a la carte - **246 rm** 1220/1615, 18 suites.

Sergel Plaza, Brunkebergstorg 9, Box 16411, S-103 27, ℘ 22 66 00, Telex 16700, Fax 21 50 70, - rm - 150. AE VISA CY **n**
M - **Anna Rella** *(closed Sunday)* a la carte 230/310 - **394 rm** 1095/1825, 12 suites.

Frösundavik , N : 2 km by A 4, Exit Frösundavik, S-171 03, at Solna ℘ 624 55 00, Telex 14196, Fax 85 85 66, park - rm - 250. AE VISA
M 161 (lunch) and a la carte 265/365 - **202 rm** 1075/1310, 12 suites.

Globe, Arenaslingan 7, Box 10004, S-121 26, S : 1 ½ km by Rd 73 ℘ 725 90 00, Telex 12630, Fax 649 08 80, - rm - 220 CZ
279 rm, 9 suites.

SAS Strand, Nybrokajen 9, Box 16396, S-103 27, ℘ 678 78 00, Telex 10504, Fax 611 24 36, ≤, - rm - 30. AE VISA CDY **x**
M 115/165 and a la carte - **120 rm** 1550/2150, 18 suites.

Amaranten, Kungsholmsgatan 31, S-104 20, ℘ 654 10 60, Telex 17498, Fax 652 62 48, - rm - 170. AE VISA BY **c**
M 145/185 and a la carte - **404 rm** 850/1295, 6 suites.

Continental, Klara Vattugränd 4, corner of Vasagatan, S-101 22, ℘ 24 40 20, Telex 10100, Fax 11 36 95, - rm - 70. AE VISA BY **e**
M *(closed Sunday)* 175/250 and a la carte - **235 rm** 1175/1375, 2 suites.

Diplomat, Strandvägen 7c, Box 14059, S-104 40, ℘ 663 58 00, Telex 17119, Fax 783 66 34, - rest . AE VISA. DY **m**
closed 4 days at Christmas - **M** *(closed Saturday dinner and Sunday)* 125/165 and a la carte - **130 rm** 1062/1910, 3 suites.

Anglais, Humlegårdsgatan 23, Box 5178, S-102 44, ℘ 614 16 00, Telex 19475, Fax 611 09 72 - rm - 250 CX **a**
161 rm, 9 suites.

Stockholm Plaza, Birger Jarlsgatan 29, Box 7707, S-103 95, ℘ 14 51 20, Telex 13982, Fax 10 34 92, - rm - 40. AE VISA. CX **e**
closed 23 to 27 December - **M** *(closed Saturday and Sunday lunch and Bank Holidays)* 200/450 and a la carte - **147 rm** 995/1440, 4 suites.

Berns, Näckströmsgatan 8, Berzelii Park, S-111 47, ℘ 614 07 00, Telex 12132, Fax 611 51 75, « Modern interior decor » - rm rm - 500. AE VISA. CY **b**
closed 5 to 26 July and 23 December-10 January - **M Roda Rummets** 170/230 and a la carte - **60 rm** 1440/1740, 3 suites.

Park, Karlavägen 43, Box 5055, S-102 45, ℘ 22 96 20, Telex 10666, Fax 21 62 68, - rm - 120. AE VISA. CX **t**
closed 23 to 28 December - **M** *(closed lunch Saturday and Sunday)* 250/350 and a la carte - **194 rm** 1175/1720, 8 suites.

City, Slöjdgatan 7, Hötorget, Box 1132, S-111 81, ℘ 22 22 40, Fax 20 82 24, - rm - 70. AE VISA. CY **c**
closed 22 December-9 January - **M** *(closed Saturday and Sunday)* (unlicensed) (lunch only) 60/190 - **300 rm** 890/1100.

Birger Jarl without rest. (unlicensed), Tulegatan 8, Box 19016, S-104 32, ℘ 15 10 20, Telex 11843, Fax 673 73 66, - - 150. AE VISA CX **z**
closed Christmas-New Year - **226 rm** 930/1200, 6 suites.

Malmen, Götgatan 49-51, Box 4274, S-102 66, ℘ 22 60 80, Telex 19489, Fax 641 11 48, - rm - 110. AE VISA CZ **d**
M *(closed Sunday lunch)* 170/212 and a la carte - **280 rm** 940/1369, 2 suites.

Wellington without rest., Storgatan 6, S-114 51, ℘ 667 09 10, Fax 667 12 54, - . AE VISA DY **p**
closed 23 December-3 January - **48 rm** 850/1100, 1 suite.

Freys, Bryggargatan 12b, Box 70439, S-107 25, ℘ 20 13 00, Telex 16750, Fax 24 22 24 - rm BY **u**
99 rm.

XXXX **Operakällaren** (at Opera House), Operahuset, Box 1616, S-111 86, ✆ 676 58 00, Fax 20 95 92, « Opulent classical decor » – AE ⓓ E VISA CY
closed Sunday lunch, 5 July-1 August and 25 to 26 December – **M** 195/595 and a la carte 360/550.

XXXX **Franska Matsalen** (at Grand H.), Södra Blasieholmshamnen 8, Box 16424, S-103 27, ✆ 611 52 14, Telex 19500, Fax 611 86 86, ≤ – AE ⓓ E VISA CY **r**
closed Saturday, Sunday, 12 July-6 August – **M** (dinner only) a la carte 350/700.

XX ✿ **Paul and Norbert** (Lang), Strandvägen 9, S-114 56, ✆ 663 81 83 – AE ⓓ E VISA DY **m**
closed Saturday, Sunday, 21 June-30 July, 24 December-3 January and Bank Holidays – **M** (booking essential) 150/840 and a la carte 380/555
Spec. Foie gras de veau mariné et truffe pochée au porto et champagne (Nov-Feb), Rumsteck de renne farci aux baies de genièvre, sauce vin rouge (Oct-Mar), Le parfait à la mûre du cercle artique et sa confiture (Sept-Jan).

XX **Coq Blanc,** Regeringsgatan 111, S-111 39, ✆ 11 61 53, Fax 10 76 35 – ▤. AE ⓓ E VISA
closed Saturday lunch, Monday dinner, Sunday, 24 June-16 August and Bank Holidays – **M** 195/295 and a la carte. CX **n**

XX Teatergrillen, Nybrogatan 4, S-114 34, ✆ 611 70 44, Fax 611 32 06, « Theatre atmosphere » CY **e**

XX **Nils Emil,** Folkungagatan 122, S-116 30, ✆ 640 72 09 – ▤. AE ⓓ E VISA DZ **a**
closed Saturday lunch, Sunday, 1 July-5 August and Bank Holidays – **M** (booking essential) 180 (lunch) and a la carte 270/370.

XX **Ulla Winbladh,** Rosendalsvägen 8, S-115 21, ✆ 663 05 71, Fax 663 05 73, 佘 – AE ⓓ E VISA DY **a**
closed 24-25 December and 31 December-1 January – **M** 170 (lunch) and a la carte 295/410.

XX **Clas På Hörnet** with rm, Surbrunnsgatan 20, S-113 48, ✆ 16 51 30, Fax 612 53 15, « 18C atmosphere » – |‡| TV ☎. AE ⓓ E VISA. ✻ CX **f**
M *(closed lunch Saturday, Sunday and Bank Holidays)* 185/270 and a la carte – **10 rm** ☐ 750/1850.

XX **La Brochette,** Storgatan 27, S-114 55, ✆ 662 20 00, Fax 622 37 75, 佘 – ▤. AE ⓓ E VISA DY **e**
M – **Ma Cave** ✆ 60 25 28 (basement, with cellar) (closed lunch Saturday and Sunday, 1 June and 31 August) 160/350 and a la carte – **Brasserie** *(ground floor).*

XX **Wärdshuset Stallmästaregården,** Norrtull, S-113 47, N : 2 km by Sveavägen (at beginning of E 4) ✆ 610 13 01, Fax 32 27 40, ≤, 佘, « 17C inn, waterside setting », ⇌ – Ⓟ. AE ⓓ E VISA by Sveavägen BX
closed Saturday lunch, Monday dinner and Sunday except 1 May-30 August and December – **M** 197/495 and dinner a la carte.

X **Mikael,** Karlvägen 73, S-114 37, ✆ 662 2262, Fax 662 2263, bistro – AE ⓓ E VISA DX **r**
closed Sunday – **M** (dinner only) 165/195 and a la carte.

X ✿ **Wedholms Fisk** (Wedholm), Nybrokajen 17, S-111 48, ✆ 611 78 74, Seafood – AE ⓓ E VISA CY **s**
closed Sunday, 4 weeks July and Bank Holidays – **M** 120/235 and a la carte 200/565
Spec. Tartar of salmon and salmon roe with crème fraîche, Steam boiled turbot with melted butter and horseradish, Fricassé of sole, turbot, lobster, and scallops with a champagne sauce.

X ✿ **KB,** Smålandsgatan 7, S-111 46, ✆ 679 60 32, Fax 611 82 83 – AE ⓓ E VISA CY **u**
closed Saturday lunch, Sunday, mid June-mid August and Bank Holidays – **M** 395 (dinner) and a la carte 210/460
Spec. Assorted marinated herring, Rack of lamb with artichoke and creamed morel mushrooms (Oct-Feb), Cloudberries with vanilla ice cream.

X **Greitz,** Vasagatan 50, S- 111 20, ✆ 23 48 20, Fax 24 20 93 – AE ⓓ E VISA BY **a**
closed Saturday lunch, Sunday and 1 July-14 August – **M** 156 and a la carte.

X Riche, Birger Jarlsgatan 4, S-114 34, ✆ 611 70 22, Fax 611 05 13 – ▤ CY **e**

Gamla Stan (Old Stockholm) :

🏨 **Reisen,** Skeppsbron 12-14, S-111 30, ✆ 22 32 60, Telex 17494, Fax 20 15 59, ≤, « Original maritime decor », ≘s – |‡| ⇹ rm ▤ rest TV ☎ – 🔬 60. AE ⓓ E VISA AZ **f**
closed Christmas – **M** *(closed lunch Saturday and Sunday)* 130/190 and a la carte – **111 rm** ☐ 1295/2080, 3 suites.

🏨 **Victory,** Lilla Nygatan 5, S-111 28, ✆ 14 30 90, Telex 14050, Fax 20 21 77, « Swedish rural furnishings, maritime antiques », ≘s – |‡| ⇹ rm ▤ TV ☎ – 🔬 90. AE ⓓ E VISA. ✻ AZ **v**
closed 23 December-6 January – **M** (see **Leijontornet** below) – **44 rm** ☐ 1490/2090, **4 suites.**

🏨 **Gamla Stan** without rest., Lilla Nygatan 25, S-111 28, ✆ 24 44 50, Telex 13896, Fax 21 69 83 – |‡| ⇹ TV ☎ – 🔬 25. AE ⓓ E VISA **c**
closed 23 December-3 January – **51 rm** ☐ 880/1495.

🏨 **Lady Hamilton** without rest., Storkyrkobrinken 5, S-111 28, ✆ 23 46 80, Telex 10434, Fax 11 11 48, « Swedish rural antiques », ≘s – |‡| TV ☎. AE ⓓ E VISA. ✻ AZ **e**
34 rm ☐ 1150/1650.

Mälardrottningen, Riddarholmen, S-111 28, ☎ 24 36 00, Telex 15864, Fax 24 36 76, « Formerly Barbara Hutton's yacht », – AE E VISA AZ n
closed 23 to 28 December – **M** *(closed Saturday lunch, Sunday, 1 May, 26 June, 22 to 27 December and 9 to 12 April)* a la carte approx. 342 – **58 rm (cabins)** 885/995, 1 suite.

Lord Nelson without rest., Västerlånggatan 22, S-111 29, ☎ 23 23 90, Telex 10434, Fax 10 10 89, « Ship style installation, maritime antiques », – AE E VISA.
31 rm 975/1400. AZ a

XXX ✿ **Eriks (at the Green House)** (Lallerstedt) with rm, 1st floor, Österlånggatan 17, S-111 31, ☎ 23 85 00, Fax 796 60 69, Seafood – AE E VISA. rest AZ u
closed Sunday, July and Bank Holidays – **M** 515/650 (dinner) and a la carte 338/638 – **2 rm** 2100, **4 suites** 2900/3500
Spec. Sweet pickled herring soufflé with a lightly smoked cod's roe sauce, Fish and shellfish, Fried duckling in two servings.

XX **Leijontornet** (at Victory H.), Lilla Nygatan 5, S-111 28, ☎ 14 23 55, Telex 14050, Fax 20 21 77, , « Remains of a 14C fortification tower in the dining room » – AE E VISA AZ v
closed lunch Sunday and Bank Holidays and July – **M** 220/520 and a la carte.

XX **Den Gyldene Freden,** Osterlånggatan 51, Box 2269, S-103 17, ☎ 24 97 60, Fax 21 38 70 – AE E VISA AZ s
closed Sunday and July – **M** 180/298 and a la carte.

XX **Källaren Aurora,** Munkbron 11, S-111 28, ☎ 21 93 59, Fax 11 16 22, « In the cellars of a 17C house » – . AE E VISA AZ x
closed Sunday – **M** 195/240 and a la carte.

XX **Fem Små Hus,** Nygränd 10, S-111 30, ☎ 10 87 75, Fax 14 96 95, « 17C Cellars, antiques » – . AE E VISA AZ r
M 145/355 and a la carte.

to the E :

at Djurgården E : 3 km by Strandvägen DY – ✉ 08 Stockholm :

XXX **Kallhagens Wärdshus** with rm, Djurgårdsbrunnsvägen 10, S-115 27, ☎ 667 60 60, Fax 667 60 43, ←, « Waterside setting, garden », – rm – 40. AE E VISA. rest DY
closed 23 December-6 January – **M** *(closed Monday dinner in winter)* 169/295 and a la carte – **18 rm** 1095/1250, **2 suites.**

to the NW :

at Solna NW : 5 km by Sveavägen - BX - and E 4 – ✉ Solna – 08 Stockholm :

XXX ✿ **Ulriksdals Wärdshus** (Krücken), 170 71 Solna, Exit E 18/E 3 from E 4 ☎ 85 08 15, Fax 85 08 58, ←, « Former inn in Royal Park », – . AE E VISA.
closed dinner Sunday and Bank Holidays and 24 to 26 December – **M** 545/595 and a la carte 450/585
Spec. Papillon d'avocat avec oeufs d'ablette, Perdrix de neige, sauce genièvre, Fausse-mûres chaudes et glace vanille.

XX **Finsmakaren,** Råsundavägen 9, 171 52 Solna, ☎ 27 67 71 – AE E VISA
closed Saturday, Sunday, 1 to 31 July, 20 December-8 January and Bank Holidays – **M** 220/375 and a la carte.

at Sollentuna NW : 15 km by Sveavägen - BX - and E 4 – ✉ Sollentuna – 08 Stockholm :

XX ✿ **Edsbacka Krog,** Sollentunavägen 220, 191 47, ☎ 96 33 00, Fax 96 40 19, « 17C inn » – . AE E VISA
closed Saturday lunch, Monday dinner, Sunday and 11 July-9 August – **M** 250/585 and a la carte 230/410
Spec. Grilled scallops with a lemon butter sauce and basil, Roast saddle of roe deer with a black-currant sauce, potatoes and leek cake, Cloudberry parfait with almond biscuits.

at Upplands Väsby NW : 29 km by Sveavägen and E 4 – ✉ Upplands Väsby – 08 Stockholm :

Scandic Crown, Kanalvägen 10, S-194 61, E 4 - Bredden Exit ☎ 590 955 00, Telex 10565, Fax 590 955 10, , , – rm – 320. AE E VISA. rest
M 49/175 and a la carte – **228 rm** 1121/1345, 8 suites.

at Arlanda Airport NW : 40 km by Sveavägen - BX - and E 4 – ✉ Arlanda – 08 Stockholm :

SAS Arlandia, Box 103, 190 45 Stockholm - Arlanda ☎ 593 618 00, Telex 13018, Fax 593 619 70, , – rm – 245. AE E VISA. rest
M 185/210 and a la carte – **334 rm** 1315/1750, 8 suites.

To find your way in the capital, use the Michelin street plans of Paris
10 sheet map, 12 sheet map with street index,
11 atlas with street index and practical information,
14 atlas with street index.

GOTHENBURG (GÖTEBORG) Sverige 985 O 8 - pop. 429 339 - ☎ 031.

See : Art Gallery★★★ (Konstmuseum) CX **M1** - Castle Park★★★ (Slottsskogen) AX - Botanical Gardens★★ (Botaniska Trädgården) AX - East India House★★ (Ostindiska Huset) BU **M2** - Liseberg Amusement Park★★ (Lisebergs Nöjespark) DX - Natural History Museum★★ (Naturhistoriska Museet) AX - Röhss Museum of Arts and Crafts★★ (Röhsska Konstslöjdmuseet) BV **M3** - Älvsborg Bridge★ (Älvsborgsbron) AV - Kungsportsavenyn★ CVX **22** - Maritima Centre★ (Maritime Centrum) (Viking★) BT - Maritime Museum★ (Sjöfartsmuseet) AV - New Älvsborg Fortress★ (Nya Älvsborgs Fästning) AU - Götaplatsen (Carl Milles Poseidon★★) CX - Seaman's Tower (Sjömanstornet) (※★★) AV - Masthugg Church (Masthuggskyrkran) (inside★) AV.

Envir. : Northern and southern archipelago★ (Hönö, Öckerö, Vrängö) - Kungsbacka : Tjolöholms Castle★, S : 40 km by E6.

Albatross, Lillbagsvägen Hisings Backa, R 15 ☎ 55 04 40 - Delsjö, Kallebäck, H 7 ☎ 40 69 59 - Göteborgs, Golfbanevägen, Hovås, R 23 ☎ 28 24 44.

Scandinavian Airlines System : Norra Hamngatan 20-22 ☎ 94 20 00/63 85 00 Landvetter Airport : ☎ 94 10 00.

To Denmark : contact Stena Line A/B, Telex 20886, Fax 24 10 38 - To continent : contact Scandinavian Seaways ☎ 65 06 00, Telex 21724.

Basargatan 10 (vid Kungsportplatsen), ☎ 10 07 40 - Kungsportsplatsen 2 ☎ 17 11 70.

Copenhague 279 - Oslo 322 - Stockholm 500.

Plans on following pages

Sheraton and restaurant Madeleine, Södra Hamngatan 59-65, Box 288, S-401 24, ☎ 80 60 00, Telex 28250, Fax 15 98 88, rm - 450. AE E VISA. BU **b**
closed Christmas-New Year - **M Madeleine** *(closed Sunday and Monday)* (dinner only) 495 and a la carte - **Frascati** *(closed lunch Saturday and Sunday)* 175/198 and a la carte - **323 rm** 1550/1750, 17 suites.

Park Avenue and restaurant Belle Avenue, Kungsportavenyn 36-38, Box 53233, S-400 16, ☎ 17 65 20, Telex 2320, Fax 16 95 68, rm - 350. AE E VISA CX **f**
M 130/210 (buffet lunch) and a la carte 245/510 - **301 rm** 1792/1992, 17 suites.

Scandic Crown, Polhemsplatsen 3, S-411 11, ☎ 80 09 00, Fax 15 45 88, rm - 200. AE VISA. rest. CU **d**
closed Christmas - **M** *(closed Sunday lunch)* 173 (lunch) and a la carte 240/380 - **310 rm**, 1030/1345, 10 suites.

Europa, Köpmansgatan 38, Box 264, S-401 24, ☎ 80 12 80, Telex 21374, Fax 15 47 55, rm - 110. AE E VISA BU **a**
M 49/150 and a la carte - **455 rm** 940/1225, 5 suites.

Gothia, Mässans Gata 24, Box 5184, S-402 26, ☎ 40 93 00, Telex 21941, Fax 18 98 04, ≤, « Panoramic restaurant on 18th floor » - rm - 40. AE E VISA
M - **Gemini Sky** 150/300 and a la carte - **290 rm** 1070/1470, 2 suites. DX **k**

Rubinen, Kunsportsavenyn 24, Box 53097, S-400 14, ☎ 81 08 00, Telex 20837, Fax 16 75 86 - rm - 60 CV **c**
184 rm, 1 suite.

Panorama, Eklandagatan 51-53, Box 24037, S-400 22, ☎ 81 08 80, Telex 27716, Fax 81 42 37, rm - 120. AE E VISA DX **s**
closed 18 December-10 January - **M** *(closed Saturday lunch and Sunday)* 200/300 and a la carte - **341 rm** 990/1590.

Opalen, Engelbrektsgatan 73, Box 5106, S-402 23, ☎ 81 03 00, Telex 2215, Fax 18 76 22, rm - 180. AE E VISA. rest DV **u**
closed 20 to 27 December - **M** 155/395 and a la carte - **237 rm** 1010/1228, 4 suites.

Riverton, Stora Badhusgatan 26, S-411 21, ☎ 10 12 00, Telex 21590, Fax 13 08 66, « Roof garden restaurant with ≤ harbour », rm - 300. AE E VISA. AV **c**
M *(closed Sunday)* 165/390 and dinner a la carte - **190 rm** 795/1220.

Victors, Skeppsbroplatsen 1, S-411 18, ☎ 17 41 80, Fax 13 96 10, ≤ harbour, rm rm - 30. AE E VISA AU **b**
M *(closed Saturday and Sunday)* (dinner only) a la carte 183/309 - **35 rm** 950/1150, 9 suites.

Windsor and Brasserie Lipp, Kungsportavenyn 6-8, S-411 36, ☎ 17 65 40, Telex 21014, Fax 11 34 39, rm - 40 CV **e**
91 rm.

Tidbloms, Olskroksgatan 23, Box 6162, S-416 66, NE : 2 ½ km ☎ 19 20 70, Telex 27369, Fax 19 78 35, rm - 80. AE E VISA. rest
closed Christmas and New Year - **M** *(closed Saturday lunch, Sunday and Bank Holidays)* 196 (lunch) and dinner a la carte 161/318 - **42 rm** 930/1080. by Redbergsvägen DT

Novotel, Klippan 1, S-414 51, SW : 3 ½ km ☎ 14 90 00, Telex 28181, Fax 42 22 32, ≤, - rm - 150. AE E VISA by E 3 AV
M (buffet lunch) 105 and a la carte 190/370 - 52 - **145 rm** 955/1085, 4 suites.

Eggers without rest., Drottningtorget, Box 323, S-401 25, ☎ 80 60 70, Group Telex 27273, Fax 15 42 43 - rm - 25. AE E VISA BU **e**
closed 23 to 27 December - **77 rm** 945/1260.

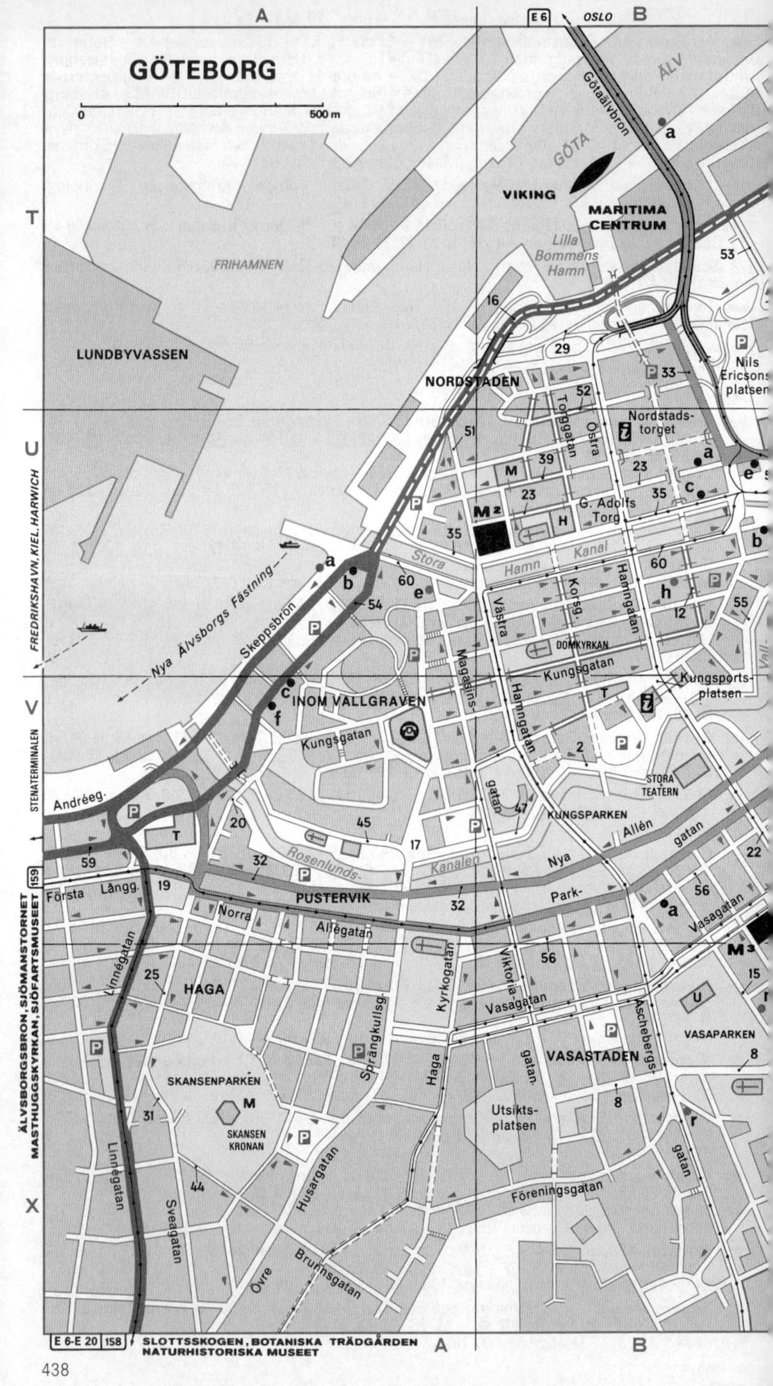
GÖTEBORG
0
500 m
E 6
OSLO
GÖTA ÄLV
Götaälvbron
VIKING
MARITIMA CENTRUM
Lilla Bommens Hamn
FRIHAMNEN
LUNDBYVASSEN
NORDSTADEN
Nordstads-torget
G. Adolfs Torg
Stora Hamn Kanal
DOMKYRKAN
Kungsgatan
Kungsports-platsen
INOM VALLGRAVEN
Skeppsbron
Nya Älvsborgs Fästning
FREDRIKSHAVN, KIEL, HARWICH
STENATERMINALEN
Andréeg.
STORA TEATERN
KUNGSPARKEN
Nya Allén
Rosenlunds-Kanalen
PUSTERVIK
Park-gatan
Första Långg.
Norra Allégatan
Vasagatan
HAGA
Linnégatan
Sprängkullsg.
Kyrkogatan
Viktoria-gatan
Aschebergs-gatan
VASASTADEN
VASAPARKEN
Utsikts-platsen
SKANSENPARKEN
SKANSEN KRONAN
Husargatan
Sveagatan
Föreningsgatan
Övre Husargatan
Brunnsgatan
Haga
Magasins-gatan
Västra Hamngatan
Korsg.
Östra Hamngatan
Torggatan
Nils Ericsons platsen
ÄLVSBORGSBRON, SJÖMANSTORNET MASTHUGGSKYRKAN, SJÖFARTSMUSEET
E 6-E 20
158
159
SLOTTSSKOGEN, BOTANISKA TRÄDGÅRDEN NATURHISTORISKA MUSEET

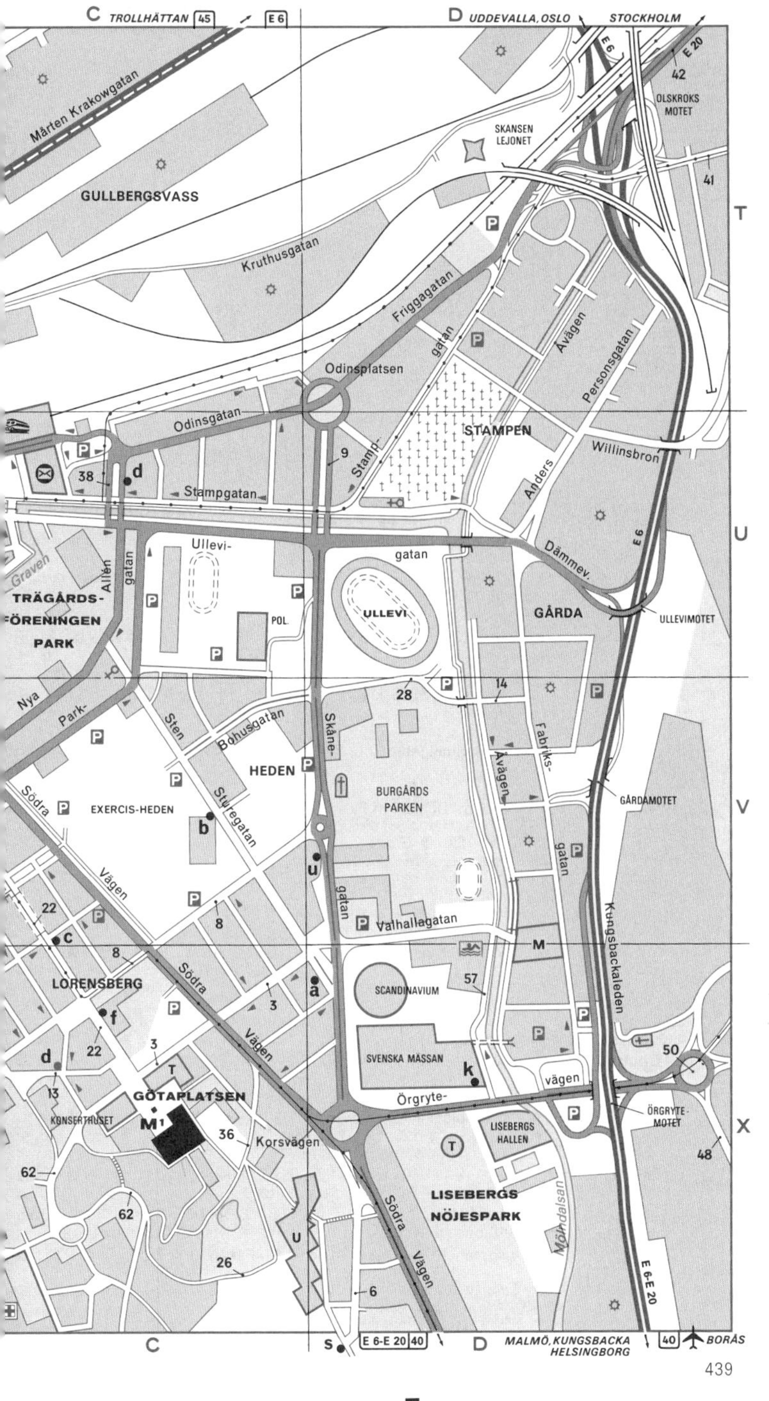

C TROLLHÄTTAN 45
E 6
D UDDEVALLA, OSLO
STOCKHOLM
E 20
E 6
42
OLSKROKS MOTET
SKANSEN LEJONET
Mårten Krakowgatan
GULLBERGSVASS
41
T
Kruthusgatan
Friggagatan
Åvägen
Personsgatan
Odinsplatsen
Stampgatan
Odinsgatan
STAMPEN
Willinsbron
9
Stamp-
38
d
Stampgatan
Anders
E 6
U
Ullevi-
gatan
Dämmev.
Graven
Allén
gatan
TRÄGÅRDS-
FÖRENINGEN
PARK
POL.
ULLEVI
GÅRDA
ULLEVIMOTET
Nya
Park-
28
14
Sten
Bohusgatan
Skåne-
Fabriks-
HEDEN
Åvägen
GÅRDAMOTET
Södra
EXERCIS-HEDEN
Sturegatan
BURGÅRDS
PARKEN
V
b
u
gatan
gatan
Vägen
22
c
8
Valhallagatan
M
Kungsbackaleden
8
LORENSBERG
Södra
3
a
SCANDINAVIUM
57
f
Vägen
22
SVENSKA MÄSSAN
k
50
3
d
T
vägen
13
GÖTAPLATSEN
Örgryte-
M1
ÖRGRYTE-MOTET
KONSERTHUSET
36
Korsvägen
X
LISEBERGS HALLEN
62
48
62
LISEBERGS
NÖJESPARK
Södra
Mölndalsån
U
Vägen
26
6
E 6-E 20
C
S
E 6-E 20 40
D
MALMÖ, KUNGSBACKA HELSINGBORG
40
BORÅS

STREET INDEX TO GÖTEBORG TOWN PLAN

Fredsgatan .... BU 12
Korsgatan .... BU
Kungsgatan .... ABV
Köpmansgatan .... BU 23
Postgatan .... BU 39
Spannmålsgatan .... BTU 52
Torggatan .... BTU

Anders Personsg .... DTU
Andréegatan .... AV
Basargatan .... BV 2
Berzeliigatan .... CX 3
Bohusgatan CV
Brunnsgatan .... AX
Drottningtorget .... BU 5
Dämmevägen .... DU
Eklandagatan .... DX 6
Engelbrektsgatan .... BCVX 8
Fabriksgatan .... DV
Folkungagatan .... DU 9
Friggagatan .... DT
Föreningsgatan .... BX
Första Långgatan .... AV
Geijersgatan .... CX 13
Gustaf Adolfs Torg .... BU
Gårdavägen .... DV 14
Götabergsgatan .... BX 15
Götaleden .... BT 16
Götaplatsen CX

Götaälvbron .... BT
Haga Kyrkogata .... AX
Hvitfeldtsplatsen .... AV 17
Järntorget .... AV 19
Järntorgsgatan .... AV 20
Korsvägen .... CDX
Kruthusgatan .... CT
Kungsbackaleden .... DVX
Kungsports Avenyn .... BCUX 22
Kungsportsplatsen .... BV
Landsvägsgatan .... AX 25
Lennart Torstenssonsgatan .... CX 26
Levgrensvägen .... DV 28
Lilla Bommen .... BT 29
Lilla Risåsgatan .... AX 31
Magasinsgatan .... ABV
Masthamnsgatan .... AV 32
Mårten Krakowgatan .... CT
Nils Ericsonsgatan .... BT 33
Nils Ericsonsplatsen .... BT
Norra Allégatan .... AV
Norra Hamngatan .... ABU 35
Nya Allén .... BCV
Odinsgatan .... CU
Odinsplatsen .... DT
Olof Wijksgatan .... CX 36
Parkgatan .... BCV
Polhemsplatsen .... CU 38

Redbergsvägen .... DT 41
Riddaregatan .... DT 42
Risåsgatan .... AX 44
Rosenlundsgatan .... AV 45
Sahlgrensgatan .... BV 47
Sankt Sigfridsgatan .... DX 48
Sankt Sigfrids Plan .... DX 50
Skeppsbron .... AU
Skånegatan .... DV
Smedjegatan .... AU 51
Stadstjänaregatan .... BT 53
Stampgatan .... CDU
Sten Sturegatan CV
Stora Badhusgatan .... AU 54
Stora Nygatan .... BU 55
Storgatan .... BVX 56
Sveagatan .... AX
Sven Rydells Gata .... DX 57
Södra Allégatan .... AV 59
Södra Hamngatan .... ABU 60
Södra Vägen .... CDX
Ullevigatan .... CDU
Valhallagatan .... DV
Viktor Rydbergsgatan .... CX 62
Willinsbron .... DU
Västra Hamngatan .... BUV
Åvagen .... DTV
Örgrytevägen .... DX
Östra Hamngatan .... BU

Liseberg Heden, Sten Sturegatan, S-411 38, ☎ 20 02 80, Telex 27450, Fax 16 52 83, – rm TV ☎ & P – 80. AE ① E VISA — CV **b**
closed 23 December-3 January – **M** *(closed lunch Saturday and Sunday)* 154 and a la carte – **157 rm** ☐ 875/1120, **2 suites.**

Ekoxen without rest., Norra Hamnagatan 38, S-411 06, ☎ 80 50 80, Fax 15 33 70, – TV ☎ – 15. AE ① E VISA — BU **c**
closed Christmas – **74 rm** ☐ 975/1175, **1 suite.**

Onyxen without rest., Sten Sturegatan 23, S-412 53, ☎ 81 08 45, Fax 16 56 72 – TV ☎ P — DX **a**
34 rm.

Poseidon without rest., Storgatan 33, S-411 38, ☎ 10 05 50, Telex 27663, Fax 13 83 91, – TV ☎ P. AE ① E VISA — BV **a**
49 rm ☐ 480/990.

Klang without rest., Stora Badhusgatan 28b, S-411 21, ☎ 17 40 50, Fax 17 40 58 – TV ☎. AE ① E VISA. — AV **f**
49 rm ☐ 600/890.

XXX ✿ **Westra Piren,** at Eriksberg, Docks (on Pier No 4), S-402 79, NW : 3 km by Götaälvbron or by boat from Lilla Bommens Hamn BT ☎ 51 95 55, Fax 23 99 40, « Dockside setting, overlooking the harbour » – AE ① E VISA
closed 22 December-10 January – **M** *(closed Sunday, 5 July-3 August and Bank Holidays)* (booking essential) 219/550 and a la carte 420/510 – **Brasserie** *(lunch only Monday to Friday September-April)* 155/250 and a la carte
Spec. Soupe d'étrilles parfumée à l'anis, flan d'ail (autumn), Médaillons de sole farcies de homard et pistache (summer-autumn), Charlotte aux châtaignes, sauce mokka.

XXX ✿ **The Place** (Wagner), Arkivgatan 7, S-411 34, ☎ 16 03 33, Fax 16 78 54 – AE ① E VISA
M *(closed Sunday, 1 and 12 April, 1, 20 and 31 May, 28 June-9 July, 6 November and 23 December-10 January)* (booking essential) (dinner only) 395/595 and a la carte 460/624 – **Bakfickan** (grill rest.) (dinner only) 225/345 and a la carte — CX **d**
Spec. Lobster salad with a papaya vinaigrette, Grilled tournedos of deer with a mustard sausage and red port sauce, Herb baked halibut with lobster and scallops on a bed of artichoke hearts.

XX **Le Chablis,** Aschebergsgatan 22, S-411 27, ☎ 20 35 45, Fax 20 82 01, seafood – AE ① E VISA — BX **r**
closed Saturday lunch, Sunday and July – **M** 149/395 and a la carte.

XX **S/S Marieholm,** Skeppsbroplatsen, Stenpvien, S-403 20, ☎ 13 88 80, Fax 13 38 65, ←, seafood, « Converted Ship » – 120. AE ① E VISA — AU **a**
closed Sunday – **M** 60/175 (lunch) and a la carte 253/332.

XX **Fiskekrogen,** Lilla Torget 1, S-411 18, ☎ 11 21 84, Fax 774 04 83, seafood – AE ① E VISA
closed Sunday and Bank Holidays – **M** 250 and a la carte. — AU **e**

XX Sjömagasinet, Klippaus 1, S-414 51, SW : 3,5 km ☎ 24 65 10, Fax 24 55 39, ←, « Former East India company warehouse » – P — by E 3 AV

XX ✿ **28 +** (Lyxell), Götabergsgatan 28, S-411 34, ☎ 20 21 61, Fax 81 97 57, « Cellar » – AE ① E VISA — BX **n**
closed Saturday lunch, Sunday, 9 to 13 April, 25 June-2 August, 22 December-6 January and Bank Holidays – **M** 195/495 and a la carte 312/491
Spec. Crayfish roll in a salsify soup, Cumin flavoured turbot with an aquavit sauce, Cloudberry and vanilla bavaroise with a sabayon.

XX Stallgården, Kyrkogatan 33, S-404 25, ✆ 13 03 16, Fax 11 59 39, « Interior courtyard » BU **h**

X **Eriksbergsfärjan,** Gullbergskajen Plats 212, S-411 04, ✆ 15 35 05, ⛱ - AE ⓓ E VISA BT **a**
closed dinner Monday to Friday and Saturday - **M** (buffet lunch) 169 and lunch a la carte 219/358.

at Landvetter Airport E : 30 km - ✉ **S-438 02** Landvetter

Landvetter Airport Hotel, Box 2103, ✉ S-438 02, ✆ 94 64 10, Telex 28733, Fax 94 64 70, ≘s - |‡| ⇆ rm TV ☎ ♿ P. AE ⓓ E VISA. ✻ by Rd 40 DX
M *(closed Saturday and Sunday)* 190 and a la carte - **37 rm** ☐ 785/895, **7 suites.**

Switzerland

Suisse
Schweiz
Svizzera

BASLE – GENEVA – ZÜRICH

PRACTICAL INFORMATION

LOCAL CURRENCY

Swiss Franc: 100 F = 67.70 US $ = 56.80 Ecus (Jan. 93).

LANGUAGES SPOKEN

German, French and Italian are usually spoken in all administrative departments, shops, hotels and restaurants.

AIRLINES

SWISSAIR: P.O. Box 316, 1215 Genève 15, ✆ 022/799 31 11, Fax 022/799 31 59. Hirschengraben 84, 8058 Zürich, ✆ 01/258 30 21, Fax 01/261 51 76.

AIR FRANCE: Chantepoulet 1-3, 1201 Genève, ✆ 022/732 16 00, Fax 022/738 85 28. Talstr. 70, P.O. Box, 8039 Zürich, ✆ 01/211 05 94, Fax 01/212 01 35.

ALITALIA: rue Lausanne 36, 1201 Genève, ✆ 022/732 15 20, Fax 022/732 40 29. Thurgauerstr. 39, 8050 Zürich, ✆ 01/306 91 11, Fax 01/306 91 44.

AMERICAN AIRLINES: Lintheschergasse 15, 8023 Zürich, ✆ 01/211 06 70, Fax 01/212 04 21.

BRITISH AIRWAYS: Chantepoulet 13, 1201 Genève, ✆ 022/731 21 25, Fax 022/798 84 25. Talacker 42, 8023 Zürich, ✆ 01/211 40 90, Fax 01/212 06 35.

LUFTHANSA: Chantepoulet 1-3, 1201 Genève, ✆ 022/731 01 35, Fax 022/738 96 55. Gutebergstr. 10, 8027 Zürich, ✆ 01/286 73 00, Fax 01/286 72 07.

POSTAL SERVICES

In large towns, post offices are open from 7.30am to noon and 1.45pm to 6pm, and Saturdays untill 11am. The telephone system is fully automatic.
Many public phones are equipped with phone card facilities. Prepaid phone cards are available from post offices, railway stations and tobacconist's shops.

SHOPPING

Department stores are generally open from 8.30am to 6pm, except on Saturdays when they close at 4 or 5pm and Monday morning.
In the index of street names, those printed in red are where the principal shops are found.

TIPPING

In hotels, restaurants and cafés the service charge is generally included in the prices.

SPEED LIMITS - MOTORWAYS

The speed limit on motorways is 120 km/h - 74 mph, on other roads 80 km/h - 50 mph, and in built up areas 50 km/h - 31 mph.
Driving on Swiss motorways is subject to the purchase of a single rate vignette (one per car) obtainable from frontier posts, tourist offices and post offices.

SEAT BELTS

The wearing of seat belts is compulsory in all Swiss cantons for front seat passengers.

Town plans of Basle, Geneva and Zürich : with the permission of Federal directorate for cadastral surveys, 2 January 1993

BASLE (BASEL) 4000 Switzerland 166 ⑩, 216 ④ – pop. 171 036 alt. 273 – Basle and environs from France 19-41-61 from Switzerland 061.

See: Cathedral (Munster)** : ←* CY – Zoological Garden*** AZ – The Port (Hafen) ☼*, Exposition* CX – Fish Market Fountain* (Fischmarktbrunnen) BY – Old Streets* BY – Oberer Rheinweg ←* CY – Museums : Fine Arts*** (Kunstmuseum) CY, Historical* (Historisches Museum) CY, Ethnographic (Museum für Völkerkunde)* CY M1 – Haus zum Kirschgarten* CZ, Antiquities (Antikenmuseum)* CY – ☼* from Bruderholz Water Tower S : 3,5 km.

18 private ✆ 89 68 50 91 at Hagenthal-le-Bas (68-France) SW : 10 km.

✈ Basle-Mulhouse ✆ 325 31 11 at Basle (Switzerland) by Flughafenstrasse 8 km and at Saint-Louis (68-France) ✆ 89 69 00 00.

Office de Tourisme Blumenrain 2/Schifflände ✆ 261 50 50, Telex 963318 and at Railway Station (Bahnhof) ✆ 271 36 84 – A.C. Suisse, Birsigstr. 4 ✆ 272 39 33 – T.C.S. Steinentorstr. 13 ✆ 272 19 55.

Paris 554 – Bern 95 – Freiburg 71 – Lyons 401 – Mulhouse 35 – Strasbourg 145.

Plans on following pages

Trois Rois, Blumenrain 8 ✉ 4001 ✆ 261 52 52, Telex 962937, Fax 261 21 53, ←, – | – 80. AE GB BY **a**
Rôtisserie des Rois M 73/105 – **Rhy-Deck M** 21/36 – 23 – **80 rm** 250/510, 8 suites.

Plaza M, Riehenring 45 ✉ 4058 ✆ 692 33 33, Telex 964439, Fax 691 56 33, , – | rm – 50. AE GB. rest DX **r**
Rôtisserie Plaza *(closed 11 July-30 August, Saturday lunch and Sunday)* **M** 65/120 – **Grand Café M** a la carte 25/50 – **243 rm** 320/460.

International M, Steinentorstrasse 25 ✉ 4001 ✆ 281 75 85, Telex 962370, Fax 281 76 27, , – | – 240. AE GB JCB. rest BZ **b**
Steinenpick M 14/27 – **Rôt. Charolaise** *(closed Saturday and Sunday from 1 July-15 August)* **M** carte 60/95 – **210 rm** 230/430, 5 suites.

Euler, Centralbahnplatz 14 ✉ 4002 ✆ 272 45 00, Telex 962215, Fax 271 50 00 – | rm rest – 150. AE GB. rest CZ **a**
M *(closed Saturday lunch)* a la carte 90/120 – 17 – **55 rm** 305/445, 9 suites.

Hilton M, Aeschengraben 31 ✉ 4002 ✆ 271 66 22, Telex 965555, Fax 271 52 20, , – | – 50 - 300. AE GB JCB. rest CZ **d**
Le Wettstein *(closed Saturday)* **M** 49/75 – **Marine Suisse M** 15/46 – **207 rm** 200/390, 10 suites.

✿ **Europe and rest. Quatre Saisons** M, Clarastrasse 43 ✉ 4005 ✆ 691 80 80, Telex 964103, Fax 691 82 01 – | rm – 100. AE GB JCB. rest CX **k**
M *(closed Sunday)* 75/160 and a la carte 106/138 – **170 rm** 230/330
Spec. Mousseline de pommes de terre truffée et médaillon de foie d'oie. Feuilleté à la mozzarelle et ragoût d'olives et tomates. Saint-Pierre "alla gremolata" sur risotto au citron vert. Wines Maispracher, Argovie.

Mérian, Rheingasse 2 ✉ 4058 ✆ 681 00 00, Telex 963537, Fax 681 11 01, ←, – | – 25 - 100. AE GB CY **b**
M 28/45 – **63 rm** 170/250.

Basel, Münzgasse 12 ✉ 4051 ✆ 261 24 23, Fax 261 25 95, – | rest . AE GB BY **x**
M 53/93 – **71 rm** 155/210.

Schweizerhof, Centralbahnplatz 1 ✉ 4002 ✆ 271 28 33, Telex 962373, Fax 271 29 19, – | rm – 100. AE GB. rest CZ **n**
M 25/33 – **75 rm** 160/250.

Admiral M, Rosentalstrasse 5 ✆ 691 77 77, Telex 963444, Fax 691 77 89, – | rm – 25 - 60. AE GB JCB. rest DX **m**
M 19 dinner a la carte – **130 rm** 150/280.

Wettstein without rest, Grenzacherstrasse 8 ✆ 691 28 00, Fax 691 05 45 – | rm . AE GB DY **q**
closed 24 December-2 January – **45 rm** 132/225.

Métropol without rest, Elisabethenanlage 5 ✉ 4002 ✆ 271 77 21, Telex 962268, Fax 271 78 82 – | – 40 - 120. AE GB JCB CZ **a**
46 rm 205/275.

Muenchnerhof, Riehenring 75 ✉ 4058 ✆ 691 77 80, Telex 964476, Fax 691 14 90 – | . AE GB JCB CX **u**
M 14/60 – **40 rm** 65/275.

XXXX ✿✿ **Stucki,** Bruderholzallee 42 ✉ 4059 ✆ 35 82 22, Fax 35 82 03, , « Flowered garden » – . AE GB by Münchensteinerstr. CDZ
closed 24 to 30 December, 1 to 9 March, Sunday and Monday – **M** 100/165 and a la carte 108/148
Spec. Fricassée de légumes au jus de truffes et champignons sauvages. Blanc de turbot aux gousses d'ail. Filet de bœuf poché au raifort et à la moelle. Wines Pinot noir de Pratteln, Riesling de Kaisten.

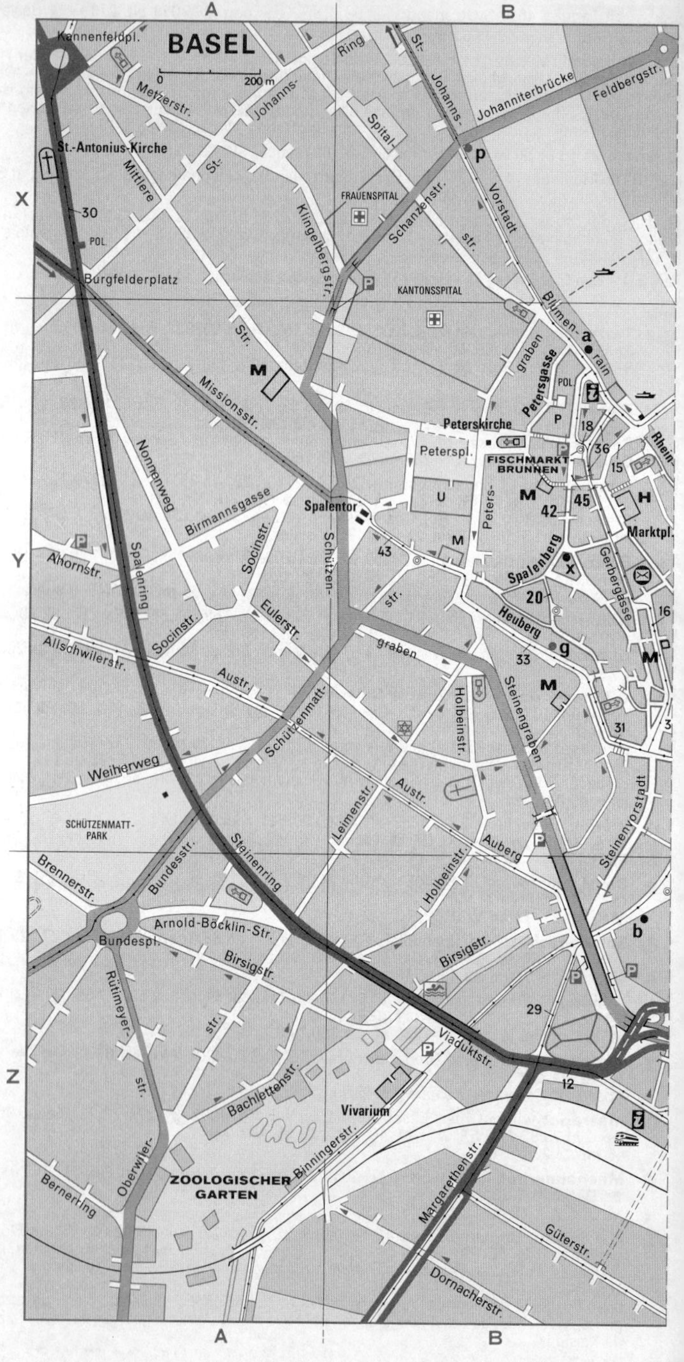
BASEL
0
200 m
Kannenfeldpl.
Metzerstr.
St.-Antonius-Kirche
Mittlere
St.-Johanns-Ring
Spital
Klingelbergstr.
FRAUENSPITAL
Schanzenstr.
St.-Johanns-Vorstadt
Johanniterbrücke
Feldbergstr.
p
POL.
Burgfelderplatz
KANTONSSPITAL
Blumenrain
a
Petersgraben
Petersgasse
Missionsstr.
M
Peterskirche
Peterspl.
FISCHMARKT-BRUNNEN
Rhein
Nonnenweg
Birmannsgasse
Spalentor
U
Peters-
M
42
45
H
Marktpl.
18
36
15
Ahornstr.
Spalenring
Socinstr.
Schützengraben
43
Spalenberg
x
Gerbergasse
20
Heuberg
g
16
33
Allschwilerstr.
Austr.
Eulerstr.
Steinengraben
Holbeinstr.
Schützenmattstr.
Weiherweg
Leimenstr.
Austr.
31
Steinenvorstadt
SCHÜTZENMATT-PARK
Auberg
Brennerstr.
Bundesstr.
Steinenring
Holbeinstr.
b
Arnold-Böcklin-Str.
Bundespl.
Birsigstr.
Birsigstr.
Rütimeyerstr.
29
Viaduktstr.
12
Bachlettenstr.
Vivarium
Binningerstr.
Oberwilerstr.
ZOOLOGISCHER GARTEN
Bernerring
Margarethenstr.
Güterstr.
Dornacherstr.
A
B
X
Y
Z

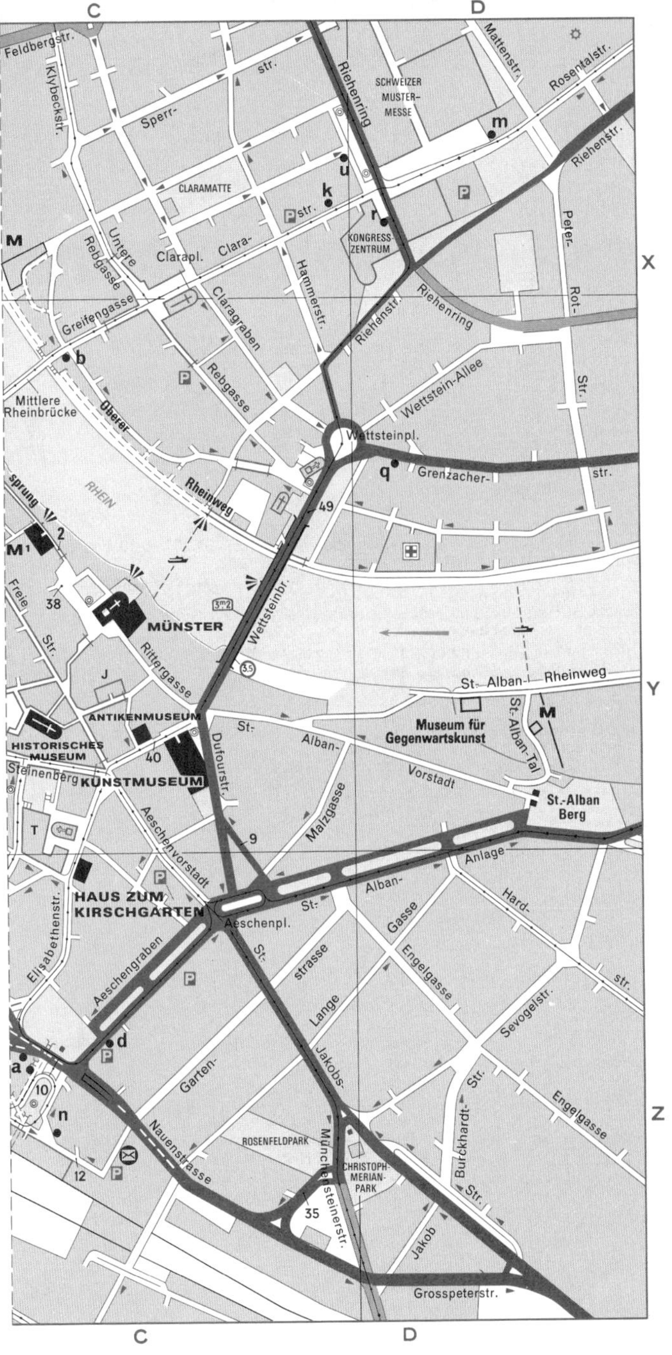

C
D
Feldbergstr.
Klybeckstr.
Sperr-
str.
Riehenring
SCHWEIZER MUSTER-MESSE
Mattenstr.
Rosentalstr.
Riehenstr.
CLARAMATTE
KONGRESS-ZENTRUM
Clarapl.
Clara-
str.
Untere
Rebgasse
Greifengasse
Claragraben
Hammerstr.
Riehenstr.
Riehenring
Peter-
Rot-
Str.
X
Rebgasse
Wettstein-Allee
Mittlere Rheinbrücke
Oberer
Rheinweg
RHEIN
Wettsteinpl.
Grenzacher-
str.
sprung
M¹
MÜNSTER
Wettsteinbr.
Freie
Str.
Rittergasse
St.-Alban-Rheinweg
Y
ANTIKENMUSEUM
HISTORISCHES MUSEUM
Steinenberg
KUNSTMUSEUM
Dufourstr.
St.-
Alban-
Vorstadt
Museum für Gegenwartskunst
St.-Alban-Tal
St.-Alban Berg
Malzgasse
Aeschenvorstadt
HAUS ZUM KIRSCHGARTEN
Aeschenpl.
St.-
Alban-
Anlage
Hard-
str.
Gasse
Elisabethenstr.
Aeschengraben
strasse
Lange
Engelgasse
Sevogelstr.
Jakobs-
Garten-
Burckhardt-
Str.
Engelgasse
Z
Nauenstrasse
ROSENFELDPARK
Münchensteinerstr.
CHRISTOPH-MERIAN-PARK
Jakob
Grosspeterstr.
C
D

STREET INDEX TO BASEL TOWN PLAN

Aeschenvorstadt . . . . **CYZ**
Barfüsserpl. . . . . **BY** 3
Centralbahnpl. . . . . **CZ** 10
Clarapl. . . . . **CX**
Eisengasse . . . . **BY** 15
Falknerstr. . . . . **BY** 16
Freie Str. . . . . **CY**
Gerbergasse . . . . **BY**
Greifengasse . . . . **CY**
Marktpl. . . . . **BY**
Steinenvorstadt . . . . **BY**

Aeschengraben . . . . **CZ**
Aeschenpl. . . . . **CZ**
Allschwilerstr. . . . . **AY**
Arnold Böcklin-Str. . . . . **AZ**
Auberg . . . . **BYZ**
Augustinergasse . . . . **CY** 2
Austr. . . . . **ABY**
Bernerring . . . . **AZ**
Birmannsgasse . . . . **AY**
Blumenrain . . . . **BY**
Brunngässlein . . . . **CY** 9
Bundespl. . . . . **AZ**
Bundesstr. . . . . **AYZ**
Burgfelderpl. . . . . **AX**
Centralbahnstr. . . . . **BCZ** 12
Claragraben . . . . **CY**
Clarastr. . . . . **CX**
Dufourstr. . . . . **CY**
Elisabethenstr. . . . . **CZ**
Engelgasse . . . . **DZ**
Feldbergstr. . . . . **BCX**
Fischmarktpl. . . . . **BY** 18
Gemsberg . . . . **BY** 20
Grenzacherstr. . . . . **DY**
Grosspeterstr. . . . . **DZ**
Güterstr. . . . . **BZ**
Hammerstr. . . . . **CXY**
Hardstr. . . . . **DZ**
Heuberg . . . . **BY**
Holbeinstr. . . . . **BYZ**
Innere-
Margarethenstr. . . . . **BZ** 29
Jacob Burckhardt-Str. . . . . . **DZ**
Johanniterbrücke . . . . **BX**
Kannenfeldpl. . . . . **AX**
Kannenfeldstr. . . . . **AX** 30
Klingelbergstr. . . . . **AX**
Kohlenberg . . . . **BY** 31
Leimenstr. . . . . **BY**
Leonhardsgraben . . . . **BY** 33
Lindenhofstr. . . . . **CZ** 35
Margarethenstr. . . . . **BZ**
Marktgasse . . . . **BY** 36
Mattenstr. . . . . **DX**
Metzerstr. . . . . **AX**
Missionsstr. . . . . **AY**
Mittlere-Rheinbrücke . . . . . . **CY**
Mittlere-Str. . . . . **AXY**
Münchensteinerstr. . . . . **CZ**
Münsterpl. . . . . **CY** 38
Nauenstr. . . . . **CZ**
Oberer-Rheinweg . . . . **CY**
Oberwilerstr. . . . . **AZ**
Peter Rot-Str. . . . . **DXY**
Petersgasse . . . . **BY**
Petersgraben . . . . **BY**
Peterspl. . . . . **BY**
Rebgasse . . . . **CY**
Rheinsprung . . . . **BCY**
Riehenring . . . . **DY**
Riehenstr. . . . . **DY**
Rittergasse . . . . **CY**
Rosentalstr. . . . . **DX**
Rutimeyerstr. . . . . **AZ**
St-Alban-Anlage . . . . **CDZ**
St-Alban-Graben . . . . **CY** 40
St-Alban-Vorstadt . . . . **CDY**
St-Jakobs-Str. . . . . **CDZ**
St-Johanns-Ring . . . . **ABX**
St-Johanns-Vorstadt . . . . . . **BX**
Schanzenstr. . . . . **BX**
Schneidergasse . . . . **BY** 42
Schützengraben . . . . **ABY**
Schützenmattstr. . . . . **ABY**
Sevogelstr. . . . . **DZ**
Spalenberg . . . . **BY**
Spalenring . . . . **AY**
Spalenvorstadt . . . . **BY** 43
Sperrstr. . . . . **CX**
Spitalstr. . . . . **BX**
Stadthausgasse . . . . **BY** 45
Steinenberg . . . . **CY**
Steinengraben . . . . **BY**
Steinenring . . . . **AYZ**
Untere-Rebgasse . . . . **CX**
Viaduktstr. . . . . **BZ**
Wettsteinallee . . . . **DY**
Wettsteinbrücke . . . . **CY**
Wettsteinpl. . . . . **CDY**
Wettsteinstr. . . . . **CY** 49

XXX ✿ **Der Teufelhof** [M] with rm, Leonhardsgraben 47 ✉ 4051 ✆ 261 10 10, Fax 261 10 04, « Rooms decorated by contemporary artists » – ☎. AE GB — BY **g**
closed 11 June-8 August (except hotel) and 23 December-6 January – **M** *(closed Sunday and Monday)* 95/165 ₰ – **8 rm** ☐ 195/265
Spec. Filet de St-Pierre aux Saint-Jacques, beurre au Noailly-Prat. Poularde rôtie au Gruyère, sauce aux champignons. Parfait aux mirabelles.

XX **Donati,** St-Johannsvorstadt 48 ✉ 4056 ✆ 322 09 19, 🏠 — BX **p**
closed July, Monday and Tuesday – **M** Italian rest. 30/38.

at Binningen SW : 8 km – ✉ 4102 :

XXX **Schloss Binningen,** Schlossgasse 5 ✆ 421 20 55, Fax 421 06 35, 🏠, « 16C mansion, elegantly decorated, garden » – Ⓟ. AE ⓓ GB
closed 12 to 26 September and Sunday – **M** 58/80 ₰.

at the Basle-Mulhouse airport : NW : 8 km :

XX **Airport rest,** 5th floor in the airport, ← – ▤.

Swiss Side, ✉ 4030 Bâle ✆ 325 32 32, Fax 325 32 65 – AE ⓓ GB
M 20/50 ₰.

French Side, ✉ 6830 St-Louis ✆ 89 69 77 48, Fax 89 69 15 19 – AE ⓓ GB
M (in FF) 59/175 ₰.

Prices For full details of the prices quoted in this Guide, consult the introduction.

GENEVA Switzerland 74 ⑥, 217 ⑪ – pop. 167 167 alt. 375 Greater Geneva 395 238 – Casino – ✆ Geneva, environs : from France 19-41-22, from Switzerland 022.

See : The Shores of the lake ←★★★ – Parks★★ : Mon Repos, la Perle du Lac and Villa Barton – Botanical Garden★ : alpine rock-garden★★ – Cathedral★ : ✳★★ FY – Reformation Monument★ FYZ **D** – Palais des Nations★ ←★★ – Parc de la Grange★ GY – Parc des Eaux-Vives★ – Nave★ of Church of Christ the King – Woodwork★ in the Historical Museum of the Swiss Abroad – Museums : Art and History★★★ GZ, Ariana★★, Natural History★★ GZ, Petit Palais – Modern Art Museum★ GZ **M1** - Baur Collection★ (in 19C mansion) GZ, Old Musical Instruments★ GZ **M3.**

Exc. : – by boat on the lake. Rens. Cie Gén. de Nav., Jardin Anglais ✆ 311 25 21 – Mouettes genevoises, 8 quai du Mont-Blanc ✆ 732 29 44 – Swiss Boat, 4 quai du Mont-Blanc ✆ 736 47 47.

⛳18 at Cologny ✆ 735 75 40 ; ⛳18 Country Club de Bossey ✆ 50 43 75 25, by road to Troinex.

✈ Genève ✆ 717 71 11.

ℹ Office de Tourisme gare Cornavin ✆ 738 52 00 - Telex 731 90 56 A.C. Suisse, 21 r. de la Fontenette ✆ 342 22 23 - T.C. Suisse, 9 r. P.-Fatio ✆ 737 12 12.

Paris 538 ⑦ – Bern 154 ② – Bourg-en-B. 101 ⑦ – Lausanne 63 ② – Lyons 151 ⑦ – Turin 252 ⑥.

Right Bank (Cornavin Railway Station - Les Quais) :

Richemond, Brunswick garden ✉ 1201 ☎ 731 14 00, Telex 412560, Fax 731 67 09, ←, – 250. AE ⓓ GB FY u
M see Le Gentilhomme below - Le Jardin M a la carte 60/90 – 29 – **67 rm** 320/630, 31 suites.

Rhône, quai Turrettini ✉ 1201 ☎ 731 98 31, Telex 412559, Fax 732 45 58, ←, – rm – 40 - 150. AE ⓓ GB JCB. rest EY r
M see Le Neptune below - Café Rafaël M 39/65 – 25 – **224 rm** 280/710, 10 suites.

Les Bergues, 33 quai Bergues ✉ 1201 ☎ 731 50 50, Telex 412540, Fax 732 19 89, ← – rm – 40 - 350. AE ⓓ GB JCB FY k
M see Amphitryon below - Le Pavillon M a la carte 50/80 – 27 – **113 rm** 290/550, 10 suites.

Noga Hilton M, 19 quai Mt-Blanc ✉ 1201 ☎ 731 98 11, Telex 412337, Fax 738 64 32, ←, – rm – 850. AE ⓓ GB JCB GY y
M see Le Cygne below - La Grignotière M a la carte 55/80 – Le Bistroquai M a la carte approx. 30 – 26 – **376 rm** 460/590, 36 suites.

Beau Rivage, 13 quai Mt-Blanc ✉ 1201 ☎ 731 02 21, Telex 412539, Fax 738 98 47, ←, – rm rest – 30 - 300. AE ⓓ GB JCB FY d
M see Le Chat Botté below - Le Quai 13 ☎ 731 31 82 M a la carte 50/75 – 23 – **104 rm** 330/660, 6 suites.

Président M, 17 quai Wilson ✉ 1211 ☎ 731 10 00, Telex 412328, Fax 731 22 06, ← lake – rm – 25 - 80. AE ⓓ GB. rest GX d
M a la carte 75/110 – 22 – **183 rm** 300/450, 29 suites.

Paix, 11 quai Mt-Blanc ✉ 1201 ☎ 732 61 50, Telex 412554, Fax 738 87 94, ← – – 70. AE ⓓ GB – M 40/60 – 27 – **85 rm** 260/530, 15 suites. FY s

Forum Hôtel, 19 r. Zürich ✉ 1211 ☎ 731 02 41, Telex 412557, Fax 738 75 14 – rm – 100. AE ⓓ GB JCB FX s
La Cortille M 50/95 – Café Ragueneau M 50/95 – 23 – **212 rm** 240/335, 7 suites.

Pullman Rotary M, 18 r. Cendrier ✉ 1201 ☎ 731 52 00, Telex 412704, Fax 731 91 69, , « Fine antique furniture » – rm rm . AE ⓓ GB. rest FY t
M *(closed 25 December-2 January, Saturday and Sunday)* a la carte approx. 60 – 24 – **84 rm** 250/270.

Warwick M, 14 r. Lausanne ✉ 1201 ☎ 731 62 50, Telex 412731, Fax 738 99 35 – rm – 25 - 300. AE ⓓ GB JCB. rest FY n
Les 4 Saisons *(closed 1 to 15 August, Saturday and Sunday)* M 41/80 – 22 – **169 rm** 310/365.

Bristol, 10 r. Mt-Blanc ✉ 1201 ☎ 732 38 00, Telex 412544, Fax 738 90 39, – kitchenette rest – 30 - 100. AE ⓓ GB JCB. rest FY w
M 18/64 – 20 – **93 rm** 255/420, 5 suites.

Cornavin without rest, 33 bd James Fazy ✉ 1211 ☎ 732 21 00, Telex 412548, Fax 732 88 43 – . AE ⓓ GB JCB EY t
115 rm 140/275.

Ambassador, 21 quai Bergues ✉ 1201 ☎ 731 72 00, Fax 738 90 80, – rm – 40. AE ⓓ GB. FY p
M 46/55 – 14 – **86 rm** 145/313.

Berne, 26 r. Berne ✉ 1201 ☎ 731 60 00, Telex 412542, Fax 731 11 73 – – 30 - 100. AE ⓓ GB JCB. rm FY x
M 14/40 – **84 rm** 200/280, 4 suites.

Carlton, 22 r. Amat ✉ 1202 ☎ 731 68 50, Telex 412546, Fax 732 82 47 – kitchenette rest . AE ⓓ GB JCB FX a
M *(closed 1 to 9 January, Sunday lunch and Saturday)* 19/42 – **123 rm** 165/305.

Grand Pré without rest, 35 r. Gd Pré ✉ 1202 ☎ 733 91 50, Telex 414210, Fax 734 76 91 – kitchenette rm – 30. AE ⓓ GB JCB EX s
80 rm 175/250.

Strasbourg et Univers M, 10 r. Pradier ✉ 1201 ☎ 732 25 62, Telex 412773, Fax 738 42 08 – – 25. AE ⓓ GB JCB. FY q
M 22 – **53 rm** 140/190.

Le Montbrillant M, 2 r. Montbrillant ✉ 1201 ☎ 733 77 84, Fax 733 25 11, – . AE ⓓ GB – M 20/25 – **58 rm** 120/170. EY b

XXXX ✿ **Le Cygne** - Hôtel Noga Hilton, 19 quai Mt-Blanc ✉ 1201 ☎ 731 98 11, Telex 412337, Fax 738 64 32, ← – . AE ⓓ GB JCB. GY y
M 90/145 and a la carte 95/135
Spec. Baluchons de tourteaux en tempura (winter). Bar de ligne à la vinaigrette de truffes. Selle d'agneau en feuille de vigne et croûte de sel (summer). Wines Lully blanc, Satigny.

XXXX ✿ **Le Neptune** - Hôtel du Rhône, quai Turrettini ✉ 1201 ☎ 731 98 31, Telex 412559, Fax 732 45 58, – . AE ⓓ GB JCB. EY r
closed 24 July-16 August, Saturday, Sunday and Bank Holidays – M 105/155 and a la carte 90/130
Spec. Escalope de foie gras de canard poêlée et croûtons de polenta. Risotto de blanc de turbot et langoustines. Tarte tiède aux pêches blanches, glace au lait d'amandes.

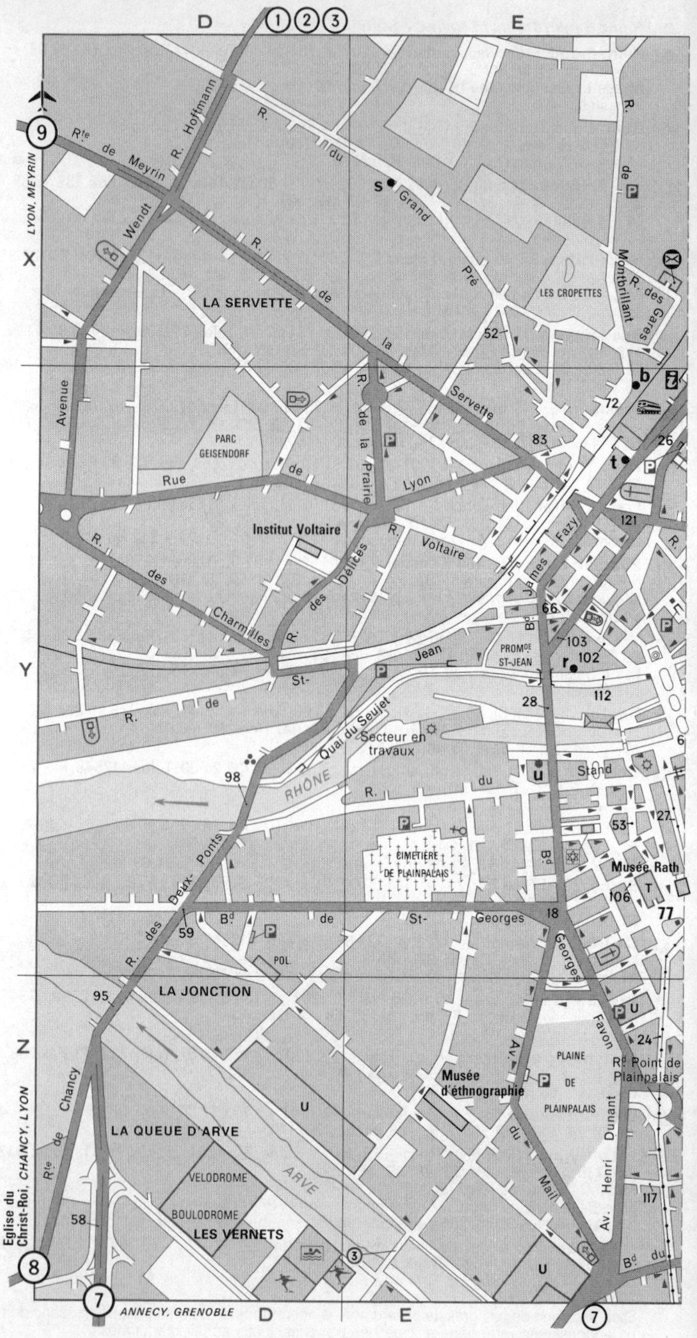
D
E
LYON, MEYRIN
Rte de Meyrin
R. Hoffmann
Wendt
R. du Grand Pré
LA SERVETTE
R. de la Servette
LES CROPETTES
R. de Montbrillant
R. des Gares
Avenue
PARC GEISENDORF
Rue de Lyon
R. de la Prairie
Institut Voltaire
R. Voltaire
R. des Charmilles
R. des Délices
Bd James Fazy
PROMDE ST-JEAN
R. de St-Jean
Quai du Seujet
Secteur en travaux
RHÔNE
R. du Stand
CIMETIÈRE DE PLAINPALAIS
Musée Rath
R. des Deux-Ponts
Bd de St-Georges
POL.
LA JONCTION
Bd Georges Favon
Rd Point de Plainpalais
PLAINE DE PLAINPALAIS
Musée d'ethnographie
Av. du Mail
Av. Henri Dunant
Rte de Chancy
LA QUEUE D'ARVE
VELODROME
BOULODROME
LES VERNETS
ARVE
Bd du
Eglise du Christ-Roi, CHANCY, LYON
ANNECY, GRENOBLE
X
Y
Z

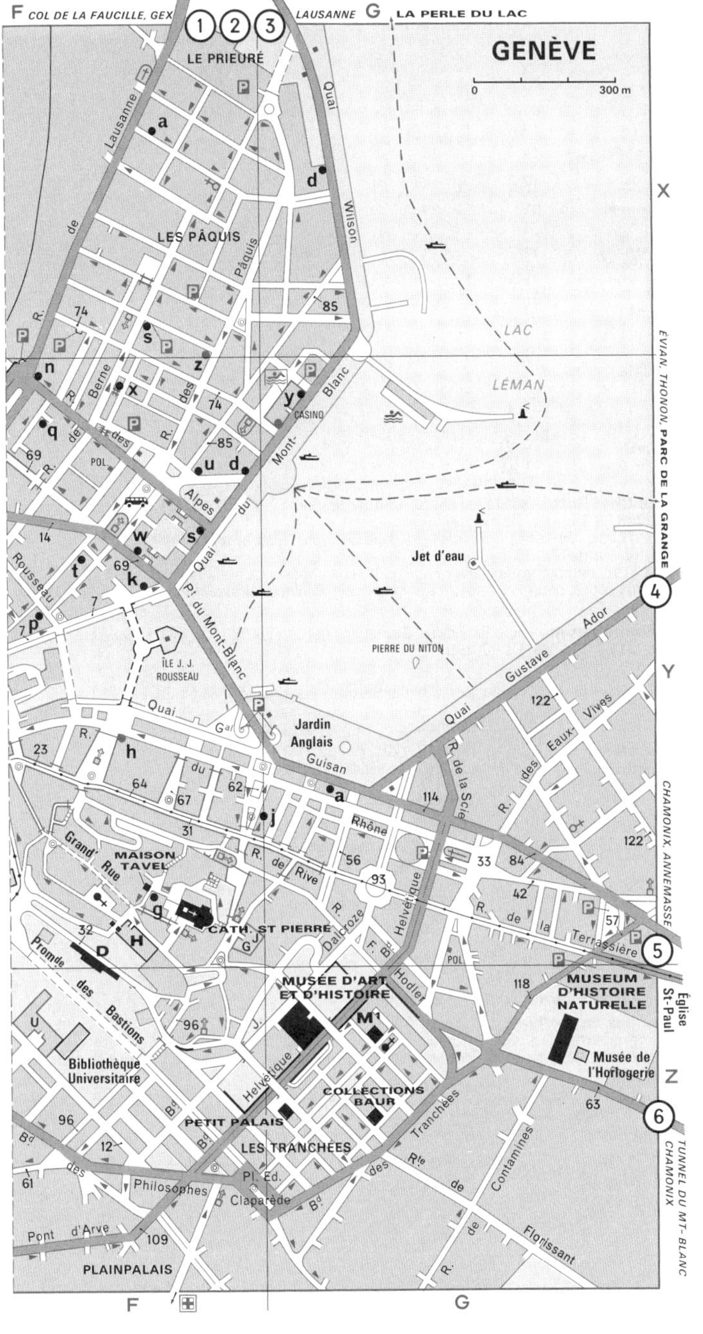
GENÈVE
0
300 m
F
COL DE LA FAUCILLE, GEX
1
2
3
LAUSANNE
G
LA PERLE DU LAC
LE PRIEURÉ
LES PÂQUIS
Quai Wilson
Quai du Mont-Blanc
LAC
LÉMAN
ÉVIAN, THONON, PARC DE LA GRANGE
X
Y
Z
CASINO
Jet d'eau
ÎLE J. J. ROUSSEAU
Pt. du Mont-Blanc
PIERRE DU NITON
Quai Gustave Ador
Jardin Anglais
Quai Gal Guisan
R. du Rhône
R. de Rive
MAISON TAVEL
Grand' Rue
CATH. ST PIERRE
Promde des Bastions
Bibliothèque Universitaire
MUSÉE D'ART ET D'HISTOIRE
COLLECTIONS BAUR
PETIT PALAIS
LES TRANCHÉES
MUSEUM D'HISTOIRE NATURELLE
Musée de l'Horlogerie
Église St-Paul
CHAMONIX, ANNEMASSE
TUNNEL DU MT-BLANC CHAMONIX
4
5
6
R. de la Scie
R. des Eaux-Vives
R. de la Terrassière
R. Dalcroze
Bd Helvétique
Bd des Philosophes
Pl. Ed. Claparède
Rte de Florissant
R. de Contamines
Bd des Tranchées
Pont d'Arve
PLAINPALAIS
R. de Lausanne
R. de Berne
R. des Pâquis
R. des Alpes
Rousseau
POL

XXXX ✿ **Le Chat Botté** - Hôtel Beau Rivage, 13 quai Mt-Blanc ✉ 1201 ☎ 731 65 32, Telex 412539, Fax 738 98 47 – ▤. AE ⓓ GB JCB FY **d**
closed Easter Holidays, Christmas Holidays, Saturday, Sunday and Bank Holidays – **M** 95/125 and a la carte 70/110
Spec. Filets de perches en salade, vinaigrette aux appétits (June-April). Noix de St-Jacques poêlées aux cèpes, beurre aux épices (October-April). Poulet de Bresse rôti en cocotte. Wines Peissy, Satigny.

XXXX **Le Gentilhomme** - Hôtel Richemond, Brunswick garden ✉ 1201 ☎ 731 14 00, Telex 412560, Fax 731 67 09 – ▤. AE ⓓ GB FY **u**
M 98.

XXXX **Amphitryon** - Hôtel Les Bergues, 33 quai Bergues ✉ 1201 ☎ 731 50 50, Fax 732 19 89 – ▤. AE ⓓ GB JCB FY **k**
M *(closed July, August, Saturday lunch and Sunday)* a la carte 75/95.

X **Bœuf Rouge,** 17 r. A. Vincent ✉ 1201 ☎ 732 75 37 – GB FY **z**
closed Saturday and Sunday – **M** Specialities of Lyons 50/68 ₰.

Left Bank (Commercial Centre) :

🏨 **Métropole,** 34 quai Gén. Guisan ✉ 1204 ☎ 311 13 44, Telex 421550, Fax 311 13 50, 🍽 – |☰| ▤ TV ☎ – 🏃 50 - 200. AE ⓓ GB. ✗ rest GY **a**
M see **L'Arlequin** below - **Le Grand Quai M** a la carte 65/100 ₰ – **121 rm** ☕ 260/435, 6 suites.

🏨 **La Cigogne,** 17 pl. Longemalle ✉ 1204 ☎ 311 42 42, Telex 421748, Fax 311 40 65, « Tastefully decorated and furnished » – |☰| ▤ TV ☎ – 🏃 25. AE ⓓ GB JCB. ✗ rest FGY **j**
M 85/105 – **42 rm** ☕ 255/355, 8 suites.

🏨 **Armures** 🐎, 1 r. Puits-St-Pierre ✉ 1204 ☎ 310 91 72, Telex 421129, Fax 310 98 46 – |☰| ▤ TV ☎ – 🏃 25. AE ⓓ GB FY **g**
M 40/48 ₰ – **24 rm** ☕ 270/360, 4 suites.

XXXX **Parc des Eaux-Vives,** 82 quai G. Ador ✉ 1207 ☎ 735 41 40, Fax 786 87 65, « Pleasant setting in extensive park, attractive view », 🍽 – Ⓟ. AE ⓓ GB by ④
closed late December-mid February, Sunday (except lunch 15 April-October) and Monday – **M** 80/150 ₰.

XXXX **L'Arlequin** - Hôtel Métropole, 34 quai Gén. Guisan ✉ 1204 ☎ 311 13 44, Telex 421550, Fax 311 13 50 – ▤. AE ⓓ GB. ✗ GY **a**
closed August, Saturday, Sunday and Bank Holidays – **M** 90/110 ₰.

XXX ✿✿ **Le Béarn** (Goddard), 4 quai Poste ✉ 1204 ☎ 321 00 28, Fax 381 31 15 – ▤. ⓓ GB EY **u**
closed 17 July-22 August, February Holidays, Saturday (except dinner from October-April) and Sunday – **M** 115/145 and a la carte 90/140
Spec. Croustillant de truffe et foie gras (mid December-mid February). Oursin fourré aux coquilles St-Jacques (winter). Gaufrette de grenouilles à l'échalote mauve (spring). Wines Satigny, Coteau de Choully.

XXX **Baron de la Mouette (Mövenpick Fusterie),** 40 r. Rhône ✉ 1204 ☎ 311 88 55, Fax 310 93 22 – ▤. AE ⓓ GB FY **h**
closed Sunday in July-August – **M** 45 ₰.

Environs

to the N :

Palais des Nations :

Intercontinental M, 7 petit Saconnex ✉ 1211 ☎ 734 60 91, Telex 412921, Fax 734 28 64, ←, terrace, gym, pool - lift ▤ TV ☎ garage P - 25 - 600. AE ⓓ GB JCB. rest by ①
M see **Les Continents** below - **La Pergola M** a la carte 60/85 - ☐ 23 - **271 rm** 340/490, 60 suites.

XXXX ✿ **Les Continents** - Hôtel Intercontinental, 7 petit Saconnex ✉ 1211 ☎ 734 60 91, Telex 412921, Fax 734 28 64 - ▤ P. AE ⓓ GB JCB. by ①
closed Sunday lunch and Saturday - **M** 88 and a la carte 90/140
Spec. Sauté de langoustines et fricassée de petits haricots blancs. Symphonie de poissons et crustacés aux élans de cannelle et d'harissa. Pigeon rôti dans ses sucs au laurier et pastilla de béatilles. Wines Peissy, Saint-Saphorin.

XXX **La Perle du Lac,** 128 r. Lausanne ✉ 1202 ☎ 731 79 35, Fax 731 49 79, ← lake, terrace - P. AE ⓓ GB. by quai Wilson GX
closed 23 December-24 January and Monday - **M** 95/140.

at Palais des Expositions : 5 km - ✉ 1218 Grand Saconnex :

Holiday Inn Crowne Plaza M, 26 voie Moëns ☎ 791 00 11, Telex 415695, Fax 798 92 73, gym, pool - lift rm ▤ TV ☎ ♿ garage - 40 - 140. AE ⓓ GB JCB
M 35 - ☐ 22 - **303 rm** 250/330.

at Bellevue by ③ and road to Lausanne : 6 km - ✉ 1293 :

La Réserve M, 301 rte Lausanne ☎ 774 17 41, Telex 419117, Fax 774 25 71, ←, terrace, « Set in a park near the lake, marina », gym, pool, pool, tennis - lift ▤ TV ☎ garage P - 80. AE ⓓ GB JCB
M see **Tsé Fung** below - **La Closerie M** a la carte 60/85 - **Chez Gianni** - **Italian rest M** a la carte approx. 75 - **Mikado** Japanese rest. **M** a la carte 70/120 - ☐ 25 - **114 rm** 360/450, 9 suites.

XXX **Tsé Fung** - Hôtel La Réserve, 301 rte Lausanne ☎ 774 17 41, Telex 419117, Fax 774 25 71, terrace - ▤ P. AE ⓓ GB - **M** Chinese rest. 75/125.

at Genthod by ③ and road to Lausanne : 7 km - ✉ 1294 :

XX ✿ **Rest. du Château de Genthod** (Leisibach), 1 rte Rennex ☎ 774 19 72, terrace - GB
closed 15 to 23 August, 20 December-10 January, Sunday and Monday - **M** 65/85 and a la carte 50/75
Spec. Salade de homard à la nage. Matelote de mer au safran. Pêche au sabayon de vin blanc. Wines Pinot noir.

to the E by road to Evian :

at Cologny by ④ : 3,5 km - ✉ 1223 :

XXXX ✿ **Aub. du Lion d'Or** (Large), au Village ☎ 736 44 32, Fax 786 74 62, ←, terrace, « Overlooking the lake and Geneva » - P. AE ⓓ GB
closed 9 to 18 April, 20 December-17 January, Saturday and Sunday - **M** 130/165 and a la carte 95/140
Spec. Rosette de langoustines et poissons crus. Dos de loup rôti aux gousses d'ail et vieux vinaigre. Mitonnée de langues et pieds de veau à l'ancienne. Wines Lully, Pinot noir du Valais.

to the S :

at Petit-Lancy by ⑧ : 3 km - ✉ 1213 :

✿ **Host. de la Vendée,** 28 chemin Vendée ☎ 792 04 11, Telex 421304, Fax 792 05 46, terrace - lift ▤ TV ☎ P - 40. AE ⓓ GB
closed 24 December-6 January - **M** *(closed Saturday lunch and Sunday)* 72/115 and a la carte 75/105 - **33 rm** ☐ 145/245
Spec. Homard en nage au Pineau des Charentes. Brochette de rognon de veau grillé. Coquelet en pie aux truffes et Champagne. Wines Aligoté, Dôle.

at Grand-Lancy by ⑦ : 3 km - ✉ 1212 Lancy :

XXX ✿ **Marignac** (Pelletier), 32 av. E. Lance ☎ 794 04 24, Fax 794 34 83, terrace, park - ▤ P. GB
closed Saturday lunch and Sunday - **M** 50/115 and a la carte 75/115
Spec. Tartare de saumon sur salade de saison. Escalopes de foie gras de canard sur pommes en l'air. Wines Dardagny, Peissy.

to the W :

at Peney-Dessus by road to Peney : 10 km - ✉ 1242 Staigny :

XXX ✿ **Domaine de Châteauvieux** (Chevrier) with rm, ☎ 753 15 11, Fax 753 19 24, ←, terrace, « Old manor farmhouse », - TV ☎ P - 30. GB
closed 1 to 16 August and 23 December-12 January - **M** *(closed Sunday and Monday)* 95/130 and a la carte 90/105 - ☐ 16 - **18 rm** 125/195
Spec. Suprêmes de grouse rôtis au chou vert et foie gras de canard (October-November). Canette de Bresse rôtie aux petits navets confits (June-October). Croustillants de queues de langoustines et champignons sauvages. Wines Satigny.

at Cointrin by road to Lyon : 4 km - ✉ 1216 :

Mövenpick Radisson M, 20 rte Pré Bois ✉ 1215 ✆ 798 75 75, Telex 415701, Fax 791 02 84, – | rm TV ☎ ♿ – 250. AE GB JCB
M a la carte 40/60 ♂ - **La Belle Époque** *(closed Saturday lunch)* **M** a la carte 55/90 - **Kikkoman M** 75/100 ♂ - 20 - **344 rm** 220/335, 6 suites.

Penta M, 75 av. L. Casaï ✆ 798 47 00, Telex 415571, Fax 798 77 58, – | rm TV ☎ ♿ P - 700. AE GB JCB. rest
La Récolte M 18/36 ♂ - 21 - **308 rm** 200/450, 6 suites.

Plein Ciel, (at the airport) ✆ 717 76 76, Telex 415775, Fax 798 77 68, < - . AE GB
M 39/62.

ZÜRICH 8001 427 ⑥ 216 ⑱ - pop. 380 000 - 01.

See : The Quays★★ BYZ - Fraumünster cloisters★ (Alter Kreuzgang des Fraumünsters) BZ **D** - View of the town from the Zürichhorn Gardens★ V - Church of SS. Felix and Regula★ U **E** - Church of Zürich-Altstetten★ U **F** - Zoological Gardens★ (Zoo Dolder) U - Museums : Swiss National Museum★★★ (Schweizerisches Landesmuseum) BY - Fine Arts Museum★★ (Kunsthaus) CZ - Rietberg Museum★★ V **M2** - Buhrle Collection★★ (Sammlung Buhrle) V **M3**.

Kloten ✆ 812 71 11.

Offizielles Verkehrsbüro, Bahnhofplatz 15 ✉ 8023 ✆ 211 40 00, Telex 813 744 - A.C.S. Forchstrasse 95 ✉ 8032 ✆ 55 15 00 - T.C.S. Alfred-Escher-Strasse 38 ✉ 8002 ✆ 201 25 36.

Basle 109 ⑥ - Bern 125 ⑥ - Geneva 278 ⑥ - Innsbruck 288 ① - Milan 304 ⑤.

Plans on following pages

On the right bank of river Limmat (University, Fine Arts Museum) :

Dolder Grand Hotel , Kurhausstr. 65, ✉ 8032, ✆ 251 62 31, Telex 816416, Fax 251 88 29, < Zürich and lake, , , 9, park, - | TV ☎ P - 200. AE E VISA. rest V **f**
M 80/90 and a la carte 95/170 - **La Rotonde** a la carte 98/159 - **165 rm** 290/500, 11 suites.

Zurich et la Residence, Neumühlequai 42, ✉ 8001, ✆ 363 63 63, Telex 817587, Fax 363 60 15, <, , , - | rm TV ☎ ♿ - 250. AE E VISA. rest U **b**
M - **Tourne Broche** - **White Elephant** *(Thai rest.)* - **263 rm** 340/390 Bb, 10 suites.

Eden au Lac, Utoquai 45, ✉ 8023, ✆ 261 94 04, Telex 816339, Fax 261 94 09, <, - | TV ☎ P. AE E VISA V **a**
M 120 and a la carte 72/95 - **52 rm** 265/500, 3 suites.

Waldhaus Dolder , Kurhausstr. 20, ✉ 8030, ✆ 251 93 60, Telex 816460, Fax 251 00 29, < Zürich and lake, , , , 1g, - | rest TV ☎ P - 35 V **r**
97 rm, 3 suites.

Central Plaza, Central 1, ✉ 8001, ✆ 251 55 55, Telex 817152, Fax 251 85 35 - | TV ☎ - 45. AE E VISA BY **z**
M Cascade *(closed Saturday and Sunday)* 32/42 and a la carte - 18 Bb - **94 rm** 250/370, 4 suites.

Pullman Continental, Stampfenbachstr. 60, ✉ 8035, ✆ 363 33 63, Telex 817089, Fax 363 33 18 - | rm TV ☎ ♿ - 70. AE E VISA U **a**
M Diff (dinner only) 46 and a la carte - **Coq d'Or** 40 and a la carte - 24 - **177 rm** 210/280.

Opera without rest., Dufourstr. 5, ✉ 8008, ✆ 251 90 90, Telex 816480, Fax 251 90 01 - | TV ☎. AE E VISA CZ **b**
closed 21 December-8 January - **67 rm** 210/310.

Europe without rest., Dufourstr. 4, ✉ 8008, ✆ 261 10 30, Telex 816461, Fax 251 03 67 - | TV ☎. AE E VISA CZ **a**
40 rm 235/450, 2 suites.

Tiefenau, Steimweisstr. 8-10, ✉ 8032, ✆ 251 24 09, Fax 251 24 76, - | rest TV ☎ P - 35. AE E VISA CZ **h**
closed 17 December-2 January - **M** 26,50 and a la carte - **25 rm** 170/350, 3 suites.

Ambassador, Falkenstr. 6, ✉ 8008, ✆ 261 76 00, Telex 816508, Fax 251 23 94 - | TV ☎. AE E VISA CZ **a**
M 30/50 and a la carte - **45 rm** 210/310.

Wellenberg without rest., Niederdorfstr. 10, ✉ 8001, ✆ 262 43 00, Fax 251 31 30 - | TV ☎ ♿. AE E VISA BY **s**
46 rm 155/310.

Helmhaus without rest., Schiffländeplatz 30, ✉ 8001, ✆ 251 88 10, Fax 251 04 30 - | TV ☎. AE E VISA. BCZ **s**
25 rm 165/250.

Zürcherhof, Zähringerstr. 21, ✉ 8025, ✆ 262 10 40, Telex 816490, Fax 262 04 84 - | rest TV ☎. AE E VISA CY **q**
M *(closed Saturday and Sunday)* 19,80/38,50 and a la carte - **35 rm** 180/280.

Rütli without rest., Zähringerstr. 43, ✉ 8001, ✆ 251 54 26, Telex 816037, Fax 261 21 53 - | TV ☎. AE E VISA. CY **a**
62 rm 160/235.

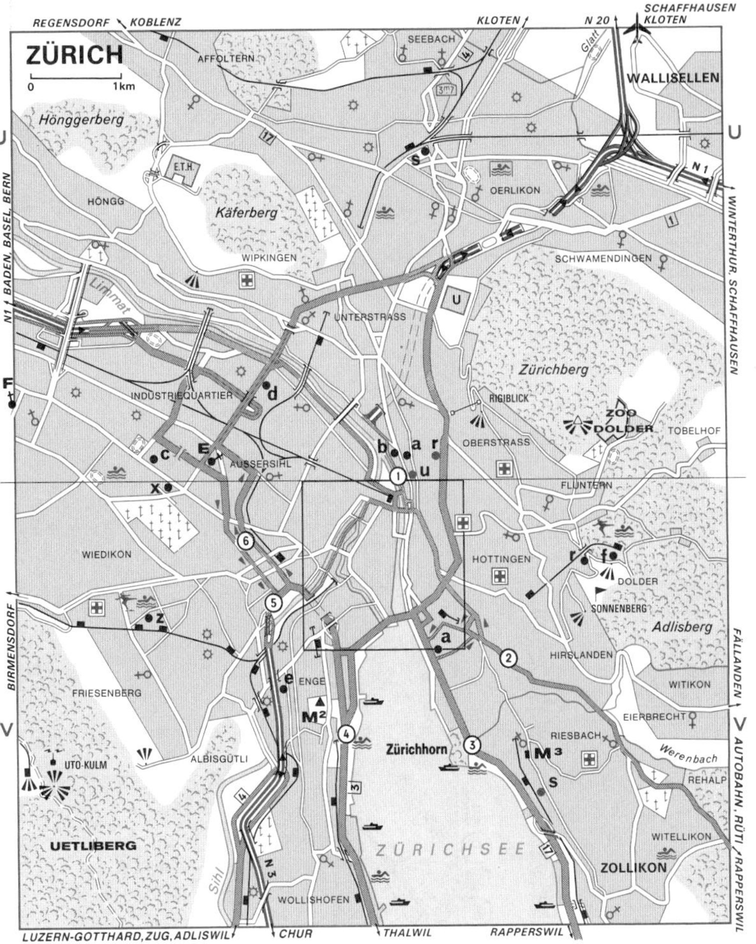

Franziskaner, Niederdorfstr. 1, ✉ 8001, ✆ 252 01 20, Telex 816431, Fax 252 61 78 – TV ☎ – 100. AE ⓓ E VISA BY **x**
M 15/32 and a la carte – **20 rm** 160/230.

Ammann without rest., Kirchgasse 4, ✉ 8001, ✆ 252 72 40, Telex 817137, Fax 262 43 70 – TV ☎. AE ⓓ E VISA BCZ **n**
closed 2 weeks Christmas and 4 days at Easter – **22 rm** 170/262, 1 suite.

XXX **Agnès Amberg,** Hottingerstr. 5, ✉ 8032, ✆ 251 26 26, Fax 252 50 62 – AE ⓓ E VISA CY **d**
closed Sunday, 4 weeks July-August, 25 December-1 January and Bank Holidays – **M** 53/150 and a la carte 63/107

XXX **Zunfthaus Zur Schmiden,** Marktgasse 20, ✉ 8001, ✆ 251 52 87, Fax 261 12 67, « 15C blacksmith's guild house » – rest. AE ⓓ E VISA BY **f**
closed 24 July-22 August – **M** 28/73,50 and a la carte 55/86.

XX **Kronenhalle,** Rämistrasse 4, ✉ 8001, ✆ 251 66 69, « Café de luxe, fine art collection » – . AE ⓓ E VISA CZ **r**
M 45/55 (buffet) and a la carte.

XX **Wirtschaft Flühgass,** Zollikerstr. 214, Riesbach, ✉ 8008, ✆ 381 12 15, Fax 422 75 32, « 16C inn » – P. AE ⓓ E VISA V **s**
closed Saturday, Sunday and 10 July-9 August – **M** (booking essential) 60/120 and a la carte.

ZÜRICH

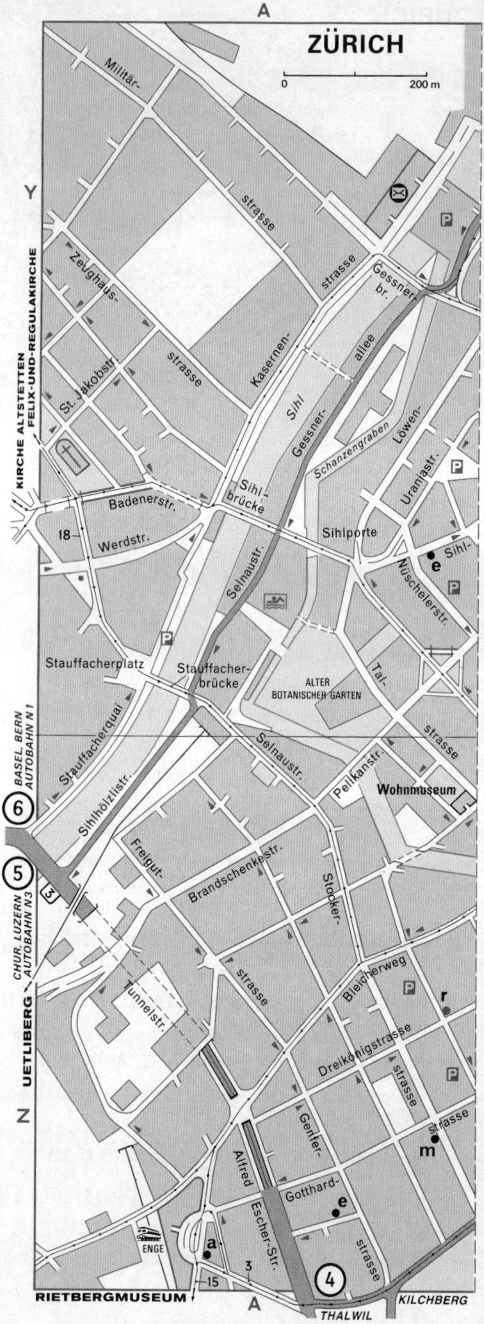

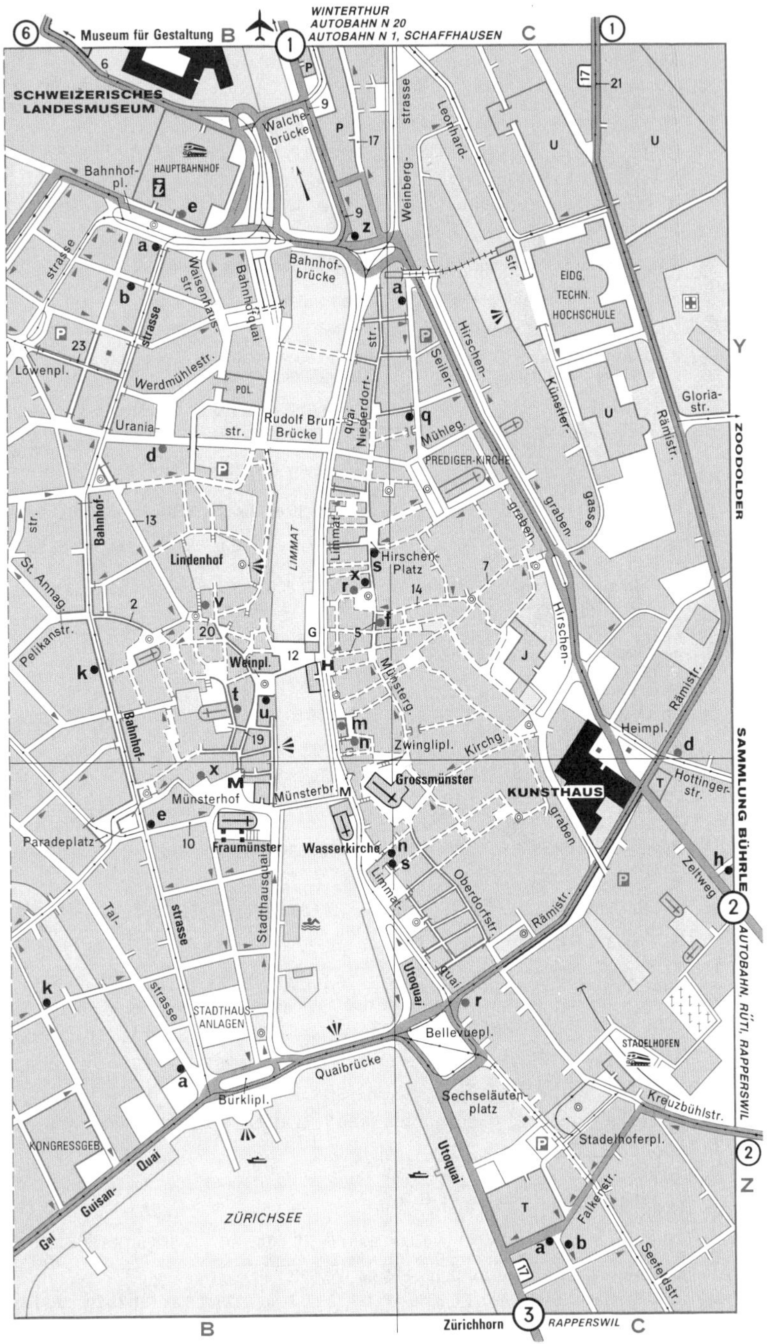

Museum für Gestaltung
WINTERTHUR
AUTOBAHN N 20
AUTOBAHN N 1, SCHAFFHAUSEN
SCHWEIZERISCHES LANDESMUSEUM
HAUPTBAHNHOF
Bahnhofpl.
Walchebrücke
Weinbergstrasse
Leonhardstrasse
Bahnhofbrücke
EIDG. TECHN. HOCHSCHULE
Waisenhausstr.
Bahnhofquai
Löwenpl.
Werdmühlestr.
POL.
Seilergraben
Hirschengraben
Künstlergasse
Rämistr.
Gloriastr.
ZOODOLDER
Uraniastr.
Rudolf Brun-Brücke
Niederdorfquai
Mühleg.
PREDIGER-KIRCHE
Bahnhofstrasse
St. Annag.
LIMMAT
Limmatquai
Lindenhof
Hirschenplatz
Pelikanstr.
Weinpl.
Münsterg.
Heimpl.
SAMMLUNG BÜHRLE
Zwinglipl.
Kirchg.
Grossmünster
KUNSTHAUS
Hottingerstr.
Münsterhof
Münsterbr.
Paradeplatz
Fraumünster
Wasserkirche
Zeltweg
Talstrasse
Stadthausquai
Oberdorfstr.
AUTOBAHN, RÜTI, RAPPERSWIL
Utoquai
STADTHAUS-ANLAGEN
Bellevuepl.
STADELHOFEN
Quaibrücke
Bürklipl.
Sechseläutenplatz
Kreuzbühlstr.
KONGRESSGEB.
Stadelhoferpl.
Gal Guisan-Quai
ZÜRICHSEE
Falkenstr.
Seefeldstr.
Zürichhorn
RAPPERSWIL

XX **Haus Zum Rüden,** Limmatquai 42 (1st floor), ✉ 8001, ℘ 261 95 66, Fax 261 18 04, « 13C guild house » – |‡| ▤. AE ⓓ E VISA BY **m**
M *closed Saturday lunch, Sunday and Bank Holidays* 150 and a la carte.

XX **Königstuhl,** Stüssihofstatt 3, ✉ 8001, ℘ 261 76 18, Telex 816431, Fax 252 61 78 – AE ⓓ E VISA BY **r**
M 98/130 (dinner) and a la carte approx. 98.

XX **Jacky's Stapferstube,** Culmannstr. 45, ✉ 8033, ℘ 361 37 48, Veal and beef specialities – ▤ Ⓟ. AE ⓓ E VISA U **r**
closed Sunday and Monday – **M** 30 (lunch) and a la carte 58/161.

XX **Zunfthaus Zum Zimmerleuten,** Limmatquay 40, (1st floor), ✉ 8001, ℘ 252 08 34, Fax 252 08 48, « 18C guild house » – AE ⓓ E VISA BY **n**
closed Sunday – **M** 40/90 and a la carte.

X **Casa Ferlin,** Stampfenbachstr. 38, ✉ 8006, ℘ 362 35 09, Italian rest. – ▤. AE ⓓ E VISA U **u**
closed Saturday, Sunday and mid July-mid August – **M** a la carte 61,50/81,50.

On the left bank of river Limmat (Main railway station, Business centre) :

Baur au Lac, Talstr. 1, ✉ 8022, ℘ 221 16 50, Telex 813567, Fax 211 81 39, ⛱, « Lakeside setting and gardens » – |‡| ▤ TV ☎ ⇐ Ⓟ – 🏛 150. AE ⓓ E VISA. ✻ BZ **a**
M Le Pavillon 55/69 and a la carte 55/130 – **Le Grill** – **123 rm** ☐ 330/540, 16 suites.

Savoy Baur en Ville, Paradeplatz, ✉ 8022, ℘ 211 53 60, Telex 812845, Fax 221 14 67 – |‡| ▤ TV ☎ ⇐ – 🏛 135. AE ⓓ E VISA. ✻ BZ **e**
M Orsini (Italian rest.) 62/98 and a la carte – **Savoy Grill** 72/98 and a la carte – **104 rm** ☐ 360/700, 8 suites.

Schweizerhof, Bahnhofplatz 7, ✉ 8023, ℘ 211 86 40, Telex 813754, Fax 211 35 05 – |‡| ▤ TV ☎ – 🏛 40. AE ⓓ E VISA. ✻ rest BY **a**
M La Soupière *(closed Saturday lunch and Sunday)* a la carte 58/73 – **115 rm** ☐ 300/850.

Atlantis Sheraton ♨, Döltschiweg 234, ✉ 8055, ℘ 463 00 00, Telex 813338, Fax 463 03 88, ≤ countryside and city, ⛱, 🏋, ≘s, 🏊, park – |‡| ⇔ rm ▤ rest TV ☎ ⇐ Ⓟ – 🏛 200. AE ⓓ E VISA V **z**
M 70/118 and a la carte – **159 rm** ☐ 350/440, 2 suites.
Annexe Guesthouse ♨, ℘ 463 00 00, Telex 813338, Fax 463 03 88 – |‡| ⇔ rm TV ☎. AE ⓓ E VISA
61 rm ☐ 210/240.

St. Gothard, Bahnhofstr. 87, ✉ 8023, ℘ 211 55 00, Telex 812420, Fax 211 24 19, ≘s – |‡| ⇔ ▤ TV ☎ – 🏛 40. AE ⓓ E VISA BY **b**
M 95/56 and a la carte – ☐ 25 – **128 rm** 240/430, 7 suites.

Ascot, Tessinerplatz 9, ✉ 8002, ℘ 201 18 00, Telex 815454, Fax 202 72 10 – |‡| ▤ TV ☎ – 🏛 50. AE ⓓ E VISA AZ **a**
M Jockey Club *(closed Saturday and Sunday)* 60/120 and a la carte – **73 rm** ☐ 200/470.

Splügenschloss, Splügenstr. 2, ✉ 8002, ℘ 201 08 00, Telex 815553, Fax 201 42 86 – |‡| ⇔ rm ▤ TV ☎ Ⓟ – 🏛 20. AE ⓓ E VISA AZ **e**
M 150/200 and a la carte – **49 rm** ☐ 200/450, 1 suite.

Neues Schloss, Stockerstr. 17, ✉ 8022, ℘ 201 65 50, Telex 815560, Fax 201 64 18 – |‡| TV ☎ Ⓟ – 🏛 25. AE ⓓ E VISA. ✻ rest AZ **m**
M Le Jardin *(closed Saturday and Sunday lunch)* 55/90 and a la carte – **57 rm** ☐ 190/400, 1 suite.

Zum Storchen, Weinplatz 2, ✉ 8022, ℘ 211 55 10, Telex 813354, Fax 211 64 51, ≤ River Limmat and city, ⛱, « Riverside setting » – |‡| TV ☎ – 🏛 40. AE ⓓ E VISA BY **u**
M a la carte 60/85 – **77 rm** ☐ 220/450 Bb, 1 suite.

Stoller, Badenerstr. 357, ✉ 8040, ℘ 492 65 00, Telex 822460, Fax 492 65 01, ⛱ – |‡| TV ☎ ⇐ Ⓟ – 🏛 50. AE ⓓ E VISA V **x**
M 16,50/49 and a la carte – **79 rm** ☐ 200/280.

Glockenhof, Sihlstr. 31, ✉ 8023, ℘ 211 56 50, Telex 812466, Fax 211 56 60, ⛱ – |‡| ▤ rest TV ☎. AE ⓓ E VISA AY **e**
M 23/55 and a la carte – **108 rm** ☐ 190/280.

Glärnischhof, Claridenstr. 30, ✉ 8022, ℘ 202 47 47, Telex 815366, Fax 201 01 64 – |‡| ▤ rest TV ☎ Ⓟ – 🏛 35. AE ⓓ E VISA BZ **k**
M 42 and a la carte – **70 rm** ☐ 260/500.

Carlton Elite, Banhofstr. 41, Nüschelerstr. 6, ✉ 8023, ℘ 211 65 60, Telex 812787, Fax 211 30 19, ⛱ – |‡| ▤ rm TV ☎ Ⓟ – 🏛 240. AE ⓓ E VISA BY **k**
M 60/75 and a la carte – ☐ 15 Bb – **73 rm** 170/360.

Nova Park, Badenerstr. 420, ✉ 8040, ℘ 491 22 22, Telex 822822, Fax 491 22 20, ⛱, 🏋, ≘s, 🏊 – |‡| ⇔ rm ▤ rm TV ☎ ⇐. AE ⓓ E VISA U **c**
363 rm ☐ 210/390.

Senator, Heinrichstr. 254-256, ✉ 8005, ✆ 272 20 21, Fax 272 25 85, – rm
– 35. AE ⓓ E VISA U d
M 22/45 and a la carte – 15 Bb – **102 rm** 170/210.

Engematthof, Engimattstr. 14, ✉ 8002, ✆ 201 25 04, Fax 201 25 16, –
– 25. AE ⓓ E VISA V e
M 35/68 and a la carte – **79 rm** 150/290.

Baron de la Mouette (Mövenpick Dreikönighaus), Beethovenstr. 32, Dreikönigstr., ✉ 8002, ✆ 286 53 23, Fax 286 53 55 – . AE ⓓ E VISA AZ r
closed Saturday, Sunday and 17 July-28 August – **M** a la carte 70/101,50.

Au Premier, Bahnhofbuffet, Hauptbahnhof, ✉ 8023, ✆ 211 15 10, Fax 212 04 25 – AE ⓓ E VISA BY e
M 80 (lunch) and a la carte 46.00/68.50.

Zunfthaus zur Waag, Münsterhof 8, ✉ 8001, ✆ 211 07 30, Fax 212 01 69, « 17C weavers' guild house » – AE ⓓ E VISA BZ x
M (booking essential) 150 and a la carte 44,50/99,10.

Veltliner Keller, Schlüsselgasse 8, ✉ 8001, ✆ 221 32 28, Fax 212 20 94, « 14C house » – AE ⓓ E VISA BY t
closed Saturday, Sunday and 12 July-15 August – **M** 65/80 and a la carte.

Brasserie Lipp, Uraniastr. 9, ✉ 8001, ✆ 211 11 55, Fax 212 17 26 – AE ⓓ E VISA BY d
closed Sunday 1 July-31 August – **M** 45/55 and a la carte.

Environs North

at Zurich-Oerlikon : by ① – ✉ **8050** Zurich-Oerlikon :

International, Am Marktplatz, ✉ 8050, ✆ 311 43 41, Telex 823251, Fax 312 44 68, – rm – 650. AE ⓓ E VISA. U s
M – **Panorama** (30th floor) ≤ Zurich *(closed Sunday and Monday)* 45/90 and a la carte – 21 Bb – **334 rm** 220/290, 11 suites.

at Zürich-Kloten (Airport) : 10 km by ① :

Ramada Renaissance, Talackerstr. 1, ✉ 8152, Glattbrugg ✆ 810 85 00, Telex 825003, Fax 810 87 55, – rm – 300. AE ⓓ E VISA
M 55/75 and a la carte – **Asian Place** *(closed Saturday, Sunday and Monday lunch)* 20/30 (lunch) and a la carte 32/76,50 – 25 – **197 rm** 235/275, 7 suites.

Hilton, Hohenbühlstr. 10, ✉ 8058, ✆ 810 31 31, Telex 825428, Fax 810 93 66, – rm – 280. AE ⓓ E VISA
M – **Harvest Grill** 60/100 and a la carte – **Taverne** 50/70 and a la carte – 27 – **276 rm** 255/395, 10 suites.

Novotel, Talackerstr. 21 ✉ 8152 Glattbrugg, ✆ 810 31 11, Telex 828770, Fax 810 81 85, – rm – 150. AE ⓓ E VISA
M 38/42 and a la carte – 18 – **256 rm** 155/175, 1 suite.

Fly Away, Marktgasse 19, ✉ 8302, Kloten ✆ 813 66 13, Fax 813 51 25, – . AE ⓓ E VISA
closed 24 to 26 December – **M** 13/20 and a la carte – 9,50 – **42 rm** 139/172.

Welcome Inn, Holbergstr. 1, ✉ 8302 Kloten, ✆ 814 07 27, Fax 813 56 16, – – 13. AE ⓓ E VISA
M a la carte approx. 51,50 – 9 – **96 rm** 105/140.

at Unterengstringen : 7 km by ① – ✉ **8103** Unterengstringen :

✿ **Witschi's,** Zurcherstr. 55, ✉ 8103, ✆ 750 44 60, Fax 750 19 68, – . AE ⓓ E VISA
closed Sunday and Monday – **M** 150/180 and a la carte
Spec. Raviolis d'huitres et langoustines aux truffes blanches, Poitrine et boudin de faisan aux poires rôties et zestés de citron, Mille-feuille de pommes sautées avec sa glace caramel.

at Dielsdorf : NW : 15,5 km by ① and B 17 – ✉ **8157** Dielsdorf :

Bienengarten with rm., Regensbergerstr. 9, 8157, ✆ 853 12 17, Fax 853 24 41, , « Modern lithographs », – . AE ⓓ E VISA
M 40/110 (dinner) and a la carte 42/90 – **8 rm** 160/320.

at Nürensdorf : 17 km by ① via Kloten – ✉ **8309** Nürensdorf :

✿ **Gastof Zum Bären** with rm, Alte Winterthurerstr. 45, ✉ 8309, ✆ 836 42 12 – rest . AE ⓓ E VISA
closed 24 December-3 January – **M** *(closed Sunday and Monday)* 59/139 and a la carte 63/94 – **14 rm** 140/200
Spec. Tartare tiède de turbot sur carpaccio de Zucchetti, Suprême de poularde avec champignons shiitake, sauce soja et sherry, Gratin et parfait d'oranges.

Environs South

at Küsnacht : 6 km by ③ – ✉ **8700** Küsnacht :

🏨 ✿ **Ermitage,** Seestr. 80, ✉ 8700, ✆ 910 52 22, Telex 825707, Fax 910 52 44, ≤ lake, 🍽, « lakeside setting, terrace and garden » – |♦| TV ☎ P. AE ⊕ E VISA
M 55/108 and a la carte – ☕ 15 – **20 rm** 140/260, **6 suites**
Spec. Fresh and smoked salmon tartar on a chive cream, Fillet of venison with endives and roasted polenta, Warm chocolate cake with almond sauce.

XXX ✿✿ **Petermann's Kunststube** (Petermann), Seestr. 160, ✉ 8700, ✆ 910 07 15, Fax 910 04 95 – ▤ P. AE ⊕ E VISA. ✂
closed Sunday, Monday, 13 to 27 February and 15 August-6 September – **M** 65/150 and a la carte 80/126
Spec. Cannelloni fourrés aux herbes, sauce légère, aux fruits de mer, Cabillaud sauté sous sa peau croquante, sauce choucroute, Ragoût de queue de bœuf au Barolo, carottes glacées au laurier.

at Gockhausen E : 9 Km. via Gloriastr. and Keltenstr. – ✉ **8044** Gorkhausen

XX **Rosa Tschudi,** Tobelhofstr. 344, ✆ 821 03 95 – AE ⊕ E
closed Monday, Sunday and 19 to 28 December – **M** 48/150 and a la carte.

at Rüschlikon : 9 km by ④ – ✉ **8803** Rüschlikon :

🏨 **Belvoir** ⛰, Säumerstr. 37, ✉ 8803, ✆ 724 02 02, Fax 724 11 76, ≤ lake, 🍽 – |♦| ▤ rest TV ☎ 🚗 P – 🏛 150. AE ⊕ E VISA. ✂ rest
M 48/75 and a la carte – **25 rm** ☕ 160/300.

at Gattikon : 13,5 km by ⑤ – ✉ **8136** Gattikon-Thalwil :

XXX ✿ **Sihlhalde,** Sihlhaldenstr. 70, ✉ 8136, ✆ 720 09 27, 🍽 – E VISA
closed Sunday, Monday, 20 July-10 August and 20 December-4 January – **M** 48/52 and a la carte approx. 52
Spec. Saumon Choucroute, Chasse d'été (June-October), Agneau.

at Wädenswil : 22 km by ⑤ – ✉ **8820** Wädenswil :

XX **Eichmühle,** Neugutstr. 993, by N3, exit Richterswil, ✆ 780 34 44, Fax 780 48 64, ≤, 🍽 – AE E VISA
closed Sunday dinner, Monday, 2 weeks February and 2 weeks October – **M** 65/125 and a la carte 75/87.

United Kingdom

LONDON - BIRMINGHAM - EDINBURGH
GLASGOW - LEEDS - LIVERPOOL
MANCHESTER

PRACTICAL INFORMATION

LOCAL CURRENCY

Pound Sterling: £ 1 = 1.49 US $ = 1.25 Ecu (Jan. 93).

TOURIST INFORMATION

Tourist information offices exist in each city included in the Guide. The telephone number and address is given in each text under 🅱

FOREIGN EXCHANGE

Banks are open between 9.30am and 3pm on weekdays only and some open on Saturdays. Most large hotels have exchange facilities, and Heathrow and Gatwick Airports have 24-hour banking facilities.

SHOPPING

In London: Oxford St./Regent St. (department stores, exclusive shops)
Bond St. (exclusive shops, antiques)
Knightsbridge area (department stores, exclusive shops, boutiques)
For other towns see the index of street names: those printed in red are where the principal shops are found.

THEATRE BOOKINGS IN LONDON

Your hotel porter will be able to make your arrangements or direct you to Theatre Booking Agents.
In addition there is a kiosk in Leicester Square selling tickets for the same day's performances at half price plus booking fee. It is open 12-6.30pm.

CAR HIRE

The international car hire companies have branches in each major city. Your hotel porter should be able to give details and help you with your arrangements.

TIPPING

Many hotels and restaurants include a service charge but where this is not the case an amount equivalent to between 10 and 15 per cent of the bill is customary. Additionally doormen, baggage porters and cloakroom attendants are generally given a gratuity.
Taxi drivers are customarily tipped between 10 and 15 per cent of the amount shown on the meter in addition to the fare.

SPEED LIMITS

The maximum permitted speed on motorways and dual carriageways is 70 mph (113 km/h.) and 60 mph (97 km/h.) on other roads except where a lower speed limit is signposted.

SEAT BELTS

The wearing of seat belts in the United Kingdom is compulsory for drivers, front seat passengers and rear seat passengers where seat belts are fitted. It is illegal for front seat passengers to carry children on their lap.

ANIMALS

It is forbidden to bring domestic animals (dogs, cats...) into the United Kingdom.

London

404 folds (42) to (44) - pop. 7 566 620 - ☎ 071 or 081.

✈ Heathrow, ☎ (081) 759 4321, Telex 934892, Fax 745 42 90 - Terminal : Airbus (A1) from Victoria, Airbus (A2) from Paddington - Underground (Piccadilly line) frequent service daily.

✈ Gatwick, ☎ 0293 (Crawley) 535353, Fax 59 50 10 and ☎ 081 (London) 668 4211, by A 23 and M 23 - Terminal : Coach service from Victoria Coach Station (Flightline 777, hourly service) - Railink (Gatwick Express) from Victoria (24 h service).

✈ London City Airport, ☎ (071) 474 55 55.

✈ Stansted, at Bishop's Storford, ☎ 0279 (Bishop's Stortford) 680500, Telex 818708, Fax 66 20 66, NE : 34 m. off M 11 and A 120.

British Airways, Victoria Air Terminal : 115 Buckingham Palace Rd., SW1, ☎ (071) 834 9411, Fax 828 71 42, p. 16 BX.

🚗 Euston and Paddington ☎ 0345 090700.

ℹ British Travel Centre, 12 Regent St. Piccadilly Circus, SW1Y 4 PQ, ☎ (071) 930 0572, Fax 839 61 79.
National Tourist Information Centre, Victoria Station Forecourt, SW1, ☎ (071) 730 3488.

Sights

HISTORIC BUILDINGS AND MONUMENTS

Palace of Westminster★★★ p. 10 LY – Tower of London★★★ p. 11 PVX – Banqueting House★★ p. 10 LX – Buckingham Palace★★ p. 16 BVX – Kensington Palace★★ p. 8 FX – Lincoln's Inn★★ p. 17 EV – London Bridge★ p. 11 PVX – Royal Hospital Chelsea★★ p. 15 FU – St. James's Palace★★ p. 13 EP – South Bank Arts Centre★★ p. 10 MX – The Temple★★ p. 6 MV – Tower Bridge★★ p. 11 PX – Albert Memorial★ p. 14 CQ – Apsley House★ p. 12 BP – George Inn★, Southwark p. 11 PX – Guildhall★ p. 7 OU – Dr Johnson's House★ p. 6 NUV **A** – Leighton House★ p. 8 EY – The Monument★ (✳★) p. 7 PV **G** – Royal Opera Arcade★ p. 13 FGN – Staple Inn★ p. 6 MU **Y** – Theatre Royal★ (Haymarket) p. 13 GM.

CHURCHES

The City Churches

St. Paul's Cathedral★★★ p. 7 NOV – St. Bartholomew the Great★★ p. 7 OU **K** – St. Mary-at-Hill★★ p. 7 PV **B** – Temple Church★★ p. 6 MV – All Hallows-by-the-Tower (font cover★★, brasses★) p. 7 PV **Y** – St. Bride★ (steeple★★) p. 7 NV **J** – St. Giles Cripplegate★ p. 7 OU **N** – St. Helen Bishopsgate★ (monuments★★) p. 7 PUV **R** – St. James Garlickhythe (tower and spire★, sword rest★) p. 7 OV **R** – St. Margaret Lothbury p. 7 PU **S** – St. Margaret Pattens (woodwork★) p. 7 PV **N** – St. Mary Abchurch★ p. 7 PV **X** – St. Mary-le-Bow (tower and steeple★★) p. 7 OV **G** – St. Michael Paternoster Royal (tower and spire★) p. 7 OV **D** – St. Olave★ p. 7 PV **S**.

Other Churches

Westminster Abbey★★★ p. 10 LY – Southwark Cathedral★★ p. 11 PX – Queen's Chapel★ p. 13 EP – St. Clement Danes★ p. 17 EX – St. James's★ p. 13 EM – St. Margaret's★ p. 10 LY **A** – St. Martin in-the-Fields★ p. 17 DY – St. Paul's★ (Covent Garden) p. 17 DX – Westminster Roman Catholic Cathedral★ p. 10 KY **B**.

STREETS – SQUARES – PARKS

The City★★★ p. 7 NV – Regent's Park★★★ (Terraces★★, Zoo★★★) p. 5 HIT – Belgrave Square★★ p. 16 AVX – Burlington Arcade★★ p. 13 DM – Hyde Park★★ p. 9 GHVX – The Mall★★ p. 13 FP – Piccadilly★★ p. 13 EM — St. James's Park★★ p. 10 KXY – Trafalgar Square★★ p. 17 DY – Whitehall★★ (Horse Guards★) p. 10 LX – Barbican★ p. 7 OU – Bloomsbury★ p. 6 LMU – Bond Street★ pp. 12-13 CK-DM – Charing Cross★ p. 17 DY – Cheyne Walk★ p. 9 GHZ – Jermyn Street★ p. 13 EN – Piccadilly Arcade★ p. 13 DEN – Queen Anne's Gate★ p. 10 KY – Regent Street★ p. 13 EM – St. James's Square★ p. 13 FN – St. James's Street★ p. 13 EN – Shepherd Market★ p. 12 CN – Strand★ p. 17 DY – Victoria Embankment★ p. 17 DEXY – Waterloo Place★ p. 13 FN.

MUSEUMS

British Museum★★★ p. 6 LU – National Gallery★★★ p. 13 GM – Science Museum★★★ p. 14 CR – Tate Gallery★★★ p. 10 LZ – Victoria and Albert Museum★★★ p. 15 DR – Courtauld Institute Galleries★★ p. 6 KLU **M** – Museum of London★★ p. 7 OU **M** – National Portrait Gallery★★ p. 13 GM – Natural History Museum★★ p. 14 CS – Queen's Gallery★★ p. 16 BV – Wallace Collection★★ p. 12 AH – Imperial War Museum★ p. 10 NY – London Transport Museum★ p. 17 DX – Madame Tussaud's★ p. 5 IU **M** – Sir John Soane's Museum★ p. 6 MU **M** – Wellington Museum★ p. 12 BP.

Alphabetical list of areas included

LONDON CENTRE

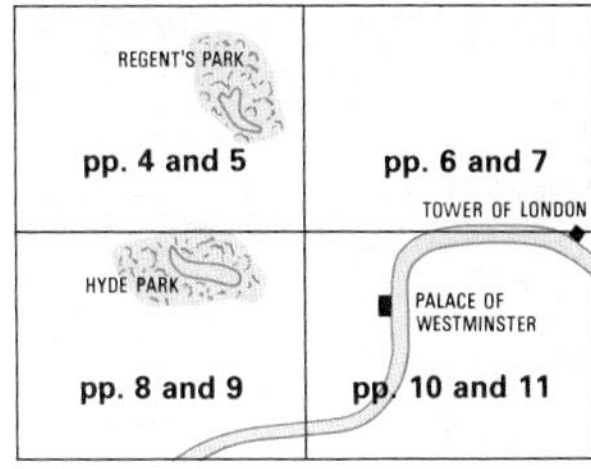

STREET INDEX TO LONDON CENTRE TOWN PLANS

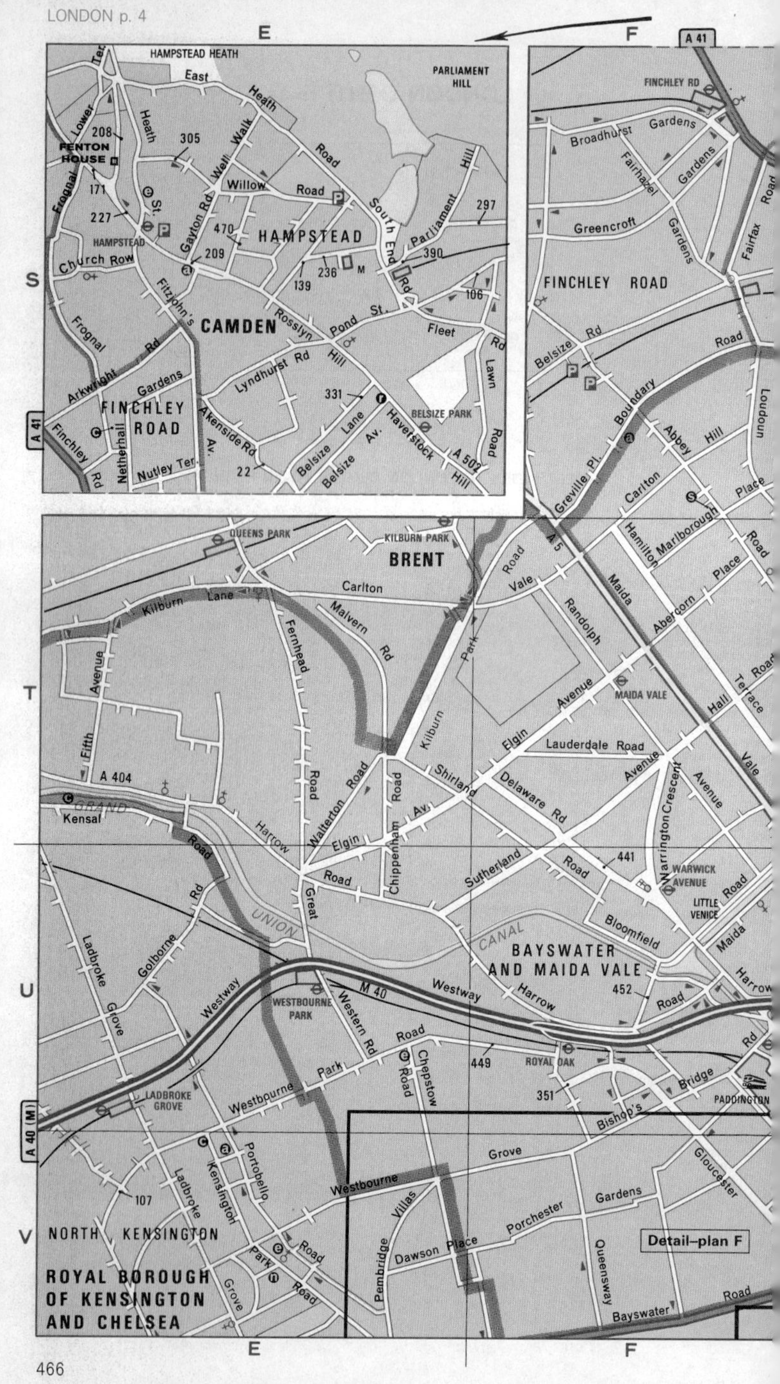
HAMPSTEAD HEATH
PARLIAMENT HILL
FENTON HOUSE
HAMPSTEAD
CAMDEN
FINCHLEY ROAD
BELSIZE PARK
FINCHLEY RD
FINCHLEY ROAD
QUEENS PARK
KILBURN PARK
BRENT
MAIDA VALE
WARWICK AVENUE
LITTLE VENICE
BAYSWATER AND MAIDA VALE
WESTBOURNE PARK
ROYAL OAK
PADDINGTON
LADBROKE GROVE
NORTH KENSINGTON
ROYAL BOROUGH OF KENSINGTON AND CHELSEA
Detail-plan F
GRAND UNION CANAL
Westway
M 40
A 41
A 5
A 404
A 502
A 40 (M)

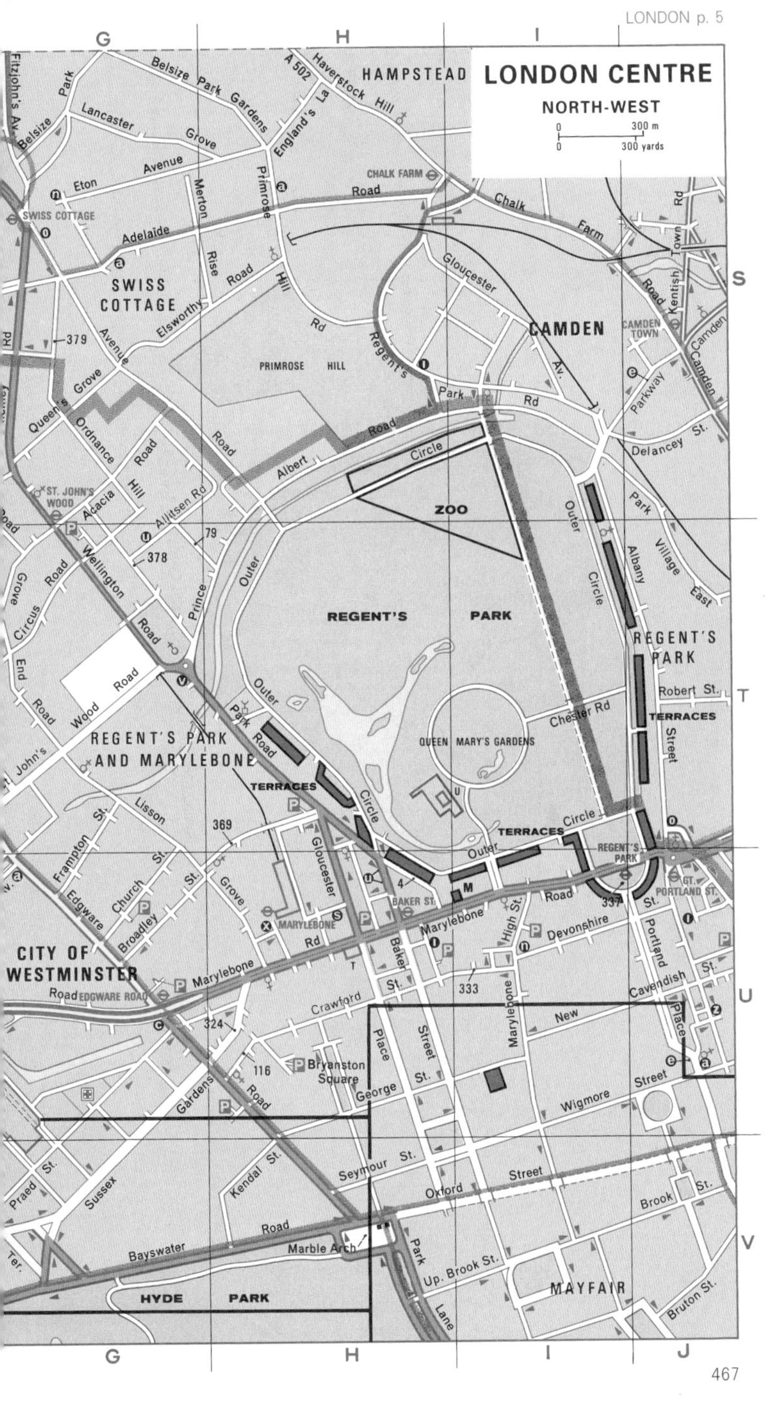
LONDON CENTRE
NORTH-WEST
0 300 m
0 300 yards
HAMPSTEAD
SWISS COTTAGE
CAMDEN
PRIMROSE HILL
ZOO
REGENT'S PARK
QUEEN MARY'S GARDENS
REGENT'S PARK AND MARYLEBONE
TERRACES
CITY OF WESTMINSTER
HYDE PARK
MAYFAIR
CHALK FARM
SWISS COTTAGE
CAMDEN TOWN
ST. JOHN'S WOOD
BAKER ST.
MARYLEBONE
REGENT'S PARK
GT. PORTLAND ST.
EDGWARE ROAD
Marble Arch
Belsize Park Gardens
Haverstock Hill
England's La
Lancaster Grove
Avenue
Eton
Adelaide Road
Primrose Hill
Elsworthy Road
Regent's Park Rd
Gloucester Av.
Chalk Farm Road
Parkway
Delancey St.
Albert Road
Outer Circle
Park Village East
Albany Street
Robert St.
Chester Rd
Prince Albert Road
Wellington Road
Acacia Road
Allitsen Rd
Circus Road
Grove End Road
St. John's Wood Road
Lisson Grove
Frampton St.
Church St.
Broadley
Edgware Road
Park Road
Gloucester Place
Baker Street
Marylebone Road
Marylebone High St.
Devonshire St.
Portland Place
Crawford St.
New Cavendish St.
Bryanston Square
George St.
Wigmore Street
Seymour St.
Oxford Street
Kendal St.
Sussex Gardens
Praed St.
Bayswater Road
Park Lane
Up. Brook St.
Brook St.
Bruton St.
A 502
Merton Rise
Queen's Grove
Ordnance Hill
Kentish Town Rd
Camden
379
378
79
369
4
337
333
324
116
G
H
I
J
S
T
U
V

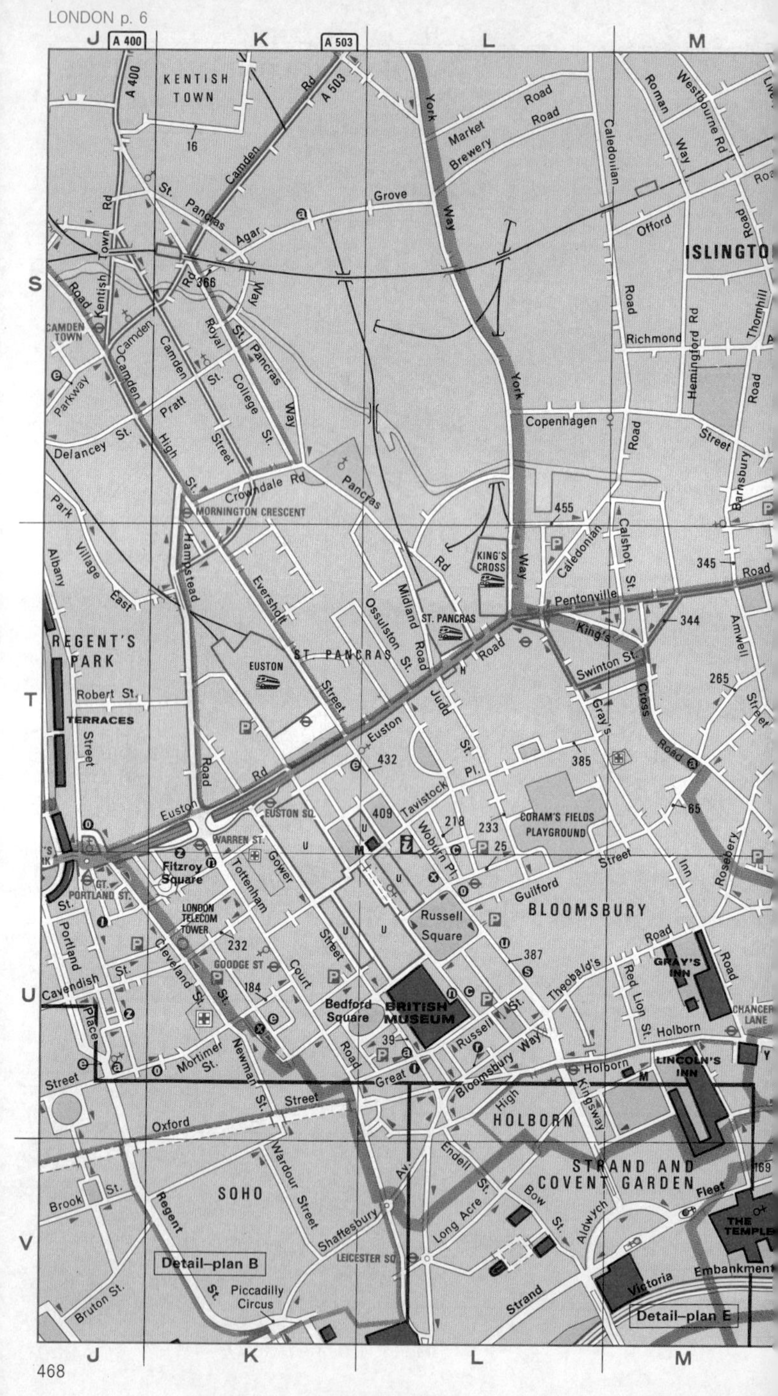

J
K
L
M
A 400
A 503
S
T
U
V
KENTISH TOWN
ISLINGTON
CAMDEN TOWN
MORNINGTON CRESCENT
KING'S CROSS
ST. PANCRAS
EUSTON
REGENT'S PARK
TERRACES
EUSTON SQ.
WARREN ST.
Fitzroy Square
GT. PORTLAND ST.
LONDON TELECOM TOWER
GOODGE ST
Bedford Square
BRITISH MUSEUM
CORAM'S FIELDS PLAYGROUND
BLOOMSBURY
Russell Square
GRAY'S INN
CHANCERY LANE
LINCOLN'S INN
HOLBORN
STRAND AND COVENT GARDEN
THE TEMPLE
SOHO
LEICESTER SQ.
Piccadilly Circus
Detail-plan B
Detail-plan E
Camden Rd
St. Pancras Way
York Way
Market Road
Brewery Road
Caledonian Road
Roman Way
Westbourne Rd
Agar Grove
Offord Road
Richmond
Hemingford Rd
Thornhill Road
Copenhagen Street
Barnsbury
Kentish Town Road
Camden Road
Camden High St.
Royal College St.
Pratt St.
Parkway
Delancey St.
Crowndale Rd
Pancras Rd
Calshot St.
Caledonian
Pentonville Road
King's Cross Road
Swinton St.
Amwell Street
Gray's Inn Road
Rosebery
Park Village East
Albany Street
Hampstead Road
Eversholt Street
Ossulston St.
Midland Road
Judd St.
Euston Road
Robert St.
Tavistock Pl.
Woburn Pl.
Guilford Street
Gower Street
Tottenham Court Road
Cleveland St.
Portland Place
Cavendish
Mortimer St.
Newman St.
Oxford Street
Great Russell St.
Bloomsbury Way
Theobald's Road
Red Lion St.
Holborn
High Holborn
Kingsway
Wardour Street
Regent St.
Brook St.
Bruton St.
Shaftesbury Av.
Endell St.
Long Acre
Bow St.
Aldwych
Fleet
Strand
Victoria Embankment
16
366
455
345
344
265
385
432
409
218
233
25
65
232
184
387
39
169

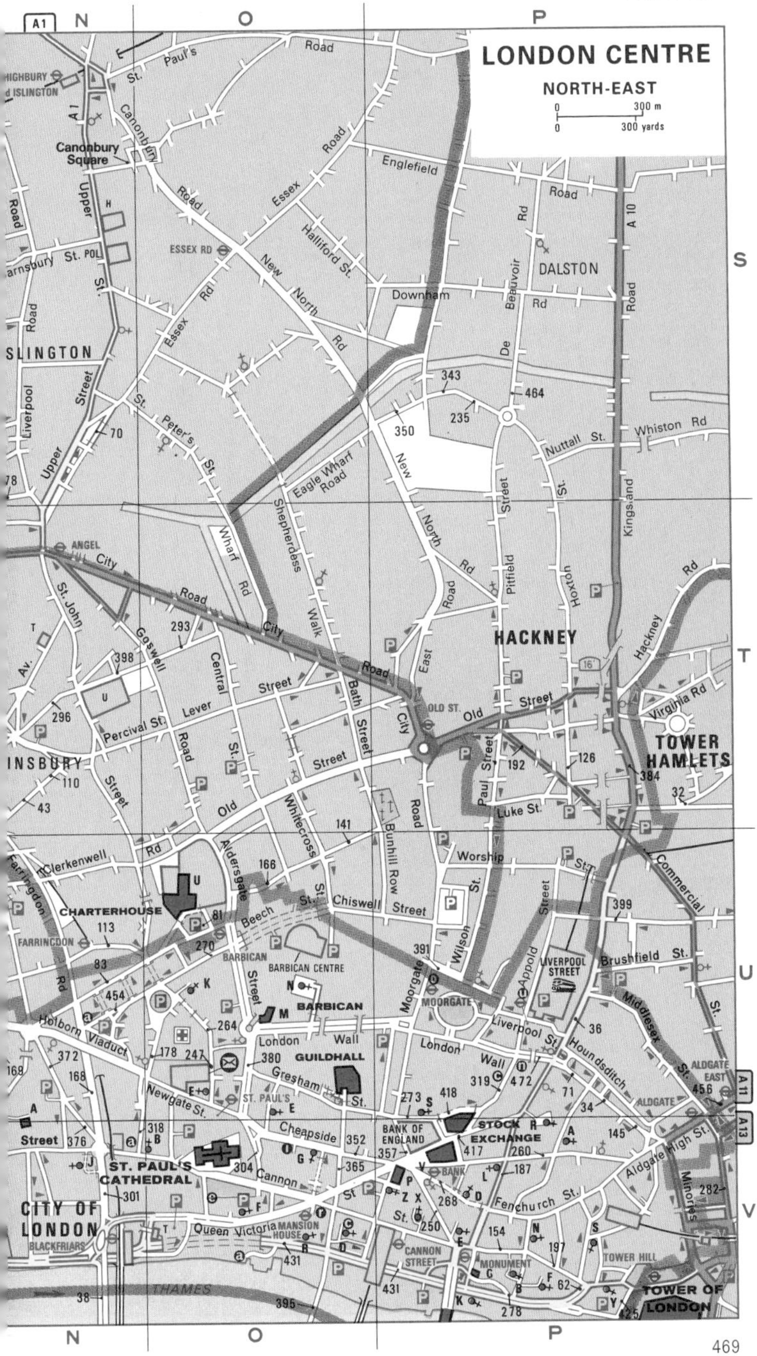

LONDON CENTRE

NORTH-EAST

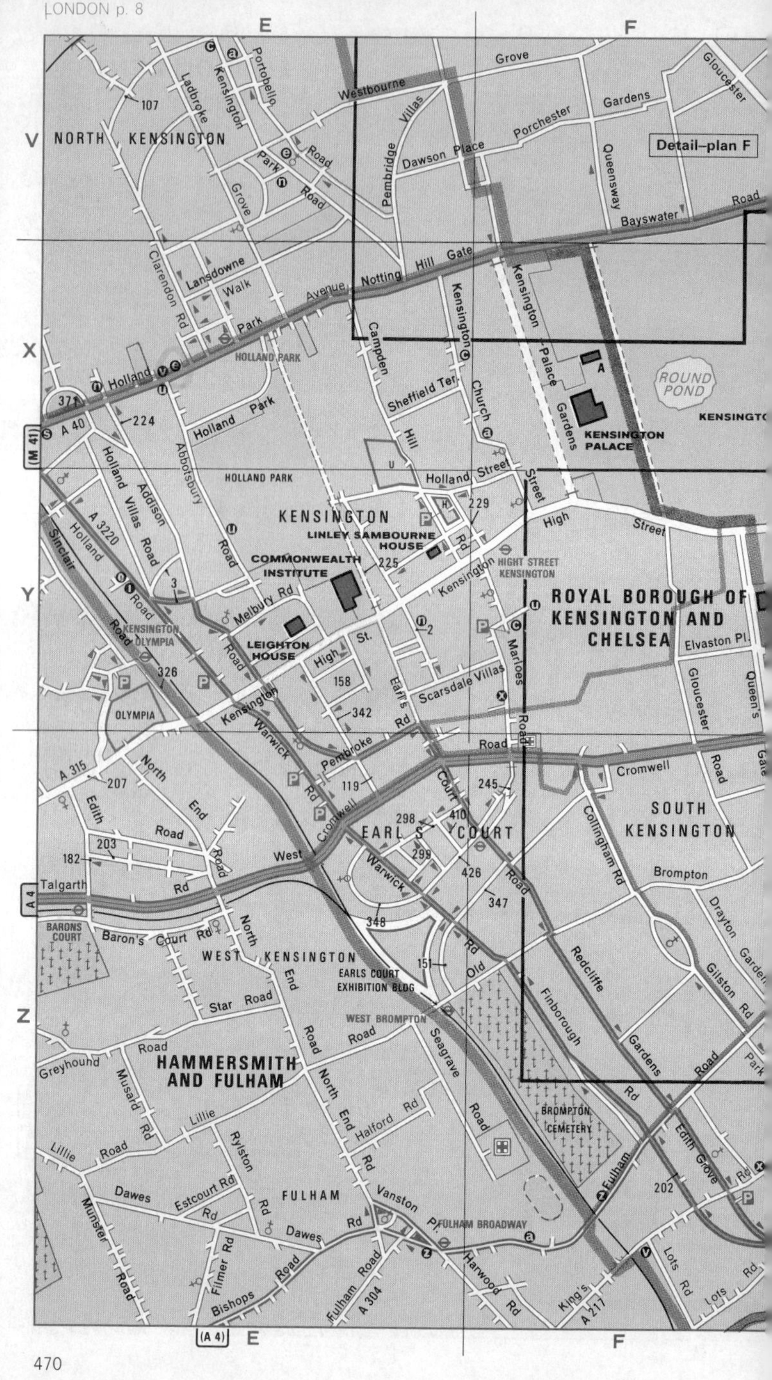
NORTH KENSINGTON
Detail-plan F
HOLLAND PARK
KENSINGTON
LINLEY SAMBOURNE HOUSE
COMMONWEALTH INSTITUTE
LEIGHTON HOUSE
KENSINGTON PALACE
ROUND POND
ROYAL BOROUGH OF KENSINGTON AND CHELSEA
SOUTH KENSINGTON
EARL'S COURT
WEST KENSINGTON
EARLS COURT EXHIBITION BLDG
HAMMERSMITH AND FULHAM
FULHAM
BROMPTON CEMETERY
OLYMPIA
KENSINGTON OLYMPIA
HIGH STREET KENSINGTON
BARONS COURT
WEST BROMPTON
FULHAM BROADWAY

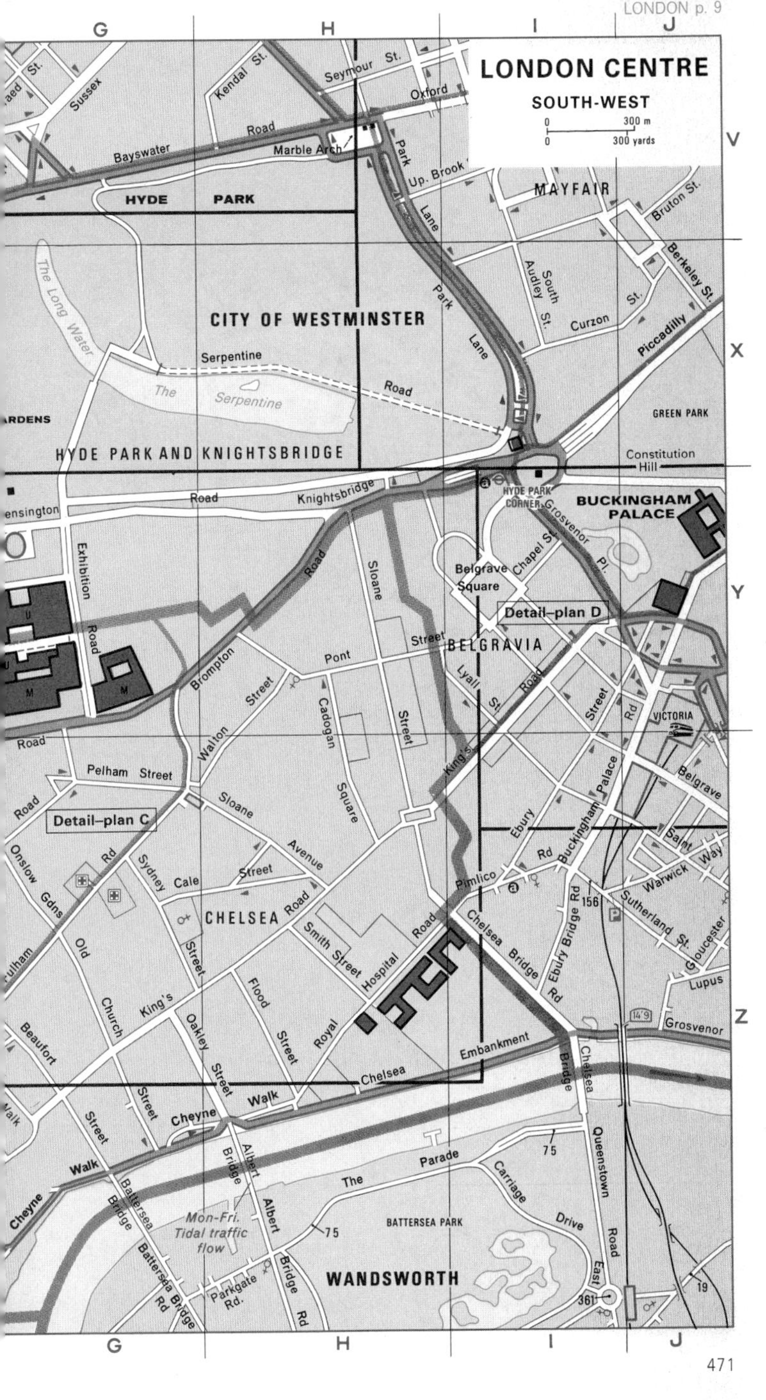
LONDON CENTRE
SOUTH-WEST
0 300 m
0 300 yards
G
H
I
J
V
X
Y
Z
Sussex
Kendal St.
Seymour St.
Oxford
Bayswater
Road
Marble Arch
Park
Up. Brook
Lane
HYDE
PARK
MAYFAIR
Bruton St.
Berkeley St.
South Audley St.
Curzon
St.
Piccadilly
The Long Water
CITY OF WESTMINSTER
Park
Lane
Serpentine
Road
The Serpentine
GREEN PARK
Constitution Hill
HYDE PARK AND KNIGHTSBRIDGE
Road
Knightsbridge
HYDE PARK CORNER
Grosvenor
Pl.
BUCKINGHAM PALACE
Exhibition
Road
Belgrave Square
Chapel St.
Detail-plan D
Sloane
Street
BELGRAVIA
Pont
Brompton
Road
Lyall
St.
Road
Street
Rd
VICTORIA
Walton
Street
Cadogan
Square
Street
King's
Pelham Street
Sloane
Avenue
Belgrave
Palace
Buckingham
Detail-plan C
Onslow Gdns
Rd
Sydney
Cale
Street
Ebury
Rd
Saint
Way
Warwick
Pimlico
CHELSEA
Road
Smith Street
Hospital
Road
Chelsea
Bridge
Road
Ebury Bridge Rd
156
Sutherland St.
Gloucester
Lupus
Old
Church
King's
Flood
Street
Royal
Oakley
Street
Beaufort
Embankment
Grosvenor
Chelsea
Walk
Street
Street
Cheyne
Walk
Bridge
Chelsea
Queenstown
Road
75
The
Parade
Carriage
Drive
Walk
Cheyne
Albert
Bridge
Albert
Battersea
Bridge
Mon-Fri. Tidal traffic flow
75
BATTERSEA PARK
Battersea
Rd
Battersea Bridge
Parkgate Rd.
Bridge
Rd
WANDSWORTH
East
361
19

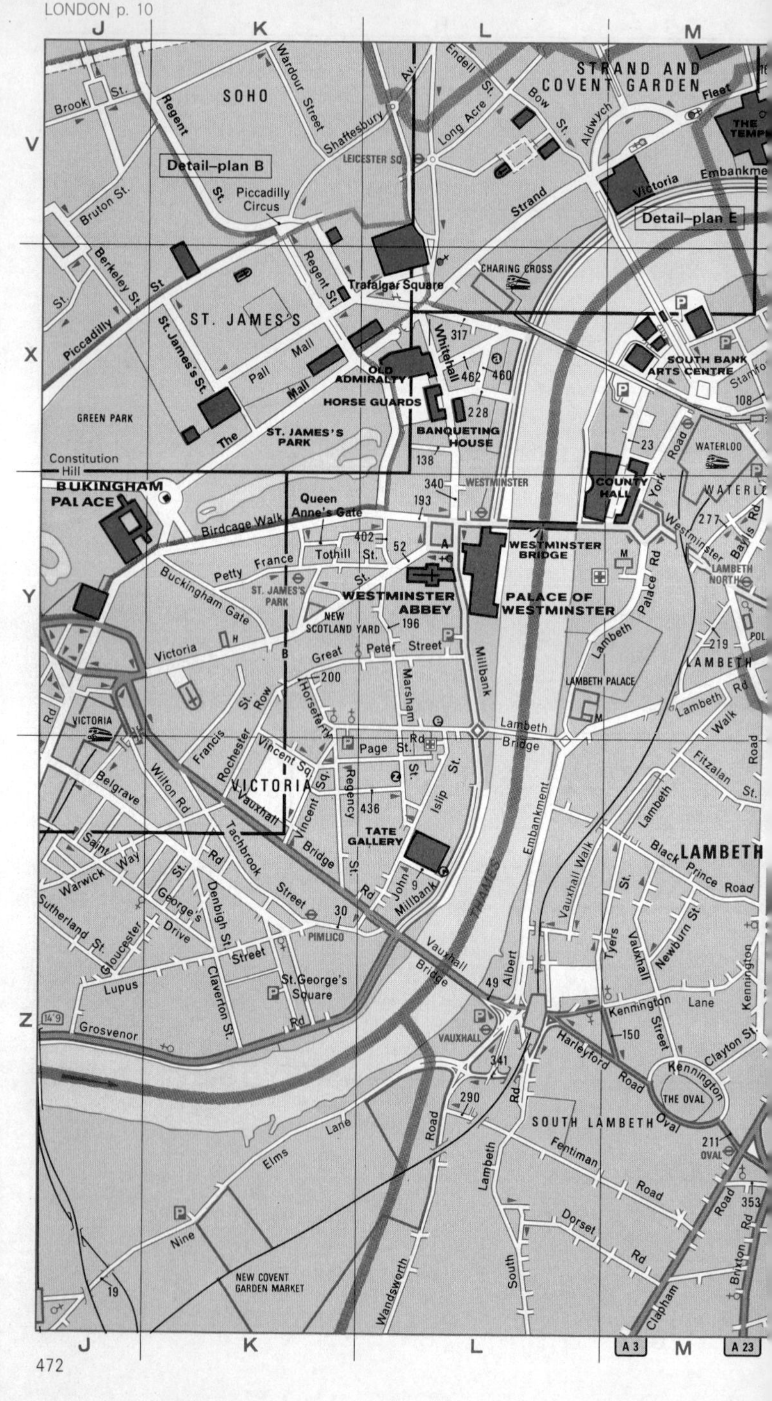
J
K
L
M
V
X
Y
Z
SOHO
STRAND AND COVENT GARDEN
Detail–plan B
Detail–plan E
Brook St.
Regent St.
Wardour Street
Shaftesbury Av.
Endell St.
Long Acre
Bow St.
Aldwych
Fleet
THE TEMPLE
LEICESTER SQ.
Piccadilly Circus
Bruton St.
Strand
Victoria Embankment
Berkeley St.
Piccadilly
St. James's St.
ST. JAMES'S
Regent St.
Trafalgar Square
CHARING CROSS
Pall Mall
The Mall
Whitehall
317
462
460
OLD ADMIRALTY
HORSE GUARDS
228
BANQUETING HOUSE
SOUTH BANK ARTS CENTRE
Stamford
108
23
Road
WATERLOO
GREEN PARK
ST. JAMES'S PARK
Constitution Hill
138
340
WESTMINSTER
BUKINGHAM PALACE
193
Queen Anne's Gate
Birdcage Walk
COUNTY HALL
York
WATERLOO
277
Baylis Rd
402
52
A
Tothill St.
Petty France
WESTMINSTER BRIDGE
Westminster
LAMBETH NORTH
M
Buckingham Gate
ST. JAMES'S PARK
WESTMINSTER ABBEY
PALACE OF WESTMINSTER
Palace Rd
NEW SCOTLAND YARD
196
Lambeth
219
LAMBETH
Victoria
Great Peter Street
Millbank
LAMBETH PALACE
200
Marsham
Horseferry
Row
Francis St.
Lambeth Bridge
Lambeth
Walk
Rd
VICTORIA
Page St.
Rochester
Vincent Sq.
Regency
St.
Fitzalan St.
Road
Belgrave
Wilton Rd
VICTORIA
Vauxhall
436
Islip St.
Embankment
Lambeth
TATE GALLERY
Vincent Bridge
Saint
Way
Warwick
Tachbrook
Rd
Street
Denbigh St.
St. George's
Drive
John
9
Millbank
THAMES
Vauxhall Walk
Black Prince Road
LAMBETH
Sutherland St.
Gloucester
30
PIMLICO
Street
Tyers St.
Vauxhall
Newburn St.
Kennington
Lupus
Claverton St.
St.George's Square
Vauxhall Bridge
49
Albert
Kennington Lane
Rd
Grosvenor
VAUXHALL
150
Street
Clayton St.
Harleyford Road
341
Kennington
THE OVAL
Oval
290
Rd
SOUTH LAMBETH
Lane
Road
211
OVAL
Elms
Fentiman Road
Lambeth
Road
353
Dorset
Rd
Nine
Rd
NEW COVENT GARDEN MARKET
19
Wandsworth
South
Clapham
Brixton
A 3
A 23

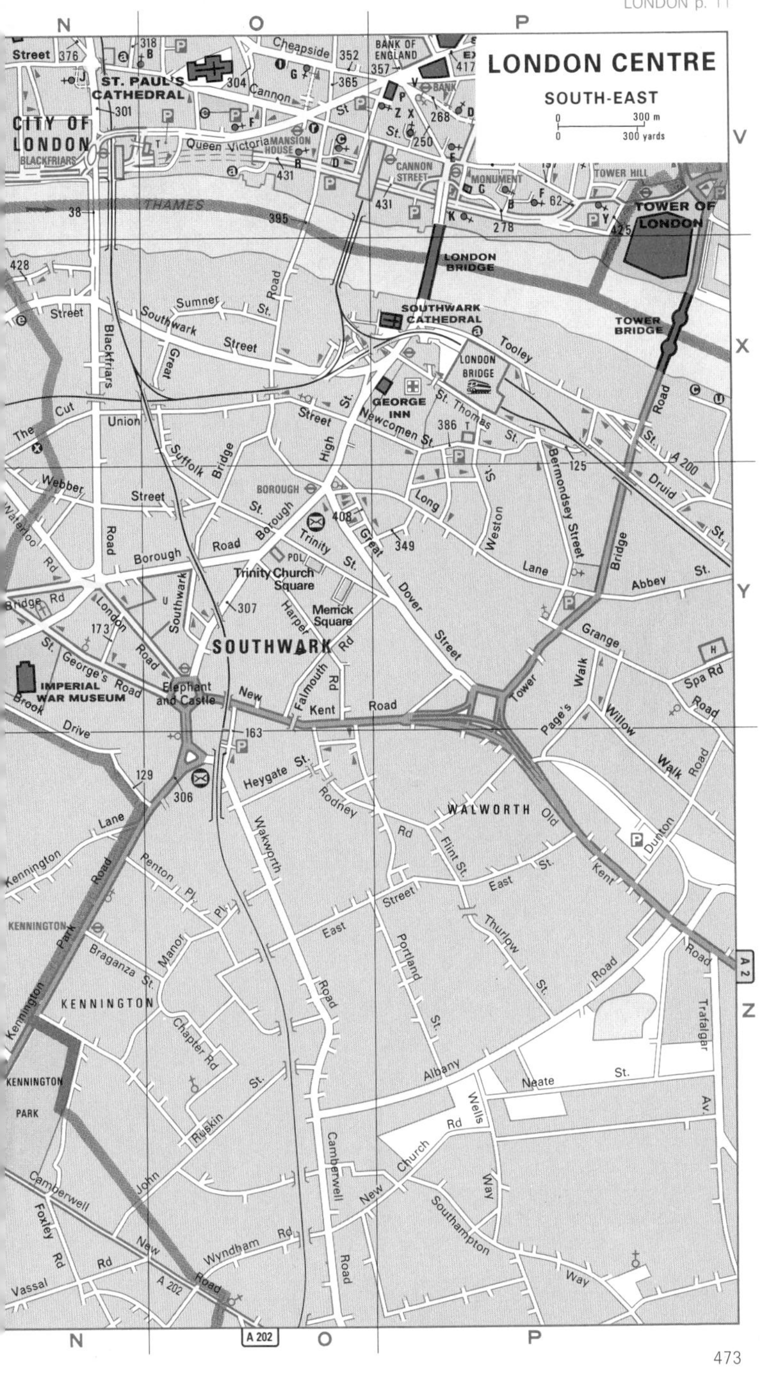
LONDON CENTRE
SOUTH-EAST
300 m
300 yards
ST. PAUL'S CATHEDRAL
CITY OF LONDON
BLACKFRIARS
BANK OF ENGLAND
Cheapside
Cannon St
Queen Victoria
MANSION HOUSE
CANNON STREET
MONUMENT
TOWER HILL
TOWER OF LONDON
THAMES
LONDON BRIDGE
SOUTHWARK CATHEDRAL
TOWER BRIDGE
Tooley
LONDON BRIDGE
GEORGE INN
Sumner St.
Southwark Street
Great
Blackfriars
The Cut
Union Street
Newcomen St.
St. Thomas St.
Bermondsey Street
Druid St.
Suffolk
Bridge
Webber Street
BOROUGH
Borough
Long Lane
Weston St.
Trinity St.
Great Dover Street
Borough Road
Trinity Church Square
Merrick Square
Harper Rd
SOUTHWARK
Abbey St.
Grange
Walk
Spa Rd
Willow Walk
Page's Walk
Tower Bridge Road
IMPERIAL WAR MUSEUM
St. George's Road
London Road
Elephant and Castle
New Kent Road
Falmouth Rd
Brook Drive
Heygate St.
Rodney Rd
WALWORTH
Old Kent Road
Flint St.
East St.
Thurlow St.
Dunton Road
Lane
Kennington
Renton Pl.
Walworth Road
East Street
Portland St.
KENNINGTON
Braganza St.
Manor Pl.
Chapter Rd
Kennington Park Road
KENNINGTON PARK
Albany Road
Neate St.
Trafalgar Av.
Wells Way
Church Rd
New Church Rd
Camberwell Road
Southampton Way
Ruskin
St.
John
Camberwell New Road
Foxley Rd
Wyndham Rd
Vassal Rd
A 202
A 200
A 2
N
O
P
V
X
Y
Z

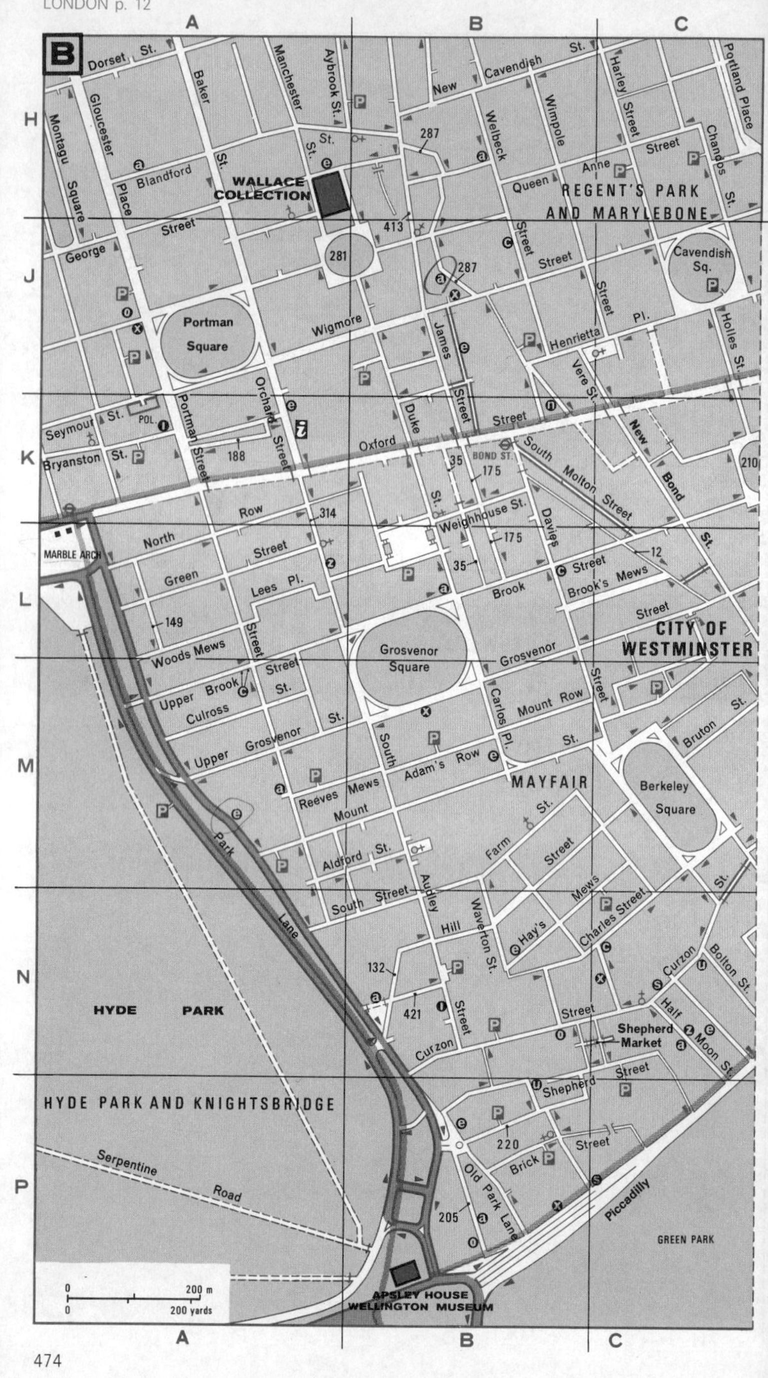

B
A
B
C
H
J
K
L
M
N
P
Dorset St.
Gloucester Place
Montagu Square
Baker St.
Manchester St.
Aybrook St.
New Cavendish St.
Harley Street
Portland Place
Welbeck
Wimpole
Chandos St.
Blandford
WALLACE COLLECTION
Queen Anne Street
REGENT'S PARK AND MARYLEBONE
George Street
Cavendish Sq.
Portman Square
Wigmore Street
James Street
Henrietta Pl.
Vere St.
Holles St.
Orchard Street
Duke St.
Seymour St.
POL.
Bryanston St.
Portman Street
Oxford Street
BOND ST.
South Molton Street
New Bond St.
North Row
Weighhouse St.
Davies Street
MARBLE ARCH
Green Street
Lees Pl.
Brook Street
Brook's Mews
Grosvenor Square
Grosvenor Street
CITY OF WESTMINSTER
Woods Mews
Upper Brook Street
Culross St.
Carlos Pl.
Mount Row
Bruton St.
Upper Grosvenor St.
South Audley Street
Adam's Row
MAYFAIR
Berkeley Square
Reeves Mews
Mount St.
Farm Street
Park Lane
Aldford St.
South Street
Hill St.
Waverton St.
Hay's Mews
Charles Street
Curzon Street
Bolton St.
Half Moon St.
Shepherd Market
Shepherd Street
HYDE PARK
HYDE PARK AND KNIGHTSBRIDGE
Serpentine Road
Brick Street
Old Park Lane
Piccadilly
GREEN PARK
APSLEY HOUSE WELLINGTON MUSEUM
0 200 m
0 200 yards

Street	Grid	No.
Arlington Street	DN	6
Avery Row	CL	12
Bateman Street	FK	18
Berwick Street	FK	26
Binney Street	BL	35
Carlton Gardens	FP	74
Deanery Street	BN	132
Denman Street	FM	133
Denmark Street	GJ	134
Duke of York Street	EN	143
Duke Street ST. JAMES	EN	146
Dunraven Street	AL	149
Gerrard Street	GL	174
Gilbert Street	BL	175
Glasshouse Street	EM	179
Granville Place	AK	188
Great Castle Street	DJ	189
Greek Street	GK	198
Hamilton Place	BP	205
Hanover Square	CK	210
Hertford Street	BP	220
Leicester Square	GM	261
Manchester Square	AJ	281
Market Place	DJ	286
Marylebone Lane	BJ	287
North Audley Street	AK	314
Old Burlington Street	DM	322
Old Compton Street	GK	323
Panton Street	FM	336
Romilly Street	GL	368
Thayer Street	BJ	413
Tilney Street	BN	421
Warwick Street	EM	444

Oxford Street is closed to private traffic, Mondays to Saturdays : from 7 am to 7 pm between Portman Street and St. Giles Circus

C
A
B
C
HYDE PARK AND KNIGHTSBRIDGE
KENSINGTON GARDENS
ALBERT MEMORIAL
ROYAL ALBERT HALL
ROYAL COLLEGE OF MUSIC
IMPERIAL COLLEGE OF SCIENCE AND TECHNOLOGY
SCIENCE MUSEUM
ROYAL COLLEGE OF ART
GEOLOGICAL MUSEUM
NATURAL HISTORY MUSEUM
KENSINGTON
SOUTH KENSINGTON
EARL'S COURT
GLOUCESTER RD
SOUTH KENSINGTON
BROMPTON CEMETERY
The Boltons
Kensington High St.
Kensington Road
Kensington Gore
Young St.
Kensington Square
De Vere Gardens
Palace Gate
Victoria Rd
Queen's Gate
Prince Consort Rd
Exhibition Road
St. Alban's Grove
Victoria Grove
Queen's Gate Terrace
Elvaston Place
Gloucester Road
Cornwall Gardens
Queen's Gate Gardens
Lexham Gardens
Lexham Gdns
Grenville Place
Cromwell Road
Stanhope Gardens
Ashburn Place
Knaresborough Place
Courtfield Gdns
Courtfield Road
Harrington Gdns
Harrington Gardens
Wetherby Place
Bina Gdns
Collingham Gardens
Bramham Gdns
Earl's Court Rd
Bolton Gardens
Old Brompton Road
Roland Gardens
Cranley Gdns
Drayton Gardens
Onslow Gardens
Onslow Gdns
Onslow Square
Sumner Place
Fulham Road
South Parade
Redcliffe Gardens
Redcliffe Square
The Little Boltons
Harcourt Ter.
Tregunter Road
Hollywood Road
Gilston Road
Evelyn Gdns
Elm Park Gdns
Elm Park Road
Elm Park Gardens
Beaufort Street
Elm Park Road
Park Walk
The Vale
Old Church Street
Finborough Road
Ifield Road
241
242
259
363
360
120
420
215
59
180
101
14
99
170
300
356
Q
R
S
T
U

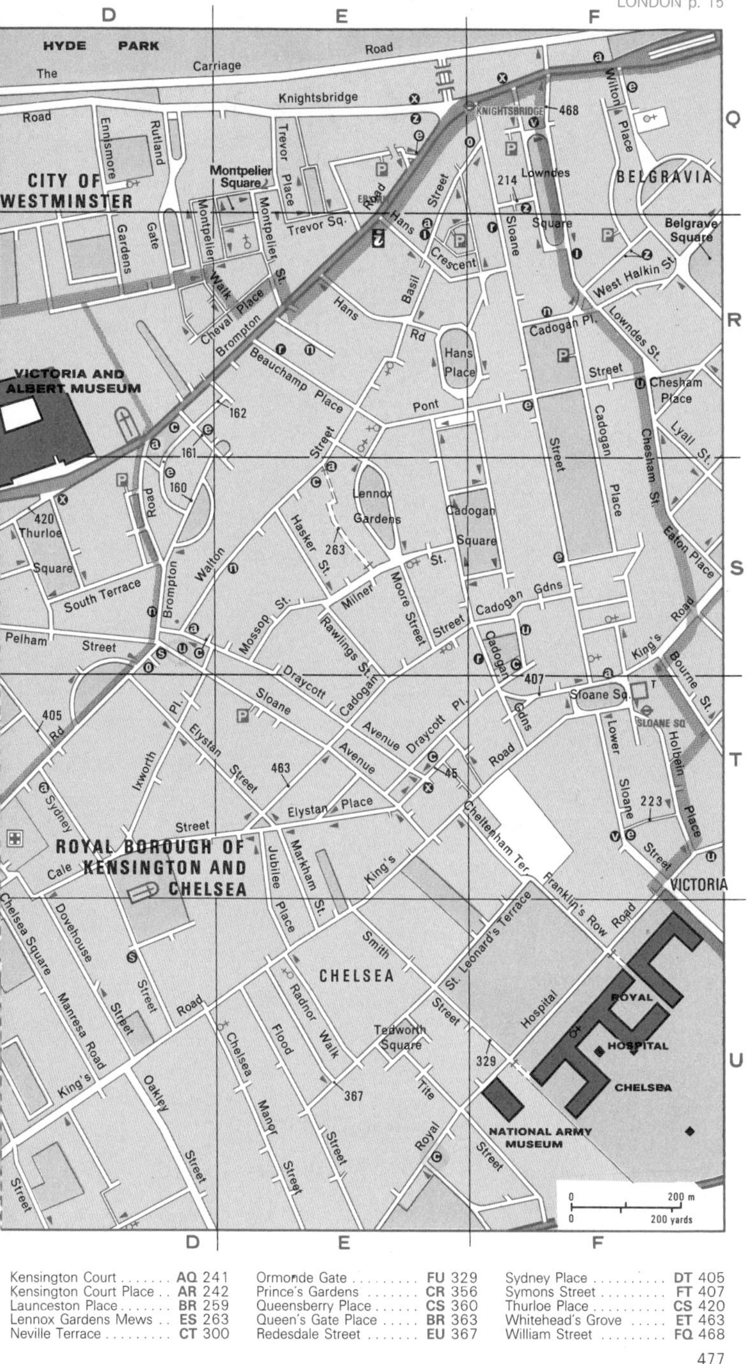

HYDE PARK
The Carriage Road
Knightsbridge
CITY OF WESTMINSTER
Montpelier Square
BELGRAVIA
Belgrave Square
VICTORIA AND ALBERT MUSEUM
ROYAL BOROUGH OF KENSINGTON AND CHELSEA
CHELSEA
ROYAL HOSPITAL CHELSEA
NATIONAL ARMY MUSEUM
VICTORIA
SLOANE SQ
KNIGHTSBRIDGE

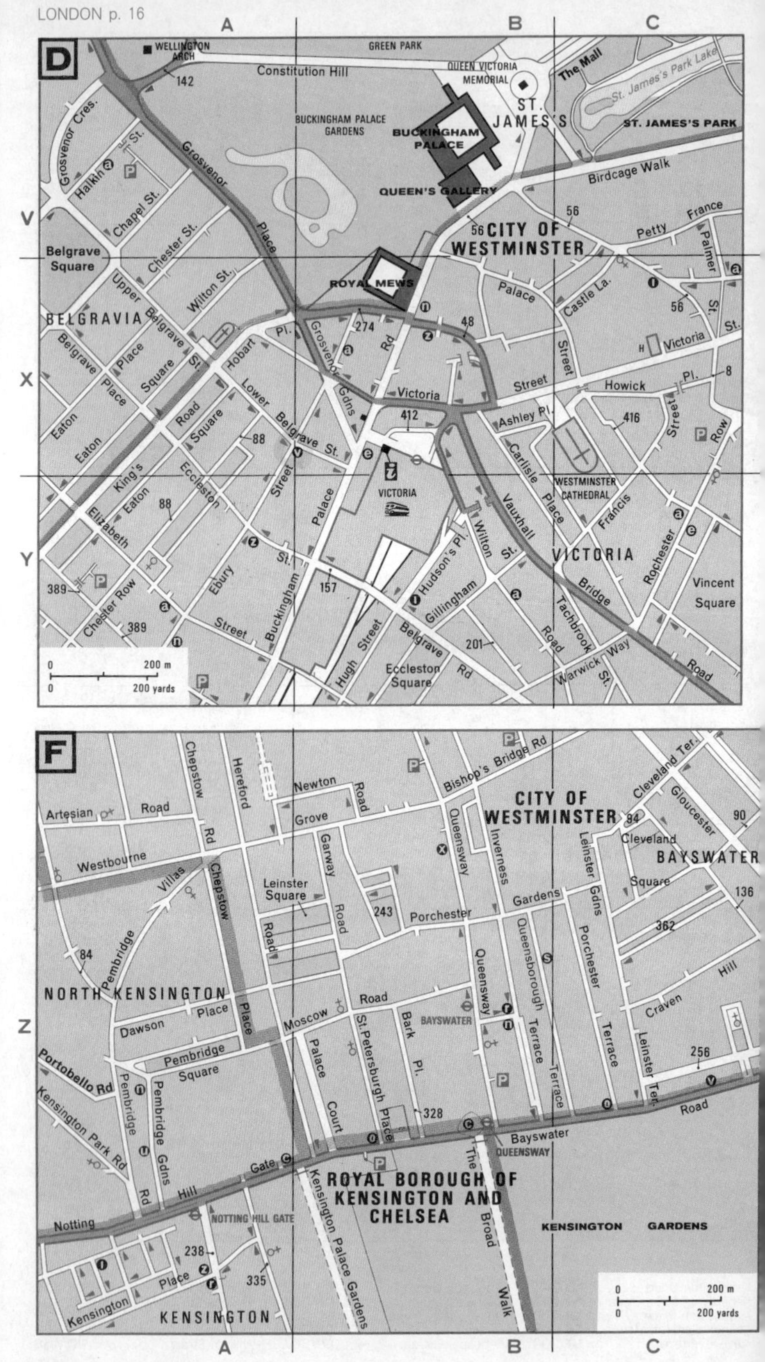
D
A
B
C
V
X
Y
WELLINGTON ARCH
GREEN PARK
Constitution Hill
QUEEN VICTORIA MEMORIAL
The Mall
St. James's Park Lake
ST. JAMES'S
ST. JAMES'S PARK
BUCKINGHAM PALACE GARDENS
BUCKINGHAM PALACE
QUEEN'S GALLERY
Birdcage Walk
CITY OF WESTMINSTER
Petty France
ROYAL MEWS
Grosvenor Place
Grosvenor Cres.
Halkin St.
Chapel St.
Chester St.
Belgrave Square
Upper Belgrave St.
Wilton St.
BELGRAVIA
Belgrave Place
Eaton Place
Eaton Square
Hobart Pl.
Lower Belgrave St.
Grosvenor Gdns
Victoria Street
Palace Street
Castle La.
Palmer St.
Victoria St.
Howick Pl.
Ashley Pl.
Carlisle Place
WESTMINSTER CATHEDRAL
Francis Street
Rochester Row
VICTORIA
Vincent Square
King's Road
Eccleston Square
Elizabeth St.
Eaton Square
Chester Row
Ebury Street
Buckingham Palace Rd
Hugh Street
Belgrave Rd
Eccleston Square
Hudson's Pl.
Wilton Rd
Gillingham St.
Vauxhall Bridge Road
Tachbrook St.
Warwick Way
0 200 m
0 200 yards
F
Z
Artesian Road
Chepstow Rd
Hereford Road
Newton Road
Grove
Bishop's Bridge Rd
Cleveland Ter.
Gloucester Ter.
CITY OF WESTMINSTER
BAYSWATER
Westbourne Grove
Villas
Chepstow Place
Leinster Square
Garway Road
Porchester Gardens
Queensway
Inverness Terrace
Leinster Gdns
Cleveland Square
Queensborough Terrace
Porchester Terrace
Craven Hill
Pembridge Villas
NORTH KENSINGTON
Dawson Place
Moscow Road
St. Petersburgh Place
Bark Pl.
BAYSWATER
Pembridge Square
Portobello Rd
Pembridge Rd
Pembridge Gdns
Palace Court
Leinster Ter.
Bayswater Road
QUEENSWAY
Kensington Park Rd
Notting Hill Gate
NOTTING HILL GATE
ROYAL BOROUGH OF KENSINGTON AND CHELSEA
Kensington Palace Gardens
The Broad Walk
KENSINGTON GARDENS
Kensington Place
KENSINGTON
0 200 m
0 200 yards

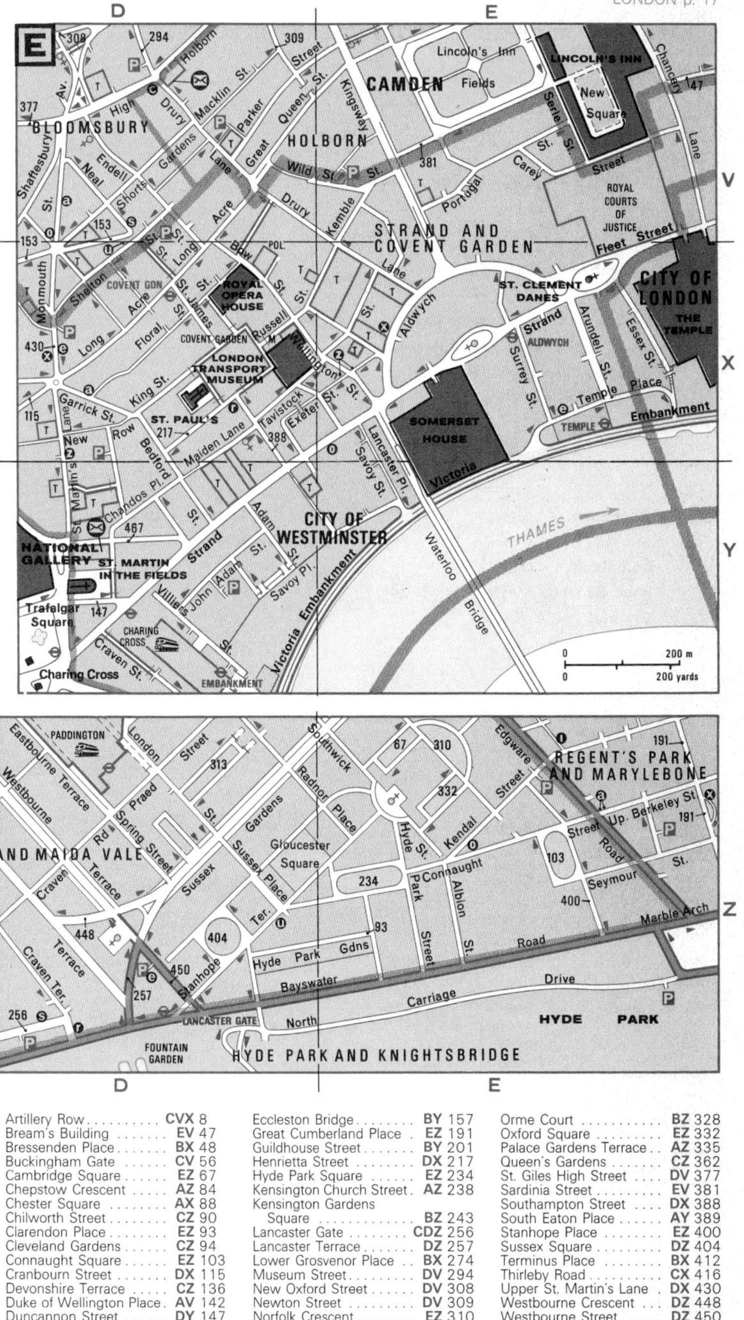

Artillery Row .... **CVX** 8
Bream's Building .... **EV** 47
Bressenden Place .... **BX** 48
Buckingham Gate ...... **CV** 56
Cambridge Square ...... **EZ** 67
Chepstow Crescent ..... **AZ** 84
Chester Square .... **AX** 88
Chilworth Street .... **CZ** 90
Clarendon Place .... **EZ** 93
Cleveland Gardens ...... **CZ** 94
Connaught Square ...... **EZ** 103
Cranbourn Street .... **DX** 115
Devonshire Terrace ..... **CZ** 136
Duke of Wellington Place. **AV** 142
Duncannon Street ...... **DY** 147
Earlham Street .... **DV** 153

Eccleston Bridge .... **BY** 157
Great Cumberland Place . **EZ** 191
Guildhouse Street .... **BY** 201
Henrietta Street .... **DX** 217
Hyde Park Square ...... **EZ** 234
Kensington Church Street. **AZ** 238
Kensington Gardens
Square .... **BZ** 243
Lancaster Gate .... **CDZ** 256
Lancaster Terrace .... **DZ** 257
Lower Grosvenor Place .. **BX** 274
Museum Street .... **DV** 294
New Oxford Street ...... **DV** 308
Newton Street .... **DV** 309
Norfolk Crescent .... **EZ** 310
Norfolk Square .... **DZ** 313

Orme Court .... **BZ** 328
Oxford Square .... **EZ** 332
Palace Gardens Terrace .. **AZ** 335
Queen's Gardens .... **CZ** 362
St. Giles High Street .... **DV** 377
Sardinia Street .... **EV** 381
Southampton Street .... **DX** 388
South Eaton Place ...... **AY** 389
Stanhope Place .... **EZ** 400
Sussex Square .... **DZ** 404
Terminus Place .... **BX** 412
Thirleby Road .... **CX** 416
Upper St. Martin's Lane . **DX** 430
Westbourne Crescent ... **DZ** 448
Westbourne Street ...... **DZ** 450
William IV Street .... **DY** 467

Starred establishments in London

✿✿✿

		Area	Page
XXXX	**La Tante Claire**	Chelsea	26

✿✿

		Area	Page
XXXXX	**Nico at Ninety**	Mayfair	34
XXXX	**Le Gavroche**	Mayfair	34
XXX	**Harvey's**	Wandsworth	31

✿

		Area	Page
	Connaught	Mayfair	33
	Capital	Chelsea	26
XXXXX	**Oak Room**	Mayfair	34
XXXX	**Four Seasons**	Mayfair	34
XXXX	**Oriental**	Mayfair	34
XXX	**L'Arlequin**	Battersea	31
XXX	**Suntory**	St. James's	36
XXX	**Tatsuso**	City	25
XX	**Pied à terre**	Bloomsbury	23

Further establishments which merit your attention

M

XXX	**Al Bustan**	Belgravia	32
XXX	**Bibendum**	Chelsea	26
XXX	**Chutney Mary**	Chelsea	26
XXX	**Zen Central**	Mayfair	34
XX	**Caprice (Le)**	St. James's	36
XX	**Hilaire**	South Kensington	30
XX	**Nico Central**	Regents Park and Marylebone	36
XX	**Simply Nico**	Victoria	38
XX	**Spice Merchant**	Bayswater and Marylebone	32
X	**Chinon**	Shepherd's Bush	25
X	**Vijay**	Kilburn	23

Restaurants classified acording to type

Bistro

Seafood

Chinese

English

French

- XXXXX ✿ **Oak Room** (City of Westminster - *Mayfair*) 34
- XXXXX ✿✿ **Nico at Ninety** (City of Westminster - *Mayfair*) 34
- XXXXX **Terrace** (City of Westminster - *Mayfair*) 34
- XXXX ✿✿✿ **Gavroche (Le)** (City of Westminster - *Mayfair*) 34
- XXXX **Boulestin** (City of Westminster - *Strand & Covent Garden*) 37
- XXXX **Chateau (Le)** (City of Westminster - *Mayfair*) 34
- XXXX ✿ **Four Seasons** (City of Westminster - *Mayfair*) 34
- XXXX **Saveurs (Les)** (City of Westminster - *Mayfair*) 34
- XXXX ✿✿ **Tante Claire (La)** (Royal Borough of Kensington & Chelsea - *Chelsea*) 26
- XXX ✿ **Arlequin (L')** (Wandsworth - *Battersea*) 31
- XXX **Auberge de Provence** (City of Westminster - *Victoria*) 38
- XXX **Jardin des Gourmets (Au)** (City of Westminster - *Soho*) 37
- XX **Candlewick Room** (City of London - *City of London*) 25
- XX **Chez Moi** (Royal Borough of Kensington & Chelsea - *North Kensington*) 28
- XX **Escargot Doré (L')** (Royal Borough of Kensington & Chelsea - *Kensington*) 28
- XX **Estaminet (L')** (City of Westminster - *Stand and Covent Garden*) 38
- XX **Gavvers** (Royal Borough of Kensington & Chelsea - *Chelsea*) 27
- XX **Mon Plaisir** (Camden - *Bloomsbury*) 24
- XX **Poissonnerie de l'Avenue** (Royal Borough of Kensington & Chelsea - *Chelsea*) 27
- XX **Pomme d'Amour (La)** (Royal Borough of Kensington & Chelsea - *Kensington*) 28
- XX **Poulbot (Le)** (basement) (City of London - *City of London*) 25
- XX **P'tit Montmartre (Le)** (City of Westminster - *Regent's Park & Marylebone*) 36
- XX **St. Quentin** (Royal Borough of Kensington & Chelsea - *Chelsea*) 27
- XX **Sous-Sol (Le)** (City of London - *City of London*) 25
- XX **Suquet (Le)** (Royal Borough of Kensington & Chelsea - *Chelsea*) 27
- XX **Truffe Noire (La)** (Southwark - *Southwark*) 30
- X **Bubb's** (City of London - *City of London*) 25

Hungarian

- XX **Gay Hussar** (City of Westminster - *Soho*) 37

Indian & Pakistani

- XXX **Bombay Brasserie** (Royal Borough of Kensington & Chelsea - *South Kensington*) 30
- XXX **Chutney Mary** (Anglo-Indian) (Royal Borough of Kensington & Chelsea - *Chelsea*) 26
- XX **Delhi Brasserie** (Royal Borough of Kensington & Chelsea - *South Kensington*) 30
- XX **Gaylord** (City of Westminster - *Regent's Park & Marylebone*) 36
- XX **Gopal's** (City of Westminster - *Soho*) 37
- XX **Kanishka** (Camden - *Bloomsbury*) 24
- XX **Memories of India** (Royal Borough of Kensington & Chelsea - *South Kensington*) 30
- XX **Nayab** (Hammersmith - *Fulham*) 25
- XX **Nizam** (Royal Borough of Kensington & Chelsea - *South Kensington*) 30
- XX **Red Fort** (City of Westminster - *Soho*) 37
- XX **Spice Merchant** (Westminster - *Bayswater*) 32
- XX **Tandoori Nights** (Hammersmith - *Hammersmith*) 25
- X **Vijay** (Brent - *Kilburn*) 23

Irish

- XX **Mulligans** (City of Westminster - *Mayfair*) 34

Italian

Japanese

Lebanese

Oriental

Thai

Greater London *is divided, for administrative purposes, into 32 boroughs plus the City: these sub-divide naturally into minor areas, usually grouped around former villages or quarters, which often maintain a distinctive character.*

of Greater London: ***071*** *or* ***081*** *except special cases.*

LONDON AIRPORTS

Heathrow Middx. W : 17 m. by A 4, M 4 **Underground** Piccadilly line direct – 081.

759 4321, Telex 934892, Fax 745 4290 – **Terminal** : Airbus (A 1) from Victoria, Airbus (A 2) from Paddington.

Underground station Concourse, Heathrow Airport, TW6 2JA (071) 730 3488.

Edwardian International, Bath Rd, Hayes, UB3 5AW, 759 6311, Telex 23935, Fax 759 4559, – rm – 500. – **M** (light lunch Saturday) 18.50/23.50 **st.** and a la carte – 11.00 – **442 rm** 153.00/215.00 **st.**, 17 suites.

Sheraton Skyline, Bath Rd, Hayes, UB3 5BP, 759 2535, Telex 934254, Fax 750 9150, « Exotic indoor garden », – rm – 500.
M 21.00/34.50 **st.** and a la carte 6.00 – 10.25 – **347 rm** 140.00/170.00 **st.**, 5 suites.

Excelsior Heathrow (Forte), Bath Rd, West Drayton, UB7 0DU, 759 6611, Telex 24525, Fax 759 3421, – rm – 700.
M *(closed Saturday lunch)* 13.95/15.50 **st.** – **Wheelers** 18.50 **t.** (lunch) and a la carte 18.45/31.40 **t.** 5.65 – 10.50 – **523 rm** 95.00/175.00 **st.**, 16 suites – SB (weekends only) 118.00 **st.**

London Heathrow Hilton, Terminal 4, TW6 3AF, 759 7755, Telex 925094, Fax 759 7579, – rm – 240.
M 16.95/29.95 **t.** and a la carte 7.50 – 10.75 – **391 rm** 145.00/165.00 **st.**, 4 suites – SB (weekends only) 108.00 **st.**

Holiday Inn, Stockley Rd, West Drayton, UB7 9NA, 0895 (West Drayton) 445555, Telex 934518, Fax 445122, – rm – 150. – **M** 15.90/16.95 **t.** and a la carte 5.95 – 9.95 – **378 rm** 127.50/142.50 **st.**, 2 suites.

Forte Crest, Sipson Rd, West Drayton, UB7 0JU, 759 2323, Telex 934280, Fax 897 8659 – rm – 200
563 rm, 6 suites.

Heathrow Penta, Bath Rd, Hounslow, TW6 2AQ, 897 6363, Telex 934660, Fax 897 1113, – rm – 450.
M 15.60/16.90 **st.** and a la carte 5.75 – 9.55 – **627 rm** 105.00/142.50 **st.**, 9 suites.

Sheraton Heathrow, Colnbrook bypass, West Drayton, UB7 0HJ, 759 2424, Telex 934331, Fax 759 2091 – rm – 70.
414 rm, 1 suite.

Novotel, Cherry Lane, West Drayton, UB7 9HB, 0895 (Uxbridge) 431431, Fax 431221, – rm rest – 200.
M a la carte approx. 13.50 **st.** 4.75 – 8.00 – **178 rm** 69.50/79.50 **st.**

Heathrow Park (Mt. Charlotte Thistle), Bath Rd, Longford, West Drayton, UB7 0EQ, 759 2400, Telex 934093, Fax 759 5278 – rm – 500.
M *(closed Sunday)* (carving lunch)/dinner 14.25 **t.** and a la carte 5.25 – 7.25 – **306 rm** 80.00/125.00 **st.** off A 4

Forte Posthouse, Bath Rd, Hayes, UB3 5AJ, 759 2552, Telex 21777, Fax 564 9265 – rm – 40. – **M** a la carte 12.70/23.15 **t.** 4.50 – 6.95 – **175 rm** 53.50 **st.** – SB (except Christmas) (weekends only) 82.00 **st.**

Yiewsley – Middx. – 081.

L'Esprit, The Arena, Stockley Park, UB11 1AA, 573 7333, Fax 561 0550 – .
closed Saturday lunch, dinner Monday to Wednesday, Sunday, 24 December-1 January and Bank Holidays – **M** 16.25 **st.** and a la carte 6.50.

Gatwick West Sussex S : 28 m. by A 23 and M 23 - **Train** from Victoria : Gatwick Express 404 T 30 – West Sussex – 0293 Gatwick.

535353, Fax 595010 and 081 (London) 668 4211.

International Arrivals Concourse, South Terminal, RH6 0NP 560108.

London Gatwick Airport Hilton, Gatwick Airport, (South Terminal), RH6 0LL, 518080, Telex 877021, Fax 528980, – rm – 360.
M 18.00/38.00 **st.** and a la carte 5.50 – 12.95 – **547 rm** 125.00/135.00 **st.**, **3 suites** – SB (weekends only) 134.00/184.00 **st.**

Gatwick Penta, Povey Cross Rd, ✉ Horley (Surrey), RH6 0BE, ✆ 820169, Telex 87440, Fax 820259, squash – rm – 150. VISA
M *(closed Saturday lunch)* 15.50/17.75 **st.** and a la carte 4.60 – 8.75 – **255 rm** 100.00/115.00 **st.**, 5 suites.

Forte Crest, Gatwick Airport (North Terminal), RH6 0PH, ✆ 567070, Telex 87202, Fax 567739, – rm – 300. VISA
M 13.00/15.00 **st.** and a la carte – 10.25 – **454 rm** 80.00 **st.**, 14 suites – SB (weekends only) 98.00 **st.**

Forte Posthouse Gatwick, Povey Cross Rd, ✉ Horley (Surrey), RH6 0BA, ✆ 771621, Fax 771054, – rm rest – 120. VISA
M a la carte 12.70/23.15 **t.** 4.50 – 6.95 – **210 rm** 53.50 **st.** – SB (weekends only) 82.00 **st.**

BRENT.

Kilburn – ✉ NW6 – 071.

Vijay, 49 Willesden Lane, NW6 7RF, ✆ 328 1087, South Indian rest. – VISA
M a la carte approx. 10.00 **t.**

CAMDEN Except where otherwise stated see pp. 4-7.

Bloomsbury – ✉ NW1/W1/WC1 – 071.

35 Woburn Pl. WC1 ✆ 636 7175.

Holiday Inn Kings Cross, 1 Kings Cross Rd, WC1X 9HX, ✆ 833 3900, Fax 917 6163, <, squash – rm – 200. VISA MT **a**
M *(closed Saturday lunch)* 17.50/19.50 **st.** and a la carte 7.25 – 11.50 – **397 rm** 105.00/154.00 **st.**, **8 suites.**

Russell (Forte), Russell Sq., WC1B 5BE, ✆ 837 6470, Telex 24615, Fax 837 2857 – rm – 450. VISA LU **o**
M (carving rest.) 16.95/17.95 **t.** and a la carte 5.00 – 10.25 – **325 rm** 105.00/140.00 **st.**, **3 suites** – SB (weekends only) 118.00/138.00 **st.**

Mountbatten (Edwardian), 20 Monmouth St., WC2H 9HD, ✆ 836 4300, Telex 298087, Fax 240 3540 – rm rest – 75. VISA p. 17 DV **o**
M *(bar lunch Saturday and Sunday)* 14.00/20.00 **st.** 6.50 – 12.00 – **121 rm** 163.00/181.00 **st.**, **6 suites.**

Marlborough (Edwardian), 9-14 Bloomsbury St., WC1B 3QD, ✆ 636 5601, Telex 298274, Fax 636 0532 – rm rest – 200. VISA LU **i**
M 16.95 **st.** 6.00 – 10.95 – **167 rm** 80.00/110.00 **st.**, **2 suites** – SB (weekends only) 74.95/132.95 **st.**

Grafton (Edwardian), 130 Tottenham Court Rd, W1P 9HP, ✆ 388 4131, Telex 919867, Fax 387 7394 – rest – 100. VISA KU **n**
M 15.50 **st.** and a la carte – 10.00 – **319 rm** 135.00/180.00 **st.**, **4 suites.**

Montague Park, 12-20 Montague St., WC1B 5BJ, ✆ 637 1001, Telex 23307, Fax 637 2506 – – 80. LU **c**
109 rm.

Kenilworth (Edwardian), 97 Great Russell St., WC1B 3LB, ✆ 637 3477, Telex 25842, Fax 631 3133 – rest – 100. VISA LU **a**
M 16.95 **st.** 6.00 – 10.00 – **191 rm** 85.00/110.00 **st.**, **1 suite** – SB 74.95/132.95 **st.**

Forte Crest Bloomsbury, Coram St., WC1N 1HT, ✆ 837 1200, Telex 22113, Fax 837 5374 – rm rest – 700. VISA LT **c**
M (carving rest.) 14.95 **st.** 5.25 – 10.25 – **281 rm** 95.00 **st.**, **3 suites** – SB (weekends only) 118.00 **st.**

Portland, 7 Montague St., WC1B 5BP, ✆ 323 1717, Fax 636 6498 – rest VISA LU **n**
M *(closed Saturday lunch and Sunday)* (Italian rest.) 13.50 **st.** and a la carte – **25 rm** 50.00/120.00 **st.**, **1 suite** – SB (weekends only) 90.00/150.00 **st.**

Bonnington, 92 Southampton Row, WC1B 4BH, ✆ 242 2828, Telex 261591, Fax 831 9170 – rm rest – 120 LU **s**
215 rm.

Kingsley (Mt. Charlotte Thistle), Bloomsbury Way, WC1A 2SD, ✆ 242 5881, Telex 21157, Fax 831 0225 – – 100. VISA LU **r**
M *(closed lunch Saturday, Sunday and Bank Holidays)* 7.50/15.25 **t.** and a la carte 4.50 – 8.95 – **98 rm** 85.00/110.00 **st.**, **2 suites** – SB (weekends only) 92.00 **st.**

Bloomsbury Park (Mt. Charlotte Thistle), 126 Southampton Row, WC1B 5AD, ✆ 430 0434, Telex 25757, Fax 242 0665 – rm – 30. VISA LU **u**
M *(closed Friday to Sunday and Bank Holidays)* (dinner only) 13.95 **t.** and a la carte 4.50 – 8.25 – **95 rm** 75.00/110.00 **st.**

XX ❀ **Pied à Terre** (Neat), 34 Charlotte St., W1P 1HJ, ✆ 636 1178 - ▤. AE VISA
closed Saturday lunch, Sunday, last 2 weeks August, 2 weeks December-January and Bank Holidays - **M** 19.50/36.00 **st.** KU **e**
Spec. Tagliatelle of langoustines with an asparagus bouillon, Fillet of John Dory with peas and a foie gras sauce, Caramelised pears with a Calvados parfait.

XX **Neal Street,** 26 Neal St., WC2H 9PS, ✆ 836 8368 - ▤. AE VISA p. 17 DV **s**
closed Saturday, Sunday, Christmas-New Year and Bank Holidays - **M** a la carte 27.00/42.00 **t.** 8.00.

XX **Mon Plaisir,** 21 Monmouth St., WC2H 9DD, ✆ 836 7243, French rest. - AE VISA p. 17 DV **a**
closed Saturday lunch, Sunday and Bank Holidays - **M** 13.95 **t.** and a la carte 4.90.

XX **Poons of Russell Square,** 50 Woburn Pl., WC1H 0JE, ✆ 580 1188, Chinese rest. - ▤. AE VISA - *closed 24 to 26 December* - **M** 20.00 **t.** and a la carte. LU **x**

XX **Kanishka,** 161 Whitfield St., W1P 5RY, ✆ 388 0860, Indian rest. - ▤. AE VISA
closed lunch Saturday and Bank Holidays, Sunday and 25-26 December - **M** a la carte 16.10/20.85 **t.** KTU **z**

X **Smith's,** 23 Neal St., WC2H 9PU, ✆ 379 0310, Fax 836 8395 - AE VISA
closed Sunday and Bank Holidays - **M** a la carte 14.50/24.75 **t.** 4.00. p. 17 DVX **u**

Camden Town - ✉ NW1 - ☎ 071.

X **La Bougie,** 7 Murray St., NW1 9RE, ✆ 485 6400, Bistro KS **a**
M (dinner only) a la carte 13.50/15.50 **t.** 4.00.

Euston - ✉ WC1 - ☎ 071.

Scandic Crown, 17/18 Upper Woburn Pl., WC1 0HT, ✆ 383 4105, Fax 383 4106, - rm ▤ TV ☎ - 135 - **149 rm,** 1 suite. KLT **e**

Hampstead - ✉ NW3 - ☎ 071.

Forte Posthouse Hampstead, 215 Haverstock Hill, NW3 4RB, ✆ 794 8121, Telex 262494, Fax 435 5586 - rm TV ☎ P - 30. AE VISA ES **r**
M a la carte 12.70/23.15 **t.** 4.50 - 6.95 - **138 rm** 53.50 **st.**

Swiss Cottage, 4 Adamson Rd, NW3 3HP, ✆ 722 2281, Telex 297232, Fax 483 4588, « Antique furniture collection » - TV ☎ - 60. AE VISA. GS **n**
M *(closed Saturday and Sunday)* (bar lunch)/dinner 25.00 **st.** and a la carte 5.45 - **78 rm** 73.00/85.00 **st.**, 3 suites.

Clive (Hilton), Primrose Hill Rd, NW3 3NA, ✆ 586 2233, Telex 22759, Fax 586 1659 - TV ☎ P - 300. AE VISA. HS **a**
M *(closed Saturday lunch)* 9.95/13.50 **st.** and a la carte 5.30 - **93 rm** 58.00/68.00 **st.**, 3 suites - SB (weekends only) 87.00/152.00 **st.**

Langorf without rest., 20 Frognal, NW3 6AG, ✆ 794 4483, Fax 435 9055 - TV ☎. AE VISA. - 6.00 - **31 rm** 63.00/90.00 **st.** ES **c**

XXX Benihana, 100 Avenue Rd, NW3 3HF, ✆ 586 9508, Fax 586 6740, Japanese Teppan-Yaki rest. - ▤ GS **o**

XX **Carapace,** 118 Heath St., NW3 1DR, ✆ 435 8000 - AE VISA ES **e**
M (dinner only and Sunday lunch)/dinner 29.90 **st.** and a la carte 4.00.

XX **Zen W3,** 83-84 Hampstead High St., NW3 1RE, ✆ 794 7863, Chinese rest. - AE VISA
M a la carte 9.30/15.50 **t.** ES **a**

Holborn - ✉ WC2 - ☎ 071.

Drury Lane Moat House (Q.M.H.), 10 Drury Lane, High Holborn, WC2B 5RE, ✆ 836 6666, Telex 8811395, Fax 831 1548 - rm ▤ TV ☎ - 100. AE VISA.
closed 23 to 27 December - **M** 15.45 **t.** and a la carte 5.95 - 9.50 - **151 rm** 117.00/165.00 **st.**, 2 suites - SB (weekdays only) 120.00/130.00 **st.** p. 17 DV **c**

Regent's Park - ✉ NW1 - ☎ 071.

White House, Albany St., NW1 3UP, ✆ 387 1200, Telex 24111, Fax 388 0091, - rm ▤ rest TV ☎ - 100. - **560 rm,** 15 suites. JT **o**

XX **Odette's,** 130 Regent's Park Rd, NW1 8XL, ✆ 586 5486 - AE VISA HS **i**
closed Sunday dinner - **M** a la carte 17.00/27.50 **t.**

XX **China Jazz,** 29-31 Parkway, NW1 7PN, ✆ 482 3940, Chinese rest. - AE VISA JS **e**
closed 25 to 27 December - **M** 16.00/20.00 **t.** and a la carte.

Swiss Cottage - ✉ NW3 - ☎ 071.

Regent's Park Marriott, 128 King Henry's Rd, NW3 3ST, ✆ 722 7711, Telex 267396, Fax 586 5822, - rm ▤ TV ☎ P - 400 GS **a**
295 rm, 8 suites.

XX **Peter's,** 65 Fairfax Rd, NW6 4EE, ✆ 624 5804 - AE VISA FS **i**
M 11.95/13.95 **t.** and a la carte 4.00.

CITY OF LONDON - ☎ 071 Except where otherwise stated see p. 7.

XXX ✿ **Tatsuso,** 32 Broadgate Circle, EC2M 2QS, ☎ 638 5863, Fax 638 5864, Japanese rest. - ▤. AE VISA PU **u**
closed Saturday, Sunday and Bank Holidays - **M** (booking essential) 60.00/65.00 **t.** and a la carte 29.10/49.10 **t.** 9.00
Spec. Toban Yaki, Flambléed lobster on a teppan-yaki grill, Sushi.

XX **Le Quai,** 1 Broken Wharf, EC4V 3QQ, off High Timber St. ☎ 236 6480, Fax 236 6479 - ▤. AE VISA OV **a**
closed Saturday and Sunday - **M** 32.50/19.50 **t.**

XX **Candlewick Room,** 45 Old Broad St., EC2N 1HT, ☎ 628 7929, French rest. - AE VISA PU **n**
closed Saturday, Sunday and Bank Holidays - **M** (lunch only) 22.50 **t.** and a la carte.

XX **Le Poulbot** (basement), 45 Cheapside, EC2V 6AR, ☎ 236 4379, French rest. - ▤. AE VISA
closed Saturday, Sunday, 24 December-2 January and Bank Holidays - **M** (lunch only) 33.00 **st.** 5.75. OV **i**

XX Corney and Barrow, 109 Old Broad St., EC2N 1AP, ☎ 638 9308 - ▤ PU **c**

XX **Corney and Barrow,** 118 Moorgate, EC2M 6UR, ☎ 628 2898 - ▤. AE VISA
closed Saturday, Sunday and Bank Holidays - **M** (lunch only) 26.95 **t.** 8.50. PU **o**

XX **Corney and Barrow,** 44 Cannon St., EC4N 6JJ, ☎ 248 1700 - ▤. AE VISA OV **r**
closed Saturday, Sunday and Bank Holidays - **M** (lunch only) 14.95 **t.** and a la carte.

XX **Le Sous Sol,** 32 Old Bailey, EC4M 7HS, ☎ 236 7931, Fax 248 6872, French rest. - AE VISA NV **a**
M 15.50/24.50 **t.** and a la carte 6.00.

XX **Miyama,** 17 Godliman St., EC4V 5BD, ☎ 489 1937, Japanese rest. - ▤. AE VISA
closed Saturday dinner, Sunday and Bank Holidays - **M** 30.00/50.00 **t.** and a la carte. OV **e**

X Bubb's, 329 Central Market, Farringdon St., EC1A 9NB, ☎ 236 2435, French rest. NU

X **Whittington's,** 21 College Hill, EC4R 2RP, ☎ 248 5855 - ▤. AE VISA OV **c**
closed Saturday, Sunday and Bank Holidays - **M** (lunch only) a la carte 21.45/25.70 **t.** 4.75.

HAMMERSMITH AND FULHAM p.8.

Fulham - ✉ SW6 - ☎ 071.

La Reserve, 422-428 Fulham Rd, SW6 1DU, ☎ 385 8561, Fax 385 7662, « Contemporary decor » - rm TV ☎. AE VISA. FZ **a**
M a la carte 10.00/17.00 **t.** - 3.00 - **38 rm** 65.00/95.00 **t.**

XX **Blue Elephant,** 4-6 Fulham Broadway, SW6 1AA, ☎ 385 6595, Fax 386 7665, Thai rest. - ▤. AE VISA EZ **z**
closed Saturday lunch and 24 to 27 December - **M** (booking essential) 25.00/28.00 **t.** and a la carte.

XX **Mao Tai,** 58 New Kings Rd, Parsons Green, SW6 4UG, ☎ 731 2520, Chinese (Szechuan) rest. - ▤. AE VISA - **M** 17.50 **t.** and a la carte.

XX **Nayab,** 309 New Kings Rd, SW6 4RF, ☎ 731 6993, Indian rest. - AE VISA
closed 25 and 26 December - **M** (dinner only) a la carte 12.75/15.40 **t.** 4.50.

Hammersmith - ✉ W6/W12/W14 - ☎ 081.

XX **Tandoori Nights,** 319-321 King St., W6 9NH, ☎ 741 4328, Indian rest. - ▤. AE VISA
closed 25 and 26 December - **M** 9.95/15.00 **t.** and a la carte 4.95.

X **Snows on the Green,** 166 Shepherd's Bush Rd, Brook Green, W6 7PB, ☎ (071) 603 2142 - VISA
closed Saturday lunch, Sunday dinner, 16 to 30 August, Easter, 25 December-9 January and Bank Holidays - **M** 12.50 **t.** (lunch) and a la carte 12.75/23.75 **t.** 4.00.

X **Brackenbury,** 129-131 Brackenbury Rd, W6 0BQ, ☎ 748 0107 - AE VISA
closed Saturday and Monday lunch, Sunday dinner, Easter, Christmas and Bank Holidays - **M** a la carte 12.00/15.00 **t.**

Shepherd's Bush - ✉ W12/W14 - ☎ 071.

X **Chinon,** 25 Richmond Way, W14 0AS, ☎ 602 5968 - ▤. VISA
closed lunch Saturday and Sunday, Easter and last 2 weeks August - **M** a la carte 20.00/30.00 **t.**

KENSINGTON and CHELSEA (Royal Borough of).

Chelsea - ✉ SW1/SW3/SW10 - ☎ 071 - Except where otherwise stated see pp. 14 and 15.

Hyatt Carlton Tower, 2 Cadogan Pl., SW1X 9PY, ☎ 235 5411, Telex 21944, Fax 245 6570, ≤, , , , - rm ▤ TV ☎ - 300. AE VISA. FR **n**
M - **Chelsea Room** 21.00/29.00 **st.** and a la carte - **Rib Room** a la carte 7.25 - 13.50 - **194 rm** 230.00 **s.**, 30 suites.

Sheraton Park Tower, 101 Knightsbridge, SW1X 7RN, ✆ 235 8050, Telex 917222, Fax 235 8231, ← - |$| ⇎ rm ▤ TV ☎ ♿ P - 🚶 80. AE VISA. ⚘ FQ **v**
M 16.00/20.00 **t.** and a la carte 🍷 7.50 - ☕ 12.75 - **267 rm** 195.00/215.00, 22 suites.

Conrad Chelsea Harbour, Chelsea Harbour, SW10 0XG, ✆ 823 3000, Telex 919222, Fax 351 6525, ←, 🏋, ≘s, ⛾ - |$| ⇎ rm ▤ TV ☎ ♿ P - 🚶 150. AE VISA
M 19.50 **t.** (lunch) and a la carte 17.00/29.50 **t.** - ☕ 15.00 -, **157 suites** 200.00/255.00 **s.** - SB (weekends only) 400.00 **st.**

Durley House, 115 Sloane St., SW1X 9PJ, ✆ 235 5537, Fax 259 6977, « Tastefully furnished Georgian town house », 🌳, 🎾 - |$| TV ☎. AE VISA. FS **e**
M (room service only) a la carte - ☕ 10.50 -, **11 suites** 250.00/300.00 **t.**.

✿ **Capital,** 22-24 Basil St., SW3 1AT, ✆ 589 5171, Telex 919042, Fax 225 0011 - |$| ▤ TV ☎. VISA. ⚘ ER **a**
M 22.00/25.00 **st.** and a la carte 25.00/44.75 **st.** 🍷 10.00 - ☕ 12.50 - **48 rm** 175.00/300.00 **st.**
Spec. Mousse of girolles draped with mushroom oil and wild fungi, Emincé of farmyard chicken with olives, tomatoes and spinach noodles, Tarte tatin, Calvados sorbet and crème anglaise.

Draycott, 24-26 Cadogan Gdns, SW3 2RP, ✆ 730 6466, Fax 730 0236 - |$| TV ☎. AE VISA. ⚘ FS **c**
M (room service only) - ☕ 9.95 - **25 rm** 100.00/250.00 **t.**

Chelsea, 17-25 Sloane St., SW1X 9NU, ✆ 235 4377, Telex 919111, Fax 235 3705 - |$| ⇎ rm ▤ TV ☎ - 🚶 120. AE VISA. ⚘ FR **r**
M *(closed Sunday lunch)* a la carte approx. 19.50 **st.** 🍷 6.75 - **218 rm**, 6 suites.

Cadogan, 75 Sloane St., SW1X 9SG, ✆ 235 7141, Telex 267893, Fax 245 0994 - |$| ⇎ rm ▤ rest TV ☎ - 🚶 30. AE VISA. ⚘ FR **e**
M *(closed Saturday lunch)* - **60 rm**, 5 suites.

Basil Street, 8 Basil St., SW3 1AH, ✆ 581 3311, Telex 28379, Fax 581 3693 - |$| TV ☎ - 🚶 55. AE VISA FQ **o**
M (carving lunch Saturday) 14.75 **t.** (lunch) and a la carte approx. 22.80 **t.** - ☕ 9.75 - **91 rm** 105.25/149.00 **st.**, 1 suite.

Egerton House, 17-19 Egerton Terr., SW3 2BX, ✆ 589 2412, Fax 584 6540 - |$| ▤ TV ☎. AE VISA. ⚘ DR **e**
M (room service only) a la carte - ☕ 12.50 - **27 rm** 98.00/190.00 **st.**, 1 suite.

Fenja without rest., 69 Cadogan Gdns, SW3 2RB, ✆ 589 7333, Telex 934272, Fax 581 4958 - |$| TV ☎. AE VISA. ⚘ FS **r**
☕ 11.75 - **13 rm** 97.75/195.00 **st.**

Sloane, 29 Draycott Pl., SW3 2SH, ✆ 581 5757, Fax 584 1348 - |$| ▤ TV ☎. AE VISA. ⚘ - **M** (room service only) - ☕ 9.00 - **12 rm** 110.00/160.00. ET **c**

Sydney House, 9-11 Sydney St., SW3 6PU, ✆ 376 7711, Fax 376 4233 - |$| TV ☎. AE VISA DT **a**
M (room service only) - ☕ 9.50 - **21 rm** 95.00/195.00 **st.**

Beaufort, 33 Beaufort Gdns, SW3 1PP, ✆ 584 5252, Telex 929200, Fax 589 2834, « English floral watercolour collection » - |$| ▤ TV ☎. AE VISA. ⚘ ER **n**
closed 22 December-2 January - **M** (restricted menu) (room service only) - **28 rm** (room service included) 110.00/250.00 **st.**

Royal Court, Sloane Sq., SW1W 8EG, ✆ 730 9191, Telex 296818, Fax 824 8381 - |$| ▤ rest TV ☎ - 🚶 40. AE VISA FST **a**
M *(closed Saturday lunch)* a la carte 16.70/21.50 **st.** 🍷 5.50 - ☕ 9.25 - **102 rm** 115.00/145.00 **st.** - SB (weekends only) 102.00 **st.**

Eleven Cadogan Gardens, 11 Cadogan Gdns, SW3 2RJ, ✆ 730 3426, Fax 730 5217 - |$| TV ☎. AE VISA. ⚘ FS **u**
M (room service only) - ☕ 10.00 - **56 rm** 89.00/200.00 **st.**, 5 suites.

L'Hotel without rest., 28 Basil St., SW3 1AT, ✆ 589 6286, Telex 919042, Fax 225 0011 - |$| TV ☎. AE VISA. ⚘ ER **i**
☕ 4.00 - **12 rm** 125.00/145.00 **st.**

XXXX ✿✿✿ **La Tante Claire** (Koffmann), 68-69 Royal Hospital Rd, SW3 4HP, ✆ 352 6045, Fax 352 3257, French rest. - ▤. AE VISA EU **c**
closed Saturday, Sunday, Christmas-New Year and Bank Holidays - **M** 23.50 **st.** (lunch) and a la carte 53.50 **st.**
Spec. Coquilles St. Jacques grillées, sauce encre, Assiette canardière, Pied de cochon.

XXX **Waltons,** 121 Walton St., SW3 2HP, ✆ 584 0204 - ▤. AE VISA DS **a**
closed 25 and 26 December - **M** 14.75/19.75 **t.** and a la carte 🍷 4.50.

XXX **Turner's,** 87-89 Walton St., SW3 2HP, ✆ 584 6711, Fax 584 4441 - ▤. AE VISA ES **n**
closed Saturday lunch and 25 to 30 December - **M** 18.50/29.50 **st.** and a la carte 🍷 9.00.

XXX **Bibendum,** Michelin House, 81 Fulham Rd, SW3 6RD, ✆ 581 5817, Fax 823 7925 - ▤. VISA
closed Easter Monday and 24 to 28 December - **M** 24.00 **t.** (lunch) and dinner a la carte 32.00/43.00 **t.** 🍷 5.25. DS **s**

XXX **Zen,** Chelsea Cloisters, Sloane Av., SW3 3DW, ✆ 589 1781, Chinese rest. - ▤. AE VISA
M a la carte 9.50/17.00 **t.** ET **a**

XXX **Chutney Mary,** 535 King's Rd, SW10 0SZ, ✆ 351 3113, Anglo-Indian rest. - ▤. AE VISA
M 13.00 **t.** (lunch) and a la carte 14.75/23.75 **t.** p. 8 FZ **v**

XX La Finezza, 62-64 Lower Sloane St., SW1N 8BP, ✆ 730 8639, Italian rest. - ▤ FT v

XX **English Garden,** 10 Lincoln St., SW3 2TS, ✆ 584 7272, English rest. - ▤. VISA ET x
closed 25 and 26 December - **M** 14.75 **t.** (lunch) and a la carte 18.50/30.75 **t.** 4.50.

XX **Gavvers,** 61-63 Lower Sloane St., SW1W 8DH, ✆ 730 5983, French rest. - ▤. VISA FT e
closed Saturday lunch, Sunday, 25 December-2 January and Bank Holidays - **M** 14.75/28.25 **st.** and a la carte 5.60.

XX **Argyll,** 316 King's Rd, SW3 5UH, ✆ 352 0025, Fax 352 1652 - ▤. AE VISA CU e
closed Sunday dinner and Monday lunch - **M** 15.75 **t.** (lunch) and a la carte 18.40/25.75 **t.** 5.75.

XX **Eleven Park Walk,** 11 Park Walk, SW10 0AJ, ✆ 352 3449, Italian rest. - ▤. AE VISA
closed Sunday dinner and Bank Holidays - **M** 12.50 **t.** and a la carte 4.00. CU r

XX Salotto, 257-259 Fulham Rd, SW3 6HY, ✆ 351 1383, Italian rest. - ▤ CU i

XX Scalini, 1-3 Walton St., SW3 2JD, ✆ 225 2301, Italian rest. ES c

XX **St. Quentin,** 243 Brompton Rd, SW3 2EP, ✆ 589 8005, Fax 584 6064, French rest. - ▤. AE VISA DR a
M 12.50 **t.** (lunch) and a la carte 16.40/18.25 **t.** 5.70.

XX **Poissonnerie de l'Avenue,** 82 Sloane Av., SW3 3DZ, ✆ 589 2457, Fax 581 3360, French Seafood rest. - ▤. AE VISA DS u
closed Sunday, 24 December-2 January and Bank Holidays - **M** a la carte 17.75/23.25 **t.** 4.50.

XX **Magic Dragon,** 99-103 Fulham Rd, SW3 6RH, ✆ 225 2244, Fax 373 6621, Chinese rest. - ▤. AE VISA DS o
closed Monday and Bank Holidays - **M** 10.00/15.00 **st.** and a la carte 4.50.

XX **Busabong Too,** 1a Langton St., SW10 0JL, ✆ 352 7517, Thai rest. - ▤. AE VISA
closed Bank Holiday lunch, 24 to 26 December and 1 January - **M** (booking essential) 19.95 **t.** and a la carte. p. 8 FZ x

XX **Nakano,** 11 Beauchamp Pl., SW3 1NQ, ✆ 581 3837, Japanese rest. - ▤. AE VISA
closed Sunday lunch, Monday, Easter, last week August and Christmas-New Year - **M** 18.00/42.50 **t.** and a la carte. ER r

XX **Toto's,** Walton House, Walton St., SW3 2JH, ✆ 589 0075, Italian rest. - AE VISA
closed 2 days at Easter and 2 days at Christmas - **M** a la carte 23.00/35.00 **st.** ES a

XX **Good Earth,** 233 Brompton Rd, SW3 2EP, ✆ 584 3658, Fax 823 8769, Chinese rest. - ▤. AE VISA DR c
M 16.50/22.50 **st.** and a la carte 4.00.

XX Penang, 294 Fulham Rd, SW10 9EW, ✆ 351 2599, Malaysian rest. - ▤ BU e

XX Le Suquet, 104 Draycott Av., SW3 3AE, ✆ 581 1785, French Seafood rest. DS c

XX Sandrini, 260-262a Brompton Rd, SW3 2AS, ✆ 584 1724, Italian rest. DS n

XX **Dan's,** 119 Sydney St., SW3 6NR, ✆ 352 2718, Fax 352 3265 - AE VISA DU s
closed Saturday lunch, Sunday, Christmas-New Year and Bank Holidays - **M** 14.50 **t.** (lunch) and a la carte 17.00/21.25 **t.** 4.50.

Kensington - ✉ SW7/W8/W11/W14 - ✆ 071 - Except where otherwise stated see pp. 8-11.

Royal Garden, Kensington High St., W8 4PT, ✆ 937 8000, Telex 263151, Fax 938 4532, ≤ - rm ▤ TV ☎ - 800. p. 14 AQ c
M - **Royal Roof** - **383 rm**, 15 suites.

Halcyon, 81 Holland Park, W11 3RZ, ✆ 727 7288, Telex 266721, Fax 229 8516 - ▤ TV ☎. AE VISA. EX u
M 15.00 **t.** (lunch) and dinner a la carte 18.00/33.00 **t.** 5.00 - 11.00 - **40 rm**, 3 suites - SB (weekends only) 310.00 **st.**

Copthorne Tara, Scarsdale Pl., W8 5SR, ✆ 937 7211, Telex 918834, Fax 937 7100 - rm ▤ TV ☎ ♿ - 500. AE VISA. FY u
M 14.00/23.00 **st.** and a la carte - 9.40 - **817 rm** 99.00/140.00 **st.**, 8 suites.

Kensington Park (Mt. Charlotte Thistle), 16-32 De Vere Gardens, W8 5AG, ✆ 937 8080, Telex 929643, Fax 937 7616 - rm ▤ rest TV ☎ ♿ - 120. AE VISA.
M 14.75 **t.** and a la carte 6.50 - 10.50 - **325 rm** 110.00/175.00 **st.**, 7 suites - SB (weekends only) 129.00/267.00 **st.** p. 14 BQ e

London Kensington Hilton, 179-199 Holland Park Av., W11 4UL, ✆ 603 3355, Telex 919763, Fax 602 9397 - rm ▤ TV ☎ ♿ - 200. AE VISA. EX s
M (carving lunch) 17.95/18.95 **st.** and a la carte 7.00 - (see also **Hiroko** below) - 12.50 - **596 rm** 115.00/135.00 **st.**, 7 suites.

Kensington Palace Thistle (Mt. Charlotte Thistle), 8 De Vere Gdns, W8 5AF, ✆ 937 8121, Telex 262422, Fax 937 2816 - rm ▤ rest TV ☎ - 180. AE VISA. p. 14 BQ a
M 12.50/16.50 **st.** and a la carte - 9.70 - **297 rm** 95.00/135.00 **st.**, 1 suite - SB 118.00/194.00 **st.**

Kensington Close (Forte), Wrights Lane, W8 5SP, ✆ 937 8170, Fax 937 8289, squash - rm rest 150. FY **c**
M (carving rest.) 15.95 **st.** and a la carte 5.50 - 8.00 - **530 rm** 90.00/125.00 **st.**

The Milestone, 1-2 Kensington Court, W8 5DL, ✆ 917 1000, Telex 290404, Fax 917 1010, - **M** 18.50/22.50 **t.** and a la carte 5.50 - 3.50 - **50 rm** 180.00/210.00 **st.**, 6 suites - SB (weekends only) 358.00 **st.** p. 14 AQ **u**

XXX **Belvedere in Holland Park,** Holland House, off Abbotsbury Rd, W8 6LU, ✆ 602 1238, « 19C orangery in park » - EY **u**
closed Sunday dinner and 25 December - **M** (booking essential) 15.00/30.00 **t.** and a la carte.

XX **Clarke's,** 124 Kensington Church St., W8 4BH, ✆ 221 9225, Fax 229 4564 -
closed Saturday, Sunday, Easter, 2 weeks summer, Christmas-New Year and Bank Holidays - **M** 26.00/37.00 **st.** EX **c**

XX **La Pomme d'Amour,** 128 Holland Park Av., W11 4UE, ✆ 229 8532, French rest. - EX **e**
closed Saturday lunch, Sunday and Bank Holidays - **M** 16.50 **t.** and a la carte 5.00.

XX **L'Escargot Doré,** 2-4 Thackeray St., W8 5ET, ✆ 937 8508, French rest. -
closed Saturday dinner, Sunday, last 2 weeks August and Bank Holidays - **M** 15.50 **t.** and a la carte 4.50. p. 14 AQR **e**

XX **Shanghai,** 38c-d Kensington Church St., W8 4BX, ✆ 938 2501, Chinese rest. - FX **a**
closed Sunday and Bank Holidays - **M** 16.50/23.00 **t.** and a la carte.

XX **La Fenice,** 148 Holland Park Av., W11 4UE, ✆ 221 6090, Fax 221 4096, Italian rest. - EX **v**
closed Saturday lunch, Monday and Bank Holidays - **M** 16.50 **t.** (dinner) and a la carte 13.60/20.10 **t.** 4.75.

XX **Launceston Place,** 1a Launceston Pl., W8 5RL, ✆ 937 6912, Fax 938 2412 -
closed Saturday lunch, Sunday dinner and Bank Holidays - **M** 12.50/15.50 **t.** and a la carte 4.50. p. 14 BR **a**

XX Hiroko (at London Kensington Hilton H.), 179-199 Holland Park Av., W11 4UL, ✆ 603 5003, Japanese rest. - EX **s**

XX Peking Garden, 11 Russell Gdns, W14 8EZ, ✆ 602 0312, Chinese rest. EY **i**

XX **Phoenicia,** 11-13 Abingdon Rd, W8 6AH, ✆ 937 0120, Fax 937 7668, Lebanese rest. - EY **n**
closed 24 and 25 December - **M** 8.95/26.20 **st.** and a la carte.

XX **Boyd's,** 135 Kensington Church St., W8 7LP, ✆ 727 5452, Fax 221 0615 -
closed Sunday - **M** 14.95 **t.** (lunch) and a la carte 18.20/30.45 **t.** p. 16 AZ **r**

XX **La Paesana,** 30 Uxbridge St., W8 7TA, ✆ 229 4332, Italian rest. - p. 16 AZ **i**
closed Sunday, Easter, Christmas and Bank Holidays - **M** a la carte approx. 15.00 **t.** 3.80.

XX **Sailing Junk,** 59 Marloes Rd, W8 6LE, ✆ 937 2589, Chinese rest. -
M a la carte 11.00/16.00 **st.** 3.50. FY **x**

X **Kensington Place,** 201 Kensington Church St., W8 7LX, ✆ 727 3184, Fax 229 2025 - p. 16 AZ **z**
closed 24 to 27 December - **M** 12.50 **t.** (lunch) and a la carte 15.00/27.50 **t.** 3.95.

X **Cibo,** 3 Russell Gdns, W14 8EZ, ✆ 371 6271, Italian rest. - EY **o**
closed Sunday dinner and 4 days at Christmas - **M** 17.95 **t.** and a la carte 5.90.

North Kensington - ✉ W2/W10/W11 - 071 - Except where otherwise stated see pp. 4-7.

Abbey Court without rest., 20 Pembridge Gdns, W2 4DU, ✆ 221 7518, Telex 262167, Fax 792 0858, « Tastefully furnished Victorian town house » -
9.00 - **22 rm** 82.25/130.00 **t.** p. 16 AZ **u**

Pembridge Court, 34 Pembridge Gdns, W2 4DX, ✆ 229 9977, Telex 298363, Fax 727 4982, « Collection of antique clothing and fans » - rest
M *(closed Sunday and Bank Holidays)* (dinner only) 12.00 **st.** and a la carte 4.65 - **21 rm** 85.00/160.00 **st.** - SB (November-March) (weekends only) 120.00/250.00 **st.** p.16 AZ **n**

Portobello, 22 Stanley Gdns, W11 2NG, ✆ 727 2777, Fax 792 9641, « Attractive town house in Victorian terrace » - EV **n**
closed 22 December-2 January - **M** (residents only) 15.00/20.00 **t.** and a la carte - **24 rm** 70.00/120.00 **st.**, 1 suite.

XXX **Leith's,** 92 Kensington Park Rd, W11 2PN, ✆ 229 4481 - EV **e**
closed 29-30 August and 24 to 27 December - **M** (dinner only) 26.50/47.50 **st.** 7.25.

XX **Chez Moi,** 1 Addison Av., Holland Park, W11 4QS, ✆ 603 8267, French rest. - p. 8 EX **n**
closed Saturday lunch, Sunday, 1 week Christmas and Bank Holidays - **M** 14.50 **t.** (lunch) and a la carte 19.75/28.00 **t.** 4.50.

XX **Park Inn,** 6 Wellington Terr., Bayswater Rd, W2 4LW, ✆ 229 3553, Chinese (Peking) Seafood rest. - p. 16 AZ **c**
M 30.00/60.00 **st.** 3.90.

192, 192 Kensington Park Rd, W11 2ES, ✆ 727 3573 - VISA EV **a**
closed Monday lunch and Bank Holidays - **M** a la carte 17.50/25.00 **t.**

L'Altro, 210 Kensington Park Rd, W11 1NR, ✆ 792 1066, Fax 602 1371, Italian rest. - VISA EV **c**
closed Sunday dinner - **M** 17.95 **t.** 5.90.

Canal Brasserie, Canalot Studios, 222 Kensal Rd, W10 5BN, ✆ (081) 960 2732 - VISA ET **c**
M a la carte 16.50/18.25 **t.**

South Kensington - ✉ SW5/SW7/W8 - ✆ 071 - pp. 14 and 15.

Blakes, 33 Roland Gdns, SW7 3PF, ✆ 370 6701, Telex 8813500, Fax 373 0442, « Antique oriental furnishings » - rest . VISA BU **n**
M a la carte 33.25/55.20 **t.** 8.00 - 16.65 - **45 rm** 155.00/295.00 **st.**, 7 suites.

Pelham, 15 Cromwell Pl., SW7 2LA, ✆ 589 8288, Fax 584 8444, « Tastefully furnished Victorian town house » - . VISA CS **z**
M 12.50/13.50 **t.** and a la carte 8.50 - 7.50 - **34 rm** 115.00/165.00 **t.**, 3 suites.

Gloucester, 4-18 Harrington Gdns, SW7 4LH, ✆ 373 6030, Telex 917505, Fax 373 0409 - rm - 400. VISA. BS **r**
M 14.95 **t.** (dinner) and a la carte 13.15/46.60 **t.** 9.00 - 12.50 - **542 rm** 115.15/143.35 **st.**, 6 suites.

Rembrandt, 11 Thurloe Pl., SW7 2RS, ✆ 589 8100, Telex 295828, Fax 225 3363, , , - rm rest - 250. VISA. DS **x**
M 15.95 **st.** and a la carte 6.50 - 9.25 - **195 rm** 115.00/140.00 **st.**

Swallow International, Cromwell Rd, SW5 0TH, ✆ 973 1000, Telex 27260, Fax 244 8194, , , - rm rest - 200. VISA AS **c**
M 15.00/18.00 **st.** and a la carte 5.00 - 9.75 - **415 rm** 100.00/125.00 **st.**, 1 suite.

Holiday Inn, 94-106 Cromwell Rd, SW7 4ER, ✆ 373 2222, Telex 911311, Fax 373 0559, , - - 125. VISA. BS **u**
M 14.00/17.50 **st.** and a la carte 5.00 - 10.50 - **143 rm** 129.00/144.00 **st.**, 19 suites.

Gore, 189-190 Queen's Gate, SW7 5EX, ✆ 584 6601, Telex 296244, Fax 589 8127, « Attractive decor » - . VISA BR **n**
closed 25 and 26 December - **M** (only members and residents may book) a la carte 18.30/38.50 **t.** 5.00 - 10.50 - **54 rm** 89.00/118.00.

Regency, 100 Queen's Gate, SW7 5AG, ✆ 370 4595, Telex 267594, Fax 370 5555, , - rm rest - 100. VISA. CT **e**
M *(closed lunch Saturday and Sunday)* a la carte 17.70/25.90 **st.** 5.00 - 12.50 - **194 rm** 119.00/139.00 **st.**, 6 suites - SB (weekends only) 95.00/150.00 **st.**

Cranley without rest., 10-12 Bina Gardens, SW5 0LA, ✆ 373 0123, Fax 373 9497, « Tasteful decor, antiques » - . VISA BT **c**
11.45 - **32 rm** 104.00/177.00 **st.**, **4 suites.**

John Howard, 4 Queen's Gate, SW7 5EH, ✆ 581 3011, Telex 8813397, Fax 589 8403 - . VISA. BQ **i**
M 12.50/16.50 **st.** and a la carte 4.50 - 9.50 - **48 rm** 97.00/170.00 **st.**, 4 suites.

Vanderbilt (Edwardian), 168-186 Cromwell Rd, SW7 5BT, ✆ 589 2424, Telex 946944, Fax 225 2293 - rest - 120. VISA BS **v**
M 12.50/14.50 **st.** and a la carte 5.00 - 9.50 - **223 rm** 92.00/165.00 **st.**

Baileys, 140 Gloucester Rd, SW7 4QH, ✆ 373 6000, Telex 264221, Fax 370 3760 - - 70. VISA. BS **a**
M (dinner only) 24.00 **st.** and a la carte - 9.25 - **162 rm** 105.00/165.00 **st.**

Onslow, 109-113 Queen's Gate, SW7 5LR, ✆ 589 6300, Telex 262180, Fax 581 1492 - rest - 80. VISA. CT **i**
M 8.00/15.00 **st.** and a la carte 5.15 - 3.00 - **171 rm** 105.00/175.00 **st.** - SB (weekends only) 120.00/140.00 **st.**

Park International, 117-125 Cromwell Rd, SW7 4DS, ✆ 370 5711, Telex 296822, Fax 244 9211 - - 45. VISA. AS **e**
M (dinner only) 12.50 **st.** and a la carte 4.25 - 7.50 - **117 rm** 65.00/120.00 **st.** - SB (weekends only) 70.00/100.00 **st.**

Norfolk (Q.M.H.), 2-10 Harrington Rd, SW7 3ER, ✆ 589 8191, Telex 268852, Fax 581 1874, , - rest - 60. VISA. CS **e**
M (dinner only and Sunday lunch)/dinner 18.00 **t.** and a la carte 6.50 - 9.50 - **93 rm** 115.00/145.00 **st.**, 3 suites - SB (weekends only) 130.00 **st.**

Embassy House (Jarvis) 31-33 Queen's Gate, SW7 5JA, ✆ 584 7222, Telex 914893, Fax 589 8193 - . VISA. BR **e**
M (dinner only) 16.50 **st.** and a la carte 7.25 - 5.50 - **68 rm** 90.00/100.00 **st.**, 1 suite - SB (weekends only) 79.00 **st.**

Kensington Plaza, 61 Gloucester Rd, SW7 4PE, ✆ 584 8100, Telex 8950993, Fax 823 9175, - - 50. VISA BS **e**
M 7.50/12.50 **st.** and a la carte 4.50 - 1.75 - **88 rm** 65.00/80.00 **st.** - SB (weekends only) 77.90/97.90 **st.**

Number Sixteen without rest., 14-17 Sumner Pl., SW7 3EG, 589 5232, Telex 266638, Fax 584 8615, « Attractively furnished Victorian town houses », - VISA. CT **c**
8.00 - **36 rm** 70.00/160.00 **t.**

Alexander without rest., 9 Sumner Pl., SW7 3EE, 581 1591, Telex 917133, Fax 581 0824, « Attractively furnished Victorian town houses », - VISA. CT **a**
36 rm 85.00/157.00, 1 suite.

Cranley Place without rest., 1 Cranley Pl., SW7 3AB, 589 7944, Fax 225 3931, « Tasteful decor » - VISA. CT **o**
6.75 **10 rm** 80.00/135.00.

Five Sumner Place without rest., 5 Sumner Pl., SW7 3EE, 584 7586, Fax 823 9962 - VISA. DR **a**
13 rm 58.00/84.00 **s.**

Aster House without rest., 3 Sumner Pl., SW7 3EE, 581 5888, Fax 584 4925, - VISA. CT **u**
12 rm 55.00/87.00 **s.**

Cranley Gardens without rest. 8 Cranley Gdns, SW7 3DB, 373 3232, Telex 894489, Fax 373 7944 - VISA BT **e**
4.50 - **85 rm** 63.00/89.00 **st.**

XXX **Bombay Brasserie,** Courtfield Close, 140 Gloucester Rd, SW7 4UH, 370 4040, Indian rest., « Raj-style decor, conservatory garden » - VISA BS **a**
closed 25 and 26 December - **M** (buffet lunch) 13.95/35.00 **t.** and dinner a la carte 5.50.

XX **Hilaire,** 68 Old Brompton Rd, SW7 3LQ, 584 8993 - VISA CT **n**
closed Saturday lunch, Sunday, 1 week August and Bank Holidays - **M** (booking essential) 24.00/26.50 **t.** and dinner a la carte 23.50/34.50 **t.** 5.50.

XX **Nizam,** 152 Old Brompton Rd, SW5 0BE, 373 0024, Indian rest. - VISA
closed Christmas Day - **M** (buffet lunch Sunday) a la carte 11.15/18.55 **t.** BT **a**

XX **Tui,** 19 Exhibition Rd, SW10 0JQ, 584 8359, Fax 352 8343, Thai rest. - VISA
closed Christmas and Bank Holidays - **M** a la carte 13.00/19.00 **st.** 3.95. CS **u**

XX **Delhi Brasserie,** 134 Cromwell Rd, SW7 4HA, 370 7617, Indian rest. - VISA AS **a**
closed 25 and 26 December - **M** 14.95 **t.** and a la carte.

XX **Memories of India,** 18 Gloucester Rd, SW7 4RB, 589 6450, Telex 265196, Fax 581 5980, Indian rest. - VISA BR **s**
M 14.50 **t.** (dinner) and a la carte 11.70/17.65 **t.**

MERTON

Wimbledon - SW19 - 081.

Cannizaro House (Mt. Charlotte Thistle), West Side, Wimbledon Common, SW19 4UF, 879 1464, Telex 9413837, Fax 879 7338, « 18C country house overlooking Cannizaro Park », - 45. VISA.
M 16.95/25.75 **t.** and a la carte - 10.25 - **44 rm** 102.00/165.00 **t.**, 2 suites.

SOUTHWARK

Bermondsey - SE1 - 071.

XXX **Pont de la Tour,** 36d Shad Thames, Butlers Wharf, SE1 2YE, 403 8403, Fax 403 0267, « Riverside setting » - VISA p. 11 PX **c**
M 24.50 **t.** (lunch) and dinner a la carte 28.50/40.75 **t.** 5.25.

X **Blueprint Café,** Design Museum, Shad Thames, Butlers Wharf, SE1 2YD, 378 7031, Fax 378 6540, « Riverside setting » - VISA p. 11 PX **u**
closed Sunday dinner and 21 to 28 December - **M** a la carte 18.50/23.00 **t.**

Dulwich - SE19 - 081.

XX **Luigi's,** 129 Gipsy Hill, SE19 1QS, 670 1843, Italian rest. - VISA
closed Saturday lunch and Sunday - **M** a la carte 15.70/20.50 **t.** 4.90.

Rotherhithe - SE16 - 071.

Scandic Crown, 265 Rotherhithe St., Nelson Dock, SE16 1EJ, 231 1001, Fax 231 0599, - rm rest - 350. VISA.
M 14.95 **st.** and a la carte 5.00 - 9.50 - **374 rm** 80.00/100.00 **st.**, 12 suites.

Southwark - SE1 - 071.

XX **La Truffe Noire,** 29 Tooley St., SE1 2QF, 378 0621, Fax 403 0689, French rest. - VISA p. 11 PX **a**
closed Saturday, Sunday and Bank Holidays - **M** 21.00 **t.** (lunch) and a la carte 20.00/44.00 **t.** 6.00.

WANDSWORTH

Battersea - ✉ SW8/SW11 - ☎ 071.

XXX ✿ **L'Arlequin** (Delteil), 123 Queenstown Rd, SW8 3RH, ☎ 622 0555, Fax 498 7015, French rest. - ▤. AE VISA - *closed Saturday, Sunday, 3 weeks August, 1 week Christmas and Bank Holidays* - **M** (booking essential) 21.50/28.00 **st.** and a la carte approx. 36.00 **st.**
Spec. Petit chou farci à l'ancienne, Gibier de saison, Filet de loup aux épices.

XX **Chada,** 208-210 Battersea Park Rd, SW11 4ND, ☎ 622 2209, Thai rest. - ▤. AE VISA *closed Saturday lunch, Sunday and Bank Holidays* - **M** a la carte 12.30/24.35 **t.** 3.75.

XX Lena's, 196 Lavender Hill, SW11 1JA, ☎ 228 3735, Thai rest. - ▤.

X **Brasserie Faubourg,** 28 Queenstown Rd, SW8 3RX, ☎ 622 6245 - AE VISA *closed lunch Monday and Saturday, Sunday, last 3 weeks August, 25 and 31 December and Bank Holidays* - **M** 15.00/27.00 **t.** and a la carte 4.25.

Wandsworth - ✉ SW17 - ☎ 081.

XXX ✿✿ **Harvey's** (White), 2 Bellevue Rd, SW17 7EG, ☎ 672 0114 - ▤. VISA *closed Sunday dinner, Monday and 2 weeks December-January* - **M** (booking essential) 24.00/48.00 **t.** 12.00
Spec. Loup de mer poêlé au caviar, Ris de veau au jambon de Parme rôti aux fèves et girolles, Tête de cochon au miel et clous de girofle.

WESTMINSTER (City of)

Bayswater and Maida Vale - ✉ W2/W9 - ☎ 071 - Except where otherwise stated see pp. 16 and 17.

Royal Lancaster, Lancaster Terr., W2 2TY, ☎ 262 6737, Telex 24822, Fax 724 3191, ← - rm ▤ TV ☎ P - 1 400. AE VISA. DZ **e**
M *(closed Saturday lunch and Sunday)* 22.50/25.75 **t.** and dinner a la carte 7.25 - 13.50 - **400 rm** 99.00/135.00 **s.**, 18 suites - SB (weekends only) 124.00/144.00 **st.**

London Metropole, Edgware Rd, W2 1JU, ☎ 402 4141, Telex 23711, Fax 724 8866, ←, , , - rm ▤ TV ☎ - 1 200. AE VISA. p. 5 GU **c**
M (see **Aspects** below) - 12.75 - **721 rm** 125.00/155.00 **st.**, 26 suites.

Whites (Mt. Charlotte Thistle), Bayswater Rd, 90-92 Lancaster Gate, W2 3NR, ☎ 262 2711, Telex 24771, Fax 262 2147 - rm ▤ TV ☎. AE VISA. CZ **v**
M *(closed Saturday lunch)* 17.50/21.50 **t.** and a la carte 7.15 - 9.95 - **52 rm** 135.00/225.00 **st.**, 2 suites - SB (weekends only) 336.00 **st.**

Plaza on Hyde Park (Hilton), 1-7 Lancaster Gate, W2 3NA, ☎ 262 5022, Telex 8954372, Fax 724 8666 - rm TV ☎ - 30. AE VISA DZ **r**
M 14.00 **st.** (dinner) and a la carte 12.20/24.40 **st.** 4.95 - 9.45 - **402 rm** 69.00/130.00 **st.**

Coburg, 129 Bayswater Rd, W2 4RJ, ☎ 221 2217, Telex 268235, Fax 229 0557 - TV ☎. AE VISA. BZ **c**
M (see **Spice Merchant** below) - **131 rm** 87.45/142.45, 1 suite.

Hyde Park Towers, 41-51 Inverness Terr., W2 3JN, ☎ 221 8484, Group Telex 263260, Fax 221 2286 - ▤ rest TV ☎ - 40 BZ **r**
115 rm.

Eden Park, 35-39 Inverness Terr., W2 3JS, ☎ 221 2220, Group Telex 263260, Fax 221 2286 - rm ▤ rest TV ☎ BZ **n**
M (lunch by arrangement) - **137 rm.**

Queen's Park, 48 Queensborough Terr., W2 3SS, ☎ 299 8080, Telex 21723, Fax 792 1330 - ▤ rest TV ☎ - 70. AE VISA. BZ **s**
M a la carte 12.50/16.20 **st.** 5.00 - 7.50 - **86 rm** 86.00/90.00 **st.**

London Embassy (Jarvis), 150 Bayswater Rd, W2 4RT, ☎ 229 1212, Telex 27727, Fax 229 2623 - rm ▤ rest TV ☎ P - 60. AE VISA. BZ **o**
M (carving rest.) 16.00 **st.** and a la carte 6.00 - 9.00 - **192 rm** 98.00/135.00 **st.**, 1 suite - SB (weekends only) 176.00/216.00 **st.**

Hospitality Inn (Mt. Charlotte Thistle), 104 Bayswater Rd, W2 3HL, ☎ 262 4461, Telex 22667, Fax 706 4560, ← - rm ▤ TV ☎ P - 40. AE VISA CZ **o**
M (bar lunch)/dinner 13.95 **st.** and a la carte 4.95 - 8.50 - **175 rm** 75.00/105.00 **st.** - SB (weekends only) 74.00/88.00 **st.**

Mornington without rest., 12 Lancaster Gate, W2 3LG, ☎ 262 7361, Telex 24281, Fax 706 1028, - TV ☎. AE VISA DZ **s**
closed 23 December-2 January - 3.00 - **68 rm** 75.00/108.00 **st.**

Pavilion, 37 Leinster Gdns, W2 3AR, ☎ 258 0269, Telex 268613, Fax 723 7295, - TV ☎ - 80. AE VISA CZ **u**
M (dinner only) 16.25 **t.** 3.95 - 5.00 - **97 rm** 91.00/109.00 **t.** - SB 70.00/119.00 **st.**

XXX **Aspects** (at London Metropole H.), Edgware Rd, W2 1JU, ☎ 402 4141, Telex 23711, Fax 724 8866, ← London - ▤. AE VISA p. 5 GU **c**
closed Sunday - **M** 19.95/29.50 **t.** and a la carte 8.75.

XX **Spice Merchant** (at Coburg H.), 130 Bayswater Rd, W2 4RJ, 221 2442, Fax 229 0557, Indian rest. - AE VISA BZ **c**
closed Christmas Day - **M** a la carte 15.35/23.10 **t.**

XX **Poons,** Whiteleys, Queensway, W2 4YN, 792 2884, Chinese rest. - AE VISA
closed 3 days at Christmas - **M** 12.00/19.00 **t.** and a la carte 5.50. BZ **x**

XX Hsing, 451 Edgware Rd, Little Venice, W2 1TH, 402 0904, Chinese rest. - p. 5 GU **a**

XX **San Marino,** 26 Sussex Pl., W2 2TH, 723 8395, Italian rest. - AE VISA DZ **u**
closed Bank Holidays - **M** a la carte 18.20/33.20 **t.** 4.50.

X **Al San Vincenzo,** 30 Connaught St., W2 2AE, 262 9623, Italian rest. - AE VISA EZ **o**
closed Saturday lunch, Sunday and 2 weeks Christmas - **M** a la carte 18.25/26.50 **t.** 6.50.

Belgravia - SW1 - 071 - Except where otherwise stated see pp. 14 and 15.

Berkeley, Wilton Pl., SW1X 7RL, 235 6000, Telex 919252, Fax 235 4330, - 200. AE VISA. FQ **e**
M - **Restaurant** *(closed Saturday)* 19.50/21.00 **st.** and a la carte 28.35/41.60 **st.** - **The Perroquet** *(closed Sunday)* 15.00/21.00 **st.** and a la carte 19.95/28.40 **st.** - 16.00 - **133 rm** 150.00/240.00 **s.**, 27 suites.

Lanesborough, 1 Lanesborough Pl., SW1X 7TA, 259 5599, Telex 911866, Fax 259 5606 - rm - 70. AE VISA p. 9 IY **a**
M - The Conservatory 20.50/26.50 **st.** and a la carte 7.50 - (see also **The Dining Room** below) - 15.00 - **86 rm** 190.00/275.00 **s.**, 9 suites.

Halkin, 5 Halkin St., SW1X 7DJ, 333 1000, Fax 333 1100 - rm - 25. AE VISA. p. 16 AV **a**
M - **Gualtiero Marchesi at the Halkin** *(Italian rest.) (closed Saturday lunch and Sunday)* 24.00/28.50 **st.** and dinner a la carte 9.00 - 12.50 - **37 rm** 200.00/245.00 **s.**, 4 suites.

Sheraton Belgravia, 20 Chesham Pl., SW1X 8HQ, 235 6040, Telex 919020, Fax 259 6243 - rm . AE VISA. FR **u**
M *(closed Saturday lunch)* 27.80 **t.** (lunch) and dinner a la carte 20.00/29.50 **t.** 5.00 - 11.75 - **82 rm** 165.00/185.00, 7 suites - SB (weekends only) 113.00 **st.**

Lowndes (Hyatt), 21 Lowndes St., SW1X 9ES, 235 6020, Telex 919065, Fax 235 1154 - rm - 25. AE VISA. FR **i**
M 17.50/21.50 **st.** and a la carte 6.50 - 10.25 - **71 rm** 160.00 **s.**, 1 suite.

XXXX **The Dining Room** (at Lanesborough H.), 1 Lanesborough Pl., SW1X 7TA, 259 5599, Telex 911866, Fax 259 5606 - . AE VISA p. 9 IY **a**
closed Saturday lunch and Sunday - **M** 24.00/29.50 **st.** and a la carte 27.00/44.50 **st.** 7.50.

XXX **Al Bustan,** 27 Motcomb St., SW1X 8JU, 235 8277, Lebanese rest. - . AE VISA
closed 25-26 December and 1 January - **M** a la carte 18.75/29.75 **t.** 7.50. FR **z**

XX **Motcombs,** 26 Motcomb St., SW1X 8JU, 235 6382, Fax 245 6351 - . AE VISA
closed Bank Holidays - **M** 15.50 **t.** (lunch) and a la carte 13.00/23.00 **t.** 4.00. FR **z**

Hyde Park and Knightsbridge - SW1/SW7 - 071 - pp. 14 and 15.

Hyde Park (Forte), 66 Knightsbridge, SW1Y 7LA, 235 2000, Telex 262057, Fax 235 4552, - rm - 180. AE VISA. FQ **x**
M - **Park Room** *(Italian rest.)* 29.50 **st.** and a la carte 8.50 - **Grill room** - 14.00 - **166 rm** 205.00/290.00 **s.**, 19 suites - SB (weekends only) 298.00 **st.**

Knightsbridge Green without rest., 159 Knightsbridge, SW1X 7PD, 584 6274, Fax 225 1635 - . AE VISA. EQ **z**
closed 3 days at Christmas - 8.50 - **10 rm** 75.00/100.00 **st.**, **14 suites** 115.00 **st.**

XXX **Pearl of Knightsbridge,** 22 Brompton Rd, SW1X 7QN, 225 3888, Fax 225 0252, Chinese rest. - AE VISA EQ **e**
closed 25 and 26 December - **M** 12.50/40.00 **t.** and a la carte.

XX **Lucullus,** 48 Knightsbridge, SW1X 7JN, 245 6622, Fax 245 6625, Seafood - . AE VISA FQ **a**
closed 25 and 26 December - **M** 15.50 **t.** (lunch) and a la carte 24.25/36.25 **t.**

XX **Dell Arte,** 116 Knightsbridge, SW1X 7PJ, 225 3512, Italian rest. - AE VISA
M 20.00/30.00 **t.** and a la carte 7.50. EQ **x**

Mayfair - W1 - 071 - pp. 12 and 13.

Dorchester, Park Lane, W1A 2HJ, 629 8888, Telex 887704, Fax 409 0114, - rm - 500. AE VISA. BN **a**
M - **Grill** 20.00/28.00 **st.** and a la carte 25.80/40.30 **st.** 9.00 - (see also **Oriental** and **Terrace** below) - 12.50 - **195 rm** 180.00/240.00 **s.**, 55 suites.

Claridge's, Brook St., W1A 2JQ, 629 8860, Telex 21872, Fax 499 2210 - - 60. AE VISA. BL **c**
M 26.00/34.00 **st.** and a la carte 42.00/65.50 **st.** 5.80 - **Causerie** 18.50/30.00 **st.** and a la carte 36.00/48.75 **st.** 5.80 - 16.00 - **137 rm** 175.00/265.00 **s.**, 53 suites.

Four Seasons, Hamilton Pl., Park Lane, W1A 1AZ, 499 0888, Telex 22771, Fax 493 1895 – rm – 400. BP **a**
M – **Lanes** 24.95/25.00 **st.** and dinner a la carte 29.00 **st.** – **Four Seasons** (see also below) – 13.75 – **209 rm** 200.00/245.00 **s.**, 19 suites.

Le Meridien London, 21 Piccadilly, W1V 0BH, 734 8000, Telex 25795, Fax 437 3574, squash – – 200. EM **a**
M – **Terrace Garden** 18.50 **t.** (lunch) and a la carte approx. 25.60 **t.** 7.00 – (see also **Oak Room** below) – 12.75 – **219 rm** 190.00/230.00 **s.**, 41 suites.

Grosvenor House (Forte), Park Lane, W1A 3AA, 499 6363, Telex 24871, Fax 493 3341, – rm – 1 500. AM **a**
M a la carte 12.95/23.00 **st.** – (see also **Nico at Ninety** below) – 12.75 – **384 rm** 190.00/205.00 **st.**, 70 suites – SB (weekends only) 238.00 **st.**

Connaught, Carlos Pl., W1Y 6AL, 499 7070, Fax 495 3262 – rest BM **e**
M (booking essential) a la carte 27.50/61.30 **t.** 5.50 – **66 rm**, 24 suites
Spec. Galette Connaught aux diamants noirs, salade Aphrodite, Homard et langoustines grillés aux herbes, Crème brûlée d'un soir.

Fortyseven Park Street, 47 Park St., W1Y 4EB, 491 7282, Telex 22116, Fax 491 7281 – AM **c**
M (see **Le Gavroche** below) – 16.50 – 52 suites 225.00/430.00 **s.**

Brown's (Forte), 29-34 Albemarle St., W1A 4SW, 493 6020, Telex 28686, Fax 493 9381 – rm – 70. – **M** 23.50/26.50 **t.** and a la carte 7.50 – 13.75 – **114 rm** 185.00/255.00 **t.**, 6 suites – SB (weekends only) 280.00 **st.** DM **e**

Britannia (Inter-Con.), Grosvenor Sq., W1A 3AN, 629 9400, Telex 23941, Fax 629 7736 – rm – 80. BM **x**
M 21.30 **t.** and a la carte 6.10 – (see also **Shogun** below) – **305 rm**, 12 suites.

Park Lane, Piccadilly, W1Y 8BX, 499 6321, Telex 21533, Fax 499 1965, – rm – 300. BP **x**
M 17.00/23.00 **st.** and a la carte 6.00 – 8.50 – **268 rm** 130.00/150.00 **s.**, 52 suites.

London Hilton on Park Lane, 22 Park Lane, W1A 2HH, 493 8000, Telex 24873, Fax 493 4957, « London from Window on the World Restaurant », – rm – 1 000. BP **e**
M *(closed Saturday lunch)* 26.95/39.00 **t.** and a la carte 14.00 – **396 rm** 180.00/295.00 **t.**, 52 suites – SB (weekends only) 170.00/232.00 **st.**

Inter-Continental, 1 Hamilton Pl., Hyde Park Corner, W1V 0QY, 409 3131, Telex 25853, Fax 409 3476, – rm – 700. BP **o**
M 25.00/43.00 **t.** and a la carte 6.00 – (see also **Le Soufflé** below) – 14.95 – **437 rm** 190.00/240.00 **s.**, 29 suites – SB 190.00/480.00 **st.**

May Fair Inter-Continental, Stratton St., W1A 2AN, 629 7777, Telex 262526, Fax 629 1459, – rm – 270. DN **z**
M (see **Le Chateau** below) – 12.00 – **263 rm** 175.00/225.00 **st.**, 24 suites.

Marriott, Duke St., Grosvenor Sq., W1A 4AW, 493 1232, Telex 268101, Fax 491 3201 – rm – 600. BL **a**
M *(closed Saturday lunch)* 23.00/35.00 **t.** and dinner a la carte – 10.50 – **212 rm** 100.00/250.00 **s.**, 11 suites.

Athenaeum, 116 Piccadilly, W1V 0BJ, 499 3464, Telex 261589, Fax 493 1860 – rm – 55. CP **s**
M *(closed Saturday lunch)* 25.50 **st.** and a la carte 9.50 – 14.00 – **106 rm** 165.00/205.00 **st.**, 6 suites – SB (weekends only) 165.00/290.00 **st.**

Westbury (Forte), Conduit St., W1A 4UH, 629 7755, Telex 24378, Fax 495 1163 – – 116. DM **a**
M *(closed Sunday lunch)* 18.50/21.50 **st.** and a la carte 8.40 – 11.50 – **229 rm** 155.00/180.00 **st.**, 14 suites – SB (weekends only) 178.00 **st.**

Washington, 5-7 Curzon St., W1 8DT, 499 7000, Telex 24540, Fax 495 6172 – rm – 80. CN **s**
M a la carte 19.90/30.00 **st.** – 10.25 – **169 rm** 148.00/178.00 **st.**, 4 suites.

Holiday Inn, 3 Berkeley St., W1X 6NE, 493 8282, Telex 24561, Fax 629 2827 – rm – 70. – **M** (bar lunch Saturday) 17.00/21.00 **st.** and a la carte 6.25 – 10.95 – **179 rm** 164.00/185.00 **st.**, 6 suites. DN **r**

Chesterfield, 35 Charles St., W1X 8LX, 491 2622, Telex 269394, Fax 491 4793 – rm – 100. CN **c**
M 17.50/19.50 **t.** and a la carte 6.75 – 9.95 – **106 rm** 115.00/170.00 **st.**, 4 suites.

Green Park, Half Moon St., W1Y 8BP, 629 7522, Telex 28856, Fax 491 8971 – rm rest – 70. CN **a**
M 15.00 **st.** (lunch) and a la carte approx. 27.15 **st.** 4.95 – 9.75 – **161 rm**.

London Mews Hilton without rest., 2 Stanhope Row, W1Y 7HE, 493 7222, Telex 24665, Fax 629 9423 – – 50. BP **u**
71 rm 119.00/138.00 **t.**, 1 suite.

Flemings, 7-12 Half Moon St., W1Y 7RA, 499 2964, Telex 27510, Fax 499 1817 – rest – 40. CN **z**
M 15.00/30.00 **st.** and a la carte 6.25 – 10.20 – **132 rm** 104.00/193.00 **st.**, 11 suites.

XXXXX ✿ **Oak Room** (at Le Meridien London H.), 21 Piccadilly, W1V 0BH, ✆ 734 8000, Telex 25795, Fax 437 3574, French rest. – ▤. AE ⓓ VISA EM **a**
closed Saturday lunch, Sunday and Bank Holidays – **M** 24.50/46.00 **t.** and a la carte 47.50/50.00 **t.** ♁ 10.00
Spec. Gaspacho de langoustines à la crème de courgette, Suprême de bar au beurre de truffe, Canard sauce Arabica.

XXXXX ✿✿ **Nico at Ninety** (Ladenis) (at Grosvenor House H.), Park Lane, W1A 3AA, ✆ 409 1290, Fax 355 4877, French rest. – ▤. AE ⓓ VISA AM **e**
closed Saturday and Sunday – **M** (booking essential) 25.00/40.00 **st.** and a la carte 48.00/58.00 **st.** ♁ 14.50
Spec. Bouchées de rouget, sauce piquante aux pousses d'épinards, Pintade aux abricots à la farce de boudin blanc (2 personnes), Crème Caramel aux fruits frais.

XXXXX **Terrace** (at Dorchester H.), Park Lane, W1A 2HJ, ✆ 629 8888, Telex 887704, Fax 409 0114, French rest. – ▤. AE ⓓ VISA BN **a**
closed Sunday, Monday and 2 weeks August – **M** (dinner only) 25.00/48.00 **st.** and a la carte 27.00/48.50 **st.** ♁ 9.00.

XXXX ✿✿ **Le Gavroche** (Roux), 43 Upper Brook St., W1Y 1PF, ✆ 408 0881, Fax 409 0939, French rest. – ▤. AE ⓓ VISA AM **c**
closed Saturday, Sunday, 24 December-4 January and Bank Holidays – **M** (booking essential) 30.00/60.00 **st.** and a la carte 43.50/81.60 **st.** ♁ 13.00
Spec. Soufflé suissesse, Tournedos gratiné aux poivres, Sauté de St. Jacques aux épices et légumes frits.

XXXX ✿ **Oriental** (at Dorchester H.), Park Lane, W1A 2HJ, ✆ 629 8888, Telex 887704, Fax 409 0114, Chinese (Canton) rest. – ▤. AE ⓓ VISA BN **a**
closed Saturday lunch, Sunday, 2 to 15 August and Bank Holidays – **M** 20.00/35.00 **st.** and a la carte 25.00/42.50 **st.** ♁ 9.00
Spec. Sesame prawns with lemon sauce, Medaillons of beef Cantonese style, Shredded coconut tarts.

XXXX ✿ **Four Seasons** Hamilton Pl., Park Lane, W1A 1AZ, ✆ 499 0888, Telex 22771, Fax 493 1895, French rest. – |♦| ▤ 🚗. AE ⓓ VISA BP **a**
M 25.00/40.00 **st.** and a la carte 32.50/58.50 **st.**
Spec. Délices du Sud-Ouest, Homard à l'étouffée, pommes et curry, Fondant de chocolat, glace pistache.

XXXX **Le Soufflé** (at Inter-Continental H.), 1 Hamilton Pl., Hyde Park Corner, W1V 0QY, ✆ 409 3131, Telex 25853, Fax 409 7460 – ▤ 🚗. AE ⓓ VISA BP **o**
closed Saturday lunch – **M** 25.50/43.00 **t.** and a la carte 31.80/42.50 **t.** ♁ 9.00.

XXXX **Les Saveurs,** 37a Curzon St., W1Y 8EY, ✆ 491 8919, Fax 491 3658, French rest. – ▤. AE ⓓ VISA BN **o**
closed Saturday, Sunday, 8 to 24 August, 24 December-10 January and Bank Holidays – **M** 21.00/39.50 **t.** and a la carte ♁ 8.00.

XXXX **Le Chateau** (at May Fair Inter-Continental H.), Stratton St., W1A 2AN, ✆ 629 7777, Telex 262526, Fax 629 1459, French rest. – ▤. AE ⓓ VISA DN **z**
M 23.50/27.50 **st.** and a la carte.

XXXX **Mirabelle,** 56 Curzon St., W1Y 8DL, ✆ 499 4636, Fax 499 5449 – ▤. AE ⓓ VISA CN **u**
closed Saturday lunch, Sunday and Bank Holidays – **M** 25.00/45.00 **st.** and a la carte – **Bon** *(Japanese-Teppanyaki rest.)* 36.40/58.00 **st.** and a la carte.

XXX **Princess Garden,** 8-10 North Audley St., W1Y 1WF, ✆ 493 3223, Fax 491 2655, Chinese (Peking) rest. – ▤. AE ⓓ VISA AL **z**
closed 9 April and 25-26 December – **M** 33.00 **t.** (dinner) and a la carte 22.50/35.50 **t.** ♁ 8.00.

XXX **Zen Central,** 20 Queen St., W1X 7PJ, ✆ 629 8089, Chinese rest. – ▤ Ⓟ. AE ⓓ VISA CN **x**
M 12.00/20.00 **t.** and a la carte.

XX **Greenhouse,** 27a Hay's Mews, W1X 7RJ, ✆ 499 3331, Fax 225 0011 – ▤. ⓓ VISA BN **e**
closed Saturday lunch, Sunday dinner and 24 December-2 January – **M** a la carte 16.50/26.00 **t.** ♁ 6.50.

XX **Ho-Ho,** 29 Maddox St., W1R 9LD, ✆ 493 1228, Fax 408 0862, Oriental cuisine – ▤. AE ⓓ VISA DL **x**
closed Sunday and Bank Holidays – **M** 23.00 **t.** and a la carte ♁ 5.00.

XX Langan's Brasserie, Stratton St., W1X 5FD, ✆ 491 8822 – ▤ DN **e**

XX Mr Kai, 65 Audley St., W1, ✆ 493 8988, Chinese rest. – ▤ BN **i**

XX **Mulligans,** 13-14 Cork St., W1X 1PF, ✆ 409 1370, Irish rest. – ▤. AE ⓓ VISA DM **c**
closed Saturday lunch, Sunday and Bank Holidays – **M** a la carte 17.25/30.00 **t.** ♁ 5.95.

XX Shogun (at Britannia H.), Adams Row, W1Y 5DE, ✆ 493 1255, Japanese rest. – ▤ BM **x**

XX **Miyama,** 38 Clarges St., W1Y 7PJ, ✆ 499 2443, Japanese rest. – ▤. AE ⓓ VISA CN **e**
closed lunch Saturday and Sunday and Bank Holidays – **M** 16.00/36.00 **t.** and a la carte.

Regent's Park and Marylebone - ✉ NW1/NW6/NW8/W1 - ☎ 071 - Except where otherwise stated see pp. 12 and 13.

Churchill, 30 Portman Sq., W1A 4ZX, ☎ 486 5800, Telex 264831, Fax 486 1255, ✗ - |♦| ⇔ rm ▤ TV ☎ P - 🔔 200. AE ① VISA. ✗ AJ **x**
M 19.00 **t.** (lunch) and a la carte 25.00/40.00 **t.** 6.50 - ☐ 14.35 - **406 rm** 170.00/225.00 **s.**, 42 suites.

Portman Inter-Continental, 22 Portman Sq., W1H 9FL, ☎ 486 5844, Telex 261526, Fax 935 0537, ✗ - |♦| ⇔ rm ▤ TV ☎ ♿ P - 🔔 380. ✗ AJ **o**
259 rm, 13 suites.

Langham Hilton, 1 Portland Pl., W1N 3AA, ☎ 636 1000, Telex 21113, Fax 436 1604 - |♦| ⇔ rm ▤ TV ☎ ♿ P - 🔔 320. AE ① VISA p. 5 JU **e**
M 29.00/39.00 **t.** and a la carte 12.50 - ☐ 13.50 - **363 rm** 165.00/185.00 **s.**, 20 suites - SB (weekends only) 120.00/232.00 **st.**

Selfridge (Mt. Charlotte Thistle), Orchard St., W1H 0JS, ☎ 408 2080, Telex 22361, Fax 629 8849 - |♦| ⇔ rm ▤ TV ☎ - 🔔 220. AE ① VISA. ✗ AK **e**
M *(closed Saturday lunch and Sunday)* 19.75 **st.** and a la carte 5.50 - ☐ 10.20 - **294 rm** 135.00/160.00 **st.**, 2 suites.

Berkshire (Edwardian), 350 Oxford St., W1N 0BY, ☎ 629 7474, Telex 22270, Fax 629 8156 - |♦| ⇔ rm ▤ TV ☎ - 🔔 45. AE ① VISA. ✗ BK **n**
M 19.00/24.00 **st.** and a la carte 6.50 - ☐ 13.50 - **145 rm** 158.00/245.00 **st.**, 2 suites.

Clifton Ford, 47 Welbeck St., W1M 8DN, ☎ 486 6600, Telex 22569, Fax 486 7492 - |♦| ⇔ rm ▤ TV ☎ 🚗 - 🔔 150. AE ① VISA BH **a**
M *(closed Saturday lunch and Sunday)* 25.00/40.00 **st.** and a la carte 5.00 - ☐ 12.95 - **196 rm** 130.00/145.00, 4 suites.

Berners Park Plaza, 10 Berners St., W1A 3BE, ☎ 636 1629, Telex 25759, Fax 580 3972 - |♦| ⇔ rm ▤ rest TV ☎ ♿ - 🔔 120. AE ① VISA. ✗ EJ **r**
M *(closed Saturday lunch)* 13.50/15.75 **t.** and a la carte 6.50 - ☐ 9.75 - **230 rm** 110.00/130.00 **st.**, 3 suites.

London Regent's Park Hilton, 18 Lodge Rd, NW8 7JT, ☎ 722 7722, Telex 23101, Fax 483 2408 - |♦| ⇔ rm ▤ TV ☎ P - 🔔 150. AE ① VISA p. 5 GT **v**
M a la carte 17.25/29.75 **t.** 6.75 - **Kashi-Noki** - ☐ 11.30 - **376 rm** 99.00/125.00 **st.**, 1 suite - SB (weekends only) 152.00 **st.**

Montcalm, Great Cumberland Pl., W1A 2LF, ☎ 402 4288, Telex 28710, Fax 724 9180 - |♦| ▤ TV ☎ - 🔔 80. AE ① VISA. ✗ p. 17 EZ **x**
M *(closed Saturday lunch and Sunday)* 18.25/21.95 **t.** and dinner a la carte 6.00 - ☐ 12.95 - **101 rm** 175.00/195.00 **st.**, 14 suites.

St. George's (Forte), Langham Pl., W1N 8QS, ☎ 580 0111, Fax 436 7997, ≤ - |♦| ⇔ rm ▤ rest TV ☎ - 🔔 35. AE ① VISA p. 5 JU **a**
M 15.95/18.00 **t.** and a la carte 6.60 - ☐ 10.95 - **83 rm** 95.00/120.00 **st.**, 3 suites - SB (weekends only) 138.00 **st.**

Marble Arch Marriott, 134 George St., W1H 6DN, ☎ 723 1277, Fax 402 0666, 🏋, ≘s, 🏊 - |♦| ⇔ rm ▤ TV ☎ ♿ P - 🔔 150. AE ① VISA p. 17 EZ **i**
M 14.95/17.50 **st.** and a la carte 7.00 - ☐ 11.85 - **237 rm** 160.00/180.00 **s.**, 2 suites.

Forte Crest Regents Park, Carburton St., W1P 8EE, ☎ 388 2300, Telex 22453, Fax 387 2806 - |♦| ⇔ rm ▤ rest TV ☎ - 🔔 600. AE ① VISA. ✗ p. 5 JU **i**
M 6.50/14.95 **st.** and a la carte 6.50 - ☐ 11.25 - **315 rm** 95.00 **st.**, 2 suites - SB (weekends only) 118.00 **st.**

Dorset Square, 39 Dorset Sq., NW1 6QN, ☎ 723 7874, Fax 724 3328, « Attractively furnished Regency town houses », 🌳 - |♦| ▤ TV ☎. AE VISA. ✗ p. 5 HU **s**
M *(closed Sunday lunch and Saturday)* 14.50/27.00 **t.** 7.50 - ☐ 9.50 - **37 rm** 90.00/165.00 **st.**

Durrants, 26-32 George St., W1H 6BJ, ☎ 935 8131, Fax 487 3510, « Converted Georgian houses with Regency façade » - |♦| TV ☎ - 🔔 50. AE VISA. ✗ AH **e**
M 17.00 **t.** and a la carte 5.50 - ☐ 8.50 - **93 rm** 85.00/99.00 **st.**, 3 suites.

Londoner, 57 Welbeck St., W1M 8HS, ☎ 935 4442, Telex 894630, Fax 487 3782 - |♦| ⇔ rm TV ☎ - 🔔 90. AE ① VISA. ✗ BJ **c**
M (carving rest.) 12.95 **st.** and a la carte 4.50 - **144 rm** ☐ 115.00/130.00 **st.**

Rathbone, Rathbone St., W1P 1AJ, ☎ 636 2001, Telex 28728, Fax 636 3882 - |♦| ⇔ rm ▤ TV ☎. ✗ p. 6 KU **x**
72 rm.

Langham Court, 31-35 Langham St., W1N 5RE, ☎ 436 6622, Telex 21331, Fax 436 2303 - |♦| TV ☎ - 🔔 80. AE ① VISA. ✗ p. 5 JU **z**
M *(closed lunch Saturday and Sunday)* 12.50/30.00 **st.** and a la carte 7.00 - ☐ 8.50 - **56 rm** 75.00/124.00 **st.**

Mostyn, 4 Bryanston St., W1H 0DE, ☎ 935 2361, Telex 27656, Fax 487 2759 - |♦| TV ☎ - 🔔 150. ✗ AK **i**
118 rm, 3 suites.

Harewood, 1 Harewood Row, NW1 6SE, ☎ 262 2707, Fax 262 2975 - |♦| ▤ rest TV ☎ - 🔔 80. AE ① VISA. ✗ p. 5 HU **x**
M (dinner only) 13.50 **st.** 4.95 - ☐ 7.75 **92 rm** 60.00/94.00 **st.**

XXX Odins, 27 Devonshire St., W1N 1RJ, ✆ 935 7296 p. 5 IU **n**

XX **Nico Central,** 35 Great Portland St., W1N 5DD, ✆ 436 8846 - ▤. AE VISA DJ **c**
closed Saturday lunch and Sunday - **M** a la carte 20.20/33.90 **st.**

XX **Martin's,** 239 Baker St., NW1 6XE, ✆ 935 3130 - ▤. AE VISA p. 5 HU **u**
closed Saturday lunch, Sunday, Easter, Christmas and Bank Holidays - **M** a la carte 15.50/20.50 **t.** 4.50.

XX Masako, 6-8 St. Christopher's Pl., W1M 5HB, ✆ 935 1579, Japanese rest. BJ **e**

XX **Gaylord,** 79-81 Mortimer St., W1N 7TB, ✆ 580 3615, Indian and Pakistani rest. - ▤. AE VISA p. 6 KU **o**
M 10.50/12.50 **t.** and a la carte 4.50.

XX Maroush III, 62 Seymour St., W1H 5AF, ✆ 724 5024, Lebanese rest. - ▤ p. 17 EZ **r**

XX **Stepen Bull,** 5-7 Blandford St., W1H 3AA, ✆ 486 9696 - VISA AH **a**
closed Saturday lunch and Sunday - **M** a la carte approx. 26.50 **t.** 5.50.

XX Mon, (at Cumberland H.), Marble Arch, W1A 4RF, ✆ 262 6528, Fax 706 2531, Japanese rest. - ▤. AK **n**

XX **The Restaurant and Arts Bar,** Jason Court, 76 Wigmore St., W1H 9DQ, ✆ 224 2992 - ▤. AE VISA - *closed Saturday lunch, Sunday dinner, Christmas and Bank Holidays* - **M** 18.50 **t.** (lunch) and a la carte 14.50/22.75 **t.** 4.50.

XX **Asuka,** Berkeley Arcade, 209a Baker St., NW1 6AB, ✆ 486 5026, Fax 262 1456, Japanese rest. - AE VISA p. 5 HU **u**
closed Saturday lunch, Sunday and Bank Holidays - **M** 25.00/55.00 **st.** and a la carte.

XX **Le P'tit Montmartre,** 15-17 Marylebone Lane, W1M 5FE, ✆ 935 9226, French rest. - ▤. AE VISA - *closed Saturday lunch, Sunday, Easter, 4 days at Christmas and Bank Holidays* - **M** 15.95 **t.** and a la carte 4.50. BJ **a**

XX Fontana Amorosa, 1 Blenheim Terr., NW8 0EH, ✆ 328 5014, Italian rest. p. 4 FS **s**

XX Tino's Garden, 128 Allitsen Rd, NW8 7AU, ✆ 586 6264 p. 5 GT **u**

XX **La Loggia,** 68 Edgware Rd, W2 2EG, ✆ 723 0554, Italian rest. - ▤. AE VISA p. 17 EZ **a**
closed Saturday lunch, Sunday and Bank Holidays - **M** a la carte 18.50/27.50 **t.** 4.20.

St. James's - ✉ W1/SW1/WC2 - 071 - pp. 12 and 13.

Ritz, Piccadilly, W1V 9DG, ✆ 493 8181, Telex 267200, Fax 493 2687, « Elegant restaurant in Louis XV style » - ▤ TV ☎. AE VISA. DN **a**
M (dancing Friday and Saturday) 26.50/39.50 **st.** and a la carte 28.00/41.00 **st.** 9.00 - 13.50 - **115 rm** 190.00/265.00 **st.**, 14 suites - SB (weekends only) 200.00 **st.**

Dukes, 35 St. James's Pl., SW1A 1NY, ✆ 491 4840, Telex 28283, Fax 493 1264 - ▤ rest TV ☎ - 35. AE VISA. EP **x**
M *(closed Saturday lunch)* 19.95/28.50 **t.** and a la carte 34.85/43.35 **t.** 7.50 - 11.75 - **38 rm** 180.00/275.00 **t.**, 26 suites.

22 Jermyn Street, 22 Jermyn St., SW1Y 6HL, ✆ 734 2353, Fax 734 0750 - TV ☎. AE VISA. - **M** (room service only) a la carte 22.00/26.50 **t.** 6.00 - 13.00 - **5 rm** 160.00 **s.**, 13 suites 210.00/245.00 **s.** FM **e**

Stafford, 16-18 St. James's Pl., SW1A 1NJ, ✆ 493 0111, Telex 28602, Fax 493 7121 - ▤ rest TV ☎ - 40. AE VISA. - **M** 29.50/40.00 **st.** and a la carte 7.50 - 12.50 - **67 rm** 185.00/253.00 **st.**, 7 suites - SB (weekends only) 170.00 **st.** DN **u**

Forte Crest St. James's, 81 Jermyn St., SW1Y 6JF, ✆ 930 2111, Telex 263187, Fax 839 2125 - rm ▤ rest TV ☎ P - 90. AE VISA. EN **i**
M 18.50 **st.** (dinner) and a la carte 15.50/27.95 **st.** - 10.25 - **253 rm** 115.00 **st.**, 3 suites - SB (weekends only) 158.00 **st.**

Hospitality Inn Piccadilly (Mt. Charlotte Thistle), 39 Coventry St., W1V 8EL, ✆ 930 4033, Telex 8950058, Fax 925 2586 - rm TV ☎. FGM **a**
M (room service only) - **92 rm.**

Royal Trafalgar Thistle (Mt. Charlotte Thistle), Whitcomb St., WC2H 7HG, ✆ 930 4477, Telex 298564, Fax 925 2149 - rm TV ☎. AE VISA. GM **r**
M 12.50/18.75 **st.** and a la carte 6.00 - 9.75 - **108 rm** 99.00/130.00 **st.** - SB 98.00/196.00 **st.**

XXX ✿ **Suntory,** 72-73 St. James's St., SW1A 1PH, ✆ 409 0201, Fax 499 7993, Japanese rest. - ▤. AE VISA - *closed Sunday and Bank Holidays* - **M** 49.80/90.00 **st.** (dinner) and a la carte 33.30/86.00 **st.** 7.50 EP **z**
Spec. Kaiseki, Suki-yaki, Teppan-yaki.

XX **Le Caprice,** Arlington House, Arlington St., SW1A 1RT, ✆ 629 2239, Fax 493 9040 - ▤. AE VISA DN **c**
closed 24 December-1 January - **M** a la carte 18.00/30.25 **t.** 6.25.

XX **The Square,** 32 King St., St. James's, SW1Y 6RJ, ✆ 839 8787 - ▤. AE VISA
closed Saturday lunch, Sunday dinner and Christmas-New Year - **M** a la carte 20.50/27.00 **t.** 4.75. EN **v**

XX **Green's,** 36 Duke St., SW1Y 6DF, ✆ 930 4566, Fax 930 1383, English rest. - ▤. AE VISA
closed Sunday dinner, Christmas, New Year and Bank Holidays - **M** a la carte 19.50/28.00 **t.** 5.00. EN **n**

Soho - ✉ W1/WC2 - ☎ 071 - pp. 12 and 13.

Hampshire (Edwardian), Leicester Sq., WC2H 7LH, ☎ 839 9399, Telex 914848, Fax 930 8122 - |‡| ▤ TV ☎ - 🏛 80. AE VISA. ✻ GM **s**
M 21.00/27.50 **st.** and a la carte 6.50 - ☕ 13.00 - **119 rm** 184.00/220.00 **st.**, 5 suites.

XXXX **Grill Room at the Café Royal** (Forte), 68 Regent St., W1R 6EL, ☎ 439 6320 - ▤. AE VISA EM **e**
closed Sunday and Bank Holidays - **M** 19.50/28.00 **st.** and a la carte 8.00.

XXX **Au Jardin des Gourmets,** 5 Greek St., W1V 5LA, ☎ 437 1816, Fax 437 0043, French rest. - ▤. AE VISA GJ **a**
closed Saturday lunch, Sunday and Bank Holidays - **M** (booking essential) 17.50/20.50 **st.** and a la carte 3.90.

XXX **Lindsay House,** 21 Romilly St., W1V 5TG, ☎ 439 0450, Fax 581 2848 - ▤. AE VISA
closed 25 and 26 December - **M** 14.75/18.00 **t.** and a la carte 4.50. GL **i**

XX **Red Fort,** 77 Dean St., W1V 5HA, ☎ 437 2115, Fax 437 2525, Indian rest. - ▤. AE VISA FJK **r**
M 14.00/16.00 **st.** and a la carte.

XX **Brasserie at the Café Royal** (Forte), 68 Regent St., W1R 6EL, ☎ 734 0981 - ▤. AE VISA EM **e**
closed Bank Holidays - **M** 13.50/16.50 **t.** 5.00.

XX **Soho Soho** (first floor), 11-13 Frith St., W1, ☎ 494 3491 - ▤. AE VISA FK **s**
closed Saturday lunch, Sunday and Bank Holidays - **M** a la carte 21.35/28.35 **t.** 4.40.

XX **Ming,** 35-36 Greek St., W1V 5LN, ☎ 734 2721, Fax 435 0812, Chinese rest. - AE VISA
closed Sunday and 25-26 December - **M** 12.00/19.50 **t.** and a la carte 6.50. GK **c**

XX **Gopal's,** 12 Bateman St., W1V 5TD, ☎ 434 0840, Indian rest. - ▤. AE VISA
closed 25 and 26 December - **M** 15.75/18.50 **t.** and a la carte. FK **e**

XX **Gay Hussar,** 2 Greek St., W1V 6NB, ☎ 437 0973, Hungarian rest. - ▤. AE GJ **c**
closed Sunday and Bank Holidays - **M** 15.00 **t.** (lunch) and a la carte 17.30/23.60 **st.** 4.00.

XX **Gallery Rendezvous,** 53-55 Beak St., W1R 3LF, ☎ 734 0445, Chinese (Peking) rest. - ▤. AE VISA EL **a**
closed 25 December and New Year - **M** 12.00/45.00 **t.** and a la carte 8.75.

X **dell 'Ugo,** 56 Frith St., W1V 5TA, ☎ 734 8300, Fax 734 8784 - AE VISA FK **z**
closed Sunday and Bank Holidays - **M** a la carte 12.50/17.20 **t.** 4.00.

X **Sri Siam,** 14 Old Compton St., W1V 5PE, ☎ 434 3544, Thai rest. - ▤. AE VISA GK **r**
closed Sunday lunch, 24-25 December and 1 January - **M** 9.00/14.95 **t.** and a la carte 3.95.

X **Alastair Little,** 49 Frith St., W1V 5TE, ☎ 734 5183 - AE VISA FK **o**
closed Saturday lunch and Sunday - **M** (booking essential) 18.00 **t.** (lunch) and a la carte 25.00/38.00 **t.** 5.00.

Strand and Covent Garden - ✉ WC2 - ☎ 071 - p. 17.

Savoy, Strand, WC2R 0EU, ☎ 836 4343, Telex 24234, Fax 240 6040 - |‡| ⇔ rm ▤ TV ☎ 🚗 - 🏛 500. AE VISA. ✻ DEY **a**
M - **Grill** 32.00 **t.** (dinner) and a la carte 28.90/42.10 **st.** 5.50 - **River** 27.00/38.50 **st.** and a la carte 32.00/50.00 **st.** 5.50 - ☕ 16.75 - **152 rm** 158.00/240.00 **s.**, 48 suites - SB (except weekdays 10 May-11 July and 4 September-22 November) 300.00/560.00 **st.**

Howard, 12 Temple Pl., WC2R 2PR, ☎ 836 3555, Telex 268047, Fax 379 4547 - |‡| ▤ TV ☎ 🚗 - 🏛 100. AE VISA. ✻ EX **e**
M 25.00 **st.** (lunch) and a la carte 27.45/44.05 **st.** 8.15 - ☕ 13.85 - **133 rm** 200.00/226.00 **st.**, 2 suites.

Waldorf (Forte), Aldwych, WC2B 4DD, ☎ 836 2400, Telex 24574, Fax 836 7244 - |‡| ⇔ rm TV ☎ - 🏛 450. AE VISA. ✻ EX **x**
M 17.50/21.50 **t.** and a la carte 6.75 - ☕ 12.95 - **273 rm** 140.00/170.00 **st.**, 19 suites - SB (weekends only) 178.00 **st.**

XXXX **Boulestin,** 1a Henrietta St., WC2E 8PS, ☎ 836 7061, Fax 836 1283, French rest. - ▤. AE VISA DX **r**
closed Saturday lunch, Sunday, last 3 weeks August, 1 week Christmas and Bank Holidays - **M** 18.75/22.50 **t.** and a la carte 6.25.

XXX **Simpson's-in-the-Strand,** 100 Strand, WC2R 0EW, ☎ 836 9112, Fax 836 1381, English rest. - ▤. AE VISA EX **o**
closed Bank Holidays - **M** (booking essential) 18.50 **t.** and a la carte 5.25.

XXX **Ivy,** 1 West St., WC2H 9NE, ☎ 836 4751, Fax 497 3644 - ▤. AE VISA GK **z**
closed Bank Holiday lunch and 24 to 28 December - **M** a la carte 16.25/33.75 **t.** 6.25.

XX Christopher's, 18 Wellington St., WC2E 7DD, ☎ 240 4222, Fax 240 3357 EX **z**

XX **Gritti,** 11 Upper St. Martin's Lane, WC2H 9DL, ☎ 836 5121, Italian rest. - ▤. AE VISA DX **e**
closed Saturday lunch, Sunday and Bank Holidays - **M** 20.75/23.75 **t.** and a la carte 4.25.

XX **Orso,** 27 Wellington St., WC2E 7DA, ☎ 240 5269, Fax 497 2148, Italian rest. - ▤ EX **z**
closed 24 and 25 December - **M** (booking essential) a la carte 23.00/25.50 **t.** 5.00.

XX **L'Estaminet,** 14 Garrick St., off Floral St., WC2, ☎ 379 1432, French rest. – AE VISA
closed Sunday and Bank Holidays – **M** a la carte 20.60/25.10 **st.** DX **a**

XX **Sheekey's,** 28-32 St. Martin's Court, WC2N 4AL, ☎ 240 2565, Seafood – ▤. AE ⓓ VISA
closed Saturday lunch, Sunday, 25 December-2 January and Bank Holidays – **M** 16.50 **t.** and a la carte 5.65. DX **z**

Victoria – ✉ SW1 – ☎ 071 – Except where otherwise stated see p. 16.
Victoria Station Forecourt ☎ 730 3488.

Royal Horseguards Thistle (Mt. Charlotte Thistle), 2 Whitehall Court, SW1A 2EJ, ☎ 839 3400, Telex 917096, Fax 925 2263 – |♦| ⇔ rm ▤ rest TV ☎ – 60. AE ⓓ VISA. p. 10 LX **a**
M *(closed Saturday, Sunday and Bank Holidays)* 17.50/24.50 **t.** and a la carte 5.75 – ☐ 9.75 – **375 rm** 99.00/165.00 **st.**, 1 suite.

Stakis St. Ermin's, 2 Caxton St., SW1H 0QW, ☎ 222 7888, Telex 917731, Fax 222 6914 – |♦| ⇔ rm ▤ rest TV ☎ – 150. AE ⓓ VISA CX **a**
M (carving rest.) 15.00/21.00 **st.** and a la carte 6.50 – ☐ 9.75 – **282 rm** 109.00/174.00 **st.**, 8 suites – SB 120.00 **st.**

St. James Court, Buckingham Gate, SW1E 6AF, ☎ 834 6655, Telex 938075, Fax 630 7587, – |♦| ⇔ rm ▤ rest TV ☎ – 180. AE ⓓ VISA. CX **i**
M (see **Auberge de Provence** and **Inn of Happiness** below) – ☐ 12.50 – **375 rm** 125.00/150.00 **s.**, 18 suites.

Goring, 15 Beeston Pl., Grosvenor Gdns, SW1W 0JW, ☎ 834 8211, Telex 919166, Fax 834 4393 – |♦| TV ☎ – 50. AE ⓓ VISA. BX **a**
M 18.50/24.00 **t.** and a la carte 6.50 – ☐ 10.50 – **75 rm** 115.00/155.00 **s.**, 5 suites.

Royal Westminster Thistle (Mt. Charlotte Thistle), 49 Buckingham Palace Rd, SW1W 0QT, ☎ 834 1821, Telex 916821, Fax 931 7542 – |♦| ⇔ rm ▤ TV ☎ – 150 BX **z**
134 rm.

Grosvenor (Mt. Charlotte Thistle), 101 Buckingham Palace Rd, SW1W 0SJ, ☎ 834 9494, Telex 916006, Fax 630 1978 – |♦| ⇔ rm TV ☎ – 150. AE ⓓ VISA. BX **e**
M (carving rest.) 15.35 **st.** and a la carte 5.30 – ☐ 8.75 – **363 rm** 98.00/120.00 **st.**, 3 suites.

Rubens, 39-41 Buckingham Palace Rd, SW1W 0PS, ☎ 834 6600, Telex 917575, Fax 828 5401 – |♦| ⇔ rm ▤ rest TV ☎ – 60. AE ⓓ VISA. BX **n**
M (closed lunch Saturday and Sunday) (carving rest.) 13.95/14.95 **st.** and a la carte 4.50 – ☐ 8.95 – **188 rm** 92.00/116.00 **st.**, 1 suite.

Scandic Crown, 2 Bridge Pl., SW1V 1QA, ☎ 834 8123, Telex 914973, Fax 828 1099, – |♦| ⇔ rm ▤ TV ☎ – 200. AE ⓓ VISA. BY **i**
M *(closed Saturday lunch)* 17.50 **st.** (lunch) and a la carte 5.75 – ☐ 9.50 – **205 rm** 105.00/145.00 **st.**, 5 suites.

Rochester, 69 Vincent Sq., SW1 2PA, ☎ 828 6611, Telex 8813164, Fax 233 6724 – |♦| ▤ rest TV ☎ – 60. AE ⓓ VISA. CY **e**
M 17.50/25.00 **st.** and a la carte 6.95 – ☐ 9.50 – **70 rm** 85.00/145.00 **st.** – SB (weekends only) 170.00 **st.**

XXX **Inn of Happiness** (at St. James Court H.), Buckingham Gate, SW1E 6AF, ☎ 821 1931, Telex 938075, Fax 630 7587, Chinese rest. – ▤ Ⓟ. AE ⓓ VISA CX **i**
closed Saturday lunch – **M** a la carte 13.75/33.50 **t.**

XXX **Auberge de Provence** (at St. James Court H.), 41 Buckingham Gate, SW1E 6AF, ☎ 821 1899, Fax 630 7587, French rest. – ▤ Ⓟ. AE ⓓ VISA CX **i**
closed Saturday lunch, Sunday, 2 weeks August and Bank Holidays – **M** 21.50/45.00 **t.** and a la carte.

XXX **L'Incontro,** 87 Pimlico Rd, SW1W 8PH, ☎ 730 6327, Fax 730 5062, Italian rest. – ▤. AE ⓓ VISA p. 15 FT **u**
closed Saturday lunch and Sunday – **M** a la carte 22.40/39.50 **t.**

XXX **Santini,** 29 Ebury St., SW1W 0NZ, ☎ 730 4094, Fax 730 0544, Italian rest. – ▤. AE ⓓ VISA ABX **v**
closed lunch Saturday and Sunday – **M** 16.50 **t.** (lunch) and a la carte 22.40/39.00 **t.**

XX **Green's,** Marsham Court, Marsham St., SW1P 4LA, ☎ 834 9552, Fax 233 6047, English rest. – ▤. AE ⓓ VISA p. 10 LZ **z**
closed Saturday and Sunday – **M** (booking essential) a la carte 15.25/41.75 **st.**

XX **Simply Nico,** 48a Rochester Row, SW1P 1JU, ☎ 630 8061 – ▤. AE ⓓ VISA CY **a**
closed lunch Saturday and Bank Holidays, Sunday, 4 days at Easter and 10 days Christmas-New Year – **M** (booking essential) 23.00/25.00 **t.**

XX **Mijanou,** 143 Ebury St., SW1W 9QN, ☎ 730 4099, Fax 823 6402 – ⇔ ▤. AE VISA AY **n**
closed Saturday, Sunday, 1 week Easter, 3 weeks August, 2 weeks Christmas-New Year and Bank Holidays – **M** 21.00/34.50 **t.**

XX **Hunan,** 51 Pimlico Rd, SW1W 8NE, ☎ 730 5712, Chinese (Hunan) rest. – AE VISA
M 11.20/18.50 **t.** and a la carte 4.00. p. 9 IZ **a**

XX **Eatons,** 49 Elizabeth St., SW1W 9PP, ☎ 730 0074 – AE ⓓ VISA AY **a**
closed Saturday, Sunday and Bank Holidays – **M** 12.80 **s.** and a la carte 4.50.

XX **L'Amico,** 44 Horseferry Rd, SW1P 2AF, ☎ 222 4680, Italian rest. – AE VISA
closed Saturday, Sunday and Bank Holidays – **M** (booking essential) a la carte 19.50/33.20 **st.** 4.00. p. 10 LY **e**

XX **Gran Paradiso,** 52 Wilton Rd, SW1V 1DE, ☎ 828 5818, Fax 828 3608, Italian rest. – AE VISA BY **a**
closed Saturday lunch, Sunday and Bank Holidays – **M** a la carte 15.50/19.80 **t.** 3.30.

X **Olivo,** 21 Eccleston St., SW1W 9LX, ☎ 730 2505, Italian rest. – AE VISA AY **z**
closed Saturday lunch, Sunday, 3 weeks August and Bank Holidays – **M** 15.00 **t.** (lunch) and a la carte 17.50/20.00 **t.**

X **Tate Gallery,** Tate Gallery, Millbank, SW1P 4RG, ☎ 834 6754, Fax 834 7736, English rest., « Rex Whistler murals » – VISA p. 10 LZ **c**
closed Sunday, 11 April, 3 May, 24 to 26 December and 1 January – **M** (lunch only) (booking essential) a la carte 18.45/23.15 **t.** 5.70.

Bray-on-Thames Berks W : 34 m. by M 4 (junction 8-9) and A 308 404 R 29 – pop. 9 427 – 0628 Maidenhead

XXXX ✿✿✿ **Waterside Inn** (Roux) with rm, Ferry Rd, SL6 2AT, ☎ 20691, Fax 784710, French rest., « ≤ Thames-side setting », – rest TV ☎ P. VISA.
closed 26 December-5 February – **M** *(closed Tuesday lunch, Sunday dinner from 3rd weekend October-2nd weekend April, Monday and Bank Holidays)* 28.50/56.50 **st.** and a la carte 47.50/62.00 **st.** 11.50 – **6 rm** 115.00/155.00 **st.**
Spec. Tronçonnettes de homard poêlées minute au porto blanc, Filets de laperau grillés aux marrons glacés, Soufflé chaud aux framboises (summer).

Reading at Shinfield Berks. W : 43 m. on A 327 403 404 Q 29 – pop. 194 727 – 0734.

XXX ✿✿ **L'Ortolan** (Burton-Race), The Old Vicarage, Church Lane, RG2 9BY, ☎ 883783, Fax 885391, French rest., – P. AE VISA
closed Sunday dinner, Monday, last 2 weeks February and last 2 weeks August – **M** 29.50/55.00 **t.** 8.50
Spec. Caille glacée et haricots verts à l'huile de truffe, Ballotine de pied de cochon, sauce gribiche, Dôme de mousse caramel brûlée.

Oxford at Great Milton Oxon NW : 49 m. by M 40 (junction 7) and A 329 403 404 Q 28 – 0844 Great Milton :

✿✿ **Le Manoir aux Quat' Saisons** (Blanc) , Church Rd, OX44 7PD, ☎ 278881, Telex 837552, Fax 278847, ≤, « Part 15C and 16C manor house, gardens », heated, park, – rest rest TV ☎ P – 40. AE VISA.
M 29.50/59.50 **st.** and a la carte 55.00/75.00 **st.** 12.00 – 14.50 – **16 rm** 165.00/325.00 **st.**, 3 suites – SB (weekdays only) 255.00/340.00 **st.**
Spec. Poêlée de cèpes, escargots et cuisses de grenouilles, Pomme de ris de veau braisée au sabayon truffé, Fleurs d'ananas croustillantes, parfait glacé au Kirsch.

BIRMINGHAM

BIRMINGHAM W. Mids 403 404 O 26 **Great Britain G.** – pop. 1 013 995 – ECD : Wednesday – 021.

See : City★ - Museum and Art Gallery★★ JZ **M2** – Barber Institute of Fine Arts★★ (at Birmingham University) EX – Museum of Science and Industry★ JY **M3** – Cathedral of St. Philip (stained glass portrayals★) KYZ.

Envir. : Aston Hall★★ FV **M.**

18 Cocks Moor Woods, Alcester Rd, South King's Heath ☎ 444 3584, S : 6 ½ m. by A 435 FX – 18 Edgbaston, Church Rd ☎ 454 1736, S : 1 m. FX – 18 40 Tennal Rd, Harborne ☎ 427 1728 EX – 18 Hilltop, Park Lane, Handsworth ☎ 554 4463 – 18 Hatchford Brook, Coventry Rd ☎ 743 9821 HX - 18, 9 Vicarage Rd ☎ 427 1204, SW : 3 m. EX – 18 Chapel Lane ☎ 357 1232, NW : 6 m. - 9 Warley, Lightwoods Hill, ☎ 429 2440, W : 5 m. by A 456 – 18 Brand Hall, Heron Rd, Oldbury ☎ 552 7475.

Birmingham Airport : ☎ 767 5511, (flight information) 767 7145, Telex 335582, Fax 782 8802, E : 6 ½ m. by A 45.

Convention & Visitor Bureau, 2 City Arcade, B2 4TX, ☎ 643 2514, Fax 616 1038 – Convention & Visitor Bureau, National Exhibition Centre, B40 1NT ☎ 780 4321, Fax 780 4260 – Birmingham Airport, B26 3QJ, ☎ 767 7145/7146, Fax 782 8802.

London 122 – Bristol 91 – Liverpool 103 – Manchester 86 – Nottingham 50.

Plans on following pages

Hyatt Regency, 2 Bridge St., B1 2JZ, ☎ 643 1234, Telex 335097, Fax 616 2323, ≤, , , – rm TV ☎ – 180. AE VISA JZ **a**
M 12.75/17.00 **t.** and a la carte 8.00 – 11.00 – **315 rm** 118.00/140.00 **st.**, 4 suites.

Swallow, 12 Hagley Rd, B16 8SJ, ☎ 452 1144, Fax 456 3442, , – rm TV ☎ P – 30. AE VISA FX **c**
M – **Langtrys** a la carte 29.00/40.00 **st.** 7.00 – (see also **Sir Edward Elgar's** below) – **94 rm** 110.00/130.00 **st.**, 4 suites – SB (weekends only) 135.00 **st.**

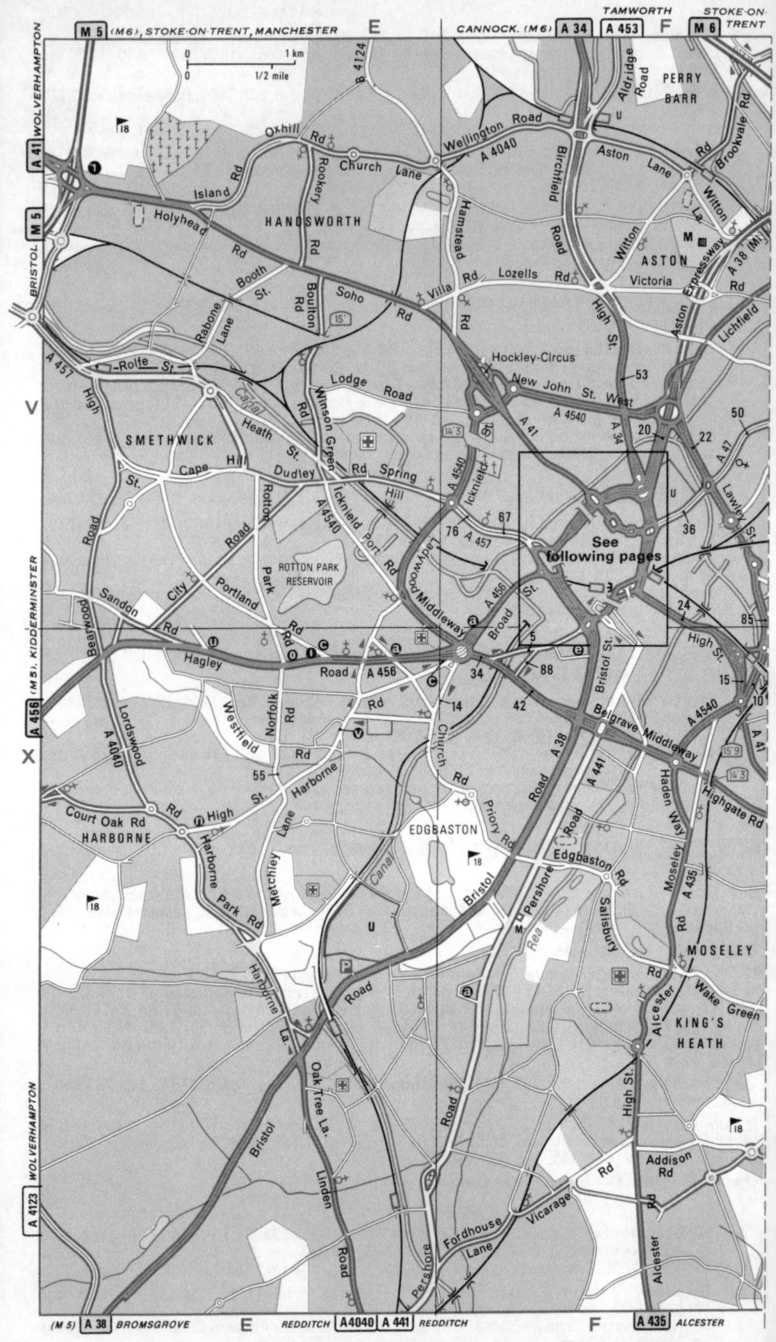

M 5 (M6), STOKE-ON-TRENT, MANCHESTER
CANNOCK. (M6) A 34 A 453 TAMWORTH
M 6 STOKE-ON-TRENT
A 41 WOLVERHAMPTON
M 5 BRISTOL
A 456 (M5), KIDDERMINSTER
A 4123 WOLVERHAMPTON
(M 5) A 38 BROMSGROVE
REDDITCH A4040 A 441 REDDITCH
A 435 ALCESTER
HANDSWORTH
PERRY BARR
ASTON
SMETHWICK
HARBORNE
EDGBASTON
MOSELEY
KING'S HEATH
ROTTON PARK RESERVOIR
See following pages
Hockley-Circus

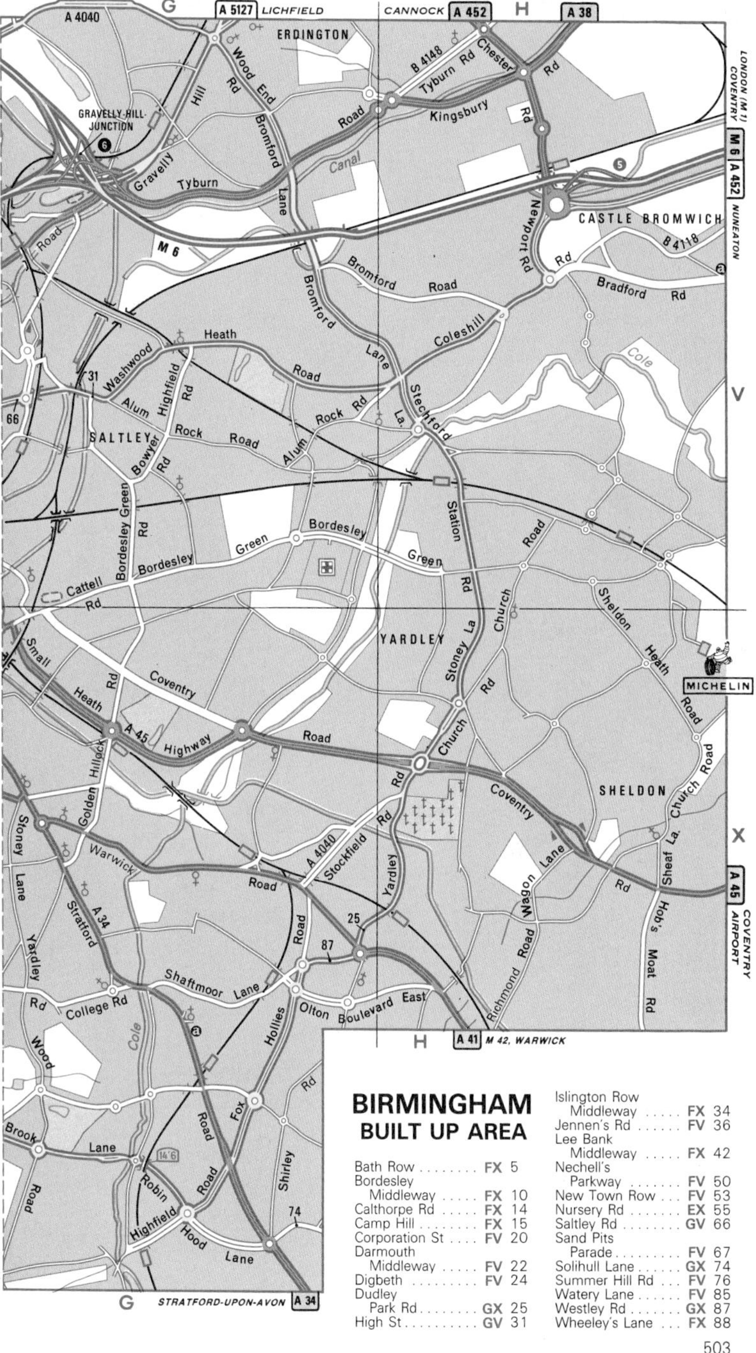

BIRMINGHAM
BUILT UP AREA

Street	Grid	No.
Bath Row	FX	5
Bordesley Middleway	FX	10
Calthorpe Rd	FX	14
Camp Hill	FX	15
Corporation St	FV	20
Darmouth Middleway	FV	22
Digbeth	FV	24
Dudley Park Rd	GX	25
High St	GV	31
Islington Row Middleway	FX	34
Jennen's Rd	FV	36
Lee Bank Middleway	FX	42
Nechell's Parkway	FV	50
New Town Row	FV	53
Nursery Rd	EX	55
Saltley Rd	GV	66
Sand Pits Parade	FV	67
Solihull Lane	GX	74
Summer Hill Rd	FV	76
Watery Lane	FV	85
Westley Rd	GX	87
Wheeley's Lane	FX	88

BIRMINGHAM
CENTRE

Street	Grid	No.
Albert St.	KZ	2
Bull St.	KY	13
Dale End	KZ	21
Hall St.	JY	29
Holloway Circus	JZ	32
James Watt Queensway	KY	35
Jennen's Rd	KY	36
Lancaster Circus	KY	39
Lancaster St.	KY	41
Masshouse Circus	KY	43
Moor St. Queensway	KZ	46
Navigation St.	JZ	49
Newton St.	KY	52
Priory Queensway	KY	57
St. Chads Circus	JKY	62
St. Chads Ringway	KY	63
St. Martin's Circus	KZ	64
Severn St.	JZ	69
Shadwell St.	KY	70
Smallbrook Queensway	KZ	71
Snow Hill Queensway	KY	73
Summer Row	JY	77
Temple Row	KZ	80
Waterloo St.	JZ	84

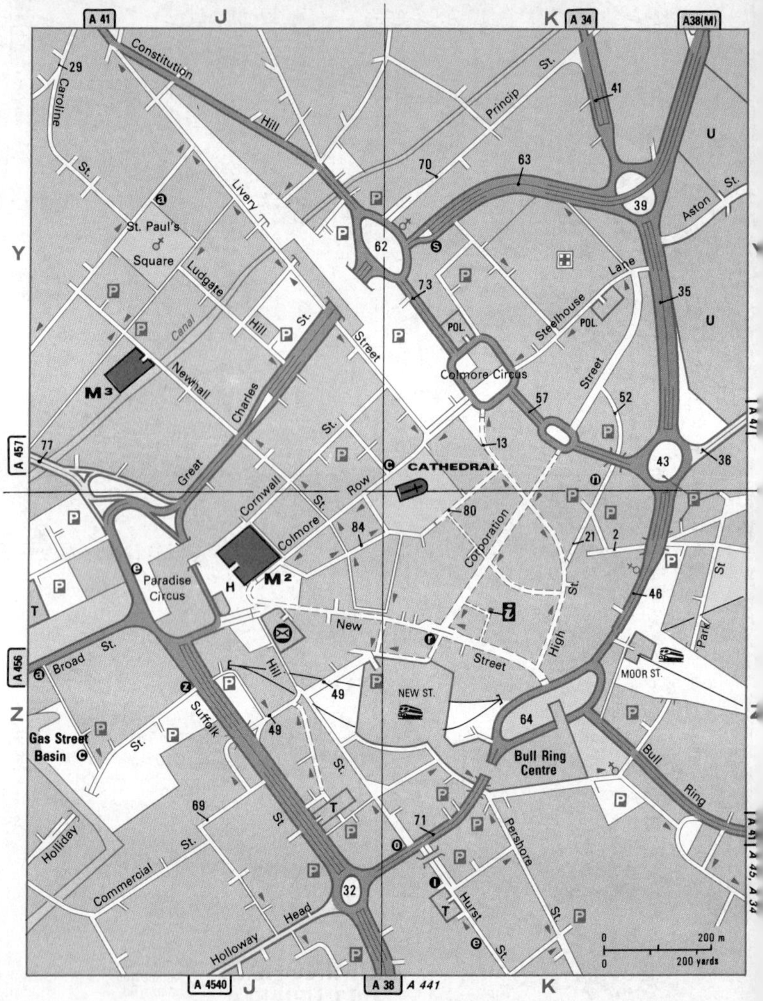

GREEN TOURIST GUIDES

Picturesque scenery, buildings

Attractive route

Touring programmes

Plans of towns and buildings.

STREET INDEX TO BIRMINGHAM TOWN PLANS

Street	Plan	No.
Bull Ring Centre	KZ	
Corporation St.	KYZ	
New St.	JKZ	
Addison Rd	FX	
Albert St.	KZ	2
Alcester Rd	FX	
Aldridge Rd	FV	
Alum Rock Rd	GV	
Aston Expressway	FV	
Aston Lane	FV	
Aston St.	KY	
Bath Row	FX	5
Bearwood Rd	EV	
Belgrave Middleway	FX	
Birchfield Rd	FV	
Booth St.	EV	
Bordesley Green	GV	
Bordesley Green Rd	GV	
Bordesley Middleway	FX	10
Boulton Rd	EV	
Bowyer Rd	GV	
Bradford Rd	HV	
Bristol Rd	EX	
Bristol St.	FX	
Broad St.	FV	
Bromford Lane	GV	
Bromford Rd	HV	
Brook Lane	GX	
Brookvale Rd	FV	
Bull Ring	KZ	
Bull Ring Centre	KZ	
Bull St.	KY	13
Calthorpe Rd	FX	14
Camp Hill	FX	15
Cape Hill	EV	
Caroline St.	JY	
Cattell Rd	GV	
Chester Rd	HV	
Church Lane	EV	
Church Rd EDGBASTON	FX	
Church Rd SHELDON	HX	
Church Rd YARDLEY	HX	
City Rd	EV	
Coleshill Rd	HV	
College Rd	GX	
Colmore Circus	KY	
Colmore Row	JZ	
Commercial St.	JZ	
Constitution Hill	JY	
Cornwall St.	JY	
Corporation St.	FV	20
Court Oak Rd	EX	
Coventry Rd	GX	
Dale End	KZ	21
Darmouth Middleway	FV	22
Digbeth	FV	24
Dudley Park Rd	GX	25
Dudley Rd	EV	
Edgbaston Rd	FX	
Fordhouse Lane	FX	
Fox Hollies Rd	GX	
Golden Hillock Rd	GX	
Gravelly Hill	GV	
Gravelly Hill Junction	GV	

Street	Plan	No.
Great Charles St.	JY	
Hadden Way	FX	
Hagley Rd	EX	
Hall St.	JY	29
Hampstead Rd	FV	
Harborne Lane	EX	
Harborne Park Rd	EX	
Harborne Rd	EX	
Heath St.	EV	
Highfield Rd	GX	
Highfield Rd SALTLEY	GV	
Highgate Rd	FX	
High St.	KZ	
High St. ASTON	FV	
High St. BORDESLEY	FX	
High St. HARBORNE	EX	
High St. KING'S HEATH	FX	
High St. SALTLEY	GV	31
High St. SMETHWICK	EV	
Hill St.	JZ	
Hob's Moat Rd	HX	
Hockley Circus	FV	
Hockley Hill	JY	
Holliday St.	JZ	
Holloway Circus	JZ	32
Holloway Head	JZ	
Holyhead Rd	EV	
Hurst St.	KZ	
Icknield Port Rd	EV	
Icknield St.	FV	
Island Rd	EV	
Islington Row Middleway	FX	34
James Watt Queensay	KY	35
Jennen's Rd	FV	36
Kingsbury Rd	HV	
Ladywood Middleway	EV	
Lancaster Circus	KY	39
Lancaster St.	KY	41
Lawley St.	FV	
Lee Bank Middleway	FX	42
Lichfield Rd	FV	
Linden Rd	EX	
Livery St.	JY	
Lodge Rd	EV	
Lordswood Rd	EX	
Lozells Rd	FV	
Ludgate Hill	JY	
Masshouse Circus	KY	43
Metchley Lane	EX	
Moor St. Queensway	KZ	46
Moseley Rd	FX	
Navigation St.	JZ	49
Nechell's Parkway	FV	50
Newhall St.	JY	
New John St. West	FV	
Newport Rd	HV	
New St.	JZ	
Newton St.	KY	52
New Town Row	FV	53
Norfolk Rd	EX	
Nursery Rd	EX	55
Oak Tree Lane	EX	
Olton Bd East	GX	

Street	Plan	No.
Oxhill Rd	EV	
Paradise Circus	JZ	
Park St.	KZ	
Pershore Rd	FX	
Pershore St.	KZ	
Portland Rd	EV	
Princip St.	KY	
Priory Queensway	KY	57
Priory Rd	FX	
Rabone Lane	EV	
Richmond Rd	HX	
Robin Hood Lane	GX	
Rolfe St.	EV	
Rookery Rd	EV	
Rotton Park Rd	EV	
St. Chads Circus	JY	62
St. Chads Ringway	KY	63
St. Martin's Circus	KZ	64
St. Paul's Square	JY	
Salisbury Rd	FX	
Saltley Rd	GV	66
Sandon Rd	EV	
Sand Pits Parade	FV	67
Severn St.	JZ	69
Shadwell St.	KY	70
Shaftmoor Lane	GX	
Sheaf Lane	HX	
Sheldon Heath Rd	HX	
Shirley Rd	GX	
Smallbrook Queensway	KZ	71
Small Heath Highway	GX	
Snow Hill Queensway	KY	73
Soho Rd	EV	
Solihull Lane	GX	74
Spring Hill	EV	
Station Rd	HV	
Stechford Lane	HV	
Steelhouse Lane	KY	
Stockfield Rd	GX	
Stoney La MOSELEY	GX	
Stoney La SHELDON	HX	
Stratford Rd	GX	
Suffolk St.	JZ	
Summer Hill Rd	FV	76
Summer Row	JY	77
Temple Row	KZ	80
Tyburn Rd	GV	
Vicarage Rd	FX	
Victoria Rd	FV	
Villa Rd	FV	
Wagon Lane	HX	
Wake Green Rd	FX	
Warwick Rd	GX	
Washwood Heath Rd	GV	
Waterloo St.	JZ	84
Watery Lane	FX	85
Wellington Rd	FV	
Westfield Rd	EX	
Westley Rd	GX	87
Wheeley's Lane	FX	88
Winson Green Rd	EV	
Witton Lane	FV	
Witton Rd	FV	
Wood End Rd	GV	
Yardley Rd	HX	
Yardley Wood Rd	GX	

Pleasant hotels and restaurants
are shown in the Guide by a red sign.

Please send us the names
of any where you have enjoyed your stay.

Your **Michelin Guide** will be even better.

Forte Crest, Smallbrook Queensway, B5 4EW, 643 8171, Fax 631 2528, squash – rm – 630. AE VISA KZ **o**
M 13.50/15.00 **st.** and a la carte 5.00 – 9.95 – **252 rm** 90.00/100.00 **st.**, 1 suite – SB (weekends only) 86.00/96.00 **st.**

Midland, 128 New St., B2 4JT, 643 2601, Telex 338419, Fax 643 5075 – 200. AE VISA KZ **r**
M 13.95/17.95 **st.** and a la carte – 9.50 – **109 rm** 85.00/99.00 **st.**, 2 suites.

Copthorne, Paradise Circus, B3 3HJ, 200 2727, Telex 339026, Fax 200 1197, – rm rest – 150. AE VISA. JZ **e**
M 12.00/15.00 **t.** and a la carte 6.50 – 9.95 – **209 rm** 102.00/110.00 **t.**, 3 suites.

Holiday Inn, Central Sq., Holliday St., B1 1HH, 631 2000, Telex 337272, Fax 643 9018, – rm – 150. AE VISA JZ **z**
M 13.50/15.95 **t.** and a la carte – 9.95 – **284 rm** 86.40/113.00 **t.**, 4 suites.

Plough and Harrow (Forte), 135 Hagley Rd, Edgbaston, B16 8LS, 454 4111, Fax 454 1868, – rm – 60. AE VISA EX **a**
M 9.95/18.00 **t.** and a la carte – 7.95 – **42 rm** 75.00/85.00 **st.**, 2 suites – SB (weekends only) 98.00 **st.**

Jonathan's, 16-24 Wolverhampton Rd, B68 0LH, W : 4 m. by A 456 429 3757, Fax 434 3107, « Authentic Victorian furnishings and memorabilia » – . AE VISA
M (English rest.) 25.00/30.00 **st.** and a la carte 4.95 **15 rm** 69.00/80.00 **st.**, 11 suites – SB (weekends only) 96.00 **st.**

Grand (Q.M.H.), Colmore Row, B3 2DA, 236 7951, Telex 338174, Fax 233 1465 – rest – 450. AE VISA JKY **c**
closed 1 week Christmas – **M** 12.95/18.50 **st.** and a la carte 4.25 – **173 rm** 45.00/100.00 **st.**, 3 suites – SB (weekends only) 80.00 **st.**

Royal Angus Thistle (Mt. Charlotte Thistle), St. Chad's, Queensway, B4 6HY, 236 4211, Telex 336889, Fax 233 2195 – rm – 140. AE VISA. KY **s**
M *(closed Saturday lunch)* a la carte 13.50/21.50 **t.** 6.10 – 8.50 – **131 rm** 75.00/95.00 **st.**, 2 suites.

Strathallan Thistle (Mt. Charlotte Thistle), 225 Hagley Rd, Edgbaston, B16 9RY, 455 9777, Telex 336680, Fax 454 9432 – rm rest – 170. AE VISA EX **i**
M *(closed Saturday lunch)* 12.25/17.25 **st.** and a la carte 5.25 – 8.75 – **163 rm** 75.00/85.00 **st.**, 4 suites – SB 90.00/132.00 **st.**

Novotel, 70 Broad St., B1 2HT, 643 2000, Telex 335556, Fax 643 9796, – rm rest – 220. AE VISA FV **a**
M a la carte approx. 13.50 **st.** 4.75 – 7.50 – **148 rm** 67.00/77.00 **st.**

Apollo (Mt. Charlotte Thistle), 243 Hagley Rd, Edgbaston, B16 9RA, 455 0271, Telex 336759, Fax 456 2394 – rm rest – 150. AE VISA EX **o**
M *(closed Saturday lunch)* 12.80/14.95 **st.** and a la carte 4.75 – 8.50 – **124 rm** 70.00/85.00 **st.**, 2 suites – SB (weekends only) 64.00 **st.**

Asquith House, 19 Portland Rd, off Hagley Rd, Edgbaston, B16 9HN, 454 5282, Fax 456 4668, « Attractive furnishings », – . AE VISA EX **c**
closed Christmas and Bank Holidays – **M** 11.95/13.25 **st.** and a la carte 3.50 – **10 rm** 50.60/61.80 **st.**

Westbourne Lodge, 27-29 Fountain Rd, Edgbaston, B17 8NJ, 429 1003, Fax 429 7436, – . VISA EV **x**
M (bar lunch)/dinner 12.50 **t.** 4.40 – **17 rm** 30.00/58.00 **t.**

Copperfield House 60 Upland Rd, Selly Park, B29 7JS, 472 8344, Fax 472 8344, – rest . VISA FX **a**
M 14.95/16.95 **st.** 3.75 – **17 rm** 44.00/65.00 **st.** – SB (except Christmas) (weekends only) 120.00/170.00 **st.**

Fountain Court, 339-343 Hagley Rd, Edgbaston, B17 8NH, 429 1754, Fax 429 1209, – . AE VISA EX **u**
M *(closed Saturday, Sunday and Bank Holidays)* (bar lunch)/dinner 12.50 **st.** 4.95 – **25 rm** 30.00/55.00 **st.**

XXXX **Sir Edward Elgar's,** (at Swallow H.), 12 Hagley Rd, B16 8SJ, 452 1144, Fax 456 3442 – . AE VISA FX **c**
M 23.50/28.50 **st.** and a la carte 7.00.

XXX **Sloans,** 27-29 Chad Sq., Hawthorne Rd, Edgbaston, B15 3TQ, 455 6697, Fax 454 4335 – AE VISA EX **v**
closed Saturday lunch, Sunday, 26 to 31 December and Bank Holidays except Christmas Day – **M** 19.50/25.50 **t.** and a la carte 4.75.

XX **Maharaja,** 23-25 Hurst St., B5 4AS, 622 2641, North Indian rest. – . AE VISA KZ **i**
closed Sunday, 2 weeks July-August and Bank Holidays – **M** 12.50/15.50 **t.** and a la carte.

XX **Purple Rooms,** 1076 Stratford Rd, Hall Green, B28 8AD, SE : 4 ¼ m. by A 41 on A 34 702 2193, Fax 702 2520, Indian rest. – AE VISA GX **a**
closed lunch Monday to Thursday – **M** 15.00/20.00 **t.** and a la carte.

XX **Henry's,** 27 St. Paul's Sq., B3 1RB, ℘ 200 1136, Chinese (Canton) rest. – ▤. AE VISA
closed Sunday and Bank Holidays – **M** 13.00 **t.** and a la carte 4.00. JY **a**

XX **Henry Wong,** 283 High St., Harborne, B17 9QH, W : 3 ¾ m. by A 456 ℘ 427 9799, Chinese (Canton) rest. – ▤. AE VISA EX **n**
closed Sunday and Bank Holidays – **M** 13.00 **t.** and a la carte 4.00.

XX **Days of the Raj,** 51 Dale End, B4 7LS, ℘ 236 0445, Indian rest. – ▤. AE VISA
closed lunch Saturday and Sunday and 25-26 December – **M** (buffet lunch)/dinner a la carte 15.55/21.30 **st.** KY **n**

XX **Dynasty,** 93-103 Hurst St., B5 4TE, ℘ 622 1410, Chinese rest. – AE VISA KZ **e**
M a la carte 15.20/19.60 **t.**

at Birmingham Airport SE : 9 m. by A 45 – ✉ 021 Birmingham :

Novotel, Passenger Terminal, B26 3QL, ℘ 782 7000, Telex 338158, Fax 782 0445 – rm ▤ rest TV – 30. AE VISA
M a la carte approx. 13.50 **st.** 4.75 – 7.50 **195 rm** 64.00/74.00 **st.**

Forte Posthouse, Coventry Rd, B26 3QW, on A 45 ℘ 782 8141, Fax 782 2476 – rm TV – 150. AE VISA
M a la carte 12.70/23.15 **t.** 4.50 – 6.95 – **136 rm** 53.50 **st.** – SB (weekends only) 82.00 **st.**

at National Exhibition Centre SE : 9 ½ m. on A 45 DU – ✉ 021 Birmingham :

Birmingham Metropole, Bickenhill, B40 1PP, ℘ 780 4242, Telex 336129, Fax 780 3923, squash – rm ▤ TV – 2 000. AE VISA
M 21.00 **t.** and a la carte 7.25 – **787 rm** 120.00/186.00 **st.**, 15 suites.

Arden, Coventry Rd, B92 0EH, ℘ 0675 (Hampton-in-Arden) 443221, Fax 443221, – TV – 130. AE VISA
M (bar lunch Saturday) 11.45 **t.** and a la carte – 7.00 – **146 rm** 65.00/72.50 **t.**

at Kings Norton SW : 7 m. by A 441 FX – ✉ 021 Birmingham :

Norton Place (at The Patrick Collection), 180 Lifford Lane, B30 3NT, ℘ 433 5656, Fax 433 3048, « Collection of classic motor cars », – TV – 140. AE VISA. – **M** (see **Lombard Room** below) – 9.00 – **9 rm** 99.00/175.00 **st.**, 1 suite – SB (weekends only) 160.00 **st.**

XXX **Lombard Room** (at The Patrick Collection), 180 Lifford Lane, B30 3NT, ℘ 451 3991, Fax 433 3048, « Collection of classic motor cars », – ▤ . AE VISA
M 14.75/18.50 **t.** and a la carte 6.00.

at Great Barr NW : 6 m. on A 34 – ✉ 021 Birmingham :

Forte Posthouse, Chapel Lane, B43 7BG, ℘ 357 7444, Fax 357 7503, – rm TV – 120. AE VISA
M a la carte 12.70/23.15 **t.** 4.50 – 6.95 – **192 rm** 53.50 **st.** – SB (weekends only) 82.00 **st.**

Great Barr, Pear Tree Drive, Newton Rd, B43 6HS, W : 1 m. by A 4041 ℘ 357 1141, Fax 357 7557, – TV – 120. AE VISA. – **M** *(closed Bank Holidays)* 13.00/17.00 **st.** and a la carte 6.00 – 7.00 – **114 rm** 55.00/95.00 **st.**

at West Bromwich NW : 6 m. on A 41 – ✉ 021 Birmingham :

West Bromwich Moat House (Q.M.H.), Birmingham Rd, B70 6RS, ℘ 553 6111, Telex 336232, Fax 525 7403 – rm ▤ rest TV – 180. AE VISA
closed 24 to 31 December – – 5.95 – **180 rm** 59.50/69.50 **t.**

EDINBURGH Midlothian. (Lothian) 401 K 16 Scotland G. – pop. 408 822 – 031.

See : City★★★ - Edinburgh International Festival★★★ (August) – National Gallery of Scotland★★★ DY **M4** - Royal Botanic Garden★★★ - The Castle★★ DYZ : site★★★ – Palace Block (Honours of Scotland★★★) - St. Margaret's Chapel (※★★★) - Great Hall (Hammerbeam Roof★★) - ≤★★ from Argyle and Mill's Mount DZ – Abbey and Palace of Holyroodhouse★★ (Plasterwork Ceilings★★★, ≤★★ from Arthur's Seat) – Royal Mile★★ : St. Giles' Cathedral★★ (Crown Spire★★★) EYZ - Gladstone's Land★ EYZ **A** – Canongate Talbooth★ EY **B** – New Town★★ (Charlotte Square★★★ CY **14** - Royal Museum of Scotland (Antiquities)★★ EZ **M2** – The Georgian House ★ CY **D** - National Portrait Gallery★ EY **M3** - Dundas House★ EY **E**) – Victoria Street★ EZ **84** - Scott Monument★ EY **F** - Craigmilar Castle★ – Calton Hill (※★★★ from Nelson's Monument) EY - Royal Observatory (≤★).

Envir. : Edinburgh Zoo★★ – Hill End Ski Centre (※★★), S : 5 ½ m. by A 702 – Ingleston, Scottish Agricultural Museum★, W : 6 ½ m. by A 8.

Exc. : Rosslyn Chapel★★ (Apprentice Pillar★★★) S : 7 ½ m. by A 701 and B 7006 – Forth Bridges★★, NW : 9 ½ m. by A 90 – Hopetoun House★★, NW : 11 ½ m. by A 90 and A 904 – Dalmeny★ (Dalmeny House★, St. Cuthbert's Church★ - Norman South Doorway★★) NW : 7 m. by A 90.

18 Silverknowes, Parkway ℘ 336 3843, W : 4 m. by A 90 – 18 Liberton, Gilmerton Rd ℘ 664 8580, SE : 3 m. on A 7 – 18 Craigmillar Park, Observatory Rd ℘ 667 2837 by A 68 – 18 Carrick Knowe, Glendevon Park ℘ 337 1096, W : 5 m. – 18 Swanston Rd, Fairmilehead ℘ 445 2239, S : 4 m. by A 702 – 18 Lothianburn, Biggar Rd ℘ 445 2206, S : 4 ½ m. by A 702.

Edinburgh Airport ℘ 333 1000, Telex 727615, Fax 335 3181, W : 6 m. by A 8 – **Terminal** : Waverley Bridge. – ℘ 0345 090700 – Edinburgh & Scotland Information Centre, 3 Princes St., ℘ 557 1700 – Edinburgh Airport ℘ 333 2167.

Glasgow 46 – Newcastle upon Tyne 105.

EDINBURGH

Street	Square	No.
Castle Street	DY	
Frederick Street	DY	
George Street	DY	
Hanover Street	DY	
High Street	EYZ	37
Lawnmarket	EYZ	46
Princes Street	DY	
St. James Centre	EY	
Waverley Market	EY	
Bernard Terrace	EZ	3
Bread Street	DZ	6
Bristo Place	EZ	7
Candlemaker Row	EZ	9
Castlehill	DZ	10
Chambers Street	EZ	12
Chapel Street	EZ	13
Charlotte Square	CY	14
Deanhaugh Street	CY	23
Douglas Gardens	CY	25
Drummond Street	EZ	27
Forrest Road	EZ	31
Gardner's Crescent	CZ	32
George IV Bridge	EZ	33
Gassmarket	DZ	35
Home Street	DZ	38
Hope Street	CY	39
Johnston Terrace	DZ	42
King's Bridge	DZ	44
King's Stables Road	DZ	45
Leith Street	EY	47
Leven Street	DZ	48
Lothian Street	EZ	51
Mound (The)	DY	55
North Bridge	EY	61
North St. Andrew Street	EY	66
Raeburn Place	CY	69
Randolph Crescent	CY	71
St. Andrew Square	EY	73
St. Mary's Street	EY	75
Shandwick Place	CYZ	77
South Charlotte Street	DY	78
South St. David Street	DEY	79
Spittal Street	DZ	83
Victoria Street	EZ	84
Waterloo Place	EY	87
Waverley Bridge	EY	89
West Maitland Street	CZ	92

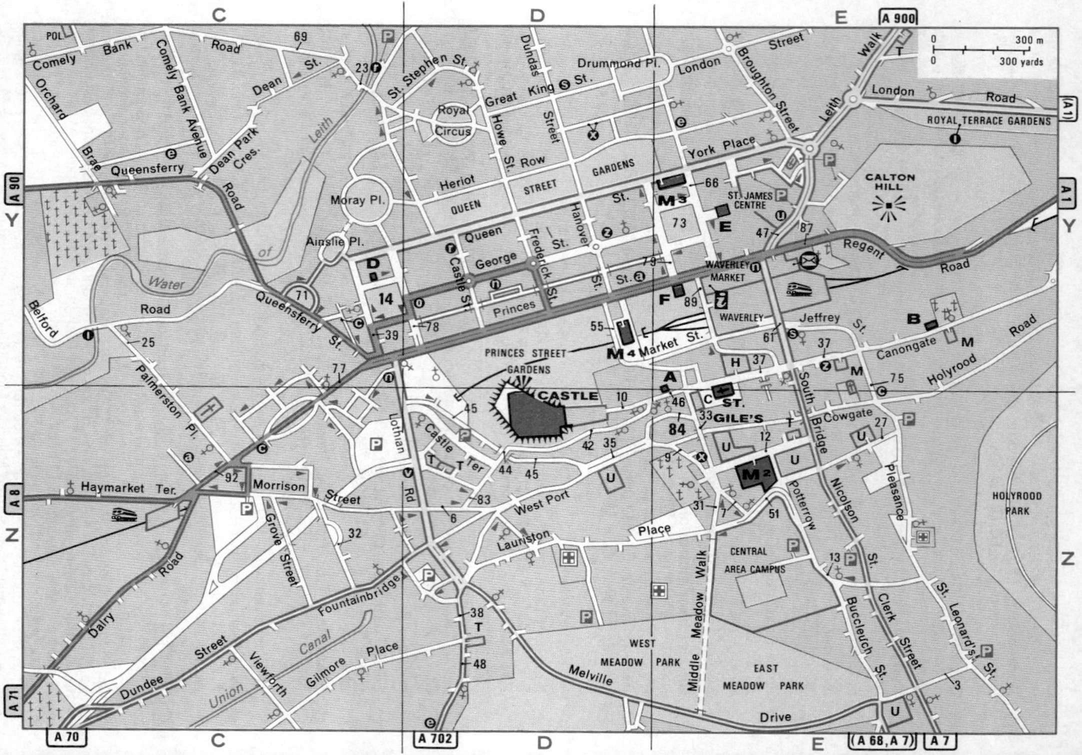

Caledonian (Q.M.H.), Princes St., EH1 2AB, ✆ 225 2433, Telex 72179, Fax 225 6632 – |♦| ⇔ rm ▤ rest TV ☎ ♿ P – 🏛 300. AE ① VISA. ⚘ CY **n**
M – **Carriages** 17.50/25.00 **t.** and a la carte 6.50 – (see also **Pompadour** below) – ☐ 14.50 – **228 rm** 145.00/250.00 **t.**, 11 suites – SB (except Christmas-New Year) (weekends only) 170.00/210.00 **st.**

Balmoral (Forte), Princes St., EH2 2EQ, ✆ 556 2414, Telex 727282, Fax 557 3747, Fō, ≘s, ⊠ – |♦| ⇔ rm ▤ TV ☎ ♿ ⇐ – 🏛 200. AE ① VISA. ⚘ EY **n**
M a la carte 19.50/41.50 **st.** 6.25 – (see also **Grill** below) – ☐ 11.25 – **167 rm** 116.00/165.00 **st.**, 21 suites – SB (weekends only) 198.00 **st.**

Sheraton Edinburgh, 1 Festival Sq., EH3 9SR, ✆ 229 9131, Telex 72398, Fax 228 4510, Fō, ≘s, ⊠ – |♦| ⇔ rm ▤ TV ☎ ♿ P – 🏛 450. AE ① VISA. ⚘ CDZ **v**
M 18.75/28.00 **st.** and a la carte 6.00 – ☐ 12.00 – **257 rm** 105.00/175.00 **st.**, 6 suites.

Carlton Highland, 1-29 North Bridge, EH1 1SD, ✆ 556 7277, Telex 727001, Fax 556 2691, Fō, ≘s, ⊠, squash – |♦| TV ☎ ♿ – 🏛 300. AE ① VISA EY **s**
M 11.50/19.90 **t.** and a la carte 4.75 – **193 rm** ☐ 107.00/150.00 **t.**, 4 suites – SB 100.00/120.00 **st.**

George Inter-Continental, 19-21 George St., EH2 2PB, ✆ 225 1251, Telex 72570, Fax 226 5644 – |♦| ⇔ rm TV ☎ P – 🏛 180. AE ① VISA DY **z**
M 14.75/29.95 **t.** and a la carte – **193 rm** 125.00/165.00 **t.**, 2 suites – SB (November-March) (weekends only) 115.00/170.00 **st.**

Dalmahoy H. Golf & Country Club ⛰, Kirknewton, EH27 8EB, SW : 7 m. on A 71 – ✆ 333 1845, Fax 335 3203, ≤, Fō, ≘s, ⊠, 18, park, ⚘, squash – |♦| ⇔ rm ▤ rest TV ☎ ♿ P – 🏛 200. AE ① VISA. ⚘ CZ
M *(closed Saturday lunch)* 14.95/22.00 **st.** and dinner a la carte 7.95 – **114 rm** ☐ 95.00/130.00 **st.**, 1 suite – SB (weekends only) 98.00/178.00 **st.**

Howard, 32-36 Gt. King St., EH3 6QH, ✆ 557 3500, Fax 557 6515, « Georgian town houses » – |♦| TV ☎ P – 🏛 40. AE ① VISA DY **s**
M 14.95 **t.** and a la carte – **16 rm** ☐ 110.00/255.00 **t.**

Scandic Crown, 80 High St., EH1 1TH, ✆ 557 9797, Telex 727298, Fax 557 9789, Fō, ≘s, ⊠ – |♦| ⇔ rm ▤ TV ☎ ♿ P – 🏛 200. AE ① VISA. ⚘ EY **z**
M 14.95 **st.** and a la carte – ☐ 9.95 – **228 rm** 94.00/155.00 **st.**, **10 suites.**

Swallow Royal Scot, 111 Glasgow Rd, EH12 8NF, W : 4 ½ m. on A 8 ✆ 334 9191, Telex 727197, Fax 316 4507, Fō, ≘s, ⊠ – |♦| ⇔ rm ▤ rest TV ☎ P – 🏛 250. AE ① VISA CZ
M 14.50/17.75 **st.** and a la carte – **255 rm** ☐ 92.00/117.50 **st.**, 4 suites – SB (weekends only) 115.00 **st.**

Capital Moat House (Q.M.H.), Clermiston Rd, EH12 6UG, ✆ 334 3391, Telex 728284, Fax 334 9712, Fō, ≘s, ⊠ – |♦| ⇔ rm TV ☎ ♿ P – 🏛 300. AE ① VISA
M (buffet lunch)/dinner 14.95 **st.** and a la carte – ☐ 7.50 – **110 rm** 81.00/97.00 **st.** – SB (weekends only) 99.00 **st.**

Hilton National, Bells Mills, 69 Belford Rd, EH4 3DG, ✆ 332 2545, Telex 727979, Fax 332 3805 – |♦| ⇔ rm TV ☎ ♿ P – 🏛 120. AE ① VISA CY **i**
M (bar lunch Saturday) 12.50/15.25 **st.** and a la carte 5.00 – ☐ 10.50 – **144 rm** 97.50/190.00 **st.**

Mount Royal (Jarvis), 53 Princes St., EH2 2DG, ✆ 225 7161, Telex 727641, Fax 220 4671, ≤ – |♦| TV ☎ – 🏛 50. AE ① VISA DY **a**
M 8.50 **st.** (lunch) and dinner a la carte 15.00/26.00 **st.** – ☐ 8.75 – **160 rm** 85.00/125.00 **st.** – SB 158.00/228.00 **st.**

Royal Terrace, 18 Royal Terrace, EH7 5AQ, ✆ 557 3222, Telex 727182, Fax 557 5334, Fō, ≘s, ⊠, 🌳 – |♦| TV ☎ – 🏛 50. AE ① VISA. ⚘ EY **i**
M *(closed lunch Saturday and Sunday)* 21.50/22.50 **st.** – ☐ 10.00 – **94 rm** 98.00/185.00 **st.**, 1 suite.

King James Thistle (Mt. Charlotte Thistle), 107 Leith St., EH1 3SW, ✆ 556 0111, Telex 727200, Fax 557 5333 – |♦| ⇔ rm TV ☎ – 🏛 250. AE ① VISA EY **u**
M *(closed Sunday lunch)* 12.50/18.50 **t.** and a la carte 5.90 – ☐ 8.75 – **142 rm** 75.00/110.00 **st.**, 5 suites – SB 114.00/174.00 **st.**

Stakis Grosvenor, Grosvenor St., EH12 5EF, ✆ 226 6001, Telex 72445, Fax 220 2387 – |♦| ⇔ rm TV ☎ ♿ – 🏛 300. AE ① VISA CZ **a**
M (grill lunch) 13.00/15.00 **st.** and a la carte 4.50 – ☐ 8.50 – **135 rm** 79.00/99.00 **st.**, 1 suite – SB 70.00 **st.**

Ellersly Country House (Jarvis), 4 Ellersly Rd, EH12 6HZ, ✆ 337 6888, Fax 313 2543, 🌳 – |♦| ⇔ rm TV ☎ P – 🏛 70. AE ① VISA by A8 CZ
M *(bar lunch Saturday in summer)* 12.75/22.50 **st.** and a la carte – ☐ 8.50 – **57 rm** 79.00/104.00 **st.** – SB (except Christmas and New Year) (weekends only) 73.00/86.00 **st.**

Holiday Inn Garden Court, 107 Queensferry Rd, EH4 3HL, ✆ 332 2442, Telex 72541, Fax 332 3408, ≤ – |♦| ⇔ rm ▤ rest TV ☎ ♿ P – 🏛 50. AE ① VISA CY
M (bar lunch)/dinner 16.00 **st.** and a la carte 6.00 – ☐ 7.95 – **119 rm** 85.00/150.00 **st.** – SB 92.00/112.00 **st.**

Barnton Thistle (Mt. Charlotte Thistle), 562 Queensferry Rd, EH4 6AS, ☎ 339 1144, Fax 339 5521, – | TV ☎ P – 150. AE VISA by A90 CY
M (bar lunch Saturday) 9.50/15.95 **st.** and a la carte 3.00 – 8.75 – **48 rm** 75.00/85.00 **st.**, **2 suites** – SB (weekends only) 104.00 **st.**

Channings, South Learmonth Gdns, EH4 1EZ, ☎ 315 2226, Fax 332 9631 – | TV ☎. AE VISA. CY **e**
closed 24 to 27 December – **M** (light lunch Saturday and Sunday) a la carte 13.00/21.00 **st.** 4.00 – **48 rm** 79.00/115.00 **st.** – SB (weekends only) 90.00/98.00 **st.**

Bruntsfield, 69-74 Bruntsfield Pl., EH10 4HH, ☎ 229 1393, Telex 727897, Fax 229 5634 – | TV ☎ P – 70. AE VISA DZ **e**
M (bar lunch Monday) 12.00/20.00 **st.** and a la carte 4.00 – **50 rm** 65.00/105.00 **st.** – SB 90.00/144.00 **st.**

Sibbet House without rest., 26 Northumberland St., EH3 6LS, ☎ 556 1078, Fax 557 9445, « Georgian town house » – TV ☎. VISA. DY **x**
closed Christmas and New Year – **3 rm** 48.00/60.00 **st.**

28 Northumberland Street without rest., 28 Northumberland St., EH3 6LS, ☎ 557 8036, Fax 558 3453, « Georgian town house » – TV. VISA. DY **x**
closed Christmas and New Year – **3 rm** 30.00/60.00.

XXXX **Pompadour** (at Caledonian H.) Princes St., EH1 2AB, ☎ 225 2433, Telex 72179, Fax 225 6632 – P. AE VISA CY **n**
closed lunch Saturday and Sunday – **M** 25.00/40.00 **t.** and a la carte.

XXXX **Grill** (at Balmoral H.), Princes St., EH2 2EQ, ☎ 557 6727, Telex 727282, Fax 557 3747 – P. AE VISA EY **n**
closed Saturday lunch and Sunday – **M** 15.50/27.50 **st.** and a la carte 6.25.

XX **Vintners Room,** The Vaults, 87 Giles St., Leith, EH6 6BZ, ☎ 554 6767, Fax 554 8423 – . AE VISA by A 900 EY
closed Sunday and 2 weeks Christmas-New Year – **M** 12.00 **st.** (lunch) and a la carte 9.00/26.00 **st.** 4.00.

XX **Martins,** 70 Rose St., North Lane, EH2 3DX, ☎ 225 3106 – . AE VISA DY **n**
closed Saturday lunch, Sunday, Monday and 24 December-20 January – **M** (booking essential) 16.00 **t.** (lunch) and a la carte 23.55/28.15 **t.** 4.70.

XX **L'Auberge,** 56 St. Mary's St., EH1 1SX, ☎ 556 5888, French rest. – . AE VISA EYZ **c**
closed 26 December and 1-2 January – **M** 14.50/19.85 **t.** and a la carte 3.95.

XX **Raffaelli,** 10-11 Randolph Pl., EH3 7TA, ☎ 225 6060, Fax 225 8830, Italian rest. – AE VISA CY **c**
closed Saturday lunch, Sunday, 25-26 December and 1-2 January – **M** a la carte 14.20/21.50 **t.** 4.90.

XX **Lancer's Brasserie,** 5 Hamilton Pl., Stockbridge, EH3 5BA, ☎ 332 3444, North Indian rest. – AE VISA CY **r**
M a la carte 12.35/20.45 **t.** 5.95.

XX **Indian Cavalry Club,** 3 Atholl Pl., EH3 8HP, ☎ 228 3282, Indian rest. – AE VISA CZ **c**
M 10.00/17.95 **t.** and a la carte 6.00.

XX **Merchants,** 17 Merchants St., (under bridge), EH1 2QD, ☎ 225 4009 – AE VISA EZ **x**
closed Sunday, 25-26 December and 1 January – **M** (booking essential) 8.95/15.00 **t.** and a la carte 4.70.

XX **Umberto's,** 29-33 Dublin St., EH3 6NL, ☎ 556 2231, Italian rest. – AE VISA EY **e**
closed lunch Saturday and Sunday – **M** 8.50 **t.** (lunch) and a la carte 14.80/18.65 **t.** 5.25.

XX **Cosmo,** 58a North Castle St., EH2 3LU, ☎ 226 6743, Italian rest. – VISA DY **r**
closed Saturday lunch, Sunday and Monday – **M** a la carte 18.70/27.20 **t.** 5.00.

XX **Denzler's 121,** 121 Constitution St., EH6 7AE, ☎ 554 3268 – AE VISA
closed Saturday lunch, Sunday, Monday, last 2 weeks July and first week January – **M** 13.50/23.50 **st.** and a la carte 5.25.

at Ingliston W : 7 ¾ m. on A 8 - AV – ✉ 031 Edinburgh :

Norton House ,, EH28 8LY, on A 8 ☎ 333 1275, Fax 333 5305, <, , park – TV ☎ ♿ P – 250. AE VISA.
M *(closed Saturday lunch)* 17.00/22.00 **st.** and a la carte 5.50 – **44 rm** 95.00/110.00 **st.**, **2 suites** – SB 95.00/120.00 **st.**

In this Guide,
a symbol or a character, printed in red or black,
does not have the same meaning.
Please read the explanatory pages carefully.

GLASGOW Lanark. (Strathclyde) 401 402 H 16 **Scotland G.** – pop. 754 586 – ☎ 041.

See : City★★★ – Cathedral★★★ DZ – The Burrell Collection★★★ – Hunterian Art Gallery★★ (Whistler Collection★★★ – Mackintosh Wing★★★ **AC**) CY **M4** – Museum of Transport★★ (Scottish Built Cars★★★, The Clyde Room of Ship Models★★★) – Kelvingrove Art Gallery and Museum★★ CY – Pollok House★ (The Paintings★★) **D** – Tolbooth Steeple★ DZ **A** – Hunterian Museum (Coin and Medal Collection★) CY **M1** – City Chambers★ DZ **C** – Glasgow School of Art★ CY **B** – Necropolis (<★ of Cathedral) DYZ.

Exc. : The Trossachs★★★, N : 31 m. by A 879, A 81 and A 821 – Loch Lomond★★, NW : 19 m. by A 82.

18 Linn Park, Simshill Rd ☎ 637 5871, S : 4 m. by B 766 – 18 Lethamhill, Cumbernauld Rd ☎ 770 6220 – 18 Deaconsbank ☎ 638 7044, S : 5 m. by A 77 – 9 Alexandra Park, Alexandra Par. ☎ 556 3711, by M 8 – 9 Knightswood, Lincoln Av. ☎ 959 2131, NW : 4 m. by A 82 – 9 Kings Park, Croftpark Av., S : 4 m. by B 766.

Access to Oban by helicopter.

✈ Glasgow Airport : ☎ 887 1111, Telex 776613, Fax 848 4586, W : 8 m. by M 8 – **Terminal** : Coach service from Glasgow Central and Queen Street main line Railway Stations and from Anderston Cross and Buchanan Bus Stations see also Prestwick.

ℹ 35 St. Vincent Pl. ☎ 204 4400 – Glasgow Airport, Paisley ☎ 848 4440.

Edinburgh 46 – Manchester 221.

Plans on following pages

Glasgow Hilton, 1 William St., G3 8HT, ☎ 204 5555, Telex 556324, Fax 204 5004, <, Ls, ≘s, ☒ – |‡| ⇆ rm ▤ TV ☎ ♿ P – 🏆 1 000. AE ⓓ VISA. ✗ CZ **s**
M 12.50/15.00 **t.** and a la carte 🍷 6.20 – ☕ 12.50 – **317 rm** 115.00/125.00 **t.**, 4 suites – SB (weekends only) 94.00/124.00 **st.**

Glasgow Marriott, 500 Argyle St., Anderston, G3 8RR, ☎ 226 5577, Telex 776355, Fax 221 9202, Ls, ≘s, ☒, squash – |‡| ⇆ rm ▤ TV ☎ ♿ P – 🏆 720. AE ⓓ VISA. ✗ CZ **a**
M a la carte 12.25/28.00 **t.** 🍷 6.00 – ☕ 10.25 – **293 rm** 105.00 **t.**, 5 suites – SB (weekends only) 110.00/140.00 **st.**

Forte Crest, Bothwell St., G2 7EN, ☎ 248 2656, Telex 77440, Fax 221 8986, < – |‡| ⇆ rm ▤ TV ☎ P – 🏆 800. AE ⓓ VISA CZ **z**
M 9.50/14.00 **st.** and a la carte 🍷 6.50 – ☕ 8.95 – **248 rm** 95.00 **st.**, 3 suites – SB (weekends only) 98.00 **st.**

One Devonshire Gardens, 1 Devonshire Gdns, G12 0UX, ☎ 339 2001, Fax 337 1663, « Opulent interior design » – TV ☎ – 🏆 30. AE ⓓ VISA by A 92 CY
M *(closed Saturday lunch)* 20.00/35.00 **st.** 🍷 8.00 – ☕ 12.00 – **25 rm** 125.00/165.00 **st.**, **2 suites** – SB (except Christmas and New Year) (weekends only) 137.50/147.50 **st.**

Moat House International (Q.M.H.), Congress Rd, G3 8QT, ☎ 204 0733, Telex 776244, Fax 221 2022, <, Ls, ≘s, ☒ – |‡| ⇆ rm ▤ TV ☎ ♿ P – 🏆 750. AE ⓓ VISA. ✗ CZ **r**
M 18.00/24.95 **st.** and a la carte 🍷 4.50 – ☕ 9.50 – **269 rm** 65.00/117.00 **st.**, 15 suites – SB (weekends only) 85.00 **st.**

Hospitality Inn (Mt. Charlotte Thistle), 36 Cambridge St., G2 3HN, ☎ 332 3311, Telex 777334, Fax 332 4050 – |‡| TV ☎ ♿ P – 🏆 1 500. AE ⓓ VISA DY **z**
M *(closed Saturday lunch and Sunday)* 13.00/17.50 **st.** and a la carte – ☕ 9.50 – **304 rm** 80.00/105.00 **st.**, 3 suites – SB (weekends only) 88.00 **st.**

Devonshire, 5 Devonshire Gdns, G12 0UX, ☎ 339 7878, Fax 339 3980 – TV ☎ – 🏆 40. AE ⓓ VISA. ✗
M (residents only) 23.50/35.00 **st.** and a la carte 🍷 4.75 – ☕ 6.95 – **14 rm** 90.00/190.00 **st.** – SB 120.00/190.00 **st.**

Copthorne Glasgow, George Sq., G2 1DS, ☎ 332 6711, Telex 778147, Fax 332 4264 – |‡| ⇆ rm TV ☎ – 🏆 100. AE ⓓ VISA. ✗ DZ **n**
M *(closed lunch Saturday and Sunday)* (carving rest.) 14.95/15.95 **st.** and dinner a la carte – ☕ 8.95 – **136 rm** 90.00/126.00 **st.**, 4 suites – SB 90.00/126.00 **st.**

Swallow, 517 Paisley Rd West, G51 1RW, ☎ 427 3146, Telex 778795, Fax 427 4059, Ls, ≘s, ☒ – |‡| ⇆ rm ▤ rest TV ☎ P – 🏆 250. AE ⓓ VISA by A8 CZ
M *(closed lunch Saturday and Bank Holidays)* 7.75/15.25 **st.** and a la carte 🍷 4.00 – **119 rm** ☕ 77.00/130.00 **st.** – SB 85.00/95.00 **st.**

Tinto Firs Thistle (Mt. Charlotte Thistle), 470 Kilmarnock Rd, G43 2BB, ☎ 637 2353, Fax 633 1340 – TV ☎ P – 🏆 60. AE ⓓ VISA by A 77 DZ
M (bar lunch Monday and Saturday) 15.00/18.00 **t.** and a la carte 🍷 4.50 – ☕ 8.25 – **25 rm** 70.00/85.00 **st.**, 2 suites – SB 90.00/164.00 **st.**

Kelvin Park Lorne (Q.M.H.), 923 Sauchiehall St., G3 7TE, ☎ 334 4891, Telex 778935, Fax 337 1659 – |‡| TV ☎ P – 🏆 175. AE ⓓ VISA CY **a**
M 10.50/18.50 **st.** and a la carte 🍷 4.50 – ☕ 8.00 – **99 rm** 70.00/150.00 **t.** – SB (weekends only) 154.00/184.00 **st.**

Crest, 377 Argyle St., G2 8LL, ☎ 248 2355, Telex 779652, Fax 221 1014 – |‡| ⇆ rm TV ☎ P – 🏆 80 CZ **x**
121 rm.

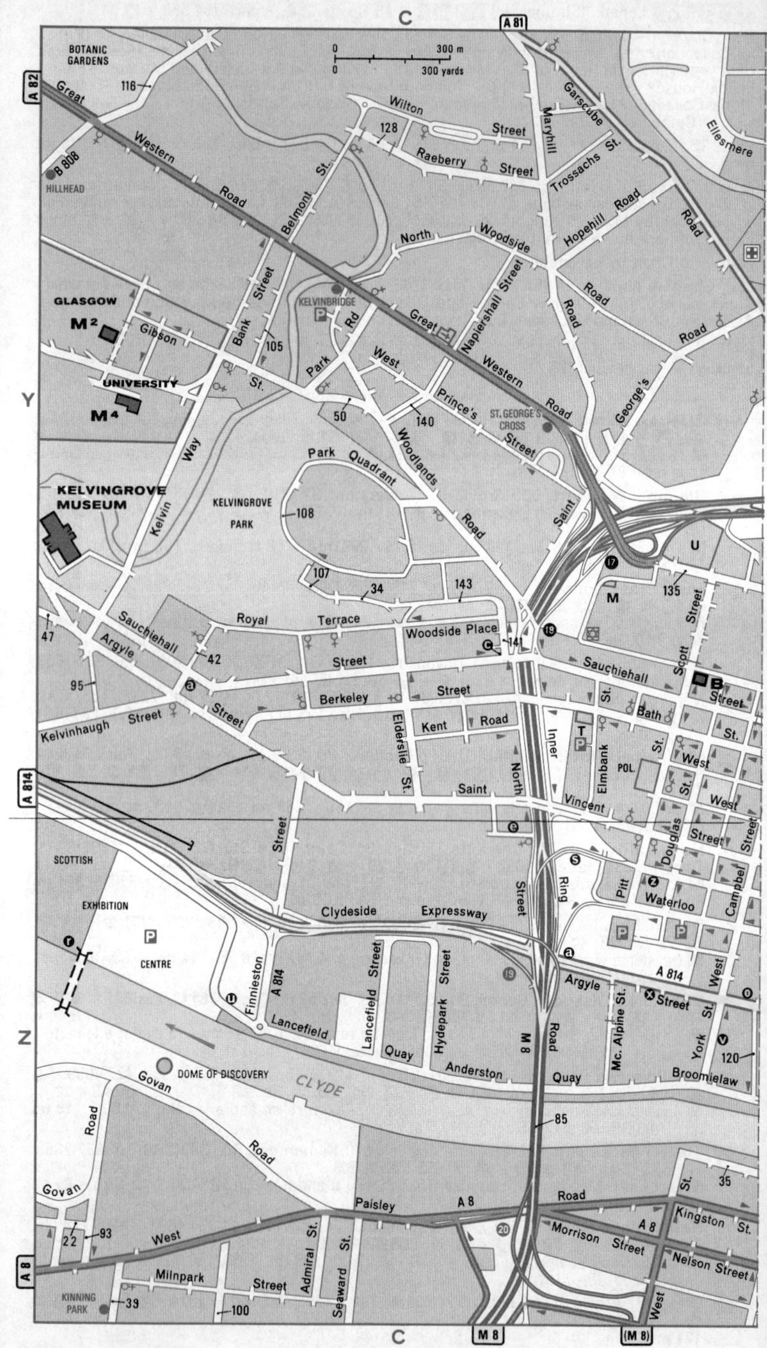

BOTANIC GARDENS
Great Western Road
HILLHEAD
GLASGOW UNIVERSITY
KELVINGROVE MUSEUM
KELVINGROVE PARK
KELVINBRIDGE
ST. GEORGE'S CROSS
SCOTTISH EXHIBITION CENTRE
DOME OF DISCOVERY
CLYDE
KINNING PARK
Sauchiehall Street
Argyle Street
Clydeside Expressway
Paisley Road West
Kingston St.
Morrison Street
Nelson Street
Broomielaw
Anderston Quay
Lancefield Quay
Woodlands Road
Maryhill Road
Garscube Road
St. George's Road
Woodside Place
Royal Terrace
Berkeley Street
Kelvinhaugh Street
Kelvin Way
Gibson St.
Bank Street
Belmont St.
Park Rd
Napiershall Street
Prince's Street
Park Quadrant
North Woodside Road
Hopehill Road
Trossachs St.
Ellesmere
Wilton Street
Raeberry Street
Elderslie St.
Kent Road
Saint Vincent Street
North Street
Inner Ring Road
Elmbank St.
Bath St.
West Regent St.
Douglas St.
Pitt St.
Waterloo St.
Campbell St.
West St.
Mc. Alpine St.
York St.
Hydepark Street
Lancefield Street
Finnieston Street
Govan Road
Milnpark Street
Admiral St.
Seaward St.
West St.
A 8
A 81
A 82
A 814
B 808
M 8
(M 8)
POL.
C
Y
Z
0 300 m
0 300 yards

GLASGOW
CENTRE

Albert Bridge . . . . . DZ 2
Brand Street . . . . . . CZ 22
Bridegate . . . . DZ 24
Bridge Street . . . . . DZ 25
Cambridge Street . . DY 32
Claremont
Terrace . . . . CY 34
Clyde Place . . . . . . CZ 35
Cochrane Street . . . DZ 36
Commerce Street . . DZ 37
Cornwald Street . . . CZ 39
Derby Street . . . . . . CY 42
Dumbarton Road . . CY 47
Eldon Street . . . . . . CY 50
Glasgow Bridge . . . DZ 60
Gordon Street . . . . DZ 65
Jamaica Street . . . . DZ 77
John Knox
Street . . . . DZ 80
Kingston Bridge . . . CZ 85
Kyle Street . . . . DY 86
Lorne Street . . . . . CZ 93
Lymburn Street . . . CY 95
Middlesex
Street . . . . CZ 100
Moir Street . . . . . . DZ 102
Otago Street . . . . . CY 105
Oxford Street . . . . . DZ 106
Park Gardens . . . . . CY 107
Park Terrace . . . . . CY 108
Port Dundas
Road . . . . DY 110
Queen Margaret
Drive . . . . CY 116
Robertson
Street . . . . CZ 120
Stirling Road . . . . . DY 126
Stockwell
Street . . . . DZ 127
Striven Gardens . . . CY 128
Victoria Bridge . . . . DZ 132
West Graham
Street . . . . CY 135
West Nile Street . DYZ 139
Woodlands Drive . . CY 140
Woodside
Crescent . . . . CY 141
Woodside Terrace . CY 143

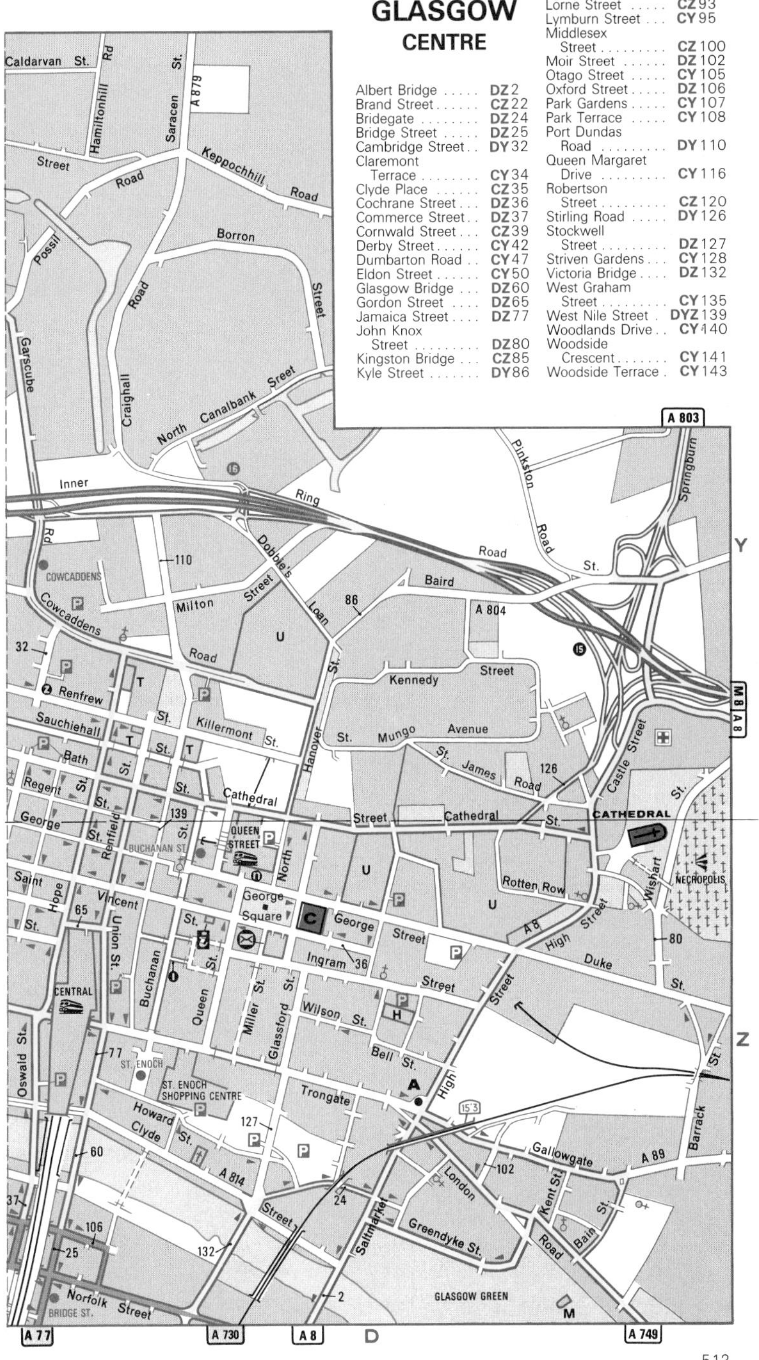

XXX **North Rotunda,** 28 Tunnel St., (2nd floor), G3 8HL, ☏ 204 1238, Fax 226 4264, French rest. - P. AE VISA CZ **u**
closed Saturday lunch, Sunday, Monday, 25-26 December and 1-2 January - **M** 10.95/17.95 **t.** and a la carte 5.50.

XXX Fountain, 2 Woodside Cres., G3 7UL, ☏ 332 6396 CY **c**

XX **Buttery,** 652 Argyle St., G3 8UF, ☏ 221 8188, Fax 204 4639 - P. AE VISA CZ **e**
closed Saturday lunch, Sunday and Bank Holidays - **M** 14.75 **st.** (lunch) and a la carte 19.75/27.50 **t.**

XX Ho Wong, 82 York St., G2 3LE, ☏ 221 3550, Chinese (Peking) rest. - CZ **v**

XX **Rogano,** 11 Exchange Pl., G46 6LT, ☏ 248 4055, Fax 248 2608, Seafood, « Art deco » - AE VISA DZ **i**
closed Sunday lunch and Bank Holidays - **M** 15.00 **t.** (lunch) and a la carte 13.25/25.90 **t.**

XX **Sepoy Club,** 62 St. Andrews Drive, Nithsdale Cross, Pollokshields, G41 5EZ, ☏ 427 6288, Indian rest. - P. AE VISA
M a la carte 10.00/20.00 **st.**

XX **Amber Royale,** 336 Argyle St., G2 8LY, ☏ 221 2550, Chinese rest. - AE VISA CZ **o**
closed Sunday - **M** 6.50/15.00 **t.** and a la carte 4.95.

X **Ubiquitous Chip,** 12 Ashton Lane, off Byres Rd, G12 8SJ, ☏ 334 5007, Fax 337 1302 - AE VISA
closed Sunday lunch, 25 and 31 December and 1-2 January - **M** a la carte 18.80/28.10 **t.**

LEEDS

W. Yorks. 402 P 22 **Great Britain G.** - pop. 445 242 - ECD : Wednesday - ☏ 0532.

See : City★ - City Art Gallery★ DZ **M.**

Envir. : Kirkstall Abbey★, NW : 3 m. by A 65 - Templenewsam★ (decorative arts★), E : 5 m. by A 64 and A 63 **D.**

Exc. : Harewood House★★ (The Gallery★), N : 8 m. by A 61.

18, 18 The Temple Newsam, Temple Newsam Rd, Halton ☏ 645624, E : 3 m. by A 64 - 18 Gotts Park, Armley Ridge Rd, ☏ 342019, W : 2 m. by A 658 - 18 Middleton Park Municipal, Ring Rd, Middleton ☏ 709506, S : 3 m. by A 653 - 18 Scarcroft, Skyke Lane ☏ 892263, N : 7 m. by A 58 - 18 Sand Moor, Alwoodley Lane ☏ 681685, N : 5 m. by A 61 - 18 Howley Hall, Scotchman Lane, Morley ☏ 0924 (Morley) 472432, SW : 4 m. on B 6123 - 9 Roundhay, Park Lane ☏ 662695, N : 4 m. by A 6120.

Leeds - Bradford Airport : ☏ 509696, Telex 557868, Fax 505426, NW : 8 m. by A 65 and A 658.

19 Wellington St., LS1 4DG ☏ 478301/478302, Fax 426761.

London 204 - Liverpool 75 - Manchester 43 - Newcastle upon Tyne 95 - Nottingham 74.

Plan opposite

42 The Calls, 42 The Calls, LS2 7EW, ☏ 440099, Fax 344100, <, « Converted riverside grain mill » - rm P - 50. AE VISA. DZ **z**
M (see **Brasserie Forty Four** below) - 10.00 - **36 rm** 95.00/125.00 **st.**, 3 suites.

Holiday Inn, Wellington St., LS1 4DL, ☏ 442200, Telex 557879, Fax 440460, - rm P - 200. AE VISA. CZ **c**
M *(closed Saturday lunch)* 14.50/18.50 **st.** and a la carte 6.25 - 9.95 - **120 rm** 130.00/145.00 **st.**, 5 suites - SB (July and August) (weekends only) 100.00/120.00 **st.**

Leeds Hilton, Neville St., LS1 4BX, ☏ 442000, Telex 557143, Fax 433577 - rm P - 400. AE VISA DZ **r**
M 11.50/17.50 **st.** and a la carte 6.00 - 9.95 - **186 rm** 85.00 **st.**, 20 suites - SB (weekends only) 105.00/125.00 **st.**

Queen's (Forte), City Sq., LS1 1PL, ☏ 431323, Telex 55161, Fax 425154 - rm rest P - 600. AE VISA DZ **a**
M 17.95/22.95 **st.** and a la carte 5.95 - 9.95 - **183 rm** 85.00/95.00 **st.**, 5 suites - SB (except Christmas and Easter) (weekends only) 118.00 **st.**

Haley's, Shire Oak Rd, Headingly, LS6 2DE, NW : 2 m. off Otley Rd (A 660) ☏ 784446, Fax 753342 - rest P. AE VISA.
closed 26 to 30 December - **M** *(closed Saturday lunch and Sunday dinner)* 14.75/23.50 **st.** and a la carte 5.50 - **22 rm** 95.00/112.00 **st.** - SB (except Christmas) (weekends only) 100.00 **st.**

Merrion Thistle (Mt. Charlotte Thistle), Merrion Centre, 17 Wade Lane, LS2 8NH, ☏ 439191, Telex 55459, Fax 423527 - rm rest P - 80 DZ **e**
108 rm, 1 suite.

Golden Lion (Mt. Charlotte Thistle), 2 Lower Briggate, LS1 4AE, ☏ 436454, Fax 429327 - - 120. DZ **v**
89 rm.

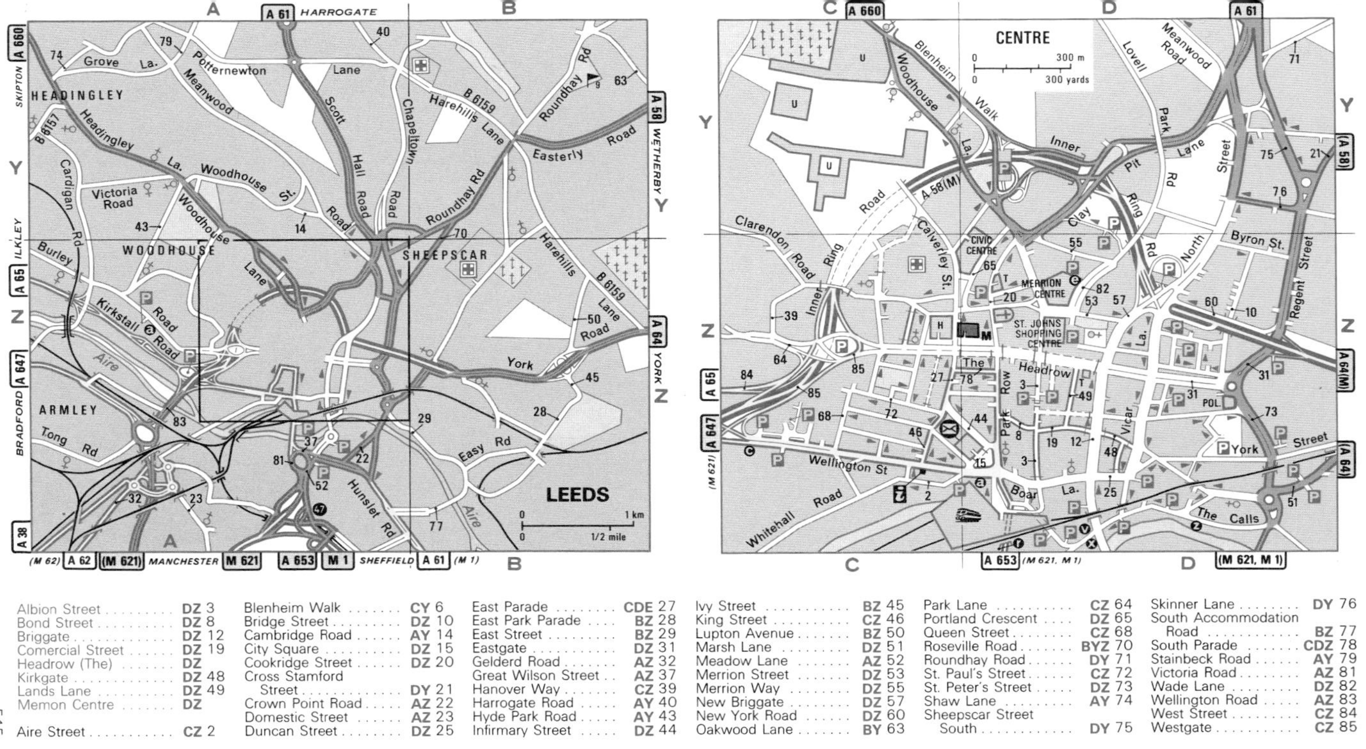

Albion Street	DZ	3	Blenheim Walk	CY	6	East Parade	CDE	27	Ivy Street	BZ	45	Park Lane	CZ	64	Skinner Lane	DY	76
Bond Street	DZ	8	Bridge Street	DZ	10	East Park Parade	BZ	28	King Street	CZ	46	Portland Crescent	DZ	65	South Accommodation Road	BZ	77
Briggate	DZ	12	Cambridge Road	AY	14	East Street	BZ	29	Lupton Avenue	BZ	50	Queen Street	CZ	68	South Parade	CDZ	78
Comercial Street	DZ	19	City Square	DZ	15	Eastgate	DZ	31	Marsh Lane	DZ	51	Roseville Road	BYZ	70	Stainbeck Road	AY	79
Headrow (The)	DZ		Cookridge Street	DZ	20	Gelderd Road	AZ	32	Meadow Lane	AZ	52	Roundhay Road	DY	71	Victoria Road	AZ	81
Kirkgate	DZ	48	Cross Stamford Street	DY	21	Great Wilson Street	AZ	37	Merrion Street	DZ	53	St. Paul's Street	CZ	72	Wade Lane	DZ	82
Lands Lane	DZ	49	Crown Point Road	AZ	22	Hanover Way	CZ	39	Merrion Way	DZ	55	St. Peter's Street	DZ	73	Wellington Road	AZ	83
Memon Centre	DZ		Domestic Street	AZ	23	Harrogate Road	AY	40	New Briggate	DZ	57	Shaw Lane	AY	74	West Street	CZ	84
Aire Street	CZ	2	Duncan Street	DZ	25	Hyde Park Road	AY	43	New York Road	DZ	60	Sheepscar Street South	DY	75	Westgate	CZ	85
						Infirmary Street	DZ	44	Oakwood Lane	BY	63						

XX **Leodis Brasserie,** Victoria Mill, Sovereign St., LS1 4BJ, 421010, Fax 430432 - VISA DZ **x**
closed Saturday lunch and Sunday - **M** 9.95 **t.** and a la carte 4.25.

XX **Brasserie Forty Four,** 44 The Calls, LS2 8AQ, 343232, Fax 343332 - AE VISA DZ **z**
closed Saturday lunch, Sunday and Bank Holidays - **M** a la carte 12.10/20.25 **t.** 4.25.

XX **Maxi's,** 6 Bingley St., LS3 1LX, off Kirkstall Rd 440552, Fax 343902, Chinese (Canton, Peking) rest., « Pagoda, ornate decor » - . AE VISA AZ **a**
M 8.00/15.00 **t.** and a la carte 7.60.

at Seacroft NE : 5 ½ m. at junction of A 64 and A 6120 - 0532 Leeds :

Stakis Leeds Windmill, Ring Rd, LS14 5QP, 732323, Telex 55452, Fax 323018 - rm rest - 250. AE VISA
M (carving lunch) 13.00/15.00 **st.** 4.50 - 8.50 - **100 rm** 69.00/89.00 **st.** - SB (weekends only) 75.00 **st.**

at Garforth E : 6 m. at junction of A 63 and A 642 - 0532 Leeds :

Hilton National, Wakefield Rd, LS25 1LH, 866556, Telex 556324, Fax 868326, , - rm rest - 250. AE VISA
M *(closed Saturday lunch)* (carving lunch) 12.50/16.95 **st.** 6.50 - 9.95 - **144 rm** 75.00 **st.** - SB (weekends only) 82.00/116.00 **st.**

at Horsforth NW : 5 m. by A 65 off A 6120 - 0532 Leeds :

XXX **Low Hall,** Calverley Lane, LS18 5EF, 588221, Fax 591420, « Elizabethan manor », - . VISA
closed Saturday lunch, Sunday, Monday, 26 October-1 November, 27 to 30 December and Bank Holidays - **M** 12.95/15.95 **t.** and a la carte 5.50.

at Bramhope NW : 8 m. on A 660 - 0532 Leeds :

Forte Crest, Leeds Rd, LS16 9JJ, 842911, Telex 556367, Fax 843451, , , , , , park - rm - 160. AE VISA
M 15.75/19.50 **st.** and a la carte 6.95 - 8.95 - **125 rm** 80.00/95.00 **st.**, **1 suite** - SB (August and weekends only) 98.00/110.00 **st.**

Parkway (Jarvis), Otley Rd, LS16 8AG, S : 2 m. on A 660 672551, Telex 556614, Fax 674410, , , , , - rm - 250. AE VISA
M 10.50/15.50 **st.** 5.50 - 8.50 - **103 rm** 89.00/127.00 **st.** - SB (weekends only) 94.00 **st.**

LIVERPOOL Mersey. 402 403 L 23 **Great Britain G.** – pop. 538 809 – ECD : Wednesday – ☎ 051.

See : City★ - Walker Art Gallery★★ DY **M2** – Liverpool Cathedral★★ (Lady Chapel★) EZ – Metropolitan Cathedral of Christ the King★★ EY – Albert Dock★ CZ – (Merseyside Maritime Museum★ **M1** - Tate Gallery Liverpool★).

Envir. : Speke Hall★, SE : 8 m. by A 561.

18 Dunnings Bridge Rd, Bootle ☎ 928 6196, N : 5 m. by A 5036 – 18 Allerton Park ☎ 428 1046, SE : 5 m. by B 5180 – 18 Lee Park, Childwall Valley Rd ☎ 487 9861, E : 7 m. by B 5178 – 18 West Derby, Yee Tree Lane ☎ 228 1540, NE : 2 m. by A 580 – 18 Liverpool Municipal, Ingoe Lane, Kirkby ☎ 546 5435 – 9 Bowring, Bowring Park, Roby Rd, Huyton ☎ 489 1901, M 62 junction 5.

Liverpool Airport : ☎ 486 8877, Telex 629323, Fax 486 3339, SE : 6 m. by A 561 – **Terminal** : Pier Head.

to Douglas (Isle of Man) (Isle of Man Steam Packet Co.) (4 h) (summer only).

to Birkenhead (Mersey Ferries) except Saturday and Sunday – to Wallasey (Mersey Ferries) except Saturday and Sunday.

Merseyside Welcome Centre, Clayton Sq., Shopping Centre, L1 1QR ☎ 709 3631 – Atlantic Pavilion, Albert Dock, L3 4AA ☎ 708 8854.

London 219 – Birmingham 103 – Leeds 75 – Manchester 35.

Plans on following pages

Liverpool Moat House (Q.M.H.), Paradise St., L1 8JD, ☎ 709 0181, Telex 627270, Fax 709 2706, ⅼ, ⅼ, ⅼ – ⅼ rm ⅼ TV ☎ & – 400. AE VISA DZ **n**
M *(closed Saturday lunch)* 16.00/18.00 **t.** and a la carte 7.00 – **244 rm** 95.50/123.00 **st.**, 7 suites – SB (weekends only) 96.00/106.00 **st.**

Atlantic Tower (Mt. Charlotte Thistle), 30 Chapel St., L3 9RE, ☎ 227 4444, Telex 627070, Fax 236 3973, ← – rm TV ☎ P – 100. AE VISA. CY **r**
M 12.95/17.25 **t.** and a la carte 4.90 – 8.25 – **223 rm** 75.00/85.00 **st.**, 3 suites – SB 66.00 **st.**

St. George's (Forte), St. John's Precinct, Lime St., L1 1NQ, ☎ 709 7090, Fax 709 0137, ← – rm TV ☎ P – 200. AE VISA DY **v**
M (bar lunch Monday to Saturday)/dinner 12.95 **st.** and a la carte 4.75 – 7.95 – **153 rm** 60.00/75.00 **st.**, 2 suites – SB (weekends only) 82.00 **st.**

Forte Crest, Lord Nelson St., L3 5QB, ☎ 709 7050, Telex 627954, Fax 709 2193 – rm TV ☎ P – 500. AE VISA DY **i**
M 10.75/13.95 **st.** and a la carte 6.10 – 8.95 – **149 rm** 70.00 **st.**, 1 suite – SB 82.00 **st.**

Campanile, Wapping and Chaloner St., L3 4AJ, ☎ 709 8104, Fax 709 8725 – rm TV ☎ & P – 30. AE VISA CZ **a**
M 7.80/10.10 **t.** and a la carte 4.00 – 4.25 – **80 rm** 37.00 **t.**

XXX **L'Oriel,** Oriel Chambers, 14 Water St., L2 8TD, ☎ 236 5025, Fax 236 2794 – AE VISA CY **o**
closed Saturday lunch, Sunday, 25-26 December and 1 January – **M** 13.95/16.95 **t.** and a la carte 4.95.

XXX Ristorante Del Secolo, 36-40 Stanley St., ☎ 236 4004 DY **e**

at Bootle N : 5 m. by A 565 – ✉ ☎ 051 Liverpool :

Park (De Vere), Park Lane West, L30 3SU, on A 5036 ☎ 525 7555, Fax 525 2481 – TV ☎ P – 100. AE VISA
M 11.00/12.00 **st.** and a la carte 3.95 – **58 rm** 40.00/73.00 **st.** – SB 66.00/70.00 **st.**

at Blundellsands N : 6 ½ m. by A 565 – ✉ Crosby – ☎ 051 Liverpool :

Blundellsands (Lansbury), The Serpentine, L23 6TN, ☎ 924 6515, Fax 931 5364 – rm TV ☎ P – 200. AE VISA.
M 9.25/13.95 **t.** and a la carte – **41 rm** 59.00/95.00 **t.** – SB (weekends only) 82.00 **st.**

at Huyton E : 7 m. by M 62 on A 5058 – ✉ ☎ 051 Liverpool :

Logwood Mill, Fallows Way, L35 1RZ, SE : 3 ½ m. by A 5080 at junction with M 62 ☎ 449 2341, Fax 449 3832, – TV ☎ & P – 200. AE VISA.
M *(closed Saturday lunch and Bank Holidays)* 12.75/15.75 **st.** and a la carte **63 rm** 35.00/119.00 **st.** – SB (weekends only) 90.00 **st.**

Derby Lodge, Roby Rd, L36 4HD, ☎ 480 4440, Fax 480 8132, – TV ☎ P. AE VISA.
M *(closed lunch Saturday and 26 December)* 12.75/15.75 **st.** and a la carte – **16 rm** 41.00/82.00 **st.**

Remember the speed limits that apply in the United Kingdom, unless otherwise signposted.

- 60 mph on single carriageway roads
- 70 mph on dual carriageway roads and motorways

LIVERPOOL
CENTRE

Bold St. . . . . DZ
Church St. . . . . DY
Lime St. . . . . DY
London Rd . . . . DEY
Lord St. . . . . CDY
Parker St. . . . . DY 103
Ranelagh St. . . . . DY 108
Renshaw St. . . . . DEZ
St. Johns Centre . . . . DY

Argyle St. . . . . DZ 6
Blackburne Pl. . . . . EZ 11
Brunswick Rd . . . . EY 19
Canning Pl. . . . . CZ 23
Churchill Way . . . . DY 25
Clarence St. . . . . EYZ 26
College Lane . . . . DZ 28
Commutation Row . . . . DY 30
Cook St. . . . . CY 32
Crosshall St. . . . . DY 36
Daulby St. . . . . EY 40
Erskine St. . . . . EY 45
Fontenoy St. . . . . DY 48
Forrest St. . . . . DZ 49
George's Dock Gate . . . . CY 51
Grafton St. . . . . DZ 53
Great Charlotte St. . . . . DY 54
Great Howard St. . . . . CY 56
Hatton Garden . . . . DY 57
Haymarket . . . . DY 58
Hood St. . . . . DY 62
Houghton St. . . . . DY 65
Huskisson St. . . . . EZ 66
James St. . . . . CY 68
King Edward St. . . . . CY 69
Knight St. . . . . EZ 72
Leece St. . . . . EZ 73
Liver St. . . . . CZ 76
Mansfield St. . . . . DEY 80
Mathew St. . . . . CDY 81
Moss St. . . . . EY 86
Mount St. . . . . EZ 88
Myrtle St. . . . . EZ 89
Newington . . . . DZ 92
New Quay . . . . CY 93
North John St. . . . . CY 96
Norton St. . . . . DY 97
Pitt St. . . . . DZ 104
Prescot St. . . . . EY 105
Prince's Rd . . . . EZ 107
Richmond St. . . . . DY 109
Roe St. . . . . DY 114
St. James Pl. . . . . EZ 117
St. John's Lane . . . . DY 118
School Lane . . . . DYZ 122
Scotland Pl. . . . . DY 123
Setton St. . . . . DZ 129
Seymour St. . . . . EY 130
Skelhorne St. . . . . DY 133
Stanley St. . . . . CDY 135
Suffolk St. . . . . DZ 137
Tarleton St. . . . . DY 139
Victoria St. . . . . DY 143
Water St. . . . . CY 150
William Brown St. . . . . DY 156
York St. . . . . DZ 157

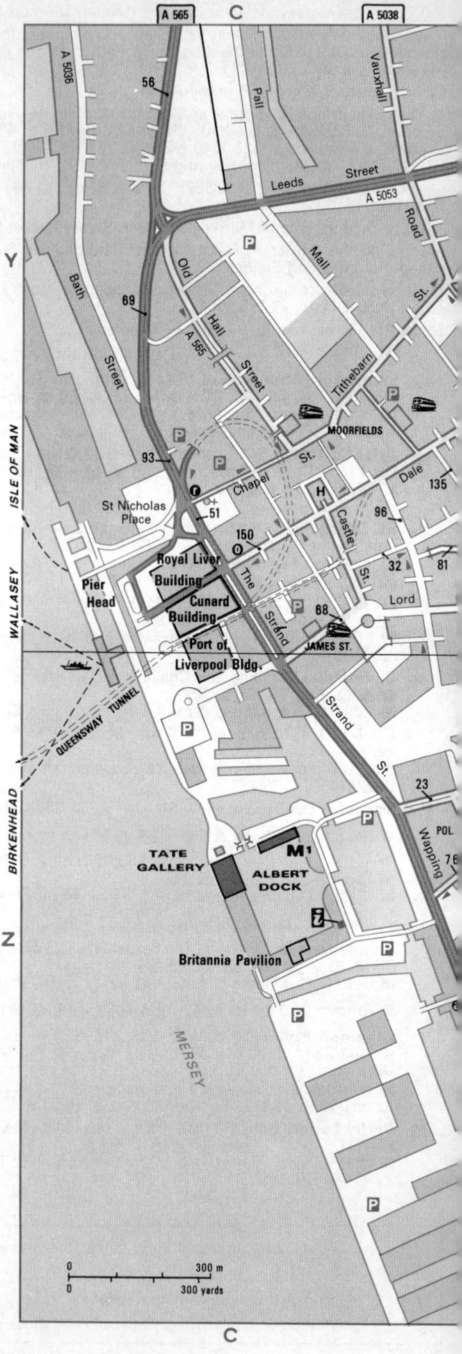

Great Britain and Ireland
is now covered
by a serie of Atlases
at a scale of 1 inch to 4.75 miles.

Three easy to use versions:
Paperback, Spiralbound, Hardback.

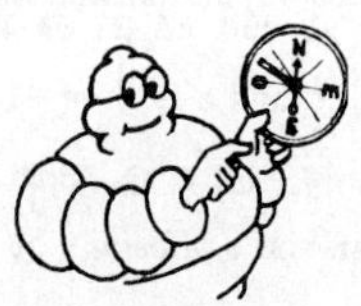

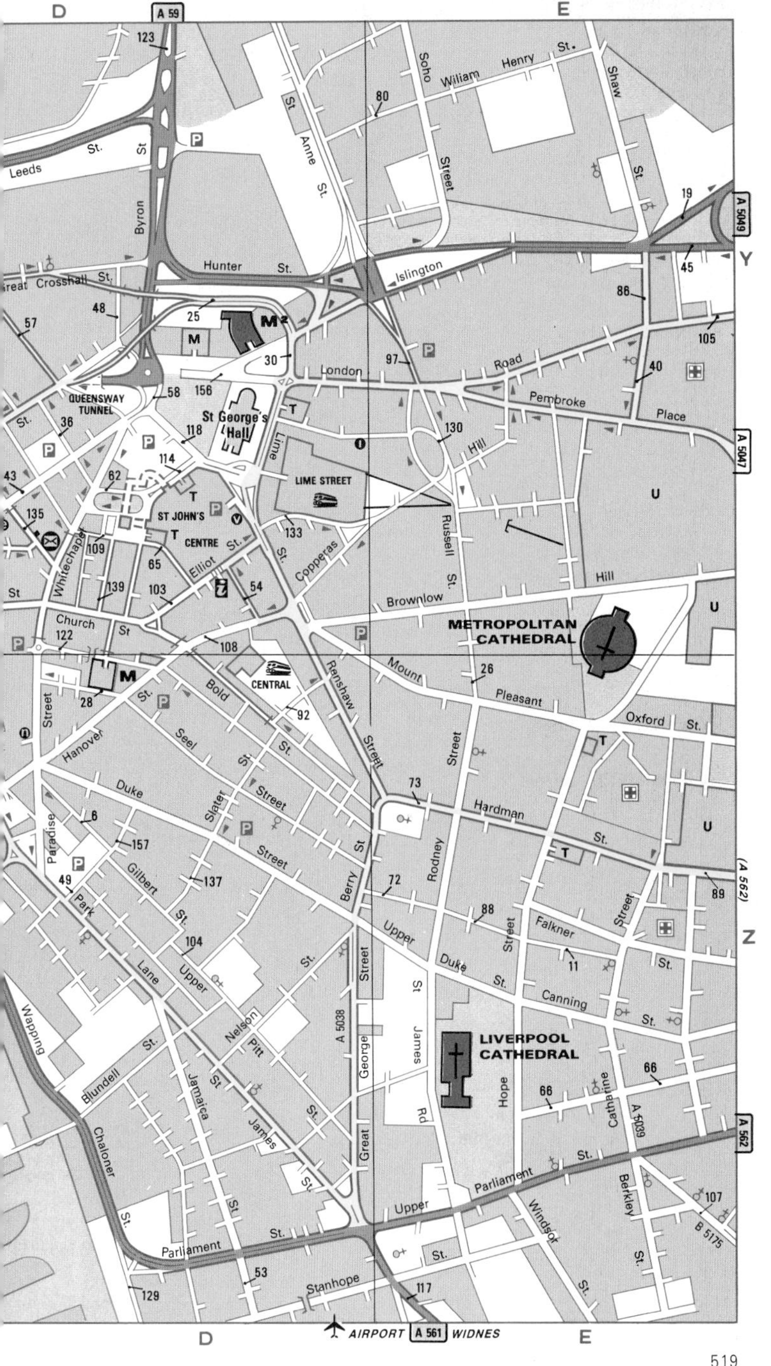

D
A 59
E
Y
Z
A 5049
A 5047
(A 562)
A 562
A 5038
A 5039
B 5175
AIRPORT A 561 WIDNES
QUEENSWAY TUNNEL
St George's Hall
LIME STREET
ST JOHN'S CENTRE
CENTRAL
METROPOLITAN CATHEDRAL
LIVERPOOL CATHEDRAL
Leeds St.
Byron St
Hunter St.
Great Crosshall St.
Islington
London Road
Pembroke Place
Soho Street
William Henry St.
Shaw St.
Anne St.
Lime St.
Copperas Hill
Russell St.
Brownlow Hill
Mount Pleasant
Oxford St.
Renshaw Street
Berry St
Rodney Street
Hardman St.
Falkner St.
Hope Street
Upper Duke St.
Canning St.
Catharine Street
Great George Street
St James Rd
Upper Parliament St.
Parliament St.
Windsor St.
Berkley St.
Stanhope St.
Whitechapel
Church St
Elliot St.
Bold St.
Seel St.
Hanover St.
Duke Street
Slater St.
Paradise Street
Gilbert St.
Park Lane
Upper Pitt St
Nelson St.
St James St.
Jamaica St
Wapping
Chaloner St.
Blundell St.

MANCHESTER Gr. Manchester 402 403 404 N 23 **Great Britain G.** – pop. 437 612 – 061.

See : City★ – Castlefield Heritage Park★ CZ – Town Hall★ CZ – City Art Gallery★ CZ **M2** – Cathedral★ (Stalls and Canopies★) CY.

Heaton Park, 798 0295, N : by A 576 - Failsworth 681 4534, NE : 3 m. by A 62 – Fairfield Golf and Sailing, Booth Rd, Audenshaw, 370 1641, E : 3 ½ m.by A 635 – Houldsworth, Longford Rd, Higher Levenshulme 224 5055, SE : 2 ½ m. by A 6 – Didsbury, Ford Lane, Northenden 998 9278, S : 4 m. by A 5103 – Northenden, Palatine Rd 998 4738, S : 4 m. by A 5103 – Blackley, Victoria Av. 643 2980, N : 5 ½ m. by A 57 off A 6104 – Stand, The Dales, Ashbourne Grove, Whitefield 766 2388, N : 5 m. by A 665.

Manchester International Airport 489 3000, Telex 665457, Fax 489 3813, S : 10 m. by A 5103 and M 56 – **Terminal** : Coach service from Victoria Station.

Town Hall Extension, Lloyd St., M60 2LA 234 3157/8, Fax 236 9900 – Manchester Airport, International Arrivals Hall, M22 5NY 436 3344.

London 202 – Birmingham 86 – Glasgow 221 – Leeds 43 – Liverpool 35 – Nottingham 72.

Plan opposite

Holiday Inn Crowne Plaza Midland, 16 Peter St., M60 2DS, 236 3333, Telex 667550, Fax 228 2241, squash – rm – 500. CZ **x**
M – **French rest.** *(closed Sunday and Bank Holidays)* (dinner only) 32.50 **t.** and a la carte 5.00 – **Trafford Room** (carving rest.) 17.95 **t.** – **Wyvern** *(closed Sunday)* a la carte 13.90/29.40 **t.** 5.00 – 10.95 – **296 rm** 118.00/134.00 **t.**, 7 suites.

Ramada Renaissance, Blackfriars St., Deansgate, M3 2EQ, 835 2555, Telex 669699, Fax 835 3077 – rm rest – 350 CY **v**
200 rm, 5 suites.

Copthorne Manchester, Clippers Quay, Salford Quays, M5 3DL, 873 7321, Telex 669090, Fax 873 7318, – rm rest – 150.
M 14.25 **st.** and a la carte – 8.95 – **166 rm** 92.00/113.00 **st.**

Charterhouse, Oxford St., M60 7HA, 236 9999, Fax 236 0674 – – 180. CZ **o**
M *(closed Saturday lunch)* 12.95/17.50 **st.** and a la carte 5.50 – 8.50 – **45 rm** 80.00/105.00 **st.**, 13 suites – SB (weekends only) 115.00/130.00 **st.**

Portland Thistle (Mt. Charlotte Thistle), 3-5 Portland St., Piccadilly Gdns, M1 6DP, 228 3400, Telex 669157, Fax 228 6347, – rm rest – 300. CZ **a**
M 10.95/30.00 **st.** and a la carte – 9.85 – **204 rm** 93.45/126.00 **st.**, 1 suite.

Victoria and Albert, Water St., M60 9EA, 832 1188, Fax 834 2484, – rm rest – 300.
M 35.00 **t.** (dinner) 6.50 – 10.00 – **128 rm** 100.00/145.00 **t.**, 4 suites.

Castlefield, Liverpool Rd, M3 4JR, 832 7073, Fax 839 0326, – rest – 70.
M 12.00/20.00 **t.** and a la carte 4.75 – **48 rm** 60.00/65.00 **t.**

Isola Bella, Dolefield, Crown Sq., M3 3EN, 831 7099, Italian rest. – .
closed Sunday and Bank Holidays – **M** 18.00 **st.** and a la carte 5.40. CZ **e**

Quan Ju De, 44 Princess St., M1 6DE, 236 5236, Chinese (Peking) rest. – . CZ **i**
closed Bank Holidays – **M** 8.95/20.50 **st.** and a la carte.

Giulio's Terrazza, 14 Nicholas St., M1 4FE, 236 4033, Fax 236 0250, Italian rest. – . CZ **r**
closed Sunday and Bank Holidays – **M** 12.50/18.50 **t.** and a la carte 5.80.

Gaylord, Amethyst House, Marriott's Court, Spring Gdns, M2 1EA, 832 6037, Indian rest. – . CZ **c**
M 13.95 **t.** and a la carte 5.45.

Yang Sing, 34 Princess St., M1 4JY, 236 2200, Fax 236 5934, Chinese (Canton) rest. – . CZ **n**
closed 25 December – **M** (booking essential) 12.25 **t.** and a la carte.

at Northenden S : 5 ¼ m. by A 5103 – 061 Manchester :

Forte Posthouse, Palatine Rd, M22 4FH, 998 7090, Fax 946 0139 – rm – 150.
M a la carte 12.70/23.15 **t.** 4.50 – 6.95 – **190 rm** 53.50 **st.** – SB (weekends only) 82.00 **st.**

at Manchester Airport S : 9 m. by A 5103 off M 56 – 061 Manchester :

Manchester Airport Hilton, Outwood Lane, Ringway, M22 5WP, 436 4404, Telex 668361, Fax 436 1521, – rm – 200
223 rm.

Forte Crest, Ringway Rd, Wythenshawe, M22 5NS, 437 5811, Telex 668721, Fax 436 2340, – rm – 200.
M *(closed Saturday lunch)* 11.50/16.95 **st.** and a la carte – **291 rm**, 2 suites.

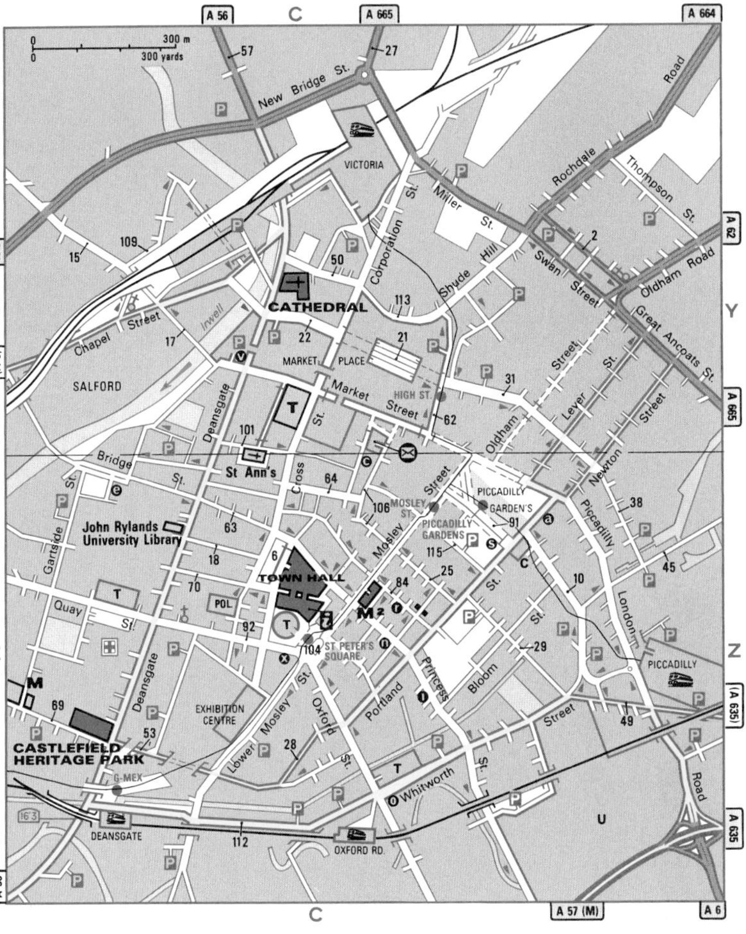

MANCHESTER
CENTRE

Street	Square	No.
Deansgate	CYZ	
Lower Mosley Street	CZ	
Market Place	CY	
Market Street	CY	
Mosley Street	CZ	
Princess Street	CZ	
Addington Street	CY	2
Albert Square	CZ	6
Aytoun Street	CZ	10
Blackfriars Road	CY	15
Blackfriars Street	CY	17
Brazennose Street	CZ	18
Cannon Street	CY	21
Cateaton Street	CY	22
Charlotte Street	CZ	25
Cheetham Hill Road	CY	27
Chepstow Street	CZ	28
Chorlton Street	CZ	29
Church Street	CY	31
Dale Street	CZ	38
Ducie Street	CZ	45
Fairfield Street	CZ	49
Fennel Street	CY	50
Great Bridgewater Street	CZ	53
Great Ducie Street	CY	57
High Street	CY	62
John Dalton Street	CZ	63
King Street	CZ	64
Liverpool Road	CZ	69
Lloyd Street	CZ	70
Nicholas Street	CZ	84
Parker Street	CZ	91
Peter Street	CZ	92
St. Ann's Street	CY	101
St. Peter's Square	CZ	104
Spring Gardens	CZ	106
Viaduct Street	CY	109
Whitworth Street West	CZ	112
Withy Grove	CY	113
York Street	CZ	115

In addition to establishments indicated by XXXXX ... X , many hotels possess good class restaurants.

Etrop Grange, Outwood Lane, M22 5NR, ☏ 499 0500, Fax 499 0790 – TV ☎ ♿ P – 70. AE VISA.
M *(closed Saturday lunch)* 17.25/31.50 **t.** 4.75 – ☕ 8.50 – **39 rm** 54.50/99.50, **2 suites** – SB (weekends only) 119.00/199.00 **st.**

XXX **Moss Nook,** Ringwood Rd, Moss Nook, M22 5NA, ☏ 437 4778, Fax 498 8089 – P. AE VISA
closed Saturday lunch, Sunday, Monday and 25 December-9 January – **M** 17.50/29.00 **t.** and a la carte.

at Worsley W : 7 ¼ m. by M 602 off M 62 (eastbound) on A 572 – ✉ 061 Manchester :

Novotel Manchester West, Worsley Brow, M28 4YA, at junction 13 of M 62 ☏ 799 3535, Fax 703 8207, heated – rm rest TV ☎ ♿ P – 200. AE VISA
M 11.50/12.50 **st.** and a la carte – ☕ 7.50 – **119 rm** 62.50/67.50 **st.**

INTERNATIONAL DIALLING CODES

INDICATIFS TELEPHONIQUES INTERNATIONAUX

INTERNATIONALE TELEFON-VORWAHLNUMMERN

国際電話国別番号

from \ to	A	B	CH	D	DK	E	F	GB	GR	H	I	IRL	J	L	N	NL	P	S	SF	USA
AUSTRIA	–	0032	05	06	0045	0034	0033	0044	0030	0036	040	00353	0081	00352	0047	0031	00351	0046	00358	001
BELGIUM	0043	–	0041	0049	0045	0034	0033	0044	0030	0036	0039	00353	0081	00352	0047	0031	00351	0046	00358	001
DENMARK	00943	00932	00941	00949	–	00934	00933	00944	00930	00936	00939	009353	00981	009352	00947	00931	009351	00946	009358	0091
FINLAND	99043	99032	99041	99049	99045	99034	99033	99044	99030	99036	99039	990353	99081	990352	99047	99031	990351	990046	–	9901
FRANCE	1943	1932	1941	1949	1945	1934	–	1944	1930	1936	1939	19353	1981	19352	1947	1931	19351	1946	19358	191
GERMANY	0043	0032	0041	–	0045	0034	0033	0044	0030	0036	0039	00353	0081	00352	0047	0031	00351	0046	00358	001
GREECE	0043	0032	0041	0049	0045	0034	0033	0044	–	0036	0039	00353	0081	00352	0047	0031	00351	0046	00358	001
HUNGARY	0043	0032	0041	0049	0045	0034	0033	0044	0030	–	0039	00353	0081	00352	0047	0031	00351	0046	00358	001
IRELAND	0043	0032	0041	0049	0045	0034	0033	0044	0030	0036	0039	–	0081	00352	0047	0031	00351	0046	00358	001
ITALY	0043	0032	0041	0049	0045	0034	0033	0044	0030	0036	–	00353	0081	00352	0047	0031	00351	0046	00358	001
JAPAN	00143	00132	00141	00149	00145	00134	00133	00144	00130	00136	00139	001353	–	001352	00147	00131	001351	00146	001358	0011
LUXEMBOURG	0043	0032	0041	05	0045	0034	0033	0044	0030	0036	0039	00353	0081	–	0047	0031	00351	0046	00358	001
NORWAY	09543	09532	09541	09549	09545	09534	09533	09544	09530	09536	09539	095353	09581	095352	–	09531	095351	09546	095358	0951
NETHERLANDS	0943	0932	0941	0949	0945	0934	0933	0944	0930	0936	0939	09353	0981	09352	0947	–	09351	0946	09358	091
PORTUGAL	0043	0032	0041	0049	0045	0034	0033	0044	0030	0036	0039	00353	0081	00352	0047	0031	–	0046	00358	001
SPAIN	0743	0732	0741	0749	0745	–	0733	0744	0730	0736	0739	07353	0781	07352	0747	0731	07351	0746	07358	071
SWEDEN	00943	00932	00941	00949	00945	00934	00933	00944	00930	00936	00939	009353	00981	009352	00947	00931	009351	–	009358	0091
SWITZERLAND	0043	0032	–	0049	0045	0034	0033	0044	0030	0036	0039	00353	0081	00352	0047	0031	00351	0046	00358	001
UNITED KINGDOM	01043	01032	01041	01049	01045	01034	01033	–	01030	01036	01039	010353	01081	010352	01047	01031	010351	01046	010358	0101
USA	01143	01132	01141	01149	01145	01134	01133	01144	01130	01136	01139	011353	01181	011352	01147	01131	011351	01146	011358	–

Calendar of main tradefairs and other international events in 1993

AUSTRIA

Vienna	Wiener Festwochen	May-June
Salzburg	Salzburg Festival (Festspiele)	3 to 12 April 24 July to 30 August

BENELUX

Amsterdam	Holland Festival	June
Bruges	Ascension Day Procession	Ascension
Brussels	Guild Procession (Ommegang)	first Thursday of July
	Holiday and Leisure Activities International Show	27 March to 4 April
	Belgian Antique Dealers Fair	27 Jan. to 7 February
	Eurantica (Antiques Show)	27 March to 4 April

DENMARK

Copenhagen	Scandinavian Furniture Fair	5 to 9 Sept.
	Future Fashions Fair	18 to 21 February 26 to 29 August

FINLAND

Helsinki	Nordic Fashion Fair	January 22 to 24 August
	Helsinki Festival	24 Aug. to 12 Sept.
	International Horse Show	22 to 24 October

FRANCE

Paris	Paris Fair	29 April to 9 May
Cannes	International Film Festival	13 to 24 May
Lyons	Lyons Fair	27 March to 5 April
Marseilles	Marseilles Fair	24 Sept. to 4 Oct.

GERMANY

Berlin	Berlin Fair (Grüne Woche)	22 to 31 January
Frankfurt	International Fair	13 to 17 February 21 to 25 August
	Frankfurt Book Fair	6 to 11 October

Hanover	Hanover Fair	21 to 28 April
Leipzig	International Book Fair	3 to 6 June
Munich	Beer Festival (Oktoberfest)	18 Sept. to 3 Oct.

GREECE

Athens	Athens Festival	From June to end Sept.
Salonica	International Fair	September

HUNGARY

Budapest	International Fair	17 to 26 September

IRELAND

Dublin	Dublin Horse Show	August

ITALY

Milan	Fashion Fair (Milanovendemoda)	5 to 9 February
Palermo	Mediterranean Fair	22 May to 6 June

NORWAY

Oslo	Nor-Shipping	8 to 11 June
	Fashion Week	2 to 5 Sept.

PORTUGAL

Lisbon	Motorexpo	3 to 12 December

SPAIN

Madrid	Fitur	27 to 31 Jan.
Barcelona	International Motor Show	15 to 23 May
Sevilla	April Fair	27 April to 2 May
Valencia	International Fair	26 Dec. to 3 Jan.
	Fallas	16 to 19 March

SWEDEN

Stockholm	Stockholm Water Festival	6 to 15 August
	International Fashion Fair	9 to 12 September
	International Boat Show	5 to 13 March 94
Gothenburg	Book & Library Fair	9 to 12 September
	International Boat Show	4 to 13 February 94

continued →

SWITZERLAND

Basle	European Watch, Clock and Jewellery Fair	22 to 29 April
Geneva	International Motor Show	3 to 13 March 94
Zürich	Züspa	23 Sept. to 3 Oct.
	International Media and Hifi Exhibition	25 to 30 August

UNITED KINGDOM

London	London International Boat Show	January
Birmingham	International Antique Fair	1 to 7 April
Edinburgh	Arts Festival	15 August to 8 Sept.
	Edinburgh Science Festival	10 to 24 April
Glasgow	Scottish Motor Show	12 to 21 November
	The Scottish boat, caravan camping and leisure Show	2 to 5 February 94

Notes

NOTES

NOTES

NOTES

This Michelin's « EUROPE » Red Guide is also available as a small laser disk, where you can promptly and easily find the information you need.
It's the « Electronic book », readable by a portable laser disk drive (EBG standard).

MANUFACTURE FRANÇAISE DES PNEUMATIQUES MICHELIN

Société en commandite par actions au capital de 2 000 000 000 de francs.

Place des Carmes-Déchaux - 63 Clermont-Ferrand (France)

R.C.S. Clermont-Fd B 855 200 507

Dépôt légal : 4-93 - ISBN 2.06.007039-2

Printed in France - 2.93-40

Photocomposition : MAURY Imprimeur S.A., Malesherbes

Impression : MAURY Imprimeur S.A., Malesherbes - KAPP LAHURE JOMBART, Evreux

Reliure : BRUN, Malesherbes

Les cartes et les guides Michelin sont complémentaires, utilisez-les ensemble.

Michelin maps and guides are complementary publications. Use them together.

De Michelin kaarten en gidsen vullen elkaar aan. Gebruik ze samen.

Die Karten, Reise- und Hotelführer von Michelin ergänzen sich. Benutzen Sie sie zusammen.

Los mapas y las guías Michelin se complementan, utilícelos juntos.

Le carte e le guide Michelin sono complementari : utilizzatele insieme.

970

EUROPE
Tourisme · Routes · Relief
Répertoire des noms
1/3 000 000 - 1 cm : 30 km

CARTE ROUTIÈRE ET TOURISTIQUE
MICHELIN